FRANZ KAFKA

Books by Frederick R. Karl

William Faulkner: American Writer (1989)
Modern and Modernism: The Sovereignty of the Artist 1885–1925 (1985)
American Fictions: 1940–80 (1983)
Joseph Conrad: The Three Lives. A Biography (1979)
The Adversary Literature (1974)
An Age of Fiction: The Nineteenth-Century British Novel (1964, revised
    1972)
C. P. Snow: The Politics of Conscience (1963)
The Contemporary English Novel (1962, revised 1972)
The Quest, a novel (1961)
A Reader's Guide to Joseph Conrad (1960, revised 1969)

EDITED:

Joseph Conrad: A Collection of Criticism (1975)
The Collected Letters of Joseph Conrad: Volume I, 1861–97 (1983),
    Volume II, 1898–1902 (1986), Volume III, 1903–07 (1988),
    Volume IV, 1908–1911 (1990) (general editor and
    volume coeditor — 8 volumes in all)
The Mayor of Casterbridge by Thomas Hardy (1966)
The Portable Conrad (Morton Dauwen Zabel's edition, revised, 1969)
The Signet Classic Book of British Short Stories (1985)
The Secret Agent by Joseph Conrad (1983)
Chance by Joseph Conrad (1985)
The Moonstone by Wilkie Collins (1984)
The Woman in White by Wilkie Collins (1985)

COEDITED:

The Existential Imagination (1963)
Short Fiction of the Masters (1963, 1973)
The Shape of Fiction (1967, 1978)
The Radical Vision (1970)
The Naked i: Fictions for the Seventies (1971)
The Existential Mind: Documents and Fictions (1974)
The Fourth World: The Imprisoned, the Poor, the Sick,
    the Elderly and Underaged in America (1976)

FRANZ KAFKA

Frederick R. Karl

Representative Man

FROMM INTERNATIONAL
PUBLISHING CORPORATION
New York

Published in 1993 by Fromm International Publishing Corporation
by arrangement with Ticknor & Fields,
Houghton Mifflin Company,
2 Park Street,
Boston, Massachusetts 02108

Library of Congress Cataloging-in-Publication Data
Karl, Frederick Robert, date.
Franz Kafka, representative man / Frederick R. Karl.
p.   cm.
Includes index.
ISBN 0-88064-146-0
1. Kafka, Franz, 1883–1924—Biography.   2. Authors,
Czech—20th century—Biography.   I. Title.
PT2621.A26Z7619   1991
833'.912—dc20   91-18562
[B]   CIP

Printed in the United States of America
Printed on acid-free, recycled paper
First U.S. Edition 1991
First Paperback Edition 1993

The author is grateful for permission to quote from the following material by
Rainer Maria Rilke:

Lines from "The Rose Interior," "The Prophet," "Buddha in Glory," "Death
Experienced," "Dance of Death," "The Coat of Arms," and "The Alchemist,"
excerpted from *New Poems (1907)*, translation copyright © 1984, and *New
Poems (1908)*, translation copyright © 1987 by Edward Snow. Published by
North Point Press and reprinted by permission.
    Lines from *Duino Elegies*, translated by J. B. Leishman and Stephen
Spender, are reprinted with the permission of W. W. Norton & Company, Inc.
Copyright © 1939 by W. W. Norton & Company, Inc. Copyright renewed 1967
by Stephen Spender and J. B. Leishman.
    Lines from *The Notebooks of Malte Laurids Brigge*, translated by M. D.
Herter Norton, are reprinted with the permission of W. W. Norton & Company, Inc. Copyright © 1949 by W. W. Norton & Company, Inc. Copyright renewed 1977 by M. D. Herter Norton.

Photographs are courtesy of Klaus Wagenbach unless otherwise specified.

To the 6 million, Europeans murdered by Europeans.

We speak of those events or lives that "may perhaps be ultimately insignificant in themselves, but nevertheless, as in a flash of lightning, illuminate a whole historical landscape, throwing even the obscurest features into sharp and dramatic relief" (Lenin).

Acknowledgments

I would like, first, to thank those individuals who proved helpful to me in the preparation of this critical biography. I am grateful to Mrs. Marianne Steiner, Kafka's niece, and Sir Malcolm Pasley, the pre-eminent Kafka scholar and textual editor; also, Dr. Klaus Wagenbach, publisher and author; Professor Siegfried Mandel of the University of Colorado; Dr. Judith Priestman of the Bodleian, Oxford University; Professor Milan Fryscak of New York University; Professor Leon Edel; Professor Mark Anderson of Columbia University; Drs. Louise and Donald Kaplan, psychotherapists; Walter Abish; Professor Martin Hilský of Charles University, Prague, and his wife, Katya; Dr. Čermák, the director of Odeon, the Prague publishing house; Ms. Sara Bershtel, formerly of Pantheon Books; Dr. Abraham Buchberg, for medical information; my oldest daughter, Deborah Karl, for mature advice and constant encouragement.

Second, I would like to acknowledge those works, both critical and biographical, which made my own work possible; without them, I am sure I would have floundered or else needed far more than the three and a half years it took me to complete this book. Many of these titles are in German and, unfortunately, unavailable to the English-language reader. But we can hope that in the future at least some of them — especially the biography by Klaus Wagenbach — will be translated.

Anderson, Mark, ed. *Reading Kafka: Prague, Politics, and the Fin de Siècle*, 1989.

Binder, Harmut. *Kafka-Handbuch*, 2 vols., 1979; *Kafka in Neuer Sicht*, 1976.

Born, Jürgen. *Franz Kafka — Kritik und Rezeption zu seiner Lebzeiten,* 2 vols., 1978.

Brod, Max. *Franz Kafka: A Biography,* 1960 (1937). Although much of his commentary and several aspects of his editing of Kafka's works are falling by the wayside, Brod will always remain a central figure in any biographical work on Kafka. Even when disputed or disproved, Brod exists.

Emrich, Wilhelm. *Franz Kafka: A Critical Study of the Writings,* 1968.

Katz, Jacob. *From Prejudice to Destruction: Anti-Semitism, 1700–1933,* 1980.

Northay, Anthony. *Kafka's Puschpuche,* 1988, translated as *Kafka's Relatives* (1991).

Pasley, Sir Malcolm. His editions of *The Trial* and *The Castle* (in German).

Pawel, Ernst. *The Nightmare of Reason: A Life of Franz Kafka,* 1984. The first serious full-fledged biography of Kafka in English, but lacking any extended discussions of the work and Kafka's background in High Modernism.

Politzer, Heinz. *Franz Kafka: Parable and Paradox,* 1966 (1962). This book began as six lectures delivered at Cornell University and has become one of the most influential critical studies on Kafka.

Robert, Marthe. *As Lonely as Franz Kafka,* 1986 (1979). This is an important psychological-psychoanalytical biography the conclusions of which are debatable.

Robertson, Ritchie. *Kafka: Judaism, Politics, and Literature,* 1985. This is one of the pre-eminent studies on Kafka, especially in areas concerning his Judaism, and it deserves a wider hearing than it has received.

Rolleston, James. *Kafka's Narrative Theatre,* 1974.

Sokel, Walter. *Franz Kafka. Tragik und Ironie. Zur Struktur seiner Kunst,* 1964. Like the Binder and Born books cited above, Sokel's study deserves an English translation.

Stölzl, Christoph. *Kafkas böses Böhmen: Zur Socialgeschichte eines Prager Juden,* 1975.

Sussman, Henry. *Franz Kafka: Geometrician of Metaphor,* 1979. This is an attempt to redirect Kafka criticism from "interpretation" into the problematics pioneered by Walter Benjamin and Jacques Derrida.

Wagenbach, Klaus. *Franz Kafka. Eine Biographie seiner Jugend, 1883–1912,* 1958. The material in this biography has been the source of several subsequent biographical studies of Kafka in English.

My interest in Kafka began shortly after World War Two, but my serious study started about twenty years ago when I delivered a paper on enclosure in Kafka before the Andiron Club of New York. I then published a paper on time and space in Kafka's novels in the *Journal of Modern Literature* and taught several courses on psychological aspects of Kafka and his fiction. After writing *Modern and Modernism: The Sovereignty of the Artist, 1885–1925*, I recognized how Kafka was located in the very center of High Modernism, and that Prague was not a backwater but a major center of modern art and literature. With this, I decided to write a Kafka biography and was helped enormously by an invitation from the Czechoslovakian University system to lecture on American literature in Prague while I pursued my Kafka research. Charles University provided me with an excellent audience for my ideas on American fiction since World War Two, gave me excellent quarters directly off Old Town Square, supplied me with a Czech interpreter, and made me feel at home in the months just prior to the civil insurrection that overthrew the existing government. I have already acknowledged my gratitude to Professor Martin Hilský, then and now chairman of the English Department at Charles University, and his wife, Katya, also a teacher and a translator; but I would like to repeat it in the context of this explanation of how I came into Kafka studies.

All Kafka scholars, critics, and biographers are indebted to the critical-text edition of Kafka's works being published by S. Fischer Verlag, of which *The Trial* and *The Castle* have already been cited.

I would like to thank Schocken Books for permission to quote passages from the following:

From *Letters to Friends, Family, and Editors*, by Franz Kafka, translated by Richard and Clara Winston. English translation copyright © 1977 by Schocken Books, Inc. Reprinted by permission of Schocken Books, published by Pantheon Books, a division of Random House, Inc.

From *Dearest Father*, by Franz Kafka, translated by Ernst Kaiser and Eithne Wilkins. English translation copyright 1954 by Schocken Books, Inc. Copyright renewed 1982 by Schocken Books, Inc. Reprinted by permission of Schocken Books, published by Pantheon Books, a division of Random House, Inc.

From "Wedding Preparations in the Country," "Resolutions," "Unmasking a Confidence Trickster," and "In the Penal Colony," from *Franz Kafka: The Complete Stories*, edited by Nahum N. Glatzer. Copyright 1946, 1947, 1948, 1949, 1954, © 1958, 1971 by Schocken Books, Inc. Reprinted by permission of Schocken Books, published by Pantheon Books, a division of Random House, Inc.

From *Letters to Felice*, by Franz Kafka, edited by Erich Heller and Jürgen Born, translated by James Stern and Elizabeth Duckworth. English translation copyright © 1973 by Schocken Books, Inc. Reprinted by permission of Schocken Books, published by Pantheon Books, a division of Random House, Inc.

From *Letters to Milena,* by Franz Kafka, edited by Willi Haas, translated by Tania and James Stern. Copyright 1953 by Schocken Books, Inc. Copyright renewed 1981 by Schocken Books, Inc. Also, expanded and revised edition (for page references), edited by Philip Boehm, translated by Philip Boehm. Copyright 1990 by Schocken Books, Inc. Reprinted by permission of Schocken Books, published by Pantheon Books, a division of Random House, Inc.

From *The Diaries of Franz Kafka 1910–1913,* edited by Max Brod, translated by Joseph Kresh. Copyright 1948 by Schocken Books, Inc. Copyright renewed 1976 by Schocken Books, Inc. Reprinted by permission of Schocken Books, published by Pantheon Books, a division of Random House, Inc.

From *The Diaries of Franz Kafka 1914–1923,* edited by Max Brod, translated by Martin Greenberg, with the cooperation of Hannah Arendt. Copyright 1949 by Schocken Books, Inc. Copyright renewed 1977 by Schocken Books, Inc. Reprinted by permission of Schocken Books, published by Pantheon Books, a division of Random House, Inc.

From *Franz Kafka: A Biography,* by Max Brod, translated by G. Humphreys Roberts and Richard Winston. Copyright 1947, © 1960 by Schocken Books, Inc. Copyright renewed 1975, 1988 by Schocken Books, Inc. Reprinted by permission of Schocken Books, published by Pantheon Books, a division of Random House, Inc.

Finally: my agent, Melanie Jackson; my editor, John Herman; Cindy Spiegel.

Contents

Preface

Kafka in a bowler (in a photo from 1906) in his early to midtwenties: the face looks at and past us. It is both jaunty and death-oriented; it is Kafka already become Kafka. It encompasses the Kafka paradox, the Kafka irony, the Kafka enigma. It asks more questions than it answers. For no matter how much we analyze and interpret and relate, we get back to that look, that pose, that combination of passivity and will set into the face and body; a Chirico of a photograph, the abstraction having taken over the object.

What creates that sense we have of both victim and conqueror? For we must emphasize the conqueror as much as the victim. History has stressed far too much Kafka as the victim, the man seeking eternal punishment. This photograph suggests the victor, the affirmation of something — for Kafka did prevail, although dead at forty and uncertain to the end of his life that he had accomplished anything. Those piercing eyes are not those of a man about to be defeated, nor of a man about to cave in, no matter what the pressures and forces upon him. We recall Kafka, not his father; the father is remembered only as Kafka's father. We recall Kafka, not even Franz Josef, with whom he shared a name. For it is the age of Kafka, not the emperor's, which prevailed. And even though Prague in the Kafka years was an artistic center, busy assimilating European Modernism as it spread from Paris and Vienna, we remember Kafka, not Prague. We see both victor and victim in the Czech Jew whose face reflects the annihilation of Eastern Europe's Jews; and, further, we see a Czech Jew who was not much of a Jew and a Czech

who wrote, not in Czech, but in German, the language of Goethe and
Schiller.

What else does this photo tell us? Although Kafka is in his twenties
(born 1883), the face is not quite that of a young man. The debonair
bowler, slightly cocked, adds maturity to the youthful face; but there
is something else, and we return to the eyes. The gaze is merciless,
pitiless: it gives no ground to the camera. From Kafka's glare, we
would hardly recognize that his photo is part of a larger one, with a
waitress to his right and a collie dog between them. From Kafka's gaze,
he seems alone, although the collie is leaning against his arm and the
waitress is quite attractive. Kafka has taken over the photo because he
has no recognition of any other existence. There is the slightest smile
on his thin lips, but that does not draw us in. The piercing eyes do it,
the heavy line of eyebrows above, the line of the bowler above the eyebrows, as if completing them. The white areas of the face appear to
exist only to set off the black lines. The face, and hat, assume a series
of planes dominated by the eyes — a face on the verge of becoming a
cubist ensemble. The upturned collar and black tie, the overwhelming black suit, with one white hand protruding, suggest a funeral. Despite the force of will inherent in the gaze, Kafka here is a death
figure. Although he is a man who triumphed over death, in fact
limned its contours, the lawyer Kafka in this photo is already closing
in on his subject.

The greatness of Franz Kafka is that he forces us to rethink everything we may take for granted. And he forces us to do this in ways we
may find repugnant, unacceptable, and inflexible. He is our twentieth-
century poet of the nether regions, our usurper of the ordinary. He refuses to be Nietzsche's "last man," that person scurrying for safety
even as everything crumbles around him. Yet Kafka did live in a period
when everything was crumbling around him — not only politically and
socially, but artistically as well. Great artists appear at historical moments of radical transformation or profound transition, and Kafka was
blessed — cursed? — to arrive at just one of those periods in history
when momentous events would change Europe and, by implication,
America. Because he saw so clearly what was happening in his era —
radical change, war, a society set on self-destruction — he is often
viewed as our prophet of later years, as a man who foreshadows the
Holocaust and Europe's destruction. In his depictions of his time, however disguised in his quasi-mysterious, quasi-mythical fictions, he assimilated all destruction, all violence and brutality. He was concerned,
among many other things, with the passing of values; if that makes
him a prophet of the Holocaust, then so be it.

But Kafka's perceptions also make him timeless. There is no need
to project his work onto specific historical moments. Kafka is, in the
Emersonian sense, our "representative" author and man of the twen-

tieth century;* that in itself makes him a prophet of doom. He needed
only to observe.

Franz Kafka: Representative Man is a critical biography. But more
than that, it will extend the reach of Kafka beyond his life and works
into a discussion of this as a Kafkan century. Previous studies, like
Ernst Pawel's and Ronald Hayman's in English, have been biographical;
in German, they have been mainly analyses of the work alone. But
there is nothing in English (and little in any other language) which relates life and works, as in a critical biography, and which also attempts
to view Kafka as the representative writer of our century. Implicit in
this historical placement of Kafka are long segments on Prague, which
rivaled Vienna in many of its cultural phases. Kafka was set in a city
that was a cultural center around the turn of the century. We can cite a
few of his Prague contemporaries: Rilke, Werfel, Hašek, Čapek, the
painters Kupka and Kubin, the composers Dvořák, Smetana, Janáček,
and Suk; not to mention Freud's background in Moravia, Mahler's in
Bohemia. Einstein was a professor of physics at the German university
in Prague from 1911 to 1912.

Observing Kafka in Prague helps us to delineate the role of Jews in
Eastern Europe. We see Jewish culture caught between Germans and
Slavs; the role of the Jew as outsider in a Czech, anti-German, anti-Jewish nationalist movement; the German-speaking enclave, inhospitable
to Jews and yet often dominated by them. Kafka was always an anxious
figure in a large, ominous drama, assimilating the social and political
anxieties of the Austro-Hungarian Empire as it was already beginning
to disintegrate. But Kafka as Jew in alien territory is only part of an even
larger cultural drama: the identification of Jews with High Modernism,
with avant-gardes, with a progressivism in the arts that inevitably
clashed with nationalism, with political ideologies, and with right-
wing, fascistic movements. This study will describe history, biography,
and the larger culture — with Kafka as the centerpiece, not only of his
own drama but of a European tragi-comedy.

Although Kafka's Jewish birth in part segregated him from the ex-

---

*Where does woman fit into "representative man"? One of the elements that so defines
Kafka for the twentieth century is his paralleling of Freudian psychoanalysis, particularly
Freud's insight into the male fear of female sexuality. Kafka's numerous "bachelors"
live on the edge of such fear. Women are everywhere, even when they are revealed
traditionally as sexual playmates, servants, kitchen slaves, or mere "connectors" to
whatever men ultimately seek. They are the ever present "other" in Kafka's male-
dominant world. He rarely socially empowers them, unless as whorish creatures who
trade in sexuality, but he makes them a profound element of male life, even when
homoerotic themes are implied. The very fact of Kafka's dilemmas and problems with
women, as we see in chapter 9, suggests what a large role they played in his imaginative
life: as the mother who failed him, as the fiancée who could never meet his needs as a
writer, as the wife who failed to stand up to the patriarchal Hermann Kafka. Women
are agents and players often by the pressures they exert. To be a bachelor is to be reminded
of how the male has failed women, not the other way around.

periences of several famous literary contemporaries, he was clearly a pivotal figure in the Central European German tradition, which reached critical intensity at the turn of the twentieth century. Kafka's coevals included, among others, both Mann brothers, Thomas and Heinrich, Robert Musil, Hermann Hesse, Rilke, and Carl Jung, as well as Freud, Karl Kraus, and Hugo von Hofmannsthal — some of them slightly older. Kafka's almost exact contemporaries were Spengler, Heidegger, Wittgenstein, Otto Weininger, Arnold Zweig, Walter Benjamin, Franz Werfel, Karl Mannheim, Georg Lukács. Among composers and painters: Schoenberg, Mahler, Klimt, Schiele. Included here are the Prague group and those born in Bohemia (where Prague is located) and Moravia.

Like the French poets Charles Baudelaire and Arthur Rimbaud, Kafka turned himself into the embodiment of the avant-garde — not only his writing, but in curious ways himself. "I am a memory come alive" (from his diary) connects him to all the great literary avant-gardes of this century, from new ideologies in Bergson and Freud to new literary achievements in Proust and Joyce. In embodying the avant-garde, he created a seamlessness between the man and the work which we associate only with those willing to die for literature; those who were more than literary priests, but suicides of a sort. Unlike the French poets, Kafka did not use alcohol or drugs, but he nevertheless saw himself as a sacrifice. His response to food (his ability to starve himself) was analogous to their indulgence in artificial substances. While they indulged, he abstained; while they tried to kill pain artificially, he found ways to intensify it. While words and language were for him almost everything, it was also necessary for him to make himself so unacceptable to a normal or an ordinary world that only his writing could reveal what he was or express what he represented.

There are, indeed, several Kafkas, for he played many roles and was in his own eyes several people, perhaps even an imposter. There is the historical Kafka, born in Prague in 1883, dead near Vienna in 1924. There is the Kafka who kept a detailed diary beginning in 1910 and who created through it, as it were, a second Kafka: the man observing the writer, the writer observing the man. Then there is the Kafka whose lengthy letters to Felice Bauer and to other friends and relatives reshaped the historical Kafka, as he play-acted for them, taking on a large variety of roles, none of which he knew he could actually play. In these letters we have Kafka's autobiography, and in the large group to Felice we have a spiritualized journey that we might call "spiritual autobiography." There is, of course, the Kafka of his novels and short fictions, who appears to observe the entire course of the twentieth century. This is the Kafka who has, so ambiguously, entered literary history. There is, still further, the Kafka of the piercing eyes that were aware of the internal disaster of his condition as his body deteriorated from tuberculosis; and through those eyes a reflection of Europe burning itself up, as though caught by a gigantic disease. There are all these seemingly conflicting Kafkas, plus the man who worked well and efficiently, gaining frequent promotions, for an accident insurance firm, who suffered terrible digestive ailments and crippling headaches, who experienced most of his sexual release with prostitutes, who tried one bogus health cure after another, and who agonized through it all over every word he wrote.

Kafka is our poet of ordinary madness. He enters into the seams between the conscious and the unconscious; a cubist, an abstractionist, a surrealist, an expressionist, a turning and twisting realist. His resonances become ours, his reverberations those of the twentieth century. In becoming our representative man, he achieves that halfway space between sanity and insanity which is the twentieth-century experience. Yet like other great intuitive and descriptive writers, he tells us what we already know, however well we have disguised that knowledge. His parables and allegories confirm our sense of how life organizes itself and us. Kafka knew that individual free will, the bedrock of an egalitarian society, was an illusion we profoundly protect to preserve our sanity; just beyond, however, is uncertainty. He moves from one to the other as a man for whom boundaries do not exist. More than any other modern writer, he tests us against ourselves. He forces us to divide and subdivide, until, like so many of his characters, we have reshaped ourselves. His mode is transformational: man to insect, animal, other forms, always reductive. His method is to purify us, himself, others, even as he purifies fiction.

The epigraphs to most chapters are from the works of Rainer Maria Rilke, Prague's other renowned twentieth-century literary figure. Although superficially he and Kafka seem opposite, the linkage between them is Prague, a link so intense that, to my mind, Rilke's poetry casts significant light on Kafka. The sense of "absence" is notable in the two writers, but it is an absence intensified, paradoxically, by the very weight of the ancient city. Like Kafka, Rilke was striving both to define that absence and to escape the heaviness of Prague. If Kafka could have had a double, he would have been Rilke.

FRANZ KAFKA

What have I in common with Jews? I have hardly anything in common with myself and should stand very quietly in a corner, content that I can breathe.

— DIARIES: 1910–1913

Sisyphus was a bachelor.

— DIARIES: 1914–1923

Introduction

F OR KAFKA, writing was all, and he willingly experienced hell so that he could, in his fashion, write. He identified strongly with other priests of the imagination, singling out Flaubert, Grillparzer, Kleist, and Dostoevsky as fellow sufferers. Only the Russian married. The others sacrificed themselves. Kafka:

> My talent for portraying my dreamlike inner life has thrust all other matters into the background; my life has dwindled dreadfully, nor will it cease to dwindle. Nothing else will ever satisfy me. But the strength I can muster for that portrayal is not to be counted upon; perhaps it has already vanished forever. . . . Others waver too, but in lower regions, with greater strength; if they are in danger of falling, they are caught up by the kinsman who walks beside them for that very purpose. But I waver on the heights; it is not death, alas, but the eternal torments of dying.

Kafka recognized that he had to torture himself with his failure before he could achieve something valuable. Achievement depended on anguish, anxiety, almost on literal self-destruction. He needed uncertainty, that dip into the valley of doubt and hell, in order to emerge with renewed strength. He uses profoundly religious terms — the journey into the desert, the harrowing of hell, the descent into self, most of all the sense of death and renewal — to describe how he must do his writing. He must impose on himself severe and drastic limitations of self in order to give the self its compressed energy; the energy then emerges as words. He is all heights and depths, little or no middle ground where normal men can live with wives and children. His sole concession to that middle ground was his position with an accident insurance company in Prague; in all else, familial matters, personal relationships to women, even ordinary social intercourse, he held himself apart. He emphasized pain, inability, uncertainty, but did so to convince himself that while he was a failure as a man he was saving himself for a higher calling. The man who described himself as lacking all ego, self, character, even personality, possessed a mountainous sense of self, an enormous ego, a striking personality — except that he withheld it all from others in order to concentrate on what mattered most to him.

"Sisyphus was a bachelor." This was for Kafka the highest praise. The man who struggled to reach the heights only to be thrown down to the depths embodied all of Kafka's aspirations; and he remained himself, alone, solitary. Kafka reveled in his solitary passion, cherished those few moments or hours when he was at his desk in the middle of the night, his household and Prague itself silent. Here his desk became a throne, and his "dreamlike inner life" could come forth, like one of those complicated dreams analyzed by another citizen of the Dual Monarchy, Sigmund Freud. Kafka was incredibly tough — not at all the man who presented himself as weak, uncertain, torn by doubt. He had developed a tremendous defense mechanism to deal with his personal as well as racial, religious, and ethnic problems.

If we move, temporarily, to another Kafka photo, one he posed for in 1923–24, near the time of his death, we can see that he is now fully Kafka. At forty, the face says it all: the eyes more piercing than ever, the jug ears, the features more set as the result of age and illness. It is a fine Central European face, the head topped with a fullness of black, healthy-looking hair. But it indicates extreme stress; the Mona Lisa smile of the earlier bowler photo has given way to both defiance and resignation. The eyes denote defiance, of whatever illness and personal vision have wreaked on the man; but the mouth denotes resignation: a sense that the game is up, not only for the wasting body, but for all those, like him, who use themselves as bellwethers of their time and place.

This later Kafka photograph is a piece of history rather than a personal item. The polarization between rebellion, or defiance, and resignation makes it representative; it becomes the prototypical face of our time, the twentieth century's "look." If the hold of the eyes were broken, the face would be ready to decompose. Kafka here is abstracting himself from the very scene he is posing for, as though a character in *The Trial* or *The Castle*.

If we are sensitive to all the crosscurrents of his time, we can see in the photo a response to what it meant to grow up in Prague: a Jew in the German-speaking minority of Czech Prague — a minority within a minority. The face in the photo yearns to break into reality, which he can identify and identify with. The question is, What reality? Kafka was perfectly positioned for the question. The uncertainty he felt whenever he contemplated reality was matched by the uncertainty of the Jew in an enemy setting, among Germans, whose language he spoke, and among Czechs, whose nationalism had no role for the Jew to play. But as a Westernized Jew, Kafka had to deal with more than anti-Semitic Germans and anti-German, anti-Semitic Czech nationalists.

There were the Jews themselves. The question of assimilation — or, rather, the question of whether assimilation was even possible, given the prohibitions of the host countries in which Jews resided — created in itself an ambiguous kind of reality, often more hallucinatory than realistic. Kafka's "reality" was interlarded in the layers of German-speaking Jews who moved among the German-speaking population; but there was little connection to ethnic Germans except at the highest professional levels. This excluded the Kafkas, who as merchants were lower middle class. The majority of people were Czechs, who resented the Germans for taking over so many professional roles, but who felt particularly hostile to the Jews, who had the double disadvantage of speaking German and of being non-Christian. Within the Jewish community itself there were those who spoke no Czech; those who regarded themselves as Zionists (like Kafka's great friend Max Brod); those who regarded themselves as socialists (like Kafka in his earlier years) and were, therefore, hostile to Zionism; those who sought assimilation as good Germans within the Czech setting; and those who, like the elder Kafka, straddled the fence and sought assimilation, or at least acculturation, within both the German and Czech sectors of the city and country. But even here language betrayed Hermann Kafka and his wife, Julie, for they spoke a Yiddish-tinged German, a kind of loutish Prague German known disparagingly as *Mauscheldeutsch.*

The "reality," even apart from any personal problems, was hard to find for a sensitive child and young man. It meant the deciphering of several codes, all of which appeared to contradict each other. For the moment we are omitting the melange of cultural changes occurring in Prague as ideas flowed in from Paris and Vienna, as Prague became a meeting point of traditional art and Modernism. We see how Kafka attempted to adjust to shifting realities in his use of halves, of divisions of self into man and beast or man and insect, of bifurcations that always occur with doubles — two assistants, two guards, two pairs, two selves. In "The Metamorphosis," Kafka's most famous example of doubling or pairing, Gregor Samsa is both young man and insect, with the body of a vermin but the consciousness and responses of a human. Kafka does not lose the self or human consciousness in the insect or animal, whether vermin, mouse, or dog. The self or "I" absorbs the life of the "other," lives both inside and outside of it — as in the "I" and the vermin in "The Metamorphosis," or the "I" and dog in "Investigations of a Dog."

Such bifurcation of human and "other" is, of course, socially, politically, ideologically, even ethnically based. It can be directly attributed to Kafka's sense of himself, to his sense of the Jew, to his sense of Germanness in Prague, as he found himself split off in one area or another from what was mainstream or "normal." Another form of marginality comes in his use of language — the strangeness he feels in writing in German, which he feels can never be *his* language since it is the language of Goethe and Schiller. In one place he writes of how even the German word *Mutter* does not express adequately what he means by Mother, and yet it is the word he must use for lack of another. Language has alienated and excluded him from some deeper experience, and yet he has nothing but German if he wishes to write, since his Czech is poor and his Hebrew, until much later, is almost nonexistent.

In one brief piece, "The Cares [or Worries] of a Family Man," he takes on language directly, with the curious word *Odradek*.* The source of *Odradek*, the narrator explains, is a point of school debate, of either Slavonic or German origin; Kafka's point here is that, like something from Lewis Carroll, *Odradek* defies derivation. And if the word is itself incapable of definition — an encoded bit of language, but whose code? — its embodiment as a "creature called Odradek" suggests even greater ambiguity.

Odradek, as language, symbol, object, represents Kafka's ambiguous, layered, difficult reality. He lurks, not walks; he is covert, not exposed; he is neither Czech nor German, and not fully Jewish. Odradek laughs, but the sound comes from a space that seems to lack lungs, the noise like the rustling of falling leaves — the dry, hacking cough of someone suffering from failing lungs. Kafka questions Odradek and its function. The writer says he may die, but anything that dies has some function or aim, and Odradek seems to have none. The narrator asserts that Odradek might continue to outlive him, but if the thing does, then he finds it painful that anything will survive him. Odradek, then, becomes an emblem of Kafka's art, which he hoped — as he informed his friend Max Brod — would die with him, become the ashes that would match his dust.

The figure of the Odradek enters into Kafka's sense of himself as a purveyor of a particular kind of art and as a tainted individual (with dying lungs) who is attempting something that feeds only vanity. But Odradek's emblem of language and art goes even further, into a nightmare of realities for Kafka, his relationship to Judaism. The Odradek spool is star-shaped, and the way it stands recalls the Menorah, or some like symbol of Judaic faith; and if not precisely that, then the star that goes back to the dawn of the Christian era, to a primitive Judaism. This short piece in which Odradek functions has implications that reveal Kafka's uncertainty about reality in every area, including his uncertain relationship to language. For in inventing an emblem that is neither

*A company that manufactured motorbikes in Bohemia was named Odradek. For more on the name, see chapter 7.

Czech nor German nor completely Jewish, he has, in the object itself, revealed his divided self, his anxiety about what is real, what is not; and he has, apparently, demonstrated how distinct he is from the ordinary run of men even while he tries to represent their lives.

Still other literary devices reflect Kafka's uncertainties about what his reality is, or which reality he should connect himself to during a tumultuous era. He repeatedly presents characters who sympathize with their captors, whose lives would be empty without the potentiality of the tormentor. The animal in "The Burrow," for example, gains its entire identity from its need to protect itself from whatever or whoever is moving toward it, possibly to destroy it. Remove that other object — if it indeed exists — and the animal snug in its burrow loses all reason for existence. The struggle for survival gives it substance, even if the struggle has to be invented. Similarly, Kafka's other protagonists live empty lives until the threat of, or actual, torment begins; and that fills them. This may be, psychologically, the need of the classic masochist, but that somewhat facile description does not adequately describe Kafka's quest. Without denying a strong masochistic tendency in Kafka, a real searching out of pain and painful situations, one should see the embrace of torment as a way of grasping reality. It is a willed event as much as an uncontrollable condition. The pain exists somewhere, and by embracing it, letting it bite into one's skin, a protagonist discovers for that time and place how things work, what reality is. Kafka differs from other writers in his uninhibited opening up of himself to every kind of bedevilment; so that while masochism may appear the most obvious interpretation of his actions, in actuality he is trying to discover how the world works, how it organizes its experience, what pain-potential has accumulated. In that ruthless quest for reality, the self takes upon itself unimaginable degradations and tortures. Gregor Samsa, in "The Metamorphosis," has little life of his own as a dutiful son and brother until he is transformed into a bug — he then gains, at the expense of his life, attention and, in some perverse way, identity.

Implied in these covert, secretive, virtually hidden activities is a kind of sexuality that has no "normal" release. The implication is that nearly all of Kafka's representations of life have a sexual component that is self-serving — that is, masturbatory. The emblems of covertness as much as the symbols of torment, whether willing or uncontrollable, are all aspects of a sexuality that could only circle back upon itself: Gregor with the woman in the picture on the wall, the hunger artist achieving orgasm through starving himself, the officer-executioner achieving ecstasy only on the needles of the machine. Kafka's distancing of himself from others, his sense of his room as a haven during the quiet hours of the night, his abstracting of himself from social activities, his near hysteria about food, especially his "fletcherizing," or masticating his food to a pulp — all these elements contain a sexual reality that disallows union with another and favors the self as the love object. Although we do not wish unduly to indulge the term *narcissism*, there is an enormous potential for the narcissistic in Kafka; and the sexual component would be self-abuse based on the need for self-inflicted pain. If we take into account his fictional emblems, as well as his diary entries and letters, we find his search for reality, or realities, embraced a sexuality that could only take, not give.

Kafka embodied disorientation; we find it in his uncertainties, sense of ambiguities, anxieties about family, sex, even language. But then he needed some structural equivalents of such psychological states, and he created them in functionaries, warders, guards, companions, assistants, potential and real tormentors. All those external forces and threats were necessary, however, not to allow him to find a position within a disintegrating Austro-Hungarian Empire, but to justify his inability to secure a solid position. To justify what he was and how he was going to live within such a sense of personal exile — which he came to interpret as the human condition — he required literary artifacts, such as *The Trial* and *The Castle*, as well as the major shorter fiction.

Kafka was a man of perpetual paradox, and one paradox was that as a man personally exiled from himself, he had to find ways to justify that exile so that he could write about it with himself as perpetual victim. For him to cure himself of his personal exile would be for him to alienate himself from the single element that nourished him. Even as he turned food into thoughts of poison, became a picky eater, a masticator of food to such an extent that even close friends could not bear him at the table, even as he became a vegetarian and a proselytizer for vegetarianism and other experiments with nourishment, and tempted fate as a "hunger artist" himself — even as he did all these things, he could not let go. Kafka was fully entrapped, no less than the prisoner strapped to the machine, his body the recipient of needles that would imprint in his flesh his crime.

For Kafka, the world of ostensible realities was the "destructive element." Only art, his writing, could transform not the realities but his way of looking at them. "I forgot," he wrote in his diaries,

> and later purposely omitted — to add that the best things I have written have their basis in this capacity of mine to meet death with contentment. All these fine and very convincing passages always deal with the fact that someone is dying, that it is hard for him to do, that it seems unjust to him, or at least harsh, and the reader is moved by this, or at least should be. But for me, who believe that I shall be able to lie contentedly on my deathbed, such scenes are secretly a game; indeed, in the death enacted I rejoice in my own death.[1]

The ultimate reality for him, which art must metamorphose, is the individual's death.

Kafka's fictions all seem to be awakenings into an incomprehensible world, which he truly wants to understand if only he could identify it. It always resides just beyond him, whether it takes shape as the law, as a castle, as America, as family and married life, as ordinary existence full of trivialities like eating, sleeping, wearing suitable clothes. Everything in Kafka becomes invested with ceremonial, almost ritualistic, fervor because it seems so unreal; for even as he breaks through his dreamlike state, he is never certain he has emerged, that he is now immersed in reality. If only he could have been certain of the breakthrough then he could have found the balance that would have nourished the man but perhaps undermined the artist. Of immense significance in understanding how Kafka structured his life is seeing how he struggled to make sure no such balance could be accomplished.

Kafka had to establish barriers to any compromise between fantasy and reality because his art depended on his uncertainty — on his depiction of that uncertainty. The multiple realities of his life in Prague, of the larger society itself, proved so rewarding to the writer because they proved to him that any balance was impossible. Resolution, if achieved, would have meant the artist was no longer needed, although the man at some superficial level may have been comforted. We gain the sense that in the period just before his death Kafka was reaching toward that balance, so that reality no longer seemed so alien and diverse, so unachievable. But we could argue that if that had indeed occurred, and he had not died, then the artistic effort might have declined or been dissipated. More than any other major creative person of this century, Kafka depended on the maintenance of an imbalance. This does not mean he had to keep himself unhappy but that he had to resist all efforts to perceive reality as something final or fixed into which he could fit himself. He needed the uncertain and unidentifiable so that his art could reflect the haze.

On the personal front, Kafka identified his father, Hermann, as keeping him outside of mainstream family life. His famous *Letter to His Father* is a tale of exclusion. The large, dull man blocked the door, insisted on his own rules, broke them in front of his son, and became a major character in Kafka's perception of life in Prague. Hermann was to be joined by those doubles, warders, and assistants who appear as representative of the "system" that excludes the protagonist. Since the protagonist can never accommodate himself to the system, that shadowy array of guards will never let him in. They are themselves undefined, not because they are allegorical or symbolic but because they are emanations of the central figure's needs and fears. Kafka is always halving himself, into the observer and the participant. The observant half sees what is occurring but can do nothing to halt it; the participant accepts his fate because there is no alternative. In the two halves, one perhaps masochistic, the other sadistic, we have the Kafkaesque archetype.

* * *

Kafkaesque (or, occasionally, *Kafkan*) has entered the English language
as an adjective used so loosely and often without clear definition that,
like many such words derived from proper names, it has lost its impact.
If it means, literally, that which belongs to Franz Kafka or that which
identifies with him, then we are thrown back to beginnings. For what
does belong to Kafka or suggest his qualities? To discover what is Kafkaesque, we must return to who and what was Kafka. The present biography departs from all previous biographical efforts in its placement
of Kafka not only in his native Prague but in the movement called Modernism. In Modernism, there is an avant-garde, a military term that
Kafka might have himself found ironic, since he, at six feet tall and 115
pounds, tried unsuccessfully to enlist in the Austrian army to fight the
Italians and/or the French.

The avant-garde is the edge of Modernism, its most defiant and resolute phase, undercutting whatever came before and ultimately itself;
yet no avant-garde fails in time to be absorbed into mainstream Modernism. That Kafka, an avant-gardist, resisted such absorption for so
long — and continues to — is an indication of his originality and elu-
siveness. But a Modernist, avant-garde Kafka takes on full dimensions
only when we see him and such movements within the framework of
Prague, in its way a contributor to Modernism almost as forcefully as
Vienna, Paris, and Berlin. Prague has mistakenly been associated with
"Eastern Europe," although it is farther west than Vienna and is almost
on a line with Dresden, Germany, and Venice to the south. In its cultural response, it has definitely faced west, and even if we cite only
Kafka and Rilke, we could make a good case for the significance of the
Prague experience.

Except in the case of Paris, Modernism seemed to thrive in places
where there was considerable turbulence — the result of an empire
wavering, crumbling, collapsing. Even Paris, we can say, experienced
its fiercest show of Modernism only when France underwent the
trauma of defeat in the Franco-Prussian War of 1870–71 and during the
ideological turmoil brought on by the Dreyfus case in the 1890s which
divided the country almost in civil war. In the wake of turbulence
comes Modernism, and Kafka's Prague was surely caught in its own
forms of turbulence: a failing empire, a growing nationalism among
ethnic Czechs, a strange rearguard action by German-speaking Jews attempting to hang on to whatever they had, a divisiveness that ran
through every aspect of the Dual Monarchy — unsettled and uncertain
conditions that were perfect not only for Kafka but for his counterparts
in Vienna (Robert Musil) and in Paris (Marcel Proust).

One area in which Modernism reveled was in readjusting our perceptions of space and time, that confusion resulting from geographical
and historical dislocations of minorities living in an empire that tried
quite the opposite, to solidify or normalize ideas of time and space. People like the Kafka family were displaced persons of a sort, and while the

parents labored hard toward acculturation and even assimilation, those of the younger generation, like Kafka and one of his sisters, Ottla, made decisions of their own. By moving outside accepted normalizing ideas, Kafka wrenched himself into temporal and spatial dimensions that made no sense to his family or society. We are confronted by a situation not too different from that which occurred in many American immigrant families, where the children broke free of their parents, often choosing ways of expressing themselves that were considered anathema to the older generation. Just as Kafka's characters move in a temporal and spatial atmosphere that breaks all rules of "realism," so too did these children of immigrants rearrange their lives so as to seem strangers to their families. Kafka played it both ways, gaining a law degree, building a professional career with an insurance company, while hiding, more or less, his writing — most of all, hiding himself behind his writing, so that he became very clearly a split person. This mosaic of choices and events depleted him personally, and his subjective life became part of that confusion characteristic of the Austro-Hungarian Empire but at the same time accommodating to the seductiveness of Modernism. It is only in Kafka that we find the juncture of virtually every dimension of the twentieth century: where personal anxiety and guilt (whatever their derivation) can cross with what was happening to racial groups, ethnic forces, entire countries — that blending of the intimate life with the political and social world.

We cannot view Kafka as separate from Prague and from Modernism. He was responsible to a particular historical-geographical configuration as well as to a more general European movement. Even when aspects of Modernism failed to penetrate to Prague in their fullness of expression, the ferment of avant-gardes and of changes in the rules of art could not be ignored by the serious writer. So much of Kafka is a question of language and narrative, two areas that were, of course, revitalized by Modernism. Kafka had to create a language that worked for him, for he could not rely on the classic lines of Goethe, Schiller, or Heine, since he was not a German; he could not fall back on the German of Prague either, since it was contaminated by local usage. And the German of Prague Jews, like that which he heard in his home, had an overlay of Yiddish or Yiddish expressions. Within what was already a minority or regional language — Czech of course being the major one — Kafka had to achieve his own kind of German, a leaner, more streamlined language, an individualized form of expression.

In matters of narrative, also, Kafka had to follow a different drummer. The encroachment into everyday thought of developments in psychology and psychoanalysis — and Prague was not immune to what emanated from Vienna — was translated for the serious writer into narrative forms. Ideas could not become stories in the same way; and stories could not unfold without regard for the disorientation of time implied by psychoanalysis. What was once simply "storytelling" had now become a battleground where protagonists fought over how their tale should be related, what should be omitted, what sketched in, what left to the imagination. Silence itself struggled to be heard against words. Repeatedly in his diary entries Kafka writes of matters that impinge on narrative: how an undifferentiated mass of language, apparently emerging from what Freud labeled the unconscious, had to be contained so that it "bears its complete organization within itself even before it has been fully formed . . ."* In another place, he speaks of himself as being involved with radii and circles, as though such tools of measurement were matters of language and narrative means.

Whatever his struggles with language and narrative, like all great artists, Kafka forces us to see as he sees. We come to accept what may appear to us to be unacceptable. We embrace the impossible because he says it is possible. His dreams, however improbable, become probable. Having sunk himself into parables and allegories, Kafka is a visionary writer. He has created for us modes we ordinarily do not embrace or find comprehensible, and yet caught in his field of force we intuit our own parables and allegories. His friend Milena Jesenská, a Czech writer and translator in her early twenties (when Kafka was thirty-eight), perhaps understood him better than anyone else, even more thoroughly than Max Brod, Kafka's lifelong friend and biographer. Jesenská told Brod that the "thing that you call Frank's non-normality — just that is his greatest trait. . . . I rather think that all of us, each and every one of us, is sick and that he is the only well person."[2]

Milena understood that Kafka was making us see the world freshly — thus his "non-normality." Kafka was able to impose on us because he saw himself as possessing powers that came from mysterious, unfathomable places. He perceived himself not as Prometheus, bringing fire to man, but as a form of Satan, descending to darkness and returning with shaded messages. Writing like this was everything to him: "This descent to the powers of darkness," he wrote near the end of his life (July 4, 1922), "this unleashing of spiritual forces normally kept under restraint, the dubious embraces, and all the other things that doubtless occur down below and which we know nothing about up here when we write our stories in the sunshine." Writing is a form of "devil worship," a process of "diabolical nature."[3] That too is what Modernism is all about.

---

*In fact, Kafka and Freud make an uncanny parallel pairing, and not only because both came from nearby geographical areas and were as German-speaking Jews part of a minority culture. Both shared intense, often difficult, and anxiety-producing relationships with their respective fathers, ambivalent attitudes toward mothers who handed them over at an early age to Czech nurses, and conflicting relationships with their respective fiancées, in which control of the "other" was paramount. Both also shared an uncertain relationship to Judaism. See Marianne Krull, *Freud and His Father* (New York: Norton, 1986). Krull does not make the connection with Kafka, focusing instead solely on Freud and *his* father.

pal conflict was clearly a theme running through the lives of both Kafka and the young Rudolf. Rudolf, unable to kill Franz Josef and succeed him, killed himself in a displacement of son-father murder; Kafka, for his part, repeatedly destroyed a surrogate self in his work, where the father figure is almost always a crushing, authoritarian, physically imposing older man.

It is no coincidence that the Modernist avant-garde nature of much Viennese-Prague art and writing has its origin in the desire to kill or replace the father. The avant-garde, or radical innovation in the arts, exists in order to question authority, order, convention, tradition, and history — it exists by breaking out and breaking through, by undermining established value systems. When Rudolf killed himself at the Mayerling hunting lodge, he acted out a drama that Kafka, less than twenty-five years later, would write about in "The Judgment," "The Metamorphosis," *The Trial*, and, not least, in his letters to Felice Bauer.

The suicide pact — in which, ordinarily, the man kills the woman, as painlessly as possible with a gun or poison, and then himself — has a certain satisfactory neatness to it, as both Rudolf and Kafka, who toyed with fantasies of suicide during much of his adult life, recognized. Its striking, even Modernist, statement established that authority could be baffled and defeated. This hatred of authority in Franz Josef's kingdom killed not only his son. If we see the suicide pact as somehow son fighting father, then we can view the various nationalities fighting to break out of the Dual Monarchy as themselves in an oedipal struggle — to defy authority, kill Vienna-Budapest paternalism, assume their own identities as Serbs, Croats, Slovaks, Czechs, and others.

Rudolf and Kafka were distant and dissimilar, yet linked by historical and personal forces. What was to Rudolf the confusion of the Dual Monarchy based in Vienna was to Kafka the ambiguity of ghostly presences in Prague. Just outside the center of power, Rudolf could fantasize about what he would be if his father died and he gained control of the empire. As far from the center of power as an individual could be, Kafka saw not the reality but the ghosts of power. One is struck by the relative paucity of his comments in fictions and in letters on events such as the European power struggle, Czech nationalism, the course of World War I, the obvious growth of a violent anti-Semitism, the Russian Revolution, even the ferment of a High Modernist culture in the very empire that was disintegrating. Except for occasional remarks, Kafka seemed almost indifferent to these occurrences, yet through his vision he captured the historic moment in his work, creatively responding to every aspect of decline, disintegration, and artistic revival.

When Kafka was born in Prague on July 3, 1883, Paris, Vienna, Nietzsche, and Modernism were far from his heritage. His immediate

Nowhere, beloved, can world exist but within.
Life passes in transformation. And, ever diminishing,
vanishes what's outside. Where once was a lasting house,
up starts some invented structure across our vision, as fully
at home among concepts as though it still stood in a brain.

— RILKE, *DUINO*, 7TH ELEGY

ONE Prague and Vienna

JUST BEFORE JANUARY 30, 1889, when Kafka was almo
six, the son of Emperor Franz Josef — after whom Kaf
was named — killed his seventeen-year-old mistress and then hims
Crown Prince Rudolf, married to the daughter of Leopold II of Belgiu
was thirty, handsome, attractive to women, magnetic, and sophis
cated. He stood near the center of Austrian power, the heir apparent
an aging monarch, who was, unfortunately for his successor, to rule
another twenty-seven years. From the age of fifteen, Rudolf had be
aware of the decline of the Dual Monarchy, that conglomeration of i
tionalities, religions, squabbling sects, and rebellious factions, whi
had its capitals in Vienna and Budapest. It was an impossible allian
held together by the military and by the imperial reach of Franz Jo
himself, but Rudolf foresaw its demise forty years before it disin
grated. The crown prince saw himself as embodying the new, his fatl
the old. He perceived, even in his teens, that the monarchy needed
newal — "spiritual development," he called it. Rudolf viewed hims
as the creator of this united kingdom, and he spent the next deca
trying to gain technical knowledge, even as the wary Franz Josef m
neuvered him offstage politically.

Politically ambitious and sexually promiscuous, Rudolf was
many respects almost the exact opposite of Franz Kafka — Rudolf's
tive nature contrasts dramatically with that of the passive, private,
tensely introspective, body-hating apolitical writer. At the same tin
Kafka and Rudolf were also precise reflectors of each other, two ve
real sides of the Austro-Hungarian Empire (the Dual Monarchy). Oe

forebears on his paternal side were a peddler and a kosher butcher; his maternal side was more genteel — settled businessmen mainly in textiles, although Kafka's maternal grandfather did own a brewery. Kafka's father, Hermann, came to Prague from a small Bohemian village, Wossek, some sixty miles south of Prague, in the district of Písek. Julie Löwy, Kafka's mother, came from a larger town, Podiebrad, on the Elbe, some thirty miles east of Prague. Her own family came from Humpoletz, in eastern Bohemia.[1]

Both Hermann and Julie, although very different personalities, were to weigh heavily on Kafka's personal and professional life, and their own backgrounds are significant in understanding the way they would handle their oldest son. The marriage was, primarily, between opposite types: Hermann, rough and ready, unable to admit being wrong, assertive, physical, although at heart something of a weakling; Julie, far more sedate, from a much more assimilated background, passive, inclined to obedience and duty to others. With her own mother dead at an early age, Julie became the "mother" in the house; further, as the sole woman serving her father and five younger brothers from her father's two marriages, she learned early on how to be a slave to men's wishes. Although pleasant looking and bright, she had little opportunity to develop personally, since her role demanded service, not independence. When Julie married Hermann Kafka, she simply extended her role to that of serving another demanding man.

Although Kafka speaks more often of his father than of his mother, and the famous 1919 *Letter to His Father* suggests that his lifelong battle was with the paternal side, we must not neglect Julie's influence. While on the surface, Kafka deeply loved and respected his mother, in the underlay of his fiction, letters, and diaries he revealed another side, based on resentment and antagonism; as he perceived it, Julie had deserted him in favor of his father. His words in fact often seem those of an abandoned child. Though Julie was gentle, just, and understanding, Kafka's relationship to her was full of hostile undercurrents. Many of the Medea and Medusa-like women he depicts in his fiction are extremely angry characterizations of Julie: not because she was a Medea but because she threw him to his father as bait in a classic family struggle. The passive mother and crafty, aggressive father in "The Metamorphosis," while not precisely a portrait of Julie and Hermann Kafka, do reflect to some extent the parental role as Kafka perceived it. In choosing Hermann in marriage, Julie not only duplicated what she had known with her five brothers and father but intensified her need for duty and obedience.

At the time Kafka was born, Prague contained about 170,000 people within its proper limits, about 300,000 if one included the sizable military presence and the (ever expanding) suburbs. Only Vienna and Budapest exceeded Prague within the Austro-Hungarian Empire; but it was in a sense odd man out in the so-called Dual Monarchy of Vienna and Budapest. The third largest city, compared with the other capitals, was incorrectly considered a backwater, and despite its size it had little pull or power within the empire. In religious-ethnic terms, the city was almost 90 percent Catholic, the other 10 percent mainly Jewish, with a small percent Protestant.* The latter were apparently not a factor in the life of the city, but the almost 10 percent Jewish minority, most of it German speaking, was considered a problem, a thorn in the side of Prague, and later something to be eliminated. With over 80 percent of the population Czech speaking, there was, besides the Jews, only a small minority who held to the official mother tongue of the empire. Everything was slightly out of kilter: the Jews were marginal in social terms and in addition spoke the language of those whom the Czech nationalists opposed. Yet — and here we observe some of the reasons for the irrational hatred directed at them and the German minority as a whole — Germans controlled much of the establishment and most of the media, as well as two German-language theaters, two technical high schools, Charles University, a technical college, two daily newspapers, and numerous weeklies and monthlies — in all, a disproportionate share of the upper-echelon life of the city. Furthermore, there were 3 million German Christians living, in resentment, on the borders of Bohemia and Moravia (the part of the country to the east of Prague and Bohemia), in Sudetenland. It was this area that Adolf Hitler would reclaim. But well before Hitler, the German-speaking Sudetenland was a source of conflict, for despite its language the area was considered part of Bohemia, even while its population was despised.

Within the German-speaking parts of Prague, Jews were themselves disproportionately represented. Czech or Bohemian allegiances were not attributed to Jews, and in truth they looked elsewhere for their rights, to Franz Josef in Vienna, whose attitudes had been tolerant (although he was personally anti-Semitic), and beyond him to Prussia's Bismarck, another anti-Semite with relatively tolerant policies toward Jews. The main problem for the German-speaking Jews was the question of assimilation when they were alien to the dominant language spoken in the country. In Poland, for example, assimilation was almost

---

*Prague Jews numbered a little over 26,000 (in 1900), most of them German speaking, although some, like Kafka's father, had sufficient Czech to handle business matters. The entire German-speaking population numbered about 60,000–70,000, making Jews somewhat more than one-third of the German-language minority. The total population of Prague, including the German-speaking population, was about 440,000. In fractional terms, Jews made up less than 6–7 percent of Prague's citizens, Germans, including Jews, about 15 percent. Since the city's expansion continued throughout Kafka's life, the Czech majority increased considerably in relation to both Germans and Jews. Numbers, incidentally, differ from one set of statistics to another. William O. McCagg, Jr., for example, in his *A History of Habsburg Jews: 1670–1918* (Bloomington: Indiana University Press, 1989), cites different figures: by his account, Prague Jews in 1900 numbered 19,000, with a total population in the city of 514,000, so that Jews formed slightly under 4 percent of the total. Jews overall in Bohemia numbered 92,000, as against 147,000 in Vienna alone.

out of the question, even when Jews spoke Polish and not Yiddish; Polish Jews therefore made little effort to assimilate. In Prague, however, assimilationist movements were quite strong and very much opposed to Theodor Herzl's Zionism. Hermann Kafka, who spoke both Czech and German, straddled what seemed to be a volatile political and social situation in Prague. He worked both sides of the street, going easy on his Jewishness, speaking Czech in his business, and moving toward a kind of no man's land in terms of ethnic and religious identification. There was in the Kafka household a definite loss of Jewish rituals, and, except for a few festive occasions, on the high holidays, Hermann seemed indifferent to Judaism as a system of beliefs.

While unacceptable in the Czech community, the Kafkas did not enter deeply into the Jewish community. They remained marginal to both, and Kafka always lamented the fact that he had been denied an anchor in any culture or ethnicity. His cry that he was an acculturated, assimilated Westernized Jew was a cry of deracination, or marginality, of a kind of isolation that began well before he was born and would control his direction.

For Kafka, Eastern European Jews, whatever else, had their faith, blind though it might be, and an easiness in their Jewish identification. They represented for him an ideal family life that Hermann and Julie were incapable of providing. Jews were pushed to the cultural margins not only by Czech nationalists but also by German Gentiles, and more generally by the hatred generated in the monarchy, despite Franz Josef.

None of this would become apparent to Kafka until he was a schoolboy. The more immediate situation was his inheritance, a marriage of opposites. Hermann Kafka's father, Jakob, was a large, powerful butcher, his wife, as dutiful as would be Hermann's Julie. Hermann was one of six children, four sons, two daughters, living in a small house with a thatched roof in a German-speaking *shtetl*, or Jewish enclave, characteristic of hundreds or thousands that existed deep within Eastern Europe or as part of the Austro-Hungarian Empire. In the empire, Jews had to decide whether to assimilate or struggle against assimilation, or else to commit themselves to Enlightenment ideas, the so-called Haskalah. The Haskalah was a late eighteenth-century radical development in Jewish thought, in which Jews attempted to enter the then modern world — that is, to shift from an isolated way of life, shunned by every government under which they lived, to a more central philosophical idea. The *maskilim*, or followers of the Enlightenment, sought to break the hold of Orthodoxy and its practice, and lead Jews into more mainstream European life. The struggle between Haskalah and Orthodoxy was, of course, bitter, and it not only split the *shtetl*, it split families; it was a kind of Jewish civil war, based on ideology, assimilation, or, at least, liberation from ancient practices that had become, for many, remote.

Within the Austro-Hungarian Empire, Galicia — where Jacob

Freud came from — was a center of the Enlightenment; and Hermann Kafka's own shtetl, while not a center of anything, was not immune to the influx of ideas that were half a century old when Hermann was born in 1852. The Enlightenment owed a great deal to the Napoleonic Code, which, while not actually favoring Jews, helped open up society for all minorities. But the European-wide revolutions of 1848, removing many of the restrictions on Jews, brought the Enlightenment-Orthodox struggle to a head, just in time for Hermann Kafka. Nearly half a million Jews benefited from the granting of citizenship rights, and this, obviously, reinforced Enlightenment ideas and weakened more traditional ones. With freedom to move around within the Habsburg Empire, with restrictions on marriage, family, and jobs stripped away, Jews began to relocate into larger cities as soon as they were able to gather their goods and leave. With their economic situation improved, they were less likely to retain much affection for the hard life of the shtetl.

A further reason for the exodus of Jews to larger cities, when not prohibited — and in the Dual Monarchy, laws directed specifically against Jews were being eased — was that anti-Semitism in small villages could be more virulent than in larger, more cosmopolitan areas. As Czech nationalism grew, fueled by Austrian anti-Semitism, in the early 1880s, life for Jews became safer in the cities, since peasants and the lower middle class in rural areas increasingly saw German-speaking Jews as the visible cause of their own downtroddenness.

Already clear in much of the Dual Monarchy when Hermann Kafka migrated from Wossek to Prague — and his siblings to other less grand cities — was the sense that even if Jews converted, they could not be absorbed. Even when Austria, through Joseph II's Edict of Tolerance in 1782, gave Jews the right to become naturalized citizens, in practice they had to become acculturated to the larger society; what seemed in 1782 to be a progressive law turned out to be far less progressive than legislation in France, Holland, Prussia, and other German states. In effect, even before the beginning of official Austrian anti-Semitism, with von Schönerer in 1882, Jews in the Dual Monarchy were caught in an ambiguous situation. The seeming way out, well before Jakob Kafka's death in 1899, was movement to those larger cities where the mix of people was greater and, so it was hoped, Jews might be able to assimilate on the surface while in other respects retaining their identity.*

Kafka's grandfather, Jakob, one of nine children, and Hermann, one

---

*Because Kafka's own life was intimately wrapped up in his parents' response to their backgrounds, his sophisticated adaptation to Prague must be measured against this relationship to his forebears' strivings. For Kafka remained friendly with his uncle Ludwig, also a merchant, who shared a common professional interest as an insurance agent; his daughter, Irma, worked for a time in Hermann Kafka's Prague shop and maintained a close friendship with Kafka's youngest sister, Ottla. Kafka also kept up ties with another of Hermann's brothers, Filip, and his wife, Klara, who, together with their children, ended up playing roles in *Amerika*, Kafka's first extended fiction.

of six, were both of generations raised under extremely difficult conditions. Furthermore, Jakob, born in 1814, was restricted by a law reminiscent of the bans placed on American black slaves: as the second-oldest child in his family, he was not permitted to marry. Jews were restricted in marriage in order to hold down the size of their families, and it was not until the revolution of 1848, which abrogated the limitations of the 1789 law, that all Jews, not only the eldest, could marry as they wished. At thirty-four, Jakob married Franziska Platowski, daughter of his next-door neighbor. Jakob was the prototypical Kafka family male: burly, extremely strong and physical, and outgoing. His wife, already thirty-three, proceeded to bear six children between 1850 and 1859, all of whom, remarkably, lived. Not of the lowest rank within the social and economic delineations of the shtetl but part of the *prosteh yid* class (simply dressed Jew), the Kafkas made do, but with tremendous struggle. Hermann was destined to be virtually a beast of burden, leaving home at the age of fourteen to peddle, since the entire family lived in a one-room shack, often with little to eat except potatoes or bread.*

Though Franz Kafka was born into much better circumstances in a sophisticated Prague, his family history actually reverberated throughout his life. Hermann would never have become an anorexic, not when food was so difficult to obtain; yet his son, with plenty until the years after World War I, turned food into an enemy and a shield against his family. Hermann, like his siblings, worked as a child, delivering meat to customers or doing other jobs. This was the hard existence of poverty-level village life: the cold, the lack of food, the physical discomfort, the absence of privacy, the roughness of a childhood the wounds of which remained forever. It was this hardship that shaped Hermann, and he held it up as a reproach to his weak, seemingly passive, dreamy son.

The name *Kafka* (or *kavka*, which is Czech for jackdaw, a kind of crow) is not an uncommon Czech surname. As several commentators have pointed out, its pronunciation could have evolved from the Yiddish diminutive for Jacob. If naming is destiny, then Kafka would have preferred *Kavka*, a bird, since the writer was drawn to presenting himself if not as a bird then as a small animal. By an act in 1787 intended to force Jews to assimilate, most Jews had to adopt German surnames. The Kafkas, however, kept their name and thus, by Hermann's time, remained rooted in both Czech and German, speaking Czech at home, but giving their children a German-language education, as mandated by the laws of the empire. Hermann had sufficient education, until four-

---

*Not all of Kafka's ancestors led such brutish lives, however. His maternal grandfather, Amschel (Adam) — after whom Kafka was originally named in Hebrew — was a Talmudic scholar, a rabbi who was deemed saintly. Unfortunately, except for his daughter Esther, who married Jakob Löwy, his family had a bad end: his wife committed suicide and one son, Nathan, was mad. Even Esther had a brief life, dying at twenty-nine.

teen, to master spoken German, although he preferred Czech. His son
was completely Germanized, although he could read and speak Czech.
The two languages, while useful for dealing with local matters, proved
divisive. Instead of creating dual allegiances, as the Dual Monarchy intended, they created fluctuating identities based from infancy on language usage. Hermann was not bothered by this conflict and in fact
gained in his business dealings through his ability to buy and sell in
Czech. And at one time, when a local nationalistic uprising led to the
Czechs' smashing of Jewish stores, Hermann's was spared because he
knew the language.

But for the son — the only one of the entire clan since his maternal
grandfather to show any literary or intellectual tendencies — the dual
languages came to mean he truly possessed none. When he started to
keep a diary, in 1910, Kafka repeatedly entered complaints against the
German language. The German of Berlin and even Vienna was not his,
could not be his, since his German was tainted by Czech and local
Prague usage, even by Yiddishisms. Kafka did not possess a pure language; and when he began to respond to Modernist ideas filtering in
from other German-speaking areas, he found himself in a strange situation: responding to the ideas, the theories, the leaps in imagination
that Modernism insisted upon, but forced to do so in a language
whose impurities and even inappropriateness he was aware of.*

The young Kafka heard endlessly about the struggles, hardships,
discomforts, uncertainties, and physical deprivations of his father's
youth. As a traveling salesman, Hermann built up his knowledge of
trade, peddling throughout Bohemia and Moravia. He then completed
his army duty, spending three years in the Austrian army where he rose
to the rank of *Zugführer*, or sergeant, in charge of a platoon. He remained a lifelong military patriot. In everything he touched — goods to
sell, the army, then marriage — Hermann moved slowly up the social
and economic scale, seemingly impervious to the blows of fortune to
which a Jew was subject. He was fortunate enough to be born after the
revolution of 1848, which removed some of the restrictions on Jews,
just as earlier, the French Revolution had taken a more kindly attitude
toward the Jewish populations of Europe. The new laws allowed Hermann to move from his village to Prague, where he lived in the Josefstadt, part of Prague's Jewish quarter, whose history, going back to
medieval days, could not disguise the fact that it had fallen on hard
times: it included a series of brothels, taverns, and sleazy joints.† For

---

*Still later, when he carried on his lengthy correspondence with Felice Bauer, his Berlin
fiancée, he found her amused at, and often correcting, his Prague German usage.
†Virtually all of this district was razed to make way for urban renewal by the turn of
the century. The new houses, with art deco overtones, were very much in the late empire
style, and several magnificent streets of apartment houses were created in modern Prague.
The most striking part of the old "Jewish Town" that still remains is the old Jewish
cemetery, with its layering of graves and its Mondrian-like gravestones. If we keep in
mind Kafka's later preoccupations, some of the houses' names in the labyrinthine Jo-

Hermann, however, it was a first step into opportunity. There he met Julie, and they married on September 3, 1882; he was thirty and Julie was twenty-six. Shortly afterward Hermann established a *Galanterie-warenhandlung*, a store for "gallants" featuring parasols, walking sticks, and articles of clothing. It was a fashionable store and represented quite a step up from peddling. He catered to customers a cut above peasants, lower-middle to middle-class Czechs, including Jews who were themselves climbing the economic ladder.

The couple went to live in a small apartment in the building At the Tower (Haus am Turm), at the corner of Maisel and Carp streets in Josefstadt in the old city — all of which is no longer in existence.* The large At the Tower had several functions before it was turned into small apartments (which in the United States would be called tenements). The building itself had a kind of historic location, forming the outermost part of the ghetto or Jewish Town, backing the Russian Orthodox Saint Nicholas Church, and facing a complex of brothels and bars, stretching out toward alien Christian Prague.

In marrying Julie Löwy, Hermann joined with someone considerably above him in social standing. Her family was prosperous, her father a dry goods merchant and owner of a brewery, and she was brought up in some expectation. Before her marriage, in fact, she lived in the Smetana House, in the Altstädter Ring. Julie and two brothers were born to their father Jakob's first wife, Esther Porias. After Esther's death, when Julie was three, Jakob Löwy married Julie Heller from Postelberg and had three more sons, all of whom, in effect, Julie raised. Her brothers were an unusual bunch: only two married, one converted to Christianity, another was considered a dark sheep. Siegfried, the youngest, was sufficiently strange to be Kafka's favorite. He was a bachelor, and his lifestyle as a country doctor caught Kafka's imagination — and there was a good deal of the uncle in the nephew, in their reclusiveness and insistence on a secret life. The oldest was Alfred, also a bachelor, who became director of several small railways in Spain, a post of considerable prestige; Joseph, also from the first marriage, founded and ran a colonial trading corporation in Paris; Rudolf, the middle son of the second marriage, converted to Christianity and remained an accountant in a Prague brewery; and Richard, the oldest of the second marriage, lived in Prague as a clerk. It was a mixed lot, but most significantly, all went their ways, and only two thought enough of family life to marry.

Julie's "slavery," since she was the sole female child in a family of

---

sefstadt seem quite ominous: "Death," "The Mouse Hole," and "The Left Glove" are not unrepresentative. Kafka described this now vanished world to Gustav Janouch, stressing the dark corners and secret alleys and emphasizing that the old Jewish town was far more ramshackle than the sanitized new area.

*Soon after the Kafkas moved out, the area was condemned, to be razed by the turn of the century.

two brothers and three half-brothers, as we have observed, would be replicated in her marriage to Hermann Kafka. In many respects, she merely exchanged men, for the role remained the same: she worked all day in Hermann's shop, cared for the family, and then played cards with her husband late into the night. She had little time for herself and, as we shall see, little time for Kafka — or so he felt. Kafka's attitudes not only toward women but also toward life in part derive from what he perceived Julie might have been under different circumstances — that is, with a different husband. Kafka's relationship to Hermann was oedipal in the classic sense — a wish to replace the father in the mother's affections — or counter-oedipal — a desire to seize the father from the mother. But even more complicating factors were at work, some of which helped turn Kafka into the kind of rebellious writer he became.

In more personal terms, while Kafka may have fantasized about replacing Hermann in Julie's affections (not an unusual dream for the oldest and only son), he also felt Julie had failed him, that she was an inadequate mother who had abandoned him to nurses, maids, and cooks. Kafka's intense desire to gain his mother's attention and affection was further complicated by his dislike of the fact that she was at Hermann's beck and call during the day and night. These hostile feelings carried over into Kafka's sexual attitudes, and, as is evident in his *Letter to His Father*, he found the idea of Julie going to bed with Hermann personally repellent. Clearly he was revolted by Julie's acquiescence to what he perceived as Hermann's animality. And he was repelled by Julie herself. There seems little doubt that Kafka's extremely troubling, minimalist sexual life evolved at least in part from his attitudes toward Julie and the role she had been conditioned to play first among brothers and then with a husband.

Now married, in 1882 Hermann Kafka was part of that large, upwardly mobile lower middle class — both Czech and German-Jewish — which was emerging in Prague (as well as in Vienna and to some extent in Budapest). When Kafka was born on July 2, 1883, the first of six children born to Hermann and Julie, the family was on the verge of the first of many moves, to new neighborhoods and to new store sites.

After two and a half years in the Tower building, the family moved to a better neighborhood, in Wenceslas Square, right at the heart of Prague life. Nowhere more than in Wenceslas Square, where Kafka spent only seven months, from May to December 1885, was the split between old Prague and newer Prague more visible. The square is dominated by the Wenceslas Monument: the figure of Václav Wenceslas, duke of Bohemia in the tenth century, on horseback. Wenceslas was a legendary figure, murdered by his brother Boleslav, then canonized as the patron saint of Bohemia, and honored thereafter as a martyr. The statue of the mounted duke is surrounded by four other figures, also patron saints, including Wenceslas's grandmother and the wife of the first duke of Bohemia to be baptized, who had been murdered by pagans opposed to her Christian beliefs. Located more or less in the center of Prague, the entire square (which is about the length of seven and a half football fields and one and a half fields wide) is a tribute to nationalistic fervor.

In the next three years the Kafkas moved to Geistgasse ("Ghost Street"), to Niklasstrasse, to 2 Zeltnerstrasse (now Celetná), near Hermann's store at Number 12 in 1888, and, finally, to larger quarters in a house called Minuta on Old Town Square in June 1889, where they remained for seven years. Hermann was desperately trying to raise himself and his rapidly growing family into respectability.

This upward striving turned the Kafka household into nightmarish uncertainty for the eldest son, and much of his fiction can be viewed as part of a rebellion against everything Hermann tried to stand for socially. Part of an upwardly mobile class, Sigmund Freud in Vienna was a parallel case: his family's frequent moves, first from Freiberg (Příbor) in northwest Moravia to Vienna, and then to several locations in Vienna itself, led Freud to experience the uncertainty and insecurity of not knowing where he would be the next year or even the next month. Freud assimilated bourgeois values and at the same time tried to subvert them, conceiving of every possible way to undermine comfort and create uncertainty. Little is more antibourgeois than his concept of the rambunctious, uncontrollable unconscious, impenetrable except through tunneling back into deepest memory.

But more than the antibourgeois feelings Kafka shared with many of his contemporaries was his sense that he was so divided because he came from such a mismatched couple: Julie's passive, deferential behavior, without any commitment to personal fulfillment, intermixed with Hermann's almost demonic drive toward getting on, moving along, working himself into a frenzy of anxiety, with not a little touch of the bully and the sadist.

These prosperous years also brought with them the deaths of Kafka's two small brothers and the births in rapid succession of three sisters: Gabriele, or Elli; Valerie, or Valli; and Ottilie, or Ottla. It is difficult to determine what the deaths of two siblings meant to Kafka and how they affected Hermann's and Julie's treatment of him. When Kafka was just past two, in September 1885, a brother, Georg, was born. He died of measles just before Kafka turned four, in the spring of 1887. When Kafka was just past four, Heinrich was born, in September 1887. He died, of otitis, when Kafka was just short of his fifth birthday, in April 1888. Before he was five, Kafka was faced with the arrival of competitive brothers, and then with their inexplicable deaths — deaths that he later told Felice Bauer were the result of medical incompetence. He became acquainted not only with death at a very early age but also, possibly, with the desire for the death of brothers who stole Julie's attention from him.

Family events were surely not the sole elements shaping Kafka, but his family's complications occurred early enough to have a distinctive and formative effect. We do know that Kafka complained bitterly to Felice Bauer that he was abandoned to the care of cooks, maids, "aging nannies," "morose governesses," and others; and this lack of attention on Julie's part must have begun to register on her oldest son's sensibilities at the time his brothers were dying. The unconscious here, however, is more significant than the conscious: the oldest child wishes to monopolize parental attention, and the advent of a sibling gives rise to survival instincts that cause him to wish the sibling out of the way.* Kafka went through two complete cycles of this condition. After the first, he must have wondered what would happen if he wished the second brother away. And when that brother died, Kafka must have felt, along with enormous guilt, powerful, indeed possessed of magic.

The "disappearance" of two brothers at such an early age, in the perception of someone not much older than the dead boys, would seem to point to some mysterious, irrational element in the world. The mysterious force would appear to function without regard for human invention. It seemed to be part of something that existed beyond individual control, and it operated — like Thomas Hardy's Immanent Will — as neither malevolent nor benevolent but *there*, outside of human reason. Such a perception on the young Kafka's part would be fine training for the future writer of *The Trial* or "The Metamorphosis."

Surrounded by threatening figures — the parents themselves, then a Czech-speaking nanny named Marie Werner ("Miss"), followed by the two brothers — Kafka turned "artist" early on in order to manage them, through disappearance and transformation.† He always held a hard, unforgiving view of his childhood, not at all tinged with nostalgia or pleasure, as though childhood were an obstacle course full of personal traps. He made it through, survived whatever they could do to him — diaries and *Letter to His Father* pinpoint his perception of that.

---

*Like Kafka, Freud was caught in a web of deaths at a time in his childhood when he was unable to understand his feelings and felt antagonism toward a young sibling. He then experienced guilt when the sibling, also a brother, born when Freud was seventeen months, died six months later. And like Kafka, Freud then had further competition with a rapid succession of siblings: a sister Anna, whom he resented, three more sisters, and then a brother, all by the time Freud was ten years old. Many years afterward, Freud commented: "I can only say ... that I welcomed my one-year-old brother (who died within a few months) with ill wishes and real infantile jealousy, and that his death left the germ of guilt in me." (Marianne Krull, *Freud and His Father* [New York: Norton, 1986], p. 135).

†In his *Letters to a Young Poet*, Rilke writes of how transformation occurs, how the artist creates himself: "It is so important to be lonely and attentive when one is sad: because the apparently uneventful and stark moment at which our future sets foot in us is so much closer to life than that other noisy and fortuitous point of time at which it happens to us as if from outside. The more still, more patient and more open we are when we are sad, so much the deeper and so much the more unswerving does the new go into us, so much the better do we make it ours, so much the more will it be *our* destiny."

We can say with some assurance that Kafka's perceptions of himself and his world were an outgrowth of the traumatic deaths of Georg and Heinrich, although we could not have predicted precisely what turns that perception and world would have taken. Kafka made himself smaller and smaller, until, like the mouse, bug, mole, dog of his fiction, he became part of a miniature world, different from that of other people.

For Kafka, the center of his world was Prague. But for the artist in him Vienna was almost as important: not the Vienna of his namesake Franz Josef, or the now dead Rudolf and his mother Elizabeth, or the soon-to-die Franz Ferdinand, but the Vienna of such cultural giants as Freud, Musil, Klimt, Wittgenstein, Weininger, Kraus, Schiele, Schoenberg, and Mahler. For Kafka was like a gigantic vacuum, gathering in the methods of others and transforming them through his own unique experience. Kafka assimilated the use of memory associated with Proust and later with Broch into his own sense of time; his Joseph K. and K., or even his Gregor Samsa, are found in the Musil method of viewing the Dual Monarchy through the eyes of a man without qualities; Freud's theories of the oedipal conflict, childhood sexuality, and sub- and unconscious, among others, were ripe ideas for Kafka.

His angles of perception distanced him from some of his closest friends in the Prague Circle, such as Franz Werfel and his future biographer Max Brod. Werfel and Brod remained unrelentingly object-oriented, whereas Kafka from his earliest writings moved toward abstraction as the crux of his paradoxes and ambiguities. Kafka, with his fierce internality, was an abstractionist both by temperament and development.

Prague's artistic circles were receptive to abstraction. We need only to note František Kupka's "Vertical Planes III," from 1912–1913, to see cubism moving toward an almost Mondrian-like geometricality. Although Kafka did not see this particular painting, it reveals how Modernist ideas had burst across Europe, reaching Prague with only a year or two lag behind Paris. The painting by Kupka, surely Czechoslovakia's finest Modernist, although by no means its only one (Kubišta and Beneš are others), not only foreruns Mondrian but also Rothko.

Kafka must be seen against the background of this and other Modernist ferment, since so much in his writing depends on his break from realism. He has often been linked to expressionism or "heightened realism," but those tags obfuscate Kafka's real effort: his denial of objects (which is not intrinsic to expressionism) and his dependence on a personal reshaping of things.*

Like Joseph Conrad's checkered history, Kafka's background im-

---

*Not the least of the seventeenth-century Golem, born in the old-new synagogue, whose presence in Kafka's writings comes in several shapes, most noticeably in Gregor Samsa and in the strange creature Odradek.

mediately distinguished him from writers born in England, France, the United States, and Russia. Kafka came from Bohemia, a region that was not a distinct national entity, a part of the Austro-Hungarian Empire, ruled from Vienna by the Habsburg dynasty. Though not a backwater, Prague was not as yet a major player in the Austro-Hungarian political power game. Nevertheless, the city was seething with discontent and nationalistic rancor. As a Jew and as a German-speaking Czech, Kafka was a marginal figure in the intense nationalism gripping Czechs.

Kafka came to his perceptions from a distinctly underclass struggle to reach into the middle class. Just the fact that by the time he was six years old he had lived in half a dozen Prague neighborhoods indicates the frantic scurrying of the Kafka family for social position. Both from the wrong class and as Jews, the Kafkas were almost certainly excluded from the mandarin class, an upper bourgeois tradition based on higher education rather than on heredity, whose men became government officials, professors, doctors, lawyers, ministers, and directors of companies.* In many respects, Kafka had to assimilate the values of the mandarinate without ever becoming part of it, despite his official's status in the insurance company. This inability to belong, and yet being positioned so that he was expected to, caused Kafka to fall through the seams of a society that was itself dissolving. The dissolution, furthermore, was not only political and social but cultural — since avant-garde art dissolves history so as to reshape it in a constantly shifting process.

It is tempting to compare Kafka's situation to that of Robert Musil in Austria. Both men, born only three years apart, were writing about "men without qualities," faceless, weightless, dimensionless figures in a dissolving, fragmenting society and empire. But because of his firm position within this society, Musil could project his vision outward. Kafka, with his fragile foothold, turned inward. Not only was Musil's family part of the mandarin serving class, with its solid historical and cultural context, but Musil was writing in a language that belonged to him. Kafka, on the other hand, was writing in the language of the alien, the Jew writing in a German tinged by Prague and Yiddish usage during successive waves of Czech nationalism, with its anti-German and markedly anti-Semitic feeling. The coordinates for Franz Kafka's world were always shifting; yet even when they appeared to hold still, they were vague, ironic, and contradictory. It was this very internality that Kafka turned into the contours of the twentieth century.

For Kafka, as well as for his most avant-garde contemporaries, it was necessary to get outside of history so as to recreate it anew. And just as history was a restricting model, so was his immediate family, which was, in its way, as deceptive, guileful, and wasteful. If we read

---

*There appears some superficial linkage to the *schlachta* in Poland, but the *schlachta* (Joseph Conrad [Korzeniowski] was the most illustrious product of this class) were a kind of landed gentry and were more dependent on heredity than on achievement. The Czechs had their own version of the *schlachta*, closed, of course, to Jews.

the highly emotional *Letter to His Father* as a political as well as personal document, we can see it as Kafka's effort to break with history: to step outside of what he was born into, to escape a father who in a myriad of ways he perceived as rejecting him, to elude a personal and political history that meant nothing substantial for him, while, of course, taunting and dogging him. The *Letter* is a completely Modernist document, not only for its oedipal dimensions, but for its defiance of authority, its establishment of different rules of conduct, and its total absorption with self.

Kafka proved a true Modernist in the egocentric sense of self that pervades the entire movement; in the personalizing of the arts, even in his concern with reforming and reshaping; and in his desire to break down classical forms and regroup them into new modes of expression. As early as "Description of a Struggle," one of his first fictional efforts, Kafka was moving across fictional and poetical genres, forging a new type of fictional experience, one based on shifting and blending modes of perception.

The redesigning of forms can be seen in other contemporary arenas of Modernist life in Prague as well. We note Rilke's poetry (and his injunction that "you must change your life"); Kupka's paintings; the music of Janáček; the satirical mode of Hašek (and his *Good Soldier Schweik*); other painters such as Kubin, Kubišta, Prochaska, Beneš, and Josef Čapek;* or Karel Čapek's "robot" figures; as well as those with Bohemian and Moravian backgrounds, like Freud and Mahler. The influential philosopher and physicist Ernst Mach lived in Prague, and Albert Einstein, whose relativity theories shattered and reconstructed our conception of the universe, was at one time professor at Prague University. Some of these forms of Czech Modernism were derivative of what was occurring in Paris and Vienna; what was unique, though, was their concern with transformation and metamorphosis. One cannot see Freud, for example, in the larger sense, unless against a background of profound experimentation in the arts, with its radical reshapings and re-creations of self and form, especially at the meeting point of consciousness with the unconscious and subconscious.

Probably the largest single influence on Prague Modernism was the Vienna Secession of 1897. Only a few hours by train from Prague, Vienna was part of a European response to nineteenth-century art and literature. Like Paris and then Munich and Berlin, Vienna made an enormous impact on those who sought to break with traditionalism both through the plastic arts and through the word.

With the Vienna Secession — literally a "going apart" — art, architecture, and literature in 1897 experienced a radical break. One could even argue that the reverberations were as much political as artistic,

---

*Josef Čapek founded the Tvrdosijini Group (the "Die-Hard" Group) as a show of avant-garde strength.

with the Vienna Secession another indication of the disintegration of
the Dual Monarchy. Vienna's position was already precarious because
of the conflicting nationalities ostensibly under its aegis, and it was
further undermined by this broadly based threat to traditional art.
Prague watched as Vienna began to seethe, with such provocateurs as
Freud (still somewhat in the shadows); Gustav Klimt (a purveyor of
so-called degenerate values); the group known as Jung-Wien (Hofmannsthal, Schnitzler, Hermann Bahr, and Stefan Zweig); the Zionist
Theodor Herzl and his own brand of secession; Musil; the architect
Otto Wagner and his ahistoric mission; and the pre-Bauhaus Adolf
Loos. The attacks on traditional values occurred on numerous fronts,
all of them very much a betrayal of fatherly values in the name of art.

One charge against Klimt and his colleagues — and against
Freud — was their alleged sexual perversity. Klimt, for example, in his
painting of Judith holding the head of Holofernes, stressed her sexual
pleasure as well as her prowess. The man is displaced not by the heroic
Judith of the Apocrypha but by a wanton woman, calling up Medea,
Medusa, or even Salomé. In this interpretation, she is part of a long line
of raging, castrating females in myth and literary history. Kafka would
himself present many women in his fiction whose wantonness and un-
predictability baffle the male. Both Klimt and Kafka caught Schopenhauer's devastating idea of the female as an irresistible life force. Like
Freud, Klimt was not interested solely in the instinctual; he had to
break through to the erotic, and then take the erotic into masochism
and sadism.

The Vienna Secession in art and architecture was part of a huge
wave of secessions, at least in their content and consequences. A listing
of these secessions takes us through nearly every radical development
in the arts and sciences, many or most of which reached Prague by way
of Vienna or, more indirectly, through Paris: symbolism, decadence,
naturalism, Jung-Wien, Die Brücke (Kirchner, Schmidt-Rottluff, briefly
Nolde), Blaue Reiter (Kandinsky, Marc, Klee), expressionism, fauvism
(Matisse, Vlaminck, Rouault, Derain, Marquet, Henri Rousseau), cubism, the "new science" (Ernst Mach in Prague, Einstein at the university), quantum mechanics, relativity, imagism, vorticism, Italian
futurism, Russian futurism, dada, surrealism, tactilism, dynamism,
Russian imagism, Russian symbolism, Orphism, serialism, constructivism and neoplasticism, abstractionism, and others. And this is only
a partial listing. Kafka responded to several of these developments, although he is not to be identified with any one or even any overlapping
movements. Many of these obviously owe a great deal to previous or
parallel forces: symbolism and naturalism nourished several movements in the later nineteenth century; and cubism and expressionism
fueled numerous others in the early twentieth. Still others are natural
outgrowths of what preceded them: futurism from the "new science"

or, later, surrealism from dada and from Freud's theories of the unconscious.

But once abstraction, as seen in Picasso, Braque, and Kandinsky, took hold, it became the measure of all visual art, and its influence appeared in a number of other areas: in literature, which became increasingly internalized as stream of consciousness, interior monologue, and related methods; and in music, which depended increasingly on "pure sound," as in the Second Viennese Group of Schoenberg, Berg, and Webern.* Growing up in Prague, Kafka was relatively isolated from a tradition of Czech literature. His reading and early growth came from German literature; and as he moved toward maturity and toward his own early writing, he was caught in the midst of that radical shift in the arts that came to be known as Modernism.

Although at the center of artistic and political revolution, Kafka remained relatively immune to political ideas or organizations. Yet he was drawn in by another avant-garde of sorts, the Zionism of Theodor Herzl. Although not an artistic avant-garde, Zionism was a form of oedipal break with the past, a rupture with the elders. Hungarian by birth, Herzl came to Vienna and identified strongly with German culture. As a correspondent for the *Neue Freie Presse* in Paris, he covered the Dreyfus trial and recognized that French — and European — anti-Semitism left little role for the Jew. His Zionism became, for Jews attempting to assimilate in Prague, as divisive an issue as anything in the arts. Zionism split the Prague Circle, with Max Brod, Kafka's best friend, among others arguing a strong Zionist case, while Kafka remained opposed or indifferent. As his commitment to secular Judaism increased, however, Kafka found in Zionism a solution for the terrible dilemmas facing Jews by the 1920s; and at one time he even fantasized about opening a restaurant in Palestine and serving as a waiter.

If some of this sounds amusing, especially given Kafka's ambivalence about food, one reason is that Zionism was as much a source of divisiveness as it was of hope for European Jews. At the center, as with Modernism in general and the avant-garde in the arts, was the sense that history and tradition — the world of fathers — were either disintegrating or ossifying, a process exacerbated by the long, tenuous life of the empire. As Franz Josef aged into his seventies and then eighties, and as his imperial rule extended beyond fifty years, then still longer (it lasted from 1848 to 1916, four years longer than Victoria's in England), the image of "a father" at the helm gave way to that of an old man attempting to keep power at any cost. And both Zionism and Modernism in the arts served to increase political and cultural pressure to put such

---

*Gustav Mahler conducted at Smetana Hall in Prague, but even more important, Alexander Zemlinsky, Schoenberg's brother-in-law and only teacher, was principal conductor there from 1911 to 1927.

fathers behind. Although many Prague (and Viennese) Jews felt they could ride out the periodic anti-Semitic outbursts and even assimilate — Kafka's father kept up his spoken Czech as a way of assimilating when the pogroms began — Kafka became aware of the impossibility of doing so. He reviled himself as an acculturated or assimilated Western Jew, completely out of touch with his history, religion, tradition; and although he did not feel religious, he did experience the pull of some "true" Jewish background. As we shall see, he looked wistfully at Eastern European Jews, slovenly and ignorant as he found them, because of their ease in their religion, their complete acceptance of what they were, their sense that whatever happened they had their Judaic tradition. Whereas he, the Westernized Jew, remained unassimilated in any real sense and belonged nowhere; he had cut himself off from his history and felt only uncertainty. When we trace Kafka's childhood in Prague, we must identify those coordinates that early on made him recognize his isolation and marginality — precisely what Herzl found was happening to Jews generally as nationalistic or folk movements left little or no place for them in Europe.

As Kafka felt a bond with his ancient heritage, he simultaneously and paradoxically answered Nietzsche's insistently Modernist call to arms for the new and innovative in human life, a call heard even by those who were not in direct touch with the texts of the German philologist and philosopher. Nietzsche's calls were like manifestos, directives that individual men must change. Nietzsche was the prophet and poet of transformation, and Kafka listened as hard to him as he did to the pessimism of Schopenhauer and the muffled cries of Kierkegaard. Written at the beginning of Nietzsche's career, The Birth of Tragedy in 1872 demanded a new form of thought that moved outside normal constraints. Particularly significant in Birth — not only for Kafka but for an entire generation of writers — was Nietzsche's division of man's existence into a "bifocal" experience, with the mind and the senses in perpetual struggle for supremacy.* In the process of structuring his dialectic of Apollonian (roughly mind and spirit) and Dionysian (sensory experience, sensuality), Nietzsche spoke of leveling or deconstructing oneself "stone by stone" until "foundations became visible." In attempting to find that "unconscious life," which he affirmed and lauded (as against Freud's later definition of the unconscious as anarchic and, therefore, something to be harnessed), Nietzsche offered the satyric chorus: a "chorus of natural beings who live ineradically, as it were, behind all civilization and remain eternally the same, despite the change of generations and of the history of nations."

---

*Robert Louis Stevenson's The Strange Case of Dr. Jekyll and Mr. Hyde (1886) was a popular example of bifocalism, as were several of H. G. Wells's science fictions, especially The Island of Doctor Moreau and The Time Machine.

In this bifocal view of man as perpetually divided and unresolved, we begin to sight Kafka territory. This "chorus of satyrs" is not in itself the spirit of Modernism; it merely helps shape Modernism because of its dialectical opposition to civilization — that is, to the Apollonian mind.* In a very rough way, Kafka's division of Jews into the Westernized, acculturated, assimilated ones, like himself, and the Eastern European ones, unassimilated and often uncouth, is an adaptation of Nietzsche's bifocalism. Nietzsche asserted that Dionysian man resembled Hamlet in that both have peered into essences, have gained knowledge, and are unable to function because "nausea inhibits action." Action, Nietzsche emphasizes, requires illusions; deep knowledge, "an insight into the horrible truth," precludes action. Nietzsche here prefigures that small army of Hamlets who will emerge in the latter part of the century and culminate in Eliot's Prufrock, Pound's Mauberly, Rilke's narrator in the *Duino Elegies*, Sartre's Roquentin, and Camus's Jean-Baptiste — and not the least in Kafka's K.'s, all twentieth-century transformed Hamlets.

Without discounting the extreme importance of Schopenhauer and Kierkegaard in Kafka's development (not to speak, also, of Kleist, Grillparzer, Flaubert, and Dostoevsky), Nietzsche's presence looms very large. His bifocalism suggests that man has passed a point of return, his will negated by a force that transcends will. Only art remains as "a saving sorceress, expert at healing." Here Nietzsche reaches out to Schopenhauer, and ahead to Mann and, of course, to Kafka, in whom art is indeed a sorceress, a satyric chorus; and it is this potentially destructive element that gets us beyond the "nausea" that prohibits action.

Nietzsche required a "leap," although one quite different from Kierkegaard's leap into faith as one confronts the abyss of dread. Nietzsche's leap involved a running jump into profound elements that lie outside rationality, a type of leap Kafka was well suited to attempt. Kafka did not move toward faith but jumped into an irrationality so profound he made it appear normal. By bending Prague around to reflect itself, he absorbed and then inverted Nietzsche. Modernism in Kafka's hands gave itself life by trafficking not with knowns but with unknowns, and the greatest of human unknowns was no longer God but the unconscious. After a century of religious worship, God had been identified as white, male, a powerful paternal figure. The unconscious upset all such identifications by substituting for such beliefs a swamp, an infinitude of time, space, and madness; a place of magical languages whose role is to intensify uncertainty. So Kafka is located.

---

*Herman Hesse's large body of work, for example, owes a great debt to Nietzsche and runs parallel to much of Kafka; compare Hesse's Harry Haller (the Steppenwolf) to Kafka's K. and Joseph K.

> . . . bone-Hebrew
> ground into sperm
> ran through the hourglass
> through which we swam, two dreams now, chiming
> against time, in the squares.
>
> — CELAN, "IN PRAG"

TWO Prague and Kafka, Kafka and Prague

PRAGUE BECAME FOR KAFKA the city he feared but could not leave; Prague also became for him a place essential to his development as a writer. What was Prague? A city of wonder and bridges, old buildings, winding streets, and demarcated neighborhoods. Until the later 1800s it was a city more German than Czech; afterward it became more Czech, as workers willing to do lower-level jobs for less money than the Germans poured into the city and its environs and swelled the native population. It was, as the third most important city of the Dual Monarchy after Vienna and Budapest, strangely ambivalent about its own character. Prague in 1883 had a population of 160,000; by 1901, 216,000; by 1922, 677,000, growing each time by incorporating other communes and districts. In the nineteenth century its German minority was as small as 5 percent. Because Jews were so prevalent Prague was called the "Jerusalem of Europe," a term not of praise but of opprobrium.

A similar ethnic shift had occurred in Vienna, where, by 1910, in a fifty-year span, the Jewish population had increased thirtyfold, but Jewish domination in several areas far outweighed Jewish population figures. Figures in both cities are difficult to estimate, since many Jews had converted, others considered themselves Austrians or Czechs, and some were the product of mixed marriages. In 1914 Jews were estimated to make up more than 25 percent of the student population at the University of Vienna and more than one-third of gymnasium (high school) students. Yet in 1910 they were only 2.9 percent of the total number of students at the School of Agriculture (Hochschule für Bodenkultur), which led to anti-Semitic claims that Jews did not prize the land, created nothing, and worked only by manipulation. In Prague Jews suffered the same accusations. Historically, of course, Jews were forbidden to own large tracts of land; the very idea of the Jewish farmer was a source of amusement, even an oxymoron.

In Vienna, by 1893 Jews made up more than half the lawyers; the same was true in Prague. Figures for medical students and university instructors in Vienna were almost equaled by Prague statistics: almost half the medical students in Vienna were Jews, as were a large minority of university teachers, although to rise in the university world was difficult for a Jew, as we can see in the case of Freud's efforts to gain academic recognition. In 1913 state figures indicated that about 75 percent of Viennese journalists were Jewish; furthermore, editors of socialist newspapers were almost always Jewish, although they were not monolithic and some even wrote for anti-Semitic papers. These statistics gave rise to the often heard accusation that Jews used and controlled the press, an anti-Semitic cry that would be heard throughout the reign of the Dual Monarchy.

In the civil service in Austria as in Prague, Jews made up about one-quarter of 1 percent of the total population. Yet in business, industry, textiles, banking, coal mining, and paper milling, Jews dominated, often overwhelming the competition from Gentiles. Since department stores were often owned by Jews and, therefore, in competition with Christian-owned smaller stores, the outcry arose that Jews not only dominated big business but were intent on undermining the small merchant. Even Jewish peddlers were viewed as unfair competition. Capitalism seemed, as someone put it, "a Jewish invention."[1] Anti-Semitism throughout the Dual Monarchy, because of the Jews' prominence, was more widespread than in Germany, despite Franz Josef's own benign policies.

In the universities, anti-Jewish sentiment was especially prevalent, with the formation of nationalistic Czech social fraternities, whose basis was anti-Semitism, both racial and religious; and the rise of Pan-Germanism — a nationalism that spread from Germany to the universities of Vienna and Graz in 1859 and called for "racial purification." Pan-Germanism, the primary tenet of which was that Slavs, Italians, and Jews were corrupting the German race, pushed to eliminate all foreign influence first from university life, then from all forms of public life, especially those related to business. Austrian prime minister Eduard Taaffe's efforts to offer Slavs even-handed treatment only reinforced the feelings of Pan-Germans that their wishes were being threatened and overridden. With the influx of Czech workers to Prague and Pilsen in the 1880s and 1890s, the conflict between Germans and Jews became a three-way struggle.

Prague was at the center of ferment. The young Franz Kafka, the German Jew without an acceptable identity, could not help but feel an exile. What he did as a fiction writer and diarist, beginning when he was in his early twenties, was to seek coordinates for his sense of exile. Part of this sense, whether it derived from the childhood trauma of his brothers' deaths, or from his place in the family as the oldest son, or from areas we cannot quite trace, meant he had to play roles. He took up different roles, playing them off against each other in turn. Many of his parables, paradoxes, and little speeches are offered to an audience as asides, the monologues of an actor staging his own persona. Some of the shorter stories — even the great story "The Judgment" — can be read as soliloquies. The longer stories are the scenes or acts in the Kafka drama, part of the larger play of events that reflect inner states of being. Kafka works through deeply personal codes and signals that ultimately curve back upon himself, revealing him in a role the way an actor taking the stage plays himself even while assuming another character. Kafka was intent on reshaping reality, a compulsion reinforced by the volatile nature of Prague and Bohemia, based as they were on the shifting sands of the Dual Monarchy. By playing roles, he could maintain that ever shifting reality, both externally and internally. And who is more exiled than the actor, condemned for life to playing roles into which he or she must subsume himself?

Everything was deceptive and illusive about Franz Josef's empire. Musil called the empire "Kakania" (Shitville), whereas Kafka presented it less picturesquely as merely "rubbish," or *kitsch*. The "stink" that Kafka breathed in his nostrils was not solely personal displacement, but the more private sense that individual lives no longer fitted into the community; that community was itself in exile from larger society; that government was in collapse and, subsequently, alien from any given social unit; that officialdom, as in his late story "The Great Wall of China," was itself so distant from the people as to exist in another time frame. This sense of displacement is evident in Kafka's use of messengers as a connection to a center that cannot be discovered. One does not find the messenger as a stand-in for the more important official, but as a divider or separator, someone who makes it impossible to come near the official; just as in role-playing, the more the individual fits into the role, the more he is removed from his own self. Messengers in *The Trial* and *The Castle*, for example, indicate not how close K. comes but how distant he will remain, how impossible any decisive action will be, how shrouded in fog and caught in mazes he really is.

Feelings of exile and displacement, the role-playing, the illusionary and ghostly vistas — all of these characteristics were set very early, played on by family life and life beyond. The awareness of exile, whose precise etiology is difficult to determine, meant Kafka had to play the stranger in both life and fiction to justify his sense of himself. Implicit in that idea is the sexual barrenness of his adult years, which fitted in with his conception of himself. While it may appear to have impoverished him, it also fed his sense of what he was, how he had to conduct his affairs, how he could maintain the many roles that nourished his sense of exile. In Kafka in Prague, with those early traumas, we discover the meeting point of several stages of physical change and emotional consciousness which constitute a post-Freudian twentieth century, those qualities which make him a "representative man."

One of Kafka's most telling images or metaphors for exile was the hole, or burrow, or maze, whose functions were to create a tension between danger and safety. The hole allowed Kafka to position the individual just beyond security, in some danger zone of potential extinction. There is, so far, a hint of paranoia, of the young child recoiling from the consequences of his wishes and seeking out a refuge, even as he knows he is not safe, that his hole can be discovered, invaded, and destroyed. Vigilance is all for the animal or person seeking to preserve the hole, or hoping to hide in the maze. The most satisfying of Kafka's hole and maze stories is one he wrote near the end of his life, "The Burrow," a suitable summation of how he started out and what, finally, he became. The story is such an astonishing performance because it permits the reader to put together several dimensions of Kafka's childhood by seeing how he arranged his fictional materials in his later years.

The paranoia is evident: the extremely sensitive mole-like animal waiting in its burrow for some destructive force to enter and devour it or destroy the maze. There is gratification in accumulating stores of food, like Robinson Crusoe on his deserted island, and for Kafka accumulating it meant more than consuming it. The mole-like creature is asexual, concerned almost solely with its maze, the construction, the safety, the art of the thing. The artist, not the person, is paramount. One must forgo intercourse in favor of an art that preserves one's sanity and physical safety. The retreat of the creature into the maze is infantile and regressive, like the means by which Kafka could protect himself against an aggressive father and a harried mother. That 1919 *Letter to His Father* was itself an act of regression, seeking understanding as a child would try to do, then withdrawing by not sending it on. Acts of fictional regression also helped Kafka nourish his sense of exile. And they paralleled his response to Prague — a place he needed for its mazes and illusions, its winding, twisting, narrow streets, and its heavy agedness, and from which he wanted to withdraw because of its lack of reality.

As many of its writers described it, Prague was a magical city. Johannes Urzidil, who wrote a brief impressionistic book on Kafka and Prague, said that it was a place where many "wondrous, conceivable things come to pass. . . . It is fertile soil for magic powers and spells."[2] Rilke, who, like Kafka, was raised on Prague's fertile soil, and along with Kafka was Prague's greatest gift to modern German literature, wrote a poem called "Magic," which describes art as the element that kindles flame out of dust. Rilke left Prague at twenty-one (in 1896);

Kafka remained in and around it all his life. Yet both were defined by the city.*

Prague was so exciting because it was a mélange of racial, ethnic, and nationalistic elements, which appeared not only in language but in conflicting styles of life. The Austro-Hungarian Empire itself stretched in several directions and subsumed ethnicities, religions, and races. The Habsburgs asserted themselves over a vast part of Central and Eastern Europe, including Croatia and Slovenia in the south, Galicia and Bukovina in the east, Erzgebirge in the north, and the Voralberg in the west. These regions included entire subempires, of Serbs, Poles, Czechs, Hungarians, Slovaks, Croats, as well as the Bohemians of Prague and the Moravians of the area to the east of Bohemia. Ethnic influences came in from every direction: heavily from Germany; almost equally heavily from the Czechs of Bohemia; from the Jews who considered themselves German as well as those who began to filter in from Eastern Europe and whose languages were Yiddish, Polish, and Russian; from Austria and, more specifically, Vienna.

But these listings make the categories seem distinct when they were often intermixed. The Sudeten Germans, for example, lived in a part of Czechoslovakia; their loyalties, however, were not to the Czechs but to the Prussians. The landed German Jews and Czechs from the countryside formed a distinctive group of their own. The Czech-Austrian nobility, who figure in Kafka's long, unfinished novel *The Castle*, were a mélange of Czech and Austrian backgrounds so intermixed that any one element was hard to extricate from another, and they turned their hopes to Vienna, not to Prague, although such groups lived on estates in Bohemia. Further, these nobles considered the Habsburgs to be upstarts, and, like the Magyars in bordering Hungary, they held on to their privileges even as the empire was sinking around them. For the writer, whether of fiction like Kafka or lyric poetry like Rilke,

---

*While Rilke turned Prague into a nightmare of maternal overaffection and overcare, for Kafka it was a vision of paternal neglect or intimidation, maternal indifference or abandonment. Rilke inveighed in several letters against his mother's presence in his life, creating out of these letters something almost equivalent to Kafka's letter to his own father. Rilke held himself back from deeper personal relationships for the sake of his art, not succumbing to the temptations of a more stable or normal life, just as Kafka withheld himself, subverting nearly every relationship, even as he entered into it. Both moved toward lasting relationships only to withdraw when the noose seemed to tighten and bourgeois life beckoned. The following words are Rilke's but they could have been Kafka's: "You [Vally, Valerie von David-Rhonfeld] know the dark story of my missed childhood and you know whose fault it was that I have little or nothing joyful to record from those early days. . . . I had love and care only from my father, but generally was left to myself, and there was no one to whom I could confide my little pleasures and sorrows. . . . What I suffered then can be compared with the worst torment known in this world, although I was but a child — or rather just because I was one, because I had as yet no power of resistance or the experience to see that this was only boyish exuberance and nothing more" (quoted in Donald Prater, *A Ringing Glass: The Life of Rainer Maria Rilke* [New York: Oxford University Press, 1986], p. 16). Not all of this is narcissistic self-pity.

the sheer variety of these racial, linguistic, and ethnic groups was both an opportunity and a source of confusion.

Yet added to the ferment of ethnicities and races in Prague and its surroundings was another factor: the ferment brought on by the advent of Modernism, and Prague's sense that it could have its own *Sezession*. The Prague Circle included Franz Werfel, Paul Kornfield, the philosopher Felix Weltsch, Hugo Bergmann, the journalist Egon Kisch, Willy Haas, and of course Max Brod, Kafka's closest friend and his future biographer.* Although many were not Modernists, all were affected if not by formal and technical changes in the arts then by the change in cultural atmosphere. Although the primary Modernist influences occurred in painting, which was truly avant-garde and adventurous and barely a year or so behind Paris, in music, the stronghold of Smetana and Dvořák, with their folk music basis, was being challenged by different kinds of musicality, such as Wagnerian influences and "new music" under the sponsorship of Alexander von Zemlinsky.[3] And in literature, the influences were Stefan George and Hugo von Hofmannsthal (in poetry) and Frank Wedekind and Gerhard Hauptmann (in drama). Karl Kraus infiltrated with scorn, irony, parody. But with all these presences affecting the tone, rhythms, and pacing of language, indeed the whole nature of narrative and continuity, Prague attempted to remain on its own. The peculiar nature of the Prague German-speaking community made it both autonomous and yet sensitive to influences from Austria, an autarchic world resistant to outside forces and at the same time a society that could not resist change. And the conflict within Prague was especially intense among its German-speaking Jews. As he was growing up, Kafka attuned his ear both to this contradictory world outside and to the struggles within him.

Throughout his life, his largest internal struggle was finding the means for expressing the most personal aspects of his life. In one respect, Kafka spent most of his mature life seeking the mode by which he could discharge what he felt as a small child, when his brothers died, his mother seemed to desert him, he was placed in the charge of Czech outsiders, and watched three sisters in turn take their part in the family drama — all of this while he, as oldest son, was expected to perform, a neomessiah of sorts. Kafka sought a method, and once again the parallel with Freud becomes apparent. For Freud, expressiveness was all: as the analysand poured out the repressed materials of his or her life, things emerged that never had before in history. Like an avant-garde artist in possession of materials that needed new forms, Freud devised a new mode for this expressiveness. The daily fifty-minute hour, in the quiet confinement of the analyst's office, was a form of artistic expres-

---

*In Hungary, a comparable — and, excluding Kafka, a more distinguished — group was the Sunday Circle, composed of Béla Bartók, Béla Balázs (the film critic and librettist for Bartók's "Bluebeard's Castle" and "The Wooden Prince"), Zoltán Kodály, Georg Lukács, Karl Mannheim, the art critic Arnold Hauser, and Karl Polányi.

sion in two ways: First, the outpouring was a creative act on the patient's part, although the material was not quite formed enough to be art. Second, while shaping that material, the analyst was performing an artistic act as well, discerning patterns, forms, and contours. Kafka needed something comparable. As both patient and analyst, he poured out and shaped. In much the same way that Freud devised a mode through which the most intimate details could be made visible, Kafka bent generic modes, of story, novel, parable, and general prose fiction, to discover the best means for personal revelation.

Freud "staged" the patient's repressions, with an audience of one, but with a setting, a director, and an act or scenic limitation. One left, usually, by an exit different from the entrance. And the patient played his revealing role only when on that particular stage; the role did not carry over into the patient's "other" life, with family, friends, or colleagues. So too Kafka shaped his personal experience, brought up from the deepest levels, to find accommodation where he had, also, a different entrance and exit and where the materials he divulged were kept quite separate from his family and professional colleagues, even from his friends. His closest friend, Max Brod, who was so significant in keeping Kafka's flame alive after the writer's death, understood he was present at something extraordinary; but even Brod, with all his intelligence and devotion to Kafka, did not comprehend what his friend was up to. Only an analyst, working along parallel lines, and an analyst as trenchant and sophisticated as Freud in his prime, might have understood — because both men were working with life in comparable ways, although in markedly different modes of expression. Both had turned language into forms of theater, although one's expression (Kafka's) was the other's pathology. Like the analysand, Kafka was always at the center of his own drama, playing the leading actor and director, as well as subsidiary roles. Freud's patients unburdened themselves of words and images and patterns that the analyst turned into relief and release once transference occurred. For Kafka, however, the release was not there — the words led only to the intense need for further release, further expression.

This does not move us far from Prague, for it was Prague that helped to generate the very lack of centeredness that gave Kafka so much of his material. Because of its location in the monarchy, north of the main axis of Vienna and Budapest, Prague suffered self-consciously from a somewhat marginal existence; and even as a large city, growing enormously during Kafka's lifetime, beautifully located and crafted, it somehow seemed, as Rilke said repeatedly, outside reality.

Part of Prague's influence on Jews was its contrast with shtetl life for those who emigrated there, like Hermann Kafka. Even in Prague, Julie and Hermann remained hinterland people. Like so many Jews who yearned for assimilation, the Kafkas sought education (for the son, not for the daughters)* and social position in general. We see Hermann, mainly, and Julie carrying over shtetl ideas into the big city, but without the shtetl values of a coherent family pattern. Although shtetl life contained several layers socially and economically, its people were certain of two things: that Jewish tradition and history should be maintained, and that Jews were not only a race but a religion. For the Kafkas in Prague, Jews became only a race, but what their son yearned for — even as he declared himself an atheist and an agnostic, a follower of Darwin's theories — was some anchor in Jewish belief or faith. Race was more or less meaningless for him as he matured, and yet he also knew the impossibility of belief for someone like himself: acculturated, assimilated, deracinated, a new kind of Jew, like intellectuals all over Europe, like someone no less significant than Freud, who was only a short train ride away.

This inability to connect to something larger than himself grew out of his family's own ambivalences, their own uncertainties about who and what they were. Given the pressures on Hermann and Julie to manage their affairs in a largely hostile Gentile and nationalistic Prague, they cannot be held fully accountable — as Kafka perhaps recognized when he decided not to send his *Letter to His Father*. Yet the letter was a culmination of diary entries and other letters that indicated how hollowed out he felt, not only in relation to his father but to fathers beyond, which meant the area of traditional belief. Community was impossible to attain, and yet he yearned, and yearned futilely, because decisions that deeply affected his childhood had already been made and acted upon.

This was the young Kafka's world in Prague: ringed by enemies, invaded by dying and dead brothers, displaced by inner and outer dictates, he himself made marginal in his perceptions of his role, hounded by a father who knew nothing but bullying, pushing, attacking his son's sensibilities with his own unrelenting needs, lost to a mother as she became an adjunct of the father's world. It was in most respects a life not too different from that of many young Jewish men growing up in Prague — Brod and Werfel, for example, from Kafka's own circle. But there was of course Kafka's supersensitivity, his utter candor when it came to what he perceived, and, an additional factor, a certain lack of balance in his perception of himself, which, while hard on the man, was glorious for the writer. In brief, Kafka had a background and childhood that promised a good deal. He might be a worthy opponent for someone's couch, perhaps Freud's, but his material was set; all he needed, as he interacted with the mysteries and ghosts of old Prague, were the details. Kafka in fact spent his entire life writing that *Letter to His Father*.

*Kafka's three sisters did not go beyond the Prague equivalent of the American elementary school.

They need no dance band;
they hear in themselves a howling
as if they were owls' nests.
Their dread oozes like a boil,
and the strong intimation of their rot
is the best of what they smell.

— RILKE, "DANCE OF DEATH"

THREE Early Life in the Austro-Hungarian Empire

L IKE THE CHINESE PEOPLE in "The Great Wall of China,"
Kafka and his circle of Jews were distant indeed from
what went on in the Austro-Hungarian Empire, and yet, in subtle ways,
they were sensitive to everything that was occurring. Even as a child
Kafka could not remain completely remote — he was both a "Chinese"
and not. As we delve into his early life (for which there is little personal
information) we discover a meeting of two documents written much
later, that famous letter to Hermann Kafka and the ironic, bitter, caustic story "The Great Wall of China." They provide, as it were, the perimeters of his expectation, the influences upon him, the shaping of his
perceptions — in brief, the way in which he grew up. We must of
course remind ourselves that both the letter and the story are fictions,
that for Kafka, perceptions, not facts, were all, and we must be careful
not to take the letter as truth any more than we would accept the story
as fact. Kafka was after all playing the role of Kafka.

In the *Letter to His Father*, in 1919, he speaks of hiding from Hermann: "I have always dodged you and hidden from you, in my room,
among my books, with crazy friends, or with extravagant ideas."[1] He
writes of their lack of communication, not only because of Hermann's
physical and emotional differences, but because of differences in their
needs which caused Kafka to find secret selves. We can assume that
when Hermann was in the family apartment and not running the business, he ranted and raved and bullied, so that the son sought out areas
in himself where the father could not enter. "From your armchair you
ruled the world." From Hermann's point of view, Kafka was little more
than a small thing whose moods and needs — communication, affec-

tion, love? — were swept aside in the larger need to survive through hard, relentless work. The boy's own experiences were negated by Hermann's stories of his struggling childhood, struggles that the son could never hope to equal. Kafka lived in relative luxury, whereas the father had lived on the edge. The boy's moods, needs, personality changes, all, had no significance in this large Darwinian sweep. Without being conscious of it, Hermann was a pure Darwinian, the most vulgar kind who could speak only of the fittest and of their survival, at least in his son's perception of him. The father was capable of great rages, and Kafka says of them that they seemed to pre-exist, that the pretext for them was slight, and that, therefore, Hermann carried around the rage merely waiting for an opportunity to let it roar.

Kafka asserts that he never knew what to expect. No matter what he did or, later, tried to achieve, Hermann retorted that little of it mattered, that it was foolishness compared with what had occurred to him in the great world: ". . . there was no opportunity to distinguish oneself in the world as you had done." Julie did provide protection, but only in relation to Hermann: "She loved you too much and was too devoted and loyal to you to have been able to constitute an independent spiritual force in the long run, in the child's struggle." Kafka then touches on what is often cited as his central concept, his sense of guilt: "Here, it is enough to remind you of early days. I had lost my self-confidence where you were concerned, and in its place had developed a boundless sense of guilt." Hermann instilled in Kafka such mistrust about any of his friends that, as in "The Judgment," he left the son no room for his own maneuvers. All movement, as in a game of chess, had to protect the king. Kafka came to fear success, and here we gain the first inkling of understanding of why he later told Max Brod to destroy nearly all his manuscripts: ". . . the more things I was successful in, the worse the final outcome would inevitably be."

If we follow Kafka's perception so far — without discounting how much of it was retributive, how much touched by vengeful paranoia, how much tinged by his own form of aggressive hostility — we see a young child fearful of taking any step for himself, afraid it is the wrong step even when it may prove to be the right one. Franz may have been named after the emperor, but it was Hermann who proved to be the ruler. "Sometimes," Kafka wrote, "I imagine the map of the world spread out flat and you stretched out diagonally across it." What he, the son, feels is that only those territories can come into his life which are beyond Hermann's reach or uncovered by him. Family life, then, from the earliest days was a kind of battlefield — Kafka uses that image in a 1921 diary entry[2] — in which either father or son, like Sohrab and Rustum, would leave as the victor, the other not only defeated but dead. Kafka looks back not simply at losses but at his refusal to leave the battlefield.

The result was that he built walls. Walls, towers, subterranean mazes, all kinds of structures implying secrets, hiding, and withdrawal characterize Kafka's mature work and must derive from early attitudes. "The Great Wall of China" preceded the *Letter* in composition by two years, coming in 1917 and itself giving the title to a volume of stories Kafka published. The story is, in one large respect, the manifestation in imperial terms of the internal struggle shaped in the *Letter*. The wall serves a dual function: it shields those who are inside, and it creates a space between those behind it and those beyond it. It is a powerful metaphor for the young Kafka and for those German-speaking Jews like him living in Prague, for it presents an image of the minority living in the Austro-Hungarian Empire, shielded by an aging Franz Josef. The story was written in the year after the emperor's death and the clear disintegration of the empire in the third year of the Great War.

A central point in the metaphor is that the Emperor is walled off from his subjects as effectively as they are walled off from him, like a family in which the father is distant and beyond communication. The Emperor whispers words to the messenger kneeling by his deathbed. The messenger is then dispatched, but he must exit through an endless series of palace chambers, and even if he does get out, nothing will be gained. For the people "out there" and beyond do not even know which emperor is reigning, and they are not even sure of the dynasty that is ruling. Despite the work of the schools to inculcate knowledge of both dynasty and ruler, much uncertainty remains; so that for the villagers well beyond the reach of the palace, long-dead emperors still rule, and old battles from history seem like recent struggles. What is alive is confused with what is dead. What is dead still seems alive.

What might seem in 1917 to be a political allegory, a satirical portrait of the last days of the Dual Monarchy, is no less a profoundly personal statement, a consequence of Kafka's caustic irony as applied to his own sense of himself and his family life. Both the *Letter to His Father* and the "Great Wall" were part of a struggle of opposite selves. Both allow us glimpses of the youthful Kafka, just beginning to shape himself in the years of constant family moves and Julie Kafka's continual pregnancies. Lack of communication is central in the young Kafka's life, but there are other similarities between his life and the events in the story, including the way in which he survives despite his father, just as the village exists without any help from the emperor, in fact not only surviving but thriving on a history that no longer makes any sense. Kafka has worked out the coordinates of his own survival.

By the time Kafka was five, his home had taken on the air of a battlefield, with two sons dead and only one left, and with the grief of the parents mourning their losses. The house was filled with adult figures: the parents, of course; the household maid, Marie Werner, a Czech-

s_eaking Jew, who served as a kind of governess; then a French governess for Kafka (although she may have arrived a little later); and other
servants who came and went. We must assume that doctors were frequently in and out of the house, first for Georg and then for Heinrich,
so that Kafka was exposed both to death and to illness, and to a sense of
the utter futility of medicine, along with the further suspicion that
medicine killed, possibly, as many as it saved.

At the age of six, according to imperial law, Kafka started school, in
September of 1889, a time that coincided with the birth of his sister Elli
(who was followed by Valli in 1890 and Ottla in 1892). Little did the
young Kafka know, while fighting the battle of the home, what another
battleground the schools would be.

Although the school system of the empire had been conceived of in
quite liberal terms, it had very different results. Well before Franz Josef,
Austro-Hungary in 1774 adopted compulsory schooling for all, based
on the Prussian precedent of eleven years earlier. Maria Theresa, who
prepared the edict, was attempting to find common ground for the diversity of her subjects — members of all those ethnic groups who spoke
different languages, Czechs, Poles, Romanians, Ruthenians, Slovaks,
Croats, and others. She hoped that a general education act would be the
means by which she could consolidate the many warring parties, all of
whom remained loyal to their particular languages, religions, and cultural beliefs. Like the United States in the 1880s and 1890s, when immigrants poured in from Eastern and Southern Europe, a homogeneous
public school system, it was thought, would turn separate factions into
citizens who, while continuing to differ, could share a common heritage. The result, Maria Theresa hoped, would be an educated "mass"
that would share more than it would struggle against, since all would
speak a common language (German) and take part in community traditions.

In a sense her plan worked — at least until the Great War broke
everything apart. Or perhaps it worked only until Prussia humbled
Austria in 1866, when various nationalities began to regroup and tear
the empire apart. In another respect, it failed miserably, in that the attempt to force a common language onto different ethnic groups only affirmed them in their sense of their own ethnicity, their own language,
their own forms of culture. Instead of becoming a common language,
German became the symbol of what had to be resisted in order to preserve one's ethnic identity. To be educated in German was to accept a
common culture; to deny German was to insist on oneself.

For ethnic groups, including Jews, various other forces were also
tearing them apart, not the least the emigration from villages and
shtetls to the larger cities and towns. For Czechs, this would bring together large numbers of people who could organize in national terms
and become a force in their own right. For Jews, it meant a breakdown

in traditional beliefs, as young people were exposed to outside temptations.* Conversion itself brought with it certain benefits.

In 1782, moreover, the Edict of Toleration (the *Toleranzpatent*) proclaimed by Emperor Joseph II created a still greater problem, even while appearing to clear the way for Jews to enter the larger society. Like the school law enforcing attendance, this edict required serious choices, this time solely for Jews. For the Edict of Toleration attempted to make Jews full-fledged citizens of Austro-Hungary by dropping all legal barriers between Christians and non-Christians. It gave Jews the same freedoms enjoyed by Christians, although full implementation of the law did not occur until after the 1848 revolution. Nevertheless, the aim of Joseph II's edict was to bring Jews into the fold — that is, to force their assimilation, either through conversion itself or through a gradual loss of their Jewish identity. On its face, the edict was a liberalizing force and, for Europe, an unusual document, preceding the French Revolution and the Napoleonic Code. Jews were to be full citizens, not outcasts living in ghettos or beyond the pale of settlement, shunned as "different," and despised.

The Edict of Toleration attempted homogeneity: Jews would have to take German names, including German first and family names. Kafka would become Franz, not František, Freud would be Sigismund, not Schlomo, and so on, with the Kafka family an exception. All legal documents, such as birth certificates, identity forms and cards, and wedding and death certificates had to be in the German language, regardless of the native tongue of the citizen. Jews became subject to military service, whereas in the past, as a marginal people, they were not sufficiently trusted to serve as soldiers. But most of all, the school system was to turn Jews into Austrians, for every Jewish community in Bohemia and neighboring Moravia was instructed to form an elementary school system in which German would be the language of instruction. In idea and shaping, as was noted earlier, this school system was not very different from what Jews found in the United States: each community with its own schools, the language of instruction English. Every ethnic and religious group was forced to learn in the language of the country. But there the parallel ends. For in Austro-Hungary Jews were not permitted separate religious schools — ever. They had not, of course, emigrated to another country but were being ordered to do something within their own settlements; and if Jewish schools failed to conform, then their students (boys) had to attend Christian schools, and in effect receive a Christian education (with conversion and assimilation as the ultimate end). For the secular, Enlightenment Jew, this was an advance; for the Orthodox, a calamity.

---

*Ottla Kafka, for example, would marry a Czech Gentile over the protests of her parents, although with Kafka's blessing.

Prague's first Jewish school, established in 1782, was presided over by Ezekiel Landau, Bohemia's chief rabbi and an opponent of the new system.[3] The Orthodox Landau opposed both the Enlightenment and its consequence, secular education. But by 1786 the Austrian government had made resistance almost impossible by establishing that an elementary school education would be the sole requirement for the issuance of marriage licenses. Many Jews of course went through their own ceremonies, by-passing the bureaucracy, but the new law served its main purpose, which was to enforce greater compliance with the original edict. For Jews, the dilemmas posed were enormous.

Furthermore, these German-speaking instructional outposts in Bohemia, where the Czech population was increasing (by the time of Kafka's birth, Czechs outnumbered German-speaking Jews and Christians by seven to one), were clearly very visible enemies. The pressure to conform and to neglect historical and traditional rites became enormous, as we see in Hermann Kafka's only sporadic celebration of Jewish holidays. By the time Franz Kafka attended the German Volks- und Bürgerschule (People's, or National, and Civic Elementary School) in 1889, it was completely secularized, having lost any of its earlier Jewish characteristics. The school was by then not Jewish but state operated, and many non-Jews from Prague also attended. In this way, the original edict served much of its function, which was to erode Jewish "difference" and to enforce greater homogeneity in the population, and it surely succeeded in that although Jews did not forsake their ethnic identification, they did pay less attention to their Jewish traditions and many of them assimilated. Some converted, especially those who sought public musical careers, like Gustav Mahler when he went to Vienna. Although they became nominal Christians, they were nevertheless not saved from anti-Jewish sentiment, and Mahler eventually gave up the Vienna State Opera because of anti-Semitic attacks. Likewise, Schoenberg and Karl Kraus were converts, but Schoenberg reconverted, as it were, back to Judaism when Jews came under attack, and Kraus made so many changeovers that it is difficult to determine what he really was.

The Kafkas assimilated, or tried to, as much as Czech nationalism would permit. Hermann Kafka's ability to speak Czech was surely a factor in his business success and had the result that his family did not suffer the usual overt bigotry. Yet the initial battleground was, in 1889, the school, appropriately located — in terms of Kafka's later perceptions of it — in a structure on a street called the Meatmarket. While this would have been good training for Chaim Soutine, who specialized in painting animal carcasses and bloody sides of beef, it proved traumatic for Kafka.

When Kafka, at six, enrolled at a German-speaking school, he was entering a political and cultural cauldron of sorts. Although the school

itself did not create extraordinary difficulties, the struggles that made
the school possible and that made its continued existence acceptable
were already dividing the larger society. How much is conveyed to a
child of six, even one as sensitive and open to persecutory visions as
Kafka? We do know he saw himself as programmed for failure, if we can
believe his later assessment of his school years. He felt he would fail at
every level; then when he passed, he considered his success anomalous
and waited for something to trip him. He asserted in 1910, when he was
twenty-seven, that his education had done him harm, and he pointed to
an entire array of people connected with it, going well beyond the
school itself.

> This reproach is directed against a multitude of people; indeed they stand
> here together and, as in old group photographs, they do not know what to
> do about each other, it simply does not occur to them to lower their eyes,
> and out of anticipation they do not dare smile. Among them are my par-
> ents, several relatives, several teachers, a certain particular cook, several
> girls at dancing school, several visitors to our house in earlier times, sev-
> eral writers, a swimming teacher, a ticket-seller, a school inspec-
> tor . . . there are so many that one must take care not to name anyone
> twice.[4]

To this list, he even adds those whose instruction he did not notice at
the time. Connected by virtue of their association with Kafka, they all
conspired to make him miserable and do him "terrible harm," as he
writes in a following entry in his diaries. Here he adds nearly everyone
he ever knew as a child, including a hairdresser, a beggerwoman, a
helmsman, the family doctor, "and many more besides."[5]

Kafka's schooling and all that went with it failed because he was a
boy who remained incomprehensible to those in touch with him. Their
mistakes occurred because they had no idea with whom they were
dealing. Even worse, his education "tried to make another person" out
of him, different from the one he became. "It is for the harm, therefore,
that my educators could have done me in accordance with their intentions that I reproach them; I demand from their hands the person I now
am, and since they cannot give him to me, I make of my reproach and
laughter a drumbeat sounding into the world beyond."[6] He feels a
"good, beautiful part" has been spoiled, and for this his reproach
"sounds the trumpet for the drummer." This assertion of his self (he is
twenty-seven, but far from independent of his parents) is followed by
further attacks. That his parents and relatives "have done me harm out
of love makes their guilt all the greater, for how much good they could
have done me out of love."

Kafka's insistence on going well beyond his education to indict an
entire population suggests that his attack on his schools and on education itself must be fitted into a much wider context. He is, at twenty-
seven, the bearer of a law degree, an insurance executive, already a

writer, so deeply caught up in his past that all of it must be perceived as negative. That negation is part of an overall depressive personality, whose sole positive elements came to the fore when he retreated from all those people and sat at his desk as a writer. The "harm" school did him, apart from the specifics of his case, is only one element in the entire question of his depression, which disallowed the memory of nearly anything even vaguely happy or pleasant. Such an attitude, unfortunate for the man but fortuitous for the writer, and particularly so for this kind of writer, turns up in another memory of school. This one is found in a long passage directed to Milena Jesenská, the Czech writer and translator with whom Kafka was romantically involved near the end of his life. When Kafka came to know Milena, he was thirty-seven, suffering gravely from tuberculosis, losing his energy, and so caught up in memories that to this woman, whom he genuinely liked, he roves back into early childhood, when school was nightmarish. If Milena read this passage correctly, she could have learned a great deal about Kafka, whom she in turn admired enormously.

> We lived in the house which separates the Kleine Ring from the Grosse Ring [in Minuta House]. Thus we walked first across the Ring, then into the Teingasse, then through a kind of archway in the Fleischmarktgasse [Meatmarket Street] down to the Fleischmarkt. And now every morning for about a year the same thing was repeated. At the moment of leaving the house the cook [described as "a small dry person," yellowish, "but firm and energetic"] said she would tell the teacher how naughty I'd been at home. As a matter of fact I probably wasn't very naughty, but rather stubborn, useless, sad, bad-tempered, and out of all this probably something quite nice could have been fabricated for the teacher. . . . School in itself was already enough of a nightmare, and now the cook was trying to make it worse. I began to plead, she shook her head, the more I pleaded the more precious appeared to me that for which I was pleading, the greater the danger; I stood still and begged for forgiveness, she dragged me along. . . . I always had the greatest terror of being late, now we too had to run and all the time the thought: She'll tell, she won't tell — well, she didn't tell, ever, but she always had the opportunity. . . . And sometimes — think of it, Milena — she stamped her foot in the street in anger about me and the coal merchant woman would sometimes be standing there, watching. Milena, what follies! And how much I belong to you with all the cooks and threats and this whole monstrous dust which 38 years have kicked up and which has settled in my lungs.[7]

In the same letter, Kafka mentions to Milena that if "you ever want to know what my early life was like I'll send you from Prague the gigantic letter I wrote my father about six months ago, but which I've not yet given him."[8]

The juxtaposition of the two, the cook and Hermann, is not by chance. The passage about school indicates that in Kafka's memory the question of power in the family was foremost, as would be revealed in the letter to his father. By threatening to tell the teachers how naughty he was, the cook gained a degree of power equivalent to that of a dominating parent. In Kafka's memory, her bullying fits well with Hermann's, both of them gaining over him a power that turned first home and then school into nightmares. What is particularly compelling about his remarks on his school situation is how the cook was able to carry over the unhappiness at home to the realm of the classroom. Because of her threat to tell the teacher of his naughty behavior at home, there was no place Kafka could escape to, at least in his re-creation of the scene. School might have been a refuge from dying and dead brothers, and then from a succession of sisters, an absent mother, a domineering, bullying father; but school as a possible refuge had now been eliminated. The consequence was that Kafka was driven back completely upon himself. Whatever guilt, depression, or anguish he felt from these early traumas had no outlet except through his own personal means. The mazes, labyrinths, secret hiding places, refuges, and even holes that characterize his writings were all being laid out at this time, however inchoately and incompletely.

What had happened to Kafka's own feelings of power, rooted as that power might be in guilt and anguish? He had felt the power to make brothers disappear, leaving Julie to him. Where was that power now, with sisters coming along, with the cook challenging him for ascendancy, with Hermann ruling the household with *his* needs, *his* self? It was power baffled at the source, and it passed into the secret byways of a creative imagination. It certainly did not vanish. Nothing in Kafka vanished. All was held together in a kind of solution for his memory to work on. He never let go, as his remarks here and elsewhere to Milena indicate. Another response was depression, deep, unresolvable depression, not the kind that makes it impossible to work but the type that excludes so much else it feeds a particular kind of talent or imagination. Depression for a young boy like Kafka could be constructive, as it was for writers like Conrad and Faulkner, in whom it rarely became acute enough to create blockage. Rather, it fed what was being stored up and became part of the material base for the writer.

Kafka was of a piece. The man of twenty-seven is caught in a reverie of what it was like when he was six and then the succeeding years as he counts them off. He is reliving the earliest school years not as the child but as the man undergoing analysis, recounting for the analyst his reproaches, hostilities, accumulated anger, and forms of anguish. The diaries, begun in 1910, served just this function, and it is therefore to be expected that the early segments are concerned with education, the formative years, the sense of memory and reverie, the reproaches for those who twisted him from what he was or might have been, and his ultimate triumph, that despite their enormous pressures he changed so little.

Kafka succeeded in school. He may have told his father in the *Letter* that he expected never to make it through first grade, that he thought he would not pass his high school entrance examinations, that once in high school he was sure he would fail. He may have added that success did not bring confidence, even when he won a prize; and he became convinced that every success simply masked a greater failure to come. He sensed what he called this "unique, this absolutely outrageous case," referring both to his incompetence and ignorance. He thought that perhaps he succeeded because he never called attention to himself, that if noticed he would have been thrown out. In this way, we see, from an early age, how he turned himself into a small object, and then hid out in holes and burrows, out of sight and, he hoped, out of mind. Yet despite the nightmarish qualities of school and the even more nightmarish dragging by the cook, Kafka excelled at this school located in the Meatmarket. He was fortunate enough to have teachers who lacked the typical Prussian severity on which the schools were founded. Most of his instructors were neither cruel nor overbearing, and many were interested in their students.

Jews overwhelmingly chose to be instructed in German, not Czech. In Kafka's final year at the Alstädter Gymnasium (high school), in 1900, about 90 percent of the Jewish students received their education in German, even though less than half of Prague's Jews admitted to using German outside the home. This disparity in figures, between those speaking Czech and the students educated in German, suggests the tremendous division taking place, the uncertainty of Jews as to what they wanted and what they should do. The pressures were equally strong to gain the education needed to be eligible for careers and professions in the empire, and yet to be associated with the Czech language in order to appease the growing nationalist movement, with its anti-Semitic slogans and calls to action.

Whatever the school pressures, and however lukewarm Jews like Hermann Kafka remained to traditional practices, Jews on the whole remained Jews. Hermann himself was not completely inactive in Jewish affairs. He served on the board of the Heinrich Synagogue, a Reform synagogue that held its services in Czech, not German. And he served as a member of the Central Organization for the Promotion of Jewish Affairs, founded in the mid-1880s to combat anti-Semitism. In the face of anti-Semitic onslaughts from the Young Czechs, membership in the organization increased dramatically, and when Jews were offered facsimile Austrian one-way railway tickets to Palestine in cattle cars, there was almost a panic to join up. Hermann, then, was not completely foreign to Judaism, but nearly all his activities in this area were directed at maintaining his place in Czech society, rather than toward identifying himself in religious terms, which is the area where Kafka attacked. The decision to convert in order to get on in life, as in Mahler's case, for example, was relatively uncommon among Prague Jews. But as increasing numbers of Jews cited Czech as their first language (figures we can glean from the language census beginning in 1880), conversion of another sort was taking place. Even as Kafka studied in a German-language school and began to read the German classics, Czech Jews were moving toward a "conversion" in terms of the language they associated themselves with. They were "Czechifying" themselves, not in religious terms but in language, loyalties, and associations. Much of this came at a time toward the end of the century when still another element entered the Jewish community, adding to the pressures of Enlightenment ideas. That was Theodor Herzl's Zionism.

The first Zionist Congress had met in 1893. The call for Zionism, for the end of the Diaspora (or the dispersion), and the return of the Jews to their homeland in Palestine meant a tremendous struggle for those who considered themselves socialists. Socialists traditionally saw Zionism or Zionist-type movements as divisive of the workers' call to order, a weakening of the structures that would lead to the alliance of all peoples against capital and owners, and an undue empowerment of those who wished to escape.*

Although he was still too young to respond to these sweeping ideologies, Kafka was early on a socialist, and he must have been aware at quite a young age of the conflicting ideas ravaging the Prague Jewish community. This is not to say that, as a schoolboy, Kafka was connected to any ideology or that he had any clear understanding of the conflicts; but rather to suggest that in every area of the young Kafka's life there was conflict, uncertainty, matters of desperate choice. There was little of a settled life for Kafka, given the shifting nature of the coordinates to which Prague Jews were subject. In yet another paradox, Prague and Bohemian Jews were moving toward forms of assimilation in an empire that was itself pulling apart, crumbling from inefficiency, disintegrating among nationalistic divisions. The Habsburg Empire was an unworkable entity that had functioned for far longer than anyone expected, and now, under the new pressures and nationalistic yearnings, it was collapsing — even as Jews linked themselves to its fortunes because of the relatively benign nature of Franz Josef's policies toward them.

This was the backdrop for Kafka's early life in the Austro-Hungarian Empire. Yet despite the emperor's benign attitude toward Jews, anti-Semitism was on the rise when Kafka was a schoolboy. Escorted by a Czech national, and therefore protected, he saw students from the

---

*Kafka's socialism and Zionism thread through this entire study, since they not only generate ideas but are aspects of Modernism, part of that entire way in which society was undergoing radical changes, politically and ideologically, as well as artistically.

Czech school located across the street attack Jewish children who were unattended and defenseless, all in the name of Czech nationalism.

Such attacks, nevertheless, were commonplace, and rumblings of nationalistic anti-Semitism long preceded Kafka's birth, going back to the youngest days of Hermann Kafka. In southern Bohemia, for instance, in 1859 workers put on an anti-Semitic demonstration aimed at Jews who were taking over jobs Czechs felt should belong to them. Just two years later, there were anti-Jewish riots in Prague, the first of their kind, and extended rioting near Wossek, Hermann's birthplace. In each instance, the Austrian army had to be called in. In addition to the advent of riots, poison-pen letters were being sent which stated that Judgment Day for Jews was coming soon. In 1866, the year of Austria's terrible defeat by Prussia, workers throughout Bohemia demonstrated and rioted, blaming Jews for Austria's defeat and for their own inability to improve their condition. With the 1867 *Ausgleich,* or settlement, between Hungary and Austria, creating the Dual Monarchy, conditions for Jews improved, as Austria adapted Bismarck's more open-minded policy toward Jews, but nationalistic fervor continued to lead to anti-Jewish incidents.

One of the basic texts helping to establish Czech anti-Semitism was a book that appeared harmlessly enough in 1871, *Talmudjude* (*The Talmud Jew*). Written by August Rohling, professor of theology at the University of Prague, it had become by the 1880s a fundamental text of theologically directed anti-Semitism. Austria and Hungary, in particular, embraced it. Rohling's point (which leads almost directly into the blood libel charges first in Kolín and then against Hilsner) was that the Talmud demonstrates Jewish hostility toward Christians, amounting to discrimination. The Talmud, in other words, instead of being part of Jewish law was an anti-Christian document. As an orthodox Catholic, Rohling made the point that Jews either had to obey Mosaic law or become adherents of Jesus, whose teachings were the valid continuation of the first revelation. The Talmud, Rohling argued, was a collection of superstitions and old wives' tales, not at all theologically valid, and yet Jews held to it as if it were gospel.

Rohling's aim, apparently, was to make Jews recognize that they were, in his view, worshipping false idols, so that they would then embrace the true religion, Christianity; but his book had the effect of poisoning the atmosphere and reinforcing anti-Semitic feeling throughout the empire. By the later 1880s and early 1890s, it was a useful text for these purposes. The Hungarian blood libel affair in 1883 was only one affair of many, led on by the Young Czech party and by the printer Skrejsovsky, who flooded Prague and its environs with anti-Semitic pamphlets in both Czech and German. The Young Czech party, which the Jews scorned, was made up of workers and the petty proletariat, those who felt left out and who blamed the Jews for it. The Old Czech party, on the other hand, which was made up of more successful farmers, upper bourgeois, industrialists, some priests, and officials, was less overtly anti-Semitic, perhaps because it had less to fear from Jewish infiltration.

Not until 1879, with Adolf Stöcker, a Berlin court preacher, do we have an organized anti-Semitic movement. The very term was coined at about this time. Stöcker's views were supported by a prestigious Czech historian, Heinrich von Treitschke, whose influence was perhaps even more insidious since he was not a professional anti-Semite and yet slid into it as it intensified in Berlin cultural life. Stöcker's attacks came only four years before Kafka's birth (and ten before Hitler's). The real motive of the anti-Semitic movement was to eliminate Jewish emancipation, because Jews were seen as playing too large a role in the economic and cultural life of the country, the very points Hitler made later in *Mein Kampf*. This attack on a "Jewification" of culture, incidentally, would become the battle cry of those opposing Modernism; anyone associated with the movement — including non-Jews like Klimt or Cézanne (himself an anti-Semite) — was identified as Jewish or Jewish tainted.

Also in 1879, with reverberations that went well beyond Germany and throughout the Austro-Hungarian Empire, where German was everyone's first or second language, came the publication of Wilhelm Marr's pamphlet *The Victory of Judaism over Germanism*. Appearing in February, it had passed through twelve editions by the fall. Its thesis was extremely popular: that Jews were not a future danger to Germany, they were a clear and present danger, having already achieved domination of the country. Marr placed the fault completely on the Germans for having permitted this to happen, and then asked what the country planned to do about it, a call to action based on anti-Semitism which would echo in Vienna, Prague, and Budapest. Marr's aim was to prevent the German fatherland from suffering "complete Judaization." Like Richard Wagner, whose attack on Jews as perpetual outsiders was well known, Marr believed that Jews were necessarily outsiders, descended from the New Testament Pharisees, ghetto dwellers who never knew anything but isolation, "scummy people." In the German perception, Jews were linked with Gypsies, both considered negative forces and marginal to the rest of humanity. Conversion of the Jew was out of the question; the only solution was to oppose Jewish hegemony with sustained opposition. In the full flush of his pamphlet's success, Marr started up a journal called *Deutsche Wache*, then an association named *Antijüdischer Verein* (Anti-Jewish Organization), until *"jüdisch"* was replaced by *"semitisch"* and the term *anti-Semite* came into being. The association was known as *Antisemitenliga*, the Anti-Semitic League. It was a great historical moment, the beginning of a dance of death, and though the idea of anti-Semitism seemed aimed at the German audi-

ence it spread rapidly and enthusiastically, reinforcing the diverse na-
tionalistic forces gathering in the many tribes of the Austro-Hungarian
Empire, and exacerbated by the special German-speaking schools that
Jews had to attend.[9]

Waves of anti-Semitism struck Hungary, based not only on fears of
Jewish domination but also on religious grounds, with attacks on Jews
growing out of the so-called blood libel. In the spring of 1881 a Russian
pogrom in the wake of Alexander II's assassination gave impetus to
strong anti-Jewish feeling right across Eastern and Central Europe.
Blood libel had historically proved a successful basis for attacks on Jews
and Jewish property. The Hungarian version at this time, in the small
Jewish shtetl of Tiszaeszlár, was familiar. A Gentile girl of fifteen disappeared. Although there was no evidence of why or where, rumors
began that she had been murdered by Jews so they could drain her blood
and bake it into holiday matzos (the so-called blood libel). The local
"crime" became a national issue when the Catholic Church saw it as a
point of attack and enthusiastically joined the anti-Jewish sentiments.
The furor that resulted foreshadowed the even more sensational Hilsner case in 1899, in Czechoslovakia. In any event, the body was found
in the river Tisza and the Jewish defendants were acquitted, but the
damage done could not be undone: anti-Semites believed in a white-
wash of justice and became more convinced than ever of Jewish culpa-
bility. It was the same story replayed, and to be replayed further.

These attacks on Jews across Central and Eastern Europe were for-
malized by a German, Georg Ritter von Schönerer, who founded the
German National party. The party's aim was to unify all elements of
the Austrian Empire, including Czechs, Poles, Hungarians, Croats, and
Serbs, under the hegemony of the Germanic peoples. Though not at
first overtly anti-Semitic, as the party evolved, it adopted blood and
race as the ticket to membership. Schönerer did not attack the Jewish
religion — he disliked all religious affiliations, Christian as well as others — but the Jewish race. That gray area between race and religion that
Kafka was to probe and come away from mainly baffled was explored in
the early 1880s, and the conclusion Schönerer drew was that Jews were
not assimilable, that in their case baptism was meaningless, since it
was race not religion that made a Jew what he was. Schönerer's brand
of anti-Semitism was joined by several other garden varieties: that of
Karl von Vogelsang (Birdsong) with his attacks on the Jewish religion,
the so-called anti-Talmud attack; and then that of the mayor of Vienna,
Karl Lueger, who used anti-Semitism as he felt it helped his political
career, and he attacked Jews without regard for the question of race or
religion and also helped those Jews who fell into his favor. Austrian
anti-Semitism, like that in Bohemia and Moravia, differed from that in
Germany. In Germany, many believed that lack of sufficient assimilation by Jews proved their marginality; in Austria, however, assimila-

tion was not the chief matter, but rather Jewish domination of the professions and of the cultural life of the various territories and tribes. In the capital of the Dual Monarchy, population figures prophesied destiny: in Vienna, Jews went from 2 percent of the population in 1860 to 10 percent of the population in 1880. In the same period just preceding Kafka's birth, Berlin went only from 3½ percent to just under 5 percent. The attack on Jews in the nineteenth century tended to be on religious grounds: the Jews' clannishness, their vaunting of Mosaic law over Christianity, their foreign practices. But toward the end of the century, various tracts on racial hygienes — that is, eugenics — began to define Jews as outlaws on racial grounds, using the ideas of racial inferiority and racial impurity. Gradually, race and religion became indistinguishable.

That Kafka was a fearful child, even though he was not in physical danger from Czech Gentiles, is apparent. In his *Letter to His Father*, he describes an incident that occurred when he was about four: his father "abandoned" him on a balcony because he had insisted on a glass of water, and then he felt cut off from his family and his own needs. This incident, which in retrospect for many older men would seem amusing, remained for Kafka pivotal. It was equivalent in his development to the blacking factory incident in Charles Dickens's life, when the boy was twelve and, it seemed, forgotten by parents and the entire world. The reverberations in Dickens's life are endless, and, although we cannot be so certain about Kafka's balcony incident, we can say that it reinforced what was already an unsteady social personality, especially since it occurred around the time his first brother died.

In an interesting exchange with Gustav Janouch, a young friend, Kafka revealed something about himself in relation to his family. His remark is disguised in that it applies to Janouch's parents, who were entering a bitter separation and divorce, which would lead, ultimately, to the father's taking his own life. Yet it is apparent Kafka was relating his own experience, one, we can assume, he had early on. When Janouch says he cannot bear family life, Kafka, whose written remarks assert his own inability to bear it, replies that Janouch should try merely "observing" his family. Then the

> family would think that you were sharing their life and were content. And in fact this would be partly true. You would be living with your family, but on different terms from them. That would be all. *You would be outside the circle, with your face turned inwards towards the family, and that would be enough* [my italics]. Perhaps now and then you might even see your own image reflected in your family's eyes — quite small and as if drawn on a glass ball in the garden.

When Janouch retorts that this indicates a course of spiritual acrobatics, Kafka agrees that such are the acrobatics of everyday life, and they are dangerous because the individual may not be conscious of what he is doing. Such antics may break "not one's neck, but the soul itself. One does not die of it, but continues to exist as one of life's deserving pensioners."[10]

While his future lifelong friend, Max Brod, was being educated at a Catholic elementary school by Czech priests, Kafka was at least in a setting where Jews dominated, although his teachers were both Czech Christians and Jews, presided over by Franz Fieger, a German-speaking Christian. Kafka gained a prize in the first grade and seemed respected by his teachers and by the other students. That year he formed a great friendship with Hugo Bergmann, and they remained close for the rest of Kafka's life, despite huge ideological differences between them: Bergmann was committed to Judaism and Zionism when Kafka was still relatively indifferent. In this setting, Kafka learned to read and write, to do arithmetic, and to handle the Austrian curriculum, which was based, as in most of Europe, on the memorization of facts, the ingesting of detail, and the training of the mind so that, in disciplined fashion, it could spew back these facts and details accurately.

Yet even as Kafka seemed to glide easily through what was required, he was transforming school into a nightmarish experience. The reason must have been in what he brought to the school, that weight of his earliest childhood that had already shaped his perceptions, which were deeply rooted in depression, not to speak of guilt and anguish. For Kafka, from the earliest years what was important to him was what occurred to him, rather than what actually occurred. In reality, he had a relatively easy time. The Jewish Matthias Beck, Kafka's third- and fourth-grade teacher, must have scrutinized the young boy with particular care — possibly he sensed something special, or saw some sensitivity that alerted him to personal difficulty despite academic achievement — for he asked Hermann and Julie to hold Kafka back for what was an optional fifth year at the elementary school. The alternative was to allow him to move on, in 1893, when he was ten, to the high school, for which he had to prepare himself.

Kafka's parents chose to advance him, perhaps at his own insistence, since some stigma was attached to that fifth year of elementary school, and in the spring of 1893 Kafka prepared for the examination that would lead to a September entrance. He was of course apprehensive about the entrance examination, which was more fitting for an adult than for a child; and Matthias Beck may have noticed the anxiety and depression such examination taking meant for the young boy. The selection process was severe, intended to pare down a large class to a more manageable group. European education was and is elitist, preparing a largely uneducated class for the work force, while providing higher education only for those who show an early talent for it.

Kafka excelled at this system, even as he withdrew into anguish and apprehension at its inexorable exams, both written and oral, all requiring an accurate memory — which meant no foggy brain, no faking it, no creeping paralysis at the sight of the examining teacher or board. Kafka faced each ordeal expecting the worst, passed through, and then foresaw that success was only a harbinger of even greater failure. It was an unhappy situation for the boy, but it helped to create a writer who would come so close to transforming the human unconscious into literature. In addition to the ordeal of examinations for the gymnasium was the further apprehension connected to his family's frequent moves.

Although none of them was then a chic address, the regularity of the moves, plus the change of nurse for Kafka, indicates that Hermann and Julie were driven to improve their condition. Few of the moves suggest a real step upward, but the mere fact that they were mobile indicated to them that they were not standing still socially. What is remarkable, given the constant changes of address in his earliest years, is how immobile Kafka became in his mature years: he held on to his parents' quarters, unable to move, even when his accommodations were noisy, unsatisfactory, repellent.

It was during their last move, when Kafka was almost six, that Hermann and Julie engaged Marie Werner, a Czech-speaking Jew, to help run the household, a position she kept during the rest of Kafka's childhood and adolescence. She was kind and gentle, fearful of Hermann (she always sided with him), and in most respects unable to control the willful, determined, unhappy boy. The prescient Hermann wanted his son to learn Czech, and in addition to Marie Werner he hired a young Czech woman to teach him, but the home language remained German for the most part, with some occasional Czech, which Kafka learned to speak and read. However, Kafka rarely felt fully comfortable with the language, and it remained, along with his French, Italian, and English, tentative.

By the time he entered the German National Humanistic Gymnasium, located in the Kinsky Palace on Prague's Old Town Square,* the patterns were firmly set. Kafka was expected to become, or remain, a learning machine. The school Hermann chose for him was in the traditional mold, offering a classical education, with drilling in Latin and Greek, little of practical use, and an emphasis on memory and rote learning. Nothing could have been further from Hermann's own background. Prague, with its mysteries and ambiguities of old and new, of traditional and modernistic, was well complemented for Kafka by this tiny enclave of the gymnasium with its own entrance, its own rules, and disciplines. It was, in this respect, a refuge from home, but it proved for Kafka a dubious reward, since he hated much of what he was forced to do, while doing it well. But the pattern was set in other ways

*Hermann's store would later be located there, on the ground floor.

as well. The intensely ambitious Hermann, with his desire for social and economic upward mobility, had no time for the amenities. While remaining coarse and crude in his habits — if we can believe Kafka's indictment in the *Letter*, his father engaged in spitting and cursing, and had uncouth table manners — Hermann ran a genteel store of gentlemanly and ladylike products, and he put into his business his considerable energy, as well as that of the ever present Julie. The pattern then was of absentee parents, particularly Hermann, except at dinner time, and then after dinner, when Kafka was sent off to his studies, Hermann and Julie played cards until bedtime, a pattern that continued through Kafka's eight years of gymnasium.

The divisions within him continued: the linguistic separation from the rest of Prague, as German became his major language; his further separation as a Jew in an increasingly non-Jewish city; the relative absence of his parents, and the sudden appearance of baby sisters; the constant coming and going of household people (with the exception of Marie Werner); and the urgent need to succeed at school, as the oldest son, the only son, on whom everything depended. Kafka constantly had to "live up to" something, to become the benefactor or savior in some mystical, traditional way. Yet the torment was almost palpable, and the disgust for his parents was beginning to build: for their unkempt, soiled bedclothing, for Hermann's crude habits, for Julie's obeisance before her godlike husband, for what became for Kafka a kind of primal scene — not that (as far as we know) he observed his parents in intercourse, but what he made of the soiled bedclothing, the onslaught of pregnancies and sisters, the noise and turmoil, some of it sexual, all within the confines of a small apartment, where his room was centrally located. That was the pattern, excellent preparation for the man who would be a writer, less than that for the man who wanted to be more ordinary.

Janouch quotes Kafka as saying that he was even more lonely than Kaspar Hauser (the mysterious German foundling of the early nineteenth century); that he was, in fact, as lonely as Kafka. The remark indicates a loneliness bred in the bone and returns the grown man (he made the remark when he was thirty-seven) to his earliest days. One of the few areas where he was not completely lonely was in the dubious one of language, his Germanism, with its roots in Goethe, Schiller, and Heine. Germanism was a protection for Jews, but what a paradoxical protection! Located in enclaves of their own, the Jewish neighborhoods, outposts of sorts against periodic Czech Gentile assaults, they had their own language. But their desire to assimilate into Germanism through language simply meant they were attempting to be absorbed into something that justified their own uprootedness. Kafka later on recognized this when he said that the German language, which he helped to transform in his writing, could never be his personally, that

the German *Mutter* was not an expression of his mother but was somehow detached from him.* Even Kafka's sense of connection and lessening of individual isolation through language had its disadvantages;
and we see this more generally among Prague Jews in the high rate of
suicide, the eccentric forms of behavior, and the dreams of escaping
from the Prague Jewish community.

Yet Kafka was not entirely passive. If we accept his words as reported by Janouch, then he had another side as a young boy, at the time
when he was still attending elementary school. Janouch brings up in
1920 the name of the French anarchist and murderer Ravachol (Franz
Augustin Königstein), and Kafka tells him a story of when he was tarred
with the name Ravachol by the family cook (though not the same one
who dragged him to school). Kafka says that between 1891 and 1894
(when he was between eight and eleven and attending school at the
Meatmarket), he was quite an active boy. When the cook was late to
pick him up, Kafka says he joined a gang "of the biggest guttersnipes in
the class" and went off with them in the opposite direction from which
the nursery maid might come. Nearly every time, he says, there was a
roughhousing, and when Janouch laughs at the idea of the puny Kafka
becoming part of it, the answer was that often he would "come home
after outings in tears, dirty, but buttons off my jacket and my collar
torn." The maids would keep it quiet, and they destroyed the evidence
of his battles. But the cook once said, "You're a real ravachol." Kafka
asked his parents what that meant and was told by his father that Ravachol was a criminal and a murderer. When Kafka fell sick with an in-
flamed throat, he asked the cook why he was a criminal. She told him
right away that *ravachol* was simply a Czech expression, "just something people say." Kafka's throat inflammation quickly disappeared
and he became well. But inwardly he continued to think of himself as a
criminal, an Ishmael, an outcast, and he discontinued the after-school
fights in order to return home on time.

Although the association of the ten-year-old Kafka with Ravachol
may seem amusing to us, the assimilation of the French anarchist's
name into Czech usage, so that even the cook used it, implies just how
close Prague was to all areas of rebellion and anarchism, whether coming from Paris or Vienna. At the time Kafka was a ravachol, Europe was

---

*Almost ten years later, Kafka commented on the tortured relationship between German
and Jew in the Jewish poet Heine: "An unhappy man. The Germans reproached him
and still reproach him for being a Jew, and nevertheless he is a German, what is more
a little German, who is in conflict with Jewry. That is what is so typically Jewish about
him." (Gustav Janouch, *Conversations with Kafka* [New York: New Directions, 1971],
p. 96). In this remark alone, Kafka caught all the paradoxes of his own situation and
usage. Strikingly, the virulently anti-Semitic Richard Wagner was the first to point out
that as a Jew Heine could never be considered part of the pantheon of significant German
writers. Heine was of course a convert to Christianity, which only intensifies the paradoxes.

enduring an epidemic of anarchist assassinations of major political figures, and a series of artistic secessions in Munich, Berlin, and of course Vienna. What all this activity suggests is that anarchism, assassinations, secessions, and avant-gardism were not isolated phenomena but associated movements. The assassinations of heads of state had reverberations in rebellions that led to artistic secessions and to ever newer avant-gardes. Europe in the 1890s was caught in episodes of sons rebelling against fathers, and we can view Kafka's guttersnipe activities after school, which led to the ravachol label, as directed against parental wishes. For Hermann, all that counted was upward mobility, socially and economically; for the young Kafka, what counted was some individual expression that, directly opposed to Hermann's wishes, led to the ravachol joke.

Within a period of just a few years, Czar Alexander II of Russia, President Carnot of France, Franz Josef's wife Elizabeth, King Humbert of Italy, and President McKinley of the United States were assassinated. At the same time, we have a series of secessions, and Karl Kraus's *Die Fackel*, whose intention, as its name implies, was to torch the old by burning out all that was false and hypocritical. We also see Kropotkin's anarchist cells and artistic rebellions or separatist movements across all of Europe. Ravachol, a French Jew, was simply part of the landscape, fitting himself in as an anarchist, but in fact he was a psychopathic murderer, responsible for the Raskolnikov-like killing of an old miserly man and his housekeeper. Even Kropotkin came to repudiate Ravachol; but the end of the century was ripe for avant-gardism, whether in forms of political anarchy, in more artistic shapes, or even as nationalistic movements.

It seemed that a witches' brew had been created, and Prague and especially Prague Jews were not left unaffected. For the many avant-gardes, in fiction, painting, and music, found themselves on a collision course with the nationalistic movements, especially the Young Czechs. Nationalism and radical innovation in the arts, while perhaps part of the same spirit of rebelliousness, did not go hand in hand, and in fact the popularity of Smetana and Dvořák in music helped bolster the anti-Modern feeling of the nationalists. That in turn entrapped the Jews, who were identified with avant-gardes as well as with anarchism, assassination, and all other forms of radical rebellion.

If my fear were not so great, I should console myself with the fact that it is not impossible to see everything differently and yet to live. But I am afraid, I am namelessly afraid of this change. I have, indeed, hardly got used yet to this world, which seems good to me. What should I do in another? I would so gladly stay among the meanings that have become dear to me; and if anything has to change at all, I would like at least to be allowed to live among dogs, who possess a world akin to our own and the same things.

— RILKE, *THE NOTEBOOK OF MALTE LAURIDS BRIGGE*

FOUR Prague and the Schoolboy

K AFKA'S ENTRANCE into the German National Humanistic Gymnasium in 1893, when he was ten, occurred at an auspicious time in European history not only because of the radical artistic movements but also because of the enormous shifts in power. A great part of this shift was caused by a surge in industrialization and the threat that it posed for what was still a medieval type of order in the Austro-Hungarian Empire. Prussia, which had quickly embraced industry and modern capitalism, had become the largest player in central Europe, while in the empire, older forces, whether in Poland, Czechoslovakia, Austria, or Hungary, were trying to retain their power despite the threat of radical change posed by industry and growth capitalism. Although Franz Josef was sensitive to political matters, hoping to keep together a disparate group of ethnic forces, in terms of growth, capitalization, and industry he was backward, permitting the rest of Europe to surpass him easily.

In the empire itself, Austria lagged badly, whereas Bohemia (with Prague as its center) and neighboring Moravia surged ahead, accounting in time for almost two-thirds of all the industrial output in the empire. "Progress," not only in industrial matters but in all areas of human endeavor, became a catchword — and for the empire that was threatening. For progress, in its way, challenged the very ground rules established in 1815 at the Congress of Vienna, then re-established after the 1848 revolutions; and it was upon these rules, however loosely interpreted and followed, that the monarchy depended.* Progress, in this

---

*Progress was as threatening as the depression of 1873, which fueled resentment of Jews,

respect, weakened everything, even when it took the form of advances in technology, in the building of railroads, in the development of the electric telegraph, the telephone, photography, the phonograph, x-rays. Scientific developments were even more threatening and were expanding so rapidly that their practical applications would not be far behind: the molecular theory of gases, the measurement of the velocity of light and experimental proof of the earth's rotation, theories on the nature of meteors and comets, the discovery of the function of dust, the proof of humanity's great antiquity (which contradicted much speculation based on the Bible), the theory of organic evolution, cell theory and re-capitulation theory in embryology, germ theory of the zymotic (infec-tious or contagious) diseases, the discovery of white blood corpuscles, and dozens of others.

Although not all these advances penetrated into Prague or Bo-hemia, such experimental daring was itself a form of avant-garde, and along with the rebelliousness of the new art, such progress was an at-tack, implicit and explicit, on the old and the traditional. As all these developments in theory, in practical science, in the arts, and in culture generally came together or ran parallel to each other, they had reverber-ations with an ominous undertone. Prague was not Paris, and Bohemia was not Germany or France, but the momentum of the new was every-where, and it led to new alignments, new struggles, new forms of eth-nic clashes.

For a Jew like Kafka, all this was bad news, even if the avant-gardes in the arts would eventually nourish his imagination. It was bad news because the entire social structure was opening up. As new classes formed, Jews found intense competition at every level, and the conse-quence was the resurgence of active anti-Semitism. As Bohemia went from being an agricultural and rural society to an urban one, as people poured into the larger towns and cities to work in industry or factories, they created a large lower middle class, and that inevitably meant com-petition with Jewish shopkeepers and small businessmen. In this light we can understand Hermann Kafka's intense work habits as a way of holding his own against Czech competitors. Jews had done fairly well under the Habsburgs, and they aligned themselves overwhelmingly with Franz Josef. But now with the ground shifting under them as a re-sult of so many changes, they found themselves adrift, caught between Czech Christians and German Christians, but the Czechs were espe-cially antagonistic as they became increasingly nationalistic. The Czechs perceived their country as controlled by Jews, although this was a vast exaggeration, and they saw their own way up blocked by Jewish prosperity. Few Jews could be considered fat cats, but a dispro-

---

for they competed in the lower-middle-class sector of shopkeepers, small businesses, clerks, artisans, and others. Czechs said, "Buy Czech," or "Don't patronize Czech trai-tors," meaning Germans, but especially Jews.

portion in the population existed, and the small number of Jews who had done extraordinarily well became ever more visible.

Thus, Kafka at ten was poised on the edge of a maelstrom. All the old racial hatreds, the ethnic clashes, the irrational attacks based on blood libel and other fantasies were further exacerbated by the assault of the new, in which Jews were perceived as playing a disproportionate role. We see the early formulation of the fantasy Hitler wrote about in *Mein Kampf,* that Jews controlled the very hearts and minds of Germany.

Furthermore, the Czechs and Germans had been in conflict with one another for five hundred years, from the time of the Hussite Rebellion at the end of the fourteenth century.* Confrontations continued from then on, with Bohemians suffering repeated defeats, Czechs as a whole not doing any better, and Germans dominating militarily, even while the Czechs, like the Poles, survived to return to the fray. By the 1890s, the balance was tipping, although not until after World War I would the independence of Czechoslovakia become a fact.

Particularly galling to Bohemians was that although their share of the industrial output of the entire monarchy was well over 50 percent, this was not reflected in per capita returns.[1] The return was in fact only about half of Germany's, leaving Bohemia and Moravia relatively poor despite their concentration of industry. By the decade or so before the turn of the century, about two-thirds of the population was working in industry, with the other third in agriculture; and this was of course a sharp increase, bringing people to the cities for work and increasing the potential for political discontent. A large work force, an underpaid population, Viennese neglect of the Czechs as a whole, ethnic hatred, the memory of old prejudices, and the seeds for nationalism were all there. The consequence was that Germans were forced to draw together under the protection of the monarchy; Czechs looked for their own forms of salvation in the various nationalistic groups; and Jews became the focus of everyone's discontent.

Economic issues, though not paramount, were significant, especially after the Viennese crash of 1873, in which the stock market plunged and a recession followed. Nearly all of Europe suffered, but Austro-Hungary as an undeveloped entity suffered more and did not pull out of the recession until decades later when its own industrial

---

*Though events of the fourteenth and fifteenth centuries might seem tangential to the life of Kafka, they are not irrelevant since they poisoned relations between Czechs and Germans in a lasting way. John Hus, in the fourteenth century, attacked the abuses of the clergy and allied himself with the nationalistic yearnings of the Bohemians against German elements in the region. This led to what have been called the Hussite Wars in the fifteenth century, and what had started out as a religious struggle (Hus is usually seen as a forerunner of the Protestant Reformation, especially in his condemnation of profligate priests) became a nationalistic one. This was one of the roots of Czech-German antagonism in Kafka's time.

output increased. The monarchy had always lagged behind Germany, France, and England, and despite a surface appearance of political stability, the monarchy was falling farther and farther behind economically. Bohemia was becoming increasingly frustrated in its attempt to challenge more successful societies, and the consequence was an intensification of attacks on Jews.

In 1893, a critical year for Kafka, a blood libel case occurred in Kolín, in central Bohemia. Hermann Kafka had relatives there, so that the case was not isolated or distant. When a young Czech servant girl was murdered, a nationalistic paper took up the usual cry that she had been killed by Jews so that her blood could be used to bake matzos. The murder was trumpeted as a Jewish ritual, recalling the medieval charge against Jews that they were plotting to kill Christians as they had once killed Jesus. Although that particular paper was seized, the news was out, and it spread throughout Bohemia, including Prague. The result was a series of anti-Semitic riots, demonstrations, and small-scale pogroms that lasted through the later 1890s. The riots took the same form of the later Nazi *Kristallnacht:* shops were looted, their owners molested, synagogues were desecrated and even burned.

Hermann Kafka's shop was very close to where the rioting took place, but it remained untouched since Hermann had so strongly identified with the native Czech population and spoke the language. The shop was threatened but not looted, and so Hermann was able to weather these outbursts of hate. In this way the still very young Kafka may have been lulled into believing he was safe.

We don't know at quite what age Kafka began to form secret and then open sympathies with the Czechs, whose anti-Semitism he recognized but also with whose aspirations he could identify. The young Kafka observed how imperious and tyrannical Hermann was in his store, how he berated the Czech employees and mocked them as listless and worthless. And since Kafka had early on set himself against his father, he empathized with the employees and on occasion interceded when they all threatened to walk out.* The "exploited" child, in his own perception of events, sided with the exploited enemy of his own people: another paradox for the youthful Kafka. Brought up with a father who paid only lip service to a religion and race he did not honor except occasionally, Kafka found himself forced to consider himself a Jew, and he never considered himself anything else. Yet in the Czech-Jewish wars, he became a secret sympathizer with the persecutor of his

---

*With some consistency, when he was an official at the Workers' Accident Insurance Institute, Kafka placed himself on the side of the workers against their employers and the state itself. One area in which he helped workers was in their filing of injury claims; another was in his organization of a hierarchy of danger zones in the workplace, so that employees in more dangerous jobs could better justify their claims. All these actions can be seen as opposition to the father.

people because he saw his father as an imperialist in his dealings. There were dilemmas here within paradoxes, and while the freight of this was heavy, perhaps too heavy personally, it provided the writer with yet another example of conflicting attitudes that only literature could hope to resolve. In his support of the Czech employees, he either consciously or unconsciously saw a way for Hermann to be eliminated. His sympathies were clearly oedipal. Strike down Hermann in the name of the newer generation, and then suffer the guilt of wishing the Jewish patriarch killed by his Christian rebels. He flirted with being Absalom. It was a twisted and anguished scenario, and it occurred early, although just how early we cannot tell. We do know Kafka was being driven ever further into his personal hole, which became both refuge from murderous thoughts and a place where he was constantly threatened.

Prague, at large, was a hostile place for a young Jewish boy, but except for periodic outbursts by the Young Czechs Kafka remained relatively untouched by events. That he was aware of the street demonstrations at their worst is clear from a comment he made to Gustav Janouch: "They [the street demonstrations] have in them the terror of godless wars of religion which begin with flags, songs and music and end in pillage and blood." When Janouch protests that such demonstrations all end peacefully, Kafka counters that that's "only because things go slowly here. . . . Such things will soon happen."[2] He accurately points out how the nationalists speak of "our homeland" when in fact they have already been uprooted by modern civilization. The demonstrations were for Kafka responses to conditions that were inevitable and had no basis either in fact or belief, part of that specter world he said he had attempted to catch in *The Trial*.

At ten, Kafka was already beginning to find specters, some of which had begun to exist in his own home. The rapid arrival of sisters — September 22, 1889, Elli (Gabriele); September 25, 1890, Valli (Valerie); October 29, 1892, Ottla (Ottilie) — of course meant that on the one hand he was displaced from the family center, at least while they were infants; but on the other hand, their advent meant he was the sole and oldest son on whom all hopes lay. The girls were considered lesser beings in terms of available educational opportunities, expectations of them, and what they were prepared for.

There was, however, an alternate way open to them educationally if their parents chose to support them, in private, not public, schools, which fell outside the traditional curriculum. But Kafka's sisters were not exposed to this kind of secondary education — they were given the traditional upbringing, receiving only elementary school education. The early years of the three girls could not have been particularly happy ones; they surely were not for Kafka or his mother. Kafka made few references to the presence of the babies; his mother, already harassed by Hermann's need for her in the store, as well as in the evenings over cards, must have found herself with even less time for other domestic or personal details. Although stable, Julie amidst her heroic exertions was subject to depression, since her life, from childhood, had turned her into a slavey. What this meant to Kafka when he was ten or so remains speculative, but the distance he put between himself and his parents, and especially Julie, in clear response to her absence, must have derived from about this time. Hermann was another matter. Even if the son removed himself emotionally from the father, Hermann's presence dominated: he clearly ruled. Whatever the son's response, there was bulky, demanding, bullying, needful Hermann.

This emotional distancing, which becomes so significant in the mature Kafka, possibly developed when the girl children arrived, although it could have occurred much earlier, when his brothers died. Kafka's feelings probably remained inchoate — with equal amounts of guilt, empowerment, and experiencing of the divine — until he felt abandoned as family grief followed by pregnancies and births left little time or attention for him. Whatever the exact sequence, Kafka set himself on a collision course with his family and transformed every difference into a larger social or political issue. He took differences with his parents, whether religious, social, or personal, and turned them into much broader matters that could feed his imagination. The distancing we note here is a foreshadowing of how he would position himself outside all social bureaucratization, outside a culture in which individual striving became frustrated and meaningless. From his own position in his family, Kafka was able to extrapolate a vision of what society was becoming, or had already become. This vision was of course reinforced by his career in the Workers' Accident Insurance Institute, work he hated because of its facelessness, inhuman procedures, and lack of attention to individual need — in other words, its bureaucratic nature.

In nearly all ways, Kafka could extrapolate those larger questions from his own situation. In his perception of Hermann's relationship to Judaism — loose, almost incoherent, with celebration only of the high holidays, and that tepidly — Kafka found the much larger question of the Western Jew who was assimilating to something that would not assimilate him, who was acculturated to a culture that intensely rejected him. A slim perception from childhood, his observations of Hermann and Julie maneuvering among Gentiles for acceptance, for Kafka became a whole question of identity, of individual expression. Unlike the Eastern European Jew, he was bureaucratized, a weak, pale copy of the real; *other* Jews were alive, valid, however debauched by their poverty and dirt. How early he witnessed this hypocrisy, in Hermann, in particular, but also in Julie, we cannot determine; but we can assume he saw while quite young his father's half-hearted attempts to remain what he was while climbing socially and economically. That distancing Kafka practiced from childhood did not only make him suffer marginality, it

gave him an angle of perception that enabled him to observe what others would miss.

Distancing served a function, especially for his development into a
writer, but for the moment, it created depression based on absence, on
what he lacked. Early evidence of this comes in his sense that he was a
failure, or that he would fail in the next situation despite his success in
the previous one. He saw around him at the prestigious Altstädter
Gymnasium students he believed to be his superiors, and he deferred to
strict teachers who, he felt, thought he was an imbecile. In no actual
instances was any of this true. Kafka passed and usually passed well in
a highly competitive, highly achieving environment. Many of the students came from much more economically privileged homes than his
own, and several were on scholarships based on intellectual ability. We
can only explain Kafka's self-assessment, in part, by seeing him as suffering from an "absence" of what he required, that support system
young people take for granted, which led to his poor estimation of his
abilities and of his chances in school.*

The Altstädter Deutsches Gymnasium was reputedly the academically toughest secondary school in Prague.† Kafka was one of eighty-
four boys who were divided into two groups. In his class, called 1a, Jews
made up three-quarters of the group (thirty out of thirty-nine), eight
were Catholic, one Protestant. We do have a contemporary view of
Kafka (by Emil Utitz), although Kafka's exact age is undetermined.

> There was nothing striking about him. He was always clean and tidy, un-
> obtrusive and solid, but never elegantly dressed. For him school was al-
> ways something that failed to reach through to the innermost self. . . . We
> could never become really intimate with him. Something like a glass
> wall constantly surrounded him. With his quiet, kindly smile he opened
> the world up for himself, but he locked himself up in front of it. He never
> joined in our conversations. He only once came with us to a pub that was
> out of bounds. There, too, he was just the same as usual — a guest who

---

*Marthe Robert (in her book *As Lonely as Franz Kafka*) catches this aspect of Kafka
better than any other commentator. Her discussions of his "self-hatred," lack of identification, and envy of those Jews he cannot himself be are all handled with keen psychological insight into the boy who would become Kafka.
†The German gymnasium is not the equivalent of the American high school; it covers
a much longer period of time. Basically, in American terms it encompasses the fifth
grade through high school, a total of eight years, and its function, accordingly, is quite
different. The American system presupposes certain stages of development, a progression
that attempts to lead the child through education gradually, with each promotional stage
geared to emotional and sexual development. In the German system, which of course
included Kafka in Prague, there was no effort to cater to a child's maturity. By ten, he
(not "she") was thrust into the big league academically speaking, with a curriculum
aimed at an adult mind. The gymnasium would, in effect, provide the educational level
we associate not just with the high school years but also with at least the first two years
of university. By age eighteen, the Prague gymnasium student would be prepared for
professional school, not university, in American terms.

looked with interest at the unfamiliar surroundings, smiled at them, whilst keeping himself at a distance.[3]

Kafka later characterized himself as hopelessly indifferent, "almost ridiculous, brutally self-satisfied indifference — that is a self-sufficient but coldly whimsical child." He says that indifference was his sole protection "against the nervous disturbance that came from anxiety and guilt feelings."[4] Recalling his years at the gymnasium, he describes the "wretched clothes" his parents provided for him, made by a tailor with no eye or sense of style. He says he let the dreadful clothes affect his posture, and he walked around "with my back bowed, my shoulders drooping, my hands and arms at awkward angles"; he feared mirrors "because they showed in me an ugliness which in my opinion was inevitable."[5] His description of himself, in these miserable clothes, reflects a reshaping: he viewed himself as bowed, all awkwardness from limbs at strange angles, his lean, tall body drooping, becoming something different from what it might have been in more suitable clothes. He wonders if he could have seemed strange to others, and if he did, why they didn't remark it, or show him more attention.

While Kafka, in looking back, saw himself as lacking courage, he cites two of his schoolmates who possessed it, both of whom shot themselves. In this witty, trenchant remark, Kafka indicates that he who is fearful, cowardly, and anguish-ridden can save himself through those qualities, while the brave man challenges the very things that will defeat him. Kafka remained low-keyed, distanced, speaking of himself near the time of his death as combining shyness and garrulousness. He tells of a weakness that kept him from going mad; and with shrewd insight into how he used illness, withdrawal, and inadequacy as effective weapons against a life he feared, he indicates that he tried little for fear of going mad.

Although religious teachers no longer dominated in the schools, Kafka had a Piarist brother as one of his instructors. The Piarists* ran their own school, which Brod and Werfel attended, and it was considered less rigid and more leisurely in its approach to education. Nevertheless, Kafka found himself subjected to a particularly rigid Piarist teacher at the Altstädter Gymnasium and subjected as well to an extremely demanding curriculum. The priest, Emil Gschwind, was a Latinist who insisted that the existing curriculum, already heavily loaded with Latin, was insufficient, and therefore assigned additional reading. In the case of Kafka, Hugo Bergmann, and the other leading students, Gschwind asked for further work, translations, and presentations, all to be checked in private visits to the monastery where he lived. In this disciplined, somewhat harsh atmosphere, Kafka excelled. Gschwind con-

---

*A Roman Catholic teaching order instituted in Rome in the early seventeenth century.

sidered him one of the better Latinists, although if we seek Latin references, or even classical references, in Kafka's diaries and letters we come up short. His resistance to what he had to learn did not, apparently, diminish his classroom ability, but his memory screened it off. Only in his mastery of German did Kafka demonstrate what Latin had helped him to do, since German, like Latin, is an inflected language in which, except for the verb, the position of words can vary depending on case endings. It is very possible that, although Kafka never admitted it, Latin helped him to tighten and organize his use of German, to make it a distinctive usage of his own, not indebted to any predecessors in particular.*

As he advanced in the gymnasium, the curriculum shifted somewhat: the introduction of Greek, with the need now to learn long passages from Homer, the reduction of the time spent on German, the added study of geography, then, later, history. Places, dates, dynasties, battles, emperors, pretenders all had to be memorized and spewed forth in class, so that these subjects, which Kafka seemed to like, never really caught his imagination. Surprisingly, at a time when advances in science were enormous, becoming an avant-garde in themselves, both science and mathematics received relatively short shrift. Kafka disliked mathematics, and fortunately for him the school didn't appear to place much value on it, since in eight years of instruction, three hours weekly, the curriculum did not proceed beyond elementary algebra and geometry. As for science, it was barely touched upon in any serious way, considered perhaps too dangerous a force, possibly subversive of both the Roman Catholic and Orthodox Jewish view of the world. Darwin, in particular, was viewed as perilous stuff, and the work of biologists and physicists was considered disruptive of received wisdom. A precarious empire did not need new theories of humanity and the universe to upset traditional ideas.

The basic curriculum was obviously heavily oriented toward languages, classical and German. Religious instruction also was required, two hours weekly, and other courses were offered in French, Czech, and physical education. Almost nothing was offered in the arts or in broader culture, whose very areas were bursting with new ideas and new formulations. In his first three years, Kafka was graded *Vorzugschüler*, or "Excellent Student," showing deficiencies only in mathematics, which would continue through most of his school years.

Ferdinand Deml, Kafka's German literature teacher, was a significant influence, for he took German language study seriously, and here Kafka absorbed his lessons. Deml left his own record of what he consid-

---

*The hatred of Latin, not its beneficial uses, comes through in *Amerika*, when Kafka's protagonist recalls a Dr. Krumpal, his Latin teacher, who created a harsh and unpleasant classroom atmosphere.

ered important in good German usage, and his rules helped to clarify Kafka's own German, which was *Prager Deutsch*. This was a Prague form of German cut off from the outside world, an inbred language, with some borrowings from both Czech and Yiddish. Not a dialect or a patois, *Prager Deutsch* was a rendering of traditional German where idioms had been worn away and replaced by Czech and Yiddish forms, while still presented as German.[6] It was linguistically corrupt, not mainstream German, and Kafka's tendency toward it, especially with a faint overlay of Yiddish from Hermann, was held at bay by Deml's insistence on clarity and accuracy in the use of idiom. Gustav Janouch reported that Kafka's German had a hard accent, like German spoken by Czechs. This was one type of German that Karl Kraus, in Vienna, railed against.

Deml caught up with Kafka in his first three years, from ten to thirteen, very impressionable years when language becomes more than forms and takes on imaginative shapes. Insistent on idiomatic usage, Deml often used Grimm's fairy tales as exemplary, and then insisted that students write out their own sentences and do exercises to give them a more limber and yet precise sense of the language. He also insisted, and this we would expect, on grammatical correctness, a particularly important element in a language whose sentence formation depends not on position (except for the verb), but on correct case and gender endings. Models, exercises, syntax — Deml hammered away, and by using Goethe to teach narrative, he gave Kafka an author he would venerate for the rest of his life. Goethe became such a literary god to him in fact that Kafka often showed bitterness that a Czech Jew, for whom German was somewhat alien, could never really "own" Goethe. He belonged only to ethnic Germans.

Language study took up a good many hours of Kafka's early years, whether Latin and Greek, German, or later Czech and French, in lesser degrees. Although he never considered himself adept in foreign languages, by the end of his life Kafka had a good hold on Czech, French, and English, a lesser, mainly reading, knowledge of Hebrew, some knowledge of Yiddish, which he could understand, and of course the Latin that stayed with him for some time. The classical Greek appeared to have drifted away as rapidly as it had been force-fed.

School offered little respite from the rigors of a father-dominated culture, and that was probably the point: to create a continuity of discipline and rigor between home and school so that in some way the student was prepared for life. Intellectually, except in language, Kafka kept little of what he learned, and none of it was intended to spark the imagination, prod innate talent, or provide intellectual sustenance. The system simply was not geared for that, although in that original class of eighty-four (only twenty-four, incidentally, survived to obtain a certificate in the eighth year) there were several talented and intellectual

students. The aim was standardization, not the furtherance of originality. Kafka toed the academic line, feeding himself with distaste for it,
undermined by that ever present sense of failure he saw looming at
every turn.

Kafka's sense of failure was not paranoid. Students failed, as the
small number with certificates indicates. Although the school was run
by rules, there were some Franz Lehar–like operetta settings during
end-of-the-year celebrations. At that time, the staid gymnasium teachers, all of them officials of the empire, dressed up in their imperial uni-
forms, with swords by their sides, plumed hats or helmets set firmly on
their heads. The scene was farcical, especially for the Jewish students,
for whom none of this display had any significant meaning. Franz Josef
felt this Austrian celebration, held throughout the empire, to be a way
of holding the Dual Monarchy together. It was, instead, a source
of amusement or folly for most. Robert Musil, in Vienna, mocked its
operetta nature in *The Man Without Qualities*, and Kafka himself
touched upon it in "A Report to an Academy." School was made up of
extremes: from firm, disciplined classrooms to displays of ostenta-
tious, pompous emptiness. Peering at his strict teachers uniformed like
Lehar hussars, Kafka could only have honed his parodic sensibilities.

In Kafka's third year at the gymnasium, the family moved to Celetná Street (once the Street of Bakers), in the Zeltnergasse, quite close
to Hermann and Julie's store. It was also close to the Teyn church, and
from his room (as *the* son, Kafka was given his own room) the student
could hear hymns, organ music, even prayers. From his window, he
could even peer through a high window of the church. At school, religious instruction was in the Hebrew language, but written work was
mainly in German excerpts from the Bible and the Talmud, little of
which made a deep impression on the indifferent Kafka. But it was
necessary for him to prepare for bar mitzvah, his initiation as a
thirteen-year-old into Jewish manhood. For that, he would have to
memorize a passage in Hebrew and chant it in the Zigeuner Synagogue.
We recognize what little effect the Hebrew had on Kafka at this time,
for when he studied it seriously much later in life, he started at the beginning. The bar mitzvah, for the nonbelieving young man, was pro
forma, what every Jewish boy went through for the sake of his family,
even when the family, like Hermann's, placed little emphasis on a religious education. Except as stories, the Bible and Torah remained quite
alien to Kafka's thinking, and he resisted attendance at the synagogue
in preparation for the event. Hermann, as the father of the bar mitzvah
candidate, had also to read from the Torah, and he saw this as an auspicious event, as a man doing his social, rather than religious, duty. To
be able to afford the expense of such a celebration was a sign of one's
upward mobility.

One teacher who proved the exception to Kafka's "harmful" education impressed him without becoming an object of fear. A disciple of Ernst Mach, the influential physicist and philosopher Adolf Gottwald served as a good part of the science department, instructing in physics, botany, natural history, astronomy, and other subjects. Kafka was under his instruction for five of his first six years at the gymnasium, and Gottwald's point of view was quite important for the young boy at this critical developmental stage. Gottwald tried to teach his students to think, not merely to absorb material by rote. As a follower of Mach's philosophy, he emphasized the importance of sensory impressions as the means by which the individual connected himself to the physical world. Mach's synthetic and all-inclusive point of view attempted to associate Darwin's evolutionary theories with the mental processes of the individual, so that a single theory could hold true for both the objective and subjective worlds. Mach was a Prague citizen, but his philosophy spread out to Vienna, Berlin, and other centers of developing Modernism.

If we seek a key idea in Kafka's early intellectual development, it would not come from science as such but from Gottwald's philosophy, and from him back to Ernst Mach, one of whose most famous disciples was Robert Musil, who wrote his doctoral thesis on the philosopher. We find in Mach's views a good deal of the resonance we discover in various avant-gardes, since Mach criticized nineteenth-century science as full of frozen concepts that were to be swept away by his theory of an impressionistic mode dependent on sensory impressions. Mach sought a unified theory, not a number of disparate ideas that explained one thing or another. His influential *Analysis of Sensation and the Relation of the Physical to the Psychical* (1886) stressed human sensations as the entirety of experience. If "substance" was unnecessary, then all was "becoming," and man needed only a language to ground what he sensed. Mach's philosophy was so significant because it supported, paralleled, and influenced similar theories, all of which undermined rationality. Mach relied upon correspondences, associations, tangential moments, revelations, antirational processes, nonlogical linkages, unconscious drives, mad moments, extremes of subjectivity, demonstrations of ego and self. These were new forms of "thought," not antithought or nonthought. Thought itself as a concept was being redefined, whereas earlier, as in Immanuel Kant, Mach asserted, it had been frozen.

Gottwald offered a trimmed-down version of this theory, but its import was quite effective in reaching the young Kafka. He would, in a few years, begin to read Darwin and attempt to blend evolutionary theory with his own subjective approach to phenomena. The theories outlined in class permitted Kafka to seek associations between two warring worlds, that of science and that of pure knowledge, blending spirit, soul, mind. In their efforts to undermine traditional frozen concepts of thought or knowledge, Modernist artists emphasized the subjective, but in point of fact they were merely addressing one imbalance with another. Modernism becomes, in one of its phases, an effort to bring back intellect and spirit from intellectual limbo. In this, Kafka played a large role.

Of course, even after his bar mitzvah certified him as a man, Kafka was still a child. Unresolved were his feelings about being dragged through school, his feelings about his parents (fear of Hermann, hostility toward Julie for her acquiescence), and his sense of displacement as his sisters grew from infants into people with needs and desires of their own, a kind of female club united against him, the one brother.

What was shadowing him as he moved toward his teenage years was a combination of sensory experiences, intellectual forms, stirrings of puberty, and slowly shaping angers, all of which remained isolated from each other and each of which felt like some form of warfare that he had to do battle against. Within these terms, the very educational system, the system that devoured most of his time and energy, was part of the enemy force. Unlike several of his contemporaries at the Altstädter Gymnasium, such as Hugo Bergmann, Kafka did not find school coherent; rather, it joined all the other elements to reinforce his feelings of dividedness and uncertainty. His method, even when he was as young as five or six and beginning in the lower school, was defensive, a withdrawal into whatever he considered to be his own; and later, as we follow him through the school system, despite the friends he made, he remained shy, withdrawn, isolated.

Later on, when he complained about the wishy-washiness of Hermann Kafka's religion, Kafka was not lamenting the loss of religious life as such, but the community that religious belief could bring to the entire family. He saw it as social empowerment, not as a matter of faith, tradition, even history. When he looked longingly at Eastern European Jews, he saw not the Old Testament or Moses or the Torah, but a community shaped by acceptance of certain received ideas, ideas less significant than the forms of acceptance. He tells us repeatedly in diary entries and letters how he missed some principle of coherence; days, weeks, months, years passed by while he waited for something that, within, he knew would never arrive. He learned (how early we cannot tell) that whatever coherence there was to be he would have to create, and that would come only in his writing, where transformation of all the uncertainty was the sole certainty.*

The ideal was Hugo Bergmann, and if Kafka measured himself against that student, first in his class, a scholarship boy, and a tutor on the side, then young Franz was lost. Bergmann was every other student's nightmare. He not only did it all, he made it look easy, a student

---

*He spent his life composing the idea that, as he put it in "On Parables," the "incomprehensible is incomprehensible, and we know that already."

seemingly unruffled by the inconsistencies and pitfalls life sets up for the young adolescent. Bergmann avoided them all, and yet although he had an important career as a scholar and archivist, he somehow did not leap into the kind of fame his early career suggested for him. Kafka, the far greater figure, found everything eating into him. He played off his religion teacher, Nathan Gruen, against his teacher of logic, the ever present Gschwind, and both of them against Gustav Effenberger, one of those strict teachers who can make science and mathematics into memorably unpleasant experience. Bergmann assimilated it all, and it seemed to make sense for him; but for Kafka, whom Bergmann helped with mathematics, it all remained discrete and troubling.

In a diary entry for December 1911, he reminisced about his time at the gymnasium, when, in good Talmudic style, he argued with Bergmann over the existence of God. "At the time I liked to begin with a theme I had found in a Christian magazine . . . in which a watch and the world and the watchmaker and God were compared to one another, and the existence of the watchmaker was supposed to prove that of God." This was of course one of the most basic proofs of God's existence, offered up in religious school to young children as an indisputable "proof." Kafka continues: "In my opinion I was able to refute this very well as far as Bergmann was concerned, even though this refutation was not firmly grounded in me and I had to piece it together for myself like a jigsaw puzzle before using it." He adds that he had no other motive than "the desire to distinguish myself and my joy in making an impression and in the impression itself."[7] As an intellectual argument, it held little interest for Kafka other than the desire to win.

The talk with Bergmann took place while they were walking around the tower of the Town Hall, which includes an astronomical clock, a view of which Kafka could enjoy from his bedroom window when the family lived in the Altstädter Ring. The tower was a dominant presence, and when the hour struck, with bell chimes, a procession of apostles marched out of one doorway and into another, a reminder to the overwhelmingly Catholic population of Prague that the church, even in the tower, was always present. The tower must also have fed into Kafka's sense of alienation from a Prague full of Christian mysteries, mysteries that he was forced to confront hourly.

His isolation is caught in another diary entry, also in 1911, and it appears to reflect the entire shadow of Kafka's life, not merely his experience at twenty-eight, when he wrote the entry.[8] He speaks of how "dreadful" it is to be a bachelor,

> to become an old man struggling to keep one's dignity while begging for any invitation whenever one wants to spend an evening in company, having to carry one's meal home in one's hand, unable to expect anyone with a lazy sense of calm confidence, able only with difficulty and vexation to give a gift to someone, having to say good night at the front door, never being able to run up a stairway beside one's wife, to lie still and have only

the solace of the view from one's window when one can sit up, to have only side doors in one's room leading into other people's living rooms.

He continues the litany, moving along into the bachelor's alienation from his family because of his failure to marry, being forced to admire others' children, not even being able to say one has none of one's own.* This plaint is not something that just occurred to a man in his later twenties; it is the lament of someone who has experienced being a "bachelor" from childhood, certainly from his early teenage years. It is, for Kafka, at least a fifteen-year-old condition, and if not centered on marriage itself when he was in the gymnasium, then centered on his feelings of marginality, his superfluity. He was, as the Russian authors wrote, a superfluous man.

In 1888, the Neue Deutsche Theater opened in Prague and produced plays by Ibsen and Hauptmann, as well as Wagner and Verdi operas. Kafka would become enraptured by the theater and was part of a group of friends who wrote plays, which they read to the assembled group. Kafka did not read, apparently, and none of his plays survives, but the titles indicate a far-ranging interest, including "The Juggler," "Georg of Podiebrad" (his mother's birthplace), and "Photographs Talk." Though Kafka neither read nor performed his own plays, from his earliest teens he wrote them for birthday parties and other celebrations. At school, he loosened up sufficiently to act Mark Antony in *Julius Caesar*, in German translation, and did other classroom readings in the classics — translations from Homer, for example, which he performed before his school.

With this interest in the theater, we have the first insight into how books or forms of art were beginning to act as a shield from his "bachelor" isolation, as well as from fears generated at school and at home. The "perception" of fear, which in another could have meant paranoia, meant for Kafka a way into a world where paranoia could be transformed, whether in reading or in writing. Paranoia, we recognize, became essential for him, for he learned how to deal with it through a lifestyle uniquely his own: antisocial eating habits, chronic lateness, repressed sexuality. Like Flaubert, he considered himself a monstrosity, and this perhaps "perverse" sense of self nourished him.

What also nourished him as a teenager during the obstacle course

---

*In an early 1915 story, "Blumfeld, an Elderly Bachelor," Kafka treats the subject not only imaginatively but surrealistically. Compare Flaubert's sense of superfluity with that "bachelor" whom Kafka came to admire and respect. Flaubert: "If you participate in life, you don't see it clearly: you suffer from it too much or enjoy it too much. The artist, to my way of thinking, is a monstrosity, something outside nature. . . . So (and this is my conclusion) I am resigned to living as I have lived: alone, with my throng of great men [books] as my only cronies — a bear, with my bear-rug for company" (quoted by Julian Barnes in *Flaubert's Parrot* [New York: Knopf, 1984], pp. 49–50). For Kafka, the bachelor, like Sisyphus, was the prototype and emblem of the artist.

of the gymnasium, as he moved along from course to course and examination to examination, was his sense of a destiny already shaping itself: "From the fact that as a child I had a great nervous fear of waiting
one would conclude that I was destined for something better and that I
foresaw my future."[9] He explains this remark by saying lateness allowed him to try out new possibilities with the people waiting for him,
another way of asserting that he changed shapes so as to breathe new
life into relationships. What he omits is the hostility that continual
lateness for appointments demonstrates; how it becomes a testing of
other people's affection; how it makes the waiter tolerate unforeseen
and uncertain changes of direction in the given situation.

Kafka's shame at his body, long, gangly, almost skeletally thin, undeveloped, unmasculine in his own perception of it, was in part responsible for his desire, or need for transformation:

> Nothing can be accomplished with such a body . . . I was so incoherent
> this morning [because of lack of sleep and wild dreams], felt nothing but
> my forehead, saw a halfway bearable condition only far beyond my pres-
> ent one, and in sheer readiness to die would have been glad simply to
> have curled up in a ball on the cement floor of the corridor. . . . My body
> is too long for its weakness, it hasn't the least bit of fat to engender a
> blessed warmth, to preserve an inner fire, no fat on which the spirit could
> occasionally nourish itself beyond its daily need without damage to the
> whole.[10]

Somehow that body must become "an other," or he will suffer from
going out of bounds, running out of control.

In another diary entry he described food as a means of changing
himself into something others would find repellent. "I shove the long
slabs of rib meat unbitten into my mouth, and then pull them out again
from behind, tearing through stomach and intestines." While food
serves as a form of purgative, it also rips up his insides, and when it
reappears, as excrement, he is a changed person. The foreshadowing of
Gregor Samsa in the 1912 story is clear, and it appears to run back well
into Kafka's earlier years, when the body, and its disproportionate relationship to the body of his father, was clear to him.

Part of his feeling of monstrosity lay in his ambivalence toward his
body. For as Kafka became a teenager in his middle years at the gymnasium, he found his body wanting, even while his yearning for women
began. That he yearned we know from his experiences with prostitutes,
and here too the components are of interest. For in most instances, the
prostitutes were all Czech Gentiles; intercourse, if it had been possible
with a Jewish girl, would have seemed like incest.

This may seem distant from the teenager grinding his way through
the gymnasium, but at an early age Kafka recognized that he could not
be what was expected of him, that inner dictates struggled against
outer goals set for him by others. In that context, he needed to change

not the outer expectation but the inner dictate: *the transformation was from the inside out.* The question was not how others perceived him but how he perceived himself. The transformation, when it occurred, was downward in the evolutionary scale. He never became heroic, a warrior, a fighter; he was always a reduced object that triumphed through its ability to turn others against it. In some ways, Kafka's transformation was allied to suicidal impulses, with suicide the ultimate transformation and victory. Yet he never actually tried suicide — although he once thought of jumping from the fifth floor of the Maison Oppelt — perhaps because he was able to take the impulse and transform it into fictions, where bug, mouse, dog, ape, and other forms served the same function: the death of the author as he is metamorphosed into a new, reduced object.

Eventually, all roads lead back to Kafka's unique situation in Prague near the turn of the century. As Czech and German animosities heated up, with students fighting it out in the streets, the clashes bled over into attacks on Jews. Patriotic German fraternities in 1897, when Kafka was fourteen, felt victorious after the downfall of Prime Minister Badeni, whose inability to unify the various ethnic factions led to his resignation.* When German students celebrated, Czech students rioted and attacked them, at the same time destroying Jewish shops and houses. In this pitched battle, the only shield for Jews was the Prague police, made up mainly of course of Czech Gentiles who were not eager to let off either Jews or Germans. It was at this time that Hermann Kafka's shop was spared; his attention to the Czech language and his low profile as a Jew finally stood him in good stead. In "The Merchant" ("Der Kaufmann"), Kafka mentions police on horseback chasing after the mobs and dispersing them. These clashes became so violent, with the police weighing in with their own brand of brutality, that martial law was needed to put an end to the rioting.

But these clashes are only a small part of the story. The Dreyfus affair from France had spread its poison against Jews, and the blood libel cases occurring at intervals kept the nationalistic right in a turmoil of ethnic, racial, and religious fury. The fact that Germans and German Jews controlled so much of the commercial life of the city, as well as its professional life, was still another factor. Furthermore, the 1899 Hilsner case became the Czech parallel to the Dreyfus affair in France, for it penetrated every part of society like a kind of poison gas. In the village of Polna, in Bohemia, a nineteen-year-old Christian girl, Agnes Hruza, was found murdered, on Saturday, April 1, which was the day

---

*Not unexpectedly, Badeni's failure occurred over language. He had hoped that by elevating Czech to the same level as German in the empire he would placate the Czechs. But the Germans within the Dual Monarchy exploded and brought Badeni down.

before Easter Sunday. The time of year was significant, since Easter and the Jewish Passover usually coincide or overlap. Leopold Hilsner, a shoemaker's assistant from Polna, was charged with the murder, for the purpose of draining the girl's blood to use it in the preparation of Passover matzos. In addition, he was accused of raping her. In a brief time the entire Jewish population of Polna was accused of complicity: it was not an individual crime, but a Jewish crime against an innocent Christian girl. The Prague newspapers became particularly virulent in their attacks on the Jewish population of Polna, playing an active role in the case, as did the press in the Dreyfus affair in France. One could in fact argue that without the press spreading its invective, fanning the flames of arson-minded Czechs, the case would not have achieved its notoriety.

Dr. Karel Baxa, the prosecutor, would later use his prominence in the case to become lord mayor of Prague. In the atmosphere that prevailed, it was relatively easy for him to gain a conviction against Hilsner, who was sentenced to death. The sentence would have stood without the interference of one of the truly great men of Czechoslovakia, Tomáš G. Masaryk, later a democratic president of the country. Masaryk, then a philosophy professor at the Czech University in Prague, laid out the errors made in the case and gained a retrial, a move for which he suffered enormous calumny, including cancellation of his lectures and attacks on him from every direction, especially from the Catholic Church. The retrial proved no better than the original, and Hilsner was again found guilty and sentenced to death, although the sentence was commuted to life imprisonment in 1901, two years after the case began. But Masaryk, despite his pariah status, rallied the Social Democrats and several leftist groups, including many Jews, so that even after the second conviction, Hilsner was pardoned in 1916. The years of his life lost in the case (seventeen) almost equaled Dreyfus's.

The murderer was never found, and lingering doubts or certainties among the anti-Semites remained. Such a case never clears the air, no more than the Dreyfus affair convinced many French that the army had in fact lied, deceived, forged, tricked, or proved itself totally unworthy of trust. The mere fact of the charge, the sentence, the idea of blood libel, remained in the minds of many as part of that continuous blasphemy to be expected from the Jews in their dealings with Christians. The results of the Hilsner case, rather than clarifying Jewish innocence, only proved to anti-Semites that there was a Jewish conspiracy, although the further charge that the newspapers were controlled by Jews would have been hard to prove given the anti-Semitic and riot-instilling nature of the media attacks.* The rapidly growing Young

---

*As part of the continuum of which the Hilsner case formed a part, we find the Beilus affair in Kiev. Mendel Beilus was accused of murdering a Christian child, kept in prison

Czechs found in such cases, as in the earlier ones, perfect justification for their racial and ethnic rhetoric and their periodic riots against Jewish stores and other properties.

Although Kafka on only a few occasions referred directly to these riots, his glancing allusions are telling. Kafka's attitude toward German literature reflects his early sympathy toward Czechs in their clashes with Jews. Rather than dealing with the issue directly in political terms, however, he reroutes his argument through language and literature. His line of reasoning, completely in keeping with his withdrawal, shyness, and desire to be absolutely his own man, is that he can revel in his ethnic strangeness to the German language. He who is held in thrall to Goethe, Schiller, and Heine has discovered a form of escape, a means of evasion. In this view, Kafka's own use of the German language, directly related to *Prager Deutsch,* was an advantage, a way by which he could gain confidence in himself. He could honor Goethe as a literary forebear and yet break away into his own peculiar usage, neither German, Czech, nor Jewish.

If we follow this argument, we are led back into his diaries to an entry for Christmas Day of 1911. There he writes that a "minor literature" has distinct advantages over a major one: a Jewish or Czech literature is not yet penetrated "by a great talent" and "has no gap through which the irrelevant might force its way. Its claim to attention thereby becomes more compelling. The independence of the individual writers, naturally only within the national boundaries, is better preserved." In a major literature, what is of importance takes place "down below, constituting a not indispensable cellar of the structure," but in a minor literature, everything "takes place in the full light of day." In the latter, we are not concerned with the few, but with the many; it "absorbs everyone no less than as a matter of life and death."[11] The implication — and here Kafka is defending his own kind of writing, his own way of seeing — is that a major national literature absorbs everything into history or into a historical perspective. It remains untouched by "the taste of the day," whereas a minor literature is responsive to the needs of the people and their times.

In this formulation, we see Kafka's shaping of his entire life, and we must assume it began to form not when he was twenty-eight, the time of the writing, but in his earliest days, when he was transforming himself into what he knew he had to be. As we work through his com-

---

for two years, then acquitted; but not before the case generated anti-Semitic riots in Russia. Kafka was himself aware of this case and in fact near the end of his life wrote about it in a story that was destroyed by Dora Dymant, with whom he was living. In "The Judgment," Kafka alludes to demonstrations in Kiev, which could have referred to the Beilus case, including a deleted line that makes a direct reference. The Beilus incident became the basis for Bernard Malamud's 1966 novel *The Fixer,* in which Beilus becomes Bok. The Russian Black Hundreds persecuting Jews found their slightly less virulent parallel in Bohemia's Young Czechs.

ments, we note how positive and affirmative he is. This is not the Kafka of "Kafkaesque" anguish or anxiety, but a Kafka who becomes a very important critic of literature, even while defining what was workable for himself. Literature stirs minds; it provides a coherence of national consciousness and gives support to national aspirations in the face of hostile surroundings. So far, Kafka's ideas seem clearly derived from Johann Gottfried von Herder's sense of a folk literature that unites a people and gives them a national purpose, an extremely influential theory in the nineteenth century. But Kafka's game is not quite the same. A minor literature, he says, allows for the spiritualization of broad areas of public life. It creates respect for those active in it, and it awakens the younger generation to higher aspirations. In a typical Kafka statement, such a literature provides a matrix for discussing the antithesis between fathers and sons and allows for the revelation of national faults. All of this is possible because a minor literature allows lesser talents to flourish, whereas a major literature silences the majority.

Goethe, to whom Kafka returned repeatedly, was for him as much devil as god. The great poet and figure, he felt, retarded the development of the German language, paradoxically, "by the force of his writing." Prose style in German may move away from him, but in the end it "returns to him with strengthened yearning and even adopts obsolete idioms found in Goethe but otherwise without any particular connection with him." For Kafka, the German language belongs not to him, but to Goethe; he himself must break the cycle of Goethe worship even while writing in German, Goethe's language.

As Kafka went through the German curriculum at the gymnasium, with its emphasis on the German classics, he recognized how alienated he was from it and from what it stood for, as literature and as language; and yet he also yearned for it. This back and forth, of rejection and desire, created ambiguities in him that we find in every aspect of his career, the foundation for works as seemingly dissimilar as "In the Penal Colony," *The Trial*, and "A Hunger Artist." Kafka alternated between wanting to seize and wanting to be seized. In sexual terms, there was a kind of Manichaean pull between one element and another, in this instance between a dominant masculine strain and a less dominant, but present, feminine line. The feminine, in Kafka's perception of it in his fiction, was manifest in passive acceptance, in some instances a kind of masochism; the masculine, again in his sense of it, was more active, often sadistic and overbearing. In one of his key stories, the pivotal "The Judgment," the feminine side of the son, Georg Bendemann, allows him to become victimized, whereas the masculine side is manifest in the father, who sadistically castigates his son and finally orders his suicide.

We cannot quite determine when Kafka formed these alternative

sides of himself, although it is tempting to see them developing in puberty, with younger sisters who were considered lesser figures in the
household. As he grew up, if we extrapolate from the *Letter to His Father,* Kafka found himself in a strange bind. On one hand, he was the
only sibling with his own room, and the family counted on him, as the
eldest, to further its fortunes. He was the traditional messiahlike presence, the oldest son in a Jewish family; and he was given all the advantages. Yet even as he was vaunted as the "savior," Kafka felt his inadequacy. They expected so much, and it was clear that every day he
let them down. With so much expectation placed on him as a male figure, he felt more like a female — again, within his perception of male
and female. Much of that famous *Letter* suggests his argument that he
is a different kind of male from what Hermann expected, that even if he
seemed female, he was still a man. His ambivalence was not only of a
sexual nature but also a mental and emotional concept: two sides that
could not join because each was out of shape in relation to the other —
a problem he could resolve only through his fiction. In one story or
novel after another he creates opposites: the dominant male figure who
rules the universe, and the weak, feminine figure, who may be a man as
well as a woman. And often a female is the dominant "male," a whip-
master, frequently sadistic and destructive, almost a Medea.

Kafka was more interested in this active-passive ambivalence than
he was in the actual gender role of the characters. His responses to
women in his life and in his fiction were always difficult, and he is not
kind to his female characters. He saw them, as Freud put it, as possessing a *vagina dentata.* Felice Bauer, an innocent bystander in her two engagements to Kafka, becomes one of his archetypal fire-eating women.
Kafka's imagination needed such images and emblems, and much of
this can be traced to his complicated relationship to Julie Kafka. In his
Letter he writes, "It was true that Mother was illimitably good to me,
but all that was in relation to you [Hermann], that is to say, in no good
relation. *Mother unconsciously played the part of a beater during a
hunt* [italics mine]." In claiming that Julie drove young Franz toward
Hermann as if she were beating the woods for game she could flush out
so the hunter could then kill it, Kafka sees her as the real killer; Hermann simply finishes off the job she begins. Kafka argues further that
even if he had responded with defiance and thus set himself on his feet,
Julie's kindness would have "driven [me] back into your orbit, which I
might perhaps otherwise have broken out of, to your advantage and to
my own."[12]

In Kafka's perception of his relationship to his parents, Julie, in an
oedipal reversal, feeds her son to the lionized husband to keep him
happy even while sacrificing the son.* This is, clearly, not an insight

---

*Or in another version of this oedipal twist, Kafka wishes to be "taken" by the father
even while protesting his fear of him and castigating the mother for her role.

that occurred to Kafka in 1919, when he wrote the *Letter*, but was a snowballing of perceptions starting very young, in the earliest stages of Julie's mixture of kindness and neglect. All those cooks, housemaids, and governesses the Kafka family employed simply became stand-ins for the indifferent mother, who used them as surrogates for bringing him up, all the while devoting her energies and attention to the "other" man in the house, Hermann. For every hunter and victim, there is the beater. Without the beater, there is no flushing out the prey. The prey, as Kafka perceived himself, would recur in nearly everything he wrote, where he could revenge himself on that archetypal woman, Julie.

In an "Octavo Notebook" entry, perhaps in 1917, Kafka speaks of one of his favorite books, *Don Quixote*. Once again, the masculine-feminine ambivalence is established, here between the Don and Sancho. "Don Quixote's misfortune," Kafka writes, "is not his imagination, but Sancho Panza."[13] What this suggests is that the Don's flights of imagination, his fantasies of self and world, his projections of self onto the world, are inhibited by the socially based realities represented by Sancho. We should not, Kafka says, condemn the Don's flights, but those who restrain him and force him back to the realities of the world, as Sancho does. The feminine side, here represented as the Don, is held back by the masculine "real world," here emblematized by Sancho. The struggle between the two, although played out between Sancho and the Don, represents personal clashes within Kafka, as we can see from his repeated use of such dualities. They suggest, further, that in his quest for some kind of wholeness from the younger years on, he was inhibited by not finding clearly demarcated feminine and masculine roles: that Julie's playing of Hermann's game did not allow her feminine side, as mother, to manifest itself, and that, as a consequence, Kafka, while developing male sexual tastes, sensed within himself a feminine side that had to be equated, usually, with weakness, or else with sadistic, Medea-like strength. Women could not be what they were. Felice Bauer never had a chance as his fiancée, since she flitted through his imagination either as a failed woman or else as a maenad fixed upon tearing him to pieces when his guard was down.

Another way to read these comments and to relocate them in Kafka's development as a teenager is to see him drawing the worst possible scenario in order to fulfill his perception of himself as isolated, alone, victimized. That is, he spent much of his writing life role-playing, reinforcing what he knew himself to be, and rather than having been truly victimized, he assailed himself as a kind of symbolic Saint Sebastian. In this regard, Kafka needed that rueful, dangerous relationship to women, regardless of the truth of each affair, as a means of nurturing that part of him that could write only if he maintained such a view. He would become, then, in a role he relished, a martyr to his writings, dependent on nothing but those magical moments in the middle of the night when he could sit at his desk with Prague quiet all around him.

At those moments, he recovered an Edenic experience; and for that experience, for those moments, he was willing to sacrifice everything else. Perhaps he had no choice.

The *Letter*, the diaries, and other correspondence are a catalogue of his compensations for his sacrifices, the so-called "perversities" that he developed early on as a means of controlling his environment. His body would be his guinea pig. Food would become one of his dominating perversities because through it he could offer up his body as a sacrifice to his difference from others. In another respect, by selecting his food so carefully, going beyond kosher practices into vegetarianism, emphasizing dairy products and excessive mastication, he could make himself special — or at least a compensatory center of attention. He speaks in one place of how abhorrent his oldest sister Elli's miserliness was to him, since he "had it to an, if possible, even greater extent." He associates miserliness with food: "Miserliness is, after all, one of the most reliable signs of profound unhappiness; I was so unsure of everything that, in fact, I possessed only what I actually had in my hands or in my mouth, or what was at least on the way there, and this was precisely what she, being in a similar situation, most enjoyed taking away from me."[14] His ability to hold his food in his mouth, that system of "fletcherizing," was part of a larger personality trait that Freud labeled the anal personality. In Kafka's case, it meant a total withholding, including chronic constipation, indigestion, poor as well as unusual food habits, a steady undermining of his health in order to meet a psychological need. One can infer from his remarks that masturbation was his preferred means of release; he could, literally, hold sex in his hands and without external interference choose the moment of release. He did not distinguish between intake and excretion but saw them as one process. In this profoundly personal compensation he had found an early way to hang on, as later he would do in his writing.

In commenting directly on his school experience, Kafka speaks of his anxieties making everything else "a matter of indifference to me." He writes of Jewish schoolchildren as an odd lot, but his own "cold indifference, scarcely disguised, indestructible, childishly helpless, approaching the ridiculous and brutishly complacent, the indifference of a self-sufficient but coldly imaginative child, I have never found anywhere else."[15] His view of himself here is ungiving. Part of his distrust of himself he felt was physical. For in a contiguous passage, he expresses his anguish about his digestion, his hair falling out (he had enough for three heads), spinal curvature, and all sorts of abnormal gradations. He speaks of his body as shooting up tall and spindly, his imbalance as the result of lankiness, his back becoming bent, so that while young he had the silhouette of an older man. He says he was open to every kind of hypochondria, beginning, most likely, with his sudden growth in height in his teenage years. Attuned as he was to illness, any sign of good health, such as adequate digestion, amazed him.

So much of Kafka was shaped early, it is tempting to have him observe everything, when in fact we are not really sure of what he observed, what he intuited, what came later with experience.* Marriage — but how early? — torments him. Here we must assume he saw marriage, bleakly, as composed of a powerful figure and a subservient one doing his bidding, a master and his slavey. Marriage, he wrote, is barred to me because "it is precisely and peculiarly your [Hermann's] most intimate domain." We recall the image of a herculean Hermann straddling the map of the world, leaving only slim geographical pickings for the son: "not many and not very comforting territories, and above all marriage is not among them."[16] Since marriage is beyond reach, Kafka can never gain Julie. She remains Hermann's property, and much as he may yearn for her, the son is an insufficient explorer. The image may be geographical, but the import is sexual, oedipal.

With marriage banned, children are out of the question, and Kafka is doomed to remain, all his life, a son, not a father or husband. He foresaw this doom early, of course; these are not late career musings, but well-digested antagonisms. Although Hermann becomes a handy peg on which Kafka can hang all of his own personal feelings and misfortunes — his inability to hang on to Felice Bauer or anyone else — there is also the sense that perceptions of marriage in small Prague (or Vienna!) apartments did not lead to exalted views of the institution. Close observation, perhaps traumas from the primal scene, views of soiled bedclothing, incestuous longings after half-undressed (or dressed) sisters would jeopardize the desire for marriage, or else make it seem unachievable for someone of fastidious taste.

What Kafka in growing up failed to recognize is that by living at home during his school years, as he was expected to do, and then long after he was economically able to afford his own place, he helped create that map of the world that Hermann controlled. What the son could not admit to himself was how this kind of experience, with all its anguish and pain, was necessary to him. The continued experience of Hermann's tirades was, for the young Kafka, another one of those "perversities" by which he could regulate himself and his surroundings. Hermann was not a foreign, alien agent but a necessary reinforcement of Kafka's needs, as the torture machine is to the military man in "In the Penal Colony." Kafka did not need the oedipal situation to "get at" the father; he needed the father to create the oedipal situation.[17] He required the neurosis to justify his feelings and to make possible his counterattack in the shape of perversities of behavior, digestion, choice of style of life, ultimately his writing. In a letter to his parents in 1914,

---

*For example, how far back does his 1914 remark to Ottla revert? "I write differently from how I speak, I speak differently from what I think, I think differently from the way I ought to think, and so it all proceeds into deepest darkness."

Kafka fully admitted he had grown up in comfort and dependency, and that while he gave his parents no "cause for lasting joy," he gave himself none either.[18]

For Kafka, everything converged. To become a writer, he had to synthesize what occurred to him personally with what was occurring externally: this is the essence of the representative writer and man. He started slowly, with observation, and moved early on to theatrical efforts with homemade plays for family presentation. A housekeeper, Anna Puzarová, who had often acted together with the three Kafka sisters in his productions, usually for family birthdays, reported on his directorial style and suggested he was something of a dictator. But he was of course still far from reaching into what became his reason for becoming an artist: "Art," he said, "flies around truth, but with the definite intention of not getting burnt. Its capacity lies in finding in the dark void a place where the beam of light can be intensely caught, without this having been perceptible before."[19]

And to do this in German: the ever present dilemma of language confronted every Czech Jew who wanted to express himself in words. Just as Kafka had to face every aspect of the oedipal situation in Hermann, family arrangements, nationalistic movements in the streets, the advent of avant-gardes in the arts, so he had to confront "oedipalization" in his use of language. Language, in brief, is linked to everything else; it is not a separate commodity.* The German that Kafka inherited from Hermann and Julie was as much part of parental territory as it was part of the "parent" country, Austria, and beyond that, Germany. The problem for the son, as a writer, was how to dissociate himself from *their* German and as well from Prague German, and at the same time resist classic German. And yet prepositional use in German — for one — controls significant meaning, not simply grammatical accuracy. As prepositional usage becomes slack or careless, the language, as in English, becomes slangy, colloquial, or inaccurate.

Common Prague German examples of loose usage exist in Kafka's writing.† He was not immune to them simply because he was so aware of language. But because of his awareness that his German needed "cleansing," Kafka could compensate by taking language from slack-

---

*Although my arguments about Kafka and presentation of his career differ from those of Gilles Deleuze and Félix Guattari (*Kafka: Toward a Minor Literature*), their reading of his life and career is often compelling. The authors see Kafka not as pursuing oedipal antagonism against the father, but as creating the terms by which he could avoid the oedipal situation; by "deterritorialization," or breaking away from the father's territory, Kafka hoped to realign his own needs separate from the bourgeois family, represented by Hermann. Their argument, however complex, does not take sufficiently into account Kafka's confusion in just this area.

†Such as overuse of adverbial modifiers — that is, words or phrases that are unnecessary but creep in as part of slack usage. "Nothing at all happened": the *at all* is redundant, since *nothing* means "nothing happened." Or "Nothing happened at all," where the redundancy becomes even more apparent. The German usage is, once again, comparable.

ness and carelessness to new heights of intensity. Just as he was concerned with personal forms of metamorphosis, so he was concerned with transformation of language. To disguise or negate what was happening to German in Prague, he stretched it, creating a language within a language.

But this was only the beginning of Kafka's struggle with language. Czech words had to be wrestled out of his language, since it was natural they would "pollute" the German and eventually become part of daily usage. Unlike American English, which glories in its absorption of words from other languages, classic German, like classic French, was too aware of its tradition to accommodate absorption. Kafka also had to deal with echoes of Hebrew. Although he didn't know the language until much later, the idea of Hebrew was present once the Zionist plan became significant in Prague. Yiddish was also a presence, never very far from those shtetl Jews like Hermann Kafka and Julie who when they came to Prague carried with them the whiff of the Yiddish-speaking past. However attentive Hermann Kafka was to his German, it was tinged with Yiddish, and if not with actual words, then with Yiddish intonations and inflections.

Yiddish in fact came to have mysterious or magical properties for Kafka. Although impure and impractical, it seemed in his view somehow truer than German; and while he did not want it to replace German, he longed for it as if it were some part of a memory he had lost. He did not measure it in religious terms, but in terms of community, as part of theater, which for him was a bond among people. He recognized it only as a spoken language, never as a written language, and here we encounter still another dilemma. What appealed so much to him as speech, in Yiddish, as forging a bond, could never replace German as the written language, which had so many deficiencies as a spoken language for a Prague Jew.

Everywhere Kafka turned, language created mounting difficulties. Yiddish picked away at his sensibilities, just as it picks away at German itself from within. Once allied to Middle High German, it took off on its own but remained close enough to German — with its alphabet the same as Hebrew — that it effectively subverted German for those who knew Yiddish. In a talk Kafka gave on the Yiddish language,* he

---

*This talk takes on intense subjectivity when we describe the setting for it. Kafka's little speech preceded a dramatic reading in Yiddish in 1912 by Yitshak (Jizchak) Löwy, the Eastern European actor whom Kafka sponsored and helped. The audience, at Prague's Jewish Town Hall, was made up of bourgeois Jews who considered themselves not only Germanized but acculturated or assimilated. Germanized as they were, they condescended to be charitable to Jews from Poland and Russia, and they also condescended to *Yiddishkeit*, the world of Yiddish, as something from which they had themselves escaped, either on their own or in preceding generations. Thus, although they were Jews, they were predisposed to be hostile, and even if they understood some Yiddish, they did not like to be reminded of it. Yet they had come to the reading, which was in itself a

described it as the language of the heart: "Then you will come to feel
the true unity of Yiddish and so strongly that it will frighten you, yet it
will no longer be fear of Yiddish but of yourselves. Enjoy this self-
confidence as much as you can!"[20] His choice of words is astounding:
Yiddish as therapeutic. It gives the Jew the opportunity to express himself and to be proud of that expression.*

Given all these options and temptations, Kafka could have followed Brod and Werfel, among others, the so-called Prague Circle, and
used language to express a kind of dreamy or loose symbolic vision. He
resisted this, and while his work has been misinterpreted as "symbolic" or "allegoric," it is in fact pitilessly realistic, and at its most extended, expressionistic. The vagaries of Czech or Prague German may
have permitted Kafka a certain laxity, but instead he worked to tighten
language, structure it, give it unique substance. Clearly, he could have
used his minority status to validate a Prague German, to demonstrate
how an "outsider" could reforge a Goethe-like language. He chose instead to make language serve him, rather than letting himself serve it.

These forays into language were only part of the whole, not the
whole. Speech was, for him, an act of considerable anguish, and it was
connected inevitably to his attitudes toward other matters, especially
toward food. Kafka experienced what we might call a triangular need,
made up of speaking, writing, and eating, for him arranged uniquely.
Two come from the mouth and were, for him, contradictory — one
cannot speak while eating or eat while speaking. Writing also is contrary to eating and speaking, and by choosing to write, Kafka chose not
to eat, or chose to make eating into a "perversity." Thus, the triangle
was not a matter of symmetries but a series of opposites. His horror at
eating, at mouths, and especially at teeth was another form of sacrifice,
for just as eating and writing were contradictory activities in his
strange equation, so speaking was wasting what should have percolated
into the written word. What he heard, what he ate or did not eat —
these were all means by which he could control his future career as a
writer.

The languages Kafka's animals and insects use indicate his preoccupation with verbal expression. His animals sing, cough, bark, cry,
slaver, and crackle — strange sounds that approximate speech — and

---

recognition that some part of them could still be touched by the East European experience, and in that respect they recalled Kafka's own position. The entire experience,
then, at the Jewish Town Hall was fraught with anxiety, nervousness, and some antagonism, even while it promised something quite rare: a return to roots, as Kafka intuited
in his opening remarks, about Yiddish cleaning "out all the foulness of a Jew using a
language which does not belong to him."
*Kafka's attitude was very possibly modeled on that of Chaim Zhitlowsky, a socialist
and a key figure in the late nineteenth-century development of *Yiddishkeit*. Zhitlowsky
saw Yiddish as the shaping force of Jewish philosophy and life, the basis for a national
existence, a bonding agent for the Diaspora Jew.

in their approximation of speech, we hear Kafka's effort to glean meaning out of a polluted language, or to make sense of sounds that are on the edge of verbal communication. His ear is attuned, his senses alive. The Kafka "sound" is of his own making but in some curious way allied to the sounds of those animals and insects striving to make themselves known in a language others do not quite understand.

He became a master of sounds. We know of his extreme sensitivity to noise. Those levels of noise we take for granted — street sounds, coughs, low conversation, the movement of objects — he transformed into active attacks on his sensibilities. Noise, or sound itself, became so oppressive he sought ever more reclusive retreats, but sound of course found him out. Later, he wrote to Ottla, "The amount of quiet I need does not exist in the world, from which it follows that no one ought to need so much quiet."[21] He chose solitary recreations, where talk was unnecessary (swimming, rowing, gardening), and was able to write only under the most silent and isolated conditions. In order to overcome noise from outside, he wrote during the middle of the night when Prague and his own house quieted; the works he turned out during this time indicate his triumph over sound. Those large ears we find in Kafka photographs were more than funny appendages. They brought in what he knew he had to overcome, regular sounds; yet at the same time they brought in language(s) that he had to hear and transform. The paradoxes are there. Even as Kafka pursued sound, he recoiled from it. Language and its sounds did not afford him accommodation to the majority culture but on the contrary made him hear his distinction, his difference.

How do such struggles and confrontations resolve themselves? In Kafka personally, they never did; he fought them out virtually to the end of his life. But in his writing there were ways in which unresolvable elements could be maneuvered into place, so that although they are not resolved in any final sense, they are confronted in narrative terms. Kafka found fictional means of joining what might otherwise have torn him apart.

Kafka must always be read in at least "double" terms. Whenever we read meaning in his stories and novels, we must also read what is omitted or repressed. *Kafka is our novelist of what is lacking.* Accordingly, in whatever a protagonist says or does, the perspective of the fiction is not necessarily his, and may in fact derive from several other directions, as the German critic Walter Benjamin first noted. Therefore we should not emphasize one particular meaning in Kafka, since we will then miss what is repressed.

In "The Metamorphosis," Gregor Samsa, once transformed into a large bug, has a particular liking for a framed picture on his wall of a woman in furs. When agitated, he crawls on the picture, pressing his hot body against the cool glass and leaving a stain behind, the stain apparently a sign of masturbation or some orgasmic response. Who is she? What does she represent? Why is she in furs? Is she, somehow, a substitute for Gregor's sister, Grete, whose similar name would indicate twinning? Is the woman a mother substitute, through whom Gregor can reveal his desire to replace his father as family head? Is she a sign, perhaps, not of his desire but of his weakness, of his impotence, so that he can have a sexual response only to a picture? Is the fur somehow a sexual symbol, vaginal "fur" in the shape of a muff? The scene's potentialities have meanings not in themselves but only as part of the larger narrative that is filled with other, not dissimilar, ambiguities. Is the apple thrown by Mr. Samsa which becomes embedded in Gregor's back and festers there original sin or, possibly, a sacrifice of some sort?

The point of these examples is to demonstrate not Kafka's obscure symbolism or cloudy thinking, but his deliberate use of ambiguous, open-ended images of sex and guilt. By creating scenes so full of potentiality and possibility, he suggests hidden areas where silence becomes significant, where objects are made to seem other than what they are. In such configurations, he found meaning and reconciliation.

Near the end of his studies, in his eighth year at the gymnasium, Kafka had to deliver a brief lecture, and his subject was Goethe — safe, predictable, once again a defensive shield against the hard choices. His later interest in Kleist and Grillparzer, among classic German writers, was of a different kind, devoted as he was to their craft, their sacrifice of self for the sake of writing, and, in Kleist's case, his self-destructiveness. Kleist's suicide pact with a young woman was made to order for Kafka's own romantic sense of self, destroyed by guilt and anguish and ready to sacrifice itself on the altar of a doomed love. But he was also boning up for the *Abitur*, that series of examinations that would come at the end of the final year. Rote learning was the requirement for advancement and the opportunity to go on to the university, and Kafka was propelled along by a system already alien to his sensibilities — just as later, after his law degree, he spent his mature years in a bureaucratic organization he deplored. This creation of dualisms, between what he was inclined to do and what he was forced to do by the laws of upward mobility, was, paradoxically, a fortunate situation for Kafka: it drove him to express his outrage and bafflement in works that sought ways to comprehend the divisions. Yet for the young boy, the fear was palpable, the fear of authority so great it made suicide seem preferable to life.

In 1920, when he was thirty-seven, he wrote Milena Jesenská about what, he felt, was the abiding presence in his imagination of those early school years. The sense of humiliation had never left him. By this time, he was ill with tuberculosis, and sensing that it was terminal he could unburden himself without repressing anything. It was to Milena that he told the story of being dragged to school by the cook who threatened to tell his teacher of his naughtiness. And it was to Milena that he would speak of his sexual disgust when he was with prostitutes, and how sex itself was never, in his feelings, far from filth, even when he was riven by desire. It was to Milena that he revealed his fear of *all* sexual contact, an unburdening that may have been easier for him since she was not Jewish, though married to a Jew, since as the exogamous object, she would understand where a Jew would condemn. It was to Milena that he seemed on the edge of even greater confessions, possibly touching on sexual tastes, perhaps suggesting that he had always been suspicious of his sexual direction since he had sensed homoerotic tendencies he had repressed — except in his work, where they are rife. It was to Milena, then, that he revealed his desperation as a student:

> . . . we also share the death wish, the wish for an "easy" death; but that, after all, is a child's wish, rather like myself back in school, during math, as I watch the teacher leaf through his notebook looking for my name, the very image of strength, terror, and reality as against the total insignificance of my knowledge. And, half dreaming with fear, I wish that I could rise like a ghost, as unsubstantial as my knowledge of math, make my way ghostlike among the school benches, pass through the door somehow, collect myself outside and be free in that beautiful air which, in all the world known to me, did not contain as much tension as that room. Yes, that would have been "easy." But it was not to be. Instead, I was called up to the blackboard and given a problem, whose solution required a logarithm table which I had forgotten at home. I told a lie, said that I had left it in my desk — thinking that the teacher would just hand me his own. Instead of which he sent me back to my desk, whereupon I discovered to my horror — genuine horror; when it came to being scared in school, I never had any need to pretend — that it wasn't there, after all.[22]

The moment ended without tragedy, with Kafka receiving an "unsatisfactory," a mere formality, but in memory he saw death everywhere: "given favorable circumstances, one could 'disappear' even in the classroom itself, the possibilities were endless, and one could also die in life."

Kafka boned up on the classics, history, geography, mathematics, physics, and introductory philosophy. He would take the *Abitur* examination in the spring of 1901, along with his good friends Hugo Bergmann, Oskar Pollak, and Emil Utitz. But well before that, in the previous summer (1900), when Kafka was seventeen, he visited his maternal uncle, Dr. Siegfried Löwy, who lived in a small village in the western part of Moravia, Triesch. Like Kafka's two other maternal uncles, Löwy was a bachelor, and there is some possibility, although no proof, that he was homosexual. Because of his girlish voice, birdlike in its sound, Kafka himself called him "twitterer." He was Kafka's favorite, perhaps because he was a free spirit, unencumbered by wife and family. The "bachelor" idea recurs so frequently in Kafka's fiction that it comes to take on personal meaning, someone not only liberated from wife and children but a man whose hostility to women is apparent. This visit to Dr. Löwy, like all future visits, was calming, a good antidote to life in a crowded Prague apartment. It was full of sunbathing, walks in the woods, haying, and other physical activities Kafka enjoyed throughout his life. Almost at this same time, in 1900, Kafka supported the Boers in their war with England, and his socialist sympathies made him unique in his gymnasium class, as nearly all the others had become fervent Zionists.

That same summer Kafka spent some time with his parents at Roztok, just north of Prague, where the family rented from the chief postmaster, Kohn. Kohn's daughter Selma provided pleasant company. Brod quotes her letter to him in which she tells how she and Kafka flirted with each other, how he read Nietzsche to her, and how they met secretly in the evenings.[23] Kafka tried to encourage her to go to school and study, but her father was against it, and the summer idyll ended on that note.

As his gymnasium days wound down, Kafka solidified his friendship with Oskar Pollak. It was, however, through Hugo Bergmann, who was familiar with the avant-garde *Der Kunstwart*, edited by Ferdinand Avenarius, Richard Wagner's nephew, that Kafka became interested in Hofmannsthal and Nietzsche, especially the most appealing of Nietzsche's work for a young man, *Also sprach Zarathustra*. Back in school, in the *Abitur*, Kafka passed, as did all but two of his classmates. But his pass lacked distinction, whereas Bergmann, clearly the most academically oriented of what would become the "Kafka Circle," did gain distinction on the examination.*

At the time of graduation, Kafka was at another point of self-examination. He was, in 1901, eighteen years old, somewhat younger but more troubled than most of his classmates. Even without decisions about university and career, he was caught up by seemingly contradictory forces. There was of course the ever present family antagonism, where he felt such an outsider he was already plotting strategies for outmaneuvering his parents and keeping his sisters at bay. In ideological terms, he was caught in a frenzy of conflicts, between the Zionist fervor of his friends and his own somewhat tepid socialism. There was as always the question of assimilation. From Hermann he received dual signals, with his father dictating assimilation so as to do business with

---

*The so-called circle expanded to become the Prague Circle: Oskar Pollak, Oskar Baum, Franz Werfel, Max Brod, Johannes Urzidil, Rudolf Fuchs, and Egon Erwin Kisch, a considerable concentration of talent, both literary and academic, although several dropped in and out. With their favorite meeting place the Café Arco, they were dubbed by Karl Kraus "Arconauts." The group was distinctly Zionist, with Kafka remaining the sole socialist, until he too changed his mind, but quietly and without incorporating such views directly into his fiction.

the rapidly changing situation caused by nationalism, but also suggesting that the Kafkas remain defiant Jews. Hermann had taken on some of the "anti-Semitism" of the German Jews, or the German-speaking Jews, who patronized those from the East, while believing that Jews could be Germans; and yet, in this bind within a bind, he was himself an Eastern European Jew who had failed to assimilate. Kafka was, for the time being, trapped in this macabre ballet.

In the *Letter to His Father,* after asserting that he, Kafka, had reproached himself for not attending services often enough, for not fasting, and for failing to carry out the other requirements mandated by Judaism, he says he felt guilt at having wronged his father. But then, later, as a young man, "I failed to understand by what right you, with that farce of Judaism you indulged in, could reproach me for not making an effort . . . to act out a similar farce. It really was a big nothing, as far as I could see, a joke. Not even a joke." He says that Hermann attended synagogue four times a year.

> Patiently you went through the formalities of prayer, sometimes you amazed me by being able to point to the passage in the prayer book that was just being read. As for the rest, just as long as I was in the temple — the only thing that mattered — I could do as I pleased. And so I yawned and dozed away countless hours (I've never been so bored in my life, I believe, except later on at dance lessons) and did what I could to enjoy the small distractions that were being offered, such as the opening of the Ark, which always reminded me of a shooting gallery where, when you hit a bull's-eye, a door flips open the same way, except that out there something interesting popped out, while here it was only the same old dolls without heads.[24]

This indictment is not directed at Hermann's lack of religious fervor or at his indifference except for intermittent practices; rather, it is directed at his hypocrisy in challenging his son's religious commitment when his own was merely a series of formalities. The attack on Hermann here reveals how Kafka could never be certain what he was supposed to do, and yet he was expected to show certainty and decisiveness about it. He adds that his boredom was not interfered with, except by the bar mitzvah,

> which, however, required just some ridiculous memorizing and amounted to no more than passing a ridiculous test. . . . This, then, was the faith that was passed on to me; at best, one might add to it the outstretched finger pointing at the "sons of the millionaire Fuchs," who attended synagogue with their father on the High Holidays. I failed to understand what better use I could possibly put this faith to than to get rid of it as fast as possible; getting rid of it seemed to me precisely the most reverential of acts.[25]

In retrospect, Kafka saw that his duty to himself was to divest himself of as much as possible. What we note in and around 1901, at the time of his gymnasium graduation, is an effort to transform himself through rejection or divestment of religion, family, ambiguities of background, the old self. The theme of a metamorphosis which so dominated his fiction was already immanent in his attitude toward self and others. Kafka saw that Hermann's small obeisance to Judaism was more a matter of class than of belief:

> At bottom, your guiding faith in life consisted of the belief that the opinions of a certain Jewish class were unassailably correct; since these opinions were also part and parcel of your own personality, you actually believed in yourself. . . . a child hyperacutely observant out of sheer anxiety could not possibly be made to understand that the few insipid gestures you performed in the name of Judaism had some higher meaning.

The indictment intensifies:

> For you, they had their meaning as token reminders of an earlier time; that was why you wanted to pass them on to me. But since even for yourself they no longer held any intrinsic value of their own, you could do so only by threats or persuasion.[26]

If anything, the boredom Kafka felt in the synagogue prepared him for the boredom he felt at the university, but even more, what he felt later in his office. The insights into the bureaucracy that made him such a representative author of the twentieth century can be traced back to those early experiences with religion, when boredom, yawning, and the disappointment of the Ark all foreshadowed his career in the mazes and labyrinths of bureaucratic organizations, and beyond that, of the Habsburg heritage. The "yawn" in the synagogue was a response to the role the assimilated, bourgeois Prague Jew was expected to experience, all part of upward mobility and efforts to relocate oneself and one's family socially. Later in life, when writing to Felice Bauer, who became part of that yawn, he looked back on that boredom and saw it as somehow indicative of his entire forward thrust into life.

Whatever Jewish history Kafka picked up was in a rather lax class with Rabbi Nathan Gruen, who was responsible for Jewish studies, readings from the Old Testament in German, with some elementary instruction in Hebrew. Gruen was an uninspired instructor and seemed to the young Kafka little more than an extension of the yawning synagogue experience. Yet even as we trace Kafka's growing hostility and then indifference to Jewish practices, his fate lay with Jews just at a time when they were undergoing one of their periodic harsh rejections by the surrounding culture. Despite occasional outbursts, especially the vicious three-day street attacks when he was fourteen,* Kafka had

*The 1897 street riots were motivated by new language laws, giving the German language new standing as against Czech. Thus, the street struggle over language was not merely a literary affair, but one that cut across all ideologies, signaling an empowerment the nationalists could not tolerate.

considered Prague a place that would offer him justice once he gained the right credentials. He believed in a just society, even an egalitarian one, at the very moment when forces were forming to make a mockery of that optimism. Even the large contribution of Jews to Prague cultural life would backfire, once Czech nationalists began to attack Jews as parasites on their city. Kafka may have wished to withdraw from all the religious crosscurrents, but his desire to do so paralleled a period when withdrawal was impossible; special commitment was called for, and here Kafka could not come forth.

In 1901 he slid away from religion and chose philosophy as his university course of study. His great friend Oskar Pollak chose chemistry, and Hugo Bergmann opted for law. Philosophy was a no man's land for any Jewish student, since university positions were virtually closed to them — Einstein and Philipp Frank (Einstein's later biographer) were, not without difficulty, exceptions. Chemistry and law, however, offered openings in industry or in private practice. Kafka did not have to worry about military service, since Jews were not conscripted (their loyalty was considered suspect), and if a Jew wanted an army career — an unusual turn of events — he would have to convert to Christianity, preferably Catholicism. The usual administrative careers in the civil service were also closed to Jews. When Kafka worked for the Workers' Accident Insurance Institute in Prague, he was one of two Jews in the entire organization. Banking, the larger law offices, much of industry, the military, and civil service, among other careers, were all closed to Jews, and so Kafka's choice of philosophy seems oddly self-indulgent or perhaps attractively self-defeating, leading as it did to nothing available to him.

But tell me, who *are* they, these acrobats, even a little
more fleeting than we ourselves, — so urgently, ever since
childhood,
wrung by an (oh, for the sake of whom?)
never-contented will? That keeps on wringing them,
bending them, slinging them, swinging them,
throwing them and catching them back; as though from an
oily smoother air,
they come down on the threadbare carpet, thinned by their everlasting
upspringing, this carpet forlornly
lost in the cosmos.
Laid on there like a plaster, as though the suburban
sky had injured the earth.

— RILKE, *DUINO*, 5TH ELEGY

FIVE Turn of the Century —
Late Adolescence and Fin de Siècle

IN A LETTER to Oskar Pollak, his former classmate at
the gymnasium, postmarked December 20, 1902, Franz
Kafka transformed himself into a writer.[1] Only one year and a few
months after his graduation from the gymnasium, he made up a little
story that he called the "Tale of Shamefaced Lanky and Impure in
Heart," a tale of outrageous potentiality, with "Shamefaced Lanky"
surely Kafka himself and "Impure in Heart" Oskar Pollak, not Emil
Utitz, a former classmate so identified by Max Brod. Although Kafka
and Pollak were pursuing different academic disciplines, Kafka philosophy, Pollak chemistry, they continued their close friendship. They
discussed artistic matters, among them the publication *Kunstwart*
("Keeper" or "Curator"), a cultural monthly founded in 1887 and edited
by Richard Wagner's nephew, Ferdinand Avenarius. Its main source of
ideas during the years Kafka was influenced by it was Nietzsche, and it
forcefully argued for serious literature, art, and ideas, opposing the de-
preciation of values it saw routinely occurring in a more egalitarian
time. Kafka and Pollak were quite elitist, peering down from their van-
tage point of intellectual superiority, feeling the anguish, pretending
terrible boredom, yawning at humdrum events. Pollak would go on to
become an art historian, but his intellectual interests were broad, from
science (chemistry) to philosophy and archaeology. He would be killed
at the front in 1915 at the age of thirty-two.

Kafka's letters to Pollak, dating from 1900, when Kafka was seventeen, are full of Weltschmertz, anguish or implied agony. They have the

tone of love letters written by a young man to a young woman, skirting deep feelings, but implying a whole range of common sensibilities. Clearly, Pollak was more than an intellectual companion, rather some kind of secret sharer for the young Kafka when he entered the university; as the letters indicate, their friendship took on overtones of Freud's more than casual feeling for Eduard Silberstein. In the December 20 letter, Kafka found a way of developing earlier feelings into a brief episode that is significant for the future writer as well as for the moment itself. The tale of Shamefaced Lanky foreshadows a much more developed piece of fiction, "Description of a Struggle," in 1904–5, but it also looks back to Kafka the adolescent and older student. A brief tale, it embodies the whole.

"Shamefaced Lanky," it begins, "has crept off to hide his face in an old village, among low houses and narrow lanes." Lanky possesses Kafka's long, thin frame, and "shamefaced" indicates his shyness and desire for withdrawal. But the German word *Scham*, for shame, in *schamhaft* (shamefaced), also has other meanings, connected to sexual anatomy: genitals, vagina, and several variations thereupon. The word is loaded; shamefaced means not only bashful but shameful in sexual terms. And as the tale unfolds, this sexual dimension grows. Lanky is associated with the village, with narrow lanes, low rooftops, and small, boxy rooms. Impure in Heart comes from a big city and is "drunk" on "the joy of cities." The linkage of the two has something in it of a pre-Brechtian dialectic. One day just before Christmas, Lanky is sitting stooped at a window, his long legs thrust outside, dangling. "With his clumsy, skinny, spidery fingers [like Kafka's own] he was knitting woolen socks for the peasants." A knock at the door produces Impure in Heart, to Lanky's astonishment. He immediately is ashamed "of his height and his woolen socks and his room." Yet he does not blush but in fact remains his usual "lemon-yellow" and greets his visitor, though shyly. Impure in Heart sits down on a flour sack and smiles. Lanky sees how well dressed the visitor is, with "glistening waistcoat buttons." Then words emerge from the mouth of Impure in Heart. "Those words were fine gentlemen with patent-leather shoes and English cravats and glistening buttons; and if you furtively asked them, 'Do you know what blood is?' one would answer with a leer, 'Yes, I have English cravats.'" Then those little gentlemen stood on tiptoe and were tall, and skipped over to Lanky, "climbed on him, tweaking and biting, and worked their way into his ears."

Lanky becomes restive, sniffs the foul air of the room, and listens to Impure in Heart tell stories about himself, about waistcoat buttons, about the city and his feelings. As he speaks, he "incidentally kept stabbing the pointed cane into Lanky's belly." All the while, Lanky trembled and grinned, but Impure in Heart stopped, now content. Lanky, still grinning, leads his guest to the door, shakes hands. Lanky is alone again, and he weeps, for he knows he cannot tell anyone. "But sick questions crawled up his legs to his soul." He wonders if Impure in Heart came to him because he is lanky, or "because I . . . ?" Is he weeping out of pity for himself or for Impure in Heart? Does he like or hate him? Has his god or his devil sent him? "The question marks throttled Shamefaced Lanky." He sets to work once again on his socks. "He almost pierced his eyes with the knitting needle. For it was even darker."

This is the entire story, little more than a page. But it is, nevertheless, an astonishing performance for its literary potentialities and for its personal revelations. Kafka has created, by 1902, one of his discontinuous narratives, with a point of view that seems to come and go. He is already both within his tale and beyond it. The material is outside the terms of realism, while not neglectful of realistic situations and confrontations. The nature of the treatment is already broadly expressionistic or broadly symbolic in its implications but cannot be pinned down by any label. Furthermore, it has some of the sadism and masochism that characterize Kafka's mature fiction, where suffering — here tears, stabbing, almost blinding oneself with a knitting needle — is always a concomitant of experience.

In more personal terms, the story is like a slightly disguised nightmare, that of a patient telling Dr. Freud his dreams while seeking some resolution to a sexual malfunction or pathology. What the tale plays with in personal terms is Kafka's reaching out to Oskar Pollak to find more intimate grounds for their friendship, a desire on his part to offer himself up as a kind of not-too-attractive bait, but willing to be the victim while Pollak would be the aggressor, even the stabber, if he so chose. Kafka would be the "female" in the relationship and take the punishment; Pollak would be the impure male and dish it out. Impure stabs repeatedly with his pointed cane at Lanky's belly, an act of aggression that Lanky accepts, trembling and grinning. There is both more and less than a boyhood crush here: on one hand we see the desire to be violated, on the other the need to be accepted for what one is. The designations of *Shamefaced*, with its strong sexual connotations in German, and *Impure*, with an almost equally strong sexual intimation, suggests a desirable relationship that has, already built in, a distaste, a fear, a shame, a sense of its pollution. Consummation must come in the silences between the words, not in overt acts; the unstated provides the arena. Even the stabbing in the belly with the cane is a bit of foreplay, not the real thing. The unimaginable does not occur, but Lanky must nevertheless punish himself. He almost loses his eyes out of shame, the archetypal symbol of self-punishment for a sexual transgression, Oedipus's ultimate action.

In an earlier letter to Pollak that same year, Kafka had spoken of the difficulty of language making the writer tread over words "as if they were rough pavement. The most delicate things acquire awkward feet and we can't help it." As a result of the hardness of words, he and Pollak bump into each other, and they take turns falling silent. Language is already an issue between the friends, and so is silence; not only the lack of sound but the lack of overt meaning. All of this recurs in the Shamefaced Lanky tale; and reading back to the earlier letter, we wonder what Brod excised before publishing that letter. Kafka writes, just after the missing lines, "The fear creeps over me that you won't understand this whole letter — what's its aim? . . . When we talk together we're hampered by things we want to say and cannot say just like that, so we bring them out in such a way that we misunderstand, even ignore, even laugh at each other."[2] As a consequence, they become bored, they yawn, their jaws stiffen. The implication of this letter, which foreshadows the Lanky one, is that their hesitations have taken over. Since they cannot be candid, Kafka can achieve expression only in the dream-fantasy of Shamefaced Lanky and Impure in Heart, where he posits a relationship that cannot be put into words.

Is the story homoerotic? Or is it a desperate attempt on Kafka's part to create a relationship at such a deep level that it overlaps with a homoerotic impulse? Has Kafka attempted to open himself up to the kind of punishment he takes for granted in any relationship so that he can establish the affair with Pollak more intensely? The needs suggested here require satisfaction, or if not satisfaction then an attempt or reaching out.

How Kafka felt can be observed in half a dozen places, where he suggests that what has occurred between him and Pollak cannot be interrupted by anyone else. In a February 4, 1902, letter, he writes of Pollak's keeping company with "that girl" but says she means nothing to him, Kafka. "You talk with her, and in the middle of a sentence somebody jumps up and makes a bow. That is me with my untrimmed words and angular faces."[3] He asks if they are enemies, and ends with "I am very fond of you." In subsequent letters, he writes about Goethe and other subjects, as if they shared a common joke inaccessible to others. It was to Pollak that Kafka spoke of Prague as an old crone with claws; "One has to yield or else." To jump slightly ahead, the letter of September 6, probably 1903, is almost a love letter in its intimacy but "purely out of selfishness, plain selfishness."[4] Kafka wants Pollak to read what he has been writing, "even if indifferently and reluctantly. . . . what is dearest and hardest of mine is merely cool, in spite of the sun, and I know that another pair of eyes will make everything warmer and livelier when they look at it." He adds that he is sending "a piece of my heart" and "packing it neatly in a few sheets of inscribed paper." This early material may be sketchy parts of the later "Description of a Struggle."

"Description" also has strong homoerotic overtones, but they are caught within a far more ambitious narrative design — a narrative designed, in fact, to negate narrative. The story, which has two parallel

versions, is made up of disconnected elements. The main part concerns
the narrator and an acquaintance he meets at a party, who asks to be
rescued from an indiscretion with a woman. We have, with this, the
messenger figure so beloved by Kafka, and the remainder of the story is
structured, however tentatively, on the narrator encountering messengers from various worlds. The entire piece seems like a stream
emanating from a middle ground between consciousness and unconsciousness, where the language of the latter can never be uttered and
the language of the former is too precise.

His height makes life miserable for the excessively tall narrator, a
"poor stick" and obviously an outsider. The fellow to be rescued has
young women falling over him, a source of envy and hostility for the
narrator. The narrator tries to make himself seem shorter by putting
his head on his trouser seams, becoming someone bent and crooked.
Carrying a knife, he expects to be murdered at any time but with his
own weapon; he is the victim of someone or something, although his
self-hatred is clearly displaced from the other person. He feels indifference, but that turns into attachment that has no clear basis, and the
narrator avoids investigating further. After several episodes of a surreal,
dreamlike, nightmarish quality, which while not fully definable seem
a description of inner struggle, the acquaintance is still caught up with
his women but is disturbed by the laugh of one, who is "sly and senile."
Here we catch a glimpse of the turn-of-the-century view of women: the
fin de siècle vampire, sensual Salomé, wily Eve, menacing Lulu. The
narrator himself speaks of girls' sensuality but also of their dangerous
and forbidding quality. Then, after an argument in which the narrator
feels he may have to kill himself, they enter into a competition for
most developed chest.

When it comes to chests, of course, there is no match. The narrator
is like Tonio Kröger in the Thomas Mann story, a physical weakling
surrounded by blond young men who love and are loved, Siegfrieds and
Vikings who are contrasted with the absurdly tall but weak Jew. The
narrator speaks of the young healthy people at a hotel who sat "in the
garden at tables with beer and talked of hunting and adventures," and
then drops the information that he is himself engaged. Yet his engagement seems a deception for the sake of defense against the fine figure of
the acquaintance: "the round head on a fleshy neck in a sharp curving
line, as was the fashion that winter." The sole defense against that expressive physicality is a bragging lie. They sit, disturbed, again with
homoerotic intimations, the acquaintance pleading for the narrator to
put his hand on his forehead to give him relief. Suddenly, the acquaintance pulls out a knife and stabs himself in his upper arm, without
withdrawing the blade. The narrator pulls it out and binds the wound
as best he can; he even sucks it. He runs for help, finds none, returns.
He says to the acquaintance that the latter wounded himself for his
sake, and yet he, the acquaintance, seems in such a fine position to do

whatever he wants, to make himself happy in so many ways. For him, "there'll be shouting and barrel organs will be playing in the avenues." Nevertheless, that is insufficient for happiness. The story ends with a scene recalling an impressionist painting: a lantern, tree trunks, a road, white snow, shadows of branches lying bent, as if broken.

Although we are jumping ahead three or four years after Kafka's graduation from the Altstädter Gymnasium, "Description of a Struggle" is so compelling as a sequel to the Shamefaced Lanky tale that it belongs here, as well as later. Often, "Description" has been dismissed as little more than a quarry for later tales, especially for *Meditation* (or *Reflection, Betrachtung*) in 1913, just after his mature writing career began, yet it is remarkable in itself, even more astonishing for having been written just after the turn of the century. For Kafka, still in his university days, had assimilated several aspects of the Modern spirit, bringing to the story interior monologue, scenic distortions, discontinuities of narrative and character. Further, the story in its fullness has a dramatic shape that makes it possible to be staged as a kind of expressionistic-surrealist drama, what we find in Kokoschka, Wedekind, and other contemporaries. This suggests, further, that a good deal of Kafka has dramatic potential, in the way Samuel Beckett's monologues and dialogues lend themselves to the stage. The wit and irony are already there.

Yet as early as 1901–2, at the time he was prepared to write about Shamefaced Lanky to Oskar Pollak, we observe many of the typical Kafkan characteristics already in place: the victimization of the self; the stabbing and knife play;* the taking on of unspecified guilt; the depiction of self as unappetizing, clumsy, unwanted; the comparison of one's unpresentable self with the healthy outside world; the mysterious coming and going of figures in an individual's life; the inability to find meaning within the patterns of one's own life; the broken, discontinuous nature of experience, especially for anyone who feels or intuits deeply; the movement toward the interior as the battleground of the struggle; the inability to identify what is essential in a mass of events or experiences; the breaking up of self and scene into small, isolated elements, as if in a cubist or nonrepresentational painting; the loss of melody in one's life, as if atonality had entered one's spirit or soul and recognizable chords had slipped away — all this and the sense of self as waste, excess, garbage, as marginal, cast-off material.

In this letter to Pollak, Kafka was already beginning to strain against the acceptable, in the name of a different degree of experience. "We were expelled from Paradise," he wrote much later, "but it was not destroyed. The expulsion from Paradise was in one sense a piece of

---

*Kafka writes in the "Octavo Notebooks," "The main thing, when a sword cuts into one's soul, is to keep a calm gaze, lose no blood, accept the coldness of the sword with the coldness of a stone. [Then] by means of the stab, after the stab, become invulnerable" (p. 73).

good fortune, for if we had not been expelled Paradise would have had
to be destroyed."[5] Although this statement contains the paradoxes and
caustic irony of the mature writer, it loops back to the young man at
the turn of the century. Paradise *is* lost; it cannot be regained. Paradise
remains *because* man was expelled from it. Man pollutes or contaminates whatever he touches, and even Paradise would not have been
spared if man had not been expelled. "Description of a Struggle" at one
level can be read as the impossibility of man's re-entering Paradise;
likewise, Shamefaced Lanky is doomed to perpetual expulsion, a victim himself, so that Paradise might exist. Yet even as we should be
grateful for the survival of Paradise despite the machinations of man,
we should weep for our exile from everlasting life. Shamefaced Lanky
is left there — full of guilt that could lead to stabbing his eyes out with
knitting needles.

Kafka found in Pollak a confidant, someone of equal intelligence
and already of considerable taste. He also needed what he thought was
a mirror image of himself: a reflection of the same anguish he felt, although Pollak, as it turned out, was really quite different. Still looking
ahead, we find in a November 9, 1903, letter Kafka speaking to Pollak
words drenched in Weltschmertz:

> We are as forlorn as children lost in the woods. When you stand in front
> of me and look at me, what do you know of the griefs that are in me and
> what do I know of yours. And if I were to cast myself down before you and
> weep and tell you, what more would you know about me than you know
> about hell when someone tells you it is hot and dreadful. For that reason
> alone we human beings ought to stand before one another as reverently,
> as reflectively, as lovingly, as we would before the entrance to hell.[6]

"Children lost in the woods," "standing before the entrance to hell":
here the youthful Kafka is attempting to make sense of a whirl of ideas
and feelings, and using Pollak as his resource.

Kafka used the letters to serve another purpose besides communicating: to create a persona for himself. We see in these inchoate por-
trayals something of the beginning of the Kafkan "representative
man." The letters, first to Pollak and later to Felice Bauer, became the
means by which he could play act or play roles, and these roles all became parallel to the roles his fictional characters played. In one clear
example, even as Kafka wrote to Felice Bauer of the entrapped Joseph K.
in *The Trial*, he portrayed himself as entrapped in the relationship to
her. Pollak here, Felice Bauer later: Kafka needed a correspondent with
whom he could try out various selves. Ultimately, the selves come
down to one: that marginal individual trapped within his own perceptions of deterioration and within the equally disintegrative elements of
the bureaucracy.

*   *   *

As we have suggested, Kafka was a repository of everything coming together in the arts at the turn of the century. For him, Prague was full of dread, and it also, in his infamous description, had claws. It contained its own ghosts, silences, memories, and it could be devastating to the young man who listened to the contradictions it offered. For the would-be artist or writer who listened to the siren songs of Modernism, Prague could prove to be a very ambiguous place.* The art and architecture it officially honored was traditional, for the people, folk oriented, embedded in the disasters of Czech history. In music, Smetana and Dvořák were its heroes, and they clearly represented not Modernism, despite Dvořák's occasional daring, but a folk-based musical composition, especially in Smetana's tone poems and in their operas celebrating village life. More of the nineteenth than of the twentieth century, the two composers helped reinforce the nationalists, who were on an inevitable collision course with Modernism. Modernism was Europewide, as much of Paris as of Vienna, as much of Berlin as of Prague, whereas nationalists of course favored the native spirit and native aspirations. Modernism cut across everything, sweeping out old style, proclaiming the new.

Freud, Marx, Bergson, and others on a lesser level were also threats to the nationalists, each in his own way. An unreconcilable divisiveness resulted, for even as the nationalists attempted to win over the workers, the latter were themselves forming labor unions, showing allegiance to the Czech Social Democratic Party (founded in 1878), and then moving to shape their own party in the late 1880s. The Social Democratic Party was oriented not toward nationalism but toward Marx, although it was not strictly Marxist. Certainly its economic policies were Marxist in nature. But, ironies within ironies, the Social Democrats also appealed strongly to Jews, especially the intelligentsia, and Jews became active in the party. At the same time, the workers and their unions were being appealed to by the nationalists, who represented an anti-Semitic position. The lines of demarcation here were as confused as any in a Kafka bureaucracy.

The appeal to Jews of Marxism and its socialist derivatives came in the idea of a classless society, possibly an egalitarian one in which Semites and anti-Semites could join on economic and social issues. Also, a socialist unity of Jews and Christians would weaken the hold of the clergy, particularly in segments of the Austro-Hungarian Empire where the Catholic clergy had often encouraged riots, demonstrations, and pogroms against Jews. Withal, the socialist idea, Marxist or otherwise, penetrated deeply into the Jewish community, not only taking over the intelligentsia but entering into the middle class, where socialism

---

*One is tempted to compare Joyce in Dublin; though there are similarities, Joyce left, while Kafka remained. Each, nevertheless, wrote and rewrote his respective city.

would appear to be anomalous. But because of the precariousness of Jewish life in countries always near the edge of anti-Jewish activity, and because of the nature of a succession of riots based on blood libel accusations, socialism seemed like a political panacea. Necessarily, Jews supported some system in which civic life could be detached from clerical and religious life; for Jews had always found themselves safer and more prosperous in societies moving toward the secular than in societies in which civil and clerical functions coincided. Yet even here, as in so much else, Jews were caught in a paradox: for as they poured into socialist parties in Europe, such parties became identified with Jewish interests, and the very working classes that socialism was intended to help turned on them and moved increasingly into nationalist groups that indicted Jews as perpetual outsiders.

Kafka was of course caught in this familiar spiral: a socialist when his friends were turning from it to Zionism, and ultimately a Zionist, which was, for Jews, its own form of nationalism and a definite outgrowth of the entire nationalist trend. Although socialism was perceived initially as a binding force, a Pan-European movement and even an international movement, it fragmented in country after country, giving way to nationalist hopes and dreams. "International brotherhood" became international fratricide. Part of the problem in the Dual Monarchy was the patronizing attitude German-speaking socialists had toward those in Bohemia, Moravia, and Hungary. The dislike and condescension German-speaking Jews felt toward those Jews from the eastern provinces was paralleled by the dislike German-speaking socialists had toward their Czech and Hungarian colleagues. Racial and ethnic divisions created chaos in the various labor movements, so that the Czechs, in defense of their own interests and their own chauvinistic yearnings, broke away in 1896. This break preceded by one year one of the largest outbreaks of street demonstrations, when, as we have seen, Czechs roamed the old town of Prague and attacked Jewish stores, homes, and individuals, a kind of early *Kristallnacht*.

Marxism in pre–Russian Revolution days showed no clear path to brotherhood of humanity, and perhaps that is the way it should have been, since Marx had himself been so ambivalent about Jews and the Jewish question. Although heir to a long line of rabbis, Marx was the son of a Jewish convert and himself demonstrated virulent anti-Semitic feelings. His fundamental theory, attacking capitalism, was meant to excise haggling or Mammon, which he equated with Jews, and by extirpating both he could cleanse society. He called the influential and distinguished German socialist Ferdinand Lassalle "a Jewish nigger." If he had lived longer, Lassalle was possibly the one man who could have consolidated socialist groups in Europe, but he found himself in competition with Marx. Lassalle's plan, for various groups in the Dual Monarchy, favored the role of the state. In his theory, the state would contribute capital outlays to allow workers to establish producers' co-operatives, and this would lead to large bodies of workers incorporated into a capitalist system while remaining loyal to their own small units or unions. Lassalle played a major role in establishing the influential General German Workers' Association in 1863, the year before he died in a duel over a love affair; and through this association he created a major element in Bismarck's Prussia. Such groups, had Lassalle's plans gone forward, would have found fertile soil in the Dual Monarchy since his smaller units could have been unionist, nationalistic, and capitalistic.*

By the time Marxism came to Bohemia, it was unrecognizable, and the socialist fervor of young men like Kafka, including those who were incipient Zionists, was more a generational affair than a matter of ideology. Like Modernism and its various avant-gardes, socialism afforded the young a chance to rebel. It too became absorbed into an oedipal response to the older generation; it too allowed for a way of removing the fathers in the name of innovation, novelty, refreshing and energizing society. As Franz Josef aged toward eternality, he became increasingly remote for the generation coming of age at the turn of the century; and the enormous creative activity, signaled by secessions and avant-garde movements, was as much a response to an aging society as it was a response to radical changes in the genres of music, painting, and literature.

Unfortunately, Prague did not have a socialist leader as dynamic as Viktor Adler, in Austria proper. Adler, a Jewish convert, tried to combine socialist and nationalist sympathies. Having started as a devoted follower of Wagner, he veered to Marxism, but his Marxism was for labor unity rather than specifically for the withering away of the state. Opposed to capitalism and a proponent of inevitable revolution, he nevertheless tempered his views and saw his primary goal as evolutionary, as consolidating and gaining preparedness for power. Adler came close to a form of radical liberalism that was not at all anathema to many levels of Austrian society. Bohemia lacked that kind of leadership and that kind of rational approach to change, most likely because it was not the center of the empire but somewhat on the periphery.

Though Kafka was an early socialist, Marx does not seem to have entered his consciousness; Darwin, however, did, and only a little later, Nietzsche. Through the work of Ernst Heinrich Haeckel,[7] Darwin was

---

*Such state-oriented outlays, however sincerely intended, would have fitted well into Robert Musil's characterization of the Dual Monarchy as *Kakania* (Shitville), in which the *K*-sounds derived from *kaiserlich-königlich* (imperial-royal) and *kaiserlich und königlich* (imperial and royal). Whichever one chooses, "K. K." or "K. u. K.," the result is a cacophony of royal, Caesar-like ideas, all of which deserved ridicule. Musil's play on words had its basis in Franz Josef's insistence on Habsburg supremacy in all matters, called *Hausmacht* — the Habsburgs as God's voice and instrument on earth.

particularly appealing to the nonbelieving Jew or the Jew who was
seeking some rootedness in a world in which any sense of God had disappeared. If Nietzsche undermined the idea of God or the possibility of
God, Darwin's disciples, like Haeckel, offered a tempting alternative, a
mechanistic, deterministic, ungiving universe that made sense to
those who had been educated on classical ideas of destiny, fate, and related theories. One became totally responsible for oneself, and while
such a view is difficult to fit alongside socialism, Kafka was not about
to become consistent. At the turn of the century and shortly thereafter,
he was flailing around, seeking what seemed workable for the moment,
something, clearly, that could anchor him as he drifted from family.

Even as a young man, just on the edge of his university career,
Kafka found himself flowing with huge changes taking place not only
in the Dual Monarchy but all over Europe. Revolutionary ideas, as part
of Modernism or as part of the advances in science and technology,
were eating away at every traditional idea and government. It was in
fact Franz Josef's inability to recognize change, to bend with it, to compromise more than he was willing to do, to absorb what could be absorbed that doomed his empire. But it is also very possible the same
forces that made innovation in the arts so inexorable were also driving
nationalistic forces; so that whatever was old, whether a literary genre
or a whole empire, was not impervious to change. When we speak later
of Kafka's ability to transform himself, or to transform his material, we
must recall that transformation was the keynote of the entire era in
which he came of age.

But even as Kafka, in 1900 and shortly thereafter, was becoming the
repository of radical events in Berlin, Munich, and Vienna, not to speak
of Paris, he was being buffeted intellectually by other forces, some of
them in direct opposition to avant-gardes, innovations, Modernism and
all its works. These countering elements were the forces of scientific
and technological advances that fall under the umbrella of "progress."
The idea of progress was clearly part of a rational endeavor, offering in
many instances a better material life, and undercutting in its assumptions the very notion of an avant-garde in the arts and culture generally.
"Progress" assumed that people were interested in quality of life based
on creature comforts, health, and ameliorism, whereas the avant-
gardes sought a deeper, more spiritualized response in which material
well-being was a secondary consideration. This is putting the matter
simplistically, but the two elements were not resolvable; they operated
if not in direct opposition then on parallel lines that could never meet.

These developments led Alfred Wallace, whose work on evolution
paralleled Darwin's, to call this period the "wonderful century." He
made this announcement in 1899, and it was directed not only to the
past but to what the future held. Wallace was not concerned with humanistic studies, or with the creative avant-garde, but with another

kind of cutting edge: science, technology, material well-being, and what that meant for mankind as the new century turned. Yet he also warned about greed, militarism, unhealthy types of work, and imperialistic plunderings of the world. That a man who was as much humanist as scientist, and who would later become a spiritualist and supporter of séances to communicate with the dead, could solidly favor rational betterment through scientific discovery indicates how strong the pull from the "other side" of Modernism could be. For from the artists' point of view, the scientific miracle workers had failed society miserably; they believed that for all of science's advances, life was not intrinsically improved, that human greed, desire for power, and self-serving needs superseded humanism; that art and literature were on an inevitable collision course with the scientists and their work. From the scientists' position, the artists were not relating to the needs of society but were indulging their own egos, and in the process creating a culture based on decadence and decay.

Wallace's point was that nineteenth-century advances added up to more than the total development of all preceding eras: ". . . that to get any adequate comparison with the nineteenth century we must take, not any preceding century or group of centuries, but rather that whole preceding epoch of human history."[8] Wallace lists among the gains the railroads, steam navigation, the electric telegraph, the telephone, friction matches, gas lighting, photography, the phonograph, roentgen rays, spectrum analysis (determining relative heat and chemical composition of stars), and the use of anesthetics and antisepsis.

By 1900, the avant-garde in the arts had set itself against everything Wallace's "wonderful century" stood for; and, perhaps more importantly for the way things turned out, that "wonderful century" of progress set itself against everything the arts stood for. At issue was far more than the artistic voice versus the rational, logical, or scientific spirit. It was a cultural war of the deepest kind, cutting into how people perceived themselves, how they defined their lives, what they wanted to be. Within a few years of each other, we find Durkheim's "suicide," Freud's "unconscious" and "dreams," Max Weber's "charisma," Bergson's "memory," Nordau's "degeneration," Mallarmé's "*ptyx*," Marx's "alienation," Ibsen's "gyntian self," Schoenberg's "atonality" ("pantonality," as he preferred to call it), Yeats's "imagism," Jarry's "pataphysics," Kandinsky's "line and point." All these ideas were widely different from each other in implication and emphasis and yet nevertheless were associated with each other as part of the movement in opposition to ideas of scientific and material progress. Even Max Nordau, whose degeneration theory was aimed at the very artistic movement we are limning, recognized that natural sciences offered salvation and rationality, that there were forces, such as those he observed at the Dreyfus trial, which fell outside of scientific solution.

Yet such was the nature of the cultural war that anyone coming of age in an artistic capacity in or around 1900 had to absorb these conflicting elements and adjust himself or herself to contradictory forces that made equal sense. The annus mirabilis, as 1900 was often called, was not only a gathering together of great adversary talents in the arts, it was also a meeting point of several philosophical ideas that undermined at every stage Wallace's sense of that wonderful century. So great was the crisis in perceiving data that the great sacred subjects of Wallace — science, discovery, progress, human amelioration, experimental research — became sources of ridicule in the hands of the artists even as they became holy matters in the hands of the politicians, scientists, and social planners. It is hard to think of any other time in history when the confrontational clash between opposing cultural forces was greater. Everything that the nineteenth century thought it stood for in reason and rational planning found itself refuted by twentieth-century Modernist culture.

In fact, 1900 was a marvelous or miraculous year because so much was undergoing alteration; a virtual reconstruction was taking place. Marxist as well as Darwinian theories were large forces for change, and Freud's ideas while deterministic nevertheless placed tremendous weight on the individual and his ability to clarify his role and his relationship to it.

Another form of secession that swept into Prague and directly into Kafka's consciousness was Theodor Herzl's Zionism. For while Zionism had political and racial overtones, reaching back deeply into history, it cannot be separated from other forms of rebellion or withdrawal from the major society. Hungarian by birth, and thus from an outlying region of the empire, Herzl came to Vienna, the heartland, and identified strongly with German culture. Like Kafka in part, he saw in the German language and its poetry and music an alternative to his Jewishness. He wanted to be not a Hungarian Jew but a Jewish German, much as Kafka early on hoped to be a crossbred Jew and German. One of the striking ironies of Herzl's Zionism is that if the host culture had been less hostile, he would have embraced it fully and Zionism would have perhaps derived from a later era. Herzl's stay in Paris, as correspondent for the *Neue Freie Press*, showed him another side of European anti-Semitism, especially in the Dreyfus affair and in the writings of Drumont, whose words were an incitement to destroy the Jews. At this point, Herzl felt a Jewish secession was the answer to all political solutions. Nationalism or folk movements left no place for the Jew in Europe (as Kafka would himself come to perceive) and Herzl's response was a return to Palestine as a way of resolving the Jew's estrangement. Legend has it that Herzl's moment of conversion to Zionism took place during a performance of Wagner's *Tannhäuser:* here he first recognized that German nationalism excluded the Jew, that in fact the Jew would always remain alienated, foreign, and scapegoated in such an environment.

No one, however, was more influential at this time than Nietzsche, the German philologist and classicist turned philosopher. Everything Nietzsche touched spoke of the new man, new attitudes, new forms of response to old and tired ideas or old and tired governments, states, figures. Nietzsche, as Freud would do later, drove home man's internality, and that meant transformation. Far from the marketplace or the commonplace, where every decision must be yes or no, man's real responses lay. In *Ecce Homo,* "Here Is a Man," we have Nietzsche's call for a new creature for our times, a new man. On the edge of madness, Nietzsche saw himself as Jesus' new man, as would a generation of writers after him who connected their vision to the unique self. In *Thus Spake Zarathustra,* Nietzsche describes man as "becoming," as a bridge, "a bridge and no end: proclaiming himself blessed in view of his noon and evening, as the way to new dawns."[9] According to the German philosopher, man's existence is like a bark heading into the unknown, heading perhaps into where the great nothing lies. One must, however, make the journey even if it means extinction. World-weariness or surrender is the way of the "last man," the man who wants to live forever, who, by denying "becoming," chooses a living death.

Nietzsche's parables, apothegems, and paradoxes, his aphoristic way of presenting philosophical ideas, were like a tonic. And we can see his influence on Kafka even from Kafka's use of parables and paradoxes, some of them embedded in his diary entries, others as lists, as in the "Octavo Notebooks." Kafka fell in with Nietzsche's thought in so many ways that any effort to disentangle particular themes must be selective. One way to read Kafka, beginning with his earliest work, such as "Shamefaced Lanky and Impure in Heart" and "Description of a Struggle," is as a form of spiritual autobiography, a genre typified by Nietzsche's *Ecce 'Homo* (1888). In such a reading of Kafka's work, everything must be read against everything else, in what may be called cross-textuality or, in more technical terms, contextuality. In this reading, Kafka's works are a gigantic mosaic, and each piece touches upon another, so that it is unwise and misleading to discuss one work as isolated from the rest. While such readings are valid for nearly every major writer, they are more relevant to Kafka, whose works, long and brief, are part of a cross-hatched, cross-textured whole, characterized by spiritual autobiography.

Spiritual autobiography was particularly prevalent at the turn of the century, influenced as it was by Nietzsche, Freud (a little later), Darwin, and other major thinkers and forces in both the literary and scientific community. It was a reshaping of an older form, the *Bildungsroman,* or novel of formation, education, or building, in which a young man (or woman) apprentices himself to life, meets various obstacles, overcomes them or is overcome, and goes on his way. *David Copperfield* and *Jane Eyre* are characteristic of this type. Kafka's first major effort at longer fiction was an attempt at this form, his incomplete *Amerika*, whose title in German, *Der Verschollene* ("The Man Who Vanished" or "The Forgotten One") is more evocative of the genre. But even before that, his first significant stories, "The Judgment" and "The Metamorphosis," were themselves forms of spiritual autobiography. In the traditional example of the genre — *Jane Eyre*, for example — generational conflicts are serious and often crushing for the younger person, whether the oppositional older person is a father, mother, aunt, uncle, or stepparent. The welfare of the young person frequently depends on acts of rebellion, secession, withdrawal, putting herself or himself on the edge. The individual finds himself at odds with social needs, particularly if sexual urges are strong, as they are in Jane Eyre.

Traditionally, acts of rebellion and sexual needs are met by career or marriage; one finds one's place in society, becomes part of some establishment, while remaining critical of hypocrisy and cant. But this traditional novel of "growing up" or of education and formation could not withstand the onslaughts of Modernism. By the turn of the century, the usual nexus between the individual and society begins to shift, moving from the socially stable individual to matters of spirit, soul, self. Under pressure from developments in general psychology, from Freud and Nietzsche, and from the sciences, physical well-being, individual happiness, and social usefulness give way to intangibles like mental health, sexual discovery, and, chiefly, spiritual needs. The protagonist, now a mere shadow figure for the author, no longer shapes him- or herself into a social unit but exists almost solely for the self. Self is all. Narrative itself reflects the change, with straight plotting becoming convoluted, incidents occurring simultaneously or in memory, present tense giving way to levels of pastness, ends implicit in beginnings — with surreal episodes long before surrealism. The changes were not only literary. Parallel spiritual journeys are numerous, for example, in Mahler's and Bruckner's long, expressive symphonies, where self in Mahler and spirit in Bruckner are primary; in Edvard Munch's deeply introspective paintings; in Strindberg's spiritual dramas of self and destruction; in Wedekind's creation of the Lulu figure and an expressionistic-spiritual drama that buries realism.

Freud's great journey into the unconscious was, in this respect, another form of spiritual autobiography, foreshadowed as it was by his own self-analysis in the midsummer of 1897 and by the shattering trauma of his father's death. Self-analysis becomes a key, since it uncovers layers of formative material and then reassociates these memories in the development of the individual, as we see in Hesse, Gide, Mann, Joyce, Proust, and Musil at the end of the century or shortly thereafter. The years 1895–1900 were, as we know, the period of

Freud's great journey. We have here an avant-garde in action, new methods and modes based on the recognition of irrational impulses from an unconscious that serves as a source for behavior.

An artist usually supplies the shaping force for his art, using materials available to anyone who can observe or hear or feel them. In Freud's case histories, the raw material derived from another's psyche, from the unconscious dreamworld — whether that of the Wolf-Man or Anna O. or Dora — but in drawing out that material Freud was committing a creative act. What Modern artists were doing with color, arrangement, deployment on canvas, distortion of reality, Freud was attempting with sex: using sex not as associated with love or physical relief, but with sex in an almost entirely new role as connected to neurosis and hysteria, to repression and shame, as we see shaded later in Kafka's mature work. Freud's sense of mission here, to find coherence in what appeared to be incoherent materials, placed him with the Modern avant-garde: "The description," he said, "of such early phases and of such deep strata of mental life has been a task which has never before been attacked; and it is better to perform that task badly than to take flight before it." Even his forceful metaphors — "attacked," "take flight," "perform that task" — suggest, once again, his alliance with the language of the avant-garde, which was associated with military and militant functions.

The "new man," unlike the striver in naturalism/realism, is disaffected, effete or aesthetic, outside social coordinates, himself a coordinate of emptiness, often a "nil" man or one striving not to be "nil" or annihilated, like Kafka's Georg Bendemann, Gregor Samsa, Joseph K., or K. He is a person for whom the outside world, however defined, has ceased to function, for whom it has become a dark place. For many of these new men, Mallarmé and Nietzsche were prototypes, and their deaths in 1898 and 1900, respectively, reinforced their legends as disaffected creatures, as Poe and Baudelaire had been for an earlier generation of poets. In this equation, Nietzsche's *Ecce Homo* becomes a key document, a major turning point in how we look at semiautobiographical fiction, where we locate it in the scale of fiction or nonfiction. The title, with its ironic reference to Jesus, suggests the extreme self-consciousness characteristic of the genre, that aspect of Modernism that would emerge despite numerous impersonal devices in the arts to disguise or blunt the self. In Kafka, the use of double-layered narrators, of an external narrator and a subjective character, and of messengers carrying information all became devices to disguise or highlight the intense emphasis on self.

What characterizes Nietzsche's confessions more than anything else is the obsessive need to clarify his own position and, once it is defined, to use it to make the world fall into place as a consequence. The reality of the world, as well as its resurrection and resurgence in human terms, depends on the individual recreating it in his mind as he wishes it to be. Although Nietzsche's theory of *amor fati* (literally "love of fate") seems to contradict the mind's ability to recreate anything, it actually nourishes that position.

Although *amor fati* would appear to lead to a kind of blind determinism, as it did for the Greeks, for Nietzsche it meant that man must work within his own fate, that he must embrace and "love" it, since he cannot attack what is outside. Nietzsche's philosophy was solidly rooted in a world of will, where *that* power allows the individual to assert himself despite a fate imposed from without. It establishes a radical dialectic not within the society but within the individual, who must struggle on as a sign of good will, indeed of good faith. By so doing, he negates that dismal "last man" philosophy of trying to survive regardless of what one becomes.

For Kafka, *amor fati* meant a brutal interplay between a destiny that the individual has already had worked out for himself and that individual's own striving to transform the way in which that world can be perceived. Kafka's "pain" resulted from his inability to bring together two seemingly conflicting ideas: that our destiny has been written for us, and yet that our inner urge, an obsessional need, rages to change our very perception of destiny. His many comments on paradise, on its loss and our efforts to regain it, nonetheless are aimed at how we have been predefined even as we seek to break from that design into a transformation of the self. Nietzsche and Freud provide essential ingredients here, and Kafka made them representational ideas.

Associated with Nietzsche's directiveness for free will is his willingness to assume the mantle of the fool: "I do not want to be a holy man; sooner even a buffoon — Perhaps I am a buffoon. — Yet in spite of that — or rather *not* in spite of it, because so far no one has been more mendacious than holy men — the truth speaks out of me." But his truth is, admittedly, "terrible," for "so far one has called *lies* truth."[10] That revaluation of all systems, the reversal of truth and lies, and acts of "supreme reexamination on the part of humanity" all become "flesh and genius" in him. He asserts he was the first "to *discover* the truth of being," as well as the first "to experience lies as lies — smelling them out." The Garden of Eden is effaced in favor of the garden of contradictions. What was divine order becomes, when reorganized by Nietzsche, divine disorder. "I contradict," he says, "as has never been contradicted before and am nevertheless the opposite of a No-saying spirit. I am a bringer of glad tidings like no one before me. . . . It is only beginning with me that the earth knows *great politics*."[11]

This is followed by a key passage for the genre of spiritual autobiography, for Modernism in general, and most certainly for Kafka at his most subversive: "And whoever wants to be a creator in good and evil, must first be an annihilator and break values. Thus the highest evil belongs to the greatest goodness; but this is — being creative." This statement goes well beyond the usual *épater les bourgeois,* or spiting the public, since it is based on that disordering of the perceiver, virtually a conscious madness, that will enable him to reverse values and seek truths. Like the doomed clan of nineteenth-century French poets, doomed or cursed by their very talent, Nietzsche declared, "I am by far the most terrible human being that has existed so far,"[12] but he sees in his terrible aspect the chance of salvation for mankind, a benefactor from below. As an "immoralist," the name André Gide gave to his destroyer of conventional values, he takes on all the nausea one must feel for man. There is, in this romantic stance, a good deal of inverted Christianity: martyrdom restated in terms of Satan, a sacrifice of self that was so appealing to the young Kafka when he conceived of himself as a victim on the altar of literature.

Nietzsche's use of negative energy — in effect, hibernation, hiding, withdrawal as positive denial — connects him to Kafka, as well as to many others of his generation writing in German: Hesse, Broch, Musil, and Rilke,* among others. Crawling into bed or into a hole is not necessarily a rejection of life, but a renewal of oneself on grounds other than those an activist can comprehend. Nietzsche sees that such so-called negativism — what becomes dicing with death in Kafka — is not a rejection but an acceptance on other terms. Hibernation is not a final stage; it leads not toward death but toward renewal on terms different from the original premise. In this "disordering" Neitzsche discovers life. For Kafka, Nietzsche's celebration of life based on negating all contemporary standards of progress and success becomes attuned less to rebellion and more to metamorphosis, in that shifting of ground so as to find alternate values by which one can survive. Kafka was more concerned with outmaneuvering than was Nietzsche, who went directly to the individual problem and forced confrontation. Kafka repeatedly slid off and away, outflanking those who would suffocate him, whether in the family or the bureaucracy.

Kafka was not a pure Nietzschean, any more than he was pure Freudian later or Darwinian earlier, or Marxist at any time. Instead, as he readied himself to enter the German University, he was a young man open to all those intellectual forces that appealed to the apostate

---

*That great poem "In Prag" by Paul Celan, a Romanian writing in German in the generation after Kafka, catches that same sense of negative energy. Prague: "That half-death, / suckled big with our life, / lay around us, a true ashen image — ." This ashen image links up later in the poem with "bone-Hebrew / ground into sperm / ran through the hourglass. . . ." Death here becomes revitalized as it is transformed into negative time. And in Rilke's "The Panther," the panther contains energies that are "like a dance of strength around a center / in which a mighty will stands numbed." And yet while this energy that the animal exudes is extinguished in the heart, it still puts to shame, in its negativism, our most active selves.

Jew. He was not, however, seeking alternatives to religion or alternatives to anything in particular. He was seeking whatever could nourish his sense of marginality, something that could sustain his feelings of intense withdrawal and that could provide him with justification for his awareness of his differences from others. The struggle in him between Nietzschean will and Freudian/Darwinian determinism, while surely not the sole struggle he was undergoing, helped him find his own measure of things.

That Kafka was flailing around for something to believe in we can see in his interest not only in Darwin but in Spinoza.[13] Spinoza's rationalistic approach to questions of belief; his weighing of its advantages and disadvantages; his monism, in which all reality is grounded in one principle; his careful structuring of truth; his mathematical approach to experience; his closing of the gap between mind and body, between ideas and the physical universe; his use of logic in positing the universe as a single substance capable of infinite attributes; his placement of God within, not outside, nature — all or some of these were very appealing to a young man seeking to make sense of what had hitherto been discrete, uncertain, incohesive. Kafka did not remain a dedicated Spinozan, nor did he remain a devout Darwinian or Machian. He absorbed all these intellectual elements and ultimately transformed them into his own shapes and elements. But for the time being, Spinoza could be very significant to a young man who felt his confidence slipping, for Spinoza spoke repeatedly of the need to preserve the self, to maintain one's pride of being, the power of what one stands for. One finds freedom, in fact, in following the laws of one's own nature; slavery, on the contrary, means bowing to ignorance or confusion.

Such rationalism did not really conflict with Mach's positivism or Darwin's own form of rationalism implicit in evolutionary theory. For Spinoza, all thinking was action, and all thought, reciprocally, led back to action. Ideas were themselves active, and in this Spinoza met up with an unlikely ally in Nietzsche and his caustic call to intellectual arms. Spinoza in this sense empowered the individual, here Kafka, to pursue ideas, to reject others' perception of him or of the world, to find infinite attributes in a universe where God is, pantheistically, within, not beyond. Kafka later, as imaginative creator, became dubious about Spinoza's monism, for he moved toward dualism (Nietzsche's bifocalism) or toward even more multiple forms from which principles could be derived. But before the artist was the mind trying to make sense of a turbulent mass; the ideas of Spinoza, Nietzsche, Mach, Darwin, and later Freud became an unlikely mix that served its purpose for the young Kafka.

Mach,* whose ideas were filtered to Kafka through the student's

*Einstein ultimately had to dispute and negate Mach's physics to prove his own "economy of nature."

science teacher Gottwald, emphasized the mind's organizing powers to such an extent that he believed mathematical formulas were merely expressions in simpler form of what the mind had already ordered for itself. The primacy of mental activity as against all other forms of knowledge deeply impressed Kafka, if we look ahead to his devastating attacks on bureaucracy, on social structures, on progress itself. Kafka's protagonists seem passive and even retrograde because they function on another level of experience from that expected of them in office and career. They expect the external world to follow principles similar to what they sense: Spinoza's monism and Mach's positivism. When the equation does not work, or works against them, they succumb, not passively, but like Jews of a later generation caught in a bureaucratic web whose operating principles and destructive threads escape them. Like Mach, Kafka tried not to divide elements into good or evil, right or wrong, or any kind of meaningless Manichaeism, but into what worked, what failed to work, what was useful, what had ceased to be useful. According to Mach, and Kafka followed here, whatever functions for the individual is itself a solution to practical problems. All depends on our intention and motivation, and from that springs our own economical way of ordering experience, whatever its consequences, whatever its ultimate "rightness" or "wrongness."*

The ideas of Sigmund Freud, whose own background and development, as we have noted, paralleled Kafka's, could not be avoided, certainly not for a German-speaking Jew of intellectual pretensions. While Kafka was not in any sense a Freudian — although early on he was aware of the Oedipus complex and the role of the unconscious and dream interpretation — he was part of that entire generation saturated with Freudian possibility. After Freud, even if one opposed everything he was describing, nothing could remain the same. But before Freud, there was Bergson, and although we do not note any direct response of Kafka to the French philosopher, no serious avant-garde writer could be unaware of him. Through his imitators and in German translation, Henri Bergson permeated the intellectual atmosphere of the Dual Monarchy, especially since so many of its writers migrated to Paris and Berlin, then returned, or else became acquainted with a kind of watered-down Bergson.

A central figure in the later transition from impressionism into Modernism, the French writer warned that the logical mind created continuities where none really existed; that this logical mind shaped mechanistic theories of existence because it had no other way of deal-

---

*Although the consequences of Mach's ideas in later intellectual thought are not our concern here, it is of interest to note that he deeply influenced language theory, not the least that of Ludwig Wittgenstein, in his *Tractatus Logico-Philosophicus*. Kafka was not a language theorist, but we will see that he too was caught up in many of the arguments about language, its philosophical functions, and its strengths and weaknesses as a form of perception.

ing with life; but that, besides this mechanistic impulse, there was another that tried to grasp vital phenomena. This impulse Bergson attributed to intuition, what would be redefined by Freud as the unconscious
in one of its attributes and by Mach as part of sensory perception. As
Modernism develops in this early phase, in the 1880s and 1890s, the nature of reality or matter drifts not only toward abstraction but toward a
void that contemporary life seems to have created especially for things.
This void or vagueness was very close to how the unconscious was
perceived in the years before Freud, and very close indeed to how the
layman still perceives the unconscious. The shadows, hazes, and
ambiguities one associates with poets like Mallarmé, Jarry, Maeter-
linck, and Yeats, or composers such as Wagner and pre-1900 Mahler —
and, not the least, Kafka — are, given their contexts, comparable to the
mists one associates with an unconscious process.

In *Time and Free Will* (1889), Bergson spoke of concepts as inter-
rupting the flow of reality without giving us anything "of the life and
movement of reality." They substitute for reality a "patchwork of dead
fragments," an "artificial reconstruction." By the time of *Matter and
Memory* (1896), the conscious mind has become a lie: "The brain state
indicates only a very small part of the mental state, that part which is
capable of translating itself into movements of locomotion," while ne-
glecting all other important functions. Bergson stressed *becoming*, not
being; the living reality, not associations that end up in conscious
memory. He inveighed against associationism, that relationship between large blocks of information: "The capital error of associationism
is that it substitutes for this continuity of becoming, which is the living
reality, a discontinuous multiplicity of elements, inert and juxtaposed." This *becoming* is a philosophical unconscious. As against associationism, a specious mental state, there is "duration," that sense of
"the real, concrete, living present," which occupies the ground between past and future. Matter is always becoming, a psychological idea
that links Bergson not only to Freud's later synthesis of the unconscious but to physical theories of energy impacted and ready to explode
into being.

Since Kafka's earliest writing in "Description of a Struggle" is so
close in form to stream of consciousness, we must note how the
stream, a flow rather than sharply plotted narrative lines, had entered
rather effortlessly into Prague thinking. Once again, the route was
Bergson and Freud, and through them the whole thrust of avant-garde
Modernist art. When the unconscious entered the vocabulary of every
major artist, it became apparent that the inevitable goal of Modernism
was, in one sense, stream of consciousness and, in another sense, abstraction. Abstraction is a stream in which method and matter are inevitable aspects of the same thing.

Bergson's *Matter and Memory* became a holy text of Modernism. In it he argued that once we actualize the past and turn it into "image," it leaves pure memory and becomes a "present state, and its sole share in the past is the memory whence it arose." Bergson here overturns the traditional view that memory and pastness are indistinguishable. For him, pastness is the enemy of pure memory. Consciousness is continuity of existence in which pastness is part of a flow or stream — that sense we receive in Kafka of everything moving along without regard for distinctions between consciousness and pre- or unconsciousness,* as if the author had harrowed the unconscious, brought it to the surface, and revealed that it clings to the conscious.

Kafka's entire development from "Shamefaced Lanky" to *The Castle* was an effort to achieve that stream associated with spirit, memory, intuition. In that final, incomplete novel, Kafka found that every outer detail of the individual life, K.'s, had its counterpart in the inner life. Scene must equate to language; external event to mind projecting it. K. hopes that if he finds the order of his own existence (that is, the right language for expressing his thought), he will divine the pattern and order, even the fundamental idea, of what lies beyond. He is, in this respect, separating process from memory, matter from mind. He can forsake no detail; for that, like the homunculus, may contain the whole. In the little world he enters, all people and all information are a language, connected in some grammatical, syntactical way, although their particular pattern of relationships is not apparent. It is as if a visitor knows the vocabulary of a foreign language but cannot figure out grammatical relationships. He must remain ever vigilant, for the missing clues may surface, and then he will learn precisely how to respond. He must, however, not only understand the maze as a whole, he must not lose any fragment of it.

For the means by which to present K.'s journey through mazes, which may or may not lead to the castle, Kafka devised a very deceptive narrative. His tale seems to be the ordinary story of a young man caught in a problem, a third-person narrative with a traditional omniscient author. But the confusion of realms — the disruption of time and space, the enclosure or labyrinthine images, the succession of bizarre characters and meetings — relocates narrative very close to interior monologue or deeper, to stream, even though the narrative derives from the author, not from the protagonist. The method seems close to what one reader has shrewdly designated "psychonarrative,"[14] in which the protagonist's deepest thoughts are presented not through him but through a third-person narrative, a kind of refracted interior monologue that was Kafka's response to Bergson, Freud, and all those others emphasizing interior lives. But Kafka even goes beyond psychonarrative in what

*What was once known as the "subconscious" is now called the preconscious in the vocabulary of psychology.

he accomplished. In effect, he transforms all external phenomena into psychological recesses — that is, he carries the world inward, as if everything derived from K.'s consciousness. We know, of course, that it does not, but Kafka through an uncanny precision confuses borders between real and unreal.

Once again, Bergson lies behind all this. The French philosopher's thought was vague, his language imprecise and ambiguous, his views surely not prescriptive. Yet he did illuminate something we accept as a given of Modernism: that distinction between a conventional ego (the social, outward-turning ego) and a fundamental self (something uniquely individual). That conventional ego is demarcated spatially or in linear modes, based as it is on clearly defined memories and perceptions, stimuli, and responses, whereas the fundamental self is temporally oriented, operating in the resonances of its own definitions. As early as "Description," Kafka was struggling to find the correct form for that distinction, and one meaning of a "description of a struggle" can apply to the author's conflict within himself about the ways inner and outer, while linked, can be differentiated from each other.

In resolving this conflict, Kafka comes close to *reverie*, which suggests an opening up the sense of wonderment. Reverie removes us from reality, entering areas even more intense than interiority. In this respect, reverie has phenomenological overtones: through reverie and poetic image we gain insight into the very workings of mind and imagination, what Shelley meant when he said that imagination is capable of "making us create what we see." For Kafka, as for Proust and Hermann Broch, reverie negates pure representation and transcription. It struggles against fact and data. It is an effort to burrow into what Bergson refers to as pure memory, which he carefully distinguishes from sensation, which is "extended and localized." Pure memory is intensive and powerless, beyond movement and beyond sensation. It allows penetration into spirit, into intuition. What is necessary, above all, is to separate memory from cerebralism. Cerebralism leads to the adoption of reference points, objects, relationships; what emanates from pure memory allows one to possess objects, surely to transform them.

As we shall see, Kafka envisioned his art, however modestly he stated his aims, as peeling back layers of existence. By so uncovering, in a kind of archaeological dig, he hoped to regain from the unconscious what was latent, to make it partially visible, to open up the jungle, forest, depths to others' eyes; and by so doing, to provide for himself a kind of therapeutic function, in which art became the medium by which he could maintain his sanity. He saw so profoundly into the impenetrable he had no choice but to play the role of a priest of the imagination. He had to forsake what one writer called the "dream of peace,"[15] which for most people represents a conventional and ordinary existence, the support of friends and relatives, normalcy of a kind. By forsaking this, as any martyr would, Kafka left himself exposed and naked; and yet only through this means could he hope to move toward that impenetrable world beyond the party and the salon.

For Kafka, the impenetrable darkness and shadows are much more: not only the collapse of the empire, not only the collapse of his own personal hopes, but the sense that life itself had so altered itself that shadows and darkness are destiny. His method of working had to approximate the vision of such blackness: in his room late at night while Prague lay black outside, or in the dungeonlike study that he envisages for himself once he and Felice Bauer are married, or in burrows, holes, mazes, and labyrinths where he cannot be found out. His request near the end to Max Brod that his friend destroy all his manuscripts and books, with a few exceptions, was part of that scheme, to approximate the blackness that had entered into his vision and possessed him. He was not psychopathological — because he evidently found suitable socially meaningful outlets for his energies — but he paralleled psychopathological behavior in the vision of bleakness and blackness that remained for him just outside all so-called normal activity.

Blackness has precedents. Mallarmé's protégé René Ghil tried to penetrate the unconscious by way of colors and words, as Rimbaud had attempted earlier and as the impressionists would continue to do. Ghil stressed that the vowel *u* corresponded to the color yellow and, there, to the sound of flutes, and castigated Rimbaud for equating the *u* sound with the color green. What seems somewhat remote and even ludicrous has serious overtones, for we find Josef Breuer, Freud's collaborator and correspondent, using language analogously. Ghil may have been somewhat mad, but he comes close to a truth. As early as 1880–82, when he was treating Anna O. (Bertha Pappenheim), Breuer discovered what would prove momentous: that if he repeated to his patient when she was experiencing autohypnosis the hysterical words she had uttered during her daytime "absences," she could recall the language and detail of her hallucinations. With this recall, couched in the language of hallucination and the unconscious, she experienced catharsis, and her destructive symptoms receded.

Such a discovery in the early 1880s was a definite link between language and the unconscious, an association among words, memory, and senses, what Freud would later label the unconscious (*das Unbewusste*), and the recreation of the patient's self, a redoing of the past by way of a present act. Freud coined the term *freier Einfall* to indicate that severe pressure of the pre- and unconscious upon the conscious. We translate the phrase as *free association*, but Freud's sense is not chiefly of liberation, as *free association* appears to indicate, but pressure and weight, a kind of determinism that traps the consciousness.

The closeness of Freud's strategies to what Kafka thought and did leads to the inevitable question of whether Kafka would have chosen this path without Freud spread out before him. With "Shamefaced Lanky" coming so soon after the turn of the century, before Freud's theories could have penetrated into Prague, did Kafka need the Viennese's ideas at all, or would he have developed them in parallel fashion on his own — in the way that Alfred Wallace and Charles Darwin developed comparable ideas of evolution independently?* Kafka was very possibly responsive to the same developments in psychology and literature which influenced Freud. Freud had his Pierre Janet, Breuer, and Fliess, but Kafka had Nietzsche and the adversarial, sexually revealing literature of the fin de siècle. Pre-Freudian psychology was not innocent of sexual etiology, of course, with studies on hysteria and probes of something close to the Freudian sense of the unconscious available. Early on, Kafka did not need Freud; and even later, when he showed some hostility to the analyst, he developed independently of Freud, all the while revealing in his work, perhaps more than any other writer, a justification of Freud's theories.

Freud's breakthrough cut deeply into forbidden subjects: the public revelations of one's most secret life, sexual practices, desires, fantasies, and failures. Sex was no longer the triumph or the cry of victory but the source of frustration and defeat; *one became a hero of sexual deprivation, not of sexual conquest.* The entire relationship between men and women had to be redefined in this new light, not the least in Kafka's fictions, where the sexual battle is relocated and redefined as shame and defeat. His long sequence of letters to Felice Bauer and later to Milena Jesenská are those of a patient under analysis.

A critical parallel between Kafka and Freud comes in the respective faces they presented to the world: unthreatening, gentle, calm, bourgeois in attitude and practice. Yet despite their ostensible commitment to bourgeois values, whether family and profession in Freud's case or bureaucratic position in Kafka's, their sense of order veiled a view of the world as disordered, discontinuous, ultimately anarchic. However undeveloped and slight, "Shamefaced Lanky" already points to Kafka's awareness of the disorder underlying surfaces, and his greatest long fiction, *The Trial*, is testament to how an orderly surface is simply a snare for the unwary. Both Kafka and Freud had to develop a language for the unconscious and for a relocated kind of sexuality. A new vocabulary was needed for a new order.

Kafka seemed to recognize this early: that the experience, the phenomena, the emotional waves were all beyond what he could find in

---

*Kafka's early use of the bachelor theme, for example, foreruns the whole gamut of Freudian possibilities: repression, sexual dislocation, displaced energies, psychoneurotic behavior, and other qualities.

German; that even as he attempted to redefine German itself, it was, as were all languages, an inadequate vehicle of expression. In music, Wagner, and then Mahler, were trying to find some musical notation that could reach beyond the ordinary and the expressible to the inexpressible. Wagner's musical language was always one of striving or yearning to get beyond the limitations of notes, keys, chords. His use of the leitmotif was in some way an expression of this quest, and the leitmotif is in one respect an insight into the unconscious through repetition and determinism, through what is inescapable. All avant-gardes and secessions, for their part, are connected in this same search for languages, a quest that reaches beyond the meaning of words into the meaning of things themselves.

All of this threatened order; in fact, it encouraged disorder, because the languages of the creative arts became a language within a language, and that internal language was uncontrollable from without. It was, in its way, a far greater threat to Franz Josef's Vienna and Prague, Bismarck's Berlin, and the French Third Republic's Paris than any overt political activity, even the assassinations that had become so fashionable. By reaching into so-called forbidden or foreign territories, the artist demonstrated there was no real order, only the illusion of it.

Fritz Mauthner was a Bohemian Jew whose *Dictionary of Philosophy* (1901) was both a philosophy tract and a dictionary of words, forerunning in some respects Wittgenstein's method in his *Tractatus* (1921).* Mauthner's importance was that as part of an entire movement, beginning with Ernst Mach and continuing with Nietzsche, his work was concerned with the way philosophical ideas impinged on language usage. Mauthner was interested in the psychological origins of words; he felt we can derive the origins of words not from purely philological backgrounds but from "sense data." Mauthner's significant point was that we can never know "truth" or "reality" because the words we assign to such "objects" are arbitrary; they do not correspond to the properties of the object. Sense data and words, as we observed in Bergson, do not meet, and therefore all metaphysical speculation is based on an intellectual flaw. Language, in this view, cannot exist apart from the person using it. We note how relevant Mach's ideas are here; yet not only Mach and other philosophers, but the entire movement of avant-garde art moved toward a displacement of objects in favor of the languages that express it.

In *Contributions to a Critique of Language*, also published in 1901, Mauthner argued that language as a form of social communication can

---

*Mauthner was himself a Christian convert, and the entire family of Mauthners — Fritz's brother Ludwig as a professor of medicine, another brother as president of the Kreditanstalt — demonstrates how conversion led to entitlements. By the end of the century, the extended Mauthner family had gone into the munitions industry and banking, with branches in Bohemia, Budapest, and even Trieste.

never express what individual emotions and sensations mean. Nor can individual feeling ever approach communicatively the social function of language. Meaning, the individual expression, remains mystical and is best caught in fantasy and metaphor. All expression in fact is metaphorical, since particularized expression, even that employed by science, is only an approximation.

The attractiveness of this theory to both Wittgenstein and Kafka is apparent. Without knowing Mauthner's work directly, Kafka moved almost immediately into forms of fantasy, denying science and logic, even reason.

Once one believes that only fantasy, metaphor, parable, or fable are adequate expressions of human sensations, then one concludes that only art expresses truth of any kind. Both Kafka and Wittgenstein reached this conclusion, each coming from a different direction but traveling a comparable path. For both, reason becomes the enemy, not because it is demonic but because it cannnot serve the purpose of revealing values. It distorts, perverts, subverts. As soon as one tries to put sensations into reason, language forces an impasse. Reason can be expressed only in action: good men or women do good things. Statements are all subject to the errors implicit in expressive language. Both Kafka and Wittgenstein came to believe (Kafka early, Wittgenstein by the time of the *Tractatus*) that the unsayable and the ineffable were of genuine value, since they were the very elements that *cannot* be verified by language.[16] In this formulation, language serves its function as a kind of litotes: affirming itself by virtue of what it cannot do. This works well with Kafkan irony, paradox, and parable as vehicles of expression; they penetrate deeply into fantasy and fable, and they undermine realism. They also help displace objects as "unseeable." For both, once again, we see a powerful repudiation of positivism (or belief purely in scientific fact), although for some time the philosopher was interpreted, incorrectly, as a positivist rather than as a subverter of it. The Dual Monarchy, which housed Freud, Kafka, and Wittgenstein, was in a sense harboring an alternative language that became adversarial to the state, denying even its solidity as an object, no less as an empire.

As he turned to writing, in his earliest phases Kafka tried to avoid the insistent pressure of what came to be called "decadence," with its apotheosis of art as a singular calling. If he felt that art was the highest expression of language, then he had to be wary of theories of art for itself, which were the underpinning of the decadent development. Decadence was equated in the minds of many with degeneration, and the idea of degeneration fed readily into racial theories, which nearly always blamed Jews and Jewish artists and middlemen for cultural breakdown. When Hitler, in prison, came to write *Mein Kampf*, his argument was precisely that Jews had through decadent and degenerative art undermined the racial purity of the German race. Richard Wagner had offered a similar argument much earlier in his "Jews in Music." All of this winds back to Kafka, as he found himself on the threshold of so many conflicting elements, so many artistic choices, including decadence itself.

Decadence is not really a separate movement or an identifiable school, although there are aspects of several writers, painters, and composers which are often identified as decadent: Gautier, Verlaine, Huysman, Wilde, the French Poe, Richard Strauss, Gustave Moreau, Odilon Redon, among others. But these artists became swept up in the larger movement of symbolism, best represented by Mallarmé, and both decadents and symbolists in turn became part of the still larger mainstream movement of Modernism. We can see decadence — forms of exhaustion, efforts to outrage, creation of a "dreaming language," a narcissistic preoccupation with self — as simply one avant-garde among several.

The decadents focused so closely on the "I," what Max Nordau, a medical doctor who became a reviewer of cultural degeneration, termed *Ichsüchtigen*, or egomania, that the subjective became virtually an object in itself. They were post-Darwinians who felt that man was so caught by evolution, and thus by heredity, that the sole expression for the individual was through subjective excess.

The decadents hoped that through their revelations of the individual's depths they could break through the material universe, and their methods were often outlandish, demonic, destructive. Fueled by drugs, more so than alcohol, they reached into the unconscious well before Freud. Yet their attachment to the unconscious had no biological grounding. Theirs was an unconscious little different from Nietzsche's anarchic and uncontrollable Dionysus.

A large part of that anarchy was of course sexual — sex as dynamic energy, as neurotic drive, as illness more than health. We can see how Kafka could be drawn to certain decadent postures, especially that association between unconscious urges and sexual imbalance or anxiety. For many of the decadents, hetero- or homosexual, sexuality becomes obsession and compulsive behavior. Proust's Charles Swann and his ungovernable passion for Odette de Crécy, whom he does not even like, is an example of this. But also we note Gregor Samsa in "The Metamorphosis" with his love-longing for the picture of the woman in furs, his orgiastic association with her, until he masturbates brown juice on the glass protecting her image. In his own life, Kafka found himself in a Swann-Odette situation — his five-year obsession with Felice Bauer.

It was the sexuality of the decadents that helped to give them a bad name among the anti-Modernists, those dedicated to a "healthy" or normal society, as Modernism came to be associated with decadence and degeneration in most minds.

Yet the critics of degeneration and decadence were concerned —

obsessed! — not only with women (inferior creatures given too much power by the decadents) and sexuality but, even more virulently, with race. It was precisely this alliance of racism and anti-Modernism that Nietzsche endeavored to combat. Yet even Nietzsche, who advocated an alliance of Jews and Prussians as a way of infusing intellect into martial Germans, was as much a prophet of decline as he was an advocate of "overmanning" or overcoming it. Decline was for him, as for Nordau, Otto Weininger, then Oswald Spengler, associated with decadence,[17] that forbidden word that lost its power as a meaningful cultural term as soon as it was linked to sensuality. So too Modernism, a tremendous force for purification and transcendence, lost its meaning as revitalization or transformation as soon as it was associated with decadence. The word *modern* itself became interchangeable with corruption when allied in the public's mind with breakdown; its next stage, that of structuring or rebuilding, was dismissed. Just when it reached Kafka and other Prague writers, Modernism was regarded as the quintessential "deconstructor." Of the immediate circle of Prague wits and intellectuals, only Kafka pursued the Modernist line, embracing decadence in some phases, rejecting it in others, particularly on moral and ethical grounds; Brod, Werfel, and others remained traditionalists.

By lumping Modernism with elements the larger society had agreed to oppose — feminism, racial justice, social and political agitation — critics of degeneration could whip Modernism as a way of reestablishing historical traditions. These critics often parted ways on the kind of society they wanted, or even if they wanted any kind of society. Otto Weininger, for example, was so consumed by hatred of women and by self-hatred as a Jew that he seemed beyond social goals. Nevertheless, their agreement came on opposition to a word, a method, a point of view, and a culture deriving from that. Much of the real hatred of Dreyfus in the 1890s, apart from that of the diehard anti-Semites (about half of the French writers and artists), was displaced hatred of Modernism: whether the state should run on traditional lines or be infiltrated and nourished by foreign ideas. If the former, one wanted Dreyfus destroyed; if the latter, then one wanted Dreyfus found innocent and the French army (and state) condemned as repressive. Once the lines hardened, degeneration, not Dreyfus, was the issue. Not for nothing were Proust, Zola, and Clemenceau allied, associated in the public mind with degeneration, even treason.

Joseph Arthur Gobineau provided the theoretical grounding for racial theories leading to degeneration. A clear line can be drawn from the French diplomat and writer to Adolf Hitler's *Mein Kampf*. His essay on the inequality of the races, in 1853–55, did not speak of extermination, but it did provide justification for eradication as a way of preserving certain racial values. "Societies perish," he wrote, "because they are degenerate, and for no other reason." By perceiving humanity within racial constructs, Gobineau insidiously did for racial theory what Darwin would do for evolutionary species. His view was that since the individual is trapped within a deterministic pattern created by race, he counts for little or naught and therefore lies outside moral designations. Here is, in one respect, a foreshadowing of Nietzsche's "beyond good and evil." Although we have no evidence Kafka was familiar with Gobineau's work, the ramifications of it were clear. The ideas, whether assimilated directly or indirectly, passed into racial theories Kafka had to relate to; and, more likely, to cultural theories of degeneration that fueled those opposed to everything Kafka came to stand for. They were, in large part, the matrix of his development and maturation.

Gobineau's theory of racial degeneration has its later parallel in Krafft-Ebing's *Psychopathia Sexualis* (1886), which connected race and sexual practices, that combination which would dog Freud as a practitioner of a Jewish psychology polluted by pathological intrusions. Richard von Krafft-Ebing perceived life as based not on chance but on what he called "the hidden laws of nature which are enforced by a mighty, irresistible impulse."[18] Man's sexual nature must be sufficiently developed so that sensual indulgence is not his sole aim but rather manifests some higher motive, such as his desire to perpetuate the species. This sounds like an updated version of Schopenhauer sifted through Darwin. Krafft-Ebing saw in sexual desire both the lowest (degeneration) and the highest forms, when sex serves "ideas of morality, of the sublime, and the beautiful." This is precisely the bourgeois Victorian ideal that Freud and Kafka sought to undermine as a superficial facade for attitudes that called for quite different responses and languages.

Psychopathia's contemporary importance was its identification of certain energies with degenerative behavior. Pleasure, pain, emergence or absence of the sexual drive, its length, overabundance, or underuse — well shadowed in Kafka, Proust, Mann, Joyce, Hesse, and Musil, among others — all become associated with forms of either degeneration or health. Either/or, no middle ground. The individual was himself fitted into a larger cultural pattern, so that his sexual needs could be identified in terms of a society either declining or strengthening its resolve. Thus, sex and race blend, in that healthy sex and a healthy race free of taint will allow a society to prosper, not decline. From this to an Aryan view of racial superiority is not far to go.

The terms *sadism* and *masochism* became common coinage from Krafft-Ebing's use of them, with masochism deriving from humiliation and mistreatment at the hands of a woman, and not from the physical pain thereof. Krafft-Ebing viewed all sexual practices that were not socially sanctioned as part of pathology, and in subsequent editions of his book he provided an itemization of perversions, including homosexuality, autoeroticism, and fetishism. He was, it appeared, collecting the sexual predilections and hidden desires of the creations of that entire generation's avant-garde artists and writers — including Kafka, whose characters run the entire gamut of what Krafft-Ebing condemned as pathological.

Kafka's route into this company came from his need to make visible what lay beneath layers of disguise and deception. He was always seeking some latent reality: Aberrant sexuality? Pathological responses to other people and society? Hidden desires for pain and punishment — Krafft-Ebing's masochism? The need to be insulted and injured? By making this latent reality at least partially visible to us, he opened up new levels of our conscious life, expressing the inexpressible, while barely skirting the pathological, and by so doing sharing a hitherto buried knowledge.

Krafft-Ebing's cautionary tale of sexual perversities, sanctioning only the "missionary position" between a married man and woman, for example, ran parallel to insidious attacks on women. While Nordau (in both his *Degeneration* and the earlier *Conventional Lies of Our Civilization*) and Otto Weininger (in *Sex and Character*, which Kafka knew) diverged in their attacks on society, they agreed that degeneration in modern civilization could be traced to degenerate relationships between the sexes. What Nordau denied to modern culture as a whole, Weininger denied to modern woman. For both, the foundation of culture was a stable, traditional, unchanging relationship between a superior male figure and a subservient, childbearing female figure. This belief resembles Nietzsche's view that women were naturally suited for house and kitchen. It indicates a fierce rejection of the emancipated woman, who was viewed as destructive.

Once Modernism began to define itself in the last fifteen years of the century, one of its fiercest battles occurred over women. Here it was not a question of women's participation in Modernism — only a few female writers or artists were associated with the avant-garde — but rather a question of their portrayal in Modernistic works. One can say the conflict was not over women, but over Woman. We note a profound paradox: that while Modernism stressed the individual achievement and the unique artist, its chief male figures and many of its theorists denied individuality to women. Freud would of course become central here, with his studies on hysteria based on women and their inability to achieve sexual harmony — and then grouped by him and his circle into some composite "woman" fit for kitchen and children. In this regard, Freud was following Nietzsche, who, despite his relationship with the progressive and intellectual Lou Andreas-Salomé, was even more insidious.

Along with Nietzsche and Freud was the large number of poets, novelists, painters, playwrights, and composers whose three views of woman all converged in the 1890s. First was woman as keeper of the hearth, loyal, supportive, patient, like Freud's fiancée Martha Bernays. Second, a woman could be seen as earth mother, robust, sensual, the figurative creature of man's desire; Yeats sought her in Maud Gonne, Lawrence married her in Frieda von Richthofen, and everyone seemed to find her in Alma Mahler Gropius Werfel, who had also been involved with among others, Klimt and Kokoshka. And finally, woman could be seen as a destructive Eve, as in Wilde's Salomé, Wedekind's Lulu, Klimt's Judith, and in Alban Berg's opera based on two parts of the Lulu plays or Strauss's *Salomé*. Lulu, moreover, was prefigured by several strong women in Ibsen and by the Strindbergian "monster," and was paralleled by female characters in work by Kokoshka and others. Kafka's own torturous relationship with Felice Bauer fits neatly into these patterns.

Although several kinds of material, literary, social, anthropological, and psychological, fed into these three divergent views of women, some ideas were more significant and influential than others. Certainly among "mythic" sources the work of J. J. Bachofen, along with that of Darwin and Frazer, was critical. Bachofen's importance for us is that he established that "mother right" or a matriarchal era is "not confined to any particular people but marks a cultural stage."[19] In his sense of "mother right," we can see the outlines of the later nineteenth-century struggle over woman's role. For those like Weininger, Strindberg, and Nordau who viewed femaleness as actually or potentially demonic, woman was a creature who swirled up out of the underworld, a figure analogous to Mephisto in her capability for subversion. Strindberg cast his demonic women in swirls and mists, so that they seem protected by Satan himself. And even Ibsen has his strong women — Hilda Wangel, Rebecca West, and Anitra, for example — come from nowhere in order to tempt men to what may prove their doom. The destructive woman is almost always a figure who has traveled a long distance or is surrounded by a haze suggesting underworld connections, an emanation from irrational depths, from the unconscious.

Bachofen, however, also emphasized woman's vocation for devotion and justice, and for similar qualities that have been given feminine names. He repeats throughout that matriarchy grew out of women's conscious and continued resistance to concubinage — which suggests that to counter men's lusts, women needed a more regulated ethical order, one caught by a purer strain. Bachofen cites this development as equally degrading to men, placing them ethically and morally below women, and with this he reveals his Victorian view of female as purity, male as polluter.

For Bachofen, marriage served men's functions and debased women. Yet women also welcomed Dionysus, the great adversary of chastity and motherhood, after first resisting him, since he provided them a modicum of safety in sanctioned marriage. Here we have one of

Bachofen's critical ideas, where he is working both sides of a paradox and establishing a point that is of considerable interest to us after his death, especially in the period when avant-gardists perceived women in many destructive roles. Dionysus is both demeaning and threatening to women, yet the Dionysian cult also protected them against concubinage, although in roles subservient to men. Thus, women are trapped in roles defined not by them but by men.

This is, according to Bachofen, woman's tragedy, even though we would go too far in identifying him as a champion of women's rights in the modern sense. He perceived the bind into which women were forced but at the same time saw their sensual life from a male point of view. We catch some of his dilemma in Kafka's relationship with Felice Bauer, as well as in his general sense of women in his fiction. Bachofen identifies clearly the dilemma: forced to forgo the "chaste, Demetrian character of a life grounded in strict order and morality," woman must accept the "new form essentially rooted in the Aphroditian principle of carnal emancipation." The older order offered "lofty virtue" and a well-directed life; the new order, despite a rich material life, "concealed a diminished vitality, a moral decay," which Bachofen felt contributed to the dissolution of the ancient world.

Kafka's own ambiguous relationship to Julie Kafka allowed him to observe several aspects of the female dilemma, while unable himself to break free into a clear perception of his relationship to women.* Given his distaste for physical contact, he nevertheless desired lower-class women, Czech Gentiles whom he could buy, while disdaining sexual relationships with women of his own class, chiefly Jews. The Jewish woman, on one hand, recalled his mother and called attention to the traditional role his mother played, as workhorse, parent, and, most of all, wife. This dimension Kafka found not only distasteful but wasteful, and he rejected it. On the other hand, he could not tolerate emancipation. Felice became "the enemy" because her view of life was so different from his that it seemed to suck from him all his creative energy. He was able to produce mainly in the interstices of his alternating acceptance and rejection of her. That is, by exploiting his own ambiguities.

Kafka's Felice, however, as we view her from his letters, was quite different from the Felice we extrapolate from his siege. Rather than being a vampire or seductress intent on undermining him with her bourgeois views, she was, we note, courageous, loyal, willing to bend, somehow able to penetrate Kafka's obsessive needs to something important she found underneath. That she did not bend all the way was to her credit, but that she did not reject Kafka out of hand was also in her

---

*The newly discovered batch of thirty-two letters Kafka wrote to his parents near the end of his life documents the ambivalence he felt toward Julie: an alternating desire for her love and the rejection of her as a person.

favor. She had become his "image" of woman, and she had to accept the fact that he recreated her according to his needs. That she survived this recreation and bending indicates a woman of considerable spirit and substance; and that she not only survived but saw in Kafka what was valuable is another indication of her qualities.

In the 1890s women were attacked as lacking spirit or soul and as having voracious, vampirish appetites. Scientific "evidence" was offered to support these distinctions. It was claimed that a woman's brain, since it was six ounces lighter than man's, was not educable, unless one wanted her hysterical. Women who did achieve were called lesbians, and by that label assigned to pathology, by Carl von Westphal as early as 1869, and later by Krafft-Ebing, who asserted that lesbianism was the result of "cerebral anomalies" and a functional sign of degeneration. Such ideas nourished men as different as Havelock Ellis and Strindberg, or Weininger and Nordau, or Freud and some of his followers. Woman's uselessness for intellectual and/or spiritual achievement made her suitable only for maternity, whereas the father's "heroism" makes him the authority. This is, in effect, what Freud wrote to Martha Bernays. It was women's failure to heed this categorization that made end-of-the-century male writers so uncomfortable.

Karl Kraus, the influential Viennese journalist and preserver of German linguistic purity, whose influence extended well beyond Vienna to Prague, said that while man has sexual urges, "woman is sexuality itself." Lacking rationality, she brings the disorder of her sexuality into everything. How remarkably close Kraus's woman is to Freud's sense of her as hysterical. Or to Kafka's view of her as devouring, relentless in her urges and needs.

There was, of course, some response to this onslaught upon women as destructive elements, but the various books and tracts failed to capture the imagination in proportion to the attacks. Olive Schreiner (*The Story of an African Farm*, 1883) was one such figure in the counterassault, as were the women who developed politically in czarist Russia as nihilists, anarchists, and socialists. But although these figures offered an alternative view, their activities often simply added fuel to the men who raged against the sex, and frequently they seemed to fit into categories already devised by Weininger, Nordau, Nietzsche, Strindberg, and others. The "liberated" or strong woman who pressed for independence — Chernyshevski's *What Is to Be Done?* in 1863 was a driving force here — only seemed to add to the danger, especially since many of these women spoke of changing society through revolutionary means — that is, overthrowing the patriarchy in social and political life.

The sexual conflict really had three dimensions to it, and Kafka, as we shall see, would be enfolded by all three parts: the new woman, whether politically oriented, as in Russia, or insistent on avoiding do-

mestic slavery, as in the West; theories of degeneration, which were
chiefly based on deterioration of traditional values, embodied in part in
the growing liberation of this new woman; and finally, the identification of emancipation, deterioration, and voracious sexuality with the
advent of Modernism. We have in fact a triangular-shaped movement,
wherein the three sides are of unequal length, although critics tended
to make them equal so as to better assail Modernism and, indirectly,
women, Jews, and other "rebels" as enemies of the established order.

By attacking women and attempting to keep them in their place,
anti-Modernists could turn aesthetic issues into social and political
ones. Further, they could strike at elements that were, they felt, disruptive of civilization itself, that revolutionary war between the sexes.
Strindberg is well placed here and particularly germane inasmuch as
Kafka was a great admirer of his work. We can, in fact, through Kafka's
admiration for Strindberg, help to locate him in this area of women
feared, hated, and yet often triumphant. Strindberg, who is often perceived as a Modernist in his techniques, was in reality concerned with
feminism as part of a process of disintegration. As such, he explored
Modernist themes even as he opposed them. In *A Madman's Defense*
(1887–88), Strindberg offered up the idea that God is dead and that
Woman has replaced him. Strindberg is creating of course the edifice
that will prove false to his view of it. Once Woman replaces God as an
object of worship, she must fail, just as God failed; only Woman fails
even more completely since through personal experience Strindberg
can cut her down. He writes — and we should think here also of Kafka
with Felice Bauer — that he wanted to adore, to sacrifice himself, to
suffer hopelessly "without any reward but the ecstasies of worship and
suffering."[20] He will immolate himself on the idea of woman's purity.

Misogyny was inevitable. Once cited as angelic, women would
prove faithless and corrupted, creatures who should remain imprisoned
since, lacking reason or logic, they were incapable of dealing with reality. Strindberg writes, "I surpassed myself in heaping insults on the
head of my Madonna." For Strindberg, man existed to be deceived and
seduced, so that madness becomes his defense against women, since a
madman can escape what would otherwise entrap him. As Felice Bauer
became more set in Kafka's perception as the enemy — that is, bourgeois, insistent on certain formalities — he stepped up his "mad act,"
becoming increasingly inaccessible and reclusive. As she became larger
and larger in his imagination, he made himself ever smaller — until finally he could speak of himself as an underground man whose contact
with her, once married, would be about an hour a day. For Strindberg,
his wife Siri "sucked my brain dry, consumed my heart [her surname
was von Essen]. In exchange, she looked upon me as a garbage can into
which she threw all her rubbish, all her troubles, all her cares." Food
imagery persists: he is the foodstuff, she the consumer. After eating his

matter, she excretes him and then refills his empty husk with herself. Kafka: "Strindberg is tremendous. This rage, these pages won by fist-fighting."[21]

Kafka was not of course the sole recipient of this tradition, whether literary or personal in nature. This new concern with woman as devourer and hysteric as well as earth mother influenced narrative itself. Since, as many assumed, women were irrational and "total sexual beings," or fixed in their roles as nourishers, their reflection in narrative needed innovative techniques, techniques that could enter the "irrational" pre- or unconscious. The developing use of stream of consciousness was one way of capturing that sense of women, what we find in Joyce, Woolf, Ford, Dorothy Richardson, and Faulkner, among others. Molly Bloom's soliloquy at the end of *Ulysses* has its origins at the turn of the century in Weininger, Nordau, Kraus, Wedekind, Strindberg, Kokoshka, Wilde, and Strauss. Bertha in Joyce's *Exiles* and Yeats's various portraits of Maud Gonne fit into the genre: stream women. An idea that was deeply European becomes international, extending as far as the United States in Dreiser's Carrie or, somewhat later, in Hemingway's Lady Brett. We are reminded of Wagner's Venus or Isolde, when drugged, his Kundry in *Parsifal*; as well as Schopenhauer and Nietzsche's view of women's role as that of a Venus's-flytrap.

But stream of consciousness or some version of it is not the sole narrative response to such definitions of woman. In Kafka's case, the use of a wandering or an indistinct narrator, *someone seemingly there as author, but just outside the author*, is a response too, especially when women are involved. In "The Metamorphosis," Gregor Samsa becomes a "voice" on the subject of his sister Grete, a devourer, even though he has become an insect and thus lost his voice as such. Kafka had to devise ways of presenting information, and he moved outside traditional forms of narrative to do so. *The Trial* and *The Castle* provide examples of narrative methods that depend on disruption of traditional forms of storytelling, a technique that, in part at least, was a response to the question of "woman" at the end of the century.

This shift in narrative line along with the shift in perception of woman is not found solely in Kafka or Proust or a few other practitioners of the art of fiction. We could argue that the entire focus of literature, as well as that of poetry and painting, shifted under the pressure of the woman issue. Subjects were no longer love and attainment or rejection but meditations on impotence, contacts with mysterious sources of strength, abstractions about human relationships, explorations of the unconscious — what we see already in Shamefaced Lanky's slinking away from ordinary experience into some unfathomable, unreachable area. If we compare Ibsen's *A Doll's House* to Strindberg's *Miss Julie*, we see the theme shifting from a woman insisting on her personal rights to woman as devourer, with narrative means and language shifting analogously toward the symbolic, ambiguous, and mysterious, from the physical and cognitive to the unconscious. This shift is not merely the question of the way that experience is presented; rather it suggests an entrance into that ambiguous, indistinct area where Kafka would locate his own fictions.

That denial of everyday reality we find so insistent in Kafka from his earliest work is connected to another aspect of Modernism: the desire for purification. Whereas purification once had, almost solely, religious significance, it now connoted the cleansing of the arts, part of the swing from religious to aesthetic experience. Wagner "purified" opera of its Meyerbeerian and Verdian or broadly Italian aspects (Bellini and Donizetti, for example). Schoenberg's twelve tones would purify music of its Wagnerian grip, returning it to fundamentals. Kandinsky's abstractionism was nothing if not purification, toward a spiritualization of art.

At about the same time, Wittgenstein saw himself as "freeing" philosophy from depleted forms and theories and from exhausted language, somewhat like Kafka's effort to "cleanse" German to fit the needs of his particularly angled vision. In another verbal medium, Mallarmé had perceived of himself as purifying poetry of the romantic excesses of Victor Hugo and others, as had Baudelaire before him. The great cubist experiments in the first decade of the century, from late Cézanne through Picasso, Braque, and Gris, similarly, began that early abstractionism that was to purify painting of its representational excesses, as, earlier, impressionism attempted to liberate light and color from academic realism, the so-called genre school. With abstractionism, the last remnants of heroism are vanquished, and with it, nature, even, action; everything is purified, except motion, space, field.

With its basis in both religion and chemistry, purification fitted well into theories of decomposition, into deconstructing elements and objects that had become "too present," too evident. Modernism prided itself on simplification, although its purifications of commonplaces and narrative elements created immense difficulties for readers. Kafka's work is often so purified, so brought down to essentials, that simplicity becomes another form of complication and ambiguity. This is observed best in his briefer works, in the parables and paradoxes, for example, or in the one- or two-page stories.

Purification has its own paradoxes: authority of style was based not on the assimilation of other styles, as we might expect, but on the expression of honest feeling which is then transformed into individuality of style. Authority, tradition, even movements all become secondary to individual style, one-man avant-gardes in many instances. In Berlin, a new magazine called *Pan* was founded in 1895, its name intended to indicate its direction: panic, uniqueness, disruption. It would serve in modern society as Panurge had served as an exploding force in Rabelais's time. The magazine suggested the cannibalization of whatever preceded it. In this regard, those who broke with previous art forms had to maintain the act of disruption, had to move along with *Pan* as iconoclast, or else find themselves lambasted and abandoned.

Art forms passed into fads within years of their iconoclasm. Not only did movements rarely have the opportunity to form into schools, but individuals had little chance to form into movements. In Prague, the "Circle" was more a matter of friendship than of art, and among that circle of friends, Kafka was unique, having more to do with Paris or Berlin groups than with the writers who drank coffee and beer in the local cafés. Surely he was more attuned to Robert Musil in Vienna than to Max Brod, his closest and most devoted friend, or to Werfel, or any of the others. Crossing genres, he was more closely linked to someone like Arnold Schoenberg than to Prague writers, or to a Czech painter like František Kupka than to those who practiced traditional forms of literature.

One of the several paradoxes of Kafka's career is how a man who was so conservative in his ideas about progress, development, modern advances, technology, nearly all of which he decried, could also have been so innovative in his fictional modes, so readily responsive to virtually everything that was being thrown out onto the world from Paris, Vienna, and Berlin. Yet profoundly connected to ideas of purification and to proliferation of styles is the question whether the development of avant-gardes in the arts really does negate ideas of progress or is aligned with them. Can we say that the avant-garde, however antisocial it may appear, is part of the same impulse that nourishes ideas of social progress? Progress is, after all, an act of purification, primarily in its subversion of earlier ideas and practices, even in its adversariness to society and state. If we suggest that acts of purification, the avant-garde, and progress are aspects of the same impulse, then developments in art are not unique but elements of a universal process in which everything moves along, although at different paces and in different contexts.

We could argue, however, that from about 1885, when Modernist thought was shaping itself in sociopolitical and psychological areas as well as in the arts, the avant-gardist was creating unique instants: revelations and privileged moments. The idea of progress is of course connected to the future becoming the present. The avant-garde artist does partake of that meaning, but he embodies in himself a significant extension of the idea, the sense that utopia has arrived purified of pastness and historical entanglements, His work, whatever shape it takes as poetry and fiction, or as musical composition, painting, or dance, is the utopian moment. It is far more than the "future is now," and it has leaped beyond progress. Baudelaire saw that gleam early, in the gaze of a cat who returns his gaze: "I see with awe the fire of its pale pupils, luminous beacons, living opals, which gaze on mine relentlessly."

The avant-gardist (and here Kafka enters) in his desire to purify is always seeking a still moment or a spiritualized moment in which time and space are disconnected from past, present, or future. One key ingredient of developing Modernism was the need for artwork to move "outside," not merely into Bergson's sense of durational time but into a temporal component that belies the needs of human reality. In an interview, Mallarmé, always the spokesman for that disconnected moment beyond, said that to his mind "the case of the poet in this society [the Third Republic in France] is the case of the man who cuts himself off from the world in order to sculpt his own tomb,"* or, in Kafka's case, his own burrow. That moment outside time became Kafka's greatest, most intense moment, *because* it was outside and beyond. As he pictured himself alone at his writing desk, late at night, or immured in a basement during marriage, he sought desperately for those still moments. They came at all periods of his life, faintly intimated in "Shamefaced Lanky" and in "Description of a Struggle," but more firmly anchored in "In the Penal Colony," "The Burrow," and "A Hunger Artist." The latter is a capstone of the Kafkan vision: the still moment taking over from all ideas of progress, with their debasement of truth and beauty.

In "A Hunger Artist," Kafka's epitaph, the artist achieves his purification when he reaches toward that exact moment when life and death touch. For the prisoner being endlessly punctured in the writing machine of the "Penal Colony," the still moment begins in the sixth hour, when he grows quiet, rejects food, and begins to radiate with enlightenment. At this point, the prisoner deciphers the script with his wounds; they are part of him, he part of the machine, the words and the total situation realized. After that sixth-hour revelation or enlightenment, the prisoner needs another six hours or so to die. Yet the point is not his death but the moment when he reaches toward purification, when progress — for after all, the machine is antiprogressive, a remnant of the old ways, and itself always breaking down or malfunctioning — is stilled. Kafka was uncanny at revealing how one entombs oneself and, in the process, is transformed into someone purer, at least for that moment.

This is not a religious moment; no revelation is attained when the worshipper "sees" or senses his deity. Rather, it is the flowering moment of ego. An artist as Kafka represents him is an egomaniac in his need for attention, in his refining of his technique, in his emphasis on appearance to an audience. When ego blends with some external moment, the within and the beyond merge with each other. The hunger artist has been warned that forty days of fasting is permissible, but he

*Consider another Mallarméan expression of separation: "As for me, Poetry takes the place of love because it is in love with itself and the pleasure it takes in itself drops deliciously into my soul" (*Selected Letters of Stéphane Mallarmé*, edited and translated by Rosemary Lloyd [Chicago: University of Chicago Press, 1988], p. 76).

wants to go beyond that biblical number to reach for the unattainable, which he senses will be the perfect moment. His desire for an absolute is not for a perfect God, but for a perfect meeting of self and beyond. The achievement occurs, if and when it does, through an act of purification, which for Kafka was connected, obsessively, to food, especially its denial.

It is interesting to note how close death, or suicide, was to ideas of progress or "perfect" moments. We discover a bizarre interlocking of death-suicide-progress-purification ritual, a suitable blend of the seeming contradictions that ripple through Kafka's early and more mature work. The association of suicide and purification, further, demonstrates that even the most final of adversary positions — saying no to one's life — had for the Modernists a sense of expanding energy. To oppose was so strong an ideology that purification, as in some religious ritual, could be achieved only by suicide.

The route we have charted so far — creating the context in which Kafka would find himself even in his earliest work — combines several seemingly disparate and divergent elements. The quality of life defined in these early Modernist purification rites involves a spiritual crisis that can be ameliorated only by negation of past history and exploration of new temporal sequences having little relationship to daily routine activities. When Freud moved from hypnosis and cocaine to self-analysis and analysis, from disorderings to reorderings, from displacement of time and even space to a renewal of self, he followed, in brief, the same path as the avant-garde artist. When Kafka created the neutral time zones of a work like *The Trial*, where time both moves forward and yet seems static, he approached hypnotic time; just as, later, in *The Castle*, he created a static space, one that stretches before us and yet rarely seems "beyond." In both instances, as well as in several shorter fictions, his aim was not only to redefine time and space for the reader, but to suggest new ways of defining matter, of recreating reality, or relocating objects in our imagination. He had become, in these respects, a great philosopher of things, a theorist of temporal and spatial considerations, a purifier of language, and an avant-garde artist at the very edges of what Modernism was all about.

There are of course few clear congruences between a movement and an individual. The avant-garde is an amorphous, unshapely element, only imperfectly defined, whereas individual effort is more clearly formed. It was Freud's genius to perceive that the individual psyche went through stages that allow for generalization followed by particular elements: his now-famous ontogeny (the individual organism) recapitulating phylogeny (the evolution of the type). So too the avant-garde in an individual's particular work. It mutated far more rapidly than in Haeckel's formulation of biogenetic law or in Darwin's

natural process of selection, and it created fossils as fast as it recapitu-
lated; but it entered that process of renewal at the heart of every major
nineteenth-century philosophy, whether that of Darwin, Nietzsche, or
Freud, or Wagner, Gobineau, and the racial purists who followed them.
What is most astonishing about avant-gardism is its consistency with
mainstream nineteenth-century thought even as it insisted on its sui
generis quality.

Connected to these diverse acts of purification, in a profound way,
is the preponderance of "mad" figures in Modernism: the actually mad
and the mad pretenders, real people as well as characters in poems, novels, and paintings. A culmination of this is the clown figure in Picasso,
Rilke, Stravinsky, and others, but the clown is merely a tame version
of the mad outsider, the spectacle rather than the actual thing. The real
thing involved the Pierrot figure: naive and mad, innocent and lacking
the ability to live in the world. The Pierrot figure shadows nearly everything that Kafka presented in his K. and Joseph K., his Gregor Samsa,
together with his other transformed creatures, those animals, for example, with human sensibilities. *Folie* in its various guises served as an
antidote for the worst excesses of rationality, as a purification of reason. With positivism, science and technology, and pragmatism offering
up logic and rationalism as the new religion, the countermovement
tendered a particularly savage and bitter god, the madman, as arbiter of
taste, sensibility, and, often, ideology. It is this mad dimension that
makes so much of Kafka seem witty, the parodic element so embedded
in his perception that the mad or semimad gives us new perspectives
on experience.

We are familiar with Lear and Lear's Fool, with the mad Don, and
others in this cast who offer madness as a higher or alternative order of
perception unknown or impenetrable to those devoted to reason. Lines
between madness and so-called sanity are blurred; real and illusory in-
terpenetrate each other. Kafka's work in Prague, Musil's *The Man
Without Qualities* in Vienna, Proust's *Remembrance* in Paris, all demand that the reader redefine the rational. Yet madness is not simply a
blithe element, not solely a contrast with sanity; it involves threat,
danger, subversion, menace, and mockery. These forms dominate so
forcefully in avant-gardism because, in this regard, the madman and his
vision are in such adversarial relationships to the larger society that the
author's only form of discourse is parody, irony, wit, burlesque. All
these latter forms of discourse are acts of purification, efforts to cleanse
a marketplace culture of *blague*, kitsch, and false illusions.

Some writers have tried to create madness through drugs (Rimbaud, or Baudelaire with his "artificial paradise"), others through alcohol. There are other madmen's means: the haze and bloodscream of Poe
or the white discourse of Mallarmé's various personae, the masks we
find in Jarry (Ubu and others), the early clowns of Picasso and Rilke, the
pigment frenzies of Van Gogh, later of les Fauves, the lunatic, antiso-

cial acts of several pre- and early Modernists (Borel, Lautréamont, Rimbaud, Verlaine). Though part of this tradition, Kafka worked differently. His individual does not subvert the system or society; rather, the system subverts the individual. Madness is transferred from the protagonist to what lies beyond, and then in a frenzy of survivalism, the individual must deal with whatever mad existence chances to enfold him.

Madness, accordingly, serves as a great weapon of discourse, since it can be given shape, gesture, demonstration, even an ideological frame of reference. As menace, the madman or what he represents is like a wild beast, the painterly equivalent here conveyed by Le Douanier Rousseau's beast inset in the jungle, peering, menacing, immobile, *there*, always there. That beast is contained within the confines of a framed setting, but its primitive nature serves as purifier for spectator and *his* frame of reference. That beastly image returns us to a menacing Garden, a full circle of threat. We encounter a curious phenomenon, in which madman, fool, or radically primitive creature has taken on a shamanistic function, beyond rationality and civilized values. In this distant territory, that world embodied by *The Castle*, the traditional lunatic and fool are portrayed as mad bureaucrats and functionaries. In a purely comedic sense, Hašek's *The Good Soldier Schweik* is a perfect example.

To bring the idea around full circle, and even closer to Kafka's point of entry, we see how much of this madness is connected to women: not to female authors, but to the presence of women in both fiction and nonfiction who drive men mad. Here madness is not only purification but also contamination. For these women, nearly all condemned by their male authors, drive men mad through their sexual needs. What follows helps us understand the deep domestic dynamics of a story like "The Metamorphosis" and much of the byplay of Kafka's mature fiction. The point of so much male masochism in Kafka and others was not the pleasure principle, but the humiliation the protagonist could suffer at the hands of a woman who would abuse and betray him, in time show him only cruelty. The male achieves orgasm, or what passes for it, from being subservient, but the matter of who is controlling whom becomes complicated. By insisting on this type of relationship, it would appear that the woman is the dominatrix, and this is in part true; but also the man is in another respect controlling the woman, since he is creating a level of "sexuality" in which he is forcing her to play a role. The role he chooses for her is one in which she must act out his own debased view of what a woman is. She, accordingly, loses whatever identity she may have in that particular relationship, and takes on role-playing that justifies the man's debased view of women as destructive, abusive, cruel, traitorous creatures.*

_____

*Such use of women connects to racial theories. For as this marginal man sees the

In Gregor Samsa's response to the "pinup" on his wall, we can see that the woman in furs holds some totemic value for him that goes beyond her obvious sexual appeal. He responds to her coldness to him (she puts a plate of glass between them and remains immobilized) by "controlling" her, which he does by squirting his life juice on her image. There is mutual humiliation as well as mutual control. Gregor's great satisfaction goes beyond orgasmic release, touching on areas he must seek because of his precarious position within his family. Those who seem to love him are ready to desert him, whereas the furred lady offers him a modicum of personal control, even while she reinforces all his worst attitudes toward women. As a bourgeois, even rich, woman, she represents to Gregor everything that is inaccessible to his family, dependent as it is on his relatively modest income. His isolation from the mainstream because of his travels, his marginal situation within the family, and his need for control precipitate his transformation and his use of the furred woman.

Gregor will eventually come to see that his family, especially his sister Grete, is vampirish, for to further her own skills and aims, she sucks his lifeblood. Although gentle in appearance, her linkage of money, power, and sexual development identifies her as parasitical. Likewise, the seemingly gentle mother betrays Gregor by siding with her husband, or remaining acquiescent to his fierce behavior, and by so doing, she too joins the ranks of women who "kill" their prey by abandoning them. In this regard, Kafka has replicated a psychological drama very close to his own domestic perceptions: the mother who sides with the father and, while passive, is a traitor to the son and his needs. As a recipient of Gregor's hard work she lives off him and reinforces his marginalization. In return, Gregor perceives her and his sister as bloodsuckers who reinforce his view of women as destructive.

Women's greed negates man's potential nobility, and the hostility that results implies a kind of suicidal act on the part of the male. By allowing himself to be debased and then attempting to counter control through transformation, he sacrifices himself. A related aspect of Gregor's plight is that despite his hard, demeaning work and contribution of salary, he has not gained control over his family. Instead, they are in effect controlling him by accepting his contributions as commonplace. Not only is his sacrifice unappreciated, it is in fact used against him, causing him to appear in others' eyes as a weak, exhausted, marginal

---

weakness of his own position and needs to debase women within his fantasies, so he can debase other races and force them into roles that reinforce his sense of their intrinsic inferiority. There are, in fact, several levels of crossover from sex to race: one of these is questions of money. Women's insatiable desire for money, for the gold of the realm, can be transferred easily to Jews and their desire to control a Gentile society through seizing its money supply or money flow. The marginalized man can see in this a form of personal control that he must struggle against, not by dealing with his marginalization, but by attacking those who have sought to fill the vacuum of power.

drone. In his perception of his role, he senses only hostility, so he seeks revenge, which transformation often involves; and, at the same time, he seeks escape from an untenable situation in the bureaucracy that attempts to mold his every activity, professional and personal. Thus, Kafka has created a many-sided trap, with women insistently part of it, in which the protagonist accedes to his role, seeks to evade it, finds it self-destructive, and, hoping to escape, transforms himself into a reductive element.

It is a premise of Modernism that each avant-garde is a kind of suicidal charge. Its thrust is a kamikaze attack in which both the art and artist are burned up or burned out. Tradition is the element that the avant-gardist must move against, until he himself proves expendable. The avant-gardist indeed does not forsake tradition but uses it to demonstrate its expendability and disposability. Each avant-garde movement incorporates what it must replace. The personal reserve we associate with earlier literatures, even with Romantic period artists, has vanished, and the artist to survive in the avant-garde must put his entire being on the line, become a willing sacrifice or suicide. That desperation we observe in the mature Kafka is the anguish of the writer who makes himself a sacrifice to his calling. Perhaps that is why he and his work finally meet at the end of his life in "A Hunger Artist," that perfect fusion of writer and protagonist, each moving toward his ultimate sacrifice, each willing his death as an emblem of art.

In literary terms, as acts of suicide of a sort, Kafka creates protagonists who have no past, no history. Completely severed from family history, as well as from social and political events, they come to us only with presentness. Isolated from all context, social or personal, they are born only in Kafka's handling of them — as though they had died in a previous existence and are being brought back only for the role he has assigned to them: to face the court, transform themselves, or seek whatever castle officials offer. They are a "new race" in fiction precisely because they come to us so lacking in psychological weight, so missing social freight.

When Kafka's protagonists do have a birthplace, it remains merely a place, without description, without social context. It belongs in the past as a dot, lacking focus or causation. That the protagonist came from that place and not another does not appear to affect him: he is what he is regardless of roots. In *The Castle*, it is mentioned that K. is married,* but that fact — which would provide some pastness in his life — has no bearing on him, nor do we learn what he was like as a husband, who his wife is, what they plan to do together. K. is, as it were,

---

*Not only married, but with children, a point made in the German edition but fudged in the English translation.

created like Frankenstein's monster, who begins when the book opens, and his history coincides with the history of the book. Joseph K. in *The Trial*, similarly, has no lived life that we can associate with him, no context into which we can enter that would explain, psychologically or emotionally, what has created the circumstances whereby he can suddenly be arrested. We are thrust into the novel, as if Joseph K. had been catapulted from some previous life into this one, as if he were a newly discovered body, a suicide, from some era for which we have no information, no sense of history or pastness.

Modernism has as one of its paradoxical tenets its own death. Implicit in the larger movement and its ideologies is the principle of self-destruction. Each exploration into the new or avant-garde lasts for perhaps only five years, so that exploration is itself a potential act of termination. Further, since each aspect of Modernism derives from rejection, subversion, the need to remake, it is based on denial: of history, pastness, even presentness. With avant-gardism always a thrust into the future, every venture is doomed by its very nature, and, by extension, so is every artist. Even as he or she works, something else rolls over, envelops, and transforms it.

Part of the unease felt by critics of Modernism, aside from the usual reasons of honoring and preserving the past, was its "all or nothing" quality, its lack of flexibility, its insistence on extremes. The artist was forsaking all safety nets. For someone like Kafka, in particular, there was no return, no point at which he could say he would do it differently. Once he had defined himself, even as early as "Shamefaced Lanky," he was committed to whatever personal anguish and misery his direction created for him. Since he could not extricate himself, he was literally seeking suicide: that taking of the self to such an extreme that only death could resolve it.

The theme of suicide in Modernism touches nearly every major phase and most writers except James Joyce. It can also be found in several painters, in the German expressionists, most apparently, but earlier as well, in Van Gogh; and in musical composition, in Mahler and his songs, Debussy's *Pelléas*, Schoenberg's early impressionistic musical dramas. *Erwartung*, the monodrama from 1909, is an interior monologue about the death of expectation, but, even more, the scenario of a suicidal venture. *Gurrelieder* is more closely allied with suicide, since the love of Waldemar and Tove combines ecstasy and a longing for death, a Wagnerian *Liebestod*. The theme is abundant in Baudelaire and in his interest in Poe, in the group loosely affiliated with symbolism, in Lautréamont, Laforgue, Rimbaud, Verlaine, in aspects of Mallarmé. It emerges later in Rilke, Woolf, Gide, Hesse, Musil, Broch, Eliot, and, of course, Kafka, and seemed in several to be connected to forms of madness.

In starker terms, Conrad attempted suicide at twenty with a revolver; Hesse attempted suicide; Mahler thought of suicide, and his brother, Otto, succeeded in it; later, Alban Berg attempted it, as did his sister, Smaragda. Wittgenstein, whose three older brothers all killed themselves, himself played on the edge of madness and suicide. In the public sphere, the apparent suicide at Mayerling Lodge, near Vienna, of Crown Prince Rudolf in 1889 was, as we have seen, the most sensational of what seemed an epidemic of self-destructiveness. To this list, we can add another group of notables: Otto Weininger, Walter Benjamin, Stefan Zweig, Georg Trakl, Ludwig Boltzmann, Kurt Tulcholsky, Ernst Toller, and others of lesser fame.

Émile Durkheim argued that his statistics showed suicide as the product of social forces; madness, however, is more closely connected to personal temperament. With madness and suicide so closely associated in Modernism, it is almost impossible to note where social forces leave off and personal temperament begins. The very nature of avant-gardism, both the type of work done and the type of artist involved in doing that work, blurs distinctions between madness and suicide, as it blurs distinctions between sanity and madness. Nevertheless, in all this, suicide was itself a form of power, when either exercised or held as a threat.

If we follow Durkheim's theories near the end of the nineteenth century, then any phenomenon that increased potentiality and expectations of power or promised energy would also lead to suicidal impulses. Freud's emphasis on the id in his mature dream interpretation, in 1900, led him to a force that had almost limitless potential for self-destruction, its energies pulsating to escape and create personal chaos. Modernism was a component of those social forces that worked reciprocally with suicide and death itself. One of the major themes of this study of Kafka is that his preoccupation with death, dying, hovering near death, waiting for death, living with death, the fact of death as a presence for him — all alongside a witty, ironic, parodic literary surface — makes him so representative of our century. It is not that Kafka embodied death, no more than most people living in pre-Holocaust Europe awaited immediate death, but rather the fact that he was sensitive to how immediate death was to everything in life. And even more than that, how close death was to the greatest thing life had to offer, the making of literature itself.

A further reflection: if Modernism with its reliance on suicide and death was a mirroring of the deepest levels of what was occurring in the social/political sphere, then Modernism was not just a causal factor but a symptom. Like the Austro-Hungarian Empire, the Third Republic of France eventually capitulated because of its schisms, in which antidemocratic forces helped bring it down. As the Habsburg Empire was becoming unglued when Kafka reached his majority, Modernism fed into those antidemocratic elements — not in any crass or direct political way, but as energies that kept alive the schisms in society and pressed both right and left to extremes. Even though the France of Modernism was superficially a republic and a democracy, the government was itself a chimera, since the National Assembly elected in 1871, as an aftermath of the Commune, was two-thirds monarchist, not democratic. In the Dual Monarchy, while Vienna kept making concessions, especially in the uses of native languages and in language usage in schools, political democracy was only a patina. The real government remained royalist, although not with tight censorship. In France, what kept the republic together was not its assembly, but the fact that its assembly could not agree on which monarch it wanted, whether the Comte de Chambord, the legitimate Bourbon heir, or the Comte de Paris, the Orléanist pretender. In the Dual Monarchy, Franz Josef instituted some reforms, but they were all aimed at preserving or regaining the status quo, not as directives toward a more egalitarian society. His concessions were merely means to play off contending nationalistic groups, with the Hungarian Magyars gaining the most, while Prague and Bohemia as a whole were held back.

We find in both Austro-Hungary and in France a type of state or governmental suicide, a national condition that, if brought down to individual terms, could be diagnosed as self-destructive. It all came to a head in France, of course, in the Dreyfus affair in the 1890s, when national suicide seemed direct and straightforward; when even as the truth about Dreyfus began to become apparent, army, state, and influential individuals pulled the country apart racially and ideologically. In the Dual Monarchy, the Vienna Secession of 1897 served something of the same function, a withdrawal that was a form of civil war, both a cause and a symptom of national suicide.

The end of the century, despite its progressivism, had become a culture of death. The avant-garde as the avatar of revolution or civil war turned the arts into elements that had to die or self-destruct in order to make way for the new, whatever its characteristics. While this had always been true, with one movement or school succeeding another, never before had successions been so rapid or so lacking in commonality. We observe that Modernism moved along in its avant-garde phases well before schools could form, certainly before traditions could be established. Inherent in this rapid exchange of one development for another, in which movement has been replaced by individual effort, is the end of things as they were known. Certainly some of the opposition to Modernism resulted from Modernism's insistence on the indeterminancy of existence, its obsessive need to break down without regard for reconstruction. For Kafka, there was the sense of an ending, his perception that whatever had existed no longer functioned sufficiently for adequate human life. One could, he observed, no longer breathe within the empire, and if writing was a form of prayer, it was prayer not for the grace of God but for the right to find one's own space. The empire, however, had pre-empted all space; Kafka felt suffocated, and his writing was an effort to ward off choking by identifying the stranger and finding survival techniques, even as one succumbs.

In Kafka's writing the beleaguered individual, insect, or animal always awaits the enemy, who, whether human or not, is always raging at the door. The victim is besieged; the enemy is far stronger and capable of destruction, at least within the victim's imagination. In nearly all of Kafka, the protagonist struggles against an internalized conception of state, empire, enemy force; the artist sets out to slay Goliath, returns injured to his lair, licks his wounds, and then once partially recovered returns to battle.

Whether the state and the arts were actually vying each to out-destroy the other in a kind of competitive heat is very possible, but not provable. A Marxist could argue that conditions of capitalism, technology, industrialization, the role of the worker vis-à-vis his job, disparities in wealth, and everything associated with progressivism had generated a suicidal impulse. But such a theory, while partially cogent, says nothing unique about Prague and Bohemia and does not help us understand Kafka's emergence. In point of fact, the avant-gardes that proliferated after 1885 were forms of ideology. Technical developments in uses of language, color, sound, movement were indistinguishable from ideological statements; they assimilated into art forms the way one looked at the state, society, community, nature. Innovation and ideology were wedded, and if revolution in the arts was the artist's aim, then he or she opened up the possibility for revolution, or secession: in style of life, attitude toward culture, ultimately in the relationship of the individual toward the state. The artist from Baudelaire and Mallarmé to Kafka and Proust was a special sort of ideologue whose means of expression was, in these instances, apolitical. Whether the language was a recessive symbolism or an expressionistic surrealism, its import in the larger sense was profoundly ideological in its subversion of the larger culture.

A related aspect of subversion and suicidal impulses is the secularization of life implied in Modernism, its rejection of formal institutions, and its embrace of its own value system as an end in itself. One example that leads into Kafka is relevant here: the ways in which a system can be so enclosed that no foreign substance can enter. In 1902, half a generation before Kafka, in Prague, the popular writer of exaggerated or fairy tales, Gustav Meyrinck, published a story called "The Burning Soldier." In this satire of the military, a soldier suffers from a fever that keeps rising, until it reaches the temperature at which water boils. When this occurs, everything around him begins to burn; he becomes, as it were, a human torch. Everyone of course runs from him, as he becomes transformed into a strange and monstrous creation — pos-

sibly the Golem is the archetypal figure here in Meyrinck's imagination. Although we have no indication that Kafka read Meyrinck, this
idea of transformation is similar to that in "The Metamorphosis," written only ten years later. Each story contains itself in its own matter;
what the character becomes through transformation pre-empts everything else. There is no value system outside of the story, surely no society, government, or state. It is self-enclosed, part of its own circuitry.

Both Kafka and his contemporary Jaroslav Hašek, the creator of
Schweik, possibly the most popular character in Czech literature, were
such critics of the Habsburg bureaucracy that preservation of the individual against organizations characterizes nearly all their work.* Kafka
went after faceless organizations, such as banks and the state, which
were modeled, apparently, on his own experience at the Workers' Accident Insurance Institute but also on his perception of life in the Kafka
family. Hašek modeled his bureaucracy on the military, and its relation
to the state. *The Trial* begins with words that have become quite famous: "Someone must have slandered [maligned] Joseph K., for without having done anything wrong he was arrested one fine morning."
Hašek's *The Good Soldier Schweik* (Švejk) begins: " 'And so they've
killed our Ferdinand,' said the charwoman to Mr. Švejk, who had left
military service years before, after having been finally certified by an
army medical board as an imbecile, and now lived by selling dogs —
ugly, mongrel monstrosities whose pedigrees he forged." The two
worlds are obviously different, and yet they overlap as responses to the
monarchy. Mysterious forces emanate from somewhere, in the first, to
place Joseph K. within a gigantic bureaucratic maze, in the other, to
begin a sequence of events for Joseph Schweik that leads to his confrontation with another bureaucratic maze, the military. The two Josephs,
however different, enter comparable worlds, linked by their facelessness and their need to play the imbecile or fool in order to survive in
them.
    Kafka began to acquire some sense of the bureaucracy when he en-
tered the gymnasium. University work would only increase his recognition of that facelessness that would become his preoccupation and
subject. One of Kafka's close friends, in fact, brought him close to other
forms of bureaucracy. He came to know a strange young man named
Ewald Felix Příbram, a Jew by background but an atheist by profession.
His father had abjured Judaism, as a means, surely, of getting on in the
business world: the elder Příbram became chairman of the board of directors of the Workers' Accident Insurance Institute and was eventually able to hire Kafka and see to it that he was treated well. All of this

*Kafka and Hašek met at the Klub Mladých, and Kafka was also present when Hašek
gave a satirical, parodic election speech.

would have proved impossible for a professing Jew; but what made it more attractive to Kafka was that young Příbram, whose father had led the family from Judaism to bourgeois comfort in the Gentile world, had also become a socialist, to which he tried to tempt Kafka.

That early interest Kafka had in socialism, as later in anarchism, would become one part of his more general rebellion against Hermann and Julie. These were antibourgeois beliefs that, while never gaining much of a grip on the young man, at the time helped to separate him from family and home. In an August 24, 1902, letter to Oskar Pollak, Kafka, writing from the Elbe town of Liboch, twenty-five miles from Prague, speaks of some inner torment and the desire to change his situation. It is unclear what "torments me now," but what is evident was his desire to break away. "My uncle from Madrid (railroad manager)* was here; I came to Prague because of him. Shortly before his arrival I had the weird, unfortunately very weird notion of begging him, no, not begging, asking, whether he mightn't know some way to help me out of this mess, whether he couldn't guide me to someplace where at last I could start afresh and do something."[22] That effort failed, as Julie's brother simply comforted his nephew, "nicey-nicey." Yet that yearning for something new and different, whatever shape it took, was part of Kafka's flirtation with socialism; a chance to cut away from family and Prague, that "old crone" with claws.

Opportunities to learn about socialism were of several kinds, not the least from an older classmate of his named Rudolf Illový, whose career spanned editorship of a social democratic journal (*Pravo Lidu*) and banking. Like Kafka, he straddled two seemingly opposing worlds, and, like Kafka in his assessment of himself, he seemed to call up equal amounts of admiration and distress. Much later, Kafka spoke disparagingly of him to Janouch; and from that and other matters, we can assume that Kafka's flirtation with socialism could not possibly have taken real hold since it coincided with other needs that proved much stronger, that need to write and to make of literature a total commitment in which socialism or any other ideology would have little room. Rather than socialism whole, he carried away bits and pieces, enough to help shape what he wanted to make of himself, however difficult that task would prove to be.

As we assess Kafka's school career on the threshold of his admittance to the university, we sense someone so absorbed in himself that full application to school or any other form of prescribed learning could not possibly take hold. Even this early, Kafka was curling back upon himself, finding in the circuitry of his own needs whatever nourishment he required, picking and choosing his way among courses and in-

---

*Of several small lines; he was not the director of Spanish Railways as he has often been presented.

structors. He came away not as an educated young man but as a young
man with an education. It was just as well, for those who were prodigious in their studies, like Hugo Bergmann, had honorable careers but
were programmed, also, for relatively safe results. Kafka's quest was far
more difficult, obviously, since his real education depended on what he
could project from himself, how he could develop, how he could walk
the minefield between his own needs and those required by his social
context.

As for minefields, although it is difficult to pinpoint the dimensions of Kafka's sexual involvements, it is possible to conjecture that
since we have no evidence of venereal disease, he indulged only inter-
mittently. Prostitutes, however, were everywhere, and unless one frequented supervised houses, where some measure of hygiene existed,
there was a good chance of syphilis or gonorrhea from chance pickups,
which seemed to be Kafka's preference.* It was, surely, difficult for all
older teenagers at a time when proper young women did not offer themselves until they were married, and sexual activity resulted from street
soliciting or in the demimonde of clubs, parties, and dancing establishments.

Yet given that, it was particularly difficult for Kafka, since for some
internal reason sex was connected to disgust, and that in turn to forms
of dissolution, disintegration, even death. Sex was rarely something
freely enjoyed. It took on for him heavy, even ritualistic, patterns, most
of them associated with obsessions about bodily cleanliness, the elimination of waste matter, the dirt resulting from perspiration, urination,
and other bodily fluids.† Kafka's obsessive personal hygiene made it
impossible for him to dissociate sexual activity from bodily functions.
Sex, food, and excrement in some forbidding alliance were never far
from his mind. Sex, in fact, was always intermixed with diabolic internal workings — intestines, bowels, the dirty cavities of the body's labyrinths — and his fear was not unlike that of those men who thought
the vagina would castrate them, fears that Freud explored in his psychoanalytic practice. Part of Kafka's distrust and wariness with sex —
but only part — derived from his distrust of anything he could not control himself. He feared giving himself up to something "beyond," and
he feared that sharing of an act with someone who might make de-

---

*Turn-of-the-century municipal statistics put the number of prostitutes in Prague at
between 6,000 and 7,000 (*Prager Tagblatt*, November 18, 1906), but that appears to be
an underestimation if one adds part-time freelancers like shopgirls, clerks, secretaries,
typists, and their like. Also, many clubs and cafés, like the Trocadéro, had a large number
of part-timers who did not fall into any official number and yet who were readily available
to young men like Kafka, Brod, and their circle. The high number of illegitimate births,
almost half of all births in Prague, would surely be linked to the large number of prostitutes, although we should not discount economic instability, which brought on later
marriage for men and meant early liaisons without benefit of clergy.
†Dirt generally was rarely distant from Kafka's imagination, and he often sought it out
so that he could justify his perception of human and bureaucratic pollution.

mands on him. He had, in this area, little to give, as well as little give.

When he wrote his letter to his father in 1919, he used the oedipal struggle as a way, both directly and indirectly, of commenting upon sex. He measures his body against his father's in the bathing hut where they changed and found himself wanting; the assumption is that his father's penis was more potent, as was the rest of his body. In other respects as well, the father is always larger, more commanding — "From your armchair you ruled the world."[23] In the image of his father spread out across the map of the world is the sense that the father can seize all women, in that atavistic Freudian struggle between father and son. This struggle was of course the very subject of Kafka's first major work, "The Judgment," in 1912, a story that reveals a protagonist extraordinarily inconclusive in sexual matters. Georg Bendemann describes how his father always bested him: "Between us there was no real struggle; I was soon finished off; what remained was flight, embitterment, melancholy, and inner struggle." When he was about sixteen, Kafka asked his father about the forbidden subject. Hermann responded with what his son considered "the filthiest thing in the world," that his son should check out a whorehouse and see for himself.[24] Whereas most young men might have been amused or pleased that their father could be so down-to-earth, for Kafka Hermann's response was tasteless and insensitive. Hermann's advice, in itself not startling, becomes part of the "filth" Kafka brought to the subject.

That same sense of "filth of the bedroom" is present in his several observations that the sight of his parents' marriage bed made him weak with disgust. The smell of bodies having grappled with each other, the leakage of bodily fluids, the mere fact that his mother could be bedding down with such a gross creature all created a strong sexual repugnance in the young Kafka.

Kafka's description of himself while growing up has within it more than the usual uncertainty of a young person. He speaks of his own body becoming "insecure." He says he "shot up, tall and lanky, without knowing what to do with my lankiness, the burden being too heavy, the back becoming bent."[25] And this faltering, plus the strain of "the superhuman effort of wanting to marry," forced blood to come from the lungs. All this, we can assume from his description, was the result of a willed process: consumption as part of his personality makeup, not biological or genetic. And this too is linked to his sexuality. His psychological concern with malfunction made the sexual act and all its attendant attitudes so unappealing to him. Immediate relief after an orgasm, whether with a prostitute or through masturbation, brought terrible self-hatred, as he saw himself polluting his body and mind. All the disgust at a body that seemed to be moving in several different directions came back to that one focal point: that with such a body, it was hard enough to live and work, much less to function sexually.

Kafka probably did not experience his sexual initiation, with a prostitute, until he was twenty, in 1903, an experience he found distasteful, even disgusting. The alternatives to professional hookers were shop-girls and others in low-level jobs who picked up extra money through occasional prostitution. Kafka's first experience appeared to have been with a young woman of that kind, who sold herself to a man or two at night but who was otherwise a working girl during the day. Kafka de-scribed this initial experience to Milena Jesenská in a 1920 letter. That he was describing his unpleasant initiation to a woman with whom he felt romantically involved must be kept in mind, for he was not only relating his early encounter, he was warning her of his unfitness sex-ually for anyone, even for someone like Milena whom he greatly ad-mired, even loved. He tells of how while he was studying, in 1903, for his state boards, he noticed a shopgirl who always stood in the door of a dress shop across the way, on Celetná Street. As he tried to absorb "dis-gusting Roman law" in the unbearable heat of the summer, he and she managed to communicate by sign language. When he descended to pick her up at eight that evening, another man was already there. Kafka sloughs that off by saying he was afraid of anyone being there, so that even in the man's absence, he would have been afraid. The girl mo-tioned the law student to follow, and when the man left her, the girl and Kafka went to a hotel in the Malá Strana (the Lesser Town area). Kafka says that even "before we got to the hotel, everything was charm-ing, exciting, and disgusting." The experience seemed no different, and he comments that he was happy the "whole experience hadn't been even filthier and more disgusting." Two nights later, Kafka went with the girl again, for the final time. He says that after his summer vaca-tion, when he returned to Prague, he could not bear the sight of the shopgirl. He considered her his "bitter enemy," and yet, he admits, "she was, in fact, a good-natured and friendly girl who kept haunting me with her uncomprehending eyes."[26]

Kafka admits that a large, although not sole, contributing factor to his hostility was "a tiny repulsive something the girl committed in all innocence in the hotel (not worth mentioning), a trifling obscenity (not worth mentioning)." The memory of this lingered, indeed festered: "That very instant I knew I would never forget it, and at the same time I knew — or thought I knew — that while outwardly this smut and ob-scenity were not necessary, inwardly they are indeed an indispensable part of the whole experience, and that it was precisely this smut and obscenity (of which her little gesture and her little remark were the only little signs) that had drawn me with such force into this hotel, which otherwise I would have shunned with my last remaining strength."

What is striking, in addition to the confessional attitude of this to another woman, is Kafka's equation of sex and death, a virtual *Liebes-tod* in the trivial confines of a small hotel renting out a room to an obscure shopgirl and an equally obscure law student. That equation of the erotic and death, or Eros and Thanatos, as Freud called them, which gripped so many elements in the Vienna Secession did not travel wholly into Prague. The presence of the main seat of the Dual Monarchy in Vienna evidently encouraged themes and preoccupations with love and death, especially with the sounds of Wagner's music in one's ears. But Prague had its own forms of Eros and Thanatos, and Kafka was not far behind — in his very conception of the city, as a city of death in which Eros lurked. We must not ignore the fact that while Prague was essential to Kafka's development and formation of his literary ideas, it was also, in his mind, a necropolis. And in this necropolis, which pulled its more sensitive citizens toward a sense of final things, toward bureaucracy and machines that destroy, there also prowled another form of destruction, Eros.

Kafka's meeting with the shopgirl should have been, all in all, an event with little substance, a trivial occurrence for any young man in Prague with enough money to pay for a quick bedding down. Yet Kafka invests this event with ceremonial qualities in which interment is not distant. What the girl said or how she gestured — although we would like to know what the twenty-year-old Kafka considered so obscene and repulsive — is less relevant than the fact that the sex act left such a profound impression, so profound that Kafka describes it in such detail seventeen years later, when he is himself thirty-seven and only four years from death. It becomes, in this respect, a key scene for him: solidifying in his imagination what sexual intercourse is or might lead to; creating for him that great fear of what regular intercourse with a woman would entail, whether wife or mistress; suggesting, further, that lurking in this distasteful scene is a shadowy scenario of what possibly went on between Hermann and Julie Kafka. The revulsion is complete, final.

If this were any other young man, not Kafka, we would say that his episode with the prostitute perhaps created temporary sexual disturbance but in the long run was not of great concern. Men get over such episodes, or else they carry them through their lives in a kind of low-grade unhappiness or sexual dysfunction. But since this is Kafka, we are of course tempted to make more of it: his equation of sex and death, his ritualization of his early encounter, his ceremonial way of relating. All these elements must be taken into account in his development, into determining the kind of writer he became, why he felt that only literature counted and all the rest was trivial. An enormous amount of sublimation occurred, or if not sublimation then displacement of sexual energy into plans, dreams, fantasies, ideas for books and stories. Kafka, in this respect, becomes one of Freud's exemplary figures — the dysfunctional young man (or woman) for whom sexuality is imbued with disgust and for whom there can be no sexual joy or pleasure. These are people whose lives may be of great success but who always feel, as Kafka felt, incomplete. The sublimation or displacement, however, was not so final that he was unaware of what he missed; on the contrary, the more intensely he threw himself into his work, the more he clarified his untenable position. He was unique, and while being unique itself provided some pleasure, he recognized that he remained unfinished, not a full man. He existed in a self-made limbo. The 1919 *Letter to His Father* is as much a confession of his incompletion as it is a cry of anguish that his father helped make him that way. Yet Hermann was only a factor, perhaps a pawn, not the reality of it.

There is another factor, one fraught with speculative possibilities: as the oldest child in the family, the only son, Kafka observed the birth and growth of three young sisters. By the turn of the century, Elli was eleven, Valli ten, Ottla eight. To what extent, we are forced to ask, was Kafka's attitude toward young women, prostitutes or otherwise, affected by his observation of three young sisters and the fear of incestuous longings? We must ask this especially since once the girls were old enough to participate in family activities, Kafka devised plays for the four of them. With Julie almost totally given over to the father, Kafka was left with female servants and three sisters. Was there provocation from the servants toward the young man of the house? From Freud's and others' case studies, we know that many middle-class young men were played with or even initiated into sex by young female servants. But even without this occurring — and we have no proof that it did* — Kafka's daily dealings with young girls in various states of dress and undress could have created such a fear of incestuous longing that he carried it over to all women. As the oldest in the family, Kafka was expected to fulfill certain expectations; and one was that because he had the favored room, he was head of the roost when the father was away, a kind of second-in-command. And since the household was mainly women, he was in effect given a harem of sorts and told to keep it in line.

Just what effect all this had on Kafka sexually cannot be pinpointed; as we noted, with him we have coordinates but few certainties. He had the kind of middle-class background and upbringing which Freud, in his analytic practice in Vienna, found stifling, suffocating, full of repression and sexual imbalance, creating sexual dysfunction, hysteria, hypochondria, headaches, poor digestion, and other dysfunctions that sometimes immobilized the individual. By virtue of his background and his perceptions of it, Kafka was a ready patient for the analytic couch — for in addition to sexual dysfunction, he suffered from

---

*Or should we make biographical matter of the fact that in Kafka's first prolonged fiction, *Amerika*, his Karl Rossmann is initiated into sexual play by a servant woman, whom he gets pregnant?

many of those disabilities Freud enumerated. The headaches started early and were excruciating. Digestive problems intensified, worsened by his own strange diets. He was, very probably, a secondary anorexic, turning food and the experience of it into a form of warfare, which he could fight and win but at the expense of his well-being. He was close to hysteria, and several of his works are themselves manifestations of a hysterical personality, however *seemingly* controlled they are in language and shape. And finally, he was a lifelong hypochondriac, completely self-absorbed in his bodily functions or malfunctions, willing to write about them to friends, relatives, and even a potential wife. He was not immobilized, since he functioned well in his various positions at the insurance company, but he did so without ease and, like Gregor Samsa, had to force himself to perform daily or routine duties. He hated himself for doing his job and hated the time given over to it to the point that, in his own eyes, he slowed down almost to immobility. He felt that his work looked impressive only because everyone else's was worse. In his near abulia condition, he refused to accept that he could be functioning well, although he received the praise and respect of his superiors, in a company that did not welcome (or hire) Jews.

Male friends, as for so many Praguers and Viennese, filled the need for companionship. It was a time of great friendships, of circles of men, of inner groups that no women could penetrate, the blood brotherhood of the universities and the dueling fraternities. It was a male world conceived of and carried through as a way of dealing with both the "monstrous woman" and the "nesting woman." A few women like Lou Andreas-Salomé managed to break through on intellectual grounds, but even these women were perceived of as outside the "circle," whether the Prague Circle, so dubbed by Max Brod, or the Viennese and Berlin circles, the famous Stefan George *Kreis,* for example. Kafka, as we shall see, had his circle, which sustained him even as he sought isolation from everything except his literary work.

With a twisted smile the lab assistant
shoved the flask away that smoked half-calmed.
He knew at last what he still needed
to make the venerable thing
spring up inside it.

— RILKE, "THE ALCHEMIST"

SIX The Advent of High Modernism: Prague, Vienna, Berlin, Paris, Munich

K AFKA'S ENTRANCE into university life coincided with
momentous cultural events: the annus mirabilis, or
"marvelous year," of 1900–1901; the meeting of various secession
groups with the establishment; the running together of cultural life as
experienced in cities seemingly as diverse as Paris, Berlin, Munich, Vienna, and Prague. Implicit in these events, in the cultural secessions
and rebellions and in the personalities behind these movements, was
the deterioration of the Dual Monarchy, whose bureaucratic nature
was anathema to an entire generation of artists. Kafka was the inheritor
and benefactor of this demise, as well as its most expressive representative. Having graduated from the Altstädter Gymnasium in July 1901,
with the *Reifezeugnis* certificate (evidence of maturity, or evidence of
having achieved matriculation standards), in mid-November of that
year he matriculated at the German Ferdinand-Karls University, with
philosophy as his subject of choice. Along with Bergmann and Pollak,
he also signed up for chemistry, very possibly more to be with friends
from the gymnasium than because of any calling in the sciences. It
would soon become clear, though, that Kafka was incapable of continuing chemistry, one of the few vocations open to Jewish graduates; his
laboratory work was not good enough. As Bergmann indicated, his
hands weren't sufficiently skilled. He then dropped philosophy to take
up law, which he felt might lead to a position in the bureaucracy. Yet
from his remarks we can sense that by this time he had already determined what he would do with his life. In fact, Kafka had conceived of

writing as a serious pursuit early in his gymnasium years. We recall that indifference to education that he indicated to his father so many years later, in his *Letter*. If we follow through on his remarks that he had already tried his hand at writing (examples of which do not survive), then we can assume chemistry, philosophy, law all made little difference. He needed to find a means by which he could support himself and satisfy his family's reliance on him. Dependent as he was on his family emotionally and psychologically, he would not be economically dependent. A position in a bank or in the state bureaucracy would enable him to remain dependent without being a financial parasite. Such dualism, in which he was caught between conflicting needs, would characterize his entire adult life. He could successfully divide himself into halves, one half for professional work, the other for his artistic quest — but only at tremendous cost to his personal life, in his day-to-day anguish and unhappiness, his loss of viable sexuality, and his almost constant hypochondria.

Later, he commented on this duality in his typically ironic, caustic way. In "The New Attorney," with all heroes and heroics having vanished from the world, Alexander the Great's horse, Bucephalus, has no real role and must become an attorney in order to live. "Do as Bucephalus has done and bury oneself in the law books. Free, his flanks unpressed by the thighs of a rider, under a quiet lamp, far from the din of Alexander's battles, he reads and turns the pages of our old books." Robbed of his destined role, he now settles for a dusty life. "Many, of course, still know how to murder; nor is there any lack of skill at stabbing your friend over the banquet table with a lance . . . no one can lead us [anymore] to India." Kafka says that "many hold swords, but only to flourish them, and the glance that tries to follow them becomes confused."[1]

And in a related parable, about Poseidon (or Neptune), the former ruler of the seas is now a supervisor or manager of the waters. Poseidon is both tamed and bored in the very role that the pursuit of law will lead to in Kafka's life. "Since he took his job very seriously, he would in the end go over all the figures and calculations himself, and thus his assistants were of little help to him." Confronted by the possibility of changing his job, Poseidon refuses, since "he had been appointed God of the Sea in the beginning, and that he had to remain." Bored with the sea, "with now and then a trip to Jupiter [on Mount Olympus] as the only break in the monotony," Poseidon sits silently on the rocky coast, while a gull, dazed by his presence, "described wavering circles around his head."[2] Resigned to his fate, Poseidon "was in the habit of saying that what he was waiting for was the fall of the world." All the high and mighty in this brief tale fall to the needs of the bureaucracy. The seductive sirens no longer want to seduce: "they knew they had claws and sterile wombs, and they lamented this aloud. They could not help it if their laments sounded so beautiful." Claws and a sterile womb, with beautiful laments — with these images Kafka created metaphors of the bureaucracy that paralleled his own transformation into an attorney.

Even as we find the youthful Kafka entering a university course of study, with his brief failures and then his overall success, we see him trying to make sense of the divisions life was forcing upon him. Chemistry, philosophy, law — none of them cohered in his university years, and nothing really cohered in his personal life. As we read his letters, diaries, and other cries into the darkness he felt closing in, we see how he was entrapped by words, even as he became convinced words were the only things that could save him.[3] He conceived of art in Romantic terms, as a beam of light, what Shelley suggested when he wrote of art as a live coal. Kafka: "Art flies around truth, but with the definite intention of not getting burnt. Its capacity lies in finding in the dark void a place where the beam of light can be intensely caught, without this having been perceptible before." Words are the agency of that beam. He would come to recognize how isolated he was, and how within his perception of self only language, the written word specifically, was salvation. In fact by 1901 Kafka found he could express himself better in the written than in the spoken word. His 1919 *Letter to His Father* is not a late-life anomaly but part of his ongoing tendency to substitute letters and fictional works for oral communication. Even with Oskar Pollak Kafka found it more advantageous to express himself in letters.

In one of his common plaints, he speaks of how, given the alien nature of the Jews in Prague, given the elusive nature of a city that seduces and transforms, he feels "the lack of ground underfoot, of air, of the commandment. It is my task to create these, not in order that I may then, as it were, catch up with what I have missed, but in order that I shall have missed nothing."[4] Yet while freeing himself through words, Kafka sensed he was also chaining himself to their dominion. He relates one of his paradoxes. A young prince visits a prison where he asks who has been there longest. He is told of a man who murdered his wife and has been serving a lifelong sentence. The prince insists on seeing him and is conducted to his cell. This should be a great moment for the prisoner — having an audience with the prince, perhaps now able to express his feelings, his sense of his crime and the punishment. But "as a precaution the prisoner had been put in chains for the day."[5] Any glimpse of freedom is balanced, or unbalanced, by a greater degree of imprisonment. Similarly, Kafka wrote of an ever present "tormenting demon," smaller than the smallest mouse, invisible to the scrutinizing eye. The demon hides in a corner, so that whatever it fears cannot find it. But although its tininess protects it, it must hide to have the advantage of its smallness. For the moment it is safe, but it suffers from anxiety, fear, suspicion — like, later, the mole in "The Burrow," whose safe hole in the ground entraps it as enemies, real or imagined, come

closer. Kafka observes the demon from inside and outside. It must protect itself from destruction, and it also destroys whomever it inhabits.
The demon attempts to stay alive, but so does the individual tortured
by its presence.

Although these parables, paradoxes, and ironic perceptions occur
later, there is good reason to believe, on the basis of the letters to Oskar
Pollak, that Kafka had by this time already assimilated these positions
and attitudes. We do know that while he was uncertain about his direction for a career, writing had become both support and demon. Consequently, by the time of university matriculation, he was divided in
ways that separated him from his Prague Circle, all the members of
which wanted to write. For Max Brod, for instance, writing was essential; he started to publish far sooner than Kafka, and his output was
enormous. Yet his investment of energy in writing was never so complete as Kafka's, nor was his agony over composition. A far lesser writer
than his anguished friend, Brod, like Werfel, seemed to turn the writing
process on and off like a faucet. He obviously did not seek that martyrdom to writing, to Prague, to words themselves, that Kafka felt in himself. Brod married, had innumerable affairs, carried on extensive Zionist activities, wrote for periodicals, and lived a long life, although not
without periods of depression and feelings of uselessness.

Kafka was seduced by Prague in ways his group of friends was not,
and in order to understand that seductive and often destructive city, he
had to conceive of, for himself, a different dimension of time and space.
When we relate Kafka to the twentieth century, or think of his shadow
as falling over the entire epoch, our consideration goes well beyond
content or attitude. We must investigate how, like great painters, ar-
chitects, and poets, he has rearranged time and space as experimental
modes for us.

Any city, as we know, which is fully lived in takes on its own spatial and temporal significance. Its variety and diversity provides a kaleidoscope and creates temporary confusion. One of the strange elements
in a foreign city for the visitor is that he or she is unaccustomed to that
city's particular temporal and spatial arrangements; this is not just a
question of knowing or not knowing where places are, but of entering
the spirit a strange place generates, and if it is a large city with a long
national history, then it generates many conflicting kinds of spirit, as
Prague did. Kafka tried to assimilate into his work, and as well into his
personal life, everything that Prague meant to him, its temporal and
spatial density, as much as its insistence on its history and its heroes
and villains. One reason that Kafka seems so strange, whether read in
German or in translation, is that he was always trying through the use
of language to grapple with what he knew was beyond language; language is simply incapable of finding the correct angle of perception, the
precise visionary quality. Prague remains, all in all, a great mystery,

an old crone with claws, perhaps, but also a tradition-ridden place obsessed with its religious, political, and artistic history. Kafka saw Prague as both trap and release; it gave him his opportunity, yet it would not let him go. Especially telling is that it would never release its meanings to any German-speaking Jew; for him, Prague was sealed at its deepest levels. *That* Kafka knew, wrote about, suffered through.

Kafka's search for meaning, certainty, and identity through his own efforts or those of his marginalized protagonists would always be defeated by the nature of Prague. The significance of this is immense, because it put him into the role of Sisyphus: always striving to reach beyond the very thing which would block him off from attaining it. Doubly damned, as Jew and German-speaking, he could not unlock what Prague meant, and so he sought it out in ways no one had ever tried to do before. While marginalization gave Kafka his greatest weapons, it also provided for his ultimate defeat. And in his efforts to make headway against the spirit of a city that would not yield to him, he became the ultimate twentieth-century figure: the man for whom words can never suffice; the figure who must carve out an inner existence by displacing parents and society, or else absorbing them; the essential loner and isolated individual who seeks in anguish, pain, and even martyrdom all those roles that a great bureaucracy tries to negate.

Before entering the German university in Prague, Kafka from July through November took a vacation in which to ponder his course work and the direction of his personal life. It would prove to be one of his longest stretches of free time, free from both school and insurance work. Unfortunately, we do not know much about these four months, when he was eighteen, for this period was surely more than a transition from secondary school to university study. This was a tumultuous time, especially since he did not feel free to study what he wanted, if he indeed knew what he wanted. In addition, Kafka felt the pressure of Hermann. His father was typical of upwardly mobile bourgeois Jews: even though he seemed to give his son free choice, in effect the young man felt he had no choice but to conform to middle-class aspirations. As he wrote in his *Letter*, "Real freedom to choose a career, therefore, did not exist for me." All this was on Kafka's mind when he set out for Norderney, a North Sea island about seven miles off the German coast. Hermann had given Kafka a three-week vacation at this resort, which was popular with Prague Jews. Norderney was one of the several East Frisian Islands, just across the border from Holland. The trip from Prague, Kafka's first, was lengthy, involving travel by train across Germany to Bremen, then to the coastal city of Norden, and finally by boat to Norderney.

The young Kafka, as would be true throughout his life, was not a good traveler, nor was he happy when he was away from Prague, unless he was in his sister Ottla's peasantlike house. He went on an excursion from Norderney to Helgoland, to the northeast, and suffered seasickness. Several commentators have suggested that Kafka responded negatively to vastness, to open sea and sky, which made him feel defeated and overwhelmed. But on the contrary, although he would say the dimensions of nature (sea and mountains) were too heroic for his taste, he was better able to measure Prague against immensity and come away with his compartmentalized sense of spatial arrangements. Since so much of his writing was concerned with the disproportion of smallness and immensity, we must understand his response to nature as one of the meaningful measurements of his life. Prague may have been confinement, cubbyholes, old buildings, narrow streets, and various enclosures, but such confinement must be measured against something else; for Kafka, this was a "beyond," a largeness or immensity. His first exposure to that size, we must speculate, brought him back to Prague even more convinced of *its* confining qualities, qualities, indeed, which he embraced.

Shortly after his return — we have no other evidence of what happened to him in Norderney — Kafka began his studies, finally settling on his third choice, law. This would prove to be a cross he had to bear since he had little interest in the law as such and was pursuing it, apparently, only to placate that Fury in the home.

Entrance into the univesity in November further polarized Kafka's Prague experience, for he entered the German wing of the university. Prague University was over 550 years old (dating back to 1348), but only recently, in 1882, it had been divided into its Czech and German parts. The division was not a sign of German strength but an emblem of Czech insistence that the mother country be separated from interlopers and foreigners. Thus, the division, which ostensibly would appear to demonstrate German empowerment, was in actuality a sign of German inferiority. Not that the Germans were any less nationalistic than the Czechs, but their nationalism was directed more toward Vienna and Berlin than toward Prague, whereas Czech nationalism was part of that large-scale rebellion and secession that led to the First World War. Caught in all this ferment, Kafka was casually indifferent, if we accept his own words, intent as he was on finding the career "that would best indulge this indifference without hurting my vanity too much."[6] Kafka's socialistic ideas placed him above the "indifference" to the warring factions of nationalism.

Although the university forced students to register in either the Czech or German wing, they could, if they wished, attend lectures in either one. The division, nevertheless, was quite real, and functioned like something out of Hašek's *The Good Soldier Schweik*. Kafka entered the law building, the Carolinum, through one of two streets, the Eisengasse being the one used by the Germans. Study areas like the library and archives were used by Czechs and Germans on alternate days, as was the place where degrees were conferred. On examinations, students had to choose which language to use — German on one hand or a combination of Czech and German on the other. This crazy quilt of entrances, study areas, examination languages, and the rest was not confined to studies, but extended into the streets and back alleys of the city, where Czechs and Germans could fight their nationalistic wars with more than words. The Germans of Prague were in most respects true Germans, with their dueling scars as marks of honor, their fraternity rituals and initiations, their drinking parties, their holiday outfits.

Politically, most Germans were on the far right, opposed to social and political change, anti-Czech and antinationalistic for other minorities, and anti-Semitic in most of their manifestations — the one area where their views overlapped with those of the Czech nationalists. But the wonders of all this went much further: Kafka and Bergmann joined an organization that was, in its organizational rules, anti-Semitic. This was simply one of the many paradoxes of Kafka's university career, as he veered from one set of beliefs to another, from one course of study to the next. The arena was the Hall of Reading and Speech for Prague's German students, intended to further German culture. But the Hall, with its regularly featured speakers and lecturers, had become part of a Pan-German nationalist group in 1892, with anti-Semitic overtones. Yet by Kafka's time, this group of almost five hundred students included many Jews. Not all these Jews were "Jews," for several were converts, and others identified with Pan-Germanic movements or were socialists, like Kafka, who thought in terms of international brotherhood rather than, like Brod, in Zionist terms. There was a natural struggle in the Hall among various cultural groups, some of them involving Kafka, Pollak, and Brod, over the role Jews should play in an organization that tried to further purely Germanic spiritual goals.

Although there was no outright violence, there was a good deal of maneuvering to prevent a Jewish takeover, and the struggle here both paralleled and foreshadowed what was occurring in the larger Prague world, beyond the German university. The Hall's board of governors tried repeatedly (in 1904 and 1907) to rid itself of the Zionist element, and on the whole there was a desire to purge the organization of Jewish influence. This attempt mirrored the increasing attacks in the larger Prague and Bohemia world on Jewish domination, in which Jews were accused of controlling Czech society through banking, merchandising, and other subterfuges. As Ernst Pawel points out, an additional irony arises in that Kafka's second cousin Bruno Kafka (they shared a common great-grandfather) headed the board of governors. As Kafka sought to escape Hermann in his university career, he ran into a powerful and domineering family figure in Bruno, although the two did not personally associate with each other. Whatever else Kafka felt, it was clear Bruno was everything he was not: forceful, dominating, powerful in his dealings, self-confident, sure of capabilities and direction — he would become a lawyer and politician.

In any comparison, Kafka appeared weak and uncertain, whereas Bruno was the "true" son of Hermann, if the latter had had the opportunity to choose his genetic inheritance. The anti-Semitic, Teutonic flavor of the Hall apparently did not concern Bruno, who was, like Karl Kraus, caustic and negative toward Judaism. Baptized a Christian, he could control both sides of the Hall, the anti-Semitic side, which he represented in his baptism, and the Semitic side, as a Kafka. In other ways as well Bruno contrasted with his cousin in his knowledge of how to thread his way through the maze of Prague and Czech professional and political life. While Kafka would stumble repeatedly and create a nightmarish personal life for himself, Bruno married a wealthy Christian girl, the daughter of a copper magnate, Max Bondy, himself a baptized Jew. In fact, he was knighted, as Elder von Bontrop, an indication of how baptism and money could open the way for Jews willing to renounce their heritage. When Bondy in later years acquired the magazine *Bohemia*, Bruno became editor and publisher, and then went on to become head of the German National Democrats, as well as a member of the Czech parliament. No position of power seemed beyond the reach of this shrewd manager of his talents, in every way different from Kafka, whose surface presented uncertainty. Kafka's inner life was of course far richer, but in his university days Bruno was the family success.

What Kafka lacked was any degree of ruthlessness, the very quality needed to survive well in this labyrinth of bureaucratic and hypocritical byplay. As Bruno and Max Brod, his canny adversary, advanced on the public front, with repeated clashes over questions of power, Kafka retreated increasingly to questions of art and the artist in an inhospitable and inaccessible society. He also fell back on an ineffective socialism, ineffective not because of its noble doctrines but because it was for Kafka merely an interim position, as was, possibly, his attraction to anarchism and nihilism.[7] What muddied the waters even further was that Bruno's university group needed Jewish support, even as it ridiculed the Zionist aspirations of Jews like Brod. Brod's vision was a dreamy one, of course, in the early 1900s, when a Zionist success in Palestine seemed as distant as the moon. Bruno's vision of empowerment here and now, however, was not idealist but power politics, at which he excelled and at which not even Brod could compete, much less Kafka. Further, although Bruno was shrewd and intelligent, he was no intellectual, and he possessed the contempt of the powerful and confident for those who wallowed in idealism or who offered up literary responses for political ones. Through control of funds for various activities and through the fixing of elections, Bruno could control the monies used for funding Brod's and Kafka's literary enterprises.

Kafka's chief activities took place in a group organized as "Section for Literature." It was through this section that he came to meet Max Brod, on October 23, 1902, after Brod, himself only eighteen, lectured on Schopenhauer and Nietzsche, one of Kafka's early gods. Their subsequent disagreement began the relationship that continued until Kafka's death, and then well after as Brod began to release the treasure trove of works his friend had left in his care and told him to destroy. Brod's development was much more rapid than Kafka's: he was a year younger and had emerged much sooner into what he wanted to be, having developed not only literarily but musically and generally artistically. By his midteens he seemed fixed in what he was, and, among other things, his fervent Zionism never wavered and was the source of many disagreements with Kafka. When they finally met, in the Section for Literature, Kafka was moving from chemistry to law after two semesters at the university, and Brod was beginning his law studies.

Although not supremely talented in any one area, as was Kafka, Brod was a miracle of will, determination, and almost first-rate talent in a number of areas. There was, first, his physical handicap. Small and unprepossessing in appearance, as against the six-foot Kafka, he had developed a humpback condition in early childhood. Besides his literary gifts as novelist and poet (although he was not of the first rank), Brod excelled in musical studies as a composer and pianist, and was also a gifted translator and student of languages. Furthermore, his taste was usually excellent, and though not himself an advocate of innovation, Modernism, or the avant-garde, he recognized it in others — not only in Kafka but in Leoš Janáček, the great Moravian composer whose works he publicized. Janáček's work is now widely recognized, in particular his operas *Jenufa, Katya Kabanová, The Cunning Little Vixen, The Makropulos Affair,* and the culminating masterpiece of his career, *From the House of the Dead,* based on Dostoevsky's *The Diary from the House of the Dead.* But at that time, Janáček's music was not easy to assimilate, not after the household gods of Smetana and Dvořák, whose folk motifs he retained while using a far more Modernistic orchestration, especially in his original use of chord progressions. Brod was also a strong supporter of Carl Nielsen, the Danish composer of more traditional compositions. Brod wrote endlessly on a variety of topics, publishing more than seventy-five books, plus thousands of articles and essays, as well as translations between Czech and German. He was, besides, despite his unattractive physical appearance, an unwearying ladies' man, marrying, having affairs, finding himself in and out of romantic entanglements that left Kafka marveling. His advocacy of *The Good Soldier Schweik,* Hašek's comic masterpiece of life under the Dual Monarchy during the war years, places in focus how attuned he was to a writer who in many ways paralleled Kafka: in caustic wit, irony, the awareness of the entrapment life brings, in the sense of the labyrinthine ways in which human behavior works itself out.

But there are other ways in which the Brod-Kafka relationship created its own kind of magic, not as influence but as example. Brod had far more reason than Kafka, it would appear, to sink back upon himself and become the caustic butt of his own predicament. His early life compared with Kafka's seems hellish, almost the opposite in fact of Kafka's situation. By viewing them as opposites, we can highlight Kafka's condition more precisely than we can by isolating it.

Brod's father was a Micawber-like figure whose presence in the home provided no real male role model, although professionally he was more successful than Dickens's character. Brod's mother was the dominant figure around whom the household ran, mainly because of her virtually psychotic condition: a hysterical nature that demanded its way, a near suicidal, paranoiac quality to her demeanor, a home life with few amenities, always drifting toward pathology. Compared with Brod's mother, Kafka's father was a model of decorum.

Brod, further, had to grow up with a spinal condition, at first a curvature, then a humplike growth that appeared when he was about four, and for which a corset or harness was devised that he had to wear day and night. The curvature was to some extent controlled, but it gave Brod a physically unbalanced look. Photographs of him reveal a large, almost macrocephalic head, perched on top of a deformed, curved body. The combination of family pathology and his own deformity should have created quite the opposite of what Brod turned out to be. Very possibly, he discovered early on what compensatory qualities he would require to overcome his condition, ways that, fortunately, Kafka did not discover. But whatever the exact process that occurred emotionally and psychologically, Brod used his wits, his intellect, and his great optimism to charm generations of women, to impose himself on the world through his writings, and to lead the fight for Zionism in days when it was still an ideal and a dream. Zionism would save him from the Nazis, for by the time of their accession he was in Palestine, an escape that did not occur for Kafka's three sisters, all of whom perished in German camps.

Brod sought personal happiness and found areas of it in the adjustments he willed himself into. As a consequence, or perhaps he had no other choice, his creative work lacks the bite and depth of Kafka's. Possibly Brod went as far as he could with his talent, but there is evidence in his poetry and fiction that he deliberately avoided the worst aspects of the pain and anguish he must have experienced while growing up under such negative conditions. Kafka, on the other hand, did not will himself from his past or from his perception of a past that had few of the overt traumas Brod experienced. Kafka's health was fragile, but until he developed active tuberculosis he seemed deliberately to make himself more ill than he needed to. His family life, while gruesome in his perception of it, and not lacking in severe emotional setbacks, had a normalcy to it that Brod could not claim. Kafka surrendered to his perceptions; he abjured the idea that will and determination can make anything different or less burdensome. In that surrender, he found his material. His perceptions of a living hell were far more profound than Brod's actual hell. It was, all in all, a matter of imagination, a dimension of achievement Brod could not aspire to.

The two, then, cemented their friendship through disagreement, at first over Nietzsche, then over the writers Gustav Meyrinck and Hofmannsthal, finally over contrasting views of life, a diametrically different perception of where real life lay. The idealist Brod pitched against the anguished, huddled, secretive Kafka protecting his own brand of pessimism. Literature springs from humiliation, the poet Auden suggested, perceived or actual. It is perhaps because Brod was so different, almost an alien creature to Kafka's thinking, that Kafka could be so open and trusting with him. Brod became, in this respect, Kafka's "wife" or "mistress," Kafka sharing with him, as he would with a lifelong mate, his deepest feelings. What is of the greatest irony is that, with all their closeness and trust, neither had much understanding of the other, as we see especially from Brod's side when he wrote about Kafka, presenting his friend to the world after Kafka's death in 1924. Brod's version of Kafka was just that, a version that fitted Brod, not Kafka. After Kafka's death, the two remained as far apart in spirit as they had in life, although in his way Brod had been more necessary to Kafka's emerging needs than anyone else. Surely no one more than Brod believed in Kafka's genius.

What perhaps helped deepen the relationship, besides their shared passion for literature, however much they disagreed, was that Kafka was fleeing from chemistry into law, which Brod had come to study without any indecision about philosophy or science. As with so much else in him, he knew where his interests lay. For Kafka, the position Brod presented was one of solidity, of a young man who knew his own mind, even at eighteen. This certainty in Brod in the face of so much of Kafka's own uncertainty possibly had as much to do with the early stages of the friendship as any commonality of interests. Or possibly Kafka was cheered by a young man who was already so accomplished when he had so many reasons for defeat. It is also quite possible that the very contrasts that nourished their relationship attracted Kafka from the first.*

*To which we might add that Kafka should have been everlastingly grateful for what Hermann and Julie provided, since without them he would have been bereft of the rebellion that made him so fearsome an adversary in print. Brod's dreadful childhood turned him into a compensatory optimist, at whatever cost to his literary talents; whereas Kafka's far less daunting childhood was turned by him into a whiff of hell. More

Before meeting Brod, Kafka had passed through a turbulent year full of starts and stops: the entrance into chemistry and his giving it up after two weeks, his tentative movement into law, his attendance at lectures on art history, all culminating in the defensive story of "Shamefaced Lanky" in his December 20, 1902, letter to Pollak. Although we are tracing Kafka in 1901–2, we can move ahead, for the moment, to another transformational process that was described in a sensational 1903 publication, Daniel Paul Schreber's *Memoirs of My Nervous Illness*. Schreber's transformation — he began as a lawyer and chairman of the state court in the Saxon city of Chemnitz — took on radical psychotic features we do not associate with Kafka, but the parallelism is nevertheless uncanny. One of the ways Schreber changed himself was bodily, by way of emaciation. He was in several respects a kind of hunger artist, using food as a means of controlling not only himself but those around him. He wrote that instead of a "healthy natural stomach [he was given] a very inferior so-called 'Jew's stomach.' "[8] He speaks of existing without a stomach, of hypersensitivity to noise (Kafka's affliction as well), of a fixation upon digestion and elimination, intake and outgoing — like all of Kafka's concerns with diet and excretion. He suffered from sleeplessness — Kafka was a lifelong insomniac. Schreber attempted suicide on at least two occasions, and though Kafka did not actually attempt suicide he did entertain the idea.

Schreber's schizoid-paranoia engaged Freud, who took up his case; and it involved repressed homosexuality (Schreber was married, with children) and other sexual dislocations. His psychosis made him believe, as part of the transformation, that he had been changed into a woman, that his male sexual organ would have actually retracted if he had not set his will against it. He became, like a pincushion, sensitive to what he felt were rays or energies from beyond which penetrated and entered him. His case was far more radical than Kafka's, but it demonstrates what is involved in transformation, a process we can assume Kafka was beginning as he moved toward his twentieth birthday. Like Schreber, he would torture himself by his difference, but also like Schreber, he would exalt in that difference. He might complain to Pollak that he yawned and sat at his desk while his friend frolicked, but in the complaint is the writer's sense of his superiority.

Kafka attended a series of three lectures on literature given by August Sauer. Sauer was a strong, even powerful lecturer, but he was also a hidebound Pan-Germanist who believed that Teutonic culture was

---

of Julie's love or Hermann's sympathetic attention would have undercut whatever ironic or caustic bite developed, with a commensurate lessening of his powers. As George Bernard Shaw said repeatedly, he was grateful for his unloving childhood because it forced him into himself, into independence, whereas a loving home would have smothered him in sentimentality.

the high point of European civilization. He was an early Aryan-racialist proponent, using the Germanic race as an indication of how exalted a particular culture could become if it remained untainted by foreign blood. Echoing Gobineau, Sauer decried the Czechs, arguing that their culture was bastardized and inferior; he was of course anti-Semitic in his implications as well as his remarks. His literary lectures, which were well attended because of his charismatic presence, were really political events, inasmuch as he used the university forum as a way of striking at Czech pretensions and exalting German accomplishment. He made Kafka uneasy in his assumptions while reinforcing his sense of the value of Goethe, Kleist, Grillparzer, and others. Sauer in fact helped intensify the trap Kafka was in culturally: a Jew forced to embrace a literary culture that was not really his but for which he had no viable alternative. Sauer, moreover, was no mere lecturer; he also edited the journal *Deutsche Arbeit (German Work)*, a complement to his views in the classroom.

Franz Brentano's pupil Anton Marty was a philosophy lecturer at the university. Brentano was a considerable figure in German philosophy, with Edmund Husserl, among others, one of his disciples. His main theory, published in his 1874 book *Psychologie vom empirischen Standpunkte (Psychology from an Empirical Point of View)*, was an effort to establish psychology as an independent science, based on the assumption that mental processes were not passive but acts in themselves. Brentano used his notion of intentionality as a way of bridging the gap between individual consciousness and things, and as an ex-priest (by now married) he encouraged judgment, acts of will, determination, and individual effort. Clearly anti-Kantian and anti-Hegelian, he introduced disturbing ideas into German philosophy, for which he was exiled from the University of Vienna to Prague. His was a magical name, however, even in Prague, and his pupil Anton Marty helped form a Brentano circle, which met every two weeks at the Café Louvre in Ferdinandstrasse. Kafka became part of that circle, although how frequently he attended we cannot know.

To what extent this particular philosophy affected Kafka is difficult to measure. Still caught up by Nietzsche and Schopenhauer, Kafka seemed more attuned to pessimistic or apocalyptic theories than to ideas that encouraged judgment and will based on strength of character. Furthermore, Nietzsche's appeal was heightened by his corrosive irony, his underlying wit, his satirical mode, an outsider's view of man and society that would become Kafka's own stance. We pick this up as early as "Shamefaced Lanky." Nevertheless, the Brentano Circle was valuable in that it helped to take Kafka out of his self-imposed shell, brought him into contact with other bright young men, and kept him refreshed with philosophical ideas, even as the law (or its idea) was deadening him.

Boredom more than anything else would characterize his law studies, which represented the Germanic method at its worst, even though most of the lecturers were Jews, not Teutons. Several of the Jews, like Heinrich Singer, who lectured on canon law, were converts to Christianity, and many were of course assimilated Jews, who considered themselves pure German. The study of law, methodically presented and based in theory and history, took up Kafka's fall semester. In the spring, he turned to literary study and, in particular, Germanic literature (the course with Sauer). Despite his misgivings about Sauer and the literary curriculum as a whole, he continued with Germanic philology through the summer, in a sense imitating Nietzsche. Kafka studied syntax, New High German as well as grammar, Middle High German poetry, and other subjects that, he knew, were a cul-de-sac for a Jew who could not go on to a university career, something that even without the religious prohibitions would have been impossible for the shy, withdrawn Kafka. Nevertheless, the literary curriculum, dry as it was, attracted him, especially since he considered, temporarily, transferring to Munich to continue there — not only to gain a better grounding but to escape Prague and family. Ahead of him, if he remained in law, were the first state examinations in July 1903, only one year away.

In one respect, we should not make too much of something that is quite common among university students: their indecision about course and career choices, the fact that many, if not most, do not really know what they want when confronted by a broad menu of selections. Kafka was surely part of the large number of indecisive students. But there are the additional factors of his minority status in a society rapidly becoming nationalistic and exclusionary, and the paramount fact of his need to find time for what was building up in him, his desire to write. When we have a university student whose interests remove him or her from career choices to more or less personal decisions, and when that student is at the edge of a major development, then we have something unique, rather than the general instance. Furthermore, with secessions, avant-garde innovation, and forms of Modernism edging into Prague from all sides, Kafka alone was not changing, but the very nature of culture was about to change. He was blessed, or cursed, to be at the meeting point of several choices that twenty years earlier he might not have considered making. There was still another factor, of an intimate nature, that may have been a large-scale ingredient in the mix— Kafka's peculiar sexuality, which was on occasion ordinary in its drive for release, and on other occasions so full of hesitation, uncertainty, trepidation, vacillation, and even distaste that it needed a manager or trainer of its own. Precisely how his sexuality drove Kafka we cannot be sure, but writing did provide an opportunity for sacrifice and dedication, which in turn meant the repression of sexual energies into something he considered far more significant. No other career choice, unless in the other arts, could have given him that same sense of sacrificial self, of the martyred individual, of priestly devotion. We do not know if he was fully conscious of the eccentricities of his sexual needs, but we do know of his distaste for human touch, his excessive cleanliness, his horror of human smells, none of which bodes well for a full sexual life.

Still cracking his jaws and bending his brain over German syntax, grammar, and philology, still pondering the work of Hartmann von Aue, the poet, and other abstruse matters, Kafka finished his term and went off to Liboch, about twenty-five miles north of Prague, on the Elbe. He arrived on August 12, 1902, and then, as we have seen, wrote Pollak that he had returned to Prague because his Uncle Alfred Löwy, who was a manager of Spanish railways, had returned for a visit. For Kafka, this was an opportunity to release himself from law studies, family, and Prague all in one motion, if Uncle Alfred would "help me out of this mess."⁹ What Kafka wanted was guidance to someplace where he "could start afresh and do something." But Uncle Alfred, while gentle and pleasant, offered nothing tangible. Kafka then went through a whole series of plans: to return to Liboch, then go on to Triesch (where another uncle, the country doctor, Siegfried Löwy, lived, about eighty miles southeast of Prague), then return to Prague before heading for Munich, to attend the university. The plans were extravagant, especially the Munich idea, as if his problems were to be solved by his giving up Prague. In one way, his separation from the family might have been beneficial; but Prague was so much a part of Kafka's inner need that his removal from it might have had severe reverberations in his literary career.

The rest of the odyssey did take place. Uncle Siegfried's home was always a relaxing place for Kafka, particularly since his uncle was a confirmed bachelor and something of an odd creature in his hermitic ways. If ever a man marched to a different drummer, while practicing a "sociable" profession like medicine, it was this uncle, whom trouble seemed to roll off. He ended his life in suicide in 1942 before deportation to a death camp. If there is inheritance of personality and attitudes, then Kafka was more a product of Uncle Siegfried than of Julie and Hermann. Uncle Siegfried was like a resting place for Kafka during his entire life, a man of many complications, possibly homosexual, possibly a lifelong depressive, a man of harsh wit, sound advice, and considerable understanding of his equally difficult nephew.

For the fall term of 1902, Kafka, whatever the internal struggles, was back in law; his plans for German literary studies, for training in philology, for career alternatives to law, for fleeing permanently to the University of Munich had all been discarded. The reality of his position was beginning to become apparent: Kafka tried Munich and then returned to Prague, as he would do for the rest of his life, no matter where he went temporarily and no matter how fondly he looked at other cities, whether Berlin, Paris, or Munich itself. Prague may have been an old crone with claws, but it contained all the ingredients he needed to oppose; and without that opposition, hatred, anguish, he could not possibly define himself.

Munich would have offered something well beyond a leavetaking of his family. More advanced at this moment than Prague in the Modernist movement, Munich, like Vienna and Berlin, was beginning to act out its rebellion. By 1896 the city had hosted several writers and artists who would go on to great accomplishment. In that year, Wassily Kandinsky left Russia for Munich, where a thriving arts and crafts movement helped influence his movement toward abstraction, a movement that filtered into Prague by 1911–12 in the work of František Kupka, Josef Čapek, Emile Filla, Bohumel Kubišta, Vincent Beneš, and others. Munich was by then well known for its assortment of cultural activities, its museums, and its responsiveness to artists and liberal ideas. In and around this time, the city enjoyed visits from Rilke, Thomas and Heinrich Mann, and Frank Wedekind. It saw the development of the periodicals *Simplicissimus* (cofounded by Wedekind) and, more importantly, *Jugend.* The latter would become associated with the style we identify as art deco, *Jugendstil,* and then play an important part in the Vienna Secession only shortly later. These magazines, preceding the Viennese Secession by a year, published work by Hofmannsthal, Richard Dehmel (whose poetry entered into several Schoenberg works, including *Verklärte Nacht*), Rilke (some of whose poems Schoenberg also set to music), Ricarda Huch (German novelist and poet), and others of note. When Karl Kraus started his satiric *Die Fackel* in Vienna three years later, he had the Munich magazine as precedent.

But Munich was only one of several places Kafka might have gone to seek out whatever he needed at this early stage in his inner life. Berlin would also have served, and its "secession" in 1897 had affinities with the one in Munich, although it differed broadly from Vienna's. It hinged on a great innovative and disturbing painter, Edvard Munch, who had been invited in September 1892 by the Verein Berliner Künstler to exhibit in its headquarters. Munch hung the fifty-two paintings and etchings himself, and when the members of the Verein saw his work the majority of them voted to close the exhibition. The traditionalists opposed Munch on the basis of several factors: color, content, morbidity, lack of "beauty," however they defined it. But more than that, the Verein, mainly conservative artists, saw in Munch an iconoclast little different from those anarchists and assassins who had spread fear throughout Europe in the nineties. He was, like so much else in Modernist art and fiction, an apparent avatar of disorder and chaos, and was dangerous on these grounds alone — not so much as an artist but as a conveyor of dangerous ideas.*

---

*This was not unlike the unsettling effect the early impressionists had. Now seeming so harmless, now so totally absorbed into our historical sense of painting, impressionism

Such typical responses to Modernism, as we saw in Munich and will see paralleled in Vienna and then Prague, are followed by a chain reaction. From the Verein membership of about 225, 70, almost a third, voted to secede and to form their own rump group. Without actually leaving the Verein — the tentativeness of the early secession differed in this respect from Vienna's — they decided to form what they called "a free association of artists," what in Paris would be an artistic milieu. The aim was not primarily to further Munch's type of painting, which would have been an aesthetic goal, but to insist on the right of Munch to be exhibited, which was more a social and political issue. This first stage of the Berlin Secession became the model for later withdrawals, until the one in Vienna, which questioned not only the right to exhibit but style and matter.

In Vienna, rebellion occurred on a broad front, with *Jugendstil* modes fitting themselves into the seams of a society already shredded. The official withdrawal came when Gustav Klimt led nineteen students from the academy to form the secession. Their idea was that twentieth-century painters needed their own style and that such styles could not develop in the stifling atmosphere of the academy.* At stake, in reality, was the entire culture, and critics of the secession perceived the threat to the state in the development of a countering splinter group. In Franz Josef's Vienna, as in Europe in general, the subsidization of the arts meant an official aesthetic line, and a threat to it was a blow at the very life of the state.

Other aspects of the Vienna Secession included numerous battles over the architecture of the city, struggles among Otto Wagner, Camillo Sitte, and Adolf Loos.[10] The actual building that took place, based on conflicts between modernizing and retaining traditional values, carries minimally into Prague. Otto Wagner's interest in traffic flow, even before the advent of the automobile, possibly influenced the razing of the Old Town in Prague, beginning in 1893, and the increasing modernization of that part of the city. Wagner's idea was that vehicles would have precedence over pedestrians, a recognition that "modern life" meant rapidity of movement, as against the slower pace of a more traditional society. Sitte, on the other hand, was attuned to the spiritual needs of the people and to their folk-nationalistic aspirations. He stressed the neighborhood (the square) as an intimate living area, rather

---

was a devastating attack on realistic values. Its breakdown of formal scenes into areas of color patterns expressed social and political breakdown and, at the same time, challenged expressed realistic versions of that dissolution of social forms. Since a public could not fight light and color, it restricted exhibitions or hooted at what it saw.

*Perhaps ironically, perhaps by chance, the secession preceded by one year the celebration of the Imperial Jubilee, which had been long in the planning. The period is covered with all due attention to matter and tone in Robert Musil's masterpiece, *The Man Without Qualities*, which is truly representative of the death throes of a stagnant monarchy and a dying culture.

than the city as a whole, and he planned small, self-contained communities, in actuality small urban areas in themselves. Whereas Wagner was more in keeping with a broader European Modernism, Sitte played to the nationalistic aspirations of those who eschewed Modernism in favor of family and national values. Sitte sought community entities and values; Wagner, beauty as motion, flow, rhythms. The Prague housing renewal near the end of the century favored Wagner but tried to retain the spirit of Sitte.

Possibly the most significant of the three, because his work flowed over into the secessionist journal *Ver Sacrum* was Adolf Loos, architect and benefactor of Oskar Kokoschka. Loos was an iconoclast who used the pages of *Ver Sacrum* to lambaste the stylistics of the Ringstrasse, the massive buildings that dominate the heart of Vienna. Loos sought a total rejection of the empire's taste, as linked to a decaying and dying time, and unresponsive to present-day needs. Loos was an early functionalist, an early proponent of what would become the Bauhaus style, a kind of architectural minimalism. His aim was purification: cutting through that equation of Eros and Thanatos into something "clean" — clearing out the debris of an ossified Dual Monarchy and its works. Loos denied history, the past, and favored remaking what existed in the image of what people wanted now; people, he believed, had the ability to remake themselves. He became the architect of transformation, rejecting adornment, decoration, and stylistics, removing art from architecture and architecture from art. Although Loos's architectural ideas had no real appeal in Prague, his sense of minimalism, his desire to clear away debris, his insistence on remaking oneself and one's environment, his use of *Ver Sacrum* for his ideas all penetrated in their way. If we apply the Loosian method to literature, in Kafka's case, we may look to his spare use of German, his often minimalist method of dealing with characters and scenes, his withholding of background information on his characters. "Loosianism" not only applied to architecture, but to an entire social and political spectrum.

As we track these major secessions, in Berlin, Munich, and Vienna, we should not lose sight of the fact that art was being defined by more than secessionist groups. In addition, at the turn of the century and shortly thereafter, there were assertions of independence by many other movements and groups — all avant-gardes of varying degrees of intensity. Each had its own self or defining characteristics, and each attempted to destroy or subvert whatever preceded it, which is what avant-gardes do. Nearly all had their own manifestoes, also — journals, magazines, and publications that might appear only infrequently which helped identify a movement or an innovation. Some of these manifestoes were only broadsides; some, like Vienna's *Ver Sacrum*, were in themselves works of art. As Kafka came of age in Prague and readied himself as a writer, or shortly thereafter, he was to inherit a fifty-year span of the most effervescent time in cultural history. Within this time period, we can list symbolism, decadence, naturalism, Jung-Wien, Die Brücke, Blaue Reiter, expressionism, fauvism, cubism, the "new science" of quantum physics and relativity, imagism, vorticism, Italian futurism, Russian futurism, dada, surrealism (foreshadowed well before the actual movement in the 1920s under André Breton), tactilism, dynamism, Russian imagism and symbolism, Orphism, serialism, constructivism, neoplasticism, and abstractionism, among others. Many of these movements obviously owe a great deal to previous or parallel forces, with symbolism and naturalism nourishing several movements in the later nineteenth century, cubism and expressionism fueling numerous others in the early twentieth. Still others are natural outgrowths of what preceded: futurism from the "new science" or, later, surrealism deriving from dada and from Freud's theories of the unconscious and dream interpretation. Once abstraction with Picasso, Braque, and Kandinsky took hold, it became the measure of all plastic art, and its influence appeared in a number of other areas: in literature, which became increasingly internalized, in streams of consciousness and related methods, in disruption of traditional narrative and characterization; in music, which depended more and more on "pure sound," as in the schools of Stravinsky, Schoenberg, Webern, Berg. These influences would continue well through the century, except in literature, which began to lose much of its secessionist emphasis by the time of the Second World War.

Many of these movements, groups, and new forms reached into Prague: into literature by way of Kafka, in music through Janáček, in art through Kupka, among others. In Kafka's work, we note symbolism, expressionism in many of its forms, certainly aspects of naturalism, a good deal of input from Freud (his use, for example, of the unconscious and dream literature), and something, perhaps indefinable, that seems indebted to developments in cubism and abstraction. The latter is difficult to pinpoint since even as we attempt to perceive and discuss it, so much of Kafka slides and floats away. But there is little doubt that his establishment of scenes and his angular approach to characters and images owe a good deal to movements in art that defined cubism and abstraction. In abstraction, objects could not be portrayed as they once were, but had to be seen as blending into line, color, plane — shapes that went to the essence of objects, not to their forms. Well before he wrote *The Castle* near the end of his life, Kafka saw objects and places as indeterminate, as lacking the actual dimensions we associate with such things. His rearrangement of spatial proportions was part of that need to present objects even while de-emphasizing them. He was uncomfortable with objects, as he was with "real people" in his fiction, and he stylized elements in such ways that they drift out of focus even while he ostensibly focuses on them. That "drift," if we can call it that, was part of his painterly eye for the abstraction of the thing, not the thing. If we look at Kupka's cubist/abstractions at about the time Kafka wrote "The Judgment" and "The Metamorphosis" in 1912, we find several overlapping features, the main ones being their common aim to deconstruct the scene, deconstruct the objects in it, deconstruct our expectations of what occurs.

Movements were only part of the matter filtering into Prague; there were also the manifestoes, as apart from publications like *Kunstwart*, which presented current cultural ideas in the German world. Under its editor, Ferdinand Avenarius, *Kunstwart* was distinctly Germanic in its intent and reach, narrowly focused on what made the Teutonic tradition so great (Avenarius, not surprisingly, was a folklorist). The manifestoes were quite different in that they did not play to tradition or to the past, or to any chauvinistic ideal. The manifestoes were subverters in many instances, certainly forms of rebellion, and often full of the anger that goes into secessions or withdrawals from the mainstream. Before the chief manifesto for the empire's readers, *Ver Sacrum*, appeared in 1898, there were several others, and then came an avalanche.

Prague itself never had a secession proper, perhaps because it was always slightly behind the other cities in its absorption of the new, and also because several of its major figures had left Prague: Rilke for good, Kupka for a stay in Paris, for example. But Prague experienced something comparable to secession in that its ideological struggles mirrored what was occurring in high culture. The political battles between the nationalistic/folklorist groups and those (several of them Jews) attuned to broader European culture were a reflection of the struggles between cultural traditionalists and those eager to embrace many or all aspects of Modernism.

Even at this time, in his earliest work, Kafka was struck by the tremendous effervescence of the artistic and cultural scene. There was never any question of his writing traditional pieces. He could not be like Thomas Mann, who had recently completed a long, traditional novel, *Buddenbrooks*. The comparison is appropriate, for Mann was fully aware of cultural changes and incorporated them into his novel, but the book was itself written within an established and traditional genre, without any of Kafka's disruptive techniques in narrative and character. Mann's theme was a suitable one for 1900, the struggle between the artistic figure and the business world represented by the Buddenbrooks banking interests. Mann's novel is about the decline and fall of earlier nineteenth-century German values, but it has resonance also for the Austro-Hungarian Empire, and specifically for Vienna and Prague. Hanno, who dies as a schoolboy, is the foreign element that represents whatever disease is eating at the Buddenbrooks soul, just as the Vienna Secession would expose every weakness and fatuity of the creaking empire.

Mann chose to depict the family and its decline as the artistic milieu began to take hold of the younger generation. But there is little left to the imagination, little left unsaid; whereas Kafka in his earliest fictions eschewed traditional forms of fiction and moved directly into oblique, difficult, innovative ways of penetrating to areas beyond. Mann's turn-of-the-century novel, for all its panoramic magnificence, its extraordinary eye for detail, skims surfaces and rarely penetrates. Kafka, at virtually the same time, was concerned almost solely with subsurfaces, with secret forces that draw the individual into shadows. Perhaps none of this could have occurred had Kafka not been aware of the innovations which the manifesto-journals were advocating. Of all of these, Karl Kraus's *Die Fackel* (*The Torch*), with its tortured views of Modernism, would become the most significant.

What all these journals — *Ver Sacrum, Der Sturm, Die Aktion* — had in common was a secessionist spirit. Theirs was the oedipal battle of generations, and in the case of *Die Aktion* a struggle that stressed political ideology, an undoctrinaire left-wing point of view. Their shared intention, regardless of focus, was renewal and regeneration of a perceived moribund society. In this line of thought was Kraus's *Die Fackel*, for Kraus in his caustic, cynical way saw himself as a contemporary Diogenes torching out the misapprehensions and deceptions of the past in order to purify his times. His emphasis was on purity of the German language, but his desire for purification spread further, into nothing less than a cleaning out of social and political decay.

Kafka was of course familiar with *Die Fackel*, whose fame spread throughout the German-speaking empire and was well known in Bohemia. Kraus was more polemical than the others, his journal more heuristic and pedagogic in its intentions. He believed he represented a higher or more sacred form of purity than they, and, therefore, whatever he offered was a critique not only of what Modernism was against but also of Modernism. His importance is less as an avatar of Modernism, although he overlaps with it, than as a caustic, parodic voice insisting on truth, as *he* perceived it.* Such an ironic figure, one who saw German usage in decline, a prophet of something beyond any particular movement or group, was for someone like Kafka intensely significant. Kraus reinforced his own perception of how the world organized itself, basically outside formal lines in ways that reached toward some mysterious center or some secret rays of power.

Kraus began *Die Fackel* one year after *Ver Sacrum*, in 1899, also in Vienna. Although he was a poet and dramatist, his name was con-

---

*For example, Kraus later directed his harsh wit at a promoter who was providing comfortable trips for tourists to Verdun and other battlefields. Kraus picked up the vulgarity, bad taste, and incongruities of such endeavors — bourgeois tourists visiting blood-soaked scenes — and titled his piece "Promotional Trips to Hell," an attack on all desecrations of what should be hallowed experiences.

nected to the thirty-seven years of *Die Fackel* until his death in 1936. The journal was completely his brainchild, and virtually every issue represented his point of view, with only occasional contributions from the outside. Since he opposed and misunderstood Klimt, it is clear he began his journal as a way of casting doubt on both sides of the cultural struggle, secessionists and conservers alike. Kraus took an active role in the running conflict between Klimt and his opponents over his depiction of Philosophy in his university ceiling paintings. Like Schnitzler's *La Ronde,* Klimt's "Philosophy" is almost a sexual daisy chain, with intimations less of love or learning than of sex, birth, and death: a kind of Brueghel-inspired *Liebestod* and definitely intended to dare or defy the bourgeoisie. The painting consists of an ascension, in which we are drawn not to angelic or wise faces, but to sizable buttocks and haunches.

Kraus was a great ironist, a critic of the same deceits and hypocrisies Musil would write about in *Young Törless* and *The Man Without Qualities,* and Mann in his early stories, a quality greatly admired by Kafka. But even as ironist, Kraus lacked the self-understanding that would have allowed him to see irony and wit in others. He was no simpleton, of course, but he was so attached to his own vision of purifying language and fortifying rationalism that he missed much of the larger historical surge. The enemy was not aesthetics or "ugly art" but the very forces of rationalism — what was called "progress." In brief, he hated the wrong things: aesthetes, Zionism, feminism (and women), Freud and psychoanalysis, and his own Jewishness, since he renounced Judaism eventually to enter the Catholic Church at the same time he founded *Die Fackel.* Yet even as we follow the inconsistencies of Kraus's career, we can see how many of his bêtes noires overlapped with uncertainties in Kafka: the attacks on Zionism, the rejection, early on for Kafka, of Judaism proper, the wariness in the face of psychoanalysis (even while using it in his fiction), the ambiguities about women, the response to rationalism and progress. We also see how, given the nature of such a volatile period in culture at the end of the century, it was possible to hold several conflicting views at once, or else maintain several ambiguities, without any chance of resolution. Even Kraus's insistence that German was being polluted by Yiddishisms and jargon, an argument recalling Wagner's diatribe in "Jews in Music," foreshadows Kafka's own sense that German was not really his language. But since Yiddish was not either, he was left truly bereft of a mother tongue.

In the fall of 1902, Kafka, who turned nineteen in July, was a rather lowly university student, just making up his mind about his course of study in law, and attempting to find escape routes from Hermann, the family in general, and trying to do it with words, words, words. He had,

in the spring of 1902, continued with philosophy courses taught by
Brentano's pupil Anton Marty, and during the summer, as noted earlier, had been invited to join the so-called Brentano Circle, which met
every two weeks at the Café Louvre. Marty gave an oral examination
on Brentano's philosophy and related material in psychology, but Kafka
failed it. Then he was off to Liboch, returned to Prague for his uncle,
Alfred Löwy, then went back to Liboch, still with Munich in mind.
After that, he spent a week with Uncle Siegfried, the country doctor, in
Triesch. In October he visited Munich, finally putting it behind him as
a place to escape to, and returned to the university in Prague, where in
October he met Brod. It was after this summer, on December 20, that
he outlined to Pollak his extraordinary idea of "Shamefaced Lanky,"
that disjointed and disruptive tale that seems, already, to be Kafkaesque.

From Liboch, he wrote Pollak, "It is a strange time I've been spending here." What is strange is that Kafka has abstracted himself from the
larger world, has entered into a kind of reverie, in which he says he
lies for hours "on a vineyard wall and stare[s] into the rain clouds . . .
or into the wide fields." He observes colors, the "brown and mournful fields," how the "late-summer shadows dance on dark, turned-up
earth," how the shadows "dance physically."[11] He is mesmerized by
the way light and soil affect each other. The reverie quality of his observations is an important step toward the reshaping of materials so as to
make them suitable for creative recall. He is slowly remaking himself,
or else dividing himself between his career goal and his real enterprise,
writing. Further, the images he describes to Pollak are painterly, part of
a shifting impressionism with its emphasis on light and altering colors.
This painterly quality is not something we associate with Kafka, since
he has become our representative creator of enclosed places, mazes and
labyrinths, or distant attics and cellars. Yet here we see him responding
to other stimuli, and responding in such a way that he has relocated
himself in dream or fantasy. The next letter to Pollak concerns
"Shamefaced Lanky," and then within a year (on November 9, 1903) we
note he was working on a book, *Das Kind und die Stadt* (*The Child and
the City*), whose passages he promises to send on shortly. This fragmentary manuscript was apparently lost.

In the fall of 1902 Kafka settled into the drudgery of law, a subject
that never appealed to him, and whose torturous pursuit gave him only
anguish and bitterness. Now with Brod as his friend, although not close
as yet, he settled in, especially since the Munich option, after his October visit, had fallen through. The law degree was obtained by means
of two strategies: the pupil should not fall ill and become unable to attend the lectures, and the pupil should leave behind everything except
his powers of memory. Law was not an intellectual degree. It was, in
fact, precisely what it became for Franz Kafka: a means of transforming

himself into a petty bureaucrat who could function within the confines of the empire. Since the bureaucracy was itself at a low level of performance, it was not necessary to be brilliant, original, or inventive. It was enough to have weathered the tedium of the degree and then to have found a niche in the system. A good example of how this works can be found not only in Kafka's several depictions of the Czech bureaucracy but also in Tolstoy's graphic *The Death of Ivan Ilych*, which portrays the rise of a provincial Russian judge who comprehends precisely the balance needed to have a successful career.

Kafka of course kicked against the traces, but not in his administrative side, where he played by the rules of the game. It was from his "other side" that he attacked the system. But the system did not intend for him to be a writer. It asked only for memorization of the codes of canon law and civil law, and it demanded attendance at large lectures that were not broken down, except occasionally, into smaller, more manageable groups. It was, in many ways, a parodic version of the Germanic brand of schooling, without the high standards Bismarck's Prussia insisted upon. It insisted on the rules but failed to compensate with quality performance. Since administrative posts were the intended destiny of most students, even for Jews who might find it difficult to become placed, there was no need to provide entertainment or intellectual sustenance in the lectures. One was expected to take extensive notes and spit them back on the examinations; what the instructor said mattered, not what the student thought about it.

Kafka pursued this course of study for six semesters, with only now and then some relief. International law was followed by civil law, canon law, commercial and constitutional law, statistics and economics (some relief), the Austrian civil code, and so on. It was up to Kafka, the lawyer-to-be, to carve out some sense of life for himself from this program, or else go under in a career that meant little or nothing to him. We should not feel, however, that every moment was one of anguish or agony, although he later complained that it was. He had a circle of friends, the Brentano Group at the Café Louvre, he had occasional encounters with prostitutes (like the one in July 1903 he described to Milena Jesenská), he had the first stirrings of his imagination and some fruits of it in 1904 with "Description of a Struggle," he had Max Brod, Oskar Pollak, and other friends to whom he began to confide more and more. Most of all, he had that dualism that had already begun to shape itself: the transformation of Franz Kafka, son of Hermann and Julie Kafka, into lawyer and writer, *littérateur*.

In 1903, coinciding with his first sexual encounter, which he found tolerable because it was not more vile and filthy than he had expected, he experienced nervous anxiety over Roman legal history, a subject in which he had to take a comprehensive examination at the midpoint of his legal studies. The tension caused by the legal material possibly created a sexual crisis, since he connects them fully seventeen years later, in writing to Milena. Roman legal history leads to his assignation with a shopgirl, because of the "constant whining" of his body, then again with the same shopgirl two nights later. This experience is followed by a distaste for her when he returns after the summer, because of something vile and filthy she said, along with a "small gesture" she made. It is a curious mix of ingredients: the desperate need for physical relief, the growing pressure of a coming examination that he is certain he will fail, the dependence on Gentile Czech shopgirls for sex, the disgust after the second coming, the long memory of it that compels him to unburden himself as a mature man.

After that unfortunate experience, he spent the summer with his parents at Zálezly, near Aussig (now Usti, about halfway between Prague and Dresden, Germany). There he played tennis with a local girl, flirted, went for bicycle rides, and generally enjoyed himself. What is missing from all this, however, is one important piece of information: that after passing the examination, Kafka suffered a nervous collapse that necessitated a two-week cure at a sanatorium (the White Deer) outside Dresden. Now twenty, Kafka for the first time entered a sanatorium, his entrance coinciding with the pressures of university work and that unsettling sexual experience with the shopgirl.

Although it is tempting to speculate, we should not, however, see his sexual initiation or the burden of the examination as the sole contributors to his breakdown; nor should we see the stay at the sanatorium as Kafka's regression into some earlier pattern when, he hoped, a mother figure would care for him, as the nurses did. Rather, whatever its degree of intensity and volatility, the breakdown was linked to an entire array of problems, some sexual, some family-oriented, some university-connected, some linked to his inability as yet to resolve exactly what he wanted and what his timetable would be.

Still, in that late summer, on September 6, 1903, Kafka wrote Pollak that he was putting together a bundle for him, "everything I have written up to now, original or derivative," some of it going back well before that year, when he says he wrote little or nothing. He also intimates that there are things "I cannot show even to you, for we shudder to stand naked and be fingered by others, even if we have begged on our knees for that very thing."[12] The breakdown, then, did not detract from Kafka's movement into serious and fairly extensive writing. Only two months later,[13] he told Pollak about the abortive novel mentioned earlier, *The Child and the City*, which sounds ominously autobiographical. It is this conjunction of events and experiences — not solely the sexual initiation, nor the need to regress into maternal comfort, nor the distaste of both sex and law — which Kafka had to confront; and in the face of his inability to resolve what were disparate experiences he did the best thing he could: he sought treatment. Whenever we note Kafka entering a sanatorium, we must be careful not to mark it as a signal of defeat or an act of infantilism, but as a way he could renew himself for the next stage of whatever the battle happened to be.

He emerged from the sanatorium better able to confront the unresolvables of his twenty years, and even be reasonably happy, as he told Pollak. How intimate he became in these letters we cannot determine, since Pollak excised portions and they have been lost. We can assume, however, that Kafka divulged far more than Pollak wanted published, so that the excisions included intimate matters of perhaps a more intense or more revealing kind than what Pollak did permit to stand.

The November 9 (1903) letter to his friend stated that Kafka had fragments of a book in hand, that while "God doesn't want me to write," he had to. This coincided with the beginning of his new law school semester. But also included in the letter is a poem, which he offers for Pollak's scrutiny. Pollak had by this time left Prague to work as a tutor. The poem is not particularly strong and does not suggest any poetic gift, but biographically it does offer some interesting lines. Kafka writes of people congealing, of footsteps sounding metallic "on brazen pavements," lines that seem to foreshadow passages in *The Trial*, among other works. A man walks in silence in the snow, and people pass without any connection to each other — the typical Kafkan scene of noncommunicative people, even when they speak to each other. The three-stanza poem closes with an individual leaning on "the squared stone railing, looking into the evening waters, hands resting upon ancient stone." Solitary, without relationships, mixed textures of flesh and stone, waters that give nothing back: all of these are intimations of what is to come, however inchoately and in whatever shadowy form they appear here.

In a follow-up letter in December, Kafka writes of how important letter writing is for him.[14] He uses the metaphor of a rope as a way of describing how people keep themselves from falling into an abyss: one end of that rope is connected to Pollak, the other to Kafka. "People keep themselves at a tolerable height above an infernal abyss toward which they gravitate only by putting out all their strength and lovingly helping one another. They are tied together by ropes, and it's bad enough when the ropes around an individual loosen and he drops somewhat lower than the others into empty space; ghastly when the ropes break and he falls. That's why we should cling to the others."*

The need for ties and linkages is clear, but then school had re-

---

*Although this letter is postmarked December 21, 1903, there is internal evidence that questions the dating. Kafka mentions being in Munich, but not writing Pollak from there; there is no evidence of a 1903 Munich trip. Kafka did go to Munich in October 1902, but why would he mention Munich to Pollak more than a year later? It is possible Kafka was taking the long view, and explaining even fourteen months later why he did not write from Munich.

started, and Kafka was back into it. He was fortunate to study Austrian civil law with Horaz Krasnopolski, who made a real effort to teach, using actual examples for illustrations and lecturing in an engaged, even passionate, voice. Another influential lecturer, this time on criminal law, was Hans Gross, and his presence in Kafka's life takes on additional interest because of the relationship of the elder Gross to his son, Otto. Gross was a noted magistrate and criminologist, one of the first to emphasize not the crime alone but the criminal behind it. Gross wrote extensively on criminal psychology and on his belief that law must take the individual into account — hence the nurturing environment of his classes. Gross had only recently published, in 1893, his landmark study, *Handbook for Investigative Judges, Policemen, and Gendarmes*. But though he achieved great fame in Europe in his time — the book was widely translated — he is better known to us for the way he handled his son. Here we find a shadow relationship for Kafka's own sense of how Hermann handled him, although Gross's treatment of Otto bordered on the criminal. After a brief period spent with Freud and his group in Vienna, Otto became schizoid, suffered from morphine addiction, and was obviously in need of intense help, which Carl Jung offered to provide. But while the Freud circle offered him help also, his father put pressure on the courts and on the authorities to have his son committed to asylums for the insane. He was relentless in his persecution of Otto and in his use of authoritative power. It was, for him, a case history in which he went after the "criminal." Kafka actually did meet Otto Gross, but not until 1917, and by then Otto was the product of his father's persecution and of those attempting to save him from his father. Unstable, uncertain, lacking direction, he was no longer himself, and five years after his father's death, in 1915, he committed suicide by letting himself starve to death.

The matter did not end here. After Otto's suicide, Franz Werfel wrote a play called *Schweiger*, named after the main character, a mass murderer released from an insane asylum and then, once free, persecuted by a Professor Viereck, the asylum director. Viereck in turn is stalked by a university instructor named Ottakar Grund, who shoots the professor in the name of breaking free of his tyranny. Grund allies himself with Schweiger in a call to organize the "diseased" people of the world. When Kafka and Werfel met in 1922, Kafka was quite upset at Werfel's portrayal of Otto Gross as Grund. Kafka saw the tortured young man as a sympathetic figure and identified with him in his struggle against his tyrannical father. He even went so far as to write a letter of protest to Werfel, which he did not mail, in which he accused his friend of betraying their generation. He implied that Werfel distorted Gross's real value as a man seeking liberation and the destruction of all hateful authority. Yet even within these strained circumstances, Kafka and Werfel remained friends.

Although Kafka was not aware of these developments at the time he was a student of Gross, the man's fanatical belief in himself could well have reminded Kafka of Hermann, and in Gross's pursuit of authority and authoritarian standards of behavior, Kafka could have recognized how his own household was organized. In some curious way, Gross and Hermann Kafka bled over into one another.* The Gross case illustrates what Kafka would later write to his father: that authority, when allowed its full run, can destroy utterly, although Gross himself, true to his code of the imperial self, never relented or admitted wrongdoing. He died convinced that what he was doing, the destruction of his son, was according to the rules of father-son relationships. Gross had an enormous impact on Kafka in the lecture hall, especially since Kafka took three courses with him and learned from him a good deal about human nature. Gross's emphasis on the criminal, rather than solely on the law, was certainly good training for the future writer; and Gross's own great fame as a criminologist carried over into the classroom in his ability to dissect and analyze a crime. His mind ran to the surgical, precisely what Kafka needed. Whenever Kafka writes about the wasteland of his education, both at the gymnasium and then in the university law school, we should keep in mind the enriching experience he had with Gross, an experience that was more intellectual than legalistic.

Kafka was now, by the end of 1903–4, moving toward the middle point of his legal studies. He was also moving toward what would prove to be the first of his longer efforts in fiction, in the autumn of 1904, "Description of a Struggle," not at all misnamed for someone as sensitive to authority as Kafka was. He had become active in the Hall university group, with closer relationships to Max Brod and Ewald Felix Příbram, whose father would eventually offer Kafka a position with the Workers' Accident Insurance Institute. Kafka was indeed socially alive, in the Hall's cultural events, in the meetings of the Brentano Circle, and in his summer forays into flirting with local girls wherever he or his family vacationed. His life was definitely not monotonous, nor was it all grind. His university work, in fact, began to fall, almost precipitously, as he rebelled increasingly against the curriculum and its expectations of the student. Whenever we note a change of attitude in Kafka,

---

*The parallels between Otto Gross and Kafka are often startling, but perhaps not so surprising considering that both Hans Gross and Hermann Kafka were typical Germanic authority figures. Like Kafka, Otto had food phobias and let himself starve to death, just a short time before Kafka wrote "A Hunger Artist." Otto was also obsessed about his body, ashamed of it, and fearful of exposing any parts to others — a physical distaste for himself that struggled against strong sexual urges. One commentator points out that Kafka wrote *The Trial* in the general period after Otto was imprisoned at his father's insistence, which had created a general scandal even among patriarchal Germans. While this may make too much of Otto and Kafka as "secret sharers," the point is that such fathers — to whom we may add Milena Jesenská's Gentile patriarch — caused all kinds of perversities in their children in the name of order, discipline, and authority.

a slippage of attention, a loss of certainty in his direction, whenever these periods occur — and he often needed sanatorium care during such crises — they must be attributed to his sense of urgency as a writer. His need to fulfill this other "half" was so enormous that he generated breakdown, slippage, loss of direction as ways of signaling to himself that his primary function in life was being neglected or not being fulfilled.

There is, further, the question of Kafka's reading. He was reading a good deal outside the curriculum, books that provided sustenance for him and that, obviously, took time away from his studies. A man truly intent on his studies would have concentrated on working with the system, excelling, and then making his mark. Kafka was not motivated in that way; legal studies were a means to an end, but not to *his* end. He read, among others, Marcus Aurelius, the Roman emperor-philosopher; Meister Eckhart, the medieval mystic; Gustav Theodor Fechner, the recently deceased German natural philosopher and experimental psychologist; Friedrich Hebbel, the nineteenth-century German dramatist whose four-volume journal was published in 1903 and became a favorite of Kafka's; then Plato's *Protagorus*, which he, along with Brod, attempted in Greek with the help of a translation and a dictionary; Flaubert, at about this time, in French, also with Brod; and Thomas Mann's stories as they appeared in *Neue Rundschau* (he was especially fond of "Ein Glück," or "Some Luck"). Some of this reading spilled over into later years, but its range indicates how diverse Kafka's tastes were. The common bond for all of them was use of language, whether Eckhart and Hebbel in German or Flaubert in French. Kafka sought careful, precise prose, and even the grinding work on reading Plato in Greek, supported by external aids, was part of his quest for language, for expression. This list is by no means complete, since Kafka also felt himself almost a disciple of Goethe and Grillparzer, the nineteenth-century Austrian dramatist and lyric poet.

The relationship with Brod developed over words, from the reading they did together, just as, later, Kafka's relationship with Felice Bauer would be mainly words, and we might add that with his famous *Letter*, Kafka turned his tie to his father into words. Brod's description of their "reading parties" deserves repeating, although it is by now well known.

Our reading parties generally took place in Kafka's little room in his parents' house (in Zeltner Street) and sometimes at my place. Over Kafka's desk there hung a copy of the picture by Hans Thoma [German painter and lithographer, influenced by Courbet], "The Ploughman." On the wall at the side there was a yellowing plaster cast of a little antique relief, a maenad brandishing a piece of meat — a leg of beef, to be precise. The graceful folds of her dress danced around the figure, which had no hand. . . . This modest furniture accompanied Franz to all his lodgings in Prague: a bed, a wardrober, the little, old, dark brown, almost black, desk, with a few books and a lot of unarranged notebooks. His last room (in Niklas Street) had at least a second entrance which Kafka generally used, through the kitchen and the bathroom. Otherwise he didn't live apart from the rest of the family, which was certainly not healthy for the conflicts that were ever inwardly consuming him.[15]

Some of these conflicts, as we shall note, are revealed in the drawings Kafka made during lectures at the university.

What strikes us about Brod's description is how Kafka's own hothouse atmosphere filters into his work. The room is enclosed in the family apartment, with not even a private entrance of its own, so that Kafka had to rub against everyone. And even when he and Brod read together, they had to make their way to Kafka's room without enjoying the privacy of adults; rather, they were like children going to play in a room the parents can supervise. Yet before we see this as infantile or regressive behavior on Kafka's part, something that should not, of course, be dismissed, we must observe that he needed such an atmosphere in order to function. He required, as Brod failed to perceive, the very elements of claustrophobic environments in order to nourish his particular vision. Not until *The Castle* was he an open writer; he thrived on closing down, on limiting spatial areas, on creating mazes and labyrinths, secret places and holes, from which one might temporarily emerge, but only to rebury oneself. His was a narrow base of conceptualization.

Even his arrangement of the German language is narrowly conceived, without the wide swings of possibility already "opening up" the language for other writers. Some of this can be attributed to a closed-down personality, but more of it was a need to remove himself to such basics that nothing remained but his mind. For that he did not need spacious quarters. He found a room embedded in the parental apartment the perfect retreat, despite the intrusions, the almost constant annoyance of sounds, card playing, spitting, and, worse, sexuality.

Kafka did not doodle. He drew, mainly, in the margins of those hallowed lecture notes passed out by the professor indicating what the student had to master for his examinations. Kafka's drawings, as we might assume, are parodic: caricatures, squiggly lined and "hunger artist" types. The drawings contain a certain paradoxical spatiality, in which individuals are distant from each other, like the messengers in his later work attempting to go from sender to receiver and finding almost infinite space between them. The message is one of lack of communication, a parodic feature in that Kafka was drawing while the lecturer was speaking. Lecturer and student are separated by unbridgeable distances. The receivers of the information, unlike the senders, are small, discrete, solitary. The drawings are not unrelated to those Kafka also made in the diaries he kept. Thin, squiggly lines, hollowed out or emaciated figures, undefined faces are constant, even in the diary drawings in the

final year of his life. One is struck by the indefinite nature of these
drawings, some of them not much more than random scribblings, and
yet they incorporate a point of view, of the separation of everyone in a
kind of swampy environment. The drawings, if we can so characterize
the early ones (later ones became more defined and linked to an event
or activity), are primitive to the extent that they bring us back to ele-
mental or atavistic times.*

With Pollak now away, Brod became Kafka's closest companion, although their intimate friendship would not be sealed for some time.
Kafka's schedule looked like this: classes in the morning, study and
rest in the afternoon, then meetings with Brod and others of the Café
Louvre circle, or discussions at the house of Berta Fanta in the Altstädter Ring. Berta Fanta was a chemist's wife, a member of the Café Louvre
circle, and a patron of the arts and of good discussion. In a sense, she
turned her home into a salon, although its members were young and
still developing rather than rich and famous. For Kafka, it was a welcome respite both from law courses and from his own family. When he
wasn't busy in the evenings with these social and intellectual enterprises, he was apparently writing, the earliest of his tryings-out which
would, in autumn of 1904, lead to "Description of a Struggle," although
its exact dating is difficult to determine. It is that work, a kind of quarry
for his later fiction but also for Kafka himself, which marks a turning
point in his development. At twenty-one, in an inchoate, incomplete,
often incomprehensible piece of fiction, he found a good deal of what
would turn Franz Kafka into Kafka and Kafkaesque, the inheritor of
Modernism.

---

*I will comment further on the drawings in their time frame.

The shield is like a mirror, which draws things in from far away
and soundlessly absorbs them. . . .

— RILKE, "THE COAT OF ARMS"

SEVEN   Young Kafka and Modernism

I N 1904 Kafka's letters to Pollak began to reveal a certain
intensity and application to ideas missing earlier. His
discovery of Hebbel's diaries at this time meant a great deal to him, not
only intellectually but creatively, since he felt a certain affinity with
the writer. It is not always clear what Kafka actually felt for Christian
Friedrich Hebbel, the German tragic dramatist who died in 1863, but
one point of agreement was the struggle Hebbel portrays between old
and new, between generations. They also share the Hebbelian sense of
the heroic. For the dramatist, the hero or heroine arrived at an exalted
state not through grand deeds but through suffering and degradation. In
this area, Hebbel fitted into a kind of Kierkegaardian world, Kierkegaard being another figure who fascinated Kafka.* Pain, suffering, degradation, transformation: all of these can be found in Hebbel, and the
appeal may well have lain there.

The four volumes of Hebbel's diaries reinforced this affinity. Kafka
tells Pollak (January 27, 1904) that he read their 1,800 pages,

---

*But not to the exclusion of very different kinds of reading. Marcus Aurelius, for example,
had become indispensable: "I think I could not live without him now, for reading two
or three maxims in Marcus Aurelius makes me more composed and more disciplined,
although the book [Meditations — Kafka called his own first, brief book Meditation] as
a whole only shows a man who with prudent speech and a hard hammer and sweeping
view would like to make himself into a controlled, steelly, upright person." Kafka adds
as an admonition to himself, "It's fine if we can use words to cover ourselves up from
ourselves, but even better if we can adorn and drape ourselves with words until we have
become the kind of person that in our hearts we wish to be" (to Oskar Pollak, Letters
to Friends [January 10, 1904], p.14). The fundamental idea is transformation: Kafka's
emblem of self.

all at once, whereas previously I had always just bitten out small pieces
that struck me as insipid. . . . At first it was just a game, but eventually I
came to feel like a caveman who rolls a block in front of the entrance to
his cave, initially as a joke and out of boredom, but then, when the block
makes the cave dark and shuts off the air, feels duly alarmed and with remarkable energy tries to push the rock away. But by then it has become
ten times heavier and the man has to wrestle with it with all his might
before light and air return.

What Kafka means is that he used Hebbel for enlightenment,
gained it, but could not himself write at all during the reading and the
experience. He feels that Hebbel rises to heights and creates such a
level that he, Kafka, is unable to work. But he praises "big wounds,"
because "that makes it more sensitive to every twinge. I think we
ought to read only the kinds of books that wound and stab us." He repeats: "We need the books that affect us like a disaster, that grieve us
deeply, like the death of someone we loved more than ourselves, like
being banished into forests far from everyone, like a suicide. A book
must be the axe for the frozen sea inside us. That is my belief."[1]

By the end of this letter to Pollak, Kafka is evidently writing about
himself, not about Hebbel. We observe the hardening of his language,
the forsaking of the earlier, more romantic and wispy prose in his letters, and the creation of a tougher, harder sensibility, steeling itself for
Kafka's own descent into the "frozen sea inside us." The images are appropriate for this writer who circles death so closely and avidly:
"wound and stab us," "grieve us deeply," "like a suicide," and of course
the final image, of the book serving a biting, cutting function to un-
freeze us, if it can. Here, not yet twenty-one, Kafka was positioning
himself. In a letter to Brod in August, just before beginning to write
"Description of a Struggle," he suggests one of his great themes, one of
the overriding themes of the twentieth century: that disparity between
surface appearance and what goes on beneath. It is the struggle between
the conscious and unconscious, although in Kafka's terms, the unconscious is somehow revealed to us even as we smother it with surface
appearances or consciousness: "It would be the fulfillment of our daily
prayer that the consistency of our life may be preserved as far as external appearances go." That is the strength of being disappointed. But
there is more to it than that. For in reality, we "burrow through ourselves like a mole, and emerge blackened and velvet-haired from our
sandy underground vaults, our poor little red feet stretched out for
tender pity."[2]

At some time in the same year, Kafka wrote Brod he had reread
Thomas Mann's "Tonio Kröger," a short story about a young man torn
between his commitment to an artistic life and his desire to enter fully
into other forms of social life denied him by his priestlike calling. His
name, half southern European, the other half northern, indicates the

antithesis and division in him. Kafka tells Brod that Brod's "Excursions into Dark Red" (later expanded into a novel of that name) recalls the Mann story. Kafka indicates that for him the value of "Tonio Kröger" is not his discovery of the antithesis in the young man "but in the peculiar profit to the artist (to quote the post in *Excursions*) of infatuation with this antithesis."[3] Kafka's angle of vision reveals how he perceived the struggle within himself between career and writing: that the antithesis in Tonio will help reinforce the creative side, not debilitate or negate it. He was, in this respect, fitting himself into his skin, and finding in his reading whatever he needed to strengthen himself.

"Description of a Struggle" is aptly named, since from Kafka's letters in 1904 we can see the internal struggle that had begun. "Description" is archetypal Kafka, a quarry, as we have noted, for later work and a quarry in many respects for his own life in the 1904–5 period when we assume he wrote the piece. In more specific terms, "Description" leads directly into *Meditation* (*Betrachtung*), Kafka's 1912–13 brief book whose title refers to Marcus Aurelius's work of the same name, and, as well, into *The Castle* at the very end of Kafka's life. The story, which has two parallel versions, appears to be made up of disconnected elements, but many of these disconnections shadow aspects of Kafka's own inner life and are disturbing to the reader and obviously disturbing to Kafka himself. The main element concerns the narrator and the acquaintance he meets at a party, who asks to be rescued from an indiscretion with a woman. We have, with this, the messenger complex, and the rest of the story is structured, however tentatively, on the narrator's encountering messengers from various worlds. This idea works only if we see the story as a kind of stream emanating from that middle ground between consciousness and unconsciousness, in which the language of the latter can never be articulated and the language of the former, consciousness, can be too precise. In that reflection of a linguistic "middle ground," we can locate Kafka's distinctive fictional voice. Not real, not surreal, just eerie and hooded.

In the initial episode, the narrator and his acquaintance walk out into the freezing night, to climb the Laurenziberg. The acquaintance seems to possess all the social graces, whereas the narrator is a lonely outsider, the side of himself Kafka identified with the artist Tonio Kröger in Mann's story. The other fellow has young women fighting over him, and he becomes the source of the narrator's envy and hostility. The episodes are very comic, particularly when the narrator, fearing his extreme height bothers the other man, puts his head on the seam of his trousers to make himself seem small and crooked. The act is one of deference, but it is also bizarrely sexual, in that the narrator plays something of the traditional female role in a developing relationship.

Meanwhile, the narrator expects (hopes?) to be murdered: he expects the dagger to emerge, the "handle of which he is already holding in his pocket," and to feel it plunged into himself. His desire, apparently, is to murder, to pillage, but it is displaced to himself. Yet there is also the sense that in every encounter exists both a victim and an aggressor. Once again, we sense a shadowy sexuality, but also the hostility at being victimized. Victim and aggressor: they become major players and themes of the story.

The narrative contains many bizarre, surreal acts: early on an act of violence in which the narrator leaps on the back of his acquaintance and rides him, cruelly, like a horse. The acquaintance trots along, his neck crushed by the narrator's hands, his belly pummeled by his boots. When the acquaintance collapses, the narrator leaves. Another surreal scene introduces a fat man who is being transported across a river on a litter borne by four naked men. The entire passage is a shaped meditation, the verbalization of inner states of being. This is perhaps close to what we might call a "scenic stream," the joining of words and scene. The narrator views the fat man and then observes himself from both without and within; all the while Kafka hovers about. The narrator addressed the landscape: "It makes my reflection sway like suspension bridges in a furious current. It is beautiful and for this reason wants to be looked at."

The narrator accompanies the fat man on his journey, until the latter speaks, urging his listener not to rescue him as this is the water's and wind's revenge upon him. The section "Beginning of a Conversation with the Supplicant" contains the fat man's story of how he used to kneel in church every day awaiting the arrival of the girl he was in love with. While there, he notices a young man flinging his emaciated body on the ground, clutching his skull, and moaning loudly. The fat man detains the youth, who pleads innocent: "I don't know what you suspect me of, but I'm innocent." We have now the basic Kafka situation: A proliferation of messengers or voices who move us ever closer to the mystery of meaning, without getting us there; the presumption is guilt, even as one protests innocence or insists that guilt is not even the issue. Throughout this indirect discourse, related by the fat man, we note that the fat man begins to merge with the narrator of the outer story.

The narrative moves to the young man's or "Supplicant's Story." Textually and even thematically, these inserted segments are elements of the larger tale, in that they create a spatial reaching-out that will help supplement the narrator's association with the acquaintance of the opening scene. Some of this may not be quite apparent to the reader, but Kafka was such a consistent writer that his themes recur even when they appear to be discrete. Here we find the attempt of the Supplicant to explain his experience of a series of personal, comic disasters.

While speaking to a young lady, the Supplicant notices his "right thigh had slipped out of joint. The kneecap had also become a little loose." As he tries to disguise his physical condition, the girl is unimpressed by his words. He then decides to play the piano, although he does not know how, until two men pick up the piano bench and whisk him away. Out in the cold, he wonders what makes him behave as though he were real. As Kafka burrows within a series of narrators whose function is to relay information that derives, ultimately, from within the imagination of the Supplicant, "truth" is decentralized or deconstructed. Objects themselves, as in some cubist or abstract painting, are dissolved or made to vanish into distant perspectives. The method is as painterly as it is consciously literary.

The Supplicant detains a drunkard, addresses him as a noble gentleman, and then experiences a series of surrealistic images: great ladies, decorated trains at the "dissolute Court of France," against a background of Paris streets in which "eight elegant Siberian wolfhounds come prancing out and jump barking across the boulevard." In some curious cross-referencing of works, Kafka's story prefigures Apollinaire's great poem "Zone," which appeared in *Alcools* (1913). Although we do not wish to make more of Kafka's early work than it can sustain, it is nevertheless obvious he was working along a kind of sensibility reaching back to Mallarmé, ahead to Apollinaire. He had, of course, the poetry of Stefan George, in German, before him, and George, head of his own circle, had been part of the Mallarmé Tuesday evenings; he also translated Baudelaire's *Les Fleurs du mal* into German. In a sense, George carried over the entire French *symboliste* tradition back into German, not only Baudelaire and Mallarmé, but Rimbaud, Verlaine, and, of course, the "French Poe." His *Kreis* (circle) became quite famous, with the following figures moving in and out of it at one time or another: Rilke, Buber, Hofmannsthal, Stefan Zweig, Thomas Mann, Kandinsky, and several lesser figures in literature, music, and painting. Thus George becomes the link between Kafka and French traditions, and helps us to understand how both symbolistic and surrealistic Kafka's first efforts in literature were.*

This leads in "Description" to the section before the return to the narrator and his acquaintance, in which the fat man and the Supplicant merge, once again, with the narrator himself. Kafka is clearly experimenting with narrative means so that he can diminish the space between subjective voice and objective details — or, in this instance, between the spoken voice and the matter voiced. This is an attempt at stream of consciousness, before the stream, and abstraction, before ab-

---

*Brod tells us that Kafka gave him two volumes of Stefan George, one on each of his, Brod's, two birthdays (*Franz Kafka: A Biography*, 2d ed. [New York: Schocken, 1963], p. 64). Although George still lives in literary history, modern readers are possibly not aware of what an enormous force he was in twentieth-century poetry, both as a writer and as a charismatic figure.

straction. The next-to-final subdivision turns from the Supplicant to "Drowning of the Fat Man." The fat man suddenly disappears into the roar of the waterfall, and the narrator is both too small and too large to help. In his helplessness, the narrator is entangled in huge arms and "impossible legs." No matter what his size is, it is the wrong one. Kafka's considerable height, in this shadowy version here, is measured against his perception of himself as miniature and helpless; and in the process he discovers that disproportionate space and time characterize the disoriented inner world from which words emanate.

Finally, we return to the narrator and his acquaintance, having plunged through words and structure deep into a surrealistic dreamlike reality in which the narrator lives. The entire experience is, apparently, a manifestation of his state of mind, the description of a struggle raging within himself. After all the turmoil of his inner struggle, the narrator is brought back to conflicts within his acquaintance. The latter discusses the beauty of girls but is disturbed by his girl's laugh, which is "sly and senile," and we catch a glimpse of the turn-of-the-century view of woman as vampire, wily Eve, menacing Lulu. The narrator speaks of the lovely curve of girls' bones, their attractive muscles and smooth skin — sexually attractive but somehow dangerous and forbidding. He likes women, but fears woman. He tells his acquaintance that he at least is loved, even if he suffers from savage dreams. Then the acquaintance repeats his gravest apprehension, and the narrator agrees his friend may have to kill himself. To this, the acquaintance strikes the bench and says that he, the narrator, goes on living even though nobody loves him. "You don't achieve anything. You can't cope with the next moment. Yet you dare to talk to me like that, you brute. You're incapable of loving, only fear excites you. Just take a look at my chest." The physical disparity foreshadows all Kafka's later references to body shapes, with his own a living disaster.

"Description of a Struggle" has drawn little serious attention in the Kafka canon (relative to the more famous and sensational pieces), or it has been dismissed as a foreshadowing of later writing. Remarkable in itself, it is even more astonishing for having been written just after the turn of the century. For Kafka, still in his university days, had assimilated every sense of the Modern spirit: interior monologue blended with its scenic equivalent, so that objects are shaded or negated. Further, the story has a dramatic shape that makes it stageworthy in a stylistic production, as a kind of expressionistic-surrealistic dream, what we find in Kokoschka's *Murderer, Hope of Women* or Wedekind's *Lulu*, even Jarry's *Ubu*. This suggests that a good deal of Kafka has a dramatic potential, in the way Beckett's monologues and dialogues lend themselves to the stage.

In "Description of a Struggle" we see Kafka's extraordinary blending of subjective and objective. Its impetus does not depend on Freud, or on any other theoretician; it is, instead, a concomitant of several elements, of which human psychology is only one. Perhaps the key to such work is the recognition that physical characteristics are themselves abstractions, dependent on other, invisible qualities; that what is unseen (although not necessarily spiritual) is more important than the visible; that human development is so much more complicated than the nineteenth-century model suggested that only abstraction will suffice. All these points were being made in the larger culture, in all areas of knowledge, not solely in literary or other artistic work. Exploration and exploitation of exotic lands (political imperialism, for example) found their equivalent in the exploration of the most exotic of all phenomena, man's interiority. The real underground was, of course, sex.

But "Description" signifies more than Kafka's ability to assimilate strategies and modes of Modernism. It is an archetypal Kafka presentation of himself as both victim and assailant, as both debilitated figure and aggressor. It became part of that dualism so prevalent then (Jekyll and Hyde, Count Dracula, several H. G. Wells protagonists, and others) and which continued into the twentieth century, not only in fictional characters but in the writers themselves as they displayed both secret and public selves. The public writer of the nineteenth century was transformed into the tortured, underground, arcane writer of the twentieth, whose anguished person was revealed in an anguished prose or narrative, or in the conception of objects as skewed and distorted. Kafka reveals a good deal of himself here: performing as needed at school, attending various intellectually stimulating groups (especially at Berta Fanta's), and writing more or less secretly, for his own consumption, or else for Max Brod's.

What Kafka reveals more than anything else is his personal sense of physicality: the "deformed normal man" — that is, the individual who functions normally but is a physical freak. In the story, the narrator has Kafka's height — at almost six feet he was quite tall for a Czech Jew of that day* — his frail leanness and sunken chest, his awkward manner of holding himself with shorter, stockier people, his sense of vulnerability, both physically and emotionally. This marks the emergence of Kafka's great persona: the mask he would wear for the rest of his life in his fiction, and the form he takes on that necessitates transformation. We recognize from this single story that Kafka saw the transformation of self (physically and otherwise) as essential to survival — otherwise he would simply waste away in his emaciated, awkward body. Kafka's great discovery, even as a university student, was how close to extinc-

---

*The average Czech man was about five feet five inches to five feet six inches tall, but the average Slavic Jew was shorter; men of five feet or five feet one inch were quite common. Kafka's mother had the typical small size of the Czech Jewish woman.

tion the individual is, even when he fights back. The landscape of this
story is the landscape of a physicality that is always on the edge of losing the struggle. The goal is not to make one's way but to prolong survival.

In these acts of transformation, we also observe Kafka's form of anorexia. One part of severe change of self is the pursuit of rituals, with
Kafka a series of food rituals — the insistence on excessive mastication, vegetarianism, the horror of meat and blood, for example. But
even more than ritual was his truly clinical obsession with food, which
he used not for weight loss but as a form of control. Kafka knew this
recurring impulse to be "different," even inappropriate, but he continued acting on it because the obsession protected him from a conflict or
disaster he feared even more. As a secondary anorexic, he was anxious
about possibly contaminated food; he suffered loss of appetite (part of a
more general depression); he turned meals, or even the thought of
them, into rituals calculated to shift the focus from food itself to him.
In brief, in transforming himself, he made hunger secondary to ritual,
obsession, fear of shadowy disaster.

In "Description of a Struggle," the narrator, tormented by the idea
that "his long body" displeases his acquaintance, bends his back while
walking until his "hands touched my knees. But in order to prevent my
acquaintance from noticing my intentions I changed my position only
very gradually: and tried to divert attention from himself."[4] The acquaintance tells him to stand up, but, the narrator continues, "my face
[remained] close to the ground." His repositioning of his body with his
head on his acquaintance's trousers is, as we have noted, a form of
transformation, a precondition for an actual bodily change. The physical details of the narrator's body all point to an obsessional need to deny
his structure and to assume the pose of another. The story is saturated
with physical gestures, of touching, watching, planning physical forays
to kiss, kneel, defer to the other; stroking is commonplace between the
two men. At one point amidst tenderness and deference, the narrator
remarks that "this is the time for the murder." He observes that he expects the acquaintance to draw the dagger: "I won't scream, I'll just
stare at him as long as my eyes can stand it."[5]

This sudden move toward murder and acquiescence to it on the
part of the narrator appears to have come from nowhere in the story,
and seems to have no place here unless we see Kafka from a distance,
along the lines of his later career. It then begins to make sense as a Kafkan strategy, if not as an element that fits here. It has of course a homoerotic component: the two men are in a partially loving relationship,
and then suddenly one plunges a blade into the other, as part of what
the narrator fears and yet fantasizes as a way of drawing them more
closely together. He treats "the time for the murder" as a convention,
as something that had to occur.

But aside from the homoerotic and phallic dimension, we glimpse the typically Kafkan masochistic victim, fearing what he secretly wishes, fantasizing the unspeakable, and willing to accept it. The shadow element comes in Kafka's structuring of the situation: the aggressor, imagined or real, and the victim, who is trying to get the situation right, or to find some way of surviving in what may prove to be a losing struggle.

> If nobody comes, then nobody comes. I have done nobody any harm, nobody has done me any harm, but nobody will help me. A pack of nobodies. But it isn't quite like that. It's just that nobody helps me, otherwise a pack of nobodies would be nice, I would rather like (what do you think?) to go on an excursion with a pack of nobodies. . . . Just look at these nobodies pushing each other, all these arms stretched across or hooked into one another, these feet separated by tiny steps![6]

The "nobody" passage occurs right after the narrator has, inexplicably, jumped on his acquaintance's shoulders and ridden him like a horse. It suggests an area of survival based on the negation of survival, a form of litotes in which nobody replaces somebody, in which the negation of desire is expressed in order to create a neutral situation wherein the narrator can survive. The "nobody" repetition is almost a form of reverie, a suicidal reverie, a fantasy of negation that will, somehow, open possibilities that an affirmation could not. With this passage, the acquaintance is left behind; the narrative takes turns and curves around itself, without regard for continuity or even plausibility. The "nobody" passage somehow liberates the narrator for his own foray into adventure, whatever it may be.

A reverie state dominates the remainder of the story, surreal in its implications and yet a projection for Kafka of many of his fears, forms of anguish, and plans. In an indirect way, the story is about writing itself: the fantastic images a writer experiences and his difficult task of arranging them into a meaningful sequence, all the while aware of how resistant they are to any orderly arrangement. In this respect, the materials of the fantasy or reverie or daydream struggle against the formal nature of the story shape, and Kafka endeavors to present that struggle between inchoate experiences and the need to find patterns for them. *That he is incapable of finding that formal pattern as the material pushes everything out of shape becomes Kafka's major theme.*

That struggle of material against form is an emblem of the internal struggle in Kafka himself: full of ideas, fantasies, plans, possible directions, and yet lacking the shape or form to his life that could contain them. Accordingly, like the story, his life moves in several directions, all of them in a kind of blur or haze, or behind a scrim so that he is unable to grasp his identity. The story becomes the means by which he hopes to discover what he is. As a consequence, the story cannot be

clear even to him, and certainly not to the reader, because it is serving
not a narrative but a personal function. It is a means for self-discovery,
a personal confrontation or dialogue between writer and materials,
without any hope of reconciling them. The key for Kafka here is control
of his material, of the direction for his life, and of the way he can shape
the rambunctious material of his imagination.

His developing eating habits must also be likened to this obsessive
need for overall control. At some point in his childhood or adolescence,
Kafka felt he was excluded, either through material neglect, the domination of his father, or some sense of himself as inferior, unworthy, or
insignificant. From this feeling of exclusion, whether imposed from
without or dictated from within, he created a strategy, consciously or
not, to re-enter. He may even have felt unentitled to re-enter; he may
even have desired to be rejected, as a way of identifying what made him
in his own eyes unique. But another part of him also needed some form
of acceptance from family, society, or the larger environment. Yet even
this equation is not sufficiently complex for Kafka, since he felt superior to what he wanted to enter and be identified with.

Through a vegetarian diet, he could maintain this moral superiority. A vegetarian does not chew on flesh, does not deal in blood, is not
responsible for death. But for Kafka even vegetarianism was not sufficient, and he would on occasion eat meat anyway, usually to validate
his hatred of it. What he required was a regimen of eccentric food habits
that were at odds with the "normal" dinner table habits of his family.
From his *Letter to His Father*, we learn how tense mealtimes were, how
demanding Hermann Kafka became about the protocol of the dinner
table, even while he himself broke all the rules and acted piggishly (according to his observant son). Kafka's form of anorexia — not to lose
weight but to use food ritualistically as a form of superior statement —
was a way of bridging the gap between himself and his family, while at
the same time insisting on his uniqueness, his superiority, his sense of
rejection. Food became, in one respect, the way in which he could avoid
the deeper aspects of the estrangement. Through food, he employed a
strategy or means by which he could disguise his deeper needs, which
might lead to the kind of estrangement he could not face — linked to
sex, for example.

The food metaphor both for reflecting estrangement and expressing
the desire for bridging that estrangement was lifelong for Kafka. It became not only a response to his family but a way of life. Early on, he
discovered the twin polarities of control for himself: what he put into
his mouth, and what he did with a pen in his hand. Whatever his professional destiny as an insurance agent called for, mouth and hand determined his willed fate. It was a remarkable drama. We catch some of it
in "Description of a Struggle," with the narrator's impulse to change
his shape through crouching, negating his height, or disguising his
leanness.

Kafka's inner struggle suggests terrible conflicts. For the anorexic, the "resolution," such as it is, involves measures that shield one from the real sources of alienation and estrangement; and the struggle is always to maintain the shield while disguising the reality. This forced Kafka into role-playing, and one way to read his work is to be aware of that fact: that every aspect of his presentation of material, and not the least his *Letter to His Father*, was role-playing, in which whatever the real Kafka is or was could hide or be disguised. Denial of others may have been a source of strength, even a way of going on — but it could only take place at a tremendous cost because it negated whatever were the real causes of the denial. In Kafka's case, whatever mechanism enabled him to get his work done must be applauded, but even as we applaud, we must observe the huge human sacrifice.

However Kafka felt about "Description of a Struggle"* — except for two segments that appeared in *Hyperion* in 1909 the story remained unpublished during his lifetime — he had become a writer and a serious one at that. He had before him virtually his entire landscape, both external and internal. Through writing, at only a little past twenty-one, he had found almost immediately his unique form of control, the way in which he could observe others and perceive himself so as to maximize his peculiar sense of self. Of course, "Description" did not quite contain the breakthrough we find in Kafka's next longer work, "Wedding Preparations in the Country," some three years later. In that work, which appears to be the remaining fragments of a novel never completed, Kafka made an enormous discovery, an act of transformation that would become revelatory for him. Kafka here is still trying to discover new selves to replace his own, which he perceived as insufficient; Kafka the jackdaw becomes in the naming Raban the raven, and then, in a further transformation, the fantasy figure of the beetle with little legs and bulging body.

As his university career moved past its midpoint and his academic

---

*Kafka referred to "Description" in a letter to Brod (March 18, 1910): "The thing that pleases me most about the short story is that I have got rid of it" (*Letters to Friends*, p. 64). He meant that *Hyperion* for the March–April issue had published "Conversation with the Supplicant" and "Conversation with the Drunk." The story was written in two parallel versions, which Brod published in 1969, as *Beschreibung eines Kampfes: Die zwei Fassungen (Description of a Struggle: The Two Drafts)*. What is of particular interest is how Kafka streamlined his German prose for the *Hyperion* versions of these two "Conversations." As Klaus Wagenbach (in his biography of the young Kafka) points out, he simplified the later versions to the point where the originals became almost unrecognizable. Kafka's reason was apparently part of his strategy to avoid the overblown German of the Prague German writers, whose inflated prose — and his own early usage — was an attempt to compensate for the fact that Prague German, somewhat like Latin, had become a dead language. The whole question of the Prague influence on German syntax and vocabulary receives an excellent airing in Wagenbach's book, which, inexplicably, has not been translated into English. For an accessible part for the non-German reader, see Wagenbach's "Prague at the Turn of the Century," in *Reading Kafka: Prague, Politics, and the Fin de Siècle*, ed. Mark Anderson (New York: Schocken, 1989).

performance began to slide, he deeply feared failure and suffered from the kind of frantic or hysterical condition that dogged him for most of his life. His literary work, his attendance at the Hall with Brod and Příbram, and his university course work did not resolve themselves. Predictably, he began to unravel, so that, midsemester, in July 1905 he spent a month of rest and quiet at a sanatorium at Zuckmantel, in Moravian Silesia. The need for rest interrupted his semester and created a complete break in his routine, so that we must view it not as a debilitating collapse but in a sense as the way he could restore himself for the kind of life he planned to lead. He stayed for about four weeks, and apparently he took up with an older woman, whose name Brod pieced together as something like "Ritschi Grade" from her signature on a postcard. Kafka would himself much later, in 1916, refer to this "affair," which was renewed the following summer when he spent another month in Zuckmantel. He spoke of being on "intimate terms" with the older woman, but this does not necessarily mean sexual consummation — rather a close companionship or sharing of ideas and emotions. On the other hand, *intimate* could imply consummation, which would suggest that as long as Kafka's women were exogamous — Czech shopgirls or an older woman — he was sexually capable. This almost month-long interlude at Zuckmantel of course interrupted his studies and required, upon his return in the late summer of 1905, a reimmersion in what he was always trying to escape.

Furthermore, he was up against an extremely important examination, so important for his professional future it was very possibly the imminence of this ordeal that sent him spinning into near hysteria and the need for relief from the pressure. What he faced was worse than a written examination, for it was an oral, the so-called *Rigorosa*, as ominous as the Latin word itself. It was required for the doctoral degree, which in Europe was not a Ph.D. but a university degree. As it turned out, his apprehension was well founded, for on November 7, 1905, he received only three of four votes on the *Rigorosum* II; and on March 6, 1906, only three of five votes on the *Rigorosum* III. Brod apparently helped him considerably, since for Kafka's friend the tests were approached with the usual determination and inner sense of success.* Kafka probably felt sufficiently reinforced by these passing grades, however slim, to take the *Rigorosum* I on June 13, 1906, and he passed all five of the five graders.†

---

*Writing to Brod, in a letter postmarked March 16, Kafka said, "There's no doubt you saved me three months of my life for some other purpose than learning finance. Only your notes saved me, for thanks to them I shone to M. as his own reflection, even one with an interesting Austrian hue; and in spite of the fact that he was still wrapped up in the masses of stuff he has lectured on this semester, and I had only your small slips of paper in my memory" (*Letters to Friends*, p. 20).
†The irregular numbering of the *Rigorosa*, II, III, I, went back to medieval practice.

At this point, approaching twenty-three, Kafka presented a figure of many contradictions. While he hated his own body and saw it as skeletal and unappetizing, he cut a figure of considerable charm and courtesy in the presence of others. Oskar Baum, who was blind in one eye from childhood and lost the other in a street fight when he was eleven, first met Kafka in the fall of 1904. After commenting that Kafka knew he was in the presence of a blind man, Baum (in Brod's transcription) continued,

> As Brod was introducing him, he bowed silently to me. It was, you might say, a senseless formality in my case, since I couldn't see it. His hair, which was smoothed down, touched my forehead for a moment as he bowed, probably because the bow that I made at the same time was a little too violent. I was moved in a way that for the moment I could see no clear reason for. Here was one of the first people in the world who had made it clear that my deficiency was something that concerned nobody but myself — not by making allowances or being considerate, not by the faintest change in his bearing. That was what he was like. He stood so far from the accepted utility formulas that he affected one in this way. His severe cool reserve [what nearly everyone misunderstood as lack of emotion or passion] was so superior in depth of humanity to the ordinary run of kindness — which I otherwise recognize when I am first introduced to people in a pointless increase in warmth of words, or tone of voice, or shake of the hand.[7]

Baum goes on to say that Kafka somehow seemed integrated, despite the impression he might give of disconnectedness:

> This co-ordination of every involuntary movement, of each everyday word with his whole personal outlook on life made his behavior, his outward appearance, unusually full of life, despite the abstract battles that continuously dominated his mind. When he read aloud — and that was his particular passion — the emphasis on each separate word was completely subordinated, although every syllable was perfectly distinct — with his tongue sometimes working at a speed which almost made one giddy — to a musical breadth of phrasing, with enormously long breaths, and mightily swelling crescendos of the dynamic levels — just as you find them in his prose.

Baum's comments about the meeting late in 1904 create a picture of Kafka somewhat at odds with the way he presented himself in his earliest fiction and in his few extant letters from this period. Baum's remarks, however, reinforce our sense of his inner divisions: what he was beginning to present in his deepest reaches through his fiction; the mask he put on for his friends, Brod, Baum, and others; the way he presented himself to his family, bowing his head and deferring to what was slowly driving him mad; and finally, his university self — his moving along on a degree he appears to have detested and feared. In these respects, he was a characteristic twentieth-century figure, taking on selves, discarding them, making up faces to present to others, hiding himself as much as he could, separating surface from subsurface.

From regular meetings, established for friends to read from their works, Brod would seem to know Kafka best. They also attended the Hall lectures by, among others, Gustav Meyrinck and Hugo Salus; or themselves discussed Grillparzer, Nietzsche, and Heine. As a consequence, Brod cast Kafka as Garta in his novel *Zauberreich* (*Magic Kingdom*, also translated as *The Kingdom of Love*), as follows:

> What he does is read to you over and over again this or that passage from his favorite authors in his rapid, unemotional voice that, at the same time, creates a sense of rhythm and climax, with a throbbing chant in the background, with his eyes flashing, surrendering himself utterly to joy in human greatness. . . . Anything forced, in any artistic expression, he always thrusts as far away from him as possible, unless it be that as an effort it is at least genuine, and the writer cannot avoid it, in which case it admittedly betrays his occasional weaknesses and demands only sympathy with what his other deeds show him capable of.[8]

As part of this encomium, Brod perceived Kafka as unified in his mind and expression, so that there was never a gap. He "never spoke a meaningless word. Everything that came from him came in a way that became less and less forced as the years went on." All derived from his special way of looking at things: "patient, life-loving, ironically considerate towards the follies of the world, and therefore full of sad humor, but never forgetful of the real kernel." Brod adds that at Berta Fanta's, Kafka spoke little, but by virtue of his personality what he did say carried with it remarkable authority, so much was it a part of the man. "There was no need of his works [no one as yet knew he was writing], the man produced his own effect himself, and despite all the shyness of his behavior, he was always quickly recognized by men of worth as someone out of the ordinary." In fact, at all periods of his life "women felt themselves drawn to Franz — he himself doubted he had this effect, but the fact cannot be disputed."[9]

Brod's praise is well taken, but it reveals only a part of the whole, for however close he was to Kafka during their adult and mature years, Brod missed Kafka's role-playing. The social side Kafka presented was very much at odds with the Kafka of his letters, or the Kafka of his diaries, started a few years later. In his remarks, Brod picked up only one side of Kafka, not the totality of sides that reflected much of the twentieth century. Those piercing eyes Kafka presented to his photographers suggest his ability to see what others missed. Kafka was in his early twenties when, reinforced by his reading, he could describe a kind of journey very different from anything Brod could comprehend or accept. And yet Brod, to his everlasting credit, saw genius in Kafka as soon as he read excerpts from his work, saw the differences between his friend and other members of their discussion circles. But finally what he saw in the writing and what he saw in the person did not fit together, and so he, perhaps unknowingly, blurred Kafka, describing what he saw in the man as distinct from what was implicit in the work.*

In the summer of 1905, Kafka spent one month in Zuckmantel and then went with his three sisters, at the end of August, to Strakonitz, to stay with an aunt. Strakonitz was directly south of Prague, on the river Wotawa, in a relatively isolated area, whose nearest large town was Budweis (now České Budějovice). He needed the break, spending the time in Zuckmantel in a sanatorium (a kind of rest home or pension, not what later were the sanatoriums for tubercular patients). The departure from school was a way in which he could recharge himself for the coming ordeals of law school work. As he told Brod (on October 21) when he returned, he was "almost pleased to be studying at last." He even begs off going to the café that week because relaxation might impair his studying for the next day.

By November 7 he was past his first hurdle on his examinations and was now preparing himself for the second, on March 16. This test, along with the final one on June 13, 1906, made up a strange sequence of three caught between his efforts at literary work. The bifurcated life Kafka had marked out for himself could not have been more split than it was during this 1905–6 university span. His support here was not family, but Brod, not only for the notes he supplied but for simply being "there." At Kafka's June 13 examination, one of the five examiners was Alfred Weber, brother of the more famous Max Weber, the sociologist; and it was Alfred Weber who gave Kafka his doctor of law degree on June 18, following the examination.

With his degree, he had come through, although as he later wrote his father he had expected to fail at every stage. In actuality, he had become stronger at the end and apparently passed the *Rigorosum* I with ease. His performance is all the more praiseworthy since during the three months after his second examination, in March, he had been working in the law office of Dr. Richard Löwy (unrelated to Kafka's maternal side). Kafka drafted legal documents, the usual kind of monotonous work a beginning lawyer can expect to find.

In those months, he found himself lacking time for any outside activities. Furthermore, he faced the move of Hermann Kafka's business from Zeltnergasse 12 to the Kinsky Palace on Altstädter Ring, a loca-

---

*Brod also was not beyond distortion. "Wedding Preparations" contains a passage that Kafka later worked into an independent sketch and which Brod published in the volume *Description of a Struggle* as "Give It Up!" It appears in the *Complete Stories* under that title. Yet Kafka had himself left the page simply titled "A Commentary," which Brod altered, adding the exclamation point. It is only a paragraph that begins "It was very early in the morning," and which ends with a policeman telling the narrator to "Give it up, give it up," when the narrator asks the way to the train station. Brod's change, while not enormous, adds drama and urgency to what is, for Kafka, an ordinary event.

tion where Kafka had once attended school. Forced to combine office work with preparation for his final examination, which one of his professors suddenly moved forward, he did no literary work. Having passed well, he continued to work in Löwy's office, spending six months there in all: a dead end, deadening kind of position Kafka saw as stretching into the future for anyone who received a law degree. The pressure took its usual toll, and in July he left again for Zuckmantel, there to re-encounter the older woman he had mentioned the previous summer. It is speculative but perhaps fair to say this episode became the impetus for "Wedding Preparations," which Kafka wrote a year later, although it is doubtful Kafka himself contemplated marriage with her or anyone else at this unsettled time.

He remained at the sanatorium until September 1906 and was, in a sense, forced to rethink his entire position. True, he had received his doctor of law degree, but he did not know what he wanted to do with it. He had saved a little money — he mentions having a secret bank account, a sign of his independence from his parents, with whom he still lived and on whose income he depended — yet he was many years away from any kind of financial independence. The major decision at hand was connected to the kind of work he wanted to do, or could obtain, and since he really wanted no particular work, he was backed into a corner of his own creating. If he tried to find employment with the state (unlikely because of his own attitudes and the fact of his Jewishness), he would need to donate his services, unpaid, for the year; and even if, as it turned out, he chose not to work for the state, he could not expect wages as an apprentice lawyer, also for a year or more. There was, then, despite his small savings account, little opportunity for independence, although he was now, in 1906, twenty-three years old.

No matter what his final choice, he needed a work permit for the state, a document from the police attesting to his good conduct (the *Wohlverhaltungszeugnis*, or certificate of good behavior). Such a police form put him on record as having good conduct, and being single and Jewish — the racial identification was useful when the state wanted to reject candidates. On September 19, with the police seal of approval that there were "no grounds for objection," Kafka passed. He was, in theory, hirable, and did not belong to any objectionable clubs or groups that were deemed antistate or antiempire, any anarchist organization, for example.

The question of anarchism is raised because Gustav Janouch, in his 1951 book on Kafka, *Conversations with Kafka*, refers to the possibility of his friend trafficking with members of the Klub Mladých (Club of Youth), one of whom was the poet Michal Mareš. Mareš in 1946, twenty-two years after Kafka's death, reported that Kafka was involved in anarchist activities, not only as an onlooker but as a participant in demonstrations, disruptions, and other public shows. In one such demonstration, when Mareš was arrested in 1909 — Kafka was already employed at the Workers' Accident Insurance Institute in Prague — Kafka allegedly bailed Mareš out at the police station. Janouch was aware of the story well before Mareš published it, of course, and writes of the time when Kafka saw Janouch carrying a little book of poems by Mareš and then exchanged some words on anarchism with him. According to Janouch, Kafka said he knew Mareš, a "fierce anarchist" whom they endured as a curiosity in *Prager Tagblatt*; then he went on to add that it was hard to take anarchists seriously. Janouch quoted Kafka as saying, "These people, who call themselves anarchists, are so nice and friendly, that one has to believe every word they say. At the same time — and by reason of the same qualities — one cannot believe that they are really such world destroyers as they claim."[10]

From this statement, Janouch understood that his friend knew anarchists personally, and Kafka allegedly responded, "A little. They are very nice, jolly people." According to Janouch, Kafka then recalled the street fights in Prague in the early 1890s, which somehow in his memory, or in Janouch's reporting, became intermixed with anarchist activities. Kafka said he studied the murderer and anarchist Ravachol's life, as well as the lives of Godwin, Proudhon, Stirner, Bakunin, Kropotkin, and Tolstoy. Then he specifically says he took part, in 1910, in the meetings of the anarchist Club of Youth, which, disguised as a mandolin club, met in the inn Zum Kanonenkreuz (at the Cannon Cross) in Karolinenthal. Zum Kanonenkreuz was indeed a well-known meeting place for anarchists — well known not only to them but also to the police. According to this story, Brod accompanied Kafka to meetings and, in fact, captured its atmosphere in his novel, *Stefan Rott, or the Year of Decision* (*Stefan Rott oder das Jahr des Entscheidung*), where he mentions Michal Mareš.

What, then, do we have, since Janouch is often such an unreliable reporter? Very possibly, Kafka's initial clearance by the police with "no grounds for objection" preceded any anarchist activity. But there is the point that in subsequent years Kafka's file was clear of adverse judgments, and any anarchist activity would have been evidence against him. The fear of anarchism among the various departments of the empire was stronger than the fear of communist infiltration in the 1950s in the United States. Anarchist assassinations, bombs, and other forms of insurrection, lethal as well as comedic, were plentiful, and in many instances quite successful at eliminating particularly odious officials or administrators of the government. How, then, did Kafka slip through their net of informers and others eager to curry favor with the government? Or is anarchism so alien to Kafka's temperament we must dismiss the entire episode, if it ever did in fact exist, as part of a legend begun by Mareš and continued by the overeager Janouch? Who would believe in Kafka as a fellow-traveling anarchist?[11]

Subsequent police clearances, after the first when he had not yet become interested or involved in anarchism, could be explained by the fact of his low profile in such circles, his failure to speak up or be counted. There is also the real possibility that while Kafka's sympathies were with the anarchists, he met with or even saw them infrequently, that his involvement, as related by Mareš and repeated by Janouch, was social — Mareš lived nearby, as we know. These social occasions might have become blown up in Mareš's mind when he wrote about Kafka in 1946, at a time when Kafka had become famous and to have known him intimately bestowed credit on oneself. In the same way, Janouch would repeat Kafka's own statements, but puffed up. A third possibility is that Kafka's sympathies with anarchy were interpreted as active participation. Kafka's early socialism, for example, could, with some embroidery, be taken to mean he believed in international upheaval or even revolution.

This latter point is worth examining, inasmuch as several of Kafka's later ideas, set down as parables and paradoxes, have within them the kernel of anarchy, disruption, and mockery of existing order, especially of the emperor and the empire. This is not to suggest Kafka was a supporter of assassinations and bombings, or of any violence; but the cast of his mind, with its dislike of authority, paternal or otherwise, can be viewed as anarchistic. This would help explain Mareš's assumption that Kafka was one of them and Janouch's transcription of Kafka's words about anarchists — suspect anyway for Janouch's claim that they were repeated verbatim almost thirty years after his friend's death.

If we take one late piece, "The Animal in the Synagogue" (written around 1920),[12] we can observe how Kafka's outlook embraced the thin line between order and disorder. While the Jews in the synagogue go about their ordinary business, a marten living there suspects something is going to happen. Avoiding the men, the animal hangs around the women's section, and the women fear it, although in time they become more or less accustomed to its presence. But it is like some silent, meek Fury, insistent on itself, saying nothing, simply waiting, sinking in. A kind of Cassandra, it waits for the collision of the Jewish experience with something else, so that it can explode. Withal, the congregation is getting ever smaller "in this little town of ours in the mountains," and if the marten waits long enough it will have the place to itself — once the synagogue no longer functions and turns into a granary or something comparable. Little by little, the synagogue ceases to function (like the empire? the state? the government in Vienna?), even as the marten sits there as a witness to something the worshippers are unconscious of. At the end of the short piece, someone sets out to catch the marten, but we know the effort fails, and the story trails off in ellipses. It remains there, like a dybbuk. Along the way, Kafka writes, "And yet there is this terror. Is it the memory of times long past or the premonition of times to come? Does this old animal perhaps know more than the three generations of those who are gathered together in the synagogue?"[13]

This is a visionary piece, but also one that subsumes an anarchic view of the world. For the marten, whatever its specific designation, is an emblem of disruption, whereas the synagogue represents Kafka's sense of the frail ordered world. Kafka's vision here is so apt, so penetrating, that he appears clairvoyant. For encapsulated in this brief fiction is the fate of the Jews in the twentieth century: victims of what was perhaps the greatest stretch of anarchy any civilization has known. Disorder exists side by side with order, with the implication that disorder, in the marten, will eventually triumph, or make order impossible to maintain.

We might further speculate that Kafka's emotional or psychological response to his developing illness (even when it was undetectable medically) colored his attitude toward himself, his family, friends, work, and aspects of everyday living.[14] That "marten in the synagogue" which we see as anarchic could be the illness itself, a disruptive force eating away at both physical and mental health and leading to a visionary sense of destruction for all. In an October 1, 1907, physical examination, a light congestion in the upper lobe of the lung was detected but dismissed as negligible, the result of "rachitic deformation." Kafka's illness, however disguised within the confines of his lungs, we can speculate, was already working to transform him emotionally. Further, we do know of his lifelong hypochondria, which was connected to his digestion, his headaches, his fastidiousness about food. This hypochondria, which gradually became a major factor in his life and eventually combined with actual physical illness when his tuberculosis began to develop, was part of an entire personality, part of an acute sensitivity and surely linked to episodic depression. It was this episodic depression, combined with feelings of failure, and the accompanying hypochondria, that signaled the end of things, or else the potential for disruption in everything other people might take for granted. It was a force for anarchy.

Part of Kafka's hypochondria was connected to his lability or mood swings; it was not a psychosis but a deep neurosis that helped reinforce his intellectual awareness of disorder. His depression was of the kind that had few external causes. Until he fell ill, we can say he responded to an "inner illness," which may have been his initial reaction to the onset of a still undetectable disease. Of course, Kafka cultivated his hypochondria and depression for the marginality they afforded him, but that marginality also helped feed the very depression and hypochondria. Within that cycle of what he was responding to and what he was consciously choosing for himself, he was never distant from feelings of disorder and the end of things, and this difference from others helped give him his visionary quality.

In 1907 Kafka needed a physical examination for his position with an Italian insurance company, the Assicurazioni Generali, with offices in Prague, in the Wenzelsplatz, and in Trieste, where he hoped to be transferred. He was considered a healthy man by Dr. Wilhelm Pollak, who examined him, although his bodily frame should have alerted the doctor to Kafka's potential for consumption. At 61 kilograms, or 133 pounds, he was unusually slender for someone of 1.82 meters in height, which is slightly under six feet tall. But further than this slenderness was his bodily structure, a concave chest, the so-called tubercular chest, a source of much embarrassment to him when he had to undress to swim, an activity he particularly enjoyed and which he often indulged in only when everyone else had left the area. His shame at his body was well taken, for it involved not only slenderness but little musculature, with undeveloped arms and legs. His already considerable height, for the time and for a Jew, was even greater: he appeared a wraith, a specter, a phantom of sorts.

But before this physical examination, in October 1907, Kafka completed his year at the district and criminal court, which had begun the previous year.[15] Kafka felt little benefit from this work — he told Brod it was futility itself — but it did thrust him into the world of courts and procedures which would affect his future development as a writer. There has been some misunderstanding among commentators, with most agreeing that Kafka's outlook and even material derived from his work in the courts and then in insurance companies. There is little doubt that his knowledge of bureaucracies, and his hatred of them, were the result of his many years of work and his efforts to deal with administrative foul-ups and stupid personnel. But other factors must be considered — the main one being that Kafka had found his ideas and direction well before he entered the bureaucracy. For someone like him, the details of his work may have proved valuable, but his overresponse to bureaucracy was preconditioned by his already negative response to authority, and that response had been nourished by his relationship to Hermann Kafka. Kafka knew what bureaucracy was well before he had any direct knowledge of it; what it did was provide data he could use, as well as direct experience. Yet even without Hermann, there was the Dual Monarchy, with its clumsy administrative arrangements. The empire, as we have noted, while located in Vienna, had to administer vast lands that stretched away from it in every direction. This was bureaucracy at its worst, and Kafka had only to observe how Franz Josef attempted to consolidate power in Vienna even as it slipped farther and farther away in Prague and Budapest, to mention only two centers of rebellion. Kafka observed how a central court, the imperial one, was dissipating its energies, even as it attempted to unify its holdings: what better definition of bureaucracy and its incapacities than that? Well before he encountered the red tape that drove him nearly crazy with futility, he had encountered two levels of bureaucracy, at home and in the empire.

In early 1907, while in the midst of his "free year" in the courts, Kafka was caught in an amusing episode with Max Brod, attesting to Brod's extravagant belief in his friend's literary distinction. In a book review in *Die Gegenwart* (*The Present*), a Berlin monthly, Brod included Kafka and praised his style, combining him with three well-known and published writers, Heinrich Mann, Frank Wedekind, and Gustav Meyrinck. What makes this amusing is that Kafka, as far as Brod knew, had not published anything, although Brod may have felt that Kafka in 1906 entered a story pseudonymously in *Zeit*, a Viennese newspaper. But Brod had not read it, and no such story has turned up. Thus, the praise for Kafka's style in the *Die Gegenwart* article was Brod's way of encouraging his friend to continue to write and eventually to publish.

Kafka wrote Brod at length, both amused and slightly annoyed, himself considering the group of names like "a curled up hedgehog": that strange group of Meyrinck, the author of *The Golem*, Mann, a socially based writer, and Wedekind, author of the Lulu plays. "A pity, though — I know you did not mean it that way — that it will now become an indecent act for me to publish something later, for that would blast the delicacy of this first public appearance. And I would never achieve an effect equal to the one assigned me in your sentence." But then Kafka sees the amusing side and says he is interested in "establishing the radius of my present fame, since I am a good child and a lover of geography,"[16] and he fantasizes about the people he will reach. Brod's prodding apparently made some difference because in the spring or thereabouts of this year Kafka wrote the fragments of "Wedding Preparations in the Country," what began as a novel and ended as one long and one much shorter manuscript segment.

The breakthrough in "Wedding Preparations" is momentous. Kafka had foreseen in the three years between that work and the earlier "Description of a Struggle" that his physical and emotional stress had to lead away from human forms, into reshapings, and that such reshapings had to be on the lower end of the evolutionary scale — not into tigers or lions, but into smaller forms, like an insect, then later domestic animals. As Eduard Raban, a kind of pre-Prufrock figure, hesitates about journeying into the country, he fantasizes about himself: "As I lie in bed I assume the shape of a big beetle, a stag beetle or a cockchafer, I think." He continues: "The form of a large beetle, yes. Then I would pretend it was a matter of hibernating, and I would press my little legs to my bulging body. And I would whisper a few words, instruction to my sad body, which stands close beside me, bent."[17] Kafka here is still trying to discover new selves to replace his own, which he perceived as insufficient. Raban fantasizes assuming the beetle's shape without actually becoming it. Gregor Samsa, in 1912, will complete the transformation. For Raban, the transformation is still a matter of the mind; for Gregor, it is the final process, the only way he can control his role in the Samsa family.

At the beginning of "Wedding Preparations," Raban is going through a typical Kafka panic attack when confronted with a journey or with a new experience.

> The journey will make me ill. I know that quite well. My room won't be comfortable enough, it can't be otherwise in the country. And we're hardly in the first half of June, the air in the country is often still very cool. Of course, I've taken precautions in my clothing, but I shall have to join with people who go for walks late in the evening. . . . That is where I'm sure to catch cold. On the other hand, I shall make but little showing in conversation.[18]

Raban's panic or near hysteria reflects Kafka's own ambivalence about moving to escape his parents' apartment. Desperate to leave, yet knowing that leaving would not resolve his problem of escape, he somehow required that suffocating, hothouse, enclosed condition of the apartment, in which he had an inner room where all the noise seemed to gather. Yet his anxieties extend to virtually every aspect of his life. A good part could well be sexual anxiety, since in the story Raban is heading for the country to visit his fiancée, who is described in terms that recall the "older woman" with whom Kafka had "intimate relations" in the summers of 1905 and 1906 at Zuckmantel.

The Kafka we find in these fragments is a Prufrockian figure, that prototypical modern man caught in doubt, uncertainty, and personal anguish:

> But they're expecting me in the country. . . . Won't they be wondering about me by this time? . . . So they'll end up by imagining that even my appearance is quite different. They may be thinking that I burst forward when I address a person, yet that isn't my way at all, or that I embrace people when I arrive, and that's something I don't do either. I shall make them angry if I try to pacify them. Oh, if I could only make them thoroughly angry in the attempt to pacify them.[19]

Prufrock's "Do I dare?" cannot be far behind.

But beyond the personal dimension to the story, which is not to be discounted, is the shaping of the material in Modernist fashion. More than anything else, Kafka is indebted to Modernist narrative; for most of the story is an interior monologue, in which Eduard Raban fantasizes, contemplates, meditates, and doubts. His subject is himself, not the upcoming wedding, not his fiancée, not even the stay in the country, but his perception of what such a venture means in terms of the journey there. Caught up in the mechanics of the trip, not the destination, he is entrapped by his own speculations and his own predictions of personal failure. Insofar as we can judge from such fragments, the story is narcissistic in its insistence on reflections of Raban — not on the person, but on the various personae he can conjure up for himself and thus hide behind. The story is all disguises and defenses, offerings that are really withdrawals.

Kafka could hide and peek through Raban and the story's narrative shaping; the sides of him revealed in the story were apparently not disclosed to Brod or his other friends, surely not to his family — though in these reshapings, Kafka is clearly still feeling his way, since "Wedding Preparations," like the earlier "Description of a Struggle," is inchoate and inconclusive, regardless of how much it reveals. Almost the only one, in fact, who became privy to this dimension of Kafka was his fiancée, from 1912 on, Felice Bauer, to whom he poured out what and who he was in a quarter of a million words in letters intended to control her without the need to possess her. Much later in his life, when he was suffering from tuberculosis, he revealed to Brod how he feared all travel and turned his fear of a journey to Georgenthal into a virtual saga of defeat: "It is a fear of change, a fear of attracting the attention of the gods by what is a major act for a person of my sort."

In "Wedding Preparations," Raban's trip is not an enjoyable occasion, not even a neutral event, but a source of great displeasure and pain. Furthermore, the story is a sequence of enclosures, from the temporal limitations of a fortnight's journey to the boxed-in spaces of endless carriages and trains. The story is, in this respect, about a man's attempt to escape his shell, a body caught in a chrysalis, attempting to break through. "I don't even need to go to the country myself, it isn't necessary. I'll send my clothed body," Raban meditates, speaking to no one but himself. "If it [his body] staggers out of the door of my room, the staggering will indicate not fear but its nothingness. Nor is it a sign of excitement if it stumbles on the stairs, if it travels into the country, sobbing as it goes, and there eats its supper in tears."[20] As his body travels, he will continue to lie in his bed and then assume the shape of a big beetle.

What significance could Brod have attached to a friend who writes that he'll "send my clothed body," so that his staggering body indicates not fear "but its nothingness." Kafka here is on the edge of a great discovery about himself, something intrinsic to nearly every dimension of Modernism — how close madness or forms of disorder are to our social disguises and social poses; how the unconscious pokes through to turn our seeming order into its opposite.

The intensity of Raban's anxiety must of course be keyed in to his desire not to be engaged, not to see his fiancée, and, ultimately, not to marry. The story, in one sense, is a foreshadowing of Kafka's courtship of Felice Bauer: the social desire to marry, but the intense personal wish not to be married, not to be tied to any woman, with her expectations, desires, individual needs. The great correspondence Kafka carried on with Felice is really one of his "novels," the only one he completed, and it must be seen as continuous with the interior monologue of "Wedding Preparations," written five years earlier. *Kafka becomes the master of anticipatory dread.* He foresees problems overwhelming any relationship, and he senses that sexual expectation, among other matters, will drive him to impotence. What may be desirable in the mind becomes undesirable as the mental image takes on female embodiment. He always recognized that what was socially correct was entirely wrong for him. Raban must live through this nightmare of heading into the very thing he wants to delay or postpone.

The story fragments, then, are the opposite of what they seem: not a journey, but an antijourney, the way in which the mind can negate the journey before it even begins. "Wedding Preparations" becomes a story of inaction, what Kafka would fashion more fully in his longer fictions. But for Kafka, stasis does not mean loss of intensity. As with Proust, Kafka could concentrate passion in the negation of movement or activity; he could stop time while the interior world worked through its doubts and uncertainties. Even this early, in 1907–8, he had begun to master a Modernist mode that would become uniquely his. It was no less than to transform spatial ideas into static inactivity, to change temporal modes into a stoppage of time, and to make external events secondary to the internal mechanism of the individual protagonist.

In the train carriage, Raban concentrates so on details of his environment that he loses contact with his destination. The trip becomes for him not the means by which he will see his fiancée, but the vehicle that brings him into contact with the backs of people's heads, the upturned faces of passengers on the opposite seat, the smell and curl of smoke from pipes and cigars, the momentary movement of individuals as they change places or exchange seats, the transfer of luggage from one seat to another, the ways in which suitcases are straightened out or left askew, a contemplation of the kinds of people who travel, merchants and commercial travelers, others who remain unidentified. He listens in on others' conversations but hears only the hum not the substance, which, he says, he would not understand anyway, since one would need preparation to comprehend their questions and answers. He is struck by the villages the train approaches and then rushes past, how they vanish into the depths of the country. He tries to penetrate into the unfathomable depths of people's lives, how life goes on, how we are shaped. Ultimately, all thoughts lead toward death, or at least toward unknowns: "Raban was now pleased that the train was going so fast, for he would not have wanted to stay in the last place. When it is dark there, when one knows no one there, when it is such a long way home. But then it must be terrible there by day. And is it different at the next station or at the previous ones or at the later ones or at the village I am going to?"[21] The rush to "get there" is apparently a rush to-ward finality, perhaps death, more likely toward the mystery at the heart of every trip.

Yet for Raban, and we can assume for Kafka, there is some comfort in this mad rush, even as there is terrible uncertainty. The comfort comes from the details themselves and from the awareness that the vil-lage he is going to has no more reality than any of the places he has left behind. When Raban enters the station, at the village of his destination, he is like K. in *The Castle*, trying to arrive and yet forewarned by the desolation of the place that having gotten there is no solution to the un-certainties he feels. The entire piece lies on the edge, not within actual-ity, not quite outside of it. It is a terrain Kafka was to make uniquely his own: that intermediate or indeterminate location that one cannot reach.

"Wedding Preparations" was, in one respect, a trying-out for Kafka of marriage itself, and before that, of courtship and engagement, with all the attendant complications of a drawn-out sexual relationship. It is only in these terms that we can assess the story, since in its fragmen-tary form it offers little of aesthetic appeal. Like "Description of a Struggle" it is apprentice work, desperately significant in personal terms, but less important as a final expression of art. When Raban ar-rives at the village and thinks of Betty, he cannot even be certain she has ever spoken of her fiancé; and the esteem or lack of it in which she is held there will determine how he is received. "But of course," Raban thinks, "he knew neither what people felt about her nor what she had told them about him, and so everything was all the more disagreeable and difficult." He worries about the rain and getting through the mud; he worries about dying of homesickness, and eating some "dreadfully fat dish — they don't know I have a weak stomach."[22] He even worries about the light from the lamp, that he may not be able to read a news-paper, itself unfamiliar. His entire routine has been wrenched apart by this trip and the engagement; and he yearns to return to his regular life, however exhausted he was from his feverish work at the office. A shad-owy Gregor Samsa floats through his plaints.

It seems here that Kafka is using interior monologue in order to carry on a dialogue with himself. Early in the fragments, Kafka recog-nized he was becoming too subjective and tried to explain his position by way of pronoun use. After deploying *one* all along — "one" does this, "one" does that — he says that "so long as you can say 'one' in-stead of 'I,' there's nothing in it and one can easily tell the story; but as soon as you admit to yourself that it is you yourself, you feel as though transfixed and are horrified."[23] He does not really solve the problem, for the narrative moves through several contortions, indicating that this early in his writing career he had not resolved the question of narrative voice. The Kafka "voice" moves back and forth between first *one* and *he,* or Raban; then between *he* and *I.* Once again, as with "Description of a Struggle," this story, or novel fragment, is concerned with writing itself. We are struck repeatedly by Kafka's mechanics of telling, his difficulty in finding the right means of propelling the story forward. Much of the interrupted or discontinuous sense of narrative comes from his uncertainty of voice or of correct pronoun; and the result, often, is more of lines and planes and angles associated with abstract painting than with the process of writing:

> Then it seemed to Raban that he would get through the long bad time of the next fortnight, too. For it was only a fortnight, that was to say, a limited period, and even if the annoyances grew ever greater, still the time during which one had to endure them would be growing shorter and shorter. Thus, undoubtedly courage would increase. "All the people who try to torment me, and who have now occupied the entire space around me, will quite gradually be thrust back by the beneficent passage of these days, without my having to help them even in the very least."[24]

In this characteristic passage, we have three modulations of voice. The first sentence is clearly the author's voice. But the second sentence has shifted slightly and become part of Raban's thoughts, a mutation between author speaking and character intruding with his own point of view. With the material in quotation marks, we experience direct access into Raban's mind. As we read the passage, we arrive by stages ever deeper into Raban, a journey itself of sorts, starting with third person narrative, then moving into a position halfway between *he* and *I,* followed by a muffled *I,* which is the interior monologue itself.

What is compelling about this is that Kafka has assimilated, however shakily as yet, the significance of narrative voice, the cornerstone of Modernist innovation. Only a few Modernists would actually use interior monologue, free association, or stream of consciousness, but the method hovered over many others, and Kafka was already moving toward his first interior monologue in 1907–8. If he was going to write something unique, he needed his own methods, not those that had traditionally proved effective. By his midtwenties, he was experimenting with how to tell what he had to tell, and very possibly the experimental narrative quality of "Wedding Preparations" was sufficient for him as far as it went, and he did not need the full novel he had originally planned to write. On the other hand, he might have been caught in the indecision he described to Brod (September 22, 1907): "I make decisions from moment to moment, like a boxer, without doing any boxing."* Overall, Kafka was clearly absorbing what was pressing in from

---

*These comments have been based on the first manuscript, one of the two fragmentary pieces. The second manuscript or fragment is a parallel document, beginning with Raban's indecisive start of his journey. It is unclear from this second document, because of its inferiority to the first, what Kafka had in mind; also, the narrative is much more traditional, with little of the introspection we find in the first.

Paris, Vienna, Berlin, Munich, and other centers of Modernism. Although Prague was not itself as yet a center of innovation, Kafka was attuned to the entire process and by 1907–8 he was demonstrating how traditional narrative strategies had to be abandoned, how he could carve out what would be uniquely his own means — the results of which we see, finally, in 1912, with "The Judgment" and "The Metamorphosis," as well as some of the brief pieces in *Meditation*.

The Kafka family moved on June 20, 1907, from their eleven-year residence in Zeltnergasse to 36 Niklasstrasse, which gave Kafka a view of the Moldau (present-day Vltava). But the nature of his room is of interest, for this twenty-four-year-old was desperate for privacy and yet still living in a crowded family residence. Kafka's room had a good view of the river, but it was a thoroughfare in the layout of the apartment. He described it as an unheated hallway between the living room and his parents' bedroom; each time they headed for their room they had to pass through his. Besides the lack of personal privacy was the agony, for Kafka, of hearing through the walls everything that went on in his parents' bedroom as well as family activity in the living room. His sensitivity to noise created in him a kind of madness until the house quieted down and he could listen to the silence while he wrote. Additionally, he had to be careful with his possessions — letters received or still being written, his manuscripts, his personal effects — since anyone coming or going had access to his desk. In a still more intimate note, it made any secretive sexual activity on his part, such as masturbation, an adventure in the light of the potential and actual traffic. Kafka railed against his lack of privacy and particularly against the noise: the card playing, spitting, raucous laughter, the slap of hands against limbs, and, of course, the disturbing noises from the bedroom.

But even before the move, Kafka was extremely unsettled. This was one of the most uncertain times of his life, as he swayed between an unpaid, unpleasant job and writing, between a certain definition of himself that he held and the reality of drift. His letters to Brod reveal desperation: "I have a headache [not an unusual event], my teeth are rotting away, my razor is dull; it adds up to an unpleasant sight."[25] The description suggests acute depression, especially the fact that this meticulously groomed young man has left his face unshaven. He adds, "My future is not rosy and I will surely — this much I can foresee — die like a dog."[26] The image of dying like a dog is one he will repeat, and it speaks not only of depression but of suicide, since *The Trial* ends with the thrust that makes him die like a dog.

In the meanwhile, he was with his favorite uncle, Siegfried, in Triesch, until August, and his descriptions sound idyllic. As we follow Kafka's activities in Triesch, we observe how he was able to relax when distant from family and job:

... am riding around on the motorbike a good deal,* swimming a lot, lying nude in the grass by the pond for hours [he favored nudist camps, but remained clothed when others were around], hanging about the park until midnight with a bothersomely infatuated girl, have already tended hay in the meadow, have set up a merry-go-round, helped trees after a storm, taken cows and goats to pasture and driven them home in the evening, played a lot of billiards, taken long walks, drunk a lot of beer, and I have been in the temple too.[27]

His activities sound natural and enjoyable, a man liberated from himself temporarily. He then mentions he has been spending a good deal of time with two girls, "very bright girls, extremely Social Democratic, who have to keep their teeth clenched lest they come out with a conviction, a principle, on the least provocation." Of the two, Hedwig Weiler caught his particular attention, and his subsequent correspondence with her becomes for him quite important.

Hedwig Weiler, at nineteen, Jewish, with a full, rather fleshy face, blondish-brown hair, youthfully attractive, a socialist politically, studied languages at the University of Vienna. She was energetic, idealistic, forward-looking, a "new woman" with plans for herself. When Kafka met her at Triesch, she was staying with her grandmother but, like him, trying to liberate herself, in her case from Vienna, and to move to Prague. She was, in this respect, planning at cross-purposes with Kafka, who would have liked to leave Prague and move to Vienna, where he hoped to study at the Export Academy. Nothing came of his plan, as nothing came of hers. Kafka did try to find a position in Prague for Hedwig and advertised in two newspapers (*Tagblatt* and *Bohemia*) for her. He described her as a young woman who had studied French, English, philosophy, and education at the University of Vienna, and who was now at the University of Prague (not so), available to give lessons to children. Since Hedwig was not in Prague, Kafka collected the responses (two) himself. Whether they became intimate at Triesch remains an open question.

Just as later the correspondence with Felice Bauer gave him free rein to his imagination, so the one with Hedwig allowed him to try out many of his fictional ideas within the framework of a romantic relationship. It would prove to be typical Kafka: the use of the letter sequence as a way of honing his skills as a writer, his use of certain images and ideas that he could then transfer to his fiction with few alterations, his immersion in a relationship that meant far less to him

---

*Motorbikes were, of course, still scarce, with only about five thousand registered in the empire in 1907, when registration became compulsory. What is of interest is that the model of motorcycle built in Jungbunzlai (which later became known to the world as Škoda Works) was called "Odradek," that strange word that Kafka co-opted for his story "The Cares of a Family Man." The word, clearly, was not his invention, but a company product; the use to which he put it was, however, uniquely his.

than the words imply, since he had little intention of bringing it to any conclusion. With the possible exception of his fully mature correspondence with Milena Jesenská, his idea was to throw himself into letter writing and gain the recipient's sole attention, for her to reply in kind, and then for him to toy with the nature of the relationship, and especially his dubious role within it. His letters to young women, first to Hedwig, later to Felice, became not missives of love, or even of attachment, but the means by which he could keep them under surveillance and ultimately win them over to his own peculiar form of courtship. As we read the letters, we see Kafka playing one of his shrewdest roles: observing himself as he writes the letters so as to pinpoint his responses to himself, and then in turn transforming that response to his fiction, or, in Hedwig's case, into those brief prose poems that would appear in *Hyperion* in 1908 (later collected as *Betrachtung*, or *Meditation*).

None of this implies that he wasn't physically attracted to Hedwig, whom he describes as short, with boundlessly red cheeks and an attractive gesture of placing a pince-nez on her nose because of nearsightedness. He found her nose particularly admirable: "[The] tip is really beautifully composed of tiny planes." But in his fantasies, her nose gives way to parts lower down, and he tells Brod he dreamed the previous night "of her plump little legs. Such are the roundabout ways by which I recognize a girl's beauty and fall in love." Kafka indicates he plans to read to the two girls from Brod's *Experiments* (*Experimente*, 1907), a collection of four stories, including one, "The Island of Carina," in which Kafka is thinly disguised as the character Carus, an aesthete. There was, perhaps, not a little vanity in his reading from a collection in which he is a character. What better way of impressing a nineteen-year-old university student!

A letter to Brod in mid-August from Triesch reveals Kafka's world before he returned to Prague to face the realities of his situation, the necessities of finding a paying position and hanging on to whatever it ultimately brought him. He tells Brod he knows all about indecision, that he keels over from contemplating the pros and cons of anything, so unable is he to make up his mind. He again indicates he is wasting his time at his job and insists that if his prospects do not improve by October he will take an advanced course at the Handelsakademie (Commercial School) to learn Spanish to add to his French and English. He has his uncle in Spain in mind and even thinks that both he and Brod could be employed there: "My uncle would have to find us a position in Spain, or else we would go to South America, to the Azores, or Madeira."[28] These castles in the air are similar to his much later dream of traveling to Palestine and becoming a waiter, the fantasies of someone trying to break out of a losing situation and temporarily forfeiting reality in the process.

Back in Prague by late August (1907), still at his unpaid position,

which would end on September 30, Kafka began his correspondence
with Hedwig, clearly the more desirable to him of the two girls. The
opening of his first letter on August 29 is quite intimate, as though they
had progressed quite far in the few days spent together, giving credence
to the idea of a possible sexual consummation. His words about how
everything about him in the office is subject to her, table, pen, paper,
desk, clock, suggest he was wooing her quite seriously with language.
Hedwig could not know Kafka was preparing his own version of the Venus's-flytrap. There is the familiar wit, in which he uses his own ailments as a way of commenting upon the general scene: "I transfer my
headaches from one firm resolution to another equally firm but of an
opposite sense. . . . like rifle bullets I fly from one [resolution] to the
other, and the accumulated excitement that soldiers, spectators, rifle
bullets, and generals distribute among one another in this struggle of
mine is quite enough to make me tremble."[29] He says he has no social
life but spends his evenings reading the Social Democratic *Arbeiterzei-
tung* (published in Vienna, founded by Viktor Adler in 1889) and is "not
a good person." He is, in fact, "a ridiculous person," adding, ". . . if you
are a little fond of me, it's out of pity; my part is fear." He says letters
are "like splashings near the shore by two who are separated by an
ocean," and he laments he must go to "an empty bed."

     If this, so far, does not sound like the man who would write "The
Metamorphosis" in five years, we should not be put off. For Kafka's
rhetoric here is theatrical, full of play-acting and role-playing. He is
trying out words, feeling his way through emotions, seeking the modes
by which he can both express himself and expunge such expressions.
These letters served somewhat the same function as his prose-poems,
which would appear in 1908 in *Hyperion* and then make up the slim
volume *Meditation*. Tryings-out, they were intended to purify him, rid
him of certain verbal and emotional baggage, prepare him for the really
important stuff. Hedwig was part of that experiment, although we cannot dismiss Kafka's emotional involvement, her physical attraction
(those plump little legs, among other parts), even the idea of becoming
engaged. But the reality was to be quite different. A barrage of letters
follows in September, at least seven, possibly eight, since dating is difficult to determine. Her responses are lost.

     In one missive, Kafka writes a complex statement of their relation-
ship, calling himself "A" and Hedwig "X."[30] In his algebra of emotions,
A is bombarded by letters from X, who denies his existence in that X is
apparently unaware of the complexities in A. A sees that X is a good
person, the best in the world, and yet A feels that X is destroying him
with her letters. What X does not recognize is that such attention
causes grief and forgets "that a light once lit sheds its illumination indiscriminately."[31] Of course, in the algebraics of Kafka's strange assignment of X and A to the correspondents, it is possible to reverse the

designations, so that X is Kafka and A is Hedwig. Such a reversal is in keeping with Kafka's point of view that all relationships partake of shifting sands, of indiscriminate illumination, of hidden factors that bubble to the surface casually only to vanish. Hedwig had quoted a line from the Danish writer Jens Peter Jacobsen, to the point that every castle of happiness is built on sand, which runs out, grain by grain, and that love is not a rock, although we like to believe it is. She too is full of uncertainties, and Kafka counters with his own response to the Jacobsen line, by asking whether the person who sees the sand flowing is in the castle or not, and where the sand is flowing to. In other words, he wants more complications, not simply the sentimentality of the Jacobsen passage and Hedwig's rather young romantic offering up of it. Kafka refuses an easy passage for either of their feelings.

He does feel nostalgic about their days in Triesch and recalls walking with her, and he mentions love, only hers, however, not his. He expresses his wish to be in Vienna, although we know his plan to enter the Export Academy fell through. They were, however, moving in cross directions, with neither as yet aware of it, unless we read beneath Kafka's words that from the beginning it was all play. In the next letter, he expresses how she looks best, a foreshadowing of his detailing to Felice Bauer of what she should wear. He says he wants her, and that her letters are only ornamental wallpaper in comparison. In this letter (dated early September), he notices that just as she wishes to come to Prague, he would like to visit her; but she is coming to this "damned city."[32]

He then offers up what their future relationship could be like if he came to Vienna to study at the Export Academy: up to his neck in "unusually strenuous work," no time even to read newspapers. He is, characteristically, warning her off, even as he offers himself. Kafka is alternately opening up the trap to let himself escape, and then closing it so as to make certain Hedwig cannot escape. The engine has a kind of alternating movement: if she comes too close, he exists, and if he comes too close to her, he finds reasons for putting her off. While she comes on in a steady movement, if we can extrapolate from his answers, he zigzags his way into constantly shifting positions, so that she can never draw a firm bead on him or what he wants. It was this sliding, slippery mechanism in his letters that carried over so well into his fiction, highlighting his sense of uncertainties and of unknowns, the source of his great contribution to Modernist literature.

One form of control Kafka rarely let go of was his insistence on knowing every detail of how Hedwig arranged her life, what she wore, where she went, whether she laughed at a particular party, when she became tired, where she sat — insignificant details for anyone except Kafka. On September 8, he openly declared a form of love, saying he wished she were there with him in the room so that he could lay his neck against hers. Then he says he is suffering from fever, is unhappy, has written a "dainty fever-letter" to her, but decided to tear it up. The details of his own situation suggest complete self-absorption and his recognition that they "have danced a quadrille between Prague and Vienna, one of those figures in which couples bow so much they do not come together"[33] — precisely what Kafka was seeking. He needed a breakdown in their arrangements in order to consolidate his control over her movements and to protect his own. He was hardly prepared for a serious relationship leading to engagement and marriage, and yet Hedwig's physical, and perhaps intellectual, appeal affected him.

In a subsequent letter one week later, he offered another impossible solution: that she get away from Vienna and he from Prague by spending the year in Paris. His unpaid position would end in two weeks, and Paris beckoned. But to what end? He knew nobody in Paris, although there could be a Czech network there; he had no means of support, although he did have a good command of the language (Flaubert was one of his great literary loves), and she too did have the language, but little else. Would they marry? Where would they live? Would his little bank account suffice? Paris sounds like a castle in the air, or else one of those sand castles he ridiculed where the grains run out more rapidly than one can recoup. As he told Brod a week later, he was like a boxer, "without doing any boxing."[34] By then, September 22, his decision to remain in Prague was firm. He would never get too distant from that city, not until near death.

But even before using the boxing metaphor with Brod, Kafka suggested it to Hedwig: his indecision was like a boxer's. He tells her he will remain in Prague, that he has obtained a position with an insurance company. Ironically, all of his plans to find work through his uncle in Madrid led to his employment in Prague, with the Assicurazioni Generali, an Italian insurance company whose main office was in Trieste. The position was no sinecure, but mere drudgery, with daily hours from 8:00 A.M. to 6:00 P.M., low pay to begin with and no pay for overtime; chances of advancement were small for a Czech Jew with no Italian. The job was to prove another cul-de-sac for Kafka, simply adding on another year with no opportunity for movement — the beginning of the design of a life composed of such years.

While informing Hedwig of his final plans to remain in Prague, Kafka wonders when she will come and touches on the advertisement he has placed, mentioned earlier. But his next letter to her, on September 24, suggests she is having second thoughts, or else was put off by the uncertain tones in Kafka's letters, as Felice Bauer would come to feel five years down the road. "What's this now, you want to run away from me again, or are at any rate threatening that? Is it enough for me to stay in Prague to discourage you about your plans?" Now that he feels her slipping away, he becomes firmer in his request to have her come. "Just before your letter arrived I thought how lovely it would be for us to meet on Sunday mornings and read that French book I am in the midst of reading (I have so little time at present), which is written in a chilling yet tattered French, the way I love it, so come, please."

The appeal sounds genuine, but in just a short time or at this very time, Kafka was writing a brief prose-poem full of hostility, called "The Encounter" ("Begegnung") and later retitled "Rejection" ("Die Abweisung") in his book *Meditation*. The "I" (narrator) meets a pretty girl and begs her to come with him, but she walks past without answering him. He provides words for her: she is thinking that the narrator is no duke with a famous name, is not an American with an Indian's figure, has no outdoor look, has never journeyed to the seven seas, and, therefore, why should a pretty girl like herself go with him? The narrator responds that she is not herself in any great demand, and her clothes do more to hide her ungainly body than one might be led to believe. She is, in a word, no more of a prize than he. And since they size each other up that way, wouldn't it be better for them just to "go our separate ways home?"[35]

Kafka sent this on in a November letter to Hedwig, and it obviously applies to both of them. That he should present himself as so unappealing is clear: that was his way, and it had to do with his own sense of self-worth, or lack of it. But that he should present such an image of himself *to her* implies a deep hostility, given that he was five years older and she still a university student. That short prose-poem seems to have doomed the relationship, and with it we observe the correspondence dwindling to one letter a year (what is extant — Hedwig may have destroyed others). The problems were not only logistical, he coming to her, or she coming to him, but Kafka's desperate need now to clear away time so that he could write; and Hedwig, whatever her attractions and needs, did not fit into his already overloaded schedule.

He nevertheless kept up the pretense of her coming to Prague and indicates that his advertisement received two responses, one "reassuringly Jewish." The first letter for October, still a month before he sent on the "Rejection" prose-poem, already begins to sound gloomy and defeated. He is preparing her: "My life is completely chaotic now." He works eight or nine hours a day, devours his free hours, is trying to learn Italian, and attempting to spend some time out of doors. As he sits in his office, he fantasizes about someday "sitting in chairs in faraway countries, looking out of the office windows at fields of sugar cane or Mohammedan cemeteries. . . ."[36] He says that the world of insurance does interest him, although his present work is dreary. He ends this letter with one of his characteristically strange images, in which the body takes on a bizarre life of its own. It is, he says, very nice to imagine laying "down the pen" and placing her hands "one atop the other and enclosing them in one of my hands, knowing that I would not let go even if my hand were unscrewed from my wrist." He would write comparably to Felice Bauer, using anatomy as part of a transformational process toward self-destruction or disintegration.

Intermixed with these long letters to Hedwig are very brief ones to Max Brod, usually with indifferent remarks or with plans for meeting. In one, Kafka speaks of people looking at his body "for the fun of it."[37] In November (very probably), Kafka told Hedwig, already beginning to recede from his mind and letters, that he would like to transfer right out of the firm, or at least be transferred far away, to Trieste. Although he did not know of what was building up in his body, the southern climate would surely have been better for him than cold and damp Prague. It was in this letter that he sent along what he called "a poor trifle," the prose-poem "Rejection," with its hostile paragraph about "her." By this November letter, we note Kafka's interests leading him elsewhere; he even tells her he has suddenly gotten mixed up with a "whole crowd. Army officers, Berliners, Frenchmen, painters, cabaret singers, and they have taken away my few evening hours in the merriest fashion."[38]

Early in 1908, Kafka sent his only letter to her for that year, a long one, but neutral in its feeling for someone he had once sought in romantic terms, however muffled and disguised. Very possibly, he began to let the correspondence run down because he was writing the intended novel "Wedding Preparations in the Country," and the short pieces that would appear in *Hyperion*. Or else the momentum was simply gone, as both he and she recognized that a summer idyll could not be stretched into a winter romance. One tries to read his intention from the tone of the early 1908 letter, as he begins to find the ironic, parodic, self-deprecating mode that he so successfully cultivated in his letters to Felice Bauer and that is continuous with his fictional writing as well: "You know, I've had an abominable week, a terrible lot to do at the office. Perhaps that will always be so; I suppose one must earn one's grave"; "Last week I really belonged in this street I live on [Niklasstrasse, 36], which I call 'Suicide Lane,' for the street traces a broad path down to the river. . . ." He then moves into praising her studies and telling her she has a right to be nervous; he comforts her that she is making visible progress. His advice is not that of an equal; rather, it is that of a protector. He predicts that her having a goal will ultimately make her happy, "whereas I shall remain one of those humming tops forever, for a while distressing the eardrums of a few people who may come too close to me, that's all."[39]

That this was a signal of the end we pick up immediately in the letter for January 7, 1909. Not only has the tone changed — Kafka very tellingly has moved from the familiar *du* in addressing Hedwig to the formal pronoun — but he is returning all of her letters, "including today's card," saying he no longer has a single line of hers in his possession. He insists he would like to talk with her, possibly about whatever has occurred out of sight to create this final, and somewhat unpleasant, split. She has apparently refused to see him, although he insists that a meeting between them would be a pleasure for him. He even invites her to the Kafka house for lunch on the eighth, when they can meet during his lunch break from the office. It is not clear whether she came, although perhaps she did, for in mid-April, Kafka wrote to her very tenderly, and his tone is not ironic, but full of the intimate revelations he would in time transfer to Felice Bauer. His use of the letter form as a way of honing his style never becomes clearer than in this mid-April correspondence with Hedwig.

Kafka's theme is loneliness, at which he is an expert: "Lonesomeness looks bleak when viewed from outside, when someone sits confronting himself as we often do, but inside the walls, so to speak, it has its comforts." He commiserates with her for having to study: "That's dreadful, especially when one is still upset about other things." Then comes one of his finest lines: "In such states we imagine — I remember that so well — that we are forever stumbling through unfinished suicides. . . ." "Unfinished suicides" — clearly he is writing about himself, cultivating his own sense of loneliness, its deficits, of course, but also its benefits. He says he found it hardest in winter, when he sat resolutely at his desk, "black through and through with unhappiness, only to stand up after all, having to cry out, and while standing raise my arms as if about to take flight."[40] In spring and summer, he says, it is better: "You no longer thrash about in hell within the four walls of your room, but occupy yourself like a living person between two walls." He assures her about her studies: "And you will surely manage to, if I could, who can only manage to do anything while literally plunging to my doom." He then alludes to family problems: mother facing an operation, father declining; at the same time, he wrote to Brod that his "family is practically a battlefield."

What resonates here is a certain *Schadenfreude*, a joy in the injuring of oneself or another, here mainly oneself. One gains a malicious pleasure in painful or damaging incidents or remarks. One creates a scenario of destruction and from that finds personal satisfaction. In his relationship with Hedwig, and then with Felice, Kafka roamed through a particular kind of romance, which is best exemplified in the courtship and marriage of Proust's Charles Swann and Odette de Crécy. Here we have *Schadenfreude* at its most Modernistic: the coming together of two people based on the obsessive passion of one to cement a relationship that gives the other little but pain; and, in fact, as Proust comments, Swann does not even like Odette. The relationship takes on a masochistic and sadistic life of its own, quite apart from the lives of the two people. Kafka and Hedwig are only a shadow of this; Kafka and Felice Bauer become the real thing — a "modern romance" based on the pain one can sustain from what is usually assigned to pleasure.

Kafka remained at the Italian insurance company for only nine months. His job was truly a dead end, in terms of promotional possibilities, working conditions, and salary. But it did serve some purpose, in that his unhappiness at his position seemed to work well for him creatively. For in the month before he left the company, he submitted eight short prose-poems to *Hyperion*, where they became his first publication, in March 1908. *Hyperion*'s first issue, edited by Franz Blei and Carl Sternheim, was quite ambitious. What other new magazine could boast of publishing eight pieces by Franz Kafka, plus contributions from Heinrich Mann, Rilke, and Hugo von Hofmannsthal? Blei was introduced to Kafka's work by Brod, who was now beginning his role as promoter of his friend's fiction. Kafka's eight pieces are little more than a paragraph or a page, all arranged under the title *Meditation*, which was also the name of the volume published in 1913, where eighteen of these prose-poems appeared. The original eight were "The Tradesman," "Absent-Minded Window-Gazing," "The Way Home," "Passers-by," "Clothes," "The Passenger," "Rejection," and "The Trees." Their titles were added later.

The reader may not make too much of these as individual pieces, but they served an important function for Kafka. In a curious parallel instance, in 1925, we find William Faulkner publishing very similar pieces in New Orleans — not distinguished work, but brief observations that helped him develop fictional strategies and tones. Kafka's work was similar, and it seemed to derive in part from the kind of thing found in Robert Walser, a Swiss-born writer who lived mainly in Zurich and Berlin. He too worked as a clerk, in a bank and a government unemployment office, and did other odd jobs as well. His first poems and prose-poems appeared near the end of the century, in 1898 and 1899, and this prefigured his career as a writer of over one thousand short prose-poems or proselike narratives. Possessed, driven, near madness on many occasions, Walser suffered from schizophrenia and hallucinations, and attempted suicide several times, until he was committed to a sanatorium near Bern and then to a hospital in eastern Switzerland. With that, he stopped writing, although he lived to be seventy-nine.

Although in a 1908 letter Kafka asserts that he does not know Walser's work, Walser was someone Kafka could have appreciated, in the line of German writers like Kleist and Nietzsche who were self-destructive. Among his thousand short sketches, Walser even has a piece called "Kleist in Thun." What he did was to establish a particular genre — which Kafka, without knowing it, followed and which we find, strangely, in Faulkner in 1925. This was the piece that roamed inside and outside, blurring lines between subjective and objective, between conscious and unconscious. Walser tried to find a middle ground that psychoanalysis still cannot identify, just below consciousness, but not sub- or preconscious, and not of course really unconscious. It was an area Kafka would probe himself, all as part of the larger Modernist movement. In such work, the detail is so clear one feels the world created is completely realistic, but then that detail becomes so intensely insistent that the world created suddenly takes on different shapes. A shadow or another shape of some indistinct sort begins to form itself behind or beneath the insistent detail; and then perspective and perception shift, from objective data to subjectivity.

In a 1914 review, the ever perceptive Robert Musil, himself no stranger to this method in his novel *Young Törless*, grouped Kafka and Walser. Musil would also highly praise Kafka's thin volume *Meditation*, in a review in December 1920, in *Selbstwehr*.[41] The Kafka pieces are deceptive, with the "prose" part suggesting a certain realism of detail and the "poetry" part assuming an intensity lying below the casual deceptiveness of the words. Things are alternately charged and lightened.

One of the most effective pieces is "The Tradesman" ("Der Kaufmann"), the longest in the group, running to two pages. "The Tradesman" (or "The Merchant") could easily be a portrait of Hermann Kafka, or else of someone in his position. Problems immediately enter his consciousness: "My small business fills me with worries that make my forehead and temples ache inside yet without giving any prospect of relief, for my business is a small business."[42] Kafka was probably writing this during Hermann's decline, in the 1908–9 period when he told Brod and Hedwig Weiler that the family was a battlefield and his father on the downgrade. Kafka knew Hermann's business from his intermittent work in it himself and lists some of the problems: the mistakes made, the need to puzzle out next year's fashions, the arbitrariness of the peasants' tastes. Furthermore, the tradesman's money is in the hands of strangers (Hermann's notions and accessories store was alternately retail and wholesale), and he fears that ill luck might overwhelm his investors, something he cannot foresee or avert. They may be spending extravagantly, and it is inevitably his money they are wasting. What is compelling about the brief piece so far is how Kafka has blended his own fears about his future with those of his father's about the business, so that we cannot really tell where one begins and the other ends. "The Tradesman," accordingly, becomes as much Kafka's inner life as Hermann's.

What Kafka has done here is break away from conventional story lines, splitting his portrait of the tradesman into small units, with the barest of linkage to hold the parts together. He moves in and out of the man's mind, using some remnants of narrative, but on the whole dividing the two pages into subunits. The method presupposes a cubist approach to literature, foreshadowing cubism in painting in its insistence on the lines and planes, or geometry, of the experience, rather than any definitive meaning. There is a swiftness to the portrait, with fantasies moving in and away, so that the reader is denied any fixed stance. While keeping to realistic detail, Kafka blurs lines. The tradesman is himself barely conscious of what is happening to him; in what seems to be simply another normal day, he is undergoing profound interruptions in his life, profound moments of rebellion against the entire process, before he must defer to the expected course.

In "The Way Home," merely four very short paragraphs, Kafka moves directly into the kind of prose-poem we find in Baudelaire's *Paris Spleen*, composed between 1855 and 1867. Baudelaire wrote about his effort, "Which one of us, in his moments of ambition, has not dreamed of the miracle of a poetic prose, musical without rhythm and without rhyme, supple enough and rugged enough to adapt itself to the lyrical impulses of the soul, the undulations of reverie, the jibes of conscience?"[43]

Less a poet than Baudelaire, Kafka's prose-poems are necessarily prosier. But in "The Way Home" his opening line has the concision and ambiguity we associate with compelling poetry: "See what a persuasive force the air has after a thunderstorm!" The air quickens Kafka's spirit and overpowers him. With the air in his face, he strides the streets like a king or emperor, its tempos his, its activities his responsibility. He feels he has nothing "to grumble at save the injustice of providence that has so clearly favored me."[44] But when he enters his room, he becomes meditative; even opening the window to the street does not relieve him. However similar their methods and their exploration of this relatively new genre of fiction, Kafka's plan is apparently quite different from Baudelaire's. The latter is interested in examining perversities so as to integrate them into normalcy, to deny their contrary or perverse nature. Kafka is interested in opposites, so that the street, with its liberating air, is contrasted with the confines of his room, where his work must be done and where he must confront his family. In the street, he has a body, in the room a mind, and the two, somehow, do not cohere or resolve themselves.

Three of the *Hyperion* pieces derive from "Description of a Struggle," and one, "Children on a Country Road," comes from a version of the story not usually printed. The other two "Description" sketches are "The Trees" and "Clothes." Like several of the other very brief pieces, "The Trees" seems like a paragraph from one of Kafka's letters, in that entire passages of the letter are prose-poems of sorts, somehow disembodied from the details communicated. In "The Trees" he compares "us" to "tree trunks in the snow," for it seems that a small push will get them rolling. But it can't be done, for they "are firmly wedded to the ground," a firmness, however, that is "only appearance."[45] Kafka takes his image, develops it slightly into a metaphor, and then turns upon it. While "The Trees" is only a brief paragraph, it does foreshadow some of Kafka's characteristic work and parallels many Modernist developments, not the least of them imagism — that use of an image or metaphor to carry the entire meaning of the poem.

In "Clothes," an observer tries to define the wonder of girls. When he sees complicated clothes, with pleats, frills, and appendages, he marvels at how they can be kept smooth; how they can avoid creases and dust and other elements that will destroy their value. But while day keeps them fresh, night brings out the worst. Kafka is turning over what constitutes freshness, what makes up weariness and dustiness. The night turns life around, revealing the truth in the murky darkness, whereas the daylight reveals little. The half-page "Passers-by" is characterized by the conjectural "perhaps"; it contains a night scene in which a whole undertow of fantasies is "perhaps" possible. It is all blending, merging of subject and object. "Children on a Country Road," with its elements of escape or liberation for a child, seems like an earlier episode in the life of the narrator of "Description of a Struggle," who himself sounds unmistakably like Kafka himself.

In this three-and-a-half-page fragment, a young child is spending an idyllic time in his parents' garden, but he is terribly weary as he eats his snack of bread and butter. A gang of boys calls to him to join it, and he and they run rapidly from the house area, "full tilt into the evening," as if happy to be liberated from the confines of what once appeared to be an idyll. At a ditch, he lies on his back and lets sounds and movement pass him by, losing his anxiety about being alone. The child is both part of the gang and independent of it, another Tonio Kröger–like figure who cannot quite link himself to the pleasures of others. The child gets up and joins the group, whooping and shouting, joining hands. Suddenly, their time is up. Time to return, the moment over. But the child runs off alone, into the forest, to make "for that city in the south," which the villagers say is full of "queer folk." They never get tired, the villagers assert, because they are fools.

The story is quite inconclusive, as it was intended to be part of a much larger structure. But Kafka did choose to include it in the *Hyperion* group, which meant he viewed it as possessing independent status. We must see it in terms of movement: moments of liberation, displeasure even within that phase, the desire to be alone amidst crowds, even friends, and then the ultimate desire to break away, to turn from village pleasures to the excesses of city life. Kafka has in a sense reversed his own priorities, since city life stifled him — so he asserted repeatedly — while village life, especially with his Uncle Siegfried, seemed to release him. But his ostensible need to get away from the city is belied by the fact that the city, Prague, always Prague, reinforced all the anxieties and forms of anguish he needed, that sense of himself as a solitary being, which he nurtured for his writing. We must, then, view this fragment not as a symmetrical view of Kafka's needs, but as a shadowy presentation, his desire to be a marginal person, the reverse of his need to

find salvation in an idyllic village. He recognizes the city as the repository of what he ultimately must be or become, whatever the personal
misery.

While Kafka corresponded with Hedwig Weiler, he carried on, as
noted earlier, a parallel correspondence with Max Brod. His relationship to Brod became especially intense in 1908 with the death of Brod's
closest friend, Max Bäuml, which in some ways made Kafka a protected
figure in Brod's life. In the friendship, Brod appeared to enjoy the greater
achievement, but he recognized that Kafka was the greater writer.
Kafka was champing at the bit in his position with the Italian insurance
company, his first real taste of what life in the outside world might be
like, and he wanted to leave even as he showered praise on those who
found the post for him. He had been expected "to remain," as he says,
"with the company forever."[46] Since Brod had been deeply involved in
securing the position, Kafka was concerned with the consequences for
his friend if he suddenly pulled out for "a job in the post office." He saw
himself as a minor functionary, doomed to this type of work.

In May 1908, just two months before he left the Assicurazioni Generali (on July 15), he told Brod he was sending him a pebble, which he
should keep in his pocket to protect him. This pebble takes on some
totemic value for Kafka, who indicates he will send one on to him as
long as they live. The pebble is akin to a blood-brotherhood ritual or
ceremony. Kafka swears his love and fidelity: "For you know, Max, my
love for you is greater than myself and I dwell in it rather than it dwells
in me." He elaborates the metaphor: the pebble becomes an emblem of
a rock, of which Brod will occupy a part. The metaphor is continued:

> ... and right now, when I am more puzzled about myself than ever and
> when fully conscious I feel about half asleep, but so extremely light,
> barely existing — I go around as though my guts were black, you know —
> at such a time as now it feels good to throw a pebble like this into the
> world and thus divide certainty from uncertainty. What are books com-
> pared with that![47]

Kafka asserts that his pebble cannot bore Brod, that it cannot disintegrate, and that he cannot forget it because he is not supposed to remember it. Also, he cannot lose it for good, since he can always find it
again on any old gravel path. It is "just any old pebble," which cannot
be harmed even by greater praise. This is, for Kafka, the finest of birthday presents for his friend. And as the metaphor winds down, we recognize that the pebble offering is the sole way Kafka can offer himself,
his friendship, without falling into sentimentality. Kafka offers himself, but something quite reduced, inconspicuous, and downgraded: he
is *that* pebble, itself an offering and yet at the same time something so
familiar it can be replaced if lost.

The diminution of an object is in keeping with his reduction of himself as an observer or spectator in the brief pieces that make up *Meditation*. But, more importantly, the pebble prefigures Kafka's animals and insects, that transposition of himself into something so small and repulsive he gains a post of observation otherwise denied him. The pebble, for whatever else it was worth, becomes the element that cements the friendship.

By this time, he had joined the Workers' Accident Insurance Institute* and had seen eight of his pieces appear in *Hyperion*. He now had a reasonable position, part of the administration of the Dual Monarchy, and all thanks to Ewald Příbram's father, Otto. It was an odd position, as we shall see, since although Příbram was himself a Jew, companies of this kind did not hire unconverted Jews. Kafka had obtained the post only because of Příbram's high position as board chairman. Yet there appears to have been no disinclination on the part of the upper administration to promote Kafka and to provide him with every consideration for frequent leaves, vacations, absences, almost always with pay. He was, of course, "protected," but there appears to have been complete satisfaction with his work, and he was given increasingly heavy duties and responsibilities. He traveled often for the institute to other parts of Bohemia, since the organization was responsible for the kingdom of Bohemia. Kafka was fortunate in knowing Czech as well as German, since one test of the applicant was that he submit his application in both languages. His salary jumped from a pittance at the Italian insurance company to 90 kroner a month, plus an additional bonus of 10 percent. While still insufficient to live on independently, this amount at least gave Kafka some spending money and a degree of independence, although he remained in his parents' apartment. Within two months of taking the position, in September, Kafka went on institute business to Tetschen and Černošic, followed by a week's vacation in Spitzberg.

The institute, whose main office was on what is now Pořič Street, was a sinking business and had been going steadily downhill mainly because of mismanagement and, possibly, indifference. Some of the coasting, inevitable in the long reign of Franz Josef, was bound to affect businesses and, especially, government institutes and offices. If we believe the satirists — Kraus, Musil, Schnitzler, Hašek — then calcification was setting in, or already had, a kind of enervation relieved only by raucous celebrations, what Musil catches so well in his epic novel. In order to revitalize the institute, Robert Marschner was appointed as director shortly after Kafka began working there, and Kafka was himself appointed to make the congratulatory speech for Marschner. Kafka's fortunes in a sense rose with Marschner's; the now budding writer was

---

*Arbeiter-Unfall-Versicherungsanstalt für das Königreich Böhmen in Prag — the Workers' Accident Insurance Institute for the Kingdom of Bohemia in Prague. Besides Kafka and Příbram, the sole other Jew (unconverted) was a Dr. Fleischmann. Příbram was himself not a practicing or observant Jew.

given heavy responsibilities virtually from the beginning. This side of
Kafka must be emphasized: his considerable success as a bureaucrat
within a very rigidly run organization, an insurance company in which
injured and maimed workers were pitted against a government that
would pay or deny compensation based on the kind of case Kafka could
mount.

The initiator of workmen's benefits was Bismarck, in Prussia, and
the Dual Monarchy adapted some of these activities. Their aim, as in
Prussia, was to keep the workers down, not to benefit them, to find a
means of holding down or placating the unions; for socialism, anarchy,
and syndicalism, among other movements, were giving workers ideas.
Also, as mechanization increased, industrial accidents were on the rise,
and even an indifferent regime had to recognize that the maimed and
injured needed some form of insurance. The problem with such social
legislation was that it created fiefdoms in each regional center, and
these fiefdoms did not always benefit those for whom money was intended. Graft, embezzlement, and malfeasance of office — the whole
range of white-collar crime — were common, especially once health
insurance was added to the package in 1887. These regional offices
were self-governing, although they were under some state regulation in
that their employees were considered civil service workers.

The institute that Kafka went to work for had the grandiose job of
covering the "Kingdom of Bohemia," an enormous region, and doubly
grandiose in its use of the ancient, legendary kingdom. By 1908 its work
force had quintupled, and its duties had increased many times that.
With few inspectors to check violations, and with paperwork well behind, along with inattentive and uncaring clerks, the system was not
working. Employers of course tended to report fewer workers than they
had in order to decrease the benefits payments they were responsible
for. Consequently, as Ernst Pawel demonstrates, an enormous deficit
began to accrue in the fifteen years before Kafka came to the institute.
A changing of the guard was in order, and Dr. Robert Marschner, with a
background as a professor of insurance at the Prague Institute of Technology, took charge and immediately instituted new procedures.

Kafka was already familiar with Marschner from the Technology
Institute, and the two, however different in outlook, complemented
each other very neatly. Not suited for the lax Viennese or Austrian
model, Marschner was a stickler for efficiency and a proponent of all
kinds of advanced management techniques. While Kafka railed against
such procedures in his fiction, he in fact thrived on them at work. Indeed, Kafka's welcoming speech to Marschner was a tribute to his seriousness at the job, which he had held only a brief time, and to the firm's
recognition that he had a way with words.

Marschner and Kafka were an unlikely duo, but the director soon
put the future author of "The Metamorphosis," *The Trial*, and "In the

Penal Colony" in charge of accident prevention. A new department, its goal was to cut down on insurance costs to the employer by trying to find ways of training workers to better operate their machines in order to protect themselves. This unlikely appointment, it would seem, turned out to work quite well to Kafka's benefit, since it gave him stature at the institute and at the same time forced him to come out of himself. Without this position, it is quite possible that Kafka's self-effacement and self-absorption would have turned him into even more of a hermit, and with that, there is no assessing how he would have proceeded. As it was, the running of such an operation gave him insight into bureaucracies, of course, but also into the needs of others who were injured, maimed, in some cases damaged for life. His socialist sympathies were reinforced by what he saw, and he could take comfort in the fact that he was doing work which actually helped people and had a social benefit.

Marschner meanwhile reshaped the entire institute, not only altering procedures but changing the philosophy of workers' benefits.[48] He introduced controls that prevented fraudulent claims; he created a hierarchy of benefits based on risk factors; and he policed employers in order to force compliance. And, as mentioned earlier, he introduced a campaign for safety factors. Toward this end, Kafka would in a short time write several reports of a technical nature all in line with accident prevention. By 1910 Marschner's controls had resulted in a positive balance sheet, although the large deficit from past years of poor management still remained. It is important to keep in mind that Kafka worked not in some dead end of a bureaucracy, but in a progressive segment of a forward-looking company, however tedious his job would become.

As we can see from the diary entry on October 10, 1911, Kafka probably wrote Marschner's press release in the *Tetschen-Bodenbacher Zeitung*. The prose does have echoes of his mordant wit. The institute's annual reports, he says, up to 1909 succeeded "in scuttling all hope for the future of the institute, which seemed to resemble nothing so much as a dead body sprouting an ever-proliferating deficit as its sole surviving limb." Kafka points out that things have changed, but the public must make certain that "these promising changes will become permanent."

Once Kafka was put in charge of accident prevention, which involved investigations, analysis, and the writing of reports, he became increasingly involved with the rights of workers. His sympathies for the Czechs (who reciprocated with stepped-up pogroms against Jews) made him wonder, Brod reports, why they didn't storm the institute and tear it to pieces. But after centuries of suppression, they accepted their lot, while taking out their anger not on Dual Monarchy institutions but on Germans and Jewish businessmen and professionals.

Kafka's success, in time, can be measured in his series of promotions, his being granted full civil service tenure in 1910 (which brought a pension and other benefits), his being made junior secretary in 1913, secretary in 1920, and two years later senior secretary. He retired on full disability and was given numerous paid vacations and leaves well beyond what other employees enjoyed.

At first, Kafka was not involved in industrial-related injuries but was assigned to provide the written sections on compulsory insurance in the building trades and also on motor insurance. Motorized transportation was beginning to increase, and since registration of cars had been instituted, the government had to keep track of ownership. In Kafka's first assignment, the 1907–8 bulletin, we note that his writing ability — not quite "The Metamorphosis" or "In the Penal Colony" (although close) — was tested, and he apparently acquitted himself satisfactorily. After this, he was assigned to workers' insurance and to the protection workers should receive in industry — whether their cases deserved a hearing, and finally how much compensation they should receive for fractures, eye loss, lost fingers, toes, hands, legs, and other disfigurements. The nature of his role here is of interest, inasmuch as he became known in the institute as a supporter of compensation for those ill-treated by their companies or else unprotected against accidents. While not exactly a crusader, Kafka became the workers' friend within the institute, making certain not only that the law was followed but that it was known.

In writing about maimings and injuries, in traveling to scenes of industrial accidents, in assessing amounts for compensation, in reporting to the institute on his decisions, then on seeing his decisions through to completion — in all of this, we glimpse the Kafka we know. We may be surprised at how enterprising he was in work that did not always appeal to him, but we should not be surprised that he took avidly to work that concerned legalities, justice, individual rights, and mainly those victimized by a large system. This also thrust Kafka among a broad range of types, mainly Czech workers, since the German population tended to be not in blue-collar but in white-collar work. Kafka was forced to travel often, trips he detested but which at the same time enlarged his range of experience and brought him into touch with those who fell by the wayside in the empire. As a German Jew, which means as someone twice removed from the mainstream, he did identify with those maimed and injured workers, whose only hope was himself, in his assessment of their accidents and in his recommendations for compensation.

In another respect, although at this stage it did not pay well, the position conferred on Kafka a kind of power out of proportion with the level of job he held in his early years with the institute. Having identified with the insulted and the injured — and his sympathies never faltered, even when he considered the worker a stupid victim — he was also in a position to set things right. He was, further, a witness to pain and misfortune, which surely fed his own sense of himself and at the same time conferred some worth on him as the assessor. But most of all, it gave him the opportunity to write at a time when he was not writing much personally, except for the pieces that would appear eventually in *Meditation* in 1913. While his writing for the institute was not "creative," a few specimens reveal he took great care with his prose and that it was both concise and precise. There is to it a hard economical edge, the distinctive voice of his fictional efforts, and also a logic to it, so that one finds, sentence to sentence, an almost obsessive clarity.

> An extremely cautious worker could probably take care not to allow any joint of his fingers to project over the lumber either during the work or while moving the wood away from the cutter head, but caution is irrelevant to the major danger. Even the most careful worker must be drawn into the cutter space area when it slips or when the lumber is thrown back, as it happens quite often, when he is pressing the piece he is planing with one hand against the machine-table, and with the other feeding it to the cutter spindle. It is impossible either to foresee or to prevent that wood from rising and sliding back, for this would occur when the wood was gnarled or knotty in particular places, when the blade was not moving fast enough, or moved itself out of position or when the pressure of the hand on the wood was unevenly distributed. Such accidents would occur rarely without the amputation of several finger joints or even whole fingers.[49]

Kafka might have added other incidents: the amputation of entire hands at the wrist or even higher, with severing of veins and arteries, severe blood loss, and even death without quick attention to the accident victim.

We note in the description how closely Kafka has observed the process of planing, a process that he, as a city boy, would have no direct experience of. Yet he has entered completely into the worker's situation, followed through his actions, and observed how at nearly every phase even the careful worker may fall victim to badly planned machinery and the vagaries of the industrial workplace. What is also remarkable about just this description is how Kafka could, with some imaginative projection, move from this planing machine to the infernal machine of "In the Penal Colony," where we find another kind of victim, but a victim nevertheless. There too the machine runs away with itself, just as here the combination of lumber and machine becomes the unpredictable element. In the story, dating from 1914, the prisoner gains enlightenment from the machine, whereas in the industrial accident, there was no enlightenment, simply compensation from the institute if Kafka's report was favorable to the victim. But the cases curiously parallel each other, for in each we have a "god" figure: the one manipulating the machine and ultimately becoming its final victim, and Kafka himself in his office or in the field "creating" the terms by which he can arrange what the machine has done. Obviously, the two cases are not symmetrical, but we glimpse in this and other reports the shadowy presence of the Kafka fictional effort, the set of his mind, the movement of his prose, the shaping of his outlook. However much he came to hate his position and the sheer boredom of it, it was superb training for someone who was slowly going to emerge as Franz Kafka.

In only a year at the institute, Kafka had become a man on whom responsibility could be loaded and who would acquit himself well. Yet Kafka was inside the very monstrous structure he would try to bring down. It is tempting, even this early in his employment, to see him as both the "good son" and the "bad son" in his relationship to his work. As the good son, he worked well and found favor with his employers. Since he did everything required of him, and did it with more than usual efficiency, he was apparently forgiven for being a Jew and was moved along. At the same time, the good son did not betray those among the working force who depended on him, for he found compensation for them, made sure it was in keeping with their injury, and even, later, tried to formulate policies that would minimize the number of accidents. The good son worked hard, bearing up under often intolerable conditions of boredom, and carving out an administrative position for himself that brought credit to the Kafka family. Gustav Janouch's father, who knew Kafka at work, remarked, according to his son:

> Kafka personifies patience and kindness. I cannot remember an occasion when there was trouble in the Institution on his account. Yet his approachability is not a sign of weakness or a desire to please. On the contrary, he is easy to get on with because, by being completely fair, just and at the same time understanding toward others, he commands a similar response from everyone around him. People speak freely to him, and if they find it hard to agree with him, they prefer to say nothing rather than disagree.[50]

Janouch senior points out that Kafka was not a yes-man at the insurance institute, for he often went against accepted opinion, but this did not make him unpopular. Many on whose behalf he worked hard considered him a saint. He often found against his own organization, discovering honorable ways to lose a case so that an injured worker could be adequately compensated. Kafka clearly played the role of good son at work to the hilt.

But the bad son was also working parallel with this, all as part of Kafka's dualism. The bad son was storing up images, characters, situations, and other factors that were subversive of the very structure he was helping to support. As he began to write seriously in 1912, his sense not only of the bureaucracy but of any individual's role within it was devastating. The bureaucracy could literally kill, as well as maim. One way to evade it was through transformation.

Kafka as the bad son of course dominates our imagination. That image is reinforced not only in the creative works, but in the wild, aggressive, hostile act of rebellion that comes in the 1919 *Letter to His Father*, in its way a culmination of the bad-son syndrome. This attitude can be found even earlier in his intimate letters to Brod, but especially in the great sequence to Felice Bauer, where all his hatred and fear of the bureaucracy carry over into still another kind of bureaucratic arrangement, engagement followed by marriage, followed by family. Although not much if any attention has been paid to this question, there is little doubt that Kafka's attitude toward the bureaucracy bled over into his personal life. It is clear in his imaginative works, but also in his response to engagement, marriage, and children: all of them part of that bureaucratic trap that extends in a kind of chain of being from the Dual Monarchy itself, down to Prague, down to the institute, down to the individual who moves toward creating his own family. In this chain of being, there is no room for Franz Kafka, who, while observing himself as part of the gigantic mechanism, also sees himself not as participant but as someone marginal to it. Kafka was so harsh to Felice, both in his comments directly to her and in those to friends about her, because in all her innocence, she was little different from those machines that chop off fingers, joints, or entire limbs. Kafka may or may not have felt his sexuality sliced off, but he nevertheless viewed her as a dangerous force, like that planing machine when the lumber begins to buckle and the operator is at the mercy of uncontrollable forces.

When we attempt to identify Kafka's Modernism, we must move in several directions, not merely toward his relationship to European literary Modernism. His response was much broader, obviously, when we consider his personal life as itself an embodiment of Modern individuality akin to anarchy. The surface of his life was placid enough: work for six hours a day, home to nap, dinner with family, evenings in cafés with close friends, then home again to read and write, when he did write; but below was a turbulence that made him part of a cycle of poets and novelists who were "cursed" or "damned," like Baudelaire, Rimbaud, and several of their contemporaries. He did not sink into desolation and ruin because of drugs or alcohol or sexually debilitating practices, but he nevertheless organized his personal life so as to place himself beyond normally accepted society. That bad-son response was part and parcel of his desire to reshape himself as separate from all demands put upon him, and in this way he became the successor of many of those "damned poets" of the nineteenth century.

The surface, meanwhile, gained his immediate attention, and it was orderly and efficient. Gustav Janouch described Kafka's office:

The office in which Franz Kafka worked was a medium-sized, rather high room, which nevertheless seemed cramped; it had something of the dignified elegance of the senior partner's room in a prosperous firm of solicitors, and it was furnished in the same style. It had two black, polished double doors. One opened into Kafka's office from a dark corridor, crammed with tall filing cabinets and always smelling of stale tobacco smoke and dust. The other, in the middle of the wall to the right of the entrance, led to the other offices at the front of the Workmen's Accident Insurance Institution. To the best of my knowledge, however, this door was never opened.[51]

Kafka's soft manner is contrasted with that of his partner, whose comment upon hearing someone knocking was a peremptory "Come in," whereas Kafka's was a gentle "Please." Yet behind this gentle manner and this neat, efficient office was a man capable of murderous remarks, such as his comment that the "hangman is today a respectable bureaucrat, relatively high up on the civil service pay roll."[52] He adds that there may be a hangman concealed in every conscientious bureaucrat. This is of course the bad son in Kafka emerging even in his office, where he plays the solid and respectable bureaucrat. If Janouch can be credited with accuracy here, then Kafka was always ready to find in any situation his kind of irony and scorn for surfaces. His act of rebellion was, we can conclude, never far from that placid surface, always ready to burst forth with some sharp image or scornful comment. When Janouch protests that bureaucrats don't "hang" anyone, Kafka demurs, saying that they "transform living, changing human beings into dead code numbers, incapable of any change." How much of that remark Kafka meant for himself, in 1920, we cannot determine, but one way in which he escaped becoming a "dead code number" was through his writing, an act of supreme rebellion and expression of individuality. And any women who got in his path were left by the wayside.

With his shift to assessment of workers' claims, Kafka was more or less set in his professional life until, because of illness, he left the institute. Those early trips, first to Tetschen and then to Černošic in northern Bohemia, an industrialized area with plenty of accidents and victims, would be repeated often as he settled into his job and took on increasing responsibilities. And even the vacation that followed, for a week in the forest, would become a regular occurrence, as the institute bent its rules to give him vacation and sanatorium time almost for the asking. Because of Brod's insistence, prodding, and even nagging, Kafka maintained a decent, if sporadic, level of creative output, at a time when such a depressed man could have let himself drift. Kafka did feel the creative urge, but he also felt the need to let reverie take over, and Brod played on him expertly, forcing Kafka to express himself. Besides almost daily walks together — Brod returned to Prague and became a post office functionary — they corresponded whenever one or the other was away. Even something so small as Kafka's inability to meet his friend because he had to work in Hermann's shop brings forth a letter of explanation. With Hermann unwell and a clerk also sick, Kafka, after his six hours at the institute, had to take over for the remainder of the afternoon and then on into the evening.

Such eventualities took a tremendous toll on him, since he despised everything about his father's store; furthermore, as a man of education and position in the bureaucracy, he did not take well to the more traditional idea of the Jewish merchant selling goods, mainly to Czech peasants. But it was time more than anything else he begrudged. He had to hoard his time, especially since because of his insomnia he felt prolonged languor and exhaustion. His insomnia was connected to his living quarters, centrally located and exposed in his parents' apartment. Thus, within a cycle of his own making, he felt trapped; and within that entrapment, lack of time became his key enemy. Working in Hermann's store, as, later, with other business ventures into which he was drawn, meant that as he grew older, he was not escaping but becoming besieged. By November 21, however, some of that depression had lifted, and he told Brod he was feeling very good.

During this time, Kafka and Brod were reading Flaubert in French (*The Temptation of Saint Anthony*), and Kafka was himself reading Diderot's *Rameau's Nephew* (translated by Goethe into German over one hundred years before); Kafka also turned to Rudolf Kassner, quite well known in his day, a friend of Rilke, Paul Valéry, and Oscar Wilde, among many others. Kassner was a critic and an aesthetician born in Austria and now in the main forgotten. The combination of Diderot, Flaubert, and Kassner led Kafka into a philosophical foray, his brand of depressing prophecy.

> There are things we have never seen, heard, or even felt, whose existence moreover cannot be proved — although no one has as yet tried to prove them — which we nevertheless run in pursuit of, even though the direction of their course has never been seen, and which we catch up with before we have reached them, and into which we someday fall with clothes, family memories, and social relationships as into a pit that was only a shadow on the road.[53]

The passage is consistent with Kafka's sense of dread, which was quite different from Kierkegaard's, though Kierkegaard remained, nevertheless, a great favorite. Unlike the latter, however, Kafka was not prepared to make any leap or jump into faith. His sense of dread, which became prophetic of the fate of European Jewry, was not a social or political comment. It was connected to his awareness of how disappointment, frustration, and the unexpected and uncertain combined to cast a shadow over everything; and this sense of dread could well have been the early effect of a developing tubercular case.

He closed out 1908 by telling Brod he preferred to spend New Year's Eve by himself rather than with a crowd of people at Brod's place. He insists he wants to sleep, read Flaubert's *Temptation* and his friend's own still incomplete *Die Glücklichen* (*The Fortunate Ones*, which Brod once wanted to title *The Thousand Amusements*). Some of the party crowd included Baum and Weltsch, who with Kafka made up a close reading circle.

During this period leading up to the writing of "The Judgment" in 1912, Kafka worked on that group of short pieces, eight of which had appeared in *Hyperion*. In all, from perhaps 1902 to 1912, he wrote eighteen that he put together in the volume called *Meditation*, published in 1913.* The volume was named after what Kafka had called the *Hyperion* group, "Meditation." What is striking about the title for both the group of eight and then the eighteen published later is the singular title, not *Meditations* but *Meditation*, as though it was Kafka's reflection of a state or condition, not an act on the part of the author. He does not meditate but provides meditation, something directed more at the reader's sensibilities than an expression of the writer's. Here are the eighteen pieces as they appeared in the 1913 volume as arranged by Kafka: "Children on a Country Road" (from "Description of a Struggle"), "Unmasking of a Confidence Trickster," "The Sudden Walk" (see *Diaries*, January 5, 1912), "Resolutions" (see *Diaries*, February 5, 1912), "Excursion into the Mountains" (from "Description of a Struggle"), "Bachelor's Ill Luck" (see *Diaries*, November 14, 1911), "The Tradesman," "Absent-minded Window-gazing," "The Way Home," "Passers-by," "On the Tram," "Clothes" (from "Description of a Struggle"), "Rejection," "Reflections for Gentlemen-Jockeys," "The Street Window," "The Wish to Be a Red Indian," "The Trees" (from "Description of a Struggle"), and "Unhappiness."

Nearly all the sketches, including those in *Hyperion*, can be read as directly or indirectly connected to Kafka's own situation. In the single-paragraph "The Wish to Be a Red Indian" (perhaps influenced by Karl May's Indian stories), he writes of dropping things as he races along on a horse: first the spurs, then the reins, finally the horse's very neck and head. As it is divested of its own body parts and all of its other encumbrances, the racing horse seems headed also toward the death of the rider — if not death, then his flirtation with a suicidal ride that will, somehow, free him as he feels wind and sees land fall away beneath the horse's hoofs. The story is a striking reminder that Kafka could find bizarre images to reveal an inner need: the need to achieve independence of some kind, or else to seek destruction in the process, or a combination of both.

Betrachtung (Leipzig: Rowohlt Verlag, 1913); later appearing in *Erzählungen* (*Stories*, published by Schocken) and *Penal Colony* (also Schocken). In most critical analyses or biographies of Kafka, whether in German or in English, they have not received much attention.

The other side to "Red Indian" is "The Street Window," a tale (one slightly longer paragraph) of stillness; a person peers out a window, solitary yet unable to resist the movement and vitality of street life. In the juxtaposition of these two pieces, we have Kafka's own internal struggles: between the solitariness he knew he needed to fulfill the major part of himself, and that part that relates to external phenomena and yearns for attachment. Kafka writes, "And if he is in the mood of not desiring anything and only goes to his window still a tired man, with eyes turning from his public to heaven and back again, not wanting to look out and having thrown his head up a little, even then the horses below will draw him down into their train of wagons and tumult, and so at last into the human harmony."[54] The solitary man yearns to connect to someone or something, even to movement itself. Yet he must do so indirectly, through a window, through a reflection. The ambiguity of Kafka's struggle within himself is borne out in this brief piece, as in so many of these sketches that may seem mere throwaways.

"Bachelor's Ill Luck," which appears three years later in his 1911 diaries, nevertheless helps define Kafka earlier as well. Here the solitary Kafka appears, perhaps with his Uncle Siegfried in mind, the eternal bachelor. "It seems so dreadful to stay a bachelor, to become an old man struggling to keep one's dignity while begging for an invitation whenever one wants to spend an evening in company, to lie ill gazing for weeks into an empty room from the corner where one's bed is."[55] The bachelor lacks all amenities, wife, children, a real place to live, and he is even deprived of speech, for no one cares to hear what he lacks. At best he can model himself on other bachelors whom he knows. The vision of the bachelor's life is of someone smiting his forehead, in a sense cursed by his situation. Kafka probes deeply, and we recognize his positioning of himself.

Gustav Janouch touches on the subject of solitude in 1920, in a remarkable interchange with his much older friend, if we can believe Janouch's transcription. Kafka indicates he would like to run to the poor Jews of the ghetto to kiss the hem of their coats, if only they would endure his presence in silence. Janouch asks if he is so lonely as that. Kafka nods. "Like Kaspar Hauser?" Janouch inquires, and Kafka laughs. "Much worse than Kaspar Hauser. I am as lonely as Franz Kafka."[56] Kaspar Hauser was an early nineteenth-century German foundling, a near idiot or psychopath who claimed to have lived in caves or holes and who died of a stab wound at twenty-one. Thus the bachelor in 1920 looks back to the bachelor in the 1911 diaries, and before that, in 1908–9. We can explain Kafka's desperate pursuit of Felice Bauer, whom he did not wish to marry and whom, possibly, he did not even like, only in terms of his loneliness and his need to express some link with mankind.

Some of Kafka's sense of loneliness and his desire for "meaning" was of course linked to who and what he was, but some was also the result of his Prague background. Although both thrived in the arts, Vienna and Prague were distinctly different in the ways they directed social and individual feeling. The Viennese, and their writers, were concerned with their feelings in a direct hedonistic way; and often, as in Kafka's view of Schnitzler, they seemed frivolous, urbane, overly sophisticated, even effete. For the sterner observer, the Viennese appeared overindulgent of their own needs and pleasures, with a literature that reflected this. Praguers were concerned more with "meaning" — transcendental truths, the meaning of existence — and less with a sophisticated surface. Viennese Jews saw themselves as assimilated to German culture; Prague Jews recognized the division and remained doubters, visionaries, pessimists, ahedonistic. The Prague Circle and those moving beyond it — Rilke, Werfel, Brod, Urzidil, Perutz, Kafka himself — saw themselves as "engaged," to use Camus's later term, but in their case not only with the society at hand but with the meaning of it all.

Kafka's response to Arthur Schnitzler and his work is a good example of how the Praguer viewed the Viennese. In one of Schnitzler's books, *None But the Brave*, his Lieutenant Gustl is slighted by a lowerclassman when a baker accidentally touches his saber at a cloakroom and calls him a "silly boy." The flare-up is only momentary, but it becomes the center of the story, for Gustl would like to redress the insult with a challenge to a duel. However, according to his and the gentlemanly code, he cannot fight a lowerclassman. He contemplates suicide because his sense of honor has been breached, and because of circumstances he cannot redress it. But he is saved from suicide by the baker's unexpected death, and after this, Gustl gains his revenge by railing against Slavs, Jews, socialists, intellectuals, women, and virtually everyone who is not in military uniform. Only the army can be trusted to be honorable (what Hašek turned into a momentous joke in *The Good Soldier Schweik*).

Schnitzler's point here is the vapidity of Gustl's attitudes, their potential danger for a society, and the lieutenant's lack of any intellectual or ethical center. Kafka approved of Schnitzler's handling of Gustl and praised the story. But he nevertheless suspected the Viennese writer of arguing for an utterly indefensible point of view: that the Jews of the empire could really assimilate or be accepted as assimilated when men like Gustl were challenged or removed. Kafka abhorred Schnitzler's *Professor Bernhardt* and his *The Path to Freedom* (or *The Path to Openness*) because the latter argued seriously for assimilation and asserted that Palestine, some unknown country without significance for the sophisticated Viennese, was only for Eastern European Jews, who had no place or job and so would find emigration attractive. Schnitzler's point was anathema to Kafka because he felt that Western European Jewry, like himself, was depleted, enervated; but that to consider oneself an assimilated Viennese or Praguer was nonsense. Even the German language did not belong to the Jew.

In Kafka's rejection of Schnitzler, we observe a major division between the Viennese and Prague points of view. As we have already observed, Prague lay heavily over Kafka, ever present. Janouch reports that his friend knew the city intimately, writing of "Kafka's wide knowledge of all the varied architectural features of the city."[57] He knew not only the palaces and churches, but the most obscure alleys of the Old Town. He knew the historical background for the buildings and pointed out to Janouch, among other things, the almost inaccessible courtyard with the inscription that Johannes Kepler once lived there and wrote his famous book on astronomy there. Janouch says that Kafka loved the streets, buildings, and gardens of the city, emphasizing that his attachment to Prague was unbreakable. This being so — Kafka himself supports this — we must see him as saturated with the city's values. Such values carry over into his own receptive imagination the sense of immensity, the tragedy of existence, the historical backgrounding for city life, the uncertainties awaiting the individual.

One of the *Meditation* pieces, called "Unhappiness," seems directly linked to Kafka's Prague. It is significant that he ended the eighteen pieces with the four-page "Unhappiness," a cry from the dark, somewhat akin to Edvard Munch's great painting "The Scream." The narrator of Kafka's piece also screams:

> When it was becoming unbearable — once toward evening in November — and I ran along the narrow strip of carpet in my room as on a racetrack, shrank from the light of the lit-up street, then turning to the interior of the room found a new goal in the depths of the looking glass and screamed aloud, to hear only my own scream which met no answer nor anything that could draw its force away, so that it rose up without check and could not stop even when it ceased being audible.[58]

With this, a door opens toward the narrator, and "a small ghost" of a girl appears. As they speak, the child begins to take on mature qualities, and the narrator regresses, his scream and loneliness having apparently enervated him. In the narrator's paranoia, he perceives that he has done something wrong. The piece hangs on an indeterminate or apparitional existence, in that the narrator is as much of a ghost as the young girl. When the narrator sees a rather hostile tenant, he explains quietly that he has just had a ghost in his room. He says he is not fearful of the ghost, but of what caused the apparition. "These ghosts seem to be more dubious about their existence than we are, and no wonder, considering how frail they are."[59] As his neighbor walks up the stairs, the narrator begs him not to steal his ghost, or else all is over between them.

"Unhappiness" has some correlation to the piece that opens the sequence, "Children on a Country Road." In the latter, the sketch ends with the child heading for the city, despite warnings that it was a place for fools. By "Unhappiness," Kafka has apparently arrived at the city — this is definitely a Prague experience — and he must live with the ghosts of his past and present. But there is more than symmetry between the two pieces. The land or country represents something solid, even if the child feels he must escape it, whereas the city is all ambiguity, all metaphysics. Lacking solidity, the urban experience is indeed populated by ghosts and apparitions. Yet there is more. The narrator of the final piece has become paranoiac, to the extent that he *seeks* ghosts and apparitions to relieve his loneliness, to interrupt his scream or even to embody it. When he cautions his neighbor not to try to steal his ghost, he fears losing that "presence." With this sketch, Kafka indicates he has assimilated Prague: its long history, its celebration of ghosts, its creation of a prototype like the narrator, or Kafka, as himself an apparition, its replacement of something substantial with something evanescent, a scream extended to a hallucination. The city lies heavily everywhere, a place where the Golem has returned.

"Resolutions" is also linked to unhappiness and loneliness. It begins with the narrator's advice on how to lift oneself out of a "miserable mood." But even after his advice, which involves some strengthening of will and welcoming of those who might cause pain and disagreement, he falls back on what comes perilously close to a form of suicide. The condition he recommends is virtually catatonic:

> So perhaps the best resource [if some slip stops the entire process] is to meet everything passively, to make yourself an inert mass, and, if you feel that you are being carried away, not to let yourself be lured into taking a single unnecessary step, to stare at others with the eyes of an animal, to feel no compunction, in short, with your own hand to throttle down whatever ghostly life remains in you, that is, to enlarge the final peace of the graveyard and let nothing survive save that.[60]

"Throttle down whatever ghostly life remains in you" — Kafka's advice is to stand by silently, observe, store up and assimilate, and then to present ordinary life as the nightmare the observer experiences. In these few words, which make up almost half of the overall piece, we hear the distinct cadences of Kafka's ironic pessimism: the pessimism and irony that enabled him to gain perspective on that ordinary world he perceived as ghostly, which, in turn, made the observer, himself ordinary, into someone apparitional. Like Kierkegaard, Kafka needed to embrace dread, but when it came time to leap into faith, he leaped instead into ghosts. Only by bringing himself close to a programmed observer, inactive and passive, could he find the silence and stasis necessary for his imagination to function fully.

Further linked to this sense of self as dread and uncertainty was the realization that victory is itself polluted by other considerations, that triumph is never clear or straightforward. In "Reflections for Gentlemen-Jockeys," Kafka catches victory in a horse race as a metaphor for victory in any activity. Fame is an intoxication the individual cannot resist, and it brings a response the day after which reverberates in his life. His opponents of course feel envy, and even friends are out of step with him. They did not bet on him for fear they would become angry if he lost; and now that he has won, they are annoyed they are out of the money. His rivals are nursing their wounds, angered at losing, full of self-pity that bad luck and injustice have befallen them. As for the ladies, whom one had hoped to impress, there is a sense of the ridiculous: the individual "is swelling with importance and yet cannot cope with the never-ending handshaking, saluting, bowing and waving."[61] At the end of it all, the sky is overcast and rain begins to fall. Triumph has collapsed around one, done one in.

A more compelling piece, and one more central to Kafka, is "Unmasking a Confidence Trickster," which fits into the 1911–12 period, but which has central significance earlier. It has affinities with "Description of a Struggle" in that the narrator is caught up with another man, this time a stranger who prevents him from going in to attend a party. They walk for two hours, and the narrator recognizes that the stranger is a "confidence trickster." The narrator knows all about such people, how they slink around the streets, how they attempt to play their tricks on the innocent, how their hands are always outstretched, how they seem to spy on people so as to take advantage of them, how "persistently they blocked our way, even when we had long shaken ourselves free." Kafka adds:

> How they refused to give up, to admit defeat. . . . And the means they employed were always the same: they planted themselves before us, looking as large as possible, tried to hinder us from going where we purposed, offered us instead a habitation in their own bosoms, and when at last all our balked feelings rose in revolt they welcomed that like an embrace into which they threw themselves face foremost.[62]

As Kafka writes his way into the world of the "confidence trickster," we recognize that the latter has become a doppelgänger or double for the writer. The trickster notion is a perfect emblem for the writer, and the "confidence" part embraces the trickster's need to inspire trust so that he can undercut the individual with his strategies. Kafka indicates how his narrator can begin to feel in himself the trickster's "ruthless hardness": he is becoming like the person he must reject. What is of interest in this brief episode is how Kafka dramatized, as he would do in so many of his letters, the inner conflict, but through ordinary or commonplace metaphors. As a double of the trickster, the writer must engage in all kinds of Modernist subterfuge: Kafka was, with this, almost ready to move into a major phase of his work.

Where for this Inside is there
an Outside?

— RILKE, "THE ROSE INTERIOR"

EIGHT Early Years of Achievement in an Age of Hostility

ALTHOUGH IN CHAPTER 7 we jumped ahead so as to see *Meditation* as a unit, we now return to 1909, a time critical for Kafka as he tried to coordinate the various threads of his life to provide working time for himself. As we shall see, the age itself, not just family, Prague, or Czechs and their nationalism, was hostile. Kafka would have to struggle on several fronts. In the few years after 1909 he embarked on several projects that in their way cohered, and he began to put into practice Modernist modes and ideas from both literature and painting.* Music remained outside his experience. From 1909 to 1913 Kafka underwent a transformation from a brooding, pessimistic, uncertain young man into a mature writer. Through the diaries, the writing of "The Judgment," "The Metamorphosis," and parts of *Amerika*, his correspondence (in its early phases) with Felice Bauer, and other letters to friends and relatives, he probed deeply into himself.

This period was also the time of Kafka's great discovery of something in Jewishness that appealed to him. He recognized that, for him, the Western Europeanized Jew, what Hermann Kafka aspired to, was a

---

*At an exhibition of French painting at a Prague gallery, Kafka peered at several Picassos, cubist still lifes and some postcubist work. Janouch remarked that the painter was a "wilful distortionist," to which Kafka retorted that Picasso did not think so. "He only registers the deformities which have not yet penetrated our consciousness" (*Conversations with Kafka*, p. 143). Kafka added that art is a mirror that, like a watch, goes fast, suggesting that Picasso reflected something that one day would become commonplace — not our forms but our deformities.

false yearning, that the only "real" Jew was the Eastern European Orthodox Jew, who took his race and religion for granted, spoke Yiddish, and did not care what Gentiles thought of him. This Jew existed for himself. Kafka's type of German-speaking Czech Jew existed to be accepted and assimilated, an effort wasted before it began, as he came to realize. None of it was as simple as that, of course, but Kafka's identification began to shift during this period, not only because of the appearance in Prague of a traveling Yiddish theater group, but from his own awareness of Jews' precariousness in a sea of hostility. As he wittily reported to Janouch, Jews and Germans had something in common: besides being energetic, able, and industrious, they were "thoroughly detested by everyone else. Jews and Germans are outcasts."[1]

Kafka made this statement after the Great War, but part of his earlier view of what a Jew is or should be came with recognition that Germanized Jews were a form of mutant, lacking identity, a language, a country, wallowing in self-hatred. It was not something generated only from within, but was the result of social and political forces that made all Germanized Jews into self-haters — and made them, even more, haters of those Jews who did not come up to the mark of German Jewish gentility.*

In early 1909 (mid-April) Kafka wrote to Hedwig Weiler and Max Brod about worsening conditions within his family. "We are forever struggling through unfinished suicides," he told Weiler.[2] Julie Kafka was due for an operation, Hermann was on the downgrade, and his grandfather had collapsed in the store that very day. To Brod: "Our family is practically a battlefield."[3] The terminology is clever, with undertones of irony, but there is little question that Kafka was being challenged by a situation that seemed irreversible and unresolvable. Some of this, however, must be understood as Kafka preparing the trap by which he can be snared, so that whatever he does or even says comes under a curse. He must perceive himself as someone so caught in a labyrinth of the family's making that he can justify his response, which is that he must sacrifice himself to accomplish what he needs to do.

Some critics have wrongfully seen these moves as masochistic, or

---

*His comments on the great German poet Heinrich Heine are apt in the light of the way Kafka felt about himself. Kafka called him an unhappy man, the Jew who converted to Christianity. "The Germans reproached and still reproach him for being a Jew, and nevertheless he is a German, what is more a little German, who is in conflict with Jewry. That is what is so typically Jewish about him" (Janouch, *Conversations with Kafka*, p. 68). Kafka's irony is tinged by compassion, for this is the Westernized Jew's dilemma. Speaking of the Old Synagogue in Prague, Kafka offered up similar feelings: that like the synagogue isolated among the modern houses, an anomalous institution, so is the Jew "an alien body." Curiously, Kafka sees the ghetto as a place of liberation for the Jew, who wanted to separate his environment from the unknown; in the ghetto, he could defuse the tension that existed outside. The ghetto walls gave him a chance to seek himself.

as part of a pattern of self-hatred. But they are really quite the opposite: they were moves of entrapment that were Kafka's strategies for surviving. As some writers use mental or physical illness as a way out, he used the family's unsolvable problems, dilemmas, and controversies as a way of making life seemingly so impossible for himself that he could justify his path only by his resistance to it. His process of transformation, through which in these years he reshaped himself as survivor, was the means by which he could identify with the life of art and leave behind the detritus of family life. Kafka may have twisted and turned on the family rope, but he was not weakened; rather, he was, with the loss of domestic happiness, strengthened to do his work.

By early 1909 the affair with Hedwig Weiler was finished, when she requested the return of her letters, although she wrote Kafka again a few months later saying she felt tired and lonely. At work, Kafka wrote a report on car insurance, which appears to have stabilized his position. He was found to be adaptable, full of zeal for his work, willing to work beyond office hours, and was rated overall an "excellent member of the staff." We should not underestimate this high recommendation from Eugen Pfohl, a senior inspector at the institute. Kafka not only passed muster, but he was considered an important part of the organization: whatever his personal misgivings about the work, he had proved he could handle it at a high level of achievement.*

The good report was all the more welcome because, with his family in ill health, Kafka was forced to spend time in the family store. His plans for settling in and writing went on hold, as we see in his early June 1909 comment to Brod: "The novel ["Wedding Preparations in the Country"] I gave you is my curse, I see; what should I do?" He adds, "I see that I'd like to go on writing forever only in order not to have to work. I really shouldn't."[4] Novel writing was to wait while he wrote the brief *Meditation* pieces. His next long work would be the unfinished *Amerika*, in three years, at the end of 1912, and then the breakthrough in 1914, *The Trial*. Kafka paid heavily for the postponement of literary gratification: "I have that pressure in my stomach, as if the stomach were a person and wanted to cry. . . . In general this sublime pressure in the stomach is something whose absence I don't have to lament; if only all other pangs were on the same level."[5]

During the summer of 1909, Kafka became involved in something we may find alien to his temperament, séances, along with Brod, Werfel, and Paul Kornfield, a poet. Seated at a table, they would attempt to

---

*Yet despite his abilities, he rarely spoke well of the work he did, and particularly to Janouch, he sounded his warning about the "end of things" in the bureaucracy. "I'm just a bit of waste matter and not even that. I don't fall under the wheels, but only into the cogs of the machine, a mere nothing in the glutinous bureaucracy of the Accident Insurance Institution" (*Conversations with Kafka*, p. 169). Perhaps the machine that draws blood with needles in "In the Penal Colony" is modeled on the insurance institute.

communicate with spirits through a concerted concentration that led to the table's moving. Since Kafka did not become a spiritualist, this phase was temporary, somewhat akin to sitting in cafés — more for the company than for any desire to communicate with the other world. On another level, however, this could have been for him the beginning of some effort to reach beyond the realistic and the ordinary into another level of experience, a spiritual experience for someone who could not believe in God.*

Throughout this period, the spring and summer of 1909, Kafka proved a willing and an apt critic of Brod's work. The friendship had now moved to another plane where both young men trusted each other's opinions and could tolerate criticism. They entered deeply into each other's lives, at a personal level, with Kafka making ironic remarks about one of Brod's girlfriends; Brod, for his part, tolerated Kafka's inability to meet appointments, with last minute cancellations, no-shows, or else excuses without explanation. Brod also became the recipient of some of Kafka's best epistolary prose:

> For I've got so much to do! In my four districts — apart from all my other jobs — people fall off the scaffolds as if they were drunk, or fall into the machines, all the beams topple, all embankments give way, all ladders slide, whatever people carry up falls down, whatever they hand down they stumble over. And I have a headache from all these girls in porcelain factories who incessantly throw themselves down the stairs with mounds of dishware.[6]

Amusingly told, the passage reveals Kafka's sympathies for these unfortunate people, part of a work force that must lose the battle in one way or another. These sympathies, an expression of his own humane feelings, were also surely part of his rebellion against his father's value system. Hermann Kafka was peremptory in his dismissals, not a kind employer, in fact something of a tyrant over his Czech (and, from his point of view, incapable) help. Kafka undermined the father by helping those in need: those crazy fools who dropped things, had things dropped on them, or fell into or under the machinery. The picture Kafka draws here is close in its satirical, mocking mode to the portrait

---

*The séances were surely an outgrowth of the meetings at Berta Fanta's. An affluent matron, she had moved from Nietzsche via Madame Blavatsky and Rudolf Steiner to forms of spiritualism and occultism that fitted quite well into Prague mysticism. Kafka seemed willing to experiment here without committing any part of himself; it was even less than a passing phase, it was a lark, and he drifted out of séances as rapidly as he moved into them. The Fanta "Tuesdays," evenings modeled on Mallarmé's famous ones, were given over to a variety of activities, not merely occultism. Once she opened up her salon to those beyond the Louvre Café crowd, she reached many representatives of the Prague intelligentsia, which included Albert Einstein during his tenure at Prague University. None of Kafka's rejection of occultism here, incidentally, denies his interest in Jewish mysticism, something quite different from Berta Fanta's spiritualism and séances.

Hašek would sketch of the army in *The Good Soldier Schweik*. Schweik's plight in the army is to act somewhat like those unfortunate workers in Kafka's description, but Schweik comes through, a survivor in a land of fools and idiots. For his part, Kafka seems the only wise man in an industrial complex of stupid workers.

But Kafka's verbal cheerfulness was superficial. Pressures were increasing, so he pleaded, through a doctor's note, the need for rest[7] and received a week's leave of absence from the institute. The buildup to his request can be seen in his frequent cancellation of meetings with Brod or with other friends, and, somehow, in the undertone of his letters, which reveal a life slowly moving out of control. His nerves were giving way under external pressures as well as from those resulting from his own unmet needs.

Kafka took advantage of the free week to go with Brod and Brod's brother, Otto, to Riva, on Lake Garda in the Italian lake country, a spot Otto was familiar with. Riva was and is a popular bathing resort at the very northern tip of Lago di Garda, in the district of Italy called the Trentino. Riva was accessible by train from Prague, and the vacation turned out quite well for Kafka. It led eventually to his writing the first piece on airplanes to appear in German literature, "The Aeroplanes of Brescia," in *Bohemia* (September 28, 1909).* It also led to a good deal of plain fun, horseplay, laughs, and the kind of escape they all needed from the cloying, enclosed atmosphere of Prague.

There is reason to believe Brod when he says that the visit to Brescia during their Riva vacation encouraged Kafka to write, or at least loosened his imagination. Brod perceived that Kafka, while blocked by work and family cares, was ready to break through if the opportune moment or material became available. The scene at Brescia was the perfect medium. Brod:

---

*In his book *Tatlin!* Guy Davenport exquisitely renders Kafka's experience in Riva and Brescia, in his own piece called "The Aeroplanes of Brescia." Davenport brings alive not only the episode but Kafka himself in a chiseled prose that makes of the experience a kind of palimpsest. Beneath his retelling lies Kafka's story; beneath Kafka's story lies the episode itself; and lying somewhere beneath both is what really occurred, not in Kafka's expressive reporting of it but in terms of the actual event. Davenport's recreation of Kafka is worth repeating, since it catches the magic of the subject: "Without paper, he conceived stories the intricacy and strangeness of which might have earned a nod of approval from Dickens, the Pentateuch and Tolstoy of England. Before paper, his imagination withdrew like a snail whose horns had been touched. If the inward time of the mind could be externalized and lived in, its aqueducts and Samarkands and oxen within walls which the Roman legions had never found, he would be a teller of parables, graceless perhaps, especially at first, but he would learn from more experienced parablists and from experience. He would wear a shawl of archaic needlework, would know the law, the real law of unvitiated tradition, and herbs, and the histories of families and their migrations, to which stock of tales he might add his own, if fate hardened his sight. He would tell of mice, like Babrius, and of a man climbing a mountain, like Bunyan. He would tell of the ships of the dead, and of the Chinese, the Jews of the other half of the world, and of their wall" (*Tatlin! Six Stories* [1974; Baltimore: Johns Hopkins University Press, 1982], p. 58).

I had a secret plan. At the time Kafka's literary work was lying fallow ["Wedding Preparations"]; for months he had not produced anything, and he often complained to me that his talent was obviously seeping away, that it had completely and utterly gone from him. Indeed he sometimes lived for months in a kind of lethargy, in utter despair; in my diary I find note after note on his sadness. *Le coeur triste, l'esprit gai* [sad heart, gay spirit] — this description fits him excellently and explains how it was that, even when he himself was in the most depressed state, he never, except perhaps in the hour of extreme intimacy, had a depressing, but rather a stimulating effect on those with whom he went about.[8]

We must always be careful of these assessments, since they were after Kafka's death in the form of a eulogy; Brod was helping to transform Kafka into a legend, and we must suspect the hagiography, as well as the romanticization. Brod's Kafka is playful on the exterior, wounded and depressed within. Some of this is true, but the playful exterior was not part of a division — rather it was a natural consequence of what Kafka felt, it was his way of handling people's expectations and creating a facade behind which he could do his work without intrusion, even from Brod. Kafka's role-playing was intended to make him inscrutable and unreachable to everyone, including his closest friends like Brod, Baum, Weltsch, and, at one point, Weiss.

What caught Kafka's attention more than anything else in Brescia was his recognition of cultural differences: Italian disorder versus German regularity. Italy proved an opening up for him in the sense that it showed him, however momentarily, an alternate way of living, ultimately unacceptable to someone like him, but sufficiently intense so that he could write "The Aeroplanes of Brescia." The piece is as much about the Italian character as it is about airplanes, beginning with the fear the travelers had of the way Italians organized such undertakings. Kafka speaks of the station at Brescia as a "black hole," with people screaming "as if the ground were on fire under their feet." Their fear extends to being separated; they vow to stick together, as though in a military campaign. The tone of anxiety is necessary for Kafka to convey their penetration into a strange land with strange forms of behavior.

When the travelers reach their hotel, the dirt — for a German — is overwhelming: it is "the dirtiest we have ever seen." But what would be unacceptable elsewhere becomes sympathetic here, for it is dirt "which is just there, that's all, and about which no more is said; dirt which will never change any more, which has made itself at home, which in a certain sense makes life more tangible, more earthly."[9] In this unlikely passage, Kafka rhapsodizes about dirt, which ordinarily would horrify him, with his fanatical cleanliness, his need to wash his hands repeatedly, his passion for swimming and baths, his often-stated distaste for the sexual act since it must follow a path of dirt. The rhapsodic passage on dirt is a metaphor for Kafka's entire experience in Brescia. Accepting dirt is a sure sign of his opening up.

In "The Aeroplanes of Brescia," the aerodrome is itself a kaleidoscope of sensations, full of a circuslike atmosphere, an "araby" or bazaar. As Kafka gazes in awe, one thinks of James Joyce's story "Araby" where a young boy looks on in wonderment. "Order and accidents seem equally impossible," Kafka comments, as people, carriages, horses plunge by. With this, he recalls the mixup he had when they came to Brescia and a cab driver wanted three lira, and they offered one, then settled on one and a half. The episode angered the driver and put the visitors off; they recognized that they had behaved badly, and the trip, until the aerodrome itself, had been tarnished. The planes provide the magic, as they read the names of the aviators and see the colors of their countries. The names are already hallowed: Rougier, Curtiss, Moucher, Cobianchi; but where is the most famous of all, Blériot? Insistently, Kafka asks, where is Blériot? as though the entire excursion depended on finding that man and his plane. Louis Blériot was now world famous, having become, just that July, the first to cross the English Channel in a machine heavier than air. Blériot was also an inventor, of the automobile and of the headlight; he had used the money from his inventions to pioneer in airplanes. Sight of the Frenchman would justify the entire trip.

Kafka describes the aviators: Rougier, then Curtiss, building up for his first view of Blériot. But Curtiss was himself no slouch, although his most famous exploits were still ahead of him (he was only thirty-one). He had already established the first American flying school, and in a short time would invent the aileron, which replaced the single-unit wing and made aerodynamics possible. Kafka is in wonder, Keats's Cortez. Then the friends see Blériot's hangar, then Blériot himself, trying to work with a recalcitrant motor. His plane is tiny compared with Curtiss's, and Kafka wonders if the Frenchman really plans to go up in that tiny contraption. The friends walk along the grandstands where the notables have gathered. They sight Princess Laetitia Savoia Bonaparte, Princess Borghese, then Gabriele d'Annunzio, and finally the "strong face of Puccini, with a nose that one might call a drinker's nose."

But all this is prelude to the race itself. Blériot flies in the plane that crossed the Channel. Kafka is filled with wonder: "Here, above us, there is a man twenty meters above the earth, imprisoned in a wooden box, and pitting his strength against an invisible danger, which he has taken on of his own free will. But we are standing below, thrust right back out of the way, without existence, and looking at this man."[10] By "without existence," Kafka means awe, ecstasy, being beside oneself: flying is turned into an artistic experience even when one is only a spectator. The winner of the Brescia Grand Prix is not the legendary

Blériot, but the American Curtiss in his large biplane. Somehow, the deck seems stacked against the Frenchman, since his plane is so much smaller than the American's; skill seems to give way to technological superiority. But just as Curtiss passes overhead in his winning effort, Blériot takes to the air, and it is unclear whether people are applauding one or the other, or both.

A slight piece, "The Aeroplanes of Brescia" is, nevertheless, a significant one, not in the sense of course of Kafka's great fictions, but rather as an expression of human will and determination just at the time when he needed a display of those qualities. Brod was more on target than he could have hoped, for Kafka took to the experience wholeheartedly, demonstrated suitable awe and astonishment, and turned the episode into a lean, underplayed report. Brod handed the finished piece to Paul Wiegler, then editor of the daily *Bohemia*, and with cuts it appeared on September 28 (1909). It was to be republished, without cuts, in Brod's book *On the Beauty of Ugly Pictures*, along with his own essay on the same theme. Kafka's piece was not an essay, as Brod suggests; it was a mutant or crossbred narrative, caught halfway between short story and essay, in an area Kafka was already exploring in the brief sketches to be published as *Meditation*. Kafka's appearance in Brod's book would have been his first publication in book form, but the publisher deemed the book too long and both Brod's and Kafka's essays were deleted.

Possibly this episode at Brescia had further reverberations in Kafka's life, for it is more than speculative that he decided to start a journal to capture such experiences, or else to set down passing reveries and fancies. In the following year, 1910, he began his diaries. The first dated entry is July, but other undated entries precede it. Not only did the diaries give Kafka the opportunity to describe events and to make comments that later ended up, directly or otherwise, in his fiction, they also allowed him to put down ideas and thoughts that could take no other shape and yet were essential to his working mind. The entries helped him feel he was writing even when he was blocked on more important projects, enabling him to clear away some of the clogging before it became solid waste matter. Psychologically, Kafka needed tangible results even when he was not writing, since his difference from others resided in that urge. The diaries, like his letters, finally, gave him an intimate entrance to himself. This too was necessary: that access to himself, part of that narcissism that underlay his seemingly giving temperament. Underneath was an enormous ego, a stupendous sense of self, that demanded outlets of every kind — if not fictions, then letters and diary entries, even doodles in the margins. It was a temperament bursting with the need for expression.

On September 15 Kafka was in Prague and back at work. He enjoyed a promotion from assistant to probationer, and he remained under Pfohl, who gave him excellent reports for loyalty and hard work. He was now involved not in accidents but more technical aspects of the business, for which he was expected to write analytic papers. The knowledge needed for this was considerable, but he tried to make up for his shortcomings by studying mechanical technology, a form of engineering, in lectures given at the German Technical University. If all this sounds strange — the Kafka of technical material or the Kafka of accident insurance — we must keep in mind that he was trained not in the arts, as a contemporary writer might be, but in law. The general expectation for a European writer was a background in some professional or technical area — Musil, for example, was adept at both mathematics and engineering — with writing as an added accomplishment. Kafka was little different, pursuing what seemed divergent aims but in some sense polishing his prose, even if it was technical prose. We already noted his skill in writing about accidents resulting in limb loss, but we can also observe his ability in writing about machines, their tolerance for error, the problems of human engineering, and related topics. That he excelled should not surprise us, since whatever he attempted to do, from swimming to rowing to gardening, he handled skillfully. A perfectionist in his activities and in his writing, he was cursed with the same quality in his personal life, making demands on himself that he could not meet.

It was at this time, also, upon his return from Riva and Brescia, that Kafka reportedly became involved in some way in anarchist affairs. Briefly, he met the Czech anarchist and poet Michal Mareš, who imitated the Italian anarchists in his style of dress (Caribiniere hat, a Verdian butterfly bow). Mareš introduced Kafka, so the story goes, to anarchist meetings at the Klub Mladých, while Kafka also attended some meetings of the Realists, Jan Masaryk's less extreme party. Kafka's role appears small, if he participated at all, and at most he may have handed out leaflets. It would be wishful thinking to place him more centrally in anarchist circles; as someone sympathetic to anarchists, and he may have been so, along with his socialist ties, the pattern of rebellion from family and from traditional literary forms would provide a uniform sense of how he thought and responded.

Yet such tidiness, though perhaps desirable, was not there. Kafka much preferred the cafés of Prague, as well as Berta Fanta's social evenings, to anarchist or even socialist events. When he did not frequent the cafés, he planned outings with Brod and others down to the last pleasurable detail: paprika goulash at 10:00 A.M., after a 7:15 departure; followed by lunch at noon; after that some wandering in the forest to the rapids, with rowing on the river (one of Kafka's real joys); and then the return to Prague at 7:00 P.M.[11] Dinner would follow, or some hours over coffee and beer in the cafés. This is hardly the portrait of a young man taken up by political commitment. On the other hand, if we en-

large the scope of politics to include the way we live, the way we respond, the assumptions we make about our society, the ways in which
we perceive state and government, then Kafka was deeply political, no
less than his contemporary Hašek and his politicized Schweik.

In the long run, it didn't matter much one way or another how
Kafka responded to anarchism in late 1909, since he remained his own
man in everything he did, and anarchism or any other ideological position, except for one, would make little difference. The one exception
involved his relationship to Judaism, and that crisis, if we can call it
that, occurred in 1910 when he made the acquaintance of a traveling
theater group from Eastern Europe, with their performances in Yiddish
and their manifestations of Jewishness so different from his own. Here
Kafka was deeply moved, not the least because he felt himself falling
deeply in love with one of the actresses (married, a mother), but going
further than that by becoming intrigued and then possessed by the idea
of a Jewishness that did not defer to Gentiles, or depend on acceptance
into genteel (that is, Germanized) society.

Reality, however, meant working in the office or traveling for the
institute to inspect businesses and to calculate their insurance risks.
Postcards sent regularly to Brod toward the end of 1909 indicate his displeasure at these trips: "Again, I have a few terrific days behind me!"[12]
He complains of feeling bad, his days spent between morning milk and
the evening's rinsing of his mouth. He was moving through northern
Bohemia to Maffersdorf, Gablonz, Johannesberg, Grenzendorf, Reichenberg, finally to Röchlitz and Ruppersdorf* and back to Prague. It
was so exhausting it would take an effort, he said, to write about it.
Kafka was also unable to take care of himself or else indifferent to his
needs, for he tells Brod in amusing terms that "I am treating myself to
having my stomach pumped; I have a feeling that disgusting things will
come out."[13] We have here early glimpses of hypochondria, his obsession with health and the need to find an alternate menu to what his
family served. Meanwhile, with Julie ill, the household went on, held
together by the very Czech help Hermann could rail against.

The year 1910 brought Kafka to many avenues of expression: as
noted, the diaries began; he found an outlet for emotions in the Yiddish
theater troupe that came through Prague; his letters deepened, taking
on the dark tones of his mature fiction; and he published *Meditation*.
With this year, we have a leap of sorts, not into original and unique
creativity — that would come two years later — but into a deeper comprehension of himself through writing his way into understanding. If
we jump ahead briefly to the spring of 1910, we find a letter to Max Brod
that is breathtaking in its potentialities for Kafka's developing sense of

---

*These are, of course, the German names for towns and cities that have since been
renamed in Czech.

himself and how that self can be portrayed in fiction. He starts by complaining about stomach pains, feelings of enervation and peevishness.
He tells Brod to stop complaining about girls, informing him that while
the pain they inflict on him is either good or bad, he must deal with it.
But the real focus of the letter is Kafka himself. "But what about me?"
he writes.

> Everything I possess is directed against me; what is directed against me is
> no longer a possession of mine. If, for example — this is purely an exam-
> ple — if my stomach hurts, it is no longer really my stomach but some-
> thing that is basically indistinguishable from a stranger who has taken it
> into his head to club me. But that is so with everything. I am nothing but
> a mass of spikes going through me; if I try to defend myself and use force,
> the spikes only press in the deeper. Sometimes I am tempted to say: God
> knows how I can possibly feel any more pain, since in my sheer urgency
> to inflict it upon myself I never get around to perceiving it.[14]

We note the "mass of spikes" going through him, an image or metaphor that re-emerged in "In the Penal Colony" in 1914, but also in *The
Trial* in the same year, both pieces depending on a perception of life in
which the self is the ultimate victim. The idea of a spike pressing in
ever deeper is an emblem for Kafka's need to feel victimized so he could
express what humanity was really like. To become representative, he
had to seek out what he thought was a universal pain, but which only
he, as an individual, could express fully. And to express it fully, he had
to experience it, whether in reality or in fantasy. In Freudian theory, we
find a shifting between what is real and what is fantasy, especially in
cases involving possible childhood sexual molestation. As we know,
Freud shifted his position from the actuality of the patient's feeling to
his, Freud's, perception that the patient was fantasizing such acts. This
opened the way for a more universal theory, the Oedipus complex
being the most significant, and it allowed Freud to move among intangibles in the unconscious.

The Freudian example is appropriate, for once Kafka, by 1910,
began to move into his years of achievement, it is unclear whether the
hostilities he describes are real or fantasized. Several hostilities were
clear: anti-Semitism, a stagnating government in which Prague played
a secondary role, the animosities created by Hermann in the Kafka
household, a workplace whose bureaucratic ways were, for Kafka,
forms of inhumanity. But given all that, Kafka fantasized other hostilities that were greater than those we can cite as historically real. In *Letter to His Father*, for example, he voiced those fantasies, turning a
difficult and uncouth father into a monster worthy of the son's rebellion against him. Hermann becomes the Golem as destroyer, not savior.* In the office, Kafka imagined a boring, rather deadening job into

---

*The argument throughout will be twofold: that Kafka had to recreate Hermann as a

one that completely exhausted him, brought him close to emotional death. In his personal life, he fantasized illnesses that while quite real for him in his imagination showed few if any external symptoms.

So much of Kafka seems to be role-playing because he cultivated his fantasies as essential to his play of imagination, while at the same time he cultivated his hold on a real world that disallowed fantasy. Prague allowed both sets of rules. Kafka could achieve this only by dividing himself, although how consciously he did it we cannot tell. The fantastic world he created, of spikes pressing into him, was probably an unconscious desire to find the medium by which he could live most explosively, how he could live in his internal life rather than the external one that he tried to exorcise through fantasy.

The listing of health problems continued through 1910: "You don't know all my ailments," he told Brod. He mentions a dislocated big toe, a bad leg, the foot in particular swollen badly; he announces a little later that five new abscesses have appeared on his backside, but that condition is secondary to a skin eruption "which is worse than all the abscesses."[15] All this, he assures Brod, will take a long time to heal and will be a big source of pain. He cannot walk because of the tight bandage, and he cannot sit because of the discomfort. This listing of ailments, chiefly to Brod, cannot be disconnected from the conditions Kafka needed to stimulate his imagination. At the time he was complaining about ailments — and we can only conjecture how much, if at all, the invisible early stages of tuberculosis made him particularly sensitive to ailments and pain — he was also establishing his memory of the past.

Though he later made disparaging remarks about his past to his father, he was already playing with the ideas in his early diaries, where he comments, "When I think about it, I must say that my education has done me great harm in some respects." He then details all the people who harmed him early on, including the "particular cook" who accompanied him to school for a year, a reproach, he says, which "twists through society like a dagger." Then he uses an image that fits well with that of the spike twisting into him: "And no one, I repeat, unfortunately no one, can be sure as to whether the point of the dagger won't suddenly appear sometime in front, in back, or from the side."[16] The diary entry continues with only a slight variation of the attack, and then still again in a third passage, with almost the same words. He repeats all this in the confidentiality of his diary as a way of justifying his own position vis-à-vis others, and possibly as a way of interpreting who he is, all as the result of his fantasies about what was done to him. "And

---

god so that he could become a suitable opponent for the son; but also that the son had to prove to himself that the father was too frail to be a god. That the two elements do not cohere was precisely Kafka's point.

how to expect it to be of any use to throw up to people in such a condition the mistakes they once made in earlier times in educating a boy
who is as incomprehensible to them now as they to us."

Kafka wore that incomprehensibility like a shield, or a suit of
armor. He reveled in it as an emblem of his uniqueness. While rejoicing
in his marginality to others, he was seeking the way to use that positioning of himself positively. Before he could enter the deepest reaches
of his talent, he needed to locate himself in the eyes of others but
through his perception of himself. He desperately needed his comment
that his education was negative and "tried to make another person out
of me than the one I became. It is for the harm, therefore, that my educators could have done me in accordance with their intentions that I
reproach them; I demand from their hands the person I now am, and
since they cannot give him to me, I make of my reproach and laughter
a drumbeat sounding into the world beyond."[17]

If we read these passages within the larger scope of Kafka's development, we see the enormous ego that demanded for itself the totality
of what Kafka was, negating anyone else who might have influenced
him. He needed to reinforce his perception that he was self-made, self-
shaped, and had, like Sisyphus, become so against tremendous opposition. His listing of "enemies" is almost paranoiac in his wish to seem
strong against those who would debilitate him, a struggle to maintain
himself against all those adversaries. But mere paranoia is not a useful
way of perceiving Kafka, since whatever shape he took and however he
felt about that shape was part of his creative talent. Whoever knew
him, whether family, friends, or fiancée, had to tolerate what might
seem pathology in someone else. The roles he took on were part of the
sacrificial element in him, his priestly devotion to his task, a kind of
Saint Sebastian of the desk. If we agree on that, then his sense of outrage in his diaries directed at the army of family, friends, and functionaries who tried to thwart him, all villains of his childhood and young
manhood, are forms of perceptions, not actualities; and the perceptions
served a solid function, to confirm in him the sense that despite them
he had reshaped himself. Whatever then accrued to Kafka, in his eyes,
was *his* only.

The early parts of the diaries, accordingly, with their repeated assaults on those who brought him up, can be explained less as malicious
or pathological detail than as strategy. "That they [parents and rela-
tives] have done me harm out of love makes their guilt all the greater,
for how much good could they have done me out of love." This is quite
an indictment, one that Kafka needed regardless of its validity, since it
reassured him that he emerged *despite* the burdens of a lost or cursed
childhood, the same message as in the later *Letter*. That the harm was
done to him out of love rather than hate makes the indictment even
stronger, since it suggests family blindness and supports his strength in

escaping. The entire performance is artistic, suggesting a kind of Method acting in which the actor finds precedents in his or her childhood or background to give emotional force and shaping to a present role. None of this indicates that Kafka did not suffer. In his assumption of roles, he did not separate the part that suffered from the part that needed to see itself as suffering. He was left only with the ultrasensitivity of a young man whose responsiveness to whatever occurred to him became reinforced not by the act but by the perception of it.

In still another diary entry for 1910 (around late summer), Kafka gives another clue to his thinking when he writes about time and what it means to him.

> We . . . are held in our past and future. We pass almost all our leisure and how much of our work in letting them [past and future] bob up and down in the balance. Whatever advantage the future has in size, the past compensates for in weight, and at their end the two are indeed no longer distinguishable, earliest youth later becomes distinct, as the future is, and the end of the future is really already experienced in all our sighs, and this becomes the past. So this circle along whose rim we move almost closes. Well, this circle indeed belongs to us, but belongs to us only so long as we keep to it, if we move to the side just once, in any chance forgetting of self, in some distraction, some fright, some astonishment, some fatigue, we have already lost it into space.[18]

Kafka's sense of time here obviously includes the Freudian unconscious, but just as certainly has within it Bergsonian and Proustian memory. What is remarkable is how Kafka was trying to find some way in which space could be temporalized, transformed into a temporal dimension. In his mature work, he would attempt blending what he intuited from cubism, abstraction, and Einsteinian physics, as can be seen most obviously in *The Castle* near the end of his life. When we come upon such a passage in the diaries, we recognize how he was beginning to assume the shape of the writer ready to probe deeply into himself and into his relationship to shapes outside him. The autobiographical works of 1912 are imminent: "The Judgment," "The Metamorphosis," and the incomplete novel that Brod titled *Amerika*, especially the first part called "The Stoker," which Kafka was willing to publish. Now in middle to late 1910, he was like an army storing up supplies for a later foray or for a defense against opponents, or like an animal stocking its stores for the coming winter. He was laying in imaginative fat, but more than that, remaking himself to become neither a better lawyer nor a better employee of the institute but a writer.

January began with Kafka's review of Felix Sternheim's *The Story of Young Oswald*, which appeared in *Bohemia*. Kafka's review is more lyrical than penetrating, and its quality is less significant than the fact of his appearance in *Bohemia*. That Prague daily, along with the *Prager Tagblatt*, was the regular conduit for cultural information to the German-speaking population of Prague and, in fact, all of Bohemia. Since we are speaking of a group of about 35,000–40,000, a good proportion of them Jews, we recognize that the two dailies must have been highly competitive for a relatively small readership. That perhaps explains why the cultural resources of each were abundant. Furthermore, they reached well beyond Bohemia and even Europe for news of cultural and intellectual importance. *Bohemia* also included a segment called *feuilletons* (short stories, brief pieces), in which imaginative work was published and where only shortly before Kafka's "The Aeroplanes of Brescia" had appeared.

The importance of such an outlet for a developing writer cannot be precisely measured. In Kafka's case, it gave him the opportunity to see in print some of his slightest work. Furthermore, it meant for someone as literarily fastidious as Kafka that he was making some progress, that while he may not have achieved the perfection he sought, he felt he could continue in a somewhat innovative format.

Cultural Modernism was now pouring into Prague through several mediums, not only newspapers. It was being performed in theaters, at least in the form of plays by Strindberg and Wedekind; while Czech theater itself, always strong, with assertive playwrights, was performed at the Czech National Theater,* as well as performances of Smetana and Dvořák, home-grown products, and a large repertory of symphonic and operatic music, both traditional and innovative. These public performances were reinforced by the literary salons, exemplified by Berta Fanta's, which was quite high-toned and not at all frivolous, and by the philosophical, political, and literary circles that met in cafés and coffeehouses, especially the Louvre and the Arco.† The Prague and Viennese coffeehouses were serious places. Newspapers and magazines in several languages were available, and tables were established for lengthy

---

*As we shall see below, Kafka tried his hand at drama, with the fragmentary "The Guardian of the Tomb," in 1916. The fragment has considerable significance in the period of *The Trial* and several of his expressionistic-symbolistic longer stories and fables.
†The Arco was so successful in drawing in not only the Kafka circle but also the Bohemian avant-gardists in painting, music, and literature that it was attacked by Karl Kraus. This guardian of Germanic culture could not miss any opportunity to attack those who showed an innovative or avant-garde spirit in the arts. His criticism was always based on their so-called mangling of the German language, whose purity, and, by inference, culture, Kraus watched over. At one point, he accused Kafka of "Kafka-ing" the German language and Brod of "Brod-ing" it, and so on down the list, including Werfel, Kisch, and others. With satirical intent, he called them Arconauts, and as was characteristic of this megalomaniacal, Jew-hating Jew, he missed every work and movement of importance coming from the Dual Monarchy. Kraus has re-emerged recently as a kind of watchdog, a man of integrity, incorruptible in a highly corruptible society; but in fact he was unreliable and subject to personal whims, with an inner life that does not convey confidence to anyone trying to follow his thought. In an era of immense egos, the man who called his magazine *The Flame* (*Die Fackel*) — that is, the organ of truth, that which burns through the dark — outdistanced his competitors in self-aggrandizement.

discussions that waiters did not attempt to break up. Of course, the coffeehouses served other functions as well as discussion: families came, particularly on Sunday, assignations were arranged, and in some of the seedier places, prostitutes were available.

It is incalculable how much Kafka derived from the regular sessions at the Arco, as he did earlier from the Louvre, not solely in intellectual terms but also in more personal ones. For these café and coffeehouse evenings became for him as for many others alternatives to home and family. We are here on the edge of a large sociological change, one already in the process of development, and now ready to burgeon: the need on the part of both sexes to put behind them unsatisfactory family life and to remake that family amidst friends with similar interests. Prague lent itself well to this change, especially for those young Jewish intellectuals who came from nonintellectual, lower-middle-class families, where art, literature, music, and culture in general were all missing, or were actually reviled as useless pursuits.

Given Hermann Kafka's ignorance of and disdain for the arts, Kafka needed to seek a family outside of his family (except, later, for his sister Ottla). The equivalent in Paris and Berlin was the *artiste milieu*, that environment created by artists and closed off to others, as a place where a particular kind of socially marginal creativity could flourish. That too was an alternative to the family, and a peculiar need of modern times, when artist and family were pitted against each other. Once the avant-garde began to dominate artistic endeavor, then family could not be expected to support or even to comprehend the artist, and he or she needed to seek an alternate form of reinforcement. This is precisely what Kafka did.

This is not to suggest that such groups or *artistes milieux* were homogeneous. They were, frequently, a warren of conflicting factions. For every avant-gardist, there was a traditionalist; and there were Zionists, Marxists, socialists, anarchists of both the violent and the gentle stripe. There were democrats, monarchists, republicans, and communists. They were, in the main, Jews, but also some Catholics, practicing and fallen away, other religionists, many agnostics and atheists. There were those with residual family ties, others who never wanted to see their families again, and those, like Kafka, caught between intellectual ties and family linkages. Their intellectual backgrounds composed a kaleidoscope of interests: philosophy, politics, law, language and literary studies, psychology, and then the breakdown of each discipline into warring categories. Even in Kafka's immediate circle, there were large differences, between Zionists and socialists, for example, a differing ideology of some significance and one that went well beyond politics and race to the very nature of how one felt about society and history. Discussions and arguments in the coffeehouses were not intended to reach solutions, but to defend what one believed against the onslaughts of others. Kafka apparently was silent through much of this vigorous dialogue.

The newly edited *Diaries* in German,* in which material omitted in Brod's original edition has been reinserted, reveals a much more active Kafka than we may be accustomed to. Quite frequently he attended lectures, plays, and films and visited art galleries. He was intellectually curious and active — especially considering he was a constant reader — although these activities, with the exception of Jewish theater, did not appreciably change his intellectual outlook. Kafka's outlook remained constant throughout his life, with the exception of the influence of Judaism on his emotional and, to a lesser extent, his intellectual life. This new information is useful, however, as a way of reinforcing our premise that Kafka's fictional practices absorbed whatever was new, whether in painting, reading, or theater. Yet despite his activity at this stage, he had believed from the beginning that art was all, and that belief remained his guiding intellectual beacon as long as he lived. All the rest was, in some ways, filler.

Having published in *Hyperion* and now in *Bohemia*, he was entering the lists as a full-fledged writer. On January 28, Max Brod, who kept pushing his friend, lectured to the Prague chapter of the Progressive Women's League and read from Kafka's manuscript of "Wedding Preparations in the Country." Kafka was himself present, but Brod carefully avoided mentioning his name or identifying him in the audience, perhaps a calculated move to force Kafka to work on the book by publicizing it. Kafka did attempt to make some sense of the material, but it was proving intractable, and on March 14 he told Brod it was no use, he was going to destroy it. He gave the manuscript to Brod as part of that mass of material he later told his friend to burn, but Brod held on to it and Kafka did little else with it.

It is also very possible that Kafka was suffering depression or some severe letdown in the winter and spring of 1910. His correspondence trailed off drastically, and in the spring letter already cited, he spoke of how everything was directed against him. Quite probably his inability to move along on "Wedding Preparations" threw him into a malaise, although the reverse is also possible — that the malaise made it difficult for him to concentrate on the novel. In either case, it is also possible that preliminary stages of tuberculosis were creating small changes in him physically, which would then affect his outlook, fueling a depressive state that was never far from the surface even under good conditions. In still another possible scenario, the depressive state, if we are

---

*Edited splendidly by Hans-Gerd Koch, Michael Müller, and Sir Malcolm Pasley. This edition not only reintroduces material from Kafka's notebooks deleted by Brod, but it redates some entries, corrects previous copying errors, clarifies Kafka's syntax, and establishes alternate readings. I have included details from this wealth of data where appropriate.

correct about it, was providing Kafka with a staging area, a way of defining what he was, and in his unique way, preparing him for major work. All of the above, or none, are possible. Certainly the spring letter suggests physical as well as mental pain, and while Kafka regularly engaged in physical exercise, he had little to help him on the mental side, except his creative resources.

So we find him in the fall of 1910 complaining to Max and Otto Brod about his skin eruption, which sounds very much like a psychological condition with physical manifestations, along with the five new abscesses, which also could have had psychological derivation. If we move later into the year, into December, we find not only doubts but despair: "Almost every word I write jars against the next, I hear the consonants rub leadenly against each other and the vowels sing an accompaniment like Negroes in a minstrel show. My doubts stand in a circle around every word, I see them before I see the word, but what then! I do not see the word at all, I invent it."[19]

Here his depression reaches right into language. We know he was reading Goethe and Kleist, for in an earlier diary entry, he mentions Goethe's *Iphigenie auf Tauris*, in which the verse "lifts every word up to the heights where it stands in perhaps a thin but penetrating light." As for Kleist, in early 1911 Kafka speaks of the writer filling "me as if I were an old pig's bladder."[20] Words and language were now doing more than merely playing their ordinary functions. Kafka was considering them freshly, as forms of expression, and that, perhaps, made him so depressed about his own usage when he compared it with that of Goethe and Kleist, whom he venerated.

But this veneration for the two German writers reveals still another side of Kafka: his desire to keep the German language purified of usages that proliferated around the turn of the century. A hyperventilated romanticism turned German into a florid or decadent impure form, in the view of some, and Kafka, no less than Kraus, attempted to keep its line uncontaminated by Viennese and Prague usages. Kafka's cry later that as a Jew in Prague not even German was his, was part of his desire to make it his and to see himself in some way as the inheritor of the German language practiced by Goethe and Schiller, but also by Kleist, Hebbel, Stifter, Fontane, and other nineteenth-century prose writers.

Kafka's reading was of several kinds, and he was, in his way, multilingual. His French was quite sufficient for reading one of his favorite authors, Flaubert, as we have seen. Among Germans, besides those mentioned above, he read Thomas Mann, Hermann Hesse, and Hugo von Hofmannsthal. Beyond this group, he read Dickens, Kierkegaard, Dostoevsky, Gogol. As an adolescent, he had become familiar with James Fenimore Cooper, Knut Hamsun, Arthur Conan Doyle, and Jules Verne. A little after that, he read Nietzsche, as did his entire generation, and he loved Czech folk and fairy tales, as well as contemporary novels written in Czech. Kafka read the American and English authors in translation, although he claimed on his 1907 job application that he had what he called a "fair" knowledge of the English language. Kafka learned what English he did know from Emil Weiss, a relative of Brod's; Weiss had fallen outside the Czech Jew's love of Germanics and turned to England. He favored Shakespeare, Byron, and the now emerging George Bernard Shaw, and it was his example that led Kafka to try to master English as a reading language at least, in 1906. Along with Felix Weltsch* and Oskar Baum, Weiss was one of the young men who made up the Brod circle.

Kafka also read a quite different author, Gustav Meyrinck. Meyrinck was part of that group that helped support guruism, spiritualism, and the occult, and met regularly at the Café Continental. He wrote a feverish prose, and he turned out one immediately popular book, *The Golem*, about Jewish Prague, even though he was not himself a Jew either by birth or choice. Meyrinck's *The Golem* was only one of several Golem pieces being written in and around the turn of the century; in fact, one can trace Gregor Samsa's metamorphosis into a gigantic beetle as some shadowy form of the Golem legend. The Golem belongs very much to Prague history: although it goes back to the Bible, the legend did not pick up momentum until medieval and Renaissance times. In the latter period, we find Rabbi Judah Loew of Prague, a contemporary of Shakespeare, creating a Golem that would protect the Jews of Prague. The Golem was both a protector, a defender of a minority, and simultaneously a monster that is an affront to God.

As the Golem develops, he becomes Frankenstein's monster, then later various robotic figures, and other metaphors of what the artist creates when he attempts to play God. For our purposes, in 1897 a Golem was created by a Czech artist, Mikoláš Aleš, a non-Jew, as part of the interest in the Golem in Bohemian legend and folklore. While the Golem was being transformed in other countries, in Bohemia it remained very much what it had been in earlier times, although it was no longer specifically Jewish. A Golem created in 1915–16 by the Czech Jewish artist Hugo Steiner looks amazingly like Kafka: almost ghostly in its appearance, a pale, lean figure, well-defined, with high cheekbones and slanting eyes. All it lacks is the Kafka hair. Surely Kafka grew up with the Golem story, although what it meant to him specifically we cannot determine. But more than likely, it caught his imagination as an "unformed substance" that could be transformed and reshaped to fit any situation and any time period, as his Gregor Samsa would come to do.

---

*Besides becoming a leading Zionist and a well-known cataloguer-librarian, Weltsch wrote a book on Kafka called *Religion and Humor in the Work of Franz Kafka*, as well as books on philosophical subjects (such as *Perception and Concept*, in 1913).

Kafka had run into Meyrinck's work before, at the Hall, where Meyrinck (born Meyer), his disciple Paul Leppin, and Hugo Salus, who posed as the local literary dictator, gave regular readings of their work. Meyrinck was not an important literary figure, but he was representative of the kind of oddball writer who turned up in Prague literary circles. Of an earlier generation (born in 1868), he came from Vienna not Prague, wrote about Jews but was Gentile, was a staff member of *Simplicissimus*, the parodic-satirical journal that influenced generations of writers, and until *The Golem* in 1916 seemed no different from dozens of other plodding journalist-writers. After the striking success of that novel about Prague Jewry and an artificial man who runs wild, he moved toward surrealism for his novel *Walpurgisnacht* in 1927.

Kafka was only marginally drawn to Meyrinck and in fact saw the writer as a proponent of the kind of prose that, once confronted, had to be rejected. When Brod quoted a passage from Meyrinck's *Purple Death*, Kafka "turned up his nose." "That sort of thing," Brod continues, "he considered too farfetched and much too importunate; everything that suggested that it was planned for effect, intellectual, or artificially thought up, he rejected — although he himself never used labels of this kind."[21] Except for *The Golem*, Meyrinck's reputation faded, as did the reputations of most in that generation who attempted to dictate literary policy — men like Hugo Salus, Paul Leppin, and Friedrich Adler, another would-be literary dictator. What in effect occurred was that this generation was incapable of responding to the demands of Modernism, and when Modernism flourished, their influence faded rapidly. To a large extent, both Brod and Werfel also suffered the same fate, although Werfel's reputation remained from his marriage to Alma Mahler, who flourished by wedding famous men, and from his status as a kind of midcult writer of *The Song of Bernadette* and *The Forty Days of Musa Dagh*.

We must attribute Kafka's depression, or part of it, to family matters as they crossed with writing problems. Neither was ever very distant from his outlook and perception of others and himself.

> Now that I've been keeping watch over myself for a week [he tells Brod], I am in such a rush of feeling that I am flying. I am simply drunk with myself, which is hardly to be wondered at under the circumstances, given even the weakest wine. Yet little has changed for the past two days, and what has is for the worse. My father has not been quite well. He is at home. When the breakfast clatter ceases on the left, the lunch clatter begins on the right. Doors are now being opened everywhere as if walls are being smashed. But above all, the center of all the misery remains. I cannot write. I have not done a line I respect.[22]

He has excised everything he wrote after a trip to Paris. "My whole body warns me against every word; every word, before it lets me write it down first looks around in all directions. The sentences literally crumble before me; I see their insides and then have to stop quickly."

The pressures of Hermann, of the apartment, of still living with his parents, and of the writing itself creates a constant sense of anxiety and concern. If Kafka could escape the apartment, perhaps he could write; but he cannot really afford a place of his own on his institute salary. Further, he does not want to give up whatever "home" means to him: that alternating feeling of need and rejection which became so significant in his perception of himself. And finally, if he did clear away the time to write more easily, then how would he support himself, since it was only the position at the institute that allowed him sufficient income to write at all?

Having been promoted, Kafka along with two colleagues, in April of 1910, had to appear, dressed in formal black, before the president of the institute, Otto Příbram, to offer their thanks in person. The situation was, of course, made to order for Kafka: the exact opposite of everything he wanted to do or could handle and, thus, a prod to his subversive self. He did not have to make the speech expressing gratitude but was expected to stand quietly with grave mien while the address was read aloud.

Příbram was the archetypal top executive, waiting for the expressions of gratitude from underlings and possibly only half listening to what were, by now, expected platitudes. Uncontrollably, Kafka began to descend from giggles toward near hysteria. It is quintessential Kafka, but also quintessential Schweik, the wise fool who cannot tolerate pomposity and idiocy. The episode stuck in Kafka's memory, almost three years later, and he hyperventilates as he relates it to Felice Bauer. Can Kafka laugh? he asks. "I can also laugh, Felice, have no doubt about this; I am even known as a great laugher, although in this respect I used to be far crazier than I am now."[23] He then launches into his story at the "gratitude" ceremony.

Kafka builds up Příbram's importance, likening him to an emperor whom the average clerk never had contact with, in fact barely saw. We hear the footsteps of those messengers in Kafka's stories radiating out from the emperor, who have not seen the source, nor even known of him. Kafka notes that like everyone "exposed to clear and careful scrutiny whose position does not quite correspond to his achievements, this man invites ridicule," but laughter was of course another dimension, left to Kafka to experience. The most dignified of the three promoted men — Kafka was the youngest — was designated as speechmaker. The emperor took his funny little posture, suitable for the occasion: legs slightly crossed, left hand clenched, head lowered, so that his white beard rested on his chest, his large protruding stomach swaying. When, as the ceremonies start, Kafka begins to giggle, the president does not seem to notice. But when the president begins his own speech, "in the imperial mold, delivered with great conviction, a totally meaningless and unnecessary speech,"

... I could no longer restrain myself and all hope that I should ever be able to do so vanished. At first I laughed only at the president's occasional delicate little jokes; but while it is a rule only to contort one's features respectfully at these little jokes, I was already laughing out loud; observing my colleagues' alarm at being infected by it, I felt more sorry for them than for myself, but I couldn't help it. . . . And now that I was in full spate, I was of course laughing not only at the current jokes, but at those of the past and the future and the whole lot together, and by then no one knew what I was really laughing about.[24]

Kafka's laughter causes one of his colleagues, who must now embark on a serious speech, to lose his composure. "No, the president in all innocence had said something to which this colleague of mine took exception." In the meanwhile, Kafka continues his laughter, which only made his colleague bring forth even more absurd and childish views. "It was too much: the world, the semblance of the world which hitherto I had seen before me, dissolved completely, and I burst into loud and uninhibited laughter of such heartiness as perhaps only schoolchildren at their desks are capable of. A silence fell, and now at last my laughter and I were the acknowledged center of attention."[25]

Demonstrating to Felice that he is a man who can laugh, Kafka admits to near hysteria. His knees, he says, shook with fear, and his colleagues, protected by his outburst, joined in to their hearts' content, although they could not match his "long-rehearsed and -practiced laughter." But by now the president was disconcerted and "in a manner typical only of people born with an instinct for smoothing things out, he found some phrase that offered some reasonable explanation for my howls — I think an allusion he had made a long time before. He then hastily dismissed us. Undefeated, roaring with laughter yet desperately unhappy, I was the first to stagger out of the hall." Kafka says that by writing a letter to Příbram, and with the consideration that the president's son (Ewald) was his friend, he was not disciplined, and the entire matter blew over. Certainly his position at the institute was not affected, since he continued to be held in high regard. He ends by telling Felice, "I may have behaved in this fashion at this time simply in order to prove to you later that I am capable of laughter."[26]

The episode occurred in April 1910, and he told Felice about it almost three years later (not two, as he says). It is an episode of considerable interest, especially as it coincides so closely with several of Kafka's complaints about living at home and about family illness. Příbram here, in one respect, is surely a substitute for Hermann Kafka: the posturing, the ridicule of his manner, the contempt Kafka shows in calling him the "emperor," the sense that he is the final authority, the ultimate patriarchal figure. Consider the situation itself. Because of this man, Kafka has been promoted, and he is expected to be honored: more pay, more responsibility, recognition in the company despite his being a Jew. Instead of Příbram playing Abraham to Kafka's Isaac, the president not only has not sacrificed him, he has deigned to praise him. And how can Kafka respond? Surely not with gratitude, because the father figure has acquired too much negative weight for that; he must ridicule the source from which the praise comes even though his response carries with it great fear and real danger of loss of position. Kafka, then, is working through all the alternating attitudes associated with Hermann and which he cannot reveal to his father, not until *Letter to His Father*, of which this laughter scene is an indirect foreshadowing.

Here was the perfect opportunity, when all his desires lying beneath his conscious wishes were unleashed, and he could mock, ridicule, parody while under the protection of his two other colleagues. Even though he regarded his colleagues deprecatingly, they were a defense behind which he could act out his hysterical strategy and make Příbram pay for finally recognizing Kafka's worth in this little ceremony that would never have been forthcoming from Hermann.

Kafka turned all father-son feeling into such a negative response that any act of authority, patriarchal or governmental, sent him into hysterical convulsions. His laughter is a cry of outrage, for even with a promotion he will not be governed or directed. What he offers to Felice in this little tale is another piece of evidence of his unsuitability as a potential husband, another warning to her that he is ungovernable, that his individual will cannot abide authority, whether Hermann's, Příbram's, Franz Josef's, or a wife's.

The other side to this outburst of laughter, however, is even more personal and intimate: a signal of deep depression. Kafka was not laughing out of self-gratification or gratitude but from despair. Since even laughter no longer functions as catharsis or therapy but becomes part of fear, anxiety, an uncontrollable and impulsive will, Kafka's near hysteria is a perfect emblem of anguish and depression. His letter to Brod about the mass of spikes driving ever deeper into him coincides roughly with the laughter episode. Kafka's very mental survival seems at stake. He will either succumb to what he later called his dread of the office, his dismay at family matters, his inability to write freely, or else will recover from despair and depression sufficiently so that he can return, renewed, to the living.[27]

Theatrical performance began to engage his imagination, and he measured human attractiveness against some ideal: that of the dancer Eugenie Eduardova (of the Russian Ballet), of Salcia Weinberg of the Yiddish theater troupe that passed through Prague, and, ultimately, against his own attractiveness, or lack of it. As for his appearance, he imagined his tall, wraithlike body to be quite the opposite of what it was: short "and a little stout." While reshaping or transforming himself in his imagination, he wondered how women would treat him. "I still please many [people], even girls. There is nothing to be said about that. Only recently one of them said something very intelligent: 'Ah, if I could only see you naked once, then you ought to be really pretty and kissable.' " To which Kafka mentally responded: "But if I lacked an upper lip here, there an ear, here a rib, there a finger, if I had hairless spots on my head and pockmarks on my face, this would still be no adequate counterpart to my inner imperfection." He explains that his imperfection is not congenital but his own; although birth gave him a center of gravity, he no longer has the corresponding body. But he also claims this imperfection "is not my own." The imaginative act of reshaping himself has led to a monologue of despair — and he resolves his lack of shape by saying he tolerates it "by means of a great labor of the imagination."[28]

We observe in this period Kafka's growing interest in the body, especially his own and that of the dancer Eduardova, a painterly perception in which solid objects or features begin to dissolve. The dancer will be described in Kafka's "dream" in dissolving terms, as a cubist figure liquefying into an abstraction, or an expressionistic painting becoming so stylized it is all symbolism and no longer objectified. The dancer:

> Her faded color, her cheekbones which draw her skin so taut that there is scarcely a trace of motion in her face and a real face is no longer possible, the large nose, which rises as though out of a cavity, with which one can take no liberties — such as testing the hardness of the point or taking it gently by the bridge and pulling it back and forth. . . . She looks like one of my aunts, an elderly lady.[29]

In the open air, he says, "Eduardova really has nothing to compensate for these disadvantages; moreover, aside from her very good feet, there is really nothing that would give occasion for enthusiasm, astonishment or even for respect." Yet she is the toast of Europe, a woman at whom men throw themselves, her girdle stuck with flowers. As Kafka asks her to dance one more czardas, he has reshaped her in his dream, and in the reshaping he turns her into a 1910 woman whose reality is secondary to the Picasso-like rearrangement of her features and to the perception of the observer.

Besides his attendance at the Russian Ballet at Prague's German theater, on May 4 he went with Brod, who had been attending their performances regularly, to see a Yiddish troupe from Lemberg, which played at the Savoy. Here Kafka sees Salcia Weinberg, whose image he calls up more than a year later when he becomes enthralled by Mania Tschissik, a woman whose "beauty" was purely in the eye of the beholder, Kafka. Salcia's chief "attraction" was the way she would bump her fellow players with her "large behind."[30] This gesture evidently caught Kafka's imagination, because Salcia came to mind when he became infatuated with Mania, or the idea of Mania. That episode will be covered later in full detail, but we can say at this time that Kafka's infatuation with her cannot be disentangled from her placement in Yiddish theater and his questioning of himself as a Westernized European Jew. She became not only the lover of his imagination but true family: that mother, sister, aunt who did not cheat on her heritage, as his family did.

But aside from such ideological positions, Kafka was re-examining the human figure. In his December 26, 1910, diary entry, he speaks once more of reshaping: "My interior dissolves (for the time being only superficially) and is ready to release what lies deeper. A slight ordering of my interior begins to take place and I need nothing more, for disorder is the worst thing in small talents."[31] This need to dissolve and regroup is connected, in some way, to Kafka's need for the diary form, where he can, apparently, reshape himself out of sight of others. "I won't give up the diary again. I must hold on here, it is the only place I can."

In March, Kafka's five *Meditation* pieces appeared in *Bohemia*, but this did not appear to relieve the anxiety and despair that were making him ill. Besides the comments on shapes and reshapings, during this time he wrote about Japanese jugglers who made a ladder based "on the raised soles of someone half lying on the ground, and which does not lean against a wall but just goes up into the air."[32] The jugglers move with a ghostly weightlessness; here, indeed throughout the year 1910, Kafka seems to be attempting to penetrate a hallucinatory world of his own making.

Toward the end of the summer, Kafka tried to assert himself, with a request for a salary increase to 2,400 kroner annually, which was still insufficient for him to become independent but was a start toward that goal. In October he gained 2,100 kroner, but before that he left Prague with Brod and his brother Otto, for Nuremberg and then Paris. The three left on Saturday, October 8, despite all Kafka's ailments, including a dislocated big toe and a bad leg that "doesn't look very pretty." This was to be a trip on which he would try out his French, a language he could read but had had no opportunity to speak. The Paris journey, followed by a shorter one to Berlin six weeks after the return to Prague, was an attempt to recover his equanimity by traveling. Paris proved a deep disappointment, however, possibly because Kafka had built up such high expectations. He walked the streets alone, which is not a bad tonic in Paris, but he carried with him his Prague depression. The result was Job-like boils Paris doctors could not treat, and in nine days Kafka retreated to Prague. Brod testifies to his friend's gloominess, and Kafka himself in three postcards to the brothers after his return speaks of being pale, apparitional, even suffering a brief fainting spell. Travel did not prove therapeutic, in fact, and Berlin, which he had looked forward to visiting for the first time, also offered no respite. However enticing Paris and Berlin might have been under different circumstances, Kafka had removed himself to some area beyond friends and places. This re-

moval of himself from beyond the reach even of Brod and his journeying now into his own regions of mind and imagination are the most significant aspects of his life in late 1910. The diaries indicate how deep
that journey could be, where he put on paper words and ideas he could
not communicate in any way until he moved into his major phase of
work; and then that work became the vehicle of his removal. Even in
the slight *Meditation* pieces, he was entering realms usually unreachable, realms full of ghosts, memories, and hallucinations. By moving
"beyond," he could put to use all those ailments, imagined and real,
from which he was suffering, for ailments and sickness gave him a further remove from the ordinary world of his literary colleagues, family,
and fellow workers. It was in this carved-out territory, where there
were no frontiers, no boundaries, no literary rules, that Kafka would
find his place. Exploration of the Arctic and Antarctic was capturing
the world's imagination, even as Kafka was moving out into his own
whited place.

Berlin, then, like Paris, proved disappointing. Everything seemed
dreary, the "architecture is nothing," and yet he senses some contentment. But this is followed by: "I still feel very bad, but how will I feel
tomorrow?" He does find the vegetarian food good: semolina pudding
with raspberry syrup, lettuce with cream, a cup of strawberry-leaf tea.
Berlin was, for Kafka, virtually a culinary orgy. He saw a performance
of *Hamlet* with Albert Basserman, the German stage and film actor,
but the experience proved unsettling: "Every so often I had to look
away from the stage into an empty box, in order to compose myself."[33]
On December 9, he returned from Berlin for the wedding of his sister
Elli, now twenty-one, to a twenty-seven-year-old merchant, Karl Hermann, from Zürau. For a brief time, he felt at ease, since he still had ten
days until his return to the institute. But this feeling was mixed with
images of a rampage and of great fear of returning to the office: "The
dread hit me so hard that I felt like hiding under the table," an image
and idea that recurred in "The Metamorphosis." In his December 15
letter to Brod, continued on the seventeenth, his mood swings are enormous, almost manic and then despairing; Kafka's emotions are on a
roller-coaster of his own making. He asserts he almost never quarrels
with his parents, and even Hermann is acting normally, only annoyed
when he, Kafka, works too late at his desk. He says he and the family
are well, the wedding is over, the "new relatives are being digested,"
and even the piano-playing young lady downstairs has vanished for several weeks.

But by the addition to the letter on the seventeenth, Kafka is raging
again, "simply drunk" with himself, and, furthermore, Hermann is
home, ill. We have already noted Kafka's sensitivity to the clatter of
breakfast and lunch dishes, and other noises in the apartment. He tells
Brod he wants to spend as much time by himself as he can so that he

can enjoy the general excitement solitude brings him, and with that he sends on a fragment "of the novella," which was probably "Description of a Struggle." That "being alone" that he insisted upon meant he could cultivate his own needs beyond the prying eyes of others: his obsessive cleanliness and neatness, his finicky eating habits, his use of the night when others were asleep, and his sensitivity to noise, to the point of madness when he waited for and then picked up ordinary sounds, especially the grunting of his parents in bed.

The year 1910 was most significant for Kafka, not so much for his achievement, which was small, as for the recognition of what was to be his life in its remaining years. The beginning of the diaries is no small matter here. Kafka had also begun to come to terms with his isolation from others; with the pain and anguish of ailments, minor or major, imagined or real; with his peculiar response to noise, disorder, the claims of work. Not that he found peace here; on the contrary, he rioted within himself, rampaged with his emotions. But he discovered within himself, and especially through his diaries, that he could bear these experiences and then transform them, even as he transformed himself into the person he had to be. The day after Christmas in 1910 he revealed part of his new credo, "that disorder is the worst thing in small talents."[34] His strength, he adds the next day, is running down; it no longer "suffices for another sentence."

The year 1911 was not particularly eventful, except for several trips Kafka undertook for the institute and some he took on his vacation time, including a return to Paris. The overwhelming event in that year was his experience of the Yiddish theater troupe, his friendship with Jizchak Löwy, and the strange, almost inexplicable attraction he felt for Mania Tschissik. Here Kafka loosened up significantly from the tightly wound, highly anxious, deeply neurotic young man who walked the edge and became open to an experience that offered easy access to his emotions and a world of responses that were all new. He observed another form of life, and it is not an exaggeration to say that this experience, along with the beginning of his strange affair with Felice Bauer in August of the next year, opened up his imagination to his first major work. Although the two events appear unrelated, they are significant in tandem because they came at Kafka from opposite sides.

Each experience represented something so different from the other: one, emotional, piercing in its undermining of the Westernized Prague German; the other (Felice), so clearly a part of that ordinary Prague-Berlin German-Jewish world, controlled, ordered, organized, not at all open to large emotions. Felice and her world drew Kafka back to parental expectations and to work opportunities at the institute, away from the kind of writing he eventually hoped to do. The Yiddish troupe drew him into a re-examination of everything he was and had done.

Mania Tschissik, inaccessible but an apparition of desire for Kafka, and Felice, whom he found unattractive, with her "normal" needs for a husband light years away from what Kafka was — the two women, so opposite in their persons and attractions, helped create Kafka's world for him from 1911 onward, either in terms of his major work or in terms of the sensational correspondence he carried on with Felice.

The internalization was almost complete.

> I haven't written down a good deal during these days [he wrote in his diaries], partly because of laziness (I now sleep so much and so soundly during the day, I have greater weight while I sleep), but also because of the fear of betraying my self-perception. This fear is justified, for one should permit a self-perception to be established definitively in writing only when it can be done with the greatest completeness. . . . For if this does not happen — and in any event I am not capable of it — then what is written down will, in accordance with its own purpose and with the superior power of the established, replace what has been felt only vaguely in such a way that the real feeling will disappear while the worthlessness of what has been noted down will be recognized too late.[35]

The privatization of experience here is overwhelming, and Kafka's words indicate how fearful he is that perception and performance will not form an equation. He does not feel quite in equilibrium between what he is capable of and what he can produce at present and is positioning himself, waiting for precisely the right moment when the equation will occur, when everything will feel right.

Near the end of January, the institute sent him on company business to Friedland and Reichenberg, in picturesque northern Bohemia. Ostensibly a business trip, the journey took on far more profound implications for Kafka as he observed in Friedland a castle that had once belonged to Wallenstein, the Bohemian general in the Thirty Years War. He wrote about it in "Travel Diaries"* and to Brod, describing it as "smothered in ivy." He sent on a picture postcard to Brod showing the drawbridge and other features. It apparently made a considerable impression upon him, and several Kafka critics associate his experience of this castle with the one he wrote about in his final novel. Observation of a castle was surely a source for Kafka's recreation of one in *The Castle*, but without minimizing the importance of this Friedland experience, we should not make too much of it, or else we restrict Kafka to a realism at odds with his procedures. Another, much more accessible castle was Hradčany Castle, which dominates every view in Prague: the official residence of the Czech president since 1918, but dating back to the ninth century and evolving into its present state through medieval and Renaissance times. That castle would have been sufficient for

---

*The "Travel Diaries" ("Reisetagebücher") are appended to both the English and German editions of his *Diaries*. In Czech, Friedland is Frýdlant and Reichenberg is Liberec.

a writer seeking in it forms of power, magical forces, mystical, even apparitional associations, emblems of history and memory, and all the rest Kafka infused it with.

Nevertheless, we should not slight Friedland, especially this diary entry with its castle:

> The different ways there are to view it: from the plain, from a bridge, from the park, through bare trees, from the woods through tall firs. The castle astonishes one by the way it is built one part above the other; long after one has entered the yard it still presents no unified appearance, for the dark ivy, the dark grey walls, the white snow, the ice covering the slate-colored glacis enhance the heterogeneity of its aspect. . . . I went up by a road, slipping all the time, while the castellan, whom I encountered farther up, came up without difficulty by two flights of stairs. A wide view from a jutting coign.[36]

He then describes the park, laid out in terrace fashion on the slope. There is a magical, scrimmed look to it, with its pond, swans, various vistas. Kafka found little to see or do in Friedland, although he tried the "Emperor's Panorama," an indoor amusement area of elegant proportions and dulling potentiality. The high point was a magic-lantern slide show of Italy; later even the bookstore seemed as forlorn as the rest of the place.

Reichenberg, less than an hour away, where he had the opportunity to attend the theater, offered more. Kafka noted scurrying people and wondered what real object they could have in this relatively small town, a question as to people's activities, since he considered himself outside the mainstream of life. He wanted to attend an exhibition at the Workers' Sickness Benefit Office, but the policemen on the street could not direct him.

Before embarking on this business trip, which brought with it an entire host of problems associated with traveling to relative backwaters, he entered his thoughts in his diaries proper, apart from the "Travel Diaries." He speaks of being "completely finished — during the last year I did not wake up for more than five minutes at a time — I shall either have to wish myself off the earth or else, without my being able to see even the most moderate hope in it, I shall have to start afresh like a baby." He writes of having projected a novel "in which two brothers fought each other, one of them went to America while the other remained in a European prison. I only now and then began to write a few lines, for it tired me at once."[37] We hear in this a shadowy beginning of *Amerika*, or "The One [or Man] Who Vanished" in its original German title.*

Der Verschollene connotes several meanings, including the one who disappears into the void, or the one who is never heard of again. *Amerika*, Brod's title, sparkles but sacrifices definition.

When he returned to Prague on February 12, Kafka was completely exhausted, and his description sounds like Gregor Samsa's plaint: "When I wanted to get out of bed this morning I simply folded up. This has a very simple cause, I am completely overworked. Not by the office but my other work." The journey to northern Bohemia was no small contributor to his enervation: the long hours on the road, the boredom of a strange city, the disruption of his schedule, his inability to collect his thoughts for writing when absent from Prague, his finicky eating habits, which made each restaurant an adventure, his sensitivity to noise; and the work itself, the meetings with strange people, the need to unravel problems on the spot, to investigate, interrogate, analyze, and resolve. Even for a much more hard-headed salesman or company officer, such a life was wearing; for Kafka, it was almost suicidal. "The office," he wrote in his diaries, in a draft letter of resignation, "has an innocent share in it only to the extent that, if I did not have to go there, I could live calmly for my own work and should not have to waste these six hours a day which have tormented me. . . . In the final analysis, I know, that is just talk, the fault is mine and the office has a right to make the most definite and justified demands on me. But for me in particular it is a horrible double life from which there is probably no escape but insanity."[38] So he wrote on February 19, 1911.

Yet however truly exhausted and enervated he was, we must not take him at his word. For he was able to drive himself into different levels of responsiveness and sensitivity by his need to hoard his time. Without the insurance work on his back and his desk, Kafka is unimaginable. It was the time burden of the work that drove him to his greatest anger and anguish, and from that he could compact himself into a small bundle of nerves. He could only flame up because his life was almost snuffed out. Nor should we neglect the fact that the office job gave him a definition in the real and ordinary world, and however much he railed against that world, a significant part of him needed that entrance into what other people did. While backing off from marital commitments, he longed after the stability of married life, children, a comfortable home. So the office, whatever its disadvantages and chilling boredom, was a necessary part of the way he looked at himself.

In his resignation letter to Eugen Pfohl, he tells Herr Pfohl he loves him as a son does, but resign he must, so that when he comes to the office the next day "the first thing I hear will be that you want to have me out of your department."[39] The letter was never sent, nor should we ever believe Kafka intended to send it when he wrote it. It was therapeutic, it met his need to throw the stone, but certainly not to take final responsibility for it.

The stone having been thrown into his *Diaries*, he plodded on, laying the groundwork, whether consciously or not, for "The Judgment,"

and then for "The Metamorphosis." He was also beginning in some indirect and shadowy way to move toward the material of "The Stoker,"
with a young man's desire for independence, his trouble with his family, and his ultimate escape into an unknown territory. Some of Karl
Rossmann's exploration of America in *Amerika* can be an emblem of
Kafka's exploration of his own territory, not abroad but within his own
imagination, a searching out of those materials that would become the
substance of his work. Parts of *Amerika*, admittedly incomplete and
unrevised, read like exploratory forays into foreign lands. Kafka's
America is not close to the actual country, although it is a good fantasy
land, an approximation of an approximation, America behind a scrim
of sorts. All this, then, was preparation.

So as to solidify his ghosts, Kafka was immersing himself in Kleist.
As was noted earlier, Kleist was particularly compelling to Kafka because of his tortured personal conflicts (leading to suicide at thirty-
four), his struggle to resolve adversarial positions (feeling and thought,
divine and human law, the real and the spiritual), and his lean, dynamic
prose style. Kleist led easily into a short fiction Kafka embedded in his
Diaries, "The Urban World," which in turn, as several critics have observed, leans toward "The Judgment." The seven-page fragment involves a young man's struggle with his father: Oscar M., "an older
student," and the dictatorial, fleshy-faced father, who turns Oscar into
a nonentity. " 'I simply won't put up with your good-for-nothing existence any longer. I'm an old man. I hoped you would be the comfort of
my old age, instead you are worse than all my illnesses.' "[40] Here we
have Abraham and Isaac, with Abraham more than willing to sacrifice
Isaac rather than any substituted sacrificial ram. This is Kierkegaard's
retelling of the biblical story.

Oscar's father defends his yelling at his son: " 'I do it not in the
hope that it will improve you, I do it only for the sake of your poor, good
mother who perhaps doesn't yet feel any immediate sorrow on your account, but is already slowly going to pieces under the strain of keeping
off such sorrow.' "[41] In "The Judgment," Kafka makes the scene more
nakedly son and father, for the mother is dead, and the two go at it
mano a mano within the confines of a small apartment, like a boxing
ring where the gladiators must struggle to the death. "Description of a
Struggle," never completed, leads into this "description of a struggle,"
however different. Not only "The Judgment" is foreshadowed here,
but the situation between Gregor and Herr Samsa in "The Metamorphosis."

Oscar tries to tell his father of his plans for the future, but Mr. M.
knows that such plans will come to nothing. He asserts that this can't
be his real father, that his real father would have embraced him; some
kind of change must have taken place. Oscar leaves to find Franz, an
engineer, to seek his advice. Franz is asleep, but Oscar props him up and
demands he come with him, advise him, support his case. The frag-

ment ends with Oscar pressing Franz, insisting he must get up, that he will communicate his information when Franz is dressed.

The fragment does not go further into motivation, resolution, or even narrative line. What Kafka had in mind was a situation, not a way as yet of bringing the various elements together. He examined his own position very clearly, but the part with Franz is inconclusive, in which Franz is used as Kafka used Brod, as a prop and support through letters and personal attention. That Oscar is Isaac seeking to escape Abraham's wrath is also clear. That Oscar cannot believe this is his real father, a switch on the Kierkegaardian retelling of this story, is another element Kafka could not resolve at this time. The materials, certainly, were there, but how to shape them could not occur in the *Diaries*, which served as sketches, not as artistic endeavors.

Diary entries for March 1911 suggest Kafka was seeking something supportive for his lonely sense of himself.[42] His slight movement toward Jewish questions and Zionism was revealed not in letters but in private diaries: Kafka speaking to himself. One extended entry concerns Max Brod's new novel, *Jüdinnen* (*Jewesses*), and then after that, his meeting with Dr. Rudolf Steiner, a guest at one of Berta Fanta's evenings. Kafka was responding to an attack on the novel for its having failed to put the complicated questions of Judaism into an individual viewpoint. But his own position was quite different: he criticized the novel for not providing a solution, when Zionism offered one, and for not providing "non-Jewish observers" who could draw out, by contrast, the Jewishness of the Jews. Kafka then makes an analogy that does not exactly reflect well on Jews. He says a lizard starting up under our foot startles us greatly and we bow down to it, but hundreds of lizards seen crawling at a dealer's leave us vacant. One Jew attracts attention; many become invisible.

Rudolf Steiner does not fare much better. When Kafka sought ideas outside of his literary favorites, he was usually quite hard on them. Steiner was a kind of faith healer of his day. When Kafka made his acquaintance, Steiner was fifty, an occultist, a leader in the German Theosophic Association, a man who, abandoning theosophy, developed anthroposophy, a philosophy in his terms that interpreted the world not through the senses but through spirituality. His role in occultism, spiritualism, theosophy, and other such matters fitted in well with Berta Fanta's intellectual evenings, in which God's essential nature was taken for granted and from which believers deduced the spiritual nature of man and his world. Kafka's involvement in this group is merely an indication of his curiosity, for he remained, until near the end of his life, an agnostic, a secular being, a hard-headed ironist and realist. When he did become a Zionist, he was like so many other early Zionists, agnostics and atheists who saw Palestine as a social experiment, a homeland for like-minded Jews.

Kafka begins his comments with an edge that comes close to parody. He describes some of Steiner's methods: curing people with colors or sending invalids "to the picture gallery with instructions to concentrate for half an hour or longer before a certain painting."[43] Kafka then proceeds to describe his consultation with the doctor, who scatters advice in all directions.

Steiner asks Kafka if he has been interested in theosophy for long, to which the latter responds with his prepared address, that a great part of his being "is striving toward theosophy," but that at the same time he has great fear of it. He is apprehensive it will result in "a new confusion which would be very bad for me, because even my present unhappiness consists only of confusion." He assumes, here, a parodic tone, the edge of burlesque. He says his confusions are linked to his literary endeavors, and here, he dares to say, he has experienced states that correspond closely to "the clairvoyant states described by you, Herr Doktor." Still in this near parodic tone, he continues: "Only the calm of enthusiasm, which is probably characteristic of the clairvoyant, was still lacking in those states. . . . I conclude this from the fact that I did not write the best of my works in those states."[44]

Kafka warms to his prepared address — half true perhaps, half imagined — like a plaintiff laying out his case and seeking legal advice, only to change his life, not to win a point. He declares that because of the slow nature of his maturation, he cannot live by literature alone, and he is prevented by his health and character from devoting himself to something so uncertain. As a consequence, he has become an official in a social insurance agency. But "the small good fortune in one becomes a great misfortune in the other. If I have written something good one evening, I am afire the next day in the office and can bring nothing to completion." As he awaits some thunderbolt from above, some paternal advice, some wisdom from a father figure, he wonders whether to these two unreconciled endeavors he can add a third — theosophy? "Will it not disturb both the others and itself be disturbed by both? Will I, at present already so unhappy a person, be able to carry the three to completion?" This is what he has come to ask the Herr Doktor, the former faith healer and occultist, now the theosophist and anthroposophist. Tablet ready, Kafka awaits his word.

Steiner listened attentively, without looking at his would-be disciple. He nodded, as an aid to the speaker's concentration. "At first, a quiet head cold disturbed him, his nose ran, he kept working his handkerchief deep into his nose, one finger at each nostril." End of diary entry, and, apparently, end of Kafka's bowed knee before Steiner. Like all father figures, Steiner has failed. More intent on his nose than on Kafka, he has let anthroposophy scatter to the winds. The parodic style of the entry is now explained by the final paragraph: Steiner is not a problem solver but an attentive nose-picker.*

---

*Kafka's parodic remarks on Steiner are among several other such comments later that

Putting noses behind, Kafka and his friends enjoyed regular Sunday hikes into the countryside outside Prague, hikes that often became endurance tests in which Kafka showed no mercy to laggards. A Sunday jaunt of twenty to twenty-five miles or more was not unusual. He had become beguiled by Jens Peter Mueller, a Danish bodybuilder, who recommended daily exercise, which Kafka proceeded to do or outdo by exercising naked before an open window in winter as well as in summer. To make himself hardy, or perhaps to prepare himself for a polar expedition, Kafka wore summer clothes in the harshest winter weather, a light summer suit, no hat or gloves, or else a light summer hat, no overcoat, and jauntily made his way along Prague streets, oblivious to the stares of those who recognized, they were sure, a crazy man.

Much of this *muellern* — the practices named after Mueller — was part and parcel of a German-inspired culture that was supposed to have little to do with Jews. It was a Prussian and German form of body building designed to prepare soldiers for when war came, against all German neighbors, but especially against the physically undeveloped French — and to ensure that Aryan youth (before that term was explicit) did not end up looking like inner-city Jews. Bodily muscle was the Prussian answer to Jewish sensibilities and achievement, and the cult of the body became part of the culture: physical exercise camps, long hikes, exercise classes, state-organized events and state-directed school activities. These body cults and their groups were, further, connected to nationalistic movements, and thus, in this respect, they seemed clearly to exclude Jews, or to show Jews in a poor light. What occurred, however, was that Jews, as well as those of other nationalities, including the Young Czechs, pre-empted some of this ideology, and clubs and organizations for body health cropped up everywhere. Nationalism and some racism permeated most of the organizations run by Gentiles, so Jews formed their own groups, the Maccabees, for example, and groups connected to Zionism. By linking Zionism and body building, Jews could work on two problems at once. For just as the Germans used such outfits as a preparation for war, so Jews could build bodies as a preparation for the settlement of Palestine.

But Jewish health clubs served other purposes as well. When nationalism intensified among the Young Czechs and other groups, an increasing number of hostile acts against Prague Jews occurred. Attacks were made on Jews on the streets or in back alleys by roving gangs, attacks sufficiently isolated that they did not make the newspapers, nor did they coalesce into pogroms. As nationalistic groups sought scapegoats for their own frustrations within the empire, Jews on Prague

---

year, many of them deleted by Brod. One concerns a visit to the art connoisseur Anton Pachinger which Kafka made with Brod. Kafka describes Pachinger: his life is made up of "sammeln und koitierin," of collecting and screwing; then he goes on to list some of Pachinger's sexual indulgences (November 26, 1911; *Tagebücher* [Frankfurt: S. Fischer, 1990], p. 272).

streets were becoming an endangered species. Body building, therefore, served defensive purposes, giving Jews some opportunity to fight back successfully, at least in individual actions when mobs were not involved.

Pawel quotes from the Prague Zionist *Selbstwehr*, in 1912, when it appealed to young Jews to shed their "intellectual preeminence. . . . and our excessive nervousness, a heritage of the ghetto." It advised, on the German model, a sound mind in a sound body: to cast off the ghetto mentality, which had meant intellectual effort, and seek balance, "harmoniously balanced personality." We spend, it said, "all too much of our time debating, and not nearly enough in play and gymnastics. . . . What makes a man a man is not his mouth, nor his mind, nor yet his morals, but discipline . . . what we need is manliness."[45] This was the new call to action, and though Kafka did not achieve the *Selbstwehr* sense of manliness, he attempted to remake a frail, concave body into something he would not be ashamed of when he undressed. In *Letter to His Father*, we note how shame at his concave figure still dominated his imagination and how it helped shape his outlook. The hostility he felt toward anyone physically well defined was not mitigated by his own efforts to achieve a more shaped body.

Physical exercise, however, was only the beginning for Kafka. Whatever pains he took with his external body, he doubled in dealing with the internal aspect. Not that it did much good, for he suffered from headaches his entire adult life, usually on a daily basis, and even though aspirin was beginning to become available (recently introduced as the first "wonderdrug") he refused all medication and insisted on organic, natural means. This insistence made him and nearly everyone around him miserable, which was, very possibly, the underlying aim of his practices. He developed an eating regimen that eliminated all meat, although it was almost impossible to hold to this when he made trips for the institute. The elimination of meat is of some interest, since one of his complaints against his father was the latter's sloppy way with food, and the association, somehow, that Kafka made between Hermann and meat. It seems certain that Kafka's distaste for meat, animal flesh, was linked to his disgust with robust Hermann's propensity for it and, further, his disgust for Hermann's father, as a ritual slaughterer. Vegetables, nuts, fruits, milk: all of these were clearly "feminine" foods in this strange gender division of what was to be eaten; and here Kafka rejected Hermann not only in person or in his famous letter, but in the very substances he put into his digestive system. And he rejected not only Hermann, the father, but all father figures; for the rejection of meat as somehow manly or masculine was, for Kafka, the rejection of all authority. By creating his own eating patterns, he was creating himself as a unique creation that he could himself shape, whatever possible harm such eating habits might hold for someone with his delicate frame. It seems now that Kafka, in a pretubercular condition, might have benefited from a diet that included more iron and protein than he was perhaps getting much of the time.

But vegetarianism was only the beginning when it came to Kafka's approach to food. He went much further, with the process, noted earlier, called "fletcherizing." Watching someone chewing food until it was reduced to a pulp was obviously disgusting for anyone else eating at the table. It disgusted Hermann, who held up a newspaper to shield himself from whatever God had wrought in his son, and friends, as well as relatives, could barely tolerate Kafka at the table.

Fletcherizing was ostensibly an aid to digestion, making the food easier to assimilate. But since much of Kafka's diet consisted of foods already easy to digest, like yoghurt, milk, bread, fruit, jellies, and vegetables, the excess of chewing seems all the more unnecessary. He was, once again, carving out a unique role for himself, whereby the social act of eating became a solitary one. And while we may see in this pathological tendencies — it is difficult to avoid noting how close to the edge Kafka was in most of his practices — we must keep in mind that his eating habits were part of the restructuring he needed to maintain his controlled sense of himself. On the surface, he might have been miserable, and he brought some of that misery to those close to him, but all that was secondary to his main purpose: to reshape himself, using whatever means at his disposal.

Kafka did not seek God through his selection of foods, but he did seek himself — and in that, some privatized God — through manipulating food and his digestive track. We can never lose sight of the fact that *he* remained the beginning and end of everything in his perception of what he wanted to be. He, not family or society, chose what went into his mouth; he selected the times when it would emerge, rarely, and only under duress; he went to prostitutes for his sex, rejecting the more socially acceptable form, marriage. All of his procedures were ways of warding off what was to his perception a hostile atmosphere, whether the hostility came from Czech thugs roughing up Jews, from well-meaning friends and self-absorbed family members, or from his own imagined sense of a negative world. To separate his judgments based on what was actual and what was imagined is always difficult, since he seemed to move equally in both worlds and to divide himself as the situation demanded. But nearly all his defenses were conceived to struggle against hostility, even to the degree that his responses were not advantageous but subversive of his health and well-being. The bottom line, however, always remained his need not to play by anyone else's rules, not to be won over by others' arguments, not to succumb to whatever hostility might have brought another person to bended knee. And within that formulation of who he was and how he would behave was his constant search for something in himself, that moment perhaps when he could make contact with a perfection, an ultimate, a uniqueness. It wasn't God he sought, but Kafka.

In April 1911 he went on a tour of Zittau (in the Kingdom of Saxony), then to Warnsdorf, where, as Brod tells it, he met Moriz Schnitzer.[46] Kafka was by now deeply immersed in his plans for health cures, and he was willing to listen to every quack who had a scheme that might help him (mainly his imagined illnesses, along with real headaches and real constipation). Schnitzer preached a "nature cure," which Kafka found to be the work of a magician. Brod is the sole source: Kafka returned to Prague from his tour depressed and enervated, his stomach out of order. He told Brod about this magician (Schnitzer was an industrialist, not a physician) who had looked at Kafka's throat in profile, from the front. Brod reports that Schnitzer "then talked to him [Kafka] about poisons in his spinal marrow and almost up to his brain already, which had developed through living on the wrong lines. To cure them he recommended sleeping with the windows open, sun-bathing, working in the garden, joining in the activities of a club for natural healing and subscribing to a magazine published either by the club or by the industrialist himself."

This sounds like an old pitch for tonic that will restore hair, or an elixir that will bring back sexual potency. Schnitzer "speaks against doctors, medicines, and injections. He explains the Bible from a vegetarian standpoint; Moses led the Jews through the desert so that they might become vegetarians in these forty years. Manna is a meatless diet." The fleshpots of Egypt, which are attacked, indicate how flesh was reviled; and even Jesus, a relative newcomer to this, insisted that this bread he pointed to was his body. Kafka saw some of the fun in these remarks, but he was easily taken in by anything that was natural or organic, and which, evidently, meant a rejection of his family's eating habits.

"Fundamentally," Brod writes, "he saw in the efforts to create a new healthy man, and to use the mysterious and freely proffered healing powers of nature something extremely positive which agreed with a man of his own instincts and convictions, and which he widely put into practice too." As we have noted, Kafka slept with the window wide open in the winter and went without meat or alcohol. Even when he was evidently ill and required more sophisticated treatment, he preferred primitive care in private houses to sanatoriums with more experienced methods. Yet even as we look askance at some of Kafka's practices, we must acknowledge that if he had been healthy he was on the track of a particular form of health treatment — food, exercise, natural and organic means — which we now know to be beneficial. But Kafka carried the entire process too far, and he was, of course, heading toward an incurable disease.

Schnitzer may have caught his imagination, but Brod was right in thinking Kafka was dispirited. His correspondence fell off, and his diary is blank except for a casual notice of Brod's birthday. The lack of energy is clear, perhaps brought on, in part, by his failure to win an increase in salary to the 2,400 kroner he had requested. His efforts to find some shape that his body could take had failed, and he possibly sensed that his efforts to find a form for his art could also fail. Kafka's struggle throughout his mature years was not to triumph over the father, but to find the correct form for his fiction and then to triumph over that. He was far more intent on discovering the right container for his ideas than he was in winning the battle of Abraham and Isaac. He had long ago turned the field over to Abraham and accepted Kierkegaard's formulation that the son will be sacrificed even if a substitute for him is offered. That may have been the battlefield once, as it would be in *Letter to His Father*, but by the time Kafka wrote this document, in 1919, he had transferred his energies to the shape of fiction, the form for ideas, the container for his anxieties and tensions. To speak of him as involved in a perpetual struggle with Hermann is to lose sight of the fact that Kafka, by means of his writing, had long since relocated Hermann. This is not to deny the large place Hermann assumed in Kafka's thought, but by the time of 1911–12, when Kafka was preparing for his foray into literature, Hermann was only one of many problems and conflicts.

As a kind of metaphor of his own battle to achieve form, the right container for his fictional ideas, Kafka created a parable, "An Imperial Message." A messenger sets out on his journey to bring the emperor's message to the people. Yet he cannot leave the palace; he is like the man from the country unable to penetrate the law, in "Before the Law" in *The Trial*. Kafka writes of the messenger "how vainly does he wear out his strength; still he is only making his way through the chambers of the innermost palace; never will he get to the end of them; and if he succeeded in that nothing would be gained; he must fight his way next down the stair; and if he succeeded in that nothing would be gained; the courts would still have to be crossed; and after the courts the second outer palace; and once more stairs and courts; and once more another palace; and so on for thousands of years."[47] And even if he ultimately breaks through, which is, we know, impossible, he could not fight through the refuse of the world, not the least "with a message from a dead man."

This parable of a messenger with a message he cannot deliver can be interpreted as an example of the Dual Monarchy's bureaucracy. The attempt to get anything out of Vienna is strangled before it can develop, and the people waiting for the word never receive it. In this view, information cannot flow; it is eternally impeded, bottled up well before it can be imparted. Yet a more personal view of the scene is that it serves as a parable of Kafka's struggle to cast his material and his recognition that it may not find the form that best serves it, that it will be bottled up as information that never gets past the inner court of his own imagination. It is, then, an emblem of his own conflict. Even though he has the message and intends to send it, his words as messenger will not find the means by which they can be communicated. Or if communicated, they will never reach the people for whom they are intended.

The other side to this metaphor, really a parallel case, is the parable called "Pekin and the Emperor." Here the villagers doubt there is such a place as Pekin, where houses and people go on row after row. The people hear that Pekin sends out edicts, but the edicts don't arrive and the people do not believe that their source even exists. The village survives independently of any authority, and the village's morals are pure because they rely not on contemporary law but on older times. The huge gap between information and those waiting to receive it is, in this reading, the divide created in the writer, certainly in someone like Kafka. What he conceives of does not enter the minds of those who are his potential audience. They not only do not receive the information in a form they can comprehend, but they doubt the very existence of the source of that information.*

Here was Kafka's dilemma. The great conundrum of "Before the Law," which appears in *The Trial* and also as a separate parable, is part of this information gap. In it, an individual comes to a door, through which only he can be admitted, since the door was intended only for him. But the doorkeeper is about to shut it, and thus the man for whom it was intended will not be able to enter. Kafka has created a conundrum within an enigma wrapped around by a paradox, as an emblem of the imaginative process that can never discover precisely what is right for it. The "law" here, which resists the individual's entrance, is the material that must be contained in the writer's imagination. All questions of freedom here — who is freer, the man from the country or the doorkeeper? — are subsumed under the larger heading of what value we put on the law itself. The sole value that makes sustained sense for Kafka is connected to the creative process, whereby the "law" becomes the experiential mass that must be transformed into a fictional form. Before that dilemma, the individual is barred by the doorkeeper who represents the intractability of the material, regardless of what is in the imagination.

An August 20, 1911, diary entry reinforces the sense that Kafka was

---

*As we know from *The Trial* and *The Castle*, this "gap" between sender and receiver becomes a common theme for Kafka. In another parable, "The Refusal," what is called "our town" (Prague?) is far from the frontier, but even farther than the frontier is the capital. While great things are said to occur in the capital, with dynasties deposed or annihilated, nothing changes in the town. Once again, this gap is the problem of the writer whose communication system fails because he cannot find the correct form, or whose language remains problematic.

girding himself for a large-scale creative effort to discover the right mix of material and form.

> I have been reading about Dickens [a biography, as well as the works of Dickens]. Is it so difficult and can an outsider understand that you experience a story within yourself from its beginning, from the distant point up to the approaching locomotives of steel, coal and steam, and you don't abandon it even now, but want to be pursued by it and have time for it, therefore are pursued by it and of your volition run before it wherever it may thrust and wherever you may lure it.[48]

This description is, in one respect, a search for the imaginative process that can transform that experience of a story; and those approaching locomotives of steel, coal, and steam are the elements that may make the writer want to abandon the idea, but he must press on, even if pursued by the very powers which try to force the abandonment.

Entries now are quite spare and far between, as are the letters to Brod. To the outsider, this seems an empty period. But if we extrapolate from Kafka's internal situation, it is not at all empty but full of potentialities simmering toward fulfillment. There are personal revelations. Kafka has, for example, stopped being ashamed of his body in the swimming schools in Prague, Königssaal, and Černošic. He jots down (on August 20) a few lines of what may be a story, and at the same time complains to Brod that he has no time for good work, no "time to expand myself in every direction in the world, as I should have to do."[49] He was planning a vacation, to leave on August 27 for Italy, when Hermann started to use familiar Kafka methods: illness as a form of control. Hermann's shop had not been doing well, the result of many factors, not least the anti-Jewish boycott, the strife in the streets, and the general turn of events in which Czech nationals were beginning to squeeze all Jews, shopkeepers and others. Hermann regressed, so that the man of the house became the child: he was unable to sleep, caught up in worries about his business, vomiting, suffocating, sighing as he walked back and forth, needing wet cloths on his heart (to slow down the palpitations).

Julie Kafka was filled with anxiety, saying that her husband who had always been so energetic was now caught in a spiral of worry and illness. The pathology of the household became circular, from son to father, now from father to son, with mother as intermediary. "He walks up and down, sighing and shaking his head." He gains attention, becomes the center — Herr Samsa of "The Metamorphosis." "By his frequent yawning or his poking into his nose (on the whole not disgusting) Father engenders a slight reassurance as to his condition, which scarcely enters his consciousness."[50] Yet the need is real, since Kafka mentions that his younger sister, Ottla, his favorite, confirmed that "poor Mother will go to the landlord tomorrow to beg."

The nose picking, which we also recall from the Rudolf Steiner episode, was one way for Kafka to gain moral authority, and the remark that it was not disgusting is simply another way of saying he was inured to the physical disgust Hermann engendered in him. By denying disgust, Kafka affirmed its presence. Yet the affirmation was for him something positive, for it enabled him to go off on vacation in defiance of Hermann's sighing and heaving, and Julie's need to beg for a postponement of the rent. As he knew, he had to escape, especially now that Hermann was stealing his scenario.

The vacation was part of Brod's ongoing plan to get Kafka writing, or at least to inspire him toward the idea of writing. Brod's diary is itself full of comments on his friend's depression and enervation. They kept parallel diaries, noting down what they saw on the trip to Italy, Paris, and Erlenbach on Lake Zurich, and then comparing what they had written. The premise was a completely false one: that Kafka could move to the same drummer as Brod, when in fact they were so completely different. Brod's depressions were acute but brief, and the very nature of his optimism and high energy for work resulted in a kind of observation very different from Kafka's. Brod hugged surfaces, favored narrative, picked up from contemporary topics, and was not overly careful in his use of the German language, giving himself the kind of freedom of usage that Karl Kraus condemned as *Yiddishkeit.** Yet Kafka initially went along and kept a diary of the affair. It is not particularly distinguished, but it served, mainly, as a prod to writing. From the beginning he says it was a poor idea for them to describe the trip and their feelings toward each other.

They departed for Zurich on August 28, 1911, meeting "Alice R." at Pilsen, where she boarded the train; she ended up as Dora Lippert in "The First Long Train Journey." Kafka merely listed what he saw, little of it caught in any distinctive way: "Back and forth on a bridge in indecision as to the order in which to have a cold bath, warm bath and breakfast."[51] Breakfast is mentioned again; the cathedral is viewed; the swimming pool, for men only, is toured and presumably used; a free concert by the Officers' Tourist Club is attended. Kafka mentions "No Jews." Lunch is described: the Kafka special of pea soup, beans with baked potatoes, a sweet, sterilized wine made of fresh grapes. Apparently the Swiss water is deemed unfit to drink. In midafternoon (at three), Kafka and Brod left for Lucerne. At the casino, they decided to lose ten francs: "The loss of ten francs was not enough temptation to

---

*The problem, clearly, was Kraus's, not Brod's. In his attempt to keep German pure, Kraus was denying his own Jewish background (he converted to Roman Catholicism in 1911 and then denied the conversion, later returning to Judaism). In much the same way, Richard Wagner, who feared being part Jewish, had inveighed against so-called Jewishness in German music. Kraus's Jewish self-hatred entered into nearly every phase of his cultural criticism, pointed and trenchant as it was.

go on playing, but still, a temptation. Rage at everything." Kafka seemed well contained and more relaxed than usual, despite the "rage."

Kafka was impressed by the beauty of Lucerne, the lake of Zug, the Jungfrau in the distance. His hips are tickled by a woman in their train compartment. They follow a route from Vitznau to Flüelen-Gersau. On August 29 they boarded the Gotthard Tunnel train for Lugano. They traveled around the environs, taking in the ordinary sights, none of them particularly exotic, although Kafka expressed some wonderment at the fresh look of it: loggias with colored cloths stuck in, cypresses, a donkey, the noise of shouting and other activities, the passage to the pissoir, soldiers on their bicycles, hotel employees dressed up as sailors. He measures his own stale and ill-learned Italian against the fluency of the spoken language and realizes the "great void of one's own ignorance."[52] Still in Lugano, when they hear of cholera, they move on to Milano. Kafka observes a young Italian woman "whose otherwise Jewish face became non-Jewish in profile. . . . Her father, near by, had a hooked nose whereas hers, at the same place, curved gently, was therefore more Jewish." The nose becomes the telltale object. He retreats before a "tall, stout, perfumed woman," hears her "scattering her scent into the air with her fan," so that he felt himself "shrivel up next to her."

When the cathedral proves a little tiresome, they discuss going on to Paris, even though their money is running short; they somehow would like to be compensated for the cholera fear which sent them on. The Galleria in Milano has its desired effect of dwarfing people in its immensity; and then with that whiff of perfume from the stout woman still in his nostrils, Kafka and Brod head for a brothel — *Al vero Eden*, as he says. Brothels lined the street, and Kafka says he was lighthearted and, "as always in such moods, felt my body grow heavier." Brod is the one who becomes apprehensive. Kafka notices a French prostitute: "A girl with a belly that had undoubtedly spread shapelessly over and between her outspread legs under her transparent dress while she had been sitting down; but when she stood up it was pulled in, and her body at last looked something like what a girl's body should." Kafka does not say what happened but does list what he had been drinking; the effect seems to have been a vomiting session. The diary has little more than these spare details. Fearful of the cholera epidemic, the two head for Paris on September 8. He notices women's fat behinds, parted legs, and will, he knows, end up in a brothel there as well.

The Paris trip appeared to start with some bad feeling between Kafka and Brod over inconsequentials: whether to wash up or to get right out to see Paris. It was Kafka who had wanted to get going, and then he kept Brod waiting while he himself washed up. It was vintage Kafka — if not late for appointments, then indifferent to time and to schedules. He recognized how out of weariness he could retreat into himself, becoming completely indifferent "and without a trace of guilt." Tired as he was, he decided to make up for the last trip to Paris, which was cut short by boils and rashes. They took in the Parisian sights, cafés and parks, as well as the Opéra Comique (*Carmen*), bookstalls, then the Comédie Française for Racine's *Phèdre*. Kafka was dissatisfied with the lead actress, having read of the great Rachel when she was a member of the Comédie Française. And then he went to the brothel, which struck him as "sensibly conducted," with a woman concierge instead of the man he had expected. In Prague he "had often taken casual notice of the Amazonian character of brothels,"[53] and here it seemed no different, female concierge and all. The two, Brod and Kafka, were escorted upstairs and received by "two respectable-looking women." When the light went on in the adjoining room, the unengaged girls "stood around us, drawn up in postures calculated to reveal them to best advantage." When one girl came forward and the madam urged him on, Kafka felt himself "impelled toward the exit."

On the street, the girls were packed like sardines, so close he found it almost impossible to escape. He speaks of them as dangerous, as sharks trying to get at him. "One would have had to keep one's eyes wide open, and that takes practice. I really only remember the one who stood directly in front of me. She had gaps in her teeth [like a shark], stretched herself to full height [Amazonian], her clenched fist held her dress together over her pudenda [*vagina dentata*], and she rapidly opened and shut her large eyes and large mouth [shark again]. Her blond hair was disheveled." Kafka is caught between fear of her and a desire to bow and take off his hat. "Lonely, long absurd walk home." Even the easy atmosphere of a French brothel could not relieve the anxiety or uncertainty that made his sex shrink.

He attempted to work out some psychology of the subway, then a new phenomenon in Europe, and he was especially taken with the lights and darks of the cars and the stations, and how people seemed indifferent to tunnels, where he, Kafka, always felt oppressed. He worried about his diet, about all the pastry he was eating, and started to consume yoghurt, one container after another, fearful that his digestive tract would clog up, as it did when he returned to Prague and needed to consult a doctor.*

Brod then departed, and Kafka continued on by himself to the Erlenbach Sanatorium in Switzerland. Just why Kafka did this is unclear. Digestive troubles, constipation, general feelings of unwellness, surely depression, an anxiety attack that could not be relieved? Any or all of

---

*In his *Diaries*, Kafka described one possible treatment picturesquely: "The artist [Alfred] Kubin recommends Regulin [a seaweed extract] as a laxative, a powdered seaweed that swells up in the bowels, shakes them up, is thus effective mechanically in contrast to the unhealthy chemical effect of other laxatives which just tear through the excrement and leave it hanging on the walls of the bowels" (*Diaries: 1910–1913*, p. 67).

these are possible. Once again, he went into lists of things he had seen, none of them remarkable: morning setting-up exercises, a fat little girl "who was always picking her nose" (a favorite image), the doctor leaning over and listening to his heart and unable to make up his mind, as if he couldn't locate it, or else wasn't sure it was functioning correctly. Kafka is witty about the possible ambiguity. He is aware of languages: French based on German, or else the speech of a Jewish goldsmith from Cracow who was caught among languages, English, German, Yiddish. "His German was disturbed by an English pronunciation and English expressions; his English was so strong that his Yiddish was given a rest." Under it all was Polish.[54] Kafka's sensitivity to interrelated and overlapping languages, mentioned repeatedly in his travel diaries, was probably linked to his own hesitation about writing in a language, German, that he felt did not belong to him.

He is aware of the patchwork nature of Switzerland: an Italian district, Ticino, that wants to secede to Italy; a German city, Biel, overrun by Frenchmen; a German school taken over by Italians, who want Italian officials to run it. Switzerland, two-thirds German, the remaining third French and Italian, reminds him of the patchwork Austro-Hungarian Empire: straining at the seams, still workable but ready to explode into nationalistic entities, and only a few years away from its final extinction after seventy years of attempts at unification.

His "misery is always present," and he remained completely by himself. While group games were going on in the dining hall, he stayed apart because of his "lack of skill." Even though he felt he was writing badly, if at all, he "still had no feeling for either what was ugly or degrading, sad or painful in this lonely state of mine, a loneliness, moreover, that is organic with me — as though I consisted only of bones." He felt the trace of an appetite "above my clogged intestines," but fell into apathy and indifference when an old lady peppered him with questions about his writing. He found nothing to answer. The scene is one of a wasteland, the emptiness of sanatorium life for Kafka, although during some stays he was luckier and met pretty young women. At meals, he sat in utter boredom, and he approached his food mechanically.

His interest in body structures suggests his move toward transformation and metamorphosis. He writes of one person as embodying "a new human type," a Mr. Fellenberg. And that gives Kafka his subject: "People with thin skins, rather small heads, looking exaggeratedly clean, with one or two incongruous little details (in the case of Mr. F., some missing teeth, the beginning of a paunch), a greater spareness than would seem appropriate to the structure of their bodies, that is, every trace of fattiness is suppressed, they treat their health as if it were a malady, or at least something they had acquired by their own merit."[55]

Although these are only passing remarks, they foreshadow that preoccupation with sickness, health, and bodily types in another writer about the European condition, Thomas Mann, in *The Magic Mountain*. But they also foreshadow Kafka's own preoccupation with the body na- ture gave him — in his eyes, a kind of joke, what we note in some of the earliest photographs. He poses for the camera, bowler pitched smartly on his head, as though the entire image-making process were some kind of joke and the reality lay elsewhere. As Kafka stared at bodies, and as a swimmer he observed uncovered masses of bodies, he saw configurations that went well beyond "pretty" or "attractive" or "hand- some" or "ugly." He moved beyond the human figure to some archety- pal image, which might be human or animal or insect. He saw in the human figure the potential for other forms of life, including a gigan- tic bug.

At about this time, according to Brod, he and Kafka embarked on another project, less competitive, but nevertheless matching their tal- ents against each other, a cooperative venture to write a novel together, called tentatively "Richard and Samuel," later renamed "Robert and Samuel." Kafka made several remarks about this venture, and from his point of view it seemed doomed almost from the start. Just before he left for Switzerland with Brod, Kafka noted the beginning of what the story might be.

> It had already become a custom for the four friends, Robert [Richard], Samuel, Max and Franz, to spend their short vacations every summer or fall on a trip together. During the rest of the year their friendship con- sisted mostly of the fact that all four liked to come together one evening every week . . . to tell each other various things and to accompany it by drinking a moderate amount of beer.[56]

In this brief scenario for what seems to be a novel completely an- tithetical to everything Kafka had become, Franz is described as "an employee in a bank," which looks forward, of course, to Joseph K. in *The Trial*. Max is said to be, as he was, a civil service official (in the post office). Among other things, Max plays the piano, while Franz, "who understood nothing of music, stood alone at the table and looked through Samuel's collection of picture postcards or read the paper." The details make the novel sound like a realistic picture of young men in Prague, somewhat on the order of George Gissing's *New Grub Street*, with special attention to the figure of the writer in that book whose passion is to capture every detail of ordinary life. If the descrip- tive of the novel sounds uninventive, the book's fate was to be still- born.*

The plan for the novel, whatever shape it was eventually to take,

---

*One chapter of this aborted novel did appear in print, in the Prague magazine *Herder- blätter* (a newspaper for the folk), in May 1912.

did not draw Brod and Kafka closer together but appears to have created considerable hostility on Kafka's part as he came to realize how different their talents were and how distinct their literary goals were. In a later diary entry, on October 30, well after the decision on the collaboration, Kafka was full of barely suppressed rage. We know he was upset because he vents his feelings on food. When he was anguished or anxious over other matters, what he put into his mouth and then excreted (or withheld) became of dominant importance to him. He writes that when he feels healthy, he has a craving to

> heap up in me notions of terrible deeds of daring with food. . . . If I see a sausage that is labelled as an old, hard sausage, I bite into it, in my imagination with all my teeth and swallow quickly, regularly and thoughtlessly, like a machine. The despair that this act, even in the imagination, has as its immediate result, increases my haste. I shove the long slabs of rib meat unbitten into my mouth, and then pull them out again from behind tearing through stomach and intestines. I eat dirty delicatessen stores completely empty. Cram myself with herrings, pickles and all the bad, old sharp foods. Bonbons are poured into me like hail from their tin boxes. I enjoy in this way not only my healthy condition but also a suffering that is without pain and can pass at once.[57]

This entire passage, which continues with equally compelling comments, moves eventually into Kafka's feelings about the collaboration with Brod. The interrelationship of food and the Brod "competition" is not without interest, especially since Kafka's violence about food is mainly about "Jewish" food. Kafka's body here becomes an alien machine dictating what enters and what exits. Kafka now tries to analyze his response to this violence toward food, and from this transitional explanation he moves on to another source of repressed violence, his response to Brod's effort to make him write.

In the linkage, Kafka seeks some explanation of his behavior:

> It is an old habit of mine, at the point when an impression has reached its greatest degree of purity, whether of joy or pain, not to allow it to run its salutary course through all my being, but rather to cloud and dispel its purity by new, unexpected, weak impressions. It is not that I evilly intend my own harm [although self-inflicted harm *was*, indeed, one way he energized himself], I am only too weak to bear the purity of that impression. Instead of admitting this weakness, which alone would be right, because in revealing itself it calls forth other forces to its support, I rather quietly and with seeming arbitrariness try to evoke new impressions in an effort to help myself.[58]

In due time, Kafka came to what is of greatest importance: his declaration to Brod "that nothing can come of 'Richard and Samuel.' "[59] He says it took not a little courage, for Brod objected to stopping; but since the idea of continuing was far from Brod's own mind, Kafka was left confused. He failed to find "the right answers," which is understandable since they were buried deep in hostilities he could not possibly admit to. "But later, when I was alone," he writes in his *Diaries*, "and not only the disturbance of my sorrow by the conversation but also the almost effective consolation of Max's presence had disappeared, my hopelessness grew to such an extent that it began to dissolve my think-ing."[60] A more direct linkage between food and the writing of this ill-ventured novel becomes clearer when we read Kafka's letter to Brod from Erlenbach Sanatorium on Lake Zurich. Brod had asked his friend to work on the novel while at the sanatorium, and this Kafka found im-possible to do: "You only showed your ignorance of the arrangements in a sanatorium, whereas when I promised to write it I must somehow have forgotten sanatorium life."[61]

He then describes the activities, the familiar sequence of bathing massages, gymnastics, meals, resting to recuperate; and then the cycle recommences. Kafka is attentive to the meals: applesauce, mashed po-tatoes, vegetable and fruit juices. "If you like, they can be taken quite unnoticeably, but also can slide down enjoyably and only slightly de-layed by whole-grain breads, omelettes, puddings, and above all nuts." He details a few other activities and then returns to writing, but says that like the time at Stresa he "felt wholly like a fist with the nails pressing into the flesh,"[62] and regrets that the activities cannot be so easily put behind him while he retreats to his room.

The entire regime is antithetical to writing, *his* kind of writing; not, apparently, Brod's kind, which could be done under any and all cir-cumstances. Behind Kafka's explanation of his inability to write is a considerable amount of anger, directed not only at himself (obviously!) but also at his friend's insistence that they could work at something as complicated as a novel on equal terms. By this time, Kafka knew his talents and interests lay at cross-purposes to Brod's. In a November 19, 1911, diary entry, he finally spelled it out: "I and Max must really be different to the very core. Much as I admire his writings when they lie before me as a whole, resisting my and anyone else's encroachment (a few small book reviews even today), still, every sentence he writes for 'Richard and Samuel' is bound up with a reluctant concession on my part which I feel painfully to my very depths."[63]

He spent a week at the sanatorium, from the time Brod left on Sep-tember 13 to the twentieth, and then returned to Prague, where he met Alfred Kubin. He found himself fascinated by the famous artist but also captivated by Kubin's fascination with constipation. Kubin told stories about Munich, and he described "the most varied things" without showing much facial expression. Yet all "evening he spoke often and — in my opinion — entirely seriously about my constipation and his." When Kubin caught sight of Kafka's hand hanging over the edge of the table, he cried out, "But you are really sick."[64] After that, he says, Kubin treated him more indulgently and protected him from others who wanted to talk Kafka into going to the brothel with them. As they parted, Kubin called out, "Regulin" (the laxative).

The fall of 1911, which seemed so precarious for Kafka, so full of indefinite preparations and yet so lacking in certainties or performance, took on a hodgepodge quality. He was interested in Goethe's diaries, and measured his own mentality against Goethe's, and met Kurt Tucholsky, who was passing through Prague. Tucholsky was a German political satirist and journalist, less hateful than Kraus, but also, like Kafka, deeply despairing: Tucholsky would commit suicide in 1935. Interestingly, he wrote under four pseudonyms, each signifying a different aspect of his character: Ignaz Wrobel (a contemporary satirist), Peter Panter (a theater and literary critic and travel writer), Theobald Tiger (a poet), and Kaspar Hauser (a figure of despair and loneliness, named after the nineteenth-century German foundling). Tucholsky was a man of many parts, with the satirical mode his dominant form of expression. Only twenty-one years old but, as Kafka wrote, "an entirely consistent person," Tucholsky immediately caught his attention. The young man wanted to be a defense lawyer, was full of plans, and saw no obstacles. Kafka was interested in the melancholy that lay beneath the surface of such energetic optimism.

From his observation of Tucholsky, Kafka roamed into another topic close to him:

> The artist Szafranski, who grimaces, reminds me that I too have a pronounced talent for metamorphosing myself, which no one notices. . . . Yesterday evening, on the way home, if I had observed myself from the outside I should have taken myself for Tucholsky. The alien being must be in me, then, as distinctly and invisibly as the hidden object in a picture-puzzle, where, too, one would never find anything if one did not know that it is there. When these metamorphoses take place, I should especially like to believe in a dimming of my own eyes.

Kafka also says that he imitates Brod.

That the meeting between the two was memorable is reinforced by Tucholsky's recognition of Kafka's unique talent, although as a writer the German was very different from the Czech. Tucholsky's criticism of Kafka's "In the Penal Colony," in 1920, gets right into the crevices of the writer and the book.*

> *In the Penal Colony* is a work of art so great that it defies all labels. It is definitely not an allegory, but something altogether different. The officer in charge explains the precise mechanism of the torture machine and comments with pedantic expertise on the victim's every convulsion. Yet he is neither crude nor cruel, but something much worse: he is amor-

---

*In the June 3, 1920, issue of the left-wing journal *Weltbühne* (World-Stage). By this time, Tucholsky had converted to Lutheranism, whereas Kafka had gone from indifference to a fervent Zionism.

al. . . . His delight in the manifestations of the victim's six-hour agony merely demonstrates his boundless, slavish worship of the machine, which he calls justice and which in fact is power. Power without limits. To be able for once to exercise power without any constraints — do you still remember the sexual fantasies of early adolescence? What stimulated them was not just sex but the absence of constraints. To be able to impose one's will, without any limits. . . . This is the dream that Kafka's story is about, and the obstacles in the way of perfect wish fulfillment are part of it. For the torture is eventually cut short not because society, the state, or the law indignantly rise up in protest and put a stop to it but because the spare parts for the machine turn out to be defective; the apparatus, though still tolerated by the higher echelons of bureaucracy, no longer enjoys full support at the top. . . . And all of this told with incredibly, understated, chilling detachment. . . . Don't ask what it means. It means nothing. The book may not even be of our time. It is completely harmless. As harmless as Kleist.

That fall the meeting with Tucholsky seemed to open a floodgate for Kafka, in which he needed support from all directions.* On October 1, he attended services at the Altneu Synagogue, on the Jewish Day of Atonement, Yom Kippur. The attendance was not for him, apparently, a religious event; there was little in his life so far to indicate any hidden desire for faith or any move toward it. Instead, it was the need for some atmospheric support, something from outside, like Tucholsky and others during this time. It was as though Kafka had worked himself so deeply into a spectral role he needed reinforcement from outside to convince him of his reality. The synagogue experience, as he presents it, is a series of brief episodes: three pious Eastern European Jews, two crying; a little boy without any conception of what was going on; the family of a brothel owner seeking respectability. Kafka ends the epi-

*The two had similar backgrounds as sons of poverty-stricken fathers who through business acumen moved up into the lower middle class and to a respectable social status. Like Kafka, Tucholsky had struggled against a strong-willed father, had gone through an educational system that he considered disgraceful and meaningless, but both became doctors of jurisprudence — Tucholsky in 1914, eight years after Kafka. Both wanted to be writers, not lawyers, and both were troubled about their Jewishness: Kafka vacillating about who and what he was, then turning on his Westernized Germanic Judaism toward a more open and committed Eastern form, though without any faith; and Tucholsky converting to Lutheranism, part of that self-hating Jewishness to be seen in Kraus, Weininger, and an entire generation of Semitic wanderers. Both were involved in the bureaucracy, and both satirized it, although Tucholsky — and this sounds strange describing a man who went to Sweden to commit suicide — remained optimistic about Germany and its place in the world. Both were ironists, satirists, mockers, Tucholsky more openly, Kafka more subtly and incisively. Tucholsky was a writer for the here and now, never a complete artist; whereas Kafka aimed for eternity. Finally, in his confusion, Tucholsky hated the kind of Jew who, he felt, created the grounds for anti-Semitism, the victim creating the terms for his victimization; and while Kafka was drawn to the idea, he rejected it when he felt the passion and warmth of the Eastern European Jew. Running parallel to this, as we shall see, was Theodor Herzl, a product of the Enlightenment, full of condescension toward vulgar Jews, an elitist who early on sought both acculturation and assimilation, a fervent believer in German ideals.

sode: "I was stirred immeasurably more deeply by Judaism in the Pinkas Synagogue."[65] What we find is a beginning, an attraction to the very kind of Jewry his father was attempting to escape from, the shtetl experience. It was only shortly after this that Kafka began his involvement with the Yiddish theater troupe and with the actor Jizchak Löwy, and, from a distance, with the actress Mania Tschissik.

As Kafka, at twenty-eight, looked out at a world of hostility, surely at a hostile but beguiling Prague, he was moving toward some form of support. With Buber's ideas before him, he would meet the Yiddish acting troupe, the very people Hermann Kafka reviled. Hermann thought that even Brod was a "crazy-nut" (*meshuggener ritoch*), but that was kind compared with the way he felt about Löwy and his crowd. Kafka's diary entries reveal how much he needed some connection.

In early November: "This afternoon the pain occasioned by my loneliness came upon me so piercingly and intensely that I became aware that the strength which I gain through this writing thus spends itself, a strength which I certainly have not intended for this purpose." Or on November 2: "This morning, for the first time in a long time, the joy again of imagining a knife twisted in my heart."[66]

This characterized the fall of 1911, including his dreams. He recalls some and notes how sleeplessness has overtaken him: "After an hour I wake up, as though I had laid my head in the wrong hole. I am completely awake, have the feeling that I have not slept at all or only under a thin skin, have before me anew the labor of falling asleep and feel myself rejected by sleep." When he awakens, "all the dreams are gathered about me, but I am careful not to reflect on them." Nevertheless, they accumulate, including one of a blind child, with a nightmarish quality. "This blind or weak-sighted child had both eyes covered by a pair of eyeglasses, the left under a lens held at a certain distance from the eye, was milky-gray and bulbous, the other receded and was covered by a lens lying close against it."[67] To achieve optical correctness, the girl's eyeglasses must be attached to a lever whose head is connected to the child's cheekbone, "so that from this lens a little rod descended to the cheek, there disappeared into the pierced flesh and ended on the bone, while another small wire rod came out and went back over the ear." He associates this unfortunate child with the daughter of an aunt in Leitmeritz, but this aunt, he knows, has no daughters, only sons.

So troubled was Kafka by this dream he told his immediate superior, Pfohl, about it. But he also associated his sleeplessness and nightmarish dreams with his writing. And this was as it should be, because the dreams are connected in some way with images he will create in his writing. The physical transformation of the blind or near blind girl, with a rod sticking from her cheek, into images from Kafka's stories is clear, as is the self-imposed torture of the rod supporting the lens. What he has created is a typical condition for him, in which the individual to gain one benefit (here sight through a lens) must tolerate a terrible pain or torture. Kafka saw his writing this way: unable to live without it, it drove him close to madness, certainly to sleeplessness. As he says in a slightly later entry: "Finally I say it, but retain the great fear that everything within me is ready for poetic work and such a work would be a heavenly enlightenment and a real coming-alive for me, while here, in the office, because of so wretched an official document [a long report to the district chief of police], I must rob a body capable of such happiness of a piece of its flesh."[68]

Just as the ability to write something meaningful appeared to be gathering strength, so did the opposing powers, as Kafka perceived the situation. He had become, as it were, a walking example of Freud's sense of antithetical elements working in the conscious and unconscious. Obstacles appeared everywhere — in the office, in nightmarish dreams, in paranoid fantasies — and yet it was precisely because of the obstacles that he had to find a way through. Any intrusion created extreme anger: for himself and for what he hoped to become. "Rage at my sister who comes into the room and sits down at the table with a book. Waiting for the next trifling occasion to let this rage explode."[69] When she departs, he feels a "dawning relief and confidence," and begins to work. As we read the diary entries for the fall of 1911, we observe Kafka describing the worst that can happen to him as a way of dealing with how he can counter it, or else assimilate it into his work. Even as he was struggling to stay afloat so that he could do his work, he was attempting to position himself as a representative or emblematic man for the twentieth century. Until the works themselves reveal him, this delicate balance is found in several diary entries and in letters.

In the October 5 diary entry, Kafka mentions that on the previous evening he attended, at the Café Savoy, a performance by a Yiddish acting troupe. This experience is usually treated as a central episode in Kafka's intellectual and emotional development, and there is little question it was significant. We must, however, also see it as a terrible challenge to everything he was: it was not an experience easily assimilated. On the contrary, it had to be confronted and meditated over before it could be understood; and then, once it was understood, Kafka could perceive it not as a reassurance but as a testing mechanism for him. His entire life was on the line as he began to move into the intimate affairs of this troupe, with Löwy, its director, becoming his friend, while he worshipped Mania Tschissik, a principal actress, from a distance.

From his first observation of them, he was thrown into a quandary over what to make of this exotic and troubling vision on stage, from Mrs. K., as a male impersonator, to her husband, who could be anyone.

He says that if he had to explain them to someone, he would consider them "notorious lazybones with whom the community has come to terms, privileged schnorrers [beggars] for some religious reason," but people who, because they have been set apart, are very close to their community's life. They see clearly "to the core the relationship of all the members of the community . . . people who are Jews in an especially pure form because they live only in the religion, but live in it without effort, understanding, or distress."[70] Here, right from the start, Kafka verbalizes the terrible challenge these Jews present: so different from himself, so reviled by Prague's German Jews, including Hermann Kafka, and yet embodying something Kafka knew was lacking in his own despondent, marginal existence. What Kafka experienced here, and continued to develop in diary and letters, is the sophisticated, urbanized, more or less genteel individual, the product of a quasi-capitalistic society, suddenly confronted with a contemporary version of the noble savage, simple in his responses, close to his own kind of community, at ease in his religious beliefs, certain about who and what he is. Kafka had stumbled into a universal conflict, and, of course, his way of expressing it was by personalizing it.

The play at the Savoy, *Der Meshumed* (*The Apostate*), was by Joseph Lateiner, a well-known Yiddish playwright who lived from 1853 to 1935. The two actors in caftans observed by Kafka as having extended arms and snapping fingers possibly foreshadow the two assistants in *The Castle*. Clearly, images from the play remained in Kafka's mind, since the performers remained fixed in his imagination. He was touched deeply: "Some of this woman's acting (who, on the stage, because she is a Jew, draws us listeners to her because we are Jews, without any longing for or curiosity about Christians) made my cheeks tremble."[71]

Kafka was especially attracted by the two men in caftans, who at times appeared to travel on air. In continued entries in the *Diaries*, he describes elements of the Yiddish play, particularly the elements of celebration through song, dance, swaying, chanting, even forms of moaning. He is alive to the sentimentality of the performance, the obvious gestures, the broadness of the acting, and the evident insincerity of the feelings expressed. Yet he is also taken with the passion and warmth lying behind the performance. He details the convolutions of the melodrama, including the unresolvable case of a Gentile woman who, unable to marry a Jew, according to civil law, cannot get the approval of her father to convert. But this is only one element in a complicated Jewish-Gentile drama, in which conversion and baptism have so blurred the religious lines we have a kind of French farce, with religion replacing bedroom.

His meditation on his experience remains horror-filled. "If I reach my fortieth year," he writes, "then I'll probably marry an old maid with protruding upper teeth left a little exposed by the upper lip." To this he adds,

> I'll hardly reach my fortieth birthday, however; the frequent tension over the left half of my skull, for example, speaks against it — it feels like an inner leprosy which, when I only observe it and disregard its unpleasantness makes the same impression on me as the skull cross-sections in textbooks, or as an almost painless dissection of the living body where the knife . . . splits still thinner the paper-thin integument close to the functioning parts of the brain.[72]

Once again, while voicing personal pain and suffering, Kafka enters into transformations of the physical state, here in terms of the brain as a case study, or as the matter through which a knife slices. In some shadowy way, the body is being reshaped. This is soon followed in the *Diaries* by a dream in which brothels play a large part. Kafka sees two prostitutes, one with her head hanging down through a break in the wall, and this is the one Kafka, in the dream, occupies himself with. Max is with the other, at her side. Kafka fingers his whore's legs and presses the upper parts of her thighs; in a kind of reverie he finds a beautiful entertainment. But then the dream takes on another dimension, one out of a Poe story, and full of Kafka's hostility:

> Then the whore, without moving her legs, raised the upper part of her body and turned her back to me, which to my horror was covered with large sealing-wax-red circles with paling edges, and red splashes scattered among them. I now noticed that her whole body was full of them, that I was pressing my thumb to her thighs in just such spots and that there were these little red particles — as though from a crumbled seal — on my fingers too.[73]

Kafka breaks stride on his private dreams to mention that he had written "a sophistic article": for the *Tetschen-Bodenbacher Zeitung* "for and against my insurance institute."* His point of view had always made him sympathetic to the workers and quite sensitive to the fact that the institute did not wish to pay out monies if it could help it. Kafka's job was to explain how the system worked, with its new equations of casualties and payments, its estimates of risk, and all the other elements that create such a division between insurance promises and actual benefits. The "sophistic" part was Kafka's recognition he was expected by the institute to keep certain realities under cover; not to lie outright, but not to tell the entire truth; not to disguise, but not to re-

---

*The *Tetschen-Bodenbacher Zeitung* for September 18 had carried an unsigned article criticizing the running of the Workers' Accident Insurance Institute, and it fell to Kafka to respond. The question was one of fraud, mainly on the part of employers who were expected to contribute toward workers' compensation in the event of injury claims. Kafka's response of five thousand words appeared on November 4, in the newspaper supplement, called "The Workers' Accident Insurance and the Employers."

veal. In walking that edge, and still trying to be partisan to the workers, Kafka was of course involved in other areas of hostility: the hostility he felt toward the institute for its procedures, toward himself for being the intermediary in these matters, toward the workers for being beguiled by his words and by the institute, and toward a system that made such divisions between promise and actual outlay. While it was good training for the writer, it was, in a shadowy way, an indication how "the Jew" was being used to trick the Czech; or how the Jew could be fitted into a plan whereby Czechs deceived Czechs. He felt the manipulation, unquestioningly, as well as the bureaucratic dishonesty and corruption, the sense of being used.

On October 14, Kafka entered in his diary his impression of another schmaltzy play in Yiddish, this time A. Goldfaden's *Sulamith*. The play, however, took second place to Kafka's meeting with Löwy and his first sight of Frau Tschissik, who played the part of Sulamith, a girl who, lost in the desert, throws herself into a well, only to be saved by the "hero," who subsequently abandons her for a rich Jerusalem girl.

Löwy was so different from Kafka as to seem to come from another planet. From Löwy's point of view, Kafka was a middle-class Praguer who might be able to help him and his troupe, although he was devoted to Kafka the man; from Kafka's point of view, as already noted, Löwy was a discovery, a yardstick against which he could measure how far Jews like himself had gotten away from what gave them identification and community. For Kafka, Löwy provided both an ideological and a sociological study, or even an archaeological dig, in which the writer could keep uncovering layers of deception from the Jew's Germanic disguises. There is little question the association with Löwy and the infatuation with Mania Tschissik helped open up Kafka for complete honesty, and thus gave him the energies to write unrestrainedly.*

---

*The actual meeting occurred through Brod. Brod had written a review of Löwy and the Yiddish troupe in the *Prager Tagblatt*, and because of that Löwy wanted to meet the reviewer, something arranged by the company manager at a restaurant. Along with Brod were Kafka, Werfel, Hugo Bergmann, Oskar Baum, and Otto Pick; and from this, Kafka moved ever closer not only to Löwy but to the entire troupe. Löwy (or Levy) was flouting his ultra-Orthodox background by appearing on the stage, something absolutely forbidden in Jewish law and practice. There was considerable rebellion in his act of family defiance. When he met Kafka, Jizchak (or Yitzhak) Löwy was twenty-four, but with a lifetime of running in his background. Part of his fascination for Kafka may have been his decisiveness in leaving home, religious strictures, and family ties. Warsaw-born, Löwy went to Paris at seventeen and became involved in acting, followed by tours throughout Europe. None of these efforts proved successful, and Löwy by twenty-four was a rolling stone dependent on sympathetic people like Kafka to get through. He seemed genuinely to have liked that strange Prague Jew, but he also saw Kafka as a needed benefactor; for someone like Löwy, it was impossible to separate feeling from need. After the troupe left Prague in 1912 and toured Bohemia, it broke up and Löwy settled in Berlin, remained in touch with Kafka in Prague until 1917, then returned to Warsaw as a journalist, and, finally, suffered the fate of most Polish Jews, in German ovens.

But intermixed in this development was a crisis in Hermann's shop: a walkout by the entire staff. Individuals had given notice before, but never everyone at once, all in protest against Hermann's crudeness, his invective, his lack of sympathy for employees' needs, his resentment at their Czech sympathies (perhaps on his part a pre-emptive strike, not allowing their anti-Semitism to get to him). He had disregarded the fact that as the nationalist movement grew, pressure was put on Czechs not to work for Jews — a condition Hermann might have understood had he been a more kindly employer. But he intended to rule the shop the way he ruled the household, by physical domination, strong words, and disregard for everyone else's feelings. Kafka sympathized with the shopworkers and indicated this when he entered into negotiations with at least one of them. In the meanwhile, Hermann cajoled them back, through what Kafka called "effective use of his illness, his size and former strength [anticipating Herr Samsa], his experience, his cleverness." Kafka went to see the bookkeeper, who had promised the manager to leave. The meeting was embarrassing for all, since Kafka found himself in a delicate relationship with a man whom he had regarded little in the past, a man, furthermore, who was alternately deferential and defiant, eager to keep his promise to the manager, but not wishing to anger the gentle and forebearing Kafka. It was a situation of contraries bound to give Kafka sleepless nights, a shock to his nerves and a blow to his sensibilities. He adds his regret that for the sake of this futile mission he is forced to miss his first meeting with Löwy.

This involvement in Hermann's shop, however, was only a taste of what lay in store for Kafka as Hermann conceived of beginning an asbestos works, in conjunction with Elli's husband, Karl Hermann. Like most family businesses, it was established in good faith, but then when family rifts grew, they inevitably spread to the business, which failed in 1917. On the surface, Hermann Kafka's aim seemed relatively simple: to provide a good business opportunity for his son-in-law and to find a safe investment for Elli's dowry, within the family itself. The new company was called Prager Asbestwerke Hermann & Co. — the Hermann here being Karl Hermann, not Hermann Kafka, although the latter could not have been oblivious to the title. In some shadowy, inexplicable way, Kafka became involved as a kind of silent partner, although several observers of the fiasco attributed more direct responsibility to Kafka as an initiator of the project.* In any event, he borrowed

---

*New evidence from the German edition of the *Diaries* suggests strongly that Kafka was not the innocent bystander he pretended to be but was a registered partner with his brother-in-law Karl Hermann. The draft of a letter from Kafka to Paul Hermann (Karl's younger brother) indicates Kafka had helped to plan the asbestos works and had even persuaded his father to lend Karl the funds for investment in the company. When the papers for the transaction were drawn up in the fall, Kafka was present. We must exercise

money from his father to give himself equity as a silent partner; perhaps here he hoped to fulfill Hermann's expectations of him as a "success," or perhaps Hermann Kafka put tremendous pressure on his son to make something of himself (that is, increase his income). The reciprocity here between pressure from one and need to fulfill his promise from the other is the sole element we can give credence to.

The factory was located in suburban Žižkov, an enterprise of twenty-five workers, started up in November 1911. The machinery was primitive, and most of the help was female, probably based on Hermann Kafka's assumption that female workers would be easier to browbeat. But Kafka's idea that he would be a silent partner and therefore not responsible for day-to-day operations was not what his father had in mind. No matter that he considered his son a business failure, he wanted Kafka to supervise and act as watchdog. Since Hermann had no interest in or comprehension of his son's writing, he did not think it was too burdensome to ask him to work at the institute until early afternoon and then at the asbestos works from midafternoon into early evening, returning for dinner and sleep, and then beginning the cycle again. Having himself worked this hard, Hermann formed the same scenario for his twenty-eight-year-old son. Further, from Hermann's point of view, Kafka was wasting his evenings in attending lectures, sitting around cafés with his other wastrel friends (including that "crazy nut" Brod), or sitting up late at night scribbling in his room. Kafka's fragility, in fact, could be attributed to this regimen; what he needed was a man's steady work.

In his diary entries, Kafka fought back, as early as December, barely a month or two after the operation of the works began.[74] He writes that when his father attacked him for malingering at the factory, Kafka responded that he had wanted to draw out profits, not spend his time there while he still worked at the institute. But this no more convinced Hermann than if his son had written the most famous book in Europe. Hermann saw everything through his own eyes and was completely conditioned by his precarious childhood. Every minute spent away from work was, for him, a form of treachery to the family and, furthermore, jeopardized the food on the table.

When father and son headed for a collision course over the asbestos factory, they had very different assumptions. Unless in some non-Euclidian universe where parallel lines cross, there could not be a meeting of minds or points of view. The hostility that had crept up so overwhelmingly on Kafka in this critical year was, if anything, intensified, as it derived now quite directly from his family. Even as he sensed escape in his new relationships at the Yiddish theater, people whom Her-

---

some caution, however, because this draft of a letter is our sole evidence of Kafka's active participation.

mann assailed as the dregs of society, he was being forced back into a
hostile environment. Kafka's immediate response was to move toward
a purgatory of his own, where no one could approach, like the animal's
underground hiding place in "The Burrow." The mental distress took a
familiar course: skin eruptions and sensitivity and digestive problems.

> I am probably sick, since yesterday my body has been itching all over. In
> the afternoon my face was so hot and blotched that I was afraid the assis-
> tant giving me a haircut, who could see me and my reflected image all the
> time, would recognize that I had a serious disease. Also the connection
> between stomach and mouth is partly disturbed, a lid the size of a gulden
> [coin] moves up or down, or stays down below from where it exerts an
> expanding effect of light pressure that spreads upward over my chest.[75]

Kafka had absorbed the whole psychosomatic scenario, and, in his case,
it served him well, forcing him to confront everything, all at once, in
the late fall and early winter of 1911. Confrontation made him ill, but
it also motivated him for writing.

In a revealing diary entry, he confessed how contradictory impulses
in him could work to provide a still center or a launching pad. He had
moved from his business worries to his involvement with Löwy, who
was desperately poor and in need even of food. Yet Kafka had spent
money on expensive seats for himself and Löwy at the National Theater, to see *Dubrovačka Trilogijia* by Ivo Vojnovič; the play and production turned out to be hopeless, and Kafka felt he had thrown away
money that could have benefited Löwy.

> I had again demonstrated the misfortune that follows every undertaking
> that I begin by myself. But while I usually unite myself individually with
> this misfortune, attract all earlier cases of misfortune up to me, all later
> ones down to me, I was this time almost completely independent, bore
> everything quite easily as something that happens just once, and for the
> first time in the theater even felt my head, as the head of a spectator,
> raised high out of the collective darkness of the seat and the body into a
> distinct light, independent of the bad occasion of this play and this pro-
> duction.[76]

Yet his diary entries and, finally, a letter to Brod, in which he contemplates suicide, suggest his confusion and despair. Near the end of
the year, to continue with his purgatorial response to the asbestos factory, he began to draft segments of what became *Letter to His Father*,
not completed until 1919. Part of it is a complaint: "The torment that
the factory causes me. Why didn't I object when they made me promise
to work there in the afternoons. No one used force to make me do it,
but my father compels me by his reproaches, Karl [Hermann] by his silence and I by my consciousness of guilt. I know nothing about the factory, and this morning, when the committee made an inspection, I
stood around uselessly with my tail between my legs."[77]

Running parallel to this, the activities of the Yiddish troupe fill his diary. There is a schizoid quality to Kafka, or an unbridgeable duality, between the pleasure he feels, particularly from Frau Tschissik, and the anguish he experiences at both his jobs, but especially at his father's enterprise. By October 22, Kafka declared to his diary his love for Frau Tschissik. "I enjoy writing the name so much." He liked to peek in: "You can get in under her eyelids with your glance if you first carefully look along her cheeks and then, making yourself small, slip in, in doing which you don't even first have to raise the lids, for they are raised."[78] He is captivated by her acting, her soft voice, her joyful looks, her solid body, the "striking smoothness of Mrs. Tschissik's cheeks, alongside her muscular mouth." Yet even as he writes so fancifully, he admits that his "love" for the actors deceives him and falsifies what they are; he somehow is protecting them against what they are. Even when he was infatuated with Mania Tschissik, he was not blind to her considerable imperfections. In his eyes, her full figure, which so attracted him, was clumsy, too broad, lacking in grace, and her features were hardly exemplary. He notes quarrels between Tschissik and Löwy, and this returns him to his own childhood, as if he had made the two into parental substitutes.

Now twenty-eight, Kafka regresses into childhood images, associated somehow with the motherly (yet tempting) Mania Tschissik. He longs for the days when his mother would return from business "and with her concerns and hurried instructions once more causes the day, already so late, to begin again and rouses the invalid [Kafka] to help her in this." He says he wishes he could once again be weak and dependent, and "therefore convinced by everything my mother did, and could enjoy childish pleasure with age's keener capacity for gratification." He recognizes that he cannot even love his mother as he wishes, for the German language itself prevents it: *Mutter* is not the Jewish mother, but the German. "I believe that it is only the memories of the ghetto that will preserve the Jewish family, for the word 'Vater' too is far from meaning the Jewish father."[79]

The ramifications of all this are enormous. Not only was Kafka somehow intermixing Julie Kafka with Mania Tschissik, he was meditating on how language itself affects one's relationships. In his example, language provides divisions, impeding him from getting closer to his mother since it lacks an adequate word for her. His stated belief that only the ghetto and its memories hold the Jewish family together suggests an abdication of all other linkages, whether affection, love, business, or other commonalities. The remark underscores his alienation even as it attempts to move him closer. And the entire passage foreshadows how difficult it will be for him to form any relationship with a woman; for not only is Julie in the way, his entire conception of family intervenes.

In the final months of 1911, Kafka revealed his immersion in the Yiddish troupe by recounting the plots of numerous plays, plots so complicated and full of melodramatic turns that one play seems to blend into another.* With its break from its own home and prohibitions, the troupe leads him back to how indebted he is to his family for housing him; and he quotes George Bernard Shaw, to the effect that rather than struggle for a livelihood, he let his mother support him and he hung on his old father's coattails. Being well past the age at which Shaw depended on others, Kafka concludes this is no consolation for him. "I lead," he says, "a horrible synthetic life and am cowardly and miserable enough to follow Shaw only to the extent of having read the passage to my parents. How this possible life flashes before my eyes in colors of steel, with spanning rods of steel and airy darkness between!"[80]

Kafka watches Mania Tschissik closely, while trying to avoid her eyes; we do not know how much of his attention she observed. He follows her movements, her agitation when she errs in her lines, or when she clumsily almost falls. She was not a gifted actress; in fact, under different circumstances, Kafka would have ridiculed an actress of her meager talents. Only in melodrama, where the overall line was outrageous, could she survive her inadequate stage presence. Kafka picks up how others felt about these performers when he accompanied the group to the Prague cafés. There, they are despised "as starvlings, tramps, fellow Jews, exactly as in the past. Thus, the headwaiter wanted to throw Löwy out of the hall, the doorman, who used to work in a brothel and is now a pimp, shouted little Tschissik down when she, in the excitement of her sympathy during *Der Wilde Mensch* [*The Savage Man*, by Jacob Gordin], wanted to pass something to the actors."[81]

He was now reading the stories of Wilhelm Schäfer, a German novelist who later became an ardent Nazi. This is juxtaposed, in Kafka's diary, with Hermann's calling him "a bad son," probably because of his association with literary wastrels and, even worse, because of his

---

*We know from more than one diary entry that Kafka did not overrate these plays, that he was beguiled by the actors, not by the performances or the content. The majority of the plays by the leading Yiddish writers, Sigmund Feinman (Kafka's Feimann, or Faynman), Josef Lateiner (perhaps the best known in the United States), Abraham Goldfaden, Abraham Sharkansky, were poorly crafted, loosely plotted, and emotionally fervid — quite the opposite of Kafka's own cool approach, and showing the difference not only between German and Yiddish expression, but between differing sensibilities. "Yesterday *Vizekönig* [*The Vice King*] by Feimann. My receptivity to the Jewishness in these plays deserts me because they are too monotonous and degenerate into a wailing that prides itself on isolated, violent outbreaks. When I saw the first plays it was possible for me to think that I had come upon a Judaism on which the beginnings of my own rested, a Judaism that was developing in my direction and so would enlighten me and carry me farther along in my own clumsy Judaism, instead it moves farther away from me the more I hear of it. The people remain, of course, and I hold fast to them" (see *Diaries: 1910–1913*, p. 112, for further comments on Yiddish playwrights).

friendship with the acting troupe. Hermann's complaint was that such relationships were useless, but his underlying motive in the attack was that he feared contamination from the very people he had put behind him. He feared not their presence, but the memories; and it was precisely this that Kafka said was leading him to hatred of his father: that artificial pose taken by Jews like Hermann to disguise their background and pollute their memories through a false sense of assimilation.

Faced by all these attacks on Eastern Jews — not only in Prague, but in Vienna and Berlin, other outposts of gentility — Kafka began to read voluminously in Jewish histories: *History of the Jews* by Heinrich Graetz, mentioned on November 1; followed by Meyer Pines's classic but unwieldy study, *Histoire de la Littérature Judéo-Allemande*, a history of Jewish-German literature written in French by a Russian with a sympathy for Hasidism; then Jacob Fromer's *Organism of Jewry*. But this was only the beginning; Yiddish entranced Kafka, and then he moved to the study of Hebrew and became a moderate Zionist. These positive elements in his life always gave way to doubts, to knives that tore through him as an act of joy, or the pain of loneliness so severe and piercing that all strength left him. He had to listen to repeated attacks by his father on Löwy and his ilk: " 'Whoever lies down with dogs gets up with fleas.' "[82] When Kafka answered with "something uncontrolled," Hermann said that he, the older man, must not get excited and should be treated with consideration. Guilty at having almost brought on a heart attack, Kafka restrained himself.

Through it all he wanted to write but had to deal with apartment noise.

> I sit in my room in the very headquarters of the uproar of the entire house. I hear all the doors close, because of their noise only the footsteps of those running between them are spared me, I hear even the slamming of the oven door in the kitchen. My father bursts through the doors of my room and passes through in his dragging dressing gown, the ashes are scraped out of the stove in the next room, Valli asks, shouting into the indefinite through the anteroom as though through a Paris street, whether father's hat has been brushed yet. . . . The house door is unlatched and screeches as though from a catarrhal throat, then opens wider with the brief singing of a woman's voice and closes with a dull manly jerk that sounds most inconsiderate.[83]

Kafka is distracted even by the two canaries singing, so that "with the canaries it comes back to me again, that I might open the door a narrow crack, crawl into the next room like a snake and in that way, on the floor [like Gregor Samsa], beg my sisters and their governess for quiet."

The apartment noise is not unusual; in fact, it is quite ordinary, with people living their lives according to individual dictates. If we attempt to "hear" this scene not from Kafka's attempt at self-aggrandizement but from off center, we listen to something different from what he describes. Kafka has decided to remain in the apartment, probably because he cannot make a definite break or needs the presence of others, or for reasons even he could not fathom. But once he has decided to stay, his assumption was that since he was special, the household should heed his needs, not its own. In these diary entries, Kafka makes himself the center of a hostile empire.

Beyond this is his distaste for others, his quasi-revulsion at Valli's voice, his repulsion at his father's appearance in his dressing gown; in other passages of his *Diaries*, his revulsion at bodily sounds, the possibility of sex between Hermann and Julie (a repulsion we are made to share, even at this distance), the smell of dirty bedclothes and bodily fluids, and other sights, sounds, and smells. Kafka's response to his needs left him with little feeling for others, and when others did diverge slightly (or broadly) from what he felt was the norm, then he struck. And strike he did, for this passage about his disgust, in an act of supreme hostility, appeared in print, in the October 1912 *Herderblätter*, Willy Haas's literary monthly published in Prague for German readers. Kafka did not change anything, neither incidents nor names. He quite simply laid out for all literary Prague to read his hostility to family and household. He was on the road to his *Letter* to his father. We find way-stations at numerous intervals in the *Diaries* and in letters, where we recognize he had learned to strike back.

His method of putting together a fictional piece disturbed him, since he realized he did not follow the usual means of shaping it; his approach to a fictional idea left parts hanging. He was, in time, to accept the very element he now considered a limitation. "If I were ever able to write something large and whole, well shaped from beginning to end, then in the end the story would never be able to detach itself from me and it would be possible for me calmly and with open eyes, as a blood relation of a healthy story, to hear it read, but as it is, every little piece of the story runs around homeless and drives me away from it in the opposite direction."[84] This explanation of his method and fears helps us understand why all his longer works were incomplete: from the early *Amerika* (even though he revised and rewrote it), then *The Trial*, and finally *The Castle*. And even several of his shorter pieces, stories, parables, and others, have an incomplete quality to them. Yet with this unfinished quality, Kafka was establishing what was uniquely his: the loose strands, the infinity implicit in the ending, the lack of ultimate coherence in characters or events, the inability to discover any dominant theme, the paradoxes and ironies that keep the material open, the seeming lack of a center or pivot, the driving need to seek conflicts where none had been observed before. Kafka's fears stated in his November 5, 1911, diary entry are, in reality, directional guides to what would become his strengths, not his deficiencies.

The unstated and unreturned feeling Kafka had for Mania Tschis-

sik continued throughout the fall of 1911. Since we do not have any indication of what her response, if any, was, it is difficult to define it. Did
Kafka find that, in some guarded way, this married woman with two
children was impressed by his attention? His shyness with women
meant he underplayed all situations, barely looking at them openly
while of course sneaking looks. He finds her movements beautiful in
some of her parts and builds her up into a far more skillful performer
than observers say she was. He sees her as the leader of the troupe, or,
as he puts it, "the mother of a family." He offers her flowers: "I had
hoped, by means of the bouquet of flowers, to appease my love for her a
little, it was quite useless. It is possible only through literature or
through sleeping together. I write this not because I did not know it,
but rather because it is perhaps well to write down warnings frequently."[85] Surely Löwy was aware of Kafka's feelings for Tschissik,
and, very possibly, he drew on that infatuation as a way of cementing
his relationship with Kafka, who, he felt, might be of help to him in
Prague.

We do not know how much Kafka suspected of that larger drama
that lies just beneath the surface of his diary entries, in which Löwy,
and very possibly Tschissik, were quite aware of Kafka's feelings and
encouraged them as a way of ingratiating themselves in order to use his
connections in the city. We learn Tschissik just happens to be with
Löwy when Kafka comes along, just happens to thank Kafka for his
bouquet, just happens to run into Kafka at the coffeehouse. Kafka comments on how lightly dressed she is — November in Prague could be
quite chilly — and she says she has a shawl. Kafka: "I could not tell her
that I was not really concerned about her but was rather only happy to
have found an emotion in which I could enjoy my move, and therefore
I told her again that I was worried."[86]

Kafka is not unaware that he cuts a strange figure, in fact, one out
of a nineteenth-century French farce. He sees the disproportion between what he feels and what others must see, and he meditates on
human absurdity, where he is the prize example.

> A young man whom everyone takes to be eighteen years old declares in
> the presence of the evening's guests at the Café Savoy, amidst the sur-
> rounding waiters, in the presence of the table full of actors, declares to a
> thirty-year-old woman whom hardly anyone even considers pretty, who
> has two children, ten and eight years old, whose husband is sitting beside
> her, who is a model of respectability and economy — declares to this
> woman his love to which he has completely fallen victim and, now
> comes the really remarkable part which of course no one else could have
> observed, immediately renounces the woman, just as he would renounce
> her if she were young and single.

To that trenchant insight into himself, Kafka adds, "Should I be grateful or should I curse the fact that despite all misfortune I can still feel
love, an unearthly love but still for earthly objects."[87]

That final remark, that he would renounce her even if she were
young and single, is reassuring. His renunciation of her was a necessary
part of his plan. He would renounce a whole succession of women,
until his very final years when physical breakdown altered the rules of
his game. He renounces because she tempts him away from his declared intention, which is to sacrifice all for art. Kafka's relationship to
Tschissik, then, is enwrapped in role-playing on his part, and very possibly on her and Löwy's part as well. Kafka entered their personal
drama, not as their lure, but as someone who could calculate just how
much he could give. He offered up love but would run if it were returned; he would offer admiration but could not bear that it might lead
to anything more. It was an act of role-playing at which he excelled;
and we must note how the Tschissik "affair" became for Kafka preparation for the ballet he danced with Felice Bauer only shortly afterward.

Everything led toward his infatuation and everything led away
from it. Even at the factory, when the lawyer read out to Kafka an agreement about shares in the enterprise, a passage touches on Kafka's "possible future wife and future children." He sees across from him a table
with two large chairs and a smaller one around it, and he thinks, "At
the thought that I should never be in a position to sit in these or any
other three chairs myself, my wife and my child, there came over me a
yearning for this happiness so despairing from the very start in my excitement I asked the lawyer the only question I had left after the long
reading, which at once revealed my complete misunderstanding of a
rather long section of the agreement that had just been read." Kafka
wrote this at twenty-eight, not at all an advanced age for a Prague man
to marry; in the profession-oriented German-Jewish sector, one postponed marital gratification. And yet Kafka had *already* firmly forsaken
it, although he would madly pursue the future in courting Felice Bauer.
The contradictory impulses were everywhere in his response to whatever came along, whether in the person of Mania Tschissik or in the
factory lawyer reading out an agreement on shares.

Kafka's despair about himself must be viewed in terms of time and
place, as well as in personal terms. Although Bohemia as a whole was
thriving, the source of most Czech industrial advances, we can find in
Kafka's response to it a way of seeing beyond economic welfare into the
reality of the situation: an empire barely held together from Vienna but
now subjected to enormous pressures from without on the eve of World
War One; a feuding among nationalities which pitted Austrians against
Czechs and both against Hungarians, with further divisions within
each nationality; national movements setting various groups against
Jews; Germans in the empire identifying increasingly with Vienna or
even with Germany, as it was asserting itself in the years before the
great conflict; the uncertainty of the Jewish question amidst several

signs that things could only get worse for Jews (except, ironically, in Germany itself); the flimsiness of economic survival when signs pointed toward conflagration or unforeseen disaster based on collapse; and the advanced age of the emperor (Franz Josef had ruled since 1848) and people around him were either being assassinated, or were agitating, or were playing out a comedic farce for their own purposes. Within this scenario, and Kafka was quite aware of the threads and directions, it was inevitable that an ultrasensitive, hypercritical person would shape his life on the configuration of collapse.

Kafka was in one respect our modern-day Theseus attempting to find his way out of the labyrinth with a thread provided not by Ariadne but by his own imagination. His novels and shorter fictions would be, if not a way out, then at least a guide to its byways and diverging paths. Unlike Stephen Dedalus, who pledged to forge the conscience of his people, Kafka had no such grandiose scheme: his was not to forge, nor even to locate, but merely to lay out the intricate patterns by which the maze could be comprehended. Kafka saw no way out, and he barely saw a way in; and his work, beginning soon, in 1912, was to capture the inexplicability of endless byways, pathways, patterns viewed behind a scrim. He was, in this area, like Robert Musil, creating *The Man Without Qualities*, with its Habsburg shadows, or like Marcel Proust piecing together in his *Remembrance* a mosaic of French decay.

He grasped at books, as he looked out at a wasteland around him, exemplified by the "dismal life of my married sister," Elli, the oldest. The greed for books, as he calls it, is linked to his need "to group everything certain in me, later the credible, then the possible." He needed books to convince him of their actuality, not even to own or read them. Books become anchors of sorts in a reality so shifting he felt he was incapable of hanging on as he was pulled one way or another. "It is as though this greed came from my stomach, as though it were a perverse appetite."[88] Once again, uncertainties connect to food or digestion, and behind it all is a sexual uncertainty, undefined, but pressing on him.

On November 12, French poet, novelist, and dramatist Jean Richepin lectured on "The Legend of Napoleon." Napoleon had long ago attracted Kafka, possibly as the pull of opposites or as the fascination with power that the powerless might have.* Kafka stared at Richepin's face, until it became transformed from that of a fifty-year-old man's to that of an elderly Italian woman "wearing a very natural, definitely not false beard." But Kafka is so captivated he experiences virtually a sexual delight at the experience. "I gave no thought," he writes, "to my

---

*The newly edited *Diaries* indicate how fascinated Kafka was with Napoleon. Two of the five references are quite extensive, revealing how he was intrigued by military strategies and how carefully he had thought about Napoleon's campaigns.

pains and cares. I was squeezed into the left corner of my chair, but really into the lecture, my clasped hands between my knees. I felt that Richepin had an effect upon me such as Solomon must have felt when he took young girls into his bed."[89] As though he had actually stepped out of the wood of the podium, Napoleon dominates the hall. Kafka is seized by the experience, measuring himself against the great conqueror, the man of destiny; whereas he, he felt, was being buffeted by destiny, forced to do its bidding.

Forebodings catch his imagination, he seeks something to hang on to; the factory experience is dragging him down. He says he appears "dry, wrong, inflexible, embarrassing to everybody" around him. "Blindly and arbitrarily I snatch handfuls out of the stream so that when I write it down calmly, my acquisition is nothing in comparison with the fullness in which it lived, is incapable of restoring this fullness, and thus is bad and disturbing because it tempts to no purpose."[90]

The powers of the universe appear to be working against him. He ponders the mystery of the city; he wonders how different people are only thirty minutes' walk from the center of Prague, what strangers they prove to be even though they share common interests with him. He is isolated, so strong is his sense of overwhelming destiny and of his marginality. There are moments in the fall of 1911 when Kafka seems so close to the edge of madness (or, alternately, to pure sanity) that we cannot believe he will pull back. This mode of living on or close to the edge, for him a mode of preparation, was particularly dangerous: he could utterly fail and sink into real madness. His inner life is saved from insanity by its ability to be assimilated into writing. But the proximity to madness is startling; not depression, but madness.

His hostility is immense. When his former governess (Marie Werner) comes to see him, he pretends he is out. As a child, he was obedient, and yet he feels she brought him up badly; he wonders why she didn't prepare a better future for him. Her view of him is of a healthy gentleman "at the beautiful age of twenty-eight who likes to remember his youth and in general knows what to do with himself." Her lack of perspicuity makes him wild with anger. "Now, however, I lie here on the sofa, kicked out of the world, on the lookout for the sleep that refuses to come and will only graze me when it does, my joints ache with fatigue, my dried-up body trembles toward its own destruction in turmoils of which I dare not become fully conscious, in my head are astonishing convulsions." He adds, "And there stand the three women [the former governess, the cook, and governess] before my door, one praises me as I was, two as I am. The cook says I shall go straight — she means without any detour — to heaven. Thus it shall be."[91] Placing the blame on those who brought him up is, of course, further preparation for the attack on his father in *Letter*.

That attack on those responsible for raising him is undeniably connected, also, to his sense of transformation.* His reasoning was that since no one knew what he was and what he was undergoing, he had changed from what they expected into something invisible to them. In that same November 21 entry in which he mocks his former governess, he also mocks his body. This too is linked to his recognition of bachelorhood: his body is somehow the guilty party that will relegate him to those who must live alone. The body has failed him, not the head.

> Nothing [he writes on November 21] can be accomplished with such a body. I shall have to get used to its perpetual balking. . . . I was so incoherent this morning, felt nothing but more forehead, saw a halfway bearable condition only far beyond my present one, and in sheer readiness to die [he wrote Brod, shortly, about suicide, a letter Brod showed to Julie Kafka] would have been glad simply to have curled up in a ball on the cement floor of the corridor. . . . My body is too long for its weakness, it hasn't the least bit of fat to engender a blessed warmth, to preserve an inner fire, no fat on which the spirit could occasionally nourish itself beyond its daily need without damage to the whole. How shall the weak heart that lately has troubled me so often be able to pound the blood through all the lengths of these legs. . . . Everything is pulled apart throughout the length of my body. What could it accomplish then, when it perhaps wouldn't have enough strength for what I want to achieve even if it were shorter and more compact [with Brod's compact, hunched-over figure perhaps in mind].[92]

Now, in November 1911, Kafka revealed the twin aspects of what would be his most important works the following year, what led into "The Judgment" and "The Metamorphosis." In the first, in which Georg Bendemann's life is invaded by his father and then condemned by this tyrant, we find Kafka's "solution" to the problems he was suffering from: suicide. "The Judgment" creates an unambiguous resolution to what his body cannot accommodate, the fact he is unable to create for himself a life that on a daily basis is bearable. The other pole of this condition would be for him to reshape himself, so that that long body, with the insufficient heart laboring to pump blood along such a length, could become compact and more functional. Here we have not death directly, but a reshaping of what is so personally disturbing into a form that will disturb not him but others.

Self-hatred here becomes reshaped into hostility toward others. He will make them feel pain for his condition, while relieving himself of the burden. As a giant bug, Gregor Samsa will shame his family, while allowing himself to escape. Accordingly, by the end of 1911, Kafka was moving almost directly toward his major vision of 1912, the beginning

---

*Reshaping was now a near obsession. When the Klugs, other actors, left Prague, Kafka dreamed about Frau Klug as being inordinately short and, beyond that, virtually legless. Then, later, he daydreamed about "the upper half of a wax woman" resting on top of him, her face pressed close to him.

of his significant career as a writer. And as an additional matter of great importance, he would make halfhearted attempts to relieve his bachelorhood loneliness by courting, from a distance, Felice Bauer; in so doing he would turn that personal anguish into writing, shaping that relationship into one of his incomplete "novels."

By November 6 the Yiddish troupe had left Prague, taking with them Mania Tschissik and her husband, an argumentative socialist for whom no one, including Kafka, had much regard. Kafka brought flowers for her, but she received them only shortly before leaving, thanking him; Kafka was nevertheless angry that Löwy had not informed her earlier who her benefactor was. The troupe would in time return to Prague, but without Frau Tschissik, who with her husband left the troupe after a quarrel. Running on a shoestring, it seemed to go wherever it had someone, like Kafka, who might help. Tschissik reappeared before Christmas, briefly, but Kafka now had to deal mainly with her loss. His grief is possibly linked to his steady attacks on his body's weakness, and to his deepening despair over bachelorhood.*

He continued to attend Yiddish theater, including Jacob Gordin's Shechite, about a man learning the art of ritual slaughtering, a throwback to Kafka's own paternal grandfather. Kafka thought Gordin was the best of the lot. The continuing collaboration with Brod on "Richard and Samuel" was no relief, since subtle indications of hostility toward Brod appear in the diary entries; Brod's facile manner of meeting problems and writing about them was so antithetical to Kafka's brooding nature that the opening of a divide between them was unavoidable. Brod was necessary, loyal, a support, but he was also an accomplice of those who did not understand that he, Kafka, was moving in a considerably different time scheme. The distance he came to perceive between himself and Brod was simply another example of his isolation.

The diary entries in late November and into December are concerned increasingly with Jewish subjects. Kafka quotes from the Talmud and even refers to the Cabala, the collection of esoteric doctrines developed by rabbis from the seventh to the eighteenth century. All the same, Kafka withholds himself; he maintains an ironic distance. He is too much the Enlightenment Jew, the assimilated Praguer, to give himself over.

He is interested, he says, facetiously or not, in the education of girls, so that they do not turn away when a man speaks to them and they can relate to ideas and even to jokes. Even with the recent changes in their attitudes and education, they still "come toward us with mournful faces when we meet them unexpectedly, to put their hands

---

*In the November 23 Diary entry: "How would I live through [the distant future] with this body picked up in a lumber room? The Talmud says: A man without a woman is no person. I had no defense this evening against such thoughts except to say to myself: 'It is now that you come, evil thoughts, now, because I am weak and have an upset stomach. . . . You have waited for your advantage' " (see Diaries: 1910–1913, p. 162).

flatly in ours and with slow gestures invite us to enter their homes as though we were business acquaintances."[93] Kafka's desire to see greater equality in social situations connects to his desire to find some social condition in which he can function seriously — that is, to be able to speak to a woman. So far he had found no such woman, in his estimation, and even Felice Bauer, to whom he would speak almost endlessly in his letters, never responded as an equal, but as a bride-to-be. Not until Milena Jesenská, near the end of his life, did he discover this kind of woman, not a German, not a Jew, but a Czech,* just the kind of woman his parents had always warned him against and, thus, very possibly his attraction.

As he tries desperately to remake himself into someone he can trust and even respect, he thinks of Schiller's remark, of transforming emotion into character, a process he hopes to emulate. Frau Tschissik (he never uses her given name) comes to mind: she has been accepted into a Berlin company, in Kafka's view, out of pity, as an "insignificant singer of duets in an antiquated dress and hat."[94] Her diminution on the stage must be juxtaposed to Kafka's vaunting of her memory; he is dismayed that someone he has built up to gigantic size in his imagination is, in reality, a kind of clownish figure in her new role. The Yiddish troupe is now back in Prague, with the Liebgolds replacing the Tschissiks, but Frau Liebgold is no replacement for the woman constantly being recreated in his memory. When he runs into the Tschissiks in the Graben, Kafka's response is one of tremulous wariness as he attempts to efface himself and view them from a distance, without being seen. His strong desire to remain out of sight indicates shame or embarrassment; possibly, and this is of course speculatory, she had served as a masturbatory fantasy for him and now her physical presence with her husband was something he could not face.

He describes her and, in the process, his peculiar perception: "She was wearing the hussy's dress she wore in *Der Wilde Mensch*." Kafka says that when he breaks down her appearance into its details, she becomes improbable. "She seemed much smaller than usual, her left hip was thrust forward, not just at the moment, but permanently, her right leg was bent in at the knee, the movement of her throat and head, which she brought close to her husband, was very quick, with her right arm crooked outward she tried to take the arm of her husband."[95] Kafka's description is odd, since it concentrates on extensions of her body, not on her face. Her appearance is to him all arms and legs, angles, planes, as though he were composing a cubist canvas, with limbs coming and going from every direction. Furthermore, his mode of perception is to abstract her: she becomes not the woman of his memory or the obsessive image that infatuated him, but some strange appari-

---

*And not merely any Czech but one with a bitterly anti-Semitic, tyrannical father, the very vanguard of the Czechs who did business with the Germans under Hitler.

tion, the ghost of the woman. He is seeing her, not as she is actually there, across the way, but as she moves in and out of his reverie or dream.

Not surprisingly, the next passage in his diary is a dream, and Mania Tschissik is in it, while her husband is whipping "a shaggy, blond St. Bernard which stood opposite him on its hind legs." Juxtaposed with that image is a comment on Kafka's ability, or inability, to work: "I can take nothing on myself as long as I have not achieved a sustained work that satisfied me completely."[96] The conglomeration of sensations and images leads us both everywhere and nowhere. What it finally communicates, if we can use such a word with Kafka, is the extreme turbulence of his mind and the uncertainty of his position. Anything that might give pleasure, such as the sight of Mania Tschissik, intensifies his sense of her inaccessibility, and this leads in turn to his statement about his frustration with his writing. His work, such as it was, consisted of completing the brief pieces that would appear in *Meditation*, his first published book. He speaks of the need to write all his anxiety out of him, "write it into the depths of the paper just as it comes out of the depths"[97] of his life. On December 13, he sees Moses Richter's *Der Schneider als Gemeinderat*, but with the Liebgolds, the "two new terrible people," replacing the Tschissiks. The Liebgold woman cannot read and is rehearsed by her husband — Kafka appears to offer this as some final condemnation on how bad it all is.

His introspection extends to an analysis of why he is so lacking in punctuality, and he locates it in the fact that he does not feel the pains of waiting. "I wait like an ox." Yet he knows it is more complicated than that.

> I have been late for appointments partly out of carelessness, partly out of ignorance of the pains of waiting, but also partly in order to attain new, complicated purposes through a renewed, uncertain search for the people with whom I had made the appointments, and so to achieve the possibility of long, uncertain waiting. From the fact that as a child I had a great nervous fear of waiting one could conclude that I was destined for something better and that I foresaw my future.[98]

Reshaping is refreshing, he says.

For Kafka, waiting for someone or having someone wait for him accedes to a sense of time unmeasurable by the clock. "My good periods do not have time or opportunity to live themselves out naturally; my bad ones, on the other hand, have more than they need." Time is more than out of joint; it heeds only some inner dictate that he cannot quite get right. The disjointedness he feels in nearly all aspects of his life is part of a deeper maladjustment, linked to time itself. If we are correct, this means he lived on two levels simultaneously: getting into the office on time, meeting his business appointments and deadlines for reports; but also living a different kind of temporal life — late for appointments, unreliable, willing to wait for others, dawdling at his desk, his personal freeing up of time. This dualism is an extension of his temporal awareness: one by clock and calendar, when it suited him, one by a kind of Bergsonian flow rooted in mystery, when that suited him. The brilliance of his major fiction was that in his imaginative work he was able to communicate both kinds of time. What seems so unsettling is that as both persons he moves in and out of his work, conveying the mysterious depths of some temporal maladjustment while also communicating at the level of a more expected temporal frame of reference.

Kafka continues to moon around Mania Tschissik.

> Yesterday her body was more beautiful than her face, which seemed narrower than usual so that the forehead, which is thrown into wrinkles at her first word, was too striking. The beautifully rounded, moderately strong, large body did not belong with her face yesterday, and she reminded me vaguely of hybrid beings like mermaids, sirens, centaurs. When she stood before me then, with her face distorted, her complexion spoiled by make-up, a stain on her dark-blue short-sleeved blouse, I felt as though I were speaking to a statue in a circle of pitiless onlookers.[99]

Astonishingly, Kafka has reshaped her, so that in his perception face and body do not match, and he can relocate her body, as it were, with dissimilar forms, whether sirens, centaurs, mermaids, or others. So strong is his awareness of transformation now that as he looks at familiar objects, he sees them in a different guise, or as posing with shapes different from what others see. We note a process of creativity not unlike what cubists and abstractionists were beginning to do in Paris and elsewhere, what Kupka was already attempting in Czech painting.

Speaking to Frau Klug, Kafka sees Mania Tschissik, and, pardoning himself to Klug, he turns away "as though I intended to spend the rest of my life with Mrs. Tschissik." Then while speaking with her, "I observed that my love had not really grasped her, but only flitted about her, now nearer, now farther. Indeed it can find no peace." From this, his diary moves to a talk he had with his mother, a chance conversation about children and marriage, and this leads to his recognition that the oldest son living in the Kafka household is stranger to them than the strangest person could be. Julie, his devoted mother, knows nothing about him. He exults, to some extent, in his strangeness and difference, hugging it to himself as a justification of his existence. He says he saw for the first time how "untrue and childish" her conception of him is. "She considers me a healthy young man who suffers a little from the notion that he is ill."[100]

In Julie's more primitive sense of medicine, whatever did not break out into desperate sickness was not really illness. She feels, he says, that his "notion" of illness "will disappear by itself with time; marriage, of course, and having children would put an end to it best of all. Then my interest in literature would also be reduced to the degree that is perhaps necessary for an educated man." Kafka expected his mother to have deeper psychological insight than would be humanly possible. She was, in his eyes, an observer of surfaces, and given her furious activities as manager of a large household, worker in Hermann's shop, and caretaker of a moody, illness-prone, demanding husband, one should not have expected more serious attention from her.

She felt that once her son was married, with a family to support, his interest in his profession or in the asbestos factory would emerge, and, therefore, she had no reason for long-range or permanent despair about his future. She does worry when his stomach is upset, or when he can't sleep, but that is temporary, she feels, ready to be alleviated by a more "normal" life. The most probable solution "is that I shall suddenly fall in love with a girl and will never again want to do without her. Then I shall see how good their intentions toward me are and how little they will interfere with me." Julie's response is perhaps typical. But she also feels that if, like his Madrid uncle, Kafka remains a bachelor, there will be no misfortune "because with my cleverness I shall know how to make adjustments." But then Kafka could not afford to be understood too well or too closely; he desperately required that inner world that did not belong to anyone else.

The diary had, by now, in December 1911, overtaken Kafka's imagination, and probably was the reason he did not write more fiction, so satisfactory did he find his entries. "One advantage," he wrote, "in keeping a diary is that you become aware with reassuring clarity of the changes which you constantly suffer and which in a general way are naturally believed, surmised, and admitted by you, but which you'll unconsciously deny when it comes to the point of gaining hope or peace from such an admission." Further: "In the diary you find proof that in situations which today would seem unbearable, you lived, looked around and wrote down observations, that this right hand moved then as it does today, when we may be wiser because we are able to look back upon our former condition, and for that very reason have got to admit the courage of our earlier striving in which we persisted even in sheer ignorance."[101]

On December 24 Kafka attended his nephew's (Elli's son's) circumcision. Kafka's disgust is apparent, as though his paternal grandfather, the ritual butcher, were slashing at an animal. The infant is set up like a sacrifice, awaiting the knife, one of Kafka's obsessive images. The boy (aged sixteen days) lies on his grandfather's lap, while the *mohel* (the one performing the circumcision) must whisper prayers and cut at the same time. The sacrifice is readied: "First the boy is prevented from moving by wrappings which leave only his member free, then the surface to be operated on [the foreskin] is defined precisely by putting on a perforated metal disc, then the operation is performed with what is almost an ordinary knife, a sort of fish knife. One sees blood and raw flesh, the *moule* [*mohel*] bustles about briefly with his long-nailed, trembling fingers and pulls skin from some place or other over the wound like the finger of a glove." There remains a short prayer during which time the *mohel* drinks some wine "and with his fingers, not yet entirely unbloody, carries some wine to the child's lips."[102]

The scene carries great power because Kafka has turned the way Jews celebrate the covenant with their deity into a ritual sacrifice. He perceives circumcision as castration: the *mohel* is an executioner who has already performed, we are told, 2,800 circumcisions. Kafka is appalled and fascinated by what "real" Judaism involves. He finds it barbaric. The bloodstained fingers of the *mohel*, the wine intermixed with blood, the mixture on the infant's lips, so that he imbibes, however slightly, some of his own blood, all communicate an alien people. The scene tortures Kafka and results in further negative comments on what occurs later in the day. He sees in the two grandfathers such incomprehension as they listen to the *mohel*'s assistant's prayers that Kafka recognizes that Western European Judaism is in transition "whose end is clearly unpredictable." His comment is trenchant, expressing his disdain at the use of rituals that no longer have any meaning apart from historical significance. "It is so indisputable that these religious forms which have reached their final end have merely a historical character, even as they are practiced today, that only a short time was needed this very morning to interest the people present in the obsolete custom of circumcision and its half-sung prayers by describing it to them as something out of history."[103]

Questions of what lies in history and what lies outside lead Kafka into what really counts: not history, not religion, but literature, and what it can do. His comments are lengthy but so appropriate to his state of mind in late 1911 they bear quoting in full.

What I understand of contemporary Jewish literature in Warsaw through Löwy, and of contemporary Czech literature partly through my own insight, points to the fact that many of the benefits of literature — the stirring of minds, the coherence of national consciousness, often unrealized in public life and always tending to disintegrate, the pride which a nation gains from a literature of its own and the support it is afforded in the face of the hostile surrounding world, this keeping of a diary by a national which is something entirely different from historiography and results in a more rapid (and yet always closely scrutinized) development, the spiritualization of the broad area of public life, the assimilation of dissatisfied elements that are immediately put to use precisely in this sphere where only stagnation can do harm, the constant integration of a people with respect to its whole that the incessant bustle of the magazines creates, the narrowing down of the attention of a nation upon itself and the accepting of what is foreign only in reflection, the birth of a respect for those active in literature, the transitory awakening in the younger generation of higher aspirations, which nevertheless leaves its permanent mark, the acknowledgment of literary events as objects of political solicitude, the dignification of the antithesis between fathers and sons and the possibility of discussing this, the presentation of national faults in a manner that is very painful, to be sure, but also liberating and deserving of forgiveness, the beginning of a lively and therefore self-respecting book trade and the eagerness for books — all these efforts can be produced even by a literature whose development is not in actual fact unusually broad in scope, but seems to be, because it lacks outstanding talents.[104]

Thus, even a narrow literature may produce widespread results. But there is more, and Kafka's range here is both social and historical, reaching back to Herder and the benefits of a folk literature and forward into a modern sense of literature as something transcending human ordinariness and pettiness. "A literature not penetrated by a great talent has no gap through which the irrelevant might force its way. Its claim to attention thereby becomes more compelling. The independence of the individual writer, naturally only within the national boundaries, is better preserved." Kafka is obviously arguing for a Yiddish literature on one hand, a Czech on the other, and implicitly condemning himself for writing in a language he has always deplored as not his. "A small nation," he says, "is not smaller than the memory of a large one and so can digest the existing material more thoroughly."[105] He of course fears he will be swallowed up by the historical greatness of German literature, where he must be measured against Goethe, Schiller, Kleist, Heine, Hebbel, and others. The writer in Yiddish or Czech, however, does not fear such absorption into a great literature. Literature can accordingly become a matter of the people, not of the critics, historians, or academicians. The individual must defend his literature, unlike the great literatures whose historical nature is their defense. They have lasted, they will continue to endure.

The significance of these remarks is clear. Not only was Kafka measuring himself against what he considered literature to be, he was also trying to find a reason for its existence and for *his* existence within it. In a great literature, everything goes on "down below, constituting a not indispensable cellar of the structure," whereas in a lesser or more narrow literature, everything occurs in the "full light of day," absorbing everyone "no less than as a matter of life and death."[106] With that, Kafka had come full circle, by the end of the year 1911: justifying his role, reinforcing what he felt literature can do, and somehow excusing himself for writing even in German. He cannot resist saying that one of his literary heroes, Goethe, "retards the development of the German language by the force of his writing." Prose style, Kafka says, returns to

Goethe with additional strength, even adopting obsolete idioms found in him, but without any organic linkage. "In Hebrew my name is Amschel,"* Kafka announces, as if defying Goethe, or dissociating himself from him.

The asbestos factory had not gone away — it would not fail until 1917 — and Kafka rues his promise to work there in the afternoons. This sense of being enclosed and entrapped, with no escape, led in time to his writing to Brod about possible suicide, a letter Brod showed to Julie Kafka so as to make her relieve her son of his duties. In a sense, with the factory position, Kafka was replicating, without the poverty and open leg sores, Hermann's privations: all of the father's talk about hardships had created in the son sufficient guilt that he put himself into this condition. In actuality, without the asbestos position, Kafka had a good deal of time on his hands, and his claim that even without the factory he was "hedged in" is inaccurate. Working only six hours a day at the institute, he had ample time of his own, which he chose to fill with the theater troupe or with long hours in coffeehouses and cafés, or in related social and cultural activities. However hard his position at the institute was on his nerves, he nevertheless had time. Of course if we factor in his constant and continuous insomnia, we can figure that his brain could not function well throughout the day; and given the nature of his imagination, he needed hours of reverie and daydreaming, lying on a sofa, letting images filter through and possibly take hold.

He considered himself, "in view of my contemptible, childish appearance, unworthy of forming a serious, responsible opinion of the great, manly future which usually seemed so impossible to me that every short step forward appeared to me to be counterfeit and the next step unattainable." Kafka headed into 1912, when he accomplished the following: decided to write a novel; met Felice Bauer; started the correspondence with her which we can characterize as "Franz, Felice, and the Great War"; wrote "The Judgment," his first major piece; wrote "The Stoker," part of the eventual *Amerika*; wrote much of that *Amerika*, called in manuscript "Der Verschollene"; and wrote "The Metamorphosis," one of the two or three most characteristic pieces of his maturity. It was, all in all, a wonderful year for Kafka, and for literature it was a miraculous year — an annus mirabilis. As for himself, it seemed not to make him any happier. "The Great War," Kafka's own, two years before the better-known one broke out, would dominate his life.

---

*That name, like Kafka or *kavka*, is not neutral, also having associations with a blackbird. In chapter 10, name resonances will be associated with bodily changes in "The Metamorphosis."

To think, for instance, that I have never been aware before how many faces there are. There are quantities of human beings, but there are many more faces, for each person has several. There are people who wear the same face for years; naturally it wears out, it gets dirty, it splits at the folds, it stretches, like gloves one has worn on a journey. These are thrifty, simple people; they do not change their face, they never even have it cleaned. It is good enough, they say, and who can prove to them the contrary? The question of course arises, since they have several faces, what do they do with the others? They store them up. Their children will wear them. But sometimes too, it happens that their dogs go out with them on. And why not? A face is a face.

— RILKE, *THE NOTEBOOK OF MALTE LAURIDS BRIGGE*

NINE Franz, Felice, and the Great War

PART I: SKIRMISHES

Although the Kafka side of the correspondence with Felice Bauer, the only side we have, seems bizarre, eccentric, even mad, it helps us focus on him as a representative figure for the twentieth century. Kafka discovered he could manipulate and control people, whether Felice Bauer, or her friend Grete Bloch, or even his Golem-like father, by making himself appear abject, despairing, vile. By debasing himself, he forged a weapon by which people were drawn to him — not out of pity, but from the intensity of his own lowly vision, or by virtue of their own weaknesses, which did not permit them to overpower him. He found levers of power — and he was always seeking empowerment — through striking at others' weaknesses, their faults, or their temporary lapses, all the while hiding behind a pose of enervation and exhaustion. He was not necessarily consciously deceptive, although he could be that too. He was, however, ready to gain control through self-debasement, and by that create a defense behind which he could hide. Disguising a difficult sexuality, the contours of which even he was not certain of, Kafka found the means to assert himself: not as a sexual being or mature man, but as a person whose inner life was so tormented that the physical dimension could be dismissed.

We recall Dostoevsky's protagonist in *Notes from the Underground* and a long line of abject Russian literary figures (in Gogol, Tolstoy, Goncharov, and others) whose means of empowerment seem vile, passive, unsocial, or pathological. Kafka has placed himself in this tradition, and his use of poses, disguises, role-playing, shields, and defenses — all while ostensibly carrying on a courtship — foreshadows our sense of twentieth-century relationships, whether before, during, or after marriage.* Becoming monstrous himself at times, he played so many roles, touched on so many nerves, presented so many choices for his intended that he made her, a very different type of person from himself, dance to his particular music. In one guise, he was the ultimate male chauvinist, but in another he was so sensitive to her needs that he seems to be living inside her skin. Kafka never posed as a "real man": a social being, a man capable of a mature relationship, or someone who could be counted on in marriage. He knew it was impossible for him, very likely an impossibility in modern life altogether. He acted antic, like Hamlet, to get at greater truths, even when such truths were obviously subversive of the very relationship he doggedly pursued.

The "greater truth," as we glean it from these frantic letters, is a view of life from its unhappy moments; it is these moments that Kafka sees as dominant. Happiness, such as it is, lies in the interstices of unhappiness; and while other men laud and encircle in memory the happy times, he, Kafka, sees them as momentary, so fleeting that like everything else they are ghostly presences. Not that he rejected happiness, or failed to seek it in his effort to create a relationship with Felice; but he recognized — and this is part of his "representative" nature — that for the sensitive or ultrasensitive person the joys given to ordinary people are a chimera, a hoax, even a defense against the truth, whatever that may be. Part of this perception goes with Kafka's role as an artist, a role he insists upon to Felice, who takes it somewhat lightly, as did Kafka's mother. But an equal part goes with what made him the man who could transform himself into the person ready to be sacrificed for some greater goal. Kafka's character includes elements of martyr, savior, sacrificial figure, and artist, and in his view, all these roles are interconnected. Such a man is so responsive to the filaments of life that he cannot possibly present a social side to his fiancée. Kafka instead presented what lay inside, which is to say, his madness.

*   *   *

*Søren Kierkegaard's "Diary of a Seducer" foreshadowed several aspects of the Kafka-Bauer correspondence. Who, for example, wrote the following, Kafka or Kierkegaard: "What I must principally impress upon my mind is that the whole affair is only a fictitious move. I have held several rehearsals in order to discover which one would be the best approach" ("Diary of a Seducer," in Either/Or [New York: Anchor, 1959], p. 367). Or: "Our relationship is not the tender and loyal embrace of understanding, not attraction; it is the repulsion of misunderstanding. My relationship to her is simply nil; it is purely intellectual, which means it is simply nothing to a young girl" ("Diary of a Seducer," p. 347). Or: "When I have brought her to the point where she has learned what it is to love, and what it is to love me, then the engagement breaks like an imperfect mold, and she belongs to me. This is the point at which others become engaged and have a good prospect of a boring marriage for all eternity" ("Diary of a Seducer," p. 372).

In his "Fifth Octavo Notebook," the precise dating of which is difficult to establish, Kafka wrote a reprise of his life, at a time when he believed it could be ending:

> For the eventuality that in the near future I may die or become wholly unfit to live — the probability of it is great, since in the last two nights I have coughed a good deal of blood — let me say that I myself have torn myself to shreds. If my father in earlier days was in the habit of uttering wild but empty threats, saying: I'll tear you apart like a fish — in fact, he did not so much as lay a finger on me — now the threat is being fulfilled independently of him. The world — F. is its representative — and my ego are tearing my body apart in a conflict there is no resolving.[1]

The "F." is Felice Bauer, whom Kafka met August 13, 1912, at Max Brod's. In Kafka's strange way of dealing with something momentous and important, she became the center of his emotional life, but not as a loved object, rather as a curious being whom he had to shape and re-shape so that, eventually, she could prove unsuitable for him. But since she was unsuitable from the start, the reshaping was Kafka's need to control her and the situations in which she moved, so he could recognize how forbidding she was for him and he for her. The statement above is a death statement: a man reviewing his life and seeing that because of the nature of things it can come to nothing. Felice becomes part of that "death" sentence because she offers a choice that he cannot accept, much less decide upon. She becomes life and death themselves.

Kafka's enormous file of letters to Felice Bauer, from 1912 to 1917, along with his letters to her friend Grete Bloch concerning Felice, forms two kinds of work: an epistolary novel of sorts, in which he and Felice are the sole major characters, with Grete as a significant "other"; and an autobiography, running parallel to the extensive diary entries.*

*Elias Canetti has written an extremely shrewd and incisive brief study of the relation-ship, called *Kafka's Other Trial: The Letters to Felice* (1969; 1974 in English translation). Canetti's basic premise is correct, that Kafka could pursue someone like Felice or Grete only through letters, and his insights along the way are indisputable. But the title of the relationship, as Kafka's "other trial," is misleading. The relationship for Kafka was not a "trial" (either court trial, general process, or illness, as the German would suggest), but a way for him to discover a medium, through words, for dealing with what was pushing upon him so oppressively. Felice was not his trial, but a creature in a kind of experimental laboratory — it was as if he had suddenly acquired a trusting animal he could put through its paces. While he did suffer, like someone being tried or on trial, he does maintain the initiative in the relationship, does control Felice, and, therefore, does seem the laboratory director rather than part of the exhibition.

Pietro Citati (*Kafka*, 1987; in English, 1990) also writes sensitively about the Kafka-Felice correspondence and relationship, noting "the intellectual and spiritual tension" revealed in every line of the letters and every shift in tone. But he is overheated and hyperbolic in his commentary, speaking of Kafka as a man full of dreadful desires, as someone who "surrendered to the illimitable, wavelike imagination that flowed through him at night," as having produced a text comparable to "a great lava flow," as having suffered the "shadows of the unconscious" invading him, as a man who "possessed a

The letters to Felice form a body of work that can stand alone, the most revealing of Kafka's personal efforts, perhaps rivaled only by his later letters to Milena Jesenská and by a few diary entries; and, at the same time, a shaped, conscious sequence, written with full awareness of manipulation, shaping, control. The fact that the letters to Felice coincided with an opening up of imagination is further revealing: in some bizarre way, she both drew him back into himself and yet made him more open so that he could write, and write masterfully. While simultaneously forcing him to find strategies for rejecting her even as he advanced his suit, she acted as catalyst for his creativity. The sequence of letters is so compelling because it is balletic, a Modern *pas de deux*: Kafka is literarily moving from one defense position to another in order to hold Felice off, while at the same time he is offering himself up to her as a sacrifice. And she, in her literal, often undemanding way, insists on normalcy, ordinariness, relatively few prerogatives of the courted female.

Felice Bauer was four years younger than Kafka, born on November 18, 1887, in Neustadt, Upper Silesia. She had four siblings, of whom one, Erna, plays some role in the drama with Kafka. Felice's father was from Vienna; he married a Neustadt woman, and when Felice was twelve he moved the family to Berlin. Herr Bauer worked as an agent for a foreign insurance company but lived apart from his wife for many years of Felice's childhood, from 1904 to 1910; consequently, her schooling ended in 1908 — it would have been unusual in any case for a young woman to attend the university — so that she could help her mother with the support of the family. She worked as a shorthand-typist with the gramophone record firm of Odeon, at first, and the following year, in 1909, moved on to Carl Lindström A. G., which manufactured dictating machines and Parlographs. She rose to executive secretary and was apparently a valued member of the company, just as Kafka became virtually indispensable at his Workers' Accident Insurance Institute. When Felice met Kafka in August 1912, she was then executive secretary at Lindström's. Two years after the meeting, her father died.

She was practical, commonsensical, self-confident about her qualities and abilities, and singularly lacking in the degree of sensitivity and imagination which made Kafka so miserable and so creative. There was absolutely nothing in their personalities, needs, or outlooks that would appear to make them suitable for each other. Felice was by no means ordinary: she was independent, knew her own mind, and was well

---

torrential imaginative wealth" (p. 57).

The letters themselves were sold by Felice Bauer, by then Mrs. Marasse and living in the United States. After the death of her husband in 1955, she decided to pass the large collection on to Schocken Books, which published them in German and then in English translation.

ahead of her time in her business abilities, but she seemingly lacked any qualities, including, apparently, appearance, that should have appealed to Kafka. Her type of person was strong, doughty, generous, not particularly attractive, whereas Kafka was hypersensitive, well educated, finicky, impractical, driven, good-looking (if one discounted his unmuscular frame), and so deeply self-absorbed he seemed to have little or nothing to give. How could two such different people, he now twenty-nine, she almost twenty-five, have come together?

Apparently they didn't. Even the two engagements are not indications they were ever joined. Kafka played at marriage, whereas Felice held out for her kind of union with a man who constantly denied everything she was seeking. But the courtship plays on several variations. At twenty-nine, Kafka was frantic at not ever having had a serious girlfriend; he was ready to buckle under to the pressures on him to marry, have children, and begin a family life. Even the semblance of that would suffice to placate the inner demons and the external pressures from his father and mother. He played desperately at what was expected of him, tried on various roles, stretched them out as needed, and found them horrendously wanting.

Felice, at almost twenty-five, was getting on for an unmarried young woman of her time, especially since she wanted children. Her life consisted mainly of work she excelled at, but it was not her desire to continue with it indefinitely, especially since her home life was not particularly joyful. Kafka came from a compelling circle of friends, was himself a social notch above her, as a university graduate in law, was interesting looking, shy, seemingly marriageable to the ordinary eye. What he truly represented was not apparent to her, since she looked at young men with the same practicality with which she looked at herself. And even for a more experienced young woman, Kafka would have proved an enigma until well into the relationship. Each came to the event, such as it was, with a different agenda: Kafka's based on the image he felt that he, as a no longer young Jewish man, required to hold his place in society; hers on the need to find a suitable husband and settle down into a conventional, bourgeois marriage, with children, a pretty home, and the usual amenities. That she hit on Kafka for this was ludicrous; that he entertained the idea of a possible marriage with her was no less ridiculous. That the cat and mouse game continued for five years is, if not farcical, certainly remarkable.

Kafka's first letter to Felice, on September 20, 1912, foreshadows, from his side, how the relationship would develop. We should, incidentally, keep in mind that almost the entire affair was carried on through the mails — the two saw each other infrequently — and it is clear Kafka preferred correspondence (words, language, writing) to personal acting out. He avoided meeting Felice on every occasion he could. The meeting at Brod's on August 13 came about during a family social gathering. At this time, Brod and his brother Otto lived with their parents (Brod's father was president of the Prague Union Bank, his mother a housewife) at 1 Schalengasse (renamed Skořepka). The elder Brods' daughter, Sophie, was married to a businessman, Max Friedmann, whose cousin was Felice Bauer. She was, then, related by marriage to Brod.

In his diary entry for August 20, 1912, Kafka memorialized the event with the following description of the woman he would pursue for five years: "I was not at all curious about who she was, but rather took her for granted at once. Bony, empty face that wore its emptiness openly. Bare throat. A blouse thrown on. . . . Almost broken nose. Blond, somewhat straight unattractive hair, strong chin. As I was taking my seat I looked at her closely for the first time, by the time I was seated I already had an unshakable opinion."[2] The sole positive thing Kafka can say about her is that while at first look she seemed "very domestic in her dress," she later turned out not to be so. But the rest of the first impression is both condescending and condemnatory.

Kafka began his siege on September 20, when he wrote to Felice that she might not have "even the remotest recollection of me. I am introducing myself once more: my name is Franz Kafka, and I am the person who greeted you for the first time that evening at Director Brod's in Prague, the one who . . . held your hand, the one which confirmed a promise to accompany him next year to Palestine."[3] He says that if the journey is to take place — Kafka had no intention of making such a trip! — then he and she should start discussions right away. In his intense way, he states that since they will want to make use of every minute of the journey, they must prepare themselves as thoroughly as possible. Then immediately he turns to a matter that will become an obsession, by denying the very thing that will obsess him. He tells Felice he never expects "a letter to be answered by return; even when awaiting a letter day after day with renewed anticipation, I am never disappointed when it doesn't come and when finally it does come, I incline to be startled." He admits to being an erratic letter writer himself — he will become a fanatical correspondent — and makes a final plea: that if she has practical doubts about him "as a traveling companion, guide, encumbrance, tyrant, or whatever else I might turn into,"[4] she might not object to him as a correspondent, and she should give him a trial.

The letter is a case of litotes, of sorts: whatever affirmation is accomplished takes place by the negative of its opposite. The litotes analogy will hold for the entire correspondence; for everything Kafka offers seems to be negated by its opposite, and then when he denies the opposite, he has found his only way to affirm something. The twisted, tortured Kafka is already apparent. Hesitation and uncertainty lie in every line and crevice. He has begun his autobiography: a twentieth-century

man's representative journey into the minefields of any human linkage, Charles Swann with Odette, Leopold Bloom and Molly, Hans
Castorp and Clavdia.

The next letter, eight days later, on September 28, is consistent
with the negative aspects of the first. It is full of negated phrases: a
"nicht-ing" of the typewriter, of his sense of belonging, of writing itself. He "doesn't" use, he "doesn't" belong, he "doesn't" write fast
enough, he "hadn't" done something, he "hadn't" come — all of these
"nots" suggesting his withdrawal. Even as he is opening up to the most
significant personal relationship of his adult life, his language suggests
retreat, holding back, withdrawing into his familiar hole. He must, apparently, find an emotional exit from the growing affair — it is now
only eight days old — and his language reveals how he hopes to achieve
a defensive posture. His major fear is that somehow this relationship
will stifle his writing ability, although, in actuality, letter writing
helped in self-discovery.

In his own eyes, he was an imposter. While playing the role expected of a suitor, he knows differently, that this is only an act, a pose,
at best a trying out. Language reinforces his sense of himself as an imposter, at the same time providing him with a shield against the real
thing, the physical Felice. Letters can postpone confrontation. But even
more, he can turn something threatening into something he understands well: words, language, phrase making; he is becoming a writer
by way of having found the medium for personal expression that serves
as a shield against intimacy. This is, in many respects, the way in
which his major fictions eventuated.

Even by now, he is already demonstrating anxiety that Felice has
not written to him frequently enough, a denial of his earlier statement
that he did not expect a rapid response. Yet this growing anxiety over
anything less than an immediate reply is connected to his feelings of
unworthiness in areas involving commitment. His doubts are stated in
such frantic terms that he appears to be on the verge of breakdown. "A
hail of nervousness pours down upon me continuously. What I want
one minute I don't want the next. When I have reached the top of the
stairs, I still don't know the state I shall be in when I enter the apartment. I have to pile up uncertainties within myself before they turn
into a little uncertainty or a letter." He apologizes for chattering on and
tells Felice how much her return letter to his first has meant to him,
"which has made me absurdly happy and upon which I am now laying
my hand to be conscious of owning it."[5]

"But why haven't you written to me?" comes soon after, on October 13. He feels he has said something foolish to disconcert her and
speculates that the letter may even have been "kept from her" because
of the "frowned-upon trip to Palestine." As his paranoia grows, he does
not consider that Felice was not, like him, driven, manic, or anxiety-

ridden. In an amusing aside, Kafka wrote Sophie Friedmann, the elder Brod daughter, that he, Kafka, by chance read in a letter to her parents that "Fräulein Bauer and I are in lively correspondence."[6] Kafka then explains it is not a "lively correspondence" but a rather desultory one, and that although he had actually written two more letters, he did not send them. What is doubly amusing is that Kafka is writing letters, both to Sophie and to Felice, not about content but about letter writing itself. What is now an aside becomes a motif.

In the meanwhile, and hardly incidentally, Kafka had written "The Judgment," his first major piece of fiction, and a short story clearly connected to his own situation.* He tells Felice that when Rowohlt publishes it in the *Yearbook of Poetry* edited by Brod, it will be dedicated to her. Further, he says that her initials appear in the name of Frieda Brandenfeld, but "the substance of the story has not the remotest connection with you." Familiar resonances are there: the father-son struggle, the father's dominance, the son's struggle to escape, the young woman as pawn, the fact that Felice is clearly Frieda, just as later Felice becomes, in small part, the model for Fräulein Bürstner in *The Trial*. Kafka indicates he realized only later that the initials *F.B.* fitted both names. The dedication, he insists, is his effort to be worthy of her. But it is, of course, far more, and in fact is an attempt at this early stage in the relationship to control her through his writing.

The next two letters are emblematic of the entire correspondence. Kafka is on a manic roll toward some kind of verbal consummation, and offers a "self" so absorbed in itself it seems fully contained. The first letter, on October 31, is typical in that it is about letters and letter writing.

> I read the letter [hers] once, put it aside, and read it again; I pick up a file but am really only reading your letter; I am with the typist, to whom I am supposed to dictate, and again your letter slowly slides through my fingers and I have begun to draw it out of my pocket when people ask me something and I know perfectly well I should not be thinking of your letter now. . . . That is what you call the "little pleasure" your letters give me. This answers your question, whether it is disagreeable for me to get a letter from you every day at the office.[7]

---

*Written in one sitting, Kafka says. His diary: "This story, *The Judgment*, I wrote at one sitting during the night of the 22nd–23rd, from ten o'clock to six o'clock in the morning. . . . The fearful strain and joy, how the story developed before me, as if I were advancing over water. . . . The conviction verified that with my novel-writing I am in the shameful lowlands of writing. Only *in this way* can writing be done, only with such coherence, with such a complete opening out of the body and the soul. . . . Many emotions carried along in the writing, joy for example, that I shall have something beautiful for Max's *Arkadia* [the poetry yearbook edited by Brod], thoughts about Freud, of course; in one passage of *Arnold Beer* [Brod's novel]; in one, of Werfel's giantess; of course, also of my 'The Urban World' " (a diary entry foreshadowing the father-son conflict of "The Judgment"; see *Diaries: 1910–1913*, pp. 275–76).

His response to letters, his handling of hers at the office, his slip-ping them in and out of his pocket, the pleasure he says he receives make of the letters something of a sexual exercise. Her *words* carry far more meaning for him than her person, or even a kiss or a larger sexual favor. Since words stir him, he is almost ecstatic in his insistence on her performance, not as an attractive woman but as a seductive letter writer. The letters displace the physical, or else become it. He does not need romantic sentiments, he needs only words. That she continue to communicate with him is the essential part of the plan, because as long as words are the medium he can control her — that is, hold sexual sway over her without any sex.

In the next day's letter, that of November 1, Kafka heralds a new stage in their relationship by going from Fräulein Bauer to Fräulein Fe-lice. His mode of address will vary from this to "dearest" and then, inexplicably, will return to Fräulein Bauer, the more formal salutation. He does not use her name, simply "Felice," for some time, nor does he use the familiar form of address rather than the Germanic formal. To go from *Sie* to *du* in German requires a long route of familiarity, unless one is addressing children, animals, or God. But the move to "Fräulein Felice" indicates Kafka is prepared to reveal himself and has chosen to establish a different level of intimacy. He announces unequivocally that his life "basically always has consisted of attempts at writing, mostly unsuccessful." In point of fact, his first volume was to appear shortly, *Meditation* (ready in 1912, published in 1913), and he had al-ready published some brief pieces, plus the forthcoming "The Judg-ment." But at close to thirty, he was well behind the efforts of many of his closest friends, like Brod and Werfel. He stresses that his energies are depleted, and to conserve himself for writing he has had to cut back on other things.* His statement of his lack of energy, however, is belied by his many activities at work and with his friends.

Kafka reveals the true Kafka: "Just as I am thin, and I am the thin-nest person I know (and that's saying something, for I am no stranger to sanatoria), there is nothing to me which, in relation to writing, one could call superfluous." But in the light of sacrifice, he adds, "Now I have expanded my life to accommodate my thoughts about you, and there is hardly a quarter of an hour of my waking time when I haven't thought about you, and many quarter-hours when I do nothing else." Nevertheless, Felice is clearly within the context of his "sacrifices,"

---

*In his diary for January 3, 1912, he had made up such a list: he had forsaken "the joys of sex, eating, drinking, philosophical reflection and above all music." On New Year's Eve, he dined on parsnips and spinach. . . . "My development is now complete and, so far as I can see, there is nothing left to sacrifice; I need only to throw my work in the office out of the complex in order to begin my real life in which, with the progress of my work, my face will finally be able to age in a natural way" (*Diaries: 1910–1913*, p. 211).

since his life "is determined by nothing else but the ups and downs of writing." Lately, he says, she has become associated intimately with his writing, but in the next lines he excludes her: "My mode of life is devised solely for writing, and if there are any changes, then only for the sake of perhaps fitting in better with my writing; for time is short, my strength is limited, the office is a horror, the apartment is noisy, and if a pleasant straightforward life is not possible then one must try to wriggle through by subtle maneuvers."[8]

When he outlines his schedule, it is difficult to see where Felice would fit as a wife. Kafka works until 2:00 or 2:30, then lunches for an hour (fletcherizing his food makes for slow going), then attempts (usually unsuccessfully) to sleep until 7:30, then exercises naked at the open window, takes an hour's walk — alone or with Max or another friend — has dinner with his family, and finally writes from 10:30 or 11:30 until 2:00 or 3:00 in the morning, sometimes until 6:00. Then he does more exercises, followed by bed, "usually with a slight pain in my heart and twitching stomach muscles." Efforts to sleep are ordinarily unavailing: his night consists of two parts, one wakeful, the other sleepless. When he reaches the office, he is half dead. "In one of the corridors along which I always walk to reach my typist, there used to be a coffinlike trolley for the moving of files and documents, and each time I passed it I felt as though it had been made for me, and was waiting for me."[9]

The images give Kafka away. The idea of a coffin as his rightful repository could not have been reassuring to a young woman seeking a suitable husband, nor could the routine he lays out, which would leave her perhaps an hour every day. But even more, his repeated declarations of how little energy he has left for anything but his writing should have alerted her to the implications: that his sexual energies were being sublimated by his writing. But Felice apparently did not pick up the plea Kafka was making, to stay with him although he was thoroughly unacceptable for what she wanted. She continued with her own agenda, to make a bourgeois marriage, have a pleasant and well-appointed home, bear children, have an attentive husband and father, and get on with what society approved and supported. Even by this time, the two principals have separate agendas, which each will pursue with equal intensity. Clearly there could be no harmony, surely no sweet music.

Kafka, however, was not finished. He relates to Felice his additional duties: not only is he a clerk (an official, not an office worker), he is a manufacturer, a partner in an asbestos factory venture — more reasons why he is inaccessible, if she should choose to put a lien on his time. But there is yet another dimension to his revelations: the amazing things he has told Felice, who is only barely within his fold, serve a therapeutic function. She becomes, in this respect, a female Brod, a silent analyst. The letters Kafka writes become sessions, he as analysand,

she as silent analyst who forces the patient to keep the words flowing.
Kafka had the need to disclose: through diaries, letters, stories, and
novels. He has reshaped Freud's therapeutic process into something
uniquely his, using written words as forms of a revealing self-analysis,
as ways of relieving internal pressures. As part of this, he wants to
know every detail of Felice's life. He feels that unless he knows all,
something will take her away from him; his knowledge will be a form
of control. Also, his uncertainty is so immense that knowledge of her
will somehow fill up his own emptiness. His interest in receiving her
letter has superseded his interest in what the letter may contain; the
physical evidence is a validation of his own existence. Words become
his sole form of salvation.

A good many of Kafka's later stories are foreshadowed in his remarks to Felice, as images, metaphors, or ideas. In speaking about living in hotel rooms, when he traveled for the institute, he says he felt
very much at ease. His following description of the hotel ambience suggests the mole and its burrow in that later story "The Burrow," one of
his most significant and ambiguous.

> To have to oneself the expanse of a hotel room with its easily surveyed
> four walls and a door that can be locked; the knowledge that specific
> items of one's belongings are tucked away into specific corners of cup-
> boards, on tables and coat hangers, always gives me a vague sensation of
> a new, unspent existence charged with vigor and destined for better
> things, which may of course be nothing but a despair driven beyond itself
> and finding itself at home in the cold grave of a hotel room.[10]

This is one of Kafka's great sentences, encompassing not only his
vision of a safe hole where he can feel secure, but also his awareness
that this very semblance of security could be a chimera, part of a despair seeking refuge and settling for an appearance of safety. He repeats
that he has always felt at ease in such rooms. His several visits to sanatoria suggest that he liked to be hidden away, taken care of, given external forms of security. Kafka's comments here wind around his
concerns, from life to death in all its rhythms. The coffin image is a familiar one, but he also uses the image of a ladder: any attempt to
achieve something only ends up with the ladder abruptly removed, or
the discovery that it is lacking in extension. What creates liberation
(security, comfort, a sense of ease) may be the process lowering one into
despair and death.

Kafka tells Felice of his love of Yiddish theater, that he has chalked
up perhaps twenty performances, and not a single one of German theater, a comment perhaps aimed maliciously at her Germanism. The letters indicate his growing comfort in opening himself up to this young
woman whom he has seen only once, about whom he knows next to
nothing, and whose education and intelligence are nowhere near his,

although she was bright, thoughtful, and resourceful. He needed a listener; she listened, and she responded, and for that Kafka was grateful. The letter-writing establishes its own rhythms, as in an epistolary novel, a kind of fletcherizing of the paper-pen-word process; it is something he can chew on until he has penetrated to her very being by way of words. He who has rejected so much in the way of food and positioned himself as a finicky eater now needs her nourishment, in fact demands it.

He attacks doctors. "I was in sanatoria only on account of my stomach [reassuring her, not for mental instability] and my general weakness, not forgetting my self-enamored hypochondria. One day I shall have to write at length about all this. No, I don't believe famous doctors; I believe doctors only when they tell me they don't know anything, and anyway I hate them (I hope you don't love one)." He is quick to warn her she will find things in him "you could not like, and what should I do then?"[11] But his letter of November 7 is hardly intended to calm her: "But I am tormenting you by my existence, my very existence." Kafka reveals his unsuitability in nearly every letter: "If I arrived in person you would find me insufferable. . . . My mode of life, though it has cured my stomach, would seem to you crazy and intolerable. For months on end, until he grew used to it [Kafka's fletcherizing of his food], my father had to hide his face behind the newspaper while I ate my supper."[12] Now almost desperate in his desire to present himself in the worst possible way, he reveals what a lunatic she is corresponding with, relieving his anxieties by telling all to someone he hardly knows. The relentlessness of his revelations is astonishing; it is an effort to put her under his control by way of making her embrace someone so unacceptable.

> For some years now my clothes have been very untidy. The same suit does for the office, the street, my desk at home . . . I can stand up to the cold almost better than a chunk of wood . . . for example, even now in November, not wearing an overcoat, neither a light nor a heavy one, walking around among well-wrapped pedestrians like a lunatic in a summer suit and little summer hat, on principle without a vest (I am the inventor of vestless attire); as for the indescribable peculiarities of my linen, the less said the better.

He asks her to imagine her shock if she ran into such a person. He adds that he neither smokes nor drinks, not even coffee and tea, and monastically stays away from chocolate; but all these healthful habits are undermined by lack of sleep. She should, he says, tolerate him "in a kindly way across this great distance."[13]

As though recognizing he is speaking to an equal and not to a parental figure, he reminds Felice he is much older than she takes him for, that he will be thirty on his next birthday (July 3) and is almost a year older than Brod, and that he must emphasize all this because he looks like a boy, anywhere between eighteen and twenty-five. The manic quality of his confession continues unabated: like Edvard Munch's figure in "The Scream," he must get it all out.

> I don't know if you have a true picture of my life, which would enable you to comprehend my sensibility, that irritability which is always at the ready, but which once it has been set free, leaves me behind like a stone. . . . Yesterday my weariness was so intense I was ready to die, and after many indecisions decided to abandon writing during the night. Instead, I walked the streets for two hours, returning home only when my hands were frozen stiff in my pockets.[14]

He indicates that Marie Werner, his former governess who stayed on as a maid in the Kafka household, burst into his room to announce the birth of a baby girl to Elli.

> Even in cases of emergency I can't be forcibly woken up, what does wake me is the general noise behind every door — trying to understand our governess' friendly interest in this birth, since I, the brother and uncle, felt not the slightest amity — only envy, nothing but passionate envy of my sister, or rather of my brother-in-law, for I shall never have a child; this is even more certain than — (I will not needlessly mention a greater misfortune).[15]

The "greater misfortune" is that he will never have a wife either.

With this, an open confession of his greatest fears, and in a sense a rejection of Felice even as he pursues frantically, he writes three letters on November 11, all filled with his fear of losing her. Kafka's state of mind, however, cannot be disentangled from a "story" he is writing, "The Man Who Disappeared" ("Der Verschollene").* Though not primarily autobiographical, the very title is appropriate to Kafka. Later that month he would write his signature story, "The Metamorphosis," with its exhausting account of personal details. Kafka's work on "The Man Who Disappeared" also cannot be disengaged from his perception

---

*"The Man Who Disappeared," later given the title Amerika by Max Brod, will be discussed in far greater detail later. Its origin is of some interest at this stage of Kafka's life: the version of the story he mentions to Felice is a revision of something he had tried to write earlier. That earlier manuscript, which is considered lost, derived from a period when Kafka was immersed in Dickens's David Copperfield (winter, 1911). In his diary (January 19, 1911) he described a novel he had started about two brothers who fought, one going to America, the other remaining behind in a European prison. Then during the spring, summer, and fall of 1912, just before and then after meeting Felice, he turned over to Max Brod about two hundred pages of what Kafka wanted to call "Der Verschollene," and which Brod referred to as Kafka's American novel. Then in November 1912, as we note in his letter to Felice (on the ninth), he overhauled the original and created a new novel, which remained unfinished, and whose eight chapters (some inconclusive) appeared posthumously in 1927 as Amerika. The only part of this work to appear in Kafka's lifetime was the first chapter, "Der Heizer" ("The Stoker"), which Kurt Wolff published in May 1913.

of the affair with Felice. In his letters to her, he plays constantly with the idea of disappearing, if not from her, then from any solid sense of himself. It is as though he has left his body, like a dybbuk, and as a disembodied soul is yearning for a reward that can never be his.

Before his surge of letters on November 11, he had even drafted a letter to Felice — never mailed, and only later revealed in Brod's biography — in which he indeed planned to disappear. He tells her not to write to him again, and he will not write to her. "I would be bound to make you unhappy by writing to you, and as for me I am beyond help. . . . If I attempted, nevertheless, to tie myself to you I should deserve to be cursed, were I not cursed already."[16] He offers to return her letters if she wants them, but he begs her to keep his. "Now quickly forget the ghost that I am, and go on living happily and peacefully as before." What level of despair and anguish brought him to write this we can see from the language itself: frantic, full of pleading, presenting himself as someone who has already vanished from the relationship before it even started. The work on "The Man Who Disappeared" surely was resonating in his private life, since the book falls broadly into what we have called "spiritual autobiography," what Kafka found in Dickens, Dostoevsky, and Nietzsche. The strain this type of fiction places on an author is enormous, since the genre depends on a marginal figure, a central character negotiating most or all of his or her life on the outside.

The author's sensibility is revealed in that crossing-over between fictional effort and letters. Kafka's first letter of November 11 is relatively calm but the next is filled with sounds of doom. "The letter in which you described one of my letters as alien to you [probably the one of November 7, in which he presents all the things he denies himself, sex being not too distant from chocolate, alcohol, and the rest], horrified me. I saw in it the unintentional, and therefore all the more decisive confirmation of doom, which recently in particular I had thought largely to have escaped, but to which, with a final blow, I had once more to submit."[17] Kafka's lack of clear identity, or his "disappearance," even as he pours himself into his writing, is never more evident than in a passage in which he mentions his mother's concern for him. She has come into his room, crying, caressing him, trying to discover what is wrong, why he has stopped talking at meals (perhaps too busy chewing?). "Poor Mother! But I comforted her in a very sensible way, kissed her, and finally made her smile." He even coaxes her to scold him for having gone without his afternoon snack. Kafka is now in his thirtieth year. He has, evidently, divided himself into the childish boy, who seeks maternal care, from Julie or from Felice, and the mature man, who can transform these regressive needs into startling fiction. Implicit in these comments on Julie is "The Metamorphosis."

As part of this regression into dependency and subservience, Kafka

offers to throw himself at Felice's feet, "to give myself to you so completely that no trace, no memory of me is left for anyone else." He outlines for her the story he is writing, which, he says, is designed "in such
a manner that it will never be completed" — it too, like its title and author, will disappear. It takes place "entirely in the United States of
America. So far 5 chapters are completed, the 6th almost." He lists the
chapters (eight in all, in the final, incomplete manuscript): "The
Stoker," "The Uncle," "A Country House in New York," "The March
to Rameses," "In the Hotel Occidental," "The Case of Robinson." He
admits that such chapter headings are meaningless to her, but he wants
her to have them for safekeeping. "After 15 years of despairing effort
(except for rare moments), this is the first major work in which, for the
past 6 weeks, I have felt confidence."[18] He asks her forebearance for he
will spend less time on his "inaccurate, alarmingly incomplete, impru-
dent, dangerous letters" to her and more time on his project. With this,
he tells her he wishes he could look into her eyes at this moment, a bit
of romantic massaging to balance his plans to vanish into his work.

As an addendum to this letter, Kafka speaks of his family. He tells
her to look at the October issue of the Prague literary periodical *Herderblätter* in which he has published his little piece on noises in the
Kafka apartment, his act of hostility revealing that he was declaring
war to protect himself. He says, additionally, that his youngest sister,
Ottla, is his best friend in Prague, closing with "It's only my father and
I who hate each other gallantly." He is overwhelmed that the *du*, or familiar form, has entered her letters, even if only as part of a quotation.

The relative calm of this letter gives way in the third November 11
letter to panic, a hyperventilation in which Kafka confesses to terrible
fears. He warns Felice to write him only so that her letters arrive on
Sunday. "I am incapable of enduring them." For after he answers one of
her letters, he lies in bed, his heart beating, his entire body "conscious
only of you." He insists, "I belong to you. . . . But for this very reason I
don't want to know what you are wearing; it confuses me so much that
I cannot deal with life; and that's why I don't want to know that you
are fond of me."[19] Before dropping his newest load of verbal bombs,
Kafka suggests here that her letters make him realize how little control
he has over her, and this he cannot bear. Underneath all is his panic
that she may be slipping away, in between letters; that he is not good
enough for her; that he is unable to handle her every move and whim
from a distance.* This is, after all, a tale of two cities: Kafka in Prague,

---

*In a shrewd psychoanalytic reading of Kafka's life, Anthony Storr, the British psychi-
atrist, sees Kafka's insistence on the details of Felice's life as a way of turning her into
a fictional character. By discovering every aspect of her life, including her mode of dress
and daily schedule, he was recreating her in his mind the way a novelist might create
a fictional character. Further, Storr feels that by keeping her at a distance — Kafka saw
little of Felice, as later he would see relatively little of Milena Jesenská — he could

Felice in Berlin, and as the correspondence develops and unofficial and official engagements follow, we recognize that Prague and Berlin are separated by more than a few hours' train ride. Different cultures are at stake.

The bombshell: "To make it short: My health is only just good enough for myself alone, not good enough for marriage, let alone fatherhood. Yet when I read your letter, I feel I could overlook even what cannot possibly be overlooked." He says he preys "like a spectre on your felicitous name."[20] Yet even if they wrote only once a week, which he both wants and cannot bear, the problem is unsolvable. He thinks of signing *dein* (the familiar "your"), but finds it false; he is forever fettered to himself, not to her, and they must try to live with that. Subsequently, his form of address is "Dearest, dearest," quite an advance over Fräulein Felice. His change is the result of Felice's having used the familiar form. The *du* remains no matter what else happens, and the *Sie* of formal address disappears. The switch in pronouns, which is quite meaningful in German, has made him delirious, especially in his protestations of calmness.

His anxiety rises when he contemplates the telephone as a way of communicating with her, revealing that "the very thought of the telephone makes me forget laughter." The telephone is an instrument of torture, an object that intensifies anxiety: ". . . sitting there for an hour, waiting to be put through, clutching the seat in anxiety, eventually being summoned and rushing all of a tremble to the telephone, then asking for you in a feeble voice, finally hearing you and perhaps not being capable of answering, thanking God that the three minutes are over.*[21] Any departure from his daily rituals and procedures sends Kafka into a depressive state, for he recognizes that nothing can make him happy. What can occur, in the best scenario, is something that can keep the demons at bay. The telephone becomes an instrument of torture not only because it is unfamiliar, but because it raises the question of almost a physical presence: *her* voice, *her* direct responses, *her* resonances; with it he could lose his visionary sense of her in the banal reality.

---

reshape her into an inhabitant of his inner, imaginative world. Storr does not slight Kafka's anxiety here; in fact, he emphasizes that his concern with Felice's comings and goings are like those anxieties a child experiences at the possible loss of a parent (a mother, in particular). The child protects itself by knowing exactly where the parent is, if and when the child needs her. Storr, however, underestimates Kafka's personal, not fictional, need for control of Felice, and since he could not, apparently, master his own family his need to control Felice became more intense. As part of this, he undoubtedly remade her into a mother figure of sorts, but the primary need was to know her so intimately that he could, like a Svengali type, enter deeply into her life and work out its direction.

*We observe how closely the language linked to the telephone approaches the language of the court case in *The Trial:* sitting, clutching, being summoned, not being capable of answering.

The anxiety over mail reasserts itself in successive letters, indicating how necessary it was for Kafka to retain communication. Affection for him means maternal love: "An image that now comes to me more and more often: of my face resting on your shoulder, of my talking, partly smothered and indistinctly, to your shoulder, your dress, to myself, while you can have no notion of what is being said."[22] Even the use of *du*, indicating the beloved, does not allay his extreme anxiety over whether she will write, and at work he frequently sends a messenger downstairs to see if the mail has been sorted, enlisting three people to watch out for and handle her letter.* In his first literary reference, he says that Flaubert's *Sentimental Education* is as dear to him as only two or three people have been. He feels, he says, "as though I were the author's spiritual son, albeit a weak and awkward one." He asks whether she reads French, but even if she doesn't, she is to tell him she does.

Julie Kafka also wrote to Felice, admitting she had read one of Felice's letters to Kafka left lying around. She apologizes for doing so, saying it was only her son's well-being that impelled her. Her comment reinforces Kafka's assessment of her as loving, well-wishing, and completely ignorant of who he is and what he is striving for. She has mother love, but no understanding, for she tells Felice that since her son has had everything he has ever wanted he should be the "happiest of mortals." Never having been denied anything, he now has short working hours in the job of his choice. As for his leisure time, which he spends writing, Frau Kafka wishes he would sleep and eat like other young men. "I would therefore very much like to ask you if you could somehow draw his attention to this fact, question him about the way he lives, what he eats, how many meals he has, and about his daily routine in general." Julie is firm that Kafka must never know she has written, but should it be "within your power to change his mode of life, I would be greatly in your debt."[23]

The distance between mother and son could not have been greater. For while Julie wrote Felice on November 16, Kafka wrote his hard-pressed Berlin correspondent on the seventeenth, mentioning "a short story that occurred to me in bed in my misery, and now troubles me and demands to be written."[24] Julie is concerned with food, sleep, her son's unusual hours, and he is beginning to write "The Metamorphosis," an annihilation of everything Julie and, by implication, Hermann had striven to achieve for themselves and their children. In a sweet, caring way, Julie observes the surface; her son, however, has

---

*On November 15 Brod wrote Felice, in response to her communication, telling her to make "allowances for Franz and his often pathological sensitivity. . . . He is a man who wants nothing but the absolute, the ultimate in all things. He is never prepared to compromise. . . . when it comes to ideals he cannot take things lightly" (*Letters to Felice*, p. 43).

sounded every weakness in the structure, rerouted it through pathology, and transformed it into a universal tale of a son's relationship to his family. What Frau Kafka would never comprehend, and it is well she didn't, is the overwhelming hostility her son felt toward her, even as he tried to shape his Berlin friend into a maternal figure, but one who might at some time understand him.

The terrible anxieties Kafka admits to, so that both Julie and Felice are worried about him, are surely connected to the story rolling around in his imagination. His conception of Gregor Samsa as a monstrous bug is a conception Kafka approximates in his sense of himself as he waits nervously for the mail, fears Felice may drop him, pours out his discontent with family life, views himself as depreciated and cheapened by work at the institute and at the factory. All of this suggests a severe depression, which perhaps precipitates the idea of transformation underlying the story. Kafka peers into a mirror, and his shameful body, still embarrassing him, even at close to thirty, has shifted its center of gravity, to just above the floor. His flailing arms and legs, scrawny and weak, have become the numerous limbs of the insect; the shameful body is turned into something that leaks not blood but a dirty brown liquid. The self-hate and shame he feels for his body had made it possible for its transformation into something abominable to all.

In his November 18 letter, Kafka reveals as much:

> I am just sitting down to yesterday's story with an overwhelming desire to pour myself into it, which obviously springs from despair. Beset by many problems, uncertain of you, quite incapable of coping at the office, my novel ["The Man Who Disappeared"] at a standstill for a day, with a fierce longing to continue the new, equally demanding story, all but total insomnia for the last few days and nights. . . . I decided quite definitely that my only salvation was to write to a man in Silesia, with whom I had made friends this summer and who for whole long afternoons had tried to convert me to Christ.*[25]

The need for maternal care from Felice builds. "Stay with me, don't leave me," he pleads. His dependence on her at this stage is quite understandable. Having started a story in which he aggressively rejects his family, making them all as repulsive in their way as he has become in his, he needs Felice as support, especially as a maternal substitute, since Frau Samsa in the story is presented as ineffectual, retiring, and under the sway of her husband. Felice becomes, as it were, his new family.

The letters about letter writing become more frequent. He admits

---

*The man in question was Herr H., a land surveyor from Silesia, and perhaps the first model for K. in *The Castle*. Kafka met him in July 1912, during his stay in Jungborn. It is unclear what he hoped to gain by writing Herr H. during this tremendously troubling time. Surely he was not thinking of spiritual uplift or conversion.

he is using correspondence to rid himself of "some of the feelings that were tearing"[26] at him; and this too is understandable, since what he was writing in the story was nothing less than destruction of everything he had grown up with and become accustomed to. He is clearly suffering from a crisis concerning his mother; the question here is one of women more than men. For if we read "The Metamorphosis" biographically, we can see that Gregor's real contempt is for his retiring, acquiescent mother. The father is a given, a tyrant, a dictator, a führer with a military bearing. All expectations derive from the female side, and first mother and then sister fail him. Felice, then, becomes doubly significant, since if she too fails him, then he has lost all. That this drama lies close to madness only increases Kafka's need for maternal affection, both personally and in terms of his writing.*

As if writing to a maternal figure, he tells Felice about his troubled eating habits. She has probably warned him, following Julie's advice, about his unhealthy schedule.

> I eat three times a day, nothing between meals, literally nothing. In the morning, stewed fruit, biscuits, and milk. At 2:30 out of filial affection, the same as the others, but on the whole rather less, less meat in particular, even less than a little, and more vegetables. Winter evenings at 9:30: yogurt, pumpernickel, butter, all kinds of nuts, chestnuts, dates, figs, grapes, almonds, raisins, pumpkins, bananas, apples, pears, oranges. Needless to say, only a selection of all these are eaten, not all mixed up as though poured from a horn of plenty. No food is more stimulating to me than this. Please don't insist on 3 extra mouthfuls, everything is eaten for your benefit, and these three mouthfuls would be to my detriment.[27]

"For your benefit": son to a mother, not man to woman. With this diet of nuts, fruit, and grainy foods, Kafka should not have suffered constipation; his chronic constipation goes beyond normal digestive difficulty into areas of psychological control of body and its wastes.

The problem of letters dips into paranoia, as Kafka conjures up persecution by the post office: "The girl who took my letter was rather careless and inefficient."[28] That is one of three letters he wrote on that day, November 21. This second letter is full of self-recrimination that he had left Felice's letter around for his mother to read. He calls his action "unforgivable and criminal" and says he normally carries her letters with him for "continuous support."[29] They make him "a better, more competent man." But the real tone of his missive comes near the end, the tone of "The Metamorphosis."

---

*The detail presented thus far in this correspondence will not continue throughout the entire relationship between Kafka and Felice. It is particularly heavy here because the letters are so closely linked to Kafka's creative efforts, particularly in the latter part of 1912, when he became, in effect, Franz Kafka, writer to the world, and was no longer František Kafka, an obscure lawyer working at a Prague insurance company.

I have always looked upon my parents as persecutors; until about a year ago I was indifferent to them and perhaps to the world at large, as some kind of lifeless thing, but I see now it was only suppressed fear, worry, and unhappiness. All parents want to do is drag one down to them, back to the old days from which one longs to free oneself and escape; they do it out of love, of course, and that's what makes it so horrible. I must stop, the end of the page comes as a warning that it might get too wild.[30]

Letter and creative work here blend, with the son's need to transform himself into an avenger who can undermine whatever remains of the family's achievement.

Felice — poor Felice! — was now bombarded with letters indicating hostilities and hatreds, first from Kafka on November 22, then from Brod, on the same day. This attack on the Kafka family is followed by another letter, telling her about his story and how it would frighten her. It should, in fact, have driven her to Lapland to escape her correspondent and all those associated with him. Kafka admits that his need for Felice has turned to hostility, an incredible insight that enables him to understand that what he is doing with her is no less than substituting her for Julie Kafka and then unloading his aggressions on her. Julie's reading of Felice's letter, in turn, is now poisoning an already poisoned, contradictory atmosphere. After spending some time with Brod, Kafka returns home convinced that if he didn't confront his mother, he would never speak to her again. But the apartment was filled with visitors, and Kafka went directly to his room. "I was amazed that the apartment didn't disintegrate, such was the tension within me." Finally he sees Julie: "I told her what I thought, told it to her in an utterly uncontrolled outburst." He feels that this openness was good for both of them. "I have never found in any family, whether of friends or relations, as much coldness and false friendliness as I have always felt obliged to show toward my parents (through my fault as well as theirs)."[31] The outburst, their first, clears the air, and Kafka sees how "pleased my mother is with our present relationship."

Brod's letter to Felice — she is now the center of a triangular situation — is intense and dramatic. In some way, she, Felice, must save Kafka: his mother "has not the faintest idea who her son is and *what his needs are.*"[32] She thinks his interest in literature is a "pastime." "My God! As though it did not eat our hearts out, willing victims though we are." Brod brings up the question of food. He says that after years of trial and error, Kafka has found the only diet that suits him, a vegetarian one; he is now, according to Brod, healthy and fit. But then his parents try, out of love, to force him back into eating meat and being ill. The same is true with his sleeping habits. Kafka has found what works for him, but his parents think he is crazy.

His parents just will not see that an *exceptional man* like Franz needs *exceptional conditions* to prevent his sensitive spirit from withering. The other day I had to write an 8-page letter to Frau Kafka about this. His parents wanted Franz to work in the factory in the afternoons; whereupon Franz firmly *resolved to commit suicide* and went so far as to send me a farewell letter. Only by ruthless intervention did I succeed at the last moment in protecting him from his "loving" parents.

Brod was indeed upset by Kafka's letter of October 7, in which Kafka writes of two possibilities open to him: either to jump out the window once everyone had gone to sleep, or to go daily to the factory and his brother-in-law's office. Although Kafka decided not to make this a farewell letter, he did stand for a long time at the window, pressed against the pane, "when it would have suited me to alarm the toll collector on the bridge by my fall." In "The Judgment," Georg Bendemann jumps from a bridge or overpass into traffic below. One reason Kafka says he decided not to jump was that staying alive would interrupt his writing less than death. Brod was not amused.

What is occurring is that Felice, becoming the repository of the Kafka saga, is being asked to mediate; her own needs are overwhelmed by those of others, primarily Kafka's. Even when he is not attempting directly to control her, she is being pressed by Brod and Frau Kafka, each asking her, in completely different terms, to look after their Franz. What had started as a romance in letters was slowly sinking into melodrama, with the two principals as far apart as ever.

Kafka, now in late November 1912, was full of his story. "I want to read it to you. Yes, that would be lovely, to read the story to you, while I would have to hold your hand, for the story is a little frightening. It is called *Metamorphosis*, and it would thoroughly scare you, you might not want to hear a word of it, for alas! I scare you enough every day with my letters."[33] He indicates they should start "a better life," and while writing that last sentence, he says he looked heavenward, hoping to catch a glimpse of her. "I am too depressed at the moment, and perhaps I shouldn't be writing at all. But my story's hero has also had a very bad time today, and it is only the last lap of his misfortune, which is now becoming permanent. So how can I be particularly cheerful!"

He follows this up, in the next letter (November 24), by saying he will put aside "this exceptionally repulsive story" to refresh himself by thinking of her. He then connects himself, Gregor, and Felice, as if to reassure her: "But now it is more than half finished, and on the whole I am not too dissatisfied; but it is infinitely repulsive, and these things, you see, spring from the same heart in which you dwell and which you tolerate as a dwelling place." Kafka has second thoughts, that perhaps this is not quite the way to court a young woman: "But don't be unhappy about it, for who knows, the more I write and the more I liberate myself, the cleaner and worthier of you I may become, but no doubt there is a great deal more to be got rid of, and the nights can never be long enough for this business which, incidentally, is highly voluptuous."[34] He declares his love amidst Gregor Samsa's repulsiveness (linked to his own), promising that if he could keep her, "I should want to live forever, but only, it must be remembered, as a healthy person and your equal."[35]

The last lines suggest an enormity: that while Kafka was immersing himself in Gregor's plight and was himself convinced that he might never extricate himself, he throws out a lifeline to Felice, asking her to save him before he, like his fictional creation, is transformed into a lower form. To be her "equal" means to be someone who can share her perspective of love, marriage, and family. He then quotes to her a poem he finds very meaningful, by the Chinese poet Yuan Tzu-tsai (1716–97), which is about a mistress who almost in wrath asks her lover to put aside his work, turn out the lamp, and come to bed. The implication is that Felice will not do this. The poem leads Kafka to other observations. "It's a pity," he says, "that my love for you advanced so fast, that there is no room left to love you more for what you eat."[36] He then approves of the fact that she too likes the window open even in the cold of winter; although he opens his only a crack, she goes all the way. "Besides I beat you in this: my room has no heating whatever, yet here is where I do my writing. . . . Now you try and compete with that!" These and similar passages indicate that however transcendent a writer may be, when it comes to romantic interludes he too touches on banality.

He worries about her health, as she appears to be taking on some of his ailments. Felice, incidentally, was not sickly, and lived a full life, dying in 1960, just short of her seventy-third birthday. But when Kafka suffered from headaches, she now had headaches; when he suffered anxiety attacks, she had attacks of nerves; when he suffered from insomnia, she reported trouble sleeping. Kafka's solution for her sudden ills: go for walks and if his letters become unpleasant, then tear them up without reading further. He says he'll replace them with ten, no, one hundred more. Keeping her informed of the progress of "The Metamorphosis," he indicates on November 25 he will need another three to four evenings. He says his preferred method of proceeding would be to write in two ten-hour sessions, so the piece can have a spontaneous flow; but he must work with constant interruptions. Yet even as Gregor becomes increasingly alienated from any part of ordinary life in house or at work, Kafka is desperately seeking acceptance. "Oh God, what I want is every moment of the whole of your life. . . . I am frightened when you tell me that you love me, and if you didn't tell, I should die."[37] He pleads that he needs her letters and her assurances because of his health: "That is what robs me of my confidence vis-à-vis you, which upsets me, and eventually drags me down." Then ambiguously he adds, "That above all, and not because I love you, is why I need your letters and all but devour them; that is why I am unable to believe all the nice things you say; that is why I cringe before you with all these sad requests."[38] He tells her of a journey he took for the institute, a "beastly journey": at the beginning "I sat opposite a repulsive woman and felt restless because I had to keep curbing my desire to ram my fist into her mouth every time she yawned." Analysand and analyst, in partnership, are closing in on each other.

Anxieties about letters received, sent, crossing, possibly straying, and paranoia about some "diabolical official who is playing with our letters"[39] bring him close to tears. And he recalls one time, two or three months earlier, when he sobbed so insistently he feared he would wake his parents next door. Yet even as he calls for more correspondence, he recognizes they are "lashing each other with all these letters. They can't create a presence, only a mixture of presence and distance that becomes unbearable."[40] Kafka understands that the very means by which he can hold on to Felice, not through physical presence but through correspondence, can be destructive in its insistence on challenge and response. He begs her to put an end to the flood of letters "that produces nothing but delusion, which makes one dizzy." He realizes that the overabundance of letters is compensation for something lacking, that the frenzy of letters is "a poison that lodges in the pit of one's stomach." Yet even as he writes this, Kafka knows he cannot bear the uncertainty of silence, since it would recall Julie's withdrawal, Hermann's rejection, and his sense of isolation and marginality, however warranted. He needed to engage Felice in an uncertainty as great as his.

Achieving transcendence in his work at hand, moving into regions of fiction no one had quite reached into before, Kafka is all dross and dust in his personal life. He seeks some transcendence there through Felice but does not find it forthcoming. By December 1, tortured by the possibility that a human relationship cannot reveal that perfect "other world" of his fantasies, he reimmerses himself in the final section of Gregor Samsa's recoil into isolation and eventual death. The suicide that Kafka had contemplated earlier, in his letter to Brod, is now achieved in Gregor's desire to see it all come to an end. What Kafka could not do in actuality — and he was not a suicidal person, despite depression and despair, and even flirtation with final things — he achieved in his fiction. The surrogate Gregor is finally rid of his family, not by moving out but by dying. Family members, then, in Kafka's perception of them, can wax strong and move on to another level of experience with the troublesome, self-destructive son out of the way. Kafka has restructured his actual life by way of an imaginary recreation of it; at the same time he pursues Felice with sentiments that belie what was occurring so intensely at his desk. Rather than unifying the disparate elements in him, the correspondence merely pointed them up as unresolvable.

But they would torture each other for several years, as though in Felice Kafka had found some way of approaching and rejecting in alternate waves his mother and all she stood for. Felice becomes the means by which he can take revenge on all those who brought him into existence, a vengeance he commits by pledging an everlasting love he knows he can never fulfill. Only a great ironist or satirist can sustain this pose. Kafka's view of a courtship is pure parody, but the parody of a great, transcendent clown, a Chaplin perhaps, or one of Picasso's painted meditative clowns. Kafka has found a means of parodying the entire process of courtship, and he has done so by using language tinged with melodrama and the irony that subverts the melodrama. By early December, he is close to the end of his "little story," as he calls it. If Felice had read Kafka correctly, and the little story, she would have known after only two and a half months of the correspondence and one meeting that the affair was effectively over. In Gregor Samsa, Kafka had signaled the end of all such relationships, whether with Felice or anyone else, until near the end of his life with Dora Dymant, perhaps. When Gregor chooses to end it all in hateful isolation, he has brought down the curtain on family life. It is, like him, dead matter.

The torture, however, must continue. Part of it is surely linked to Kafka's desire to transform Felice. If he can become in his fictional re-creation a giant bug, so she must become something else as well. He is full of advice in his December 4–5 letter, even while finishing up on Gregor; he tells her to open a gramophone shop in Paris, then another in the West End of London, or else to work in Paris, where she could sit and simply rake in the money. "I suggest this only because you could then use your other hand, the one not required for your duties, to write letters to me all day long. Dearest, what nonsense my longing for you makes me invent."[41] We must read these pleas juxtaposed with what was occurring late at night at Kafka's desk, the window open slightly, cold air pouring in, the sounds of the streets and the household finally hushed. In that work, he was plotting how to get rid of Gregor Samsa — not only how to wind down Gregor's situation, but how to lead Gregor into a life of such withdrawal that only his death can solve the Samsa problems. Killing Gregor off after his final and complete rejection by even his sister, whom he had trusted and helped, Kafka is desolate, deserted, unable to turn to anyone except the person he can reach through still more words. His life had come down to language, and he was desperate to maintain contact with himself through words even when his words might bring pain. "You will realize that the pain I caused you by letter was as nothing compared to the burden imposed by personal contact with me."[42]

He sends on a photograph of himself, taken two years earlier, and says that in reality he looks even worse. In keeping with his transformation into Gregor, he warns her of his appearance.

After all, the picture is bearable, but what will happen when the man himself appears? — You might run away from him altogether. Remember, you have seen him once, and that by gaslight and without paying too much attention to him at the time. He doesn't get out much by day, and this has given him a veritable night-face. . . . But perhaps you will get used to him after all, dearest, for don't forget, even I, the writer of this letter, whom you have treated so well, have had to get used to him.[43]

Kafka is being both witty and looney. But getting used to his own face was not eased by his completion of Gregor's journey on December 5 or 6: "The hero of my story died a little while ago. To comfort you, I want you to know that he died peacefully enough and reconciled to all." The story is not quite finished; some afterthoughts about the Samsa family remain. But he is not satisfied, feeling that with a steady pull he could have achieved a "neater, more telling, better-constructed piece of work than the one that now exists," a sentiment he repeats when the story is completed.

The thought, even of a trip to Berlin, brings out all the worst in Kafka's description of himself. "I am basically a very feeble and unhappy man; the things that are unusual about me are largely bad and sad, and consist mainly . . . of the fact that, although able to go on a pointless trip to Leitmeritz [where the widow of Kafka's paternal uncle Heinrich had remarried], I am unable to come to Berlin with the most definite objective."[44] A trip to Berlin in March 1913 would finally occur, but only for a very brief stayover.

The immediate letters in this post-"Metamorphosis" period are somewhat less frantic. Kafka says he remains "lazily sitting back, in comfortable lassitude, as though slowly bleeding to death."[45] This small touch allows him to recreate Felice as the nurse who tends his wounds, or dissipates his gloom. Yet the correspondence is not simply blood and gloom, for at times it breaks into literary discussion. Felice sends on an article by Wilhelm Herzog, "Was ist Modern?" ("What is Modern?"), which appeared in the Berliner Tageblatt (December 10). The Herzog piece, which Kafka found incoherent and weakly written, has no insight into the kind of Modernism Kafka was himself practicing; for most critical views of literary effort would have to be re-evaluated in the light of his present work. Kafka responds by praising Franz Werfel's first book, The Friend of the World, a volume of poems published in 1911, calling him "really miraculous." He finds Werfel to have "tremendous ability," and feels he is already rewarded for his talent, by living in Leipzig "in blissful conditions" as a reader for Rowohlt, Kafka's own publisher for Meditation.

Then by mid-December, Kafka begins the cycle of complaints: how tired and unhappy he has been, unfit for company. He says the novel he is bringing along, "The Man Who Disappeared," looks terrifyingly like him. "Before we met I also had these unpredictable moods; but then I seemed to lose all contact with the world; my life seemed disrupted; I rose to the surface and dived to the depths; now I have you dearest, I feel myself benevolently supported, and when I collapse I know it will not be forever."[46] Thus the maternal Felice: soft breast, kind shoulder, warm gesture, all-forgiving. He seeks her, he says, so they can be alone together: "Entirely alone, dearest, I wanted us to be entirely alone on this earth, entirely alone under the sky, and to lead my life, my life that is yours, without distraction and with complete concentration on you."[47] There is a passage in George Meredith's novel *The Egoist* when Sir Willoughby Patterne looks into Clara Middleton's eyes and wants to see only himself. Kafka's words here speak only of control: she will be Friday to his Crusoe, and their abode, like Sir Willoughby's with Clara, will be some island cut off from the rest of humankind. The little bit of Hermann in Kafka will turn her into a likeness of Julie.

Not unusually, Felice shows symptoms of illness: she who wrote that she was never ill is now going from "doctor to doctor." Kafka speaks of her as looking "like a corpse on leave" with symptoms strikingly close to his: headaches, sore throat, languor. Dr. Kafka is full of manic energy in his remedies, and he says he has sympathy for headaches and sore throats almost in line with hers. "And I suffer even more from your exhaustion, and more still from your headaches. And if you take some aspirin, then I too feel physically sick." There is a kind of defense mechanism here, whereby he uses her illness as a means of presenting something significant about himself. He sees himself, perhaps, as "just a madman who in his mind lays his hands on your temples many times, and hopes his kisses may have the power to kiss away from your forehead all the headaches, from the dimmest past to your golden future."[48] If they are one, as he wants her to believe, then if one is ailing so is the other. Inseparable, they must suffer together.

Then in a remarkable piece of self-analysis, part of the foreshadowing of his letter to his father in 1917, Kafka describes what it means to be an oldest child, as against being a "late-born" one like Felice. His indictment is devastating; he does not blame his parents for lack of love but for their lack of understanding of what they have wrought. "Of course there are disadvantages," he writes, "in being a late-born child, but the advantages compared to those of a firstborn, of which I am the sad but perfect example, are after all very great." He writes of the later-born,

> By then the family is far better equipped to deal with them; the parents, as far as it is possible for them, have learned from their mistakes (which, however, have also made them more obstinate); and automatically these late-born ones are settled more warmly in the nest; less attention is paid to them; here advantage and disadvantage fluctuate, the latter never dominating, but they don't need it, for everyone is unconsciously, thus all the more deeply and less harmfully, concerned with them.[49]

But for him:

> I am the eldest of six brothers and sisters, two brothers somewhat
> younger than I died in infancy through the fault of the doctors; then there
> was a pause; I was the only child until 4–5 years later my three sisters
> arrived, separated by one and two years respectively. Thus I lived alone
> for a very long time, battling with nurses, old nannies, spiteful cooks, un-
> happy governesses, since my parents were always at the shop.

Kafka then signs off because of the late hour.

At twenty-nine and a half, Kafka was still seeking some Eden, possible for the later-born but denied the oldest, himself. What he omits,
in a general sense, is the greater attention usually paid to the oldest
child because he or she is unique in the parents' experience. What he
omits further is the dominant place the oldest assumes, especially a
son, and especially in a Jewish family, where the boy may turn out to
be messianic. Yet Kafka views all these "advantages" as deficits. Because he was never able to seize the dominant role, he feels inadequate
to the expectations placed upon him, misunderstood from the start, neglected by his mother, martyred somehow to those two dead young
brothers.

Curiously, while writing in late 1912 at great length, Kafka avoids
discussing current events. We would not know from his voluminous
correspondence that Europe was heading toward a cataclysm, and that
the Dual Monarchy, and Prague's shaky position within it, was heading
toward disintegration.* Like so many others, Kafka took it for granted
that Franz Josef was eternal, and although his work can be read at one
level as symbolic of the disintegration to come, Kafka personally was
not politically involved. In one of his few references, he mentions that
his sister Valli's marriage (to Josef Pollak) was postponed by a war scare
to January of 1913. The "war scare" was connected to Balkan politics:
In the so-called first Balkan War, Turkey's Ottoman Empire (also tottering, like the Dual Monarchy) was defeated by an alliance of Serbia,
Greece, Bulgaria, and Montenegro. The alliance, however, had no lasting validity except as a way of beating a common enemy in Turkey.
Once the enemy was vanquished, Serbia emerged as a major power and
as a distinct threat to Austria and the monarchy. This was of course a
significant nationalist movement that undermined the Austro-Hungarian Empire and helped to destroy all liberal movements. With Serbia as
a threat, both Austria and Russia mobilized — thus the "war scare"
Kafka refers to. Further developments would follow, leading to the Ser-

---

*The very bourgeoisie as a class, which Hermann had hoped to join, saw its younger
people fading into nationalistic movements, or else was itself displaced by those who
yearned for aristocratic connections. An entire class that had once provided an alternative
to imperial power was being dissipated, as it were, before Kafka's eyes. Only later, in
The Castle, do we find his direct response to such political as well as social displacement.

bian assassination of Archduke Ferdinand, Franz Josef's heir apparent, and the beginning not of a "scare" but of the Great War. In all of this, Kafka remained a patriotic subject. In the main, Bohemian and other Jews remained extremely loyal subjects to the empire and to the German side. Hungarian Jews, in fact, had been such devoted citizens that the Magyars had rewarded them with something close to acceptance — until nationalism in Hungary, as everywhere else, led to resentment of "Jewish control" and infiltration into places of power, and Jews were scapegoated for whatever was wrong with the regime.* In the Dual Monarchy, Franz Josef out of expedience had been benign toward Jews, although most parts of the empire found even assimilated Jews (those who had converted, married Gentiles, and so forth) unacceptable during periods of high nationalism. It was a familiar story, but Kafka was curiously inattentive to all but the most overt outbursts of anti-Semitism.

Just before Christmas of 1912, the correspondence appears to settle down. Kafka continues with his cries for help, but they are somewhat muted. He speaks of his hatred of his job, where he says he slithers "out of responsibility like a snake"[50] — when in fact, he had the reputation for efficiency and hard work. He manages to keep his grip on Felice by expressing how close he feels to her, and how unhappy he is at their separation. He complains of completely collapsing at the office because his head was bursting from lack of sleep. Yet he asserts he has written nothing for nights on end. The cries he sends out, however muted, are cries of impotence, but they appear much more closely linked to his inability to write than to his feelings about Felice, or his fear, as Elias Canetti claims, of impotence if and when he and Felice came together. Sexual impotence is possibly there, but secondary to the turmoil Kafka experienced at his inability to do his main work. Also, there were impending marriages: Brod would marry early in the new year, and that inevitably would crimp their roving style. Valli's forthcoming marriage, to someone Kafka did not particularly like, was another example of the world closing in, with expectations for him to normalize his personal life. Werfel had moved away, and the circle of friends was reforming or dissipating. Constants in Kafka's life were vanishing.

Once again, Felice becomes, innocently, the repository of all his ills, and he is not even sure he likes her. There is little he can like or love, since he has shaped an idea of her, and if there is any feeling, it is for his image of her. What Felice has come to mean, and her name rein-

*Lest we think the Magyars had become soft and tolerant, we should recall an 1878 appeal by a member (Istóczy) of the Hungarian Diet for a final solution to the Jewish question. He suggested that all European Jews be resettled in Turkey, whose Ottoman Empire had not been officially anti-Semitic and which could use Jewish initiative, said Istóczy, to rebuild. Here was, in some curious sense, a foreshadowing of Theodor Herzl's Zionism.

forces this, is some ideal vision of happiness Kafka has created for himself. Within this formulation, Felice Bauer does not exist. When she does reveal herself later on, he is not pleased by what he sees and hears, since she seems to run counter to everything he is. Still, in these early stages, he can reshape her to fit his vision of what a happy courtship should be, and he can idealize her into the woman who, perhaps, might be suitable for him. Yet in nearly everything he writes, there is the deeper sense that this is an acting-out, a role-playing, a kind of dance that must end when the stakes, finally, become too high. When real commitment, apart from words, is called for, then Kafka knows he must escape. The letters to Felice are so extraordinary because in them Kafka has resolved nothing: he has simply ingested his own awareness of the coming "great war" so that he can act it out in his own terms. His "war" uncannily prefigures the actual conflict.

A photo from Felice precipitates an obsession that they enjoy a monthly exchange of these "little pictures," inasmuch as her appearance must "surely alter, the seasons advance, you wear different clothes — no, dearest, I am asking too much, I'm going too far. I must be content to possess this picture for which I should thank you again in every letter."[51] With her picture in hand, Kafka attempts to be protective, protesting Frau Bauer's treatment of Felice, "behaving so tyrannically toward you." Apparently, Frau Bauer has called the stream of letters futility itself, demanding a declaration of some kind. The matter goes around and around, Kafka circling, Felice in the center, the terms somewhat nebulous, the entire relationship caught in ambiguity — all the trappings of a Kafka fiction like *The Trial*, avant-garde and Modernistic, with no center, no steady substance, a reliance on language, and plenty of irony to undermine everything.

A particularly bad Sunday, December 29–30, brings Kafka down, and Felice must be the recipient of his disappointment and despair. He says she didn't like his book, *Meditation*, any more than she liked his photograph; but that doesn't matter so much with the book because it is "largely old stuff." Nevertheless, it is a part of him she does not know. He sympathizes with her over her home, but that is merely a pretext for him to describe his own.

> My mother is my father's devoted slave, and my father her devoted tyrant, which is fundamentally why there has always been perfect harmony, and the sorrows we have all shared, particularly in the last few years, are due entirely to my father's ill health. . . . At this very moment my father is turning over violently in bed. He is a big, strong man; fortunately he has been feeling better recently, but his illness [hardening of the arteries] is an ever-threatening one [he outlived Kafka by almost a decade].[52]

Now comes Gregor Samsa, Felice's fiancé in the making: "The family's harmony is really upset only by me, and more so as the years go by; very often I don't know what to do, and feel a great sense of guilt toward my parents and everyone else. . . . On more than one occasion in the past, I have stood by the window at night [Gregor blends again into Georg Bendemann here], feeling it almost my duty to open the window and throw myself out."[53] Not so subtly, Kafka has made Felice his salvation, and if in fact he were to commit suicide she would have to blame herself for some lessening of her love that led him to do it. Poor Felice: There is no question she must suffer nervous tension, headaches, sore throats, and other ailments, even while remaining basically healthy.

New Year's Eve, of course, depresses Kafka, and he wishes he could hide his face in her lap. Sounds from outside of people celebrating and shouting have made him feel desperate. Did Felice understand how much he needed this sense of isolation and his sense of self-sacrifice? But he does have insight: "I believe we barter our anxieties," he says with wounding precision.[54] One day he is the anxious one, another she is; and then they exchange ailments. In a sense, the marriage has been consummated at this level: that exchange of anxieties and complaints that can sustain a marriage as much as sex and companionship. He sends on three copies of his most recent photograph and warns that the mad look results from the flashlights, not from the subject. He wittily says that in larger quantities the photo "loses some of its horror."[55] He assures her that in reality he is twice as beautiful as in the picture, and he promises a better one in the future. Beneath his remarks is a desire for her to reinforce the opposite view. Once again, Kafka's irony works as a kind of litotes, whereby he negates what he wants to hear and then insists that what he wants to hear is really a negation of the truth, whatever that is. He can, then, wrap himself in an enigma that neither Felice nor anyone else can possibly interpret. In the interim, he dreams about Felice, the young woman he has already dreamed up.

He tells her of every pain and informs her when he has a cold; and he reveals how for him illness is sustaining, creating a break in "the inexorable passage of time" and allowing for a "minor rebirth, which I am now really beginning to crave."[56] In the next letter, for January 8–9, 1913, Kafka tells Felice he is a "great laugher"; here he describes the episode, mentioned earlier, in which he could not contain himself in the presence of the institute president when he and two colleagues, having been promoted, had to make a little speech. Kafka's whoops of nervous laughter sweep through the pages; he whoops and roars and howls.

Kafka indicates his love for Strindberg "in a very special way," and congratulates Felice for being under the spell of *The Dance of Death* and *The Gothic Room*. Kafka had also just been reading a piece called "Memories of Strindberg" in *Die Neue Rundschau*. While his affection for Flaubert was connected to craftsmanship, precision of language, and fidelity to vision, his feeling for Strindberg, whom he had to read in German translation, was apparently based on the Swede's tortured personality. Strindberg's misogyny went further than Kafka's fear of women, but at certain points they crossed: Strindberg's view of the destructive woman Kafka translated into fear of woman's intrusion into his most private self. Strindberg, wallowing in self-hatred and in hatred of women, associated himself precisely with those who would prove him correct, whereas Kafka found acquiescent women whom he could reject after having gained their affection.

Possibly, Kafka's attitude toward women was deeply connected not only to ambivalent feelings toward his mother but also to shame at his own body: by rejecting his body so definitively, he could gain the psychological confidence needed to pursue a woman. It was, obviously, a twisted, tortured course. So strong was his sensitivity about his body that he wrote Felice about it, saying that his thinness made him look like an orphan. He describes to her, tellingly, an episode that occurred when he frequented a bathing establishment on the Elbe, during a very hot summer. He loved water and swimming, but amidst all the gay people enjoying themselves in mixed company, he was depressed and withdrawn. "My desire to bathe was of course constant and immense — I roamed around alone, like a lost dog . . . watching the small bathing establishment for hours in the hope that it would at last be cleared and accessible to me. . . . As a rule I could only bathe toward evening, but by then the air was cool and the pleasure no longer quite as great."[57] He says that occasionally he would become reckless and take "the overcrowded bathing establishment by storm. Then I could bathe in peace and play with the others; no one paid any attention to the little boy, but I couldn't believe it."

Kafka had internalized what he thought others felt about his puny frame, and that carried over into nearly every aspect of his life. It certainly reappeared when he wrote to his father and contrasted their bodies in the dressing booth, Hermann big and burly, body-proud, Kafka puny, body-ashamed. If there were feelings of impotence in Kafka, then they can be partly attributed to his uncertainties about all bodily functions. He carried it further than most by extending it to digestion and to elimination: that poor, long, scrawny body simply would not function for him. Embedded in this is a vision not only of himself but of the world. It is impossible to join, impossible to share joy, impossible to give oneself away. Kafka was always on guard, holding back. At Valli's, he tells Felice, he found himself in this "dried-up, head-hanging condition, in which I felt inferior even to the most wretched of guests."[58]

All of this was merely a warmup for his great revelations of January 14–15, 1913, when he informs Felice of what would be awaiting her when she became his wife. If he chose to be a priest, she would have to be a nun. She had suggested that she sit beside Kafka while he wrote, in which case, he says, he would not write at all. For him, writing means revealing "oneself to excess; that utmost of self-revelation and surrender, in which a human being, when involved with others, would feel he was losing himself." But even that self-deprivation is insufficient for writing. "Writing that springs from the surface of existence — when there is no other way and the deeper wells have dried up — is nothing, and collapses the moment a truer emotion makes that surface shake. That is why one can never be alone enough when one writes, why there can never be enough silence around one when one writes, why even night is not night enough."[59]

Having created the setting in which he can write, a Carthusian monastery, where silence is complete, Kafka offers Felice his ideal:

> I have often thought that the best mode of life for me would be to sit in the innermost room of a spacious locked cellar with my writing things and a lamp. Food would be brought [Felice, presumably, being the bearer] and always put down far away from my room outside the cellar's outermost door. The walk to my food, in my dressing gown, through the vaulted cellars, would be my only exercise. I would then return to my table, eat slowly and with deliberation, then start writing again at once. And how I would write! From what depths I would drag it up! Without effort![60]

But this is not enough, for even in these optimal circumstances he might not be able to maintain this pace for long, "and at the first failure — would be bound to end in a grandiose fit of madness." Then, in an amusing addition, Kafka asks Felice's opinion of this, she who was thinking of a well-appointed apartment at a good address, heavy furniture, children, a husband with a regular position, with herself as keeper of the household. *"What do you think, dearest? Don't be reticent with your cellar-dweller."*

After offering to his future bride this monastic existence, an offer worthy of Kierkegaard or Flaubert, or even Strindberg, Kafka tells her that his mode of creative work is completely self-contained. He does not need further experience, outside contacts, or the stories one gains in friendships. Whatever he writes, he assumes, is already within him, and the sole question is of the correct circumstances and atmosphere for it to emerge. So self-contained is he, in fact, that his wife-to-be can expect at most one hour of company daily. Not unusually, after such revelations of self-containment and enclosure, Kafka suffers from that most fitting symptom of self-absorption, severe headaches: headaches lasting all day, "dreams exploding in my uneasy sleep." He blames it on the failure to write satisfactorily, from depths explored without sufficient gain, but more likely the headaches and exploding dreams were the consequence of a self-involvement so intense that body and head had to pay.

Frequent references to Martin Buber, whom Kafka had listened to in lectures before, and then met, are almost always derogatory —

dreary, he says, with something missing. Opposed to Buber is Flaubert, especially at this time his *Sentimental Education*, which was particularly appealing to Kafka, since it and Flaubert's protagonist have shadowy reference to his own Karl Rossmann in "The Man Who Disappeared" (*Amerika*). But literary references and urgings for Felice to read this or that take second place to his main topic: himself. His is not a weak ego trying to define itself, but a powerful engine attempting to influence another person. He warns her repeatedly that she must understand what she is getting into: "You must realize that you will never get unadulterated happiness from me; only as much unadulterated suffering as one could wish for, and yet — don't send me away. I am tied to you not by love alone, love would not be much, love begins, love comes, passes, and comes again; but this need, by which I am utterly chained to your being, this remains."[61]

Kafka comments on the appearance of the Russian Ballet in France, an event of considerable cultural importance, since it featured Eduardova, whom he had seen two years before, and of course Nijinsky. He describes Nijinsky and Lydia Kyast as "two flawless human beings" who are "at the innermost point of their art; they radiate mastery, as do all such people."[62] But this is cultural icing, and Kafka soon winds around to what his and Felice's relationship would be in marriage, and how distasteful and incomprehensible everything around him is. Even when Werfel came to Prague to give a lecture, Kafka missed it, saying he felt more like being buried than leaving the house. Denial even extends to feelings of inadequacy about his work on "The Stoker," writing "with such skill as might perhaps be adequate for chopping wood, not even for chopping wood, at best for playing cards."[63] This comment puts him on a level with his father, whose view was that playing cards was preferable to what he had heard of his son's writing.

Kafka was full of business schemes, in which Felice would be a key figure in getting hotels to use Parlographs. His scheme shows a very practical sense and, in fact, foreshadows several contemporary communication systems, in which major hotels provide an entire range of business services, from typists, secretaries, and machines to post office facilities. This is part of a general pattern of control that characterizes his early 1913 letters. Whether in business or food, Kafka was trying to reshape Felice. "Nevertheless, on account of my immense love, and because these reforms seem to me neither good, nor right, nor profitable, I may gladly allow you sausages, cold meats, etc.; but I still don't like the amount of tea you drink. . . . And you defend it in the way everyone defends the poison he is accustomed to."[64] Food has become grim, associated with death.

Kafka's positioning of himself *was* unique. In a particularly brilliant, but chilling assessment of who and what he was, he uses an example of a cold: "Do you know, there was a time when I thought I saw the impossibility of my catching a cold, a not insignificant sign of my increasingly rapid downfall: of the fact of this rapid downfall I was always convinced. I said to myself: (the not catching cold was of course but one sign among many) this is how I detach myself little by little from human fellowship." He desperately needs that sense of separation: "I took care to notice anything that might offer some proof; every little thing went wrong; not all fears were confirmed, but all hopes were disappointed."[65]

Kafka wrote of an excursion he and Brod took to Dobřichovice, near Prague. They stayed overnight and took two rooms. Kafka adds that out of apprehension he needed his own room. But since he couldn't sleep, he lay apathetically on a sofa in Brod's room, while Brod wrote furiously on his short novel, *A Czech Maidservant*. Brod is moving at a great pace, his pen flying across the paper, and Kafka lies there, fearful of even opening his eyes, listening to the rain falling, completely lethargic. He yearns to get up and stretch, "but actually for no other purpose than to renew my desire to throw myself once more onto the sofa and go on lying there in apathy."[66] He says that is how he has lived for several years. Yet what he describes to Felice is not a breakdown of his physical and mental abilities, but a ground plan of his imagination. Brod's great gift was his facility, but it was also what made most of his work lacking in textures and resonance. Kafka was always gathering his forces. Apathy was the way his imagination could work; it was reverie time, during which he could dream himself into a fiction. It was this side of his friend that Brod never comprehended, despite his devotion and loyalty. Not unusually, Kafka refers to himself as Felice's "hardy, chill-proof, cast-iron madman,"[67] a witty way of telling her how impossibly unsuited he is for her. Kafka did not fear impotence; he feared attachment, contamination of self, subversion of whatever he was. "There are times," he writes, "when I am convinced I am unfit for any human relationship."[68] He tries to achieve stoppage, stasis, silence: "Have you observed how, within yourself and independent of other people, diverse possibilities open up in several directions, thereby actually creating a ban on your every movement?"[69]

Conditioning Felice for what to expect, he tells her of Kleist's "Michael Kohlhaas": Kleist, one of Kafka's great favorites, was a suicide. Kafka can ask Felice why she chooses to "love such an unhappy young man, whose unhappiness in the long run is bound to be contagious." His comments on current literature are negative: Lasker-Schüler is unbearable; her poems make him feel either boredom or antipathy. Schnitzler is worse, a representative of "bad literature." Kafka comments, "For I don't like Schnitzler at all, and hardly respect him; no doubt he is capable of certain things, but for me his great plays and his great prose are full of a truly staggering mass of the most sickening drivel."[70] He accuses him of "bogus dreaminess" and "sentimentality I wouldn't touch even with the tips of my fingers," although Kafka does praise the early work (*Anatol, La Ronde, Leutnant Gustl*). He feels

Schnitzler is trying to come between them, since, apparently, Felice has praised his work, especially his *Professor Bernhardi*. Kafka suggests she is dragging him down with her tastes, and he even cautions her that Brod's review of his own *Meditation* is excessive.* Such recognition has underscored how unfit he is for praise. "I am a very unhappy human being and you, dearest, simply had to be summoned to create an equilibrium for all this misery."[71]

He returns to the notion of just the two of them inhabiting space unapproachable by anyone else. He attempts to get to the rock bottom of what they are but recognizes that words (even words!) cannot communicate fully what he means. Only certain images seem to function: their movement in space separated from all else, their connection by a cord that he is fearful she might attempt to break, the fact they seem to move in an unreal world that only their connection to each other validates with reality. He fantasizes about a trip they might take together, to Genoa, for example, and Saint-Raphaël, but he realizes he is most fit to sit alone "in the corner of a compartment, that's where I belong; that's where I should stay."[72] He perceives, however, that physical proximity would subvert their special linkage.

Letters are a delicate proof he exists. "If proof were not there before you, could you imagine, judging from your past experiences, a human being leading as useless a life as I do, and who is *alive nevertheless*, and by being alive achieves no more than to run around an enormous hole and to guard it. Doesn't this almost make you believe, dearest, that rather than a human being it is some misguided spirit that is writing to you?"[73] Kafka here foreshadows the entire theme of "The Burrow," whereby the mole seeks the security of its hole but can never feel safe because someone may be outside waiting to enter and destroy it.

Yet more than that, these constant images of being buried or of vanishing into compartments, enclosures, basements, and the like suggest a virtual suicide syndrome. Kafka was edging toward final things: a sense of extinction, possibly the result of physical changes leading to the discovery of tuberculosis in four years; a sense of worthlessness, both real and a role he had learned to play; a sense of how his ego could work — only through constant threats of annihilation could he reemerge in order to pull off another victory, in his fiction. Or, in still another phase, he needed to see himself as almost literally buried as a means of establishing his separateness from Felice and everyone else. The "hole" becomes more than a place he can retreat to; it represents his difference from others, conveying on him a certain superiority. "I run around in circles like those mad squirrels in their cages," he writes Felice, "with the sole purpose, dearest, of keeping you there in front of

---

*Titled "Das Ereignis eines Buches" ("A Book's Occurrence," or "A Literary Milestone," the review appeared in *März* (February 1913, no. 7) and was indeed excessive in its puffing up of a small work to large scale.

my cage, and to know you are near me, even if I cannot see you."[74] Kafka validates himself by locating his spirit as caged, and he cows Felice by pointing out how dependent he is on her presence, separated though they may be by cage bars.

He is almost at the stage of "A Hunger Artist," though not quite, since he is not yet wasting away. But he is caged, and he needs an attentive audience to observe his performance. Felice, even more intensely than before, is part of that performance. Presumably enclosed with this fantasy of the caged, mad Kafka is another image, involving one of his favorite emblems, the knife. It is an image of intense self-torture, and here we sense not role-playing but an effort to open himself up brutally to Felice. "To be a large piece of wood, and to be pressed against her body by the cook, who with both hands draws the knife toward her along the side of this stiff log (approximately in the region of my hip) and with all her might slices off shavings to light the fire."[75] The desire for self-sacrifice is intense, and Kafka ritualizes it with sharp instruments, as he would in his fiction, with the knife of *The Trial*, the needles of "In the Penal Colony," and other knives and cutting instruments in fiction, diaries, and letters.

Hermann having deprived Kafka of empowerment in the household, Kafka sought it elsewhere, with Felice. He was constantly relocating himself and Felice in areas where he could hold the upper hand, or at least dictate what their mutual policies would be. Like countries stalking each other before the main event breaks out, as in a Great War, they sought positions of strength. Kafka was, of course, the far greater master of repositioning, relocating, reshaping.

In this quest for reshaping of self, he could not tolerate intrusion. One such intrusion was noise. Sounds in the apartment of Hermann shouting, singing, and clapping to amuse his great-nephew or grandson were to the son like "a punch in the eye." He says such behavior is less comprehensible to him than tribal dances. All his revulsion toward his father comes to the surface, but there is more. "And yet it may not even be the shouting that puts such a strain on me; altogether it requires strength to tolerate children in the apartment. I can't do it, I can't forget myself, my blood refuses to flow, it becomes congealed, and this desire of the blood, after all, is supposed to represent love for children."[76] He says he has considered leaving home to take a room somewhere else because of the visits of his nephew and niece, but moving out proves to involve a choice he cannot handle. In effect, Kafka is telling Felice to forget plans for children, since their father-to-be cannot bear their noise, not even their presence. She appeared not to listen, for the engagement was beginning to loom. Two days later, Kafka added dessert to the menu: "Dearest, it's a miserable life, and only he who knows how to intervene with a whip can grasp it fully."[77] It is unclear whether he intends to whip or be whipped.

But something else lurks in the affair with Felice, something indistinct, a subterranean wish, a quick and final solution: the chance of mutual suicide, a suicide pact, perhaps modeled on the Mayerling affair. They have become drawn into "some unhappiness," as Kafka puts it.

> Dearest, I do wish we could be gone from here together. Why should we tolerate having been thrown upon this black prickly earth from some kind of heaven? Even as a child I used to stand in great admiration in front of a picture dealer's window, looking at a bad color print depicting the suicide of two lovers. . . . The couple stood at the end of a small wooden landing-stage, about to take the decisive step. Together both the girl's foot, and the man's, strained toward the deep, and with a sigh of relief one felt they were within the grip of gravity.[78]

Kafka does retreat from this, but his portrait of the couple on the edge of suicide cannot be ignored; nor can it be eliminated from the way he perceived the affair with Felice. It was part of that fin de siècle flirtation with death in which final things provided some resolution, somewhat on the order of a great war fought to its absurd end.

Kafka ultimately was not a suicidal person, but we can see from his words and images how close such a despairing person may be to the idea of suicide. While part of his depression, thoughts of a suicide pact went further, into some vision of an absolute consummation; what could not be consummated in life could be completed in death. Was it fear of impotence? Fear of commitment? Fear of a physical joining of oneself to another? Fear of losing the "other"? Or perhaps some other perception of the self we cannot fathom? Kafka was moving along on so many different levels, and not all of them consistent or integrated, that we cannot be certain where any drive or idea originates.

His aloneness, a form of suicide, becomes a leitmotif in the letters: "I would have had quite a lot to tell you about my being alone"; or "I should like to meet the man who, without injury to himself, could stand my way of life, above all my lonely evening walks."[79] At home, he says he speaks to hardly anyone, but he sees Felice as surrounded by people; their lives are precise opposites. "If one bolts the doors and windows against the world," he writes after spending an evening at Brod's reading part of "The Metamorphosis," one can from time to time "create the semblance and almost the beginning of the reality of a beautiful life." Headaches are, naturally, a steady torture, part of an agitation that makes him toss through the night; he says this right after his statement that Oskar Baum is reading in the Klindworthsaal on April 1 in Berlin, and he, Kafka, shall go with him. This puts him in Felice's territory: the headaches follow.*

---

*Not to be discounted is the presence in Kafka's mind of "The Judgment." In a February 11, 1913, diary entry, he speaks of the story as having come out of him "like a real birth, covered with filth and slime, and only I have the hand that can reach to the body itself

At the time, Kafka was writing in his diary (for February 28) the tale of Ernst Liman,[80] which concerns a trip in which all of the traveler's experiences become part of a phantasmagoria. The brief piece is a vision, very possibly, of Kafka's forthcoming trip, a nightmarish hodgepodge of his fear of change and his sense of unusual disruptions that follow from any break in routine, especially one as momentous as a meeting in Berlin with Felice.

Repeatedly, Kafka writes of his fear she is slipping away, and he cannot blame her, not in the light of what he is divulging to her. "And what I fear is that even if I were to become abhorrent to you — after all, you are a girl, and want a man, not a flabby worm on the earth — even if I were to become abhorrent to you, your kindness would not fail you."[81] He adds,

> I will not deny that I could very easily feed on someone else's compassion, but I certainly could not enjoy the fruits of any kind of compassion that could inevitably destroy you.... should you realize that you — a kind, active, lively, self-assured person — have nothing, save something harmful to yourself, in common with the confusion or rather the monotonous blur of my personality, would you then, dearest . . . would you, heedless of your compassion, be able to tell me so truthfully?

He has, in effect, finessed her hesitation about what she has gotten into. By appealing to kindness and compassion, he makes her embrace his presentation of a futile self, or forces her to reject him by denying her own sense of compassion for such a suffering soul as her Prague friend.

He was a bug, or, if not quite that, then another person.

> I am now a different person to the one I was during the first 2 months of our correspondence; it is not a transformation into a new state [not Gregor!], rather a relapse into an old one and no doubt lasting one. If you felt drawn to that person, you must, you must inevitably, abhor this one.... The fact that this different person — so greatly altered in every way — continues to cling to you, if anything more tenaciously than before, cannot fail, if you will admit it to yourself, to make him even more abhorrent to you.[82]

Although the correspondence has another three hundred pages to go, he has offered her as honest a view of himself as he can describe. He has, in a curious way, found the means to make her accept him at the same time he has created all the terms for her rejection.

The letter of March 6–7, 1913, evinces a great effort to be candid. Kafka examines three possibilities in her response to him. First, she feels nothing but compassion, "in which case why do I insist upon your

---

and the strength of desire to do so." He is now reading proofs, and he proceeds to chart the father-son binding; he also mentions the fact that so many of the names in the story refer to Felice Bauer, so many relationships to his own situation.

love, obstruct your every course, force you to write and think of me every day, tyrannize you with a helpless man's helpless love?" Second, she lacks true insight into his wretched personality, disregards his confessions, and unconsciously prevents herself "from believing in them, although this would be very much against your nature." In that case, he has failed to make the situation perfectly clear, and he would be forced to "step out of myself and quite ruthlessly defend you against myself." The third possibility really disturbs him: she has "a perfect understanding of my present state, but may think that at some time I might yet turn into a useful human being with whom a steady, calm, lively relationship would be possible." His judgment of that: "If this is what you think, you are under a terrible misapprehension."[83] The terms of their "great war" are set: Kafka wants her, but on his grounds, not hers; and she must accept this, if she accepts him. In a romantic gesture, he says that the best thing would be for him to come to Berlin and carry her off in his arms, but adds that if he were capable of that he would have done it long ago. How impossible it all is: "If only I could once, Felice — for once would be always — be so close to you that talking and listening would be one: silence."[84]

The intensity of Kafka's pleas foreshadows his visit to Berlin in March, and then again in May. We suspect a crisis in the relationship, since he has hitherto been hesitant about committing himself to a visit; but now on March 16–17 he suggests an Easter visit. His proposal for the visit, however, is couched in his usual weird terms. He will travel for about six hours on the train in order to see her for only an hour; he inquires if she can spare him that hour, and if not an entire hour at one time, then divided into four quarters. He would, we assume, see her in rapid fifteen-minute segments and wait by the telephone for her clearance. "So the most important question is whether you consider it a good thing, and whether you are aware of the kind of visitor to expect." He insists he does not want to see her relatives: "I am not fit for that at present, and I shall be even less so in Berlin." He adds, "In short, I shall understand perfectly if you don't have the time."[85] If this falls through, they can meet in Frankfurt in April.

Within a few days, Kafka was hedging, finding reasons why a trip may be impossible. The Czech Milling Associations and the Czech Builders from Sudetenland, with which the institute did business, were holding their convention in Prague and Brünn, and, despite his "deplorable" Czech, he may be asked to attend. His Czech, however, was quite serviceable. Kafka did arrive in Berlin on a Saturday night, having written by express letter on Friday, and he then sent a short missive to Felice on Sunday, March 23, from the Askanische Hof. He fears they have missed connections: "And now I am in Berlin, and will have to leave again this afternoon at 4 or 5; the hours are passing, and no word from you."[86] They did finally meet, under conditions which revealed Felice's vacillations. Kafka stayed over on Sunday, and they walked in the Grünewald. He left on Monday for Leipzig, where he met Löwy, and then returned to Prague on Tuesday, the twenty-fifth. He had to depart almost immediately for Aussig and had the burden of paperwork. Harassed by work with the files, unable to sleep, Kafka uses language that recalls "The Judgment" to indicate his frame of mind. "The window was open, and in the whirl of my thoughts I jumped out of the window continuous for whole quarter-hours, then trains came, one after another they ran over my body, outstretched on the tracks, deepening and widening the two cuts in my neck and legs."[87] The self-punishment foreshadows "In the Penal Colony," where pain provides some relief from anxiety and then reshapes itself into bliss.

On April 1 Kafka confessed his fear of impotence: "My one fear — surely nothing worse can either be said or listened to — is that I shall never be able to possess you. At best I would be confined, like an unthinking faithful dog, to kissing your casually proffered hand, which would not be a sign of love, but of the deeper despair of the animal condemned to silence and eternal separation."[88] Yet this expression of impotence goes well beyond physical possession, into his inability to become what she expects, into his own sense of inadequacy in all areas of life. We must not neglect Kafka's sexual fears — they were real and they rarely quieted — but we must also not embrace them as full explanations. Elias Canetti overemphasizes his mental, psychological, imaginative impotence; Kafka's fear of what woman means went well beyond fear of female sexuality. As noted earlier, he came from that generation that viewed women as destruction personified, the generation of Weininger, Strindberg, and others.

In early April, as another meeting with Felice in Berlin loomed, Kafka turned not to thoughts of immortality but to contemplation of death, and he tried to find release from office tension in gardening. This was a form of therapy through manual work: two hours a day in a garden at Nusle, south of Prague. Yet the sense of death was not so easily dissipated. He dreamed, he tells Felice on April 4–5, about teeth: "They were not ordinary teeth in a mouth, but a mass of teeth fitted together exactly as in a children's jigsaw puzzle, and the whole lot, guided by my jaw, were in some kind of sliding motion."[89] He expresses the sensation of the teeth, their movement, the gaps, their grinding and biting. Not unusually, his expression of this form of death, the teeth squeezing life from him, takes the shape of biting and chewing — that is, digestion, food entering and exiting, teeth working away in endless pulverizing. These teeth are a portent of death, later the "teeth" of the machine in "In the Penal Colony," part of a larger meaning elicited when the needles become "writers" on the victim's body. The death symbolism here becomes spelled out in images of despair: "I go about in a state of pointless despair and rage, not so much against my environment, against my destiny, against that which is above us, but only and passionately against myself, against myself alone."[90] Her mouth recurs when Kafka observes Felice's decaying teeth and is repelled.

He hoped through gardening to make contact with a metaphysical experience that could carry him outside of himself. Meanwhile, Felice went to Frankfurt for her job, on assignment, while Kafka tried to help Löwy; the actor's fortunes were at a particularly low ebb, and he was lying in a hospital with the headaches he suffered from every three months. Löwy's fall even from moderate fortune into illness, lack of money, and bankruptcy of his company made him a sympathetic figure to Kafka, who identified strongly with failure. It also allowed him to exult in the fluctuations of fortune, part of his ideological belief that at any time one could sink, irrevocably. He tries to hang on: "I could have built the Pyramids with the effort it takes me to cling on to life and reason."[91]

PART II: SOME MAJOR BATTLES

The relationship now appeared to have reached one of its periodic climaxes. Caught between sight of Felice in March and a possible resighting in May, Kafka is in panic. "In my letters it is my perpetual concern to free you of me, but when for once I seem to have succeeded, I go raving mad." As Felice meets representatives of other firms, or else a new or an old acquaintance, he perceives how far short he falls. "The representatives of all the firms undoubtedly meeting there, distinguished, well-dressed, vigorous, healthy, amusing young men — that is to say, men compared with whom, if I were to be confronted with them, for comparison, I would simply have to do away with myself."[92] He adds, "I would be precisely where I should have to and seemingly wish to be — i.e., expelled from your presence, as would be my desert, since I did not hold you by your hands, as one holds one's beloved, but clung to the feet and so made walking impossible for you." He is in effect giving her a way out but at the same time reeling her in with his pleas of weakness and need. Yet he can also tell her that writing (not she) "is the only thing that makes my inner existence possible. . . . I am awake only among my imaginary characters, but on this subject I can neither write nor talk convincingly. Nor would this be necessary, provided I had everything else."[93]

He plays with the idea of dismissal and says he would not have been surprised if she had dismissed him for not knowing him for what he was: "It was almost as though I had approached you sideways and it took some little time before we turned to face each other."[94] The letter of May 1 — they would meet at Whitsun on May 11–12 — is that panicked sort Kafka wrote when he felt cornered. He accuses Felice of not sending a letter, and then says they should make a pact for him to get but one letter per week, on Sundays, *"but without fail,"*[95] no matter what interrupts her or what disaster she may face. By the next day, when he recognizes he will have to meet her family, he is near nervous collapse, turning his anxieties into a series of insistent questions: "What is your telephone number? [The Bauers had moved, much closer to the Askanische Hof, where Kafka stayed in Berlin.] I assume it can't be in the book yet? Must I wear a black suit, or will it be good enough if I arrive as a chance visitor in my ordinary summer suit? I should much prefer the latter, or rather the former would be almost impossible. Do I arrive with flowers for your mother? And what kind of flowers?"[96] He worries how much time Felice will have for him, as her brother, Ferdinand, was getting engaged, with a reception on May 12. Kafka is all details and dates. He offers to write Herr Bauer about their plans for one another. He consoles himself that he will not be able to see her on Sunday morning (the eleventh) but he will hear her voice. When they finally did meet, they discussed marriage, for in June Kafka formally proposed, and in July he wrote to Herr Bauer asking for Felice's hand. Once back in Prague, on May 12, Kafka wrote, "I cannot live without her, nor with her," and felt something "was about to explode in my breast." In the margin of the letter, he asserts, "The request of a poor human being who cannot bear uncertainty."*[97]

With the anxiety building, Kafka wanted to ingest Felice. "Oh God, I wish you were not on this earth, but entirely within me, or rather that I were not on this earth, but entirely within you; I feel there is one too many of us; the separation into two people is unbearable. . . . Why instead do I squirm on the forest ground like one of those animals you are so frightened of?" The relationship has now reached its peak (or valley), in that Kafka was confronted with an either/or choice: what he had attempted to avoid through negative presentation of himself. He wonders if Felice can trust herself "in all that is in store for you."[98]

Nevertheless, by May 21 he had decided: the engagement was to go ahead, but first he must ask her father, by letter. Telling Felice of this, Kafka presents further problems, such as things about him she doesn't take seriously enough. "For about 10 years I have had this ever-growing feeling of not being in perfect health; the sense of well-being that comes with good health, the sense of well-being created by a body that responds in every way, a body that functions even without constant attention and care, this sense of well-being which in most people is the source of constant cheerfulness, and above all unselfconsciousness — this sense of well-being I lack."[99] Kafka of course overrates the ease

*Kafka apparently did not feel strengthened by publication of his still slim body of work thus far. In May "The Stoker" appeared, with Kurt Wolff; and in June "The Judgment" was to appear in *Arkadia*. Seeing himself in print was, for him, more derisive of his talent than neglect, since publication brought home his inability to work well and continuously.

with which "others" experience their bodies; Brod, for example, had to make do with a hunchbacked body that was hardly agreeable to the way he wanted to feel about himself. Further, that cheerfulness that Kafka sensed in others was often forced, a veneer for many of the feelings he himself experienced. Nevertheless, he was correct about himself: he was suffering from a precondition that would eventually blossom into a terminal illness. He admits he has been, apart from children's illnesses, a fairly healthy person, but, attuned as he was to psychological theory, he knew that his "sad state," as he called it, was unmistakably present.

"Just as this condition," he says, "prevents me from talking naturally, eating naturally, sleeping naturally, so it prevents me from being natural in any way."[100] In this, his pledge of allegiance to her, a "self-assured, quick-thinking, proud girl," he repeats how ill-fitted he is for the role. Once again, his is not fear of impotence in any clearly sexual way, but impotence as a husband responding to the demands of a healthy wife: an inability to respond along the full emotional range of their relationship.

Uncertainty, he asserts, makes him suffer so much "that at times I am almost out of my mind."[101] His assessment of their situation: "The more I came to know you the more I loved you, the more you came to know me, the more insufferable you thought me. If only you had realized it, if only you had said so openly." The reason is that Felice has not written for a week, and the silence has convinced Kafka she is withdrawing. He has, of course, discovered the correct formula for eliciting a response and a denial from her, the strategy of repeating his worthlessness, which immediately put her on the defensive. Even when she does write, he can indict her dilatoriness in the correspondence as making a statement of her halfheartedness, which he can then reshape into her rejection of him because of his obvious unfitness as a spouse.

By June 1, with Felice's response having been only by telegram, Kafka is frantic, saying that only his ferocious activity on behalf of Löwy's recital (on June 2, at the Prague Hotel Bristol) has saved his state of mind. His attempt to retrieve the situation: "There is no doubt that we are immensely different, that you are healthy in every sense of the word, and as a result calm in your innermost being; whereas I am ill, perhaps not so much in the generally accepted sense, but consequently in the worst possible sense of the word, hence I am restive, absent-minded, and listless."[102] He adds that perhaps they can remain together because each makes the other suffer, and that brings mutual satisfaction. This accords well with Kafka's view that all personal activity is based on some blood-letting, that pain is a natural concomitant of every foray into life.

He then takes up the question of "The Judgment," saying he finds no coherent meaning in it, but he adds that he does find certain strange things about it. He offers the names as examples of that strangeness, yet his motive is not just names, but the interweaving of Kafka and Bauer as "secret sharers."

> Georg has the same number of letters as Franz, "Bendemann" is made up of Bende and Mann, Bende has the same number of letters as Kafka, and the two vowels are also in the same place; out of pity for poor "Bende," "Mann" is probably meant to fortify him for his struggles. . . . "Friede" and "Glück" are also closely related; "Brandenfeld," owing to "feld" [field], has some connection with "Bauer" [farmer], and also starts with the same letter. And there are other similar things — all of which, needless to say, I only discovered afterwards.[103]

In a follow-up letter on June 10, Kafka now admits that his doom-filled tale is not so strange. "The story is full of abstractions, though they are never admitted. The friend is hardly a real person, perhaps he is more whatever the father and Georg have in common. The story may be a journey around father and son, and the friend's changing shape may be a change in perspective in the relationship between father and son. But I am not quite sure of this either."[104]

Since the story so clearly follows what Kafka has told Felice of his own relationship with Hermann Kafka, his hesitation to speak about it has its own meaning. In Kafka's brief comments here there is some intimation that the father and son's relationship has been interrupted by a friend who creates a sexual challenge, that there is a duel between father and friend for the affections of the son, who may be homoerotically attached to the friend, at least within the father's distorted perspective. Or else the perspective is not so distorted, and the father, in his crazily insightful way, smokes out something the son has wished to hide or disguise, and when the father reveals that Georg has no secrets from him, then Georg recognizes he has been found out and his sole recourse is self-destruction. Or else, in a slightly tilted frame, the father prefers to have a dead son to one homoerotically inclined, or even suspected of it. Kafka's comment about the "change in perspective in the relationship between father and son" suggests that Herr Bendemann has divined some secret, and that this secret is so enormous it leads to a death sentence.

The theme of a death sentence is rarely distant from Kafka's subsequent letters to Felice, leading to his proposal and her acceptance, followed in August by his writing to Herr Bauer. His letter of June 10–16, 1913, is perhaps the centerpiece of the entire sequence: an extraordinary confession on his part of what he is, even as he hopes desperately, he says, for her acceptance. The letter is so extraordinary because while it offers marriage, it also offers every reason why she should not accept. Kafka has by now perfected his technique: to convince Felice that by marrying him, she will be getting someone almost

completely abstracted from the role as husband; and yet, simultaneously, pleading that without her his life will somehow end, or else his
writing will.

"What comes between you and me is, above all, the doctor. . . . the
medical diagnosis is not the most decisive factor in these decisions; if
it were, it wouldn't be worth obtaining. As I said, I have not actually
been ill, and yet I am."[105] He recognizes that different circumstances
might make him well, but he deems these different circumstances as
impossible, a typical Kafka conundrum, into which Felice will have to
squeeze. The decision whether he is fit to marry is up to a doctor whose
view will not be decisive, and in fact a good deal will depend on which
"stupid" doctor. He follows with his proposal, what he calls a criminal
question: "But there also isn't time for endless hesitations, at least this
is what I feel about it, and so I ask: In view of the above — alas, irre-
mediable — conditions, will you consider whether you wish to be my
wife? Will you do that?"

Felice had written they were not equals, that Kafka was "ahead in
every way." He disputes this as pure fantasy. "I am nothing, absolutely
nothing. . . . Some capacity for understanding people, and for putting
myself in their place — this I have, but I don't believe I have ever met a
single person who in the long run in his ordinary human relationships . . . could be more hopeless than I." He lists all his negative qualities as a way of proving himself so impossible she need not worry they
are unequal: he has no memory either for things learned or read, or for
people and experience; he knows less than the average schoolboy; what
he knows is completely superficial; he is unable to reason, and whenever he tries he comes up against a blank wall; he is incapable of coherent or consecutive reasoning; he cannot tell a story properly — and,
in fact, he can hardly talk; when he must relate something, he feels like
a small child assaying his first steps. He does admit to "certain powers
which, at a depth almost inaccessible under normal conditions, shape
themselves into literature, powers to which, however, in my present
professional as well as physical state, I dare not commit myself, because for every inner exhortation of these powers there are as many, if
not more, inner warnings. Could I but commit myself to them they
would undoubtedly, of this I am convinced, lift me out of my inner misery in an instant."[106]

Thus Kafka has answered her objections as to his superiority, by offering up, except in this one area of writing, his inferiority. He trades
off her health and balance and stability against his hypersensitivity, his
inability to deal with life; and in this trade-off he does offer her, not the
truth of what he is capable of, but the truth of his inner world as opposed to her outer one. What he argues is that his inner world cannot
be measured in terms of equality or inequality, since it moves outside
her purview, which is external, focused on the ordinary and the normal.

He then must answer her objection that he would not be able to stand life with her, a position he finds conceivable. "Here you almost touch on the truth, but from an angle totally different from the one you have in mind. I really do believe I am lost to all social intercourse."[107] Even with Max Brod:

> During the long years we have known each other I have, after all, been alone with Max on many occasions, for days on end, when traveling even for weeks on end and almost continuously, yet I do not remember — and had it happened, I would certainly remember — ever having had a long coherent conversation involving my entire being, as should inevitably follow when two people with a great fund of independent and lively ideas and experiences are thrown together.[108]

He emphasizes that with a number of strange people, in any unfamiliar place, "the whole room presses on my chest and I am unable to move, my whole personality seems virtually to get under their skins, and everything becomes hopeless. This was what happened that afternoon at your house."*

But Kafka was not finished with self-deprecation or negation. He works out a debit and credit side for the marriage, and it appears that Felice would be the most likely debtor.

> I should lose my (for the most part) terrible loneliness, and you, whom I love above all others, would be my gain. Whereas you would lose the life you have lived hitherto, with which you were almost completely satisfied. You would lose Berlin, the office you enjoy, your girl friends, the small pleasures of life, the prospect of marrying a decent, cheerful healthy man, of having beautiful, healthy children for whom, if you think about it, you clearly long. In place of these incalculable losses, you would gain a sick, weak, unsociable, taciturn, gloomy, still, almost hopeless man who possibly has but one virtue, which is that he loves you. Instead of sacrificing yourself for real children, which would be in accordance with your nature as a healthy girl, you would have to sacrifice yourself for this man who is childish, but childish in the worst sense, and who at best might learn from you, letter by letter, the ways of human speech.[109]

Kafka relates the state of his finances, an income of 4,588 kroner a year, an entitlement to a pension, the expectation of only slight annual increases, with no hope of help from his parents, who were themselves barely hanging on. He also has no expectations from literature. He cautions her to think over all his letters, from the beginning.

What is remarkable is not the revelations themselves but Kafka's

---

*In a previous letter, that of May 15, Kafka had written, "I felt so very small while they all stood around me like giants with such fatalistic expressions on their faces. . . . It was entirely in keeping with the situation: you are theirs, so they are big, you are not mine, so I was small. . . . I must have made a very nasty impression on them" (*Letters to Felice*, p. 257).

honesty. He plays by rules different from those of other suitors, obviously, and exaggerates his incapacity for practical experience, perhaps to reinforce his calling as a writer. He was, as we know, quite effective in his insurance work, trusted by his colleagues, and beloved by workers whose cases he had adjudicated justly. And we know from his periodic reports that he could gather a good deal of material, oral as well as statistical, and shape it into a coherent document. As a civil servant, he was effective and much cherished by his superiors; they allowed him vacations and leaves with pay which few others at his level would have enjoyed. The more personal parts of his personality and character are revealed candidly, without too much exaggeration, although he did minimize his sense of humor, his sense of the absurd, his ability to enter into witty, ironic banter. He was not as mummy-like with his friends as he pretends, even though he was not effusive, like Werfel or Brod, for example.

He feared, above all, that Felice did not take sufficiently into consideration "that writing is actually the good part of my nature."[110] He says, "Without this world in my head, this world straining to be released, I would never have dared to think of wanting to win you. It is not so much a question of what you think of my writing now, but, should we live together, you would soon realize that if willingly or unwillingly you do not come to love my writing, there would be absolutely nothing for you to hold on to. In which case you would be terribly lonely, Felice." His schedule will add further obstacles to any kind of normal, or sexual, intercourse. "But what, dearest Felice, have you to say to the kind of married life in which the husband, at any rate for several months in the year, returns from the office at 2:30 or 3, eats, lies down, sleeps until 7 or 8, hurriedly has his supper, takes an hour's walk, and then starts writing and writes till 1 or 2? Could you really stand that?"

He is not finished. Fatigued, enervated, half-dead, as he characterizes himself, he has other "peculiarities" as well. "For as long as I can remember it has made me feel awkward, or at least uneasy, to have a stranger or even a friend in my room; you, at any rate, like people, perhaps even parties, whereas I should have to make a great, an almost painful effort to force myself to receive relatives or even friends in my or — dare I used the word — our apartment. Nothing, for instance, would be easier for me than to live in Prague and never see any of my relatives, though they are quite the kindest people."[111] His hope is to have an inaccessible apartment near the outskirts of town. Kafka tells Felice she will feel as isolated as her sister feels in Budapest and even more so, since she, Felice, will have him to deal with. If she ignores his warnings, she will be, he emphasizes, committing the gravest sin against herself. "You have to believe what I say about myself; which is the self-knowledge of a man of 30 who for deep-seated reasons has sev-

eral times been close to madness, thus reaching the limits of his existence, and so can see all of himself and what can become of him within
these limits."

Still a year short of the start of World War I, Kafka has laid down
the terms of the "great war" to come. He has presented marriage not as
a union of two souls (much less two bodies) but as two warring factions
in which his needs will pre-empt her defensive maneuvers once she accepts his sallies. However kindly he intends to be, he is dictatorial, tyrannical, using his defensive posture of incompetence and inability as a
great offensive weapon. Felice is, apparently, immune to his warnings,
and as the correspondence continues, we note how she chips away at
Kafka's posture, trying to establish her own position. Even so, the formal engagement does not take place until April 1914, then is broken off
three months later, almost coinciding with the outbreak of the Great
War. But in the time between these revealing letters to Felice, in June
1913, and the official engagement in April of the next year, Kafka, withdrawn and unsocial, as he presents himself, was unfaithful with at least
two women. One of them, Grete Bloch, whom Felice was using as an
intermediary in her dealings with Kafka, turned out, for a time, to be
more to his taste than Felice herself.

All else aside, writing for him is deeper than death. "What I need
for my writing is seclusion, not 'like a hermit,' that would not be
enough, but like the dead. Writing, in this sense, is a sleep deeper than
that of death, and just as one would not and cannot tear the dead from
their graves, so I must not and cannot be torn from my desk at night."[112]
This is in response to Felice's worry that their life together might be
"rather difficult." Kafka is not through. "I have always had this fear of
people, not actually of the people themselves, but of their intrusion
upon my weak nature; for even the most intimate friend to set foot in
my room fills me with terror, and is more than just a symbol of this
fear."[113] Kafka takes Felice's acquiescence to his self-flagellating admis-
sions as an acceptance and considers them informally engaged. "And
still you are prepared to risk it; either you are absurdly bold, or else
have intimations of whatever holds sway over us that I lack." He pictures them joining hands, although his don't seem very appetizing. "Do
you still remember my long bony hands with fingers like those of a
child and an ape? And you join yours to that."[114]

He tells Felice he has informed Julie Kafka of the engagement, and
his mother agreed but asked if she might make inquiries about the
Bauers, a proceeding calculated to enrage Kafka. "I don't know exactly
why, perhaps from my permanent feeling of guilt towards your parents,
but I gave in and handed my mother your father's name in writing." He
then wittily says that any information sought about the Kafkas would
turn up nothing, and "no information agency would be capable of telling the truth about me."[115] He asks Felice to give her father "The Judg-

ment" to read, on the assumption that the truth about the Kafka family lies there. Kafka's irony was rarely more corrosive.

He explores the strangeness of everything: how his letters make him more of an alien element; how his parents in a picture look like all other strangers, only "diminished by the fact that we are all Jews"; that he, Kafka, cannot get over his fear of Hermann, who, being afraid himself, becomes even more terrible; that Felice does not seem to possess fear, in fact exudes courage. "It's a miracle, there is nothing that can humanly be said about it, one simply has to thank God for it."[116]

Beginning in early July, with the engagement certain, Kafka becomes even more brutally honest. For him, whatever shreds his spirit must be shared. She becomes his analyst, as he assumes the role of analysand, and the doctor-patient relationship seems more powerful by far than that of the fiancée-fiancé. Felice has also taken on the role of a close friend, a female Max Brod, as it were; since she is strong and courageous, Kafka presumes she can listen to it all, absorb it, and continue to return for more.

What he enjoyed communicating was his disgust. He relates the story of how the entire family walked along a muddy path, but his mother, because of her clumsiness, became covered with dirt, especially her shoes. When they returned home, Julie Kafka asked her son to inspect her shoes, to show they weren't as dirty as he asserted. Kafka answers, "I was repelled, and not, as you might think, by the dirt. . . . I had come to feel some little affection, or rather admiration, for my father for being able to put up with all this — with my mother and me, my sisters with their families in the country, and the confusion in their summer home where cotton wool is to be found lying among the plates and a disgusting assortment of all kinds of objects on the beds."[117] Kafka's disgust is surely sexual, directed at people whose every movement communicates how separate he is from them. He draws a scene

> . . . where one of my sisters, the middle one [Valli], is lying in bed with some slight throat infection, while her husband sits beside her and in fun as well as in earnest keeps calling her "My Precious" and "My All"; where the little boy because he can't help himself while being played with, does his business on the floor in the middle of the room . . . where my mother insists on waiting on everyone, where bread is spread with goose-drippings which, if one's lucky, trickle only down one's fingers. I do supply information, don't I?[118]

What has been described and what follows suggest such self-loathing Kafka can represent it only in images of disgust for others. He is encircled, so to speak, by his sexual distaste for everything connected not only with family but with people themselves. Part of it is real, part an essential role he must play in order to separate himself for his work. As we examine Kafka's loathing, we must never isolate it from the stand he felt he must take to make writing possible: marginality, isolation, withdrawal, rejection, separation.

> It is not because they are relatives that I cannot bear to be in the same room with them, but merely because they are people. . . . Yesterday I was so choked with loathing that I groped for the door almost as if it were dark, and I was far from the house and out on the road before I felt better; but I had stored up so much of it that I still haven't rid myself of it, even today. I cannot live with people; I absolutely hate all my relatives, not because they are my relatives, not because they are wicked, not because I don't think well of them . . . but simply because they are people with whom I live in close proximity. It is just that I cannot abide communal life.[119]

He adds that he does not regard this as a misfortune.

These outbursts have a heuristic function for the marriage-to-come. Felice is expected, no matter what her own predilections, to share his behavior. She must experience life as he feels it, even if she, healthy and more socially oriented, finds it difficult or impossible. These are the "rules" of marriage, and he pounds away to make certain she is aware. Her response is reasonable and understanding, but part of it, we must assume, was based on her continuing misunderstanding of him, her feeling that eventually his "nervousness" would end and he would behave like all other normal husbands. While he is fighting his "great war," she is waiting for his offensive to weaken, and then, she feels, he will settle in. Her sweetness, as Kafka calls it, is founded on her reasonableness, which she thinks he will eventually come to share. Only years later did she recognize that he was immovable, that what he was telling her was a final line of defense, not something negotiable. If she had hoped to bring him to the peace table, she found herself outmaneuvered by his brutal honesty. There was no compromise in him or in his words, only a repeated request for unconditional surrender.

Kafka's assault on her defense was motivated by his need for her to discover the absolute bottom in him. He sees family life as countries undergoing civil war or revolution; every move is part of power politics. In this, he is no novice himself. "I am not a human being," he confesses to Felice.

> I am capable of tormenting you cold-bloodedly, you whom I love most, whom I love alone out of the entire human race. . . . Can I tolerate this situation when I am in a position to see it so clearly, have suspected it, find my suspicions confirmed, and continue to suspect it? If need be, I can live as I am, my rage turned inward, tormenting only by letter, but as soon as we lived together I would become a dangerous lunatic fit to be burned alive. The havoc I would create! Would have to create![120]

Now that she has accepted, his desperation and panic have caught him in endless coils. As he contemplates a regular companion, he realizes how unsuitable he is for such closeness. The defensive wall he has constructed will be constantly tested.

> To be quite frank (as I have always been with you as far as my self-knowledge at the moment allows) and at long last to be recognized by you as the madman I am, it is my *dread of the union* [Kafka's italics] even with the most beloved woman, above all with her. How can I explain to you what to me is so clear that I long to cover it, to stop it blinding me! . . . I have a definite feeling that through marriage, *through the union, through the dissolution* of this nothingness that I am, I shall perish, and not alone but with my wife, and that the more I love her the swifter and more terrible it will be.[121]

These are extraordinary words, full of insights parallel with his greatest fiction.

They are part plea — for Felice not to abandon him to his madness — part rejection — for her to leave him to work through that madness — part uncertainty — he wonders if he can be saved or if he is forever damned to separation and loneliness. Further, they are part fear of impotence in any situation requiring closeness, not just a sexual union; part egomania and narcissism, that he can somehow survive without anyone else; part of the clearing away of debris so that, as he says, he can "race through the night" with his pen; part a desire to perish, with the hope of resurrection into a new life where he can write and express himself. It is also, in part, a playing with words, using them for demonic purposes, trying them out to see how far he can push Felice without discouraging her. We must not neglect the testing-out quality of his words and ideas, the need to condition her to what he is, the intensity of his desire to find her stretching point. Only then can he measure his own worth, by the degree to which she will accept someone so extraordinarily unacceptable. There are, he concludes in the July 13 letter, "still a number of horrible recesses in me that you don't know."[122] In the same letter, he indicates that the apartment he has in mind for them cannot be occupied until May 1914. He says there is, accordingly, no need to hurry his letter to her parents (for the formal engagement), or any need for them to make plans until "February, January, or Christmas" of next year. His arrangement of dates is interesting: he works backward in time, when he would like to postpone the date.

Felice is not the only one caught by headaches. Kafka writes of headaches "that grip my head like a hood,'"[123] from fears of being abandoned. He suggests he will do something dramatic: suicide is never too distant from his response to her lack of letters. *Nothing* becomes a key word, and it indicates an annihilation of self as much as it does a paucity of mail. He repeats he is going downhill: she will have "a white-haired husband."[124] (Kafka's hair actually remained luxuriantly black until his death.) Warnings proliferate. "I say that I am absurdly afraid of our future and of the unhappiness which, through my fault and temperament, could develop from our life together, and which would be bound to affect you first and the more profoundly, for I am basically a cold, selfish, callous creature, despite my weakness which conceals rather than mitigates these qualities."[125] Very witty: he hides behind weakness, but if one penetrates it, he is even worse than if strong. He fears all people — this said after he receives a photograph of Frau Bauer, who, though no beauty queen, was a decent-looking woman. Kafka says that such fear along with indifference is his basic feeling toward people, that he is afraid of his own parents, "certainly of my father." He speaks of Frau Bauer as an agent of death, all in black, "mournful, disapproving, reproachful, observant, stiff, a stranger within her family, let alone toward me."[126] Her very presence sent shivers into him, and rightly so, for Frau Bauer was a nervous, unsettled, sad person, for whom Kafka must have appeared as a stranger from another planet. But he is mainly concerned with his own appearance in the family, and he knows that not a single Bauer will be pleased with him as an in-law. As Max Brod repeated to one and all, his friend Franz was unique and was not to be judged by others' standards.*

Well into August, Kafka was still working away at his favorite story, "The Judgment." Writing to his maternal bachelor uncle in Madrid, Alfred Löwy, he talks of his impending engagement, while sending on the issue of *Arkadia* with "The Judgment." It occurs to Kafka that by sending along the story in which Georg sends a letter to his friend, he is indicating that a good deal of Uncle Alfred appears in "The Judgment," chiefly as the friend, a parallel Kafka remarks on to Felice. He concludes this strange intrusion of the story into their relationship with an even more dire statement: "Thus we are being elevated to official status from Madrid, while your parents are still living in ignorant bliss, knowing little or nothing about the terrible son-in-law they are threatened with."[127] Given the violence of the story, perhaps Kafka was not exaggerating the threat.

Along with depicting himself as the worst possible case, he is still extremely anxious over the arrival of Felice's letters; demanding that they be regular, he writes, *"but even this is denied me."* Then amidst an apology for his insistent tone, he complains about the content:

---

*The Bauers could not, for example, have known about Kafka's ills, real or imagined. He tells Felice he was examined in June by the family doctor but says he doesn't believe what he was told. Still, doctors can serve as "natural therapy"; that is, when they say you are healthy, you feel better. Yet after receiving reassurances that his health was good, Kafka felt palpitations, followed by "stabs and pains in the region of the heart" (*Letters to Felice*, p. 296). These he ascribes to being separated from Felice. Worried, he returned to the doctor that very day, August 4, and was told that except for the sound in one area not being quite clear, there was nothing wrong. The medical advice: vacation (impossible), medicine (impossible), sleep (impossible), no swimming (impossible), and a quiet life (more impossible than all the rest). The doctor evidently did not realize he had Franz Kafka as his patient.

"With only a few superficial changes, these could be letters to a stranger, or rather this is what they couldn't be, for in that case — it seems to me — they would be less casual."[128] All this must have been exhausting to Felice. We must wonder where she found the energy to reply to so many contradictory impulses, so much anxiety, such a mountain of uncertainty. Kafka further feels she is trivializing their relationship by some frivolous remarks made in her postcard from Kampen, a picturesque village on the Sylt, north of Westerland. "If it is your wish, Felice, to take upon yourself the sacrifice of becoming my wife — I have made every effort in accordance with the truth to prove down to the last detail that it is a sacrifice — then, unless you wish to condemn us to endless misery, you mustn't take a frivolous view of your affection for me, let alone have no views about it."[129]

He shrewdly says that within her, somewhere, there must be an illusion "which from time to time stops working." He is astonished that in three sentences she had dismissed the idea of coming to Prague: not until May 1914, nine months in the future, would she come. Very possibly, his extreme annoyance as evidenced in this and subsequent letters explains his September–October affair with a Swiss girl at a sanatorium, which was then followed by his interest in Felice's friend, Grete Bloch. Since Kafka was not vengeful or promiscuous, he may have felt he had to assert himself when he sensed Felice was not taking him seriously enough.

The relationship now for Kafka is hellish. His letters are "infernal," he lives in the underworld, his spirit is demonic, Felice's role is sacrificial, her parents are threatening, both principals suffer from debilitating headaches, misery is their lot; all that is missing is the smell of sulphur. He doesn't fantasize about her body but rather about his separation from her. As he moves past the midpoint of this vast correspondence, he has, in effect, objectified her. She is no longer Felice Bauer of Berlin, with a life of her own, but a woman who is dancing at the end of the Franz Kafka string. She is, in his view, not much different from his mother; like Julie with Hermann, she will do her husband's bidding and efface herself. When Kafka says, "I have no literary interest, but am made of literature, I am nothing else, cannot be anything else,"[130] he is turning Hermann's devotion to the shop into his enslavement to his desk, with dire consequences for the woman who must serve his basic desk needs.

In August, when he writes to her parents and, thus, casts the die, he is frantic with self-deprecation. The critical moment has arrived, when his contrary needs meet on the battleground of a conflicted self. He must make himself as unappealing as possible, as though there were still areas he could criticize. He tells Felice that as she once feared having a bald-headed suitor, "now an almost white-haired man offers you his hand in marriage."[131] As for speech, talking is altogether against his nature. "For me, speech robs everything I say of its seriousness and importance. To me it seems impossible that it should be otherwise, since speech is continuously influenced by a thousand external factors and a thousand external constraints."[132]

The August 22 letter brings forth a crisis, since Herr Bauer has responded hesitantly, showing general doubts. Kafka also knows there are elements in himself that Felice's father knows nothing about, and none of that part can ever be "cleared up." "For it is I alone," he reminds Felice, "who carry all anxieties and fears within me, as alive as snakes; I alone who scrutinize them constantly, and only I know what they are."[133] What information can Herr Bauer gain that will uncover that pool of self-doubt? Kafka then directs his fire at Felice, warning her again of what their married life will be like. "The life that awaits you is not that of the happy couples you see strolling along before you in Westerland, no lighthearted chatter arm in arm, *but a monastic life at the side of a man who is peevish, miserable, silent, discontented, and sickly;* a man who, and this will seem to you akin to madness, is chained to invisible literature by invisible chains and screams when approached because, he claims, someone is touching those chains."[134] The emphasized portion reveals Kafka's heuristic attempt. He is planting the minefield within full sight of the victim and then daring her to find a path through; and, to continue the metaphor, he is daring himself to try the minefield even though he may be blown up with her.

The reply to Herr Bauer was an outburst intended to relieve him. The letter is contained in his diary entry for August 11, 1913, and was noted earlier; but some of it is appropriate here.* He contrasts his sickly, neurotic being with Felice, a "healthy, gay, natural, strong girl."[135] He insists "it nevertheless remains true that she must be unhappy with me, so far as I can see. I am, not only because of my external circumstances but even more because of my essential nature, a reserved, silent, unsocial, dissatisfied person." He emphasizes his alienation from his family, "among the best and most lovable people,"

---

*The diary entry was expanded into an August 28 letter, which Kafka sent on to Felice, to deliver to her father if she so chose. The letter is an act of such self-flagellation Kafka appears to be pleading with Herr Bauer to save him. He speaks of himself, as he has to Felice, as "taciturn, unsociable, morose, selfish, a hypochondriac," someone in poor health (*Letters to Felice*, p. 313). He sees all this as advantageous, "the earthly reflection of a higher necessity." He says he has deluded Herr Bauer's daughter with his letters and has always been aware of their incompatibility. He offers a monastic existence. She can expect a life "utterly divorced from her parents, her family, and almost any other social contact — because I, who would lock my door against my best friend, cannot imagine any other kind of married life." A Bluebeard could not have put it better, but Kafka is not through, in the event Herr Bauer dismisses all this as the ravings of a lovesick suitor. Even if Felice could stand this, what would it be for? For his writing, which is in her eyes problematic. At best, she would be living in a strange place, Prague, in a relationship of love and friendship but not "a real marriage." Kafka then assures Herr Bauer he has spoken only a minimum of what he has to say; there is much more.

asserting he rarely addresses his mother. "Everything that is not literature bores me and I hate it, for it disturbs me or delays me, if only because I think it does." And then in a final plea for Felice's hand, Kafka
adds, "I lack all aptitude for family life except, at best, as an observer. I
have no family feeling and visitors make me almost feel as though I
were maliciously being attacked." Unmailed, this missive of intense
anger, hostility, and aggressiveness toward his future father-in-law was
like a festering wound in Kafka's mind. His disdain for the Bauers is
clear. They may have produced Felice, but they have no conception of
what a Prague intellectual is like. "A marriage could not change me;
just as my job cannot change me," he throws in, pearls before swine.

All in all, it was a clean surgical job of letter writing which only a
failure of nerve kept him from posting. The August sequence of letters
suggests a Kafka even more precariously balanced than earlier. Felice
had erred in writing that he seemed to have "a bent" for literature or for
writing; and this "bent" becomes another trial for him. He insists it is
not a bent, but his "entire self." A bent man can be uprooted and
crushed, he says. "Not a bent, not a bent! The very smallest detail of
my life is determined by and hinges on it."[136] He describes their life
with such a frantic intensity he seems to feel it has been traduced even
before it has become a reality: "We will have but *one* hour a day together. . . . As a married woman, you will find loneliness harder to bear
than you can possibly imagine now from afar." He turns the screw.
"You would shrink in derision from the idea of a convent, yet you contemplate living with a man whose natural ambition (and incidentally
his circumstances, too) oblige him to lead a monastic life?" In the following sentence, Kafka winds around his entire life: "While his [Herr
Bauer's] letter is friendly and open, mine was nothing but a screen con-
cealing the most lamentable ulterior motives with which I am continuously compelled to attack you, my dearest Felice, whose curse I am."
It is all there: the kindness of others, Kafka's destructively secret nature, and the self-flagellation when he accuses himself of being a curse
on his beloved.

Much more remains in that August 24 letter, for Kafka describes
how he told his father he wants to get married and even has a candidate
for it. This begins another phase of the "great war" between him and
Felice, made up of side skirmishes that bled over into their relationship. "You know," he tells Felice, "that he is my enemy, and I his, as is
determined by our temperaments, but apart from this my admiration
for him as a man is perhaps as great as my fear of him. I can manage to
avoid him; but ignore him, never."[137] The division between father and
son existed on so many levels, it is difficult to identify them. Besides
personal differences were the cultural differences between the former
shtetl Jew who emigrated to Prague with nothing but his wits and the
sophisticated son with his law degree and literary friends. If Abraham

still lived by the old laws, Isaac, although not quite assimilated, was a native to a cosmopolitan city and its cultural values. Then there was the oedipal struggle, and here we are on familiar ground, with Kafka frequently voicing his resentment of how he had "lost" Julie to her husband, how Hermann pre-empted the women in the household, except possibly Ottla. Father and son had battled for the women, and Hermann won, as Herr Samsa was victorious in "The Metamorphosis." There was, additionally, the physical disproportion: the father sturdy, burly, muscular, large-limbed; the son with his concave chest, thin limbs, undeveloped body, and frail look.

The confrontation over marriage becomes just that, not a reasoned discussion. Hermann's irritability and his uncontrolled remarks — we assume a disdain for his son's intentions — led to Kafka's irritable response, as the two unsuited men square off with verbal blows. Hermann's chief point of attack was his son's inadequate income for marriage; but this was linked in the father's mind to what he considered to be Kafka's "lack of purpose," and that in turn to his resentment that his son had pressured him to invest in the asbestos factory, which was slowly going under. He attributed its failure to Kafka's lack of attention to it. Hermann also worried about the financial difficulties in his second daughter's marriage, and that problematic area carried over into Kafka's own plans. The reproaches were addressed to the thin air, to Julie Kafka, and to the son, indiscriminately — part of Hermann's feeling that the entire family was plotting to bring him down financially.

After about half an hour of ranting, Hermann calmed and became relatively gentle, so that "one is helpless when confronted by him, above all myself, who haven't a word to say to him that is genuinely felt."[138] Hermann finally offered to go to Berlin to meet the Bauers, further offered "irrefutable objections" to the marriage, and then if the marriage were to go ahead anyway, promised to say no more.

What we can learn from all this is clear: that if Kafka had found it in himself to stand up to Hermann from the start and disallowed his bullying manner, then he could have won virtually all the battles but perhaps lost some of his greatest themes. Hermann, clearly, was not a satanic force put on earth to make life hellish for his son, but a blowhard whose sense of his role in Prague life was uncertain, and who, as a former inhabitant of the *shtetl*, was so deprived of economic security that he saw plots and conspiracies everywhere. For such a man, his children can never be satisfactory, his financial position never secure, his hard work never fully rewarded, his wife never sufficiently devoted, and he can never be free of doubts. Hermann's own life was full of hellish fears, which he translated into verbal bullying.

Yet in still another continuation of this (August 24) monumental letter, Kafka reveals his understanding of Hermann; understanding,

however, does not lead to affection or to counteraction. Like Frau
Bauer, Kafka writes, Hermann

> foresees catastrophe everywhere. When he was younger and still had
> complete confidence in himself and health, these fears were not so pro-
> nounced. . . . But today he fears everything, and, horrible as it may be,
> these fears, at any rate in important matters, are invariably con-
> firmed. . . . my father has worked hard all his life, and from nothing has
> made, comparatively speaking, something. This progress, however, came
> to an end years ago, when his daughters were grown up, and now, owing
> to their marriages [the two oldest], it has turned out a frightful never-end-
> ing decline.[139]

Hermann feels that his sons-in-law as well as his own children are mill-
stones around his neck, and his attack on Kafka's future marriage is
part of that fear: that once he is married, his son will find he cannot
support a wife and will become an additional burden. All of this is exacerbated by Hermann's illness, hardening of the arteries.

Kafka demonstrated a mature understanding of his father's dilemma, as Hermann entered his sixties and found his world crashing
down. In the background, we must recall, are the increasing nationalist
attacks on Jewish shopowners and other commercial interests, the
aging of the Dual Monarchy, which had protected Jews, the growth in
other parts of the empire of virulent anti-Semitic elements — in Vienna and Budapest, for example — and the tightrope act between war
and peace being performed by nearly all the nations of Europe. Kafka's
final comment on all this is that he will make no claims on Hermann,
that while he may have inherited his father's avarice in little things, he
does not possess his acquisitiveness.

Yet the encounter and the steady movement toward an official engagement sent Kafka into an "insurmountable fear": he fears achieving
happiness, he says, and possesses "a desire and a command to torment
myself for some higher purpose."[140] He sees the engagement as a juggernaut that will crush both of them: "That you, dearest, should be forced
to land under the wheels of this carriage [she had written a 'suicidal letter,' as Kafka put it], which is destined for me alone, is really terrible. I
am consigned to darkness by my inner voice, yet in reality drawn to
you; this is irreconcilable." Felice had requested some respite, apparently, and Kafka answered he would like to call off everything, if he
could, but this was not what she meant at all. She has said her mother
has potential love for him, and he asks what he should do with it. "I
could never return it, who never could or wish to be equal to her love!"
He demands she "push me aside," for "anything else means ruin for us
both." But this is nothing compared to the letter three days later, on
September 2, when he produces a great "fictional" image for his condition. He is seeking nothing less than sacrificial death, having spent
Sunday (August 31) lying "in the woods with a headache."[141] He has the

following wish: "When passing a house, to be pulled in through the ground-floor window by a rope around one's neck and to be hauled up, bloody and ragged, through all the ceilings, furniture, walls, and attics, without consideration, as if by a person who is paying no attention, until the empty noose, dropping the last shreds of me when breaking through the roof tiles, appears on the roof."

The images here are truly those of a madman, and Kafka's insistence on such bloody, sacrificial death must indicate he was very close to the edge, or even over, during this sequence of events — closely linked to Felice's acceptance, his letter to Herr Bauer, his recognition he might not be able to extricate himself. In that extraordinary image of death, he is both killer of himself and victim of someone, ostensibly Felice. Shredded, lacerated, with flesh hanging from him in strips, he is preparing himself for the death machine, without even the certainty of enlightenment along the way (six hours into the torture in "In the Penal Colony"). He repeats his desire to renounce the greatest human happiness for the sake of writing; the desire is so powerful it "keeps cutting every muscle in my body."

He draws a literary analogy, of how the four men whom he considers "to be my true blood-relations" responded to marriage. Only Dostoevsky married; Flaubert, Kleist, and Grillparzer all remained bachelors. Furthermore, Kleist, who shot himself when compelled by inner and outer necessity, "was the only one to find the right solution." It was an intense idea, not more role-playing, reaching into every part of his thinking; that he stopped short may well have indicated a recognition that death would end his writing.

Meanwhile, and somewhat inexplicably, his insurance career was ongoing, and he announced to Felice that on the following Saturday (September 6) he was assigned to attend, with Robert Marschner and Eugen Pfohl, the International Congress for First Aid and Hygiene in Vienna.* After Vienna, he planned a return to the Riva sanatorium, with possibly a brief trip through northern Italy. He exulted in the fact that in Vienna he was staying at the Hotel Matschakerhof, where Grillparzer used to lunch. He attended the Zionist Congress and told Felice that he felt Zionistic in "certain respects, also for the entire concept, but not for the essential part."[142] That is, not for himself. From Vienna, he went on to Venice,† hoping that the pouring rain in Venice would completely wash away the Vienna experience. From Verona, where he kept up with the latest letters from Felice, he assured her he was there

---

*This was the second such International Congress for First Aid and Accident Prevention (Kafka's specialty), and it lasted from September 2 through the ninth, running simultaneously with the Eleventh Zionist Congress in Vienna, which Kafka attended on the eighth.

†Kafka's notebook entries on his trip to Vienna and Venice will appear in another chapter, since they reflect not on Felice but on the trip.

"in all my misery," in the event she suspected he might be enjoying himself. Kafka's trip included Trieste and Desenzano (at the south end of Lake Garda), as well as Venice and Verona.

A large gap in the extant correspondence coincided with Kafka's affair with an eighteen-year-old Swiss girl, who goes unnamed. Earlier in his July diary entries (July 21), Kafka had drawn up a debit and credit list bearing on marriage: he calculates his inability to live alone against his great desire to be alone most of the time; he measures his own marriage against what he knows of other marriages; he factors in the need for conversation with another person against his hatred of everything that does not relate to literature; he judges his occasional need of people against the boredom he feels in their company; he even measures spoken words in conversation against the real meaning of words, as in literature. This attitude, in part or whole, carried over into the brief affair with the Italian-looking Swiss girl, in some ways a forerunner of his interest in Felice's friend Grete Bloch. But the Swiss girl was also an adventure, a breakout, since she was not Jewish, much younger, and ordinarily an inaccessible type for someone like Kafka. Yet as he wrote Brod on September 28, the "idea of a honeymoon trip fills me with horror. Every honeymoon couple, whether or not I put myself in their place, is a repulsive sight to me, and when I want to disgust myself I have only to imagine placing my arm around a woman's waist."[143] The brief affair at a sanatorium, with no chance of follow-up, was the very opposite of marriage and honeymoon.

Yet like everything with Kafka, complications accrue. The affair must be viewed as an act of aggression, even rage, against Felice. A letter to Brod is conclusive for there Kafka displays real anger at what Felice has done to his life — that is, what he has done to himself because of his need to role-play at a normalized life. "If only that *one* thing [Felice] would loosen its hold over me . . . if only I did not have to think of it constantly, if only there were not those times, mostly in the morning when I am getting up, when it leaps at me like a living thing. . . . I had to say I couldn't go through with it and I really cannot."[144] This is in reference to Kafka's letter to Felice on September 16 that they "shall have to part,"[145] that he is miserable, falling to pieces, unable to write truthfully to her father, unable to confront the reality of his situation. He was, in several ways, abstracting himself from his own life to prepare the ground for a large literary effort; but at the same time, the brief affair with the Swiss girl "with a low-pitched voice" was a terrible act of hostility against Felice and her bourgeois standards. By finding a Gentile girl who would be intimate with him, he was (temporarily at least) effacing the Berlin Jewish girl who remained intractable. The entire episode has the flavor of an exogamous adventure: Kafka communicated with the Swiss girl by knocking on the ceiling of his room, below hers, even while he was being pursued by a Russian fortune-teller who would have admitted him to her bedroom. The Swiss girl was ill, and coughed often, but she was also a free spirit, singing, carrying no heavy burden of a permanent attachment.*

In his diary Kafka comments on the importance of the Riva episode. "For the first time I understood a Christian girl and lived almost entirely within the sphere of her influence. I am incapable of writing down the important things that I need to remember."[146] By effacing Felice, he could assert his independence from a bondage he had himself pursued as necessary to his salvation: he had created for himself a kind of metaphorical trap, analogous to his literary metaphors. What is pursued as salvation merely tightens the trap. In that letter to Brod, of September 28, he speaks of traveling inside a cavern, as he must contemplate returning to Prague and reimmersing himself in his self-made mess.

He is, however, unable to escape himself. As he tells Brod, although he writes no more letters and receives none, he still cannot free himself. "I cannot live with her and I cannot live without her. By this one act my life, which was at least in part mercifully veiled from myself, is now completely unveiled. I ought to be whipped out into the desert."[147] Writing to Felix Weltsch, also from the Dr. von Hartungen Sanatorium and Hydrotherapy Institute at Riva, he characterizes himself as drifting, in limbo. He explains his guilt, apparently at the impasse with Felice, asserting that the "reason why I have this sense of guilt is that it is for me the finest form of penitence." He also fears that looking too deeply into his guilty feelings would be a trip into nostalgia — a witty way of suggesting he feels so perfectly comfortable with the lifelong guilt he can vaunt it.

All this is preparation for the resumption of the correspondence with Felice. But it was also preparation for something far more momentous in Kafka's life than the brief Riva affair, which lasted only ten days. This was his meeting with Grete Bloch toward the end of October 1913, when, as a friend of Felice's, she came to Prague to act as "intermediary" in their great war. She was, if successful, to arrange an armistice, or if not that, then at least a truce during which the two conflicting sides could air their differences without actual warfare. Grete Bloch immediately appealed to Kafka, possibly because he could demonstrate hostility to his erstwhile fiancée by becoming intimate with her friend. Grete was born in 1892 and at the time of the meeting with Kafka in Prague was, therefore, twenty-one. Almost five years younger than Felice, she too was a working woman, as a shorthand-typist in Berlin, Frankfurt, and Vienna; later she became executive secretary with a Berlin office machine company. She and Felice met and

---

*With their enclosed, hothouse atmosphere, many sanatoria offered sexual diversion as part of the entertainment, a kind of Club Med for the ill and the wounded.

became close friends in April 1913, only a few months after Felice and Kafka met, in August 1912.

Grete Bloch and Kafka corresponded intensely for about a year. In a letter she wrote to a friend on April 21, 1940, which subsequently was published in part by Brod, she indicated that several years previously she had borne a child, presumably Kafka's. This illegitimate son, born in 1914, died suddenly at nearly seven years old, in Munich, in 1921. Kafka's name is not mentioned, but Grete Bloch's letter leaves little doubt she meant he was the father. At the time she wrote the letter she was in Florence, and was afterward picked up by the Germans when they occupied Italy. She died in a concentration camp. There is nothing to prove her claim of bearing Kafka's child, and none of Grete's friends thought it plausible. Further, there is nothing definite to suggest that sexual intimacy even took place, although the two did sense an intimate connection. The entire episode will be taken up elsewhere, but here it should be noted that her assertion was unlikely; possibly, she was eager to regain the past by associating herself with Kafka's growing fame and making this posthumous claim on him.

From now on, Kafka's letters to Felice thin out considerably, only to pick up again in 1914, when the correspondence with Grete Bloch had more or less run its course. But on October 29, 1913, at about the time Kafka was meeting Grete, he wrote Felice trying, as he says, "to arrive at the limits of possible understanding." He returns to his familiar litany: "How can I take my place in a new family, and then establish a family of my own, I who am rooted so loosely into my own family that I feel I don't touch anyone on any side?"[148] Kafka runs his perpetual obstacle course; having been so conditioned to misery, he cannot possibly break out or through. After more than three hundred pages of letters, he has located himself, truly, in a limbo. He is worse off now than he was fourteen months ago when he first glimpsed Felice Bauer. What a monster Felice has become! What a devastating hostility he feels! How he needs her as a way of fueling these wrenching conflicts and reinforcing his abject sense of himself!

When Grete appeared, Kafka saw someone he immediately felt was more attractive than Felice; she was full of life, fashionably slim, not at all what he had imagined. Her visit set off a series of moves: he made a two-day trip to Berlin on November 8 for his and Felice's third meeting in almost a year and a half; in late December he confessed his Riva infidelity to Felice; and he turned Grete Bloch into an intimate. Our knowledge of this brief weekend trip to Berlin comes mainly from his November 10 letter to Grete, its contents full of very damaging remarks about Felice.* First, he disarms Grete by saying he had expected

*In the middle of November, the Kafka family moved to a four-room apartment, on the fourth floor, of a house on the Niklasstrasse. The larger apartment was no longer needed

her to be "tall and strong," an Amazon perhaps. He says that since in his imagination he had pictured someone spinsterish with maternal feelings, he felt he could now speak easily to her. She had turned out to be a "slim, young, undoubtedly rather unusual girl."[149] Kafka then moved toward the jugular. Grete had told him about the trouble Felice was having with her teeth, and he responded that to him "tooth trouble (something you couldn't have known, but I didn't bother to tell you that night) is among the most repulsive ailments, which I can overlook in people most dear to me, and then only just." Kafka's revulsion over a "bad mouth" was surely connected to his ideas about the entire oral-anal system. Tooth trouble, finicky food habits, poor digestion, and constipation are surely linked by an overall revulsion for all signs of bodily malfunction, and accompanied by a fascination with such problems. Kissing a bad mouth was a form of defilement, *treyf,* or dirty.

Grete had also mentioned the breaking off of Felice's brother's engagement, and that disturbs Kafka because it brings into focus the entire family, "who frighten me in every way and whom I would prefer to forget." Then in a telling remark, he says he feels sorry for girls, his "only incontestable social sentiment." He is uncertain where this compassion comes from, but perhaps it is "on account of the transformation into women which they have to undergo."[150] Having grown up with three younger sisters, Kafka had observed their difficult puberty years, but his remark was also connected to his response to Julie Kafka — being "sorry" does not end with "girls."

He writes of the "four" Felices: one who was in Prague; the second who writes letters; the third whom he meets in Berlin; the fourth, the Felice who consorts with people he, Kafka, knows nothing about. "Well, the third has no great liking for me"[151] — that is, the Felice whom he sees in Berlin. This could be either a very shrewd observation or a sign of paranoia. He follows up this remark, still to Grete, with a long explanation of how, once he was in Berlin, a comedy of errors developed: no meeting at the station, his letter going astray, her need to accompany her brother to the station at another hour, her inability to be free in the evening, his expectation she would call, their being together for only a brief walk in the Tiergarten, her general business that in effect left no time for him. "So I left Berlin like one who had had no right to go there. And in a sense this is true." Felice was surely playing some game of her own, in which she paid back Kafka in the only way she could, by allowing him to make the trip and then cutting him off, like an enemy at the pass. His strategies had gone awry, and he had been finessed, one of the minor skirmishes of their war.

In a letter in late December 1913, Kafka accused Felice of lying

---

now that two daughters had married and only Kafka and Ottla remained at home. This may have made him even more frantic about Felice.

about having sent him letters, and says her purpose was nothing less than to inflict torment on him, "minute by minute."[152] He adds that at the merest word from her, he would write to her parents — the letter that would lead to an official engagement — even though they have broken it off. He further accuses her of being inhuman, since each promise appears to offer him hope, until the expected letters do not appear. Kafka then offered his twisted logic for why they should or should not marry. "You misunderstood if you imagined that what keeps me from marrying is the thought that in winning you I would gain less than I would lose by giving up my solitary existence. . . . For me it was not a matter of giving something up, for even after marriage I would go on being the very same person I am, and this precisely — if you so chose — is the serious problem that would confront you."[153] Thus, he has enwrapped her in his conundrum: even while offering reconciliation, he promises hell.

With that, he confessed. "At the sanatorium I fell in love with a girl, a child, about 18 years old, she is Swiss, but lives in Italy, near Genoa, thus by blood as alien to me as can be; still immature but remarkable and despite her illness a real person with great depth,"[154] referred to by Kafka only by initials G.W. He explains that given his state of hopelessness a far less remarkable girl could have captivated him. Both recognized that the love affair was temporary and could not last beyond the ten days available to them. "Nevertheless we meant a great deal to each other, and I had to make all kinds of arrangements to prevent her bursting into tears in front of everyone when we said goodbye, and I felt much the same. With my departure it was all over." He tells Felice that the young girl knew about her and about his plans to marry. Kafka leaves it at that; so Felice can "read" his confession as his failure to reconcile with her, not as his lapse. The fact of the confession appears more significant than the brief affair itself: he may have intended to wound Felice; he may have hoped to bring her closer to a decision. Either way he could rid himself of a good deal of hostility by telling her something that made him feel guilty; or he could be boasting that he was approachable, neither a lunatic nor a freak.

On January 1 the comments are more focused on what will happen to them. He admits that Felice's disinclination to lose her position in Berlin is valid. She would be exchanging her comfortable existence in Berlin for Prague, "a provincial town with a language unfamiliar to you," an official's life, a petty bourgeois household, "and instead of social life and instead of your family you would have a husband who more often than not . . . is melancholy and silent, and whose infrequent personal happiness lies solely in an occupation that, as an occupation, would inevitably continue to be alien to you."[155] Yet he insists she must decide not on the basis of loss, but on whether she feels, as he does, that both husband and wife must be equals, "in order to exist independently within this unit."[156]

The next day, within the same format, he hammers away at three possible choices facing her. Either she doesn't want to have anything to do with him and is using her sense of "loss" as a method of pushing him aside; or else her confidence in him has been shaken and she is weighing the situation for a later decision; or, the third possibility, which he cannot believe, "without deeper reason you merely calculate the losses." If the first, she is lost to him, and they must part. With the second, he is confident that once she puts her trust in him all will be well, regardless of how weak he may appear at any particular moment.

Kafka has created a large fiction, an epistolary novel in which he, as author, has become so deeply involved he now believes his own future is at stake. "I love you, Felice, with everything that is good in me as a human being, with everything in me that makes me deserving of being astir among the living."[157] He reiterates that he wouldn't think of changing her, and yet a good part of the correspondence is devoted to his desire to reshape her so that she can adapt to his vision of their future together. As we see in his letter to Grete Bloch three weeks later, in this ongoing epistolary novel he is to some extent plotting and playing roles. Kafka has written himself so deeply into this fiction he is becoming confused about what is real about him and what is role-playing.

To Grete (on January 23), he attempts to lay himself bare, for she has become his confidante and accessory, privy to his deepest feelings and strategies. We must assume that caught as he was now in his plots and given the complications of the situation he had created, he was being as honest as he could be. Sensing hostility on Grete's part, he has postponed writing to her; he then apologizes for "loathsome subterfuges" on his part, playing games with his letters even to her. He perceives how bizarre their relationship is: "I know how to appreciate the least kindness, have received nothing but kindness from you, kindness bestowed in a most unselfish way — there is no explanation for my feeling other than that my relationship with F. — unbearable, uncertain, yet forever piercingly vivid — puts me in an entirely false position with you, too."[158] He informs her he has renewed his suit, and we assume he tells her this and other intimate matters so that she can get back to Felice. She is, as in traditional fiction, the intermediary between pursuing lover and fleeing mistress. "I could understand," he writes, "F.'s behavior from my point of view, her silence I mean, her letting the uncertainty go on, but given her nature, as I imagined it to be, I don't understand it." His manipulation of Felice's friend is now under way. In interweaving one complexity with another, he was practicing his fiction. *The Trial*, begun in midsummer, is taking shape.

After Kafka's monumental letter to Felice begun December 29, 1913, and continued through January 2, forty pages in manuscript, with no reply in sight, he writes in a panic to Grete. He indicates he would have gone to Berlin at Christmas, except that Felice had said on the telephone he was not to come, then repeated it in a telegram. With this letter to Grete Bloch, Kafka suggests he sees his situation worsened by the fact Grete is herself not writing in response to his pleas for some developments. He fears he has offended her, or else she has bad news for him — omitting the possibility that this stable young woman may feel she has been drawn into a bizarre drama in which she is a useful pawn.

Kafka writes at great length about his response to Felice's last, sad letter with this sentence from her: " 'Marriage would mean that we should each have to sacrifice a good deal; let us not try to establish where the excess weight would be. It is a good deal, for each of us.' "[159] Kafka cites this sentence as so dreadful it cannot express Felice's views, although he admits it contains "much actual truth." He now shifts the weight to Grete, saying he and Felice have a "joint future" only in the letters Grete writes, and presumably in the pressure she exerts on her friend. Kafka is dominating Grete as a lifeline to Felice, as earlier he had dominated Felice as a means to penetrate his own life. His feelings for Grete are focused not on her needs, but on his. What would, of course, complete this novelistic triangle would be: Felice's letters to Kafka, now lost; Grete's letters to Kafka, now lost; and Grete's words to Felice, in person, on the telephone, or by mail, all lost. The overall relationship has in a sense been deconstructed by the paucity of materials, but deconstruction of the situation also allows us to center or ground it wherever we wish: not only, as Kafka hopes, in his needs, but in the shadowy Felice, now herself becoming more of a strategist and even a conspirator; as well as in Grete, the intermediary who is attracted to Kafka even as she tries to bring together her two friends.

The drama continues with Kafka assuring Grete that her intervention is bringing in Felice's letters to him. He says he is indebted to her not only for having done something for him, but for having "had to do something against yourself."[160] She has apparently complained of her role, of having become ill on behalf of these strange combatants. What she doesn't know is that Kafka had planned a flying visit to Felice at her Berlin office, a plan he hatched in mid-February and carried out on February 28, a Saturday morning. Thus, he was making plans for him and Felice even as he was importuning Grete to act for him without revealing to her his full strategies. Incidentally, when Grete went to Vienna, Kafka regretted once again that she had not seen Grillparzer's apartment at Spiegelgasse 21, which after the author's death had been transferred to the Historical Museum of the City of Vienna. Kafka demeans Vienna itself and agrees with Grillparzer that "one can well and truly suffer in Vienna."[161]

Kafka's frequent diatribes against the capital of the empire were both personal and ideological: personal in that Prague was a poor sister, relatively speaking, to the glittering capital; ideological in that Kafka felt that Vienna, Freud notwithstanding, was frivolous and trivial in its pursuit of pleasure, whereas Prague was mystical, weightier, with far greater gravity. None of this prevented Kafka from being sensitive to avant-gardes in Vienna, but he judged harshly the Viennese spirit, and possibly regretted he was stuck in a "backwater" city, as he called it, while Vienna ("that decaying mammoth village")[162] sparkled. Prague, of course, was anything but a backwater.

With Felice introducing "a renewed silence," Kafka confessed to Grete he had grown up to suspect that behind every silence there was "some snag that could undo me." This is one of those self-perceptions that open up entire panoramas. We sense the author of *The Trial*, the man who will suffer "Before the Law," the eventual victim of tuberculosis, the man who reshapes himself into insects and animals, and, finally, the mole who seeks silence in its burrow only to suffer from the silence. He mentions the engagement of Felix Weltsch, and he sees this as the end of an era, the last of bachelor friends now lost to him. A married friend isn't "a true one." His distrust of women is bitterly disclosed: "Anything he [the married friend] is told will be revealed to his wife either silently or explicitly, and the woman in whose head all information doesn't become distorted probably doesn't exist."[163] While Kafka rues the loss of his "bachelor fraternity," he does not assess what his own confession of the Riva sanatorium affair did to Felice.

On February 28, Kafka made a quick trip to Berlin, to catch Felice by surprise. By visiting her at her office, Kafka hoped to bypass her family's objections to him and his bizarre way of carrying on a courtship. He dropped Grete a picture postcard from Dresden, on his return, amusingly put: "Have been to Berlin. It couldn't have been worse. Next thing will be impalement."[164] The sacrificial nature of the remark befits Kafka's conception of the trip: it would be all or nothing, the suitor taking his future bride by storm within her own territory. It was a new ploy in the ongoing war.

We learn of the Berlin episode from Kafka's March 2 letter to Grete. It relates not so much a comedy of errors as a bloody skirmish in a Balkan war, where the stakes are egos rather than large property gains. Felice was surprised to see him, but not unduly, and seemed friendly. They spent an hour at lunchtime, in a tearoom, then walked for two hours after her office work was completed. That evening, Saturday, they did not spend together as Felice for business reasons had to attend a ball. On Sunday morning, they spent three hours walking and in a coffeehouse. Felice promised to see Kafka in the afternoon, when he left, but didn't appear, sending a telegram that she had to see her Aunt Marta, or "something of the kind." They did, nevertheless, have time to talk, and while Kafka was not exactly rebuffed, Felice made it clear her own life would not be interrupted by his sudden visit.

As Kafka relates what went on in their conversation, we see further evidence of Felice's good sense. He tells Grete that although Felice says

she "quite likes me," she does not feel this is sufficient for this particular marriage. "She has insurmountable fears about a joint future; she
might not be able to put up with my idiosyncrasies; she might not be
able to forgo Berlin; she is afraid of having to dispense with nice
clothes, or traveling third class, sitting in cheaper seats in the theatre
(this sounds ridiculous only when put on paper), etc."[165] He misjudges
what is "ridiculous" because he has misjudged Felice. She did not envision her future life as a sacrifice for literature, and she viewed marriage as a comfortable extension of the benefits she had enjoyed as a
working woman. Kafka nevertheless was somewhat encouraged, since
she was friendly, and they used the familiar *du* form of address, even in
front of Weiss, whom they ran into. She had retained Kafka's picture in
a locket she was given the past November, and insisted she would not
marry anyone else; nor did she ask for a return of her photograph or
choose to dispose of his letters.

Not surprisingly, Grete Bloch was suffering from headaches, a natural result of being caught between two headache sufferers. Kafka's advice to her was paternal: work less hard, get more exercise, sleep with
the window open, eat less meat, and possibly chew more thoroughly.
"In an overtired and overworked body like yours . . . meat causes nothing but devastation; the headaches are no more than the body's complaints about it."[166] He suggests a fine vegetarian restaurant on Opolzer
Strasse (the Thalisia), clean, well run, with a pleasant atmosphere. That
will, he assures her, help her get over the headaches. He then launches
into his own "situation," when his parents come to the table and he
can no longer write in peace. "My father is breathing heavily through
his mouth, he is just reading the evening paper but after that he starts
his usual game of cards with my mother, accompanied by exclama-
tions, laughter, and squabbling, not to mention whistling."[167]

Food, noises, parents: all combine to create the peculiar disgust
Kafka experienced at human contact, even as he tried to explain to
Grete how he wanted to regain Felice. That disgust carried over into a
March 4 letter, where his physical description of Felice hardly disguises
a repulsion on his part, although he denies it. "F.'s appearance varies;
out of doors she generally looks very well, indoors sometimes tired and
older, with rough, blotchy skin. Her teeth, all of them, are in a worse
condition than they used to be, each one has a filling. This Monday she
started another series of visits to the dentist who is making new gold
crowns for her. All this and more I can note, see, observe carefully, but
in no way does it alter my feelings for F."[168] Sexual disgust is never far
from his descriptions and denials.

In his diary for March 9, 1914, Kafka carried on a strange dialogue
with himself over his situation with Felice. Many of the diary remarks
are things he said on his Berlin trip, and which, he informs Grete, he
retracted in a letter to Felice six days before. How much he told her we

cannot measure, but some of what Kafka says is destructive. He states, for example, that an official's life would benefit him if he were married. Such a life would "in every way be a support to me against society, against my wife, against writing, without demanding too many sacrifices, and without on the other hand degenerating into indolence and dependence, for as a married man I should not have to fear that."[169] Balanced against this, in his inner debate, is the point that as he gets older any change seems formidable, and there is his literary work, which he must protect. Yet his present bachelor's life is also inhibiting such work: he has written nothing for a year. He ignores, of course, the fact that his sequence of letters to Felice and to Grete is a form of creative outpouring, the creation of a certain genre of fiction.

He considers how his statement of idiosyncrasies has worried Felice, and he says he loves her enough to rid himself of anything that might trouble her. "I will become another person,"[170] he tells his diary and, presumably, Felice. Yet he admits he has no prospects. To leave Prague is one way out; Vienna, he reiterates, he hates. Berlin is a possibility, where he thinks of pursuing a career as a journalist, an odd choice given his hatred of the public. He concludes the diary entry with the observation that if he went to Berlin, their being together might get her out of his blood. Those teeth!

Kafka was, nevertheless, on the right track. He had somehow empowered himself to pursue Felice more intensely by way of degrading himself. Just the next month, in April 1914, when he went to Berlin, he and Felice became unofficially engaged, with an announcement in the *Berliner Tageblatt* and the *Prager Tagblatt*. Yet even as he kept up the pursuit, he was becoming more involved, through letters and attempts at meetings, with Grete. In that same April when he saw Felice, he asked Grete to join him in Gmünd on the Austrian-Czech border. Grete, meanwhile, was concerned about Felice's reaction to her closeness with Kafka. As the triangular shape of the affair became clearer, Kafka admitted only that at one point Felice said that Grete "seems to mean a good deal to you."[171] We can speculate that one reason Felice agreed, in April, to the unofficial engagement was to regain Kafka from Grete Bloch. His power in the situation was such that he was able to drive, however small, a wedge between the two young women and establish a competition of sorts in which he, the idiosyncratic one, was the ultimate prize.

He was full of the kind of advice for Grete he once gave to Felice. Health is, of course, high on the list, but he also recommends that she forsake Vienna and even come to Prague; and if not Prague, then Frankfurt. Vienna, however, is the villain, where she works too hard and suffers from poor health: "Get out of Vienna." He asks her, on March 11 or 12, to come to Prague, not on a Sunday, when only a few hours with her would be too heavy a strain for him to bear, but on a Saturday after she leaves work at 3:00 P.M. Or else, he offers to meet her halfway, which becomes the Gmünd meeting in April, to "spend Sunday together."

On March 13, with schemes going forward on both fronts, Kafka wrote Felice, suggesting they meet in Dresden, just over the northern Czech border in Germany. "Imagine I am a stranger who has seen you but once in Prague and now asks you a favor [for Saturday, the twenty-first], which to you is a mere nothing and to him is the one thing that matters. You would not refuse him."[172] He repeated his fear of coming to Berlin as long as matters between them were unclear. Felice, however, declined. Yet on the same day, Kafka pursued the meeting with Grete, now postponed until the following Sunday. Again, he pressed Grillparzer upon her, his autobiography as well as his travel diaries. Her visit to the Grillparzer Room at the state museum will somehow make them secret sharers. He repeats, "You are not to leave Vienna until you have done this."[173] This need for Grete is complicated: it is surely part of Kafka's conscious need for an intermediary in an affair the direction of which he was uncertain; but unconsciously it was also, perhaps, a way of introducing a sister-figure into his home, someone like Ottla. Yet the complexities go further: Grete was more than sister but less than lover. She becomes the "good scout," whom one can flirt with, fantasize about, even replace the wife with as a buffer against a marriage that can never be what one wants. Also, a good deal depends on exactly what happened between Kafka and Grete, to what extent, if any, they did become intimate. Grete, we know, insisted that Kafka return her letters if the marriage took place, and he refused, asserting he was not as yet married. There is the additional factor of the son Grete claimed was Kafka's, conceived, according to her, in the spring or early summer of 1914. But her very claim, which Max Brod believed, is belied by the fact that Kafka asked her along on nearly every meeting with Felice; if she was showing pregnancy, or they had become this intimate, Grete's "betrayal" of Felice, a bulging middle, would have been difficult to explain. Further, she would have needed considerable backup support to have found a home for the boy, while keeping the entire matter a secret, at the same time supporting herself and the son on a fairly meager salary.

The son must be discounted, but intimacy or the desire for it cannot be. Although analogies can be misleading, when Dickens married Catherine Hogarth, her sister, the angelic Mary, came to live with them, and Dickens used Mary not only as a buffer against a woman he was uncertain about but as a substitute wife in his fantasy life. To what extent Kafka did this we can only measure by the letters to Grete, which make her look suspiciously like a surrogate fiancée, or wife, whose real or fantasy presence would make marriage tolerable.

Interspersed between long letters to Grete are brief ones to Felice, demanding in hectoring tones that she break her silence and respond to his questions about himself and their future. The real arena, however, was in the correspondence now with Grete, unrelenting in March 1914, when steps leading to the unofficial engagement were being taken. Kafka was marching on several fronts here, and not unusually all his writing energies were going into his personal life, not literary work. With Grete now an indispensable confidante, he even flirted with the idea of "snapping her up," saying he would not write to her office for fear someone might open the letter and think he was from a rival firm trying to compete for her services.*

We also receive the impression that pursuit has so engaged Kafka it has given him a kind of energy he did not think he had. There is something hyperactive about his succession of plans involving not only letters and telegrams, but telephones, trains, and schedules, and planning or misplanning meetings. He is sending telegrams to Felice, asking her to reply by telegram; and he is telling Grete that if he doesn't go to Berlin and she doesn't have to go (on business) to Budapest, they will meet in Gmünd. He is bombarding the two women with mail, living out his fantasy of being an active man by way of words, creating excitement with language.

On March 18 Kafka chided Felice for not even considering him "worthy of a single word."[174] He says it is his duty to find her wherever she is. His telegram to her indicated that if she didn't come to Dresden, he would arrive in Berlin on Saturday, the twenty-first. But he went further and apparently asked his mother, although she denied it, to write Felice to please "answer Franz's letter by return for I [Julie Kafka] can see how upsetting your silence is to him." Sent on March 18, as part of the bombardment, Julie says her son must not know about this request, which has as letterhead HERMANN KAFKA, FANCY GOODS. It is unlikely that Frau Kafka would write unless her son requested it, and the maternal letter became part of the strategy to wear Felice down. On the next day, Kafka postponed seeing Grete in Gmünd but held out for a future meeting. "I want to present to you a decent and more or less mature person, not the kind of person I am at present."[175] Kafka apparently recognized the madness of his pursuit, the manic quality of his personal life, the sheer depression that lay beneath. Uncontrolled, he could survive in this period just before beginning *The Trial* only by attempting to control everything outside him.

On March 19, when it is difficult to see him doing any work in the office while he contemplated his personal situation, he wrote to Herr

---

*If we jump vast divides of culture and practice, we find, nevertheless, in George Meredith's *The Egoist* an amusing analogy to Kafka's strategy. In the Meredith, the egoistic Sir Willoughby, about to be rejected by Clara Middleton, even as he strenuously pursues her, has Laetitia Dale in the wings in the event Clara falls through. He needs someone, really anyone, to snap up, as it were.

and Frau Bauer. They had acquiesced to this mad courtship, but surely without insight into someone like their daughter's fiancé, and Kafka now wanted news of Felice. He indicates he has sent four letters and a telegram since the past Saturday, the fourteenth, five missives in five days, some to the apartment, some to the office, all unanswered. He asks if Felice is perhaps ill, bypassing the real nature of her silence, which was her extreme uncertainty about her raging suitor at the other end.

In some ways, Kafka feared he was becoming even more like Kierkegaard, with whom he identified as a friend and even a brother. The Danish philosopher and theologian had been engaged, when he was twenty-seven, although to a much younger girl (of seventeen), had procrastinated as he weighed his desire to marry against the impossibility of someone like himself marrying; had kept himself in a state of torture and uncertainty for about a year; and then had ended the engagement. Kafka's identification extended to Kierkegaard's recognition that he could not do his work as a married man; that he had to suffer loneliness to expiate some privately held guilt. Kafka saw clearly into Kierkegaard's dilemma with his brutal father, and with the Dane's formulation of the Abraham and Isaac episode in the Old Testament.

The result was a mind responding at a level close to madness. On March 21, with his detailing of their missed connections — his telegram arriving when Felice was out of the office, her telegram incorrectly addressed, his letter to her parents delayed in the mails, his receiving her telephone call when he could not leave his office — we find ourselves on the thin edge between lunacy and French farce. Her most recent letter, by express mail, was full of acrimony, according to Kafka, and he hoped her telephone call at the institute would relieve some of the bitterness. But, as in a Kafka fiction, he cannot hear her well on the phone because of the raucous noise all around him, ". . . and as it happened one of the directors, a tiresome man, was standing behind me cracking jokes; I could have kicked him."[176] We are now moving toward a Marx brothers mixup. Not being able to hear properly, he says, he could not take in the meaning of her words. He was further confused by his belief that his letter to the Bauers had already arrived, which it had not. "Thus on the telephone, apart from the fact that I couldn't hear properly, I couldn't help wondering what it was you wanted, and why in fact you had called me."[177] Added to this is his fear of the telephone. "I hurried out of the office, dashed to and fro in the rain, thought it over, everything seemed so hopeless, the outward journey I could have accepted gladly, but was so terrified of the return journey that I could not make up my mind to go." When he arrived home, he found a telegram from Herr Bauer saying Felice was well and had written. The Bauers were now engaged in this round robin, as well as Julie Kafka and, of course, Grete.

PART III: WIN A FEW, LOSE A FEW

Kafka had turned a skirmish into a full-scale conflict. He had Balkanized his personal life, and as it broke into fragments, the disparate elements were leading toward their own version of the "great war." Kafka now says he decided not to go to Berlin, and has sent telegrams to both Felice and her father. If nothing else, the postal services had dipped into a bonanza.

In this same letter of March 21, with all the accusations in letters and telegrams crisscrossing each other, Kafka steps up the comedic effect by denying vehemently that he would let his mother write "so as to win my wife for me. . . . I let my mother write so as to get direct from you confirmation of what you had said to me in the Tiergarten [during their walk in Berlin, when Felice was alternately angry and silent]."[178] Then Kafka becomes Kafkaesque, his twisted logic perfect preparation for the ambiguities and tortuous turns of *The Trial*. He takes Felice's uncertain words in the Tiergarten walk to mean she would accept him and in effect sacrifice herself "because you realize 'I cannot do without you.' Am I to accept human sacrifices, the sacrifice, moreover, of the dearest of human beings? Surely you would be bound to hate me if I did, but not only that: if what you say in your letter is strictly true, then you must hate me already. Surely you are bound to hate the one whom you do not love enough to be able to share his life willingly, but who by some means . . . can force you to share his life."[179] With written words, Kafka could twist and alter meaning, or catch her in paradox and dilemma and find openings he could never do with her person or voice present. Although we do not minimize his anguish — it was real and it was intense — we must see much of this as role-playing, in which he was honing his skills on the only person who would listen now that Brod and his other friends were married or engaged. Felice, at least, listened; whether she heard was another matter.

Kafka speaks of plans, that when he first returned from Riva, he had decided to give notice at the institute, since he felt he could not keep his job unless married. If he married, he says his job would make sense, "would become almost desirable."[180] He indicates that if he doesn't marry her — he assures her there is no one else — then his job will become loathsome. He was shifting his misery so that she became the repository, in a sense the chooser of which form of misery he should embrace: a loathsome job for a bachelor or a marriage that he has already said would keep him isolated and alone. Right after this, Kafka wrote to Grete (still on March 21) about his writing, and called her "the best, kindest, and sweetest creature."[181]

On March 22, Kafka reinforced the view that he saw Grete as an alternative. He says that if by tomorrow, Monday, he does not receive from Felice some "utterly inconceivable letter . . . then we, F. and I, are free."[182] He adds that only Felice will be capable of enjoying that free-dom, although someday he may too. But he did hear from Felice. He re-sponded, on March 25, with lines and images that should have warned her away for good, but which from his point of view were conciliatory and even abject. He says he cannot give her all the information about himself that she asks for: "I can give it to you, if at all, only when run-ning along behind you in the Tiergarten, you always on the point of vanishing altogether, and I on the point of prostrating myself; only when thus humiliated, more deeply than any dog, am I able to do it."[183]

He offers a declaration of love, to the limits of his strength, and in this she can trust him entirely. One must, however, question the depth of that "love" when in mid-May we read his discovery of "realms of gold" in Felice's mouth. Writing to Grete, whose own sensibilities he now rarely takes into account, Kafka first inquires about Grete's mouth, wondering who attends her teeth, even asking if she brushes after each meal. He attacks the "infernal dentists," who make one taste misery to the bitter end. But his real goal is Felice's mouth, not Grete's, and as we read his remarks we wonder how he could love a woman who so repels him. Felice had suffered further tooth decay and needed gold caps. "To tell the truth, this gleaming gold (a really hellish luster for this inappropriate spot) so scared me at first that I had to lower my eyes at the sight of F.'s teeth and the grayish yellow porcelain. After a time, whenever I could, I glanced at it on purpose so as not to forget it, to tor-ment myself, and finally to convince myself that all this is really true. In a thoughtless moment I even asked F. if it didn't embarrass her."[184] She said it didn't.

Kafka, however, was hardly through. He had to absorb her mouth and teeth into his more general quest:

> I now no longer wish these gold teeth gone, but that's not quite the right expression, for I actually never did wish them gone. It's rather that they strike me as almost becoming, most suitable, and — this is not unimpor-tant — a very definite, genial, ever-present, visually undeniable human blemish which brings me perhaps closer to F. than could a healthy set of teeth, also horrible in its way. — This is not a bridegroom defending his bride's teeth: rather, it's someone incapable of expressing what he wants to say, who at the same time wants to encourage you, if there is no other way.[185]

All of this was written to Grete, who would eventually show some of Kafka's letters to Felice, and with passages underlined. Jealousy on her part? Revenge? Desperation? Kafka had put her in a no man's land. He was in effect telling Grete that in order to love Felice he must over-come repulsion; that to get closer to her, he must come to terms with a mouth he finds as objectionable as meat. Back in March, Kafka was stepping up his suit, especially since Felice had opened a slight gap in her resistance. "I must tear myself out of my present life," he writes, "either by marrying you, or by giving notice and going away."[186] Just as he had turned Grete into someone decisive in his life, now he returned to Felice to make the momentous decision for his future. This had become opera buffa.

Grete was returning from Budapest to Vienna when Kafka wrote her on March 26 — interweaving letters between her and Felice. "Pest [where most Jews lived] is rather better [than Buda, where Gentiles lived], but crawling with Jews and a meeting place for tradesmen."[187] It was also crawling with animals, pigs and bullocks making up one-third of the population, and seemingly indistinguishable from Jews and tradesmen. The remark suggests, beyond obvious self-hatred on Kafka's part, an overwhelming loathing for everything Hermann Kafka was and is.* Leading up to his April 11–13 visit to Berlin and the unofficial engagement, Kafka reveled in being humiliated by Felice. Anxiety-ridden once again over telegrams that did not arrive when he expected, he recalled their last meeting. "Surely no human being can ever have been more profoundly humiliated at the hands of another than I was on that occasion by you, though certainly no one could have asked for it more than I did."[188] He says the humiliation did not derive from her rejection of him, which was her right, but from her silence or her vague answers, "revealing a dull hatred and antagonism which was so terribly convincing that even the memory of our good times was affected by it." Felice had apparently stiffened, and her silence and vague answers, if real, were part of a defense, an attempt to grapple with an onslaught that had become incomprehensible.

Kafka was an ever shifting target, as if dodging a sniper attack, and his desire for humiliation left Felice little choice but to accommodate him; at the same time, the need to provide the humiliation that made him return for more only made her more uncomfortable about a relationship she was uncertain of in the first place. Her desire to be engaged and married, on her terms, had run up against a situation and a fiancé that did not fit into any of her categories; and yet she was sufficiently intrigued (or desperate, at her age) to bend just enough for Kafka still to pursue. It was a losing battle in the overall war between them: where defenses proved not quite strong enough for the offense, and then, as fortunes shifted, where offense proved insufficiently strong against a renewed defense. They moved battle lines back and forth, until one or the other wearied, then broke off hostilities for a time, only to return to

---

*This expression of Jewish self-loathing was hardly unique. Theodor Herzl, a Hungarian and the voice for a Zionist state, showed comparable contempt for vulgar Jews, whether those from the bourgeoisie (merchants, tradesmen) or the Eastern European variety who remained on the margins. Not incidentally, both Herzl's and Kafka's fathers derived from shtetls, arriving at the big city (Budapest in Herzl's case) impoverished, with little education, and only their will and determination to guide them. Their educated sons quickly Germanized, exhibiting disdain for both trade and their origins.

the fray, each testing out the offenses and defenses of the other. The
Great War itself, only a short time ahead, would prove to be little different.

What engages us in Kafka's early April letters preceding his trip to
Berlin is the question of communications themselves. It is as though he
were trying to deconstruct or even circumvent the relationship by focusing instead on how it is carried on. In an April 5 letter to Grete, he
is full of details about his clumsiness with the telephone ("new to me
and which I hardly know how to deal with") and how when Felice's
calls come, on the second floor and he is on the fourth, he must first be
found, then must make his way down, only to arrive at the instrument
breathless, while in the background is a voluble crowd of people, or individuals only too eager to listen in. What he has created is a Kafkaesque atmosphere around something as simple as receiving a call or a
letter. The description of life at the institute suggests almost a complete breakdown of order once a telephone call comes in for Franz
Kafka. And this breakdown, apparently, is linked to his panic or hysteria that a call means distressing news, or else signals some loss of
control of that small world he has created around himself.

Included in this panic at the coming and going of missives is Kafka's effort to correct misinformation (the result of crisscrossing letters,
telegrams, and telephone calls), in some ways creating his own forms of
misinformation. He enjoys changing plans, so as to create the chaos
that can then justify his panic. Even as he moved toward the Easter Berlin visit, he changed his hour of arrival from noon on Saturday (April
11) to 6:51 Saturday evening, a matter of little moment except that it
left no time for any activities on Saturday itself and rushed conversation and decisions later on in the weekend. In writing Felice about this
(on April 7), he sent out mixed signals: asking her to meet him, but
then saying that since he might arrive with the Brods and Otto Pick as
well, she might find it embarrassing to meet them all at the station. He
had, in a sense, prepared himself for the disappointment of her not coming to the station, but left an opening for her to come, so that when she
failed, he had further ammunition against her neglect of him.

They were fencing for position. In his next letter, on the ninth,
Kafka spoke of each seeking his own advantage, "that I should want
your answers by letter, whereas you should want to give them or-
ally. . . . But have you considered carefully whether this actually is to
your advantage?"[189] He admits that "after all this time, after so much
running, we are still so very far apart." They sparred to avoid being cornered, seeking better ground on which to take a stand. The movement
toward engagement can be viewed in military terms: as engaging the
enemy, but before doing so seeking an advantageous position. Also,
choice of weapons is significant. Kafka definitely favored the written
word — here he is certain of eventual victory — Felice preferred the

spoken. As the engagement loomed, they moved toward open warfare, each trying to probe the other's weaknesses, each attempting to find a better battle position, not for a moral victory, disarmament, or an armistice, but for eventual triumph. Felice was fighting back in the only way she knew, which was to keep Kafka off balance, to disallow his heavy artillery from finding her position.

With this, Kafka went to Berlin and the engagement (still unofficial) went forward, with marriage planned for September. Julie Kafka wrote to Felice to congratulate her, and signed off as "your mother, Julie Kafka." It was, all in all, an oasis of a letter amidst so much rancor and barely suppressed hostility. Meanwhile, Kafka was pursuing a double course: his letters to Grete Bloch piled up daily after his trip to Berlin and the engagement. She became not less necessary but more so. While he wrote to Felice that he thanks God they don't live in the same town just now, he told Grete he wished he were holding her hand. He admits that in Berlin he did neither badly nor well, but acted with determination, all as part of the "inevitable necessity that existed for me, not for F." These are not the words of a man sure of himself, but the language of someone seeking a way out of a trap. He stressed to Grete that their relationship "which for me at least holds delightful and altogether indispensable possibilities, is in no way changed by my engagement or my marriage,"[190] repeating the idea of a joint visit, all three, to Gmünd.

The entanglements increase when Felice plans to come to Prague, on May 1, and Kafka asks Grete to be present. "Lovely, lovely, lovely!" he rhapsodizes at the idea; once more he suggests Gmünd as a possibility. "But I just don't know whether engaged couples can do that, non-engaged couples are far better off, they can do everything, and are not obliged to do anything."[191] Nearly every aspect of his immediate future is worked out with Grete in mind.

She requested the return of her letters, to which Kafka acquiesced but asked why she should think anything had changed between them. Grete apparently feared Felice would read her letters, and Kafka assured her that would not occur, playing innocent that their content could be offensive to his bride-to-be. The open warfare with Felice has now given way to skirmishes with Grete. It is possible, and on this we must speculate, that as Kafka measured Felice against Grete, he found he preferred Grete.

The September date for the marriage was set so that Felice could complete five years, in August, at her company, Carl Lindström, or else to give her the opportunity to back out. She came to Prague on May 1, to inspect an apartment Kafka had taken an option on, but she did not like its amenities, or lack of them. In the meanwhile, Kafka wrote Frau Bauer, addressing her as "Mother": the German *Mutter*, which he had said earlier never expresses, for a Jew, the sense of mother. Admitting imperfections, he says everyone has shortcomings. To Felice, he relied on one of his favorite images: "My letters to you are not so much letters as whimpers and baring of teeth."[192] Whose teeth he does not indicate! Kafka told her he arranged for the notice of the engagement in the *Prager Tagblatt*, for Friday, April 24: "Dr. Franz Kafka, Vice-Secretary of the Workers' Accident Insurance Institute, has become engaged to Miss Felice Bauer of Berlin." Her work designation is not indicated. He complains that her notice in the *Berliner Tageblatt* makes the reception sound "as though on Whitsunday F.K. is going to give a demonstration of looping the loop in a variety show."[193] Their styles were already clashing: Kafka as severe minimalist, almost withdrawing from the engagement in his spare wording of it; Felice, the maximalist, putting it forward without hesitation. Their views of apartments and furnishings would similarly clash: he wanted simple, even spartan quarters, she wanted more commodious, bourgeois appointments, what she felt a middle-class woman deserved.

Then in combining two seemingly disparate elements of naming, Kafka makes a critical point about his relationship to Grete Bloch. He writes to Grete of "The Metamorphosis," in which Gregor's sister is named Grete, and Kafka says he anticipated the living Grete; he adds she is the heroine, who in no way discredits the living Grete Bloch he is writing to. Then: "Later on, though, when the agony becomes too great, she withdraws, embarks on a life of her own, and leaves the one who needs her."[194] The parallelism he draws is remarkable, since she can no longer be expected to play the role he has designated for her. In fact, in the story, Grete not only embarks on a life of her own, she replaces the son in the family and develops into a mature young woman when Gregor withers away and dies. Kafka excuses himself: "At that time I hadn't begun to appreciate the name Grete, learned to do so only during the process of writing." Yet his hidden implication is that she is deserting him, leaving him to a life that reaches toward death; embarking on a life of her own, she has consigned him to hell — that is, to Felice. One day later (April 22), he tells Felice they should just get married: "Let's put an end to it."[195] He offers her that beautiful and expensive apartment, which she would find wanting.*

The pressure on Grete continues right up to the time of Felice's arrival in Prague. To Grete: "I still don't know how to express it, but sometimes it seems to me almost essential that you should be present when F. comes to my place for the first time." She declined but would come to the Bauers' house on June 1 for the party that would make the engagement official. Kafka was emotionally enervated when Felice

---

*If not that, then another that he has located, a three-room apartment at the top end of the Wenzelsplatz, but it is full of smells and crowds of children. His comment: "Life in this kind of place is almost inconceivable, except as a result of a curse" (May 12, 1914; *Diaries: 1914–1923*, p. 405).

came to Prague, as the engaged couple was dragged from one place to another, which included hunting for an apartment. He tells Grete the apartment he took is precisely the one he should not have taken, and the one he rejected was the one he liked. He turned it down when he heard piano playing in the next-door apartment. He says Felice has been in good spirits and felt at ease. But then a strange warning: "My family has taken a great liking to her, rather more than I like."[196] Such a deep hesitation came to the surface in a series of "disturbances" between him and Felice, finally ending the engagement in July. Its end approximated the beginning of the Great War.

All kinds of warning signs were evident. Kafka still insisted that once he was married Grete was to come to live with them "for some time." "We shall lead a pleasant life and, in order to test me, you shall hold my hand and I, in order to thank you, must be allowed to hold yours."[197] He communes with Grete through Grillparzer, when, under his directions, she finally went to the Vienna State Museum to see the Grillparzer Room. Kafka details what makes that nineteenth-century writer so sympathetic: "He was palpable misfortune personified," perhaps because he felt such hostility toward the woman he was engaged to.

This is followed by the extraordinary letter of the next day, in which Kafka marvels at the gold in Felice's teeth. But there is still another revelation in that letter. Kafka relates that he cut his thumb so badly that his blood filled a small bucket. He is treating it, he says, by natural methods, no plaster or bandage, so that although healing is much slower it is more effective — "no inflammation, no swelling, a veritable feast for the eye."[198] The image at the end cannot disguise Kafka's attempt to make Grete maternal.

As his letters proliferate, one every day in this immediate period following the engagement and preceding the party, Kafka lets go, with teeth and food a continuing obsession. Orality, digestion, processing have overtaken him: a world created between what was taken in and what could be retained, between what the teeth chew and what the intestines hold. This fluctuation between chewing and retention is transformed into fictional terms, in *The Trial*, as a tension between the need to gather information and subsequently to withhold it. Information is caught, so to speak, between teeth and digestive system, between mouth and anus. Meat is the most obvious villain: "If the deterioration of the teeth wasn't actually due to inadequate care, then it was due, as with me, to eating meat. One sits at table laughing and talking (for me at least there is the justification that I neither laugh nor talk), and meanwhile tiny shreds of meat between the teeth produce germs of decay and fermentation no less than a dead rat squashed between two stones."[199] He adds, "Meat is the one thing that is so stringy that it can be removed only with great difficulty, and even then not at once and

not completely, unless one's teeth are like those of a beast of prey —
pointed, set wide apart, designed for the purpose of tearing meat to
shreds."

Teeth, meat, tearing and shredding: these images of a primitive life
suggest deep anger and hostility. The anger is directed at women and
transmitted through women: Felice and Grete, but also Kafka's mother
as the provider of food. Since food is of such great ceremonial importance in Jewish families, as well as the focus of an obsessive nourishment, it becomes a central symbol for Kafka. By "denying" food, by
focusing on teeth as barbaric remnants, by stressing the shredding of
meat, he expressed an unconscious force, a hatred untouchable by reason. He had already expressed such hatreds and resentments directly
toward his father, but with his mother he had to be more circumspect.
While his behavior and words toward her were correct, he belied the
words with emblems of anger centered on the digestive process, which
is, after all, a traditional concern of mothers.

Kafka's letter to Felice of May 19 for once has him sounding like a
man about to enter into marriage: he talks of plans for their apartment,
furniture, the possible arrival in Berlin of Ottla, his favorite sister. He
sounds domesticated, but does sign off coldly with "kindest regards,"
not love. Yet the tone lacks the usual contrasts of surface control
and underlying anger, and he does not seem overly concerned with
supervising her life. There is, if we continue our martial metaphors, a
kind of truce; both warring parties are exhausted and holding back,
resting, waiting for the moment when they can once again ride out to
joust.

Health becomes a preoccupation — not that Kafka neglected it before, but now that his marriage is approaching, he becomes obsessed.
To Grete he speaks of "the abomination of contemporary medicine,"[200]
a standard line with him, and his "conviction of the ugliness of the fur
stole" she wore. The fur is "a flattened object" which makes him ill at
ease.[201] The fur stole, or shawl, seems to be linked to health, as though
he were somehow placing a curse on it that was causing Grete's insomnia and general ill health. Her sickness, however, was not fur related,
but linked to her sense of exclusion, regardless of Kafka's offers for her
company in his new home. It is impossible to measure how much her
resentment led her, later, in 1940, to claim that she had had a child by
Kafka, conceived during or around this very time. To what extent did
she blur fact and fantasy, or to what extent did she need the idea of bearing Kafka's child as a way of staking her claim?

It is unclear to what degree Kafka observed these subtle fluctuations of feeling, although in his presentation, shortly, of Joseph K. he
seems to have transferred his personal life into a universal fiction. This
makes us believe he was aware of far more than he let either Felice or
Grete know about their vulnerability, humiliation, and the threats of

authority. Joseph K. would appear to be, in part at least, an amalgam of many of the attitudes Kafka was working through in his correspondence with Felice and Grete and his awareness of the cross-currents threading through their response to each other.

Yet despite the maneuvering, there is real intimacy between Kafka and Felice's friend. When Kafka wrote Grete on the eve of his departure for Berlin (on May 29), for the engagement party she was also to attend, his letter is full of unspoken sentiments. He says ambiguously, "My luggage will consist of insomnia, a queasy stomach, a twitching head, and pains in the left leg, but it won't weigh much compared to the pleasure of the reunion"[202] — with Felice or with Grete? He follows this with an early June letter, after the party, asserting that Grete "cannot be fully aware of what you mean to me, yet the little of which you are aware must make you realize that in a situation which you don't by any means wholly recognize but which emotionally you are able to share with me to the full, you probably do just about everything one human being can do for another."[203] He closes by offering to "kiss her dear hand," a bit of Czech gallantry with unspoken feeling behind it, or else manipulative intent.

In subsequent letters, and during a pause in the correspondence with Felice (or because of the loss of his letters for this period), Kafka confesses things about himself one would say only to a wife or mistress. Grete is close to him in ways Brod could never be. "I really don't know how I, being what I am, can bear the responsibility of marriage."[204] He says his is a marriage "erected on the woman's fortitude." He asks if it is bound to be "a crooked edifice," and feels it "will collapse and in so doing rip the foundation from the earth." He has, in a sense, excluded his fiancée from his view of marriage and predicted its demise well before the event.

Not unusually, this "crooked edifice" would collapse in July in the Askanische Hof confrontation in Berlin, traumatizing Kafka, although he was quite responsible. He pleads with Grete for understanding: "Each of us has his own way of emerging from the underworld, mine is by writing."[205] And: "I am far more likely to achieve peace of mind through writing than the capacity to write through peace." He adds with typical circuitry of purpose that "I surely ought to have known that I am visible and alive only when I suppress as much as possible all things concerning myself." Here he confesses how he lives by withholding, how repression and suppression characterize his perception of himself, and how this Czech-German Jew living in Prague reaches across to Berggasse 19 in Vienna.

He speaks also of how ghosts have dominated his life since childhood. The passage shows how his fiction has taken secondary place to his letters, where he squanders fine phrases such as the following:

388

FRANZ KAFKA

If one has no children, it's one's ghosts that make one realize it, and they do it all the more thoroughly. I know that when I was young I tried to lure them out, they barely showed themselves. . . . Later on they did appear, only now and then, always as exalted visitors, one had to bow to them though they were still very small. . . . But when they did come they were seldom fierce, one couldn't be very proud of them, at best they pounded on one like the lion cub on the bitch; they did bite. . . . Later, however, they grew bigger, they came and stayed at will, delicate birds' backs turned into the backs of monumental giants, they came in through every door, forcing those that were shut; huge, bony ghosts they were, namely in their multitude; a single ghost could be fought, but not all those by which one was surrounded.[206]

When he is writing, the ghosts are benevolent; when not writing, demons. And they came so close, pressed so tightly, he has literally to hold them off. He asks forgiveness for complaining, this newly engaged man, saying that everything is bearable. And "if the pain remains, the days do change, the expression of the pain changes, one's powers of resistance change, and then one is carried along more or less alive on the waves of change."[207] This is a lovely philosophy of life for a bachelor, but for an engaged or a married man it leaves little space for the woman. Ghosts everywhere, pain, change, the individual's ability to bear it all: Kafka was right on the edge of *The Trial*.

In the June 11 letter to Grete, Kafka in effect tells her that marriage for him is impossible; and, implicitly, he seeks her understanding of this strange maneuver that has found him, a totally unsuitable man, bound to a woman, that exotic apparition in Berlin.

Owing to circumstances as well as to his own temperament, a completely antisocial man in an indifferent state of health hard to determine at the moment, excluded from every great soul-sustaining community on account of his non-Zionist (I admire Zionism and am nauseated by it),* nonpracticing Judaism;† the most precious part of his nature continually and most agonizingly upset by the enforced labor of his office — a man of this kind, certainly under the deepest inner compulsion, decides to get married — to undertake, in other words, the most social of acts. For a man of this kind, that strikes me as no mean venture.[208]

These words form a kind of "life sentence," in which Kafka has put himself completely on the line, brutally open, using Grete as a means of thinking aloud. He is struck by the absurdity of his existence, but not in any Kierkegaardian sense. Kafka's awareness of dread contained no

---

*This mixture of admiration and nausea did not prevent him from attending, as mentioned earlier, a September 8 session of the Zionist Congress, and to make a commitment of a sort, in joining the Association of Jewish Officials (*Verein jüdischer Beamten*), a newly formed organization with strong Zionist leanings.
†Nonpracticing to the end of his life, but increasingly interested in and fascinated by Eastern European Jewry; ready to learn Hebrew; and identifying sufficiently with historical Judaism to want to emigrate to Palestine.

sudden movement toward faith. He had to remain poised on the edge, like Sisyphus, another of his role models, at the moment the huge boulder is about to roll back. He seemed to enjoy the suffering but could not contain it, and he could not quite define it. He sensed his health was deteriorating, and possibly he was suffering from a precondition of tuberculosis, a kind of mental enervation. "This state of health is also deceptive, it deceives even me; at any moment I am liable to be assailed by the most detailed and precise imaginings and invariably on the most inconvenient occasions. Undoubtedly an enormous hypochondria, which however has struck so many and such deep roots within me that I stand or fall with it."[209] Yet hypochondria cannot explain everything. Kafka had become so ultrasensitive about himself and others that he could not ignore signals from his body and general health that someone else might dismiss. The hypochondria might have been an intensifier; once he picked up these signals, real or imagined, he sensed more general poor health than the original impulses warranted. Kafka made himself so "representative" because he found in that blending of inner and outer a seamless existence that gave him interpretive powers.

He was seeing more of Ernst Weiss, who, he says, was pulling him "no more than an inch, out of this miserable hole of an office."[210] Weiss has been until now somewhat peripheral in Kafka's life, but he was an important presence. Born in 1882, a year before Kafka, he seemed far older, more mature, more settled. A surgeon and an author (*The Gallery*), he appeared at peace with himself as an assimilated Jew. Yet Weiss was not quite what he seemed. He suffered from tuberculosis at the time Kafka met him (he died in 1940), which gave them questions of health in common. When they met, Weiss had decided to forgo medicine for a literary career; far more able than Kafka to make decisions, he decided he had to confront each personal dilemma with a choice. He vigorously opposed Kafka's relationship with Felice — he would be present at the July breakup in Berlin — on the grounds that marriage to her would distract his new friend from a literary career. His forthright, often demanding manner finally led to a break with Kafka, not because they discovered they had little in common but because Kafka found Weiss's decisiveness incompatible with his own hesitations and uncertainty. Yet in 1914 — the break came during the war — Kafka leaned on Weiss, at a time when the situation with Felice was overwhelming him.

We have emphasized Kafka's sense of a "precondition"; he was a consumptive without consumption. To Grete: "I am beginning to fear that it's all a delusion behind which there lies in wait the real core of the real misfortune, of which I know nothing directly, only by intolerable threats."[211] He saw, with increasing clarity, the huge mistake he had made in carrying through the engagement, and he was writing to Grete, in letters no longer extant, about undefined and undetermined feelings. These letters to Grete came *before* the actual confrontation on July 12 in the Askanische Hof in Berlin, with Felice, Kafka, Grete, Weiss, and Felice's sister, Erna, in attendance, and make the break seem inevitable. We also know that Grete showed passages or entire letters to Felice, some of them underscored by Kafka when he wished to make a particular point about their incompatibility and his general unsuitability. It has become a drama worthy of eighteenth-century court intrigue, a version of *Les Liaisons Dangereuses* with its undercurrents of betrayal and ambiguous motives.

The "war" between Kafka and Felice, in the days before the break, had shifted its grounds to Kafka and Grete. He responds to Grete's charge that she perceives him not as Felice's fiancé "but as a threat to F."[212] He says she demands for Felice "a man who is her equal in various respects," and apparently she feels he does not meet that qualification. Since she has revealed parts of Kafka's letters to Felice, he feels the "two against one" has altered, and he is not the one. He excuses himself on the grounds of health: "I am dying of exhaustion," possibly more mental than physical. At this writing, he had turned thirty-one, and, to his dismay, he was in effect little different from who he was at twenty-five or twenty-six.

Against a background of Frau Kafka's writing to Frau Bauer, and the expectations of the two families, Kafka went to Berlin for a showdown with Felice. The July 12 meeting at the hotel was devastating for Kafka, less a meeting than a shootout, a trauma that in every way prepared him for the victimization of Joseph K. in *The Trial*.*

We now skip to the fall of the same year, 1914. Kafka heard from Grete that there was still some chance for the marriage, and in his subsequent letter to Felice, in late October/early November, we gain some details of that disastrous July 12 meeting. Kafka tries to explain how he suffers from his work. "You were unable to appreciate the immense power my work has over me; you did appreciate it, but by no means fully. As a result you were bound to misinterpret everything that my worries over my work, and only my worries over my work, produced in me in the way of peculiarities which disconcerted you."[213] He confesses all: "Moreover, these peculiarities (odious peculiarities, I admit, odious above all to myself) manifested themselves more with you than with anyone else. . . . You see, you were not only the greatest friend, but at the same time the greatest enemy, of my work. . . . Thus, though fundamentally it loved you beyond measure, equally it had to resist you with all its might for the sake of self-preservation."

Then he moves into the Hof scene. His attempt to justify his si-

---

*A brief diary entry on July 29, 1914, mentions a Joseph K. and there is a foreshadowing of the novel to come, although the entry does not lead us to expect the complications of *The Trial*.

lence becomes complicated. He was disconcerted initially by the presence of other people, especially Grete, who had shown Felice passages in his letters which discredited her. Further, the presence of Felice's sister, Erna, was another abrasive, since it loaded the odds against him. He explains his silence there not as an act of spite but as the result of having nothing to say. He thought he might save the situation by saying something startling but could think of nothing. Confronted by his stony silence, Felice began to make remarks that, Kafka says, "ought to be impossible for one person to say to another."[214]

In attempting an explanation of his silence and indecisiveness, he offers up "two selves" wrestling with one another. This is not a new defense but one consistent with his contention that what you see with him is not what you get, and he must convince Felice that what she gets is still not in clear focus for her. "One of them," he says, "is very much as you would wish him to be, and by further development he could achieve the little he lacks in order to fulfill your wishes. None of the things you reproached me with at the Askanische Hof applied to him."[215] That "self" is the bourgeois one Felice can relate to and which really tries to deal with society. "The other self, however, thinks of nothing but work, which is his sole concern; it has the effect of making even the meanest thoughts appear quite normal; the death of his dearest friend would seem to be no more than a hindrance — if only a temporary one — to his work." Kafka excuses his self-absorption by saying he compensates for such appearances of meanness by the fact he suffers for his work. "These two selves are locked in combat, but it is no ordinary fight. . . . The first self is dependent upon the second; he would never, for inherent reasons never, be able to overpower him." The conflict conjures up the battleground of "Description of a Struggle," one of his earliest fictions: "On the contrary, he is delighted when the second succeeds, and if the second appears to be losing, the first will kneel down at his side, oblivious of everything but him." Then in a trickily worded resolution, he adds, "And yet they are locked in combat, and yet they could be yours; the trouble is that they cannot be changed unless both were to be destroyed."

Kafka then runs through his busy schedule, here used as a justification for his lack of choice, given the way everything is arrayed against his doing his work. He is now staying in his oldest sister's apartment; her husband is in the army, and she and her child are living with the elder Kafkas. But the weakness of his argument is that a good deal of his time is taken up with traveling to his parents' apartment for dinner, followed by a long trip back to Elli's place. If he had broken with dinner at the Kafkas', which he detested, he could have found far more free time; furthermore, he ate a long lunch at home also. According to his figures, and this is part of his defense, he has only three hours to himself, although he works normally for only six and a half. With his defense in place, he is ready to proceed to other matters, failing to see, apparently, that he has given irrefutable proof of why the relationship must end, not continue.

Kafka mentions Felice's letters going back to her time in Frankfurt, when she indicated "hatred" or "dislike" of his way of life, as well as some hesitancy about his concern for her, which she rightly saw as a form of control. Yet he feels he has to protect his work and his right to live the way he does, thus bringing the differences back to the beginning, where they cannot be resolved. He agrees that what she wanted was perfectly reasonable: a pleasant and pleasantly furnished apartment, a standard of life commensurate with that of people like her and him. She wanted it in its "entirety," he accuses, including a synagogue ceremony, which he balked at and wanted canceled. And then he homes in:

> But your whole idea about the apartment, what does it show? It shows that you agree with the others, not with me. . . . These others, when they get married, are very nearly satiated, and marriage to them is but the final, great, delicious mouthful. Not so for me, I am not satiated, I haven't started a business that's expected to expand from one year of marriage to another; I don't need a permanent home from whose bourgeois orderliness I propose to run this business — not only do I not need this kind of home, it actually frightens me.[216]

In trying to placate Felice, Kafka has managed to agree with every one of her objections. He is so hungry for his work it makes him feel limp: *The Trial* was now on his desk, a story of such desperation its contours must have blinded him to everything else. Marriage, then, on her terms of bourgeois comfort would finalize a condition that was already suffocating him. He contemplates the two of them in isolation, some place untainted by incursions into his imagination. "For I loved you in your true nature, and feared it only when it met my work with hostility."[217] But the perfection he seeks is completely on his terms; if he were Adam, she would be Eve, and he would dictate that they never eat the forbidden fruit. As Kafka rambles on, and he has lost consecutive thought in his efforts at a defense, he suggests, as his vision of Eden, some perfect place, outside Prague, where they could live together, he would write, and she would, somehow, fit herself into his antic schedule. It is, as he knows well, even as he is writing about it, an impossible vision, the very kind of happiness he would on other occasions mock.

If we return to the period just after the July 12 disengagement, Kafka tells Grete he hopes to remain friends with her, even though he feels somewhat betrayed by her role. He indicates he sees things clearly, and he thinks Felice and she also do. As the mothers write back and forth to each other in commiseration, Kafka pecks away at Grete, chiding her for sitting in judgment on him. Julie Kafka is also sitting in judgment, on her son. She tells Frau Bauer she hoped an intelligent, clever woman like Felice would be able to change him but that now all her hopes are dashed. Julie, apparently, had no idea what Kafka stood for, or what he was going to do with his life; she believed the old saw that a clever, determined woman can wind a man around her finger and alter his habits. She also communicates that business is very poor, hardly existent — the shop is open, but no customers appear. By this time, World War I was a reality.

After the futile attempt at rapprochement in late October or early November, when Kafka tried to justify himself, the correspondence thins out. They did meet on January 24, in Bodenbach (Podmokly in Czech). Kafka used the meeting, for which Felice had done most of the traveling, to try to justify himself. In his letter he says he can write far more effectively, because she cannot upset him as she does when they are together. He admits "that our time together was not pleasant." Not only this time but virtually all of their time: "We may not have spent a single minute together entirely free of strain."[218] Felice had herself admitted that it was impossible to be close to Kafka, that she would like to help him, but they remain separated. Kafka agrees that this is a fact of their lives.*

If we stand back for a moment, we see that the greatness of this correspondence as a grand "fiction" lies in the way Kafka can decenter himself. He slips away from any clear focus, and even when he is explaining himself to Felice, he slides off. His approach is to avoid any interpretation that focuses him, in the same way his fiction eludes clear interpretation. Kafka's art was not to reshape life into fiction, but to understand himself so well that he could use fiction or letters to avoid clear-cut understanding, to allow the text to be itself. What Felice could not bear was that very avoidance of interpretation in the person

---

*In the January 24 diary entry, he commented on the brief stay with Felice in Bodenbach, indicating that it was impossible for them ever to unite, but that was something he dare not say either to her or to himself. "Each of us silently says to himself that the other is immovable and merciless. I yield not a particle of my demand for a fantastic life arranged solely in the interest of my work; she, indifferent to every mute request, wants the average: a comfortable home, an interest in my part in the factory, good food, bed at eleven, central heating; sets my watch — which for the past three months has been an hour and a half fast — right to the minute" (*Diaries: 1914–1923*, pp. 111–12). Kafka grants she is right but finds other things that grate, such as her correcting his "bad German" and calling his two older sisters "shallow." "She doesn't ask after the youngest at all, she asks almost no questions about my work, and has no apparent understanding of it." Their stay together sounds like two people already divorced for incompatibility: "We were alone two hours in the room. Round about me only boredom and despair. We haven't had a single good moment together during which I could have breathed freely. With F. I never experienced (except in letters) that sweetness one experiences in a relationship with a woman one loves — such as I had in Zuckmantel and Riva — only unlimited admiration, humility, sympathy, despair and self-contempt." These seemed good reasons for him to pursue the relationship.

he presented to her. What Kafka was heading for Rilke described in "Autumn Day" ("Herbsttag"):

> Who has no house now will not have one.
> Who is now alone will so remain:
> sitting, reading, writing long letters;
> restlessly wandering the avenues,
> back and forth, while brown leaves blow.

Kafka not coincidentally was under enormous strain in the early months of 1915: he was working on *The Trial*, writing several stories, toiling at the institute, spending afternoons at the asbestos factory, with his brother-in-law away in the army; plus he needed to find a place of his own, and, of course, there was the war itself, which he wanted to volunteer for. His life was beginning to lose coherence. Perhaps this loss of direction led him to be even more brutally honest with himself than before. He tells Felice his grave fault is that he makes no effort to convince and quarrel; as a result, they have no apparent quarrels, while he feels tremors that "keep running between us as though someone were continually cutting the air between us with a sword."[219] She too suffers in silence, and it is their mutual silence that makes them so merciless, so ungiving toward each other. He holds out little hope for a rapprochement, although underlying his words is some dream of a miracle, he says, that will enable them to become more compatible. He admits to winning the skirmishes but losing the war.

Two weeks later, however, he was having another go, trying to explain his position, which had become desperate. With brother-in-law Karl Hermann joined in the army by his brother, Kafka found himself responsible not just for the factory but for the warehouse too. He was frantic about his work. "All I want is peace, but the kind of peace that is beyond people's understanding."[220] He indicates he has a new room, on Bilekgasse, where his sister Valli Pollak lived. Yet even the possession of his own place brings with it problems: a quiet room has its noises, as he listens for doors opening and shutting, or else whispered words, the clock itself in his room. What he desires is absolute quiet, in the middle of Prague, and when that becomes unachievable, he waits for the slightest sounds and transforms them into bomb drops. He is so insistent on his needs he lays himself bare to Felice; she would suspect from this that children are out of the question. He stops the striking of the clock: "The half-hours are proclaimed with a deafening if melodious sound." But then he hears coughing from a lodger; the landlady apologizes for the whispering and promises to hang a heavy curtain on his door to deaden sound. Yet he plans to give notice on Monday next. He measures his misery against real misery and demands that his be recognized as real. "Don't laugh, F., don't look upon my suffering as despicable; no doubt many people are suffering nowadays, and the cause of their suffering is something more than whispers in the next room; at best, however, they are fighting for their existence, or rather for the bonds connecting their existence to that of the community, and so do I, and so does everyone. Accompany me with your good wishes when I look for another room."[221] By insisting on *his* needs, no matter how negligible they appeared in the larger order of things, Kafka was insisting on what made it possible for him to do his writing. However valiant his defense of himself, though, it became clear that Felice could not accept whispers and a striking clock as menaces tantamount to forms of extinction.

That he should be particularly sensitive now can surely be explained by the intensity he brought to the manuscript of *The Trial*.* He tells Felice on March 3 that he cannot dispatch the manuscript because it has not been typed or printed. Headaches were racking him. Although his landlady had expected him to stay until he died, "without being more specific about the date," he gave notice and moved to Langegasse 705/18 (now number 16), the house called Zum goldenen Hecht (At the Sign of the Golden Pike), with a fine view of Prague and the Moldau River. Felice had invited Kafka to Berlin, not for a visit but to stay, and her query about what will happen to them opens him up to speculation. He asks if there is a future for them in Prague; if not, it won't be the fault of Prague. He foresees the early end of the war, without too much destruction, and this will make conditions "quite favorable." But his own war is now with noise, which he hears everywhere, and all directed at him. He lies in his new room waiting for the sounds that will disrupt him, drive him close to insanity; his needs are unreconciled with those of others.

He says his new room is ten times noisier than the other but pleasant in other respects. The noise: "Someone right above my head in a studio (empty, not even let!!) stamps around all day in heavy boots and has installed some kind of pointless noise-machine to simulate the sound of a game of nine-pins. A heavy ball is rolled at great speed along the full length of the ceiling, lands in a corner, and comes slowly bumping back."[222] The landlady, who also hears the noise, Kafka says, tries to deny its existence, asserting that the studio is empty. Lying beyond Kafka's ultrasensitivity to noise is his revulsion at life in his family: his rejection of their noise; his further denial of family life altogether, everything noise is connected to, including the most repellent of noises, that indicating sexual activity between his parents. His numerous references to their grunts and groans, their card playing, their dirty bedding, the sheet stains he discerns are all linked to his effort to iso-

---

*Like Kafka's other stories and longer works, *The Trial* will be taken up in detail in later chapters, once we return to his "other" life, that outside Felice and their "great war."

late himself from them and their noise. That perfect silence Kafka sought is not disconnected from death itself, but death as he interprets it: a condition that through imaginative work enables one to become renewed. As he moves deeply into *The Trial*, he seeks death and burial as the sole locale in which he can work. We recall his speaking to Felice of a dungeonlike setting for his desk, with food brought to a far-off door. He was, in effect, burying himself in a grave so as to engage his talent.

When he writes next, on April 5, 1915, building up toward a meeting with Felice and Grete in Switzerland at Whitsun in May, he is back at home, in his own room. But the noise from outside sounds as if "they are unloading timber; one can hear a tree trunk being released from the truck, then it is raised, sighs like a living thing, then a crash! It falls and is received into the reverberations of the whole infernal concrete building."[223] Even closer, the elevator purrs and echoes through the empty attic rooms; he hears housemaids scurrying above; below is a nursery in which the children run around, scream; doors open and screech, are slammed shut; the nursemaid in the nursery shouts to enforce quiet. When the day nursery closes, people nearby chatter as if at a party. By ten o'clock, however, it is over, and Kafka says he indulges in "a most wonderful calm." His solution is to send to Berlin for some Oropax, "a kind of wax wrapped in cotton wool." He says it is messy and does not even shut out the noise but muffles it. He cites Strindberg's *By the Open Sea*, in which the hero suffers from a similar complaint and slides sleeping balls into his ears to find peace and quiet; but such balls, Kafka admits, do not exist except in Strindberg's imagination. What he fails to take into account is that a description of wax wrapped in messy cotton wool thrust into his ear would not sound too appetizing to a twenty-seven-year-old woman. Only a mother might find it exciting information.

Kafka makes one of his mentions of the war, indicating that Elli's husband (Karl Hermann) is in the Carpathians, outside the danger zone, whereas Valli's husband (Josef Pollak) was wounded, restored to health, sent back to the front, and is now recovering from sciatica. This takes Kafka back to his own lack of service, but he says his turn may yet come. Some factors, unspecified, prevent him from volunteering, but he resolves that by saying hidden factors always prevent him from doing anything. He repeats he is not in conflict with his surroundings, only with himself. After two weeks, on April 20, Kafka writes to draw a circle around himself and Felice, to demonstrate to her how impossible it all is; at the same time, he asks to see her at Whitsun (May 23–24), a meeting he cannot handle without the presence of Grete. He chides Felice as an intelligent woman who, while seeing other things clearly, cannot understand how things in Prague could be made "possible and right." He speaks of her and himself in the third person: "Today he loves her no less, though finally he may have learned his lesson: that it isn't as simple and easy as all that to win her, even if she agrees."[224]

As the time approached for their proposed meeting, in Bohemian Switzerland, Kafka tried to find some way into their problems, even calculating not the differences themselves but the "distribution of weight" within the relationship. Even so, he admits he cannot shed the complications, anxieties, and diverse considerations that attend him: "It is a burden I am forced to bear, I shiver with discontent."[225] Having traveled with Elli to visit Karl Hermann in Hungary, Kafka has wound his way back via Budapest, only to discover that Felice was probably there on the same day, a matter of missed communications.

In subsequent letters, he assumed a strange third-person character, writing to Felice using "he" or "F.'s fiancé" to indicate himself. The shift from "I" to "he" when writing to his former fiancée suggests not only a shift in perspective but also a deep change within Kafka; his "he" indicates he can stand outside himself, disengaged, dissociated from himself, and can perceive Felice and himself as objects. He is an "other." This dissociation would suggest some kind of breakdown, or else a blending of the letters with his fictional efforts. He has become, if we extend the analogy, Joseph K. of *The Trial*, an object for Kafka to write about even when the words apply directly to him. As he goes from his fiction to the letters, he is not distinguishing which is person and which is persona. This shift to writing about himself in the third person came in and around the May meeting in Switzerland with Felice, and it may signal a deep alienation or splitting of himself as a way of grappling with his predicament.

The usage is disconcerting: "The other day you [Felice] asked me a number of fantastic questions about F.'s fiancé. I am better able to answer them now, for I observed him carefully on the return journey in the train."[226] He says that since it was so crowded they both had to sit in one seat, and from his observation he could see that her fiancé "is really in bondage to F." Kafka goes on about how her fiancé cherished her memory. In the next letter (postmarked May 27), "he says he is alarmed. He says he stayed there [in Switzerland] too long. Two days had been too much." In June Kafka joined Felice in Karlsbad, and in August he resumed the third-person narrative: "I spoke to him quite frankly, as you would have done, and he also answered me frankly."[227] He then carries on a dialogue between questioner (himself) and "him" (also himself). The dialogue is less remarkable for what it says than for his division of himself, as in Diderot's *Rameau's Nephew*, into both inquisitor and responder, with strange psychological overtones. He has become someone who can step in and out of the relationship, offering her, in effect, two Kafkas, one reasonable, inquiring, thoughtful, the other uncertain and undecided about who he is and what he wants. We cannot call him schizoid in any clinical sense, for he was carrying on well — working, meeting his obligations, writing his stories and longer fictions, managing his life within social terms, and, in fact, discovering a way in which to deal with his ambiguous feelings toward her.

From a biographical point of view, it is difficult to determine whether Kafka's division of himself into "I" and "he" is a sign of terrible schisms or his way of withdrawing from the relationship by objectifying himself. Interpretation simplifies what are several levels of response. The division of self can be viewed as a clear warning he was on the edge of disintegration, that his very personality was shattering, or else as a literary device by which he could handle the relationship on more solid ground. The effect, in either instance, is eerie.

> These are his words, and his appearance confirms his state of mind. He is delirious, utterly uncontrolled and distracted. At the moment there seem to be but two possible remedies for him — not in the sense that they can wipe out the past, but possibly guard him against future happenings. One would be F.; the other, military service. He has been deprived of both. When all is said and done, I would not disagree with him about not writing. Does his writing not cause more sorrow than his silence?[228]

All the uses of *he, him,* and *his* refer to Kafka. It is signed "Affectionately, Franz."

By the end of the year (see the letter postmarked December 5, 1915) he is back as "I," but then the complaints pile up. By this time, since the August letter, he has resumed writing his diary, which for him meant letters to Felice were not so urgent, and he had completed one of his more important short pieces, "Before the Law," which Kurt Wolff published in December. He felt he had done little but drift, although the starting up of the diary was an important sign of his return to introspection. It also anticipated the conclusion to the Franz and Felice great war. On December 5 he wrote to Felice: "I believe that even the true voice of an angel from heaven could not raise my spirits; so low have I sunk. If you were to ask why, I could offer little more than extraneous explanations; even mentioning my insomnia and headaches would be extraneous — however grave and real these are."[229] He asks for Erna Bauer's address so he can send on "The Metamorphosis."* And he closes this attempt at rapprochement with the following farewell lines: "Once again, even now, I could bring you nothing but disappointment, monster of insomnia and headaches that I am." He says he will not leave Prague for his vacation but will, like Gregor Samsa, spend it "creeping along the old familiar walks."

In a strange sequence of events, Kafka came into the money given for the Fontane Prize. The original recipient of it was Carl Sternheim,

---

*"The Metamorphosis" was first published in October 1915, in magazine format, and then by Kurt Wolff in Leipzig in November, as part of a double volume in a series called *Der jüngste Tag* (appropriately, *Doomsday*).

who received it in 1915 for three stories, "Busekow," "Napoleon," and "Schuhlin." A common friend, Franz Blei, suggested Kafka for the prize money, which Sternheim, already wealthy, did not need. Kafka was, of course, pleasantly surprised. But it did not appreciably relieve his personal gloom, not about the war, or about the huge losses suffered by the German and Austrian forces (which he supported), but about himself. As he moved into early 1916, his letters to Felice, somewhat infrequent now, reopen negotiations by way of his presentation of an abject self. He makes a halfhearted offer to live eventually in Berlin but then describes himself as "a man consumed by insomnia and headaches."[230]

He says he has felt as though a tight net with thin, cutting cords were clamped on his head. "So it's as this kind of man, Felice, that I shall be coming to Berlin after the war. My first task will be to crawl into some hole and examine myself. . . . Needless to say, the living man in me is hopeful, which is not surprising. The thinking man, however, is not."[231] He depicts himself as "a naughty child, a madman, or something of the kind." He says in his next missive, "Are not my letters more terrible than my silence? . . . I would like to open a trap door under my feet, and allow myself to disappear to a place where the wretched remnants of my remaining powers could be preserved for some future freedom."[232]

These are, clearly, images of self that are already appearing in his work. They are in several respects variations of Gregor Samsa, a transformational, crawling figure, so lowly he, or it, is beyond humanity. He emphasizes his unworthiness, which is now not only a strategy for engaging Felice but an inescapable part of the Kafka landscape. He is what he was becoming or had already become in his fiction. But these warnings to Felice are merely a warmup for a fuller treatment. As we read this desperate, tortured, despairing record of his daily life,[233] we cannot escape one salient fact: that the precondition of tuberculosis was now clearly present, that it was intensifying what was already ripping Kafka to pieces, and that it was not too different from stages of the illness itself, which was discovered the following year, in August 1917, with his first major hemorrhage. Yet behind this appalling outpouring of personal malaise is a mute appeal to Felice: to understand and forgive him, reconsider him as a lost child, bring him back from the lower depths.

"For I am desperate, like a caged rat, insomnia and headaches tearing at me; how I get through the days is quite beyond description. To be free from the office is my only possible salvation, my primary desire."[234] He cites the institute, the factory, imagined and real obstacles, admitting he hasn't the strength to break free. The early stages of tuberculosis would certainly involve a lowering of will or inner determination, a loss of forward-looking reason. "It's not that I'm afraid of life outside the office; the fever that heats my head day and night comes from lack of freedom; and yet as soon as my chief begins to complain that the department will collapse if I leave . . . then I cannot do it, the conditioned official in me cannot do it. And so these nights, these days, go on."

His own indecision and uncertainty have been reinforced by her inability to recognize his suffocation in Austrian officialdom, as he puts it. He accuses her of being unable to judge these elements in him. "Instead we went to buy furniture in Berlin for an official in Prague. Heavy furniture which looked as if, once in position, it could never be removed. Its very solidity is what you appreciated most. The sideboard in particular — a perfect tombstone, or a memorial to the life of a Prague official — oppressed me profoundly. If during our visit to the furniture store a funeral bell had begun tolling in the distance, it wouldn't have been inappropriate."[235] We recognize how that "heavy furniture" becomes for Kafka what the "needle machine" is for the victim in "In the Penal Colony." In both instances, he has constructed an infernal machine for stifling his powers of expression.

Then in a postscript, he realizes he has been too severe and excuses himself, but says, "I am so thoroughly lacerated and shaken that I cannot be held entirely responsible."[236] He returns to the ghosts hanging on to him: "I am so hemmed in by ghosts from which the office prevents me freeing myself. Day and night they cling to me; if only I were free it would be my supreme delight to chase them at my will; but as it is, they gradually do me in. As long as I am not free I don't wish to be seen, and I don't wish to see you." He adds that she is very wrong if she thinks there are other explanations. Yet they do exist, although they are too complicated to be communicated even in his delicate, tortured prose. At one level, he is confused sexually, but the sexual problematics are only a part of his larger burden: his health is deteriorating, and he is unable to enter the military because of his physical condition; also, his slowness of production; the demons themselves, or ghosts, attendant upon his efforts to write; his lingering desire to lead a normalized life, and yet his perception that heavy furniture will always defeat him; and, what is perhaps the most inexplicable element of all, his recognition, finally, that he cannot connect to anyone, to society, to anything outside those demons, which, he feels, are undermining his will and subverting his spirit. Thus he is Sisyphus and Laocoön and all those figures caught in coils, punished for "crimes" hardly commensurate with the penalties. With those demons and ghosts, Kafka has now positioned himself in that no man's land beyond society, where he can be only one thing: "as lonely as Franz Kafka."

PART IV: DEFEAT OR VICTORY

After a brief journey to Karlsbad with Ottla, on business, where they visited the Villa Tannhäuser, Kafka returned to the question of furniture, writing to Felice in April 1916, "But you shouldn't deny how much furniture means to you, not those particular pieces of furniture, not furniture as such, but the things that go with it."[237] He is turning furniture into a kind of negative totem, signifying to him everything separating him from Felice, or from married life. His April letters reveal an entire range of anger: furniture, military service, even a reprise of what occurred at the Askanische Hof almost two years before, when the engagement was dissolved amidst mutual rancor and humiliation. On April 19 he mentions visiting a nerve specialist, who diagnoses cardiac neurosis, a heart irregularity, for which he suggested therapy in the form of electrical treatment. Kafka promptly canceled the appointment. His physical state was clearly linked to mental duress and appeared to the nerve specialist as a heart condition, a diagnosis not far from the truth.

Just before, Kafka indicated he had met Robert Musil, the Austrian writer whose *The Man Without Qualities* would show several analogues to Kafka's work. Musil early on recognized Kafka's talent, having reviewed *Meditation* and "The Stoker" in *Die Neue Rundschau* (August 1914) and then inviting Kafka to contribute. Musil was one of the few major writers outside Kafka's immediate Prague circle who recognized his unique qualities; but then, both were responding to similar developments: the deterioration of individual, social, and moral life in the twilight years of the Dual Monarchy.

But to Felice, Kafka only touches on this, and in the next letter, in which he mentions cardiac neurosis, he demands, "As long as I am no better, we want to have nothing to do with each other."[238] He calls it a "very sensible solution." Yet he tells Felice of his planned trip to Marienbad, in mid-May, for the institute, anticipating his July meeting with her in that resort and their unofficial re-engagement. The alternating parting and embracing in the letters suggest not only his confusion but hers. Given her common sense and her desire for a bourgeois marriage, we would expect her to drift away, but apparently there was a part of her that agreed with Brod that Kafka was extraordinary and unique, although she may not have been sure what it was. Or else, and we cannot discount this possibility, she felt such profound pity she could not simply drop him. Or, at her relatively advanced age, she wanted simply to marry. Or, further (and here we speculate), he so intrigued her as a man who would lead her into new adventures as a married woman she forsook customary caution until Kafka's health forced the break.

In mid-May, he wrote Felice of his business trip to Karlsbad and Marienbad. "There are ghosts that haunt one in company and those that haunt one in solitude; now it's the latter's turn."[239] Nevertheless, he indicates he wouldn't mind remaining in Marienbad for several months to take stock of his position. He admits his efforts to quit the office have been unsuccessful, but when he finally decided to leave, the institute bent its rules and offered him a long leave or an unscheduled vacation — as it did in May when he asked for either a long leave or exemption from military service (as an official of the empire). He tells Felice that when he made this request, leave or reclassification, the director of the institute thought the first funny and the second worthy of being ignored.

Instead, Kafka was offered vacation time. The director apparently knew something Kafka did not: that his disgruntled, despairing, bizarre employee was far too volatile to lose as the result of a whimsical request. The director, in fact, assured Kafka he was certain of his position and career, totally misunderstanding that Kafka was crumbling and that his request was intended to relieve pressure. The two carry on a Kafkaesque dialogue, which reinforces Kafka's perception that all life will be like that. Life and his fiction are inseparable. "I go on telling lies with the irresponsibility of a child, albeit under pressure. I can only cope with the simplest practical tasks by staging outrageous sentimental scenes; but how difficult this is! The lies and stratagems, the time it takes, and the remorse!"[240]

Yet even as everything seemed to have bottomed out — the institute turning him to lunacy, his own work stalled, his personal life unimproved, his health deteriorating — despite all this, he was moving toward re-engagement with Felice and was yet to write many of his greatest works. Perceiving all life around him as parody, he was able to muster satire, irony, and the grotesque* as ways of encompassing and intensifying his vision. Considering himself a "sick person" (and therefore one who should give sanatoria a wide berth), he was to make one more serious effort to live normally. On July 10, he and Felice, having met in Marienbad, wrote a common letter to Frau Bauer indicating they had reconsidered. They admit they had tackled things in the wrong way in the past and ask for her "maternal consent." The official engagement, their second, would occur fully one year later, in July 1917, just one month before Kafka suffered his first severe hemorrhage. But in that July 1916 stay in Marienbad, he and Felice spent ten days (from the third through the thirteenth) at the Hotel Schloss Balmoral and Osborne; and then Kafka remained for another ten days. He seems to have enjoyed a sharp upswing in his health, for he told Brod and wrote in his diaries that his twin ailments of headache and insomnia had vanished. He says he felt a kind of euphoria, perhaps akin to what the prisoner in "In the Penal Colony" feels in his sixth hour under the needles. To intensify the euphoria, he moved into Felice's room after she left, but noise from either side diminished what he had hoped would be a prolongation of pleasure.

---

*The ever present grotesque Golem in Prague's Jewish community as idea, symbol, defender, threat, and ghostly substance should not be forgotten.

Yet this experience, the second (unofficial) engagement, was not only nerves or euphoria. It led Kafka into a second burst of creative energy. In the near future, he wrote, along with several shorter pieces, some of the stories that appeared in *A Country Doctor*, also "The Warden of the Tomb," part of "The Great Wall of China" (the story, not the book of that name), "The Hunter Gracchus," and "A Report to the Academy" — which sums up an entire bureaucratic phase of his life and curiously foreshadows Karel Čapek's *RUR*, the play about robots, and Jaroslav Hašek's *The Good Soldier Schweik*. Just as the first engagement led to bursts of mature creative energy, so the second seemed to liberate Kafka for work at the highest levels.

We catch some of that sense of liberation in his very detailed letter to Brod (July 12–14, 1916) about this meeting with Felice.

> The cords with which I was trussed were at least somewhat loosened; I straightened out somewhat while she who had constantly been holding out her hands to help but reaching only into an utter void, helped again and we arrived at a human relationship of a kind I had so far never known and which came very near in its meaningfulness to the relationship we had achieved at the best periods of our correspondence. Basically I have never had that kind of intimacy with a woman, except for two cases.[241]

Here he mentions the older woman in Zuckmantel and the much younger girl in Riva, she "half a child" and he "altogether confused and sick in every possible way."

He admits his fears:

> Aside from other doubts, last time I was hampered by the actual fear of the reality of this girl behind the letters. When she came toward me in the big room to receive the *engagement kiss*, a shudder ran through me. The engagement trip [to Berlin] was sheer agony for me, every step of the way. I have never feared anything so much as being alone with F. before the wedding. Now all that is changed and is good. Our agreement is in brief: to get married soon after the end of the war; to rent an apartment of two or three rooms in some Berlin suburb; each to assume economic responsibilities for himself.

Felice will continue to work, while Kafka cannot say what he will do. He then presents a future scenario, full of his usual corrosive irony: "There is the picture of two rooms somewhere in Karlshorst [five miles southeast of Berlin], say, in one of which F. wakes up early, trots off, and falls exhausted into bed at night, while in the other room there is a sofa on which I lie and feed on milk and honey. So there the husband lolls about, the wretched and immoral lout (as the cliché has it)." Nevertheless, Kafka admits there is in this some "calm, certainty, and therefore the possibility of living."[242]

On July 18 (in a letter postmarked Marienbad), Kafka informs Felice that headaches have returned for the past two days. He mentions he has joined the Hasidic rabbi of Belz, who has been in Marienbad for three weeks. This was, apparently, a large moment for Kafka, for he wrote at great length about the meeting to Brod (but only briefly to Felice), and not too much later took up the study of Hebrew. Kafka's relationship to Hasidism, as noted above, was ambivalent. He felt drawn to its certainties that Jews formed a community based on common practices; he remained ironically distant from its sublime devotion to God, its ritualistic practices, its isolation from the world. What was attractive, its unworldliness, was also its disadvantage. From the Hasidic point of view, Kafka was more than a pariah; he was part of that traitorous portion of Western Jewry disinheriting itself from its traditions and history.

Kafka met the rabbi through Georg Langer, from whom both he and Brod later took Hebrew lessons. The rabbi was treated like royalty: no one could stand in front of him, and he was always to be given free passage. Kafka was impressed by his look and majesty, and told Brod he seemed like the sultan in a Gustav Doré illustration of the Münchausen stories that Kafka had read in childhood. And not only sultan, but also father, grammar school teacher, gymnasium professor. Kafka was slowly transforming him into a massive father-God figure. He was tremendously impressed by his dignity and command — we perceive a Kafka here who is willing to be subdued and seduced by a mighty presence, someone to fill him with power and strength. "Long white beard, unusually long sidelocks. . . . One eye is blind and blank. His mouth is twisted awry, which gives him a look at once ironic and friendly."[243] His dress is a silk caftan, a broad belt about his waist, a tall fur hat, white stockings, and white trousers. (Kafka is particularly impressed by the hat.) He is surrounded by an entourage ready to do his slightest bidding. His silver cane is quickly exchanged for an umbrella. Ten Jews walk behind and to either side, one of them carrying the cane and a chair on which the rabbi may wish to sit. Another carries a cloth with which to wipe the chair dry; still another carries a glass from which he might drink. A "rich Jew from Pressburg," Schlesinger, carries a bottle of spring water. There are also the *gabbaim*, employees, officials, and secretaries, the lay persons serving the rabbi's needs.

As the sightseeing continues, everyone paces himself according to the rabbi's needs. As Kafka details this brief meeting, the holy man's comments, and the succor offered by the entourage, he reveals a side of himself rarely glimpsed by Felice: an enormous hole waiting to be filled, not so much by faith or God but by some certainty of purpose. The rabbi is so sure of himself and his role that he can, like the Pied Piper, which this description resembles, draw everyone after him by sheer force of personality. Strikingly, Kafka's words to Brod about Felice, while full of feeling, are nowhere near so powerful as his recreation of his experience with the Belz rabbi. The earlier experience with Löwy and his acting troupe had tapped Kafka's imagination, forcing him to recognize that as a Westernized Jew in Prague, he had neither city nor religion nor ethnic position; he was as isolated as every Jew who thought he or she could be German.

Now that the two of them had papered over their differences and the "great war" had dwindled into temporary truce, Kafka became fixated on his health. He felt he had to communicate to Felice his coughs, headaches, insomnia, and other ills, as if she had taken over the maternal role. He even wrote of his huge appetite from the country air and offers her a menu that is, supposedly, to fatten him. There is, however, unconsciously, a sacrificial element to his speech, an assurance to his executioner that when the time comes, he will indeed be a fattened calf. The menu indicates that Kafka's "treatment" involves almost around-the-clock eating, starting at midmorning and continuing until nine in the evening.

Amusingly, while he was writing to Felice about his newly found happiness, he was negotiating with Kurt Wolff Verlag about the possibility of a volume to be called *Punishments*, which would combine "The Judgment," "The Metamorphosis," and "In the Penal Colony." Intermixed with descriptions of food, swallowing half a kilo of cherries, and giving an update on his sleeping habits is the casual mention of *Punishments* (not by name, however); as if the real matter of his life was connected to suffering, while the part communicated to Felice was marginal. So fixated on himself and his food is he that he even mentions his fletcherizing, which, apparently, he tried to interest her in.

Once he is back in Prague, his afflictions return. He is now back with his family and the institute, the twin areas of headache production. But he shows interest in Felice's activities, when in September of 1916 she begins volunteer work in the Jewish People's Home in Berlin, having been encouraged to do so by Kafka. The home was a center for Jewish relief work in Berlin and had been founded only that May by Siegfried Lehmann, in the Alexanderplatz section of the city where mainly Eastern European Jews resided. In one respect, Kafka's encouragement of Felice in this enterprise was a vicarious commitment for himself. Before undertaking her volunteer duties, she was evidently worried about what she was getting into. Kafka assured her that her help was not directly connected to Zionism, about which she had misgivings (Felice, much later, emigrated to the United States), telling her that Zionism was "but an entrance to something far more important":[244] that need to establish contact with something less trivial, perhaps, than heavy furniture.

Although the war, in midsummer 1916, was at its fiercest and most hopeless — a standstill without any cessation of the human slaughter — Kafka does not mention it. Julie Kafka does refer to the days they have all lived through, in her letter to Frau Bauer (August 9, 1916), but her son remained silent on a matter that would, in a brief time, change the history of Europe and, of course, the Dual Monarchy. History, tradition, continuity of rule — the very nature of order itself was shifting, but Kafka wisely had decided to let his fiction, not himself, speak of his times. Some of his attitude was self-absorption, but also creative, an extreme subjectivity that allowed him to transform whatever the war meant into literary forms. He was not simply self-indulgent, although that is not to be discounted, nor was he merely trying to shield himself from horrors that interfered with his own.

In a revealing letter to Felice, ostensibly about the writer Theodor Fontane, Kafka was really reverting to his earlier confessions of near madness.[245] It was, we recall, the Fontane Prize money (800 marks) that Carl Sternheim had asked be passed on to Kafka in October of 1914. Kafka paraphrases Fontane's words to Mathilde von Rohr, speaking of his three and a half months as secretary of the Royal Academy of Arts: "During the entire time I have derived not a single moment of enjoyment, experienced not a single pleasant sensation. . . . Everything galls me; everything stultifies me; everything nauseates me. I have the distinct feeling that I shall always be unhappy, could become emotionally disturbed and melancholy."[246] Kafka's years at the institute could not have been better described.

Fontane adds that one cannot strive against one's innermost nature, and "in the heart of every man lies a Something that, once it feels abhorrence, will not be pacified or overcome." Then he writes a line so close to Franz, Felice, and their great war that any reasonable young fiancée would have retreated rapidly. Fontane: "I had to decide whether to lead a dull life devoid of life and joy for the sake of material security, or etc." In the event Felice missed the point, Kafka added sardonically: "So today it was Fontane who wrote to you instead of me."[247]

Then follows the "anniversary letter" of August 15, in response to Felice's of two days earlier commemorating the fourth year of their acquaintanceship. In those four years, they had sparred, skirmished, fought a few large-scale battles, become unofficially engaged twice, broken up once, and were moving toward a second official engagement in July 1917. It was indeed an opportunity to celebrate, but through letters, since letters had become their medium. Through words, Kafka could control the affair, insofar as he could control anything; and through words, he could endlessly explain himself, in that therapeutic process for which letters served him. Further, through words, he could learn how to position himself for his mature works; he could locate himself in the letters as he would in his fictions, disguised, shielded, always talking, but so ironically that no clear interpretation was possible.* Their celebration, then, was not candy, flowers, or a meeting, but letters and words crisscrossing in the mails.

---

*Several commentators have recognized that "interpretation" always reduces Kafka's

As Felice moved toward assuming the volunteer work in the Jewish Home, Kafka became frantic that she might withdraw at the last moment: "If in order to survive the present moment one must continually have some immediate pleasure, then mine consists of knowing you have begun to be associated with the Jewish Home."[248] Through her, he could "enjoy" the Eastern European Jewish experience and feel he was abnegating his false Westernized role. He speaks of them: "As for our union, it is certain, as certain as human beings can be; the exact time is only relatively certain, and the details of our life together in days to come (excluding Prague) we must leave to the future."

Once more, in another August letter, Kafka "uses" Fontane, the nineteenth-century writer with whose despairing sensibility he identified, as a means of defining for Felice the limits of their relationship, what she could expect, how he interpreted her needs, how far he felt he could go. Kafka says Fontane's demands upon his wife were "too severe"[249] for her to defer to all his needs, but she should have trusted him, kept silent, and learned in all their years of married life how to deal with him. Kafka was showing sympathy, then withdrawing it in the face of a writer's need for his own kind of freedom, a freedom that the wife cannot possibly comprehend. It was, distinctly, a male view of the world, not merely a writer's.

On September 1, 1916, his complaints of being feverish did not speak well for his health, since headaches and fever ("from the tips of my toes to those of my hair") are signals of a tubercular condition. The warnings were all there, including enervation, despair, and the inability to maintain a sense of accomplishment. His examination by Dr. Mühl-stein leads to his usual disparaging remarks about the medical profession, although this particular doctor inspired confidence. Mühlstein found nothing but "extreme nervousness" and made some "very funny" suggestions: not too much smoking (Kafka did not smoke), not too much to drink (he did not drink), eat more vegetables than meat (he was a vegetarian), exercise in the form of swimming (his favorite activity), and get plenty of good sleep (he had tried for a lifetime). In his amusement, Kafka does find time to disparage himself: "How you could ever come to trust anything as long and thin as me is something I shall never understand."[250] The visit to the doctor was like everything else, superfluous, given the nature of the patient. Only when he produced something, like a hemorrhage, was it possible to locate his ills and complaints. Otherwise, they remained buried so deeply in his

---

work; even when the biographer is forewarned and forearmed, biographical interpretation follows this course. One way out is suggested by Henry Sussman's *Franz Kafka: Geometrician of Metaphor* (1979), a Derrida-influenced, poststructuralist reading of the major fictions, which attempts a descriptive, formal criticism. For the biographer, such criticism, while extremely valuable in itself, can go only so far since biography demands both thematic and historical considerations. At best, one attempts some middle way.

personality that physical ailments remained indistinguishable from mental.

Kafka mentions being invited to give a reading in Munich, in November, and Felice decides to meet him there. They will fall into serious disagreement, but in the meanwhile the relationship has settled into a calmer, fairly relaxed process, in which each feels out the other's positions. Kafka assures Felice she need not worry if she decides, as a result of her work in the Home, that Zionism is not for her. He tells her that Zionism is not something that separates people, and then speaks amusingly of his own synagogue experiences. "I wouldn't think of going to the synagogue. The synagogue is not a place one can sneak up to. . . . I still remember how as a boy I almost suffocated from the terrible boredom and pointlessness of the hours in the synagogue; these were the rehearsals staged by hell for my later office life."[251] He keeps going on Judaism: "Those who throng to the synagogue simply because they are Zionists seem to me like people trying to force their way into the synagogue under cover of the Ark of the Covenant, rather than entering calmly through the main door." He says that if he had to talk to the Home children, he would have to tell them that "owing to my origin, my education, disposition, and environments I have nothing tangible in common with their faith," whereas she, Felice, may have. He was rationalistic but envious of community; she was traditional, secular, but willing to pay her respects.

The letters in this period prior to the Munich meeting in November remain mature exchanges between two people exhausted by previous skirmishes, now eager to paper over differences in order to get on with their lives together. For the first time, Kafka seems to have forsaken role-playing and is instead moving toward official engagement and marriage. His only form of control focuses on Felice's reading, to some extent, and more indirectly on her work at the Jewish Home. He takes her to task for having agreed to type the annual report, "which will mean a huge additional burden for you."[252] He jokingly says that her time, even if the report were only one page, would be better spent on him. He asks her to come to Munich, indicating that for him a detour to Berlin (where all her relatives were) would be impossible. We catch the slightest note of panic: that the idyll of letters will be disrupted by her actual presence.

Kafka relates a nightmare, in which he receives a telephone call from the porter's lodge at the institute that there is a letter for him. He finds no porter but instead the department head, to whom all incoming mail is delivered first. This man examines the table, finds no letter, blames the porter for having taken the letter directly from the mailman. Now Kafka has to wait for the porter, if he wants his letter. The porter, a giant, arrives but does not know where the letter is; Kafka decides to lodge a complaint with the director, demanding a confrontation between mailman and porter. "Half out of my mind," he tells Felice, "I wander along corridors and up and down stairs, searching in vain for the director."[253] The nightmare has several possibilities. The lost letter, if it ever existed, is linked to the potential loss of Felice now that a Munich meeting is shaping up; or conversely, to a disguised desire to lose her. The situation also involves Kafka's loss of resolve now that the words of the letter are "lost" — that is, they cannot be substituted for the meeting itself. Order has given way to disorder. Still further, Kafka mourns the letter because it was his way of controlling the relationship. That frantic search for a "director," or some form of authority, is an archetypal Kafka image and situation.

The October 5 letter is a distinct warning, for Kafka feels change in his body: "The laws by which my blood rages within me are inscrutable; for some days now my whole nervous system has been in turmoil again, and not a moment's sleep is granted me."[254] His aching head makes him feel like "a condemned man." And this seeming shift in his health, from unwell to unbearable, brings with it one of his most corrosive remarks on family life, comments foreshadowing the quarrel he and Felice would have in Munich. He speaks of an exhibition in Berlin, called "Mother and Infant," which Felice had apparently praised, whereas he had recently written her in praise of being alone. He says the exhibition may be very beautiful, but it is incomplete, and what it lacks is a "Chamber of Horrors, the principal exhibit of which would have to be a group as depicted, for example, by a cousin of mine, with her husband and the baby carriage." Kafka is now "destroying" Felice in his attacks on family and on the wife.

He bites into the rotten apple of family life: "Helpless, she [his female cousin] was determined to get married, and married — admittedly with the approval of all her variously informed relatives — a man she would certainly never have married had she been in a calmer frame of mind." Kafka describes the man as not objectionable — amusing (a laugher), healthy, with passable looks — the child of this marriage is attractive, strong, and solid, seemingly a fine two-year-old. "But it is quite listless; it lies in its carriage, large and motionless, its eyes roving about aimlessly and apathetically. It can't even sit up, the mouth can't smile, and nothing can induce it to utter a word."[255] It appears retarded or autistic. Then Kafka savages the scene: when the parents walk the child and are stopped by someone, Kafka himself, for example, the mother — "saddled with that father and that child — stands there with tears in her eyes, glancing first at the acquaintance, then at the child, yet manages a smile so as not to leave her permanently contented husband all alone with his laughter — well, this too should form part of that exhibition."

This terrible indictment is indicative of Kafka's despair at any future relationship even while he pursued the official engagement. The indictment probes deeply into his fear of sex as a kind of Fury, for some sexual attraction between his cousin and her husband led to this present hopeless situation disguised by laughter. They are, perhaps without full consciousness of it, mired in hell — the future for all family life, as Kafka's vision goes.

He keeps up the barrage of family indictments, a premonition of the *Letter to His Father* in 1919. He writes of his family celebrating the Jewish New Year and the Day of Atonement (Yom Kippur), on which they fasted. "Fasting was no trouble since we have been in training for it all year."[256] Here "fasting" stands for the failing business, Hermann and Julie's shop, as well as the asbestos factory. He can't stop a few days later with these kindly words: "I fear no one except my parents; but them enormously. To sit at my parents' dinner table with you (I mean now, later on it may become quite easy) would be sheer torture for me."[257] Still, he wishes she would come to Prague so he could show it to her more thoroughly than before.

By now, Kafka was expert in sending out double signals. While pursuing Felice, he was undermining everything she stood for. While asking her to come to Prague, he tells her how dreadful their meals will be for him. While encouraging her in her Jewish Home volunteer work, he is exerting control, so that she is really doing what has significance for him. While expressing his staunch support of the relationship, he is attacking marriage as a chamber of horrors. While writing of his plans to settle eventually in Berlin, he seems increasingly focused on Prague. While promising to resign from the institute, his other chamber of horrors, he appears ready to stick it out. While offering his attention and affection, he undermines them repeatedly with avowals of his primary dedication to his craft.

In an October letter he raked over the entire relationship, leaving Felice in his wake as he sailed out into what are clearly very personal waters. He starts by saying he does not like her admitting she would find the dinner table at his home a pleasant experience, but he quickly counters this by saying he would not like it if she said that such experiences were not enjoyable. He feels the truth lies elsewhere, which enables him to launch in deeply ironical terms into the entire range of familial relationships. He restates his need for independence, his seeking self-reliance and freedom in all directions. Ostensibly speaking about family, he is telling Felice something quite significant for their future. "I would rather wear blinkers and go my own way to the bitter end, than have my vision distorted by being in the midst of frenzied family life. That's why every word I say to my parents, or they to me, so easily turns into a stumbling block under my feet. Any relationship not created by myself, even though it be opposed to parts of my own nature, is worthless; it hinders my movements. I hate it, or come near to hating it."[258] He was narrowing her role even further.

Yet he admits he is part of his family, inescapably so. But this admission only makes him sense the repellent aspect of it. The sight of the double bed, sheets that have been slept in, nightshirts carefully laid out, "can turn my stomach inside out; it is as though my birth had not been final; as though from this fusty life I keep being born again and again in this fusty room." Kafka attempts to be fair, however: "I know that after all they are my parents, are essential, strength-giving elements of my own self, belonging to me, not merely as obstacles but as human beings."[259] He sees them, somehow, as godlike, and therefore he seeks perfection from them, an unusual expectation from a man of thirty-three.

He reveals that despite his "nastiness, rudeness, selfishness, and unkindness" he has always trembled before them and does so to this day. Kafka then expresses his relationship to them in characteristically corrosive terms: "Since they — Father on the one hand and Mother on the other, have — again quite naturally — almost broken my will, I want them to be worthy of their actions."[260] After an insertion that his youngest sister, Ottla, would be the kind of mother he would like, he returns to the fray. "So I want them to be worthy of their actions. In consequence, for me, they are a hundred times more unclean than they may be in reality, which doesn't really worry me; their foolishness is a hundred times greater, their absurdity a hundred times greater, their coarseness a hundred times greater." They can't escape even with an intensification of their faults, and their good qualities, even their good qualities, are a "hundred thousand times smaller than they are in reality."

This is, of course, ammunition in Kafka's "war," and it is aimed at Felice's role. In his attack on family, he points out he cannot rebel against the laws of nature "without going mad," so the consequence is hatred "and almost nothing but hatred." Then he intermingles Felice into this recipe of attraction and repulsion. "But you belong to me, I have made you mine; I do not believe that the battle for any woman in any fairy tale has been fought harder and more desperately than the battle for you within myself — from the beginning over and over again, and perhaps forever."[261] The words suggest entrapment personified: she is his, he controls her, he has won the battle over himself, and it has all been in words, language, forms of epistolary communication. Kafka then tightens the noose of entrapment, suggesting that because of her, his relationship with the Bauer relatives "is not unlike my relationship with my own"; they constitute a bond, for good or for ill, which hampers him, and hampers them even if no words are exchanged.

He means the Bauers must not think he has become part of them, no more than his own family must feel he has joined their ranks if Felice and he gathered with them at the table. The Kafkas might also think they had gained an ally in her against his opposition; and just as they would be making incorrect assumptions based on that, so would her family be making comparably incorrect assumptions. Their failure to comprehend his alienation even in a married situation means they have failed even more in understanding than on previous occasions. The greater his expectations, the greater their failure, and, therefore, the more intense his hatred.

But he is not through. He loves his paradoxes:

"I stand facing my family perpetually brandishing knives, simultaneously to wound and to defend them."[262] He tells Felice he wants to act on her behalf with his family without her doing the same with hers. This was, in fact, merely another set of coils to entwine her in: his effort to involve her in his decision to separate himself, both from her family and his, turning the two of them into an island of rebellion. In a late October letter, his remarks on Strindberg consolidate his attitudes toward family and toward young women: "One has only to close one's eyes and one's own blood delivers lectures on Strindberg."[263]

The self-torture that Kafka experienced from circumstances and uncertainties and which he wanted to reveal to Felice is rarely relieved. The imagery is familiar, of both food and insect. "My life," he says, "is made up of two parts, the one feeds on your life with bulging cheeks and could in itself be happy and a great man; but the other part is like a cobweb come adrift: being free of tension, free of headaches is its supreme though not too frequent joy."[264] Whereas the first part is the element yearning for connection to normal life, the second is the part that writes. He asks her what he can do about that second part. He says he has done no work for two years, which is not true, since he has moved along on *The Trial* and other short pieces, and was to write two important stories ("The Hunter Gracchus" and "A Country Doctor") in coming months.

The announcement of his division into one part feeding on Felice, the other associated with insect life, was necessary since he was getting ready to meet her in Munich. In nearly every instance of their (rare) meetings, he created a scenario of his unacceptability for the encounter, and then watched the encounter unravel as he forced the circumstances that made any rapprochement impossible. This too, although a form of control and manipulation, left him emotionally devastated and despairing. Yet it was absolutely necessary for him to establish the terms by which Felice could quarrel with and/or reject him. An early November letter indicates Felice was thinking of pulling out, even though some of her hesitation was linked to the difficulty of getting travel clearances during wartime. The stay in Munich was scheduled for November 10–12, 1916, and it proved not only personally agonizing but professionally unnerving: Kafka read "In the Penal Colony" and a few Brod poems, and the audience appeared indifferent. Felice, incidentally, was not the only "celebrated" person in Munich; Rilke was there, although probably not in the audience at Kafka's reading. The poet had been taking a considerable interest in his fellow Prague writer, and he had apparently read the manuscript of "In the Penal Colony" when Kafka sent it on to Eugen Mondt in Munich.[265] Rilke tried to keep up with Kafka's work in general, though his tastes were peculiar — he preferred "The Stoker" (incorporated into *Amerika*) to "The Metamorphosis" and "In the Penal Colony."*

Kafka called "Penal Colony" his "filthy story," an attempt to condemn it after he observed audience coldness. But the larger part of his dissatisfaction came from his quarrel with Felice. She had accused him of selfishness, and he complained of her silence. He speaks of a traumatic meeting, recalling the one in Berlin. "Although I'm far from convinced that quarrels of this kind (that ghastly pastry shop) will not occur again, at least they won't have the tension of the hurried meeting, that vague nightmarish transitory feeling which adds to bitterness, and so will be borne merely as part of ordinary human misery."[266] With his plans crumbling, headaches, which had ceased for a while, had also started up. He insists on his right to selfishness, not directed at a person but at an object or an objective. Felice's headaches resume, in that cycle of dependency each had on the other's weaknesses.

After the quarrel, we receive the impression from Kafka's letters that he was writing far more than she and that he was pressing her to respond. Her silences, which seem to have been her most effective weapon against his assaults on her flaws, did serve their purpose: they intensified his anxiety and made him recognize the frailty of the relationship. He even cites his "incredible impudence" of reading in public, whereas in Prague he had not read a single word to his friends for the past year and a half. He perceived the Munich venture as an act of overweening ego, as well as a personal disaster.

Yet as 1916 came to an end, Kafka began to find some reassurance. His comments are less frantic, and he suggests that Felice read Dickens to the children at the Home. He sends on *Little Dorrit*, in German translation. One painful intrusion was the reappearance of Löwy, his actor friend, who wrote from Budapest attacking Kafka for not having done enough for him, attacks that Kafka called "wild" and "by no means justified." What he possibly did not recognize was that Löwy's life, lived so unconventionally and so close to the financial and artistic precipice, had created a dependence in him, on Kafka and others, that was translated into irrationality and rage. Kafka was suitably wounded.

In an early 1917 letter, before a long hiatus in the correspondence (to September 9, a fateful letter), Kafka writes at length to Felice about

---

*Kafka on Rilke: "After some extremely kind remarks about 'The Stoker,' he went on to say that neither *Metamorphosis* nor 'In the Penal Colony' had achieved the same effect [as 'The Stoker']. This observation may not be easy to understand, but it is discerning" (December 7, 1916; *Letters to Felice*, p. 536).

his plans for an apartment of his own. His spirits seem buoyed, although the apartment hunting itself proved frustrating. He says he had found in 1915 a comfortable place, a room "At the Sign of the Golden Pike," but the noise proved intolerable: "No possibility of peace; total disorientation; breeding ground for every kind of madness; ever-increasing weakness and hopelessness." He was indeed stretched tight as he and Ottla began to look for another place. He recognized that his "two years of suffering" were insignificant when compared to the world's suffering "but bad enough for me."[267]

Ottla found a little house in an alley, off the Malá Strana, or Lesser Town. Although it was defective in every way, she had it painted, made it livable, and kept it as a hideaway from the family. Kafka himself found a lovely place, the Schönborn Palace in the Malá Strana (Marktgasse 265/15), where he stayed for six months, from March to August. But this exceptional place had an occupant who wanted to sell the improvements for 650 kroner, which Kafka says he could not afford. He was shown another apartment, not nearly so grand, which he took, while using Ottla's hideaway for his evening meal, staying there until midnight before going to his room in the palace.

But there are disadvantages, and he warns Felice, even while offering her what he calls "the most perfect apartment imaginable in Prague." The disadvantages are considerable for someone seeking "perfection": "You would have to do without a kitchen of your own, and even without a bathroom."[268] He says that after the war he would take a year's leave of absence, and the two of them could live there, apparently while he wrote and she worked. Then we find the gap in Kafka's letters to Felice, although in early July she did come to Prague and they did announce formally their second engagement. They were now a couple, although according to witnesses Kafka's attitude and bearing recalled the manner not of a man embarking on marriage but of a criminal awaiting the block. Brod, for example, saw his friend's situation as both moving and horrifying.

Then on July 11 the couple went to visit Felice's sister Erna in Arad, Hungary, a break in their trip in Budapest, where Kafka met Löwy and suggested that the actor write an article on the circumstances of the Yiddish performer in the Austro-Hungarian Empire. Then something happened, and Kafka and Felice parted for the final time. On July 18 he went on to Vienna, and she remained in Budapest; the engagement, the relationship, the frantic correspondence, although not all letters, were finished. It was a sudden and somewhat mysterious end. What we can glean from various sources, including Kafka's own words, was that as long as they wrote to each other, they could maintain the illusion of compatibility, but as soon as they met and were forced to interact personally they both recognized, as Kafka said, that they had no future together. He wrote several letters to her when he returned to Prague which she probably destroyed; he described them as characteristic but "nevertheless monstrous."

He tells her this in his letter of September 9, which is one of the most significant documents in this already remarkable series. Kafka speaks of his hemorrhaging, the emblem of doom, and yet he sounds positively jaunty about it. Part of his jauntiness is connected to the fact that with the illness he can break from his imprisonment. The engagement is over, for good, and even though Felice visited him at Zürau, where he was recuperating, this new meeting was on different grounds from the others. It held no threat of a renewal of the relationship or the imprisonment of courtship and marriage.

In the September 9 letter, Kafka explained his silence: "Precisely 4 weeks ago, at about 5 A.M., I had a hemorrhage of the lung. Fairly severe; for 10 minutes or more it gushed out of my throat; I thought it would never stop."[269] He says he went to see a doctor the next day, was x-rayed several times, then on Max Brod's insistence saw a specialist. The verdict: tuberculosis in both lungs. Although surprised, he says he has to accept it, and one advantage is his headaches "seem to have been washed away with the flow of blood." He announces he is going to Zürau for at least three months, to Ottla's, three miles east of Karlsbad (post office Flöhau). When he asked the institute for permission to retire, the director told him that for his own good it was better not to.

He tells "poor dear Felice" that this may be the "closing phase" to his letters. Except for some sporadic coughing, he tells her, a slight temperature, some sweating at night, all the classic accompaniments of the disease, he feels positively better than at any time during the last few years. His words reveal a sense of relief that the worst is now out, that even with a death sentence, the uncertainty has been relieved.

Felice visited Zürau on September 20–21, which Kafka noted in his diary. In the entry for September 15, as he awaited Felice's visit, he was quite forward-looking:

> You have the chance, as far as it is at all possible, to make a new beginning. Don't throw it away. If you insist on digging deep into yourself, you won't be able to avoid the muck that will well up. But don't wallow in it. If the infection in your lungs is only a symbol, as you say, *a symbol of the infection whose inflammation is called Felice* [my italics], and whose depth is its deep justification; if this is so then the medical advice (light, air, sun, rest) is also a symbol. Lay hold of this symbol.[270]

This suggests strongly that with Felice gone from his life, even as she was planning to visit, he has the chance to regroup, revive, even transform himself during his remaining time.

In the September 21 entry, just after Felice had left, Kafka is contrite and self-accusatory. But we must compare these words of contrition with the very different image of himself he presented to Brod, in a letter just before her arrival. In the diary, he speaks of their thirty hours together, with his former fiancée showing the "utmost misery and the guilt is essentially mine." He does not know what to say or how to act. He says he feels she is wrong in defending her rights, "but taken all together, she is an innocent person condemned to extreme torture; I am guilty of the wrong for which she is being tortured, and am in addition the torturer."[271] The situation sounds remarkably parallel to the one Kafka described in "In the Penal Colony."

To Brod, he lists his hostilities as he awaits Felice's arrival on the twentieth. "I don't grasp her, she is extraordinary, or rather I do grasp her but cannot hold her. I run all around her, barking as a nervous dog might tear around a statue, or to present an equally true but converse picture, I gaze at her as a stuffed animal head mounted on the wall might look at the person living quietly in his room.* Half-truths, a thousandth of a truth. All that is true is that F. is coming."[272] Kafka has emasculated himself in order to present his sense of a devouring Felice. She has become in this respect the Amazon of turn-of-the-century literature, the dominatrix who gives men little quarter: Wedekind's Lulu, Klimt's tortured female figures, Wilde's Salomé, Weininger's perverted images. It is true that Kafka is ill and the arrival of any healthy person creates a contrast, but his image of the dog scurrying around is one in which more than contrast is involved: he is demeaned, reduced, transformed into that animal or insect life that is for him his sole form of escape from perceived weakness.

The intimacies he had revealed to Felice earlier are now transferred to Brod, as later they will be to Milena Jesenská. Kafka indicates his desire for deep withdrawal, probably linked to the enervation his illness was causing him, a kind of reverie in which he perceives he has no way out; he is full of false hopes and self-deceptions even about staying in Zürau or in the country forever. He daydreams of his country uncle, the doctor; he had recently written the story "A Country Doctor." He senses that his country uncle has discovered something valuable in the land experience, and Kafka wonders if he can ever find that contentment, at thirty-four, with his fragile lungs and "still more fragile human relationships." But it is quite possible his country uncle lived an isolated life because even more than his nephew he felt socially marginal, was possibly homosexual, was therefore unwilling to confront his family on that, and so found himself beyond courtship, marriage, urban ways.

Kafka speaks of the only marriage of which he seems capable: "I live with Ottla in a good minor marriage." In emphasizing that they run "a fine household,"[273] he suggests that with the overt sexual element missing (without discounting an unconscious sexuality running

---

*All that "stuffing" may be related to his need to gain weight; at thirty-four, he was just under six feet tall, weighing 61½ kilos, or 134 pounds — lean but not yet skeletal.

between him and his sisters) much of the tension is removed. His words about his life with Ottla recall Adam and Eve before the Fall: an Edenic vision, an earthly paradise. It is like some of the brother-sister relationships he had read about in one of his favorite authors, Dickens, where the household of siblings, without parents or spouses, runs smoothly and contentedly because sexual tension is missing. The undercurrent of incest gives the "couple" just enough snap to keep them happy.

Kafka, however, is not finished in his "confession" to Brod. In another mid-September letter, he speculates, "Should I give thanks that I have not been able to marry? I would then have become all at once what I am now becoming gradually: mad. With shorter and shorter intermissions — during which not I but it gathers strength."[274] In brief, tuberculosis saved him from rapid madness, consigning him to a slower process. This is not to say that Kafka was unaware of his predicament, or that Dr. Mühlstein's prognosis was favorable. In a September 22 letter to Felix Weltsch, right after Felice has left Zürau, Kafka wrote that the doctor has gradually taken a darker view of his prospects: "It is as if he had wanted to shield me with his broad back from the Angel of Death which stood behind him, and now he gradually steps aside. But neither he nor it (alas!) frightens me."[275]

At the very end of September or in early October, Kafka tried to write a final scene for him and Felice, a kind of summing up of their "great war," which was winding down even as that other Great War was reaching toward a final stage with the October Russian Revolution. Kafka's phrasing is of a war that raged in him and of a war that has continued into his relationship with her. He speaks of two combatants within him, in constant struggle; and he says the better of the two belongs to her. "By word and silence, and a combination of both, you have been kept informed about the progress of the war for 5 years, and most of that time it has caused you suffering."[276] The sentiments seem lifted from *Hamlet*, when Hamlet tries to explain to Ophelia, however full of self-hatred his explanation is, that the war within him has made her the victim.

Kafka emphasizes that he has tried to be as truthful with Felice as was humanly possible, admitting subterfuges but not lies. He further admits to being a mendacious character in other respects, for so fragile is his boat he can maintain "an even keel" only through mendacity. He admits, in this apologia to Felice, that he does not attempt to be good or to answer to some supreme tribunal. "Very much the opposite. I strive to know the entire human and animal community, to recognize their fundamental preferences, desires, and moral ideals, to reduce them to simple rules, and as quickly as possible to adopt these rules so as to be pleasing to everyone, indeed (here comes the inconsistency) to become so pleasing that in the end I might openly act out my inherent baseness before the eyes of the world without forfeiting its love — the only sinner not to be roasted."[277] He presents himself in Manichaean terms, as containing good and evil battling for supremacy, and he says she has been his human tribunal, an assumption that she has brought out the best in him, even while the worst struggles to emerge and dominate.

He applies this Manichaean conflict to their relationship, to the blood he is shedding for their wasted years together. In striving to find the metaphors by which he can explain his failure, Kafka has elevated the terms of their affair to poetic language. "Suddenly it appears that the loss of blood was too great. The blood shed by the good one (the one that now seems good to us) in order to win you, serves the evil one. Where the evil one on his own would probably or possibly not have found a decisive new weapon for his defense, the good one offers him just that. For secretly I don't believe this illness to be tuberculosis, at least not primarily tuberculosis, but rather a sign of my general bankruptcy." He then assumes the sacrificial pose: "I had thought the war could last longer, but it can't. The blood issues not from the lung, but from a decisive stab delivered by one of the combatants."[278]

But he knows it is tuberculosis: terminal for him and terminal for any hope of a relationship with a woman like Felice. It is the final stage of his weakness that he can wield as a weapon. "Has not the war [that inner war] been most splendidly concluded? It is tuberculosis, and that is the end."[279] He then moves into one of his most twisted and touching poses, that of the warrior brought down in battle and dependent on female succor. "Weak and weary, almost invisible to you when in this state, what can the other one do but lean on your shoulder here in Zürau, and with you the purest of the pure, stare in amazement, bewildered and hopeless, at the great man who — now that he feels sure of universal love, or of that of its female representative assigned to him — begins to display his atrocious baseness. It is a distortion of my striving, which in itself is already a distortion."[280]

She must understand he has not put up a barrier, and one word would bring him to her feet again. But his disease makes all that impossible. He says that in contrast his other weapons, such as his physical incapacity or his work or his parsimony, look expedient and primitive. Then he opens up completely, his final confession and effort to be truthful: "I will never be well again. Simply because it is not the kind of tuberculosis that can be laid in a deckchair and nursed back to health, but a weapon that continues to be of supreme necessity as long as I remain alive. And both cannot remain alive."[281] Their relationship is completed, ended by death.

There remained one more letter, from October 16, 1917, and a fragmentary note, undated. In the letter, he recalls their moments together when they stood in silence and they did seem to commune with each other even when they knew it was all over. She was unhappy, he says, about the pointlessness of her journey and about his "incomprehensible behavior";[282] but he was not unhappy. He says he was tormented, yet hopeful, because he saw the "whole tragedy" as having an immensity that surpassed all his strength. This knowledge gave him a calm he had lacked before. He refers to his words addressed to Max Brod, and Brod's response, that one can find happiness in unhappiness, which Kafka finds unacceptable. But in that same letter to Brod, he ends on a note of hopelessness. Cabarets, he says, are out of bounds for him. "Where would I crawl off to, when all the big guns start booming, with my toy pistol of a lung."[283] Even his damaged organs can be described in martial terms.

He ends his last (extant) letter to Felice with his immediate plans: to return to Prague, to visit a specialist, a dentist, and, inevitably, his office. The final note is worth quoting in full:

> One more thing I want to say: there were and are moments when — in reality or from my recollection, usually from my recollection — your way of looking at me — something more than what you are and, in essence, something higher seems to break through; but, as in other respects, I am too feeble to hold on to it, or to hold on to myself in the face of it.[284]

Seven years from the end, he had a vision of what marriage might have meant to him if he had been able to accommodate it. But out of strength, not weakness, he rejected it. He saw himself as weak, but in that reversal of roles that served Kafka so well in his fiction, he was acting from strength. He was the powerhouse; Felice was weak and uncertain. Kafka's uncertainties were all transformed into acts that ultimately protected him from intrusions on his personal life that most likely would have defeated him.* Using his show of weakness, he retreated and retreated, somewhat like the Russians before Napoleon, until, like the French, Felice had overextended her lines. The weaker foe had found his means of triumphing. Like all such triumphs, it was on the surface Pyrrhic; but subsurface, it was pure victory.

---

*In an interesting formulation, in an important book, Stanley Corngold speaks of Kafka's "turnings" as part of a double helix. Corngold sees Kafka as undergoing two basic turnings, first a renunciation of the body (food, sex, marriage, Felice) in order to make writing possible for him; second, a more intense turning, when writing moves to a point beyond the body and the writer, Kafka, has no more to give because he is depleted. "In the first instance, to be nothing is to be good for writing; in the second, it is to be good for nothing. Everything there was to sacrifice has been sacrificed; there was no more bodily life to harm" (*Franz Kafka: The Necessity of Form* [Ithaca: Cornell University Press, 1988], p. 109). This second turning occurs after the hemorrhaging and discovery of tuberculosis in 1917. While recognizing Corngold's distinction, I see Kafka as moving in a single direction, whereby he surrenders more and more of himself until there is nothing left except the act of writing itself, on the model of the hunger artist, who dwindles to almost nothing. As he declines through disease, Kafka becomes like his transformational objects, diminished; and all that remains is "writing," which he has apotheosized into ritual, sacrament, spiritual experience. Like the lambcat in "A Crossbreed," he awaits the knife thrust that will end his life, but before that end he becomes writing and memory.

Earth, isn't this what you want: an invisible
re-arising in us? Is not your dream
to be one day invisible? Earth! invisible!
What is your urgent command, if not transformation?

— RILKE, *DUINO*, 9TH ELEGY

TEN Kafka's Maturity and the Beginning of a New Era

ALTHOUGH THE CORRESPONDENCE with Felice Bauer has considerable intrinsic value of its own, by itself it could not have made Kafka into a world literary figure or a representative man of the twentieth century. Significant as it was, the correspondence must be viewed against the rest of his life as a man and, especially, as a writer. It must be seen as complementary to his fictional efforts, not as separated from his professional life. In his letters, Kafka carried everything — feeling, emotional response, psychological reactions, decision making — to extremes. In his role as suitor and, temporarily, as fiancé, he created almost a parody of what courtship is expected to be. Yet in that parody or near parody, he found several of his fictional weapons. He created images and symbols, he transformed himself, he brought tremendous pressure on his fiancée, tantamount to control of her life, he reached as deeply into himself as he had to do for his best works, he discovered what he was and was capable of, and he consolidated his view of himself as unhappy and despairing, a perception he desperately needed in order to fulfill his mission as sacrifice and martyr. One further reason he could not marry Felice was that he had transformed himself into a priest, of the imagination.

Most of all, however, he discovered how effective he could be in written words, as opposed to a more public forum, or even a personal discussion between engaged people. The written word revealed to him that he was a serious writer even when he was incapable of writing fiction, with the letters serving as a kind of epistolary novel. They served, further, as a means for him to play his roles, to change himself into various shapes and forms, as the situation demanded. By acting out, he could enjoy a therapeutic process, playing alternately analyst and analysand. However much pain the correspondence caused him, and evidently caused Felice, who became his guinea pig in his testing out of human relationships, the written words of the letters enlarged his imagination, stretched his abilities, and forced profound introspection. The letters helped Kafka become a great writer, but only a great writer could have written those letters.

Kafka had closed out 1911, as noted earlier, with a message to himself about the value of literature to a people and to a nation, even when the literature, like contemporary Yiddish literature, was not unusually broad in scope. Even when a great talent was absent, such a literature is compelling; and in fact the absence of an overwhelming figure, like that of Goethe in Germany, allowed each writer to be more independent and less linked to some empowered tradition. Kafka of course was being self-serving, justifying his own strange situation of writing in a language not his, while aware of the great masters of that language, which belonged to others.

As we move toward 1912, we sense revelations everywhere; even in his dissatisfaction, we note how he was shaping his feelings and ideas to his fictional recreation as insect, emigrant, or suicide. All these personal complaints, we should emphasize again, were for Kafka not signs of weakness but forms of empowerment. As he attacked what he was and how he felt, he did not sink into the despair that leads to passivity. He recharged himself by changing weakness into forms of power, the characteristic note of his letters to Felice Bauer.

In the early part of the year (1912), Kafka's immersion in Jewish matters intensified as he attended plays, read profusely, and listened to Löwy's tales of his Orthodox background. His efforts to express all his "love and devotion" for Mania Tschissik, upon meeting her and her husband, had backfired and brought their conversation to an end. The couple soon left Prague because Prague Jews — because of their hostility to Polish Jews — took so little interest in them. Mania's rendition of "Hear, O Israel," which she sang in the play *Sedernacht* (*Passover Night*), was something Kafka particularly cherished; and it might have been this song, along with other associations, that led him to ask Felice Bauer when he first met her in August to go with him to Palestine. We may think of Kafka as safe and withdrawn, but when an idea struck him he could be daring and could act quite out of character, suggesting, for instance, that he and a young woman he was meeting for the first time emigrate together.

Even while it gave him something of a direction, however, this movement toward an understanding of Jewishness and Yiddish as observed in Eastern European Jews created further divisions within Kafka: he was attracted to the trappings but unable to accept the core of faith that made these Jews into people who could take themselves for granted. What he also perceived in this, and what he brought to his fiction, was how close he was to the very thing he attacked in his parents: how incapable he was himself of bridging these gaps. And this knowledge of his own lack of base or anchor gave him particular qualities once he transferred this personal uncertainty into fictional works.

He assessed Zionism, which until recently had been for him anathema. Here we enter thickets, for Kafka's *Diaries* suggest considerable vacillation, whereas Brod, himself a dedicated Zionist, states a firmer commitment. Brod tended to see himself as a considerable influence on Kafka in this area. Repeatedly, we gain the impression that Brod saw himself as the "prime mover," with Kafka following; in fact, the evolution of Kafka's Zionism was never simple or pure, and often contained misgivings. Brod admits the influence of Löwy and says that Kafka's material on the actor amounts to a kind of autobiography, based on the conversations they had. Löwy, Brod says, revealed the more colorful and showy side of Jewry than the Zionists could, and this was certainly a valid insight. Kafka needed manifestation, not theory. Brod himself said that more could be learned from the performance of these actors than from the "philosophic deductions" of Western Jews.[1]

Kafka held back, however, from admitting that East, West, Zionism, and the Diaspora were interconnected.* Part of his diffidence on this point was his wariness of community. Brod entered in his own diary for January 18, 1913, that Kafka felt he had insufficient strength to extend beyond himself into any notion of community. But another aspect of his withholding of himself was linked to languages: that he could write in no other language but German and was, therefore, connected irreversibly to the language of Schiller and Goethe, of Hebbel, Grillparzer, and Fontane. Even later, when he came around almost completely to Zionism, he had to divide himself: into the Hebrew recommended by the Zionists, for possible emigration, and into the German he continued to write. That he did undertake seriously the study of Hebrew in the last years of his life — and supported the Jewish National Committee in 1918–19, when he was already tubercular — indicates he was trying to close the gap between what he believed and what he practiced.

Martin Buber came to represent everything Kafka resented and yet had to deal with.† Buber was an ardent Zionist when Kafka met him, remaining very active in the movement after Herzl's death in 1904; but

---

*If Kafka can be characterized as a hesitant Zionist, no one was more reluctant than the founding father of Zionism, Theodor Herzl. Unlike Herzl, Kafka at least did not become part of a German dueling fraternity while at the university or worship Bismarck and the Prussian Junker ideal.

†In one of those historical ironies that seemed to envelop Kafka even after his death, Margarete Buber-Neumann, who had been married to Martin Buber's son, Rafael, found herself in Ravensbrück concentration camp as a friend and helper of Milena Jesenská, one of Kafka's closest women friends in his final years.

more than that, he emphasized the mystical side of Judaism and built his early career on a retelling of Eastern European shtetl stories. His was a direct attack on the Westernized or Germanized Jew, and through revealing their warm literature, he mounted a defense of Eastern European Jews, who were reviled in the West for uncouth manners, bad hygiene, and mystical practices. Buber published an anthology of mystical testimonies, calling it *Ekstatische Konfessionen* (*Ecstatic Confessions*). He was principal speaker on at least three occasions at the Bar Kochba Society, an association of Jewish students, and we know Kafka was in and around this society beginning in 1910. He attended at least one Buber lecture, the third, in 1910. What Buber offered was a full-dress examination of contemporary Judaism along with a resolution of what it should be and where it should direct its energies.

As a Zionist, Buber broke with the usual socialist, agnostic-atheistic Jews who made up a good part of the Zionist movement, and instead based his desire for a Jewish homeland on mysticism. Buber's mysticism allowed him to probe the nature of the isolated individual and yet to demonstrate that even the most solitary of characters can, somehow, be joined to the world. First the self withdraws into individual expression, and then in some mystical experience reunites itself with the rest of mankind. In this process, God is a necessary vehicle but is not the ultimate reality.

Despite the mystical dimensions to his thought, Buber was basically a secular philosopher; his God was little more than a necessary fiction to get the process going. In his mysticism, there was no ultimate union with a transcendant being. Using his beliefs, Buber could attack Westernized European Jews who attempted to assimilate by denying what they were and deride those same Jews for their alienation from their real roots, in Eastern European mystical Judaism. In a sense, Buber covered all bases, from Zionism and Jewish nationalism to a denial of God but, withal, emphasized rejection of assimilation and a return to origins. Only by plumbing the depths of his own being can the Jew find in himself his Jewishness, and the means by which he makes that descent of discovery is through intuition or mystery. Only then can he end his isolation on one hand and his feeble efforts to assimilate on the other. At some point, he identifies with the "race." Even in Buber, the matter of race had become paramount; and now he offered the idea of a "Jewish race," which was his way to resolve what is still an unresolvable matter. Buber believed in blood ties: a Jew was a Jew because he had Jewish blood. Such a view, when turned on its head, could permit later German national socialists to work out a racial plan in which every drop of Jewish blood was to be expunged.

But no one yet saw these dangers of a theory of race, and Buber's ideas proved almost irresistible. One problem, however, that young men like Kafka had with Buber's thought was his failure to address democratic ideas. A theory of race based on blood ties, however Jewish, did not leave room for theories of egalitarianism or democracy. Buber, in fact, was little concerned with such matters, and was essentially working through the individual's dilemmas, not society's. Furthermore, as a Zionist, he was interested in providing the groundwork for a return to the Palestinian homeland, not for some vision of what could happen in a severely divided Europe, although some argument can be made that Buber intuited or foresaw that Jewish life had no place in twentieth-century European history. One commentator has caught most profoundly what Buber's influence was on young Jews like Kafka, and on Kafka himself.[2] He correctly sees Buber's point as an attack on capitalism, in fact on every economic system that permitted Jews to be stereotyped. Buber agreed with the "degenerationist" theorists, like Nordau and Weininger, that the contemporary Westernized Jew was degenerate, slack in his thinking, corrupt in his practices, someone who had sold out to the capitalist mode and, unthinkingly, turned his back on his true heritage.

Assimilationist or not, this Westernized Jew has cut himself off from everything that might provide sustenance. Cast adrift as a result of his self-absorption and narcissism, he has forsaken all supports, and even support from within. He is lost, wandering the face of Europe as part of the Diaspora, but unable to connect with anything meaningful, not even to himself. He is that man without a soul, the superfluous man, the unknown man. Buber was quite sensitive to this and to this kind of Jew, since for him the Jew seemed representative of the entire process, in his way a speeded-up illustration of the modern wasteland experience. Such a man is not a man at all, inasmuch as he is passive, lacking in practical knowledge, able to function only at the intellectual level, which is inadequate for modern life. We can see how Buber's indictment of the Westernized Jew (that is, Kafka and his life) underpins his Zionism; for in the return to the homeland, to the land, the Jew will exercise a different function. No longer purely intellectual, he will have to become practical. Since the Zionist dream was based on agriculture, not an urbanized existence, the Jew would have to learn practical skills and get into touch with his instincts, which had in Buber's view lost out to a contaminated rationality.

This could be appealing, and it set up in Kafka a sequence of complicated responses, responses that he worked out over a number of years, not in any given time. That it coincided with the Yiddish theater troupe's stay in Prague was more than happenstance: Kafka was opening out to something that had troubled him since schoolboy days. In effect, his conflicts and inner struggle here were not Jewish, although Buber had a Jewish cure for them, but the problems of modern man and his civilization: the loss of an instinctual life, the relationship of the individual to a larger entity, the self-absorption endemic to an urban, civilized existence, the inability of the individual to reach out beyond himself, the loss of any sustaining faith, even in oneself, the role one cast for oneself in a hostile environment.

Kafka had already taken a step in his recognition of how futile efforts at assimilation were, and how the Westernized Jew did not even have a language of his own, how German failed him, while a national language could not be his either. The idea of struggling to reach one's instinctual life has, of course, since been besmirched by racist preachers and obviously became completely contaminated by what occurred under the Nazis, when Germans of all persuasions (and a good part of Europe) embraced the Nazi creed of an instinct based on blood and race. But the lack of an instinctive life, a life in which brain dominated, was a profound issue in Kafka's time; and Zionists played upon it. It was one way of demonstrating the "degeneration" of Jewish culture as practiced in the West, with its many conversions (Heine, Marx, Mahler, Kraus, Schoenberg, Tucholsky, and an army of others), its futile efforts to assimilate, its pariah status as soon as nationalist movements and pogroms developed, its equally futile efforts toward socialism as a way of identifying with the working classes, who turned out to be more anti-Semitic and bloodthirsty than their middle-class cohorts.

One can trace Buber's analysis to a distinction made by the sociologist Ferdinand Tönnies.[3] Tönnies posed a distinction between a society based on traditional values and blood ties (what he called *Gemeinschaft*, communion or partnership), and one based on individual self-interest (*Gesellschaft*, a company or party). While useful for developing capitalist countries as they confront traditional modes in their societies, his distinction has its origin in folk and racial theories traceable to Herder and to Gobineau. Here a traditional society takes on racial overtones, even while providing some alternative to runaway individualistic, self-seeking capitalism. All of this becomes rather heady stuff given the nature of ideological struggles in Kafka's time, and there is little doubt that Kafka was caught up in it. His interest in rowing, carpentry, and gardening were all part of his effort to identify with the older forms of society and were explicitly a rejection of the capitalistic society in which he enjoyed his status and made his living. His movement toward Zionism and a personalized form of Judaism in the last ten or twelve years of his life is linked, apparently, to the ideological question of what kind of society the individual should belong to.

These ideas, however, can lead to strange decisions, as they did with Buber. For so caught up was he with "folk" and "nation" and "community" based on blood ties that he supported the emergence of German nationalism and with it the First World War. Like several others, he felt that if Jews served in the war and showed their loyalty to the Kaiser, they would become part of this community of spirit. In a sense, he was right, because when the Germans decided to kill Jews, out of gratitude former soldiers with medals were among the last to be selected for extermination in the camps.

For Buber, then — as shortly for Kafka, despite his earlier rejection of the philosopher — the way to balance was through the practices of Eastern European Jewry. His model clearly was the Hasidic movement in the eighteenth century, a form of revivalism of the religious spirit as a response to Enlightenment ideas. Hasidism represented for Kafka several fundamental ideas of religion that he could not accept, but what he found attractive in it and in its believers was their certainty of identification. The individual clearly had linkage to a large group, and the group was supportive of the individual. Kafka could not, of course, go all the way, for whatever his longing was for community values, he was, and would remain, too much a unique being to give himself over wholly to any belief or group. His irony and suspicion of all firm ideas made him an outsider, although through Zionism and certain Hasidic ideas he moved toward that ideal society that he imagined as possible and yet derided as unachievable.

Although our focus here is on Kafka, not Buber, it should be added that Buber was himself sidetracked in his youth from Zionism by Hasidism, which he demonstrated in his collection of Hasidic tales, published in 1906 and 1908. Many estranged Jews felt the power of these tales and sought identification with their backgrounds as a result: Hugo von Hofmannsthal, Walter Rathenau (the industrialist), George Lukács (whose Judaism would in time take second place to his Communism), the publisher Salman Schocken (who later became Kafka's publisher), and Arnold Zweig. Kafka himself found the study of these stories, as recounted by Buber, intolerable, by which he meant his German was excessive and sentimentalized. Whatever their stylistic excesses, as these stories became extremely popular in the Jewish community (including Prague), their point of view was taken up by several Jewish societies, not the least by the Prague branch of the Bar Kochba, with which Kafka had more than nodding acquaintance. Mysticism replaced theories of race, but the blood tie was retained, a kind of societywide blood-brotherhood. As Ritchie Robertson puts it, "Rejecting the arid rationalism often ascribed to the Jews, the writers [in the Bar Kochba] are anxious to regain access to the irrational, mythopoeic, creative depths of the Jewish soul, and agree that these faculties can only flourish in a restored Jewish community. They set youth against age, mysticism against rationalism, the Orient against the Occident, and *Gemeinschaft* against *Gesellschaft*." Accordingly, Buber's drift from Zionism toward mysticism was resolved in the blending of the two: mysticism practiced in a Jewish community, in a homeland of its own.

The significance of all this for Kafka cannot be overestimated. While he may have struggled against Buber's "intolerable" excesses, he

Hermann Kafka (1852–1931), Kafka's father and a Prague fancy-goods merchant.

Julie Löwy (1856–1934), Kafka's mother, married Hermann Kafka in 1882.

Hermann Kafka used the jackdaw (*kavka* in Czech) as his business logo.

The Kinsky Palace in Old Town Square, with Hermann Kafka's store indicated to the right. (He did not use the spelling *Herman.*) Kafka attended secondary school in the same building, from 1893 to 1901.

Minuta House, on Old Town
Square, where Kafka lived as
a young boy, from 1889 to 1896.

Sharon Spiegel

Celina Spiegel

Old Town Square, with the Jan Hus Memorial, celebrating the late
fourteenth century/early fifteenth century religious reformer. The
square, along with Wenceslas Square, is a centerpiece of Prague life.

Kafka at about age thirteen.

Kafka's youngest sister, Ottla (Ottilie), at age eighteen.

Kafka's second oldest sister, Valli (Valerie), at age twenty.

Kafka's oldest sister, Elli (Gabriele), at age twenty-one. All three sisters died in German concentration camps.

Kafka sent this photograph of himself, taken when he was twenty-
seven, to his fiancée, Felice Bauer, in December 1912. He attributed the
"visionary expression" on his face to the photographer's flash bulb.

Max Brod.

Jizchak Löwy, a Yiddish actor
who became close friends with
Kafka and helped to introduce
him to Jewish life and literature
in Eastern Europe.

Felice Bauer, Kafka's fiancée, in 1914. Her teeth disturbed Kafka throughout much of their five-year relationship.

The cover of Kafka's third book, *The Metamorphosis*, published in November 1915, in the *Jüngste Tag* series. The design is a lithograph by Ottomar Starke; Kafka had insisted that the insect was not to be drawn.

FRANZ KAFKA

DIE VERWANDLUNG

DER JÜNGSTE TAG · 22/23
KURT WOLFF VERLAG · LEIPZIG
1916

A sample of Kafka's drawings and doodles. He was an inveterate doodler, and one finds his diaries, notebooks, and postcards embellished with strange but graceful shapes. Most of these appear to come from his university years.

The famous clock in Old Town Square, which features the apostles revolving through the two windows just above the dial. Their procession occurs every hour on the hour.

The headquarters of the Workers' Accident Insurance Institute for the Kingdom of Bohemia, at 7 Pořič Street, where Kafka worked for most of his adult life. At the upper right is the official seal of the company. His office was on the top floor.

No. 22 in Golden (or Alchemists) Lane, in the Hradčany Castle section of Prague. Kafka's sister Ottla rented this house, and Kafka wrote there in the evenings. The Czech plaque to the left states KAFKA LIVED HERE, which is not true.

Kafka and Ottla, his favorite sister, around 1917.

Grete Bloch, the friend of Felice Bauer with whom Kafka may have become intimate. She later claimed he had fathered a son with her, but there is no evidence to support her assertion.

Kafka and his fiancée,
Felice Bauer, posed in
Budapest, in July 1917,
shortly before the second
engagement ended when
Kafka hemorrhaged from
his lungs.

Milena Jesenská, a Czech Christian
with whom Kafka became intimate
in his later years. She died in a
German concentration camp, where
she had been committed for political
reasons.

The last known photograph of Kafka, taken either in 1923, or in 1924, the year of his death.

Dora Dymant, with whom Kafka lived at the end of his life in Berlin. Before his fatal illness, they had planned to emigrate to Palestine together.

A bust of Kafka, just off Old Town Square. This is the sole memorial to him, except for his marked grave in the New Jewish Cemetery. The bust dates from 1965 and was designed by the sculptor Karel Hadlik.

The gravestone marking Kafka's grave, along with that of Hermann and Julie Kafka, in the New Jewish Cemetery. The grave is a leading Prague tourist stop and is virtually the only part of the cemetery maintained.

was beguiled by the vision, and it would be a vision he could assimilate into his imagination and make part of his work. While many of his subsequent short and long fictions had as their locale his own highly uncertain and anguished psyche, there is also little question that several of the works concern ideological struggles. Even a story seemingly so personal as "The Judgment," written the following year, contains many of the elements just described: Georg Bendemann's desire to break away from his father's control of him is, in one respect, his need to assert his individualism against traditional values that no longer function for him. Kafka has shifted the point somewhat to fit his own needs, but the conflict exists between Georg's desire for independence (*Gesellschaft*) and his father's insistence on a self-effacing *Gemeinschaft*. Similarly, we can view "The Metamorphosis," aspects of *The Trial*, "In the Penal Colony," several of the animal stories, and surely the pinnacle of Kafka's work, at the end of his life, "A Hunger Artist."

In the meanwhile, he learned of the Haskalah (Enlightenment) movement, whose adherents tended toward Hebrew, not Yiddish. After the 1881 pogrom (in part brought on by the assassination of Czar Alexander II of Russia), these adherents became strongly Zionist, especially when several "blood libel" cases occurred and the Dreyfus trial made it clear that Jews were not welcome in Europe. "Be a man on the street and a Jew at home," Kafka quotes one writer as saying, the very charge Freud once leveled against his father: that in giving ground to a Gentile on the street his father had surrendered his manhood. Kafka saw all the contradictions here, for the Haskalah movement in its need to reach Jews had to use Yiddish for communication, the very language it wanted to replace. In this and other divisions, Kafka saw his own situation reflected: he was continually attracted to an idea whose center, for him, did not hold.

Kafka was torn further by the clash between Yiddish literature, which he was reading about, and his education, in which figures like Goethe and Schiller were gods. He and Brod, in fact, would make a special trip to Weimar to worship at the shrine of Goethe, touching base with Schiller and Liszt along the way. All this came together in February 1912, when Goethe's name turned up repeatedly in Kafka's *Diaries* even as he was being awakened to a quite different Jewish experience. The asbestos factory was also turning into a nightmarish episode, as Kafka observed the factory girls becoming increasingly dehumanized. His description of them in his February 5 entry as ceasing to be people, as having become objects, uncannily foreshadows Čapek's *RUR*, a play about robots. And, of course, Kafka, like Hašek in his *Good Soldier Schweik*, saw the bureaucracy, whether business or army, as robotic in its reification of people and denial of their individual needs.*

---

*Kafka's parallelism to Hašek will be apparent throughout this book. Although Hašek's masterpiece was not begun until 1921, he and Kafka shared analogous experiences: one

At this time, Kafka arranged an evening for Löwy at the Jewish Town Hall, while he, Kafka, would deliver a brief introductory lecture on Yiddish.

In giving his speech, Kafka discovered something in language that moved him toward a center of meaning that German could not have for him. He tells his audience what he once told himself, that they should not fear Yiddish, that they should not feel they cannot understand it. For with their German-language background, they will "understand far more jargon [Yiddish] than you think. I am not at all worried about the effect of what we have prepared for you this evening, but I would like you to be free to properly appreciate it. And this you will not be able to do as long as some of you are so frightened by the sound of Yiddish that the fear is written all over your faces."[4] That fear, Kafka assumes, is not simply connected to language. It is linked to what Yiddish means to the German-speaking Jew who has put behind him the Eastern European Jewish experience and who considers himself assimilated, Germanized, part of Western culture and civilization.

Kafka prepared for his lecture preceding Löwy's performance with considerable trepidation; he had originally thought Oskar Baum would deliver the introduction, but Baum pulled out and Kafka was left to do it. Almost a week before the event, on Sunday, February 18, he started to prepare, and he felt his body turning alternately cold and hot. In performance, he turned out quite capable, and even he admitted it was successful, despite two weeks of fear. Reviews (including one in *Selbstwehr*, a Jewish weekly) were praiseworthy; and Löwy also acquitted himself well.*

Kafka soothes his audience, like a parent trying to get a small child to swallow a pill, warning him not to constrict his throat but to open wide and let the pill slip down easily. "You will already be quite close to Yiddish if you realize that, active within you, in addition to knowledge, are forces and junctures of forces that enable you to feel into an

---

in the army, the other in a large institutional organization. They may have even met, at anarchist functions, although that cannot be proved, but both wrote of the bureaucracy as a machine. Strikingly, when Hašek came to name Schweik, he called him Josef, like Kafka's equally famous Josef(s) and Vienna's Franz Josef.

*Kafka could not resist measuring worries against benefits. The worries made him lie in bed "twisted up," "hot and sleepless, hatred of Dr. B. [Baum], fear of Weltsch (he will not be able to sell anything) . . . the notices are not published in the papers the way in which they were expected to be." There are distractions in the office, a mixup in the stage preparations, and several uncertainties. But the benefits were there: pride and confidence in Löwy (although the evening was not a financial success), a newfound confidence in his own delivery ("coolness in the presence of the audience . . . strong voice, effortless memory"), a power he did not know he had, a certain manliness in standing up to the town hall porters who demanded more money. "In all this are revealed powers to which I would gladly entrust myself if they would remain." But Kafka could not let this burst of joy remain; he ends the entry, "My parents were not there" (*Diaries: 1910–1913*, pp. 234–35). Even a victorious evening needed that poison pill. His activities fell below their recognition because they did not make money.

understanding of Yiddish. . . . Yiddish is everything: word, Hasidic melody, and the very essence of this Eastern Jewish actor himself." Once the audience lets go of its former complacency or resistance, "you will so powerfully feel the true unity of Yiddish as to make you afraid — not of Yiddish any longer, but of yourselves. And you would not be able to bear the burden of this fear by yourselves alone if, at the same time, Yiddish did not also endow you with a self-confidence that resists this fear and is even stronger."[5] And should the memory of it fade, Kafka hopes they will also forget the fear. What is remarkable is how the speech speaks to him. The talk is peppered with the "fear of Yiddish," as if it were the poison dooming Jews everywhere, and with the conviction that Jews had to fight off the desire to deny their true selves so as to present a better face to the Gentile.

This "fear" haunted Kafka, obviously because he was brought up with it: that upbringing that insists the child may not be himself since society will accept only a transformed creature. But there was more, something uniquely Kafkan: the need to find in language a home, parents, beliefs, a center of rest, a way to relieve the ever present sense of alienation and marginality in oneself and in everything around one. The deracinated, alienated Prague Jew is Everyman in the twentieth century — or at least Everyman who tries to be someone else and, thus, loses whatever he is or has a chance to be. Through language, Kafka is speaking about several things: the loss of ceremony, the lack of tradition, the forsaking of history, the failure to achieve social solidity. Kafka was not ripe for religion; he was ripe for some kind of fulfillment.

He found this fulfillment in literature, as a writer, identifying himself with the great writers he admired, Flaubert, Kleist, Hebbel, Goethe; through that identification he mitigated the sickening marginality he felt as a person.

We can see in an early 1912 diary entry what writing was beginning to mean for him:

> It is easy to recognize a concentration in me of all my forces on writing. When it became clear in my organism that writing was the most productive direction for my being to take, everything rushed in that direction and left empty all those abilities which were directed toward the joys of sex, eating, drinking, philosophical reflection and above all music. I atrophied in all these directions. This was necessary because the totality of my strengths was so slight that only collectively could they even halfway serve the purpose of my writing.[6]

He stresses he was in the hands of some destiny or fate: "Naturally, I did not find this purpose independently and consciously, it found itself, and is now interfered with only by the office, but that interferes with it completely." He insists he has no time for a sweetheart (although Felice will sail into view this year), that he understands as

much about love as he does about music and would "have to resign myself to the most superficial effects I may pick up." In line with his sacrifice of himself for his craft, he remarks that on last New Year's Eve,
he dined on parsnips and spinach, "eased down with a glass of
Ceres. . . . My development is now complete and, so far as I can see,
there is nothing left to sacrifice; I need only throw my work in the office out of this complex in order to begin my real life in which, with the
progress of my work, my face will finally be able to age in a natural
way."

This dedication to writing, almost comparable to Stephen Dedalus's in James Joyce, is encapsulated in a short piece Kafka now wrote,
"The Sudden Walk," which appeared in *Meditation* in 1913. We have
already noted this brief sketch, but it deserves repeating here since it
involved the complex train of thought Kafka was experiencing as he entered this intense period of balancing diverse elements in his life, even
as he felt bereft of the energy to succeed in any enterprise. The brief episode is part of the conflict between lazy acceptance of what is, the
peace and quiet of one's room, and the outside, where decisions must
be made and where one's strength is realized. To get "outside" is to
take the most distant journey. The piece is an emblem of Kafka's inner
struggle: how to distance himself, finally, so that he remains untouchable within his own expectations and forms of satisfaction. Since no
one can measure what gives him joy, except himself, then he must experience it alone. The piece suggests he can.

Although Kafka's diffidence among other people remained, he revealed, nevertheless, how deeply involved he was with artistic circles,
despite his shyness or embarrassment with others. Through participation in lectures, in café talk, at meetings with writers and artists passing through Prague, he was soaking up the spirit of Modernism, *even
when* such figures were themselves suspicious of the avant-garde or
were anti-Modern. Kafka's *Diaries* for this period are full of jottings, literary ideas, some sequences, bits and pieces of dialogue that go nowhere. Though he was not heading in any clear direction, until closer
to the end of the year, he was writing.

In these months of early 1912 he became completely dependent on
the *Diaries*, with both short and long entries, some of them clearly autobiographical, but others blending fiction and fact as a form of fantasy.
He views himself (on March 12) in a sanatorium for lung cases, and
when he is unable to get the landlord's daughter to go to bed with him,
he throws her, suddenly, down in the grass, "the way lung cases sometimes act."[7] Then while she lies unconscious, stunned and frightened,
he takes her — in effect, rapes her. Awakening her with cool water, he
accepts full responsibility for his act, an impulsiveness he can partially
excuse by his "delicate lungs." The girl is too weak and embarrassed to
make trouble for him, and he recognizes that "he, the great, strong per-

son, could push the girl aside." No one would believe her anyway, so weak and plain is she. The fantasy event, full of violence and anger toward women, gave Kafka or his surrogate a masculine strength surely lacking in its creator; but it also reveals in the horrific act a side of Kafka filled with extreme hostility toward women, particularly women of the lower classes. This was, obviously, merely a simple Czech girl and, therefore, someone who could serve as a degraded vision. Other diary entries indicate a subsurface violence, directed also against men as well as boys. In Kafka's repressed feelings, there was terrible anger, and when it was not directed at himself, as it was most of the time, it emerged, particularly in the *Diaries*, as cruel and brutal acts against others.

A March publication in the *Neue Rundschau* by Arthur Holitscher, "Amerika heute und morgen" ("America Today and Tomorrow") — a number of articles describing a journey through the United States — may have influenced Kafka's own work on what became *Amerika*. One critic points out that Kafka's spelling of "Oklahama," perhaps confusing it with Yokahama, is duplicated by Holitscher. But just as likely Kafka's sense of the "Wild West" came from his childhood reading of Karl May, the German James Fenimore Cooper. Intruding into his progress on the novel and his ability to write at all with continuity was the factory business, which appeared to be making the entire family miserable. We get the impression that at each moment Kafka expected something drastic to occur which would alter the course of his life, but when he looked back, he found no change, which brought him into a deep despair about the future.

Despite his realistic perceptions about himself and his powers, Kafka maintained an implicit optimism about change; and yet each day followed the last without altering his circumstances. Kafka blamed his father, intensified his hostility toward his mother, inveighed against a situation that made him, at close to twenty-nine, as vulnerable as he had been at fifteen. He could write of himself as having, "without weight, without bones, without body, walked through the streets for two hours considering what I overcame this afternoon while writing."[8] He was of course working, and well, at the institute, but the statement indicates he felt disembodied, dispirited, lacking in connection between body and mind or between self and society.

In still another example, he contemplates the paradox of a devil who, if he possessed us, could keep us in some equilibrium with the spirit of God. But no such devil exists, no such equilibrium exists; instead, we are possessed by a "crowd of devils" who account for our earthly misfortunes. The fact that they don't exterminate each other, or consolidate into one "great devil," cannot be explained, but either way would "be in accord with the diabolical principle of deceiving us as completely as possible."[9] Kafka implies that if we could understand the demons bedeviling us, we could at least determine what they have in mind, but such is the nature of devils and demons that we cannot determine the reality even of them. It is a statement worthy of Joseph K. when he discovers that any determination of his case leaves him as uncertain as no determination at all, or all determinations taken together, or even one that appears more favorable. The argument is one of complete entrapment, in life as in fiction.

With no way out, Kafka and Brod undertook a trip, on June 28, to Weimar, the heavenly abode of Goethe and Schiller. Brod tells us Kafka, as we know from his *Diaries*, spoke with awe of Goethe: "It was like hearing a little child talk about an ancestor who lived in happier, purer days and in direct contact with the Divine."[10] Yet, Brod adds, Kafka was aware that if one quoted Goethe in a particular context, the Goethean statement would make everything around it seem lesser. Kafka left a fairly detailed account of the trip to Weimar, which extended from June 28 to July 29. Most of the journey he spent alone, for the two friends parted while Kafka went on (on July 8) to a sanatorium noted for its nudist colony.

Their first stop was two nights in Leipzig. There, Kafka saw the publisher Ernst Rowohlt, who requested a book from him, the eventual *Meditation*. Then they departed for Weimar. The days of homage had begun. Kafka describes the Goethe house as a holy place: "Touched the wall. White shades pulled part way down in all the rooms. Fourteen windows facing on the street. The chain on the door. No picture quite catches the whole of it."[11] Each item is part of a sacred dwelling that has special meaning for him. On June 30 they visited the Schillerhaus, then went back to the Goethehaus, where in fact they made repeated visits. On July 2 they combined a morning visit to the Goethehaus with an afternoon visit to the Liszthaus. But the impression of that experience was apparently matched by Kafka's observation of one Grete (not Grete Bloch); he notices the "suppleness of her body in its loose dress." He flirts with a number of girls whom he sees for brief periods. He sounds in these pages like a quite normal twenty-nine-year-old on a jaunt with his friend, worshipping the idols of his youth but not neglectful of the sexual atmosphere. Every succeeding day indicates a revisit to the Goethehaus, where Kafka examines letters, memorabilia, portfolios, geegaws, photographs, even the custodian's quarters. He soaks up the Goethean emanations from a century before, attempting to discover in Goethe and his ambience the nature of the world, then and now. Ironically, Kafka, the Prague Jew, would become heir to the greatest German master of the nineteenth century.

The visits are intermingled with frequent swimming excursions and walks with Grete. On July 7 Brod and Kafka paid a visit to Halle, just northwest of Leipzig, and then from Halle Brod returned to Prague and Kafka continued on to a natural therapy sanatorium (with nudism, a controlled diet, open-air treatment, and special drinking water) in Jungborn in the Harz Mountains, a magical place. He traveled there with four Prague Jews, one of whom reminded him of his father. Kafka was uncomfortable with the nudity: naked people exercising, sleeping, bounding about. He himself drew attention to himself by wearing bathing trunks. Yet for a man so embarrassed by revealing his unmuscular body, displaying even that much of his physique was an advance. The doctor is presented as typical of his profession: "affected, insane, tearful, jovial laughter," with a face created to be serious. He is buoyant, full of bounce, and gives Kafka a good deal of nonsensical advice, or Kafka makes it seem nonsensical: don't eat fruit, but he could disobey; certain exercises (but not masturbation) will make the sexual organ grow; nocturnal atmospheric baths are recommended, but too much moonlight is injurious. In the morning: washing, setting-up exercises, group gymnastics. "I am called," Kafka wrote, "the man in the swimming trunks."[12] The entire enterprise, in 1912, had no relationship to Freudian or any psychological doctrines, but followed a good many of the "nature theories" that preceded all psychoanalytic knowledge.

For Kafka, whose health was not yet precarious, it proved a relaxing vacation. He felt comfortable in sanatoria, which were, as he had discovered earlier, a good place to meet girls and women, an effective singles scene. A Swedish woman, however, is described as having a body like "a leather strap." He adds, "When I see these stark-naked people moving slowly past among the trees (though they are usually at a distance), I now and then get light, superficial attacks of nausea." They sneak up on naked feet. "Suddenly one of them is standing there, you don't know where he came from. Old men who leap naked over haystacks are no particular delight to me, either."[13] It is unclear whether the actual nudity is so disturbing, or the fact that people can be so unself-conscious about their bodies, when he, Kafka, is all repression and shame. He reveals his incomprehension that people with bodies as unattractive as his own — a "leather strap" open for all to view — could leap and bound without concern for staring eyes. What he neglected to observe was that in a nudist colony bodies in the mass cease to call attention to themselves and imperfections cease to matter. Yet Kafka's embarrassment and discomfort cannot be ignored, since on several occasions he frequented such sanatoria. Seeking out nudism so as to be repelled by it was far more complicated than ignoring it by choosing less natural therapeutic establishments. He had, in some part of himself, to match his discomfort against the need to open himself up, to compare and contrast himself, and to confront the very elements that repelled him. In *Letter to His Father*, one of the most telling and now famous scenes comes when as a child he must undress in front of his father, feeling the shame of it all.

One of the nudists he meets is a land-surveyor, a man from the "Christian Community," tall, sunburned, with a handsome body; a proseletizer for Christian beliefs, he gives Kafka four pamphlets. Kafka was unimpressed by the material, indicating to the surveyor that there was little prospect of grace for him at present. Another girl pops up, a rural type heading in three months to a convent. They dance, flirt a little, engage in light conversation, and then it is over, like almost all engagements at the sanatoria. The idyll itself ends on July 28. Kafka's letters to Brod from Jungborn are generally upbeat, concerned with stuffing himself, exposing himself to the sun, rolling in the grass. He recognizes, however, that his present life does not confront sadness but merely circumvents it. He indicates he is writing, although he chooses not to show any of it yet to Brod. This was the first version of what would become, in a later draft, Amerika.* He recalls their attempt at "Richard and Samuel," saying the only part he enjoyed was "sitting beside you on Sundays." He reveals how shaky his entire conception of himself is, living as he does on the edge of nervous anxiety. "This craving for people, which I have and which is transformed into anxiety once it is fulfilled, finds an outlet only during vacations."[14] He tells Brod he will spend a day and night in Dresden on his way home, take a look at the Dresden zoo, in which, he says, he belongs. On Sunday evening, the twenty-eighth, he will be back in Prague.

The publication of Meditation loomed, since Rowohlt wanted it soon. Kafka was concerned that although it was such a "little book," it would take him long to prepare. His concern was predictable: a first book was, for him, like uncovering his body to others, a different kind of nudity. His first letter to Rowohlt indicates his hesitancy about the little pieces he is collecting for the book, his hope that at first sight one will not notice their weaknesses. He observes that what makes each writer individual is his ability to conceal his bad qualities in a completely different way.

Kafka's dreams or reveries of alienation, cast as brief stories in his diary entries, suddenly took shape in a remarkable writing session during the night of September 22–23. In an eight-hour stretch he wrote "The Judgment," the first of his mature works and surely the beginning for him of a new era. Just what opened him up to this burst of creativity is difficult to determine, but one aspect may have been the meeting with Felice a month earlier, and the thought, however indistinct, of future marriage,† for that theme is certainly part of the story's meaning.

---

*This early version of Amerika ("Der Verschollene") has vanished. Written during a stretch between spring and fall, 1912, it was thoroughly revised later in 1912 and came to be known by the title Brod gave it, Amerika.
†Since the major part of this five-year relationship is discussed thoroughly in chapter 9, I will only touch upon it henceforth when it cuts across other important parts of Kafka's life. Obviously, it must run through every aspect of his life and work until the end of 1917, after the second engagement was broken off.

"The Judgment" is not a replication of Kafka's life; furthermore, it defies precise interpretation. Kafka did not commit suicide, he did not compete with his father for a young woman, he did not give in to the paternal figure, but fought him to the death and often beat him on his own turf. Like so much else he wrote, it had profound personal resonances. But here the personal resonance was part of a larger trying-out, an imaginative recreation of possibilities or potentialities.

"The Judgment" must be viewed intertextually with the other pieces Kafka wrote in this harried time: "The Metamorphosis"; the major part of "The Man Who Disappeared" (*Amerika*); the finished version of "The Stoker," the first chapter of *Amerika*. In an intertextual view, we can interpret through the relatedness of one work with another, without losing the distinctiveness of the particular piece. It enables us to see that these works, at their most complex, have no one point of entry but possess, in fact, several. The text is full of *signifiers*, pointers toward what *may be*, but no *signifieds*, which would resolve it into one meaning. We must be cautious, however: Kafka has meanings of course. But any one interpretation or reading cannot be viewed as definitive or as exhausting a story's — or even an image's — possibilities. Furthermore, any effort to pin down these possibilities to actual events blunts their potentiality.

"The Judgment" in outline may seem simple.* A young merchant, Georg Bendemann, lives with his father, his mother having died two years ago. The family business has picked up considerably since Georg has had a larger voice in it. A month earlier, the young man had become engaged to a Frieda Brandenfeld (whose initials recall Felice Bauer, to whom the story is dedicated), and Georg has just written to a friend in St. Petersburg about his engagement.

Georg reveals the letter to his father, who has the burly build we recall from Hermann Kafka. Herr Bendemann questions whether this friend even exists. Georg says that no friend, even a thousand friends, could make up for his father, and offers to shift rooms, even to close down the business if it is undermining the older man's health. Georg is in charge of all the physical comforts of Herr Bendemann, his woolen drawers, his socks, and other intimate items. He thinks of taking him into his home when he married, but the father, intuiting his son's plans, battles back, refusing to be "covered up" or dismissed. He states that this friend in St. Petersburg would have been a real son and mocks Georg's engagement to a girl who lifted her skirts and enticed him with

---

*"Das Urteil" in German has several possible meanings, of which "The Judgment" is only one. It could also denote "The Sentence," as in one is sentenced to death; or "The Condemnation," with the same sense of finality. In a broader way, beyond its judicial possibilities, it should not be viewed as merely a legal term, which *judgment* and *sentence* suggest, but as a kind of final solution to a sequence of problems. Even "The Condemnation" fails to catch that finality, since it seems to have come at the end of a trial, whereas in "Das Urteil" the sentence is passed without trial or jury, only by a judge.

her undergarments, "and mimicking her he lifted his shirt so high that one could see the scar on his thigh from his war wound."[15] Everything about Georg is a lie, including the friend in Russia, the attempt to marry, the effort to consign the old father to pasture — such is Herr Bendemann's indictment. He asserts he has been writing to the friend in Russia, who knows everything a hundred times better than Georg ever will know it. With that and other attacks, the father condemns Georg to death by drowning. Herr Bendemann crashed to the bed, on which he had been standing, as Georg rushes out to a bridge and lets himself drop into the water. Abraham has consigned Isaac to some modern-day sacrifice. The "traffic" that passes over the bridge is, in German, *Verkehr*, the word for intercourse, and it is unclear in the German text whether Georg is condemned to die in traffic or through sexual contact.*

Brod reports Kafka's comment on the last sentence: "When I wrote it, I had in mind a violent ejaculation" — bringing to mind the dual meaning of *Verkehr*, but also Kafka's assertion that the story emerged from him like some human birth, "covered with dirt and slime." Exactly how all this fits into the story's "meanings" is not easy to determine.

While the story line of "The Judgment" is straightforward, its possibilities are immense, not simply in biographical terms, but in a broader sense of the kind of fiction Kafka was creating. For in one brief period, in 1912, he demonstrated how he had assimilated the characteristics of Modernism and especially of psychological fiction. Except for its lack of a convoluted or self-directed narrative, the brief story has many of the other characteristics of Modernism: characters who exist only in the foreground; sexual battles that lie well below the surface and have little to do with eroticism; a landscape of desolation, comparable to the urban wastelands of Baudelaire; the spareness and void quality associated with Mallarmé;† a conflict that seemingly has no basis in ordinary or expected life; a geometric ordering of people and events; an outcome that while driving to an extreme appears to be insufficiently motivated or explained. Furthermore, it is unclear whether the father is correct in thinking his son has lost touch with reality; or whether he is a sadist intent on preserving his own power even at the expense of his son (the Abraham and Isaac motif); or whether the son

---

*A third meaning: a transaction, such as a business or commercial transaction. This meaning too floats through the story. The manuscript of "The Judgment," at Oxford's Bodleian Library, shows considerable agitation in Kafka's handwriting in the segment when Herr Bendemann jumps on the bed, just prior to Georg's suicide. From this point on, also, the otherwise clean pages become more revised, with crossed-out words, substitute language, some uncertainty. On the whole, however, the manuscript is remarkably clean, bearing out Kafka's claim that he wrote it at a fever pitch.

†Especially that sense of reverie or dream that Mallarmé created between events and reader, what we might call "dreamtime."

has misunderstood everything and is carrying out a punishment on himself for crimes never committed but perhaps dreamed of. Finally, the story may be reinforcing the idea that while a son does all the right things, he is nevertheless exposed as an imposter by one who has a stronger hand on reality.

If we look at the evidence of the story, it seems a paradigm of Kafka's feelings as expressed in his *Diaries*, his letters to Felice and Brod, and, finally, in *Letter to His Father* seven years later. In fact, as noted earlier, *Georg* has the same number of letters as *Franz*; the *Bende* part of the name has the same number of letters as Kafka, and the "vowel *e* occurs in the same places as does the vowel *a* in Kafka." Further, *Frieda* has the same number of letters as *Felice*, and the same initials; in fact, *Feld*, in *Brandenfeld*, or field, has something in common with *Bauer*, or farmer. As virtually every commentator has indicated, it is a struggle between father and son that imitates Kafka's battle with Hermann. In this view, the son does all the right things but becomes entrapped by the father's force anyway. But the quite "normal" aspects of Georg differ markedly from the paradigm of Kafka himself. Here, the son is not odd but obedient, the perfect Jewish boy. He becomes engaged, does well in the family business, has a good friend, takes care of his aging father, is devoted to his mother's memory. As we have seen, Kafka was quite different from the "good son," at least in his perception of the role. He becomes engaged, but cannot face marriage, he resists the family business — both the shop and the factory — he finds ways to drive Hermann nearly crazy, and he moves as much as he can on the periphery of his family. While not the prodigal son, he pursues a course quite his own, and his writing is a further emblem of his separation from family interests. What Kafka has done has been to turn himself, in the fictional treatment, into an "as if" creature: Georg is "as if" Kafka had done all the right things and yet, like Kierkegaard's Isaac, he is condemned anyway.

Kafka has recreated his own situation but without duplicating it, turning it into a "night reverie." That the piece was written throughout the night in one sitting gives it the quality of something that appears in the dark and vanishes in the morning, an apparition or a hallucination. With this dreamwork about it, it would be incorrect to see it as realistic or as autobiographical. Images of Georg's friend, of Frieda Brandenfeld, and even of the father are slightly apparitional. And once we observe this, we can see how "The Judgment" partakes of the same imaginative thrust as "The Metamorphosis," written only a short time later.

The story, in fact, is an example of wish-fulfillment, even a Freudian one, with condensation, distortion, and other aspects of the dream. As the material flows into story form, we see the process of latent dream content becoming manifest — but in doing so, the content is deformed, as it must be. Furthermore, in the distortion of the original impulse, we have a kind of free association, especially in the descriptions of Herr Bendemann. Observations of the father blend both Georg's thought and narrative form, and the lines of demarcation between inner and outer, as yet imperfectly established, are blurred, a process continued with greater maturity in "The Metamorphosis." Kafka here employs Modern narrative techniques in order to blur distinctions between what belongs to the mind and what belongs to the surface of things. Subject and object merge with each other and become indistinguishable.

Kafka wrote in his *Diaries* (February 11, 1913),

> The friend is the link between father and son, he is their strongest bond. . . . In the course of the story, the father, with the strengthened position that the other, lesser things they share in common give him — love, devotion to the mother, loyalty to her memory, the clientele that he (the father) had been the first to acquire for the business — uses the common bond of the friend to set himself up as Georg's antagonist. Georg is left with nothing; the bride, who lives in the story only in relation to the friend, that is, to what father and son have in common, is easily driven away by the father since no marriage has taken place, and so she cannot penetrate the circle of blood relationship that is drawn around father and son.[16]

Kafka writes of the story emerging from him like a "real birth, . . . and only I have the hand that can reach to the body itself and the strength of desire to do so." As a "birth," "The Judgment" takes on qualities that dissociate it from any straight autobiographical content. Kafka sees it as a distinctly separate body from his; the matter emerging is not what he is, rather something buried deeply within him, with a life of its own. Later, he wrote to Kurt Wolff, his publisher, on April 11, 1913, asking that "The Judgment," "The Metamorphosis," and "The Stoker" be combined into a single volume, to be called *Sons.** He says the three stories have an obvious connection, and even more important, "a secret one, for which reason I would be reluctant to forgo the chance of having them published together in a book." This combination suggests that Kafka perceived all three as revealing a part of himself, since we can assume he was the son of *Sons*. But in presenting three differing views of himself, he was eschewing the purely autobiographical reading of any of them — and demonstrating that although all three present viable views of the author, none is definitively he, or is even close.

Somewhat paradoxically, though the stories show strong fathers willing to sacrifice their sons, the fathers are themselves victims of surviving situations in which sons usually attempt to bury the patriarch.

---

*Nothing came of it in Kafka's lifetime, but Schocken brought out just such a volume in 1989, calling it *The Sons* and including *Letter to His Father*.

Kafka was not only measuring himself against Hermann and finding himself weak, but taking measure of a man who could function in the world of fathers, husbands, and families — that is, a man who was complete in ways sons could not be. More central than the son's sacrifice is the father's strengthening of his own position, or else his forcing the son out into another world. Karl Rossmann's being packed off to America reinforces the father's role in the family.

Several plays and stories in and around this time, many of them pieces Kafka was probably familiar with, stress the significance of the father's role and diminish the son's.* Of course, Kierkegaard's retelling of the story of Abraham and Isaac was sufficient for Kafka to understand that even when God wants to offer a reprieve and save Isaac, Abraham insists on the sacrifice to demonstrate his paternal priority. But we would be incorrect to indicate that Kafka's sympathies lie only with the son. While the narrative is presented from the son's point of view, the family, whether Bendemann here or Samsa in "The Metamorphosis," is the arena. In "The Judgment," Herr Bendemann starts up the business, which the son enters into; the father sets up the apartment where they live; the father has provided the economic opportunities for the son, as well as a home; the father is the one who feels he is host to the son's parasitism and is being slowly relegated to a secondary role.

Kafka had already worked out this conflict in his diary entry of "Die städitsche Welt" ("The Urban World").[17] There, as described earlier, Oskar is stifled by his home life and by a demanding, dictatorial father who accuses his son of laziness, wickedness, extravagance, and stupidity. "The Urban World" demonstrates what we have claimed also for the later pieces: that in the conflict the father must retain his power in the face of the son's clearly antagonistic effort to destroy him. What Kafka has done has been to turn the oedipal situation around. Without identifying with the son, he sees that the threat of displacement makes the father turn to any method to hold on. Kafka has transformed the usual paradigm: the father's strength, whether Bendemann's or Samsa's, overcomes the weakness of the son.

Yet we must emphasize that this scenario was not Kafka's situation, although it may have been his perception of it as he nearly drowned in institute and asbestos factory work. In reality, he overcame

---

*Gordin's *Gott, Mensch und Teufel* (*God, Man, and Devil*) is one, involving a condemnation and a suicide. Grillparzer's *Der arme Spielmann* (*The Poor Musician*), while not quite the same, does offer a dominant father and a passive son, who declines his role, though without killing himself. Scharkansky's *Kol Nidre* (the Jewish holiday service that looks ahead to the Day of Judgment) features a patriarchal figure who consigns both his daughter and her Jewish lover to death, a fate they evade by suicidally jumping into the flames. Other examples both before Kafka's maturity and soon after suggest that father-son struggles and the son's suicide formed a literary subgenre. Many of these works in German or Yiddish long preceded Freud and his oedipal theory.

everything his father tried to do to him, or everything Kafka thought his father was trying to do to him. But even while accomplishing that, he thought of himself as weak, passive, self-destructive, so put upon he was ready for suicide or bugdom. Leaving out "The Stoker" for the moment, the stories reveal a tremendous split within Kafka: between what he was actually accomplishing and how he perceived his role as loser in the father-son war. On the loser side, he saw the father become a giant standing on his bed, whereas he becomes a puny David to this Goliath; unlike the biblical David, however, he is overwhelmed. Comparably, the worn-out, sickly, and "retired" Herr Samsa grows in size and confidence as the son recedes into a world the father considers contemptible and repellent. Gregor too becomes part of the dust heap in the face of paternal strength; in actuality, Kafka got to Hermann, forced him to beg for relief by making him plead illness, indisposition, old age. Like his country uncle, with whom he found so much in common, Kafka insisted on what he was, despite his perception in these stories that he was being shaped by someone else.

As we probe around in Kafka's mind, we must acknowledge that he perceived weaknesses as signs of inner strength, in one of those many paradoxes that served his purposes, helping to make him such a representative author of the twentieth century. Through weakness, succumbing, deferring, even death, he asserted himself, wrapping all will and determination in disguises, deceptions, and ambiguities. Another way to consider this is to see how Kafka tested out weakness as a means of asserting strength. He created, here, the worst-case scenario, in which the son is utterly crushed by a ruthless father, in order to demonstrate how a stronger son, like himself, can survive such onslaughts, verbal and otherwise. In this view, Kafka reveals how his own weapon, his writing, enables him to compete with the great presence and physical strength of the patriarch — and compete so that whatever the older man wishes for him, he can find a means to circumvent it.

All the physical details of "The Judgment" indicate that the old man has the more powerful weapons. Standing on the bed turns him into a physical giant. His superior knowledge, of the friend, for example, gives him an additional advantage over Georg. His attack on his son's easy seduction of a girl who, he alleges, lifts her skirt, leaves Georg helpless and emasculated. The father's questioning of all the details Georg presents leaves the son with a story that may be fantastic, not at all rooted in reality. The father's claim that he can steal his son's bride is a further attempt to emasculate the son. Even the older man's use of the mother and her memory is a device to shame Georg into someone who betrays the dead. Finally, the physical facts — Georg's changing of his father's underwear, his slipping off of his dressing gown, and other such details — all undermine the son's sensibility, making the older man both repellent and overwhelming, an old warrior in preparation for deadly combat. These, then, are physical details Georg must overcome, and they are essentially the details Kafka catalogued in diary entries. The battlefield is set, but Kafka, unlike Georg or Gregor, does not back down. He grieves, he despairs, he fills himself with self-hatred, he inveighs against fortune, but he devises stratagems to fight back and, in his way, to triumph.

Within a week after finishing "The Judgment" in the kind of manic burst of creativity that often came over him (he worked in short, explosive spurts) Kafka also completed the first chapter of his novel, "The Stoker." He finished the novel on October 2, then read it to Brod, along with "The Judgment." Brod writes of this immediate period as having put Kafka in "unbelievable ecstasy." Following this ecstasy, on October 7, he wrote to Max Brod in such despairing terms that Brod showed the letter to Julie Kafka, fearing that his friend might indeed commit suicide. Kafka's brother-in-law had left on a ten- to fourteen-day business trip, but even with his brother-in-law's younger brother in attendance, Kafka was still drawn into the factory as supervisor. He fell under considerable pressure at home, from Julie, not to intensify his father's bitterness and sickness, and in some way unacceptable to Kafka, he was blamed for the very establishment of the factory. Even Ottla, his steady ally in family confrontations, deserted him, he told Brod. As bitterness overwhelmed him, he realized "with perfect clarity that now only two possibilities remain open. . . . either to jump out of the window once everyone has gone to sleep, or in the next two weeks to go daily to the factory and to my brother-in-law's office. The first would provide me with the opportunity of shedding all responsibility, both for the disturbance of my writing and for the orphaned factory. The second would absolutely interrupt my writing," leaving the prospect of his picking up in two weeks where he had left off, if he had the strength of will to do so.

Kafka writes that he stood at the window for a long time, "pressed against the pane, and there were many moments when it would have suited me to alarm the toll collector on the bridge by my fall," a suicide reminiscent of Georg Bendemann's. We already saw, in *Meditation*, the single paragraph called "Das Gassenfenster" ("The Street Window"), with its intimations of defenestration. Kafka used windows extensively, usually as an obstacle to whatever his protagonist desires, or as a reflection of his uncertainties. But windows also provide access to the outside, that other side of Kafka: the strength of purpose that made him feel "too firm to let the decision to smash myself to pieces on the pavement penetrate to the proper decisive depth." Then, wittily, he adds that "my staying alive interrupts my writing less than death."[18]

When Brod showed this letter to Julie Kafka to demonstrate to her how depressed and suicidal her son was, he covered up the final part written early the next morning. Kafka: "And yet, now in the morning, I must not conceal this, I hate them all, one after the other, and think that in these fourteen days I shall scarcely be able to summon up the good-mornings and good-evenings. . . . I am far less sure than I was during the night." The afterthought, composed at 12:30 A.M., indicates, once again, Kafka's strength amidst all the signs of weakness. As a result of Brod's intervention, Julie Kafka recognized the intolerable situation and helped lessen the pressure on her son at the factory. What she could not alleviate, however, was his guilt that, even with the burden lessening, he was still expected to "help out" the family; and when he did not, he was failing to meet expectations. It was these expectations that caused Kafka such despair, inasmuch as he wanted expectations to derive from the literary demands he made upon himself.

Yet despite Kafka's agitation and despair at this time, the manuscript of "The Stoker" ("Der Heizer") shows uncommon control. Aside from a few stylistic revisions — deletions are the most frequent alterations — and with entire pages unchanged, the manuscript at the Bodleian Library reveals a restrained and fine handwriting. The pen line is that of a tightly cautious person, with most letters quite economically formed and only a few capitals indicating a temperamental flourish. Likewise, the entire manuscript of *Amerika* reveals virtually no revisions, few words crossed out, only occasional deletions for purposes of clarification. Like "The Judgment" and the *Diaries, Amerika* is written in six-by-nine-inch brown notebooks, those of a Prague schoolboy.

The "ecstasy" and inspiration Brod cites must not be disengaged from the work at hand, nor from the manic state they suggest, giving credence to Kafka's need to keep writing or else end it all with suicide. Even if the suicide were not meant literally but rather as an emblem of his desperate feelings, it suggests he had reached some imaginative peak from which all else seemed dross. The expression that he might end it all was surely linked to the activity of the mind that created two major pieces within a short time of each other, followed only a month and a half later by an even more significant work. Having reached what was, for him, a peak of achievement, he could only see himself struck down by familial circumstances that made such work impossible to continue. How much of this Brod understood we cannot tell, although his intervention in a deeply intimate matter like a family business suggests he saw the seriousness of Kafka's dilemma.

After completing the first chapter of "The Stoker," Kafka worked rapidly, so that by November 13 he had finished the sixth chapter, which he considered "crude and bad." He was, in fact, having difficulty with the entire novel — nearly all of which he had written in this two-month period. The retitled *Amerika* would extend, incomplete, to eight chapters. Kafka tells Brod that in looking back he will need to make changes, especially in chapter 3, which he had promised to read aloud at Baum's.[19] The whole question of "The Stoker" and the larger manuscript, "The Man Who Disappeared," and its transformation into *Amerika*, has strong biographical implications.*

Part of what makes it dramatic is the large dose of secretive sex and sexual energy which underlies the narrative, some of it fairly obvious, some of it buried in sexual symbols. For starters, Karl Rossmann is forced to go to America because he had been seduced by a servant girl who then became pregnant. Then the Statue of Liberty is described as having an "arm with the sword" rising up, a transformation of the actual beacon. Further images: Karl loses his umbrella down below and in time also loses his box with everything from home in it. Finally, several scenes, especially in "The Stoker," are described with homoerotic connotations that, on the surface, seem to have little to do with the progress of the novel.

But before we explore this story and its possible significance in Kafka's inner development, we must look at *Amerika* as a whole as fitting into that loose genre of the *Bildungsroman* that we have called spiritual autobiography, with linkages to Dickens's *David Copperfield* (an acknowledged source), Dostoevsky and Nietzsche (especially *Ecce Homo*), Gide's *Immoralist*, Joyce's *Stephen Hero*, Proust's *Jean Santeuil*, and several of Hermann Hesse's early novels. Even Mann's *Buddenbrooks*, in part, and Musil's *Young Törless* fit into the general configuration. The modern development of this genre, not the least abetted by Kafka, added several qualities to the older, established form: estrangements that cannot be resolved; social coordinates submerged or altogether lost, dimensions of emptiness, or loss of direction; the creation of a "nil man," a protagonist caught by nothingness; the outside world presented as a dark place that rarely if ever lightens; a main character trapped in a spiritual crisis that takes on universal dimensions; a sense of place as surreal; a sense of time as falling outside clock or calendar. Kafka's *Amerika* shares many, if not most, of these components: America is certainly surreal, not realistic, and time is only ostensibly sequential. The protagonist is estranged in every situation he faces, in the main, an empty or nil man awaiting what can fill him; except for a mindless good will, little emanates from him. Social coordinates are missing, of necessity in a society where communities are

---

*Brod in the afterword to *Amerika* says Kafka's manuscript bore no title, and that he used to refer to it as his "American novel." Then, later, he called it "The Stoker," after the title of the first chapter, which had appeared separately in 1913. Since the original version of the novel, which is no longer extant, was called "The Man Who Disappeared," very possibly Kafka intended to use that title for the novel when and if he ever completed the revision. Since "The Stoker" was the only part published within his lifetime, he had no opportunity to use that original title. Brod's retitled *Amerika* was published in 1927, three years after Kafka's death. By November 12, when the sixth of the eight planned chapters was written, Kafka realized he might never finish the novel. He told Felice (November 11, 1912), even as he was enthusiastic about the book, that it would never be completed because of the manner in which it was conceived. As for that original title, the avant-garde composer Leoš Janáček, in 1916–19, coincidentally wrote a song cycle for tenor and piano called "The Diary of One Who Vanished."

continually reshaping themselves. No goal or direction is possible, certainly none of the nineteenth-century sense of definite paths to be discerned and then taken, only a drifting into new situations.

Kafka has turned the spiritualized autobiography into his own vision of the world. Whereas Nietzsche in *Ecce Homo* stressed that one must annihilate, break, or reverse values in order to seek truths, Kafka believed that only in victimization of the protagonist could one find truth. Without denying its general validity, he turned the Nietzschean view upside down, or inside out, in order to validate it for himself. Kafka found strength in negative energy, akin to the Nietzschean *ressentiment*. This negative energy can bring forth rancor, hostility, hatred; but it also allows for a countering effect, a miniaturized world of sickness and passivity that is a form of preservation and that permits one to bury oneself and in that seek affirmation. Such is the nature of negative energy. This stance fitted Kafka well, taking into account his withdrawal from a modern civilization (but not Modernism) that he saw as little more than decay and corruption. It validated his "solutions," in nature worship, gardening, vegetarianism, fletcherization of his food, sleeping naked with open windows, wearing summer clothes in the coldest weather. Kafka's adaptation of *ressentiment* allowed renewal on terms different from those of the world.

Kafka's hatred of the bourgeois world — Karl Rossmann's movement toward the Nature Theatre of Oklahoma as an emblem of this — derived from Nietzsche as well as from his own experiences. His growing interest in Zionism was one way of avoiding the complete self-absorption implicit in withdrawal. With Zionism, he had to balance community with the individual. We recall from above Ferdinand Tönnies's distinction between *Gemeinschaft* (a real community of shared interests) and *Gesellschaft* (a makeshift society of self-oriented individuality). Tönnies argued that the first, a real community, was based on blood relationships and inherited customs, whereas the second was an atomistic society bonded only by rational self-interests.

The dangers within such a contrast becomes obvious, and it is one of the paradoxes of such visions that Kafka held to the first, which brought danger, and rejected the latter, which might have saved. For the first, *Gemeinschaft*, or real community, was based on the *Volk*, or people: an organic society made up of peasants, farmers, craftsmen, those opposed to the liberalizing results of technology and capitalism, those who emphasized older values based on kinship, blood ties, family, the land. This way of thought was opposed to modernization and Modernism, to big cities, and, inevitably in this equation, to Jews, those associated with the very urban, capitalistic elements driving out "old values."* The end result of such *Volk* worship was, unfortunately,

---

*Even the great Czech leader Tomáš Masaryk, who dealt so liberally with the Jewish

not Kafka, but *Mein Kampf*. Tönnies's attack on *Gesellschaft* came as early as 1877, when he was only twenty-two, although he lived well into the Hitler era and could see the end results of his famous distinction between community and society. While valid in its attack on the dehumanization of industry and of bureaucracies — thus the appeal for Kafka of both Tönnies and Nietzsche — the solution, in community values, was retrograde, full of nationalism, and of course potentially devastating for those minorities who could not be assimilated to *Volk* priorities or who fell outside the blood community.

Zionism itself was based on many of these *Gemeinschaft* elements, especially in Martin Buber: back to the land, the salvational qualities of manual labor, the democracy of small communities ruling themselves, the physical benefits of hard work, the expulsion of complex ideas, and simplification of one's life. Tolstoy was not an indifferent spectator to this movement, either.* These divisions between community and society become apparent in Kafka's vision in *Amerika*. Especially in "The Stoker" chapter but also elsewhere, the novel illustrates how once community is slowly lost and taken over by society, group bonds are traduced by those interested only in the self. The unit gives way to self-absorbed individuals, while Karl Rossmann, a kind of Chaplinesque innocent, pursues his own agenda for truth, purity, meaning. There is, also, something of Cervantes's Don in Karl: the naive fool who embodies certain values coming up against a world that cannot even see him.

In the first paragraph of "The Stoker," Karl Rossmann is packed off to America because a servant girl has seduced him, and the Rossmanns do not wish to pay her alimony or child support.† A sexual act has forced him out into the wilderness and his guilt becomes manifest in the loss of familiar objects. He first loses his umbrella "down below,"

---

question once he gained power, while growing up in rural Catholic Moravia was an anti-Semite and believed fully in the blood libel accusations made against Jews. This was at a time when Jews represented only about 1 percent of the Moravian population.

*Buber's enthusiasm for community led him to become a strong German nationalist during World War One, and he saw in the war, as did Kafka, to some degree, an identification that would eliminate Jews' rootlessness and give them purpose. Buber also saw in eighteenth-century Hasidism in Eastern Jews another form of community, and here again Kafka was attracted through his association with Löwy and his acting troupe.

†The incident seems to fit Dr. Robert Kafka, Kafka's cousin, the son of Filip, who was said to have been seduced at fourteen by the family cook; she became pregnant and allegedly bore him a son. There is, however, no clear evidence making this connection. Cousins, nevertheless, did appear to enter Kafka's imagination as he wrote *Amerika*. As Anthony Northey (*Kafka's Relatives*, 1988, 1991) reminds us, Kafka had three American cousins: Otto (oldest son of Filip), Franz (Otto's younger brother), and Emil (middle son of Heinrich). He also had two maternal uncles, Joseph and Alfred, who had lived in North America. Northey argues very persuasively that these relatives (part of the Kafka *Mischpoche*, or clan) influenced Kafka's conception of Karl and the uncles in the novel. It is quite possible, even probable, but Kafka transformed them so radically into personal and imaginative creations that the originals were inevitably left far behind.

then he also loses his box, which, upon parting, his father had teased him that he might lose, and his exile is complete. Having been associated with the father, and part of the parental shame, the box was linked to the parental demand that he leave. By losing the faithful box, Karl has made a move toward independence, not only from his father but from the entire community that his family represents. He now must depend on his own ingenuity. Karl's losses suggest that he is caught in Kafka's own fear of sexual entanglement; he recognizes that sexuality can result in exile or marginality, and that castration, as in the loss of the umbrella, may not be far behind.

Once that occurs, neorealistic or surreal scenes begin to accumulate, and Karl must make decisions based on self-interest in conflict with justice. Such situations in Kafka, where the individual's welfare runs up against what he considers to be justice, are "absurd," part of the surreal circumstance one finds in a large bureaucracy. The individual appears to be pursuing realistic ends, whereas justice or law follows its own movement. The two can never really meet, although the individual may expect such a meeting. One of Kafka's ways of measuring the breakup of community, in which the individual falls into some inexplicable bureaucratic society, comes when that very individual tries to equate his interests with those of that society. The archetypical Kafka scene results: two elements sparring with each other on different planes of existence.

The stoker, caught in an impersonal bureaucracy, tries to interest Karl, a sixteen-year-old immigrant who can hardly speak English, and then watches as he is abandoned when the immigrant is led off by his influential uncle, a senator, a man of substance. The failure to redress injustice here is of course an emblem of the entire manuscript, for it will later affect Karl in his dealings as he moves around the country and is himself as exposed to injustice as was the stoker.

That cyclical, episodic movement dominates the entire story. Its tone is of someone, Karl, attempting to free himself, while he is being pulled back by forces he cannot determine. In this respect, it reveals one of Kafka's major themes, in both his life and his work: the absolute need to break free, and yet the absolutism of denial because of external, inexplicable elements. All three works from this later 1912 period can be viewed in this way, as efforts at liberation that must, somehow, be compromised by the situation itself. Of the three protagonists, only Karl still has a chance, although we never know since the novel is incomplete.

In class and caste terms, "The Stoker" illustrates how the poor man, the stoker, without influence or friends, can become victimized; whereas the man with important friends, Karl, can walk away. Given the nature of power and how it dictates justice, Karl's efforts to point out how Schubal, the chief engineer, has persecuted the stoker are unavailing. In this confrontation with three shipping officials, "justice" is created not by the circumstances of the case but by the weight of the individual's class or caste.

Karl is witness to a particular kind of injustice, just as, earlier, he had been "saved" from Johanna Brummer by being sent away, with his own responsibility in the affair inconclusive and Brummer "punished." In this ship's office, Kafka has recreated the nature of a bureaucracy, which is, evidently, the very opposite of a community held together by common interests and blood ties. It is, instead, a society in which each individual strives to achieve his or her position through self-interest, without regard for truth, justice, or basic decency. As Kafka understood its lines from the insurance institute, this is the ultimate bureaucracy. But it is also based on his sense of family, as made up not of members cohering to each other but of figures pulling against each other. While the stoker suffers the fate of the weak and disempowered, Karl moves in the opposite direction, becoming the beneficiary of a Freudian "family romance," in which he substitutes a set of weak parents for a powerful one.

When Schubal, the main link in this power play, appears, his words carry significant meaning. Assuming that the stoker's accusations of injustice have been denied, the captain puts Schubal's case to the side, allowing Karl's position to become of central importance. In this respect, a new, fantasy family is formed for the young man, on the spot, as Uncle Jacob, a senator, comes forward to claim his nephew. (This is as though Kafka's affluent Madrid uncle had come forward to extricate him from Prague.) The senator appears to know the family story, of how Karl was seduced by a thirty-five-year-old maidservant, was turned out, and came to America on this ship. Such information had come from the maidservant herself, and Uncle Jacob, accordingly, had appeared to embrace his nephew and introduce him to life in America.

As his uncle speaks, Karl thinks of Johanna Brummer, and his main memory is of disgust, sexual disgust. "[She] pressed her naked belly against his body, felt with her hand between his legs, so disgustingly that his head and neck started up from the pillows, then thrust her body several times against him," so that in spite of himself, "he was seized with a terrible feeling of yearning."[20] After the act, he departs in tears, with her plea that he return to her again. It is, all in all, quite close to how Kafka described his first encounters with Czech prostitutes.

To return to the narrative line, just as injustice and discipline are the fate of the stoker, so they are for Johanna Brummer, he in the foreground, she in the background, as parallel lives. At this juncture, Karl seems to make a homoerotic overture to the stoker. Showing his concern for the injustice dealt him, Karl "drew his fingers backwards and forwards between the stoker's, while the stoker gazed round him with shining eyes, as if blessed by a great happiness that no one could grudge him."[21] Karl follows this with an even more forceful gesture: he bursts out crying and kisses the stoker's hand, "taking that seamed, almost nerveless hand and pressing it to his cheek like a treasure which he would soon have to give up." The apparently disquieted senator is soon at Karl's side and firmly leads him away, adding that the stoker seems to have bewitched Karl in his loneliness. Shortly after, as they disembark from the ship, Karl bursts into "violent sobs," at which point the senator draws his nephew close with his right hand and with his left caresses him. Drawn close together, they slowly descend to the small boat awaiting them.

With this departure, "The Stoker," chapter 1 of the eventual *Amerika*, ends. We have witnessed, whatever we make of it, a profoundly sexually charged scene, in which Karl alternates between two experienced and older men who seem to "want" him. He has become momentarily the stoker's "boy," before he is claimed by the prestigious and well-placed much older man, the "uncle." With one, Karl does the caressing, while the other, the uncle, makes the advances. Karl is carried off by the man with money and position into a kind of middle ground between freedom and slavery. What seems like Freud's family romance, in which one wish-fulfills a more advantageous set of parents, is in fact a kind of sexual market operating in shadowy fashion disguised as parental concern.*

In chapter 2, Karl is at Uncle Jacob's, a house of six floors that is somewhat of a castle, containing even three levels in the basement. Karl's room, complete with balcony, houses an American writing desk, which is itself an emblem of life for Karl, a foreshadowing of the cubbyholes and drawers he will encounter in the future. It is described as having a hundred compartments of different sizes, fit for a president and his documents. In its curious reshaping of itself, the desk prefigures the needle machine in "In the Penal Colony"; that machine too is an emblem of life, as well as of death. By reminding Karl of Christmas memories, the desk leads back to his mother and, thus, encompasses many aspects of his few years. When the handle of the regulator is turned another notch, the entire "machine" becomes a symbol of what has been but also of what will be.

The uncle's business is a "commission and despatch agency." It does not transfer goods, say, from producer to consumer, but handles goods and raw materials, going between large manufacturing trusts. The operation involves an immense web of telephonic and telegraphic communication with clients, since keeping track of the immense purchasing, storing, transport, and sale of goods is the essential part of the business. It is, in effect, a labyrinth, perhaps less threatening than the court system of *The Trial* but no less effective. Here goods are bottled

---

*We can only speculate how Felice Bauer might be factored into this equation.

up; there, individuals. Karl's view of the operational side of the business is of a gigantic bureaucracy: not a simple buying and selling, but a gigantic spider web of activities spreading out from phones and telegraphic keys.

In his uncle's dining room, Karl sees two large, older men, Green and Pollunder. Like Uncle Jacob, they are part of a circle of older, successful men who gravitate toward the country-fresh sixteen-year-old. Pollunder has come to take Karl to his country house, which means Karl must miss his riding lesson. "They sat close together and Mr. Pollunder held Karl's hand in his while he talked."[22] Pollunder speaks of his daughter, Clara, but as their car moves from one labyrinthine area to another, Karl feels sleepy and cannot maintain his attention. With the main roads the site of demonstrations, police keep shunting the car off into side alleys and narrow lanes. The trip is itself a kind of phantasmagoria, a hallucinatory journey during which Karl becomes as though drugged, while Pollunder talks on. The entire experience, on their way to the Pollunder castle outside New York City, seems appropriate preparation for what will be an episode of synesthesia, in which the senses became disarranged and reshaped.

Chapter 3 does not relieve the ambiguous sexuality, the shadowy sense that another scenario is being played out beyond the main one. Karl meets Clara and is immediately taken with the girl's red lips, which, he observes, derived beautifully metamorphosed from Pollunder's magnificent red lips. The observation is androgynous, in that it allows Karl to be fascinated with father and daughter in turn; and then he meets another large, even gigantic man, in Green. Bulk characterizes both older men, and juxtaposed to Karl's figure, as Hermann Kafka's was juxtaposed to his son's, they take on qualities of Wagner's Fasolt and Fafner, those twin giants of potential evil. Green's way of eating at the dinner party is one that creates disgust, since, almost certainly, he fletcherizes his food. The dinner goes on, lingers, becomes interminable as Green "dissected each course, which did not keep him however from attacking each new course with fresh energy."[23]

Then comes a series of events that reinforces the implicit sexuality underlying the narrative. Karl observes a number of servants: "As they [he and Clara] passed along the corridors he could scarcely credit his eyes at first, when at every twenty paces he saw a servant in rich livery holding a huge candelabrum with a shaft so thick that both the man's hands were required to grasp it."[24] This is followed by a scene in which he and Clara have a tug-of-war that escalates into her striking him so hard on the chest he almost falls from the window. Then she seizes him and carries him "in her athletic arms almost as far as the window, since he was too surprised to remember to brace himself." Finally, he frees himself, but she does not give up, and in a succession of wrestling maneuvers "locked him in a well-applied wrestling hold, knocked his legs out from under him by some foot-work in a technique strange to him and thrust him before her with amazing control, panting a little, to the wall." She is not finished, however, for she puts him on a couch and presses her hand to his throat so strongly he can barely breathe. With her other hand, she experimentally thrusts her fist against his cheek, as if measuring him for a knockout blow. Then, like a mother with a naughty child, she threatens to box his ears for his rudeness to a lady, and says that if she lets him off tonight, he had better behave himself next time. He has, in effect, lost the wrestling match with a young woman who has practiced wrestling holds for the greater part of her life.

These two scenes, with servants holding a huge shaft with both hands followed by an immensely strong and skilled female warrior, turn Karl into a kind of girlish, powerless figure. Not only is he the object of attention for the elderly gigantic males, he is threatened in some way by the masturbatory servants, and even by a young woman who can terrorize him at will. We recall those Gothic novels of the eighteenth century in which an innocent young woman is lured to a castle and there terrorized and threatened with rape, Samuel Richardson's *Clarissa* being the archetype. Karl's exposure to the luxuries of Pollunder's castle is accompanied by an analogous sexual danger or threat, but here bisexual, from gigantic men, or men with huge shafts, or women with martial skills.*

The empty house itself, with its great corridors and blank walls, is not unlike a Gothic castle, fraught with sexual danger like a kind of enormous *vagina dentata* waiting to devour Karl. The hollow, empty space of the house is totally threatening, implying both the unknowns of his residence there and the potential peril of his future. "The house was a fortress, not a mansion"[25] — which suggests a martial, hostile dimension to it, protected against something or someone, or else a potential trap for whoever gets caught in its labyrinthine corridors and empty chambers.

The empty house as a sexual threat of some indeterminate quality gives way to another homoerotic scene between Karl and the large man, Pollunder. The latter puts his arm around the willing young man and draws him between his knees. The passage reads as though it were a father displaying affection for a son — wish fulfillment for Kafka? — except that Karl is sixteen and himself a father, of Johanna Brummer's fetus. Whereas Karl loathes Green, Pollunder continues to show the young man kindness — as if the two large men were in competition for him. When Karl talks at length about his education, or lack of it, Pol-

---

*By women quite unlike Johanna Brummer, who does not wrestle but seduces. The names — *Brummer* is "grumbler," also close to "horse-fly," and *Rossmann* is "horse-man" — indicate that the affair is one of persiflage — unlike the more deadly, intense one going on in the Pollunder castle.

lunder tightens his arm around him.[26] Green seems preoccupied with
his own business, and yet when Karl insists he wishes to return to
Uncle Jacob, Green says the young man has been disobedient and remains noncommittal about his return.

They enter into the kind of dialogue Kafka has made famous:
wherein people while seeming to address each other's needs speak at
cross-purposes. Everything misses. That lack of communication or failure to create real information flow sustains his indeterminate world,
conveys that sense of incompletion. In this regard, Mack, from the riding school, turns up while Karl is at the piano, playing one of the ten
tunes he says he knows. Like the dialogues that miss their target, the
presence of Mack suggests a series of circumstances that operate beyond human intelligence. This world has its own rules that must remain impenetrable to the individual and impervious to human need.
There is almost a Cabalistic mysticism to Kafka's fictional thought.

Furthermore, in Kafka one never knows what choices will be helpful, which disadvantageous. The individual will want to make choices
but is never certain what they are, much less where they may lead. He
never knows what is expected of him, although he is aware of expectation. This scheme fits well into the mental state not of someone path-
ologically ill or schizoid, but of a person so sensitive to human possibility he can see the futility of all decisions and choices. No final
choices can occur, and even the opportunity to know all the choices is
denied. Such a fictional condition occurs near the end of chapter 3
when Karl receives a letter from Uncle Jacob, delivered personally by
Green. Although we must be prepared to accept the letter at face value,
there is the possibility that Green has forged it. In it, Uncle Jacob
sounds like an abandoned lover, a man rejected for the comforts afforded by Pollunder and his cohorts. Uncle Jacob asserts he is a man of
principle who must send Karl away from him for having decided, this
evening, to leave against his wishes. Karl has, in effect, been condemned, in a causal chain that pulls his future back to his past. Uncle
Jacob has selected Green as his messenger because he knows Green
will find indulgent words for the situation; also, he brings with him
Karl's box and umbrella, which had been lost and which, like certain
people, inexplicably turn up.

This leads to some sharp words that Karl directs at Green for letting
him stay on at Pollunder's and failing to return him by midnight. Since
the letter is dated midnight, Karl feels Green purposely kept him from
returning so that Uncle Jacob could disown him. "Karl looked at Green
with shrewd eyes and clearly saw that shame over this exposure was
conflicting in the man with joy at the success of his designs."[27] Green's
only retort is that Karl should not speak a word more. The young man
is suddenly in the garden, cast out; the scene is of the expulsion. Karl
now has his box and umbrella and is in the same position at the end of

chapter 3 as he had expected to be in chapter 1. With the novel about one-third completed, Karl (his English improved) is on the road to Rameses (the title of chapter 4). All choices have been made for him, even while he thought he was making his own, and they have left him, after a circular movement, back at "Go."

At an inn Karl first encounters Robinson and Delamarche, and with this we have something of a European convocation, the German Karl, the Irish Robinson, the French Delamarche. Robinson attacks Uncle Jacob's firm as a "scandalous fraud,"[28] notorious throughout the United States. Karl admits he has money, and soon the three become interdependent: he for protection in a strange land, they for exploitational purposes. At the Occidental Hotel, where Karl goes for food for the three, he is constantly brushed or touched by people approaching or by objects that caress him.[29] Kafka emphasizes such scenes, in which Karl is squeezed or pressed. On several occasions, he cannot breathe, a condition repeated in *The Trial*, when Joseph K. finds himself in suffocating locations, where space is so constricted that even air has difficulty passing through.

When Karl returns to the two adventurers, he finds his photograph of his parents missing. This loss, which Karl regrets, is an indication he is on his own, that Robinson and Delamarche have in some vicarious way become his new parents, and that his separation from home and country is complete. This separation from the photograph prepares him for the next episode in his journey, his stay at the Hotel Occidental, where he is initiated into the world of injustice. By now, his relationship with the two adventurers has taken on the same overtones as that with the big men before: homoerotic behavior, mainly covert, cannot be ignored as part of Karl's appeal to them, and their appeal to him. Having replaced a father with big, older father figures, he is now moving closer to men his own age, although still older and representing knowledge of a world not yet his. Robinson will become a Fury in Karl's life, bringing him close to ruin: a dissatisfied lover of sorts, or someone vying with Delamarche for an attachment to the still innocent and fresh sixteen-year-old.

The fifth chapter, set at the Hotel Occidental, is central. This chapter becomes a clear foreshadowing of *The Trial* and *The Castle*, in that the lack of empowerment of an individual suggests the futility of all activity. Karl is located in a situation where nearly all other people are empowered and have some degree of control over him. Such a circumstance is perhaps inevitable in any "journey" novel, inasmuch as the protagonist is always going to find himself in a foreign situation where others are entrenched and know the rules. Yet in most of these other narratives — especially in *David Copperfield*, which Kafka cited as a chief source* — the protagonist learns from each experience, so that by

---

*"Dickens' *Copperfield*. 'The Stoker' a sheer imitation of Dickens, the projected novel

the end of his journey he has become wise, acclimated to the ways of the world, able to function, or else he has been completely broken by the experience. Kafka chooses neither extreme. Karl does not learn; he is not utterly destroyed, but nearly broken. He remains innocent but burdened by everyone who moves beyond his control. He is helped, for example, by the manageress, but she is not the ultimate authority, and when the time comes for his dismissal, she must back down. As he seeks "fatherly" protective figures in an increasingly dark and shadowy society, he finds that, as in the past, fathers fail him. The town where the hotel is located is called Rameses, or Ramses, the ancient king of Egypt, perhaps suggesting that as Karl moves forward in space on his journey, he is moving backward in time; or perhaps meaning nothing in particular.

The manageress is almost immediately interested in Karl when he indicates he is a German from Prague, in Bohemia. Her name is Grete Mitzelbach, also German, from Vienna, and she once worked at the Golden Goose in Wenceslas Square in Prague, for six months. The old Golden Goose no longer exists, Karl tells her, and this episode in still another way closes out the past. He is in America, where everything is presentness. He admits his age, turning sixteen next month, as young as the country he has emigrated to. He moves into the hotel and soon becomes acquainted with a hotel employee, Therese Berchtold, another German, from Pomerania, once part of Northeast Germany (now part of Poland). All these "home" linkages are necessary so that we can see their inevitable breakdown in America, where society has replaced community.

Karl works wearily as an elevator- and errand-boy. When Therese relates her story, much of it is characterized by the presence of buildings, shelters, corridors. We are, clearly, in familiar Kafka territory, where spatial arrangements are labyrinthine, the consequence being that the individual seeking his or her way out becomes even more lost. There is, apparently, some sexual dimension to this: of the individual wandering in a large shadowy or black hole–like area, fumbling to get in, straining to get out, but caught in a tentacle-like existence where in and out are no longer demarked. Therese relates just such an experience with her mother, when she was about five, but this is also Karl's awareness of space, and obviously Kafka's, since he repeats it in nearly every major work. Even as it suggests vastness and infinitude, space is nearly always denied. Inevitably, Therese's mother is de-

---

even more so. . . . It was my intention, as I now see, to write a Dickens novel, but enhanced by the sharper lights, I should have taken from the times and the duller ones I should have got from myself." Kafka saw in Dickens "opulence and great, careless prodigality," along with passages of "awful insipidity." He found the whole makes little sense. "There is a heartlessness behind his sentimentally overflowing style." He says that Robert Walser, whose work so engaged Kafka at the time of the *Meditation* pieces, resembles Dickens "in his use of vague, abstract metaphors" (October 8, 1917; *Diaries: 1914–1923*, pp. 188–89).

stroyed by a shower of bricks and a heavy plank that negate her space and crush her — an indeterminate structure has caused her death. In some twisted way, this becomes Karl's own fate within the immensities of the Occidental Hotel near the town of Rameses. America, with its vastness, is now becoming for him not the land of opportunity but the denial of it.

Chapter 6, "The Case of Robinson," begins with the reappearance of Robinson, at the hotel. Robinson is a Fury in Karl's life, a parasite who will reappear to exact whatever he can from the young man. Karl leaves his post, is found out, and the mechanism that is controlled by the Furies starts to crank out its vengeance on anyone who denies conventional wisdom.

Karl now must deal with the head waiter, who is dressed like some chief of state. Remarkable about his appearance is how close it becomes to Gregor Samsa's father in "The Metamorphosis" and Kafka's own father in Letter to His Father. The head waiter is tall and bulky, "whose splendid and richly-ornamented uniform — even its shoulders and sleeves were heavy with gold chains and braid — made him look still more broad-shouldered than he actually was. His gleaming black moustache drawn out to two points in the Hungarian fashion never stirred even at the most abrupt movement of his head."[30] Because of his heavy clothing, he could move only with difficulty, and stood with legs apart to provide balance for his weight. Obviously a caricature, the man is also a dreaded figure, whose authority is emblematized by his stage-operative qualities. He may be a figure out of Viennese light opera, or else a caricature of an Austro-Hungarian officer in his dress uniform, a Schweikian vision, but he is nevertheless more than a parodic vision to Karl. He represents terror, dread, even death, the end of hopes, opportunities, the dreaded authority of the Old World now transplanted to the New. He becomes another awesome father figure.

Karl views the situation with Kafkaesque logic. Since the head waiter is so grand, and he, Karl, so insignificant, he might escape retribution by virtue of his being little more than a gnat on the wall of a great establishment. The Kafka mode of reasoning is quite clever, and it prefigures the transformation of Gregor: to become so small in the eyes of others that he can then gain liberty of movement because he is so unimportant in the larger scheme of things. It also has sexual implications, because in becoming insignificant, the male "resolves" his sense of sexual inadequacy — that is, no expectations are held for him, and so he can escape into inconsequentiality: "Just because he was of no importance, any offence he committed could not be taken very seriously." Karl's innocence leads to still another miscalculation.

As he discovers, the head waiter does consider him to be of no consequence but dismisses him; the head porter acquiesces, and eventually the manageress must go along. Karl is struck by the rapidity with which the transaction takes place, despite his two months of hard and devoted work. In his innocence, he has not mastered the New World's methods, that the individual in a position of such insignificance is immediately replaceable. Being invisible does not help. When Karl appeals to the manageress, he hears himself attacked as profligate, undependable, absent every night, a carouser, and a no-good young man. When he attempts to redress the imbalance, the head porter at one stage grasps him by the upper arm and tightens his grip cruelly, and so immensely strong is he (another "bad father" figure) that Karl begins to lose consciousness and then faints. When Therese appears, the head porter affectionately pulls her to his chest, while with his other hand he squeezes Karl with all his might, as if he had some "unfulfilled design upon the arm he was holding."

Physical contact is, once again, not familial or pleasurable but sadistic and overbearing. The head porter, embracing both Therese and Karl, creates a tableau of some perverted family scene. In time, because of the way in which he has been treated, Karl regresses to the level of a child who has done some unacceptable thing. He finds it impossible to defend himself in an atmosphere lacking good will. The clocks in the hotel ring out, like a bell tolling Karl's doom. But there is more: the manageress (with her German background, from Vienna, having worked in Prague), something of a mother figure up to now, turns against Karl, and she becomes, along with the head waiter and the head porter, part of that forbidding authority with which Kafka invested Hermann. Like Julie Kafka, she is not cruel, but she will not jeopardize her own position to defend Karl and clearly aligns herself with the forces of empowerment and established order.

When it comes time to leave, Karl finds himself in another typical Kafkaesque situation, of space denied. In the head porter's office, he is caged. Although the office consists of enormous panes of glass through which one can see the flow of incoming and outgoing guests, "there seemed to be no nook or corner in the whole office where you could be hidden from their eyes."[31] Open to all, subject to constant movement of messengers, the locale, further, of two underporters who convey information, the office is the ultimate bureaucratic "place," the archetypal profane location. Although glass seems to offer the possibility of openness, instead it creates a sense of being closed down, imprisoned, where one is observed by all as though in a barred cage. Karl is like a hunted animal, now caught, now displayed, now being readied to be expelled once again from what he thought might be the Garden.

The sexual implications cannot be ignored. In this scenario, Karl becomes a passive victim, a de Sade–like "female" who becomes the property of those using and misusing her, and then cast her out. The sadism of the head porter extends beyond his abuse of power. While there is the bureaucratic dimension, there is pleasure. If the bureaucracy and, by implication, the state are inhospitable places, they are also the scene for stale and perverted sex. The head porter continues his physical abuse of Karl, "crushing Karl's arm until it was numb and literally dragging him to the other end of the office."[32] What is occurring without actual sodomy is a form of rape, the seizure of the person and the crushing of him or her into humiliation. Karl wonders why no one seems to notice, or if they do notice, what they think it means. He does not recognize they are all accomplices; they do notice, but they do not consider the act unusual, since empowerment means the right to humiliate: maleness exercised is a form of rape. Karl smells the "curiously depressing odor given out by the Head Porter, which he had not noticed until he had stood so close to him for so long." As he forces Karl to become physically passive — in this homoerotic pairing, he assumes the masculine role, Karl the female — he insists on his power over everyone else because he controls all the doors of the hotel.

As though to reinforce his assertion that he is the emperor of openings, the head porter rifles Karl's pockets, another aspect to the physical violation of the young man which has characterized his actions. He thrusts his hand "into one of Karl's coat pockets with such violence that the side-stitches burst." He keeps repeating that there is nothing there. What he finds — papers, some buttons, a nail file, the manageress's card, an old pocket mirror — is clearly not what he was looking for. All this is staged against a furious rush in the background, of guests, events, bells, hotel staff careening about: personal violence amidst a form of generalized war.

The accumulation of activities of course dooms Karl, and he must leave the hotel. He departs and finds himself with the drunk Robinson, whose appearance was the catalyst for Karl's firing. This ends chapter 6, completed by November 12.* With chapter 7, titled "A Refuge," we head into a much more surreal presentation of the material. This is understandable given Kafka's announcement to Felice, on November 17, that he had imagined a short story "that occurred to me in my misery, and now troubles me and demands to be written."[33]

The story is "The Metamorphosis," and it would gradually take over Kafka's imagination in November 1912. It is part phantasmagoria, the consequence of imaginative crisscrossings in Kafka's creative faculty; part a revival of the Golem tradition in Jewish literature and folklore; part a result of his reading of Buber's Hasidic tales; part a mirroring of insectlike creatures in, for example, Dostoevsky's *Notes from Underground* or *The Double*; part, obviously, from Kafka's own sense of his position in the Kafka family.† As his mind was moving toward

---

*His rapidity in writing the manuscript was paralleled by his closer verbal relationship to Felice, arriving at "Dear Miss Felice" ("Liebes Fräulein Felice"). By mid-November, he was enraptured by her use of "du," the familiar form of address and an indication they had warmed to each other.

†Kafka's famous dictum, "Coitus is punishment for the happiness of being together,"

surreal and hallucinatory material, it was not surprising that the latter parts of *Amerika* should become less realistic, more expressionistic, surreal, possibly "cubist" in their insistence on line and plane. With the last two chapters, "A Refuge" and "The Nature Theatre of Oklahoma" ("Oklahoma" in the German), Kafka moved well into Modernist strategies. His narratives become discontinuous, less focused on objects, more attuned to subjective states of being than to any effort to portray life objectively. With his tone and methodology becoming profoundly psychological, he leaves behind all traces of flat realism. Recreation and reshaping are all.

"A Refuge" is filled with surreal scenes. Karl sees a "young lad with a nose half eaten away,"[34] the first of such apparitions. Robinson, Delamarche, the grotesque woman Brunelda, even the policeman who appears are all part of a Picasso-inspired or Cocteau-created street scene, something perhaps that would come together in *Parade*.* When the policeman chases him, Karl bounds into the air like a deer, "useless bounds, too high in the air and a vain waste of precious time." Karl is always the victim in these scenes, his entrapment creating part of the surreal dimension of the chapter. After leaping and bounding, he ends up in Delamarche's arms, in still another reenactment of the young man being gathered up homoerotically by older men, here Delamarche and Robinson and their Amazonian friend Brunelda. "Saved" by the two men, Karl encounters Robinson "scantily wrapped" in the small blanket from the hotel. Karl must now reckon with Brunelda living in this menage à trois. The apartment is a typical Kafka setting: musty, dark, smelling like an armpit or a crotch, dust and decrepitude everywhere — a vision or an emblem of death. Karl has fallen not into the arms of salvation but into a trap. Seemingly saviors, these men are intruders in his life, purely destructive, like all the older men he has encountered in America.

Food and sex must come together, since they are so closely knotted in any Kafka parable. Robinson eats sardines from a can, and the oil drips from his mouth before he can mop it away with a big chunk of bread. The sardines in the open tin seem to have been lying around for some time, along with sweets squashed into a mass. Robinson reminisces about the wonders of Brunelda and begins to pinch and slap

---

directed at Felice, really characterizes his 1912 fiction. In his *Diary* entry for August 14, 1913, he added, "Live as ascetically as possible, more ascetically than a bachelor, that is the only possible way for me to endure marriage" (*Diaries: 1910–1913*, p. 296). This applied to "The Judgment," much of *Amerika*, and, of course, "The Metamorphosis." It is not only fear, however, but a willed sense of direction and control.

Parade did not appear, of course, until 1917, in a collaboration of Picasso, Cocteau, and Erik Satie, with program notes by Apollinaire; but Kafka saw some of the Ballet Russe performances, a mixture of many of the elements that later became part of the dada-surrealist theater-ballet characteristic of *Parade* and others like it. When Kafka saw Nijinsky dance, he experienced an abstracted form of voice, with bodily movement replacing words and verbal sound.

Karl's leg, until he shouts in pain. Robinson then unsheathes a dagger and begins to slice up some hard sausage; the sexual imagery is so insistent as to become a parody of Freudian symbols. Meanwhile, during this sexual foreplay, Robinson's mouth opens wide for the oily bread, "while in the hollow of one hand he caught the oil that dripped from it, making a kind of reservoir in which he dipped the rest of the bread from time to time."[35] The sexual implications are, once more, both apparent and shadowy. Robinson seems to be using food as emblematic of a sexual drama, in which he masturbates himself or Karl, or else engages in oral sex in some fantasy reshaping of himself and the young man.

The presence of Brunelda, who has "exiled" Karl to the balcony, in a replay of that traumatic scene from Kafka's childhood, is no reassurance. She is Amazonian, masculine, a mistress who demands obedience to her demands. Like so many women who will follow in Kafka's fiction, she is overpowering, masterful, unfeminine in traditional terms, the opposite of mother or yielding fiancée. Although this is speculative, it is possible that Kafka, in his early uncertain relationship with Felice, saw in Brunelda the consequence of a man's deference to a woman. Karl becomes her servant, even her slave, and must cater to her whims. He seems to enjoy this quasi-masochism, acting out with her a wish-fulfillment fantasy of subservience. With voice (she is a singer, reinforcing the Brünnhilde role she plays) and sexuality, she controls men and turns them into playthings, not a little like the legendary Circe. If Karl is to have any relationship to her, it must be as her inferior.

Yet even as this aspect of the novel is advanced, it is clear Kafka has begun to lose control of the material, or has lost interest. The *longueurs* here suggest he had no clear sense of direction and was simply putting words on paper.* As "The Metamorphosis" begins to take over his imagination, we can observe his hesitation with chapter 7. In the light of that material, *Amerika* seems shapeless and directionless. Kafka repeats himself, describing more of Robinson's homoerotic play with Karl, touching, wrestling, legs twisted around legs. Karl soon is crushed against Brunelda, near the balcony railing, and is unable to straighten himself out. First pressed by bodies, he is then ordered by Brunelda to make the bed; he feels himself unable to breathe, so much has the space allotted to him been denied. He soon finds himself locked in, a true prisoner, with no key in sight. Even as he feels suffocated by lack of air, by the press of events, he cannot escape the apartment. He

---

*Not untypical: "Now, too, one could realise the interest which the whole street took in the occurrence [the appearance of a speechmaker]. On the balconies where supporters of the candidate were packed, the people joined in chanting his name" (*Amerika*, p. 232). The passage has nothing to do with Karl and leads nowhere; it remains, merely that, a street scene.

tries to work the lock with two knives, whose blades soon break off. The lock continues to resist, and the threesome hear his efforts. The scene becomes hallucinatory, nightmarish, outside of ordinary time and space. Delamarche leaps at Karl, who tries to evade him, and the two jockey for position, then for various wrestling holds. The wrestling implies some sexual play, even as it gets increasingly violent. Karl is flung aside, and Delamarche promises further punishment, a sadistic moment in an unreal world.

What follows is extraordinary and shows how an intertextual reading of Kafka's two immediate works suggests meanings. Bloody, beaten, but conscious, Karl crawls on all fours toward the outside door. Having been treated like a bug, he assumes the form of a bug in order to bring about his escape; the overlap with "The Metamorphosis" is apparent. "Then involuntarily he turned towards the outside-door and groped his way towards it on all fours."[36] But with the door blocked, he makes for the balcony. Bleeding from his wounds, disoriented, he crawls to still another balcony, to that of a student named Joseph Mendel, who is sympathetic. Mendel mentions a job at Montly's big store, but Karl is uncertain about trying for it. He is unable to face the difficulties of choice, whether to break free entirely or to continue as a servant.

Two scenes that are part of the German text (Jost Schillemeit's critical edition, S. Fisher Verlag, 1983) were, inexplicably, omitted from the American edition translated by Edwin and Willa Muir in 1940. These scenes come between Karl Rossmann's stay in Brunelda's apartment in chapter 7 and his escape, in chapter 8, in "The Nature Theatre of Oklahoma." Both scenes suggest a mockery of bourgeois life, almost a kind of Marx Brothers slapstick as Karl is left alone with the Amazonian Brunelda, once Robinson and Delamarche desert her for better pickings. At the end of the second episode, in this parody, Karl half carries and pushes Brunelda in an ambulance-cart to a bordello, called Enterprise No. 25. The segments suggest almost a manic Kafka, as Karl becomes involved in one bit of horseplay after another; all that's missing is pie in the face.

This ends chapter 7. The final completed segment, chapter 8, with its "Nature Theatre of Oklahoma," is Kafka's first attempt to express his feel of middle America, what he probably had picked up in reading Karl May and his "Westerns." Kafka's America is a surreal place, but it has enough of P. T. Barnum and promotional values in it to ring almost true as a place where anything can occur.* Chapter 8 was written well after the other segments, in the latter half of 1914,[37] but it is in many respects

---

*Kafka was acquainted with American advertising and knew of several swindles (see Ritchie Robertson, *Kafka: Judaism, Politics, and Literature*, p. 59). Some of this he could have picked up from Dickens's *Martin Chuzzlewit*, written some seventy years earlier. More likely, since he repeated Arthur Holitscher's spelling of "Oklahama," it is quite possible he was familiar with that writer's attack on American advertising gimmicks.

of a kind with the other chapters. As "theater," the playing of roles is consistent with Karl's role-playing earlier, but where it departs, and becomes more optimistic, is in its acceptance of American openness, even when such openness is associated with parodic publicity and promotion. Brod's addition of the word *Nature* to the title of course increases the optimism of the segment, since Kafka's title was simply "Theater von Oklahoma." With Brod's emendation of the chapter heading, there is implied the inevitable clash between the mechanical world Kafka despised and the natural world he often embraced and overidealized.

The chapter appears as a mutant conglomeration of admirable openness and frivolous promotionalism. Kafka uses parody and burlesque to demonstrate American religious values; for whatever is transcendent here is part of a publicity coup, not revelatory. The opening paragraph is indicative: a placard announcing a call for stage members. "If you miss your chance now you miss it for ever!"[38] The placard promises employment for everyone, "a place for everyone!" "Down with all those who do not believe in us! Up, and to Clayton!" The Clayton racecourse is the staging area, from 6:00 A.M. to midnight. This manic beginning of the chapter catches the spirit of America, such as we find later in Dos Passos's *U.S.A.* trilogy, or, more banally, in advertising trying to sell shares in one boondoggle or another.

Kafka's view of America has religious overtones, in that the placard, a form of Providence, promises a great deal without providing any certainties. Certainty is not the only element missing; so is our knowledge of how Karl got here, a lacuna in the manuscript and probably the result of Kafka's inability to make the material cohere. When we left Karl at the end of chapter 7, he was delivering Brunelda to a bordello; suddenly, he is catapulted to a street corner and the placard. The scene is a phantasmagoria: hundreds of women dressed as angels, in robes "with great wings on their shoulders," all of them blowing on long trumpets "that glittered like gold."[39] Standing on hidden pedestals, they become, for Karl, gigantic; he is miniaturized. Sexually, the overwhelming women become one with the Amazonian Brunelda and the Hotel Occidental manageress, all of them joined with the large, powerful men. We find Karl turned passive, "feminine," unable to function fully. An "angel" named Fanny is introduced, and she knows Karl, another indication of the helter-skelter way in which Kafka was now proceeding. Nevertheless, despite the bizarre character of the Oklahoma Theater, Karl is drawn to it. The biggest theater in the world, it would seem to hold out hope for all, like some gigantic church set in the middle of a field.

The religious dimension is reinforced by the introduction of men, to counterpoint the women: the men are dressed as devils, half of whom blow the trumpet, the other half play the drums. Yet the idea of this as a "church" is undermined by the locale of a racecourse, and the use of a grandstand, an umpire's platform (for the theater leader), and booths for signing up recruits. Although it is possible to see in the "services" a parodic view of a religious ceremony, the juxtaposition of angels, devils, and racecourse as arena is far more amenable to theater than to church. In another view, the theater alternates between life and death: offering jobs, as a form of life, but creating an aura of death in the haphazard, uncaring way the individual is drawn into the organization.

When the time for engagement comes, Karl has no papers, no ID. Kafka was following here Czech and European procedures, not knowing that papers were unneeded in America. But Karl raises his hand to indicate that he too has his papers in order, and for the time being he is passed on. He is directed to the employment bureau, which is set up for each trade or profession. When he reaches this point, he admits to having no papers but says he is not yet an engineer, which leads to his being taken to the bureau for technicians. The engagement process is loosely like a slave market, with each person assigned to the role he or she is supposed to play. Karl is passed on from one booth or bureau to another, until he is almost at the end of the possibilities. His lack of papers is glossed over, and he is engaged. When they ask his name, Kafka plays one of his clever games. Hesitant about using his own name, with no reason given why, Karl decides they will learn it only when he has a place. Instead, he gives his nickname from his last post, at the hotel: Negro. The clerk writes it down, and Karl is engaged for "the Theatre in Oklahoma." His next step is to be presented to the leader as "Negro, a European intermediate pupil."[40]

Karl faces the prospect of being an actor, without knowing if he is capable of being one. "But I shall do my best and try to carry out all my instructions."[41] There is, in this, some shadowy representation of Kafka's own stoical response to work; as an insurance clerk or as a suitor for Felice, he was playing a role. Karl repeats that he would prefer to be an engineer, and is assured once his arm is tested for its strength, he will be reassigned in Oklahoma to some minor technical work. America is a gigantic maw, to be filled with laboring men, all of whom are replaceable and expendable. From actor to laborer, Karl moves along the needs of the theater, like everything a part of the bureaucracy.

In a final scene of great splendor and confusion, Karl looks upon the grandstand, where a leader is being toasted. He turns around and sees Giacomo, the elevator operator from the Hotel Occidental, who seems unchanged. Karl wonders what has happened to the manageress and to Therese. But the meeting is interrupted by the staff manager who announces that the train for Oklahoma leaves in five minutes. The trip goes on for two days and two nights, and the last view we have of Karl is of his having his legs tweaked by fellow travelers, as he attempts to evade their grasping.

*   *   *

Before we edge over from chapter 6 of *Amerika*, written in 1912, into the beginning of "The Metamorphosis," we should ask whether the presence of so many homoerotic scenes and images in the earlier work can be linked to events in Kafka's life. If so, they must be connected to his correspondence with and pursuit of Felice Bauer. In the previous chapter we noted how Kafka played a verbal game with the young woman, pursuing her desperately with words while avoiding her personally and even finding her physically repellent. Exactly what this meant to Kafka in sexual terms we cannot be certain. But most likely the measurement of himself against a young woman whom he ostensibly wanted for his wife and yet whom he found less than physically attractive created a great deal of sexual tension. If we can assess it, this tension erupted in images of sexual confusion, ambiguity, and ambivalence. Such images demonstrate how Karl is "seized" by large men and women. With his masculine assertiveness taken from him, he assumes a more passive or traditionally feminine role, letting things be done to him. Kafka's sense that an engagement and then marriage could lead to his loss of freedom, even to his loss of time for writing, might have shaken loose an entire edifice of weak sexuality, the consequence of which is the ambivalence and ambiguity of Karl's experience. Though all this depends on how we interpret *Amerika*, Kafka seemed at other times as well to demonstrate an "undetermined" or undirected sexuality when he was under great tension; or, put another way, he could relieve the tension by writing about an ambiguous sexuality.

With the *Diaries* silent and with letters pouring out to Felice, but hardly at all to friends or relatives, Kafka pressed on with his writing and with his duties at the institute. His spirits picked up when Felice used "du" in addressing him but then, as we have seen, sank when his anxiety about her became so great he wanted almost instantaneous communication, even while he detested the telephone. That Felice was employed in communications while he reviled the telephone did not appear odd to either of them. Then, as he told Felice on November 17, he was in his usual position, lying in bed, miserable, when he had an idea for a story. It was to become his greatest act of transformation, and if Kafka had not written anything else after 1912, he would have entered literary history with this single piece.

With "The Metamorphosis" ("Die Verwandlung"),* Kafka created one of the three great novellas of early Modernism, the others being Joseph Conrad's "Heart of Darkness" and Thomas Mann's "Death in Venice," possibly with William Faulkner's "The Bear" as a fourth. But of them all, Kafka's is the one that most closely represents not only the

---

*The German word covers the broad ground of metamorphosis, transformation, alteration, even conversion and transubstantiation, but also a nuance not picked up in English, of "commutation" of a sentence or punishment.

era but our very notion of what a Modernist work should and can be. It is, also, most surely the one to have changed our sensibility, the one to have transformed our entire way of "seeing." It is the most startling statement any writer has made in shorter form, and it is doubly compelling because it refuses interpretation. One can see it only as "possibilities" or "potentialities." And even the effort to link the novella to Kafka's own life uncovers several discrepancies. The most satisfactory yield comes from letting the novella do its own work, without intrusion.

We may say "The Metamorphosis" symbolizes an era of unrest and uncertainty less than two years before the outbreak of the Great War. It does that. We may say it catches the feelings and tones of Prague Jews, of all Central and Eastern European Jews as they lived on an edge that was becoming thinner and thinner. It does that also. And in that respect, it ironically recalls the Golem, that seventeenth-century artifact that was to save the Jews.* We may say it becomes one of the most perfect examples of Freudian psychology, in its use of the oedipal conflict, in its display of repressed personal background coming to the foreground as breakdown and pathology. It of course does that too. We may say, in that regard, that it embodies, then, the most significant aspects of Modernism in its pursuit of psychological truth; and it does. In more personal terms, we may say that the story is the perfect emblem of the writer's sensibilities; that it characterizes Kafka at this time when pressures were reducing him to a bug. The story obviously does that. Finally, we may say that the Gregor Samsa story is not only one of defeat and "trashing," but one of resistance, a weak person's imaginative way of finding some victory in the ashes of his life. It does that, without question. The story does so many things, represents so many ideas and points of view, is allegorical, symbolic, as well as historical and sociological, that we would be mad to "interpret" it. The novella has no clear center, which does not mean it is centerless; it enters our lives at so many points that we must, in viewing it, perform a balancing act.†

---

*The Golem surely was an inspiration for so much else in Prague's German-Jewish writers, not only Kafka's transformational creatures, but Brod's use of murderous characters, his presentation of madmen, also Rilke's and Werfel's emphasis on murderers or the insane, not to mention Meyrinck's use of ghosts, shadows, and deluded creations.
†Jürgen Kob's *Kafka: Investigations of the Consciousness and Language of His Figures* (in German) is an excellent examination of language in Kafka, in particular word order, usage, and nuances that accrue from verbal variations. Kob cites Kafka's grammar and syntax as his ways of seeing and concludes that the protagonist's perception of the world follows exactly what he sees of it. Therefore protagonist and reader must come to the same conclusions, without interference from the narrator, who lies just outside the tale. In this respect, Kafka has purged his fiction of comment. Playing off against this pure fictional existence, according to Kob, is that same narrator who lies just beyond the narrative, and who shifts the protagonist around, veering him this way or that. As a consequence, there is a kind of dialectic: the protagonist may see only what he sees,

In any story of transformation and metamorphosis, we should keep in mind the biological dictate: things in nature undergo alteration in order to adapt themselves better to their environment. Transformation is not necessarily progressive, but it is an act of survival; as one form becomes impossible, the object to survive assumes another stage of development. If this is so, then how do we account for Gregor Samsa's transformation "downward," from man to large beetle, cockchafer, or simply bug?* The explanation must lie in the level at which Kafka initially saw Gregor, at some stage lower on the scale than an insect; therefore, the transformation suggests his adaptation to his environment, a "progressive" stage, as it were. If this is so, if Gregor has sunk so low in his own estimation he perceives himself as lower than insect life, then his transformation, whatever else it may mean, indicates a way to survive, or at least a way to prolong his life. One reading of the novella, perhaps the major one, is to see Gregor's transformation as an attack mechanism: a defensive ploy intended to give himself leverage he did not possess before.

Nothing in this story works without its language: a language of simplicity, even flatness, which underscores the hallucinatory quality of the piece. The first sentence has become quite famous because of its understated horror: "As Gregor Samsa awoke one morning from uneasy dreams he found himself transformed in his bed into a gigantic insect."[42] Lying on his armor-plated, hard back, he lifts his head and sees "his dome-like brown belly, divided into stiff arched segments on top

---

but the reader has the benefit, also, of the narrator slightly outside the scene. The result is that we can trust only language. Similarly, Barbara Beutner, in *The Language of Kafka's Imagery* (also in German), points out that an image or a metaphor in any instance is more charged or more intense than what the character perceives, or what the character comprehends of that image. The image almost always appears to belong to some higher order of being, as one can judge from the whipping scene in *The Trial*. (For that and related points, see Henry Sussman, "The Court as Text: Inversion, Supplanting, and Derangement in Kafka's *Der Prozess,*" *PMLA* [January 1977]: 41–55.) The "new perspectives" on Kafka that have appeared in the last fifteen or twenty years have nearly all been linked to language, imagery, word order, syntax, grammar, diction, and usage. The tendency in contemporary Kafka criticism is to elbow out the biographer as an unwelcome intruder. And yet if we can see more broadly, we note that language theory should not necessarily preclude biographical intrusion, provided that contribution includes details of language, imagery, and overall usage, as well as historical and cultural contexts. What the language scholars have insisted upon, rightly, is that the fiction or text is always different from the author, which is indeed an appropriate caveat for the biographer.

*The German *Ungeziefer* is a generic form of "vermin," and an *ungeheueren Ungeziefer* is a monstrous vermin, a prodigious vermin, a gigantic vermin. With his "armor-plated back," Gregor is evidently a cockroach, cockchafer, beetle, or some insect associated with that family. Kafka keeps the identification unspecified, to indicate that Gregor is associated with the "bug family" in general. In another sense, the repetition of the *un* sound in German, Heinz Politzer reminds us, has a negative effect, a still further denial of Gregor. At the human level, *ein Ungeziefer* is a lowlife, as we say someone is a roach or a rat. We recall several literary predecessors: Gogol and Dostoevsky, of course, but even Tolstoy.

of which the bed quilt could hardly keep in position and was about to slide off completely." He observes numerous legs, pitifully thin, waving helplessly before his eyes. In fact, despite his unexpected transformation during the night, Gregor intends to go to the office. That it was a night change, one that occurred during dreams, nightmares, anxieties, indicates it happened deep in the unconscious, or in some allied area. Because Kafka's language seems to emanate from the unconscious, it works mysteriously at cross-purposes to the event itself — both are part of an uneven dialogue. Seemingly at odds with each other, they serve as a dialectic that blends. Unheightened language heightens; lack of rhetoric establishes the terms whereby the events can be highlighted.

Kafka is posing an expressionistic event in realistic terms: establishing what will become his major form of address. The opening of *The Trial* is similar: "Someone must have traduced Joseph K., for without having done anything wrong he was arrested one fine morning." Enormity is underscored by the ordinariness of the presentation. Intertextually, "The Metamorphosis" is an extended reading of the terms of "The Judgment." Georg Bendemann becomes Gregor Samsa, but Gregor reaches back to help elucidate Georg's life, which we have only briefly glimpsed. Karl Rossmann is not completely outside this tension, but walks the edge of it. Neither a suicide nor an insect, he is, nevertheless, a passive being, an easily replaceable part in a bureaucratic chain.

In "The Metamorphosis," Gregor is a commercial traveler. His work involves constant pressure, including traveling itself. Unlike Kafka, whose position in the institute involved relatively little traveling, he is a marginal figure who must live in hotels and eat alone in restaurants. In perpetual movement, he cannot be his own man. Gregor must cater to clients, cater to his home office, and then, when home, cater to parents who have fallen on hard times. In nearly all his dealings, he lacks an identity of his own, forced as he is to take on the noncommittal, blanked-out identity of a traveler.*

The picture in his room — the Samsa apartment incidentally

*The name *Samsa* does not appear to have any particular meaning in Czech or German, although in Czech its root is connected to *Sam*, which indicates loneliness, solitariness, the state of being alone. Naming, however, goes further, into the very conception of self and its images. To what extent, we may ask, was Kafka aware of ridicule because his name indicated a carrion-picking jackdaw, related to the crow? To what extent did schoolmates make fun of him, perhaps cawing at him? If we add Amschel, his Hebrew given name, with its linkage to blackbird, Kafka is almost ludicrously named, with both parts connected to scavengers. In "Wedding Preparations in the Country," we find Raban, or *Rabe*, crow; and he too views himself as an insect. The jackals (*Schakale*) of the story "Jackals and Arabs" are also carrion eaters. With these personal and fictional names, Kafka was associating naming and bodily changes; to go from carrion eater to vermin was only a brief step. (For an excellent dissection of these and related matters, see Clayton Koelb, *Kafka's Rhetoric: The Passion of Reading* [Ithaca: Cornell University Press, 1989].)

seems laid out like the Kafkas', with Gregor's room, like Kafka's, in the center — is of a woman with a fur cap and a fur stole, holding out to the viewer a huge fur muff into which her forearm has vanished. She is, in some way, more than a "pinup" for Gregor, filling in for the sweet-heart-wife-mother he lacks. Her outfit suggests a mature woman, and she is clearly one of Gregor's most desirable possessions. She is, in one respect, the woman he comes home to when he is not traveling.

Gregor's immediate situation at home is little different from his life on the road. The Samsa family has debts, which he must repay by working for five or six years. Since the entire household depends on his income, he fears being fired. He has become, as in a Dickens novel in which parents are so incapable of running their lives a son or daughter must parent them, the father to his father. Despite his abrupt metamorphosis, Gregor's anxiety about being late at the office brings him into conflict with authority figures. The fear of tardiness indicates a horror at disappointing others and the fear that some authority or father figure will materialize to chastise one. Sure enough, Herr Samsa pounds on the door and demands to know what ails his son, his voice gaining resonance as his anger builds.

Kafka achieves here the quality of all horror stories. While one line of development indicates a terrible change, another, here the father, proceeds as if nothing has happened. Only the reader is aware of both levels and can, from the start, respond to them. Kafka has so decentered or deconstructed the typical family or office story that its components leave the reader nowhere to settle. So too Gregor. Even as his new body is a fact, he looks forward to the moment when his morning's delusion will fall away, going as far as attempting to carry out his usual ablutions. What makes his condition so intense is that even as he hates every moment of his earlier life, all he wants to do is to return to it. The former life, which is what helped to turn him into what he is, now seems desirable. Regularized torture, as the victim of the needle machine in "In the Penal Colony" also recognizes, is preferable to random torture.

Gregor's dilemma of whether to act on his bug-ness or to insist on his ability to get the job done suggests several key questions. Although he is now a bug in body, where or what is his bug mentality? As of now, it has yet to appear. Does the transformation mean that in his unconscious or preconscious Gregor has so thought of himself as vermin that he has changed into one? Or is the alteration of body, and eventually of mind, a wish fulfillment, possibly a means of gaining revenge on a stressful and ungrateful family? Or, to shift the ground, is Kafka portraying a view of the artist or writer whose imaginative life must be subsumed to commercial needs, or to family pressures? In this view, the writer has no standing; only his bread-winning ability has. In the first two or three pages, we have nearly all the possibilities: Gregor and family, the father, work, financial pressures, Gregor's sense of himself as son and as bug, his unconscious wishes, his desire for change.

Herr Samsa calls to him through the door, as does the chief clerk, who has suddenly materialized, in that Kafka way of producing people immediately as soon as one fears them. The chief clerk keeps up a barrage of criticism, attacking Gregor for not being dependable, although he had thought he was, for failing to respond except with yes or no, for making a spectacle of himself. It is all large men — their size heightened by Gregor's new lowness — who control his present and future. Still responding as a man, not as an insect, Gregor asks for more time, for his body simply will not come around. He assures the head clerk (as before Karl Rossmann had tried to deflect the head porter's attacks) he can still collect himself for the eight o'clock train.

When Gregor tries to turn the key in the lock in order to exit the room — although lacking teeth, his jaw is powerful — he damages his mouth and discharges a brown fluid that flows over the key and drips on the floor. This brief description, one of Kafka's masterstrokes, "creates" the insect. With this, there is no doubt of the transformation. The room with a door, still another part of the Kafkan equipment, indicates a spatial enclosure opening up but in reality closing down.

In not describing Gregor as he exits the room, but instead revealing others' observation of him, Kafka leaves the bug's size, agility, and shape to the imagination.* Leaning into the living room so that only half of his body is visible, to the horror of his family, Gregor observes all the familiar sights, including a photograph of Herr Samsa in his lieutenant's uniform, his bearing proud and carefree. The photograph overmatches father, as he once was, with son, as he now is, just as earlier the woman's picture on Gregor's wall, cut from a magazine, suggested her power over him.

Gregor's announcement that he'll be dressed at once, and his fear that if he does not act swiftly he will endanger his position in the firm, reveal Kafka's logic moving forward in a situation in which logic obviously has no place.

Gregor's parents have forsaken him, so intense is their preoccupation with their place and their fortunes. Abraham willingly sacrifices Isaac. But then all along they have taken Gregor for granted; the sacrifice, in reality, occurred some time ago. Yet unconsciously, Gregor's transformation becomes an act of supreme rebellion; self-destructive as it may be, it seems destructive of all those who parasitically lived off him. Instead of returning, the prodigal son reshapes himself into a monster and demands acceptance but is, of course, turned away. Somewhat

---

*When "The Metamorphosis" appeared in 1916 (published by Kurt Wolff), Kafka insisted that the jacket illustration omit the insect altogether. In the illustration by Ottomar Starke, a figure with his hands covering his face in horror is turning away from the open bedroom door. Kafka did not want the insect shown "at all, not even from a distance."

sympathetic, his mother cannot bear what she is witnessing and backs away. Even as this occurs, however, Gregor is becoming more comfortable as a bug.

The symbolism of the scene that closes part I of the novella, in which Herr Samsa attempts to get Gregor back into his room, is based on the birth trauma but with a particular Kafkan twist. Having emerged bleeding brown fluid from his painful delivery, Gregor must now be forced back into the room — having been reborn, he must return forcibly to the womb, where he can be sequestered. The final passages of this part describe a reverse birth process. Grown too large for the door at the angle he approaches it, Gregor is pressed and squeezed. His re-entry is marked by bleeding, bodily damage, crushed members, "when from behind his father gave him a strong push which was literally a deliverance and he flew far into the room, bleeding freely. The door was slammed behind him with the stick, and then at last there was silence."⁴³ Gregor's family hopes he can be aborted before he reappears. This is a remarkable sequence for Kafka, since it represents his desire to achieve unlife without actually killing himself.

Gregor's dislike of milk and his growing finickiness about food reflect his own isolation and were ways of commanding center stage by turning food into theater. Gregor's attitude mirrors his creator's sense of food as destructive, the cause of poor digestion, hemorrhoids, sexual imbalance, overall poor health. Like coitus, food is part of the punishment one must suffer for maintaining life. Kafka's asceticism was not a means toward a holier vision, but a way of repressing the body as some form of martyrdom to his craft, a form of masochism expressing its own form of pleasure. One way of reading "The Metamorphosis" is through deconstructing the larger social elements into Gregor's attempt to question the world of food by becoming an insect. In this regard, food becomes an emblem of what he must reject in order to survive, and yet to survive as an insect, he must come to terms with it. Food here has something of the ritualistic quality Kafka attributed to "heavy furniture" in his relationship with Felice. She felt reassured by it and wanted it for their apartment; he saw in it all the evils of married life. Food becomes in the story a sign of extreme hostility, for Gregor in time will be offered garbage, representing what he feels he has always been offered by the Samsas.

The pride he asserts he feels in having provided such a fine apartment for his parents and sister is belied by his rejection of their usual food. Kafka plays on this pride, letting it reinforce the transformation: "There were old, half-decayed vegetables, bones from last night's supper covered with a white sauce that had thickened; some raisins and almonds; a piece of cheese that Gregor would have called uneatable two days ago; a dry roll of bread, a buttered roll, and a roll both buttered and salted."⁴⁴ Of course, the more Gregor relishes this food the more he can humiliate and shame his family: food becomes the ultimate weapon for degrading them. He devours the cheese, the vegetables, and sauce, leaving the fresh food untouched. He cannot, in fact, even bear the smell of it. Accordingly, his food habits have effectively removed him from the family, not by degrading himself solely, but by degrading them.

Kafka's transformation of Gregor into an insect while still allowing him to understand with human awareness is anthropomorphism of a particular kind: giving human qualities to a nonhuman, and yet insisting on the nonhuman qualities of the one experiencing transformation. Gregor's ability to understand what the Samsas are saying is accompanied by his continuing desire to help his family. He recalls how when his father's business failed — Hermann Kafka's shop was itself doing very poorly in late 1912 — he, Gregor, had become a commercial traveler instead of a clerk in order to earn more money. Life as a traveler was of course far harder, but it warmed him to see how the money he earned comforted his family; as they had become accustomed to this comfort, his contribution was never seen as a personal sacrifice.

A superficial reading of Gregor's sacrifices would find immediate parallels in Kafka's life, his sacrifice of himself at the asbestos factory, for example. But in a deeper reading, we see Gregor's need for revenge, his need to play a role at the center of things, and, finally, his need to survive a mess he has embraced. He discovers that the family has kept hidden from him certain monies they have saved, so as to keep his contribution as heavy as possible. But this "deception" could only have occurred because Gregor wanted it to, so that he could justify his revenge. His inability to find a place for himself, as in Kafka's own inability to move out into his own apartment, has consequences he is willing to accept as long as he can make his oppressors pay with shame and humiliation. The struggle between father and son takes on several aspects in this scenario: Gregor wins all the battles, but Herr Samsa wins the war. From Kafka's point of view, it was necessary to find a valid battle plan. Becoming the kind of writer he was and refusing the role of married son with children were ways he struck back at Hermann and at all authority figures. Gregor's way was more radical.

Just as Gregor's family degenerated so as to make him their sole support, so now he degenerates to make them observe him. He hides under the sofa whenever Grete enters his room and then covers the small part of his body still visible when he notes her repulsion. Leaving the cleanup duties to Grete, his parents cease to enter the room. In his newly discovered freedom, Gregor hangs suspended from the ceiling, leaving sticky stuff wherever he crawls, rocking and swinging more comfortably than when he was on the floor. He is becoming accustomed to all those little legs, and to the way insects must control their bodies and limbs. Soon, all the furniture is removed from his rooms: his transformation is taken as irreversible. The clearing out of his room is, obviously, the relegation of him to the dead.

As his room is emptied, he cherishes the lady in fur, in the picture on the wall. He presses himself to the glass and enjoys its cool against his hot belly. Nobody is permitted to remove this object. When Frau Samsa catches sight of the "huge brown mass" on the flowered wallpaper, she screams out and almost faints. The scene is one of great intensity, and it must have had special meaning for Kafka. The woman in fur, as part of a masturbatory fantasy, is some kind of replacement figure for the mother about to be lost; or else she is so close to Gregor's fantasy life he is willing to lose everything but that. The woman symbolizes life for him *outside* the family, and is perhaps the sole source of pleasure his dutiful and obedient life has brought him. Curiously, it lies beyond the family, in some unknown world of magazine art. It recalls that Kafka's sexual drive was almost always exogamous, directed at Czech Gentiles, while limited or frustrated with Jewish women.

With this, Gregor is cut off from his mother, in effect a passive or negligible figure in his drama, and Herr Samsa takes up the struggle, appearing in a "smart blue uniform," the gold buttons reminding Gregor of a bank messenger. But he is no messenger. He is an authority figure, every inch a father to be feared: large, bushy eyebrows, black eyes, hair carefully combed, and extraordinarily large shoe soles, exaggerated from the disadvantageous point of view of an insect. The father is slowly regaining the household, reasserting his traditional authority. He lobs apples at Gregor, as if tossing hand grenades in a scene recalling the original Garden, but in a scrambled form: Gregor is expelled from paradise into the reality of paternal hatred. Oedipal forces are reversed, and the father attempts to "kill" the son using the forbidden fruit as an emblem of his unnatural hatred.

Kafka was clearly toying with the Abraham and Isaac episode as related by Kierkegaard and intermixing it with aspects of the Fall of Man and the expulsion from the Garden. The scene is linked to the father's desire to rid the family of the son; and it fits Kafka's perception of Hermann but hardly the reality. In reality, Hermann acquiesced to whatever his son wanted as long as Kafka persisted, and by the time of this story, Hermann Kafka was ill and unable to fight back. Kafka's perception, however, was another matter.

Herr Samsa's attack is a turning point in the story and makes way for the third and final segment. The apple remains stuck in Gregor's back as symbolic of his father's recovery from passivity and indolence. Furthermore, even after recuperation, Gregor is impeded in his movement, so that he crawls like an old invalid; he has now become the inactive figure in the apartment. The Samsas begin to assert themselves in several ways. Grete takes a position as a salesgirl, learning shorthand and French in the evenings; Herr Samsa remains attached to his uniform and seems to be working as a bank messenger; the maid takes over Gregor's care; and the family lets out a room to three lodgers. Gregor's room itself becomes a storehouse, suggesting that his presence is no longer a consideration. Even Frau Samsa shows some initiative, spending her time sewing. As the son deteriorates, the family waxes; in Kafka's view, the son does not reinforce family values but subverts them. Of course, with this perception, Kafka has made himself, and Gregor, more important in his own eyes.

We have not yet touched upon the transformation of Gregor into a bug as emblematic of the Jew in Prague. Although the Samsas do not seem to be Jewish, their vague similarity to the Kafkas gives them some Jewish identity; but when they take in non-Jewish lodgers, they join collectively in condemnation of the hated bug. As a form of fantasy, Kafka has invented a role for the Jewish victim that fits the perception of him held by Czech anti-Semites and even Hungarian nationalists, who began to lose their more tolerant attitude toward Jews. If we extend this idea, we can see Kafka's perception of himself as victim become wedded to his view of the Jew as victim, with both turned into what people envision as a large, brownish bug. If they can get rid of the Jew, they themselves can grow, which is essentially what Hitler would write in *Mein Kampf*. Germany could only expand if it rooted out the vermin in its midst. We speculate here about Kafka's vision, but it was an aspect of his thinking as he became increasingly interested in Jewish questions and in Zionism in 1912. His movement toward a greater Jewish secular self-identification created an awareness of how the Jew repelled those who were traditionally anti-Semitic, or those who felt Jews had poisoned the atmosphere of their country.

The revulsion the lodgers feel toward Gregor is understandable, from their point of view. But if we see events from Gregor's, where the perception of the story lies, then we must assume he sees himself as a bug responding logically to his situation. The entire question of how we accept the story depends on where we feel Kafka has located himself. Yet even though Gregor engages our sympathies and most of our attention, one of the difficulties of interpretation is our recognition that he is everywhere, that the rest of the family is correct in its disgust. When the maid calls the brown bug "you old dung beetle," we realize that everyone's assessment must be taken into account, even that of the hateful lodgers. The lodgers obviously do not want to live in a place that harbors such vermin, and it is precisely the way in which they verbalize their revulsion that makes us feel they have just discovered a Jew in their midst. They cannot abide this, and they give notice on the spot.

With this, Grete takes action, saying they must get rid of "it." Gregor is now a neuter pronoun (*es* in German), a neutered man, a bug without further identity, sexuality, or sensibility.[45] Gregor of course understands everything being said, having retained his ability to comprehend at the human level, and so he sees Grete as the ultimate traitor. She who was perhaps the most parasitical on him, the violin player, the would-be humanist, now becomes his greatest persecutor. And still we accept the logic of her behavior. Gregor engages us even as we accommodate his removal. Kafka has validated all roles, all positions, all decisions. He is, we must assume, everywhere.

When Gregor re-enters his room, the door is locked behind him. He is now, like the victim in the needle machine or the hunger artist, at his final moment of isolation, where triumph and death come together. In some prophetic way, Kafka foresees his own end in a sanatorium, all exits from his bed and room blocked to him. There is a prophetic sense of the Jew driven to the final point of existence, reviled by all, and finally put to death by those he has lived among. Just before Gregor dies, sinking to the floor, Kafka shifts back and forth between first and third person, so that Gregor can assess his situation even as Kafka narrates what is left for him to consider.

Kafka's fascination with physical details does not end here. Grete notices how thin he is, that he has not eaten for some time. His body is flat and dry, clearly akin to the victim's body in "In the Penal Colony," or that of the hunger artist, as it folds together in a corner of his cage. That the body is little more than refuse is, of course, the point. It is another dimension of Kafka's sense of his long, thin, useless body devoid of substance. The son's death energizes Herr Samsa, and he throws the lodgers out of his apartment. Like Herr Bendemann in "The Judgment," he is all man once he can head his family again. The women too have revived, liberated by the removal of the awful son. Grete now can develop, her young body can blossom. Her fleshiness is a perfect antithesis to Gregor's wasted body.

A vision of self is what the novella is all about, and it can be devastating, as Kafka knew it would be. It could have been triggered by some brewing physical condition, an infection, possibly, that led in turn to an emotional storm or breakdown, of suicidal tendencies, surely of radical self-hatred. The breakdown would not necessarily impede Kafka's physical movements if he were able to transfer it to a literary creation. Thus, in this possible psychological process, he was himself becoming transformed, avoiding complete breakdown through literary creation.

Yet it would be a huge error to view the novella as little more than a portrait of Kafka in his home, or Kafka at work. It is also necessary to see something else, more than self-hatred, a striking back through literary revenge. In this respect, Kafka indeed loathed himself, but not to the degree that he was only a bug in the eyes of others. Quite the opposite. By becoming a bug in the eyes of others he could reveal their hypocrisy, their intrigue, their basic indecency, their inhumanity, along with their survival instincts. The bug may even be the classic figure of the hated Jew, but once again it is more than that: it mirrors how others are perceived as they reveal their hatred.

As we move in and out of Gregor's consciousness, we observe his sense of victory, *even* as he measures the intrigue and deception of those who have depended on him. The story is of a family and how it responds; and in the larger sense, it has political implications, since the Samsas here are a miniaturized nation, collapsing within, waiting for the death of a member, then recovering in the wake of his forgotten sacrifice. The story is more brutal than Gregor's lone demise. It prophesies collapse, disintegration, disaster. "The Metamorphosis" foretells the years of war to come, not to mention Kafka's own breakdown.

By December 6, 1912, Kafka had "The Metamorphosis" in hand, telling Felice that although it was "exceptionally repulsive," it might help cleanse him so he could be worthy of her; there remained, he added, a good deal to drain away.* There were interruptions, for example, when he traveled for the institute to Kratzau for a trial, on November 26. On his return, on the same day, he wrote one of his longest letters to Felice, full of the tensions of the unpleasant trial (of competing lawyers fighting for the highest bid), his nervousness about putting aside his writing, his ambivalence about Felice herself and his response to her love. His nerves were so tightly strung, he tells her, he wanted to ram his fist into the face of a repulsive woman sitting opposite him on the train. Christmas vacation was approaching and he would be expected to visit Berlin. He needed excuses not to go, partly out of the desire to go on writing — "The Metamorphosis" had convinced him he had not lost his touch — but equally significant was his fear of turning written words into spoken ones during a meeting with his fiancée.

The days leading up to the new year were spent in hesitation, even as the general idea of an engagement began to shape itself. Kafka was able to excuse himself from a Berlin trip because of his sister Valli's wedding, which was postponed to January 12 when war almost broke out between Austria and Russia. With the marriage of Valli and with Elli already a mother, Kafka found only Ottla as his ally in the family, and they become increasingly close in outlook and sympathies. Ottla was the only one even remotely like her brother; she was also something of a rebel against Herr Kafka's dictatorial manner, and Kafka could hide behind her refusal to defer. Ottla, however, was being tested by long hours in the store, in somewhat the same way as Julie Kafka had been. In January, Kafka acted as usher at the synagogue wedding,

---

*The idea of writing as connected to filth and as catharsis seems to have claimed him. In a February 11 diary entry, already cited, he speaks of reading proofs of "The Judgment" and recognizing that the story came out of him like a birth, "covered with filth and slime," a comment that says something not only about his writing as "filth" but about life itself, in the birth process.

and now he had two brothers-in-law he did not like or respect. More than that, he saw others marrying, having children, carrying on normal lives, all of which drove home to him, as if he needed further evidence, that he was marginal to ordinary life and would always remain so. Gregor Samsa had already made that clear.

By this time (late 1912), Kafka had in hand *Meditation*, his first published book.* In early 1913, he could look forward to further publications, "The Stoker" in May and "The Judgment" in June; but he had little on the drawing board. He would return to *Amerika* (still called "Der Verschollene") in the following year, but for the time being he was accomplishing little except the enormously long letters to Felice. Those letters had taken over his imagination to the extent that they became a kind of epistolary novel or an autobiography of sorts. He saw Brod, now planning to marry in February, and he was in touch with Werfel, whom he described to Felice as a "beautiful" twenty-two-year-old who reads aloud as if his very life depended upon it. In early February (the third), accompanied by Ottla, he went to Leitmeritz for a trial, representing the institute. These trips, frequent enough so as to interrupt the flow of his life, may have given him the idea of writing "a trial," however different his was from those he witnessed. Certainly as a lawyer himself, he became familiar with the workings of one such kind of court, with lawyers, witnesses, judges, the nature of evidence, visible defendants and plaintiffs. Even Ottla, however, made him nervous, and he told Felice that after three or four hours in her presence he felt weary and eager to be alone. His conclusion: he was unfit for any human relationship.

With Brod now married, Kafka's sense of him became more distant. Brod himself remained loyal, reviewing *Meditation* extravagantly in the Munich weekly publication *März*. Brod spoke of a force (Kafka's) working against the spirit of the age and bringing to it a medieval introspection, a new morality and religiosity. Kafka felt embarrassed, as he should have, at the overpraise for brief pieces that show flashes of interest mainly because Kafka wrote them; and because one seeks in them, as we have, intuitions of the great works yet to come. Without that hindsight, he was fortunate to have found a publisher.

By February, Kafka had returned in irregular fashion to his diaries. In a February 28 entry, we find a fragmentary piece, a four-page interlude that has a shadowy relationship to *The Trial*, still nearly a year and

---

*We can see how Kafka's correspondence with Felice was analogous to Kleist's with Wilhelmine von Menge, in which he distanced himself from the woman he pursued, even though von Menge was a virtual neighbor of his in Frankfurt an der Oder. Kafka's further intense devotion to Kleist is revealed in his request to Rowohlt to publish *Meditation* in the same format as Kleist's *Anecdotes*. The year 1911 was the centennial of Kleist's death. To parallel *Anecdotes*, Kafka wanted a large print size; *Meditation* has larger than usual type, with wide page margins, and each piece has its own page or pages, with no overlapping.

a half away. Ernst Liman, who, like Kafka, travels for business, arrives in Constantinople and heads directly for his usual hotel stop, the Kingston. He finds, however, that it has been burned almost to the ground, and the driver has taken him there fully knowing the hotel was no longer functional. Part of the ground floor remains, and the staff, unemployed, are living in the ruins. A man emerges and tells Liman to remain loyal to the hotel by staying in a private home set aside for those former guests of the Kingston. Liman declines, but the hotel representative, holding back the door of his carriage, refuses to let him go. Liman manages to break away with the help of a servant girl, Fini, who caresses his shoulder and tells him to let her arrange a place, as she tries to swing herself into the carriage. Liman is eager to get away, but Fini insists on going with him. The hotel representative tries to force Fini into the carriage, while Liman exerts all his strength to keep her out, all the while imploring the driver to move on. But his efforts fail, and she manages to climb inside, straightening her blouse and arranging her hair, as Liman says, "This is unheard of."[46] End of fragment.

We shouldn't make too much of such a brief episode, but Fini foreshadows, certainly, the powerful women of *The Trial* and later works; Liman is himself an early version of Joseph K., a man whose destiny seems thwarted by forces or circumstances he cannot begin to deal with. The tone of the piece is based on frustration, impediments, disappointment. When the hotel Liman has frequented for years is no longer habitable, "ordinary life" is suddenly and unexpectedly removed from him. With this, hallucinatory experiences become possible: a tug-of-war with the hotel representative, and then with a young woman out to gouge an older man. All his plans for a quiet five days in Constantinople are upset and undermined by this hotel episode, and Liman heads off into a completely unforeseen future, which we are led to believe he will be incapable of handling. In a small form, the typical Kafka scenario is there, although still inchoate.

After this, until early May, the diaries stop, an indication of the ferocity with which he was bombarding Felice with letters. In March, Kafka received a promotion at the institute to deputy secretary, still a fairly low-level position but an indication of how well regarded he was. At Easter, he went to Berlin, saw Felice on Easter Sunday, and returned via Leipzig (where he met Löwy, still not solidly on his feet with a new theater troupe). He returned to Prague only to be faced with still another trial, in Aussig. The *Diaries* mention the meeting with Felice but only in passing, for he was concerned with the Kafkan self: his need, in particular, to keep a diary again, to express himself. We re-encounter his clever use of knife imagery (on May 4): "Always the image of a pork butcher's broad knife that quickly and with mechanical regularity chops into me from the side and cuts off very thin slices which fly off almost like shavings because of the speed of the action."[47] A "pork butcher's" knife — a Gentile enemy to this grandson of a kosher butcher — suggests Kafka's growing immersion in Jewish matters, his withdrawal from the Gentile world where knives awaited him.

Meanwhile, Kafka drove himself to physical punishment with a daily two-hour stint of gardening, in a Prague suburb. It was volunteer work that he took on as a way of exhausting his body to get rid of torturous office images. It was, in its way, a helpful therapy, clearing his mind not only of the office but of his inevitable movement toward engagement and marriage. On May 11–12, Kafka made another quick trip to Berlin, where he met Felice's family; characteristically, he describes them as gigantic, and we know he uses the word not to denote physical size but to mean unapproachability. He sees them as "possessing" Felice. In contrast, he is small, unprepossessing, unimpressive, and hardly man enough for the Bauers' daughter. He was, in effect, acting out the bug in this confrontation with her family.

Felice's silence drove him close to madness — not because he particularly missed her, but because, as we have observed above, he could not bear losing control of someone who was "his." By this stage, when he proposed in the letter of June 16, he needed her to bolster his self-image; her acceptance at least would mean that he was more than a bug. Kafka was working through an extremely perilous scenario, touched upon in chapter 9. What we can never discover is how much of it he was aware of, and how much was so deeply embedded in role-playing that even he failed to have access to it. The peril was that he did not know where his game was taking him, and that the result could indeed be marriage, unless he found some way to withdraw before the future was sealed. For while it was overwhelmingly important for him to pursue Felice, as any normal man would, it was also overwhelmingly clear that he must not catch her.

We have already seen how Kafka was disgusted by the physical details of married life and children; how he saw his mother's figure become bloated after six children and feared Felice would end up looking the same; how he detested the mindless play with children that got them so excited they wet the floor or let their food dribble down their clothes. His sense of physical decorum and distaste for any physical aberration, such as, later, Felice's poor teeth, left him no alternative but to rage against the byproducts of a bourgeois life. Nevertheless, Felice accepted his proposal, and the unofficial engagement was on, while Julie Kafka asked to investigate the Bauer family, permission for which Kafka withdrew. That Felice would accept him after he had called himself, among many other things, her "chill-proof, cast-iron madman" is an indication of either her blindness or, more likely, her belief that she and married life would change him. Kafka knew better; he was unchangeable.* To Brod, he would speak (on August 29) of his "interior

*While writing to Felice about being a madman, he was telling Max Brod that his mind

Tower of Babel,"[48] by which he meant, we can assume, his madness. Meanwhile, Felice had shown a sample of her fiancé's handwriting to a graphologist, who said Kafka was good-natured and sensual, with artistic interests and a thrifty disposition. The interpretation, of course, made Kafka wild, especially the insight about "artistic interests," when he felt literature was not his interest but his life.

Such were the misunderstandings. Felice more or less accepted the graphologist's view and felt that "literary interests" could be contained, perhaps at some future date filed away. Although they were supposedly meeting in an engagement of interests, in actuality they were moving on parallel lines; and while in time Felice would become more sympathetic to Kafka's self-absorption, she never accepted it, insisting on her own prerogatives against his need for control. Hermann Kafka looked askance at the engagement. We learn of this response, however, from Kafka, who may have been trying to duplicate Herr Bendemann's "judgment" on Georg. In Kafka, the lines between his artistic recreation of events and actuality overlapped; and often actuality was bent to fit imaginative conception. According to Kafka, his father raised financial questions, fearing that the errant writer would remove his support, withdraw from the asbestos factory, and desert a sick man in need of sons. In this respect, Hermann reverts to Herr Bendemann and Herr Samsa. Then after grumbling, he agreed to meet the Bauers in Berlin.

As noted, Kafka wrote a most forbidding letter to Herr Bauer, demonstrating how unsuitable he was as Felice's fiancé, how all he wanted in the world was a solitary, even monastic, life; and then having revised its language, without alleviating the force, he sent the letter on, on August 28. It was everything a future father-in-law would not want to hear about a potential relative, but the Bauers, very possibly eager to marry off their not-too-young daughter, agreed. With Felice, Kafka played the "dog" or "insect," making himself imitate his fiction, as he had made his fiction imitate his inner sense of himself. Having gained the Bauers' approval, he tells Felice to cast him aside as unworthy of her, and by such rhetoric he secured her hand: offering her someone who had been so rejected by his mother he now asked her to reject him as well, but also sending a countering signal that if she leaves him, he will be nothing. It was precisely at this time he wrote Brod that his inner world is an interior Tower of Babel, "and what lies above and below is beyond the ken of folks in Babel."[49]

Just before this, in a July 21 diary entry, he offered a clerk's assess-

---

was prey to fantasies: "For example that I lie stretched out on the floor sliced up like a roast, and with my hand am slowly pushing a slice of meat toward a dog in the corner" (April 3, 1913; *Letters to Friends*, p. 95). The passage contains familiar imagery, of being cut up, of oneself as a hunk of meat, and of an association with dogs. Kafka was, once more, playing out the bug, or, in another scenario, the impotence of man when confronted by choice.

ment not of financial debits and assets but of arguments for and against marriage. Although we have mentioned some of this before, the arguments are often compelling because they reveal how Kafka's handling of his own inner life bleeds over so effortlessly into his fiction. He confronts his frustration, that while he wishes for a solitary life, he cannot bear, by himself, the "assault" of his own life, the demands of his person, the attacks made by time and old age, "the nearness of insanity." Yet even as he says this, and insists on sharing his madness, he says he cannot function except alone. He emphasizes that conversation, which accompanies marriage, takes "the importance, the seriousness, the truth out of everything I think." His courtship of Felice by letter made conversation negligible, and we note that whenever the two did come together, they barely communicated. More often than not they walked or sat in silence or else Kafka talked, while Felice listened; but her silences drove him near insanity, and at the same time he recognized her talk would undermine the "truth" of any situation. He insists he is fearless and powerful only when he writes.

Beginning in September 1913, Kafka traveled, first to Vienna on company business, accompanied by his superiors, Eugen Pfohl and Robert Marschner, for the second International Congress for First Aid and Accidents. This is a side of Kafka always present during his long tenure at the institute, that involvement in accidents, first aid, reimbursements for injuries. Those who argue, and Kafka himself so argued, that work at the institute was sapping his strength, lose sight of the fact that his immersion in others' accidents and injuries helped relieve some of his despairing self-absorption and gave him focus for feelings beyond himself. Without that, the intense self-absorption that preoccupied him could, very possibly, have taken him over the edge: a mixture of self-pity, despair, frustration at the slow pace of his writing, and other factors could have combined to halt his productive work altogether. Once in Vienna, Kafka attended a session of the Zionist Congress, an organization that had begun to meet in 1903. Although not as yet feeling himself caught up in the Zionist fervor for settlements in Palestine kibbutzim, Kafka nevertheless moved toward further Jewish identification upon his return to Prague by joining an association of Jewish officials. While not made up of fervent Zionists, this group was also not assimilationist, and favored Zionism over continued efforts to be accepted where they were clearly unwanted.*

*The so-called "Protocols of the Elders of Zion," a Russian forged document promoting the idea of a takeover of the world by Jewish interests, was alive and circulating throughout Europe. In the wake of still another blood libel accusation in Kishinev, on the Russian border, in 1903, the "Protocols" poured fire on the rumors of Jewish subversion. The following from a newspaper in Barlad, in the Moldavian sector of Romania, catches the flavor of Gentile sentiment: "The recent ritual murders committed by Jews in Austria, Bohemia, Hungary, Germany and Russia [all of them disproved and the defendants acquitted] must still be fresh in everyone's mind. And how many children have disap-

At the Hartungen sanatorium in Riva, Kafka became intimate with an ill Swiss girl of about eighteen, and this was very important to him. "For the first time I understood a Christian girl and lived almost entirely within the sphere of her influence."[50] Once again, Kafka was intrigued by exogamy, a Christian girl outside the world of his parents, and someone, he felt, who did not share his guilt at any transgression. On guilt itself, he told Felix Weltsch, "If you imagine that I derive some help, some solution, from a sense of guilt, you are wrong. The reason why I have this sense of guilt is that it is for me the finest form of penitence. But one must not look too closely into this matter lest the sense of guilt become merely a form of nostalgia."[51] On his return to Prague, he first met Grete Bloch, and the double game charted in chapter 9 was about to begin. At first, Kafka used Grete as a screen behind which he could hide while he kept after Felice, but he also used Felice as a screen behind which he pursued Grete.

Another brief trip found him in Berlin, to see Felice, but with his usual ambivalence he kept changing plans, so that when he finally arrived on Saturday, November 8, she was so put off at his last-minute and confusing arrangements her schedule was full and they barely had time for a walk in the Tiergarten. Like all their meetings, this one was full of tension, very brief, and inconclusive as far as their broad differences were concerned. If anything, this meeting, like the earlier ones, drove them farther apart. Only the ferocious exchange of letters could compensate for the troubled hours they spent together. On his return, on November 9, Kafka began to use Grete Bloch as a convenient confidante, in a sense courting her by way of complaining about Felice.* He analyzes his fiancée's dental problems, which he admits is for him one of the most repulsive ailments — since, he might have added, the mouth is the entrance not only for love but for food. Food and dogs meet in this lovely analogy: "At bottom I am an incapable, ignorant

---

peared in our own country! How many mutilated bodies have been found, while the criminals have remained undiscovered! Who are these criminals — these bloodthirsty murderers of our prattling babes? They are the fanatical Jews that infest our land. These monsters are the slayers of our Christian children. They are the criminals — the Jews who have invaded our country like locusts" (Ronald Sanders, *Shores of Refuge: A Hundred Years of Jewish Emigration* [New York: Schocken, 1988], p. 196). In all cases where the murderers were apprehended, they were members of the Christian community. A pogrom in Zhitomir, in the Ukraine, near where author Joseph Conrad had been born, led in 1905 to hundreds of Jews being killed or injured. The "Black Hundreds" operating there were paralleled by similar groups in Bohemia and Moravia and in Hungary.

*Although circumstances differ, the parallel with Freud's use of his sister-in-law Minna Bernays cannot be ignored. Earlier, we had indicated Kafka's and Freud's curiously parallel paths, and in their use of another woman as confidante and, possibly, lover we discover further similarities. Minna was Martha Freud's sister, and, therefore, any relationship would have been incestuous; yet Freud depended heavily on her in revealing his psychoanalytic theories and in this way took her into his confidence in a manner he did not with Martha. Kafka "used" Grete similarly, opening himself up so that she became a secret sharer of his life, in a way Felice could not.

person who, if he had not been compelled . . . to go to school, would be fit only to crouch in a kennel, to leap out when food is offered him and to leap back when he has swallowed it."[52] Chewing had preoccupied him, and still did, and teeth were the mechanism by which hated food could be transformed into excrement. As Kafka writes of teeth, the reader may feel he is experiencing a description not of the mouth but of the anus.

We learn, in fact, that this most recent trip was a fiasco not from Kafka's diaries, which are blank about this latest episode but from an enormously long letter to Grete. He dissects Felice into four "almost incompatible girls," including one who has no liking for him. But he adds he regards her dislike as "nothing is more natural."[53] He then outlines his approach to the visit, and it sounds less like a sequence of scheduling errors than a Marx Brothers script. Each time he expects Felice to be in a certain place at a certain time, she is elsewhere, while he uses all forms of modern communication, including a messenger on a bicycle, to try to coordinate his visit with her activities. Nearly everything fails, obviously, *because they wanted it to fail.* He could sustain the courtship only by letter, not by visits, and Felice was herself too undecided, even with the engagement (still unannounced).

The limbo quality of Kafka's existence now is underscored by a strange comment he makes in his diary for November 19, ten days after his return from Berlin. Rather than being reassured, he is less certain than ever. He says the reading of his diary moves him, but he worries it may be because he no longer possesses any confidence. "Everything appears to me to be an artificial construction of the mind. Every remark by someone else, every chance look throws everything in me over on the other side, even what has been forgotten, even what is entirely insignificant. I am more uncertain than I ever was. I feel only the power of life. And I am senselessly empty."[54] He compares himself to a sheep lost in the night, in the mountains, and he feels so lost he lacks the strength even to regret it.

In an interesting comment on his sexual interests, he says he walks through the streets where there are whores, and the experience excites him, "the remote but nevertheless existent possibility of going with one." He says he wants only the stout, older ones, "with outmoded clothes that have, however, a certain luxuriousness because of various adornments." (One recalls the picture of the woman in furs on Gregor Samsa's wall.) But then he moves to a different type, a working woman, wearing a work blouse like a cook's and carrying a bundle that might have been laundry. "No one would have found anything exciting in her, only I."[55] In the evening, he sees her dressed in a tight-fitting coat walking her beat on a street that branched off from the Zeltnerstrasse; but when she responds to his glance, he runs away from her. He connects his uncertainty to thoughts of Felice. But precisely what repels him in

Felice — her bourgeois qualities, perhaps her Jewishness, which reminded him of his sisters, her flawed features, and silence in his presence — makes the prostitutes attractive. Since they were Gentiles, they did not require conversation, and were well outside of anything associated with middle-class Jewish family life.

The uncertainty continues with a dream recorded on November 24 and a brief fictional episode later; completely inconclusive, they suggest wandering, indecisiveness, loss of direction, a need to hang on to familiar objects, inability to concentrate or make sense of things. If we did not know Kafka was still functioning, we might see him in the midst of a breakdown, or at least suffering from what the French call a *cafard*, when enervation and inability to do anything take over to create a kind of misty or foggy nothingness of existence. By November 25, the Kafkas had moved to a smaller apartment, on the Niklasstrasse, where Kafka had his own room, looking out on the Russian church and its dome. But the move was also a step down in fortunes and in class. The shop was doing poorly, Hermann was ill, Elli and Valli were married and away, and Ottla was beginning to rebel.

The move, or else just the general malaise, made Kafka consider death: "To die would mean nothing else than to surrender a nothing to the nothing, but that would be impossible to conceive for how could a person, even only as a nothing, consciously surrender himself to the nothing, and not merely to an empty nothing but rather to a roaring nothing whose nothingness consists only in its incomprehensibility."[56] In brief, to be or not to be is resolved — it is better to be because there is less nothingness involved in being than in not-being. Kafka affirmed through a negation. The ironic temper of Modernism had entered completely into him.

That uncertainty and nothingness dogged him into the new year, 1914. He questions even the quality of uncertainty, saying that the mood of the moment is influenced by a variety of circumstances, so that one falsifies by saying one is resolute yesterday and in despair today. The individual creates fantasies for himself when he tries to separate different feelings, creating what Kafka calls "an artificial life, as sometimes someone in the corner of a tavern, sufficiently concealed behind a small glass of whiskey, entirely alone with himself, entertains himself with nothing but false, unprovable imaginings and dreams."[57] He stares in the mirror to identify who and what he is, and is surprised to note it is a "beautifully outlined face," neither haggard nor childish, "rather unbelievably energetic." The mirror episode was very possibly caused by Felice's failure to answer his letters; he needed something else to validate his existence. Without her responses, he was pouring his letters, it appeared to him, into a void.

He even thinks of a Christmas visit (1913), but when he telephoned, she turned down the possibility. His despair about not hearing from her makes him think of asking Weiss to hand-deliver a letter to her in her office, demanding she respond. When a letter does arrive, he says he feels warmth in his blood. Doing no other writing, receiving few other letters, with only work at the office and in the asbestos factory at hand, Kafka more than ever needed that lifeline from Berlin. Of course his confession in December of his infidelity at Riva did not exactly warm Felice. But Kafka's determination to confess had a note of desperation in it — to force Felice to see what he was if and when she decided to back off, and at the same time to demonstrate to her he was capable of such an act, ashamed of it as he was.

By the beginning of 1914, the triangle composed of Felice, Grete, and Kafka was in place. As we saw in chapter 9, Felice and Grete discussed Kafka, while Kafka discussed Felice with Grete, while Kafka and Felice carried on their courtship. At this point, it is unclear which side of the triangle was in the foreground, which in the background. Kafka was revealing more intimate feelings to Grete than he was to Felice, while Felice was telling her friend that Kafka was a poor fellow. That this round robin of commentary created further tensions is indisputable; and Kafka's increasingly intimate correspondence with Grete, with all its sexual overtones, could not have been lost on her, and possibly not on Felice either. Certainly, Grete began to feel quite jealous, sensing that she more than her friend possessed Kafka.

These feelings of jealousy, envy, possession, or some such combination, perhaps explain why she claimed to have conceived a son by Kafka, since dates and other evidence do not support her assertion. With no child to produce — he was conveniently dead by 1921, at nearly seven years old — and no real evidence to support her story, Grete had only a fantasy. And yet it was founded on real feeling, for Kafka was revealing more sympathy for her than he was for Felice. In comparing the two women, Kafka preferred Grete but was committed to Felice; in reality, he wanted neither in any lasting relationship.

Because of the disarray Kafka felt his correspondence with Felice had fallen into, he decided to fly to Berlin, and he arrived on Saturday, February 28, without having informed her of his visit. He went to her place of work, presented a calling card with the name Gotthart on it — a mystery, that! — and found that Felice would not invite him in. They met for lunch and for a few hours the next morning, but, as on previous visits, she was occupied with a busy schedule. It was as inconclusive as ever, since although Felice promised not to marry anyone else, she did not feel she could marry someone with such eccentricities of behavior and outlook. Kafka attempted to persuade her to make a final commitment, even if she did not love him, since, he asserted, his love was sufficient for both. None of this, of course, was true, and the fact of the matter was that he needed her commitment as a way of justifying his quest. In point of fact, he found her skin blotchy and her teeth made him absolutely frantic. Since the Golem plays so fervently in and out of Kafka, in Gregor Samsa, in the strange Odradek shape, and elsewhere, perhaps it is not too outrageous to say that he perceived Felice as being somewhat Golem-like. Undeniably, his descriptions of her mouth, skin, even coloring (likened to dust) vaguely suggest the Golem. None of this is extravagant if we consider Kafka and his insects, animals, and other strange forms as a modern Rabbi Loew, creating contemporary Golems not to save Jews but to offer them perceptions of themselves.

From his diary entry of January 24, a month before his brief trip, he evokes the image of Sisyphus: "It occurred to me that my life, whose days more and more repeat themselves down to the smallest details, resembles that punishment in which each pupil must according to his offense write down the same meaningless . . . sentence ten times, a hundred times or even oftener, except that in my case the punishment is given me with only this limitation: 'as many times as you can stand it.' "[58] This punishment included his affair with Felice, although the tug-of-war obviously satisfied or completed some part of him, since he insisted on it so strongly. Each time she drew closer to him, however, he put her off with another confession of his unsuitability. Clearly, Kafka was playing puppetmaster, letting her out, then drawing her in, in alternating movements of accommodation and rejection. This latest trip to Berlin was part of puppet theater, for in subsequent letters after his return to Prague, Kafka rejected promises made in Berlin, and in fact intensified his unsuitable presentation of himself. He needed the punishment of rejection, apparently, as a means of goading himself into further self-absorption, with the hope that from this he would be able to find material for his fiction. The plan of course functioned well. He was miserable, despairing, often suicidal, but he found his material and would mine it intensely.

Since the give and take of the relationship and its details are presented in chapter 9, it is sufficient here to demonstrate how Kafka used the correspondence, apart from its daily punishment of himself, as a means of understanding where he stood, what he stood for, and how completely dedicated he was to a style of life that excluded everyone else. If nothing more, the relationship to Felice demonstrated to him that his feelings were cast in stone. Yet he did honestly fear to be alone. After Brod's marriage and announcement of Felix Weltsch's plunge into matrimony, Kafka wrote, "I remain alone, unless F. will still have me after all."[59] He follows this up with typical gallows humor, the Kafkan pose as a possible suicide: "There will certainly be one to blame if I should kill myself even if the immediate cause should for instance appear to be F.'s behavior. . . . I can't live without her and must jump [from the ledge of her balcony], yet — and this F. suspects — I couldn't live with her either."[60] Apart from romantic play-acting, his insight is correct, and it clarified for him the fact he was so entangled in life he could never kill himself. What saves him from any further move is his self-absorption: everything plays into him, everything is assimilated into his perception of reality — to the degree that a world without his perception of it would cease to exist. He is needed in order to keep it alive, just as it is necessary in order to sustain him. His eye is like a telescope into existence. Even a letter from Robert Musil cannot pick him up but "pleases me and depresses me, for I have nothing."[61]

Kafka has assumed a Modernist pose: that ability to bring himself down into such a slough of despair that only artwork can carry him out. For Kierkegaard, that slough was the point of departure for the leap into faith; for Kafka, it was quite different, since his sole faith focused on the written word that he produced not to relieve the despair but to assimilate it into the work itself. As he himself recognized, his great talent was his ability to transform his unconscious and preconscious into narrative. But he was not unique; this was the way of all great Modernists, whether they called their unconscious "privileged moments" (Proust) or "epiphanies" (Joyce).

In early March (the ninth), Kafka was caught between one recent trip to Berlin and another planned for April 12–13 (during Easter). Trying to balance himself between two equally unacceptable options — whether to marry or not — he did his usual tightrope walking act. He carries on an interior dialogue, as though he were two people, between the official who could benefit from marriage and the writer whose work would be jeopardized. Yet as he moves from one position to the other, he admits he is neither married nor writing: nothing for a year, and possibly nothing at all in the future, since he is obsessed with only one thing, marriage. He admits to having tried all kinds of self-humiliation, including his statement to Felice in the Tiergarten that his love would make up for any lack in hers.[62] What he does not add is that self-humiliation was a practice run, a kind of linkage between his work at the end of 1912 and the beginning of *The Trial* in the summer of 1914. The self-debasement, as he sees it, is not at all wasted, but part of the matter he needed to sustain his perception of himself so that it could be transformed into literary substance. Defense would become offense.

A five-page interior dialogue in the *Diaries* does not open up any startlingly new ground, but it does reveal how Kafka hugged to himself the smallest elements; each day, he states, the tiniest success is a gift. To do anything, whatever, is all to the good. He sees Prague, which he must leave (if married), and Vienna, which he hates, as the only places he can consider for making a living as a lawyer. Or else, he can imagine Berlin, where he would go as a journalist, since he feels he cannot leave the German language (a choice of profession so distant from his talents as to seem ludicrous). Like nearly all his thoughts about the future, the dialogue ends inconclusively — ends, in fact, with his realization that all he needs is a room and a vegetarian diet, "almost nothing more."[63] This bleak prospect was made bleaker by his feeling that he had heart, sleep, and digestion problems. Yet some of his greatest work was almost upon him, *The Trial* and "In the Penal Colony."

The two-day trip to Berlin over Easter led to an unofficial engagement, what was really agreed upon the previous June, when Kafka formally proposed and Felice accepted. The courtship seemed to have its own engine: the acceptance, the unofficial engagement in April, followed by the official engagement in June (1914), one year after the proposal. The plan was for a September wedding, when Felice had completed her five-year stint at Carl Lindström. Kafka's response to the April meeting in Berlin was an invitation to Grete Bloch to meet him and Felice in Gmünd, a border town; and Grete, in turn, requested the return of her letters, which he failed to see as compromising or embarrassing for her under the new circumstances of his attachment. The young women were, clearly, caught in Kafka's game plan: to keep the courtship going with unofficial and official engagements (the first was, as we have seen, broken off after only one month); to hold on to both young women and pour out his anxieties in his *Diaries* until he could transfer them to his fiction. Prior to the April Berlin meeting, his diary entries are full of trepidation, repeating Kafka's plaint that all his strength was emptying itself into nothingness, and only Felice through understanding could help him.

A meeting with Werfel, on April 8, only brought home to Kafka how his young friend was facing life so differently. Kafka's feelings about Werfel's work changed radically from one time to another, but he remained impressed by the young man's impudent and flawless attitude, his good features, his confidence in himself, his ability to function without constant unease.

Kafka confesses he hates Werfel, "not because I envy him, but I envy him too. He is healthy, young and rich, everything that I am not." Kafka could have added that besides that, Werfel was the apple of his mother's eye, the little doll on whom she lavished all her attention, and with money, brains, and boyish good looks, he waxed fat and successful seemingly without effort or introspection. Kafka senses that lack of introspection can make the individual happy; whereas with it, one is damned. "Besides, gifted with a sense of music, he has done very good work early and easily, he has the happiest life behind him and before him, I work with weights I cannot get rid of, and I am entirely shut off from music."[64] The "Tonio Kröger" condition reappears: Werfel is that talented, easy, unreflective "other," whereas Kafka is the tormented introspective creator, who must sustain his agonies. Kafka was, of course, probing a far lesser talent.

But the *Diaries* also begin to move into brief scenes or episodes, indicating that Kafka was moving toward fiction. Intermixed with personal matters were imaginative exercises: a white horse on an autumn afternoon finding sudden and unexpected freedom; a landlady who drops her skirts and hurries through some rooms; a neighbor who enters Kafka's room and wrestles with him. All this is noted in and around Felice's May 5 visit to Prague. Kafka says, mysteriously, that he is "coming closer," as though "the spiritual battle were taking place in a clearing somewhere in the woods." He hears the clash of weapons in a struggle: "Perhaps the eyes of the warriors are seeking me through the darkness of the woods, but I know so little of them, and that little is deceptive."[65] The precise meaning of this image is clouded, but the general sense is of an embattled Kafka who would like to fight but does not even know who or where the enemy is. That it might be Felice is a good guess; that it might be himself is more probable. That the "warriors" are these two is strengthened by Kafka's remark to Grete, after Felice's departure from Prague, that his fiancée's mouth was filled with teeth of such a repellent nature that to look at her was torture. Teeth, knives, and related sharp instruments were forms of self-torture for Kafka, elements he voluntarily pursued to validate his view of himself and his world. Unfortunately for her, Felice gave him ample proof of the imperfection surrounding and eating at him.

This was, approximately, the time when Grete Bloch would have conceived the child she said she was carrying. Again, the dates do not allow for such a possibility, even intimacy between her and Kafka is doubtful, although possible, and her claim, later, in 1940, of the child's existence and death in 1921 was part of her own "family romance," giving her a hold on Kafka that Felice never obtained. There is some chance that she gave birth later, in 1916, when she complained of "sufferings," but a boy born then would not have been almost seven in 1921. Her story falls too closely into the fantasy of a woman who felt spurned in turn making a claim on the man who shunned her. There is little question Kafka's treatment of her was indiscreet at least and cruel at most. He was surely inconsiderate of her feelings and was so wrapped up in himself that he failed to see her "sufferings" at being used up as confidante when she, apparently, felt *she* should be his fiancée.

The diary entry in which his neighbor wrestles with him predates the Berlin trip by only three days, and its emphasis on a struggle must have been linked in Kafka's mind to the upcoming visit. Since each trip proved unsatisfying and frustrating, Kafka might easily have envisioned it in wrestling terms — as he envisioned the entire nature of marriage. But the diary entry of the day before he leaves is far more desperate, a real preparation for *The Trial* and "In the Penal Colony," not to speak of the eighth chapter of *Amerika*. This passage of love prose is hallucinatory, as though Kafka were the object and not the subject, as though Kafka could look at the "other" as patient, client, or victim.

But as I stand here in my misery, already the huge wagon of my schemes comes driving up behind me, I feel underfoot the first small step up, naked girls, like those on the carnival floats of happier countries, lead me backward up the steps. . . . I feel myself at the farthest verge of human endeavor, and high up where I am, with suddenly acquired skill spontaneously execute a trick I had admired in a contortionist years ago — I bend slowly backward (at that very moment the heavens strain to open to disclose a vision to me, but then stop), draw my head and trunk through my legs and gradually stand erect again.[66]

On the edge of a vision, he sees

small horned devils leaping out of all the gates of the land . . . overrunning the countryside; everything gives way in the center under their feet, their little tails expunge everything, fifty devils' tails are already scouring my face; the ground begins to yield, first one of my feet sinks in and then the other; the screams of the girls pursue me into the depths into which I plummet, down a shaft precisely the width of my body but infinitely deep.[67]

This sense of infinity tempts him to "no extraordinary accomplishments," for anything he should do would be insignificant. He falls, insensible. The next day he prepares to leave for Berlin, and Felice.

Back in Prague, on June 6, he was now officially engaged, "tied hand and foot like a criminal."[68] He says that had they sat him down in the corner chained and placed policemen in front of him and let him look on, the experience could not have been worse. "And that was my engagement." He grants that everyone attempted to bring him to life, but when they failed, they simply put up with him. Felice, he observes, was deeply upset. "What was merely a passing occurrence to the others, to her was a threat." The contrast between inner and outer Kafka is compelling. Frozen in his exterior, unable to respond, caught up in the horror of his estrangement from the proceedings, incapable of comprehending his role in these family festivities, Kafka within is quite a different person, harboring schemes for his work, readying himself for a huge creative effort, digging ever more deeply into his misery to find compensation and solace in tortured images. Except for chapter 8 of *Amerika*, his work in the immediate future would concern entrapment, injustice, suffering, uncertainty: that hell the sensitive man digs for himself. His letters to Felice following his return to Prague become even more anguished; he writes of himself squirming on the ground like one of those animals she is so frightened of. He hesitates about writing to her father asking for her hand, the final stage in the engagement, and by now a mere formality. He writes to Felix Weltsch's wife, Lise, that he feels reduced to the "last remnants"[69] of his feeble strength, enervated and dispirited.

In his *Diaries*, he writes "Temptation in the Village," an inconclusive tale of a man's entrapment. The beginning, about his arrival in a village, foreshadows the fairy tale opening of *The Castle;* in many ways, it becomes the characteristic Kafka opening, of a stranger in our midst.* As he seeks a place to sleep, the "I" of the fragment goes from inn to farm, until he finds a spot in the farm attic where only the children sleep. He climbs up amidst the straw and the children and falls into a deep slumber. But it is brief, broken by the presence of a small bushy city dog who suddenly appears on the farm. The dog makes it impossible for the stranger to sleep, and he gets up and carries the small animal in his arms. But when the dog begins to protest, the stranger stumbles over a child, waking all the children, who take the animal from him. They all run out to return the dog to its owner, and the stranger is left worried about his meddling in the affairs of the house. He feels he has been nothing but a disruptive force.

The piece, describing an estrangement of such monumentality, suggests that Kafka was undergoing a severe bout of self-punishment over his Berlin engagement party. These scenes of estrangement dominate in the *Diaries,* including one in which, at about midnight, five men hold him, while a sixth raises his hand, attempting to grasp him. All of them fall back when he shouts that they should let him go, but he knows they will come after him. He warns his mother he is being pursued by a ragtag bunch of men, all of whom seem like pirates or brigands. The speaker's mother seems to accommodate this development and becomes a refuge against the outside turbulence. But the experience suggests an inner turmoil of such moment that one suspects a kind of clairvoyance, an intuition of the impending struggle that would last for the next four years. It was at the end of this month, June, that Archduke Ferdinand was assassinated by a Serb, Gavrilo Princip; and with the heir to the empire's throne killed by a nationalist, war was inevitable.

Such passages in Kafka's *Diaries,* however, were not prophetic, but hypersensitive perceptions of himself; for when the nerves of a creative genius are strung so tautly that they seem to be driving him to insanity, his own fears and doubts can appear to be prophecy. Kafka no more intuited the coming war than Dostoevsky foresaw the 1905 and 1917 revolutions. Kafka did not intuit or prophesy the Holocaust, either, but because he contains within his own disintegrating self so many of the wounds suffered historically by Jews, he can seem to be predicting the future course of Jewish history. His experiences can be applied in so many areas and directions only because he made them so intense that they burst beyond the individual.

As we have seen, the letters to Felice after the June meeting in Berlin become so agitated that the July break with her becomes inevitable.

---

*There are two possible openings for *The Castle,* with the more commonly accepted one describing K.'s arrival in the snow-covered village, with Castle Hill "hidden, veiled in mist and darkness."

Leading up to it is Kafka's hesitation about writing to Herr Bauer requesting his daughter's hand in marriage. Kafka devised the means of withdrawal, avowing ill-health in his May 23 letter. He says he lacks that sense of well-being that in most people is a source of cheerfulness. But his hesitation to mail his letter to Felice's father was connected to other concerns: that it was a final step, from which he feared there was no retreat. From the letter to the marriage bed would be a clear path. He could fight off the young woman, but not the older man.

There is also the possibility that he was troubled by Grete Bloch's role, and that he had had an affair with her, or was involved in some ongoing understanding. We have no proof of this, but a broad speculation would be that even if Kafka and Grete did not consummate the relationship physically, they had become intimate; and there is some reason to think there was a consummation, even without direct proof. Kafka's agitation, then, could be explained by the excitement of his personal situation and its difficulties. Certainly, except for diary entries with those hallucinatory fragments mentioned earlier, he was not writing; even his letters to friends and family are quite few for this period, from spring through fall of 1914. Still another assessment of his extreme agitation could be located in his preparation for a great burst of creativity, much of it coming together in November, that characteristic burst that occurred every two years or so, followed by little but the *Diaries*.

In his efforts to explain himself to Felice, Kafka makes certain she sees his unsuitability. He emphasizes his inner life (inaccessible to her), his possession of certain powers that shape experience into literature. Under present conditions, he cannot exercise these powers, he says, but if he could he would be lifted out of his inner misery. He warns that he does not fit into any friendship patterns and feels himself lost to all social intercourse. This distancing of himself, not only from Felice but even from Max Brod, was Kafka's preparation for that assault on his inner life that would produce his next burst of creative work. The language of his letters indicates a real journey he is about to undertake, into areas where Felice cannot possibly follow; and he exults in the fact that there is a part of himself that she cannot fathom or pursue. Superficially an effort to allay her fears at his strangeness, these letters between the engagement in June and its sundering in July are really acts of profound hostility. For even while he attempts to show her she has little to fear, he is establishing the terms on which she should really fear him. He is outlining the space he must occupy, which under no conditions can she enter. The letters appear to include her but in reality are exclusionary. His insistence on his inaccessibility is so forceful that if she had read him correctly — and evidence from his replies indicates she was beginning to do so — she would recognize the futility of their courtship.

As we have seen in the previous chapter, Kafka's insistence on his needs is like a juggernaut as it rolls over her objections. He turns his imaginative world into something so significant for him that without it he could not even think of trying to win her. Such was the state of events when he and Otto Pick traveled to Dresden, to an area called Hellerau, which was known for its Dalcroze eurythmics studio. They left on June 27, stayed over in Dresden, journeyed to Leipzig to see Kurt Wolff, the publisher, and Franz Werfel, and Kafka returned to Prague on the thirtieth. But this trip, which had its own tensions, was only preparation for the traumatic one in July, in the Askanische Hof in Berlin, which was indeed like a page out of the yet-to-be-written *Trial*. A great deal occurred in this brief period. Kafka was pursuing Grete, and Grete, in her uncertainty about where she and everything else stood, showed Felice passages from Kafka's letters to her. Meanwhile, Julie Kafka was writing to the Bauers about how pleased she was about the engagement. What Kafka had wrought Kafka was about to reap.

On July 11, Kafka departed for Berlin, where in the Askanische Hof he confronted a tribunal. We have previously described the face-off, with Felice, her sister Erna, and Grete. Felice's evident hostility had been building, while Kafka had apparently not noticed her jealousy of Grete. He had not understood the cumulative effect of his letters, all suggesting withdrawal even as he pressed his suit; and he had chosen to ignore the signs in Felice's letters of her hesitancy, her insistence on her own prerogatives, her tacit rejection of his way of life as he described it. Either he had missed all of this or out of his own self-absorption he had chosen to dismiss it. Or perhaps he had unconsciously baited a trap in which he could be the victim. Whatever surfaced in Berlin left him traumatized. For he who had been doing all the rejecting was now rejected; the engagement after six weeks was off.* Kafka and Felice's "great war" was now almost ready to be absorbed into the Great War.

---

*The trauma of Felice's hostility was joined by another disturbing exchange, this time over "The Metamorphosis." In a July 1914 letter to Robert Musil, Kafka revealed his annoyance at the delaying tactics of the *Neue Rundschau*. (See *Letters to Friends*, p. 109. The recipient, Musil, was identified by Harmut Binder in an article on Kafka and his relationship to *Die Neue Rundschau* — which, incidentally, did not publish "The Metamorphosis." The story was eventually published in October 1915 in *Weisse Blätter*, founded in 1913, and edited by, among others, Franz Blei; it was distributed by Kurt Wolff Verlag, in Leipzig.) Kafka was particularly exercised that Musil had accepted the story unconditionally, then delayed publication for months, and finally requested that Kafka cut the story by one-third. Kafka says that if the shortening had been requested from the beginning all present embarrassment would not have occurred, because he would not have agreed. He asserts that either the first chapter be published or else the entire story; no other alternative was acceptable. In this frame of mind, Kafka wrote to his parents that while he has not given them any lasting joy, he has not, except for this broken engagement, given them any serious anguish. He admits his dependency on them, his having grown up in comfort, but says that not all people are capable of independence. He indicates his need to break from Prague, to live, probably, in Berlin or Munich. He asks, at thirty-one, for their advice.

Kafka chose to vacation close to the Baltic Sea, at Gleschendorf, on the Ponitzer Sea. From Lübeck, he made his way to Travemünde, where he met Ernst Weiss and his companion, and together they traveled to Marienlyst, a Danish resort town. The trio was not fully compatible, as Weiss and his companion, the actress Rahel Sanzara, argued incessantly; further, the food seemed execrable. Feeling the aftereffects of the Berlin confrontation, Kafka described himself as unable to think, observe, or determine the truth of things: *"I am turning to stone, this is the truth."*[70] He adds that if he cannot take refuge in some work, he is lost. He says he shuns people not because he wants to live quietly, but because he wants to die quietly. At Marienlyst, he makes his usual uncomfortable analysis of people, getting beneath their social pose to the scruffy individuals lurking within. In his disorientation, he starts to eat meat, soon shoving it into him, as though to show Felice how normal he is, or, alternatively, to spite her, doing it when she cannot see him because he knew his vegetarianism troubled her.

The end of July brought two momentous events, perhaps disconnected, perhaps not. Austria-Hungary declared war on Serbia (with Germany on August 2 declaring war on Russia); and Kafka, on July 29, made his first mention of "Joseph K." Joseph K., the son of a rich merchant, is accused by his father of being dissipated. Joseph goes to the house of the corporation of merchants, near the harbor, where the doorkeeper makes a deep bow but gives no other greeting. Joseph makes some stinging remarks to himself about such underlings, while the doorkeeper "turned toward the street and looked up at the overcast sky."[71] The fragment ends, a dreamlike frustration or bafflement, the creation of stasis out of a potentially violent scene. While *The Trial* is not explicitly present, it is implicit in Kafka's method: the bringing down of all elements to silence and stasis.

This fragment is followed immediately in the *Diaries* by another brief piece, about a clerk who is thrown out of a store by his boss for having stolen five gulden after five years of slavish work. The clerk insists it is a mistake, that he did not commit the theft, but admits later that he had borrowed the money, intending to repay it from his salary only three days later. Since the clerk committed the act in broad daylight, he evidently intended to be caught, as he was, and thrown out. While this too was not *The Trial*, the exclusion of the clerk from his normal world, his standing accused, his sense of guilt at what he both did and did not do are all intimations of the set of Kafka's mind for the novel.

Kafka's "other trial" was going to be played out on the face of Europe. In one sense, the war bypassed him — he was rejected for military service and then held back, on further grounds, by the institute as too valuable in his critical post — but in another sense, it would permeate his imagination, reinforcing the disintegration and despair he felt individually. In still another sense, if we see history as determining individual lives, the war and its aftermath doomed all of Kafka's sisters. For what led to the transformation of Germany into bestiality was to doom Elli, Valli, and Ottla to the camps and death. But in the immediate sense, Kafka remained untouched.

Nevertheless, the alignments Czech Jews made were to be critical for their historical destiny. Closely identified with German interests, the Jews of Prague faced toward Austria and the Dual Monarchy, especially since Hungary had been particularly tolerant until it too needed scapegoats for losses and economic failures. But the Czechs of Bohemia looked toward Russia and Serbia, along with the Moravians and the Slovaks, the latter having been ill-treated by the Hungarian Magyars. Thus, Prague Jews were bedeviled two- and threefold. Cut off by their wartime sympathies from the Czech majority around them, they were not at all welcomed by German Gentiles; so that they found themselves more or less isolated as defenders of a sinking empire and opposed by the nationalists who saw in the war a means toward independence. From the Czech point of view, the Jews who supported the empire were traitors, or else expedient predators who hoped to hang on to Franz Josef's coattails.

But there were additional factors in this crazy-quilt of empire-making and empire-breaking. Jews were associated with the industrial minority that seemed to control Prague money,* whereas Czechs were linked to agriculture, and thus to the land and to its products. While this interpretation was only partially true, it identified Jews as those who stood to gain from the war: industrialists, factory owners, bankers, and so on. Omitted from this equation was the fact that the major war-making machine emanating from Vienna was hardly Jewish in origin or nature, and its military was virulently anti-Semitic. But Czech nationalists burned ever brighter when the war alignments occurred, for they foresaw the end of a monarchy that had kept them poor, and in siding with Russia and Serbia, they perceived the chance for a breakaway and the establishment of their own country.

Slav hopes historically had been encouraged by several developments, only to be dashed when they attempted to cash in on independence. The defeat of Austria by Prussia in 1866, the so-called Seven Weeks' War, created a new situation that for the moment seemed advantageous for Slav aspirations. Austria was so badly defeated and so removed outside the German orbit that it appeared it would embrace Slavic aspirations. But this was a complete misreading of the situation. Austria had no intention of looking east. It was to remain Germanic

---

*More than one-third of all industrial output in the empire came from Bohemia and Moravia, regions containing only a small percentage of the population and constituting only a small part of the land mass.

even without Germany and, if anything, became more stubborn in its identification. The terrible defeat in the war did lead to Austria's signing a pact or compromise with the Magyars in 1867, giving the Hungarians virtual sovereignty: thus the Dual Monarchy of Austria and Hungary. What this did was make the Slavs subject to the Germans in Austria and cut Czech lands off from the Slovaks, with new borders between Austria and Hungary. As a token of rapprochement, Franz Josef had given the Czechs their own schools under certain conditions, beginning in 1859, and then reinforced this edict in 1867. From 1880, Czech schools were on an equal basis with the German in organization and facilities: separate *and* equal.

With Vienna's insistence on being the center of the Habsburg monarchy and with all political arrangements in Bohemia favoring the Germans, the lower working classes and Slavs were generally left out of the political equation. In 1871 Franz Josef seemed inclined to give the Czechs sovereignty, like the Hungarians, but changed his mind. This did not dissuade the Czech nationalists but made them turn inward, toward those elements in society they considered opposed to their aspirations, and Jews, no matter what their allegiances, became scapegoated. Further maneuvering for power came during the 1870s when Germans opposed the occupation of Bosnia-Herzegovina (the western part of Yugoslavia, its capital Sarajevo) because that would increase the Slav proportion of the empire. This was still another nail in the coffin of Slav hopes. Under Eduard Taaffe, a new government head under Franz Josef, Slav hopes rose once more, especially when the annexation of land increased the Slav population and, accordingly, reduced the proportion of Germans. There were some gains: the language decree placing Czech on the same footing as German in administrative positions, and the establishment of a Czech National Theater, which became increasingly prestigious in later years.

But these so-called concessions were considered insufficient by the Young Czechs. They fought with the Old Czechs (more cautious and conservative) and with Germans, who approved of the status quo. Racial feelings, along with ethnic conflicts, exacerbated the entire situation as Georg von Schönerer's hateful anti-Semitic and ethnic attacks permeated Bohemia. His voice reinforced Pan-German feelings, which of course excluded everyone else, Slavs and Jews alike. In 1897, when Kafka was fourteen, a proposal was drawn up to make the Czech language equal with German, but under German protest the proposal was withdrawn. Much of the struggle, not so incidentally, was taking place in the area of language. The question of language penetrated the schools, the courts, the entire range of officialdom, the vote, in a sense the future of the empire. Kafka was brought up at a time when whoever controlled the language, whether German or Czech, controlled Bohemia and Moravia (the Slovaks spoke a related but different language

of their own). In some respects, language helped bring about the Great
War, since language was connected to who had power, how that power
was wielded, how it could be extended or contained, and how it could
be used to shape public opinion. While many Czechs knew some German, few Germans knew Czech (the Kafkas were unusual here); thus,
hegemony for the Germans depended on maintaining the status quo,
containing Slavic aspirations, holding back the hordes. We have here
not only elements nourishing the Great War, but the hate and filth that
would feed into the postwar years. Hitler used the term *Ungeziefer* to
designate what he considered the vermin of Europe, Jews and Slavs —
the very word Kafka used in "The Metamorphosis" to indicate Gregor's
new shape.

Czechs did gain some seats in the Reichsrat,* and by 1907 the
Czechs made up 70 percent of Moravia, easing political pressures somewhat. But in Bohemia, with Prague as its center, the situation was
bogged down in a many-sided struggle, among Young Czechs, fiercely
nationalistic, and Old Czechs, willing to evolve very slowly, with the
German-speaking part of the population, including the Kafkas, caught
between. The Germans succeeded in blocking any reforms that would
have given Czechs a larger voice, and the franchise was stymied. By
1913 the Diet was paralyzed.†

External forces, however, were pressing in from every side, and the
Russian revolution of 1905 gave a focus for Pan-Slavism. It encouraged
nationalistic movements, such as the Young Czechs, and provided ammunition for Czechs who accused Vienna of catering to Germany. The
sides for World War One were already forming. Vienna was accused not
only of courting Germany, but of being dominated by the Magyars and
showing distinct anti-Slav tendencies. When Austria-Hungary finally
did annex Bosnia-Herzegovina, it was designated "German," instead of
Slav, which its majority population would have indicated. Still another
source of division was created. The Czechs further had grievances
against the Hungarians, who, they felt, were persecuting the Slovaks.
Involved in all this were racial and ethnic hatreds, not just anti-Semitism; in fact, Jews became caught in this web almost incidentally. The
real ethnic and racial prejudices derived from German nationalistic
feelings of superiority to Slavs — Germans believed that Slavs performed at a lower level, lived inferior lives, were less educated and sophisticated, and were generally racially inferior. Vienna did not need
Hitler to instill these values.

By 1914 Czech and Slovak sympathies were clearly allied with Russia and the Serbs, against the Central Powers; whereas Germans of Bohemia supported the Austro-Hungarian empire and the German war

*The Reichsrat, or Imperial Council, of Austria really served as a kind of parliament,
on the order of the German Reichstag.
†The Diets were legislative assemblies for each province or territory of the empire,
alternately tried out, revoked, then resurrected.

effort. During the war itself, Czech and Slovak soldiers by the thousands went over to Russia, and thousands of others, civilians suspected of disloyalty, had by 1916 been shot. There were some Czech nationalists (like Karel Kramár and Tomáš Masaryk) who were at first loyal to Austria in the hope that once the war started, Vienna would recognize Slavic sovereignty, but when that did not happen, they presented their arguments against Austria and the monarchy to the Allies, in the process becoming traitors and wanted men in Vienna's view. Masaryk himself moved to put together a manifesto, which was signed by Czech groups abroad publicly announcing Czech and Slovak solidarity, a movement toward an independent state accomplished by 1915.

The buildup of pressures on Prague Jews was enormous. On every side, their loyalties were questioned, and their position was, in reality, untenable. In a real sense, the fate of Central and Eastern European Jewry was already implicit in what was occurring in the years leading up to and then during the war. Whichever way they showed their allegiance they were trapped. Loyalty to the Dual Monarchy meant going down to defeat in the war, and in 1916 they lost their "protector," Franz Josef. Further, loyalty to Vienna meant a connection to Germany, against England, France, and the United States, a loyalty that would prove foolhardy, as Jews marched off to defend the kaiser. Jewish opposition to Slavic aspirations made them easy targets for scapegoating when the name calling after the war became a matter of life and death. They would be perceived as a kind of fifth column within the Slavic state, and accused by the other side, the Central Powers themselves, of having caused the defeat of Germany.

Furthermore, the representation of Jews in the arts, their support of avant-garde movements (as dealers, for example), their identification with Modernism itself — although not all Jews by any means embraced Modernism — all categorized them as both anti-Slav and anti-German. They were the opposite of *Volk*, the opposite of *Heimat*, the enemies of "people" and "homeland." In some bizarre way, the inpouring of Modernistic art and literature from Paris, Berlin, and Vienna further entrapped Jews, for although most of this effort was made by Gentiles, Jews were nevertheless identified with the new and the rebellious. Kafka's loyalties were clearly with the empire. He rejoiced in Austrian victories, deplored their losses, although overall the war did not preoccupy him directly. That this sense of Jewish entrapment did not escape him, however, is clear, and every one of his works beginning in 1914 until his death can be read *in one respect* as part of his recognition of being trapped politically, socially, racially, and ethnically. Kafka in his work became not the emperor of ice cream, but the sovereign of "squeeze," containment, restriction.*

---

*What happened after 1914 among Czechs was that Masaryk and his group found the ear of the Allies and, in 1917, of Woodrow Wilson. His organization (called the *Maffia* —

The beginning of the war brought Kafka some immediate benefits. With both brothers-in-law in the Austrian army, and Elli and her children moving into Kafka's room, he acquired Valli's apartment in Bilekgasse, a place of his own, while she stayed with her parents-in-law just outside Prague. By August 3 he was established at Valli's. At thirty-one, he had left his parents' apartment, but he was still dependent on family quarters, now Valli's, later Ottla's. Those who argue that Kafka remained infantile in his dependency on his family lose sight of the fact that he drew tremendous strength from his proximity to the very ones who gave him his anger, hostility, and indeed material. Someone as self-absorbed as Kafka needed reinforcement from elements that justified his withdrawal into himself.

As for the coming war, Kafka stated, among other problems, "I am little affected by all the misery and am firmer in my resolve than ever" — his resolve being to write despite everything, saying that writing "is my struggle for self-preservation."[72] An August 2 entry reinforces this attitude: "Germany has declared war on Russia. — Swimming in the afternoon."[73] The next day, alone in Valli's apartment, he writes, "No longed-for wife to open the door. In one month I was to have been married." He faces the tormenting pain of solitude but resolves not to change, especially now that the idea for *The Trial* has been implanted. He feels an emptiness, which is natural given the nature of mobilization, crowds shouting in the distance, artillery rolling across the Graben, men appearing in uniform. "An empty vessel, still intact yet already in the dust among the broken fragments; or already in fragments yet still ranged among those that are intact"[74] — so he characterizes himself, on August 6. His comments are now all self-condemnatory: full of lies, envy, incompetence, stupidity, thickheadedness, laziness, weakness, helplessness. He adds pettiness, indecision, hatred; hatred "against those who are fighting and whom I passionately wish everything evil."[75] Mobilization has, if anything, intensified his sense of himself as marginal and useless; this was now no country for

---

two *f*'s) was secret, but with Franz Josef's death in 1916, it came out in the open; then abetted by the Kerensky revolution in Russia in March 1917, Czech troops began to fight on the Russian side in large numbers. By late 1917 the French government agreed to the formation of an independent Czech army on French soil; Czechs fighting with the Russians, after traveling across Siberia, were to regroup in France. The Italian defeat at Caporetto led to growing solidarity among Serbs, Croats, and Slovenes, with whom Czechs and Slovaks identified, and this also meant the withdrawal of Italy as a force in Slavic politics. Masaryk and his cohorts (including Beneš) moved rapidly toward establishment of a Czech-Slovak state, with Slovakia to retain its own language and separate parliament and courts of law. In 1918 the First Republic was formed, with 6.5 million Bohemians and Moravians and about 3 million Germans in these territories. With Germans fomenting trouble and refusing to assimilate, even Czechs and Slovaks did not make a good fit. The Slovaks were peasants, not well educated, with little or no middle class, devoutly Catholic and virulently anti-Semitic, as against a Czech group that was middle class, anticlerical, more urbanized, and only mildly anti-Semitic except during outbursts of patriotic fervor.

old men, and Kafka at thirty-one was not only old but feeling ill and useless. He relies solely on himself as a writer, that fallback into complete self-absorption that was his salvation. "My talent for portraying my dreamlike inner life has thrust all other matters into the background; my life has dwindled dreadfully, nor will it cease to dwindle. Nothing else will ever satisfy me." Thoughts of death are never distant: "But I waver on the heights; it is not death, alas, but the eternal torments of dying."

Yet through this he was not collapsing but writing at the peak of his powers. Parallel to work on *The Trial* was a short piece in his August 15 diary entry called "Memoirs of the Kalda Railroad."* It is in several respects a vessel for nearly everything Kafka would write in the next ten years. It is, of course, about solitude, but solitude of such magnitude it becomes metaphysical. It is the solitude of being and of meaning. It is Crusoe on his island, but without the lushness Crusoe enjoyed, and without the endless stores he could draw upon. The railroad near Kalda is part of a deserted region, a death town. Not surprisingly, the railroad to which he is posted is itself no longer significant; new roads are needed, so that even as he is posted he is forgotten. The narrator finds he is not suited for such solitude and becomes attached to the people in the region, although he cannot see them regularly since he must remain at the station. A typical Kafka situation arises, in which the dream work takes over and creates spatial difficulties; as one strives to be close, space separates people and things.

The narrator intends to go hunting — this was one of the attractions of the place. However, no game animals are reported in the area, only wolves and bears. But there are large rats, running in packs across the steppes. Sometimes the rats attack his provisions, and the narrator splits them with his long knife. One day he spits a rat and holds it at eye level. "The most striking feature of these rats was their claws — large, somewhat hollow, and yet pointed at the ends, they were well suited to dig with. Hanging against the wall in front of me in its final agony, it rigidly stretched out its claws in what seemed to be an unnatural way; they were like small hands reaching out to you."[76]

One day the narrator focuses on a particular rat working feverishly at its hole; the narrator decides to kill it and then protect his hut against infiltration. He turns his hut into an impregnable fortress; in effect he prepares himself for winter hibernation, like an animal. He decides to have a plank floor installed, as a way of insulating against the coming cold, but the peasant who promises the planks never brings

---

*It is tempting to speculate that this compelling work owes something to Kafka's dealings with his maternal uncle, Alfred Löwy, a director of several smaller lines of the Spanish railways.

them. But all this comes to an end when, after three months of service, the narrator falls seriously ill. His illness begins with severe coughing, so intense he has to double up during an attack. The train crew recognizes it as the "wolf's cough." After that, the narrator hears the wolf howl in his cough. So severe are the attacks, so fierce the howling of the wolf, that he waits for a blood vessel to burst. A train engineer recommends a certain tea to be drunk on the eighth day of the coughing fit, and it does relieve the condition. Yet a fever remains, weakening the narrator, leading to heavy perspiration, trembling, and loss of strength. He feels he is getting worse, not better, and decides to go to Kalda until his condition improves.

With that, Kafka ends, and then swings right back into *The Trial*, which goes forward through successes and failures. The "Kalda Railway" piece, however, is not a throwaway. It may be unformed and rough, but it lies at the center of Kafka's consciousness. The narrator seems like a coarse fellow, especially with the rat spitted on his knife, but he undertakes a position much like that of the writer or artist who seeks solitude in order to become absorbed in his work. Further, he becomes increasingly closed in upon himself, like the mole in "The Burrow" or the hunger artist — more immediately, like Joseph K. in the early stages of *The Trial*.

Kafka was trying out forms of suffocation. One can as easily suffocate in the open spaces of the Kalda railroad as in the atmosphere of courtrooms. The narrator in the story has a hut that circumscribes every aspect of his life, like Joseph K.'s law courts in the attic. The narrator becomes desperately ill, enervated, unable to function, and this too recalls *The Trial* with its allusions in German to tuberculosis as well as to a trial. The two works are hardly symmetrical, but the "Kalda Railroad" plays in and out of the longer work, each pointing up in fact the very incompleteness of any "process."

At the end of August, Kafka indicates his progress on *The Trial*: August 21 brings some effort with results; August 29, some success and some failure; August 30, despair, feelings of coldness and emptiness, limitations and narrowness. In the early fall, he moved along on the novel and then, for some reason, returned to the incomplete *Amerika*, for the final chapter, "The Nature Theatre of Oklahoma," as Brod came to call it. At first, on September 13, he tries to blame his apathy and slow progress on his sorrow over the Austrian defeats, but he recognizes the problems are more intimately personal. The war cannot engage him; only he can engage himself. He connects his thoughts about the war to his torment over Felice, and he finds he is devoured by unendurable worry. He feels he has been created, perhaps, solely to die of worry. At every turn, Furies await him, and all he can hope for is postponement of disaster, which is, not incidentally, the final of three choices confronting Joseph K. The accused remains "on trial," but he occupies a limbo area, or else a purgatory. In his *Diaries*, Kafka indicates such suspension and says that only the support of his writing enables him to go on.

Although his imaginative direction was still unclear, by October 15 he admits he has had two weeks of good work. The airy "Nature Theatre of Oklahoma" is an indication of some lifting of despair; although even with the opportunity offered Karl for work, he has entered a completely enclosed universe where workers are manipulated and directed. As we have seen, they move along as if on a conveyor belt, eat when offered food, sleep when offered shelter, line up to take the train. As suggested earlier, they become robotic, not at all unlike what Karel Čapek will demonstrate a few years later in his *RUR*. But even so, Karl's journey suggests he can at least move on, escape his family and past, remake himself to some degree within the open American atmosphere.*

Part of Kafka's sense of "good work" was linked to two factors: he had taken a week's vacation, and he had heard from Grete Bloch. Grete's letter led, in turn, to his sending a telegram to Felice on October 27, followed by an enormously long letter in late October. This letter, again not unrelated to *The Trial*, is openly confessional. As we know, Kafka speaks of his work and of the traumatic confrontation at the Askanische Hof in July, in Berlin. He identifies Felice as the greatest friend but also the greatest enemy of his work; it, his work, both loved her beyond measure and for the sake of preservation had to resist her with all its strength. As for the Hof scene, he tries to explain himself as dualistic, with twin selves always battling for supremacy: the side linked to her and wanting to please her, and the side involving nothing but his work. He sees these two selves as locked in a deadly embrace, an indication of Kafka's earnestness but also of his romanticization of himself as a kind of warrior. He may not be fighting on the eastern front, but he is fighting his own kind of war; the militaristic terms of his letters are unmistakable. The warrior side will not permit surrender, whereas the other side turns toward Felice and domesticity. Yet even as Kafka explains himself, the issue has been decided: marriage could never satisfy him, as it does others, and failure to write on his terms would make him suicidal. What he needs more than anything else is not Felice but her belief in him. With Brod married, she has become his best friend for almost two years, and now he wishes to re-enter her life, not to gain her, but to regain her belief in him.

Mid-October 1914, then, became the juncture of several important areas of Kafka's life. He hears from Grete, which leads to his writing to Felice and resuming an on-again, off-again correspondence, with a January meeting planned in Bodenbach. He is moving along fairly well

---

*Brod took the optimistic interpretation, although the outcome for Karl is not that clear.

with *The Trial*. He will write the final chapter of *Amerika*, at about the same time; and he will, more importantly, write "In the Penal Colony" the following month. Also, in December, still 1914, he will write one of the most important parts of *The Trial*, the segment called "Before the Law" ("Vor dem Gesetz"), which he incorporated into chapter 9 of the novel.

Certainly the outburst of creative work cannot be disentangled from his renewed interest in Felice and, possibly, Grete. Just how this chemistry worked is impossible to chart, but we can find in his alternating hope and disappointment in his personal affairs that extra charge he needed to open up his imagination. Rather than consuming his energies, the letter writing was part of "writing," which he carried over into his literary work; and the rethinking of his relationships helped bring him sufficiently out of his self-absorption so that he could capture himself on paper. It was a process of immense complication which ran in cycles. Once it ended and he was back in his literary hibernation, he experienced intense self-pity and a wasting away of his powers, to the degree he felt he would never recover.

The early stages of *The Trial* are both successful and victim of these alternating cycles. Even as Kafka's mind was racing along, motoring on its own, as though separated from his body, he worries that his work is only an imitation of earlier work, not independent of it. But this was clearly untrue. *The Trial* was a culminating achievement for him, even though he had not been writing much or long. Even the title (*Der Prozess*)* suggests an entire life: its reference to a trial or court case; its use of the German connotations of a case of tuberculosis; and its added dimension of an ongoing process or affair of some kind. It is, also, a testing-out. The title suggests both something that will end, such as a lawsuit or an illness, and something that goes on indefinitely. With both limitation and extension, it becomes representative of Kafka's sense of himself — as opening out with his literary endeavors toward infinity, and as closing down because of personal disabilities.

The novel also captures quite well the sense of Europe as it passed over into turbulent war and personal disasters; in particular, it is an emblem of the Dual Monarchy. "Someone must have traduced [*verleumdet*] Joseph K., for without having done anything wrong he was arrested one fine morning."[77] The German *verleumdet* can mean slandered, calumniated, as well as traduced and accused wrongfully. The "Joseph" of Joseph K. is suggestive of the biblical Joseph, vain, petted, a favorite, but hated by his brothers and sold into slavery, who eventually became the savior of his people. The "K." is not clearly Kafka, but an abstraction of the name; the use of an initial suggests the dehuman-

---

*The reader should remain aware of the greater variability and range of the German title, which means a process or trying-out rather than merely a court case.

ization of any process. Joseph K. is lacking a family name, a form of deprivation, but at least he has a given name, which means he had a family at one time. K. in *The Castle* is deprived of both; his demise is not only of a person but of the very act of naming.

The archetypal court case in the background of *The Trial* is that of Captain Dreyfus in the 1890s in France.* We are not asserting that Kafka drew directly on the Dreyfus case, nor can we claim Kafka's work was intended to reveal a Jewish victim. Nevertheless, the most famous case of victimization in Kafka's lifetime occurred in the French army's framing of Dreyfus. Kafka's generating idea was that court, lawyer, and accused were functioning in the dark, that lawyers could not be present during interrogation, that the accused could never be sure where his case stood in the courts, that the courts themselves seemed to operate by different rules at different times, and finally, that law itself had broken down since it contained impenetrable guidelines that differed for each individual. All of these factors were of course present in the Dreyfus case, so that the accused could not only not be defended, he could not even be sure of what the case was against him. If Kafka's novel has allegorical, thus representative, potentialities, then it describes a society disintegrating because its legal system has imploded. In many respects, it is a perfect emblem for the war, a form of national suicide surely for Austria, which would be devastated, and the end of the empire, with Franz Josef's death and then Austria's surrender. In comparable terms, the Dreyfus case in France, while not bringing down the country, did reveal the rot and decay lying at the heart of *la gloire* and showed that France in its persecution of Dreyfus was a mock-democracy. Kafka's use of a court case undeniably has allegorical dimensions, but it is also political, social, and cultural. Life as a "trial" becomes the representative Kafkaesque image of our time.

The shape of *The Trial* is difficult to determine. When we speak of it as being incomplete, we use the descriptive term in a certain sense. The novel does have a beginning, middle, and end, but several unfinished chapters are not included in the German or English editions.† Six of these unfinished chapters appear as an appendix, in Max Brod's arrangement of the novel, so that the remaining ten chapters lack the

---

*Possibly, Kafka also had in mind the case of *Jarndyce vs. Jarndyce* from Dickens's *Bleak House*, which went on indefinitely and destroyed nearly all the combatants. We know of Kafka's affection for Dickens's novels.

†Upon his death in 1962, Brod left the manuscript for *The Trial* to his long-time secretary and companion. It was acquired by the German State Government of Baden-Württemberg and was sold in September 1988 for $1.98 million by the estate of Max Brod and his companion, Ilse Esther Hoffe. Sir Malcolm Pasley, professor emeritus at Oxford and a leading Kafkan textual scholar, has prepared a critical edition. Efforts to examine the manuscript prior to publication of this edition have not been successful. For an informed but still speculative view of an alternate ordering of *The Trial*, see Ritchie Robertson's excellent study, *Kafka: Judaism, Politics, and Literature* (1985), pp. 88–89. See note, p. 524.

possible continuity that the unfinished chapters might have provided. Further, passages deleted by Kafka, often amounting to a page or more, appear in an additional appendix. We do not know at this stage the order of the finished and unfinished chapters, and we are furthermore unsure of even the finished chapters. It is unclear how Kafka intended to proceed, whether he would choose to complete the fragmentary chapters, where he would locate them in the text, what order the novel would finally take. From internal evidence, we do know that the opening and final chapters were written first. Certainly the novel works in its own terms, and the narrative as presented has its own integrity. What we are really unsure about is what the final shape would have been, and we worry to what extent that reworking and revising or rewriting would have appreciably changed our sense of what is presented to us.

Since so much is uncertain — both the placement of the incomplete material and the final arrangement of the completed chapters — we must for the time being accept Brod's arrangement, while recognizing that more light may be shed on the manuscript in the future. Kafka's method of working failed to achieve closure in his longer texts; he wanted his work destroyed because it was unfinished and imperfect. Given the nature of his absolutism and drive for perfection, his needs are understandable, but at the same time, we must recognize that except for *Amerika*, which is truly fragmentary, the other longer works function quite well in their own terms.* As far as leaving works unfinished, we might agree with what Maurice Blanchot, with Kafka in mind, says, that "the work of art, the literary work — is neither finished nor unfinished: it is. What it says is exclusively that: that it is — and nothing more." He adds, again referring to Kafka, "The writer belongs to a language no one speaks [recalling Paul Valéry's line, that poetry is a language within language], a language that is not addressed to anyone, that has no center, that reveals nothing. He can believe he is asserting himself in this language, but what he is asserting is completely without a self.'"[78] Kafka would have concurred.

In the fall of 1914, Kafka was generating story ideas at a tremendous rate, even for stories he would not write until much later, such as "The Burrow."† The return of his brother-in-law (Josef Pollak) from the front brought to Kafka's attention a story about a mole burrowing under the soldier in the trenches. The mole becomes a sign to him, and he flees the area just as a bullet strikes the man behind him. This is only a fragment, but its message became part of Kafka's transformation of every-

---

*The interplay between *The Trial* and Kafka's life will be picked up in chapter 11, along with further analysis of the novel itself.
†The *Diaries* also reveal many story ideas that Kafka referred to euphemistically as "horses" but did not develop.

thing he saw or heard. He felt as embattled as Austria-Hungary, now the subject of an advancing Russian army, along with pressure from France and England on its ally, Germany. We must not forget that Kafka was on the "other side" — he was a fervent supporter of the Central Alliance and was opposed to France, England, and the United States. Entrapment was a familiar theme politically and socially, and not an unlikely one for his fictional ideas. He sensed the impossibility of being able to pull himself together; and yet his imagination was soaring, with "In the Penal Colony" completed by the end of November.

"In the Penal Colony" is about levels of suffering, and Kafka notes in his November 25 diary entry that only when he becomes satisfied with his sufferings will he stop his despair. Was this sentiment merely self-pitying indulgence, or did it go further? For the ordinary person, we could call this diary entry the somewhat infantile outpourings of an immature person seeking comfort and security. But with Kafka, the contours of despair and dissatisfaction shift, for only by thrusting himself into the pit could he observe the underside of bourgeois life, of patriotic fervor (including his own), of praise of the warrior, and of the ever present societal desire for comfort and security. He envisioned the basest plan for the future, and it involved, as he was writing the final chapter of *Amerika*, devils as well as angels. He needed, for himself, the worst possible scenarios in order to capture the subsurface of what was occurring; beneath all the fervor and esprit de corps, society as he knew it was collapsing upon itself; disintegration was the final note, a *Götterdämmerung* that not even love (Wagner's solution) could help. In that November of 1914, as *The Trial*, "The Nature Theatre of Oklahoma," and "In the Penal Colony" each took shape, Kafka was establishing the terms by which the "new world" would have to be discussed. He was reshaping the meaning of "representative," whether of man or society.

"In the Penal Colony" does not turn up in Kafka's letters, and it is hardly mentioned in the *Diaries*, except briefly on December 2. But the language of several collateral diary entries recreates the ambience of the story, as Kafka sees himself as a solitary stake fixed in a plowed field, or as someone whose position in the family is a form of punishment. The "disobedience" of the prisoner in the story, for which HONOR THY SUPERIORS will be written in needles on his body, involves a threat against authority, Lucifer's challenge to God, the very "crime" implied in *The Trial*. There is compensatory suffering, what psychiatrists call moral masochism, transposed from Kafka to the victim of the needle machine, but also transferred back from the victim to him, the author of the piece. In prolonging the prisoner's agony, the machine becomes a perfect emblem of Kafka's own form of masochism. Like *The Trial*, "In the Penal Colony" is his effort to discover some ultimate or absolute truth that lies below deception. In the novel, Joseph K. must keep penetrating layers of appearance, but unlike famous diggers like Schliemann, he will never discover the source of his endeavors. Instead, the novel remains a search or journey, like "In the Penal Colony." The recording, sensitized figure in the story is called an explorer. What he seeks is that experience of darkness where sudden light might illuminate the truth lying beneath the disguises. Kafka's purpose is to bring forth some light, as is Conrad's goal in "Heart of Darkness," another journey into darkness in search of illumination.

The intensity of Kafka's quest for illumination in "In the Penal Colony" gives rise to a symbolic reading of the final days of the empire. A deeply personal statement about knowledge, truth, absolutes, illumination, the story is also a psychological profile of the early twentieth century. In its depiction of "final days," when traditions have outlasted their original function, the story depicts man's failure to accommodate what is occurring, but also recalls the grandeur that comes from hanging on to the old ways regardless of their meaning. Kafka digs into all the contradictions of a society confronting change and yet insisting on customs that are no longer meaningful, except as forms of support for individual (and twisted) belief, the willingness to sacrifice oneself and others to ideas no longer viable. It is as though Kafka had perceived in the earliest months of the war that an ending was imminent, and that the ending meant the loss of individual values and individual vision. The end of the war brings with it a technological world, in which visions and visionaries play no role, in which all is dictated, evenly, by law. No more priests; no more prophets.

The story is also an emblem of the meeting of cultures: an older culture confronting the avant-gardism of the new. Implicit in "In the Penal Colony" is the presence of the new and changeable. The surreal quality of the story is an indication that the old style of realism is no longer tenable, that a new kind of "machinery" is needed.

Like Conrad's Marlow, the explorer is located as the reader's representative in the narrative, the filter through which the material is presented. He is an outsider, as the reader is, and everything must be explained to him by the officer. The officer-executioner, who has strong parallels in The Trial,* is priestlike in his ministrations to the prisoner, conveying last rites and serving as the final figure in the soldier's life. The officer washes his hands, prepares the needle machine, anoints the act with his attention to detail — all part of a ritualistic process. The two ladies' handkerchiefs he tucks under the collar of his uniform suggest a priestly collar of sorts. He officiates at a ceremony of

*These two pieces fit well with Kleist's Michael Kohlhaas, which we know Kafka had read at least ten times by 1913, and which he particularly liked to read aloud. Kafka's interest in Kleist had been intense since 1911, the centennial of the German writer's death. All three works, the Kleist and the two Kafka fictions, are concerned with crime and punishment, law, justice, and questions of authority.

life and death, and participates in a Mass when he goes through the act of execution. The machine serves as God, as an instrument of sacred punishment when the needles imprint themselves into the prisoner's flesh, etching the "evil" into the victim. Yet before we view this story as Kafka's longing for religious faith, we must pause. The machine is an instrument of learning and knowing, a pedagogical device, and as it penetrates ever deeper into the prisoner's body, it seeks out whatever meaning lies beneath flesh, bones, and blood. It searches for the very soul of things, which is to say that it searches for whatever meaning may remain in the very world that has replaced meaning. Kafka does not make the machine and the act of torture into some avatar of the future — of the camps and gassings — it is, quite clearly, a futile gesture looking back to the past. As a farewell, it is the last cry of ritual, symbolic of the dying empire.

In the working of the machine, invented by a former commandant, we find emblems of the larger culture. The machine is divided into Bed and Designer, with the middle part called the Harrow, which contains the needles. The prisoner is laid on the Bed, and then the Designer and Bed have their own motions, while the Harrow "is the instrument for the actual execution of the sentence."[79] It is tempting to see the officer-priest-executioner as Franz Josef (whom Kafka supported), the one who consigns all young people to death in the war; the "former Commandant" can be viewed as the ultimate wise man whose wisdom is carried on by the next generation, like Jesus and his apostles. In this instance, an apostle is the ultimate killer. But all these designations are arbitrary, useful only if one views the work as allegorical. Although allegorical functions exist — the quest or journey, the godlike figure, the movement from life toward death, the question of eternal punishment — allegory is the wrong medium for the story, whose quest for truth is quite different from those of Sir Gawain or Parsifal. The end result is not the discovery of truth; rather, it is a recognition that such a quest ends in confusion and meaningless slaughter.

When awakened from his sleep, the prisoner responds that the captain had better throw his whip away or he will be eaten alive. This moment of rebellion is his death sentence, clearly a cultural and historical one, with the empire now at war. It is tantamount to the overthrow of the old order and must be suppressed with a traditional punishment: the "father" killing the son. Kafka understood the nature of punishment when one traduced the loyalties governing cultural traditions. This had been his theme since "The Judgment," when Georg Bendemann committed suicide rather than face any other kind of punitive action.

When the messy details are presented — the writing of the needles, the penetration of the skin and the profuse bleeding, the short needles for spraying water to keep the area clean, the long needles for the writing itself, the spike for the head — we are expected to be revolted. The gag provided for the prisoner, so that he cannot scream out, is the gag the reader lacks, one he seeks as he reads. The messiness and cruelty are not byproducts of the machine, but part of the story's meaning. They do not refer to anything; they *are* meaning. The spike, recalling the spike on the Hun's helmet in World War One, makes the machine into something of a crucifixion device. The process is an elaborate one, and the officer explains it with great intensity, the way the Ancient Mariner was compelled to tell and retell his story. The script is not supposed to kill the prisoner immediately but to draw out the punishment for twelve hours. In the sixth hour, the prisoner enjoys enlightenment, when his intense pain turns toward an "experience," an illumination. After two hours, because the victim is too weak to scream, the gag is removed, and he is offered warm rice pap to help him keep his strength. By the turning point in the sixth hour, the prisoner has lost all desire to eat; he may roll the pap around in his mouth, only to spit it out. "Enlightenment," Kafka writes, "comes to the most dull-witted. It begins around the eyes. From there it radiates."[80]

Although an observer may find it difficult to decipher the inscription in the wounds, the victim can do it. It has become internalized, part of his body and soul. We note how this punishment resembles several of Kafka's diary entries and his words to Felice: the internalization of all pain and suffering, punishment as a way of gaining control over oneself. It may not be too farfetched to say that the victim in the needle-writing machine has become, ultimately, the author: he is so much the wordman that bloody writing becomes an essential part of his body. Kafka had discovered a way to turn writing into the one thing he understood best, pain as a way of gaining illumination and enlightenment. After his sixth hour, the victim has another six hours or so to enjoy his "peak." In that final period, he can contemplate his career from the position of illumination; like an orgasm or a drug rush, it is a privileged moment, one that Kafka associated, clearly, with writing. Sex has been finessed.

The machine experience plays in and out of his attitudes, extending into but also beyond writing. The felt gag placed in the prisoner's mouth has been used by more than one hundred men, and the observer feels sick at the slobbered and gnawed-upon piece of cloth. It contains within it the dying moments of all these men, in the dried saliva, the smell of fear. That it is part of an oral process brings it back to Kafka, with his disgust at many foods, his distaste for whatever passed into his mouth, his revulsion for the digestive process itself. In some way, this disgust at orality is linked to the need to write, whether compensatory or otherwise. The vomit that runs over the machine, ejected by the disgusted victim, is part of a bulimia-anorexia pattern of sorts, the food brought up, or else food denied oneself. The officer's solution is to have the victim fast the day before: thus anorexia as a way of preventing bulimia.

Yet despite the disgusting manner of the present-day execution, in the past it had great significance as a ritual and ceremony. The day before the event the valley was packed with people who came to look on. When the commandant and his ladies appeared, excitement was palpable. The description of the preparation for this ritual killing contains some of Kafka's most compelling prose. The machine was freshly cleaned, glittering, with spare parts on hand for almost every execution. There were no failures or breakdowns; as people stood on tiptoe, expectations were always met. "In the silence one heard nothing but the condemned man's sighs, half muffled by the felt gag," Kafka begins.

> Nowadays the machine can no longer wring from anyone a sigh louder than the felt gag can stifle; but in those days the writing needles let drop an acid fluid, which we're no longer permitted to use. Well, and then came the sixth hour! It was impossible to grant all the requests to be allowed to watch it from near by. The Commandant in his wisdom ordained that the children should have the privilege . . . often enough I would be squatting there with a small child in either arm. How we all absorbed the look of transfiguration on the face of the sufferer, how we bathed our cheeks in the radiance of that justice, achieved at last and fading so quickly! What times these were, my comrade![81]

The day of the functioning machine and faultless ritual was a golden age, a whiff of Eden. For the officer in charge, it was analogous, on one hand, to an earthly paradise, on the other to orgasm. Not just the victim achieved an illumination, but the entire party: executioner, children, the commandant's party, and other observers. Kafka has created a transcendent experience, a transformational episode, in which a masochistic relationship is equated to writing itself.

Now the machine is worn out, undependable, and the ceremony is shabby. The public of course does not care, having turned to other things. We note how continuous this story in 1914 is with "A Hunger Artist" at the end of Kafka's life. The two pieces are in fact one, divided into branching segments. The hunger artist achieves a comparable illumination or transcendence through denying himself food, a form of suffering and pleasure that come from orality. From 1914 on, in fact, we can say Kafka was writing one gigantic work, whose parts were divided into separate branches, stories, novels, brief prose statements, diary entries, or lengthy letters to Felice or to Milena Jesenská. Kafka's imagination was a unit now, a solid mass of ideas for the next ten years upon which he could draw. However much the pieces may seem to differ, they have a commonality, all involving illumination, transformation, and transcendence, intermixed with pain, suffering, and despair. Kafka reveled in it.

The officer recognizes that with the death of the machine he will himself become superfluous. Trying to survive by bringing back the machine, he asks the explorer for his help with the present commandant. With the old world and order fading, a dying art needs resurrection. Can anything be done to recover or at least preserve the status quo, shabby though it may be? The officer, however, fears that too direct a plea to the commandant will call attention to the worn-out machine, the broken strap, the filthy gag, and executions will be banned. Without executions, he has no function, life has no meaning. When the explorer demurs and expresses disapproval of the entire proceeding, the officer frees the prisoner from the Harrow. He now chooses to have the message BE JUST written into him, the officer. Like the thousands dying at the front to prop up a moribund empire, the officer finds his mission in the machine of destruction. Whether part of war or ritual, the machine must be fed victims, and if the prisoner is not to be the victim, then the officer will replace him.*

This is an intense vision for Kafka. For while he presents the machine as inhumane, it is also something that contains desperate meaning in an age that has lost all ritualistic significance. The officer takes the prisoner's place, like the hunger artist who willingly sacrifices himself for the sake of his art, even (or especially) when no one cares anymore. The officer accepts the felt gag, shrinking from it only momentarily; he then enters the machine, not needing the broken straps. In what will be the final moment of the machine, he is a willing participant.

Everything at first seems to work quietly, but suddenly the mechanism goes crazy, as it should, given the fact that it has no present purpose in the society. The Harrow is not writing, only jabbing, and the Bed is not turning over, but bringing itself and the body against the needles. There is no writing now, only impalement, a sacrifice without significance, a torture chamber. The body is spitted, as though in its twelfth hour, with no chance of illumination or transcendence, no redemption, no sense of guilt, no sense of atonement. What others had discovered in the machine, that great privileged moment, was denied to the officer. Finally, the point of the spike goes through his forehead. The process ends, a kind of crucifixion without enlightenment. The end result is blood, gore, fragments of flesh, a mangled body: the raw meat of the wounded at the front.

The explorer visits the grave of the former commandant. He bends to see the inscription, which speaks of the commandant's one day rising to lead his adherents and recover the colony. "Have faith and wait" are the final words. When the explorer leaves, he must fight off the prisoner and a soldier who want to get away; he threatens them with a heavy knotted rope to keep them "from attempting the leap" from a

---

*Part of the futility in trying to be explicit about Kafka's "meaning" is that the story can be read equally as the pursuit of religious transcendence in a transitional age or as a parody of religion, ritual, ceremony. The prisoner gains illumination, but only at the expense of his life. Kafka's irony precludes clear lines of analysis. Yet at the same time the irony teases all possibilities. We return to Blanchot's point, that once the work is written it no longer belongs to the writer. Kafka has entered into another language.

dock to the boat that will take them away. The story ends on this ambiguous note. The significance of the "leap" is multifold. The explorer, for his part, does not want any part of this experience to accompany him. The prisoner and soldier, for their part, hope to escape a dying society to a newer one. Meanwhile, the explorer is unsure whether old or new has any validity. Is the leap Kierkegaard's step from dread into faith, from sickness into health? Or is it the leap that someone like Kafka must himself make when he sees the end of the Dual Monarchy as Austria faces far superior forces? Or is it purely personal: Kafka's envisioning the explorer as the writer uniquely having had *his* experience? The ending in all its complications is another of Kafka's "processes," in which internalized shadows and ambiguities, all unresolvable, become part of the emblem of his writing.

Kafka read "Penal Colony" to Brod, Werfel, and Pick on December 2 and found himself not "entirely dissatisfied." It did have glaring faults, he says, but he does not cite them. Six days later, he indicates he is doing good work, mentioning the "mother" chapter of *The Trial*, which appeared in the German text as appendix matter, "Journey to the Mother" ("Fahrt zur Mutter"). Then he worked on an aspect of "Before the Law" that would appear in chapter 9. All this work, however satisfactory, led him to thoughts of death: "The best things I have written have their basis in this capacity of mine to meet death with contentment."[82] He says all his fine and convincing passages have to do with the fact that someone is dying, but it seems harsh and unjust that this should be so. "But for me, who believe that I shall be able to lie contentedly on my deathbed, such scenes are secretly a game; indeed, in the death enacted I rejoice in my own death." Yet all his disclaimers, whether of working poorly or rejoicing in death, are belied by his progress on *The Trial* and his work on shorter pieces. The thought of dying spurred him on.

On December 18, within this explosion of imaginative vigor, he wrote "The Village Schoolmaster." The circumstances were propitious. Hermann Kafka had berated him for his lack of interest in the asbestos factory and accused his son of having dragged him into the enterprise, seemingly against his will. After this, in the full consciousness of his guilt, "beyond question," he says, he went home and calmly wrote for three hours. The juxtaposition of guilt concerning Hermann and the ability to write is unmistakable, especially if we take into account precisely what "The Village Schoolmaster" is about. It is, in its way, a summation of Kafka's attitude toward his family, toward Hermann in particular, toward his own inner life; a combination of his several protagonists, Gregor, the hunger artist, and the mole of "The Burrow." It presents Kafka transformed into a lower form and, once there, triumphant in his ability to penetrate intelligently and imaginatively into his situation.

"Those, and I am one of them, would probably have died of disgust if they had seen the giant mole that a few years back was observed in the neighborhood of one of our villages."[83] We recognize, in these words, a self-portrait. Only the village schoolmaster remained to write of the incident. But because of his limited abilities, he was incapable of an adequate explanation of the phenomenon. Nevertheless, although no one supported him, he made the episode his life's work. As a writer he assumes the role of the hunger artist practicing his craft, while everyone's attention lies elsewhere. The schoolmaster, however, does not accept defeat, and in a brochure that follows up a pamphlet he complains of the lack of understanding people have displayed toward his work. He is particularly disturbed by the reception of a scholar whom he consulted about the affair and who dismissed the phenomenon as nothing special. The expert advanced the notion that since the soil in the teacher's neighborhood is particularly rich, its moles will grow to unusual size.

All this is introductory to the appearance of the "I," the narrator, a businessman, who becomes interested in the affair, someone like the explorer in "Penal Colony." Kafka now splits his persona, into the schoolteacher laboring in vain, and yet refusing to give up, and the observer-narrator who decides to investigate the matter himself. The narrator realizes he has taken on a thankless task, because he knows he will not change public opinion in the teacher's favor, and also because he cannot appeal to the teacher, whose honesty, not point of view, he wants to defend. The narrator accordingly finds himself in no man's land, a typical Kafka landscape: he has discovered an area that is bound to anger everyone, yet is unable to convince the very people in whose name he has taken up the cause. Kafka has defined the Kafkaesque landscape. Even to read the pamphlet, the narrator feels, is inadequate for his purposes, since it might lead him astray. In fact, despite his desire to defend the honesty of the schoolmaster, he finds himself on a collision course with him and even develops hostile feelings. For when he does read the pamphlet, he finds he differs on many points; he is defending someone, now, with whom he no longer agrees, except that the giant mole existed.

Additionally, hostility grows between the two because the schoolmaster feels he is being displaced by the narrator. "For in his heart he was convinced that I wanted to rob him of the fame of being the first man publicly to vindicate the mole. Now of course he really enjoyed no fame, but only an absurd notoriety that was shrinking more and more, and for which I had certainly no desire to compete."[84] The question becomes one of information and disinformation. What is offered as evidence? What is embraced as opinion but has little to do with evidence? Or else, when is information perceived as disinformation and dismissed, until no one can distinguish between the two?

In the narrator's antagonism toward the schoolmaster, we find something of the Great War fought out on a smaller battlefield. The schoolmaster feels his position has become more difficult, while the narrator recognizes he is viewed as a traitor and the entire question of the gigantic mole has been blurred. The narrator's own pamphlet was not well received, perhaps because it was poorly written. Furthermore, some confuse the present pamphlet with the schoolmaster's original description of the mole, and those who laughed at the first are equally condemnatory of the second. Some even castigate the now almost forgotten schoolmaster for having been concerned with moles rather than teaching. The narrator tries to explain to the older man that although he had tried to help him, he finds he has damaged him in every direction.

In this confrontation, we have a shadowy presentation of Kafka and his father. The son apologizes for having attempted to help but in some way makes matters worse — the Kafkan sense of guilt whenever an older man is concerned. He promises to step aside, since he seems to be passing failure on to the teacher and disguising the real issue, of the mole. But the narrator recognizes that old people are mendacious: that while you live in peace with them you think you understand their ways and their prejudices, and take them for granted, only to discover when something decisive occurs that these seemingly docile oldsters have depths of iniquity in them you never dreamed possible.

Kafka was now rolling along, in his element, with both narrator and schoolmaster talking at cross-purposes to each other. Further, in a change of direction, the teacher feels he has found in the businessman-narrator a protector and hopes he will now achieve true glory for his discovery. His illusions are at a peak: he imagines that he will be dragged by this successful man from obscurity into recognition and affluence. The narrator is in the position of protecting the teacher's illusion, and to help him, he sends out a circular requesting the return of all of his pamphlets. The wording of the circular makes it clear the request does not depend on the pamphlet's contents, whether true or false, but on a personal wish. In an explanation to the teacher, the narrator mentions that if he had asked some professor to look into the affair, the discovery itself would have been lost in the larger scientific discovery. The narrator's point is that anything original, even the discovery of a gigantic, freakish mole, is easily caught up in other questions and issues until it is so disguised that it becomes absorbed. The teacher answers that he understands, and with that the story concludes.

On one level, the piece is an almost classic demonstration of paranoia, fitting well into the period that produced *The Trial* and "In the Penal Colony." Once the discovery — whether authentic or not — is made, it is caught up in the machinations of a world designed to bury it, either through ridicule, ignorance, active opposition, or recycling.

We have, in the story, some of the layers of court and justice governing Joseph K.'s case. Whatever aid the narrator tries to give (and we are not positive of his good intentions) will backfire. If successful, the narrator's pamphlet will call attention to itself, not the discovery. Or else it will capture the attention of a professor, whose students' work will bury the discovery itself. If the pamphlet is a failure, the failure will carry over to the discovery and sully it. And even if the entire enterprise catches on, at most the village schoolmaster, now a powerless bystander, can hope for some monetary reward, as others grab for the glory. In the midst of all this, the teacher experiences delusions of grandeur and glory, of being himself discovered and lauded. Kafka has managed to cover over the "truth" with all the possibilities that transform every event into something false. With such a cover-up, the story of the mole, and, by implication, any form of writing, cannot be understood because of the opposing play of forces just beyond it.

Kafka moves personally among mole, village schoolmaster, and narrator, each in turn. As mole, he is the original element, the substance that begins everything. As schoolmaster, he is the one who attempts to bring to the public his enormous discovery, as Kafka was doing with his insect and animal stories. As narrator, he remains just outside the main arena as commentator, observer, even writer; he is the one who can see everything occurring and whose own efforts only intensify the muddle. The paranoia derives from the fact that all effort, all writing, all announcements are subject to elements that distort and pervert them; there is no getting away from some "force" readying itself to do damage. Obliteration is always waiting.

In the same diary entry about arguing with Hermann Kafka and writing the story, Kafka makes one of his most meaningful remarks on writing itself. He asserts that the beginning of every story is at first so ridiculous it is barely able to make its way in the completed organization of the world. Yet every story has its own identity, its own "self," before it is fully formed, and thus it establishes a kind of conflict with the world that wants to close over it. It insists on itself, to such a degree that one should not despair about it, no more than the parents of a newborn helpless infant should despair of their child because the world can go on without it. Kafka is of course speaking of stories that have some justification for existing, and his remarks suggest he was trying to find some way in which he could make his mark in a world that seemed completely "written." It is the fear of every writer, but it was especially intense for Kafka, since the kind of story he wrote could easily for lack of audience simply vanish into that "completed organization of the world."

As the year 1914 was closing, he was clearly attempting to discover what literature meant. Brod had objected to Dostoevsky's using so many mentally ill persons in his novels; Kafka counters him by claiming they aren't ill. "Their illness is merely a way to characterize them, and moreover a very delicate and fruitful one."[85] Comparably, *his* bizarre characters, from Georg to Gregor to Joseph K., are not oddities; they are the means by which he can characterize certain elements in the world. Kafka's comment on Dostoevsky's characters reveals his sensitivity to the bizarre transformations he made of his own characters and how he felt he had not forsaken the mainstream.

Christmas he spent in Kuttenberg, with the Brods, at the Hotel Morawetz. On December 26 he says he is still working on "The Village Schoolmaster," which, he feels, he should have completed in three nights. He makes a New Year's resolution to use his time better. He observes people and images that float in and out of *The Trial:* a merchant, for example, dogged by misfortune. The merchant decides to consult a sage of *die Schrift*, law writing or scripture, but is put off by the sage's efforts to calm him. Nevertheless, he feels he has no choice; like the author, he cannot bear to live with uncertainties. On December 31 Kafka offered an assessment of his labors since August, and even he had to admit the list was not poor. Despite insomnia, headaches, a weak heart, and the overall feeling he wouldn't last long, he cited *The Trial* (worked on, but not completed); "Memoirs of the Kalda Railroad"; "The Village Schoolmaster"; a story not preserved, called "The Assistant Attorney"; the completion of "In the Penal Colony"; and a chapter of *Amerika*. Whether he was sick or not, it was a considerable list, and doubly so for a man who was working every day at a job he detested, under pressure from his family to devote more time to the factory, and with the additional burden of an anxiety-ridden personal life. In fact, had he been healthy, it is doubtful he could have created as much, or as well.

... And already in his inmost self
words are building up again,
not his own (for what would his amount to
and how benignly they'd go to waste)
but other, hard ones: chunks of iron, stones,
which he must melt down like a volcano
in order to throw them out in the outbreak
of his mouth, which curses and curses; ...

— RILKE, "A PROPHET"

ELEVEN Kafka as Prophet, 1915–1917

WITH *THE TRIAL*, begun in 1914 and continued, with several interruptions, through 1915, Kafka had found the perfect medium for becoming himself — that is, for becoming Kafkaesque.* As a lawyer, he returned to something he knew well, the courts; and into the courts he introduced something else he knew well, family life. These two elements of the story represented him as they would a later age: a society, a body politic, a set of human relationships — in brief, an entire culture. The shape of *The Trial* (or "Process") is a journey or quest, and the progression is one of uncovering

---

*Conceived of in 1917, but not fictionalized until 1926–27, Arnold Zweig's *The Case of Sergeant Grischa* has remarkable similarities to Kafka's *The Trial* and even *The Castle*. It is an excellent example of "Kafkaesque" in action. Further, in the German title *Der Streit um den Sergeanten Grischa*, the word *Streit* may also mean the "lawsuit" or the "struggle" or "contest." Even more remarkable, however, is this parable by the Chinese writer Lu Xun (1889–1936): "Once upon a time, there was a country whose rulers completely succeeded in crushing the people; and yet they still believed that the people were their most dangerous enemy. The rulers issued huge collections of statutes, but none of these volumes could actually be used, because in order to interpret them, one had to refer to a set of instructions that had never been made public. These instructions contained many original definitions. Thus, for instance, 'liberation' meant in fact 'capital execution'; 'government official' meant 'friend, relative or servant of an influential politician,' and so on. The rulers also issued codes of laws that were marvellously modern, complex and complete; however, at the beginning of the first volume, there was one blank page; this blank page could be deciphered only by those who knew the instructions — which did not exist. The first three invisible articles of these nonexistent instructions read as follows: 'Art. 1: some cases must be treated with special leniency. Art. 2: some cases must be treated with special severity. Art 3: this does not apply in all cases.'"

the truth, or what passes for it beneath layers and layers of deception, misinformation, or simply conjecture. *The Trial* concerns a man who, assuming he is innocent of any crime, is pursued by a shadowy government organization that offers him dubious legal choices, and that executes him before he ever learns what crime he is being charged with. Kafka's world, which has come down to us, somewhat prophetically, as Kafkaesque, is often little more than an intense effort to peel away protective shields, to reach some core, or else to discover there is no core. The effort is frustrated, inevitably, since the world never yields up its truths. Like everything else, truth falls victim to uncertainties, doubts, personal distortions. Yet one is driven to try to discover it. Thus the Kafkaesqueness of the Kafkan world: that insistence to uncover what is always uncoverable, or to recover what cannot be recovered.

The trappings of *The Trial* are based on misinformation — or if not quite that, then insufficient information. Joseph K.'s quest takes the shape of the innocent young man who must make a journey into an indeterminate world, often a hostile and alien one. The individual either makes his way or falls along the road, a victim of some missing link in his understanding, or some malevolence in the universe he is not attuned to. The world of Thomas Hardy may seem an unlikely analogy here, but Hardy's recognition of the ways in which layers of deception (and self-deception) can defeat one or create decisive uncertainties is not distant from Kafka's vision. The two of course differ; Kafka has the ability to make realistic scenes and activities seem extraordinary, and, conversely, to take the ordinary and engage it with his half-dream, half-magical aura. But they share common ground in their mutual recognition that there are seams or joints that disconnect humanity from the universe as much as there are linkages. The more an individual discovers as he peels away layers the more he finds himself cast off, isolated and marginal. To live with sensitivity to one's situation, to live with prescience, to try to be representative are all forms of self-destruction in this discrete universe.

In the long, incomplete chapter 8 — "Block, the Tradesman/Dismissal of the Lawyer" — Block ("log" or "boulder") is avidly pursuing his case with lawyer Huld ("grace," "graciousness"), also Joseph K.'s lawyer. Block seemingly is much further along than Joseph; he in fact expects to see a conclusion soon. But the judge thinks otherwise: "What do you think [Block] would say if he discovered that his case had actually not begun yet, if he were to be told that the bell marking the start of the proceedings hadn't even been rung?" The case becomes like a "story" that somehow must fit into an organized world, and the author of that story, here Block, really has no sense of when his story or case has begun, where it fits, even whether there is room for it in the scheme of things. The discontinuity between him and his case marks the uncertainty of his situation. Any assumptions he makes can be belied by another reality, possibly by another level of truth or misinformation altogether. He has no way of connecting to that level; at best, he can hope to strip away layers in order to get closer. But he cannot even tell whether he is approaching what he wants. For all he knows he may be further removing himself. The beauty of Kafka's world is that spatial arrangements can work either for or against the protagonist; the horror of that world is that he never knows which is happening, or when.

Block's perception of his case enfolds him in his own layers of misinformation. He makes assumptions and judgments based on incomplete data, or else not on data at all, but on his misconception of his case, or its importance, when in actuality it has little significance. In still another example of spatial arrangements, Kafka makes the accused individual the center of his universe, puffing him up into someone important enough to have a case; in another sense, the accused is part of a world that reduces him to a nonentity through the injustice of the case and its uncertainties. Thus any individual caught in the courts (that is, in the uncertainties and ambiguities of life) has to deal with two opposing forces: one that drives him into an ego-ridden world of self-centeredness, the other that pushes him farther and farther from what may save him in that world. Block's misapprehension of his case, of where he stands within it, is an emblem of all such cases, especially of Joseph's.

The case points up all the divisions and schisms within the individual and within that individual's effort to connect him to something outside. In a segment of *The Trial* separated from it and later published in *A Country Doctor* (1919), a three-page episode called "A Dream," Kafka offers a variation on the case.* Joseph K. has a dream of himself as a spectator in a cemetery as a grave mound is being prepared for the dead person by a stonecutter who is producing "golden letters from his ordinary pencil." In his most beautiful way, the cutter, or artist, is writing HERE LIES when he catches Joseph's eye and cannot go on. Joseph recognizes that in some way the sight of himself has embarrassed the cutter and made him helpless. Between them there exists some misunderstanding that is unresolvable. Joseph feels miserable because of the artist's predicament and begins to cry. The cutter, in turn, waits until the spectator calms and then continues his inscription. But he works now with great reluctance, and the letters suffer. Also, the gold leaf appears to have run out. At last, a letter emerges, a very big J. The

---

*"A Dream" ("Ein Traum") was once considered a possible alternative ending for *The Trial*, but Kafka during his lifetime strongly opposed it. If anything, this ending would have made *The Trial* even more surrealistic, and it would have softened the brutality that seems more suitable in the ending Kafka left standing.

artist stamps angrily on the ground, as if some agreement or covenant has been broken. Finally understanding the problem, Joseph digs relentlessly into the earth, which offers little or no resistance. "Everything seemed prepared beforehand; a thin crust of earth had been constructed only for the look of the thing." Immediately, a great hole opens, its sides steep, and Joseph sinks into it, "wafted onto his back by a gentle current." While he is being received into the depths of the hole, "his head still straining upwards on his neck, his own name raced across the stone above him in great flourishes." But the final lines create the real complication: "Enchanted by the sight, he woke up."[1]

The dream is of Joseph's own death, and he is enchanted by it, since it relieves the pressures of the case, but the dualism between artist-stonecutter and Joseph K. is Kafka's. He has found in this little parable-dream (part of the parable nature of several of the pieces in the collection *A Country Doctor*) a perfect example of his own division, into the hounded, persecuted middle-rank official and an artist whose very pencil can draw in gold. Once again, Kafka uses spatiality: here to indicate that space downward into the grave is a form of escape, even while it offers death. The divisions in Kafka, dramatized in Joseph K., can only be reconciled in the grave.* In life, they remain unreconcilable divisions. This brief dream episode helps us to catch Kafka's recognition of his own role in *The Trial* — not as interchangeable with that of Joseph K., but as a persona he can play off against himself. For he knows that all of Joseph K.'s efforts to discover the terms of his case and to fight it are futile; the great reconciler is the end of it all.

What, then, gives Joseph K. his energy to pursue a solution to his case? It is indisputable that he undertakes a long and arduous journey to find its key. He does not surrender to his condition, and he is not merely the "despairing" side of Kafka given over to the desire for death. The bank official fights hard to maintain his composure and to uncover information that will save him. He becomes a warrior of sorts, alternating between desperation and hope, but willing to pursue what may prolong his life and his position at the bank.

Though several episodes in *The Trial* seem especially important, the key to Kafka's thinking about Joseph K. directly and about himself indirectly can be found in two passages: the "Before the Law" segment of chapter 9 ("In the Cathedral") and the scene in Titorelli's studio in chapter 7. Each represents something different: the first, "Before the Law," presents the ambiguities of who is master, who is slave, who has power, who is subservient; the other, in the painter's attic, focuses on spatial and temporal aspects of the novel that cannot be ignored. The studio episode encompasses all of Kafka's artistry; if it is the most sig-

---

*Joseph is killed on the eve of his thirty-first birthday, at about the same age as Kafka when he wrote the bulk of *The Trial*.

nificant scene in the novel, this is because it develops several of Kafka's fictional weapons.*

The episode involves Kafka's use of an "enclosure" theme, in which all energy and activity are bottled up; and yet the enclosure of Joseph K. here does not mean he surrenders to circumstances. Although he expends energy just to get even, an inner determination keeps him going, even while he becomes convinced of the uselessness of the quest. What gives the scene its momentum is Kafka's modulation of various means: the middle ground of discourse, somewhere between conscious and unconscious; the use of spatial arrangements in which space is both denied and declared; the precise and logical presentation of elements within a setting that seems part of the unconscious, surreal or dreamlike.

The scene is introduced by a series of sensory impressions, images of hell: "disgusting yellow liquid," fleeing rats, an untended shrieking infant, a deafening din from the tinsmith's workshop, apprentices beating on a sheet of tin that casts a "pallid light," stifling air, the presence of scurrying, ratlike children led by a "slightly hunchbacked" thirteen-year-old. Salvation or relief from his case, Joseph K. had led himself to believe, lies here, and yet this seems closer to damnation than salvation. This is typical Kafka despair: deeply urban, full of the corruption of civilization and human values, replete with the loathing of artificial human progress and modernity. Neither light nor space nor expansive time enters here. Yet Joseph K. is seeking a painter, someone who usually works with light, tones, spatial arrangements.

Even before Joseph K. enters Titorelli's suffocating quarters, we observe Kafka's denial of expected time and space: in the court, which holds its sessions in attics and low-ceilinged rooms, in the lack of information, which throws experience into some ahistorical dimension. Once the scene begins, however, Kafka does not simply negate; he denies routine experience against an ironic background of the painter's "wild heathscapes," an outside world that exists somewhere as a lost paradise. Joseph K. can only obtain the wild heathscape through payment; he cannot experience it. The room itself, from which he had intended to soar beyond the confines of his case, only further confines his case. A mockery of a room for a painter, its one window allows almost no light from beyond. Titorelli is evidently part of the "case," since his means of operating have placed him outside all normal expectations.

---

*This and other scenes have led some critics, especially Heinz Politzer (1962; *Franz Kafka: Parable and Paradox* [Ithaca, N.Y.: Cornell University Press, 1966]), to argue that the focus of the novel is not Joseph K. but the proceedings; and that in "Before the Law," the central figure is the doorkeeper (mentioned twenty-three times) not the man from the country (mentioned only nine times). This is an example of how criticism when divorced from biography can lose its way. The proceedings as well as the doorkeeper are, of course, significant, but from the biographical point of view, the person who tries to enter, whether Joseph or the man from the country, is the focus in all of Kafka.

The spatial conception of the painter's attic is a standard one in Kafka. Space *up* is negated by space enclosed. Upward space may be a room at the top of something — a building, warehouse, or tower — but it is also space denied. There is no vista, no horizon, no sense of things opening out. This point is demonstrated most obviously in *The Castle* (whose German title *Das Schloss* can mean both "castle" and "lock") — the castle dominates the village and is situated somewhere in heaven, and yet its very spatiality in distance is negated by the stuffy rooms that, apparently, lead toward it, or so K. thinks. Kafka rarely gives us a true feeling of space but presents only enough of it for purposes of denial — his characteristic use of litotes. His use of space is transformational, like so much else in his work; it is offered and even described, only to be withdrawn and denied. His "theory" of space is of dimension that depends mainly on perception — that is, something very close to a Bergsonian sense of time and, by implication, space. It is all subjective, even in his use of vastness in "The Nature Theatre of Oklahoma," in *Amerika*. Space there, while not enclosed, is a concept that depends not on geography but on a size we carry in our minds.

In a curious play of spatial-temporal concepts, Joseph K. in the painter's studio is swallowed up not by immensity and endless horizons but by a "wretched little hole." Few critics have commented upon Joseph K.'s bank as a locale, and yet it too consists of a maze of rooms, a burrow, even though the end function of the bank is to convey limitless wealth and power to a seemingly unending procession of clients. Once again, we find a large, apparently ceaseless organization or function embodied in tiny stages, small rooms, cramped quarters. Joseph K. in his bank office is little different from Gregor Samsa in his position as traveler (living in small quarters) and in his room. Double doors, openings, entrances, exits, labyrinths, paths, roads, and their like dominate. The endlessness of space and sweeps of time, implied in the vastness of the case, the oceanic quality of the court system, the endless vistas of the organizations and institutions become enclosed spatially and severely restricted temporally. Kafka opens up only to close down.

In these and other ways, Titorelli's attic is the perfect setting for the choices the painter will offer Joseph. We note that Joseph's deepest insights into his case derive from the painter and take place in that stuffy attic. Block and the priest do offer insight, but they confuse him; only the painter presents the alternatives. What had before been incomprehensible chaos becomes, now, comprehensible chaos. When Joseph K. learns of his three alternatives from Titorelli, he is so uncomfortable, so near suffocation, he barely listens. Titorelli has to keep repeating them. The alternatives are themselves enclosure patterns, since the choices offered are not really choices. The three possibilities are "definite acquittal, ostensible acquittal, and indefinite postponement." The first is out of the question; the second, ostensible acquittal, calls for great but temporary concentration; whereas the last, indefinite postponement, is less taxing but requires steady application. All involve escape; all are traps. Even with knowledge, Joseph K. is in limbo. The three also have spatial-temporal dimensions, indistinguishable from their conditions: just as the choices suffocate, so do the spatial and temporal components of the choices squeeze and enclose.

Part of the suffocation we feel in Kafka's work as a whole, and in *The Trial* in particular, is not merely physical; it extends to the intimate relationship between locale and content, place and voice, initial choices and final decisions. Kafka's is a philosophy of life stretched out between points that seem to go everywhere and may go nowhere. After explaining these choices, Titorelli then opens up startling new vistas of the case for Joseph. A new arrest is possible at any time after acquittal. "Even while they are pronouncing the first acquittal [he tells Joseph] the judges foresee the possibility of the new arrest." These are spatial matters, since they extend the case to infinity. In some Modernistic way that we recognize in painting, Kafka has destroyed perspective, that dependence traditional painters have on the horizon line. He has used the forms of cubist and abstract art, dispensing with perspective and turning *his* canvas into areas of possibility. Together, the potential and actual elements along Joseph's path form a canvas not of coherent elements but of contingencies that turn his fate into absurdity. The existential language here should not, however, lead to any single interpretation of Kafka's novel: its potentialities, caught in uncertainties, are almost infinite.

As befitting a painter, Titorelli speaks of "distant" prospects and "foreshadowed" ones, "vistas" and "immediate" objects. He speaks of not letting the "case out of your sight"; he tells Joseph to keep the case going "only in the small circle to which it has been artificially restricted." He mentions that the "judges foresee" new possibilities and vast considerations, which they can deny.[2] Being caught in such uncertain dimensions reinforces the terrible loneliness and isolation every Kafka protagonist experiences despite his considerable activity and display of energy in pursuing his journey. With space and time so different from his expectations, he walks the paths of a world that lacks bright color, contrasting texture, and human affect. The landscape of a Kafka novel, here symbolized by Titorelli's attic, with its strange entrances and exits, its suffocating atmosphere, is absolutely flat, even though there are steps, buildings, and attics. The surreal effect derives from the disproportion of elements: one climbs numerous stairs, for example, in order to reach something that lacks space, or in which one must bend over so as to walk or enter.

In another sense, these enclosures, stifling and suffocating as they are, are scenic equivalents of the stream of consciousness, part of the running on of language. We may seem to be equating different elements, but once Kafka established the psychological mode of the novel, innerness tended to collapse words in time and scenes in space. We come to recognize that these phenomena, once considered separate, found a focal point in the mind; so that words, intervals, scenes, and character, along with voice, are layered and interwoven rather than differentiated.

Additionally, *The Trial* must be perceived as a huge cry, a protest, an accompanying text to "The Metamorphosis," and a work indebted to the short, bitter, final things of "The Judgment." Certainly, the longer work can be seen as somewhat like Munch's "The Scream," a cry of protest given literary shaping and form. The whipping episode in chapter 5, which creates considerable discomfort in the reader, is surely part of that scream of protest. The two men are being flogged, they cry out, because Joseph complained about them to the Examining Magistrate. Joseph tries to excuse himself, saying he only reported what had occurred in his room, when they, Franz and Wilhelm, came for him (in chapter 1). They claim they were only doing their job, that they have families to feed. Their pleas go on, and Joseph reiterates he did not intend for them to be punished. Punishment, however, is the lot of man.

What is disturbing is the sadomasochistic quality of the scene: the concentration on pain, the birch cutting into the men's fat, the healthy, brutal face of the whipper, "tanned like a sailor."[3] Strong homoerotic overtones are evident, with the men stripped and Joseph as an engaged onlooker, and instigator, since he did complain of them to the Magistrate. Also of more than passing interest is Kafka's use of his own first name for one of the warders who is being beaten on the complaint of Joseph. Almost a circular system exists, of one person being beaten by another who wants to be beaten but chooses a substitute. Even more disturbing is the implication that Joseph's pursuit of the case against him is little different from a desire for punishment. In this respect, the whipping scene is an emblem of the "trial" as a whole. The force behind the case, then, is sadomasochistic — the need for Joseph to find a suitable punishment for whatever guilt he feels. Such implications recycle the novel into Kafka's own life, since his guilt feelings at this time were especially strong, in respect to his family, to Felice, and, most of all, to himself. Yet we should not view the novel as merely an extension of Kafka's life; that would limit it and negate the enormous creativity and skill that went into his reshaping of himself into Joseph K.

"In the Cathedral," the ninth chapter, with its important parable of "Before the Law," offers a powerful statement, both sadomasochistic and spatial. It also supports one view of the novel as the working out of a ritualistic or ceremonial function. It has parallels and analogues to the primitive rites of some societies in which ritual is enacted through the agency of a priest and victim whose sacrifice enables that society to survive. The parallel to Stravinsky's 1913 *The Rite of Spring* becomes evident, and we can see in both works some response to the coming of the war. In both, an outcast or marginalized person has been selected to die, even though that individual may represent a hard worker who thinks himself assimilated to the society. Joseph K., like Gregor Samsa, shrinks from being away from his work even for a single day. His paranoia about work finds its coordinates in the cathedral scene, where he discovers his marginality amidst holiness and space.

Joseph is to accompany an Italian client to the town's cultural monuments, one of them the cathedral. The Italian does not appear but is either late or forgetful, as Kafka frequently was for appointments with friends. Caught by uncertainty about the Italian and fearful of missing time in his office, K. observes a huge armored knight, sword stuck into the ground, and speculates that perhaps the knight was placed there to observe him. K.'s uncertainty and what he sees are all part of an unsettling process in which space itself will be out of joint, as will be normal considerations of pain and suffering. The stillness and immense size of the cathedral strike K.: the voice of a priest in a small side pulpit resonates through space so vast that K. feels it tests human limits. The priest, he recognizes, is calling out "Joseph K." The sermon or condemnation is for him, and clearly the cathedral scene contains some form of sacrifice of a victim. The altarpiece itself contains a portrayal of Christ being laid in the tomb. The priest announces he is the prison chaplain and indicates that he had K. summoned here; the matter of the Italian is forgotten.

The scene recalls the Supplicant from Kafka's earliest fiction, the quarrylike figure in "Description of a Struggle." K. is to be judged here, in this immense space, and as he fears what the priest may say, he experiences that type of masochistic pain that Kafka provided for his characters — that prolongation of one's fate, that stretch of uncertainty. The priest is of course the sadistic figure, the figure of male authority, larger than life, as his voice booms through the limitless space. The priest warns K. he is too reliant on outside help, especially that of women, which is of interest since the writing of these portions of *The Trial* coincided with Kafka's involvement with Felice and Grete. But even apart from that, his attitudes toward women are questioned: that although he may rely on them, they are not to be trusted. The women in *The Trial* are as much vampires as helpers.

This exchange, in which K. strangely trusts the priest's good intentions, leads into the "Before the Law" segment, which is presented as a parable about delusion. Here the delusion concerns how the law affects a man from the country who wants entrance through a doorkeeper who blocks that entrance to him. But the "entering" dimension is common to nearly all of Kafka's protagonists: whatever they wish to enter is blocked, with the archetypal doorkeeper Hermann Kafka himself or

some other comparable authority figure. In this parable, Kafka is re-
playing his anguish of the divided self: the one who must enter (escape,
fly the coop, evade authority) and the "other," who resists all such
moves and, ultimately, makes them impossible. The doorkeeper now
assumes a major role, in blocking the entrance, but the main player remains K., who acts out the Kafka role. What is remarkable about the
basic situation, so far, is how Kafka's vision remained integrated. For
this desire to enter countered by the force that blocks is also the theme
of *The Castle*, still several years away, and looks back not a little to
Amerika. The cathedral of *The Trial* becomes the tight village, with
the vast castle in the distance, of that later novel, or the "Nature Theatre of Oklahoma" of the earlier.

The influence of Kafka's physical condition here is also clear. For
as he felt himself caught up in ever more severe symptoms of his precondition of tuberculosis — those headaches, feverish bouts, the will-
lessness and lethargy — Kafka found the boundless spaces of his life, in
his midthirties, being blocked or closed down by elements he could not
define or resolve. Breath itself was being denied him, the ultimate in
spatial denial. In this scene, as in several others, Kafka has created a
dreamlike temporal and spatial distance between events and what the
reader can experience, a kind of region somewhere between preconscious and unconscious which language can only suggest.

The law, whose secrets he wishes to penetrate, remains guarded,
but its arcane nature may open at any moment, or never. The doorkeeper is, in fact, backed by others, at further doors, each more powerful than the previous one. The man from the country, of course, waits
for the propitious moment, since it may come at any time; but he waits
futilely for days and years. His span of life is devoted to that "moment,"
that sense of "now."

Bribes are accepted gratefully, but they prove useless. The doorkeeper takes each gift as a way of making the man comfortable with his
decision to await the right moment. To reject a bribe would be to signal
that there is no hope. The man from the country curses his fate, mut-
ters to himself, and finally grows childish as he ages into dimness. His
life is ending. Before he dies, however, he condenses his entire life and
interminable wait into one final question, what a man on his deathbed
might direct to God: Why, he asks, has no one except himself come to
gain admittance? The doorkeeper replies that the door was intended
only for him. He then moves to shut it. After this story, related by the
priest, K. feels — in applying the parable to his own court case — that
the doorkeeper deceived the man. This leads to a discussion of the truth
and falsity of language, of whether the doorkeeper raised the man's
hopes or dashed them, whether life creates hope or disappointment in
equal amounts, whether language itself can become part of the dicing
with life that one must undergo. Ultimately, K. is presented with var-

ious sides of questions of free will and determinism.* The man from the country has not been *compelled* to wait; similarly, the doorkeeper has been *bound* by his duty to maintain his post. He is, after all, in the service of the law, and is, if anything, inferior to the man from the country because he must spend his entire life blocking the door. He cannot walk away. But since he is in service to the law, which lies "beyond," he too is beyond human judgment. Is he free? Is he bound? Are there any distinctions? The argument dwindles, as it must, since K. is trying to find a way into the parable that somehow provides a means of understanding his own case.

The enormity of the cathedral, the booming voice of the priest, the ineffable nature of the parable all become commentaries on K.'s situation. Enormity comes down to a fine point of argument, a nicety of language, a philosophical distinction that K. never really comprehends. Spatiality has become smallness, but smallness in turn suggests enormity. Back and forth, Kafka moves, although once the law cannot be penetrated by K. the end is clear. In the final chapter, in Brod's structuring of the manuscript,† K. is murdered, just one year after the cathedral experience. K.'s end suggests surrender, although Kafka also saw it as K.'s fight to preserve his life until he had no choice but to accept its fu-

---

*Amidst several points that help relate Kafka to Kant, Freud, and Judaic law, Jacques Derrida stresses the forbidden quality of the law: "It is the forbidden: that does not mean that it forbids, but that it is itself forbidden, a forbidden place" ("Devant la Loi," in *Kafka and the Contemporary Performance*, edited by Alan Udoff [Bloomington: Indiana University Press, 1987], p. 141). From here Derrida extrapolates that this very point is the trial and judgment implicit in the novel, an ambiguous process in which man is caught between legal injunctions and freedom to respond. We acknowledge Judaic law and the figure of Job in the not too distant shadows.

†As noted earlier, the structure of the incomplete *Trial* has led to endless speculation, especially since Kafka himself cautioned Brod that several episodes (chapters?) were supposed to be interposed between the cathedral chapter (9) and the end (10). Increasing the difficulty is the fact that Kafka left not only unfinished chapters, which may have been intended for several locations, but also numerous deleted passages that might have been restored. One restructuring that questioned Brod's order came from Dr. Herman Uyttersprot, who placed "Prosecuting Counsel," a nine-page fragment, at the beginning, before the arrest (chapter 1); then followed with Brod's chapters 4, 2, 3, adding "On the Way to Elsa," a brief interlude; then Brod's 5, 6, 9 ("In the Cathedral"), followed by 7 and 8. Before the end (Brod's 10), he intervenes with "Conflict with the Assistant Manager," "The House," and "Journey to His Mother," all three potential chapters. Uyttersprot's reformulation has its own problems, however, not the least being the disruption of what is an effective opening chapter and the re-placement of the cathedral scene to before the lawyer chapter, where its power is dissipated.

What we gain from the critical edition edited by Sir Malcolm Pasley is a volume rather close to Brod's version, with the exception that the conversation with Fräulein Montag (Brod's chapter 4) is turned by Pasley into a fragment located in the appendix. The Pasley edition indicates that Kafka probably worked on several chapters at roughly the same time, then put a completed chapter in a folder, marked it, and set it aside, until he had the bulk of a novel. The incomplete material suggests that he ran out of inspiration or energy, but these segments should not be considered "throwaways." They need to be read as part of the way we learn about K. and K.'s personal life (his relationship to his mother, for example). If we include the ancillary material in our reading, then *The Trial* seems less hermetic and, indeed, more like a process.

tility. The murderers are, perhaps, "two tenors," the ragtail scum who carry out such details. K. has recognized the uselessness of resistance, but only after resisting fiercely. If the Jew is to die, it is only after he has attempted every avenue of escape. Herzl's Zionism was becoming increasingly attractive to Kafka.

Along the way, K. fights a valiant battle against women who will either destroy or incapacitate him; strong, demanding, controlling women, who culminate, of course, in the lawyer Huld's mistress, Leni (Magdalene, the whorish Mary). But even before Leni, we find Fräulein Bürstner, a typist, who lives in Joseph's house as another boarder. In her lack of generosity toward Joseph, she represents women unable to give sympathy and compassion, and in this respect she is possibly a sideways blow at Felice. When Joseph does kiss her, his kiss is a vampire's kiss, a long and steady pressure on the throat. Joseph K. in *The Castle* will undergo the same temptations, and also succumb to women who, while appearing to offer succor, might be linked to the obstacles he cannot overcome.

At best, Kafka's presentation of the two K.'s and their women is fractured, poisonous, filled with hostility; at worst, full of sexual fear and misogyny. While men seem to be controlling the case itself, it develops that women are in collusion. Although they move on the margins of what seems to be the case, the women, beginning with the wife in the chapter 3 courtroom scene, use the case as a means of gaining empowerment. The point as K. goes from woman to woman, culminating in Leni, is that *even women* have some form of power denied to him. They provide a kind of shield behind which the man can formulate and carry out the case; they divert attention, they allow momentary, but duplicitous, pleasure, they appear to offer themselves to all. But their consolations are those proffered men about to be executed, a last meal, as it were.

They are all physical temptation: Gentile whores, not Jews, or mothers, or faithful fiancées. It may be fanciful to speculate how much of Kafka's perception of Felice has gone into these women; not the actual Felice, of course, who was courageous and faithful, but the way he perceived her so as to make her unacceptable for himself. Or, to carry the speculation backward, how much these women in his longer works are connected to that turn-of-the-century view of women as destructive elements, tempters, castrators, an irrational rush of energy that man must resist if he is to remain rational. Very likely, Kafka's attitudes toward his female characters, here and elsewhere, were conditioned by all of these views, and by his position as eldest son in a household of women — most of all, as a man who had constantly to reconstruct his feelings to make them suitable for the work he wanted to do. The one exception in *The Trial* is K.'s mother, what we see of her in the incomplete and inconclusive chapter called "Journey to His Mother."

The women are, for the most part, bait, drawing K. more deeply into his case, while themselves only tangential to it. They partake of the *danse macabre* of the novel, seeming to offer delight, while shielding death or doom — emblems of the war within Kafka and of the Great War itself. These women, but especially Leni, seek out accused men, really condemned men, finding them attractive, and they of course succumb. It is the old story, of men expelled from the Garden, of men who foolishly see in Leni an opportunity to return but who are, in reality, thrust even farther out by their associations with her. Seemingly deeply misogynist in this novel, Kafka was that but also distrustful of all forms of order, represented by the courts, by the law, by precedent and procedure, by bureaucracy; and behind that deeply resentful that marriage and family, represented by Felice and his mother, had organized society so tightly that someone like himself had to struggle to attempt to enter. So, not only men but also women make it impossible for him to enter, make it impossible for him even to grapple with what the conditions are for entrance.

By the end of 1914 Kafka felt less exhilarated than he should have, if we consider his achievements, and more entrapped. He sensed that just as "The Assistant Attorney" had, stories would slip away unless he could pursue them through the night into the morning. That was now impossible, since his free time was spent in the factory, his brother-in-law Karl Hermann having been called up for service and no longer available. Kafka speaks of time there as "my perpetual Day of Atonement."[4] Although "The Village Schoolmaster" was almost done, he abandoned the story temporarily, gave up on the now lost "Assistant Attorney," and felt himself incapable of going on with *The Trial*. He complains of continual headaches. Despite all this, he senses four or five stories within him, standing "on their hindlegs in front of me like the horses in front of Schumann, the circus ringmaster, at the beginning of the performance."[5] The reference to animals is of interest, since when he did begin to write Kafka used a wide variety of animals to populate his world.

Despite his misgivings, attendance at the factory did make Kafka feel he was indeed working, something he found missing at the institute, but nevertheless it undermined his ability to take a broad view of matters. He needed, in fact, the time for reverie, dreaming, fantasizing, the endless time in which he could conjure up his stories from that place beyond his conscious mind. His links to Modernism lie in that rejection of consciousness and in his ability to gain a voice deriving from areas other than consciousness. Feeling as if he were "at the bottom of a ravine,"[6] he planned for a meeting with Felice at Bodenbach, on the weekend of January 23–24, 1915. On January 20 he was already apprehensive, sensing he was in a bad state, and unprepared for their first confrontation since the breaking off of the engagement. Because Kafka did not know his own mind, it was a time obviously of extreme tension. Filled as his imagination was with stories in embryo and with the ongoing *Trial*, he both wanted to fit Felice back into his life and yet reject her as unsuitable to his literary aims. His diary entry on the meeting is not hopeful. He admits he thinks "it is impossible for us ever to unite, but dare say so neither to her nor, at the decisive moment, to myself."[7]

The meeting could only be disastrous: she had been traveling all night; he was, as ever, undecided and divided by his need to get back to writing. While he had his head filled with other matters, she was suspicious of this man who offered her such strange choices. "Each of us," he writes, "silently says to himself that the other is immovable and merciless. I yield not a particle of my demand for a fantastic life arranged solely in the interest of my work."[8] Indifferent to his requests, she looks forward to an average life and a comfortable home. Kafka had set his watch an hour and a half fast, and Felice reset it right to the minute: they lived not only with different expectations but in different time zones. She speaks of furnishings in her home, the "heavy furniture" that Kafka often cited as an emblem of their separateness. "Heavy furniture" symbolized for him everything he saw as destructive of his plans as a writer.

In this and other respects, he was quite in keeping with the avant-garde, in that he was suspicious of objects and saw himself in some purified location, some Mondrian grid, where lines are clean and objects banished. He had made himself into something of an abstract painting, had de-objectified himself, so to speak. He was all lines, planes, and angles — a geometric man, part cubist, part abstraction, nonrepresentative physically. In order to be a writer, he heeded James Joyce's injunction to refine himself out of existence; he joined Proust in that cork-lined room. Kafka was obviously impossible for a woman like Felice, who held on to averageness with a tenacity equal to his grip on extremity.

Yet Kafka does not blame her for her reservations toward him. As befitting someone immersed in the fate of Joseph K., he blames himself: "I am as incompetent and dreary as always and should really have no time to reflect on anything else but the question of how it happens that anyone has the slightest desire even to crook her little finger at me."[9] While realizing their separateness, he cannot surrender to his better judgment. "We haven't had a single good moment together during which I could have breathed freely." He repeats, as we have seen, that with Felice he never enjoyed that sweetness one experiences with a woman one loves, such as he had felt in Zuckmantel and Riva. He says he feels "only unlimited admiration, humility, sympathy, despair and self-contempt." But the experiences in Zuckmantel and Riva were so pleasing because they were fleeting; outside of matrimony, setting up a home, considering a family, putting lives together — they had no consequences. They recalled visits to prostitutes. At the same time, Kafka truly admired Felice, for her sense of herself, her ability to accommodate his own peculiar demands, her defense of her own values and the systems on which she depended.

In one curious respect, the struggle between Kafka and Felice was the struggle being fought out in the larger world of artistic achievement: between Modernists and traditionalists who argued for an object-oriented world, with recognizable narratives, story lines, plotting devices, characters. Such exponents of traditional forms shaped a culture entirely different from that of the Modernists. The traditionalists found themselves in the camp of nationalists, whether Young Czechs or otherwise, aligned with religious forces, those arguing from historical precedent. Above all else, they feared disorder. Such proponents of historical continuity saw in Modernism and its practices a threat to civilization itself. From their point of view, painting had become unintelligible, music (that of Schoenberg, in particular) had turned into squawks and squeaks, and literature no longer touched base with human realities and human concerns. This group was quite honorable in its way, but its views had nothing to do with Kafka's outlook or practices, which were profoundly rooted in artistic change, in avant-garde notions of time and space, in the infinite potentialities for literature now that Freud had probed beneath human consciousness, in the opportunity to deny objects and that reified world he found so fearful and confusing. It gave him the occasion to explore literature as a function of language and to replace traditional religious beliefs and customs with artwork itself.

Kafka's journey was of course torturous, since it meant confrontation with social norms at every turn: Felice herself, his family, and even several of his friends, who, like Werfel, worked traditionally and reaped the rewards. It meant living, in his imagination, as a pariah, or else in a cellar where food is brought to him, where his hours are spent in the dark outside of human contact, self-absorbed, caught up in the trajectory of his own talent. Kafka's world was a heady one, perilous at best, destructive at worst; Felice's was solid, steady, unwavering. She was a captain taking her ship through the shoals. Kafka was the mate who wanted to try out the dangerous possibilities by testing out the shoals themselves, a challenge to his ingenuity. That there was no possible meeting between them can be seen in that larger world where head-on collisions between traditionalists and avant-gardists also disallowed resolution.

As if the divisions between them were not powerful enough, Kafka read to Felice his latest "gem," the parable "Before the Law," which Brod later incorporated into chapter 9 of The Trial. If Felice had fully comprehended it, the parable would have told her that Kafka was so caught in matters of choice and indecision that he could never decide on her, much less decide on her terms. He speaks of the nebulousness of his consciousness, which makes it impossible for him to converse with people normally. This ability requires a pointed, focused, sustained coherence that he says he is lacking. It is not so much a lack — he certainly exhibited that ability in his work at the institute — but his choice was to submerge it into another dimension, his world, his imagination, his desire to see things his way.

Writing Felice after their miserable Bodenbach weekend together, Kafka admits to her that not only was their time with each other unpleasant, but they hadn't spent a single minute together "entirely free of strain." He senses that the problem lies in the fact that each is merciless toward the other; but then, twisting this observation, he states that part of the fault is his failure to argue his case and his expectation that his point will come through miraculously, without an effort to convince her. Whatever their positions, the result, as he writes in his diaries, is calamitous. Yet despite his recognition of their disparities and different levels of expectation, he tortures himself over the affair and cannot let go. He rues the fact that they have no quarrels, which might clear the air, but go on in unstated tension that keeps tremors running through them, as though "someone were continually cutting the air between us with a sword."[10]

The relationship that Kafka was suffering through with Felice strangely or not so strangely replicated his relationship with his family: no quarrels, no confrontations (except over Julie Kafka's reading Felice's letter), but tensions and tremors one could cut with a sword. Kafka turned all such connections into forms of torture, not because he could help himself but because such tortured experiences validated his own sense of reality. Without the validation of his difference and of his need to suffer self-doubt, he could not proceed. Where those feelings came from, we can only speculate, but we do know they came with a supersensitivity to modulations of experience, a feeling of being left out after his birth, his sense of desertion when his two brothers died young, the further desertion when an avalanche of sisters hit the family. But equally intense was the fictional imperative, which forced Kafka to separate himself. He was not a writer who created his fiction from "stories" or from personal activity — no Hemingway here! He was, instead, a writer who started out with a consciousness that generated its own materials; he was inevitably the subject of everything he wrote, no matter how imaginatively and creatively he was able to reshape the material. This gave him language, voice, tone, attitude, and overall expression itself.

In the aftermath of the Bodenbach meeting with Felice, Kafka was unable to concentrate on work. Conditions at the factory, however, improved when Karl Hermann's brother began to relieve Kafka at the factory, and even the institute seemed less dark and gloomy. Yet Kafka's imaginative work suffered; he started "Blumfeld, an Elderly Bachelor" but considered the first few lines "ugly" and felt they gave him a headache. He finds the beginning mechanical, like a fish breathing out its life on a sandbank. Kafka had reason to be suspicious of the story — it remained incomplete — because it was so clearly a symbol of his own life if he failed to marry. "One evening Blumfeld, an elderly bachelor, was climbing up to his apartment — a laborious undertaking, for he lived on the sixth floor."[11] Moved by his own story, Kafka himself sought out a room of his own, on the Bilekgasse, in the same house as his sister Valli (he never removed himself far from the family, even when he wished to avoid it). But he cannot bear the noise in his room, although in the main it seems quiet. He tells Felice he stops the striking-clock in his room, but then the one next door drives him to frantic worry; and there is the doorbell, the whispering of other tenants, the coughing of lodgers, and the landlady herself (who speaks softly). The landlady apologizes for the whispering, and the coughing lodger is moved to another room. Because he listens so intently to noises he knows will undermine him, Kafka hears everything. He asks Felice not to look on his suffering as despicable, especially since other people are suffering far more than he is.*

Yet this is the fate of Blumfeld, whose happy name ("Flower field") belies the loneliness of his existence. He must live out his life with other people's unfamiliar noises: their coughs, snorts, snores, and worse. Poor Blumfeld can't bear dirt in his room, and yet he would like to acquire a little dog. The problem is that a dog creates not only dirt but also fleas, illness, oozing eyes, and other ailments. As Blumfeld thinks about a dog as a companion, he can only contemplate the drawbacks of owning an animal: its demand for his attention, the fact that it too would age and need care. Even from the beginning of this incomplete piece, we can see that Kafka has used Blumfeld's reflections on the dog to parallel his own on Felice. Every disadvantage Blumfeld finds in owning a dog, Kafka has intuited in marriage. In the face of all the insurmountable problems of ownership, he decides to remain alone, and he realizes he does not need around him some submissive creature on whom he can lavish attention. Of course, the dog has the advantage over Felice in that very submissiveness. Blumfeld prefers a companion he doesn't have to pay much attention to, one who doesn't mind an occasional kick. But since this is impossible to obtain, in ownership or in marriage, he renounces the entire idea.

He is left to an existence of isolation, loneliness, and complete self-

*By March 1, he had given notice to the landlady, despite all her efforts to please him. Kafka indicates he must torture himself with continual change of his situation, all of which will prepare him for some future great change. Obviously, no landlady could deal with this.

absorption. Blumfeld is Kafka's plan for the future, the way Kafka sees himself at thirty-one and a half, as his life stretches out into middle age. But there are other factors present. When Blumfeld opens the door of his room, he sees something magical: "two small white celluloid balls with blue stripes jumping up and down side by side on the parquet; when one of them touches the floor the other is in the air, a game they continue ceaselessly to play."[12] He seeks some thread holding them, but finds none. He figures they contain other balls, causing a rattling sound. If he had been a child, this would have made a fine toy, but now he cannot conceive how someone with these two strange spheres has penetrated his retiring life. He runs after them, tries to catch them, but they elude his grasp. He finally traps one, and feels the energy in it as it attempts to escape him. To evade him, the second ball jumps even higher, until Blumfeld would have to forgo all dignity to capture it. Furious, he releases the one in his hand, and it resumes its former well-coordinated jumps. The balls have a life of their own; they do not suddenly retire to some quiet spot. They continue to jump around, until, like two pet dogs, they enter into his service.

When Blumfeld cannot turn off the jumping balls, what was momentary amusement now begins to dominate his life. Finally plugging his ears with cotton, revealing that sensitivity to noise Kafka suffered from, he goes to sleep; and in the morning before going to work, he manages to corner the balls in the wardrobe, where they are imprisoned, living objects trapped in the dark. Blumfeld gives the key to his room to some girls, who are to pass it on to the charwoman's dim-witted son, and then he proceeds to work, putting the balls out of his mind until his return in the evening. We do not know if the balls are real or part of a fantasy world of the lonely bachelor. We wonder what they represent, perhaps a kind of fate, or some element following Blumfeld, or perhaps simply a rambunctious representation of his sensitivity to noise. In their way, whether real or whether part of his imaginary world, they will take over his life, possibly serving for Blumfeld what writing itself was for Kafka.

The second part of this incomplete story concerns the bachelor at work, with inadequate assistants, a director who does not understand him, and other aspects that make the job distasteful. Although Kafka's actual position was not like this, his perception is telling: Blumfeld surrounded by incompetents. The story here bogs down in meaningless and tedious detail, of two assistants, children merely, who make life hellish for the bachelor and are themselves perhaps the office equivalent of the two jumping balls. A janitor whose job is to sweep up is another thorn in Blumfeld's side. The work itself involves some kind of minor management in a factory employing large numbers of seamstresses, so that the workplace seems more like the asbestos factory than the insurance institute.

When Blumfeld tries to make peace among the assistants and janitors, matters that have become of little concern to the reader, the story trails off. Nevertheless, the overall level of depression and despair in the story gives us a sense of Kafka's perception of his own future as a middle-aged and then elderly bachelor. There is no relief, no alleviation, simply an aging process in which a man does his job under most trying conditions and then returns to his room in a house he can barely stand. Since the story had wound itself so deeply into Kafka's predicament that he could not imaginatively see his way clear, it is evident he could not complete "Blumfeld." Having started out too close to the bone, he lost all creative reshaping of the material.

The *Diaries* reveal Kafka's complaints at every stage: incapacities, headaches, hesitations. But by March 1, he decided to move, to an airy corner room with a balcony on the fifth floor of a house on Langengasse. He had a fine view of the towers of the Altstadt and, further on, of the Laurenziberg, but one basic problem remained: noise, much greater than in the previous location. Much the same as in his parents' apartment, silence came only after 11:00 P.M. He hears everything: carts in the street, the house elevator, a party in other rooms, with the result that he cannot work; and the less he works, the more sensitive he becomes to noise, the more anxious he is that noise will make it impossible for any work to come forth. He fears he is in danger of losing everything: "Occasionally I feel an unhappiness which almost dismembers me, and at the same time am convinced of its necessity and of the existence of a goal to which one makes one's way by undergoing every kind of unhappiness."[13] The anxiety creates such a pressure, such a fear of impotence, that only work can relieve it.

Through Brod, Kafka became interested once again in Eastern European Jews and felt more than ever their contempt for the Westernized Jews of Prague and Vienna. Kafka indicates that even Brod, who was attempting to bring the two groups together, was lost in the situation and gave an inadequate and feeble speech to an assembly seeking some linkage. The failure of two such distinct groups to come together, their only commonality being their ostensible Judaism, suggests for Kafka something of the division within him: his self-hatred as a Prague Jew, but his complete inability to accept the religious faith of those of the East. He wanted their community, not their God. For Kafka, the Jewish Yahweh may betoken hope, but not for him. He was, in this respect, not a renegade but a devout kind of Jewish nonbeliever. Cosmic emptiness, the outer form of his inner terror, ultimately possessed him more than God could. Like Herzl, Freud, and other secular Jews, he found he could live with that.

He returned to "The Assistant Attorney," but a party taking place in the house shatters him; he lies on his sofa waiting for silence, but when it finally comes he still cannot work. All this gets dutifully reported to Felice.[14] The room itself is lovely, with a view that relieves some of his depressed condition; but the noise in the space above him recalls a game of nine-pins. He has sent to Berlin for some Oropax, a kind of wax wrapped in cotton wool with which he can stop up his ears, but despite its messiness and annoyance, it doesn't do an effective job, muffling rather than blocking the noise. He is somewhat guilty about complaining when the war is being fought fiercely and the factory is going under. His brothers-in-law are serving active duty, and Valli's husband has already been wounded. Kafka feels it's not out of the question his turn will come, but there are factors that he says made him decide not to volunteer. Out of place in Prague, he repeats, he would be even worse in the army, although it is doubtful the army would have taken him in. When he repeats to Felice how conflicted he is and how out of touch he is with his surroundings, he is reporting a particularly bad time. Once again, his work was on hold, with only sporadic attempts, a page or two, lines and paragraphs; and as he moved toward thirty-two, his personal life was frustrated. The war in the background reinforced his sense of helplessness: men were coming forward to fight for their side, while he dallied. Even a monthly salary raise of 100 kroner made little difference, especially since if the factory went bankrupt he would be liable. He was digging himself into a hole, as he viewed it, and foresaw no respite.

With his bold work on *The Trial*, Kafka had begun 1915 as a unique prophet of the disconnected self. Now with the novel lying on his desk in fragments, he was less prophet than wanderer between two worlds, neither of which fitted him, or he them. Under these conditions, he accompanied Elli to visit her husband in the Carpathians in Hungary, going through Budapest. After Ujhel, they spent the night in Sátoral-jaujhely and ended up in Nagy Mihály. Kafka noted in his *Diaries* that he was incapable of living with people, even of speaking. "Complete immersion in myself, thinking of myself. Apathetic, witless, fearful. I have nothing to say to anyone — never."[15] The prophet had been temporarily muted. By way of Budapest, he traveled alone and was back in Prague by April 27. Kafka's entries on the trip are for the most part lacking in sharpness; depression and inability to respond made him an indifferent observer. By May 3 he described his condition as comparable to a well gone dry. During the trip, he even went to see Felice and Grete Bloch at Whitsun. His *Diaries* indicate a limbo state: "What is there to tie me to a past or a future? The present is a phantom state for me; I don't sit at the table but hover around it. Nothing, nothing. Emptiness, boredom, no, not boredom, merely emptiness, meaninglessness, weakness."[16] Even an excursion to Dobřichovice, near Prague, did not lift the gloom.

In one respect, Kafka's "prophetic" qualities were expressed in his descriptions of emptiness and nothingness. By using his own condition as a representative one, he was acting as seer and clairvoyant. In effect, the limbo condition he described for himself was characteristic of all of Europe. The war was settling into an impasse, which did not prevent the battlefields from becoming killing grounds on both Western and Eastern fronts. The present condition of Europe was emptiness and nothingness. In the next year, Franz Josef would die, and in the year after that the Russian Revolution, first under the Mensheviks and then the Bolsheviks, would further alter the face of Europe.

So representative was Kafka that even without writing further on *The Trial* he had already moved toward prophetic history, foreseeing a process of entrapment, movement toward degradation and death, the squeezing of the individual by the state or some other bureaucracy, the disappearance of justice and justification from the world, the dessication of leadership and officialdom, the manipulation of people by some "higher" (or "lower") order. Kafka was depressed not only by his own condition, or by the condition of Europe, but by the vision he had himself started to provide as an explanation. He recognized he would have to go through life without understanding, which meant without support. Only Strindberg, who went through some of the same agony, sustained him. Even while perceiving it as impossible, he is desperate to be understood. He evaluates friends and relatives for their support, but he knows there is no relief.

He looks ahead to the Whitsun (May 23–24) meeting with Felice and Grete, admitting that his vacillations have not altered but believing he knows more about both of them now. So that Felice doesn't have any false illusions about change in him, he repeats that while he would prefer some straightforward resolution of their problems, he knows one cannot exist. He shivers with discontent. What is filtering into his letters is a morbid recognition that his course is fixed — toward the condition described as Blumfeld's elderly bachelorhood. But the planned meeting is itself some indication he wants to try again, only now more realistically. The May 6 letter to Felice shifts, and he says they must start afresh, by which he means that *he* must start afresh, since Felice was and is in the right. They must meet and try to hammer out a truce (with a war ongoing, Kafka's language is martial), followed perhaps by another engagement.

They did meet in Bohemian Switzerland, with Grete Bloch in attendance. They shared meals, stayed under the same roof, and saw each other so much that Kafka felt they had progressed toward a rapprochement. But he also feels himself divided into two, into the Kafka who would be husband and the Kafka who would be prophet. The diary entry for May 27 indicates he is falling to pieces; and he is, figuratively, fragmented. He tells Felice (May 26) that on the return trip to Prague he observed carefully her fiancé, made easy by the fact that the large crowds made them both sit in one seat. He says her fiancé, as he observed him, is in bondage to Felice and sought memories of her and her room. On the next day, he tells her that the two days they have spent together have created ties very difficult for him to break. Yet he also expresses hope he will be accepted into the military, an ambiguous hope that was dashed by his rejection.

He and Felice met again, in Karlsbad, in June; all we know about that meeting comes from two references in Kafka's letters to her. The meeting did not appear to calm him. He tells her that upon his return to Prague, things became unbearable and he had to get away. He chose a sanatorium in Rumburg (Rumburk) and went near the end of July. Easily accessible, Rumburg was second choice to the seventeen-hour journey to Lake Wolfgang. The woods and hilly country of Rumburg seemed to settle him, but only temporarily. Now thirty-two, Kafka was gaining another realistic insight, that he had entered into the only meaningful phase of his life, and it was personally miserable, uncertain, in nearly every regard unsatisfactory. From that perspective, he could write. But at these moments writing itself was too difficult, and even diary entries over the summer of 1915 vanish. There is a gap from May 27 to September 13.

Back from Rumburg, somewhat refreshed, he soon fell back into the familiar cycle. In retrospect, even the sanatorium experience seemed an act of madness. He tells Felice he has no one else he can talk to about these matters, except possibly Ottla. To Felice: "I come back and spend the first week as though beside myself, think of nothing but my, or our, misfortune, and neither at the office nor in ordinary conversation am I able to take in more than mere superficialities, and this only between the aches and strains in my head. I am in the grip of a kind of imbecility."[17] The Karlsbad episode with Felice, in June, apparently had not gone well; while expectations had been great, the actuality had not been ideal. Kafka expected Felice to respond that he had only himself to blame, expecting from her a form of guilt that fed into masochism. Meanwhile, he searched for a remedy and thought of a meeting the following week in Bodenbach, but rejected this as no remedy at all. He realized that unless other matters were clarified their meetings were futile; and since the fog cannot be dissipated, he is back at the original impasse.

The energy Kafka put into his new pursuit of Felice was consuming both mental and physical reserves. Yet we could counterargue that his need to work through the impasse with her was his way of concluding how unfit he was for marriage and forcing him to return to writing. His needs worked in cycles, and, as we saw in chapter 9, there is little question Felice served as nourishment for his work as much as she forced him to suspend all work while he tried to reach a truce with her. In the August 9 letter, he speaks in the third person, like someone detached from himself but also like someone mirroring his concerns. He has re-created himself as a fictional character, yet remained himself as the author of that character. He speaks of himself as an "other," which is fine for him as a writer and consistent with what he will write in later years. "These are his [the "other's"] words, and his appearance confirms his state of mind. He is delirious, utterly uncontrolled and distracted." He mentions two alternatives for "him," either Felice or military service. But, he says, he "has been deprived of both. When all is said and done, I could not disagree with him about not writing. Does his writing not cause more sorrow than his silence?"[18] If it does, then he writes to increase his suffering. In his offer of alternatives to the "other," however, Kafka has omitted the most important aspect of the equation: his return to imaginative writing, especially *The Trial*, that ongoing process of his life and the prophecy of his own demise from tuberculosis.

While his *Diaries* still contain significant statements and literary ideas, the entries are much thinner for the next nine years than we would expect. Partly this was because in those years he was writing again, and partly because he felt he was now beginning to repeat himself. In September, he was suicidal: the knife image returns, this time a thrust between throat and chin: "Lift the chin and stick the knife into the tensed muscles," which he describes as the "most rewarding place."[19] The image of course recalls the ending of *The Trial*, already implicit here. An entry on September 30 further links him to *Amerika* and to *The Trial*: "Rossmann and K., the innocent and guilty, both executed without distinction in the end, the guilty one with a gentler hand, more pushed aside than struck down."[20] That Kafka considered Joseph K. guilty is part of the process in which reality is altered; but Karl Rossmann, while innocent, also gets much the same punishment, pushed aside rather than stabbed. But by commingling the three, Kafka has cast guilt on all, whatever their moral or legal status. The image of stabbing, then, is not just on his part a suicidal impulse, it is an imaginative participation in the lives of fictional characters. His identification is complete: the innocent young man who gets shunted aside, the bureaucrat convicted in some vague judicial area and condemned to death, the author who feels himself drifting toward nothingness and welcomes the knife thrust.

Yet the very next day, Kafka can show us a completely different face. He had been reading volume 3 of the *Memoirs* of General Marcellin de Marbot, and he gives us a detailed explanation of the mistakes Napoleon made in his Russian campaign, including the fact that on the day of the Battle of Borodino, the French general suffered from a severe migraine. Kafka reveals a considerable knowledge of the campaign, but even more than that, a sharp sense of military strategy, a keen insight into how things go wrong. Although Napoleon and Joseph K. are far apart indeed, Kafka's understanding of human frailty and of circumstance is well integrated. In both areas he understands how one loses, how the unforeseen can enter into the situation, how what may seem within one's grasp one moment slips away the next.

None of this, however, alleviates his nervousness, and his observation that noise can no longer disturb him is barbed. It no longer disturbs him because the deeper one digs one's pit, "the quieter it becomes; the less fearful one becomes, the quieter it becomes."[21] In brief, the ultimate silence, that final avoidance of noise, comes with death. He suggests he may be dead and not know it. In his *Diaries* the next day, he continues with the same contemplation of final things. "Insoluble problem: Am I broken? Am I in decline?" Yet he finds something to balance this decline. "Almost all the signs speak for it (coldness, apathy, state of my nerves, distractedness, incompetence on the job, headaches, insomnia); almost nothing but hope speaks against it."[22]

That "hope," slight as it may be, occurs at the end of *The Trial* when two "tenth-rate actors" come to kill Joseph K. Joseph K. sees a policeman and thinks of turning to him for help; in the final version, as we know, Joseph accepts the inevitable and lets the two men stab him to death, without turning to the policeman. But in the space between his momentary desire to appeal his case to a man of the law and his acquiescence to death, Kafka found that element of hope which sustained him. The interstices of hope, we might call it — a seam or crease within ongoing events or the inexorable press of circumstance.

We could argue that by killing off Joseph, Kafka had found the means to save himself, just as earlier, by shunting Karl Rossmann aside in *Amerika* — sending him into vastness, where he will vanish — Kafka had found a way of killing off one part of himself while allowing another part to survive. Similarly, as early as "The Judgment" in 1912, he could himself come through by eliminating Georg Bendemann, and later in that same year, recreate himself by crushing Gregor Samsa. Comparably, by killing off the officer in "In the Penal Colony" and letting the prisoner escape, Kafka could act out the near miss in his own survival, while the death itself allowed that segment of him to die in order to ensure the life of the remainder. In all his major fictions up to this time, Kafka had found that crease in life through which he could sneak.

Some external events in his life now began to press on him so that he had to respond. The illustration for Kurt Wolff's new edition of "The Metamorphosis," by Ottomar Starke, included a depiction of the bug. Kafka protested vehemently that it could not be depicted, or even shown from a distance, but would have to exist only in the reader's imagination. Wolff and Starke acquiesced, and the eventual jacket design, as has been noted, shows only a folding door, slightly open, and a man in the foreground, his hands grasping at his face in anguish. Another external event difficult to avoid was the war itself. Kafka's hesitation about purchasing war bonds and his debate about whether they were a good investment created an excitement that, as his thoughts switched from bonds to writing, became the impetus for transformation. "I felt myself up to it, wanted nothing save the opportunity to write, considered what nights in the near future I could set aside for it, with pains in my heart crossed the stone bridge at a run, felt what I had already experienced so often, the unhappy sense of a consuming fire inside me that was not allowed to break out."[23]

He measures himself against a mutual acquaintance of his and Brod's, a young man named Abraham Grünberg, a refugee from Warsaw who died of tuberculosis during the war. Kafka devises a game with himself as judge: If one of them had to die, whom would he choose? At first, he thinks that Grünberg is a far more valuable person than he and, theoretically, should live, while he, Kafka, dies. But before that could occur, Kafka says he would find arguments to keep himself alive, "arguments that at any other time, because of their crudity, nakedness and falsity, would have made me vomit."[24] Kafka here recreates something of the ending of The Trial. By killing off his characters, here played by the stand-in Grünberg, he allows himself to live. The measure of difference between life and death is that small, and Kafka satisfied himself with games that left him only a slight edge. Yet such sophistry made him ill.

If we total up Kafka's list of complaints, his sense of despair, his protests about life, his edging toward death, his images of the knife in the larger context beyond the immediacy of his own survival, we observe how he has ingested the morbid meaninglessness of the war. The war was now, in late 1915, unwinnable, and yet it would continue to claim millions of lives. In his way, Kafka became the prophet of that war's endless killing. In offering up himself as a ritual sacrifice, for whatever psychological reasons, he found images and visions for what Europeans were doing to each other. Kafka discovered annihilation, extinction, temporary solutions through killing; and he responded by taking it all upon himself, in insomnia, headaches, languor, thoughts of suicide. His "representational" qualities come through his identification with the general situation and his use of his fiction to shadow that identification through fantasies, visions, specters. As Europe engaged in its dance of death, Kafka sought ways to reshape that ballet into fictional forms.

After a long respite, he wrote to Felice on December 5, admitting he has sunk so low that even an angel from heaven could not lift his spirits. He says he can't come to Berlin — he lacks a passport — and she can't come to Bodenbach — she lacks the official permit or visa. He cannot bear Prague, either. But even a meeting would resolve nothing. "I could bring you nothing but disappointment, monster of insomnia and headaches that I am." [25] His fate is to creep along the old familiar streets of Prague: Prague is his destiny, fate, circumstance; he is doomed to Prague. On Christmas Eve of 1915, he tells Felice he has plans to reorganize himself after the war and move to Berlin. He says that by then (after another three years of war, with Kafka suffering from terminal tuberculosis) he will be a man who can work for one week before reaching the end of his strength. He rues not having left in 1912, when, he felt, he had full possession of all his forces.

On Christmas Day, he says he spoke to Herr Pfohl at the institute about some course of action. His talk was quite frank: he indicated that if things went on as at present, he would go mad. He didn't want to use that as an excuse to seek a vacation, but he couldn't give notice because of his parents and the factory. Military service was hardly an option, since he could not pass the physical examination. But he also pointed out he would not use his institute position to keep his deferral from service. Ever understanding, Pfohl offered Kafka a week's vacation, asserting he was too valuable to lose. Since Pfohl was not well either, he suggested that both receive hematogenic treatment. Pfohl believed Kafka's ill disposition was the result of poor blood, and his recommendation was for a sanatorium stay. Kafka was later diagnosed as having "cardiac neurosis," an organic (not psychologically induced) heart irregularity. Neither diagnosis, whether blood or heart, was of course accurate.

But as Kafka headed into 1916, whatever the diagnosis, he was death-oriented — befitting the war, befitting what was about to happen to the Dual Monarchy, befitting the bloodletting in which death surrounded one. At the end of December, Kurt Wolff published "Before the Law," which describes perfectly the trap into which humanity has slipped, in which, whatever the guilt or innocence of the person, life and the courts both end in death. Seeking some way to position himself, Kafka divided himself once again into the living man (hopeful) and the thinking man (hopeless). "Yet even the thinking man," he writes, "maintains that though in the end I do away with myself in that hole [one that he intends to crawl into], I shall have done the best I could do at the time."[26] These lines are, of course, addressed to Felice, so that he can follow up by telling her he has no right to her until he emerges from that hole. He admits to being "a naughty child," a madman, whom she treats in a kindly manner, nevertheless. This line intensifies in his January 24 letter. He asks whether his letters are not more terrible than his silence. Then he says he would like to disappear into a trapdoor that opens under his feet, to a place "where the wretched remnants of my remaining powers could be preserved for some future freedom."[27]

A March letter to Felice, cited earlier, increases the cries of desperation. He has offered himself to her as someone beyond the pale: a caged rat, an insomniac, a creature wracked by headaches. He doesn't know how he can get through the days. In his *Diaries* a month later, he tells of a dream that shows an extremely confused individual, not just at the institute and in his work but in his inner turmoil. The dream is both homoerotic and filled with wishes for parricide: oedipal, erotic, and frustrating. This dream is preceded by another, briefly described, in which his father swings into his room from the window ledge but begins to slip away into space. The dreamer tries to grasp him but has no way of anchoring his own feet to prevent him from slipping. His dilemma is that to fasten his feet, he would have to let go of his father. In a more major dream, two groups are fighting each other, when the dreamer's group seizes one of its opponents, a gigantic naked man, once again, some eerie version of Hermann Kafka. Five of them cling to his head, arms, and legs, but they have no knife with which to stab him. They frantically seek a blade, but when none is forthcoming they drag the huge body to a red-hot oven nearby, hold one of his feet close until it begins to smoke, pull it back, and then repeat the act — until the dreamer in a cold sweat and his teeth chattering awakes.

This leads in the *Diaries* into an incomplete story of two children, Hans and Amalia, which also involves a stranger who drags Hans inside a warehouse, while Amalia hesitates to call their father to save them. The story is connected vaguely to the two other dreams, and all of them suggest a crisis in Kafka's thinking about Hermann. The famous letter to his father would not be written until 1919, but the foundation for it seems laid within those dream sequences. The fantasy of the father held outside by the dreamer's hands, even as he is himself slipping toward the ledge, has within it both a wish for the father's death and the suggestion of suicide: a replay of "The Judgment," in which the father dies, while the son retains the option to live or die, to become here the murderer.

In the second dream sequence, the father figure is captured and will be made to pay by slow, fiery torture for whatever he has done. Lacking that crucial knife, his captors make of him a human sacrifice, burned not at the stake but at the oven door. Kafka here is killing the father but also engaging in a disturbing sexual fantasy: the naked man, gigantic, recalling Hermann, is held and slowly cooked. In this great dreamwork of confusing signals, he kills the father but first tortures him, with the accompaniment of confusing sexual patterning of captors and captured, of son with father. If nothing else, Kafka's recorded dream sequences reveal the terrible disarray of his mind and imagination.

Just before this, on April 9, he went to Karlsbad for two days, on business, with Ottla. One of the first things they did was to visit Villa Tannhäuser. His brief letter to Felice about this visit sounds almost cheerful, but another one in April on her liking for "heavy furniture" makes him disconsolate. And in still another one, for April 14, he mentions, without any details, that Robert Musil, now in military service as a first lieutenant, came to see him. Musil's response to the Dual Monarchy and to the Great War in his *The Man Without Qualities* is the only other work, aside from *The Good Soldier Schweik*, to capture the ironies, paradoxes, and futilities of these years such as we find in Kafka. A planned trip to Marienbad was postponed; Kafka went there in the middle of May, while on another business trip to Karlsbad. He agrees he and Felice should not see each other until he gets better. With that, he announces his latest medical report, cardiac neurosis, or heart irregularity, and the treatment, electrical therapy. Canceling the Easter Tuesday visit to Marienbad, he says his journeys are stripped of pleasure before they even start. Despite his gloomy predictions, his mid-May trip to Marienbad was exceptionally rewarding, and he returned there with Felice in July.

On May 10, still wandering from one idea to another, he delivered a much rewritten letter to the director of the institute, Dr. Robert Marschner, in a sense a set of ultimatums. He asked either for a long leave, without pay, if the war should end by autumn, or else for his exemption to be canceled. Marschner, who was sympathetic to Kafka and his problems, thought his employee was attempting to extort three weeks of vacation. What he failed to recognize was that Kafka was attempting to redirect his life. He had even considered resigning if a long leave were not forthcoming. The director had his own agenda and told Kafka to take three weeks' vacation at once, not the six months without pay he had wanted. As for the issue of the army, which Kafka said he wanted to join, Marschner did not even acknowledge it. This led to Kafka's mid-May trip for the institute to Karlsbad and Marienbad, which he found "unbelievably beautiful." Writing to Felice from Marienbad on May 14, Kafka ran through the entire episode at the office, without considering that his plans for a long leave or for military service left little or no room for her. So intent was he on reshaping himself and the direction of his life that Felice, just two months before their second unofficial engagement, was hardly a factor.

On his return to Prague, he felt the same strangulation that had gripped him before, and there is some reason to suspect that the seeds of his illness were being planted, although they were still undetectable. The ever present headaches appear more than a concomitant of tension and seem somehow linked to physical changes. The headaches, Kafka says, made it impossible to work, read, think, or even sit still. He was certainly not writing seriously or in any sustained way. In the early summer of 1916, his condition was such that at thirty-three he had not progressed at all. He could still enter in his *Diaries* a rather ambiguous passage about being with at least six girls since the summer. He says that with all six, his "guilt is almost wholly inward."[28] They do not seem to be prostitutes, but who they were and how Kafka met them remains a mystery. He repeats he senses only emptiness, even in his own room.

Felice suggested they go to a sanatorium together, an indication of how his neurasthenia had become contagious. They would later meet in Marienbad, but his response to her is that sick people, among whom he counts himself, should give a wide berth to sanatoria. He feels that although she is making concessions to him, she is misreading his desire for rest cures in official places. Kafka did take the three-week vacation offered by the director and on July 3 spent his first day in Marienbad with Felice. They stayed in adjoining rooms, with keys on each side. It was a typical Kafka experience: full of hopes and expectations, full of recognitions and realities that dashed those expectations. Did they consummate the affair, since each had access to the other's room, and the hotel was ready to wink at what its guests did? Kafka's diary entries are ambiguous about this. He writes of the hardships of "living together. Forced upon us by strangeness, pity, lust, cowardice, vanity, and only deep down, perhaps a thin little stream worthy of the name of love, impossible to seek out, flashing once in the moment of a moment." The next day his words are equally ambiguous: "Unhappy night. Impossible to live with F. Intolerable living with anyone. I don't regret this; I regret the impossibility for me of not living alone."[29] His attitude — which could mean they came together, or did not, could not — dissolves into insomnia, headaches, a plan to jump out of a high window, but onto ground where it won't be fatal. When he considers Felice, the suicide theme is never distant.

But in that same July 6 entry, he can also admit he has never been intimate with a woman apart from the times in Zuckmantel and Riva. By "intimate," he can of course mean something more than sexually engaged — perhaps emotionally and psychologically involved. Their proximity, in fact, created a good deal of tension. Kafka closed up in Felice's presence, and she reciprocated, choosing silence and withdrawal in the face of his clamping down. They had little of the free and easy movement of two young people together, and this lack of ease in their relationship would seem to militate against any physical consummation. It is difficult to believe that with the surface so tense they could have satisfactorily come together in bed, or even attempted it, even apart from Felice's being a well-brought-up young woman and Kafka's difficulty with all women except prostitutes. Furthermore, if their aim was to see if they were compatible, as part of a movement toward a second engagement,* then physical compatibility would have taken secondary place to their emotional, intellectual, and psychological sympathy with each other. The evidence, admittedly, is sketchy and leads only to speculation.

When Felice (on July 13) left and Kafka stayed on, he wrote of his terror of noise at the hotel, of his fleeing to the park to escape domestic noises, of his horror when he returned to his room — what had been her

---

*Their move toward this second, unofficial engagement came in a joint letter to Frau Bauer, on July 10. They assure her that the relationship between the two has altered for the better, and that their coming together here is a sign of their renewed commitment. Of course "beautiful Marienbad" had created a romantic setting, far as it was from the war in Berlin and Prague, and far from where their real lives were taking place.

room — to recognize he had returned too soon. He tried other places the next day, but everything was taken. The rabbi from Belz, mentioned earlier, was a distinguished visitor, and Kafka followed him around. He wrote extensively to Max Brod about this period, one of his most tumultuous in emotional terms, revealing his fear of the actual woman, Felice, behind the letters. Some of this was discussed in chapter 9, but since Kafka tells Brod things he would not even reveal in his *Diaries*, it is worth repeating: that he had never feared anything as much as being alone with Felice before the wedding. Yet in his torment, he says all that has now changed, that they have agreed to marry after the war and rent an apartment in Berlin, with each assuming responsibility for her- or himself. Kafka attempts to visualize it, and even while presenting it as their common vision he cannot help but mock the very idea of the working woman, Felice, and the husband, himself, feeding on milk and honey, lolling in bed, and feebly trying to make a living.

Kafka also relates his experience with the rabbi from Belz, describing it in considerable detail to Brod. He was evidently very impressed not so much with the rabbi himself but with the dignity of the occasion, the commitment of the Jews attending him, and the rabbi's own unmistakable integrity in areas he, Kafka, could not accept. If anything, the encounter touched him deeply *because* it underlined his own lack of commitment to anything, although he had been moving ever closer to a Zionist point of view and to an attention to historical Judaism — not matters of faith but matters of Jewishness in terms of survival and prosperity.

In a curious diary entry, dated July 20, Kafka responded to the meeting with the rabbi from Belz with a liturgical-sounding passage.

> Have mercy on me, I am sinful in every nook and cranny of my being. But my gifts are not contemptible; I had some small talents, squandered them, unadvised creature that I was, am now near my end just at a time when outwardly everything might at last turn out well for me. Don't thrust me in among the lost. . . . If I am condemned, then I am not only condemned to die, but also condemned to struggle till I die.[30]

The rhythms of the entry sound like a prayer, a trial run at God, as it were, and suggest that Kafka somehow wanted to bare himself, in some way confess to his self-absorption and inability to connect with others. The confessional aspect of the passage is surely linked to his recent stay with Felice, their meeting with Valli and Frau Kafka, in Franzensbad, and his need to reassess himself as suitor and potential husband. It was also related to his long-standing conflict between potential happiness, brought about by marriage and family, and potential despair, the result of his rejection of everything in favor of drift.

Yet as is characteristic of Kafka, good feelings, even if temporary ones, are accompanied by their opposite. He suffers a Manichaean struggle. He tells Felix Weltsch that though his boils have gone, he feels out of sorts generally, with headaches that will not go away. And on July 22, he enters another one of his stabbing-executioner phases, in a diary entry describing how a condemned man is sitting in his cell writing when the executioner comes in and asks if he is ready. The method of execution is, of course, the knife. "Having received no reply, the executioner opens his instrument case on the cot, chooses the daggers and even now attempts to touch up their several edges here and there." When asked again if he is ready, the prisoner becomes wild and uncontrollable, screaming that he cannot be put on his cot and stabbed to death; that since the executioner is a human being, if an execution is to take place, it must occur on a scaffold, with assistants and in the presence of magistrates. Intent on his knives and planning precisely what the condemned man says is impossible to conceive of, one man simply killing another, the executioner says nothing. The victim insists the judicial procedure is a form that must be followed. He demands to be transferred to another prison, where he may stay a long time but will not be executed. To all this, the executioner, loosening a new dagger from its cotton sheath, says, " 'You are probably thinking of those fairy tales in which a servant is commanded to expose a child but does not do so, and instead binds him over as apprentice to a shoemaker. Those are fairy tales; this, though, is not a fairy tale.' "

Considering Kafka's recent stay with Felice in fairy-tale Marienbad, his peaceful overtures to his family, and his expressions of some balance in his life, the diary entry is extraordinary. It suggests several factors in his life, primarily that no matter what occurred in the "above world" of so-called happiness (relationships, family, courtship), his "subterranean world" dominated and directed his imagination. But there had to be more. The use of knives suggests the intense desire to be ripped open, as though in some ritualistic procedure. More than merely pain is operative here: we see his need to sacrifice himself to establish balance in the world. Kafka is not pure victim here, but someone who must pay so as to create normalcy. Get rid of me, he appears to be suggesting, and ordinary life will return. It is the message of Gregor Samsa's death, of course, Kafka's archetypal expression of how the death of the marginal figure can restore normalcy.

The *Diaries* remain empty for the next month. Kafka tells his publisher he is no longer keen on issuing a collection of three stories ("The Judgment," "The Metamorphosis," and "In the Penal Colony") in a collection to be called *Punishments*, but he would agree to it if Wolff so desired. His progress on *The Trial* having more or less halted, Kafka was assuming he would produce no longer work in the foreseeable future. He further tells Wolff he would like to appear in *Der jüngste Tag* series, with his favorite, "The Judgment," appearing first. Kafka preferred each story as a separate volume, since he felt "The Judgment" and "In the Penal Colony" published together would "make a dreadful combination."[31] With "The Metamorphosis" mediating between them, there might be balance, but he leaned toward separate publication of "The Judgment" because it needed "open space" around it. The format of *Der jüngste Tag* series allowed for short works, and "The Judgment" did appear in October in book form. Kafka's comments indicate he saw his work as more than a printed story but as an artistic object as well. He was interested in the overall appearance of the piece, as he had been interested in the large print and wide margins of *Betrachtung*, his first published book, and as his desire for "open space" indicates. His concern with the visual was, apparently, connected to his sensitivity to developments in Modern art, in the establishment of an entire context for a work.

Kafka's correspondence with Felice becomes particularly heavy in August 1916; he was writing a letter of some length nearly every day. On August 15 he announces the fourth "anniversary" of their first meeting. Although his observations were still mixed with characteristic despair, overall they were calmer as he headed toward their second engagement. On August 18, Dr. Mühlstein gave him a relatively clean bill of health, diagnosing only nervous strain, without further complications. His advice was for Kafka to pursue a healthier routine, one that he had, however, been following for years: no smoking or drinking, the eating of more vegetables than meat, exercise, sleeping well at night. Except for the latter, which was impossible for him, Kafka could without difficulty take to this regime, but it was, of course, quite beyond the real point, which was the developing tuberculosis, detected the following year. All of his symptoms at this time point toward a pretubercular diagnosis: headaches, extreme nervous tension, inability to sleep, a sense of disharmony in his body, occasional feverish flashes, periods of languor and lack of will.

In his more relaxed way, Kafka was still cautioning Felice about their ever having children. As we cited above, he used the nineteenth-century writer Fontane as his spokesman, a man who made severe demands on his wife ostensibly to preserve the independence he needed as a writer. Kafka's game was of several kinds: to encourage their union, to discourage children from it, to encourage Felice in her association with the Jewish Home, to discourage anything in which he did not have a hand. The signals he was giving out were not acts of cruelty, but derived from his own uncertainties and gropings. He was not working (not until November would he return to serious writing), and yet he was still attempting to re-establish their relationship based on his need to write.

He was aware, even disturbed, about Fräulein Bloch's "suffering." He tells Felice not to desert Grete now and to be kind to her.[32] The nature of this "suffering" is unclear and cannot be ascribed to impregnation by Kafka, but it could have been connected to his impending reengagement to Felice and to Grete's feelings of abandonment. But even with his more relaxed tone with Felice, Kafka's diaries reflect some of the familiar tensions. He perceives himself, still, as a battleground of conflicting forces, and he vows never to let the blows against him go unanswered. He advises himself to escape officialdom, and to "start seeing what you are instead of calculating what you should become."[33] He says he must give up the comparisons he makes between himself and a Flaubert, a Kierkegaard, a Grillparzer, a comparison he calls "simply infantile." Unlike him, Flaubert and Kierkegaard "knew very clearly how matters stood with them, were men of decision, did not calculate but acted. But in your case — a perpetual succession of calculations, a monstrous four years' up and down."*[34] He admits the comparison with Grillparzer is valid, but then adds that the writer is not a proper one to imitate, apparently because, ironically, Grillparzer was too much a sufferer.

What is compelling is how his diary entries were fighting through a battle considerably different from the one he was revealing to Felice. The two, *Diaries* and letters, appear almost as parallels, but they in fact identify different aspects of the same man. Kafka's perception of dualities is far keener in the diary entries; but in the letters his desire for balance is far more pronounced, at least in his presentation of himself to Felice. Yet both are significant. The Flaubert and Kierkegaard dimensions did not drive out the bourgeois desire, but caught it up in a morbid struggle for the possession of Kafka's imagination. Much of the writing impasse at this and at an earlier time derived from his inability to resolve the internal struggles.

If it is possible to abstract Felice — that is, view her not as a flesh-and-blood woman in Berlin, but as a phantom of Kafka's imagination — then we can see she serves as a muse for his uncertainties. Put another way, Kafka needed her desperately so that he could measure within himself what it meant to be a writer, what he must sacrifice. Without her, he had no clear measure for that "other world," from which he had always assumed he was banished. With her, he glimpsed that world, and through her he was able to perceive what he must surrender if he was to validate himself as a writer. An abstract Felice, then, meant as much to Kafka as the real one, perhaps a good deal more. He hung on to her so possessively and made her believe in him, despite his frantic, lunatic manner, because she provided something outside him he could, ultimately, reject.

---

*Kafka's internal dialogues, in which he splits into self and "other," recall, as noted, Diderot's pioneering work in this area, *Rameau's Nephew* (written between 1761 and 1774), translated from the French by Goethe in 1805.

"The bringing up of children is a conspiracy on the part of adults," Kafka intones[35] — a Rousseauistic view of education Kafka was not really interested in except as a way of criticizing his own educational background. Whatever his views, along with Pfohl, from the institute, he did help in founding a clinic for the treatment of nervous diseases acquired during military service, which was opened in Rumburg, at the Frankenstein Clinic (Kafka had himself stayed in the Rumburg sanatorium in 1915).

At the same time, shifting ground, Kafka says he would have to tell their children that "owing to my origin, my education, disposition, environment I have nothing tangible in common" with his own faith. He says it may be otherwise with Felice, and that, since her memories might make her respond, it is all right with him. He is, apparently, not worried about training their children, since both he and Felice are fully secular, Westernized Jews, although she was concerned with appearances. His focus on this matter is of some interest, since it suggests he was trying to locate children in his future, even while discouraging Felice from thinking of them. He reviles synagogue attendance, telling Felice that his hours in the synagogue "were the rehearsals staged by hell for my later office life."[36] He equally berates Zionists who attend synagogue worship as people "trying to force their way into the synagogue under cover of the Ark of the Covenant, rather than entering calmly through the main door."

Control remains very important for his stability. A fragment of a letter to Felice, in his *Diaries* for October 18, becomes quite melodramatic. "You belong to me. I have made you mine. I can't believe that there was ever a woman in a fairy tale fought for harder and more desperately than I have fought for you within myself, from the beginning, and always anew, and perhaps forever. You belong to me then, and so my relation to your people is similar to my relation to my own." But this desire for control gives way to a free-running expression of hostile feelings toward his family, and theirs toward him. "Because I confront my family unceasingly flailing about me in a circle with knives, as it were, in order simultaneously to injure and defend them."[37] The knives, once more!

This statement coincides precisely with a series of remarks he made to Felice on family life as a "Chamber of Horrors," culminating in the great letter of October 19 (misdated as September 19), cited earlier.* Here, family life is "frenzied" and disallows freedom of the individual, generating feelings of extreme disgust. He realizes how his parents have fallen so far short of what he wants them to be and uses

---

*The letter Kafka dated as "September" must be moved to October because the matter included there fits so closely with material dated in the *Diaries* for October 18. In both, Kafka has worked himself up into a near frantic fit.

the image of knives to indicate how he both defends and attacks his family. It is a letter of such vehemence, such anger and revulsion, such expenditure of emotional energy, that Kafka seemed on the edge of losing his sanity, much less his perspective. He was now over thirty-three, and each wound was as fresh as though he were thirteen or twenty-three. What was driving him mad, however, was not only thoughts of family (although that factor loomed large) but thoughts of how he had reached an impasse with nothing to show since the fall of 1913 except sporadic work on *The Trial*. With this, his diary entries end for five and a half months, from October 20 to April 5, 1917. Some of the slack was taken up by what came to be called the "Eight Octavo Notebooks," which, except for one segment dated February 19, 1917, in the "First Octavo Notebook," remained undated; such entries could have been made at nearly any time in the next few years.

Kafka was biding his time, but doing so with extreme apprehension. He had announced to Kurt Wolff, his publisher, that he was waiting for a quieter period, "in saying which I am representing myself, at least superficially, as truly a man of our times."[38] He expects to be representative, awaits his fate, and hopes his imagination will flow again, as it will toward the end of the year. He agrees that "The Judgment" should not appear in *Der jüngste Tag* and announces to Wolff he will be reading ("In the Penal Colony") at the Galerie Goltz in Munich, on November 10. In a move that was to have a significant effect upon him, his favorite sister, Ottla, was seeking a place of her own. She had a secret life that even Kafka was unaware of, her relationship with a non-Jewish suitor, Josef David, and she needed a place where she could meet him. Kafka's parents would not, of course, have agreed to such an arrangement. They feared that if she married a non-Jew, she would be absorbed into Czech life and lost, with her children probably brought up as Catholics. Since she did not have many resources, she needed something very modest, and Kafka agreed to help her, since when she wasn't using the place, he could write there. What they found was a small house, really a tiny, boxy cottage, in the Alchimistengässchen (Alchemist, or Golden, Lane, suitably named), in the Hradčany Castle area overlooking Prague. In disrepair, but very cheap, the house contained one room, a sleeping loft, and a kitchen area.* It was available in November, and it proved a happy event for Kafka. Within a short time, he would produce "The Warden of the Tomb" and "The Hunter Gracchus," not major works but signs he could still write.

This was not his sole November experience, however, for when he went for his reading on the tenth, he met Felice, for a two-day reac-

---

*It is presently a bookstore, with a plaque outside, in Czech, saying that Kafka lived there, which is technically not true. The owner, Františka Sofrová Michlová, reclaimed her house in 1917.

quaintanceship and the first since Marienbad. Here conditions were quite different, the romantic idyll of Marienbad giving way to the reality of Munich and to the anxieties Kafka suffered about reading. At such affairs, he always felt like an interloper, especially when he was not even writing. The two quarreled: Kafka on edge, Felice expecting perhaps some of the more settled atmosphere they enjoyed at Marienbad. The quarrel that stuck with them occurred in a pastry shop. Kafka tried to assure her, almost two weeks later, that it would not recur. Our quarrels "won't have the tension of the hurried meeting, that vague nightmarish transitory feeling which adds to bitterness, and so will be borne merely as part of ordinary human misery. You will strike the stone, and the stone will be only slightly scratched."[39] But the combination of events made Kafka's nerves raw. At a later time, he described the work he read as a "filthy story," the audience as cold and indifferent. Rilke, whose taste in Kafka was strange, preferring "The Stoker" to "The Metamorphosis" and "In the Penal Colony," may even have been in the audience. Kafka felt the trip was disastrous. Summing up the entire episode, a significant one because it brought him back to writing, he told Felice, "I have abused my writing as a means of getting to Munich, where otherwise I have no intellectual ties, and after 2 years of not writing had the incredible impudence to read in public, while for the past year and a half in Prague I didn't read a word even to my best friends."[40]

The main event was to take place in Ottla's tiny rented house on a narrow street, with the Castle and Saint Vitus's Cathedral in the near distance. Though Kafka planned to move from his room on Langenstrasse to something more commodious in the Schönborn Palace (the present U.S. embassy) on the Marktgasse, he remained in his unpleasant room, took dinner, still, with his parents, and wrote late at night at Ottla's, apparently without regard for her own reason for having taken the place, to see her fiancé. It seemed, for a time, to signal an upturn in his fortunes.

The work itself was full of Modernistic techniques and attitudes, deeply gloomy, ironic, morbid, hateful of self and society, and enormously meaningful for any understanding of Kafka and the twentieth century. He was reaching into the deepest part of his imaginative net, where he kept allegories, parables, paradoxes, and expressionistic forms. "The Guardian of the Tomb," at the end of November or the beginning of December, is only fragmentary, but it brings together many of Kafka's concerns. Ostensibly a play in its dialogue form, it is in words analogous to what abstract, nonrepresentational painters were attempting. In some respects it is a postcubist, predada piece of dadaism: words used as lines, planes, geometrical shapes, lacking in objective reality but profoundly linked to inner meanings through echoes and reverberations.

Although the brief fragment is often labeled "expressionistic," its real subject is time and space, not the threat to empires, although that theme is there too. The Guardian (or Warden) watches over the Prince's vault (no one, incidentally, has a name). The Prince, planning to add another guard to stand down in the tomb itself, calls him to an audience. The Prince explains that in his family the tomb or vault is the borderline between the human sphere and the other, and it is on this borderline that he wishes to place a guard. The old guard, the original "warden," at sixty is already very old and seemingly close to dying. The problem, as he sees it, is that people might want to get out of the Prince's park, not in, as the Prince himself fears. His struggle is against an unnamed Duke, about whom the Guardian or Warden says, "Only sometimes I'm afraid that the Duke might lose me between his fingers and he won't know any more that he is fighting."[41]

Located out of sight is the question of who is in and who is out, whether borders seal off those who want to enter or those who want to escape. It is concerned with victories — who really wins when both sides appear to be losing. The tomb is itself an ambiguous locale, an emblem: it makes death the focus of activity, forcing all experience "underground," yet here it often seems as full of life as death. In this respect, everything is "relocated," as it would be in *The Castle*. This fragment, in fact, suggests that *The Castle*, more than three years away, was already taking shape in Kafka's imagination.

The guard's words have a dreamlike effect, like those passages in Mallarmé's poetry where object and subject melt into each other, so that borderlines are blurred. The Guardian speaks of how sometimes, in the morning, he lies down out of breath, too weak to open his eyes, when a soft being, "moist and hairy" to the touch, a straggler, Countess Isabella, comes to him. She feels about him, puts her hand in his beard, lets her entire body glide over his neck, all the time pleading that he should allow the others in but let her out. The soft and hairy Countess Isabella is a typical Kafka creation, as much a gigantic bug as one of his transformed animals, on the borderline between animal and human life.

In the darkness of the locale, part of that dark setting characteristic of many dramas of this time, especially Kokoschka's *Murderer, Hope of Women*, the darkness denotes borderlines, frontiers, crevices between life and death or between human and other forms. We find an undefined room in an undefined castle, unnamed characters, no sense of everyday reality, only those medieval or even mythical designations like Prince, Duke, Guardian, or Warden. The entire piece seems to emerge as one of Kafka's nightmarish dreams, where dark interiors go on forever, like Chinese boxes ever receding from the human eye. The dialogue set into the play is not intended to cast light on a mysterious event, as is characteristic of most drama, but to create further obfuscation. The more the talk the deeper the mystery; language only creates additional interpretations, which themselves escape rational thought. Words are not illuminative but part of a darkening process. The Princess speaks the final words: "But I know it is getting blacker and blacker, this time it is an autumn and beyond all measure."

This is the first of a whole sequence of works in which Kafka is measuring death — his own, society's, all of Europe's — against possibilities of life, and finding death more significant. He is, as it were, on his deathbed and seeking some revelation that makes life significant. As long as people want to get out, not in, then death has triumphed. Fragmentary and incomplete as it is, "The Guardian of the Tomb" signals a new stage in Kafka's development, more surreal, more abstract, more symbolic and allegorical than before. Those two years of inactivity, we now see, were not wasted, for once he started (late in 1916), the work began to pour forth. His major revelation is that the object-filled world of "The Metamorphosis" and *The Trial* is insufficient as a portrayal of what he was seeking. Now, he had to enter seams, interstices, creases. Crawling into places where no other writer has ever gone, except perhaps Gogol and Dostoevsky, he emerges with one parable after another. All of them concern how we might seek life in a world of death, how we can maintain some hope when all processes seem hopeless, how we can yearn after absolutes in a world seemingly gone mad.

"The Hunter Gracchus" ("Der Jäger Gracchus"), in two fragments, is borderline material as well, concerning a life trying to emerge even as death is pressing to enter — or vice versa. For Gracchus is already dead, even as he speaks of being alive in a certain sense. Kafka has reshaped the legendary story of the Flying Dutchman,* in which a man is cast out to sail the seas forever unless he can gain the love of a pure woman, making it fit his own sense of the artist's journey. Gracchus is a hunter, but only in the sense that he has hunted for some truth beyond the visible, only to find death in life. Alive and dead, Gracchus can travel to that borderline experience Kafka was seeking, begun with Joseph K. and to some extent completed by K. of *The Castle* and later by the Hunger Artist.

His ship having gone off course through a "wrong turn of the wheel," Gracchus survives only to die in the Black Forest when he falls from a cliff while following a chamois. The place of the fall, given its name and reputation, is itself emblematic of deep mystery. But this hunter is after bigger game than a chamois: he is pursuing nothing less than meaning: "For nobody knows of me, and if anyone knew he would not know where I could be found, and if he knew where I could be found, he would not know how to deal with me, he would not know

---

*In an April 6, 1917, diary entry, Kafka refers to the ghostly ship, which pulls into port every two or three years, and belongs to the Hunter Gracchus.

how to help me."[42] The artist here is inhabiting his own space and time continuum, into which no one from normal life can follow. It is the artist, in a romantic sense, doomed to sail the seas, fated to wander, caught midway, always, between life and death. The fact that Gracchus has fallen into a ravine and died there is not known to anyone; he has returned, after all, only to communicate that he has left. The fate of the artist is no less ghostly: he is a specter in the life of ordinary people.*

The other Gracchus episode, called "The Hunter Gracchus: A Fragment," is, if anything, more spectral. Here a narrator emerges and somehow intertwines himself with the dead hunter. The narrator wants to understand, and Gracchus tries to calm him. The narrator plies the hunter with queries about what has occurred until Gracchus pleads, "Don't ask any more. Here I am, dead, dead, dead. Don't know why I'm here."[43] As far as he knows or says, he was loaded onto the death ship. In both pieces, the hunter wonders what he did wrong, what was unusual about his life. If he did wrong, what should he have created in its stead? Lying in that twilight zone between life and death, the writer-artist indicates he has done all he was supposed to, and yet something went wrong. Was it his own fault? Circumstance? Some historical twist he is unaware of? These will become Kafka's most insistent questions, part of that process that made Kafka Kafkaesque.

A more nearly completed piece from this general period was "A Country Doctor" ("Ein Landarzt"), which appeared during Kafka's lifetime in Die neue Dichtung, published by Wolff in 1918, and in a collection of Kafka's tales, also published by Wolff, in 1919. Although a story about a doctor, someone who saves lives, it moves us like the others toward a border between life and death. Perhaps modeled on Kafka's country doctor uncle, whom Kafka often visited, the doctor is called out on an emergency visit, but he lacks horses. Suddenly the necessary horses emerge from the pigpen. The surreal appearance of the animals sets the tone for the story, caught as it is between conscious and unconscious. At first, when he arrives at his destination, the doctor finds the sick boy relatively well, but then he discovers a wound near the hip, crawling with worms "rose-red and blood-spotted . . . wriggling from their fastness in the interior of the wound towards the light, with small white heads and many little legs."

These are typical Kafka insects, animals, transformed people, and they in some uncanny way foreshadow the disease or bacteria eating away at his own lungs, also an unforeseen "wound." The revelation of

*Yet his description has strong religious overtones, ritualistic rather than spiritual. Gracchus lies on a wooden pallet, wrapped in a filthy winding sheet, his limbs covered with a woman's shawl, a sacramental candle at his head, the pallet described as a bier, his hair and beard matted — a crucifixion of sorts. That the story is self-reflexive comes in the name "Gracchus," from the Italian gracchio, crow or jackdaw. Also, Gracchus's body comes to Riva, where Kafka vacationed with the Brod brothers.

the wound suggests the festering, hidden nature of an injury, that universal, metonymic Kafkan wound. This wound lies behind all efforts of individual will, all assertions of independent action, all choice, all attempts at happiness or at controlling circumstance. Every dimension of life must eventually come back to the hidden wound, which ends only in death itself.* One can never escape the wound, or withdraw from its inevitability; it is the "other" in all transactions, although one must hope and go forward as though no such wound exists. This particular wound has a religious dimension, since it is something of a rose, a devotional symbol, linked in some mysterious way with the stigmata, the sign that Jesus Christ has visited one. But it is a form of stigmata in another sense as well, signifying the presence not only of the Christian lord, but also of the destroyer of the individual.

Recognizing the hopelessness of his quest, with the boy's death inevitable, the doctor wants to return through a blizzard to save a servant girl, aptly named Rose, from a ferocious groom. His dilemma is terrible: to get back through horrendously foul weather, to give up on saving the rose-wounded boy, and to "save" his servant Rose from the "disgusting groom." The doctor pictures himself as stripped of all defenses, and we recognize he is actually the one dying. If he fails to cure the boy, the peasants in a dreamy, fantastic scene will strip and kill him. But the boy himself has vacillated between wishing to live and wishing to die, even as the doctor tries to reassure him he can recover, that he has seen worse wounds. The story winds down with all negatives: the horses crawl like old men; the doctor feels he will never reach home; his flourishing practice is done for; his successor is robbing him; the groom is raging, with Rose as his victim. "Naked, exposed to the frost of this most unhappy of ages, with an earthly vehicle, unearthly horses, old man that I am, I wander astray. My fur coat is hanging from the back of the gig, but I cannot reach it, and none of my limber pack of patients lifts a finger. Betrayed! Betrayed! A false alarm on the night bell once answered — it cannot be made good, not ever."[44]

The negativism of the enterprise, which started out as an act of hope and salvation, is now vintage Kafka. Not only has the mission been defeated, but life itself has been frustrated. The doctor has, as it were, thrown the dice and failed to abolish chance. His situation has, indeed, reinforced the "dicing," and his failure comes from his effort to impose choice on the situation or on himself. But such negativism was not for Kafka defeat; rather, it was merely the signal that all effort and endeavor must be made against such eventualities.

"The Bridge," possibly written a little later, in the winter of 1917, fits into this general sequence of stories beginning with "A Country

---

*The death of sex also. The wound creates a sexual image so disgusting that sex itself is made to seem maggoty, a fearful experience fraught with disease.

Doctor." It has the quality of a dream sequence in which the narrator is himself a bridge, stretched over a ravine. This bridge is not on any map, so the narrator waits anxiously for a stray tourist. He hears steps and steadies himself for the weight. The tourist comes onto the bridge, plunging the iron point of his stick into the narrator's bushy hair and letting it lie there (the familiar "stabbing motion" of Kafka's other fictions). Suddenly, the tourist jumps with both feet. The narrator shudders but cannot call out. Who was this tourist? A child? A suicide? Was it all a dream? The narrator, the bridge, turns around to see his tormentor, and with that he begins to fall, until he is torn and "transpierced by the sharp rocks."[45] Little known, "The Bridge" is a magnificent example of Kafka's simple but resonant prose, and a brilliant instance of his use of what are now his characteristic emblems. Once again, the bridge is the writer-artist, once again he is forced into an impossible role, once more he is destroyed by some ordinary act, still again he is stabbed or pierced. All this within 350 words or so!

Kafka was now off at a gallop, writing short pieces much stronger and more defined than those in *Meditation*, his earlier volume of brief prose fictions. In quick order, he wrote "Up in the Gallery," "A Fratricide," "The Next Village," "A Visit to the Mine," "Jackals and Arabs," "The Bucket Rider," "The New Advocate." One of the shortest and most compelling is "A Fratricide." This brief story (a little more than two pages) involves the familiar use of a knife as the murder weapon. The murderer, Schmar, takes up his post one night and awaits his victim, a man named Wese (*die Schmarre* is a "slash" or "cut"; *wesen* means "to be" or "to live"). Unknown to Schmar, he is being observed by Pallas, a private citizen. Pallas's name recalls Athena, goddess of wisdom and knowledge, and indeed a moral dilemma is at the story's center. Schmar awaits his victim in the cold night air, his weapon "half a bayonet and half a kitchen knife."[46] He attempts to sharpen his weapon while he waits, first against the pavement bricks and then against his boot sole.

Before the killing actually occurs, Pallas observes everything in preparation, choosing to stand by without protest. Meanwhile, Frau Julia Wese is waiting for her husband to return from his office. Kafka has drawn a dramatic scene, with its components of lurking murderer, waiting wife, observant onlooker, victim preparing for his final journey. The characteristic tone of the entire drama is silence. Kafka has managed to turn potentially brutal action into stasis. The doorbell sounds, and Wese emerges. Frau Wese, satisfied her husband is on the way, closes the window. But the bell is also a sign to the others: Pallas sets himself for the coming event, and Schmar presses himself against the pavement, expectant. The trap has been set, and all that remains is for Wese to walk into it.

Observing only the dark blue and gold of the evening, Wese is of course innocent of his coming fate: "Nothing up there drew together in a pattern to interpret the immediate future for him." Everything "stayed in its senseless, inscrutable place." Schmar stands on tiptoe as Wese approaches, cries out that his victim will never see Julia again, and stabs three times, twice into the throat and finally deep into the stomach area. "Water rats, slit open, give out such a sound as came from Wese." Schmar now is manic with joy, flinging the knife away, and crying out how blissful murder is. "The relief, the soaring ecstasy from the shedding of another's blood!"[47] He rhapsodizes over Wese's blood oozing away into the dark earth and regrets that his victim was not merely a bladder of blood so he, Schmar, could stamp on him and obliterate his body into nothingness.

Observing all, Pallas "chokes on the poison in his body." He calls out to Schmar that he missed nothing, and the two peer at each other. Frau Wese comes rushing up, her face suddenly aged, her fur coat swinging open. She falls on Herr Wese's body, her body now belonging to him, the fur coat "spreading over the couple like the smooth turf of a grave belonging to the crowd."[48] Schmar is apprehended, and, fighting the last of his nausea, is led away by a policeman. As in a Verdi opera, revenge has been played out.

Rarely has Kafka been this bloody; it is as though the blood drawn by Schmar's knife will be the blood gushing from his own throat when his tubercular condition finally emerges later in the year. Like the images in Poe's "The Masque of the Red Death," the dominating substance is blood, the dominant color red. The moral center, forsaken by Pallas, shifts to the question of how the inner rage of an individual in society can be gratified.

Kafka appears to have written a brief parable on the war. That his own rage was active is clear from his letters about his family; his letters to Felice and his descriptions of their quarrels are still another sign. The greatest indication was his repeated use of knife images, to slice, stab, shave, and ultimately kill. The rage to destroy oneself for lack of others persists, not as an act of suicide, but as some means of regaining a self that has been lost. The knife images are not only self-destructive, but part of a willed need to kill off the old so that something new will come. In this respect, Kafka was sacrificing his life so that he could return to write. Holding him back were his father, Felice, and his old self; all had to be eliminated.

There is a commonality to these brief stories or parables pouring out from Kafka's pen at this time: a bitterly ironic, mocking tone, a sense of overwhelming desolation and emptiness, an interest in metaphysical questions presented through seemingly narrow situations, a response, however veiled, to the events of the war. The man who had headed Austria since 1848 and who had been emperor of Hungary since 1867, Franz Josef, died in 1916. His death came just before the empire was to be smashed militarily, but his death itself, after so many years of rule, heralded the end for the Dual Monarchy and its attempts to hold on against the newer empire, Germany, on one hand, the Allies on the other. All this becomes absorbed into Kafka's work.

Typical is "The New Advocate," in which the advocate, Dr. Bucephalus, shares the name of Alexander the Great's horse. Difficult though his position is, as an advocate and through his association with the historical horse, the doctor is admitted to the bar. He does not walk but mounts the marble steps, so that they ring beneath his feet. Something is expected of him, but there are no more Alexanders in the world; there are, however, plenty of men who know how to murder people. The skill to reach over a banquet table and pink a friend with a lance is still practiced, but the Alexanders who can blaze a trail to India are no more. While the gates to India in Alexander's time were not breached, today's gates have receded, and no one any longer points the way. Many carry swords but only to brandish them. "So perhaps it is really best to do as Bucephalus has done and absorb oneself in law books. In the quiet lamplight, his flanks unhampered by the thighs of a rider, free and far from the clamor of battle, he reads and turns the pages of our ancient tomes."[49]

Despite the clear political allusions to the war and to the coming demise of the monarchy, Kafka's words point inward. As a writer, he feels disarmed, a potential Alexander or Samson who has been shorn of his virility and forced to retreat into law. His sword dangles, no longer an effective weapon, if it ever was. One of Kafka's related parables (or paradoxes) is called "Alexander the Great," and here the circling back to himself is clear. He says it is conceivable that Alexander, despite his excellent army, his martial successes, and his sense of power, may have been left standing on the bank of the Hellespont and did not cross it, "not out of fear, not out of indecision, not out of infirmity of will,"[50] but because there is some center of gravity that pins him, something beyond will, desire, and desire for conquest. It is the invisible force Kafka had cited most of his mature life, and it went beyond anything any doctor could diagnose. Life weighs him down so that Alexander, like Napoleon, cannot even move.

With these parables, ironic tales, and parodic forms, Kafka had become a prophet, telling and foretelling what the empire had become and was becoming. Looking deep within himself, he had found every dimension of present and future. Using his own psychological insights, he developed, as seer or clairvoyant, as conscience of his race, locating himself in a tradition that went back to Baudelaire and was being rediscovered, among Kafka's contemporaries, by James Joyce and Marcel Proust. All three, together, in fact, become the voice of the twentieth century, with Kafka as most representative, because his tragic vision, leavened by wit, mockery, and irony, became the most prophetic of all.

Appearing to be so fleeting, these brief tales are corrosive and brutal in their expression of life so far beneath the surface of most people's lives as to seem emanations from another world. In one respect, they *are* emanations, but that "other world" was Kafka's perception of collapse, disintegration, reshaping, and transformation, expressed by animals and insects, with the tone sardonic and paradoxical.

In this early to mid-1917 group,[51] "A Report [or Statement, Advice] to an Academy" ("Ein Bericht für eine Akademie") is central to Kafka's thinking. It is, in one regard, the end of an era for him, the beginning of another, and in this way prophetic of what was occurring in Europe and what would happen to it shortly afterward. It is, characteristically, a tale of transformation — not Ovid's *Metamorphoses*, in which people change into other forms, but Kafka's uniquely transformational-allegorical reshaping, here from animal into man. In this story the figure giving a report to the academy was once an ape, but has not been one for the past five years. Since he is making an evolutionary change "forward" even while trying to recall what it was like going "backward," he has difficulties in giving his report at this stage. The difficulty is that the forward stage does not seem superior to the backward one, part of Kafka's attack not only on progress but on the progressive element in evolutionary theory itself. As an ape, the creature was not free, and what he needed was a way out, crushed as he was against a wooden wall in his cell. "To get out somewhere, to get out!" is the sole demand he makes.

To gain freedom, he starts to take on the mannerisms and habits of human beings, inasmuch as that appears to be the way toward liberation. But no one promised him that if he became like them the bars of his cage would be removed. "Such promises for apparently impossible contingencies are not given."[52] As an ape, he learned to imitate people; he acquired, for example, the knack of spitting, like the crewmen on the ship. They spit in each other's faces, with the main difference being that while he licked his face clean afterward, they did not. He soon masters a pipe. Like the men, he too is fighting against "the nature of apes," only he has the more difficult task. The ape is badly wounded, in pain from a cheek wound whose red scar gives him the name "Red Peter," and a more severe wound in the hip, which has caused a limp. This, together with his desire for freedom from his cell, made him realize that life as an ape had its disadvantages. He had to become a man.

Thus the ape finds himself in the ambiguous position of doing precisely what man does: man fights against regressing into apedom, and the ape struggles to achieve manhood by denying its apeness. The potentialities of the situation are enormous, given Kafka's biting irony, which was directed not only against his countrymen but against himself. Like so many other pieces in the 1917 group, "A Report to an Academy" looks forward to "A Hunger Artist," both with caged crea-

tures, both attempting a transformation. But in larger terms the ape
trying to "ape" others recalls the position of the Prague Jew attempting
to imitate the Gentile, to acculturate or assimilate, to take on characteristics that will let him "get out" of his cage or situation. But the
irony is that those he is imitating to achieve manhood are not themselves quite men. Jews and Czechs here become intertwined in a great
evolutionary drama, about which Kafka can comment, "I repeat: there
was no attraction for me in imitating human beings; I imitated them
because I needed a way out, and for no other reasons."[53] The ape faces
only two alternatives: the zoo or the variety stage (Yiddish theater?).
But since the zoo means only a new cage, the variety stage becomes
his goal.

With that object in mind, he educates himself. "And so I learned
things, gentlemen. Ah, one learns when one has to; one learns when
one needs a way out; one learns at all costs. One stands over oneself
with a whip [Kafka's second favorite weapon, after the knife]; one flays
oneself at the slightest opposition." His ape nature begins to diminish,
and in a twist of role-playing his first teacher himself almost turns into
an ape and is taken away to a mental hospital. With several teachers, he
manages to change. "With an effort which up till now has never been
repeated I managed to reach the cultural level of an average European.
In itself that might be nothing to speak of, but it is something insofar
as it has helped me out of my cage and opened a special way out for me,
the way of humanity."[54] Of course his transformation into humanity
leaves him with man's own apelike level of intelligence and practice.
As a former ape, he gives performances, has a manager, and now is giving his report, in the language of science, German. He achieves a level
of success: the performances, banquets, scientific receptions, social
gatherings, at all of which he is a focal point. But when he comes home
from these affairs, he finds waiting for him his mistress, a half-trained
little chimpanzee, with "the insane look of the bewildered half-broken
animal in her eye," which only he sees. This chimpanzee recalls to him
his own dilemma, for the chimp is only halfway there, between apedom and manhood. She has *him* but no identity of her own.

Kafka plays in and out of his own life. He is of course, in one reading, that ape who has become human, but even as he gains success in
the human world, he is not completely removed from being an ape. The
half-trained chimp is not quite Felice, but she is the bewildered mistress or fiancée of a creature like Kafka, who lacks clear definitions:
neither ape nor man. In another sense (and no reading is definitive or
absolute), Kafka observes himself in animal-man terms as a way of revealing his division between writer and ordinary person.

In one guise, the ape is the artist-writer: communicating a report,
conveying information, himself having undergone a transformation
that affords him insight into other forms of experience. The rest of

mankind lacks that sensibility or sensitivity. In still another respect, Kafka the Jew is calling attention to the Jew's unique situation: seeking acculturation and assimilation in a city and country clearly not his, which can never be his, mirroring Kafka as a stranger to any meaningful background. This returns us, and Kafka, to his sense of the Western European Jew, who belongs nowhere, has no firm beliefs, who is, whatever his temporary refuge, an eternal wanderer. Kafka's sharply ironic story owes much to Baudelaire, and especially to his "Albatross," that ungainly bird, representative of the artist, which is so maltreated by the ship's crew, a source of mockery because of its ungainliness and inability to fit. The crew is human but closer to animals, while the bird, an animal, has the higher sensibilities of humans.

By the time of "A Report to an Academy," written probably in the spring of 1917, Kafka was able to encapsulate enormous amounts of meaning into a brief, terse story. In formal terms, his "story" is almost shapeless, often little more than an expression of sensibility or a subjective outpouring, somewhat akin to an analytic session in its pursuit of a stream of thoughts held together only by the speaker's intelligence. There is, in most instances, little outside static or interference, nothing that would answer back or create a tension. All the conflict resides in the speaker, in a kind of monodrama, what Arnold Schoenberg, in musical drama, caught in "Der Erwartung" ("Expectation"). The mode has no verifiability, no evidence, nothing but the testimony of the person responding to a condition or feeling. Seemingly formless, these stories can be self-indulgent, or they can be the product of a mind adapting Freudian analysis to all levels of experience.

"Up in the Gallery"* is barely a page in length. At a circus performance, a spectator is confronted by a dilemma. If he were to watch the "frail, consumptive equestrienne" (herself a foreshadowing of the hunger artist) being whipped around and around for months on end without respite, the spectator, perhaps a young visitor, is sure he would rush from the gallery and shout, "Stop!" But this is not the way it goes. Instead, the ringmaster is all deference to her, "as if she were his own most precious granddaughter," and shouts to her only in admiration. When her act ends, he lifts her down, kisses her on both cheeks, and finds that the audience's ovation is hardly sufficient. The equestrienne herself is full of her triumph. At this, the spectator or visitor "lays his face on the rail before him, and sinking into the closing march as into a heavy dream, weeps without knowing it."[55]

What the visitor seeks is the cruelty implicit in the artistic performance. If that cruelty is present, then he can enter into it by rushing down to stop the terrible suffering. But if the act is part of an audience-pleasing episode, in which everyone conspires to cater to spectator

---

*Surely inspired by Georges Seurat's *Cirque*, which Kafka saw in the Louvre in Paris.

tastes, then there is no sacrifice, no martyrdom, no artistic achievement. There is simply performance, a selling out. For that, the spectator can only weep, for what may have created an exalted feeling now descends into a commercial enterprise.

Food is never distant from this vision of the artist. In a story from a somewhat later date, Kafka creates an entire political parable on the barbarity of eating meat, and it too prefigures the linkage between food and artistry in "A Hunger Artist." It is remarkable to see, in retrospect, how Kafka could adapt his own response to food to the element that meant most to him, his writing and the role of the artist-writer. Like a painter with paint or a composer with notes, or a sculptor with metal and stone, Kafka "sculpted" or "painted" food into his equations. "An Old Manuscript" chronicles the memories of a cobbler who watches as nomads enter the country, despite the country's system of defense (like the Great Wall of China, in Kafka's later story of that name). The nomads are barbarians from the north, perhaps the Russians, but more an archetypal barbarian based on Kafka's perception of the Czech Gentile. They are hordes on horseback; they live outdoors and have turned the peaceful square into a stable.

The intrusion or invasion leads to the breakdown of order, the beginning of anarchy — the clash between some social routine and the habits of an alien people who are completely disruptive. In a central episode (of this two-page story), the nomads eat a live ox, tearing morsels from the living animal with their bare teeth, then lying around as if drunk. But even before that scene of ultimate desecration of food, the nomads establish themselves as voracious meat eaters, who even feed meat to their horses. Their meat eating sets off the nomads from everyone else, as it sets off their horses. Kafka even has the cobbler report that the nomads communicate with each other in a language of their own, "much as jackdaws do" (a personalizing of the matter, with the equation of *jackdaw* and his own name). These almost cannibalistic people, with the language of jackdaws, recall Kafka's paternal grandfather, a ritual butcher, and by implication they serve as an indictment of his own family. The scene of horses lying at one end of a meat joint, the nomads at the other, creates a picture of barbarism reminiscent of Bosch.

The town cannot stop the delivery of meat because it fears what the nomads might do; actual cannibalism could be the next stage. Near the end of this brief piece, we glimpse the emperor at his window, but in this situation his authority is useless. He spends all his time "in the innermost gardens." The cobbler points out that it is left "to us artisans and tradesmen to save our country; but we are not equal to such a task. . . . This is a misunderstanding of some kind; and it will be the ruin of us."[56] This is clearly a political statement, intertwined though it is with the personal: that the people, not the new emperor, will have to save the country, or at least the village. The political extension of this idea is that the nomad-barbarians are always at the gate, waiting to break through as soon as leadership is weak. "An Old Manuscript," however brief, links several of Kafka's themes and concerns. With Franz Josef dead, and his jejune successor little more than a caretaker, presiding over a disintegrating empire, with the war being lost and Russian invasion imminent, with his own personal fortunes in disarray except for these tales themselves, with a physical precondition of tuberculosis, Kafka was writing on the edge of chaos and anarchy. The cobbler's "old manuscript" is really the new manuscript chronicling the meeting of several conditions: society crumbling, individual fortunes in jeopardy, and red meat as the symbol of disintegration.

One other ramification of the story, and not uncharacteristic of several pieces in this grouping, is the lack of a father figure. What the cobbler calls out for, explicitly and implicitly, is a patriarchal figure who can seize the situation and reverse it. The emperor's vacillation — he has drawn in the nomads but cannot drive them out — is at the center of the entire pageant. Lacking his force, the cobbler can only write; he cannot act, and yet he says that only action on the part of the people can reverse the situation.*

Both "The Bucket Rider" and "A Visit to a Mine" may owe something to current events, to a coal shortage in the first, and to labor trouble, but they are far more attuned to Kafka's own sensibility than to external events. They are both of a piece with Kafka's de-emphasis of objects and his artistic reshaping of them into surreal landscapes. "The Bucket Rider" characteristically stresses details that cohere only at a level well beyond the page on which they appear. In its presentation of a frozen world in which the human will is baffled, the story is also existentialist. With its evocation of cold, the beginning indicates the lot of an individual who may perish for lack of a basic commodity, coal, and yet he cannot obtain it by normal means. For Kafka's rider, as for his country doctor in another context, the unreachable dealer becomes, as it were, a god who will dispense life-sustaining coal if only he can be reached.

In this story, in which almost nothing occurs and yet in which everything seems to exist, Kafka exposes a cruel, uncaring world where the most ordinary objects are stretched into new shapes and new meanings. Like many other Kafka protagonists, the rider must subordinate

---

*An even briefer piece called "A Common Confusion," from a somewhat later date, reinforces the idea that no one can resolve conflicts. With almost no content, only process, "A Common Confusion" reveals how one can never know anything, one can never bring things together; even when a meeting seems possible, something like a twisted leg will interfere. Energy is expended on tasks that go nowhere; all effort ends up in delay. The episode recalls the emperor who can only sit tight and wait, or the emperor so enfolded and enclosed by walls that he is irrelevant.

his will to the will of others; without the coal dealer's decision to give him fuel, he will not survive. Such is the absurdity of a universe he cannot hope to understand — an "absurdity" in the sense of elements that refuse to cohere or form a discernible pattern. Absurdity, however, goes even further, for the rider never encounters the dealer. Like K., in *The Castle*, who is intercepted before he reaches his destination, the rider finds his plea intercepted by the dealer's wife, and it is she who relays the misinformation back to her husband. Thus, the rider fails to make contact with the one person who can possibly help him. Without help, understanding, or identity, he ascends to a frozen world, locked into himself and cursing the cruelty of God's creation. The bucket rider may rebel against the order of things, but as a rebel he paradoxically makes a better victim. In Kafka's shaping, the rider's rebellion turns into absurdity when the expression of it falls upon deaf ears. He becomes a victim, a defeated rebel, a cosmic fool: a little-known figure among many better-known Kafka performers.

"A Visit to a Mine" has far less definition than "The Bucket Rider," which is itself a story that blurs at the edges. It is about displacement and dispossession, the Prague motif. The miners watch a procession of self-confident chief engineers who have come to bore new galleries; they are making the initial survey, in what seems a brief glimpse of the surveyor of *The Castle*. Most of the piece is devoted to a description of the engineers, senior and junior ones, important and less important ones. But the most cocky among them is the porter himself, although he is not even permitted to touch the delicate survey instruments. The main point of the story concerns the people for whom the mine is essential to life and yet, in Kafka's construction, play no role except as observers. The point of "Mine," accordingly, is the displacement of the main players by those who move in and temporarily take over. Into the mining-industrial complex of Bohemia, Kafka has introduced Prague marginality: Jew and miner blended.

"Jackals and Arabs" is an exercise in many of Kafka's preoccupations: teeth, whips, struggles of people or groups to maintain their separation from others, hatreds that exist among those sharing a common territory, the inconclusiveness of outcome. The story is formed as a kind of emblematic tale of Jews (jackals) and Czechs (Arabs). The latter clearly have the upper hand, but the jackals seek their own kind of justice. " 'We [jackals] want to be troubled no more by Arabs; room to breathe; a skyline cleansed of them, no more bleating of sheep knifed by an Arab; every beast to die a natural death; no interference till we have drained the carcass empty and picked its bones clean. Cleanliness, nothing but cleanliness is what we want.' "[57] The jackals ask the Northerner, who is the narrator, to help them by slitting the throats of the Arabs with a small pair of sewing scissors.

The jackals may speak of their exile among the Arabs, but they don't want to kill their enemy directly; all the water of the Nile couldn't cleanse them of that sin. But even as they speak to the Northerner, two young beasts get their teeth into his coat and shift so that he cannot get up. The older jackals explain that these are training jackals, that overall they are all poor creatures who have nothing but their teeth. In their anguish, they feel Arabs want to maintain them as slaves. When the Arabs approach the Northerner, they tell him that the jackals are fools, but they are liked anyway as dogs, as finer dogs than any of the Northerner's might be. When a camel carcass is thrown down in their midst, the jackals revert to the behavior they know best: they attack the carrion with their teeth, until they are piled so thickly on the carcass they seem mountain-high. To show their superiority, the Arabs wield whips on the muzzles of the guzzling beasts, until the Northerner stays the arm of the caravan leader. He agrees to leave the jackals to their business, and they get ready to break camp.

Kafka's presentation of the plight of the oppressed jackals is not particularly sympathetic. If they do play out the situation of Diaspora Jews living in Prague or Bohemia, the Diaspora Jew is presented as predatory. The Arabs themselves reveal little, nor need they, since, invested with power, they do not have to explain themselves. Kafka's insights into empire and bureaucracy made him recognize that such elements do not need to justify themselves; they act, they do not explain. The story, accordingly, should be read as a tale of perpetual conflict resistant to resolution. The jackals need to use their teeth, and for that they need carrion; the Arabs, in turn, will control the jackals with whips and other forms of repression. Once the Northerner departs, the two will live side by side, but they can never come together.

This burst of creative activity for Kafka in the early part of 1917 indicates just how much of an exile he sensed himself to be, and in that awareness of exile, how he conceived of himself as a prophet-artist. That quality of exile Kafka revealed, which extended beyond marginality into death itself, is revealing of his entire era. It becomes a dominant motif in the twentieth century, very possibly *the* dominant motif: exile of the individual, or alienation followed by exile, and exile of entire peoples, even those who considered themselves natives and assimilated. These pieces also demonstrate how Kafka reveled in the short burst; how he would feel uncomfortable with longer works requiring steady application. These brief works required only a sitting or two; and they contrast with his three long fictions, none of which he could complete. "A Report to an Academy," from the spring of 1917, suggests the perimeters of his experienced world, that world in which transformation and metamorphosis bring with them none of the Ovidian grandeur of reshaping, but rather the grim news that evolution itself no longer functions, that what passes for progress is not merely retrogression but the major cause of individual suffering. Kafka wished this story and "Jackals and Arabs" to be labeled "Two Animal Stories" when Martin Buber published them in successive issues of *Der Jude* (*The Jew*), a monthly periodical he edited.

In early March, Kafka took over the rather lavish apartment in the Schönborn Palace, but he continued to write at Ottla's little house. Ottla herself left Prague in mid-April to supervise Karl Hermann's farm in Zürau, in northwest Bohemia. It was, as farms went, middle-sized, at fifty acres, and Ottla's role was to keep it going until her brother-in-law returned from military service. Both Kafka and his sister had been freed from the asbestos factory nightmare when it closed in March; and with this removal from factory and Prague, Ottla achieved a liberation that did not come to her brother. But the closing of the factory did not occur peacefully. Even its end seemed like a fragment of one of Kafka's stories. Hermann Kafka, with Julie Kafka's support, accused Karl Hermann's brother, Rudl, of fraud in its running — reimbursing himself while letting the factory decline — and he was asked to leave the Kafka apartment. Needless to say, such a scene did not rest easily with the family.

Near the end of April, Kafka was energized into writing another one of his parable-allegorical stories, "The Cares of a Family Man" (also called "The Troubles of a Householder"),* in which he invented a shape called Odradek. This story has already been discussed, but it also fits well here, caught as Kafka was between a writing life that was going well and a sense that other things were precarious. His premonition of his declining physical state is captured in Odradek's laugh, which seems to originate in a chest cavity that has no lungs. His voice "sounds rather like the rustling of fallen leaves."[58] The narrator ("I") asks himself what can possibly happen to this odd creature, which resembles at first sight "a flat star-shaped spool for thread."[59] Anything that dies, Kafka writes, "has had some kind of aim in life, some kind of activity, which has worked out; but that does not apply to Odradek." The assumption, only implicit here, is that the creature has some artistic sensibility, as observer, lurker, marginal figure. It cannot be defined, nor can it be predicted. It exists outside of any temporal-spatial expectations, and it does not fit any presuppositions about shape or function. In brief, it must, for lack of any other role, be an artist, or the mysterious Golem.

Kafka was seeking ways in which to define the artist, apparently giving shape to his own sense of himself. This period was a real breakthrough for him not only because he was writing, but because the work itself was an expression of the artist forming and reforming. Like his contemporary Thomas Mann, and to some extent Robert Musil, he was

---

*"Die Sorge des Hausvaters," which might also be translated as "A Trouble to (or for) the Caretaker."

seeking the role of the artist in modern life at the same time he was trying to find out what or who the artist is. Some commentators have suggested reference to the Cabala,[60] that mystical collection of Jewish lore that concentrated on layers of linguistic meaning and inner significance beyond words. For Kafka, the artist's role was never to depict; it was instead to remain close to the sources of magic and the occult.

In the spring of 1917, with work now flowing from him, he wrote "The Great Wall of China." The story would later be incorporated into a volume of that name but was not published during Kafka's lifetime (not until 1931). It is a hermetic story that can mean almost anything: from the personal to the social to the political to the psychological, to mystical significance. The writing of the story coincides generally with Kafka's growing immersion in Jewish matters, his study of Hebrew, his interest in Jewish themes. Certainly Jewish themes are present, but most apparent are analogies with the final days of the Austro-Hungarian Empire. "Great Wall" is a commentary on political fate, on the individual scooped up by events. The ostensible subject matter is of building the Great Wall of China, but the subtext is art, language, the gaps and silences that lie between substances. When the wall was built, gangs of workers and supervisors worked on various stretches, but the gaps between these stretches are not filled in.

Parallel to this problem is the question of what the wall was intended to do. Kafka was now in his element: he could question the very nature of a wall intended to keep out an enemy by posing the counter-question of whether it was intended to keep in its own people. In this way, the wall rejects, while also becoming hermetic, enclosing. This is, however, only one of the areas of the wall Kafka questions. And from this, an almost Talmudic exercise, we ponder an outpouring of individual, artistic, political, and religious possibilities. The gaps in the wall, between parts being constructed in different areas of China, become then the gaps in our knowledge; Kafka has established from the first paragraph that whatever meaning we apply is full of comparable gaps.

In order to supervise the peasant laborers, artists were needed, men "versed in the art of building." Before the wall was started, fully fifty years before the first stone was laid, the art of architecture and masonry had been proclaimed the most significant branch of knowledge. Other arts gained stature to the extent they were measured against architecture. Yet despite this, as the story progresses, confusion exists as to what the high command had in mind, since construction is piecemeal. People in the southeast of China could not understand what it meant to protect the country against invaders from the north, since no northern people could menace them there. Every question asked poses another ambiguity to the plan for the wall, so that eventually there is only the work itself, not any discernible pattern. The sole conclusion is that the building of the wall is a timeless imperative; its absolute value is an artistic act apart from function. In fact, Kafka describes the wall as a cubist artifact.

If the high command has existed since time immemorial, then the idea for the wall has always existed, like Yeats's golden bird, outside time and space. There was never a need to protect the people of the north; they did not cause the building of a defensive protection. On the contrary: the wall had to be built regardless of circumstances. In fact, as Kafka speculates, the Great Wall would have made it possible for the Tower of Babel to have existed, by providing a secure foundation for it. Thus, language itself would have been validated by the wall, that mélange of languages that collapsed when the original tower collapsed. This new "tower," furthermore, has linkages to the Dual Monarchy, which, like the original tower, was collapsing because its foundation was unstable, its political power waning because it had become dissipated. Here Kafka comes extremely close to what Musil would write in *The Man Without Qualities*, where the empire becomes Kakania, Shitville.

In the wall itself, in its possibilities as a foundation for the tower, in its temporal-spatial aspects, the story fits well into one of Kafka's paradoxes: there is a heavenly collar and chain that pulls against gravity and chokes us if we attempt to remain on earth, and a gravitational collar, pulling at the same time, if we attempt to reach toward heaven. Either way, we find ourselves pulled back, or back and forth, by forces we cannot control: the very nature of the world is acting against us. Kafka would confront his tuberculosis in the same way. It had the advantage of presenting him with a fate he knew was always his, and at the same time it would end his life. Thus, he could be happy in his unhappiness, unhappy in his happiness: two conflicting forces that fitted the duality of his vision, both for himself and for everything in the world at large.

Within Kafka himself was a great wall holding something in and also preventing anything from getting out. It was this wall that burst, like a dam, early in August of this year, when his lungs provided their first "flow." With the wall cracked, the dam broken, he hemorrhaged. He described it as a "swimming bath," pouring out blood, but at the same time, something entered, a kind of bliss, the awareness that his destiny was encountered. That Tower of Babel that had failed to reach its goal because its foundation was insecure could not be glimpsed, a tower that in Kafka's paradoxical view was more internal than external.

When he finally arrives at the Emperor of China and his messengers, he glories in his ability to divert temporal-spatial relationships from their expected flow into his more ambiguous way of viewing them. The Emperor is himself so distant that people in the provinces, while they would like to defer to him, do not know who he is: "We would think about the present one if we knew who he was or knew anything definite about him. . . . We are always trying to get information on this subject, but, strange as it may sound, it is almost impossible to discover anything, either from pilgrims . . . or from near or distant villages, or from sailors. . . . One hears a great many things, true, but can gather nothing definite."[61]

Here is the central Kafka dilemma, what made his name into an adjective describing the human condition. In the year 1917, all of Kafka's prophetic powers came together, not least because it was the year in which his illness struck him, the precondition having transformed itself into the condition. His illness appeared to convey a kind of clairvoyance, when he saw not only into himself, in his usual self-absorbed way, but into the very heart of things. He became that messenger of bad news, but mixed with it great wit and moments of almost manic happiness. Messengers fill his vision of what we are, how information is to be transmitted, how misinformation accrues, how the truth, whatever it is, is distorted in the carrying and in the telling. All life is behind a scrim, veiled from us. Plato's parable of the cave, in which we see the image or shadow, not the truth itself, is played out in Kafka's act of becoming Kafkaesque. He has so followed the Modernist example of disguising the object, and then gradually extinguishing it altogether, that he has revealed the final message of the Modern movement: the confusion between subject and object, that interpenetration between internal and external. Kafka achieves that here with the Emperor, who recedes farther and farther away the more we and his people wish to glimpse him. The more intently we focus on the object, the more it evades us; we are presented with an equation in which the object escapes us in direct proportion to the degree we try to focus upon it.*

The Emperor sends out a messenger whose purpose is not only to communicate a message but to validate his existence. In the villages where the messenger is to come, the people worship long-dead emperors because no one has told them who the living one is. The people are intensely loyal, but the Emperor gains no advantage from that, since he has no contact with them. Peking, where the Emperor reigns, is in fact far stranger to the people than is another world. The messenger has difficulty even getting out of the palace's innermost chambers — he cannot find the right gates, he cannot make his way down all the stairs, he cannot cross the innumerable courts; he is caught in a labyrinth long before he ever reaches the people.†

---

*In one of his parables, or paradoxes, Kafka describes "Der Kaiser," or the Emperor: "A man doubted that the emperor was descended from the gods; he asserted that the emperor was our rightful sovereign, he did not doubt the emperor's divine mission (that was evident to him), it was only the divine descent that he doubted. This, naturally, did not cause much of a stir; when the surf flings a drop of water on to the land, that does not interfere with the eternal rolling of the sea, on the contrary, it is caused by it" (*Parables and Paradoxes*, p. 109).

†Another fantasy-like story based on gates comes with "The Knock at the Manor Gate," barely two pages long but full of Kafka's ambiguities about entrances and exits. The

"Nobody," Kafka writes, "could fight his way through even with a message from a dead man."[62]

This is Pirandello theater. For even if the messenger does get through, he is speaking of a dead man as if he were still alive: "This Emperor of his died long ago, the dynasty is blotted out, the good official is having his joke with us, but we will behave as if we did not notice it, so as not to offend him." But there is more, when the official leaves. "And behind the departing litter of the official, there rises in might as ruler of the village some figure fortuitously exalted from an urn already crumbled to dust."[63] The theatrical aspect exists in the people's being forced to respond to the present while eager both to "obliterate the past" and yet relate to something that no longer exists. Comic theater and *danse macabre* combine.

The great weakness of the people is their condemning all but past times. Yet this very weakness is what unifies them. Kafka has penetrated into that Nietzschean awareness of a paradox implicit in all historical reasoning. In the Modern's thrust toward presentness, the past is wiped away, and yet Modernism itself becomes part of that history that is effaced. Kafka chooses a somewhat different route. Past and present working together bring us to an edge of awareness, and at that edge we lose our ability to cope with history, to understand how pastness and presentness function to shape us. This is a dilemma not only for peasants but obviously a message for all people, especially for those living in Prague as the empire teeters on the edge of collapse, an empire that went far back beyond Kafka and his parents. Where in the death of that historical process does the individual cut himself off from pastness, declare for presentness; and what is presentness in the face of the disintegration of the sole thing one has known, the past?

While less well known than some of Kafka's other longer works, certainly less frequently anthologized, "The Great Wall of China" is one of his most trenchant fictions. It displays the honing of his greatest

---

narrator with his sister passes a great manor house, and the sister perhaps knocks on the gate out of mischief, or possibly only raises her hand threateningly, without knocking. But even that gesture is sufficient to create a disturbance as townspeople appear, terrified and deferential as though some enormous sin had been committed. Like Joseph K. in different circumstances, the narrator remains calm, feeling that in a law-abiding society a few words should straighten out any misunderstanding. In the distance, however, he sees horsemen with spears raising a cloud of dust, and he sends his sister away, so as, he says, she can appear in better clothes before these gentlemen. The riding party consists of a judge and his silent assistant, and the judge says he is sorry for the narrator. They take him to a large cell, with an iron ring fixed in the wall. As the story ends, the narrator wonders if he could still endure "any other air than prison air?" (*The Complete Stories*, p. 419). Or at least that would be the question if he still had any prospect of release.

Kafka's insight is that behind gates, any and all gates, there are elements we cannot understand, Cabalistic, as it were, in their impenetrability. If we understood those elements better, we would then comprehend the nature of the crime we have committed which requires punishment.

literary skills in these years, bringing together his ironic sense and a prose that whips across the page with complete mastery of word and sentence.* In 1917 Kafka was the complete writer, moving along the very center of his creative abilities, imagining situations and scenes that included everything he knew. The magic of the Schönborn Palace, where he was now living, is communicated in the work itself.

Momentous events were about to occur in Kafka's life, one of them being his re-engagement after Felice's visit to Prague in July. They went calling on friends and relatives, which Brod described as being horrifying for Kafka. Kafka and Felice then left Prague to visit her sister in Hungary, stopping in Budapest to see Löwy, Kafka's old friend from the Jewish acting troupe. Then after a flareup, the nature of which remains mysterious, he left Felice, in Budapest, to go on to Vienna alone. He met the poet Rudolf Fuchs, wrote two letters to Felice, which he called "monstrous," and still planned to marry after the war, or so he told Kurt Wolff in a July 27 letter. Contradictory information, all of it! The letters that he called monstrous he refers to in his letter to Felice on September 9, after he had suffered his hemorrhage and which had, in effect, ended the engagement. The letters, which we must assume he mailed, have not turned up, and they were possibly so accusatory in content that Felice destroyed them. Or else they revealed such an unexpected side to Kafka that she was too embarrassed to allow them to be sold and printed. Or, in fact, he never mailed them. What is so contradictory is Kafka's assumption that even with the sudden quarrel with Felice in July they would, nevertheless, marry after the war.

He seems to have been operating on several levels at once, on several levels of unreality. Very possibly, he was responding to a confusion of senses or a confusion of aims brought on by the intensification of his precondition: in early August the hemorrhaging would create completely new terms for his life. And very possibly that "confusion of realms" he was undergoing was part of his creative outburst. In this respect, the growing intensity of his tubercular condition sped up other aspects of his system, as the outpouring of work in the winter and spring of 1917 attested to. His own inner clocking system was telling him that time was running out. This outpouring of fiction in 1917, much of it at high levels, would be the first indication of that sense of urgency. Another aspect would be his contradictory position with Felice: his need to believe the marriage would take place, and yet the recognition it could never occur. Nor did he really want it to occur.

Between the expected breakup of the engagement, following the quarrel and the onset of the hemorrhaging, Kafka began making diary

---

*Kafka's German builds rather than beguiles. His sentences are structured as though with a motor of their own; the structure rises and falls with distinct cadences, until Kafka breaks it off in some unresolvable way. For a somewhat different view of his prose, see Wladimir Weidlé, *Les Abeilles d'Aristée* (1954).

entries once again. On August 3, just before the attack, he appeared to have a premonition and wrote a remarkable passage, revealing several dimensions of his fears and anxieties:

> Once more I screamed at the top of my voice into the world. Then they shoved a gag into my mouth, tied my hands and feet and blindfolded me. I was rolled back and forth a number of times. I was set upright and knocked down again, this too several times, they jerked my legs so that I jumped with pain; they let me lie quietly for a moment, but then, taking me by surprise stabbed deep into me with something sharp, here and there, at random.[64]

In some vicarious way, Kafka was suffering for all soldiers wounded and killed at the front, the killing fields not only growing but moving closer to home. As part of his fantasy of being abused, penetrated, and desecrated, he had found some physical equivalent, and that stabbing deep into him would begin in a few days, with his attack. The *Diaries* do not record the attack, and not until an entry on September 15 does he refer to it, telling himself he has the opportunity now to make a new beginning.* On September 4, he tells Wolff that his disease, brought on by headaches and sleeplessness, had finally broken out, and is "almost a relief."

The most dramatic rendering of his illness is found in his letter to Felice, on September 9, explaining the silence and dating the attack four weeks previously — that is, August 10. Kafka is quite graphic, and we know he presented the details so explicitly because he was secretly overjoyed that his disease ended the chance of marriage. "I had a hemorrhage of the lung. Fairly severe; for 10 minutes or more it gushed out of my throat; I thought it would never stop." On the following day, he consulted a doctor, Dr. Mühlstein, who diagnosed it as bronchial catarrh. Brod insisted he see a specialist, who diagnosed tuberculosis in both lungs. Kafka had apparently told Brod he felt the disease was psychical, since it rescued him from marriage. In descriptions of the attack to Ottla, Oskar Baum, Felix Weltsch, and then, later, to Milena Jesenská, Kafka was more matter-of-fact than to Felice, often sounding more like the examining doctor than the stricken patient. To Ottla, he joked that after the hemorrhaging stopped he slept better than he had for ages; and to Milena, he indicated that when he wanted to spit he produced something red, whenever he felt like it, until it became boring and he forgot about it, until the attack itself.

---

*Except for informing Brod, Kafka went on, business as usual. He wrote Kurt Wolff, for example, about both the title and contents of his new book, *A Country Doctor*, with the subtitle *Short Tales* (August 20, 1917; *Letters to Friends*, pp. 136–37). Contents: "The New Advocate," "A Country Doctor," "The Bucket Rider," "Up in the Gallery," "An Old Manuscript," "Before the Law," "Jackals and Arabs," "A Visit to a Mine," "The Next Village," "An Imperial Message," "The Cares of a Family Man," "Eleven Sons," "A Fratricide," "A Dream," and "A Report to an Academy."

The specialist did not appear to be alarmed, but a flower girl who had come in after the attack and seen the blood told Kafka he was done for, finished. She was, of course, correct, although the drama would be played out for another seven years. In writing to Felice, he attempted to be accepting and calm: "For years my insomnia and headaches have invited a serious illness, and ultimately my maltreated blood had to burst forth; but that it should be of all things tuberculosis, that at the age of 34 I should be struck down overnight, with not a single predecessor anywhere in the family — this does surprise me. Well, I have to accept it."[65] In one sense, he was grateful because the blood had washed away his headaches. But his use of cause and effect is compelling: the headaches and "maltreated blood" led to the tuberculosis. He assumed his attack was induced by other factors besides a physical weakness in the lungs. His mental state, his nerves, his anxieties all conspired to create the physical condition. In this, he overdid Freud himself in linking a physical ailment like tuberculosis to a mental or neurotic state.

But possibly Kafka was not entirely wrong. Possibly with a predisposition for tuberculosis, with a weakness in his lungs, a different regime, mentally and physically, might have postponed the attack. Or possibly his unconscious awareness of doom helped shape his outlook, gave him materials for his fiction, and formed his attitude toward himself and life. Incidentally, Kafka's death just short of his forty-first birthday, while absurdly early in our era, was not so unusual in his, especially if we factor in *all* young men and their chances of dying in the war or later of epidemics that swept through Europe.

Kafka announced to Felice he planned to spend at least three months in Zürau, with Ottla. Felice would visit in September, in what became their penultimate view of each other; the final meeting came in December, in Prague, and led to the disengagement. Kafka hid his attack from his parents, telling both Felice and Brod not to reveal it until he was ready to do so himself. Julie Kafka apparently suspected nothing when her son told her he was feeling nervous and was going to request a long leave from the institute. He jokingly says, with gallows humor, that Julie is always ready to give him a leave for all eternity. Near the end of this dramatic letter, he cannot avoid his favorite image. "It's not a knife that stabs only forward but one that wheels around and stabs back as well."[66] That knife, sexual, psychological, marital, had penetrated to his lungs.

Kafka's secrecy about his illness, especially with his parents, was a mixture of consideration and hostility. The disease was *his* and his alone, and he did not wish to share it. He did not seek or want advice, and he surely did not want recriminations, accusations that his crazy way of life, in the Kafkas' perception of it, had now caused a major disease. There is of course the further distinct possibility that he did not want to worry them. Most of all, the disease was like his writing: something he could hug to himself because there was no chance they would understand either condition. When, for example, "In the Penal Colony" was published in May 1919, Hermann Kafka refused a presentation copy from his son.

By keeping the disease from his immediate family and by moving toward a divestment of Felice, Kafka was in one respect clearing the way for a grand finale, in which he was the sole central character of consequence. Like the suicide-to-be, he was clearing the decks, giving away what he has, sliding into some distant region where he cannot be reached. The mole in "The Burrow" comes to mind as the archetype of this. To Felice, as the divestment neared, after she had visited Zürau, Kafka says he doesn't believe the illness to be tuberculosis but "rather a sign of my general bankruptcy. I had thought the war [his war, that is] could last longer, but it can't. The blood issues not from the lung, but from a decisive stab delivered by one of the combatants."[67] And in his closing remarks, he decides to tell her his greatest secret of the moment, one that he is not sure he believes himself: "I will never be well again." His reasoning is pure, so pure one wonders from what region he could have dragged it up: "Simply because it is not the kind of tuber- culosis that can be laid in a deckchair and nursed back to health [not the *Magic Mountain* kind], but a weapon that continues to be of su- preme necessity as long as I remain alive. And both cannot remain alive."*[68]

To Brod, he opens up differently; he writes of the wound of which the lung lesions are only the symbol. Ottla now knows everything, and Kafka will write that they live together "in a good minor marriage; marriage not on the basis of the usual violent high currents but of the small windings of the low voltages."[69] This kind of marriage is, for Kafka, the only functioning kind: sexless, but possibly full of uncon- scious longings; full of understanding he could not possibly receive from his parents, a wife, or even a fiancée. To Brod, he also wrote, "Sometimes it seems to me that my brain and lungs came to an agree- ment without my knowledge. 'Things can't go on this way,' said the brain, and after five years the lungs said they were ready to help."[70] Three years later he wrote essentially the same thing to Milena, an in- dication he still held to his theory that his brain had created the dis- ease, that his lungs were merely an accessory to a more conscious or active role of the thought process. To Milena he was witty in his for- mulation: he sees his brain as having become exhausted by the burden of worry and suffering; it is now asking for relief. "These discussions

*The final, extant letter to Felice is postmarked from Zürau, October 16, 1917. After more than six hundred pages (in the German edition), Kafka tries to say something about her pointless journey, his incomprehensible behavior, his "happiness in unhappiness," and he finds there are no words to explain any of it. After more than a quarter of a million words, they are, one hesitates to add, back to square one.

between brain and lung which went on without my knowledge may have been terrible."[71]

Great dramas were being staged in Kafka's nervous system, his emotional life, his intellectual responses as he began to prepare himself for final things. Just before the hemorrhaging, he had been working on a gloss of "In the Penal Colony."[72] It is a fantasy of sorts, with some violence, a mysterious snake, and visionary effects involving the U.S. government's fight against the Indians.* The diary entries now have a kind of delirious effect, a foreshadowing of the attack to come shortly, and a judgment on himself as well as on the victim of the needle machine. But the real drama comes in an entry several weeks later (on September 15), when Kafka attempts to probe what it all means: a death sentence, a reprieve, a chance for renewal, or the end of writing? He sounds both hopeful and despairing:

> You have the chance, as far as it is at all possible, to make a new beginning. Don't throw it away. If you insist on digging deep into yourself, you won't be able to avoid the muck that will well up. But don't wallow in it. If the infection in your lungs is only a symbol of the infection *whose inflammation is called F.* [my italics] and whose depth is its deep justification; if this is so then the medical advice (light, air, sun, rest) is also a symbol. Lay hold of this symbol.[73]

The harsh line about Felice, which is in every respect unjust, is softened by a diary entry after her visit to Zürau on September 20–21. Kafka is saddened that after traveling thirty hours to see him, she suffers from the utmost misery. He feels extreme guilt that he is unable to control himself or the situation. He analyzes her as wrong in defending what she calls her rights, "but taken all together, she is an innocent person condemned to extreme torture; I am guilty of the wrong for which she is being tortured, and am in addition the torturer."[74]

Remarkable about this insight is how close it comes to his comments the previous month which glossed "In the Penal Colony" and how close to the story itself, in which the explorer or observer feels that the prisoner in the bite of the machine is interchangeable with himself. He is victim, torturer, and the cause of whatever created the situation. This is not madness or paranoia on Kafka's part but his recognition of the impenetrability of all experience and of the interweaving of roles that occurs between people who ostensibly have no connection to each other. This is not a religious responsibility — Kafka was not about to turn into a Christ figure — but an awareness of the excessive pressure

---

*In the diary entry, the victim is not dismissed, and the officer, with a spike "protruding from his shattered forehead as if it bore witness to some truth," reappears. Further, the explorer has the sense that a "perfect solution" had been effected, with the corpse on hand, the death of the officer, and other matters. One cannot help but read these remarks as Kafka's intuition of his own situation, the perfect or final solution of his illness.

each person puts on another. In this diary entry, he admits his effort to control Felice, and he takes the blame for having brought her to this stage; his guilt here is honestly expressed, not faked. But it was, also, a guilt he could only admit once the hemorrhaging made the end of the affair clear to him.

Kafka obtained a three-month leave (with pay) from the institute, and that led to his long stay with Ottla in Zürau. He gave up his short-term apartment in the Schönborn Palace, moved back with Julie and Hermann, and on September 12 left for Zürau. This three-month leave would extend into an eight-month stay. With the collapse of his relationship to Felice imminent — Kafka's words after her visit indicate it is finished — his confidant becomes, almost solely, Brod, accompanied by his dialogue with himself in the *Diaries*. This slack will be picked up when he begins to correspond with Milena Jesenská in late 1919, a correspondence that has the same degree of intimacy he displayed with Felice and a somewhat higher intellectual level as well. When he hears that Felice will visit, Kafka tells Brod he is in a frenzy of indecision: that he runs around her barking like a dog, he gazes at her "as a stuffed animal head mounted on the wall might look down at the person living quietly in his room."[75] He finds so many things troubling him, he can find no way out. He wonders if the decision to go to Zürau, opposed by the specialist Friedl Pick because no doctor was available there, was the correct one. He feels that his decision to get far away from the city comes from the genes he shares with his country doctor uncle, and although he believes this desire for country life is a deception, he says he deserves one, at thirty-four, "with my highly fragile lungs and still more fragile human relationships." Whatever else, the proliferation of mid-September letters mainly to Brod, but also to Baum and Weltsch, suggests he was less cool and collected about his disease than he let on, that he needed human contact, especially in lieu of Felice's regular communications.

A letter to Brod at this time exemplifies the characteristic flow of Kafka wit and irony about people and also about himself, the prophetic Kafka letting his voice run on. "Should I give thanks that I have not been able to marry? I would then have become all at once what I am now becoming gradually: mad. With shorter and shorter intermissions — during which not I but it gathers strength."[76] Then he indicates that people have been excessively good to him, even self-sacrificing. But rather than feeling better about humanity, he as a result feels "more oppressed." He knows that is wrong, but something tells him that people "behave that way only to one who is altogether beyond the reach of human help. People have a special scent for cases of this sort."

There is little question the visible onset of the disease had confused him. All along, he spoke of himself as ill, as burdened with maladies, but the ills were undefined; he intuited he was a sick man, without hard evidence. When the disease finally appeared, after so many premonitions, Kafka felt eerily that by predicting it he had created it. As he had claimed all along, his fantasies were part of reality, not antithetical to it but interwoven with it. The dualities he had revealed in letters, diaries, and fictions were now upon him unmistakably; he could not deny he was being forced to struggle within himself for life even as death was reaching out. While it was not a new condition, it was a more intense stage of what he had role-played at. The theatrical part was now finished, and he was forced off stage into the arena itself.

To Felix Weltsch, he writes with his usual ironies, but here they also mask a basic confusion: he has gained a kilogram in the first week in Zürau and feels "the disease in its initial stages [is] more like a guardian angel than a devil."[77] But its further development may be the diabolic aspect "and in hindsight what seemed angelic will be the worst part of it." All the talk of angels cannot disguise from Kafka that he has been penetrated, in another one of his fatal stabbings, by no one less than the Angel of Death. In his brief tale of Odysseus and the Sirens, in October, he will mute Odysseus's ability to struggle against adversity by stopping his ears. By that means, the wily Greek misses the silence of the Sirens, whereas in any other version, he would have called up his considerable powers to resist whatever they held for him. Kafka has stripped Odysseus of his will, now a deeply personal motif.*

When Brod suggests that Kafka see the health healer Moriz Schnitzer (who in 1911 had recommended to Kafka vegetarianism, fresh air, sunbathing, and no doctors), the sick man says he will consult doctors. Brod had asked Schnitzer to write to Kafka. But Kafka also says, "All that is certain is that there is nothing to which I would surrender with more complete truthfulness than death."[78] This kind of talk disturbed Brod, who possibly missed the mental confusion Kafka suffered from as he struggled to find solid ground when he suspected he was doomed. Writing to Baum early in October, he tried to make light of his condition, saying he had never had an illness so easy to bear and so restrained, although that might be, he believed, its sinister quality. He adds he is looking so well that when Frau Kafka came to Zürau she did not recognize him at the station.† His parents still did not know of the illness.

As he attempted to find himself — and the short piece on Odysseus

---

*Kafka also mentions with some disguised pride that Wilhelm Stekel, whom he refers to as the Viennese who "reduces Freud to small change" (*Letters to Friends*, p. 145), has used five lines of "The Metamorphosis" in the second volume of his *Pathological Disturbances in the Sexual and Emotional Life* (*Masturbation and Homosexuality*).

†By this time, his weight was up to 65 kilos, or 143 pounds, a gain of 3½ kilos since his arrival. At 143, with a slender build, he was slight but not emaciated. This would be a high point in his weight; when he died, he was close to 90 pounds.

is clearly connected to his need to identify with someone strong and assertive — he discovered solace and peace in his natural surroundings. He retained his sense of humor, that saving grace that rarely left him even when he was at his lowest, although it could be corrosive. He moved among goats and bent branches for them to reach. He observed that the goats looked like "thoroughly Jewish types," mainly doctors, but some approximated lawyers, Polish Jews, and even some pretty girls among the flock. The very doctor who treated him is "heavily represented among them." When he feeds three of them, he calls it a "conference of three Jewish doctors."[79] With this slight satire on his own kind, he seems peaceful, far more at ease with goats than with people.

Having told Felice there was nothing to which he'd give himself with more confidence than death, he also wrote Brod that his tuberculosis was not a special disease, "or not a disease that deserves a special name, but only the germ of death itself, intensified, though to what degree we cannot for the time being determine."[80] With typical black humor, he adds that his weight gain will make him "a considerably heavier weight for shipment out." But this dueling with death was quite different from succumbing to it. He was testing out the limits of what might occur, and he was experimenting with the idea of dying, or being dead. In some internal working of his imagination and mind, he was attempting to discover what he could bear, and to what extent he could come back from the disease in order to fulfill his expectations of himself. There were still plenty of stories and novels to write, and his last years were in fact quite productive. But to write them, he had first to settle where he stood in regard to the disease, and where, further, he stood in regard to death itself. The letters to friends were so significant for him because he could try out his feelings, respond to their remarks, defend himself, engage in some kind of dialogue between life and death. What he had once fantasized about, the duel in himself between life and death, was not the same as the actual thing; and he needed Brod, Baum, and Weltsch, in place of Felice and family, for their support.

With the attack, Kafka, already self-absorbed, dived ever more deeply into himself. Losing Felice made him even more introspective. He no longer had to pretend. His prophecy that all was turning to death was well borne out by what was happening to him; his sense of himself as "representative" was further demonstrated by his subjectivity, his internalization of everything around him. With this, all external matter had to be reinterpreted by what it meant to an individual facing finitude. Self-absorption passed into solipsism, even narcissism. Brod had hammered away at Kafka's being "happy in unhappiness," a disturbing development, he felt, in someone so caustically opposed to normal forms of satisfaction. Kafka first contrasts himself to Cain, whose mark, he says, implied "unhappy in happiness," and then turns the entire argument around: "When someone is 'happy in unhappiness,' it follows that he has fallen out of step with the world and that everything has fallen apart for him, or is falling apart, that no clear call can reach him any longer and so he cannot follow any call with a clear conscience. Things are not quite so bad with me or have so far not been so bad. I have met with both happiness and unhappiness in full measure."[81] While praising Thomas Mann — "one of those writers whose works I hunger for" — Kafka does attack Mann's bent toward "inveterate sorrow," which he finds as false as Brod's search for happiness. He cannot, however, avoid a final caustic sally. Having told Brod he will come to hear him speak in Komotau, on October 27, he says he is not in the mood for cabaret. "Cabarets are out of bounds for me now. Where would I crawl off to, when all the big guns start booming, with my toy pistol of a lung?"[82]

Denying morbidity, expressing (to Weltsch) that he was in love for the first time, full of guilt about Felice, Kafka tried to tip himself so that he stood straight. He tells Weltsch he no more believes in nature-cure theories than he does in their psychological counterparts, but he is, nevertheless, obsessed by such psychological theories. After a November 10, 1917, entry, the *Diaries* go blank until June 27, 1919, more than nineteen months. The so-called "Eight Octavo Notebooks" take over. But there is also another series of entries similar to diary notations, the "Reflections on Sin, Suffering, Hope, and the True Way," also contained in a blue octavo notebook. They were numbered by Kafka himself and are considered separate from the more extended passages in the "Eight Octavo Notebooks."*

Numbering 109 in all, the "Reflections" reach deeply into Kafka's psyche, with several indicating how desperate he was to discover ground he could stand on once the disease took hold. They differ not only from the entries in the "Eight Octavo Notebooks" but also from the group of brief tales published under the title *Parables and Paradoxes*. The "Reflections" recall Proverbs in the Old Testament. They are, of course, full of Kafka's wit, irony, and sense of paradox. "The true way is along a rope that is not spanned high in the air, but only just above the ground. It seems intended more to cause stumbling than to be walked along."[83] This is the first, and it immediately creates a world in which ordinary elements, not unusual ones, cause the stumbling blocks. Or: "Beyond a certain point there is no return. This point has to be reached."[84] Here Kafka expresses his purity and absolutism, that inner need to achieve what is essentially unachievable, what may lead into an extreme from which there is no retreat.

Applicable to his own condition, in later 1917, was this: "One of the first signs of the beginning of understanding is the wish to die. This life appears unbearable, another unattainable."[85] Life itself picks up at

---

*These "Reflections" are called "Betrachtungen" in German, which may cause some confusion with Kafka's late 1912 publication *Betrachtung*, or *Meditation*, the German containing both meanings, which in English are slightly separated.

the awareness of death. "Leopards break into the temple and drink to the dregs what is in the sacrificial pitchers; this is repeated over and over again; finally it can be calculated in advance, and it becomes a part of the ceremony."[86] Like death itself, the leopards must be accommodated if life is to go on; since they cannot be prevented from entering, one must factor them in. "The animal wrests the whip from its master and whips itself in order to become master, not knowing that this is only a fantasy produced by a new knot in the master's whiplash."[87] The terms of Kafka's world are here: each part replaces the other in a fantasy that the "other" is superior or master; the reality is simply the replacement, not an advantage. Life resists death, thinking it is itself superior, but when death enters life finds itself neither better nor worse off.

"It is only our conception of time," Kafka says, "that makes us call the Last Judgment by this name. It is, in fact, a kind of martial law."[88] If we deny our sense of ordinary time, the Last Judgment exists always. There is, in fact, a war, between us and what that "lastness" denotes. Kafka can be intensely political: "They were given the choice of becoming kings or the kings' messengers. As is the way with children, they all wanted to be messengers. That is why there are only messengers, racing through the world and, since there are no kings, calling out to each other the messages that have now become meaningless. They would gladly put an end to their miserable life, but they do not dare to do so because of their oath of loyalty."[89]

Kafka has entered deeply into information theory and into areas of language associated slightly later with Ludwig Wittgenstein. In this respect, he has deconstructed the idea of how information is transmitted; and he has turned the world of "knowledge" and how it is transmitted into a typical Kafkan farce, of people moving rapidly back and forth without making connections. In several of his works, he has constructed circuits, usually of information or of intelligence, which resist becoming linked, so that messengers remain full of ideas, language, and political notions they have no way of delivering, like the Chinese messengers in "The Great Wall" or the more personalized messengers yet to come in *The Castle*. With the play on the German word *Schloss*, meaning either "castle" or "lock," Kafka can suggest that the messengers — who are so essential to K.'s understanding of what he has been called to do — lack the key to any final message. Characteristic of Kafka, they are messengers with messages but without the means of delivery; or, in Wittgenstein's terms, with a language unable to bridge the gap between the words we employ in everyday life and the modes of thought this language is supposed to reflect. From this, Wittgenstein extrapolated that what was unsayable, the "ineffable," was of genuine value, since it was the very element language could not verify. In Wittgenstein's rebuttal of positivism and in Kafka's reliance on messengers who cannot transmit their message, we have, in parallel terms, a recognition of abstraction and how abstract forms have carried us into worlds where language does not suffice.*

"In the struggle between yourself and the world second the world."[90] This is a typical Kafkan irony wrapped within a paradox, a paradox because Kafka only half believed it. Earlier (in Number 50), he had said man cannot live without "a permanent trust in something indestructible in himself," although both trust and the indestructible element may remain hidden from him. This undercuts the paradox that one should bet on the world when it faces off against man. But a terrible irony remains: that in the confrontation man's certainty he will win is countered by the fact that the world wins at least half the time. One cannot count on individual will triumphing; the world has its own arsenal of tricks.

"He is a free and secure citizen of this earth, for he is attached to a chain that is long enough to make all areas of the earth accessible to him, and yet only so long that nothing can pull him over the edges of the earth. At the same time, however, he is also attached to a similarly calculated heavenly chain."[91] In this design, as noted, if man wishes to reach earth, the heavenly chain chokes him; if he tries to gain heaven, the earthly chain chokes him. Yet the individual, feeling he enjoys all possibilities, refuses to acknowledge that the original chaining was a mistake. He sought freedom, he gained strangulation. This statement of what Kafka believed must be paired with Number 89, a meditation on free will, which concludes: "This is the trichotomy [the three kinds presented just before] of free will, but since it is simultaneous it is also a unity, an integer, and fundamentally is so completely integral that it has no room for any will, free or unfree."

As Kafka began to acknowledge his tubercular condition, and moved beyond the often misleading remarks he made to his friends, he was brought up against the unresolvable conundrum of the individual's free will battling forces or circumstances outside him. Can one influence circumstance? Does circumstance shape the individual? He recognized life as a labyrinth, and so tried to sidestep questions of free or unfree. His "trichotomy" left him where he started, with what he was, a sick man facing limited choices, although he had once contemplated something else.

"Test yourself on mankind. It is something that makes the doubter doubt, the believer believe."[92] Here we have the other side of the unfree will: the desire to experiment. But then there is the Kafka irony. Test

---

*Compare Kafka's Reflection Number 57 with Wittgenstein's unbridgeable gap: "For everything outside the phenomenal world, language can only be used allusively, but never even approximately in a comparative way, since, corresponding as it does to the phenomenal world, it is concerned only with property and its relations." We recognize how Kafka had assimilated that need to discover a language that can move beyond objects into reflection, thought, ideas, and still be reasonably representative.

out, and the individual discovers exactly what he has always believed; the doubter doubts, the believer believes. Nothing in mankind will alter what already is in one. Having rejected psychology in another Reflection, Kafka is committed to who and what he is. There is no salvation, no appeal to authority, hardly any to self. Yet he is concerned with sin. "Why do we complain about the Fall? It is not on its account that we were expelled from Paradise, but on account of the Tree of Life, lest we might eat of it." This is followed by a companion Reflection: "We are sinful not only because we have eaten of the Tree of Knowledge, but also because we have not yet eaten of the Tree of Life. The state in which we are is sinful, irrespective of guilt." A third Reflection on the subject indicates we were created in order to live in Paradise, but this has been changed, although we do not know what happened with what was ordained for Paradise.

Here Kafka is clearly facing the nature of our fate, of his fate. He tried to eat of the Tree of Life, he implies, and for that he was expelled from Paradise. It is a nice distinction. Only those who attempt the Tree of Life, he suggests, will be cast out; the Tree of Knowledge was not sufficient cause. Paradise was lost because of people like him, those reaching for what was forbidden, life itself; and not only have we lost Paradise, but Paradise itself has not fulfilled what it was ordained to be. It is clear Kafka is moving in and out of Kierkegaardian patterns here, assaying the nature of sin, guilt, and dread, but he backs off into ironies and paradoxes, reflecting his inability to make that "leap" the Danish philosopher saw as the sole means of salvation. Kierkegaard was "saved"; Kafka had no chance. For him, not only has he lost Paradise, Paradise is itself lost.

He was not, however, satisfied with this. He picked away at it in several succeeding Reflections, acknowledging that since the Fall we have been able to know good and evil. But we must go beyond this, for "only on the far side of this knowledge do the real differences begin."[93] He feels that settling for good and evil provides man with a deceptive point of rest: "Indeed the whole visible world is perhaps nothing other than a motivation of man's wish to rest for a moment — an attempt to falsify the fact of knowledge, to try to turn the knowledge into a goal." Kafka rejects this and argues one must make "this last attempt," which means forgoing the desire for a moment of rest. He is offering something very close to an existential idea: that in the face of the world's absurdity, its lack of coherence, its skewed experience, one must nevertheless continue to probe it and oneself. A Beckett-like voice is coming from the terminally ill Kafka — but, then, *his* was the voice that preceded both Beckett and existentialists and gave them grounding. In every way, these Reflections are the mature philosophy of a man who refuses to give up, even while he writes his friends he would welcome the embrace of death.

One might, he says in Number 103, hold oneself back from the sufferings of the world, but if so, then that holding back is the sole suffering one can avoid. There is no resolving one's own suffering, or its emanations into the individual's relationship to others. The final advice is a cautionary tale: "There is no need for you to leave the house. Stay at your table and listen. Don't even listen, just wait. Don't even wait, be completely quiet and alone. The world will offer itself to you to be unmasked; it can't do otherwise; in raptures it will writhe before you."[94] A remarkable ending, it suggests that since the world is already inside the individual, waiting to be unmasked, as Kafka puts it, there is no need to go out to meet it. He had, in effect, prepared himself for those final years. These "Reflections" are not religious statements but secular meditations on how a man facing death can ready himself not for death but for the life that remains to him; and, further, how that man can use his time for his work, without exhausting his energies on questions for which he will find no answers.

Several of these undated "Reflections" carry us beyond late 1917, but virtually all of them have significance for the Kafka pondering his condition in those final months of this year. Not all his philosophical reflections, however, could keep him from becoming morbid, and when he did, it was now Brod, not Felice Bauer, who was the recipient of his bad news. He admits to terrible failure: with city, family, profession, with the community of Jews ("our people"). In all, he says he has not acquitted himself well, and it derives from pride that "no one is as bad as I am." He reveled in his badness, in his separateness, however great the pain and suffering. He viewed himself as a stage on which mankind played out its frail drama.

He limns his desire for escape from what he was in childhood, and says that the most obvious escape was not suicide "but the thought of suicide."[95] What deterred him "was no particular cowardice, but only the thought, which similarly ended in meaninglessness." He ascribes his inability to kill himself to the same ineffectuality that made it difficult for him to do anything. Later, he says, he stopped thinking of suicide, very possibly because he had found he could use the idea in his fiction; and when the fiction took over, the author was freed. Nevertheless, in personal terms, what lay before him "was a wretched life and a wretched death." Within these confines, he sought a way out. "It consists in this, or would consist in this — that I not only privately, by an aside, as it were, but openly, by my whole behavior, confess that I cannot acquit myself properly here. This means I need do nothing but continue to follow with the utmost resolution the lines of my previous life." Here he finds a coherence that will not be dissipated. He asserts there is nothing admirable in this, although his aim is to preserve his integrity in the face of decline and death. It is, in fact, heroic, part of a warrior's journey toward what he knows must be done, regardless of the outcome.

Brod asked Kafka to send some work to be read at Frankfurt, but

Kafka felt this would be only a display of vanity. He indicates he does not respect the work but only the moments in which it was written. "What's the point of having an actress, who can find far more effective vehicles for displaying her talents, spend one moment in an evening raising them [his pieces] out of the void into which they will fall more or less swiftly. It's a waste of effort."[96] Later, Brod's wife, Elsa, read "A Report to an Academy" on December 19, 1917, at the Jewish Women's and Girls' Club in Prague, the first public reading of a Kafka work by someone besides himself. Kafka's insistence on not submitting work for reading underscores his hesitancy about the work itself, his feeling he had achieved less than perfection, and this possibly explains why he felt it should be destroyed upon his death. But there are other reasons, one of them connected to a fear of the reception, regardless of the work itself. In this regard, Kafka could not bear criticism, could not tolerate being "touched" by having his work become public. Accordingly, his need to burn or sequester his work from the public was attached to his distaste for all contact, and especially for any physical contact.

His sensitivity to noise, but especially to noises that are muted and, therefore, more penetrating, takes over his next few letters, to Weltsch and Brod. In Zürau, his room is overrun by mice, with rustling and racing around starting at 2:00 A.M. He is terrified, not only of the mice but of the disturbance, particularly when a horde of them suddenly leaped down together. He is, in a sense, penetrated by their daring to disturb him, as though they were attacking him personally. He lay in bed straining to hear them even when they quieted down, perhaps one mouse only "either finishing the work of the night before or getting a start on the next night's assignment."[97] What so disturbs him is that even while he builds philosophical defenses against his condition, he can be upset by something so insignificant. For this only proves his previous position, that small matters have an impact all out of proportion to their meaning; that larger matters can be confronted and withstood.

The mice make him frantic. He, nevertheless, can joke: "My health is quite good, assuming that mouse phobia does not carry me off before tuberculosis does."[98] This is the man about to be executed who pats down his hair neatly as he ascends the scaffold. While horrifying for him personally, these minor disturbances were advantageous for the fictional side of Kafka. What we respond to on a daily basis, he suggests, shapes our behavior and our activities. Mice, not tuberculosis, are sources of suicidal depressions.

Getting a cat, while a solution for the boldest mice, is no solution for Kafka, who dislikes its furry presence, hates its attempts to be cozy with him on his bed, and cannot bear its dirty ways. The cat is even unwell, "vomits continually,"[99] probably from a surfeit of mice or from proximity to someone who hates it. The cat, he says, comes to him thin in the evening and leaves fat in the morning — in this image alone, we catch Kafka's revulsion at eating. What is also remarkable is that the episode has so taken over his imagination that he writes about it in detail in several letters to Brod.

Even in an early December letter to Felix Weltsch, amidst all kinds of other rambling comments, he is still taken up by mice: "I control the mice with a cat, but how shall I control the cat? You imagine that you have nothing against mice? Naturally, nor have you anything against cannibals either, but if they should start crawling about in the night behind every chest and chattering their teeth at you, you surely could not bear them any longer."[100]

In the same letter, he asks Weltsch to recommend a good edition of Saint Augustine's *Confessions*. Kafka says he is interested in Pelagianism (the doctrine opposed to Augustine's, denying original sin and asserting freedom of the will), which he indicates he does not retain, not an iota. He tells his friend that when reading Maimonides (the twelfth-century philosopher who tried to reconcile rabbinical teaching with Aristotle's doctrines), he should also read Solomon Maimon's *Autobiography*, edited by Ludwig Fromer. This book, which Kafka praises, is the portrait of a man not unlike Kafka himself split between Western and Eastern European Judaism.

This interest in religious matters was a sign of Kafka's effort to consider elements that, before, he had deemed unresolvable. His mature mind had always been Talmudic, full of exegesis and questioning of meaning; and he became increasingly drawn to the Zohar, mystical readings of the Torah. This interest in turn was linked to his interest in language, and to his quest for words that would heal the split between what one felt and how that feeling could be expressed. Recognizing the huge gap, Kafka perhaps saw in the Zohar, the medieval Cabalistic work that attempts an exegesis of the Torah, some sense of language. For the Zohar emphasizes that God's words cannot be strictly defined, that exegesis can extend only so far; and because that distinction between God and man is so great, man can never hope to capture precisely what God means. Along with this, as we shall see later, Kafka was also drawn to Gnostic ideas, especially when he comments to Brod that God created the earth on a bad or off day.

The comments here coincide with some of the "Reflections" on sin, suffering, and guilt. Though Kafka's illness certainly moved him toward religious questions, the entire pattern was implicit in him from the moment he met Löwy and his acting troupe. Secular and Westernized Jew that he was, Kafka was now coming through a world war, and although it barely touched him, except for the military service of his brothers-in-law, it was a watershed in Western civilization. The killing grounds on both fronts, for which there was no precedent, called into question everything that Europeans had been taught. Like his fellow Praguers, Kafka had to assimilate a unique historical moment, especially intensified for Jews living amidst nationalistic Czechs and Germans who vowed allegiance to Germany. As was evident by late 1917, with the Russian Revolution changing the nature of the war, Vienna was coming apart. With the empire disintegrating, the future was unpredictable, and yet the massive killing continued. The historical moment called into question everything one might believe about history, politics, philosophy; it undermined any certainties about the sanctity of human life, and it jeopardized every prediction one might make about the future of the human race.

Just as the dropping of the atomic bombs at the end of the Second World War created a unique historical situation, so did the twilight year of the First World War. An in several ways that first war was even more traumatic for the West, since, with the fall of empires throughout Europe (not only Habsburgs, but Hohenzollerns in Germany and Romanovs in Russia), it meant a recarving of the continent. Centers of power were shifting, but it was inconclusive where the power was going. Everyone was exhausted, and this sense of exhaustion is reflected in secularists like Kafka trying to come to terms with more binding ideas: not belief as a source of serving a God, but belief in any certainties, in any forms or patterns deriving from the past. In historical Judaism, Kafka sought relief from insanity, not in the Judaism of practice (although his dietary regime in its ferocious devotion was almost Orthodox), but in a Judaism that because it had survived became an historical fact. In his illness, in his awareness of what chaos the war had created, Kafka needed some anchor. The brilliance of his imagination, however, was that even as his mind sought certainties, his imagination told him nothing in him could change; certainties were ideas, not elements incorporated into life.

He did not sit in Zürau all this time, having traveled back to Prague on October 28, with Brod and Ottla, ostensibly to see his doctor and dentist, but more likely to wrap himself in Prague. He needed the city in order to write, and part of his stalling now on his work was his distance from the city of his dreams and nightmares. He returned shortly after to Zürau and would remain until December 22, returning to Prague not only for the Christmas holiday but for an important meeting with Felice. In one of his rare remarks on the war, he wrote Josef Korner, a literary historian and critic, of his distaste for an illustrated monthly magazine called *Donauland:* "*D.* strikes me as an unmitigated lie. . . . the impure cannot be made pure, especially when it inevitably must go on pouring impurities from its source. By this I do not mean to say anything against Austria, against militarism, against the war, for it is not any of these that repels me in *D.*, but rather the special mixture, the studied and outrageous mixture, out of which the magazine is concocted."[101]

Kafka uses these arguments to indicate he will not associate him-

self with the publication. From his remarks, we can observe his acquiescence to the war and to Austria, explained in part by the fact Jews
considered Franz Josef (dead now since 1916) a supporter, if not a friend,
and Vienna's rule had left Jews relatively free, except for the pogroms
and outbursts associated with local nationalistic movements and
clergy. Considering what would occur after Kafka's death — what was
beginning to happen even before he died — it is one of the great historical ironies that Jews felt safest in German-speaking countries or in
those countries that had a strong German language and tradition.

In the middle of the conclusion of his affair with Felice, Kafka
found himself drawn into the marital difficulties of Elsa and Max Brod.
Elsa had accused her husband of being unsuitable for marriage, and she
was, in the main, correct. Brod was a philanderer and a compulsive
worker, so that he had little energy or will left for marriage. Kafka
wrote her on December 19, just before he left Zürau for Prague and
his showdown with Felice. He knows he is on shaky ground, and he
implores her that they must speak on the same plane, as friends of
Max's. Because of Kafka's identification with his friend's unsuitability for marriage, something he understood well, the subject was doubly
touchy. Kafka tried to finesse the entire question, saying one cannot influence another person; that while her grief springs from love, Max also
feels love as he tries to support her even as she tries to support him.
Kafka concludes he cannot advise Brod what to do, anymore than Brod
could have advised him, Kafka, not to contract tuberculosis. The inappropriateness of this analogy perhaps indicates how flustered Kafka became in an area demanding deep feelings and human relationships.

Writing to Brod in early 1918, he confronted the problem more directly. But his interpretation is, obviously, sifted through his own
needs: "You need marriage, but only in part, while the other part of
your nature draws you away from it and also tugs at your husbandly
side, and so uses it in spite of itself to shatter the foundation of marriage."[102] While devoted to his wife, Brod kept his eyes fixed on the
distance, just beyond Elsa: toward literature, to which he was also
wedded, then toward Palestine and a host of other interests. Kafka recognized that his friend had not wedded the whole world in his wife, as
would a more traditional man; and this too is Kafka's own rationale for
not marrying.*

With this problem in mind, Kafka confronted Felice in Prague, telling her in effect that they had no future together. After so many endings, it was the real end. Brod indicates that Kafka avoided all advice
because his mind was firm. Kafka himself indicates in his letter to

---

*His other close friend, Oskar Baum, had found his marriage unbearable and came to
see Kafka to discuss his problems. Kafka concluded that the impossibility of Baum's
marriage came down to the impossibility of marriage in general.

Ottla that it was a difficult time for both, but there was no other possible conclusion to what was becoming a Marx Brothers scenario of exits and entrances. With this exit from Prague, back to Zürau, he needed finality or he would never write. What was once an impetus to writing, the meetings with Felice, was now a barrier, until he could settle his affairs with her. After spending Christmas Day (a Saturday) with the Brods, and going on an outing the next day, with the Baums, Weltsches, and Brods, Kafka and Felice apparently agreed all was over. The next morning in tears she left for Berlin, and later Kafka appeared at Brod's office and himself wept, the one time Brod ever saw him weep. A little earlier, Kafka had written, "Celibacy and suicide are not on similar levels of understanding, suicide and a martyr's death not so by any means, perhaps marriage and a martyr's death."[103] He noted, "Everything difficult, wrong and yet right after all." To which he added, "Not essentially disappointed," and then, "Of his own volition, like a fist he turned and shunned the world."[104] He then launched, as we will see, into his parable about the four legends of Prometheus,[105] which apparently apply to him.

By presenting a weeping Kafka, Brod simplifies his friend's response. He misses the sense of liberation Kafka experienced. Marriage was not impossible for him solely because of the tuberculosis, but because of what his imagination had made of marriage. He had fictionalized and analyzed it to such an extent he recognized that no man with serious plans for himself should become encumbered by it; especially when he brought to this recognition his own observations of his parents' marriage, the marriages of his sisters, and now the trembling unions of two of his closest friends. But that was only a beginning. Until he became physically helpless near the end, Kafka simply could not find within himself the ability to bear the proximity of another person on a regular basis. He could not bear the physical closeness, the demands on him to show affection, to seem interested, to respond sexually to the expectations of another human being.

The attitude went further than his self-absorption; it went profoundly into sexual and physical distaste for other people, whether friends, relatives, or a potential wife. In some remote area we cannot completely comprehend, he feared the disorder an emotional and physical life entailed. He was terrified of chaos, something he could not control from his desk. He found sex itself problematic, probably because it was so closely connected with digestive processes, inlets and outlets, and food itself, which ended up as excrement in the sexual areas.

Now back in Zürau, during the first week in January 1918, he suffered from a series of foul moods, his outlook so depressive he seemed close to suicide. For some of this time, until January 13, he had Oskar Baum with him, and he had to listen to Baum's outpourings of trouble in his marriage. Kafka was full of the Fall and of Paradise lost. "We were expelled from Paradise, but it was not destroyed. The expulsion from Paradise was in one sense a piece of good fortune, for if we had not been expelled, Paradise would have had to be destroyed."[106] Man, in brief, so contaminates everything with his presence that he must be expelled. Just before this, Kafka commented on the four legends about Prometheus: Prometheus betrayed the gods and was chained to a rock, his liver perpetually devoured by eagles; he tried to avoid the agony and pressed ever deeper into the rock until he became part of it; in the course of years, his treachery was forgotten, as was everything connected with him; and, in the final legend, forgetfulness has turned to weariness: "The Gods grew weary, the eagles grew weary, the wound closed wearily." Kafka comments that "legend tries to explain the inexplicable. Since it arises out of a foundation of truth, it must end in the realm of the inexplicable."[107]

If all this sounds familiar, it is because Kafka has found another way of metaphorically describing the artist and his role. Prometheus is the archetypal artist: he betrays the gods, he is punished and must suffer agonies, he is eventually forgotten, and finally everyone wearies of him and his meaningless existence. The "inexplicable" that remains is what the artist tried to do, and that cannot be interpreted. He passes into stone. Kafka was, once more, seeking a reflection of himself as artist, and finding it only in the act of betrayal itself. All else passes into nothingness. No wonder he wanted his work to be burned when he died.

He has other, equally despondent images for himself: "The suicide is the prisoner who sees a gallows being erected in the prison yard, mistakenly thinks it is the one intended for him, breaks out of his cell in the night, and goes down and hangs himself." This is followed by "Not shaking off the self, but consuming the self."[108] Death followed by resurrection is the prescription, but he is not certain of rising. He says later that if you wish to achieve eternal life after having gained knowledge, "you will have to destroy yourself, the obstacle, in order to build the step, which is the destruction. Expulsion from Paradise was thus not an act but a happening."[109] These are all metaphors of what the artist must undergo: he must crush himself in order to achieve something; resurrection is only possible for those willing to chance death. The prisoner kills himself, and in so doing denies others the opportunity to do it to him. The artist embodies it all, the treachery, the deception, the ultimate deadly ending. Only the act of writing counts. Atlas, Kafka says, was permitted the opinion that he was at liberty to drop the earth, if he chose, and to creep away; but he was permitted only the opinion. Kafka is not sure about the "liberty." Was Atlas a potential artist? If so, he could have moved from "opinion" to liberty and accepted the consequences.

Couched in caustic irony, full of despondent and trenchant criticism of life, Kafka's metaphors are very much alive here, as he measures what is still possible against his chances of continuing. He tells Kurt Wolff — since his subject has been death — that he wants the dedication page of *A Country Doctor* to be inscribed "To My Father."[110] This was not an act of devotion or love, but of revenge. Kafka knew Hermann would judge the stories as a waste of time, the sign not of his son's success but of failure, his inability to direct his life entrepreneurially. Yet possibly he may also have seen it as a peace offering: the son ill, the father ill, the business having gone bad in the war years. It may have been an attempt to reverse "The Judgment" and "The Metamorphosis," a final gesture before writing the famous *Letter* the following year.

Kafka was still trying to deal with Brod's marital problems and his friend's involvement with another woman. He was trying, himself, to push back from the edge of despair. He tells Brod he was right in saying that "the deeper realm of real sexual life is closed to me; I too think so."[111] He says that is why he avoids judging this aspect of Brod's situation. He adds that he feels women take the lead, as was demonstrated in the Garden of Eden. Men follow and turn their lives into follies because women eventually hold the upper hand, an extension of his view of powerful and domineering women who change men into putty. But his view goes further than being merely sexist. It winds its way around into his sense that Julie Kafka failed him, that she was not one of those strong women but a weak vessel into which Hermann poured what he wished. Parallel to this is his recognition that the world somehow exists independently of our desire to destroy it. We have strayed into it, as he puts it, and when we do, the world illustrates our negligibility. Kafka is searching in apocalyptic terms, as the war begins to wind down; he views the end of a world destroyed not by renunciation of it but by means of its being carried to its logical conclusion.

"Freedom and bondage are in their essential meaning one. In what essential meaning? Not in the sense that the slave does not lose his freedom, hence in a certain respect is more free than the free man."[112] The paradox is always present: the slave, who is not free, cannot lose his freedom and, therefore, is freer than the free man, who can. The paradox also turns into a parable, of the writer seeking freedom, yet becoming more a slave to what he does, even as he seeks to break the bonds. Kafka fears the world's ephemera: "If I wish to fight against this world, I must fight against its decisively characteristic element, that is, against its transience."[113] Once again, the thrust is toward the artist and the creation of something enduring: if he "becomes" writing, then he can create something that transcends transience. He can contain the disintegration of self, of course, but also of city, country, and empire, and beyond that, the fear that Jews will be squeezed and crushed. Kafka would soon take up Hebrew again; the study of language was a symbol of his need to align himself with something old, traditional, permanent, in the face of unimaginable change. There is, also, the hope, a dim hope, that the permanence of an ancient language like Hebrew will stop the proliferation of his disease, or at least balance it: one element looking back to deepest history, the other becoming rambunctious and running amok.

All of these matters were shaping him for his final assault on literature, and they reappeared in his letters to his now one steady correspondent, Brod, until he met Milena Jesenská and started to write so candidly to her. Kafka admits to Brod he is unable to fix "the concept of freedom of will at a specific point on the horizon as readily as you do."[114] Brod's positivistic outlook allowed him to place much greater emphasis on individual will, whereas Kafka's sense of ambiguities, mysteries, and paradoxes disallowed any such easy definition. Yet he does not wish to forgo the idea, and we may see his final six years as an effort to make sense of the will and what it means when external forces thwart it. In this respect, Kafka was living out the stuff of tragedy: a man of some consequence brought down by a flaw, perhaps, or carried down by some disproportion between what he wills and what the world allows. He accepted the flaws but was not convinced that was all there was to it; rather, he felt circumstances conspired. Trying to get into the seams of that conundrum would characterize his last years of work; like other great writers of the past, Kafka knew that only art could begin to resolve that problem.

His interest in Kierkegaard, which never flagged, was now renewed. He acknowledged that the philosopher had answers, although they weren't relevant to him. "So much light radiates from Kierkegaard that some of it penetrates even to the deepest abyss."[115] Yet Kafka admits that Kierkegaard's religious position does not come across to him as it does to Brod.* He cautions that the Dane's point, that one's relationship to the divine is not subject to outside judgment, is unsatisfactory, and would make it impossible for Jesus himself to judge how far a follower of his had come. Kafka offers up his own nostrum: "Striving man must oppose this world in order to save the divine element within himself. Or, what comes to the same thing, the divine sets him against the world in order to save itself." This is, of course, a considerable reshaping of Kierkegaard's relationship between man and God, since in Kafka's formulation the divine already lies within and must, somehow, be permitted to emerge. In creating that emergence, one has committed a religious or divine act. Once again, Kafka has rerouted religious ideas to accommodate an aesthetic one: that divine spark he speaks of in the individual is part of the artistic act, the creation of something that

---

*Not that Brod was converting. In 1918 the Jewish National Council was established, and Brod became one of its leaders.

proves the divine resides in the single will. Only art allows that divinity to escape or emerge. Kafka insists a man must retain his original nature, no matter what the world is or is becoming. This does not mean peace. What it signifies is his belief that the conflict between angels and demons suggests a "soul" exists.

Just before this, in mid-February, Kafka returned once again to Prague, to check on his exemption from the army, then came back to Zürau, to recover from the inebriation of the Prague experience. In his notebooks, near the end of February, he tried an assessment of himself and his fortunes, really an attempt to recover some identity from the ashes of what he sees as his life. He must, he says, create "the commandment." "It is not inertia, ill will, awkwardness — even if there is something of all this in it, because 'vermin is born of the void' — that cause me to fail, or not even to get near failings: family life, friendship, marriage, profession, literature. It is not that, but the lack of ground underfoot, of air, of the commandment."[116] He adds that it is his task to create these. He senses that his sense of lack or void is part of the age, an age that Modernist art was helping to capture by deconstructing its various elements, deobjectifying it and emptying it out, as it were. "I have vigorously absorbed the negative element of the age in which I live, an age that is, of course, very close to me, which I have no right ever to fight against, but as it were a right to represent. . . . I have not been guided into life by the hand of Christianity — admittedly now slack and failing — as Kierkegaard was, and have not caught the hem of the Jewish prayer shawl — now flying from us — as the Zionists have. I am an end or a beginning."[117]

This powerful insight into himself and into his age leaves him only as a writer. He can limn the end of things, become the end of things or the beginning of something new. In some strange conjunction of imaginations, he is, like Whitman in America, an end and a beginning. Kafka as prophet was never more evident, because virtually everything he had written or thought was an emblem of endings, but as well a signal of beginnings. There is no clearer statement of Kafka's recognition of himself as the pivotal representative figure of the twentieth century, the representative of our time, the creature who sacrifices himself so that a beginning can emerge. That beginning was a prophetic voice of what was to come as transformation, metamorphosis, reshaping that changed the entire look of the world. Kafka was there at the recreation.

After this deep and desperate probe into himself, he found himself opposed to what Freud would soon call the "death principle" (in *Beyond the Pleasure Principle*) and itself an outgrowth of the war. Kafka: "Our salvation is death, but not this one."[118] With thoughts on death, meditation on Kierkegaard, inability to write seriously — while vaunting the artist as the only creature capable of resolving paradoxes and ambiguities — Kafka worked in Ottla's small garden. His time in

Zürau was winding down, his leave from the institute almost over; he would be back by the end of April 1918. On May 2 he was in his office and living in Ottla's room in his parents' apartment. He was now approaching thirty-five.

In an undated notebook entry, which may have been written around this time, Kafka set forth his feelings about returning to the institute and living with his parents. The passage deserves full quotation:

> For the eventuality that in the near future I may die or become wholly unfit to live — the probability of it is great, since in the last two nights I have coughed a good deal of blood — let me say that I myself have torn myself to shreds. If my father in earlier days was in the habit of uttering wild but empty threats saying: I'll tear you apart like a fish — in fact he did not so much as lay a finger on me — now the threat is being fulfilled independently of him. The world — F. is its representative — and my ego are tearing my body apart in a conflict that there is no resolving.[119]

As noted above, Felice is the vehicle in this message of hate and self-hate of a tortured soul seeking some outlet for the rancor he feels at his condition. He was not writing seriously, and that was part of the tearing apart. The passage also presents the knife imagery of laceration and ripping Kafka has so often employed.

Even Brod fell out of step with him. In the summer of 1918 Kafka made several visits to the clinic he helped found in Frankenstein, but as his health deteriorated he refused hospitalization or any stay in a sanatorium. He was slowly reaching the point at which it would be difficult for him to maintain himself at work, yet the institute refused to take him off salary. He was up for an award, in fact, from the Royal Bohemian State Office for the Welfare of Returning Ex-Servicemen: Kafka the public official, sympathizer with the wounded and the injured, the man who sided with the workers against his own organization.

In one notebook entry, Kafka mentions "K." as a great conjurer who came to the narrator's little town for the first time twenty years ago. The vignette is slight, but it resurrects K. and it has him coming to a town, the slightest beginning of *The Castle*, which Kafka did not actively work on until the late summer of 1920, two years hence. In another entry, he is dreaming in a delirium because of fever; he lies helpless and weary in his bed and lets visions wash over him. In one such vision, he has to sleep through many of his free hours, "in order to banish hunger";[120] here we have the merest trace of "A Hunger Artist," written near the very end of his life. He creates scenarios of his own condition, nearly all of them involving imprisonment or caging. In one, as we have seen, a young prince visits a prison and asks who has been there the longest. He is told it is a man who has murdered his wife and has served twenty-three years of a life sentence. The prince asks to see him, but as a precaution the prisoner has been put into chains for the day. In brief, to achieve hope, one must suffer the greater penalty. And, further, there are no guarantees: the prince may not offer amnesty, the visit may not lead to hope, and the chains, the chains remain. The parable fits well with a man who coughs blood.

For the second half of September, Kafka was in Turnau, in Bohemia, recuperating at a hotel, at best trying to remain stable. He undertook the study of Hebrew, seriously, and corresponded with Brod about usage; Kafka had been working at it since May and had reached the point of reading the language. He was also spending a good part of each day in the garden and eating well, even eating meat, which was the staple of the diet there. He was in good enough spirits to correspond with Kurt Wolff about the contents of A Country Doctor, and shortly after about "In the Penal Colony" as a separate, thin volume. At the end of September, he returned to Prague just in time to fall very ill from Spanish influenza, a killer that surfaced near the end of the war and ravaged as many people as the war had. Kafka lay near death, with a temperature that hovered at almost 106 degrees. He was in such poor shape the Kafkas moved him into their own room. His mother wept, his father wrung his hands and indicated to his son he was really affected, so that Kafka felt some joy at the gesture. On top of his tubercular condition, the influenza seriously weakened him, as would be expected, and he had great difficulty in recuperating, waiting a month before he was able to get up and around.

Strange notebook entries appear, although exact dating is impossible. A little mouse gets caught in a trap, and as its life ebbs, all the mice in the district tremble and shake. Slowly they come out to view the death scene: "There it lay, the dead little mouse, its neck caught in the deadly iron, the little pink legs drawn up, and now stiff the feeble body that would so well have deserved a scrap of bacon. The parents stood beside it and eyed their child's remains."[121] Then: "When I came home in the evening, in the middle of the room I found a large, overlarge egg. . . . I was very curious, took the egg between my legs and carefully cut it in two with my pocketknife." Out comes a featherless storklike bird. The narrator does not want to feed and keep the bird unless it can pay him back; so he dips the stork's beak in ink and writes out a contract, whereby he feeds the bird and in exchange the stork will carry him to countries in the south. Day by day, the bird fattens and develops, and he awaits the day when he can escape the cold for the warmth of the south. As the bird becomes stronger, its wings and body more muscled, they begin to practice flying maneuvers together. Acting like a stork mother, the narrator shows the offspring how to glide by jumping up and down with outspread arms, with the stork imitating him. Thus it learns how to fly away from the narrator.

In another entry, Kafka writes of "the Tormenting Devil." This devil hides out in an abandoned cabin in the forest: "Smaller than the smallest mouse, invisible even to an eye that comes very close, the tormenting demon cowers in a corner. Here it feels safe, even though the cabin door dropped off its hinges long ago. But still it gropes, as if trying to pull the door to. Then it lies down."[122] A dead mouse likened to a child; a storklike bird that, once it learns to fly, will abandon its keeper, despite their contract written in beak and ink; a tormenting devil, occupying a cabin in the woods: all three pieces have the quality of dream or delirium, and yet they apparently capture Kafka's sense of himself in late 1918.

With the war finally winding down,* with his illness in some way approximating that ending, with his major powers still dormant as he awaited a suitable idea for a longer project, Kafka used these pieces to indicate a sensibility seeking a subject. In the bird, we have Kafka's ironic view of himself and the way the world works; one trains the bird until it is ready to be itself, and then it abandons the trainer, whose hopes ride on it. Like Gregor, like other Kafka creatures, the dead mouse is a sacrifice to the family: mourned, but a victim. The forbidden food, bacon, brought it down. The tormenting demon does not need roomy or spacious quarters, and it can appear in unexpected places, in the forest, for example, where one expects peace and solitude, not in the city where it would seem to thrive. It lies in wait, like bacilli.

The end of the war was fairly swift, once it became apparent that it was, finally, lost, although the killing went on almost unabated for the two months it took to fumble toward an armistice. Even though it was clear that the empire could not survive under Emperor Karl, it was events on the Western front that finally brought home defeat. When the German counteroffensive, the second battle of the Marne, was stopped just short of Paris, Foch ordered a counterattack that pushed the Germans back to their own Hindenburg Line. With Germany on the run on the Western front, the Dual Monarchy on September 14 offered to come to the peace table. The offer was rejected, until both Germany and Austria agreed to surrender, on October 4. This was after Bulgaria was invaded by the Allies and surrendered on September 30. The entire region was caving in, war having changed to interim chaos. Austria and Germany agreed to retreat to their original borders, but the actual surrender of the Dual Monarchy was not accepted until November 4; by that time, the Ottoman Empire had collapsed and its surrender had taken place, on October 30. Germany, meanwhile, had tried to

---

*The armies of Emperor Karl I, successor to Franz Josef, were literally disintegrating, suffering retreats in the Balkans, in Italy, and in Poland. By the end of October, the armies had broken down into nationalities: Magyars, Poles, Slavs, and Czechs, whose sole desire was to head home to defend their new or emerging states. Every part of the retreat and even attempts at armistice were mishandled by Karl and his general staff. Italy, in particular, was attempting to grab as much of the old empire as it could and, toward that end, even armed Czech prisoners of war. The war that killed 20 million ended in farce, material for Hašek and Schweik.

stick it out, but a revolution broke out, leading to the armistice on November 11.

By the time of the armistice, all the weaknesses of the empire were apparent. Czech troops had defected almost from the beginning, refusing to fight for the emperor. Italy and Romania, because of their need to appeal to their minorities in Austria and Hungary, joined the Allied forces. Croats and Slovenes joined with Serbs to create a South Slavic state. Near the end, Hungary itself declared its independence, along with Poland and Czechoslovakia. When Austrian forces were decisively defeated by the Italians at Vittorio Veneto, the end was clear, and Emperor Karl abdicated. German Austria was declared a republic. That entire part of Europe, while gaining temporary independence, was literally Balkanized: each unit was its own nationality, with its own languages, its own tariffs, holding the other countries at bay. The empire was gone, and in the final five and a half years of his life, Kafka could observe the preliminary maneuvering for that greater war that would come only fifteen years after his death.

By the time he returned to work, on November 9, the state of Czechoslovakia was in the making, with the meeting of the national assembly in Prague on November 14, and the election of Tomáš Masaryk as president. On the day of the armistice itself, Kafka was involved with Kurt Wolff over the publication of a slightly shortened version of the "Penal Colony," and he announced his address as Pořič 7, Prague.* There is no mention of the armistice in letters, diaries, or notebooks. Only the dreamlike entries in his notebooks, if these entries are indeed around this time, convey some sense of the phantasmagoria he felt in the rapidly changing situation. Since many of these dreamlike pieces are expressions of anxiety-ridden narrators, we can assume Kafka was expressing in fictional episodes his response to political and social change. Even his rather long entry on Jewish theater in the final notebook could be a response to what he intuited would be a major overhaul of Jewish life.[123] After citing how his devout parents consider theater to be *treyf* (or unkosher, dirty), Kafka launches into his own intense interest in all kinds of dramatic presentation, but, later, especially in Jewish theater. What is different about this entry — since he had already written about this form of entertainment — was the presence of so many Yiddish words and so many ideas associated with Jewish tradition and ritual, probably a byproduct of his now intense study of Hebrew.

His health, meanwhile, was poor, and following his mother's advice, he traveled with her to be installed in the Pension Stüdl in Schelesen, near Liboch, in the Italian Tyrol, on November 30. This was, in a

---

*Wolff had suggested (on October 11) publishing the "Penal Colony" in a deluxe edition in the new series called *Drugulin-Drucke* and returned the manuscript for any changes Kafka might want to make (Brod was the conduit for this). Kafka excised a small section and returned the piece for publication.

sense, the beginning of the final stage, when his illness would keep him close to convalescence for much of the rest of his life. What started out as a four-week stay became four months, with an interruption for Christmas, when he returned to Prague. As before, the institute was generous with sick leave, first granting him three weeks, then four weeks, then extending that. Kafka's life now became a series of strung-out, seemingly disconnected episodes: anxieties about Ottla, who was studying at the Agricultural Economy Winter School in Friedland and was unhappy there; corresponding with Brod about Hebrew grammar; and meeting Julie Wohryzek, whom he would come close to marrying.

Julie and Kafka met in the early part of 1919, when Julie, also convalescing from illness, came to Schelesen to recover. The daughter of a shoemaker and a synagogue custodian, she seemed to Kafka a "common and yet astounding phenomenon." He was quite taken with her ability to make him laugh, to provide some way out of his self-absorption, and to be, most of all, simply a good sport. She had little education, little knowledge, but a sense of life that immensely appealed to him.

> Not Jewish and yet not not-Jewish [he wrote Brod], not German and yet not not-German, crazy about the movies, about operettas and comedies, wears face powder and wiles, possesses an inexhaustible and nonstop store of the brashest Yiddish expressions, in general very ignorant, more cheerful than sad. . . . if one wanted to classify her racially, one would have to say that she belonged to the race of shopgirls. And withal she is brave of heart, honest, unassuming — such great qualities in a person who though not without beauty is as wispy as the gnats that fly against my lamp.[124]

He says that in this and other traits she resembles Grete Bloch. The following month Kafka told Brod he had passed his time gaily and laughed more in the last few weeks than in the past five years altogether. The relationship may not have gone beyond holding hands, but we cannot be definite about that. Kafka informed Julie early on that he could not possibly marry, although he said he had a good opinion of marriage and children. Nevertheless, they did move toward marriage. While recognizing all her faults, Kafka found her accessible, amusing, a fine companion for someone as chronically despairing as himself. When she returned to Prague early in March, he followed three weeks later. In the summer (1919) an engagement was announced, with wedding plans in November. On November 24, if we look ahead, Kafka wrote an enormously long letter to Julie's married sister, explaining how they came to be engaged and then why the engagement stopped short just before the event itself.

Other factors of course existed that helped prevent the marriage, besides Kafka's usual anxiety. Since this was an important episode in his life, we must jump ahead a little. One factor was the differing atti-

tudes of both families: Julie's family was pleased; Kafka's father, at
least, was displeased about his son marrying an uneducated shopgirl
type, whose father was a shoemaker and a minor synagogue official (a
shammes). Hermann apparently wanted a genteel doctor's or lawyer's
daughter for his overly refined son. But more than that, Hermann, if
we are to believe Kafka's words about him, accused his son of falling
for a coarse girl who put on a "fancy blouse, something these Prague
Jewesses are good at."[125] If that is why they wanted to marry, then
he, Hermann, would take him to a brothel, in fact accompany him, so
that Kafka could relieve himself without taking a bride. The remark is
vile, of course, but it all depends on whether we believe Kafka's report
of it, or whether, as in so much else in *Letter to His Father* in 1919, it
fitted a pattern he wanted to believe and for which he needed ammunition.

At Schelesen itself, well before the possibility of marriage entered
seriously, Kafka and Julie spent most of their days together in an almost
deserted pension. A good part of the attraction came from the time,
place, and situation: both ill, neither attached to anyone else, each desperately lonely and seeking support; plus, of course, a genuine attraction. In spite of all his preoccupations and preconceptions, Kafka liked
this young woman. But they did not get beyond the *Sie*, or formal designation of addressing each other; and she herself indicated she did not
want to marry. Yet after they met in Prague in late March, Kafka, now
thirty-six, physically uncertain, emotionally fragile, began to pursue
the idea of marriage. In late spring or early summer, he proposed and
was accepted. But, as always, he was uncomfortable, and in a resumption of his *Diaries*, he refers to Julie on June 30 and indicates, "Uneasy
heart." On July 6 he continues with trepidation: "calmer than usual, as
if some great development were going forward the distant tremor of
which I feel."[126] It did not help that a few months before, Hermann
Kafka showed no interest in the "Penal Colony," and when Kafka presented him with a copy of the deluxe edition published by Kurt Wolff,
his father told him to put it on the bedside table — again, if we are to
accept Kafka's description of this episode.

There is some reason to believe that even if his father had supported his marriage or had been less brutally frank about its reason (urgent sexual need), Kafka would not have gone ahead. True, he did try to
rent an apartment and did permit marriage banns to be published, but
when the apartment fell through, two days before the announced wedding, he chose to break off the affair, using the loss of the apartment as
an excuse for feelings that went far deeper. His relief was immediate, as
if some order of condemnation had been rescinded, like the criminal at
the end of "In the Penal Colony" who is suddenly freed from having his
crime written into his flesh. He did not give Julie up completely, however, asking her to come live with him in Munich, but nothing came of

that or the move itself.* Kafka's long explanation to Julie's sister, whom he had met at Schelesen, is an indication of his need to relieve guilt and to present himself as he once had to Felice Bauer and to Grete Bloch. His honesty and candor demanded he hold nothing back, and he describes himself as full of warts and beset by demons.

This letter is more than explanatory — it is closer to confessional. After revealing that he and Julie laughed continually, he adds that the laughter was not pleasant, because it had no apparent reason; it was even painful and shameful. He says he was "like a person who is sore all over and gets along tolerably well as long as he does not bump into anything, but at the first really direct contact is thrown back to the worst of his daily pain . . . what lingers is the formal aspect of pain; there is literally the channel of an old wound and every new pain immediately runs up and down it."[127] He says Julie was naturally reserved, while his anxieties seemed incomprehensible to her and struck her as exceptionally strange. He praises her as a wonderful mixture of warmth and coldness, but the strain of their differing natures has created a tremendous burden on his heart. He decided, he says, he could not marry. Julie agreed that she too did not wish to marry, and Kafka believed her. The letter thus far is more descriptive of a fencing match than of a budding love affair. He says that while they agreed on not marrying, they disagreed on the reasons, and "this disparity barred us from remaining together."

This left him, Kafka says, with the choice of either going ahead with marriage plans or tearing himself away from her. In Schelesen, he managed to do the latter, however difficult it proved to be. He takes full blame for what he calls that mistake: that he had considered "the whole thing" merely "a Schelesen affair which both of us would be free of once we were back in Prague." He admits he was deceiving himself, and here we cannot doubt his candor. Julie had touched a part of him Felice never reached into. When he returned to Prague after Julie had been there for three weeks, they "flew to each other as if driven." This was, for both, an extremely happy time. They walked in the woods or late at night in the streets, or went swimming in Černošic. In this description, Kafka seems to have become much younger than his old, old thirty-six. But then the devil intervened. "It was I who insisted on marriage, I alone; I deliberately destroyed a completely peaceful life, and I don't regret it. . . . I had to insist on marriage."[128]

He admits that in the past he had had bad experiences with such plans, but this situation seemed so much more favorable. He is candid about Hermann's opposition but says that opposition, "given the un-

---

*With the end of marriage plans, Julie opened a ladies' hatshop in Prague and, we must assume, perished under the Germans, along with nearly every other woman in Kafka's life who did not emigrate to the United States or Palestine.

happy relationship I have with him, could only serve as a further strong proof of the correctness of what I wanted to do." It would be a love-marriage, but also a prudent one. There were some matters that bothered him. Like Julie's acquaintances, but he felt he could handle them as they arose. What he could not handle were the internal demons, "which [are] lying in ambush, as it were, and carefully watching developments." In all candor: "I can actually speak of them as though they were something alien to me, for they by far surpass my personal strength and I am wholly at their mercy." He dismisses financial problems as a cause of the demons. He has never had them, and they have no reality for him, so it must be something else, an "inner obstacle" that "exerts diabolical cleverness" in intermingling finances with everything else. These anxieties make him wonder if he, who has fought incessantly for inner stability, has the strength to draw on for this new condition. He tells Julie's sister that, in effect, he does not know if he can hold together under the pressure of marriage, that intrusion into what he calls his inner stability. He is too precariously balanced, perhaps, for any interruption; and such an invasion might create in him an uncontrollable condition.

He describes himself in abject terms, using self-deprecation as a means of justifying his actions, as he had with Felice. What is he? he asks. "You are not even a businessman in your inward disposition, I mean, but (probably a reject of the European professional class) a civil servant, moreover excessively nervous, one who long ago fell prey to all the perils of literature, with weak lungs, exhausted by the meager scribbling in the office."[129] Yet he wants to marry, but given these preconditions and intentions, "you also have the brazenness to want to sleep at night and afterward by day not run around half mad with headaches as if your head had been set afire." He adds ironically that this is "the morning-gift with which you hope to make a trustful, yielding, incredibly unselfish girl happy?"

In describing himself at the end of the Great War, Kafka could not have been more prophetic. His lack of balance between surface wish and unconscious need is indicative of how modern man must live in two or more worlds, with awareness of his split needs. That sense of wholeness that had been steadily eroding had now disintegrated and given way to divisions in the self that could not be resolved. The whole movement characterized as Modernism had been exploiting that split. If Freud was its analyst, Kafka was both that and its representative man, its Joshua. With those words to Julie's sister, Kafka bared the soul of twentieth-century man, as he did in his fiction; but here he does it not as a creature reshaped by imagination but in statements that become prophecy: *do not expect, he cautions, a modern, sentient being to respond in normal or ordinary ways.* That old cycle is completed, and a new phase has begun; a new rough beast is indeed slouching toward Berlin, and Kafka, like Freud, was its prophet.

He is aware that Julie's sister will ask if he did not already know these things about himself. But he has prepared his response. First, one never knows these things, "even if one has had similar experiences." Second, he had no real choice since his nature pointed toward marriage. Third, the situation was itself favorable, so that, if not deceived by the contrary forces within him, he felt he might achieve what he wanted. But then reality intervened, those internal demons. "The greatest scruples do at first creep away and hide when confronted with firm decision, but then they try to disrupt everything by all the torments of sleeplessness, although for a long while they do not dare to appear in their own form. Upon this I founded my hope. The whole thing was a race between the outward circumstances and my inner weakness."[130] He explains various phases: his doctor was away; his father's opposition provided a good distraction; a "halfway decent apartment" was immediately available; the banns had been published. But then the apartment slipped away, they could not marry on Sunday, and their plans fell apart. Kafka says that that may have been advantageous, for an even worse collapse could have followed "and buried a married couple in its ruins."

Once things fell apart, Kafka says he could not deal with the postponement: "Warnings that had hitherto been distant rumblings now thundered day and night in my ear." He recognized he could not go on; he had to tell Julie, but no one else except Ottla. Kafka's entire life is, as it were, encapsulated in this scene: he was moving outward toward some external sign of happiness, while inner demons pulled him back to what was essential about himself — his ensuing inability to create a balance that would permit him to act, followed by the decision that those demons cannot be denied because in some way they are right. With variations, it was the scenario for *The Trial*. Kafka then presented to Julie an alternative, which was in effect a relationship without marriage, whether consummated or not we cannot tell. Without his badgering her, he believes she would be satisfied with "fidelity or love outside marriage, or what is called marriage nowadays." He adds that such a relationship would not involve on her part any great sacrifice of happiness. Kafka says he would agree to their separation only if he were wrong in this conclusion. Otherwise, he asks for both of them to be left to themselves, with some future plans, in February, for him to go to Munich, perhaps to work for Kurt Wolff's newly established publishing house. "We would see another part of the world; some things might undergo a slight change; many a weakness, many an anxiety, will at least change its form, its direction."

Nothing came of this, and the engagement and any chance of a continuing relationship ended. But Kafka's words do indicate an overwhelming desire to get on with his life even in the face of a gradually worsening physical condition. He was looking ahead, and while his despondence over not being able to write continued, his words are not suicidal. He was, if anything, more conflicted, but with hope. His conflict is revealed in his diary entry for December 11. He is with Julie in Rieger Park. They do not speak; it is all too difficult. He thinks of his school years, when he was ten, and the teacher suggested he remain in the fifth grade because he wasn't strong enough to rush along. "And in fact such has been my growth, like a shoot forced too soon and forgotten; there is a certain hothouse delicacy in the way in which I shrink from a puff of wind."[131] The end of the relationship with Julie Wohryzek, which lingered on until July 1920, although effectively over before that, was a form of slow dying for Kafka. Before his illness changed the direction of his life, it was his final chance at that personal happiness he had sought since 1912. It was both an end and a beginning, the beginning of a brush with death, in the man and in the work.

... for high above, your suns in full splendor
have wheeled blazingly around.
Yet already there's begun inside you
what lasts beyond the suns.

— RILKE, "BUDDHA IN GLORY"

TWELVE Modernism and Death, Kafka and Death

WHILE MARRIAGE WITH JULIE was still a vague possibility, Kafka received a letter by way of Kurt Wolff from Milena Jesenská Polaková, a young but worldly woman who would have a profound effect on his life. Quite different from Felice Bauer, she related to Kafka intellectually and emotionally. Theirs was not an affair primarily of romantic inclinations, but of companionship between intellectual equals and anxiety-ridden individuals. Milena Jesenská was a young writer (born in 1896), not Jewish, married to a Jewish writer, Ernst Polak, an Austrian who was an inveterate philanderer. (The Polaková of her name was, in Czech, the feminine form of Polak.) Her background was completely different from Kafka's, going well beyond the ethnic-racial difference between them, into matters of class, caste, and overall status. She came from an old, patrician Prague family, with famous and brave ancestors and deep roots in Czech patriotic history. But she possessed a wild, nontraditional side that made her particularly attractive as a person in her own right and then to Kafka, always on the lookout for a "secret sharer." When Milena wrote to Kurt Wolff for permission to translate some of Kafka's work from German into Czech, she did not of course realize how sympathetic Kafka would find her as a person.

Before meeting and marrying Polak (scandalous for her father, since marrying a German-speaking Jew was both racially and socially unacceptable), Milena had had several love affairs and had been accused of stealing things from her family home to help her lovers along. She was intelligent, volatile, unpredictable. As a result of these antics, her father, himself a Czech patriot and a professor, had his daughter committed to a mental institute near Prague.* After her release, she took revenge by marrying the Jew, Polak, and going to live with him in Vienna. Polak treated her abominably, making no effort to hide his philandering and not considering her, a Czech Gentile, worthy of being admitted to his intellectual group, the Vienna Circle, a band of neopositivists, followers in part of Ernst Mach. When she wrote to Kurt Wolff, she was only twenty-three, Kafka's junior by thirteen years, but was knowledgeable in terms of experience, suffering, and opposition to bourgeois values. It is perhaps not merely chance that Kafka's first sight of Milena (briefly in a Prague café in 1919) and then receipt of her letter coincided almost exactly with his writing of *Letter to His Father*, in November 1919, at Schelesen. Kafka told Brod in May 1920 that "she is a living fire, of a kind I have never seen before, a fire moreover that in spite of everything burns only for him [Polak]. Yet at the same time she is extremely tender, courageous, bright, and commits everything she has to her sacrifice, or to put it another way, perhaps, has gained everything she has by her sacrifice. Yet what kind of man must he be, who could evoke that."[1]

That she had touched Kafka is unmistakable, and as a result a remarkable correspondence ensued. What made them more than friends, but indeed secret sharers, was that she too was ill, with poor lungs, what Kafka attributed to half of Europe. Yet they also shared autocratic fathers, fiercely antiestablishment ideas, a driven, rebellious spirit, a willingness to seek absolutes and extremes, a disregard for conventions, and an effort to break from tradition, whether in behavior or in literary work. Milena brought Kafka right up against the Modernist spirit, not only in art but in life; and she brought him up against the finality of death, since if ever a relationship were doomed, if ever a couple were on a death trip, it was Milena and Franz, Franz and Milena. They were Mayerling relived. It all came together in this period, as 1919 and 1920 met: Modernism, death, a possessive love, tyrannical fathers, doom confronting them at every turn, as personal habits and bad lungs made their futures dubious. What is most remarkable is that she, at twenty-three, should understand Kafka so well.†

With his personal feelings activated by Milena — even while the "affair" with Julie was ongoing (until July 1920) — Kafka brought himself to write one of his most important works, a combined document

---

*Reminiscent of Kafka's former teacher Hans Gross and his son, Otto, whom Kafka had met only recently, in 1917.
†The difference between Milena and Felice Bauer is clear from the following remarks that the budding Czech journalist made to Max Brod, words being her way of maintaining her sanity against Polak's indifference and cruelty. Milena writes: "I knew his [Kafka's] anxiety before I knew him. Understand it, could armor myself against it. In the four

and fiction, the now famous *Letter to His Father*. One problem with this piece is the willingness of readers to accept its tone, words, and content as autobiography. Yet *Letter* is not that. It is a fiction of sorts, shaping itself like so many other "fictions" of Kafka that fall between the cracks of designated genres. The vast correspondence with Felice, for example, was also a form of fictional creation, an epistolary novel, replete even with another correspondence, embedded in it, that to Grete Bloch. Kafka's dreamlike fantasies, furthermore, do not fit into any clear generic pattern as "poem" or "story" or "dream sequence." As mutations, his longer, as well as some short, prose works are true Modernistic artifacts: not easily identifiable. In the same way, painting and music were being transformed from their nineteenth-century assumptions: loss of objects, reliance on lines, shapes, and forms, loss of tonic in music, atonality, the use of unconventional sounds.

Since Kafka's writing was running parallel to these developments in the other arts, his *Letter* must be viewed not as a "letter" (it was not sent, it was not read by the intended recipient, it was not a form of communication from one person to another), but as a fictional representation of Kafka's perceptions. It is both autobiography and biography, both letter and fiction, both objective data and subversion of objectification. It must be read as a perception of a form of death. It is, after all, written by someone who is convinced he is facing death; and it is, as we know, an oedipal document, written by Isaac who protests that Abraham really intended to kill him. It is an effort to present a son's case against the father, not so much as a defense, however, but as a way of holding off his own death. The father attempted to kill the son, and now the son will kill the father — with words. Kafka used the only father he knew, but that is no reason we should read his "defense" as fact; it is a true Modernist fiction based on perceptions.

Once we do not expect "truth," we find a remarkable fiction cast in the form Kafka had perfected in his correspondence with Felice and would continue in his exchange of letters with Milena Jesenská. Kafka took great trouble with this document. He typed it himself, with hand

---

days (in Vienna, walking the hills, among other activities) Franz was with me he lost it. . . . When he felt this anxiety he looked into my eyes, we waited a while as if we couldn't catch our breath, or as if our feet hurt, and after a while it went away. . . . everything was simple and clear. . . . He walked the whole day, up, down, walked in the sun, didn't once cough, ate an awful lot and slept like a log, he was simply healthy, and to us in those days his illness was rather like a slight cold." The key insight is this: "I knew his anxiety before I knew him." Milena was the perfect companion and correspondent for Kafka in these days, even though he knew he was failing her too. There was, of course, another factor in their near "doubling," as Mark Anderson points out: Milena was sending Kafka her Czech translations of his work and, thus, creating in herself a mirror image of him (see Mark Anderson, "Kafka's Unsigned Letters: A Reinterpretation of the Correspondence with Milena," *Modern Language Notes* 98 [1983]: 384–98).

corrections, on forty-four and a quarter sheets of 8½-by-11-inch large-sized typing paper. Although there seems to be a gap after the larger section, continuity is clear from two and a half pages on smaller paper.[2] Whether Kafka actually intended Hermann to read this letter is uncertain, since it was never delivered directly to him; and whether Hermann, even if he had read it, would have made sense of it is still another question.

Instead of viewing it as a form of communication, we should see the long letter as a form of self-analysis for Kafka; not only a therapy, but an analysis that enabled him to reach into the creative part of himself where he could transcend the elements portrayed here. Calling it therapy is to see it as somehow curative; but to see it as a probing analysis (somewhat similar to Freud's own self-analysis in the later 1890s, leading to his *Interpretation of Dreams*) is to recognize that Kafka needed it in order to clear himself in order to be able to write. After this, he did write, not only letters to Milena, with a wild creative rush, but also *The Castle*, the following summer (1920).

The letter is premised on fear, although it omits the very real possibility that Hermann equally feared his educated, aloof, strange son. Franz Kafka would have been a burden for any family, especially one somewhere between shtetl and city, not really fitting into either. Hermann's reciprocal fear of Kafka would help explain his defenses, the bullying, building up of his past, his using whatever ammunition a basically unlettered man might use against a son whose very presence was a mockery of him. Kafka's attack presupposes not an opening up of the relationship toward some understanding, but a verdict already delivered. Only here he is the prosecuting attorney; for the first time, Kafka, the lawyer, is not on trial. The indictment and verdict are unrelenting. That alone should warn us we have fiction, or perception, not history. If we shift the angle of perception slightly, Kafka cautions us that autobiography is as fictional as fiction; in its personalizing of detail, it must reshape fact until fact and fiction blend, as in fiction itself.

"I have always dodged you and hidden from you, in my room, among my books, with crazy friends, or with extravagant ideas."[3] Here, near the beginning of the document, Kafka evokes one of his most persistent fictional images: the animal that hides, the mole in "The Burrow" that hugs its castle keep. Kafka charges coldness, estrangement, ingratitude, a motif in Hermann's treatment of him, only altered in his father's blast at him for considering marriage to Julie. That demeaning exchange, in which Hermann offered to accompany his son to a brothel rather than have him marry Julie, seems to have been a motivating factor in the writing of the *Letter*.

Kafka tries to remove blame from his father, as he also tries to remove it from himself, and yet self-blame or guilt lingers. He cannot long remain removed from the attack: "You have been too strong for me, particularly since my brothers died when they were small and my sisters only came along much later, so that I had to bear the whole brunt of it all alone, something I was much too weak for."[4] The reverse of this, which Kafka is aware of, is that a stronger son would have himself gained strength from the contest and learned how to meet the father on the father's terms. As a warrior or gladiator, Kafka concedes the field; and yet in every father-son relationship there must be some deadly competitiveness, especially with a household full of women — not only wife and three sisters, but an array of female help. In his perception of his victimization, Kafka misses the normalcy of the combat.*

He identifies himself more as a Löwy, which signifies refinement and sensitivity, not as a Kafka, with their bent for business, life, and conquest. Hermann, however, is a "true Kafka in strength, health, appetite, loudness of voice, eloquence, self-satisfaction, worldly dominance, endurance, presence of mind, knowledge of human nature, a certain way of doing things on a grand scale."[5] From this, since he is his mother's son, not his father's, Kafka can draw several conclusions, most of which make him a lackey in Hermann's empire.

Herr Kafka is not unlike Franz Josef, the late emperor. His son says Hermann ruled the world from his armchair, the image Habsburgian: "Your self-confidence was so great that you had no need to be consistent at all and yet never ceased to be in the right."[6] The observation blends into political parody, Kafka merging with Hašek. He says his father was capable of running down Czechs, Germans, and even Jews, "and finally nobody was left except yourself." This leads, later in the document, to one of Kafka's greatest images, worthy of the highest fiction: "Sometimes I imagine the map of the world spread out flat and you stretched out diagonally across it. And what I feel then is that only those territories come into question for my life that either are not covered by you or are not within your reach."[7] In keeping with the son's conception of the father's magnitude, the territories remaining are few and not very comforting, and marriage is not among them.

---

*Judge Daniel Schreber, whose case we have already mentioned, had a father who was truly repressive in his methods. Schreber's father was a famous pediatrician whose view of the home was Prussian: duty, discipline, obedience, full patriarchal control. Toward that end, in the several books and pamphlets he wrote, he stated that harnesses and other restraining contraptions should be used to enforce proper posture, bearing, and presence for children from two to twenty. In effect, Dr. Schreber was promoting the use of straitjackets on young children, probably tested on Daniel Schreber himself — so that when he became psychotic, he relived many of these childhood experiences in his fantasies. Incidentally, during the Nazi era, Alfons Ritter paid tribute to Dr. Schreber's methods as ways of controlling children, implying that Nazi methods were not far removed from Prussian authoritarianism. See the chapter "Daniel Schreber: Madness, Sex and the Family," in *A Social History of Madness* (New York: Dutton Obelisk, 1987), by Roy Porter.

These images of the great Hermann stretching across the map of the world, or making his pronouncements from his throne, all mean there is no place for his son to hide except in holes, or else transformed into a bug or small animal. In spatial terms, Hermann has grasped the upper reaches, commanding from a great height, whereas the son has been relegated to the lower levels, holes, corners, insignificant locations, where he must squeeze himself into something minuscule in order to avoid being seen. The spatial considerations here are, obviously, part of Kafka's fictional vision, those spatial arrangements in which large and small act as metaphors. In sexual terms, Hermann's presence is phallic, and his relegating his son to the lower depths is a form of emasculation. Kafka has become puny, limp, impotent, whereas the emperor grows ever more erect.

The prevailing image of the son in this arrangement is the bug. If "The Metamorphosis" in 1912 was a fictional presentiment of the *Letter*, the *Letter* is both a gloss and documentation of the earlier story. In the seven years between the two works, Kafka has remained absolutely consistent with himself. Both works should be read intertextually, with images, spatial arrangements, and metaphors sharing similar considerations. In one of these spatial metaphors, Kafka tells of a childhood experience when, after creating a fuss over a glass of water, he was placed on the balcony (the *pavlatche*) and left there. This became for him the tea and madeleine of Proust's Marcel, but instead of bringing back a memory that recreates something, it recalls resentment, hostility, the inexplicable.

Kafka turns this memory into his version of the "primal scene" — not the child's sighting of the sexual engagement of the parents, but the creation of his utter helplessness when faced with the "huge man," which has its own sexual implication. The entire confrontation has a sexual component: the desire to be squashed on Kafka's part or brutalized in order to justify his position, and the equally disturbing oedipal struggle to "kill" the father verbally when physically he is too puny and helpless to accomplish it. The balcony scene brings home to the small child how helpless he is before the "ultimate authority" figure, and since he fears that this "huge man" might come at any time during the night and carry him into the balcony, he must plan his strategy of response. Here he has only words, but different kinds of words from those of Hermann, who shouts and rants. Kafka's words are quiet but permanent.

Thus we find murderous impulses on both sides, with language the agent. Kafka paid for his feelings when he was young; Hermann will pay now, by reading about what a monster he has created in his son. As we have noted, there are the familiar descriptions of the two physically juxtaposed: Hermann burly, broad, capacious; the son skinny, slight of build, cavernous. Spatially, Hermann is convex, Kafka concave — and from that physical opposition derive all the differences. Undressing together, Hermann looms doubly huge — the sexual element not negligible — and Kafka doubly skeletal, looking far younger than his years, childlike even when an adolescent. As we know, this distress at his undeveloped body continued well into adulthood, when he looked forward to swimming in public places but felt everyone would stare derisively at his puny figure. But that physical disparity was only the beginning; their differences extended into every area: eating, opinions, the ways life was arranged. Kafka attacks Hermann for disregarding what his words and judgments did, for the suffering and shame they caused. But Hermann had expected some comeback or retort; for when Kafka does lash back, his father retreats into silence or into muttering. As a harmless bully, Hermann took whatever was handed to him and then demanded more, until he was stopped. Ottla, for one, could drive him wild with opposition, and she refused to let him frustrate her wishes.

There was, we must add, no active physical bullying. Kafka was not struck, manhandled, or abused in any way. What he is drawing from was no worse than any other European family and, in most instances, far better. As he admits, the family was successful, and Hermann had pulled it all together. Kafka must make a failure out of success, must create a fictional reshaping of experience, must personalize fact. More than any other writer of the century, Proust possibly excepted, Kafka found his material in weakness, failure, defenselessness. Because of his need to reshape these qualities into imaginative works, he could not let Hermann escape. Julie was herself too weak to sustain her son's hammering away at failure, although at another level he holds her responsible as well.

Meals are often the testing ground of whether a family is functioning well or becoming pathological. Even if we accept only part of Kafka's description of dinnertime, we discover the roots of his response to food, digestion, and, ultimately, to sexual behavior. Hermann turned meals into acts of imperialism, where he pursued hegemony at the expense of all the others, but especially offending against his son's fastidiousness. It was another form of castration. Hermann ate everything, we learn, in big mouthfuls, "fast and hot," as well as rapidly and noisily. He relished the fact that he finished first; he enjoyed cracking bones, while forbidding others to do so; he sipped vinegar noisily; he cut the bread with a knife dripping with gravy; he clipped his fingernails at the table, sharpened pencils, cleaned out his ears with a toothpick. Kafka's measure of disgust with food and, by implication, with all bodily functions, is located here, or else intensified by such practices, which reinforced an already queasy stomach and personality. His comment is labyrinthine: "Please, Father, understand me rightly: these would in themselves have been utterly insignificant details, they only became depressing for me because you, the man who was so tremendously the measure of all things for me, yourself did not keep the commandments you imposed on me."[8]

There is, here, the failure of God. Part of Kafka's bitterness comes from the fact that the man he wished to exalt above all others proved unworthy of the devotion. What should have been a sacred calling, as father and family leader, becomes a disappointment, a failure. The letter has the bitterness of a romance gone sour. Kafka now has clearly gone beyond Hermann as bully and browbeater into areas of the son's expectations of a father who has failed to live up to billings. Kafka's expectation is biblical: he is the Isaac who believes so intensely in Abraham that he could not believe his father would sacrifice him. Yet, at the same time, he would have accepted sacrifice if only the patriarch had gone through with it. Hermann's failure here, which is not Kafka's main point in the Letter, becomes enormously significant; to have let the son down is a more powerful factor than to have created a poor home for him.

Kafka's accusation is that he is precisely what Hermann attempted to make of him. In some ironic way, the son whom Hermann cannot bear is an exact product of the father's fashioning. In this respect, Kafka's mere presence is his best revenge on his father, and there was really no need for the Letter. Kafka had only to be present or make some announcement, like his engagement to Julie Wohryzek, and Hermann was being repaid in kind. He even ascribes his "hesitant, stammering mode of speech" followed by silences to the fact that Hermann was an "excellent talker."[9] Thus, whatever Hermann did produced in the son the opposite, all calculated to bring him close to collapse. Kafka adds he became dumb, cringed from his father, hid from him, and only stirred when there was plenty of distance between them. As leper, outcast, pariah, Kafka justifies himself as a bug!

"The older I became the more material there was for you to bring forward against me as evidence of my worthlessness; gradually you began really to be right in a certain respect."[10] They work in reciprocity: as Hermann attacked him for worthlessness, Kafka in his perception of himself managed to become the rightful object of such attacks. But little of this is accurate: Kafka did graduate with a law degree, did hold a responsible job (in early 1920 he was promoted to institute secretary, with a salary increase the next month), and had been publishing on and off for seven years. Furthermore, he had in his desk hundreds of pages of other manuscript materials. In the personal area, he was considered a failure only because he had set for himself a standard he could not meet. What Kafka neglects in this passage and elsewhere is how his perception of his failure became part of his view of how the world worked; that without the perception, in which Hermann was an inevitable victim, he, Kafka, would lose his most significant insights. Trying to find justification for his father's treatment of him, he has Hermann say, in a created dialogue, that his son was "not capable of living." In this imagined dialogue Hermann calls Kafka "dishonest, equivocal, parasitical"; the *Letter* is merely another example of his son's "parasitical sucking."

In this fantasy, Kafka of course validates his story "The Judgment." He also raises the interesting question of whether the *Letter* was so necessary because it reinforced what he had written fictionally, or whether, in a second possibility, Kafka was so involved in the workings of self and other that he could not distinguish between fact and fiction. In this regard, he desperately needed his perception of Hermann to validate his fiction, and as desperately he needed his fiction to validate his view of Hermann.

Kafka accuses his father of bringing children up by irony, in which everything becomes either the opposite of what Hermann really means or else an exaggeration. It is a rhetorical device adopted to create feelings of inferiority in the child who does not understand the frustration or even cruelty behind it — "Can't you do such a simple thing right?" instead of the more straightforward "I'd like you to learn to do this correctly." Or, "I suppose this is too hard for you," instead of "If this is too hard for you, let me show you how to do it."[11] Yet Hermann had neither time nor inclination for niceties. From his *shtetl* background, he was conditioned for rough and ready action. Parental superiority was demonstrated not through reasonableness, but through verbal and physical intimidation. It was, all in all, faster, and parents of that generation and background were not aware of either psychological damage or loss of respect. Hermann simply took it for granted that parental rights were written in stone. Kafka, who knew his Freud before Freud, was of another generation and had been sensitized to a different order of being.

He attacks Hermann for saying nasty things about his oldest sister, Elli, whom, Kafka admits, he disliked and enjoyed hearing attacked as a "great fat lump" or described as a piggish eater. Kafka's insight is brilliant: "The expenditure of anger and malice seemed to be in no proper relation to the subject itself, one did not have the feeling that the anger was caused by this trifle of sitting some way back from the table, but that the whole bulk of it was already there to begin with, then only by chance happened to settle on this matter as a pretext for breaking out."[12] He comprehends that Hermann had a driving need to assert himself caustically, that the father as a result of his conditioning was so filled with anxiety and dread of failing nothing could satisfy him. Kafka knows this, and yet he asks why Hermann's need could not have been curbed. Since it could not, then any action on the children's part to placate the man went unnoticed. "So you suffered and we suffered," pulled to pieces as they were by endless entanglements.

At some later point in his correspondence with Milena Jesenská,

Kafka sent on a drawing of his that is reminiscent of the needle machine in "In the Penal Colony." It is a different "machine," but basically it is the same kind of sadomasochistic process. He explains it:

> There are four poles, through the middle ones are driven rods to which the hands of the "delinquent" are fastened; through the two outer poles rods are driven for the feet. After the man has been bound in this way the rods are drawn slowly outwards until the man is torn apart in the middle. Against the post leans the inventor who, with crossed arms and legs, is giving himself great airs, as though the whole thing were his original invention, whereas he has only copied the butcher who stretches the disembowelled pig in his shopfront.[13]

It seems that Kafka is the one being torn to pieces, while Hermann is, apparently, the inventor of the contraption. But if that sounds too simple, the point is that Kafka perceives himself as both victim and victimizer. He has assigned to himself a brutal death, like that by which vile criminals or heretics were torn apart by horses tied to their limbs. For Kafka, it was not sufficient to be so bound and tortured; he had to be the designer of his own torment, as part of his role-playing. It is consistent with his presentation of Gregor in "The Metamorphosis," the father as seeming authority figure who wants Gregor dead, but also Gregor himself who has absorbed the role of victim. Kafka seeks torture in regions that go well beyond sadomasochism, beyond what he felt psychoanalysis could penetrate, into areas where one seeks emblems both for unexplored personal territory and the human condition.

With its rods and bindings, this torture machine recalls the cross on which Jesus was crucified while others looked on unconcerned. Kafka here identifies with that aspect of Jesus that, seeking redemption in torture, finds something sacred in a secular punishment. The moment the body begins to pull apart is for Kafka an artistic-poetic instant: the ecstasy felt by the believer on one hand, by the artist-creator on the other. The one way he knew how to induce such ecstasy was by suffering and pain, which he equated with the creative act. In presenting Milena with this machine for punishment, while really applying it to his relationship with his father, Kafka had produced an extended metaphor of how the artist functions, at least if that artist is Kafka. As in most Modernists, art and death are never too distant from each other.

Letter to His Father is, ostensibly, about Hermann Kafka, but the missing link is Julie; and in one respect her near absence makes her an equal player with her husband. In one of the few references, Kafka attacks Julie as unconsciously playing the part of a beater during a hunt. "Even if your [Hermann's] method of upbringing might in some unlikely case have set me on my own feet by means of producing defiance, dislike, or even hate in me, Mother canceled that out again by kindness, by talking sensibly. . . . and I was again driven back into your orbit, which I might otherwise have broken out of, to your advantage and to my own."[14] On occasion, Julie shielded her son from Hermann's wrath, but that only made Kafka more furtive and deceptive. The failure of the mother to stand up to her husband echoes back to the son's losing a vital defense against the tyranny of the father. Kafka's indictment of the mother, even when she is absent, is more poignant, since in his perception of events, the mother, the woman, the softer one, should have protected him by defying the authoritarian.

In this brief but caustic vignette of Mother as beater in a hunt, we have one of the formative stages of Kafka's attitude toward women, already mentioned but worthy of repetition. In their weakness, women contain the strength to destroy a sensitive man; thus women become dangerous creatures, whose seeming weakness is overcome by their need to destroy or subvert the male. This attitude leads, in turn, to Kafka's distaste for physical contact, his finicky eating habits, his digestive problems, his general fastidiousness, all in some way linked to the failure of the female. There is, clearly, no linear sequence of events here, and inevitably we confront mysteries whose secrets cannot be elicited. But we receive the impression from the *Letter* that if things had gone differently with Julie, in her son's perception, then he could have withstood Hermann.

Since Kafka did not know what was expected of him, he felt reduced. Hermann humiliated his children by speaking of the past, but instead of using his history as cautionary, he turned it into an offensive weapon, attacking the soft life of his children. His childhood disorders were all "lacks," from lack of food (lucky to have potatoes), lack of shoes and other essential articles of clothing, lack of space (everyone slept in one room), lack of health care (untreated open sores on his legs from insufficient clothing), to lack of understanding of who he was and where he was going. He then left for the army and contributed money for the home.

Hermann resonates like a drum, going into his act in front of his sister, Kafka's Aunt Julie. "She too has the huge face of all Kafka's relatives," Kafka writes, an indication of Kafka's revulsion in their presence. "There is," further, "something wrong and something disturbing about the set or color of her eyes."[15] She too suffered terrible privations as a child, forced out into the severe cold, so that the skin on her legs cracked, her skimpy skirt froze and only dried out at night in bed. All this was true, and Kafka saluted them for having survived such a childhood and young adulthood. But Kafka also wondered what pedagogical significance it had for him, since none of these conditions now applied. Hermann's very triumph in life had been to provide well for his children, so that none of them suffered privations. Given that, what could he gain from his pride in having come so far from his beginnings, unless it was an effort to crush his children, and especially his son?

The aim was to turn the son into an ungrateful person, so low and contemptuous he was little better than an insect. Kafka points out that there was no opportunity for him to distinguish himself as his father had done. The real alternative, he says, was to break from home, through violence or rebellion, and that of course was precisely what he was unable to accomplish. But, like Hermann, he is entrapped in his own needs. "But that is not what you wanted at all, that you termed ingratitude, extravagance, disobedience, treachery, madness. And so, while on the one hand, you tempted me to it by means of example, story, and humiliation, on the other hand you forbade it with the utmost severity."[16] What escapes Kafka is how ensnared both men are in worlds of their making: Hermann sending out mixed signals, which allow no escape and permit him no peace of mind; and the son refusing that rebellion and instead allowing himself to become caught in the father's mixed signals. Kafka would love to do something, but he does not know what, if anything, could placate the raging father.

He chooses to become a bug.* "I could enjoy what you gave, but only in humiliation, weariness, weakness, and with a sense of guilt." He is grateful the way a beggar is. He takes up the family shop as an example of how it might have worked magic within his life. It was, as he recalls it, lighted and animated; it had so much to see and hear, it was a kind of magical place in which the father held sway, made jokes, was clearly a good salesman. But all this was spoiled for the boy by the way Hermann treated the staff. "You I heard and saw shouting, cursing and raging in the shop, in a way that in my opinion at that time had not its equal anywhere in the world." He tyrannized over the workers, called them "paid enemies," said he hoped an assistant with tuberculosis would die soon, the sooner the better; and in this way, a potentially magic place, the shop, became hellish, analogous to the home.

This leads back to Julie Kafka, in the sense that she failed him when she could have been supportive. The protection she afforded the fleeing Kafka was always in reference to Hermann's needs. "She loved you too much and was too devoted and loyal to you to have been able to constitute an independent spiritual force, in the long run, in the child's struggle."[17] By trying to understand his mother's "defection," Kafka was positioning himself for his fiction. It was absolutely necessary for him to find women who would fail him, repeatedly, so that he could justify his view of Julie; and, conversely, it was as necessary for him to undermine her so that he could justify his attitude toward women. The lines describing her in the *Letter*, in lieu of any other creative writing, helped keep her insufficiency before him. As the years

---

*His later comment to Ottla, March 9, 1921, is appropriate here: "I am reluctant to return to my place in the domestic nest, where all around the little beaks are opening wide, perhaps to receive the poison that I disseminate" (*Letters to Ottla*, p. 64).

passed, Kafka accuses, his mother took on more and more of Hermann's positions, blindly adopting his judgments and condemnations, so that the two seemed to speak with one voice. Yet he feels some sorrow about her, recognizing how she, caught up in both the house and the business, was never allowed any independent life. None of this allowed her to break away into becoming herself; and she took the brunt of the children's attacks, since Hermann kept himself out of the line of fire. Kafka is describing here a war in which he could not be a warrior, or even a loyal vassal.

Then in a brilliant examination of his sister Elli, Kafka defines his own personality as fitting into what Freud called the anal type: he describes his need to hold on to everything (the ceaseless chewing of food and then constipation), his economy passing into parsimony. Elli too had suffered from some of these characteristics, but once she rebelled and left home, she became cheerful, carefree, generous, and brave — all the qualities denied to her older brother, he says. On Ottla, Kafka reaches even greater heights in his assessment. He senses that all that Hermann feels for her, when she was not in danger, is hatred, because she always seemed intentionally to be causing him suffering and annoyance. Hermann sees her as "a sort of fiend."[18] He says she "is so remote that you scarcely see her any more, but set a specter in the place where you suppose her to be." Kafka himself views Ottla as a Löwy "equipped with the best Kafka weapons," a lovely image of the monster she had become in Hermann's eyes. "Between us [Kafka and father] there was no real struggle; I was soon finished off; what remained was flight, embitterment, melancholy, and inner struggle. But you two were always in fighting position, always fresh, always energetic."

The reader should not miss the wit underlying Kafka's condemnation: gallows wit, perhaps, but also a relish in his use of words. Kafka is fighting back superbly, and he is winning because he is fighting by way of the written word. He can say anything he wishes, and his words here ring true. We can virtually overhear the splendid struggle between the proud Ottla and the overmatched Hermann: Ottla with Löwy brains and Kafka muscularity beating Hermann to a protesting pulp. Kafka loves every minute of this *danse macabre* that has taken place in his own home; it is, for him, close to the highest reaches of human endeavor, just below art itself. Of course, in that kind of balletic struggle, he was useless, unless he could retreat to the written word. When the other side was not present to shout him down, he was splendid. He even says that under different circumstances "the two of you would have become a magnificently harmonious pair."[19] Of course, then Kafka would not have had the basis for this splendid attack.

He has thought of still another possible nasty rejoinder from Hermann, who might say his son acts out of nothing but coldness and treachery toward his family, while with others he is affectionate and loyal. Kafka admits that even in different circumstances "I should probably have become a shy and nervous person, but it is a long dark road from there to where I have really come to."[20] He derives his guilt feelings as part of this transaction, starting when he, the once loyal son, lost his self-confidence where Hermann was concerned. He says part of this process occurred when his father tore to shreds every single person who was important to his son. Now comes an even larger, darker charge: "I found equally little means of escape from you in Judaism." Here we enter a region in which Kafka found such mixed signals he had no idea what to grab hold of. He found both intense Judaism in Hermann and also anti-Semitism directed toward those Jews whom he felt he had risen above. Kafka's own uneasiness about being an acculturated Jew comes to a head here, and there is little question that Hermann in going from *shtetl* and poverty to Prague and relative prosperity was also befuddled. Trying to balance race, religion, and assimilation, he found only self-hatred.

What kind of Judaism did he, the son, get from his father? As a child, Kafka reproached himself for not going to the synagogue enough, for not fasting or otherwise holding to Jewish laws. From this, he felt he was transgressing, not against himself but against his father. Hermann chastised him for not honoring his religion, when such religion was for the father only an "insignificant scrap." Hermann wanted it both ways: he did not need to maintain the laws but wanted his son to. The son sees all this as a joke, since Hermann attended the synagogue only four days of the year. Kafka then becomes quite amusing, at his own expense. He speaks of how bored he was at services, how he yawned and dozed, his boredom comparable only to that in dancing class. When the Ark of the Covenant was opened during services, he was reminded, as noted, "of the shooting galleries where a cupboard door would open in the same way whenever one got a bull's-eye, only with the difference that there something interesting always came out and here it was always just the same old dolls with no heads."[21]

Kafka finally began to recognize that with all his bluster and failure to attend regularly at the synagogue Hermann had brought traces of Judaism with him from "that ghetto-like little village community." Dissipated during military service and then again in Prague, it was still there, and Kafka proceeds deftly to analyze it. Hermann's Jewishness was connected to social ideas, certain as he was that his opinions were correct and justified because they were rooted in a particular class of Jewish society. Yet none of this belief, which was more social than religious, was sufficient to pass along; it could only be dribbled out and, thus, dissipated among the children. Yet Hermann held on as if what he had to pass on was meaningful. "For you they [his flimsy gestures at religion] had their meaning as little souvenirs of earlier times, and that was why you wanted to pass them on to me, but this, since after all even for you they no longer had any value in themselves, was something you could do only by means of persuasions or threats."[22]

The son suffers from being the typical deracinated Jew, cut off from all forms of reinforcement of who and what he is, or might have been. History has failed him. Kafka is struggling not only with the relationship between father and son, but with the very question of survival that is embedded in identity. He feels adrift, an urbanized, cosmopolitan man who can believe in nothing, who feels supported by nothing; and as he digs ever deeper into the reasons why, as he probes background and history, he runs up against the villain of the piece, his father. The *Letter* at this stage goes much further than the clash of personalities and the differing needs of father and son, but leads into areas of how the son was shaped as a result of the father's failings in matters of religion, faith, and related matters. The conclusion is devastating, and here we are tempted to accept Kafka's version of events, simply because Hermann was conflicted by matters he could not possibly understand, much less assimilate.

> I have received [Kafka writes] a certain retrospective confirmation of this view of your Judaism from your attitude in recent years, when it seemed to you that I was taking more interest in Jewish things. As you have a dislike in advance of every one of my activities and particularly of the nature of my interest, so you have had it here too. But in spite of this general attitude, one would really have expected that here you would make a little exception. It was, after all, Judaism of your Judaism that was here stirring, and thus with it the possibility too of the start of new relations between us.[23]

Yet he goes further and admits that if Hermann had showed interest in Kafka's studies, then such studies would have become suspect in Kafka's own eyes. "For I do not dream of asserting that I am in this respect in any way better than you." This is in keeping with the son's emphasis that he is exactly what the father made him. The best revenge is to remind Hermann that what he cannot bear in the son is precisely what was in the father; conversely, the self-punishment Kafka suffers from is the recognition of how much of Hermann lies in him. Everything Kafka thought about Judaism became abhorrent to Hermann, "unreadable," or it "nauseated you." From this, Kafka extrapolates that the only Judaism of meaning to Hermann was *his* Judaism, those shreds and dribbles carried over from childhood, and "beyond that there was nothing."[24] Thus in the father's hands Judaism becomes a further weapon, and the so-called nausea of Kafka's religion was directed not against the religion "but against me personally."

This leads Kafka into an even more delicate area, and, if we can accept his view, it was so deep a hatred as to pass understanding. He is like a revenging Medea with Jason, or Clytemnestra with Agamemnon. He is reversing "The Judgment" and seeking Hermann's death. The reason is the father's attitude toward the son's writing. Kafka pictures himself as a worm that, "as a foot tramples on the tail end of it, breaks loose with its top end and drags itself aside."[25] Kafka's indictment is that Hermann refused to read his son's work because he feared it meant the son's freedom. The son exalts in that as the reason for the rejection: "because to me that formula sounded something like: 'Now you are free!'" Obviously, he was not, or not *yet*. "My writing was all about you; all I did there, after all, was to bemoan what I could not bemoan upon your breast. It was an intentionally long-drawn-out leave-taking from you, only although it was brought about by force on your part, it did not take its course in the direction determined by me."[26]

To make his point, Kafka is reducing his work, simplifying it to resonate with father-son antipathies and little else; he exaggerates for the sake of the argument. For the works that seem all about Hermann are also about many other things. Very possibly the central document in any understanding of Kafka's inner world and his role as an artist, "The Metamorphosis," is about a great deal more than his struggle with his father, although that element cannot be neglected or marginalized. It is also about more than any general father-son relationship, although that too is not to be ignored. And, further, it is about more than Kafka's taking leave from parental tyranny, although such an element is present in the story also. By bringing his work down to the personal level, Kafka has made it seem more of a weapon against Hermann than it can possibly be. For in his fictions he has transformed personal and familial feelings into something representative not only of father-son conflicts, but of conflicts that range across the entire society.

"The Metamorphosis" examines the dynamics of family life in a post-Freudian era; it examines the relationship of a contemporary man to his work, to the demeaning nature of a routine job, to the tyranny of his superiors. It examines, further, the ways in which an individual plots his survival, what he feels about himself, how he creates his identity and, when it crumbles, how he reshapes it. Most of all, it examines the dread that all people feel within themselves, and how that dread cannot be ascribed simplistically to any one formula, to any one style of life. Intermixed and deeply involved in all this is the father-son conflict, but also sibling tensions, and beyond that, the son's disappointment at the mother's lack of involvement on his behalf. That dread which lies at the center of the story, and which Kafka attempted to recapture in fiction after fiction, in his diaries and letters, would exist apart from Hermann's presence, although that presence surely exacerbated an already unbearable loss of faith and nerve.

From this, Kafka moves to something else that is emotionally meaningful for parents (and an easy target to attack), the education of their children. His strategy is clear: by demeaning and debasing himself as an uneducated fellow, he can point up Hermann's folly in thinking his son received the best. After stating that "Jewish schoolchildren in our country often tend to be odd," he asserts he is the oddest of them all: "Something like my cold indifference, scarcely disguised, indestructible, childishly helpless, approaching the ridiculous, and brutishly complacent, the indifference of a self-sufficient but cold imaginative child, I have never found anywhere else, but admittedly here it was the sole defense against destruction of the child's nerves by fear and a sense of guilt."[27]

Little of Kafka's coldness and indifference, as he calls them, may really lie at Hermann's feet. The reasoning is torturous, the perception anguished, since Kafka's nature could have been shaped by forces quite distinct from Hermann's influence on him: by the early death of two younger brothers; by the birth in rapid order of three sisters; by an absent mother, responsible for working in the shop; and beyond that by the fact he was in the hands of help, of nurses and housemaids, during his formative years. Kafka is on a course to destroy Hermann by denigrating himself, but in so doing, he reshapes the past as he would do in his writing.

Kafka even blames Hermann for the way he grew tall and lanky, "without knowing what to do with my lankiness, the burden being too heavy, the back becoming bent."[28] He was left open to every form of hypochondria, "until finally under the strain of the superhuman effort of wanting to marry . . . blood came from the lung." This sequence of his "case history" is so compelling because now, at thirty-six, Kafka sounds like a child reciting a litany of complaints. The father becomes central in a drama in which he played almost no part, since Kafka's tubercular condition obviously was not connected to his failure to marry. Nor was that failure directly connected to Hermann, but to fears in Kafka himself that were only generally and indirectly reinforced by the father. Where Hermann was tangential, Kafka makes him central.

He then winds back to education, and how at every stage, as we have noted earlier, he thought he would fail, so that each passing stage was for him a sign of the failure to come. For this he blames Hermann: "I positively had the proof of it [that failure was forthcoming] in your forbidding expression — that the more things I was successful in, the worse the final outcome would inevitably be."[29] But Hermann's "forbidding expression" could as well have been his growing realization that his sole surviving son was someone he could not possibly fathom; was far more Löwy than Kafka; and was, furthermore, moving into areas of education and manner that excluded Hermann and all his past history. It was a recognition that he had no one to follow him, and he feared rejection even before it came.

Taking up his career choice, Kafka points out it was really no choice at all. "Everything would be exactly as much a matter of indifference to me as all the subjects taught at school, and so it was a matter of finding a profession that would be most likely to allow me to indulge this indifference without overmuch injuring my vanity."[30] Out of this came law, after a senseless fortnight's study of chemistry and an equally futile six months of German studies. Yet it is unclear how Kafka's indifference and his selection, finally, of law were directly linked to Hermann. Kafka is digging around in a very gray area, where he had entered and where Hermann could not have followed. The father had no knowledge of how schools or professions worked. What Kafka ascribes specifically to Hermann was a universal situation, the son exploring, the father unable even to comprehend the direction.

Kafka now moves on to marriage, saying that Hermann has ranked the failure of his near marriages with all the rest of his failures. He emphasizes that he considers marriage and raising a family to be "the utmost a human being can succeed in doing at all."[31] He neglects to say he feels this only in theory; in practice, the one marriage he did observe revolted him. The mere idea of living closely with another, physically and emotionally, was intolerable. Whenever father and son touched on such matters or on sex itself, Kafka says the advice forthcoming was "the filthiest thing possible." Perhaps Hermann had informed his son that masturbation was the safest form of sexual relief until marriage, but whatever had occurred, Kafka, with his distaste for physical details, was appalled. We recall, if we believe Kafka, that Hermann offered to accompany Kafka to a brothel rather than have him marry Julie Wohryzek. Yet whores were a fact of life in Prague and in all the cities of the empire; however distasteful to Kafka, who did nevertheless visit them, they were a bourgeois society's indispensable way of keeping its respectable women pure.

What Hermann found so unacceptable in his son's possible marriage to Julie Wohryzek was her lack of social standing. But here we note a subtle social discrimination. For Julie's father was clearly of the same status as Hermann himself, and by objecting to her family background Herr Kafka was objecting to his own. And in objecting to Julie herself, Hermann was vaunting his son, his son's education, his career at the institute, even his writing, while he saw Julie as a mere shopgirl. So in this round robin of acceptances and rejections, Hermann was denying someone not much different from himself or the woman *he* married, and was at the same time forced to build up the very son whose career he has seen as wasted.

Kafka wants to air the marriage issues thoroughly. He states that neither young woman, Felice or Julie, disappointed him; he disappointed both of them, although each case was different. He tries to be candid and explain why marriage is impossible for him: "The essential obstacle, however, which was unfortunately independent of the individual case, was that I am obviously intellectually incapable of marrying. This manifests itself in the fact that from the moment when I make up my mind to marry I can no longer sleep, my head burns day and night, life can no longer be called life, I stagger about in despair."[32] Yet this inability to consider marriage cannot be disconnected from his relationship to Hermann; in this attack, marriage and family life are linked.

Kafka's logic now becomes anguished. The way to gain independence from Hermann, "in the particularly unhappy relationship in which I stand to you,"[33] is to do something that has no association with him. Marrying is the greatest thing of all and provides the "most honorable independence." But, and the "but" alters everything, "it is also at the same time in the closest relation to you. To try to get out at this point therefore has a touch of madness about it, and every attempt is almost punished by it." One cannot escape Hermann, according to this logic, because he is stretched out flat across the entire map of the world, all-powerful, omnipresent, and inescapable.

Kafka's logic is that he cannot marry because marriage is represented to him by Hermann and Julie. Ironically, he describes their marriage as a model in terms of "constancy, mutual help, number of children,"[34] and even when the children grew up and disturbed everyone's equanimity, the marriage remained untouched and untroubled. From this example, Kafka says he formed his high regard for marriage, but with that came the recognition that a good relationship to children does not necessarily follow. Kafka fears a repetition of his own situation, "a fear that one's children would some time pay one out for the sins one has oneself committed against one's own parents." This relocates the matter from marriage, impossible because Hermann and Julie reflect the institution, to children. Yet, to shift his tactics, Kafka is not even sure of this argument since he feels his own case is special, and this tormenting feeling of uniqueness makes the idea of repetition unthinkable. Then he belittles himself further by saying that if he had a son like himself, "mute, glum, dry, doomed," unbearable, he would, as Hermann threatened to do, emigrate in order to flee from him. And this too bears on his incapacity to marry.

Yet it all comes down to the same thing: he is unable constitutionally to seek independence. Kafka is not handing the field over to his father, he is not conceding defeat, nor is he seeking bilateral disarmament. He is biding his time for a final and complete victory, but on his terms, which *are* unique. He described his inability to marry even more firmly and eloquently in a letter to Brod, later, a desperate admission on his part and surely linked to this explanation to Herr Kafka.

The fact was [he writes] that the body of every other girl tempted me, but the body of the girl in whom I placed my hopes (for that reason?) not at all. As long as she withheld herself from me (F) or as long as we were one (M), it was only a menace from far away, and not even so very far; but as soon as the slightest little thing happened, everything collapsed. Evidently on account of my dignity, on account of my pride (no matter how humble he looks, the devious West European Jew!), I can love only what I can place so high above me that I cannot reach it.*35

Kafka is right on the edge of discovering the real reasons why he can find exogamous sexuality tempting, but with anyone close to him, like Felice or even Milena, impossible. The fear of incest was there, and the bond with his mother unmistakable, not to mention his three younger sisters. The elevation of the mother to Madonna figure, or else the oedipal desire for her, created an alternating distaste for sexuality because of the fear of consequences. Furthermore, the presence of those three younger sisters might very well have led Kafka on several grounds into confusion. Their mere presence could have made it difficult for him to dissociate sexual love from forbidden feelings; and the household, except for him, was run mainly on female lines. With Hermann, the god figure, away in the shop, the apartment was overrun with sisters, housemaids, cook, nurse, governess, and the like, all women. Kafka apparently did not develop to the stage where he could disconnect the women in the house from women in general; and his visits to brothels and to shopgirl-whores in his youth were indications of how sexuality could be experienced only in settings completely opposite to the values of the home. The further fact that almost up until his death he continued to return to his parents' apartment suggests he needed the protection of those forbidden feelings in order to validate his distaste for sexuality with anyone close to him. He saw in his parents' sexuality something utterly repellent, primarily because he could not bear the thought of Hermann succeeding with the "Madonna" he created, whereas he, Kafka, lay in the next room and listened to the noise of the hated one's success.

None of this was simple with Kafka, and one should not put him in some sexual either-or situation, either Madonna or whore.† Such re-

---

*Several letters to Brod in this period, the spring of 1921, while Kafka was attempting to recuperate at Matliary, in the High Tatras in Slovakia, are deeply felt and expressive examples of his correspondence.
†In this regard, Kafka's problem might not have been unique. During his maturity, statistics indicate that fully 33 percent of Jewish grooms married Gentile women. Furthermore, by 1921, in a related matter, only 15 percent of Bohemian Jews identified themselves as Jews, 35 percent as Germans, and the other 50 percent as Czechs — another example of how Jews tried to bury themselves in the national Gentile population. As part of this new development, even as Czech clerics and politicians pointed out that Jews could never be Czechs, Jews put out magazines such as *Rozvoj*, which emphasized assimilation. Jews started to claim Czech as their language of common usage. Of course, any effort at acculturation or assimilation was futile; while German Jews hoped to be accepted as Germans, there could be no such phenomenon as "Czech Jews." In a parallel movement, even as one-third of Bohemian Jews identified themselves as Germans, the Czech German minority became strongly pro-Nazi. Bohemian Jews overall were declining in Kafka's lifetime, from close to 100,000 in 1890 to 80,000 in 1921, and to about 75,000 in 1930.

ductionism vulgarizes the subtleties of his tortured position. His complicated attitudes and complex responses, if we can pin them down, appear in his stories or parables. There is one he relates to Brod, in mid-April 1921, which plays in and out of his parents' condition, while ostensibly about the Trojan War. That "anonymous Greek" in the brief tale could be Joseph K., K., Kafka, or any one of his protagonists: the representative Kafka man.

> Sometimes for fun I imagine an anonymous Greek who comes to Troy without ever having intended to. He has not got his bearings yet when he finds himself in the thick of the battle. The gods themselves don't yet know what the issue is, but he is hanging from a Trojan chariot and being dragged around the city. It is long before Homer has yet begun to sing, but he is already lying there with glassy eyes, if not in the dust of Troy, then in the cushions of the reclining chair. And why? Hecuba [wife of Priam, king of Troy] is nothing to him, of course. But Helen too is not a decisive factor. Just as the other Greeks, summoned by the gods, set out and under the protection of the gods gave battle, so he set out, impelled by a father's kick, and gave battle under his father's curse. Lucky that there were other Greeks there, or else world history would have remained restricted to two rooms in his parental house and the threshold between them.[36]

The reverberations of this are immense, and if we peer deeply enough we see the patterns of *The Castle* embedded in this "surveyor" of the Trojan War. But it is of course Kafka who is winding back to himself, driven out by Hermann into a war he never understood, never wanted, an older man's war. How does this reflect Kafka's "historical destiny"? It presents him as that twentieth-century traveler who, without too much understanding of who he is or what he wishes, moves into one situation after another; and since it is the twentieth century, the situations are all Trojan Wars, all scenes of death, with images of victors and losers, scenes in which everyone inevitably loses. Kafka and Death: here he gives historical memory to the century, and to himself, he who is never far behind his interpretation of anything.

This moves back to the final pages of *Letter to His Father*. Kafka repeats his statement about escape — to avoid those "two rooms in his parental house" — and says that while marriage seemed to offer it, it would have jeopardized his more valid effort at escape, his writing. "Marriage is the possibility of such a danger."[37] Then, playing the serpent finding a point of attack from unusual positions, he twists himself into coils in order to strike back at Hermann. "In the face of every little thing you by your example and your method of upbringing convinced me, as I have tried to describe, of my incapacity, and what turned out to be right in the case of every little thing, proving you to be in the right, naturally could not but turn out to be tremendously right when it came to the greatest thing of all, that is to say, when it came to marriage."[38] The turning and twisting sentence registers Kafka's agitation.

Then he moves in for what is for him the kill. He puts Hermann's response to him in the form of a monologue, in which the father is given the opportunity to answer. But the answer is really Kafka's use of a reversal, for he intends Hermann's words, which are devastating, to be part of his own answer to his father, putting them into Herr Kafka's mouth because he cannot say them directly. The father says there are two kinds of fighting: "chivalrous fighting," in which independent opponents measure each other, with one winning, one losing; and the other kind, "the fighting of vermin," in which they "not only sting but at the same time suck the blood too to sustain their own life."[39] He says that is what the professional soldier is, and that is what Kafka is. "You [the son] are unfit for life; but in order to be able to settle down in it comfortably, without worries and without self-reproaches, you prove that I have deprived you of all your fitness for life and put it into my pockets."

"What does it matter to you now," Hermann says to his son, "if you are unfit for life, now it is my responsibility, but you calmly lie down and let yourself be hauled through life, physically and mentally."[40] Hermann's words clearly are Kafka's merciless way of attacking the now old man who is so ill and ineffective. It is an open question who is burying whom. Herr Kafka says his dislike of the marriage would not have prevented it but instead added stimulus to Kafka's desire to marry Julie Wohryzek. This is, of course, Kafka's own argument, turned around. In *his* response, Kafka says that this entire rejoinder can be turned against Hermann and originates in the son. If the father had ever read the letter, the irony here would have been lost; for Kafka is describing a Laocoön situation, in which it is impossible to distinguish the figure from the serpents intertwined and coiled around him. At the end of the letter, Kafka says he hopes this effort at the truth "may be able to reassure us both a little and make our living and our dying easier."[41] It would, obviously, not have done that at all, nor was it intended to. The letter was therapeutic to some degree, but more than that, it was an act of such great rebellion that Kafka had to express it in order to continue living.

The *Diaries* for 1922, when Kafka's physical condition was clearly deteriorating, contain a long entry that fits perfectly into the 1919 mental attitude of *Letter*. It is a litany of failure, of a somewhat different kind from what he presented to his father, but nevertheless part of his perception of himself when faced by death. He starts by saying his life until now has been marking time, and has progressed at best in the way that decay progresses in a rotten tooth. He tries a spatial analogy. It was as if he had been given a point "from which to prolong the radius of a circle, and had then, like everyone else, to describe my perfect circle round this point." Laboring in this respect like Sisyphus, he was forever starting his radius, only to be forced to break it off. He provides examples of efforts that, he says, went nowhere: "piano, violin, languages,

Germanics, anti-Zionism, Zionism, Hebrew, gardening, carpentering, writing, marriage attempts, an apartment of my own." He continues with the spatial metaphor: "The center of my imaginary circle bristles with the beginnings of radii, there is no room left for a new attempt; no room means old age and weak nerves, and never to make another attempt means the end." He wraps the entire metaphor in a characteristic enigma: "If I sometimes prolonged the radius a little farther than usual, in the case of my law studies, say, or engagements, everything was made worse rather than better just because of this little extra distance."[42]

Drifting toward death, Kafka could not hide. There is little role-playing here, even less than in the *Letter*, where he assumed several shapes in order to subvert paternal power. Yet even here, in this "death statement" of failure and impotence, he omits the most important part of his life, where he was eminently successful, his writing. Part of him knew he was superior to every fiction writer contemporaneous with him in the German-speaking world, with the possible exceptions of Thomas Mann and Robert Musil. He could not, however, have dreamed that along with James Joyce and Marcel Proust, he would be considered among the three most significant prose writers of the twentieth century, and even more than the other two, the writer who represented and reflected his age and who gave his name to the century.

His name has become part of our vocabulary in a way denied the other major writers of the period, and the adjective formed from Kafka reflects not only what he wrote and thought but what he was: a recording instrument of that subterranean world lying parallel to daily existence. Kafka spoke of himself as a memory "come alive," but he was also psychoanalysis "come alive." On several occasions in letters and diary entries, he spoke out against psychoanalysis, yet he had himself become psychoanalysis, as he had become memory. Nevertheless, he needed the litany of failure to drive him on, and in his final years he pushed himself relentlessly to write a new novel and several of his most exacting stories.

Kafka was always seeking spatial metaphors to express his condition, not only physically but also psychologically, even in his attitude toward language and its reach as art. In the period between the fall and spring of 1922, he wrote two pieces, "First Sorrow" and "A Hunger Artist," of which the first is a spatial metaphor of Kafka's perception of his condition. It is less well known than "A Hunger Artist," but it is no less a gem of concision and resonance. Here the artist is a trapeze performer who practices high "in the vaulted domes of the great variety theatres." So intense is his devotion to the trapeze that he refuses to come down. He practices his skills by staying aloft continually, and he maintains there his mental composure. All his needs are supplied by relays of attendants, who observe him from below and through specially constructed containers haul up and down whatever he requires. Because he is an extraordinary and unique artist, this soon becomes acceptable behavior. The management "recognized that this mode of life was no mere prank, and that only in this way could he really keep himself in constant practice and his art at the pitch of its perfection."[43]

The trapeze artist finds it quite healthy up there and especially refreshing in the spring when the windows around the dome are left open. Although he finds his social life limited, he chats occasionally with fellow acrobats, repairmen working on the roof, or firemen inspecting the facilities. "Otherwise nothing disturbed his seclusion." In his eyrie, he has the same seclusion and services performed for him which Kafka once described to Felice Bauer as his cellar experience: once married, he would live in some subterranean space, where he would write, and she would bring his meals. But there is an interruption when the trapeze artist must travel, and even though management does everything possible to get him to his new trapeze as rapidly as possible, he is miserable when on the road and when confronted by new quarters. On the train, so as not to lose his skill, he passes his time in the luggage rack.

But the artist is not satisfied, and on one trip, near tears, he demands a second trapeze for his performance. When he senses some slight hesitation in the manager, he bursts into tears, until the manager climbs on the seat to get to the luggage rack and calms the performer, assuring him of a second trapeze. Slowly, the artist is brought around, but the manager is not quite reassured himself. He keeps peering over at the performer, and as he wonders if this will be the end, he sees the "first furrows of care engraving themselves upon the trapeze artist's smooth, childlike forehead."[44]

Although this brief story moves us ahead to near the end of 1921, or even possibly 1922, it looks back to Kafka's state of mind when he wrote *Letter to His Father* and began his correspondence with Milena, at the end of 1919. The "second trapeze" that the performer demands and that upsets the manager is a typical Kafka touch: if one trapeze conveys near perfect isolation and silence, then a second will double it. And what the manager foresees, it seems, is that as the trapeze artist seeks ever greater perfection — the perfect performance, the perfect art, the perfect isolation — he will demand more and more trapezes, until his needs outrun the show itself. The care lines on the artist's face and the manager's unease are signals that the striving for a perfect art can have no end; it is in fact, to use an apposite spatial metaphor, bottomless.

This story and "A Hunger Artist" reflect each other. In the later story, the artist wastes away while the crowd rushes off to more spectacular exhibitions, the circus animals; here, the "wasting" begins in the need to acquire additional trapezes so the performer can strive for greater perfection. But the two are congruent, in that the hunger artist

wants to extend his fasting beyond the point of survival in order to justify his art, and the trapeze artist needs more and more equipment to
justify his quest for ever purer forms of art. Kafka's sense of the absolute forced him to seek extremes, and since extremes reach limits, he
was bound to come away frustrated. The perfect art eluded him, as
much as the perfect life, his ideal, had to elude him. We find still another reason why he asked Brod to burn his manuscripts after his death.

Back in November 1919, the time of the *Letter*, Kafka and Brod
spent a week together at the Pension Stüdl in Schelesen. There he met
Minze Eisner, a young woman whom he took up for a while as a correspondent, encouraging her in a fatherly way. Minze was convalescing
from a long and serious illness, and there was no question of a love affair. Rather, Kafka came to like her courage and thought she reminded
him of Ottla. His correspondence with her was fitful, but it lasted into
March of 1923, when she became engaged. The major part of it was his
attempt to help her keep going in the face of illness and personal disappointment — the opposite of his letters to Milena, which are almost
completely about himself. He repeats to her that the lungs become a
sacrifice when the head cannot take things any longer (his notion of
psychosomatic disease that makes tuberculosis a matter of neurosis).
When she complains she cannot find a place to stay, he tells her, playfully, he had no idea she could roll herself up into such a small ball. Yet
even as he gives her advice, both jocular and serious, he cannot avoid
pouring out his own view of life, which could be discouraging to a
young woman trying to fight her way out of illness. "Everyone has his
sharp-toothed sleep-destroying devil inside him [he writes], and this is
neither good nor bad, but is life. If one did not have him, one would not
live. . . . This devil is the material (and basically what wonderful material) that you have been endowed with and with which you are supposed to make something."[45]

Probably the major Kafka pronouncement comes in late March of
1921, when he was recovering at Matliary. Minze had praised fever,
writing the "faster and more beautifully to squander life, the better."
Kafka says there is no such thing as a mild fever, only "an abominable
fever," and that squandering her life that way is not at all beautiful.
"No one is squandering; he is being squandered."[46] He says that with
her fresh youth she can put up a strong fight against it. This leads Kafka
to one of his favorite authors, Schopenhauer, and with this, two wise
"old men" speak to the young, hopeful Minze. Kafka was paraphrasing
from *The World as Will and Representation* (1844). "Those who find
life beautiful would seem to have an easy time proving it so; all they
have to do is to point out the world from a balcony." However the
world might be, in bright or dreary weather, life and the world will always look hopeful from that view: "The region, whether varied or monotonous, will always be beautiful, the life of nations, of families, of

individuals, whether easy or difficult, will always be interesting and beautiful." But what does this mean, or prove? Only that the world "if it were nothing but a peepshow, would really be infinitely beautiful." It is all in the eye of the beholder, for the world is not like that at all, unfortunately. "Rather this beautiful life in a beautiful world has really to be lived through in every detail of every moment and that is no longer so beautiful, but simply toilsome."

The point by now seems commonplace in Kafka: his recognition that surfaces are for people who lack insight or prophetic powers. For those like him, those mundane details contain different meanings. But the commonplace of the idea, lovingly stated here, is directed at an eighteen-year-old who sees all life from that "balcony," where things look beautiful and fine. He tells her to look in the light of the kerosene, in the evening, when things look different. She must adjust to life as it is, not to the balcony of life. In this connection, Kafka even quotes a little story about Grillparzer, who faced the reality of existence, as against Friedrich Hebbel, the nineteenth-century dramatist, who wanted to be soothed. While the advice to Minze Eisner was only a sideshow for Kafka — Milena would shortly become the main arena — it reveals a soft, caring side. He was touched by this young woman and her optimism; and his response to her is paternal. What she felt on her side we do not know, and very possibly she saw this saturnine personality as a potential suitor. But there was something here that went beyond Kafka's usual desire for control in his correspondence with women; for moments he almost forgot himself.

Kafka returned to Prague from Schelesen but then fell ill. He was still seeing Julie Wohryzek, but that relationship was of course doomed. His promotion at the institute to institute secretary came through with a commensurate rise in salary, although in the period between the promotion and his retirement on July 1, 1922, he spent less and less time at work. He sided increasingly with workmen suing the institute for compensation, and secretly helped some to win their cases. Yet, withal, Kafka was considered an important part of the organization and very probably would have risen to quite a high position if he had stayed on for another twenty years.

This was, all in all, an exceptionally poor time for him. Except for occasional letters to Brod, Kurt Wolff, and Minze Eisner, he was doing almost no writing. His *Diaries* had become slack, with no entries for 1918, only a handful for 1919, and very few for the first half of 1920. The spare entries suggest his effort to come to terms, to grab hold of himself for some final swing into action or into writing. The confusion of realms is present, and clearly Kafka, having lost his bearings, was trying to rediscover them. "A segment has been cut out of the back of his head. The sun, and the whole world with it, peep in. It makes him nervous, it distracts him from his work, and moreover it irritates him that just he should be the one to be debarred from the spectacle."[47] Only *he* cannot look in. In another passage, he speaks of an imprisonment that continues unchanged, but then foresees that it may be the "necessary preliminary to an ultimate liberation."[48] After this, Kafka tore out several pages from the *Diaries* (the twelfth manuscript notebook), which then skip to October 1921. The correspondence with Milena helped fill in some of these gaps of creativity.

In March 1920, Kafka's colleague Janouch brought in his seventeen-year-old son, Gustav, and from this flowed a series of conversations. Since Kafka hardly ever sounds like himself in these so-called conversations — Janouch makes him sound like some benign Jewish prophet — we must be quite suspicious of his reputed pronouncements. Janouch was such a hero-worshipper that in his eyes Kafka becomes not a wise man but a saint. Accordingly, whatever is useful in the *Conversations with Kafka* (1951) must derive not from what Kafka said, but from Janouch's own observations of the office, Kafka's relationships to others, and other somewhat marginal matters; and even here, we must be cautious. Janouch put himself at Kafka's feet and missed the irony, the caustic wit, the self-abasement, although on occasion he does catch the despair and anguish.

Once we leave behind the artificial conversations with Janouch, what we find in Kafka is a serious search for an identity that can carry through his final years. In his approach to himself and to his work, or lack of it, is his sense that the world is squandering him and will continue to do so unless he can find the means to halt the process (or "trial"). He begins to doubt his own reality and questions whether he exists. Max Brod writes about this general period in Kafka's life as a crisis of faith, a faltering because he had lost his way as a Jew, and Brod tries to reincorporate Kafka back "in" by way of Judaism, by way of a direct identification with what he actually was. Brod does grant some existential dimension to Kafka's quest, in which the crisis of faith cannot be resolved, but ultimately he views Kafka as moving toward a resolution of his religious crisis. It is, I think, an entirely incorrect assumption, suiting Brod's perception but not Kafka's reality.

Brod quotes, in fact, from a February 28, 1920, conversation he had with Kafka which seems to deny the religious factor. Kafka is at his most ironic. He states, "We are nihilistic thoughts that came into God's head." Brod tries the Gnostic argument that the world is evidence of God's sinning. But Kafka will have none of that: it is too positive for him. "I believe we are not such a radical relapse of God's, only one of his bad moods. He had a bad day." Brod then asks where there would be hope. Kafka: "Plenty of hope — for God — no end of hope — only not for us."[49] These are not the words of a man seeking resolution, but of a man trying to find where he can fit in a world where everything is indifferent, patternless, directionless. Kafka's real question is where a man seeking direction can enter a world that itself lacks pattern. He moves toward the existential question of the individual's trying to fit into absurdity. Yet Kafka is not ready to test out existential waters, because, he knows ahead of time, there is no solution except in his writing itself.

He could not, however, make a religion of art, as so many of his contemporaries were doing. He needed to justify his existence. A good part of the relationship with Milena Jesenská — and it was mainly letters, as they met infrequently — concerned his effort to validate what he felt was a self being chewed up from outside. In a series of fragments called "He," he presents himself as a commentator on one Franz Kafka. He is both subject and observer, a curious example of the dualism he had practiced on and off throughout his life. As we read his comments in "Paralipomena,"* we become aware that this dualism had reached another stage: we see the living Kafka and the dead Kafka in a kind of dialogue that, as long as it can be maintained, will allow the living Kafka to continue.

> He is neither bold nor frivolous. But he is not timid, either. A free life would not cause him anxiety. Now, such a life has not been his lot, but even this does not worry him. . . . But there is a certain Someone, utterly unknown to him, who worries about him a great deal. . . . This Someone's worries concerning him, especially the continuity of these worries, are what sometimes, in a quiet hour, gives him a racking headache.[50]

That force from outside is somehow using him up, squandering him, as he says in another place.

"He lives in the Diaspora [he continues]. His elements, a horde that lives in freedom, roam about the world. And it is only because his room is, after all, part of the world that he sometimes sees them in the distance." He wonders how he can be responsible for them. But the more immediate question is how he can live amidst this freedom when his own life is circumscribed by a room. In that characteristic use of spatial relations, Kafka sees "life" from a distance; here, once again, we can see early glimmers of The Castle, which is all about spacing, peering, distancing, gauging perspectives, befitting its protagonist, a land-surveyor.

"He has a peculiar door to his apartment, once it has been slammed, it cannot be opened again, but has to be taken off its hinges. Consequently he never shuts it, on the contrary, he keeps the door permanently ajar. . . . As a result, he is, of course, deprived of all the comfort of home life." Although the neighbors are trustworthy, he must carry all his valuables with him in a briefcase; and when he lies on his sofa in his room, it is as though he were in the passage, "stuffy in the

---

*A series of aphorisms that appeared in the volume The Great Wall of China. Paralipomena are concise forms in which the preceding point or statement has been omitted. The aphorisms pick up in medias res.

summer, icy cold in the winter."[51] Kafka is the perpetual outcast, Cain, marked by his calling as a writer and artist, unable to close the door because he cannot completely cut himself off; and yet with the door open he is unable to partake fully of what he needs, privacy. As in so many of his metaphors, he is trapped in situations that point both ways and provide no resolution.

"He has [he writes] many judges, they are like a host of birds perching on a tree." With their voices commingled, individual competence cannot be ascertained. But a bird does stand out, and it recommends "that one has only once to cross over the side of the good and one is saved, without reference to the past and even without reference to the future." But this temptation to the good holds an obvious temptation to evil, and the judging bird does not recall a single case as falling within his competence. He is nevertheless surrounded by a crowd of candidates, "an everlastingly chattering mob that apes him."[52]

These roving comments in early 1920 thrust Kafka into the world presented in "Advocates," written in or around this time. It too is concerned with an area in which one's definition of self is undeterminable. "I was not at all certain whether I had any advocates. I could not find out anything definite about it, every face was unfriendly. . . . I could not even find out whether we were in a law court."[53] Yet if it were not a law court, he asks, then why was he searching for an advocate there? If the matter is a verdict, and Kafka feels on the edge of one, then one cannot have enough advocates. "Advocates galore, the best possible advocates, one next to the other, a living wall, for advocates are by nature hard to set in motion." Perhaps he should be seeking them in a huge fairground, not in corridors. He doesn't know where to look, he is confused and fearful time is running out. "The time allotted to you is so short that if you lose one second you have already lost your whole life, for it is no longer, it is always just as long as the time you lose." His advice: once you start out, continue, for you can only gain. In the end you may fall over a precipice, but if you turn back, you may fall down the steps at once. If you climb stairs, keep climbing, for as long as you climb the stairs won't end: "under your climbing feet they will go on growing upwards."

All of these remarks, whether in "Advocates" or in the diarylike "Paralipomena," are efforts to discover the arena in which the fight can go on. Kafka is not necessarily looking for victory; he is seeking the ground where the battle can begin and be continued. The dilemma can be found in a brief February 2 paradoxical entry: "My prison cell — my fortress." All the ambiguities are there, as well as the dualism of character: what keeps others out, keeps him in, a prisoner of his desire for isolation. Only extremes govern; no middle, only absolutes.

As his illness worsened, Kafka was uncertain about where he should go. He resisted the sanatorium, but applied, nevertheless, to one in Bavaria, in Kainzenbad. Meanwhile, his doctor recommended Meran in the South Tirol. His resistance to a sanatorium was part of his resistance to the inevitability of the disease; going meant full validation that he was one of "them," those who lie in the sun, watch everything they eat, and become, in effect, invalids.* The comments by "He," mentioned earlier, were part of that inner dialogue he was having with himself, about how he should arrange a future so that he was not already a dead man. At no point would he have identified more with Rilke's panther.

> The supple pace of powerful soft strides,
> turning in the very smallest circle,
> is like a dance of strength around a center
> in which a mighty will stands numbed.

At the end of February 1920, he received a six- to eight-week sick leave, the first of many such leaves and extensions until his actual retirement. He was, in effect, being supported by the institute while he recuperated — another example of how valuable an employee he was considered to be, and totally belying Kafka's own words about his ineffectuality and incompetence. When he had trouble gaining an entry permit for Kainzenbad, in Allied-conquered Germany, he decided to go to Meran, at the beginning of April, in the lovely Tirols. For many months, it became a home away from home, and it was from Meran, the Pension Ottoburg, that he began the long and extremely compelling correspondence with Milena Jesenská, who was arguably the most important figure in his life, apart from Hermann, Felice Bauer, and Max Brod. Her role, however, differed from theirs, because Kafka told her things he would not reveal to anyone else, even to Brod. The correspondence with Felice, earlier, was a kind of extended therapeutic session for Kafka; with Milena, the sessions became more than therapy — they became his movement toward the line separating life from death. For as death approached, he attempted, in a dialogue with her, to define what life was, how it could be lived, how death could be postponed, even if only temporarily.

At Meran, Kafka immediately recognized how anti-Semites had infiltrated every aspect of life in the former empire. With nationalist groups rampant and growing bolder, anti-Semitism had become fashionable. In Hungary, one of the last outposts of civility to Jews, there was a complete turnabout, with Béla Kuhn's pro-Semitic views (Kuhn was a Jew) giving way to waves of anti-Semitism under the Romanian occupation and the regime of Admiral Horthy. In the rest of the former

---

*Weight loss or gain, fever up or down, coughing blood or not, respiration heavy or normal, constant eating, special diets, temperature taken seven times a day — that was the cycle.

empire, Jews were being blamed for the loss of the war, or else for making profits on the war, and for subverting the "Germanic spirit" with an alien culture. Ideas for the earliest stages of the National Socialist Party were being hatched in Adolf Hitler's mind, and Austria itself — its rambunctious anti-Semitism formerly held in check by Franz Josef — was now bringing to the surface what had always been latent. In Czechoslovakia, and in Prague, in particular, nationalist groups were attacking both German nationals and Jews; and Germans were themselves turning on the Jews, even in the pre-Nazi era. Kafka found this in Meran, in an incident he relates to Brod, on April 8, 1920.

On his first evening in his new room, Kafka felt expansive, particularly in his observations of Jews. He says that in the past he stayed in the best hotels, with distinguished Italians, some interlopers, but mainly Jews. He attacks the baptized ones: "What horrid Jewish energies live on close to bursting inside a baptized Jew, only to be modulated in the Christian children of a Christian mother."[54] But now, in Meran, the situation is different, as all guests are German and Christian. Kafka had requested a separate table so that his vegetarian diet would draw less attention, and his slow mastication of his food would go unnoticed: "Above all one could chew better and on the whole it is safer." But one day, when he enters the dining room, he is invited to the common table by a colonel and later joined by a general. Almost immediately they pick up Kafka's German accent as "different," and "now the thing took its course." They said they were acquainted with Prague and asked if he was Czech. He said no. "So now explain to those true German military eyes what you really are." Someone else suggested "German-Bohemian," another "Little Quarter," meaning the left bank of the Moldau in Prague. They quiet down for a while and eat. But the general, who during his military days had heard so many different accents, remained inquisitive. After they had eaten (did Kafka chew his food fifty or more times in front of the German military men?), the general probed, "perhaps more bothered by what he saw than by what he heard." Kafka's intense "Middle European" looks did not necessarily fit into the stereotype of what a Jew "looked like."

At this point, he explains he is Jewish, which satisfied the general's linguistic curiosity but not his human feelings. "At the same moment, probably by sheer chance, for all the others could not have heard our conversation, but perhaps there was some connection after all, the whole company rose to leave." Out of politeness, Kafka says, the general remained, and brought their chat to an end before departing. "That hardly satisfied my human feelings either; why must I be a thorn in their flesh? But otherwise it is a good solution; I shall be alone again without ridiculously sitting off by myself, provided they do not invent some disciplinary action for me."

Kafka's final thought, of their perhaps punishing him, is not paranoia but realism. The confrontation is one with death: although these people did not as yet have the power of life and death, their response to Kafka at that table in the Meran sanatorium, in the lovely Tirol Mountains of Austria, was, in fact, a death sentence. Although Kafka died long before they could kill him, the general, the colonel, and the other dinner guests did kill his three sisters, the actor Löwy, and everyone else associated with him who had not emigrated to Palestine or the United States. And they would get Milena too, though not a Jew but with the wrong political ideas and associated with Jews.

With Milena as a correspondent, Kafka moved into one of the most important phases of his life. A good deal of energy went into the Milena letters, but they also motivated him toward writing. In August, after the first April letter, he made his first sketch for *The Castle*. From her side, Milena wrote about Kafka's qualities as a "good man," which she contrasted with the man of "sterling qualities," associated with her father, a cruel and authoritarian professor. In terms of extreme candor, she also wrote extensively to Max Brod about their mutual friend.[55] Although they considered themselves lovers, she and Kafka did not become sexually intimate. Even while being treated badly and even abused, she would not leave her husband, and of course she knew that any sexual life for Kafka was impossible. In his *Diaries* a little later, Kafka wrote, "What have I done with the gift of sex? It's been a failure, no doubt about that. But it might have been successful. M. was right. Fear was wholly to blame."[56]

To Brod, whom she told that their love found no sexual consummation, Milena explains why Kafka was afraid of love. It is, she says, because he views life differently from the way others see it. She describes him as unworldly to the extreme, as being mystified by the things of the world, although with this interpretation she would be hard pressed to explain his success at the institute. Yet she is correct in thinking Kafka was indifferent to most of the things that excite other people, such as money, possessions, properties, mechanical objects like typewriters and cars. His possessions never amounted to much: little in the way of clothing, no secret hoards, a few hundred books.* The sui-

---

*Kafka's library of about three hundred books disappeared during the Nazi era, but two hundred of them surfaced in late 1982 by way of a Munich bookseller, and they were purchased by the Institute for the Study of Prague's German Literature at the University of Wuppertal. The collection, which contains thirty volumes dedicated to Kafka from friends and admirers, is a mixed group: Schiller, Goethe, as expected, nine volumes of Shakespeare in German, a German translation of several Dostoevsky novels, including *The Brothers Karamazov*, with Felice Bauer's words "Perhaps we will read it soon together." Other volumes, from Brod and Werfel, included a life of the Zionist Theodor Herzl, a series on Jewish folklore, the memoirs in two volumes of Lilly Braun, a feminist and socialist. Two books also contain dedications by Kafka to Ottla, one a collection of poems by Ludwig Richter, the other a collection of Chinese folktales. The volumes overall do not contain underlinings or marginal comments — Kafka rarely marked up books in this way. The fastidiousness characteristic of his daily activities extended to his library.

cide, it is said, prepares for the end by giving away his possessions, including his most valuable items. Kafka prepared for an easy sliding into death by never accumulating things to give away.

When Milena told him about her unfaithful husband, as she relates this to Brod, Kafka looked at her as if baffled that a man could have mistresses and still maintain a wife. "He is incapable of living. Franz will never get well. Franz will die soon."[57] Milena speaks of how we all seek refuge in lies, to others or to ourselves, but says Kafka is incapable of lying, as much as he is incapable of getting drunk. He has left himself no refuge into which he can retreat from the truth. "His being is resolutely self-contained and self-sufficient, devoid of all artifice that might enable him to misrepresent life, either its beauty or its misery. There is nothing heroic about his asceticism — and that makes it all the greater and nobler."[58] For him, asceticism is not a means to an end, it is the thing itself. She feels he is amazing, his books amazing. She writes this when it has become clear the two can never get closer together, that their intimacy in letters and brief meetings defined the relationship.

In another letter to Brod after she and Kafka had separated, she speaks of Kafka's fear, which he lost in their four idyllic days together but which returned and will doom him. "He will never get well as long as he has this fear. And no psychological treatment can overcome his fear, because his fear will stand in the way of any treatment. His fear applies not only to me, but to everything that is shamelessly alive, to the flesh, for instance. The flesh is too naked, he can't bear the sight of it."[59] Perhaps with some self-delusion, she deceives herself that his "abnormality" in connection with flesh "makes him superior." She stresses that the women he knew were commonplace types, "capable only of a female existence." As part of this deception, she adds, "I prefer to think that all of us, the whole world and everybody in it, are sick, and that he alone is healthy, right-thinking, right-feeling, and pure."[60]

Her self-delusion was based on her certainty that she was different from other women and could have brought him out of himself, if only she had gotten to him before fear and illness had overtaken him.* De-

---

*Whatever self-deception Milena practiced, she wrote a profoundly touching obituary notice of Kafka. Among other things, she said, in 1924, that he wrote "the most important books in recent German literature." She said they "embody in untendentious form the battle of the generations in our time. They are genuinely naked and therefore seem naturalistic even when they speak in symbols. They have the dry irony and second sight of a man who saw the world so clearly that he could not bear it and had to die, for he was unwilling to make concessions, to take refuge, as others do, in intellectual delusions, however noble.... As a man and an artist he was so infinitely scrupulous that he remained alert even where others, the deaf, felt secure" (Margarete Buber-Neumann, *Milena: The Story of a Remarkable Friendship* [New York: Seaver Books, 1988], p. 72). In a follow-up, in 1926, Milena wrote about meeting Kafka in Meran, in a little book called *The Way to Simplicity*. In a chapter called "The Curse of Sterling Qualities," she speaks of the best man she had ever known, clearly Kafka, although unnamed. "He was infinitely noble, but made a secret of it, as if he were ashamed of being in any way superior to others" (Buber-Neumann, *Milena*, p. 58). There she tells the Robin Hood story of how he once gave a shilling, obtained from his poor mother, to a beggar woman;

spite her extreme sensitivity, she omits the enormous contradictions that made up his inner world and that made possible the writing she admired so much. The Kafka she imagines could never have written his novels and stories, nor the *Diaries*, nor the letters, nor the fragments of parables, paradoxes, and other sayings. She neglects the imaginative side, which needed denial, fear, anxiety, asceticism, priestly devotion to his art, isolation and marginality, the sense of sacrifice and martyrdom — in effect, all the elements that would have forced him to reject Milena even if he had been healthier and less fearful. His fear or hatred of the flesh was not some isolated phenomenon, as Milena with all her insight thinks, but was deeply embedded in the entire way he thought about life and its objects. Flesh was so ambiguous, even detestable, because even when it was rosy and delectable he saw into its rot and decay. Long before he foresaw his own impending death, Kafka saw death in everything. He had lived death, so to speak, apparently from the time he experienced the death of his two younger brothers and the withdrawal of his mother's attention.

The correspondence starts out suspiciously, with Kafka, recalling his misunderstandings with Felice, saying he wrote from Prague and Meran without receiving an answer, and he wonders if possibly he had offended her. He adds he doesn't remember her face in any detail since their one meeting in a Prague coffeehouse. When she answers and indicates she has an infected lung, he responds that "half of Western Europe has more or less faulty lungs."[61] To that, we should add influenza and other diseases of epidemic proportion. Just as the war had thinned out the male population of Europe, now disease was taking its toll on the female part. To gain some perspective on tuberculosis, we might add that two of Freud's children, Anna and Ernst, suffered from the disease, and Freud's grandson, Heinerle, died of miliary tuberculosis. Kafka rightfully saw it as a kind of vengeful God, or that "squandering" of oneself he saw as his fate.

Kafka then repeats some of his favorite stories. One of the disadvantages (or advantages!) of a sequence of affairs is the need to repeat the stories of one's life. Kafka had several he relished, especially the one of his hemorrhaging — how it was relief because after it he slept better. The other is his diagnosis of the disease: that when the brain could no longer sustain the burden of worry and suffering piled upon it, it surrendered its role, and the lungs took over "the maintenance of the whole." The dialogue between brain and lungs, he speculates, "which went on without my knowledge may have been terrible."[62] We must assume these are not as yet love letters, for Kafka's presentation of his death sentence is more an invitation to a *danse macabre* than to a Viennese waltz.

---

but since a shilling would attract attention, he changed it into pennies and gave her the amount in twelve separate trips past her.

Yet there are overtures to intimacy in his request that Milena write to him in Czech, not German; this was in keeping with his sincere admiration for her translation of "Der Heizer" ("The Stoker") into Czech. The shift in language has subtle implications. It speaks of his separation from the language in which he wrote but which he was never happy about; and it implants him more firmly in her world, Gentile, Czech, female — an adventure on his part to be everything his parents disapproved of. There is a particular rebellion in his desire to embrace her language, especially since she uses it so well.* He then shifts to his private life, and tells Milena of his two engagements, three in all, if one counts the two to Felice: "So I've been separated three times from marriage by only a few days."[63] His wording suggests they were all close calls. He hears that Felice is married, with a small son; and Julie is well, but without prospects.†

He even comments sympathetically on Milena's husband, Ernst Polak, a person for whom, Kafka says, he always had respect from what he knew of him in coffeehouse circles. Brod too had a high opinion of him. This is devilish stuff for Milena, who, while she wanted to hear good things about her husband, knew him differently as an abominable, overbearing, inconsiderate man with little or no regard for her feelings and a willingness to demean her at every turn. But Kafka did not spend long on acquaintances and soon wound back to the difference between himself and "others," presumably those more normal people. "How shall I express the difference? A man lies in the filth and stench of his deathbed and there comes the angel of death, the most beatific of all angels, and looks at him. Can this man so much as dare to die? He turns over, hides himself ever deeper in his bed, he's incapable of dying."[64] So deep into his own kind of hell has Kafka crawled, he cannot even move; he is doomed, like one of Dante's denizens of the *Inferno*, to an everlasting punishment with no hope of salvation.

Soon after the correspondence started (exact dating is difficult to determine) Kafka started using the familiar *du* in addressing Milena, but then returned to the more formal *Sie*, as if testing out the word with a woman who refused to leave her husband and yet was obviously deeply interested in Kafka. He was on familiar ground: coming close to someone who could not respond because of a situation beyond her control. Such relationships have their fictional counterpart in characters who seek personal freedom in spaces or rooms that cannot be theirs and

---

*In a later letter, Kafka spelled out his ambivalence about German: "I have never lived among German people, German is my mother-tongue and therefore natural to me, but Czech feels to me far more intimate . . . I see you clearer, the movements of your body, your hands, so quick, so determined, it's almost a meeting." Still later, he mentions the famous Czech author Božena Němcová, who wrote in the second third of the nineteenth century, her most famous novel being *The Grandmother* (*Babicka*). He calls her language musical.

†Kafka wrote that he took all blame for having put Julie through torture, he pushed for marriage, he found an apartment, he subjected her to his delusions.

who, in seeking liberation, discover only anxiety and guilt — or else, in characters who think they are in one time frame and find they are in another, where the finite and the infinite clash within the characters' perceptions.

Kafka was a master of disorientation, nowhere more than in the spatial obscurity of *The Castle*, soon to be sketched in and then started; and we find in the skewed "romances" of his life that same disorientation. Felice found he was not there when she looked for him, and now, with Milena, he will find she is not quite there when *he* looks for her; and she, in turn, will not know how to locate Kafka, as her comments to Brod reveal. Each part of the relationship seeks the other in spaces that do not belong to either; not surprisingly, they come away frustrated and anxiety-ridden.

Since Milena was pouring out her problems with Ernst Polak, she expected Kafka to respond in some sympathetic way. But his answers are not quite what she expects. In one letter, he says he stands "so far below you both that it sickens me even to talk about it."[65] Who is he, he asks, to condemn anything connected with "marriage, work, courage, sacrifice, purity, freedom, self-sufficiency, truthfulness?" When she comments acerbicly on Werfel's "fatness," Kafka counters that he sees his friend as becoming "more beautiful and lovable" as the years pass, even though they see each other only infrequently. But while he admires Werfel's ability to hang on, he is subtly ironical: "Only in these strong-walled vessels [of fat people] does everything get thoroughly cooked, only these capitalists of the airspace are, as far as it is possible for human beings, protected against worry and madness and are able to go calmly about their business, and they alone are, as someone once said, useful in the whole world as world-citizens, for in the North they warm and in the South they give shade."[66]

The anti-Semitism Kafka sensed at Meran made him particularly alert, as if he were becoming aware, suddenly, that it was more than an isolated phenomenon, with occasional outbursts, as the riots in Prague against Jewish shopkeepers had been, for example, or the more studied attacks that blamed Jews for the war and for lack of loyalty to a restored Czechoslovakia. In some disingenuous way, Milena had apparently asked Kafka if he was Jewish, a query difficult to understand unless she meant a practicing Jew. "You ask me if I'm a Jew [he replied], perhaps this is only a joke, perhaps you're only asking me if I belong to those anxious Jews, in any case as a native of Prague you can't be as innocent in this respect as Mathilde, Heine's wife [who in her naiveté did not know Heine was himself a convert from Judaism]."[67] Milena, married to a Jew, had reproached the race in general for its "specific anxiousness." Kafka counters by saying that this description does not fit most Jews, only isolated ones, like himself.

Yet he goes on to defend a certain kind of anxiousness in Jews, and we recognize how deeply he has pondered this, despite his relative removal from formal Jewish questions. "The insecure position of Jews, insecure within themselves, insecure among people, would make it above all comprehensible that they consider themselves to be allowed to own only what they hold in their hands or between their teeth, that furthermore only palpable possessions give them the right to live, and that they will never again acquire what they once have lost but that instead it calmly swims away from them forever."[68] The statement is both prophetic and a death sentence: he foresees the fragility of the Jews' position within a frame of reference that was changing radically. In Hungary alone, change for the worse came from one year to the next, and in Germany a revolutionary movement preceding Hitler would gradually descend into the rambunctious racism and nationalism that made a Hitler possible.

Precisely because Milena was both sympathetic and so innocent, Kafka was encouraged to continue. "From the most improbable sides Jews are threatened with danger, or let us, to be more exact, leave the dangers aside and say they are threatened with threats." He gives an example, that when Ottla was getting ready to marry a Czech Christian, her fiancé told a relative of Milena's he intended to marry a Jew, and the relative said, " 'Anything but that, anything rather than getting mixed up with Jews! Just think: our Milena' "[69] — herself "mixed up" with Jews, Kafka's perception of the undertow of anti-Semitism, well beneath the ranting anti-Semitism of German-Austrian political life, gave him an insight into the tightrope act of Jewish existence; and, in a sense, it validated his own anxiousness and uncertainty. In the final years of his life, Kafka was able to blend his own sense of fragility with that of the Jews in general. In another letter to Milena, he uses the Czech language, "Jste žid?" or "Are you Jewish?" to illustrate how in the "Jste" the "fist is withdrawn to gather muscle-strength? And then in the 'žid' the cheerful, unfailing, forward-flying blow? These are the side-effects which the Czech language frequently possesses for the German ear?"[70] None of this has any linguistic basis, but it reveals Kafka's sensitivity to how language can communicate a tone even when the words themselves may be neutral.

When Milena takes his remarks on Jews seriously, Kafka responds he was being witty, and then becomes so caustic only self-hatred can explain his remarks: "I could rather reproach you for having much too good an opinion of the Jews whom you know (including myself) — there are others! — sometimes I'd like to cram them all as Jews (including myself) into the drawer of the laundry chest, then wait, then open the drawer a little, to see whether all have already suffocated, if not, to close the drawer again and go on like this to the end."[71] The image is itself breathtaking. Another possible explanation for Kafka's remark might be a desire to fit himself more closely into Milena's world, in which not she but others perceived Jews in precisely that way. We must also keep in mind that by surrounding herself with Jewish intellectuals, she was getting revenge against her father.

At about this time, in the beginning of May, Kafka wrote Brod extensively about Jews, in his typically ironic, harsh way when referring to "his people." He writes of Germany: "perhaps the Jews are not spoiling Germany's future, but it is possible to conceive of them as having spoiled Germany's present. From early on they have forced upon Germany things that she might have arrived at slowly and in her own way, but which she was opposed to because they stemmed from strangers. What a terribly barren preoccupation anti-Semitism is, everything that goes with it, and Germany owes that to her Jews."[72] Kafka here sounds Nietzschean in his scorn for the German mentality, and in his inversion of the German "poison" as the result of the Jews' success. He then describes his little circle at Meran and points out that the general who had smoked out Kafka's German accent had been quite friendly; and he wonders if perhaps he has exaggerated the story to himself. But he attributes his newly found social charms to the fact he is an attentive listener and listens "sincerely and happily."

But this does not mean anti-Semitism is not rife at the table. The general considers Kafka "something like a child," and with the others does not show much consideration for this youthful fellow. "When they talk about Jewish rascality, brazenness, cowardice, they laugh with a certain admiration and, to boot, apologize to me." Kafka cites war stories circulating of so-called Jewish cowardice, one in which a sick East European Jew, the evening before his unit was to march to the front, "sprayed germs of the clap into the eyes of twelve other Jews."[73] Such stories were, of course, consistent with the forged "Protocols of Zion" and with other charges of blood libel, merely variations on the theme.* The group, however, does not apologize to Kafka for Jewish socialists and communists, who are not forgiven. "These," he says, "are drowned in the soup and cut up small with the roast." Such charges of Jewish complicity in left-wing politics would reverberate for many decades, as they were already active in Hungary under Horthy and becoming more earnest when shortly after Hitler repeated the accusation in *Mein Kampf.*

Kafka finally leaves this subject to wind back to Milena, surely in his mind as a non-Jew and part of that "other" world he is being forced to deal with. After telling Brod he has put on weight — he was over 130 pounds, very thin but not emaciated — he still complains of insomnia, and attributes this to his correspondence with Vienna, with Milena. "She is a living fire, of a kind I have never seen before, a fire moreover

---

*In 1988 a well-placed Chicago politician, a close associate of the mayor, accused Jews of spreading the AIDS virus among blacks as a form of genocide. One wonders which side of the genocide issue this politician was on.

that in spite of everything burns only for him [her husband]. Yet at the same time she is extremely tender, courageous, bright, and commits everything she has to her sacrifice, or to put it another way perhaps, has gained everything she has by her sacrifice. Yet what kind of man must he be, who could evoke that?"[74] Kafka omits from the equation Milena's fierce rebellion against everything her professorial, authoritarian father stood for, including his anti-Semitism. With Ernst Polak, a Jew, a philanderer, a man totally unacceptable to her family, she had found a weapon with which to fight her father, a man who had had her committed for mental instability. Under these conditions, for her to admit a mistake by ridding herself of Polak would be to recognize her father's view of matters. In her deep rebellion, she was, in effect, humiliating herself before Polak as earlier she had been humiliated by her father. Furthermore, she was ill, and her illness kept her system racing; she was constantly accelerating, seeking frantically for solutions, for companionship, for understanding, scattering herself in the search for answers to her personal problems.

Kafka's letters to Brod and Baum from Meran are like bulletins from the front. He tells Max that while he, Brod, is overtaken by unhappiness — difficulties with his mistress, defeat as Jewish Party candidate in the April National Assembly elections — he can nevertheless work. But he, Kafka, is different. "While I am burning up, suddenly I have nothing but a few beams; if I didn't prop them up with my head, they would collapse and the whole hovel catch fire. . . . I am not complaining. My appearance complains."[75] And to Baum, he repeats one of his favorite witticisms, how his physical illness is only an overflow of a spiritual illness. In this struggle, the head defends itself. "For the head in a time of need has spawned the lung disease and now they are trying to force it back into him, just when he feels the strongest urge to spawn still other illnesses."[76] This is not nonsense, but neither is it accurate: it is meaningful only for Kafka, who had to believe that everything derived from his head, just as everything meaningful derived from his imagination. He heard voices.*

He was writing the same thing to Milena, about the voices telling

---

*At almost the same time, the great dancer Nijinsky was considered schizophrenic, by the very man, Eugen Bleuler, who coined the word to fit the condition, and yet his "voices" were not too different from Kafka's. Nijinsky raved about how art had been degraded and emasculated by polite society; that it had become the plaything of the rich, and turned, like love and all other finer matters, into a commodity. The dancer raged against the marketplace, which encouraged, he said, lust and cruelty; and these in turn he linked to meat-eating, a form of carnality dependent on the slaughter of untold numbers of innocent animals. Further, he detested and feared doctors, as agents of death, and he opposed, violently, the taking of medications for one's condition. As we note how Nijinsky complained bitterly against the world's own madness, against its misuse of reason, against its materialism, we are reminded of course not only of Kafka but of several of his protagonists, not the least his archetypal hunger artist. Shift a few things here and there, and that hunger artist could be Nijinsky, having withdrawn his body from the world's competition as a protest against it.

him the lung had taken on the disease of his brain. He points up the disparities in their ages: he thirty-seven, almost thirty-eight, almost a generation older than she, a typical exaggeration made when he wished to establish a point about disproportion between himself and someone else. By now, he had concluded he could never recover. He relates to Milena a little parable, not only of Kafka and death but of Europe and death.

> On the balcony is a sparrow which expects me to throw some bread from the table on to the balcony, instead of which I drop the bread beside me on the floor in the middle of the room. It stands outside and from there in the semidarkness sees the food of its life, terribly tempting, it's shaking itself, it's more here than there, but here is the dark and beside the bread am I, the secret power. Nevertheless it hops over the threshold, a few more hops, but farther it doesn't dare to go and in sudden fright it flies away. But with what energy does this wretched bird abound; after a while it's back again, inspects the situation, I scatter a little more to make it easier for it and — if I hadn't intentionally-unintentionally (this is how the secret powers work) chased it away with a sudden movement, it would have got the bread.[77]

But the parable cuts even deeper. It is not only the death rattle of Europe, it is the epitome of Modernism, which often can hardly be distinguished from death. It is a tale of disconnection, separation, of subject and object disengaged: it is the very nub of Modernism and its death drift, its consciousness of discontinuity.

This carried Kafka past the spring of 1920 into the later part of the year, or early 1921. Back in May 1920, when it was clear he was not recovering, he asked for and received permission from the institute to extend his stay in Meran until the end of June. When he left Meran on June 27, he was caught in one of his usual dilemmas. Milena had insisted he meet her in Vienna, or she would cut off the correspondence and, by implication, herself. He of course feared the trip, although Vienna was quite accessible on his way back to Prague, but it made the journey somewhat longer than going through Munich. Yet despite his putting Milena through every kind of hesitation and uncertainty, as he had with Felice earlier, the meeting did take place. Only now he was so ill that a journey, however desirable in other ways, was nightmarish, made doubly so by Kafka's dislike of Vienna itself and in general of anything new. Despite his protests, the one place he felt comfortable was in his parents' apartment, where all his complaints and revulsions had a familiar ring to them. "When I survey these journeys and compare them with the condition of my head, I feel much as Napoleon would have felt if, on preparing his plans for the Russian campaign, he had known the precise outcome at the time."[78] A witty comparison, that: Kafka and Vienna, Napoleon and Moscow!

The four days with Milena in Vienna went exceptionally well. They enjoyed walks, laughs, good conversation, a kind of festival before each returned to a darker reality. To Brod, much later, Kafka spoke of it as happy fragments wrenched from the night. He felt love for Milena, accentuated by the fact of her unattainability — the perfect blend for him. When he returned to Prague, he and Julie Wohryzek broke off what had already dwindled into virtually nothing. Julie demonstrated considerable anger when Kafka told her about Milena. She warned him that Milena would never leave her husband, which was already clear to him but unacceptable. Julie threatened to write to Milena; Kafka agreed, and then feared what she might say.

In the midst of Kafka's own uncertainty when it came to the women in his life, Ottla married Josef David, on July 15, 1920, a union he had encouraged strongly. In a way, Ottla's marriage to a Gentile took some of the pressure off him in the Kafka household, since it gave Hermann something else to rage about. With Ottla entering a new phase of her life and, therefore, unavailable as before, Kafka was thrown back almost completely upon his correspondence and relationship with Milena. Brod was himself now somewhat distant, because of his multiple activities as politician, author, philanderer; and Kafka's other friends, because of marriage or their distance from Prague (Werfel), were no longer to be counted upon for intimate support. What is remarkable is how this young Czech woman, almost fifteen years his junior (of "another generation," as Kafka put it), was his chief form of encouragement, his supporter, his reason, in some respects, for living. Even as he was preparing to enter one of his most intense responses to high literary Modernism with *The Castle,* "A Hunger Artist," "The Investigations of a Dog," and many brilliant short pieces, he was almost bereft of personal friends. Milena was herself by this time spitting blood, the beginning for her of a long period of illness before her death in a German concentration camp.

In mid-August, they did meet in Gmünd, where he once had been eager to meet Grete and Felice, but this only after Milena indicated she could not separate from Ernst Polak, who, she insisted, needed her — although more likely she needed him for whatever masochistic, revengeful meaning he had for her. Kafka had already poured out to her his own forms of misery, his childhood experience with hired help who had turned his daily life into terror, especially with regard to school attendance. In one of his curious images, he speaks of that "monstrous dust" of childhood memories as having been kicked up to settle in his lungs. According to this reasoning (or fantasy), he was preconditioned to damaged lungs by childhood experiences, most notably by his mother's neglect, so that an ignorant cook could terrorize him. He has also offered to send Milena his letter to his father, so she can see what his early life was like under the sign of the tyrant.

The meeting in Gmünd, a weekend in mid-August, did not go well, since the physical presence of Milena could be, for Kafka, far less prepossessing than the correspondence. They spoke of infidelities, and she asked him if he had had sexual relations in Prague, presumably with Julie; Kafka, knowing Milena was sleeping with her husband, felt mocked. Further, he had already written her his own feelings about sexual contact. There he had described his first effort, with a Prague shopgirl, an incident already referred to, in which he felt dirty and obscene, an act of "repulsiveness and smut." "And as it was then, so it has always remained," he told Milena.[79] This did not rule out sexual desire, but desire was always mixed with distaste and disgust. He smelled sulfur, felt hell nearby. "This urge had in it something of the eternal Jew, being senselessly drawn, wandering senselessly through a senselessly obscene world."* From this, he admits he feared spending a night in Gmünd, the usual " 'fear' (oh, the usual one is sufficient) which I also have in Prague, not a special fear of Gmünd."[80]

Since he was now in his late thirties, Kafka's responses to sexual contact, which we have already commented upon extensively, demand further notice here. They resulted from a complicated amalgam of causes, one of which, of primary importance, was his priestly attitude toward writing: the need for sacrifice, which in martyrs is traditionally the sacrifice of the body, the denial of pleasures involving sex, food, and drink. And, finally, also regarding writing, Kafka had been and continued to be very much a man responding to the dominant literary modes of his day; and in his formative years, as we have observed, women were presented in fiction and on stage as vampires, Amazons, and night creatures who preyed upon men. Otto Weininger, whom Kafka admired, was the leading theoretician of the destructive woman syndrome; and Kafka's fiction often reflects this kind of female presence. While the sum total of such causes and reasons cannot predict that an individual will find sexuality difficult to consider and consummate, we can see that Kafka, rather than hiding his attitude, used it profitably as part of the landscape of his fiction. That "fear" he mentioned to nearly all the important women in his life joins with anguish, uncertainty, dread, and, also, wit to create his particular world.

In this listing, the one element we have thus far scanted in his position toward women was his attitude toward Julie Kafka; and while for some readers of Kafka, she seems critical, for others, like myself, she is only one important element among many. The maternal linkage is, of course, present in Kafka's reshaping of Milena to fit his image of her, and she accepted that role, letting herself be transformed into what she thought Kafka needed of her. As she wrote to Brod, she thought Kafka was incapable of living, and implicitly she felt she must help him —

*One recalls Kafka's two versions of "Gracchus," one type of Wandering Jew.

which means, lacking any sexual contact, mothering him back toward life. Kafka tells her both are married, she in Vienna, he to his fear in Prague, and he tugs in vain at their marriages. But it is less a marriage than a parent-child relationship that develops. Just as he had reshaped Felice Bauer into a vision he needed of her, which may or may not have been close to the real Felice, so he recreated Milena. He shaped her as a character who could fit into some fictional vision he had; she becomes, for this period when he was not writing, his "creation."

Here is the kind of throwaway he could use with her: "As in the deep sea there is no tiniest spot that isn't always under the heaviest pressure, so it is with you, but any other life is a disgrace and makes me sick to think of."[81] His association of her with deep water suggests a further maternal linkage: he wants to lose himself in her, be smothered by her, become caught up in her embrace. In another letter, he speaks of laying his face in her lap, feeling her hand on his head and remaining "like that through all eternity."[82] In confessing his deepest secrets to her, about food, childhood anguish, sexual experiences, he is using her as a mother-confessor, expecting her to understand and forgive all. Wandering between life and death in these final years, Kafka envisioned Milena as his savior: the return of a Julie Kafka–like figure in the form of this recreated young woman in Vienna. In still another manifestation of the disproportion between them, in Kafka's perception of it, he assumes the "bug" role. While she and Polak, in this fantasy, live in their "great household," all he wants to do is once a year to be allowed to run across their carpet.[83]

Even the Jewish content, which rises and falls as Kafka feels accepted or abandoned, has something of the maternal about it: the lowly Jew is the offspring of the powerful Gentile whose whims determine what can be left for this outsider. "It is not because they are Jewish that [certain stories] depress me, nor because when once the dish has been placed on the table each Jew has to take his share from the awful, poisonous but also old and essentially eternal fare."[84] He says he is not depressed by this, but implied is the condition of the Jew which makes him subservient to whoever hands out the dinner portions. The Jew lacks his own destiny; it is proffered to him, host to servant, as the parent sees suitable for the child. Some of this thinking is, of course, attributable to Kafka's worsening physical condition. Some, however, is a constant. And it did affect his fictional achievement. In *The Castle*, whose first sketches appear in August 1920, K. is reduced to a childish or adolescent role by the actions of the parental castle authority. Further, communication is by means of a sequence of messengers, which in Kafka's terms are the cooks, maids, nurses who took charge of him as a child.

These sketches are joined by other material, collected as "Fragments," themselves brief sketches, sometimes no more than paragraphs Kafka jotted down without dating. The sketches are merest traces: "Then the plane lay before K. and far away, remote in the blue distance, on a little hill, scarcely distinguishable, the house that he was striving to reach. But it still took him until evening, and many times during the day he had lost sight of his goal, until on a darkening field-path he suddenly found himself standing at the foot of that hill."[85] Although details for *The Castle* will diverge, the geography is right.

In another sketch, K. attempts to enter the family of the lord of the manor, although the so-called lord is hardly that; and in still another, Kafka presents a dialogue about a castle only vaguely visible on a hill in the distance. Many of the sketches not directly related to the novel are full of spatial dimensions, usually of a person walking toward something, or of the disproportion of the individual and the distance he has as yet to traverse. Or else, he is walking toward some distant goal, although he never arrives. There are also "reverse" spatialities: "What are you building? — I want to dig a subterranean passage. Some progress must be made. My station up there is much too high. We are digging the pit of Babel."[86]

Kafka's story "The Burrow," with its subterranean "Pit of Babel," is in some respects the other side of *The Castle*. Space up or in the distance is transferred to space beneath. Kafka is measuring life in terms of distances, possibilities or potentialities of life in dimensional terms. This is, in one respect, a response to looming death; but it is also Kafka measuring himself against his powers as a writer, not caving in to his physical discomfort and deterioration, but instead thinking heroically, spatially, in large, broad terms. When we come to the main body of *The Castle*, we must not read it only as a form of frustration or doom, but as a movement into life: *not* that K. has lost all chance of succeeding in his mission, but that in the face of so many obstacles, he continues to push on and believe in his mission.*

"Writing as a form of prayer," Kafka wrote[87] — not the words of a man succumbing to his affliction, but the language of someone fighting back, using the sole means he knows. "Where is the obstacle to success in the tremendous task? Do not spend time in search of the obstacle; perhaps there is none."[88] Whatever its other qualities, the correspondence with Milena was a form of sustenance for Kafka, even though he may have used it as much negatively as positively — "negatively" in the sense he presents a defeated warrior to the young woman; but "positively" to the extent that this negative presentation helped sustain him in the immortality of his words. As long as he had something to write, even letters, he could believe he was not dying. Even *Letter to*

---

*Along these lines, Kafka wrote, "Man's fundamental weakness lies by no means in the fact that he cannot achieve victory but in the fact that he cannot exploit his victory" ("Fragments from Notebooks and Loose Pages," in *Dearest Father*, p. 284).

His Father, which seems a surrender to past anguish, was really a refusal to fade away. Kafka's *Diaries* lack entries until October 15, 1921, at which time he gave Milena all his *Diaries* up to this point.

In another one of his problematical parable-sketches, "The Problem of Our Laws," Kafka was working in and around *The Castle*. This is, incidentally, one of his finest pieces of prose, a tightly argued paradox illustrating, among other things, that what you want is what you can never have. "Our laws are not generally known, they are kept secret by the small group of nobles who rule us." Convinced as they are that these laws are scrupulously administered, the people are worried that possibly the laws do not exist; or if they exist, no one knows about them. The problems with the law are obviously linked to the problem K. has in locating the lord of the manor, the keeper of the castle, or even discovering what the castle wants of him, since he cannot be sure there is any end to the messengers sent out to reach him. Yet even questioning whether the laws exist is a matter of presumption. "There is a tradition that they exist and that they are a mystery confided to the nobility, but it is not and cannot be more than a tradition sanctioned by age, for the essence of a secret code is that it should remain a mystery."[89] There is, indeed, a party that believes the laws that the people are trying to unravel do not exist at all. They say the law is whatever the nobles choose to do.

"We live on this razor's edge. A writer once summed the matter up in this way: The sole visible and indubitable law that is imposed upon us is the nobility, and must we ourselves deprive ourselves of that one law?"[90] That "writer" is clearly Kafka stating one of his paradoxes: that in the absence of control, we wander aimlessly; so we choose authority, whose validity we must seriously question. Whether meaningful or not, the law is all we have. Should we repudiate what gives us direction, even if the direction is not what we want? Connected to this are words Kafka directed at Brod: "There exists a theoretic possibility of perfect human happiness, that is, to believe in the determining principle and not to strive toward it."

In one of his aphorisms (Number 69) Kafka put it more boldly: "Theoretically there is a perfect possibility of happiness: believing in the indestructible element in oneself and not striving towards it."[91] While disagreeing with Brod here, as he did on so many other issues, Kafka believed that the possibility of happiness was unattainable, just as knowledge of the law lies beyond one; and yet despite its unachievability and even the blasphemy of such a belief, Kafka does not repudiate this belief. The analogy applies to the law: if one removes all belief in it, because the law may not exist, then one repudiates a belief that is sustaining. The illusion is important, not because one believes in the illusion, whether law or happiness, *but because one must believe in the belief*. The Kafka paradox is part of what makes Kafka Kafkaesque. And one can take this as a drift toward some divine authority or, quite the opposite, as a mockery of all belief.

In the fall of 1920, with his health becoming increasingly precarious, Kafka remained in Prague. At Ottla's insistence, he suffered through a careful examination of his lungs, with both apexes found to be infected and, in point of fact, incurable. Although the diagnosis was not put quite in these terms, rest cures could be only a holding action. The doctor recommended a further leave of absence from the institute and at least three months at the sanatorium. In and around this time, Kafka's letters to Milena had already become death oriented, especially after he learned she had spit blood and needed treatment. "So we seem to have drifted apart completely, Milena, and the only thing we appear to have in common is the intense desire — that you should be here and your face somewhere as near mine as possible. But of course the death-wish we also have in common."[92] He is not suggesting double suicide with Milena, as he touched upon with Felice, but he is indicating that death would somehow join them: Heathcliff and Catherine Linton, side by side in the grave. Or he combines death and need for maternal loves: "Now I want to die, then you, now I want to cry in front of you like a little boy."

The emphasis on dying, death, entombment is a natural consequence of the postwar years — not anomalous, not restricted to Kafka, not unusual in the light of four years of senseless killing. Further, this wish for death was very close to directions Modernism was taking. As Kafka was writing, Dada was giving way, blending into surrealism. In Dada, there was the death of sense, the use of nonsense syllables or images, the combination of sounds and sensations to repudiate the so-called civilization that had created the war. But Dada and surrealism, in addition, repudiated objects in favor of unconscious forces, demons creeping in from subterranean places. Both attempted to move outside history; history in traditional terms or conceptions was dead.

Kafka's insistence on death or the end of things, while surely connected to his own condition, was just as surely part of his immersion in Modernism and its condition. Shortly after Kafka's death, the two German-language writers who shared part of his vision, Robert Musil and Thomas Mann, would publish their own "death novels," *The Man Without Qualities* and *The Magic Mountain*. The first is concerned with the death of the empire. The second is Kafka territory directly, the death of a culture signified by the sanatorium, where all are sick, and those who are cured, like Hans Castorp, will find their end in the Great War, which is just beginning. Only his personal statements make Kafka appear closer to death than either Musil or Mann. All are "morbid" in the word's original sense, "sickly" or "diseased."

Death or imminent death *was* everywhere. Revolution had followed the end of the war in Germany. The Allies had invaded the Soviet Union in order to restore the Whites and drive out the Bolsheviks.

Horthy in Hungary had successfully overthrown Kuhn and set up a nationalist, anti-Semitic counterrevolutionary government. Austria was in turmoil. Rosa Luxemburg was murdered in Berlin by German fascist thugs. Hitler was beginning his anti-Semitic tirades, tied in to the signing of the Treaty of Versailles. Prague was itself the scene of rioting, mainly against Germans and Jews, with the two considered one for purposes of looting and vandalism. German newspapers were destroyed, as were synagogue documents and scrolls. The attackers were nationalists, but they were using old hatreds to even scores. The "Protocols of Zion," the forged document outlining how Jews would seek control of the world, was always in the shadows.

Not surprisingly, Kafka's letters to Milena begin to have crowded images of Jews. He speaks of luxuriating in the anti-Semitism rife on Prague streets; and he says he hears Jews called a "mangy race." He says that to stay would show no more heroism than do cockroaches when they can't be driven out. He sees the police charging the crowds, scattering them — hellish images of chaos. "When you talk about the future, don't you sometimes forget that I'm a Jew?" He adds, "It remains dangerous, Jewry, even at your feet."[93] He speaks of Milena's father and says that for the European "we both [Kafka and her husband] have the same Negro face."[94] He employs a tunnel image, almost exactly what will turn up in "The Burrow," to indicate it seems to lead toward her from a dark hole where he resides. But instead of leading to her, the tunnel heads into "impenetrable stone." This is, in one respect, the role of the Jew, who tries out a path, finds it blocked, fills in the original hole, and then makes new paths again — "old mole that one is."[95] It is also, for better or worse, the role of the writer.

Kafka intervenes in the fight between Milena and Brod over Zionism. "You have your homeland and can also renounce it and that's perhaps the best one can do with one's homeland. . . . But he has no homeland, and therefore nothing to renounce and has to think all the time of seeking or building it."[96] This indicates how far Kafka had moved toward recognizing the European Jew had no future in Europe. Dispossessed, marginal, in exile, a refugee, Kafka now sees how he and the Jew have become symmetrically allied. He has not been absorbed even in the most superficial ways. The fact that German was not his rightful language, although the only one he truly possessed, has now become a reality for life itself. Although the tone here is calm, Kafka is filled with rage — at himself, at his domestic arrangement, at the deterioration of all his plans — and this rage emerges in a murderous dream. He says he committed a murder for Milena's sake.

> Someone, a relative said [in his dream] in the course of a conversation — that this or that person couldn't accomplish something — thus this relative said ironically at last: "Well, then perhaps Milena." Whereupon I killed him somehow, came home in great excitement, my mother running after me . . . at last hot with rage I cried out: "If anyone says any-

thing bad about Milena, for instance the father (my father), I'll kill him too or myself."[97]

With that, he awakens. Brod had commented that Milena was possibly not too good for Kafka.*

The dream has such reverberations that it eventually courses through nearly every aspect of Kafka's life. It is, obviously, a dream of death; but it is also one in which he emerges as a warrior defending his rights against authority. Here he kills the father not in any direct oedipal assault but to protect his property rights. He has reversed the situation of "The Judgment," so that instead of bowing to the father's death sentence and leaving the field to the parent, he asserts himself in the dream and eliminates the obstacle to his happiness. Another Kafka has emerged, a vengeful killer, a distant cousin of Musil's Moosbrugger. Of course, it is only a dream!

Another side to this rage emerges in the brief sketch Kafka wrote in 1920 called "The Refusal." In this he uses his now familiar image of a little town so far from the country's frontier it has no connection to the capital, like the provincial towns in "The Great Wall of China." In this scenario, because the outside world has not penetrated, the town continues to operate by laws and rules with no link to anything beyond. Something of Prague of course exists here, in its separation from Vienna or even Budapest, where the emperor rules in the capitals; but the location is really closer to Kafka's sense of himself.

Each of these little towns has its own patriarch, or paternal figure, a man who deems himself the leader. "In the great capital great rules have superseded each other — indeed, new dynasties have been deposed or annihilated, and new ones have started; in the past century even the capital itself was destroyed, a new one was founded far away from it, later on this too was destroyed and the old one rebuilt, yet none of this had any influence on our little town."[98] Of course the narrator's information is contradictory, since he knows what has occurred in the distance and yet denies any knowledge of it. But this is the dualistic Kafka: watching himself observe everything while disavowing anything beyond himself.

The commander of the little town is a self-appointed colonel, a petty tyrant who rules because he produces a document that he claims gives him the right to command. His job is mainly to "refuse" when individuals or delegations petition him for something. Most of his rulings are aimed at maintaining the status quo. Each time he makes a decision, the townspeople wait in excitement and apprehension, but when the refusal comes down, they are relieved that nothing will

---

*A line followed by several commentators on Kafka, who see her as unbalanced, a morbid influence, a destructive female. My comments reveal quite the opposite. Whatever pain she caused Kafka was balanced by the intellectual and emotional support she provided him.

change their lives. "In all important matters . . . the citizens can always count on a refusal. And now the strange fact is that without the
refusal one simply cannot get along."[99] Among the young, however,
those between seventeen and twenty, there is less acceptance of the
colonel's refusals, and these young people, incapable of seeing the dire
consequences of revolutionary ideas, feel discontent.

But there is another factor, the presence of soldiers who create great
fear, not because they are violent but merely because they are there.
When they appear, the citizens become quiet and drift away from any
place the soldiers gather. The soldiers are themselves not imposing,
with the most striking thing about them "the prominence of their
teeth which almost overcrowd their mouths."[100] Children run away at
the sight of those teeth (as Kafka himself almost ran at the sight of the
metal in Felice's mouth). Furthermore, the soldiers speak an utterly incomprehensible dialect and barely understand what the citizens say.
The result is a family situation in which the authority figures speak in
one language, the lesser family members respond in a different tongue,
and neither comprehends the other.

What Kafka has created here is another version of his standard
theme, but presented with an originality that suggests political overtones. Authority always means lack of communication among partici-
pants, a failure of information. Authority brings fear, not sympathetic
contact. The teeth of the soldiers suggest barbarity, weapons to be used
against the citizenry. The image of being torn to pieces — so constant
in Kafka's letters, as well as in that drawing sent on to Milena of a victim being torn to pieces by an infernal machine — has achieved almost
legendary status in Kafka's iconography. It denotes the fear implicit in
authority, but also the rage directed against the self for having borne
such pressures.

In still another presentation of rage seeking an outlet in depictions
of a family, Kafka wrote "The Married Couple" in or around this time.
The "married couple" here is clearly based on Hermann and Julie, Kafka's perennial honeymooners. The narrator is a hapless salesman, recalling Gregor Samsa before his transformation. He must visit a client
known only as N., and since he has no time to see N. during office
hours, he visits him in the evening, at N.'s home. Already apprehensive
about making this visit under such conditions, the narrator arrives, only
to find another salesman there. This man, a rival, seems quite at ease at
the bedside of N.'s son, who is ill. N. himself stands there still in his
overcoat, a tall, broad-shouldered man who to the narrator's astonishment has grown very thin because of some malady. The description is
clearly of Hermann, once robust, now stooping, thin, and gaunt because
of a heart condition. N.'s wife is small and frail — Julie was small, not
frail, but in her deference to N. the rest of the description fits.

Pacing up and down by the sickbed as though he were in his office,
the narrator makes his usual blunders of tact and tone. Kafka captures

the embarrassment he still feels in a domestic situation. N.'s son, who is the narrator's own age, is another representation of Kafka, the sick son who is vying with the father for the mother's attention. In the hazy distance of this piece we sense "The Judgment" and, of course, "The Metamorphosis," those 1912 stories that established Kafka's fictional position. In the face of sickness, including N.'s obvious ailing, the narrator goes into his sales pitch, offering advantages for his product, making concessions in his nervousness. Suddenly, N., who is looking worse and worse, breathing with difficulty, "closed his eyes, the mark of some great strain passed over his face and vanished, and all was over."[101] N.'s lifeless hand was "so cold that it sent a chill through me." The son wildly sobs at his father's death, while the other agent remains cold and indifferent. The narrator feels it is his duty to inform the wife. Clearly, while he seems anguished, he has wished his client dead — so that he, the narrator, will not lose out to the other agent; also present here is Kafka's usual agenda about eliminating authority figures.

Yet N. is not dead, only sleeping, and he is brought back to wakefulness by the ministrations of his wife. He "endured with a mixture of annoyance and irony his wife's tender reproaches for having overstrained himself." The narrator decides to leave. "In the lobby I met Frau N. again. At the sight of that pathetic figure I said impulsively that she reminded me a little of my mother." When Frau N. remains silent, the narrator adds that his mother was a wonder worker who could make whole again whatever her children destroyed. But Frau N. doesn't hear, and she even confuses the narrator with the other agent. The narrator knows this meeting was just another business call that came to nothing, and "yet one must keep going."[102]

Only a few pages in length, "The Married Couple" recapitulates numerous Kafka motifs and shows that the rage he felt about family life was constant and was itself consistent with other views: his attitude toward Jews, among them. In crossovers, Kafka foresaw that the fragmentation of the family is linked, in some mysterious way, to the disintegrating nature of modern life and of the Jews, all against a background of radical action in nationalist politics and equally revolutionary action in the arts.

In his correspondence with Milena, he cast himself in various guises: as the Western Jew who can never be at peace with himself; as the man without a homeland; as a rebel against his powerlessness; as a creature whose "eternal bondage," presumably to her, far transcends her husband's behavior, his infidelities; as someone who values marriage so highly he knows it can never be for him; as a figure so marginal she will be fortunate if he ever presents substance to her; as an object slowly disappearing from sight, dissolving into a shade or phantom.[103] In this and other ways, Kafka has transformed himself into a Modernistic object. By decentering himself — that is, by removing himself from any focused or stable role — he has made himself into an art object whose meanings can be generated from several points. Kafka presents himself as a creature whose potentialities are immense, even as they are being denied. In becoming analogous to an art object, he has thrown his lot in with abstraction and nonrepresentation: he is not a man whom a woman can "see" in any ordinary sense. Instead, she must "read" him. Lacking an anchor in either faith or country, he has so disembodied himself that like objects in abstract painting he has receded, or exists only in the viewer's eye.

This transformation of self in person as well as in fiction was one of his triumphs. As we read his list of grievances to Milena, we recall he reveled in his denial of self, in his sacrifice of the normal, in his presentation of a creature she could not possibly embrace. That she did is testimony to her ability to see through the roles to the man, and beyond the man to his yearning for some great role. As in so much of Modernist fiction and art, Kafka's identification was through denial: denial of the object, ultimately an effort to efface even the subject. He writes to Milena about marriage, which for Kafka held such fascination not only because he yearned to relieve his loneliness but because it contained in one package all the elements he had to reject. With Felice, the choice was heavy furniture versus art; with Milena, illness and fear versus some commitment that would jeopardize the self. Apart from the sexual demands marriage might make, Kafka viewed it as the ultimate betrayal of self.

"The correspondence on this subject [marriage]," he writes Milena, "brings one again and again to the conclusion that you're united by all but sacramental indissoluble marriage (how nervous I am, my ship must somehow have lost its rudder during these last days) to your husband, and I by a similar marriage to — I don't know to whom, but the eye of this terrible wife often lies on me, I feel it."[104] He agrees that "it will never be," so they must speak only of the present, not of the future. To cement the agreement, he writes it in Czech, their secret language, as it were, two children defying their parents. At about the same time, he wrote, "I sometimes feel as though I were carrying such weights of lead that I must at any moment be dragged down into the deepest sea and the person trying to seize or even 'rescue' me would give up, not from weakness, not even from hopelessness, but from sheer annoyance."[105]

Having had great difficulty in obtaining in Prague an Austrian visa, Kafka decided he could get a resident visa in Vienna, as part of his plan to meet Milena in Grimmenstein. Granted another three-month leave from the institute (on December 13), he gave up the Grimmenstein idea and decided instead to go on December 18 to the High Tatras, in Slovakia, to a tuberculosis clinic in Matliary.* As was customary, his first

*Writing to Brod, he chides himself for not using the Grimmenstein residency permit, and announces his choice of Tatranské Matliary, but if it fails to work out, then Szon-

impressions of the clinic were unfavorable, as he told Ottla, especially since his temporary room in the annex lacked central heat and except for the bed was virtually bare of furniture. The next day everything cleared, when the maid gave him a much better room, which had been prepared for Ottla, who had originally planned to accompany Kafka. In his report to Brod about the people there, so Hungarian-looking he took most of them to be Gentiles (they were, in the majority, Jews), Kafka also referred to Felice. He remarked she did not appear at Brod's reading in Berlin, probably because of her condition, awaiting her second child. "I feel for F. the love that an unsuccessful general has for the city he could not take, but which 'nevertheless' became something great."[106]

Kafka went on a regime of milk and cream daily to settle his stomach and nerves, which had, apparently, been upset by the lung infection. The doctor also prescribed arsenic, but Kafka declined; he did gain weight, even though the treatment had little connection to what ailed him. He fell in with a twenty-five-year-old Hungarian boy, "charming in the East European Jewish sense" and a "young man to fall in love with . . . full of irony, unrest, moodiness, confidence, but also neediness." Although inviting Brod to visit, Kafka was not eager to see Milena. She in turn poured out her anguish to Brod, brooding that she was on the brink of madness because she thought she might have been the one to make Kafka suffer as he did with other women. She feels that if she did she was responsible for making his illness worse; and to decrease his anguish, he had to run away from her also. A good deal of her response to Kafka is, of course, connected to the high degree of nervousness, anxiety, and neurotic frustration she felt with her own life. That Kafka did not want to see her at this time had little to do with her specifically, but with his own inability to find direction. He hoped to become immersed in some major pieces of fiction; she would only be an intrusion.

Kafka wrote of the demise of his affair with Milena in a mid-April letter to Brod, already partially quoted earlier. He wanted to be certain that when Milena, herself consumptive, came to Prague, he would not be there. "And I would like you to inform me if M. does get to the Tatra Mountains [where Matliary was], so that I can leave here in plenty of time. For a meeting would no longer mean that desperation tears its hair, but that it scratches bloody welts on head and brain."[107] Kafka then rambles on, trying to make himself understood, and we recognize from the disorientation of his words to Brod how miserable he was made by the need to terminate the relationship. He cites his lack of vitality, his inability to encounter conflict, his desire to run away. A

---

tagh's Sanatorium in Nový Smokovec. He later went to see Dr. Szontagh for an examination.

metaphor puts it well: "But people don't always run away to save themselves; the ashes the wind blows away from a fire don't fly away in order to save themselves." Once burnt out, one has little choice.

Then in a poignant passage already cited in this chapter, Kafka indicates how the bodies of girls tempted him, until they became close to him, and then not at all. He adds, "I can love only what I can place so high above me that I cannot reach it." But this rejection is linked to his "fear of death," which intensified what was already a sexual malady. He also ascribes his condition to his being a "devious West European Jew," by which he means he is out of tune with his feelings; or else his emotional and rational lives move on parallel lines. In his assessment of his condition, his self-abuse is enormous. His shame is as strong as if Napoleon had said "to the demon that summoned him to Russia: 'I cannot go now: I haven't drunk my evening glass of milk yet'; and as if he then, when the demon asked, 'Will it take so long?' replied: 'Yes, I have to Fletcherize it.' "[108]

He asks Brod if now he understands. This withdrawal was, apparently, part of a larger frame of reference, in which Kafka was refocusing himself for his new role, for the work he was yet to do. Or at least he was attempting to clear away the mental and emotional debris of his life so as to give himself the chance to strike forth. With *The Castle* now beginning to take shape, through sketches and other references, he had to rid himself of something as enormous as Milena.

Meanwhile, mainly because of noise, life at Matliary was not idyllic. As he "writhes on his reclining chair almost in paroxysms," he hears voices above, someone singing below. Even after the director at Matliary promises him quiet if he will stay, Kafka tells Brod, on January 13, he plans to leave for Smokovec, which, he knows, will be less suitable. "I mention all this because I am so full of it, as though the world were composed of nothing but the balcony over me and its noisiness." He draws an amusing analogy between Matliary, which he otherwise likes, and old Austria: "Sometimes things went well; one lay on the sofa in the evening in the well-heated room, thermometer in mouth, the milk jug nearby, and enjoyed a certain measure of peace. But it was only a certain measure, not real peace." Then comes his point. Only a triviality, he remarks, was sufficient to make the throne in Vienna begin to sway. He cites the 1891 law that mandated use of German in the superior courts of one mixed German-Czech district, leading to Czech riots, suppression, and nationalistic fervor. Out of this reverberated the "triviality" that eventually brought down the empire. So it is with noise for him.

Kafka was increasingly caught up in Brod's adulterous relationship with Emmy Salveter, who was working as a chambermaid in a Berlin hotel when Brod met her. Brod gave her money to begin a career as an actress, and he came to incorporate her in three of his novels. Also, the character of Pepi in Kafka's *The Castle* owes something to her. Kafka words his approach amusingly: "You [Brod] want the impossible, while for me the possible is impossible. I am perhaps only a step below you, but on the same stairway."[109] Kafka's attitude is that Brod, married, with the choice still to make about having children, has enjoyed it all; but he is dissatisfied because he yearns for the impossible. Kafka, on the other hand, yearns for the possible, but is always struck down before he can attain it. There is a difference, he admits, but it does not distinguish their essential natures.

He shows tolerance for Emmy Salveter, saying that her low social role as a chambermaid validates Brod's serious interest in her: "Because of the seriousness with which you took the relationship she was able to hold her own."[110] Yet even as Kafka shows interest in such an affair — exogamous, exotic, a fantasy — he is troubled by it. "A foreigner, a guest, even a Jew, one of hundreds who take a liking to the pretty chambermaid, someone in whose serious desires she can believe, for a single night (even if he does have this seriousness). But what more can there be? A love spanning the distance between countries? A correspondence?"[111] Where can it lead? He wonders if Brod is serious about the relationship or about the woman, a sharp insight into his friend's need for diversion, his inability to settle for marriage, his need to walk the edge. Kafka foresees terrible misery in all this, in Brod's wife, Brod himself, even Emmy. He cannot avoid leading the affair back to himself, cast as a metaphor. "Every womb is fruitful and smirks uselessly at the world. And when one hides one's face, it is not in order to protect oneself from this smirk, but not to let one's own smirk be seen. Compared to this, the struggle with the father doesn't mean much. After all, he is only an elder brother, also a scapegrace son, who from jealousy is merely pitifully trying to distract his younger brother from the decisive struggle and moreover does so successfully."

With passages like this, we observe Kafka writing his way back into writing. For by taking off from Brod's position, he has in metaphorical terms reviewed his own. While Brod conquers, he, Kafka, hides his face from every smirking womb, and yet this is the most important part of his life, compared with which the struggle with Hermann over courtship and marriage is secondary. But the metaphor also returns Kafka to "The Judgment" and to "The Metamorphosis," with the father moving in and out of the son's life. Although there is no split between the friends over Emmy, Kafka's words, carefully chosen, indicate a wide gulf in sensibilities.

The caustic quality of the metaphor must be partly attributed to the fact that at Matliary he had entered a culture of death. What is striking about his surroundings as he describes them is how closely they represent the morbid world beyond, and how that world with its death orientation is reflected in the culture of Modernism. The trench warfare of the recently ended conflict was a kind of metaphor for a generalized death of mankind; and the development of Modernism in art and literature mirrored this. Modernism has often been accused of nihilism, but it did not advocate destruction, it reflected it. As Kafka well knew from his insurance experience and involvement with bureaucracies, the real nihilists were advocates of order and an ordered society. In the name of order, they destroyed human values, offering either the bureaucracy or the state as replacement. Modernist artists mirrored this, rebelled against it, offered alternatives, but without withdrawing from the death orientation of the society at large. Kafka at Matliary is a perfect image of the individual caught in a death culture. What he describes could be a Munch painting, a Rilke poem, a Schoenberg score. He speaks of one bad case, a Czech with tuberculosis of the lungs and larynx, precisely what Kafka suffered from in the final stages of his illness. When Kafka takes pity on him and visits, the Czech showed "a little mirror which he has to insert deep into his throat when there is sun, in order to expose the abscesses to the light, then showed me the large mirror with which he can look further into his throat in order to place the small mirror properly."[112] He further shows Kafka a drawing of the abscesses that had first appeared three months before.

The Czech makes Kafka handle the picture and the mirror and insists on his placing them near his eyes. Kafka begins to feel a fainting fit "coming toward me like a wave." He manages to remain conscious, but his big problem is how to get out of the room. The scene has the quality of his fictions, and it foreshadows Mann's sanatorium in *The Magic Mountain*. Kafka sees it all as a culture of death, what he is caught in and what he will represent when his creative powers return. "This whole wretched life in bed, the fever, the shortness of breath, the taking of medicines, the painful and dangerous business with the mirrors (one little awkward motion and he can burn himself) — all this has no other purpose but to slow down the development of the abscess, from which he must finally suffocate, to prolong this wretched life, the fever and so, as long as possible."[113] Yet he is not finished. Over this "slowly smoldering pyre," the man's relatives and doctors have built scaffolding, so that "without danger of contagion they can visit, cool and comfort the tormented man, cheer him up to endure further misery."

This episode was quite necessary, since it validated what had always been Kafka's view of life: the disproportion between the healthy and the sick, a reflection of a culture of dying and dead, a representation of the way in which there are sufferers and those who live beyond suffering, his sense of how imperfection in every phase of life frustrates any effort at perfection. Even as he strives for that ideal — the "striving for perfection is only a small part of my huge Gordian knot"[114] — he sees how the sensitive person is cut off and must rebuild his vision from a position of weakness. He compares himself with the skiers tearing along the slopes and telemarking in great swings, and he knows it is like a dream in which a healthy man glides from waking into sleep; a man like himself does not glide, does not swoop, does not swing wildly, does not even sleep. His life and fiction converged absolutely at Matliary.

Meanwhile, almost as if in a kind of hoax, he was gaining weight, almost a kilo a week for the first five weeks, a total gain of nine pounds. Outwardly he was looking healthier, less skeletal; inwardly, the disease was moving along at a pace that would weaken him. He did make the acquaintance of a twenty-one-year-old medical student, Robert Klopstock, a Hungarian Jew from Budapest, who became a devoted friend and helper when Kafka's condition deteriorated. Although still quite young, Klopstock had served as an officer in the war, on both the Eastern and Italian fronts; his medical knowledge was already deep, and he was a serious reader of Dostoevsky, among others. Kafka offered to lend him books. What brought them together initially was Klopstock's enthusiastic recognition of Brod's name; and what finally attracted Kafka to him was the young student's resemblance to Werfel.*

Kafka was still corresponding with Minze Eisner, mainly about the progress of his condition, while hers had cleared and she was running around the world, like Robinson Crusoe or Sinbad the Sailor, as he put it. They also had been exchanging gardening information, she from the Pomological Institute at Troja, just outside Prague, where Kafka had himself done gardening after working hours, and he from the Matliary gardens. But it was to Brod and Milena in and around this time that he expressed his most anguished thoughts. A recurring image in his correspondence with Milena is a watery grave: "How uncontrolled one is, how tossed to and fro in a sea which, only out of malice, does not swallow one up."[115] He compares himself to Robinson Crusoe: "Robinson, you see, had to sign on, make the dangerous voyage, had to suffer shipwreck and many other things — I would only have to lose you and already I'd be Robinson. But I would be more Robinson than he. He still had the Island and Friday and many things and finally the ship which took him off and almost turned everything into a dream again — I would have nothing, not even a name, this too I gave you."[116] He says he is independent of her, just because the dependency "reaches beyond all bounds." He adds that their relationship is either/or: if she is his, that is good; if he loses her, it's not just bad, it's nothing. He says there is something blasphemous about putting so much importance on one person, "and this is also the reason why fear creeps round the founda-

---

*Kafka mentioned to both Ottla and Brod that Klopstock, an anti-Zionist, was guided by both Jesus and Dostoevsky, qualities that appealed to Kafka more than his medical skills.

tions." Then comes his real sentiment: "It's not, however, so much the fear about you as the fear about daring to build like this at all."[117] Because he knows how close death is, *even when one is not ill*, he hesitates to throw himself into life. Unlike Brod, Klopstock, Werfel, Minze Eisner, even Felice Bauer, he knows that all assaults on life must be hedged with countering forces. He was, in these and subsequent lines, getting ready for "A Hunger Artist" and *The Castle*, although they were several months away.

Feeling his isolation so intensely, like the Robinson Crusoe he would have been if he were deserted, he provides his alternative: to be a small Eastern European Jewish boy in the corner of a room, unworried about his future, his father in the center of the room talking with other men, his mother rummaging in the bundles, his sisters chattering with other girls, and in a few weeks they would be in America. He knows, also, it can't be as simple as that; there is violence, hostility and anger, there is disorder and noise. But if one is a small boy like this, what can happen to him? And the food, under these conditions? "Everything is edible."[118] In his desperation, Kafka has drawn his version of a racial paradise, clearly based on his vision of Eastern European Jews and their strong sense of family and community, their unshakable belief in who and what they are, uncontaminated by a progressive civilization, people who trace their roots back hundreds of years, speak Yiddish, unpolluted by other languages and cultures. Here Kafka finds the "real mother," not the *Mutter* he was stuck with, either as language or as actual woman. Not unusually, his response involves food. Under these conditions, he would eat everything, because its source was pure.

The vision is of womb, sea, heavy wrapping that would provide protection; he could crawl in. Even as it soothes and comforts, it is a desperate image, for he knows by now it is a fantasy he has conjured up for the sake of Milena, whose own background and aspirations are completely opposite to these. He takes up one of his favorite transformations, what he could soon write about with dogs and mice, his change into an animal of the forest. Lying in a dirty ditch, he, this animal, sees her, and he cowers before her, "laid my face in your hand."[119] Still, he was only an animal and belonged in the forest. She is kind, strokes him, calms him, but she had to recognize his oddities, that he was out of his element and belonged only in the woods. It soon becomes clear to him he is an "unclean pest," an obstacle in her path; and he refers to some business he had done for her that did not turn out to her satisfaction. He feels guilt and remorse. "You ask how I live: this is how I live."[120] He moves from the animal image to another favorite: "Nor is it perhaps really love when I say that for me you are the most beloved; love is to me that you are the knife which I turn within myself."

He senses subterranean threats, which are essential if he is to keep living; it's his way, he says, of participating in life. "If it ceases I abandon life, as easily and naturally as one closes one's eyes." In the meanwhile, he lives in his dirt, and he feels remorse he has dragged her into it. At this time, he sends his drawing of the torture apparatus, with the Jesus-figure pulled apart by rods driven into his hands. And then he presents a dream, one of his most powerful, because it repeats the motif of what passed between him and Felice, the fantasy of a suicide pact.

> What happened in detail I can hardly remember, all I know is that we kept merging into one another. I was you, you were me. Finally you somehow caught fire. Remembering that one extinguishes fire with clothing, I took an old coat and beat you with it. But again the transmutations began, and it went so far that you were no longer even there, instead it was I who was on fire and it was also I who beat the fire with my coat. But the beatings didn't help and it only confirmed my old fear that such things can't extinguish a fire.[121]

The blending of the two, her disappearance in the fire, his subsequent burning — all of this suggests mutual destruction, with their differences being resolved in a conflagration. But there is more: a fire brigade arrives and she is saved. But she is spectral, and falls lifeless into his arms; he too has been saved. Yet here Kafka is uncertain, and the uncertainty comes from his unconscious recognition that the fire was intended so that no one would be saved. They were to burn up, joined.

He recognizes that she fears death but says he is only terribly afraid of pain. To want death but not the pain, he asserts, is a bad sign. Otherwise, one can risk death. "One has just been sent out as a biblical dove, has found nothing green, and slips back into the darkness of the arch."[122] He follows with a series of remarkable images of death, some of them full of sexual fantasies, like that of her love twisting in him as a knife thrust. He asks what he should do in a sanatorium. "Have the senior physician take me between his knees, choke on the lump of meat he stuffs into my mouth with his carbolic fingers and then forces down my throat?" The blending of death (carbolic), meat (the taboo object), and the sexual image (he between the doctor's legs, his mouth being stuffed) creates a recurring Kafka vision, a homoerotically oriented *Liebestod*.

He wonders why she does not find him repugnant. As a Jew alone, he might be considered repellent, since the press and political spokesmen are asserting that Jews have corrupted and decomposed everything, are "even supposed to have corrupted the flagellantism of the Middle Ages!"[123] He cites the organ of the Agrarian Party, the anti-Semitic *Venkov*, part of the nationalist-populist movement to drive out Germans and Jews.* He tells Milena to emigrate, since that is the mes-

---

*Jews were indeed leaving Bohemia, their population dropping from 94,500 in 1890 to about 80,000 by 1921. In Prague, where almost half the Bohemian Jews lived, they formed 4 percent of the population, but overall only about 1 percent of the Bohemian population.

sage of the reactionary press. She has herself called such matters reflections of illness, but Kafka sees more deeply: "All these so-called
illnesses, sad as they may appear, are matters of faith, efforts of souls in
distress to find moorings in some maternal soil; thus psychoanalysis
[which he opposes] also considers the origin of religions to be nothing
but what (in its opinion) causes the 'illness' of the individual.'"[124] Kafka
observes that illness is an easy explanation: the entire culture and its
conditioning of the individual are in question, and people lacking a
sense of religious community rally around other ideas that give them
the feeling of belonging, of empowerment.

He was, of course, moving parallel to developments in the German-
speaking world, as well as the nationalist movements in Czechoslovakia and Hungary, in which people flocked to prophets who promised
solidarity and belonging. He understood well from his own experience
that people seek a party or empowerment, and if it turns out to be hateful, unjust, hostile, that doesn't really matter as long as it fulfills its
function. Milena could not possibly pick up the caustic irony in his
seemingly innocent words, his insight that the war had changed everything and that disorder seeking hateful order was the menu for the day.
As for himself, he presents what he sees: that Western Jew who is not
granted a calm second, someone for whom everything has to be earned,
"not only the present and future, but the past too — something after all
which perhaps every human being has inherited, this too must be
earned, it is perhaps the hardest work.'"[125] But it is all madness, and any
attempt, he says, to get through this on his own strength is also madness and will be rewarded with madness.

Later on, as the correspondence wound down, Kafka's humor became almost completely death oriented. Marriage made out of despair
is simply joining loneliness to loneliness. When he moves to another
place, in May 1923, he says it is so expensive "that one should be allowed to stay here only the last days before one's death, then there's
nothing else left — and secondly I fear — Heaven and Hell";[126] but his
first fear is the expense. "Apart from this, the whole world is open to
me." He speaks of wishing to go to Palestine in October but knows he
never will. With that, Milena vanishes from his life. She will turn up in
a German concentration camp, a political prisoner, a lover of Jews, and
will die there.

To Brod, Kafka is equally intimate about his obsessions: death and
food are linked. "I was lying on my sofa, knocked out by the exertion of
eating. An agonizing lack of appetite brings sweat out on my face when
I see the horror of a full plate in front of me.'"[127] He says he has been
eating meat for the last two weeks, the result of a replacement cook
for the one who catered to his needs, and this consumption of meat
has caused his hemorrhoids to flare up, with intense pain night and
day. Accompanying this discomfort is shortness of breath and cough-

ing, which seems to get worse but is offset by weight gain and a favorable temperature. This preoccupation with death and dying, directed at Brod, continues with Kafka's announcement that the doctor has warned him a return to Prague would be a death sentence. Yet Matliary has become unbearable. The girls in the kitchen, he says, pick uneaten food from the patients' plate, patients he does not even want to sit across from. "How loathsome it is to sit opposite a larynx patient, for instance (blood brother of a consumptive but far sadder), who sits across from you so friendly and harmless, looking at you with the transfigured eyes of the consumptive and at the same time coughing into your face through his spread fingers drops of purulent phlegm from his tubercular ulcer."[128] He yearns for Prague in the spring and summer, which he thinks he could bear well. Yet he admits his health is poor, with coughing and shortness of breath worse than before. He foresees the end of his leave and contemplates his return to the office, whose work he says he can handle. He indicates that when the weather turns in the fall, he will have to go away again, while the doctor warns him that if he remains at Matliary for another four to six months he will stabilize and be better prepared for work. The subtext in all his letters is his knowledge that all choice is a dicing with death.

As we have seen, the April letters to Brod indicate Kafka's desire to leave the Tatras if Milena comes to recuperate from her own lung condition. This does not occur, and he stays on, his leave extended first to May 20 and then another three months beyond that.* He complains he is not healthy two days in succession, even apart from his lungs and hypochondria. By this time, his entire system is out of balance. The doctors are divided on whether to give him injections, and he, with his horror of medication, rules them out. He expresses his contempt for inoculations:

> The foreshortened time span in which conventional medicine deals is ludicrous, and nature therapy has nothing but contempt for it. I am willing to believe that tuberculosis will be controlled [as it would be, more than twenty years after Kafka's death, by medication]; every disease will ultimately be controlled. It is the same with wars — each will come to its end but none ever stops. Tuberculosis no more has its origins in the lungs than, for example, World War had its cause in the ultimatum. *There is only a single disease* [my italics], no more, and medicine blindly chases down one disease as though hunting a beast in endless forests.[129]

That "single disease" is the quality of modern life. It is the preoccupation with progress and industrialization, the loss of community and social solidarity, the decline of any kind of faith (not necessarily re-

---

*In the background of Kafka's extended leaves were Brod and Ottla, who was active on his behalf. At one point, the institute director suggested that Kafka move to South Africa, while Ottla pushed for Palestine.

ligious or spiritual), the rage for individual need, the impossibility of the individual ego to adjust to any social norms, the leap for self-regard. Out of all this grows tuberculosis, the single disease that expresses all of Kafka's contempt for the Faustian pact man makes in order to enjoy his futile successes. He had just recently quoted Schopenhauer to Minze Eisner, and it was Schopenhauer, as well as Kierkegaard, who was so outraged that people sitting on a lovely balcony looking out on a lovely scene should think life is beautiful. It is not that, Kafka repeats, not only not for himself but for anyone who looks beyond the scene. To Brod, he had spoken of himself as "the devious West European Jew," whose dissolution he has been predicting for a decade, because he chases a chimera. Kafka sees no hope for any of it, but in that he differs from doomsayers like Nordau, Kraus, and Weininger at the turn of the century. Unlike them, he diagnoses only; he does not tinker with the system to bring about change. In that, he is the archetypal Modernist: diagnostician of dissolution and disintegration, mocker of those who refuse to see the world as it has become, ironist and satirist about those nostalgic for the past, builder of new art forms to fit new sensibilities. For Kafka, the past is dying, the future ungiving, the present a matter of holding on.

He notices an attractive girl, and he tells Brod all the young women are called Aranka or Ilonka or Clarika; and he has had his eye on Aranka but kept his distance. He assures Brod he is not staying on at Matliary because of a woman. "No girl will ever hold me anywhere. Amazing how little discernment women have; they only notice whether they attract you, or whether you have pity for them, or finally whether you look for compassion from them."[130] What he ignores is the near desperation of women in the postwar period to find husbands after almost the entire generation of young men had been killed. But the remarks also express that blend of hostility and self-hatred he felt when women were concerned: that unconscious attribution to them of qualities he found in his mother, in her failure to nurture him. All women, in this perception, must pay; but, of course, it was not so simple as that.

Noise has followed him into the very recesses of Matliary. "I am like the father of Matliary and can only fall asleep when the last squeaking chambermaid is in bed." A workman installing stoves in adjacent rooms hammers, sings, whistles, from five in the morning until seven at night. The chambermaid tells him to stop whistling, and Kafka feels guilty that he, lying down, should forbid a workman from whistling. But he sometimes forgets and whistles, "probably cursing at me." When the workman stops his noise, everything else in the place is ready to take up the slack. Kafka has insight into it: "But it isn't the noise here that is at issue, but rather the noise of the world, and not even this noise but my own noiselessness."[131]

Yet as the letters deepen, noise may be bothersome but it is not central. He has been cut off from Prague and family for several months; Ottla has given birth to a daughter, Věra, and he has even been staying in the room intended for Ottla. Writing now to Klopstock, the young Budapest medical student, he takes up Kierkegaard's conception of Abraham and Isaac in his *Fear and Trembling*. Kafka has referred to this interpretation before, but it is particularly fitting here since it leads into his final burst of creative work. At the same time, it reveals his disorientation. He starts by discounting Abraham the patriarch who is ready to carry out God's orders. He posits another Abraham who might not even make it as an old-clothes dealer and who would carry out orders not in some divine mission but like a waiter. This Abraham would be ineffective because he couldn't get away from home; the farm needs him. Kafka wittily quotes the Bible: "He puts his house in order."[132] This Abraham is a klutz of sorts, and he represents not Hermann but Kafka himself. Such an ordinary Abraham is not worth discussing, little more than an insect or a small animal.

Yet Kafka has in mind still another patriarch who actually wants to carry out the sacrifice, as did Kierkegaard's Abraham. But Kafka's patriarch, while he is prepared to do the deed, cannot believe he is the one meant, "the repulsive old man and his dirty boy."[133] Kafka is now riding his hobbyhorse: "He does not lack the true faith, for he has this faith; he wants to sacrifice in the proper manner, if only he could believe he was the one meant."[134] His irony turns droll: "He is afraid that he will, to be sure, ride out as Abraham and his son, but on the way will turn into Don Quixote." He fears the world will ridicule him. He fears, further, that "this ridiculousness will make him still older, and more repulsive, his son dirtier, more unworthy to be really summoned." The next letter speaks of illness as filth: "This contradiction between the appearance of the face and the lungs, all of it filthy."[135] All this is linked to Kafka's imaginative processes. Through images of folly, illness, and abjectness, he was attempting to activate his creative power in the only way he knew how: by playing the abject role. This role could take several shapes, even as a disreputable Abraham or as a "dirty boy."

In the same letter to Brod, Kafka comments on Karl Kraus's attack on Werfel, who had himself previously attacked Kraus. Kafka readily admits Kraus's dominance in the narrow world of German-Jewish writing; he then moves on to questions of language, once again arranging ideas in letters which can serve him in his fiction. He wonders, first, why Jews should be so drawn to German, both its language and literature. At the center of this, Kraus insisted on the purity of the German tongue and, in keeping with his pre-eminence in the German world, was himself an anti-Semitic Jew, a convert at two points in his life. Kafka's view of Kraus is as the grandfather figure in an operetta, who instead of saying *oy* composes long tedious poems. His point here and later will be that German, even the pure form Kraus insisted upon, was a trap for the Jewish writer.

Kafka casts the next phase of his somewhat circuitous argument in oedipal terms. He says that psychoanalysis stresses the father-complex, which many find intellectually fruitful; but he prefers another version: where the issue is not the innocent father, but his Jewishness. "Most young Jews who began to write German wanted to leave Jewishness behind them, and their fathers approved of this, but vaguely. . . . But with their posterior legs they [the sons] were still glued to their father's Jewishness and with their waving anterior legs they found no new ground. The ensuing despair became their inspiration."[136]

This is such central Kafka we may feel he is parodying himself. The Jewish writer is caught in a trap of his own making, and all effort to rebel against the father through language finds itself trapped in language, German. Using a Gregor Samsa–like image of a bug caught between forward and backward legs, Kafka perceives the Jewish writer as being forced to gain energy by despair, the only way he could resolve his own enigmatic position. Yet Kafka is of course correct: to write within a language is to accept the culture that that language expresses, and no Jewish writer — and surely not even Kraus, although he may have thought otherwise — could find a true home in German. Seventy-five years earlier, Richard Wagner, starting from an anti-Semitic point of view, argued that Jews could never write "German music" because they were cut off from what Germanism meant. Kafka is arguing a similar point but from a cultural, not racial, point of view: that the Jewish writer in the West has no real language of his own. Yiddish, he felt, was not viable and was of course not the language of the Western European Jew; Hebrew had not yet gained favor as a literary language, and it too was not known by the acculturated Jew. German, then, remained the Middle European language, and Kafka saw, as was mentioned before, four impossibilities: not writing, writing German, writing differently, writing itself. As a consequence, "what resulted was a literature impossible in all respects, a gypsy literature which had stolen the German child out of its cradle and in great haste put it through some kind of training, for someone has to dance on the tightrope."[137]

Feeling isolated from language did not, however, prevent him from creating a distinct German of his own. What is at stake is less his adeptness in using his "borrowed" language than his feeling of isolation from what gives that language its powers of expression. Kafka's awareness of isolation in using language was, then, simply another aspect of his total personality of isolation; each dimension of separation fed the other, all of it deriving, he felt, from his Western European position, a Jew without Judaism, a German without German culture, a Czech without Czech identification.* Being bereft gave him energy; despair provided inspiration.

---

*Still another distinction was between those who were German by education, like Kafka himself, and those ethnic Germans, later known as Sudeten Germans, now living in

In several long letters to his oldest sister, Elli, about the education of children, hers as well as others', he tried to reshape his own early years. He speaks of a certain spirit in Prague, from which children cannot be shielded, and he calls it "this small, dirty, lukewarm, squinting spirit."[138] He hopes one's own child can be saved from that intellectual provincialism. For someone so caustic about fate or destiny, he is surprisingly Rousseauistic in some of his assumptions, speaking of the boy as "the incorruptible seeker after truth," who must then pass that truth on. He warns her how a big city can make him overindulged, overstimulated, but bored and lacking religion. "The boy reads, he learns music, he plays soccer, and all this does not have to but very possibly may contain terrible boredom and aimlessness which neither he nor others can recognize but which reveals itself by its consequences."[139] Amusingly, he tells her not to blame his advice because it comes from him; or, he might have added, because it defined him.

But all this is merely a warmup for the full blast against educational ideas. After a faulty citing of Jonathan Swift as a family man (he was unmarried and had no children), Kafka says the family is an organism, but an extremely complex and unbalanced one; and the equilibrium between parents and children, when it exists, is called education. But he charges that that which depends on the quiet, "unselfish, loving development of potentialities of a growing human being is no real education; neither is the toleration of a child's independent development." All this was much closer to Rousseau than to anything in Swift. Kafka is now on familiar ground. Family education is a chimera because of the "monstrous superiority in power of the parents vis-à-vis the children."[140] As a consequence of this, the "parents arrogate to themselves the sole right, during the childhood of the children, to represent the family, not only to the outside world but also within the intimate intellectual organization."[141] By so doing, they deny the children their "right to personality and from then on can make them incapable of ever securing this right in a healthy way." Kafka has turned his views on education into an extension of *Letter to His Father* and is, at the same time, energizing himself for some fictional effort.* "First Sorrow," discussed earlier, about the trapeze artist who never wishes to descend from his perch, comes from this time (October 1921). It is clearly very close to another one of Kafka's ideas not itself distinct from education, the care and nurturing of the artist.

Drawing out his arguments in this enormously long letter to Elli, Kafka is now off and running. Real education is a human affair, family education a family affair; and the two cannot meet, since they depend

---

what was Czech territory. Even they owned the language in a way denied Kafka. These Sudeten Germans held themselves apart, and when Hitler in 1938 annexed the Sudetenland, they welcomed him. Language played as much a role here as did politics.
*And, as we shall see, to return to his *Diaries* after a hiatus of nineteen months.

on antithetical ideas of empowerment. The growing child lacks empowerment, and if he or she fails to conform, the child is not expelled "but accursed or consumed or both."[142] He cites the archetypal father figure Kronos, in Greek mythology, who devoured his sons, because "perhaps Kronos preferred this to the usual methods out of pity for his children." Even parents who love are so selfish in their views of education that their use of power knows no bounds. Kafka then zeroes in on Hermann: when the father educates the child, he will "find things in the child that he already hates in himself and could not overcome and which he now hopes to overcome, since the weak child seems to be more in his power than he himself. And so in a blind fury, without waiting for the child's own development, he reaches into the depths of the growing human being to pluck out the offending element." Or, conversely, he recognizes that something in him is lacking in the child, and, therefore, he must pound that into the child. "Which effort is successful, but at the same time disastrous, for in the process he pounds the child to pieces."

From this, Kafka concludes that tyranny or slavery, born of selfishness, "are the two educational methods of parents." Tyranny can be expressed in great tenderness (here Kafka can and does indict the mother), and "slavery can express itself as pride,"[143] in which the parents consider the son to be their savior and thus remake him in an image unlike his own. Such methods are not education but antieducational. The son turned into savior or messiah is a son reduced to slavery. He quotes a line from a Viennese poet (Vogl) saying that when the prodigal son returns home, the mother knows him: "The mother's eye her son did know." But Kafka twists this around, so it means that if the son had not left but had remained at home, the mother would not have known him, "for her daily association with the son would have made him completely unrecognizable to her and so the very opposite of the poem would have happened."

Kafka now returns to Swift and agrees with the eighteenth-century satirist that children should be removed from their parents. In this revision of current thinking, the family's animal needs should be "postponed to a time when the children, independent of their parents, should become equal to them in physical and mental powers, and then the time is come for the true and loving equilibrium to take place."[144] This is what Elli called "being saved," or what others labeled "the gratitude of children," which is so rarely found. Kafka provides Elli with what she might not have known, since being six years younger than Kafka and a girl, she did not comprehend the dynamics of his role as the oldest and only surviving son. Within the power structure of the family, her role was completely different, and, therefore, her consciousness of education was not her brother's. He is in the main arguing for the education of sons, not daughters, and he is in his perception of events

thirty years later reviewing what was unworkable, torturous, and humiliating. Now thirty-eight years old, he finds the wounds as fresh as
they were twenty years earlier, surely as fresh as in 1919, when he
wrote the famous *Letter*. His advice to Elli about rearing her children
had little reference to reality but was, in a sense, his way of educating
her to their common past.

The autumn of 1921 was an extremely trying time. On August 26,
he returned to Prague to resume work at the institute, where he started
on the twenty-ninth. He suffered from a low-grade fever, just above
normal, rarely higher than 99 degrees, but sufficient to keep him enervated. His doctors recommended that he return to a sanatorium, Matliary or another, but he resisted. He could not work, and when he learned
that Milena was coming to Prague, he was further agitated, unable to
sleep, work, or concentrate. "The letter-writer," he tells Klopstock,
"whose sharp and even penmanship you know from her envelopes is in
Prague and so the sleepless nights begin."[145] He writes this at the end of
September. But his apprehension turns into something else: he lends
Milena his diaries on October 8 as an act of validating himself, but also
as a way of turning away from the earlier kind of diary to something
different. "I no longer need to make myself so minutely conscious of
such things, I am not so forgetful as I used to be in this respect, I am a
memory come alive, hence my insomnia."[146] These remarks (on October 15) are followed by images of death in the entries for the following
day. For now, bereft of his *Diaries*, he must create himself anew in his
present role. He may have become a "memory come alive," but he had
also become a man temporarily removed from the visible proof of those
memories.

Images of death, coffins, and ruins mingle with a resolve to do his
best. "I don't believe people exist whose inner plight resembles mine;
still, it is possible for me to imagine such people — but that the secret
raven forever flaps about their heads as it does about mine, even to
imagine that is impossible."[147] That "secret raven" calls up a flight of
death, but it is also what gives him his power. His difference from others lies there, in his insight into the culture, but also into himself,
which allows him to represent that culture. He is, here, somewhat like
the French poet Rimbaud, whose awareness of death, and of the fact it
needed a new language to express itself, became part of the structure
both of his life and of a new kind of evocative poetry. Kafka is probing,
picking away, digging in to discover that formula that will work for
him and, at the same time, mirror what he knows is true.

"It is astounding," he writes, "how I have systematically destroyed
myself in the course of the years, it was like a slowly widening breach
in a dam, a purposeful action."[148] Yet what seems like destruction also
has its magic. "It is entirely conceivable that life's splendor forever lies
in wait about each one of us in all its fullness, but veiled from view,

deep down, invisible, far off. It *is* there, though." It is all there, however, only when summoned by the right word or right name, as if by some sleight of hand. When he recognized death through tuberculosis, Kafka sought images of life in language hidden behind veils and disguises, like Keats's nightingale, like the creature who can experience joy only because he has endured pain and suffering.

He says he cannot endure the eyes of people, not from misanthropy but because of their mere presence. He compares himself to a man wandering in the wilderness, who is on the track of Canaan all his life; thus the parallel to Moses, who sees Canaan only when he is on the verge of death. Such a dying vision is intended to reveal how incomplete a moment human life is. Moses, he says, failed to enter Canaan not because his life was too short, but because it was a human life. In a fine passage of close writing, Kafka shows how close he is coming to creative work, how through despair and enervation he is revitalizing himself.

> Anyone who cannot come to terms with his life while he is alive needs one hand to ward off a little his despair over his fate — he has little success in this — but with his other hand he can note down what he sees among the ruins, for he sees different (and more) things than do the others; after all, dead as he is in his own lifetime, he is the real survivor. This assumes that he does not need both hands, or more hands than he has, in his struggle against despair.[149]

This is the credo of the Modernist artist who plunges toward the bottom in order to validate his difference from others; one who demands for his work his own temporal and spatial dimensions, who out of anguish and abnegation can find determination. Because he has once been dead or has approached death, this man is more alive. Kafka's indebtedness to Dostoevsky and Kierkegaard is evident in this passage, but completely assimilated to his own emotional and creative needs. The one who faces the firing squad returns from the experience more alive than those who have played it safe. The passage is Nietzschean also in Kafka's rejection of Nietzsche's "last man," the individual who places survival above being. Such an individual will never hit bottom and, therefore, will never experience profoundly.

Suffering, punishment, pain — Kafka repeats them to such an extent that the unwary reader might suspect self-parody when actually such words are really rallying cries: not submission, not subservience, not bending the knee, but the early sounds of triumph, the voice sensing victory. Kafka had an entire range of complaints, from abjectness to despair, from masochistic suffering to physical pain, but the complaints led to wit, irony, satire, and other positive elements. He was not only the victim, as some have charged, but the starting point for his vision. "My feeling of unhappiness lay in the fact that I welcomed so freely, with such conviction and such joy, the punishment that came, a sight that must have moved the gods, and I felt the gods' emotion almost to the point of tears."[150] His abjectness gives him a central role in the world of gods. Without punishment and suffering, he would have been ignored. Now they focus on him.

These comments (on October 18, 19, and 20, 1921) coincided with another examination, this time by Dr. O. Hermann, who, finding catarrh of both lungs, recommended that Kafka leave the institute. Instead, Kafka obtained another three months' absence, from November 5 to February 4, 1922. In his usual way, Kafka told Klopstock that Dr. Hermann was "sublimely, childishly ridiculous," in keeping with his own feeling that his condition was incurable and all the doctors had to do was to tell him that. When his father asks him to join in a hand of cards, Kafka's anger carries over into the home. He refuses, as he has always refused. He says he could have gotten caught up in the currents of life but instead chose solitary activities: his law studies and job, and "senseless" expenditures of energy on activities like gardening, carpentering, and rowing. He does not mention the most solitary activity of all, his writing. Nevertheless, a few evenings later, he does join in, to the degree of keeping score for his mother. However, it "begot no intimacy. . . . I have seldom, very seldom crossed this borderland between loneliness and fellowship, I have even been settled there longer than in loneliness itself. What a fine bustling place was Robinson Crusoe's island in comparison!"[151]

Although Kafka saw Milena in Prague, on four occasions — and had entrusted her with his *Diaries* — his emphasis now was almost completely on self. Already obsessively self-absorbed, he was, like so many seriously ill people, so caught up in *his* responses only that he observed and catalogued every detail of his life. He felt Milena was condescending to him because of his illness, and although she returned to Prague on January 22–23, they had become like strangers, moving along parallel lines destined never to come together. His *Diaries* are full of self-examination, alternating submission and defiance. He repeats how Hermann had defeated him as a child, and how as a consequence he, Kafka, had never been able to quit the battlefield, despite his perpetual defeats. On the day Milena left Prague, December 2, he makes the following notation: "Always M. or not M. — but a principle, a light in the darkness!" The remark is enigmatic: a light in the darkness, perhaps, but nevertheless another one of his "perpetual defeats."

He follows this with a meditation on writing and its dependence on other factors, so that it lacks "independence of the world." It depends on the maid who tends the fire, on the cat by the stove, on any old human being warming himself by the stove. "All these are independent activities ruled by their own laws; only writing is helpless, cannot live in itself, is a joke and a despair."[152] The comment is curious, not only because he is returning to his idea that writing is infinitely difficult to produce, but because he recognizes it cannot live in isolation from other factors and that these other factors are hindering him. He is frustrated by the very thing that has to be. Not too surprisingly, a January 16, 1922, entry indicates he has suffered something "very like a breakdown. . . . Everything seemed over."[153]

As with all details connected to his experiences, he analyzes the breakdown. He senses a complete disorder, not only in his inability to sleep or stay awake, or to endure life, but actually a breakdown in time. "The clocks are not in unison; the inner one runs crazily on at a devilish or demoniac or in any case inhuman pace, the outer one limps along at its usual speed."[154] The early pages of *The Castle* will reveal an almost complete disorientation of time and space in K.'s quest to fulfill his position as land-surveyor. Despite his breakdown, Kafka has, in one respect, assimilated the entire feel for innovative art: that Bergsonian sense of inner and outer time, the split between an inner world of abstraction and an outer world of demanding objects, that clash between perception of the world and the recognition that things exist independently. He reflects the distortions of space that such temporal clashes create, the relegation of consciousness to a secondary position, the assumption of priority by the unconscious: "Introspection, which will suffer no idea to sink tranquilly to rest but must pursue each into consciousness, only itself to become an idea, in turn to be pursued by renewed introspection." He is, indeed, a memory come alive.

He also questions his solitude, which in the past he said was in equal parts forced on him and voluntarily sought by him, perhaps compulsorily. But it is no longer what it was and is approaching its denouement. Where is it leading? he asks, and worries he may be heading toward madness. He indicates he can no longer control his desire for solitude, nor can he maintain that dualism and role-playing that allowed him to move in and out of his own world at will. The breakdown suggests he is incapable of discovering distinctions between inner and outer; the two are now smothered by his growing madness, as he perceives it.

"The pursuit [of him, by Furies] goes right through me and rends me asunder."[155] He wonders if he can manage to keep his feet and be carried along in the wild pursuit, so that he can control his own rush toward the unknown.

Pursuit, he says, is a metaphor — assault would be more appropriate. Yet all these metaphors are part of writing, part of the assault on frontiers. He is, somehow, finding emblems for his breakdown and perception of madness in writing itself; or else, conversely, he is discovering in writing the potential for such breakdown. In the new year, he tells himself (in a January 18 entry), this almost forty-year-old, "to rest content in the moment . . . the terrible moment."[156] Yet, he admonishes himself, it is "not terrible, only your fear of the future makes it so." The breakdown is clear, as he asks what has happened to his gift of sex; others will see everything about him as failure. "But it might easily have succeeded. A mere trifle, indeed so small as not to be perceived, decided between its failure and success." He agreed with Tolstoy that "trifles decide trifles."

He also agreed with Milena that fear means unhappiness, but it does not follow that courage means happiness. He says that in his class only two Jews possessed courage and both of them shot themselves while still at school or shortly after. He denies courage, but stands up for fearlessness, "with its calm open eye and stoical resolution."[157] All of this is linked in his mind to sex, which, he says, keeps gnawing at him, "hounds me day and night." To satisfy it, he would have "to conquer fear and shame and probably sorrow too."[158] Yet since he is Kafka, ill or not, he knows that no single position can explain what he feels or is responding to. He is now transformed into a Modernist protagonist: a veritable Prufrock with even greater sensitivity to the paradoxes life offers. He knows that conquering fear is not the answer, that conquest itself should not be the goal of a life. One should, instead, take advantage of opportunities, even when they are slow in coming or fail to come at all. There is a middle ground between "doing" and the "opportunity to do," and this area involves a kind of juggling act, in which one tempts opportunities, tries to draw them to one. This is what he feels he has done, and yet it too, like everything else, is unsatisfactory. He even wonders what yesterday's conclusions mean today. It is tempting to view Kafka in his final years transforming himself into an existential figure of sorts, into a protagonist so aware of life's absurdities and contingencies he foresees no way out and yet still refuses to succumb. His only consolation is that "Sisyphus was a bachelor."[159]

He wonders if Milena, in all her kindness, found some "final proof" against him. He writes about reveries filled with violence, of being dragged through the streets, pushed through a door. This is how it is in the abstract, whereas in reality there are counterforces, but only a little less violent than the forces they oppose: "The trifle that keeps life and torment alive. I the victim of both."[160] It is passages such as this which several Kafka critics cite as evidence that he prophesied the fate of the Jews at the hands of the Germans and other Europeans. Kafka, however, was not prophesying anything specific, nor was he intuiting the slaughter of the Jews. He was, instead, creating out of his own sensibility an awareness of how life at its basest arranges itself. When that is done intensely enough, it becomes prophecy.

Indulging himself, he perceived a culture of death; in this respect, he had transformed himself into a cultural guru. He did not need Nazis in reality to know that Nazis existed. His was the voice of Europe well before Europe began to close in on its Kafkas, when a Kafka was only a ripple on Europe's surface, here and there attacked. He had assimilated it all, but only because he was himself so closely linked to that culture of death that characterized the entire first half of the twentieth century in Europe. Jews happened to be in the wrong place.

The counterforce to personal violence is only slightly more bearable than the original violence. There is no respite or relief. In the diary entries leading up to his January 27, 1922, departure for Spindlermühle, a mountain resort on the Polish border, he takes dim stock of himself. It was during this period that he made his list of activities he had started without completing. He sees only desolation; but before we accept his words at face value, we must remember that in the time remaining he wrote some of his greatest works: *The Castle,* "A Hunger Artist," "Investigations of a Dog," "The Burrow," and "Josephine the Singer." In fact, just the month after this terrible assessment of his life, he wrote "A Hunger Artist" and began serious work on *The Castle.* The January 21 entry is a magnificent assessment of a man "lacking." He leads up to this by sleeping through the night, to past five, but when he thinks of his good fortune in overcoming insomnia, he sees it is really misfortune. He recognizes he doesn't deserve so much good fortune: "All the venging furies flung themselves upon me, I saw their enraged chieftain wildly spread her fingers and threaten me, or horribly strike cymbals."[161] He is, of course, attacked by Furies, which are female, and that in turn will lead into the next passage, involving women.

He now lists his "withouts." "Without forebears, without marriage, without heirs, with a fierce longing for forebears, marriage and heirs. They all of them stretch out their hands to me: forebears, marriage and heirs, but too far away for me."[162] The image calls up many associations, but mainly that of legendary Greek figures yearning for something, only to be defeated — Sisyphus and Tantalus, of course, but also Jason, after Medea has slain their children. "There is," Kafka continues, "an artificial, miserable substitute for everything, for forebears, marriage and heirs. Feverishly you contrive these substitutes, and if the fever has not already destroyed you, the hopelessness of the substitutes will." Writing, *his* substitute, is his ultimate killer; but it also saves and preserves and, accordingly, is not quite so destructive as Kafka informs his *Diaries.*

In a letter to Brod he writes his major confession. This is what writing means to him:

> Writing sustains me, but is it not more accurate to say that it sustains this kind of life? By this I don't mean, of course, that my life is better when I don't write. Rather it is much worse then and wholly unbearable and has to end in madness. But that, granted, only follows from the postulate that I am a writer, which is actually true even when I am not writing, and a nonwriting writer is a monster inviting madness. But what about being a writer itself? Writing is a sweet and wonderful reward, but

for what? In the night it became clear to me, as clear as a child's lesson book, that it is the reward for serving the devil. This descent to the dark powers, this unshackling of spirits bound by nature, these dubious embraces and whatever may take place in the nether parts which the higher parts no longer know, when one writes one's stories in the sunshine. Perhaps there are other forms of writing, but I know only this kind; at night, when fear keeps me from sleeping. I know only this kind. And the diabolic element in it seems very clear to me.[163]

Kafka then fantasizes what happens to a writer when he thinks of death, and from this we note how closely he related writing and death, how interwoven each was with the other. In one of his fantasies of what the writer experiences, Kafka sees writing as having postponed death, but now in the moment when death comes to claim him, he recognizes that he has "not bought [himself] off" by writing. "I died my whole life long and now I will really die. My life was sweeter than other peoples' and my death will be more terrible by the same degree." The scene of his role-playing as writer ends when he realizes he has not lived, that he has remained clay, that he has not blown the spark into fire but only used it to "light up [his] corpse." Kafka then questions why he is talking of dying, why he is consigning "the old corpse, the longtime corpse, to the grave." His answer: "I sit here in the comfortable posture of the writer, ready for all sorts of fine things, and must idly look on — for what can I do but write? — as my true ego, this wretched, defenseless ego, is nipped by the devil's pincers, cudgeled, and almost ground to pieces on a random pretext" — that pretext being a short trip to see Oskar Baum in Georgenthal.

But Kafka is not finished. He now presents himself in terms that foreshadow the "Hunger Artist" waiting for death, alone, ignored, betrayed by changes in the crowd's tastes. It is, however, not a new image for Kafka but one consistent with his earlier sense of himself: the perpetual hunger artist, controlling his fate with diet and bodily change, with transformations, until he becomes a miniature of himself. "This will mean," he tells Brod, "from now on I may not go out of Bohemia, next I will be confined to Prague, then to my room, then to my bed, then to a certain position in bed, then to nothing more. Perhaps at that point I will be able to renounce the joy of writing voluntarily."

He then attempts something more logical than an exposition of his innermost fears, and he tells Brod that perhaps his fear of the journey to see Baum is fear he will be kept from his desk for several days; that the writer is legitimized only by his dependence on his desk, "and if he wants to keep madness at bay he must never go far from his desk, he must hold on to it with his teeth." In the final sense, the writer "is the scapegoat of mankind. He makes it possible for me to enjoy sin without guilt, almost without guilt." The usual explanation of this function is that it belongs to the priest, but for Kafka, writer and priest are intertwined in their mission. Guilt, sacrifice, partial redemption through work, perhaps a period of grace, then the renewal of the cycle — this is Kafka's sense of himself, of the writer, of the man who will mirror life in the twentieth century.

The words sound grim but are leavened somewhat by the fact that he is carrying on a dialogue, and death, or "without," does not always triumph. He cites his resemblance to his Uncle Rudolf (Julie Kafka's half brother) — both dependent on their parents, both at odds with their fathers, both loved by their mothers, both shy and modest — but the noble goodness he identifies in his uncle he says is lacking in him. Both, however, are on the verge of insanity; with Rudolph having escaped from Jewry into the Catholic Church, where his tendencies to madness were held in check. "One difference in his favor, or disfavor," however, "was his having had less artistic talent than I, he could therefore have chosen a better path in life for himself in his youth, was not inwardly pulled apart, not even by ambition." Rudolf was probably troubled by women, also, although Kafka is not certain."In single details he was my caricature, in essentials I am his."[164]

Then comes, on January 23, the extraordinary image of his life presented in radii either broken or extending out a little, only ultimately to be broken. This leads to further dessication of spirit, to his awareness that even while contented, he yearned for discontentment. He feels he is not a crank but a man who perceives that nothing is free, that it is better to know the worst than to wait for it to occur. Yet once discontented, he wants a respite, while knowing fully that a change of fortune will be only temporary. In a remarkable entry after he arrived in Spindlermühle, he says that having legibly written his name in the register, "they have Joseph K. down in the directory. Shall I enlighten them, or shall I let them enlighten me?"[165] He was being followed by fate or Furies, and since "Joseph K." or "K." had not yet seen print, Kafka could feel he was being pursued by forces from another world.

He then begins to define himself as a citizen of that "other world." He tells of that "strange, mysterious, perhaps dangerous, perhaps saving comfort" that exists in writing; that it is "a leap out of murderer's row; it is a seeing of what is really taking place." There are, however, penalties to pay for this, as he well knows. He cannot lay hold of new weapons that might give him joy (like tobogganing, which he has just tried) because he is ignorant of their use. But more than that, he has willed himself to reject joy so that he can experience his own kind of peace; he fears to disturb the balance of his life. And for this reason, "I could not allow a new person to be born elsewhere while I was bending every effort to bury him here." Then Kafka makes a central statement of how he has perceived himself for almost his entire life, as someone wandering the desert not to lose himself but to discover something else. And he has paid the price:

... for I am now a citizen of this other world, whose relationship to the ordinary one is the relationship of the wilderness to cultivated land (I have been forty years wandering from Canaan); I look back at it like a foreigner, though in this other world it is the paternal heritage I carry with me — I am the most insignificant and timid of all creatures and am able to keep alive thanks only to the special nature of its arrangements.[166]

He winds back to how he could not have resisted his father's decree; he wonders why he was not crushed at the "border." Instead of being crushed, however, he has become a Wanderer in the Wilderness: like Moses seeking the Promised Land, or else Adam attempting to return to the Garden after the expulsion. Yet after considering that, he recognizes he is a wanderer in reverse, continually skirting the wilderness and full of childish hopes, particularly in regard to women. He says that perhaps he shall remain in Canaan: "when all the while I have been decades in the wilderness and these hopes are merely mirages born of despair." Canaan is perhaps his only Promised Land, "for no third place exists for mankind,"[167] or for himself.

Yet even while rejecting the role of wanderer, in the wilderness or elsewhere, Kafka defines himself as marginal. Like Tonio Kröger in the Mann story, he sees people congregating, part of a community, and he says he is full of astonishment at people cheerfully assembled. He rakes over the entire human condition, caught up by people enjoying life, extending themselves into others' lives. He thinks of himself as a man with the "too-great shadow,"[168] and considers himself a person who wills himself to live under this shadow, as part of the penalty he must pay. Yet he is not quite sure what he is paying for. He has been banished not by others, but by something in himself, "since I am human after all and my roots want nourishment." But he must get his nourishment "from other roots in other climes,"[169] sorry roots, but better able to sustain life.

Again like Mann, in the scene "Snow" that was to appear in *The Magic Mountain* in a few years, Kafka experiences some revelation in the snow, a reprise of his life and what was to be. If he accepted his experience in the snow, that euphoria, which is not to be his, then he would feel only menace, a kind of "present execution." "But I live elsewhere; it is only that the attraction of the human world is so immense, in an instant it can make one forget everything." Surely some of this disorientation resulted from Milena's visits to Prague early in December and then again, just before these diary entries, on January 22 or 23. Her visits made him recognize loss, not gain; and his remarks are aimed at regaining that balance he thought he had struck. "Yet the attraction of my world is too strong; those who love me love me because I am 'forsaken' ... because they sense that in happy moments I enjoy on another plane the freedom of movement completely lacking to me here."[170] He focuses on what would occur if Milena should visit at Spindlermühle: how his situation would seem brighter, how he would be esteemed by others as a human being, how they would speak to him; but he would be plunged, he says, into a world in which he could not live. "What used to be a dividing thread is now a wall, or a mountain range, or rather a grave."[171]

He has transformed himself into one of Picasso's twisted figures, facing several ways at once; or else into a surrealist image, melting and bending and completely at the beck and call of the unconscious; or, still further, into the wandering protagonist of spiritual autobiography, where all edges of the world have softened and crumbled, leaving the individual to recreate not only himself but the world in which he will live. That world, so recreated, will be for Kafka the castle — in German, of course, both castle and lock. The castle will be his key, a reprise of all the quests; just as a hunger artist is his view of himself as part of an unbalanced, unachieved world.

He is aware of the negative force in his life, in life itself: "If I have gone the tiniest step upward, won any, be it the most dubious kind of security for myself, I then stretch out on my step and wait for the Negative, not to climb to me, indeed, but to drag me down from it."[172] He bows in the direction of his mother, as representing life, as herself bending all her energies to compensate for her son's isolation. Yet this would mean he is staying alive for the sake of his mother, and this cannot be true. He wonders, further, if the only real, uncontestable truth, marred by no external circumstances, is physical pain. He finds it strange that the "god of pain" was not the primary god of the earliest religions. "For each invalid his household god, for the tubercular the god of suffocation."[173] He sees the negative strengthened by his struggle, and in the future he prophesies an imminent decision between insanity and security — surely a foreshadowing here of "A Hunger Artist," embodying insanity (art) and security (food).

As he has done many times before, he goes after his failings. He recognizes himself as a compound of timidity, reserve, talkativeness, and halfheartedness. He perceives all this as preventing him from going mad, but also as making headway impossible. He has indeed achieved balance, but at the expense of movement. Because he fears madness, he cultivates his failing(s) and thus sacrifices all advantage, "and shall certainly be the loser in the bargain, for no bargains are possible at this level."[174] He has become all innerness, all exploration of self, and has almost ceased to exist at the level of a public self. The terrible struggle is to validate himself: to discover what can justify his choices, especially in lieu of active writing. Since for the moment he lacks any form of expression, he will transform himself into various selves and shapes in order to find outlets. He assumes, once again, an aspect of Modernism, the unstable self, the self seeking expression, the balance lost while the individual attempts to extend his radii.

In a very brief insert, a short, short story, Kafka tells of a commander-in-chief who sees one soldier after another halt by his window and, pressing against it, peer in. It is a different soldier each time, but the physical characteristics of the soldiers seem the same. The commander finds he cannot tolerate this, and he lies in wait for the next soldier, throws open the window, and drags the hapless fellow into the room. He asks who he is, and the soldier answers "nobody," to which the commander responds that one could have expected as much. Then, he wonders, why the soldier looked inside. "To see if you were still here," the soldier answers.[175] The short piece is a sign of breakdown, or near breakdown, with Kafka playing a kind of game trying to validate himself, attempting even as his identity wanders off to locate himself in some time and place. The diary insert leads meaningfully into "A Hunger Artist" as well, with its captive artist, the spectators who once peered in, the question of who he is and, after his audience deserts him, for whom he performs. Kafka is not clear who the "nobody" is, the soldier peering in, or the commander who may not occupy the space inside.

Later in the winter and early spring, he will return to this theme of himself as a ghostly presence, "a wretched little person possessed by all sorts of evil spirits."[176] To Milena he writes of ghosts. Johannes Urzidil had sent on a book, *Karl Brand: The Legacy of a Young Man*, the unpublished writings of a consumptive who had died, with a preface by Werfel. The book reminds Kafka of Ivan Ilych. And what better link to "A Hunger Artist" than Tolstoy's unhappy protagonist! Ivan Ilych is not an artist, but he shares with Kafka's unnamed protagonist the fact that both observe themselves wasting away. Slow death awaits each protagonist: Kafka's from within, Tolstoy's from without (society at large). For Kafka, the emblem of "A Hunger Artist" is food, a constant in his later years, when correct diet was possible salvation; yet his portrayal of food in "A Hunger Artist" is as the enemy of "true life." For the artist, food is extraneous, since it is a form of nourishment that distracts him from his calling, or a material element that conflicts with the spirituality of art. Food is indulgence, artistry denial. The artist's happiest moment comes when he observes big eaters tucking in a huge breakfast, and he can measure his superiority from what is considered ordinary or normal. When food becomes the norm of a society, he finds happiness in starvation; and this goes beyond art into the deepest levels of Kafka's perception of himself. It fits into his secondary anorexia; in fact, even as it reveals the artist as sacrifice and martyr, the story is an emblem of anorexia. Kafka has brought together the innermost self and a conception of art that is purely romantic and Modernistic.

In another respect, the story reveals how Kafka conceived of the artist as godly; his forty days of fasting recalls the forty days Jesus experienced in the wilderness. As part of his art, the artist is even willing to extend the forty days, if the public will remain interested. In his control of the public's attention, he gains his power; and in his ability to extend beyond the forty days, if given permission by the impresario, he can reveal his power over himself. In both instances, his act has divine implications: not only as sacrifice and martyrdom but as a means of demonstrating power through control. We recognize now how close Kafka was to a hunger artist in the years he corresponded with Felice Bauer, how a hunger artist syndrome was already in place as a means of controlling her, gaining and keeping her through making himself a display piece she could not reject.

The obsession with food is not only a sublimation of the sexual drive, it is a form of intense rebellion, replacing sex as the form of rejecting family. Although food had always been part of Kafka's inner life, in his secondary anorexia, in his fletcherizing of his food, in his distaste for meat, in his fascination with digestion and excretion, and in his sense of food as somehow the enemy of his body, it has now assumed a certain place in his imagination. To deny food altogether is now obsessive. It suppresses all sexual drive: the hunger artist is monastic. It becomes part of that search for the precise line between life and death. It serves the artistic calling, the artist's quest for the perfect moment: the breaking of limits, the complete control of one's powers, the final integration of will and materials. It reveals the Kafkan need to explore others' disgust for him as a way of gaining them as his "public." The artist becomes a manipulator, choosing a medium that by establishing its limits can catch others' attention and hold them against their will. The artist is isolated, marginal to everything in society except the play of his art; he is caged, constantly observed, suspected of cheating on his art by sneaking in food. The artist has found the sole way he can justify his life, for life without justification is incomplete. The artist, finally, is savior. Without him, the public degenerates into a mob, into blood lust, into the lowest forms of behavior, identifying with the savage and the primitive.

Kafka has intuited that art, however bizarre its forms, is the means by which the public can be restrained from its atavistic tastes, from the degeneracy and disintegration implicit in what a public is. The artist's calling is not only spiritual and salvational, it has social and political implications. And the art that restrains the public is, for Kafka, an innovative art. It is grotesque, all angles and shapes, often unrecognizable. It lacks traditional forms, shocks its spectators, and uses physical forms to evoke the divine — both for the artist and for the audience. It recalls Kandinsky's insistence on the spirituality of art, ideas expressed in late 1911.

> The solitary visionaries [Kandinsky writes] are despised or regarded as abnormal and eccentric. Those who are not wrapped in lethargy and who feel vague longings for spiritual life and knowledge and progress, cry in harsh chorus, without any to comfort them. The night of the spirit falls more and more darkly. Deeper becomes the misery of these blind and ter-

rified guides, and their followers, tormented and unnerved by fear and
doubt, prefer to this gradual darkening the final sudden leap into the
blackness.[177]

Those visionaries who perceive the spiritual in art are doomed to a solitary, marginal existence, for their public fears to pursue them, preferring death itself to the implications of a spiritual art.

But Kafka in "A Hunger Artist" was not merely creating emblems
of the self. He was playing roles, as he had in his letters and in many
other of his fictional works. The role he played out was that of a man
who feared invalidation of self more than he feared death: he had to
carry through in his imagination the most extreme form of art to justify himself as an artist, although his justification led to the artist's
death. It was better to play such an extreme role, leading to certain
death, than to chance the fact that he might live without having made
that final sacrifice. Role-playing here has the typical shape of a Kafkan
paradox: one seeks sure death in order to validate a life that is worth
little unless it can confront final matters through some meaningful
gesture.

Biographically, "A Hunger Artist" is a gold mine of meaning. It permitted Kafka to flout his family, by rejecting all its ideas of food, nourishment, and health, a death blow to any family and especially an
upwardly mobile Jewish family in Middle Europe. Next, he could finalize a role he had played all his life, as finicky, panicked eater, vegetarian, fletcherizer. Further, the role gave him celebrity; he could use
his own internal dilemmas and problems as a means of exhibiting himself and gaining fame. As an exhibition, he could gain a public by becoming a pariah, a strange object, a bizarre artifact, all the elements he
had harbored in himself. Still further, as someone already sensing his
death, he could play with the edges of dying and death, approaching the
end in ever finer gradations, until, with one misstep, he would be over
the edge. And finally, and most importantly, all his obsessions with
food, sex, and his body could be channeled into a symmetrical shape,
into something he could present to the world as representing him and
yet, because of its art, transcending him. It was a final act of rebellion.
He located himself so far outside bourgeois society he became transformed, transcendent, even transfigured. All the earlier yearning to validate his "difference" now had a solid shape.

The hunger artist gloats over his difference; he vaunts his deprivation. His superiority lies in every moment of his indifference to what
others consider life-sustaining and part of their indulgence. By not eating for more than forty days, he can demonstrate not only a record for a
hunger artist, but the perfection of his art, an absolute moment that
only the highest artists can achieve. In this achievement, he finds the
artistic equivalent of orgasm: a perfection that transcends usual bodily

enjoyment, that moment when all comes together, Kandinsky's "spiritual" moment.

The hunger artist is not past his prime. What happens as his public deserts him is that it itself, now interested only in sensational experiences, has changed. In this, Kafka has caught the shift in his part of Europe, in the early 1920s, when the countries adjoining Czechoslovakia were teetering on the edge of lawlessness, disorder, their own forms of wildness. There is a profound political message in "A Hunger Artist." It is not good news either for artists or for Jews. In this respect, the artist figure is a perfect symbol of the Jew and his position. Like the artist, the Jew has not fitted, has not been part of the establishment, was considered a kind of freak of nature or clown, and, as part of his fascination for the public, was exhibited. But as "tastes" changed, the Jew was not afforded that precarious position. As the public passes the hunger artist by for wilder experiences, for the jungle animals, for example, we sense their perceptions shifting; and although there is still no "leader" in view, it is clear the spectators want blood, not refinements.

In a related sense, the artist is rejected for presenting a decadent art. The Jew as artist is an equation that many nationalists and populists made to justify squashing first one and then the other. With his art judged decadent and, therefore, as corruptive of the society, the artist observes the public moving away to more wholesome exhibitions, those fitting a folk art, a folk people, a people attuned to the blood and the senses, not to the intellect. The explosion of folk art that came with the Weimar Republic and with the Bauhaus fit well into that backlash against anarchic, uncontrollable Modernism in the social and political spheres. The relationship of the hunger artist, in 1922, to these shifts in public opinion and to the way the public was manipulated cannot be neglected. Kafka may use obsession with food as his pivot, but his meanings extend well into social, political, racial, and ethnic considerations.

In this respect, Modernism itself is on trial. The artist tries to prolong the refinement of taste on which his art depends, on the qualities of intellect, will, and definition it offers to the discriminating spectator. Modernism was, after all, a fine art, and it required dedicated artists, those who, like Kafka, would commit themselves completely to their craft. When because of shifts in public tastes that was rejected (although Modernism never had a large or particularly receptive audience), then the end not only of art but as well of a kind of civilization was imminent.

Kafka was insistent on this, as we see here and in nearly everything else he wrote in the last years of his life, including those extraordinary diary entries already cited. He was describing the end of things, the final moments of a civilization, the morbid directions of a new sensibility, all by way of manifesting these elements in himself. He was

careful to demonstrate that the hunger artist is not being abandoned because he is losing his powers. His performance does not depend on age
factors. When he is rejected, he is in fact refining his performance. As it
turns out, the audience judges him as negating life because he is rejecting food itself; his artistry does not lie solely in negation, however, but
in his assumption of a role that opens up the audience (and himself) to
great mysteries, analogous to those rituals associated with the myths
of life and death. The hunger artist is becoming a shaman, a clairvoyant, a seer, and if he is intense and successful enough, he will transmit
his "vision" to those observing him. He has questioned the very foundation of the existence of the ordinary. He opens up questions of existential experience, of the individual edging toward the abyss, of a
creature attempting to move ever closer, in asymptotic steps, toward
that forbidden borderline between life and death where the ultimate
mysteries lie.

What is outrageous about the artist is his lack of interest in that
well-being that characterizes ordinary people and is part of ordinary
life. He is tuned in to one era, they to another; and when they desert
him they have relegated him to the past, to memory, elements that
have no place in their new social and political sensibilities. They have
put history behind them, as the German-speaking world tried to put
the humiliations of the Versailles treaty behind it.

The audience seeks coarseness in its new experience, something to
gratify more sensual sensibilities. The new public enjoys the smell of
the menagerie and watches as raw lumps of meat are fed to the wild animals, an experience the very opposite, of course, of that offered by the
refined hunger artist. It is a public associated with the bread and cir-
cuses of the late Roman Empire, to the gladiatorial fights, to orgies that
left little to the imagination or intellect. With such interests, the public can gain its excitement only from sensational moments. The slow
development of sensibility required by the hunger artist is a source of
boredom and distaste. Also a source of distaste is the weak, frail, exhausted hunger artist — the Jew as pitiful, the artist as enervated and
played out, especially when compared with the wild animal, the intense and powerful figure of the present moment.

The hunger artist becomes indistinguishable from the straw he lies
in. Organic matter passes slowly into inorganic, until he is swept up as
part of the garbage pile. The artist asserts he cannot find the food he
likes, that if he had found it, he would have made "no fuss and stuffed
myself like you or anyone else."[178] These are his last words. But such
expressions make him sound like an imposter, as though he were, as
the audience has suspected, a mountebank of sorts. In the final moments, he wavers, for his denial and rejection have not depended on
"taste" but on choice. The panther who has replaced him in his cage
makes no such decisions. After the artist is cleared out, with the trash,

the young panther eats and does not seem to mourn its loss of freedom; its noble body is sleek, bursting with energy: "His noble body, furnished almost to the bursting point with all that it needed, seemed to carry freedom around with it too; somewhere in his jaws it seemed to lurk; and the joy of life streamed with such ardent passion from his throat that for the onlookers it was not easy to stand the shock of it. But they braced themselves, crowded round the cage, and did not want ever to move away."[179]

This Kafka panther is still young, still bursting with energy. Rilke's panther knows better. In time, it too will become enervated, as the strength implicit in its "mighty will" is slowly extinguished; and when that animal slows, the audience will desert it for some new sensation, leaving *that* panther to a deserted cage. The final lines of Rilke's poem would seem a fitting epitaph not only for panthers in captivity but for Kafka:

> *From time to time the curtain of the pupils*
> *silently parts —. Then an image enters,*
> *goes through the taut stillness of the limbs,*
> *and is extinguished in the heart.*

Nearly all of Kafka's works after this are comparable expressions of farewell.

We know nothing of this passing on
that so excludes us. We have no grounds
for showing admiration and love
or hatred to death, whom a mask's mouth
of tragic lament grotesquely disfigures.
The world is full of roles we act.
As long as we strive anxiously to please,
death also acts, though never to acclaim.

— RILKE, "DEATH EXPERIENCED"

THIRTEEN Kafka, Jews, and Other Solutions: The Kafka Presence

WITH "A HUNGER ARTIST" in February of 1922, Kafka began a reassessment of his work. He did not change himself so much as deepen even further his imaginative creation of a world known only to him. In the remainder of 1922, he explored both life and death in about equal measure. He wrote "Investigations of a Dog" in the spring and completed the first nine chapters of *The Castle* by just after the middle of July. By the end of the year, having decided upon the few pieces he reluctantly felt were worth keeping, he told Brod to burn all his manuscripts after his death. He was upset by everything: the "maid who forgets to bring me my warm water in the morning overturns my world."[1] Yet it is this sensitivity to almost meaningless moments of loss, his "comforts," as he calls them, which gives him his strength. Even as he complains of loss, he is empowered to probe more deeply. One diary entry simply reads "March 17. 99.3°," as though his slight fever were the dividing line itself between life and death.

He wanted only to be well again, to have those pains that passed away and made him happy. His awareness of everything was heightened. Ordinary events like a child playing, the sound of rousing music, marching feet take on magical qualities. He sees and hears and heightens them because they have ceased for him. He lives in a state in which everything he embraces is the negative of what he wants. After his return to Prague in February, he observes a fresh young couple and notes their confidence and readiness to take up the fight; and he is remorseful at their ignorance "of what awaits them, but an ignorance that inspires not hopelessness but admiration and joy in the onlooker and brings tears to his eyes."[2] He takes up the new concept of neurasthenia and wonders whether weakness and illness "induce the possession or whether weakness and illness are not rather a stage of possession, preparing a bed for rest and fornication for the unclean spirits."[3] He is certain of one thing, that the new concept makes a cure more difficult, apparently since it is itself caught up in a paradox.

He is satisfied only with ironies and contradictions. He perceives himself as ghostly, as possessed, as a phantom. In telling Klopstock, who has now become the recipient of some of his most intimate thoughts, about his becoming a phantom, he reroutes and reshapes his own condition for fiction. The beginnings of *The Castle* are in hand, even to the use of the word *key* in one of his letters: "You will quite painlessly see [he tells Klopstock] that this phantom does not exist, but only a man who is hard to put up with, who is buried in himself and locked away from himself with a strange key."[4] In that endless search for spatial meaning in *The Castle*, he was seeking some key to himself, some way of measuring inner and outer.

Writing, he repeats to Klopstock, has become his salvation, "the most important thing in the world to me . . . the way his delusion is important to the madman (should he lose it, he would become 'mad') or the way her pregnancy is important to a woman."[5] "First Sorrow" is the product of this general time, that brief story of a trapeze artist who never wishes to descend. It fits, of course, into his insistence on writing and on the solitude implicit in writing. The acrobat is clearly linked to the hunger artist and then to the dog of "Investigations of a Dog" in June of this year. Solitary and withdrawn, the dog is an emblem of that still center Kafka required so as to practice an ideal, perfect, absolute art. But he knows that is impossible, for intrusions will always occur; and yet he strives to find the conditions under which such an art can work.

"Advocates" (not to be confused with "The New Advocate") has often been cited as a bridge between *The Trial* and *The Castle*.[6] But while it does provide some linkage, it is also consistent with much else in Kafka. It derives from this general period, although it could have been written a year or more earlier. At its center is the narrator's search for an advocate, needed even more in life than in court. In court cases, an advocate is most necessary when inquiries are being made. The danger lies in what the plaintiff might discover in order to bring about a verdict. That is why the narrator is so frantically seeking advocates, but he is unable to find any, only old women who come and go. He thinks a huge fairground might be the best place to seek advocates, not the corridors of law courts. He hears droning, is drawn to the courts, but turns away, his search more frustrated than ever. "The time allotted to you is so short that if you lose one second you have already lost your whole life, for it is no longer, it is always just as long as the time you lose."[7] Even at the risk of falling over a precipice, one must walk and run. If the corridors lead nowhere, open the doors; if nothing is there, climb to another floor, reach another stage, stairs will always lead upward, they won't end, and as you climb they will go on growing upward under your feet.

The Trial and courts are obviously evoked here, as is the quest for someone in authority in The Castle, part of that unending search amidst expansion and contraction of space. But the brief story is of a piece with nearly all of Kafka: that yearning after what might save one, balanced by that inability to discover the very missing element that could have saved one. This is linked, forcefully, to Kafka's very conception of writing: the search is the drive for perfection, absolutes, for writing that omits nothing. It is a reaching toward what is unattainable, unachievable.

That search for an advocate is, ultimately, connected to how the Jew in particular and how humanity in general is to live in the modern world. Kafka is seeking norms, ways of reducing alienation — an advocate, or whoever, will draw him back into the ordinary — and yet, of course, the advocate will elude him. Marginally placed, Kafka needs advocacy to show him — the alienated Jew, the artist outsider, as well as his disoriented protagonists — how a society can function. It has ceased to function for him, not only because of his illness but because a modern society no longer has the rules that make elements cohere. Faced by incoherence, Kafka seeks an advocate to pull it all together: to prevent those "sly foxes, those slinking weasels"[8] of plaintiffs from crawling through the crevices and establishing their own terms.

In late February, as he moved toward starting The Castle, or shaping some of his salient ideas, he asked himself if there was any hope. He points to himself as having an "unnoticeable life. Noticeable failure."[9] He admits, however, that possibilities do exist within himself, close at hand and as yet undefined. He must find his way toward them. He must take up the dare. "This signifies [he writes in his Diaries] a great many things: that possibilities do exist; it even signifies that a scoundrel can become an honest man, a man happy in his honesty."

By March 15, Kafka had written enough of The Castle to read the first parts to Brod.* As we can see from a certain congested quality in

---

*Brod admits he did not know exactly when Kafka wrote The Castle. His description of the text, which has misled generations of Kafka readers, emphasizes the role of the Jew in the narrative. Although the word Jew does not appear, Brod says that Kafka "has said more about the situation of Jewry as a whole today than can be read in a hundred

the first one hundred pages, writing did not come easily. He had told Klopstock of his need to protect his writing, and in mid-April he wrote of his anxiety, which he did not find strange. "A Jew, and a German besides, and sick besides, and in difficult personal circumstances besides"[10] — from these liabilities he plans to transmute gold into gravel, the opposite of an alchemical reaction. As he moved along slowly on the novel, he took time out in the spring to write "Investigations of a Dog," a story about the artist's alienation, the Jew's marginality, the author's solitude, the animal kingdom as compensatory for human deficiencies. Like the hunger artist and like K. in the developing pages of *The Castle*, the dog is an artist.

In "Investigations of a Dog," one dog, the narrating animal, has separated himself from the rest of the canine species. Once he had thought of himself as a full member in good standing, "a dog among dogs," but now he is solitary and withdrawn, "with nothing to occupy me save my hopeless but, as far as I am concerned, indispensable little investigations."[11] Here is a definition of the artist, not in the fullness of his power but in the twilight, debilitated by illness. The long story becomes a form of spiritual autobiography, associated with "The Metamorphosis" and "A Hunger Artist."

The canine narrator speaks of the communal impulse of dogs, and yet they are all different, with distinctions of "class, of kind, of occupation."[12] Even when they choose to live together, their strange vocations force them to live separated, incomprehensible to one another. In an incident in his youth, the narrator, a mere puppy and full of life, encountered seven dogs, discovered that the canine race is capable of great music, but was rebuffed by them, as though he did not exist. "Dogs who make no reply to the greetings of other dogs are guilty of an offense against good manners which the humblest dog would never pardon any more than the greatest."[13] His rejection "robbed me of a great part of my childhood; the blissful life of the young dog which many can spin out for years, in my case lasted for only a few short months."[14] Nevertheless, his rejection and vision become the great moments of his life.

In these first few pages, Kafka appears to be writing an allegory, only thinly veiled, of his own life: his attempt to be joyous, the rebuff,

---

learned treatises" (*Franz Kafka*, p. 185). Although he recognizes that the Jewish interpretation goes along with what is common to all humanity, he singles out the Jewish dimension for discussion. His argument is based on questions of assimilation and alienation. But Kafka's use of the land-surveyor goes well beyond the role of Jews, although that aspect can be assumed to be present. The land-surveyor fits far more closely into the role of the artist, a part of Kafka more closely associated with his thought than his perception of himself as a Jew. Although artist and Jew have been linked in his mind, as twin elements of alienation and marginality, the artist-role has for most of his life pre-empted other considerations. Well before he made his commitment to historical Judaism, he defined himself through his craft. As Brod admits, all mankind is involved in *The Castle*, but the mankind most involved is that connected to those who must stand outside, its artists. Brod was, clearly, riding his own hobbyhorse.

his inability to comprehend the behavior of his elders, his withdrawal, his profound isolation. In another respect, he might be writing an allegory of the role of the Jew: the Jew's effort to assimilate, his inevitable rejection, his retreat into marginality. In still another area, the piece might appear to be a political allegory: the separation of elements within the Dual Empire, the lack of identity each element experiences, the sense of breakup and incomprehensible behavior each suffers, symbolized by the dog-narrator. And in a final sense, the story might refer to the philosophical question of how liberty can be defined — that is, how the individual artist separates himself from the general comity and still retains the human characteristics that that comity helps to define for him. Where do the self and the community part, where do they overlap? To what extent is the individual such a product of that community that no final separation is possible? And, ultimately, what happens to the community or society when individuals break away, often the most sensitive, artistic individuals?

All of these questions are pertinent. Kafka's vision had so deepened that all possibilities are present, but the overriding question pertains to the nature of art and the role of the artist. This will be a question of great concern in "The Burrow" and then in Kafka's last completed work, "Josephine the Singer, or the Mouse Folk," not to speak of *The Castle*. He probes questions of knowledge in order to establish how one becomes what one is. What has, he asks, the canine race nourished itself upon? But this question proves to be beyond the comprehension of any single scholar. He wonders why people treated him well. Was it because he was a lean dog, badly fed? But there were countless others — why him? He responds, "All knowledge, the totality of all questions and all answers, is contained in the dog." All answers must be sought within. He pursues the marrow of the bone, and he must admit that the richest marrow can be obtained only by a collective crunching of all dogs' teeth. But he wants to dismiss the others while, all alone, he laps up the marrow. "That sounds monstrous, almost as if I wanted to feed on the marrow, not merely of a bone, but of the whole canine race itself. But it is only a metaphor. The marrow that I am discussing here is no food; on the contrary it is a poison."[15]

Food, the ever present theme of food, here contains questions of individual linkage to society, the demands of individual freedom as against social needs, and, inevitably, the ways the artistic figure can make demands on the society or community not permitted to anyone else. As a young dog, the narrator tried to renounce all pleasure, and is cast out to depend entirely on his own resources. But he insists he is no different from any other dog. One thing he must make sense of, however, is the presence of "soaring dogs." These are canine musicians, and he cannot really integrate them into any pattern. "They have no relation whatever to the general life of the community, they hover in the air, and that is all, and life goes on its usual way; someone now and then refers to art and artists, but there it ends." Why do they float in the air? "Why can one get no words of explanation regarding them? Why do they hover up there, letting their legs, the pride of dogs, fall into desuetude, preserving a detaching from the nourishing earth, reaping without having sowed, being particularly well provided for, as I hear, and at the cost of the dog community too?"[16]

The question Kafka asks is why anyone would forsake the comforts and security of life in order to soar, or to make some artistic gesture, which may itself be doomed to futility. What happens when one forsakes what is considered normal and moves toward what is socially abnormal or extraordinary? What makes one fight upstream for this? Because it is embedded in the nature of the enterprise itself, the response cannot be forthcoming. To ask intellectual questions of the artist is beside the point; for artists "are not much distinguished for intellectual power, and their philosophy is as worthless as their observations, and science can make hardly any use of their utterances."[17] The soaring dogs, those artists of the canine world (Kafka calls himself merely an "ordinary middle-class dog") move in such rarified air that their existence shades off into mysteries. One thing the narrator does know is that once it exists no dog species ever dies out, or at least not without having put up a successful defense. Every effort, then, to find out who or what these soaring dogs are is doomed to futility; they simply *are*, beyond the ordinary dog's comprehension. Since all questions ultimately fail, one does not even know if they are the right questions.

In trying to compose his autobiography, one based on understanding rather than on lifestyle, the narrator finds himself baffled at every turn. The analogy of dogs to the land-surveyor in *The Castle* is clear, and the application to nearly all of Kafka's later work becomes apparent, in that intense quest that becomes circumscribed. "True, knowledge provides the rules one must follow, but even to grasp them imperfectly and in rough outline is by no means easy, and when one has actually grasped them the real difficulty still remains, namely, to apply them to local conditions."[18] Trying to find some pattern to the meaning of it all, to soaring dogs, to the existence of the species itself, to its endurance, and, most of all, to his role in this shadowy, mysterious drama, the narrator-dog goes around and around. As Kafka edges to the line between life and death, the struggle is not so much to live but to find reasons why one should live.

The narrator makes certain discoveries: that food comes "from above," and therefore it has some religious significance. Food dominates not only for the dog but because it becomes a testing ground for the battle between science and spiritual matters. He wonders if the absence of food was caused not by "unscientific preparation of the ground rather than by my experiments."[19] The dog has a splendid appetite, but he fasts, and he is concerned, as the mole will be in "The Burrow," with the storing of food, a process analogous to the digestive process and constipation. The dog realizes that if he could sleep he could fast even better and longer — sleep and nourishment, those twin enemies of Kafka's life even before the onrush of the hemorrhaging blood. The narrator pleads for science, all the while noting that his own researches might not be scientific. He begs forgiveness of science for errors of his making and hopes there is room in it for his researches, which are not researches at all, but efforts to comprehend the making of art.

He perceives an area of limbo between will (wanting food to come down) and will-lessness (to sleep away his life and let whatever will happen, happen). His so-called scientific researches leave him in even a greater quandary. He becomes his sole form of experimentation, and only fasting can be his "most potent weapon of research." "It seems to me," he says, "that it takes almost a lifetime to recuperate from such an attempt; my whole life as an adult lies between me and that fast, and I have not recovered yet."[20] Only through denial, here of food, can he locate himself in the area where art is created. Fasting becomes a form of divine behavior, that reaching toward an inner balance that is what the artist achieves with his work, which is also the dog's apotheosis. Yet when he gnaws in hunger at his hind legs and, in his distress and despair, even up to his very buttocks, then "the universal interpretation of this dialogue seemed to me entirely and completely false."[21] His extremism makes him falter.

He resolves to deny himself all smells and then cannot abide by his resolution. He drags himself to and fro, "and sniffed as if that were in accordance with my resolution, as if I were looking for food simply to be on guard against it." The typical Kafkan paradox occurs in these lines. "The fact that I found nothing did not disappoint me; the food must be there, only it was always a few steps away, my legs failed me before I could reach it. But simultaneously I knew that nothing was there, and that I made those feeble movements simply out of fear lest I might collapse in this place and never be able to leave it." The dog's desire to pursue a purely artistic life is always interrupted by a breakdown in resolve and will. For fear of a worse outcome, he pursues a chimera. "It seemed to me as if I were separated from all my fellows, not by a quite short stretch, but by an infinite distance, and as if I would die less of hunger than of neglect."[22] He recognizes the difficulty of escaping from the world of falsehood since "there is no one from whom you can learn the truth," not even from oneself, born as one is "a citizen of falsehood." The narrator's way toward art and the role of the artist is mined with countering wishes and acts, his own wishes scattered among the multiplicities of possibilities.

He imagines a hound who was already singing "without knowing it." But he cannot be certain. Yet "even if it was an error it had nevertheless a sort of grandeur, and is the sole, even if delusive, reality that I have carried over into this world from my period of fasting."[23] This act of imagining song reveals how far one may go when carried beyond oneself. The melody of the hound seems irresistible, and even as the narrator stands in a pool of blood, from his vomiting, and is tottering, he is energized by song. Carrying his researches into music, spurred by the melody, he was "careening from the spot in splendid style." The narrator's experience with musical dogs made him realize how incapable he was of responding scientifically. However much it may provide obstacles and frustrations, freedom is clearly connected to art; science must be rejected. So ends "Investigations of a Dog."

When we observe the now developing *Castle*, we can see how Kafka's transforming mind included not only the land-surveyor, but the dog, the hunger artist, the singing mouse Josephine, and the mole seeking refuge in its burrow. As Kafka was gaining visible results, his *Diaries* reveal his fear of being disturbed, and the attacks of insomnia he suffered because of that fear. Near the end of April, on the twenty-sixth, he applied for permission for a five-week vacation starting May 5, which was granted on presentation of Dr. Kodym's letter recommending further rest and treatment. Kafka was clearly in a spiral of sufficient health to write but not quite enough to live; he exists in alternating patterns of forays into his own work while dependent on others' support in sanatoria. Thoughts of Milena sent him into near hysteria: "A nightmare recently because of M.'s letter in my portfolio."[24] He recognizes and accepts his loneliness, alone except for his memories. He says he feels "more deserted" with a second person than when by himself. With a second person, he is delivered, helplessly, into his or her hand; while if alone, "all mankind reaches out for him — but the innumerable outstretched arms become entangled with one another and no one reaches to him."[25] After this, the diary entries thin to a very few over the summer months, then to one only each month for the remainder of 1922, one entry in 1923, and no more. Kafka's loss of energy undermined his interest in the *Diaries*; what little energy remained went into his writing.

As we might expect, the winding down of diary entries coincided with the end of his service to the institute. Having requested temporary retirement on June 7 — after Dr. Kodym told him he could not expect recovery in the foreseeable future — Kafka was officially retired on July 1. He had served fourteen years (minus one month), and he had risen in an organization notorious for not employing Jews, much less promoting them. All efforts by Kafka to present himself as incapable and inefficient, as unable to move ably in the real world, as withdrawn and retiring, as a helpless official or bureaucrat — all of these roles he played with different people are belied by the good work he did and by the high esteem in which he was held. No matter what the *Diaries*, letters, and fictions tell us about frustration, defeat, despair, and the rest, Kafka met his responsibilities and obligations at the office. Gregor Samsa may have so resented his drudgery at work and his lack of respect in his own home that he transformed himself into something repulsive; but Kafka could divide himself, between the efficient and effective official, and the artist who perceived himself as quite different.

His career had been honorable and exemplary, especially when he silently took up the cudgels for the injured and crippled who would otherwise have been railroaded or short-changed by the institute's policies. As noted before, Kafka intervened, on occasion with his own money, to ensure that injured workers received fair compensation and a fair hearing of their case. Although he revealed few progressive social views in his letters or *Diaries*, Kafka was clearly allied with the workers whose cases he helped to adjudicate. He was not the cold lawyer or cool administrator, but a concerned employee who, unlike his fictional protagonists, refused to get lost in a bureaucratic maze. As we survey his career, we must remark how he was able to thread his way through the labyrinth. He did not give up, he went to the office daily, and he did his job until his health no longer permitted it. Furthermore, he gained the respect of his colleagues and of his superiors, who offered him benefits and loopholes in company policy which they permitted no one else. He may have been their showcase Jew, but they acted honorably on his behalf, and he repaid them with fourteen years of devoted work.

In remarks that seem in this instance credible, Gustav Janouch tells of the cleaning out of Kafka's office.

> Frau Svátek, who cleaned Kafka's office, and also our own house in Karolinthal, told me: "Kafka came and went as silently as a mouse. . . . I don't know who cleared out his desk. In his hanging cupboard there was only Kafka's threadbare grey second-best coat which he kept there for a rainy day. I've never seen him with an umbrella. A cleaner took his coat. . . . I scrubbed the empty cupboard with soap and water. On his desk stood an old, slender glass vase, containing two pencils and a penholder. Next to it was a lovely blue-and-gold teacup and a saucer to match."[26]

An institute official, Treml, told her to take "that rubbish" away. The vase had been part of Kafka's working effects; from the cup, he often drank milk or tea. She took the "rubbish" and brought it home.

What makes even this Janouch story a little suspect is that it approximates so closely the end of "The Metamorphosis," with Gregor's effects and himself reduced to rubbish, swept away as so much garbage. Janouch was always seeking such dramatic results. In a follow-up, Frau Svátek offers the cup and saucer to Janouch, who took them, cherished them, but never used them. It is all rather neat, but what does ring true is the extreme modesty in which Kafka lived, the small number of his possessions, his indifference to what Felice had ominously liked and what he referred to as "heavy furniture."

In late June, with Prague too heavy a weight upon him, he went to Planá, to join Ottla, her husband, and their baby, Věra. Near the Austrian border, in southeastern Bohemia, Planá was a rural area that made Kafka a little apprehensive. Even in such a remote area, he was worried about noise (he was using Oropax to shut it out, including the horn playing of a peasant youth) but even more worried about his little story "First Sorrow," which was in Kurt Wolff's drawer. That tale about the trapeze artist who cannot achieve ultimate isolation Kafka calls a "repulsive little story"[27] that he would like to wipe out of Wolff's memory. Kafka seems to revel in his self-denigration, which he describes to Brod as being part of the story and Wolff's response to it. It was, nevertheless, published in Wolff's magazine *Genius* (vol. 3, no. 2, 1922). "First Sorrow" apparently was one piece Kafka would have liked to destroy, but Wolff was too fast for him.

There are two "parables" whose dating is impossible to determine but whose application to Kafka at this time seems particularly appropriate, for, despite enervation and depression, he was readying himself for a real pull on *The Castle*. One is called "The Spring," and it is characteristic in its play of paradox.

> He is thirsty, and is cut off from a spring by a mere clump of bushes. But he is divided against himself: one part overlooks the whole, sees that he is standing here and that the spring is just beside him; but another part notices nothing, has at most a divination that the first part sees all. But as he notices nothing he cannot drink.[28]

Kafka validates his division of self into parts, into roles; and he ascribes his "thirst" or yearning or hunger to an inability to put the conflicting halves together. This condition is especially true now. In the second parable, called "The Hunger Strike," Kafka tries to define a category into which he fits, those ascetics who go on a "hunger-strike in all spheres of life."

They hope to achieve a number of goals. Initially, they have denied themselves enough, so that even if they return to eating, it will not be counted as eating. Fasting, secondly, will no longer seem like a compulsion, but a joy, and denial will be sweeter than food. Next, this voice that gave the first two commandments will assure him that since he, Kafka, has conquered the world, he is released from the need to fast and eat. The final voice says that although he has not fasted completely, he has displayed good will, and that suffices. So ends the voice. Kafka has used the voice of the priest or of another godly figure to provide him with penance; he is forgiven for not having fasted fully. Partial fasting, however, has demonstrated his good will, and he is, the voice assures him, in a state of grace.

Kafka is seeking justification or validation for his course of action, the submission to fasting as a means to a more spiritualized consciousness. He is, also, through this omniscient voice, seeking the balance between himself and the world, something analogous to Moses seeking God's commandments. While Kafka is no Moses, he too is seeking direction; but more than that, he is trying to find some explanation in the external world for his choice of weapons in his battle against life. His conclusion: he has not held fast, he has slipped, he has achieved something less than perfection, he has missed the goal of absolutes; but he is forgiven for having demonstrated good will. He can go on.

Once in Planá, with Ottla and her family, at the end of June, Kafka entered deeply into every aspect of his life, with work on *The Castle* and with comments on his perception of himself. The assassination of Walter Rathenau, the well-known and highly influential German politician and industrialist (he was head of the German equivalent of Consolidated Edison) by German political thugs on June 24, 1922, evoked one of Kafka's rare political comments. The assassination was, of course, an indication of the resurgence of German nationalism in the growing power of the Nazi party; and Rathenau, a Jew, was considered a prime target as part of the German policy of cleansing the air of "foreign elements." Kafka, in fact, says he was surprised Rathenau had not been killed before, and news of his assassination had circulated in Prague two months earlier. Kafka sees this murder as the "linked destinies of Jews and Germans,"[29] although his remarks do not reveal any foreknowledge that anti-Semitic poison would make the Austrians eventually out-Nazi the Nazis in their virulence. Violence in Prague, except for occasional outbursts, was still held in check by the police, although ominous sounds were emerging from nationalist groups in Hungary and from street fights in and around the capital of the newly established state.

Jewish questions were clearly in his mind, as is evident in his reference (to Klopstock) to Hans Blüher's *Secessio Judaica*, published in 1922 in Berlin. Kafka had indicated in his diary (June 16, 1922) that he has difficulty with Blüher's assertion that he was an anti-Semite but without hatred, "sine ira et studio." Kafka grants him that but also feels he is an enemy of the Jews in his every remark, whether made out of "happy hatred or unhappy love."[30]

Blüher argued it was impossible to use the old historical arguments against Jews by appealing to statistics, for example, to claim that Jews controlled this or that, or undermined the society. Other people may be refuted in this way, but not Jews, who will have an answer for every charge leveled against them. Blüher's anti-Semitism was more fundamental, connected to Richard Wagner's mythologizing of the German people, with Jews as incapable of being assimilated to true Germanism, and, therefore, always marginal, an enemy. Kafka asks Klopstock to respond to Blüher, in either German or Hungarian, since he, Kafka, is not able to do so. He says there is no need for a refutation, but an answer must be made to Blüher's mythological appeal. "That ought to be very tempting. And there is indeed a temptation to let one's flock graze on this German and yet not entirely alien pasture, after the fashion of the Jews."[31] Kafka's irony should not be lost, nor should the twist in his argument: answer Blüher, he tells Klopstock, so that Jews can prove they can eat up the Germans and, thus, help sustain the anti-Semitic argument that Jews are parasites on the German body politic and society.

But more significant matters were at hand: his work on *The Castle* and his letters now reflect nervousness and anxiety that he may not be able to settle in without interruption. He has fear of change, as he tells Oskar Baum, who had found a suitable place for him in Georgenthal. Change, however, is somehow related to death. He says he would like to breathe different air, "a discovery which to be sure does not make the world any wider but does quiet certain gnawing yearnings."[32] Yet measured against this is his fear: "I have, to be frank, a horrible fear of this journey, of course not exactly of the journey itself, and not at all fear of the journey alone, but of every change. The bigger the change, the bigger the fear." He says that if he confined himself to the smallest changes in life, the moving of a table in his room would be no less terrifying than the journey to Georgenthal. But not only will the journey there be unbearable, so will the departure; and that departure opens up his real fear that in the last analysis "it is of course nothing but a fear of death. Partly also the fear of calling the gods' attention to me. If I just go on living here in my room [at Planá], one day passes as regularly as the last."[33]

Kafka's fear now becomes quite understandable. He is seeking a balance between power (travel, moving on, facing new situations) and the present (remaining, doing his work). He has chosen stasis, not only out of fear the gods will notice him, but from the fear he will disrupt something that is ongoing, his writing, his thin thread of life, his ability to hold off death. "Of course," he writes Baum, "someone has to look after me, but that is already being done, the hand of the gods is only mechanically holding the reins."[34] Those references to gods and to reins are Kafka's nod to the world of fate and destiny, to its presence in circumstance, and to its power against individual will, which he desperately wants to believe in. "So lovely, it is so lovely to be unnoticed." He humorously adds that if "any fairy stood beside my cradle, it was the fairy named 'Retired on Pension.' " What he wanted, from infancy, was to withdraw, and now that he finally has the opportunity — no school to face, no office to attend to, no parents to rage against — he does not wish to forsake it for a journey.

In the final sense, Kafka is using the idea of the "journey" in its direst sense, as poets have used it for centuries, as the journey toward death. He cannot risk jeopardizing his frail balance by exchanging the staleness of his situation for a more airy one. To Brod, he takes up the same question, an indication of how seriously he considered his decision. He tells Brod his fear is not weakness of will, which would involve the calculation of contingencies, which is in the main impossible to do, but a fear that if he changes, he will attract the "attention of the gods by what is a major act for a person of my sort."[35] Although he has not yet written "The Burrow," Kafka has already buried himself, and he fears, in his tomb, to make any sound for fear he will attract enemies, gods, or a nemesis.

By reading back from that story to his comments here, we can see how K. in *The Castle* is entombed, even as he attempts to move ever more deeply into castle business or tries to comprehend the thinking of the people at the castle. Kafka's idea was not to bring K. enlightenment, but to demonstrate how entombed he becomes even as he delves more deeply into his role as land-surveyor. K.'s profession is particularly ironic, since there is no land to survey, there are no spatial measurements for him to make, there is no clear assignment of what externals are at stake. Thus, while he seeks the land to survey, or those who can so instruct him, he is being buried in his quest. His journey from home and family has not been a journey into achievement or attainment, but into a negation of everything meant by journey.

Kafka probes deeply into his feelings, and Brod is the repository of his revelations. "What I had almost forgotten during the last relatively quiet time became clear to me: namely, on what frail ground or rather altogether nonexistent ground I live, over a darkness from which the dark power emerges when it wills and, heedless of my stammering, destroys my life."[36] He says it is unclear whether writing sustains him or whether it sustains that kind of life, a large distinction. He does not mean his life is better when he does not write. It is far worse, in fact unbearable, "and has to end in madness." As mentioned earlier, he says he is a writer "even when I am not writing, and a nonwriting writer is a monster inviting madness." Yet what about being a writer? What does that signify? It is, he says, a sweet and wonderful reward, but "in the light it became clear to me, as clear as a child's lesson book, that it is the reward for serving the devil."

He then reveals how he is indebted to the Modernist view of the artist, a view that extends back to the French *symbolistes* of the second half of the nineteenth century and forward to Kafka's contemporaries, Mann, Musil, and Rilke. He speaks of the writer descending to the dark powers, "this unshackling of spirits bound by nature, these dubious embraces and whatever else may take place in the nether parts which the higher parts no longer know."[37] There is a pact with Lucifer, so that all serious writing carries with it a whiff of sulphur. Kafka admits there may be other kinds of writing, but he knows only that kind. As befitting a man who honored Flaubert, Kleist, and Dostoevsky, Kafka saw writing as a journey into the night, into dreams, and nightmares. "And the diabolic element in it seems very clear to me. It is vanity and sensuality which continually buzz about one's own or even another's form — and feast on him."[38] The writer has given himself over to that other world, and he is permanently transformed by his experience; because he is changed, he can never return to the normalizing world. "The movement multiplies itself — it is a regular solar system of vanity." The writer is like the person who wishes to be dead so he can see how people mourn him. The writer, Kafka says, "dies (or rather he does not live) and continually mourns himself. From this springs a terrible fear of death, which need not reveal itself as fear of death but may also appear as fear of change, as fear of Georgenthal."

These passages are of such extreme importance because they bring together what had been implicit in Kafka since 1912, when his first serious work emerged. The "fear" expressed here has been a necessary ingredient of his imagination, now intensified, of course, by his weakening physical condition. But we should not attribute fear only to his weak state; it was a driving force in Kafka, part of the way he could reshape himself for his work. He feared death, but he feared, even more, not leaving something behind; and when he told Brod to destroy all his manuscripts, it was not because he did not want to leave a remnant of himself, but because he felt the remnant was insufficiently representative of what he had hoped to accomplish. His equation of writing and doing the devil's work is not mere pose; nor is it the romanticization of the artist we find in Thomas Mann, the Tonio Kröger syndrome. For Kafka, it was the belief that when he wrote, he descended into a state of being that was close to nonbeing, to a denial of life, even as he was intensifying life in his writing; and by so doing, he was coming close to what the devil seduces man into, into a denial of himself in order to gain something, temporarily, more rewarding. Kafka has immersed himself in the Faustian pact, which he sees as the archetypal pact of every serious artist.

He explains to Brod his fear of death, which he divides into two categories. In the first, he fears death because he has not yet lived. By this, he means that "wife and child, fields, and cattle are essential to living."[39] He yearns for the ability to move into the house, instead of admiring it from the outside or hanging garlands on it. The second reason, and the more significant, is an enormous admission that he has indeed played roles; furthermore, he now confronts what he has been playing with. "What I have playacted is really going to happen. I have not bought myself off by my writing. I died my whole life long and now I will really die. My life was sweeter than other peoples' and my death will be more terrible by the same degree." The passages that follow are equally extraordinary, and surely are a concomitant of Kafka's deep immersion in *The Castle*. As he presents K. with one bafflement after another, one paradoxical situation after another caught in the language of irony, Kafka was mining everything he had thought about life and its end.*

---

*So close is *The Castle* to death that we could argue the longueurs connected to Amalia's story were, for Kafka, a way to prolong life: that as long as he kept K. going, he, Kafka, lived.

But even more than that, he was seeking ground on which he could justify himself as a writer, something we find in another writer who died young, Keats, in *his* letters as he contemplated the end — not only death, but the end of writing. Kafka: "Of course the writer in me will die right away, since such a figure has no base, no substance, is less than dust. He is only barely possible in the broil of earthly life, is only a construct of sensuality. . . . But I myself cannot go on living because I have not lived, I have remained clay. I have not blown the spark into fire, but only used it to light up my corpse."[40] It was a burial within a burial: the writer, insubstantial as he is, consigning the "old corpse" to the grave. He wonders why he should be speaking of dying when he is sitting comfortably in the posture of a writer, awaiting all sorts of fine things. "The existence of a writer," he says, "is an argument against the existence of the soul, for the soul has obviously taken flight from the real ego, but not improved itself, only become a writer." In this complicated, witty, enigmatical formulation, Kafka is suggesting that the writer has so transformed himself, into what he is, that he cannot be judged like other people, that for him, the soul is merely another name for the writer.

He foresees the future as the downward part of the arc of his existence: he has been declining since 1912, but now even further; he is no longer the trapeze artist at the top of his art, but the mole waiting silently in its burrow for its enemies to defeat it. If he cancels with Baum, we have seen, "this will mean that from now on I may not go out of Bohemia, next I will be confined to Prague, then to my room, then to my bed, then to a certain position in bed, then to nothing more."[41] Once he had play-acted at being static, immobile, immovable; he would be immured in his dungeon while others (Felice, for example) brought his sustenance. All would come down to only his active brain and imagination. Now this is his reality; he is immobile in bed, and his fear of the journey to Georgenthal is that he will be denied that moment of stasis. He admits to Brod it all comes down to that, his fear of losing time at his desk, since the existence of the writer depends on the existence of the desk: "If he wants to keep madness at bay he must never go far from his desk, he must hold on to it with his teeth."

He defines the writer: "He is the scapegoat of mankind. He makes it possible for me to enjoy sin without guilt, almost without guilt."[42] This description is consistent with his earlier definition of the writer as not only a priest devoted to his calling, but as martyr and sacrifice, enabling other men to live. His view and Mann's have virtually converged. But further than that, he has reached down into the entire Modernist sense of the artist as devilish, dangerous, a rebel, and yet also a martyr and sacrifice; and in defining the artist this way, he has come perilously close to defining the modern Jew's role in an always alien society. The Talmud says that a Jew who has "sinned" still remains a Jew; and Kafka's Jew has sinned by trafficking with the devil, analogous to the way the artist has himself survived. Kafka has positioned himself as one of those intensely Jewish Jews who through heresy has tested out the limits of Jewishness; who, by means of heretical thought, has become the very test of what a Jew is. The company he finds himself in is distinguished: Freud, as well as Trotsky, but also Heine, Spinoza, Marx (to some degree), and Rosa Luxemburg. Some of these Jews, like Heine and Marx, were converts, but their conversion seemed in several respects only to intensify their Jewishness, or made Jewishness more of an obsession, as it did with Marx. For Marx, the Jew was associated with the God of Mammon. The role forced on the Jew by a Christian society was, inevitably, the role for which the Jew could be castigated by that society. Despite (or because of) being in a long line of rabbis (Marx's father was a convert), Marx saw Jews as major players in exploitational capitalism, and his heresy was to attack Jews as the archenemy, calling, as noted above, the distinguished socialist Ferdinand Lassalle "a Jewish nigger." Kafka did not go that far, and he came to have a kind of respect for the mercantile Jew; but by introducing the artist as someone dealing with the devil, he made the connection that a Christian society had made about the Jew: that his dealings were below ground, subversions, subterfuges, and that he gained his power from some pact, not with God, but with Lucifer.

The intensity of Kafka's feelings here, as most of his self-perceptions come together, cannot be overestimated. As he writes *The Castle*, K. becomes his modern artist wandering in a kind of wilderness of Kafka's imagination. K.'s quest to locate his job, or even to discover what its coordinates are, makes him a recognizable artist figure wandering through the maze of the material seeking suitable form. As Kafka struggled to shape the novel, K. struggles to shape his experiences. K.'s problem is somehow analogous to Kafka's effort to find his way in the book. In July letters, respectively to Felix Weltsch and to Brod, Kafka writes of the hazards of noise, those interruptions of his concentration that he thinks of as a death sentence. He speaks of noise as having something fascinating and narcotic about it — that when the circular saw across the room starts up "it makes one curse life";[43] and if he changes his room (he has two), then he hears children playing in front. We note the perfect symmetry of his expectations: that wherever he turns, he will be trapped by noise — an excellent analogue to what was occurring with K. as he searched the village, not for ways to evade noise, but to find castle officials. Both wanderers are baffled.

Kafka cites the case of Mahler, whose summers were given over to composing. Mahler would retreat to a little "composing hut" in the woods, where his breakfast awaited him and where he would work until one in the afternoon. The trees surrounding him protected him against noise. He would nap, and at four in the afternoon join his family. Kafka's yearning after this kind of routine is apparent. Yet it involved all the elements he could not control: wife, family, discipline, absolute mastery of time and goals. What characterized Mahler — an iron discipline, a clear definition of direction — were precisely the qualities Kafka struggled with. He mastered himself but not in the manner he envied in Mahler. The saw drives him close to madness. "Left to myself, I cannot get away from it: my sister has to come and with unbelievable sacrifices of her comfort vacate the other room for me (which however is no composing hut)."[44]

To Brod, however, he is even more graphic. "I have been dashing about or sitting as petrified as a desperate animal in his burrow. Enemies everywhere."[45] This is not paranoia, but the writer seeking absolute conditions for his work; and this line gives us a way of viewing his later story "The Burrow" as the mole's way of seeking perfect quiet, without even the scratching of other animals. The mole, then, is still another artist figure, and his underground keep is part of the labyrinth the artist creates to hide his tracks from others. Children, not the saw, are now the enemy, outside of both rooms. One is a nasty group, Kafka says, the other nice and lovely looking, but "the noise made by both was the same. It drives me from my bed, out of the house in despair, with throbbing temples through field and forest, devoid of all hope like a night owl." Yet we must believe the response to children goes beyond noise, to the very question of the children themselves, a morbid reminder to Kafka he had none of his own.

Yet these children are not all. Timber is being loaded at the nearby railroad station, and that results in constant hammering. It begins early and it rings through his "sleep-famished brain in quite another way than it does by day." In addition, some two hundred Prague schoolchildren have been quartered nearby, as part of their vacation. "A hellish noise, a scourge of humanity."[46] He wonders why people in the affected part of the village have not gone mad and rushed out into the woods, but even that would not help since "the whole margin of these lovely woods is infested." He has been spared the worst of this, but he looks expectantly from his window for some sign of Mongol hordes descending on him. The expectation of noise, for Kafka, was as painful as the noise itself.

The writing, nevertheless, was going forth: "less than average in quality, no more, and constantly endangered by noise." Then he employs one of his favorite images: "All this writing is nothing but Robinson Crusoe's flag hoisted at the highest point of the island."[47] That is, although his writing is an emblem of his existence, the writer remains in danger. In regard to the return of new noises, he even says that if he had been Mahler he would have been disturbed by the birds, had not the "horrible voices of the Prague children"[48] already dominated. The assessment Kafka made of his writing is on target. The opening chapters of *The Castle* are murky, often lacking that sharpness of observation that was his characteristic quality, and lacking that edge of irony or wit we have come to expect. Although the novel remained unfinished and uncorrected, and it suffers as a result, it seems even in its present state not to have been completely clear in Kafka's mind. The idea was clear, and it may be the idea we applaud rather than the details of the development. It is as though Kafka had to let a novel emerge, since the urge to write was clear, while the material was itself vague to him.* Or else at this stage in his life, he was incapable of a long work.

While he was writing the novel, news arrived that his father needed an immediate operation. Hermann had become sick while in Franzensbad and was brought back to Prague for medical attention. Kafka left for Prague on July 14. At seventy, Hermann was suffering from a strangulating hernia, not malignant, but a dangerous condition nevertheless because of his age, his record of previous heart trouble, and the still rather primitive medical care available. With his head full of K., Kafka now had to deal anew with a head full of Hermann. He felt his father might need him, but he saw that Hermann's affection for him "diminished day by day,"[49] peaking on the second day and then precipitously falling. By July 19 he could not get his son out of the room quickly enough, as Kafka perceived it.

Kafka sees Hermann's illness as yet another ordeal for his mother.

---

*The written manuscript (at the Bodleian Library, Oxford) is relatively clear of corrections, emendations, or vagueness of composition. As with so many other works of Kafka, it seems to have emerged smoothly, but that still does not mean that Kafka did not experience difficulty in developing the material. At the beginning there is some revision, indicating hesitation. The revisions involve crossing out and insertions, mainly to achieve greater clarity or more silhouetting of the castle's "foggishness" and inaccessibility. The aim, apparently, was to sharpen ambiguity, to create a confusion of the senses. After that, many pages are virtually untouched, although occasionally an entire page is deleted. Sir Malcolm Pasley, who has examined far more manuscripts than I, confirms that Kafka wrote with a flow and fluidity that reflected how he felt at that moment. Revisions, when they did occur, were apparently made at the time of the writing; there was little looking back. In Pasley's view, product and production were closely linked to writing and the finished text. Whatever failed to work for Kafka, as his notebooks reveal, he simply gave up, forsaking revisions or alternatives. (See Sir Malcolm Pasley, "The Act of Writing and the Text: The Genesis of Kafka's Manuscripts," most readily available in *Reading Kafka: Prague, Politics, and the Fin de Siècle*, edited by Mark Anderson [New York: Schocken, 1989].) Pasley's arrangement of *The Castle* provides titles (in German) for most of the chapters; but his chief readjustment is in his division of the very long chapter 15 into six separate entities, five of which he gives names to. As a consequence, the novel contains twenty-five chapters, whereas the English version has twenty. Pasley's headings follow: "1. Arrival"; "2. Barnabas"; "3. Frieda"; "4. First Conversation with the Landlady"; "5. With the Mayor"; "6. Second Conversation with the Landlady"; "7. The Teacher"; "8. Waiting For Klamm"; "9. Struggle Against the Hearing"; "10. On the Street"; "11. In the School"; "12. The Assistants"; "13. Hans"; "14. Frieda's Reproach"; "15. [broken down into six chapters] With Amalia"; "16. Untitled"; "17. Amalia's Secret"; "18. Amalia's Street"; "19. Processions"; "20. Olga's Plans"; and chapters 21, 22, 23, 24, and 25 are all untitled.

He regarded most of her adult life as having been wasted in catering to her husband, without understanding or accepting that Julie Kafka had been conditioned to serve by her adolescence. Kafka sees Hermann as becoming even more impossible than before, since he must not move. His description of the older man is an insightful blend of pity and revulsion. The man's heavy body, bulky bandages, irregular heart, coughing, and painful incision — all these call up in Kafka part of the nightmarish existence he has always constructed about his father. He sees in Hermann's gestures some desecration of the human spirit. Even when his father moves his hand at the nurse, Kafka says it is as though he had said "bitch." He says he understands each gesture in all its dreadfulness, indicating that a full three years after writing the therapeutic *Letter to His Father* he has not lost any of his revulsion.

Since obviously his presence only made his father nervous and interfered with his mother's martyrdom to this noisome lump on the hospital bed, by July 20 Kafka was back in Planá. He was ready to return to *The Castle*.[50]

The novel begins: "It was late in the evening when K. arrived. The village was deep in snow. The Castle Hill was hidden, veiled in mist and darkness, nor was there even a glimmer of light to show that a castle was there. On the wooden bridge leading from the main road to the village, K. stood for a long time gazing into the illusory emptiness above him."* From here, K. seeks quarters for the night at the inn, where there is no room but there is a bag of straw in the parlor. With that begins his effort to establish who he is, as land-surveyor, and that he has in fact been commissioned by castle officialdom.

The key metaphor for the novel, as for K.'s quest, is spatial. The paradox of *The Castle* is that while it employs a seemingly infinite space open to the sky, with the castle in the distance as part of that infinitude, it is also labyrinthine. Distancing and denial of distance are implied in K.'s role as a land-surveyor, one who deals in dimensions, horizons, measurements, proportions. Kafka had always put into geographical settings the dimensions of his inner vision. The "space" of K. is as ever a matter of limits, in the way language fails to capture spatiality and the almost temporal stream of words. We can say that despite its reach toward infinity, *The Castle* is a novel of extreme inwardness, the pit, rather than the tower, of Babel.

K. uses the spatiality surrounding the castle approaches, suggested in the first paragraph, as a means of getting from one small space to another. He lives in measured, cramped quarters, even though his mission is to survey large distances and to measure *them*. Early in the

---

*The alternate version of the opening paragraph is rather different, with the landlord welcoming K.: the novel begins *in medias res*, as it were, with K. seeking quarters. The version above seems far more attuned to Kafka's way of working, which was to lead into murkiness with certain spatial considerations.

novel, K. calls out to Barnabas, the castle messenger, and the name rings out into the night, only to echo from a great distance. Distances, nevertheless, have little relationship to human capability, for Barnabas (this "son of exhortation") has just left K.'s side and yet is already so far off that K.'s voice seems to carry for miles. The effect upon us and upon K. is disruptive of normal spatial (and temporal) expectations, so that even in this brief scene, which occurs outdoors, we are carried back into hollows and concavities, into Kafka's peculiar world of space exaggerated, distorted, denied, and then apotheosized. The result is that "confusion of realms" associated with the sense of someone enclosed, but connected also to the stream of consciousness, in which words come to us from levels we cannot quite identify.

About midway through *The Castle*, a little beyond the point Kafka had reached by the end of July 1922, K. tries to grapple with the idea of freedom and/or imprisonment, although the formulation is full of the author's typical paradoxes. He is almost completely ignored.

> It seemed to K. as if at last these people had broken off all relations with him, and as if now in reality he were freer than he had ever been, and at liberty to wait here in this place usually forbidden to him as long as he desired, and had won a freedom such as hardly anyone else had ever succeeded in winning, and as if nobody could dare to touch him or drive him away — or even speak to him; but this conviction was at least equally strong — as if at the same time there was nothing more senseless, nothing more hopeless, than this freedom, this waiting, this inviolability.[51]

This mixture of liberation and imprisonment within a restructured space and time is, apparently, the subject of *The Castle*. Certainly it would be in keeping with Kafka's own estimate of his personal condition, caught as he was between yearning for liberation from a declining body and recognizing that he was imprisoned within it; between the desire for freedom from all things that had entrapped him, and the perception that he was the sum total of those forces. We note the religious, political, and social overtones of such a passage, but we must resist seeing Kafka's position as either more or less than the tensions and conflicts themselves. As tensions, they are representative — the way in which Kafka could see his individual condition as part of a general condition. These tensions are implicit in language also, in the verbal stream that passages in *The Castle* approximate, between the content that belongs to consciousness and the content that suggests another dimension beneath or beyond consciousness.

Kafka was apparently aware of the paradoxes arising from his emphasis not on ideas as such but on the tensions between them. The tensions create that "space" between reader and subject, a kind of dreamy filler that both separates and connects. He had written to Felice Bauer, as we recall, that writing is an act akin to death, part of a sleep deeper than death; and just as one would not wrest the dead from their graves, so too he must not be wrenched from his desk. We recall also those extraordinary passages in which the artist-writer is entombed in his own cellar, where his wife brings him his food and walking to the door of his dungeon would be his sole exercise. These remarks are directed to Felice and encode Kafka's withdrawal from the relationship even as he pursued it; but more than that, such comments seek out a deeper tension within him, one that extends beyond his tenuous tie to this young Berlin woman. The deeper tensions lie in Kafka's need to seek the most inner life possible and to discover the forms of language that can capture the sense of burial and entrapment. The scenic equivalent of such language is cellars, basements, sleep and death, graves, his desk at night, and, not least, a castle that remains as inaccessible as any underground maze. As the German title suggests, K. lacks the key to the lock of the castle, meaning that the castle must remain inaccessible, even as he views it in the distance.*

Every detail of that individual life must, somehow, find the scale of the outer world; or, conversely, that outer world must find a comparable scale in the inner. Scene must equate to language, external event to mind projecting it. K. hopes that if he finds the order of his own existence (that is, the right language for expressing his thought, the right gestures to pacify the natives, the right codes to win over a strange and alien tradition), he will divine the pattern and order, even the fundamental idea, of what lies beyond. He can forsake no detail, for it, like the homunculus or the microcosm, may contain the whole. In this little world, all people and all information are a language, linked in some grammatical, syntactical way, although their particular pattern of relationships is not apparent. It is as if one knows the vocabulary of a foreign language but cannot figure out grammatical relationships; or, geographically, as if one were presented with a map of the Balkan countries but could not distinguish what each represented. One must remain ever vigilant, for the missing clues may surface, and then one might learn precisely how to respond. One must, however, not only understand the maze as a whole, but one must not lose any fragment of it. The glimmers of paranoia that enter Kafka as he awaits noise or other interruptions find expression here in K.'s need to decode the whole before he can decide how to live.

This need to fit oneself into unknowable spatial and temporal elements shrouded in fog and to master hitherto unknown languages is attached to Kafka's persistent theme of the protagonist-artist endeav-

---

*In Prague, Hradčany Castle, really an entire village, including Saint Vitus's Cathedral, looms over the city proper. At twilight in particular, it seems to hang in the air like some magical, inaccessible place, as much fantasy as actuality. Kafka's "idea" of a castle could well have derived from Hradčany, but one would be mistaken to limit his novelistic vision to this castle. Kafka's "castle" is, obviously, no fixed geographical setting.

oring to ply his art. Although K. is not a craftsman, nor a creative artist, his role is presented as being like that of the artist who must journey into unknowns in order to understand the nature of his vocation. We recall Kafka's letter in which he tells Brod the writer is a voyager through hell, or through the unconscious.[52] Here the artist encounters dark spirits, the devils lurking in the underworld; and while the writer lurks down there amidst the wreckage of civilization, the house collapses, for he has left the house at the mercy of evil forces. The imagery is of the Orphic descent into a disruptive pattern, a descent into the labyrinth or maze that, lying outside time, characterizes Kafka's measured universe.

For the means by which to present K.'s journey through mazes, which may or may not lead to the castle, Kafka devised a very deceptive narrative. His tale seems to be the ordinary one of a young man caught in a problem, a third-person narrative with a traditional omniscient author. But the confusion of realms — the disruption of time and space, the use of labyrinthine images, the succession of bizarre characters and meetings, the proliferation of duplicating figures and scenes — relocates narrative very close to interior monologue or even deeper. This develops even though the narrative derives from the author, not the protagonist. The method comes close to what one critic has called "psychonarrative,"[53] in which the protagonist's deepest thoughts are presented through a third-person narrative. But even psychonarrative is not quite what Kafka accomplishes. For, in effect, he transforms all external phenomena into psychological recesses. He carries the world inward, as though it all solipsistically derived from K.'s consciousness. We know of course that it does not, but Kafka through an uncanny precision has confused borders between real and unreal.

Kafka's ability to write about himself as an "other" suggests that he had been developing some method, close to the diary and letter modes he had been using, which denied borders between conscious and sub- or unconscious. The long correspondence with Felice Bauer, as was suggested earlier, was as much about a character named Kafka as it was about Kafka himself. And while he maintained this protracted correspondence, he was keeping a diary, in which he frequently commented on the letters he was writing, on her replies, on his response to both. And in those diary entries, he was treating Franz Kafka (often called K.) as a character in a dream, from which he could remove himself at will. While all of Kafka's novels are about him, they are also about a person *from whom he can remove himself.* That playing of roles noted earlier entered into his very conception of his fictions.

The reuse of K. — and the dropping in, playfully or not, of Joseph K. — indicates not only an extension of *The Trial,* but also a desire to re-enter life after having died. Even as Kafka senses the end of his own life, he resurrects Joseph's. But naming enters into other dimensions of

the novel as well. The central position of someone named Klamm
(*klamm*, or compact, narrow, tight, stiff, numb, close, even clammy)
cannot be ignored, especially since for K. he becomes a key figure. Kafka's use of Joseph K. for K., as suggested, may be playful, or may be
merely his dropping a distraction, another figure into the maze, turning
The Castle into a *Trial*. Although K. and Joseph K. differ in some ways,
both are caught in a common fate: to seek egress from a labyrinth
whose function is to paralyze them; and to create for Kafka some
boundaries for his life, or else to indicate to him its limits, beyond
which he cannot pass without death itself. Further, name confusion is
evident with other characters: Sortini, who persecutes Amalia, and Sor-
dini, who becomes part of K.'s affairs; a little girl named Frieda and K.'s
mistress, Frieda; a brother, Hans, and the landlord Hans; and several
others. Naming is less for purposes of identification than to create emblems of confusion.

An artist figure whose situation is already compromised by his association with people who understand no art, a man himself cut off,
alienated from home and family, forsaking his past, now apparently
rootless, K. journeys to the village to take up a post the precise nature
of which he does not foresee. From the first paragraph, we must also
suppose that the journey is not outward, to a real place, but inward to a
state of mind, that Kafka is hallucinating, as it were, fantasizing an inward journey, like the voyage in Rimbaud's "The Drunken Boat," for
example. K. is a dedicated man, a bachelor who, having once mentioned a family in the old country, never refers to it again. The very in-
distinctness of his goal becomes significant if we judge him as an artist;
for he has come to measure, contemplate, imagine, and then to try to
resolve the elements. In his role as artist, his encounter with labyrinths
is not unexpected, since to penetrate into the intricacies of the maze is
to embrace mysteries invisible to common sense. That labyrinth or
maze, in fact, is the testing ground for the artist, for the Orphic figure
must encounter a different, possibly deranged space and time when he
descends. In this manner, Kafka approximated the descent into the
middle ground of consciousness where stream, which suggests freedom, and enclosure, which suggests entrapment, overlap or cross. By
the end of July, with nine chapters completed, Kafka had brought K.
into every one of Kafka's own concerns.

While the sexual components of penetration and the labyrinth are
inescapable and psychologically revealing, a more fruitful area of in-
quiry into the novel can be found in those myths akin to the making of
art. None of this denies that Kafka's mazes and his protagonists' inability to find their way run parallel to his own sexual disorientation — his
alternating desire to penetrate the female and his trepidation over the
threatening coils at the female center; his attraction to exogamous
women, his withdrawal from Jewish women. In his balletic correspon-

dence with Felice Bauer, he maintained the relationship while in every word pulling away from its implications.

None of this denies, further, that the circuitous routes Kafka plots both above and below ground are tubes, canals, vaginal walls, to which entrances are blocked. And, finally, none of this denies that such places contain Eleusinian mysteries, terrible rites of initiation, locales of death, and indeed seem protected by the *vagina dentata*. To recognize all this, however, is to observe that the sexual component, which is not at all a contradictory note, is subsumed in the artistic process. Both lead to that Kafkan no-man's-land where terrible energies are transformed into passivity and inertness, where rage and hostility are subverted by enervation. This too is what we mean when we call something Kafkaesque, although this particular sense has become secondary to the meaning of the word as embodying frustration and entrapment.

Despite all his movement and activity, K. never leaves the periphery of the village, he never finds the path leading to the castle or the castle compound, and he never discovers clues to the labyrinthine process in which he finds himself. Even the time sequencing of *The Castle* throws K. (and the reader) off balance. The expectation is of temporal infinity: the castle as a mythical place shrouded in mystery seems caught in endless time. It has always existed and will continue to be veiled by fog and mist long after K.'s quest — whatever *that* is! — has ended. That is one line of temporal expectation. Set alongside or against that is the actual time span of the novel, in all, seven days, the biblical and magical seven. Thus far, then, we encounter a temporal duality in which parts cannot possibly harmonize. Further, the first three and a half days take up approximately one-seventh of the book's total length and the other six-sevenths describe the final three and a half days. K. and the reader, moving along rapidly, suddenly come up against a pace in which a day takes almost one hundred pages.

Temporal factors become increasingly complicated: the castle remains an unfocused place somewhere in the haze, while the foreground shifts from concentrated to extended time, with neither meeting our expectations of pacing. Language itself takes on the role of approximating an unconscious that must remain inexplicable. The novel has that expansiveness and withdrawal associated with dreams; and yet K. moves in what is routine time. One played off against the other creates a dissociation of sensibility, all narrated by a logical, rational voice, which even further disturbs the realm of order. Like Proust in many of his passages, Kafka has used the same method to speed up time that he has used to slow it down. In one respect, he has created external expectation; in another, subverted it for interior time.

If we locate the novel in Kafka's life in the summer of 1922, we find that his experience of his disease had created in him several levels of experience, and among them, there is no clear demarcation between what is exterior and what is interior. Kafka not only personifies a memory come alive, he is a living reminder of everything that can occur to an individual of extreme sensibilities. In this frame of reference, there is no clear division of self; the experience of the disease has made him so open to phenomena he becomes the embodiment of all things. The idea of a split between body and mind, or body and soul, or sacred and divine, no longer holds for Kafka. In some Nietzschean transformation of self, he has made himself into the representative man who absorbs all, a kind of Prague Golem, but a human one.

But these calculations fail to take into account the village with its own temporal expectations and its relationship to castle eternality. When K. enters into village life, there is virtually no way he can carry over clock, calendar, or empirical time from his earlier life. Like the artist when he inserts himself into the temporal dimensions of his work or the analyst when he tries to fathom a patient's unconscious, K. must attempt to balance time sequences that define his own experience with those that exist in village and castle. With village time an unclear factor, castle time mysterious and ahistorical, and K. himself living in empirical time, K. must discover a formula, which consistently eludes him. This formula is more than a way of reaching Klamm or any other of the castle officials; it is no less than how to grasp distorted forms of experience, unexpected states of mind, and different levels of time. With this, Kafka has brought the reader to the very crossroads of narrative modes as they try to reflect modes of experience. He is desperate to make us understand. Yet what we must understand is unclear to Kafka himself, especially since there is so much he feels he must communicate even as his time dwindles.

With time a labyrinth, space is also a maze of possibilities. Spatially, Kafka uses the various emissaries and minor officials — Erlanger, Bürgel, Barnabas, the two Assistants — as ways of increasing distance between K. and the castle. In realistic or representational fiction, the presence of an intermediary indicates that the protagonist has approached the seat of power; he can then negotiate with the functionary, who acts as a stand-in for the principal officer. By making the intermediary separate K. even further from officialdom, Kafka scrambles this spatial concept. Despite K.'s hopes, the functionaries indicate not how close he has come, but how distant decisive action may be, how shrouded in fog that principal officer really is. Accordingly, space, like time, is opening up and closing down, alternating resolution and frustration, becoming the labyrinthine way that is Kafka's metaphysical principle.

In still another respect Kafka was a master of the modern mode, which, depending on the destruction of expectation, exposed the dissociation of self. He could have absorbed this mode from nonrepresentational painting, which had become familiar in Prague art circles, or derived it from his own sense of himself as he grew up, or, more likely, developed it from a combination of personal feeling and experience of experimental methods. Kafka became the master of receding frames, the equivalent in fiction of the internal frame of the cubists, a device clearly linked to the negation of spectator expectation. What the viewer sees is so dislocated from what he expects that the self, for the time, splits.

Even while he identified Prague as a city associated with the past, Kafka assimilated new modes to an imagination already sympathetic to the novelty of experimentation. Internal reshapings, silences, pauses, and absences were forms of secular worship, responses to spiritual malaise. We are familiar with how art became a religious substitute, how when the avant-garde assumed successive waves of spirituality the artist posed as a god. Many of Kafka's diary entries, in fact, while pretending debasement and self-degradation, are really expressions of an elitist, a superior being whose powers give him a force denied others. Kafka knew that his imagination gave him a certain divine empowerment. Less familiar, perhaps, is the fact that culture was itself ready to accommodate these reshapings, not out of a desire to welcome change but because it was so enervated that only change could infuse energy.

In most instances, the larger culture embodied a state ready to collapse from its own dead weight, or a state that had so lost its bearings (the Weimar Republic, for example) that it was merely holding on to a counterfeit nationalism. Politics took on the illusions of dreams; Mann would quarry this theme later with his Joseph tetralogy. The avant-garde found all the seams in such shaky structures and squeezed through. By way of irony, paradox, parable, and satire, Kafka and Musil discovered their own method of dealing with such matters.

At the same time, the state and its institutions were sealing themselves off, hoping that by isolating themselves from the new they could control their destiny. In *The Castle*, Kafka has sealed off an institution, a state, a government, and a people by surrounding the castle with a "moat" of messengers and other functionaries who make it impossible for communication to take place. The mystery surrounding the castle is lightened somewhat if we recognize the place as illusory: as powerless power that must disguise itself as though it were an empire, impregnable and unassailable. The so-called power of the castle derives not from its innate force, but from its ability to provide an illusion of power. It sits up there like a painting whose strength is associated not with any specific content, but with *trompe l'oeil*, the illusions of the perspectives it commands.

Kafka's castle had its counterpart in Proust's use of the Dreyfus case. For Proust's characters, the danger of Dreyfus was his intimation of a new order, even though the victim by choice really belonged to the old. It was a question of perception. Dreyfus simply was not supposed to exist. By sealing themselves off into factitious chauvinistic groups — whose nationalistic fervor resembles that of the villagers protecting the image of the castle and its people — several groups hoped to isolate the old and block out Modernism (a situation analogous also to the way Franz Josef's propped-up empire tried to maintain its disintegrating hegemony by banning Gustav Klimt's university ceiling paintings of Medicine and Jurisprudence). The great historians of this dialectic between old and new, traditional and avant-garde, trivial and iconoclastic, are, evidently, Proust, Musil, and Kafka. *The Castle* is Kafka's "summa" of these developments. Now with the empire gone, with the Dual Monarchy subdivided into nationalistic states, Kafka can see how the old multinational order had tried to isolate itself from being "surveyed" or measured or evaluated anew.

The key to such evaluation is, in Kafka, transformation or metamorphosis, the altering not only of experience but of shape itself. It is evident in the novel at hand, in that the castle is not in any respect the solid domain of our expectations. Shrouded, veiled, disguised, it is a confluence of elements rather than the heavy stone structure we associate with castles. Nor does it have the expectation of the castles of our fantasies, "castles in the air." In Kafka, transformation is a form of control. So it is in *The Castle*. By never appearing distinctly to the eye, the castle looms larger than it ever could physically.* Kafka's conception of the castle owes so much to the modern painterly eye that the entire novel must be viewed as an antirealist, antiexpressionist drama, with strong affinities to the kind of abstraction in which all objects are problematical because they are unidentifiable.

The women of *The Castle*, like most other fictional women in Kafka, are of a special sort. Marriage and children, the traditional female concerns during his lifetime, are eschewed, even irrelevant. Women are mistresses, whores, companions, and rarely if ever wives, except marginally. Kafka's women keep no homes, tend no hearth, mother no children; they are temptresses, abstractions of life forces with only sexual curiosity. As noted, they fit well into that pattern of turn-of-the-century women, those from Ibsen and Strindberg, but even more so of those "monsters" of sexual consumption. Such women are part of Kafka's reorganization of life to fit the castle's demands; socially normalizing events like marriage and child bearing are out of place when time and space themselves are under revaluation.

Several questions about *The Castle* remain, all of them focused on Kafka's attempt to resolve disparate elements as he wrote ever more obsessively and frantically into the novel. Clearly in one respect, he

---

*One recalls the numerous ways in which Monet "saw" Rouen Cathedral, until he almost abstracted it out of existence; or Cézanne's Mont Saint-Victoire.

had lost direction in the final chapters — we know that Brod omitted several end chapters altogether in his first edition, and the first English translation reflected that omission. Brod's edition ended before K.'s encounter with Bürgel, which is in many ways critical. But even before the final chapters, in the fifteenth, when Olga retells Amalia's woeful story of having rebuffed Sortini's sexual overtures, we find Kafka wobbling stylistically. Sortini, in his plan, must be opposed to Klamm,* that much is clear, but Kafka is so circuitous in his prose here that entire segments of this almost interminable chapter are caught up by uncertain prose. *Perhaps, possibly, maybe, so to speak, as it were, in this respect, to a certain extent* — all these qualifiers indicate uncertainty and loss of direction.

These stylistic uncertainties continue into the critical scene between K. and Bürgel, when the latter seems on the edge of opening up the case, allowing K. some insight into the workings of the castle or into his pursuit of castle directions. Yet K. is so sleepy he is unable to take advantage of Bürgel's potential help. The scene reads as though Kafka's own inability to find suitable direction, beyond merely writing itself, has found its analogy in K.'s inability to hear Bürgel and his potential advice. K. closes down in somewhat the same way Kafka has closed down: he is unable to go any further and yet is obligated to go on, to find some resolution or ending.

Bürgel advises that the individual, or his vital spark, reaches limits, and those limits, however one defines them, are part of the balance the world insists upon. K. has in effect reached those limits, and if he recognizes that, then in one respect his mission is accomplished. Bürgel offers a certain sardonic wisdom: "Who knows what awaits you over there? Everything here is full of opportunities, after all. Only there are, of course, opportunities that are, in a manner of speaking, too great to be made use of, there are things that are wrecked on nothing but themselves."[54] The import for Kafka is that by having taken the journey in the guise of K., to seek out castle instructions, to discover what his role should be, he has reached the boundaries of what is possible; after that, there is only an ending.

All this indicates that the castle is not a real place but a dreamspace in a world of distorted or dream time. All efforts to find a real castle as model must give way, not to allegory but to Kafka's placement of it as part of a journey, not for spiritual salvation as in Bunyan, for example, but for what is possible if one does not succumb to paralysis of will. One critic, Ronald Gray (in *Franz Kafka*, 1973), ingeniously cites a work by Kafka's seventeenth-century Czech countryman Komensky (better known as Comenius), his *Labyrinth of the World and the Para-*

---

*Klamm represents yet another of Kafka's roles: arcane, withdrawn, operating in shadows, empowered by invisible forces, as the writer is.

dise of the Heart (1631), in which a castle leads to a false trail. But whether or not Kafka was familiar with Komensky, it is clear that his castle is different. It is not death, it is not an end; it is its unachievability, even as one tries to close the distance. Kafka always sought success in defeat.

The inner turbulence created by the reshaping of *The Castle* material did not lessen Kafka's sensitivity to external noise. Children had become the bane of his existence, to the extent one begins to wonder if the absence of children in his fiction is not in itself his way of revenging himself on the noise they had made, or else a reflection of how, by excluding them from his fiction, he could somehow exclude them from his life. Not that he disliked children as individuals, but collectively they became for him no better than mobs — or rampaging insects: "It is as though I had pried up a stone and saw underneath the obvious, the expected, and yet the dreaded, the wood lice and all the creatures of the night. But this is obviously a transference. It is not the children who are the night's creatures, rather it is they who in the course of play pry up the stone from my head and 'favor' me with a glance into it."[55] But Kafka is not through with his extended canvas of himself and the children playing out some deadly game. He says the worst thing "of which they are innocent and which ought to render them loved rather than feared, is that they represented the last stage of existence. Whether they appear terrible by their noise or delightful by their silence, beyond them begins that chaos invoked by Othello." Here Kafka suggests still another dimension: that children because of their vitality and energy call into question existence itself.

It is clear that even as he was writing well and at a good pace, he was confronting questions of life and death and trying to prepare himself. When he hears that Felix Weltsch's father had seen "pride and flashing eyes" in Hermann Kafka when the latter discussed his own son, Kafka discounts the report and presents his own view, which is death oriented. He asks Brod what there is to make a father's eyes light up. His response is a list of the ways in which he "died" for his father.

> A son incapable of marriage, who could not pass on the family name; pensioned off at thirty-nine, occupied only with his weird kind of writing, the only goal of which is his own salvation or damnation; unloving, alienated from the Faith, so that a father cannot even expect him to say the prayers for the rest of his soul [by predeceasing Hermann, Kafka was spared from saying Kaddish]; consumptive, and as the father quite properly sees it, having got sick through his own fault, for he was no sooner released from the nursery for the first time when with his total incapacity for independence he sought out that unhealthy room at the Schönborn Palace. This is the son to rave about.[56]

Although he did suffer hemorrhaging at the palace, the place could hardly be blamed for his tuberculosis; however, Kafka loved clever exaggeration that belittled him.

Curiously, this passage, like *Letter to His Father*, is rerouted from an attack on the father to an attack on the self. Its presence here forces us to look once again at the famous *Letter* as directed not primarily toward Hermann but, at least equally, as we have seen, toward the writer. That much is obvious. Less obvious is the fact that even as early as that *Letter*, Kafka was death oriented. In another letter to Brod from Planá, at the end of July 1922, Kafka was offering a dead son to Hermann's alleged praise. Once again, he was reshaping. Kafka was always turning over the coin.

Kafka's thirty-two letters to his "Liebste Eltern" ("Dearest Parents") from July 27, 1922, to June 2, 1924, near the time of his death, are mainly intended to resolve the wars of the past. While terminal illness has not burned out the inner vision (we can cite "A Hunger Artist"), his deteriorating physical condition has turned him toward reconciliation with those who might help him. Most immediately, he needed material support while in inflationary Berlin with Dora Dymant, but these letters also reveal Kafka's desire for familial healing. His parents may not have known the full extent of his physical decline, but they were made aware, through the letters, that their only son was living precariously. Then, by April 1924, they finally learned how ill he really was, when in that month alone one-third of the extant thirty-two letters were written, all from one sanatorium or another. Kafka focuses on his weight (50 kg., almost skeletal), temperature, medication, coughing, extreme thirst, and other bodily matters. A chart printed in this Czech edition of letters* reveals the wide fluctuations in his fever curve at the Hajek-Klinik, a curve that was a form of doom.

He spares them little in what is for him his first effort to present himself as he is. These terminal letters are in one respect an effort to balance the anger and hostility expressed "secretly" in *Letter to His Father*. While Kafka does open himself up, much of his commentary centers intensely on the need of a terribly ill person to justify or defend himself, so that he becomes the center of the world. He laments bad doctors (tyrants), praises helpful ones. In return, Hermann and Julie wrote back and sent foods they thought their son might like, incapable as they were of recognizing that he was entering a phase not unlike his hunger artist. Food had become the enemy, even while, of course, it remained his only chance to hang on. Kafka's concentration on himself is complete; his letters spare no sick-room details. Like reports from the

---

Briefe an die Eltern aus den Jahren 1922–1924 (*Letters to His Parents from 1922–1924*), ed. Josef Čermak and Martin Svatoš (Prague: Odeon, 1990).

front, they sound like pseudomilitary communiqués. He sees himself arrayed against forces trying to annihilate him in what is clearly a losing battle. As the letters wind down — one in May, the final one in June — Kafka cannot hide his deterioration, especially since several letters are started by Dora, with only his brief additions. But even apart from the context, his handwriting indicates how weak he has become. The final letter, in parts almost illegible, remained incomplete, with Dora supplying the last few words. This same Dora — who stayed by Kafka during these last two years — would be ignored by his parents when he was buried. It remains unclear how much of a reconciliation between Kafka and his "Liebste Eltern" actually took place.

With each act of self-deprecation, Kafka reinforced his presence. It was a method he revealed in his letters to Felice Bauer, by which he empowered himself through self-deprecation, whimpering, self-humiliation. His sole way of controlling his life, as it slowly ebbed, was to degrade whatever was left of him, so as to reveal something even lesser than what met the eye. Kafka strengthened his presence by becoming unknown, invisible, by shrinking, as K. does whenever confronted by a castle presence. Presenting a persona who has given up or withdrawn, Kafka freed himself for writing, the sole form of empowerment left to him. When Janouch thoughtfully brought him a specially bound volume of "The Metamorphosis," "The Judgment," and "The Stoker," in rich, dark brown leather, Kafka felt that it should all be burned and reportedly told Janouch his work should not have been printed at all. When Kafka spoke of writing as being everything to him, he meant literally the process of writing, not the printed word.

When Martin Buber planned to leave the editorship of the magazine *Der Jude* (*The Jew*), Felix Weltsch suggested Kafka as the successor, to which Kafka responded that it must have been a joke that his name should come up. "How could I think of such a thing, with my boundless ignorance of affairs, my complete lack of connection with people, the absence of any firm Jewish ground under my feet? No, no."[57]

He returned to Prague near the end of July for four days, and then came back to Planá, where his stay would be interrupted by Ottla's plan to leave for Prague in early September. As he sees the continuity of his life disrupted by the actions of others, and continuity on his novel interrupted by the need to formulate new plans, his comments take on a frantic quality. In his confusion, he even writes to Emma Salveter, whom Brod had made his mistress when she was a chambermaid and who was now pursuing an acting career in Leipzig. Kafka's series of remarks indicate a precarious hold on his existence, perhaps made possible only by the manuscript on his desk, but even that he saw as almost perpetually threatened. The beginnings of his troubles (he called them "breakdowns") came in succession: the trip to visit the Baums was canceled; the children's noise was unresolved; a new threat appeared in

Ottla's return to Prague; and finally, he feared remaining alone in Planá, but he also feared returning to Prague. Only this last matter was resolved when Ottla, out of sympathy for her brother's anxiety (and Kafka speaks of being caught like Gulliver between two gigantic women, his sister and the landlady, who offered to cook for him), stayed on through the month of September.

Gulliver was much on his mind, as were young women. The disease may have been ravaging his lungs, but it piqued his sexual interest, especially now, in summer, when women were scantily clad. In Prague, he observed "half-naked women," against whom "one could hardly put up a longer resistance." He says, "Not until summer does one really see their curious kind of flesh in quantities. It is soft flesh, retentive of a greal deal of water, slightly puffy, and keeps its freshness only a few days. Actually, of course, it stands up pretty well, but that is only proof of the brevity of human life."[58] Then Kafka makes one of his characteristic "turns," so that succulent flesh, which activates the male libido, or at least his, is linked to corruption and decay — that is, to death. How close all flesh and sex are to rot!

> How short human life must be if flesh one hardly dares to touch because of its perishability, because its shapely contours last only a moment (which contours, as Gulliver discovered — but most of the time I cannot believe it — are disfigured by sweat, fat, pores, and hairs) — how short human life must be, if such flesh will last out a good portion of that life.[59]

Kafka's citation of Swift here, as well as in other places, locates his sexuality as part of a desperate gamble or as a conflict between sex and decay, or sex and excrement. He describes the women who visit the village as being altogether different, as repulsive in their fatness, dressed "like a fine poisonous toadstool" and smelling "like the best edible mushrooms."[60] The comparison is not quite clear, but the revulsion behind it is, although he says he admires the native, as apart from the visiting, women. He praises one hired girl as having breasts that she sends "into battle." He finds such women dry, however, and one can probably fall in love with them, he comments, only from a distance. At least they do not seem dangerous, they appear even magnificent, and their dryness is not of the urban kind but is brought on by wind, weather, work, child bearing, worries.

Kafka sees country virtues, especially in a large family that lives next door. He admires their ability to survive, their strategies for overcoming difficult situations, their endurance in the face of problems Kafka himself would have succumbed to. He is full of self-pity but is not without compassion and consideration for others. Women upset him, but he knows how delusionary it is to think about them. Fantasies are all that is left to him. He is saddened, he says, by his father's persistent suffering, his discomfort and fear; and he is sad about his mother, also, whose bravery and strength of spirit cannot disguise the fact she is destroying herself in looking after her husband. He is sad, further, about other things, oppressed by his thoughts, full of ideas of self-destruction, not only for himself, but for everyone, including Brod.

He returns to his friend's involvement with Emmy Salveter, "the letter-writer who is working to destroy you, and *at the same time denies that she has any such intention.* There are too many contradictions here." For while Brod has spoken of her as a wonderful friend, even as a goddess, Kafka says, "She does not add up to a person and so I do not know who walks at your side."[61] Is there envy, even jealousy, in these words? Possibly Kafka envies Brod's ability to juggle wife, mistress, work; possibly he envies his friend's refusal to surrender, as a succession of mistresses would show; and possibly he sees female companionship as a way of postponing death, even while it undermines one.

Kafka could not leave the Emmy Salveter affair alone. Brod was clearly unhappy about it, but Kafka was intrigued at the idea of a married man having the energy and initiative to keep a mistress. Citing the legendary Count of Gleichen, a medieval figure who set up a menage à trois, Kafka suggests the same for Brod, for them to live as a threesome in Berlin, perhaps. "Then almost all the previous evils would vanish (though new and unknown evils may appear)."[62] Kafka says he will lose Brod under those conditions, but adds that if there is room for two women, then there must be some sort of room for him, an indication he suspects slow exclusion from his friend's feelings.

Then, in response to her card and letter, Kafka writes to Emmy Salveter. He indicates he would like to meet her and attempts to dissipate any suspicion he is hostile. He says that Brod's happiness depends on her well-being, and therefore he, Kafka, could not possibly want to drive them apart. He sees them as a threesome, "a perfect unity." Yet Brod is tormented, and Kafka does not spare her his friend's pain and sleeplessness, his emaciated look, a description that easily fits Kafka as well. He adds that if she could see Brod like this, she would rush to his side; it is a pity she is not there when he needs her. Yet Kafka describes a meeting in a café with Felice some time ago as "one of the most meaningless incidents of my life."[63]

This was a precarious time for Kafka, when, needing support, he felt that Ottla was deserting him for Prague and he would be left with the landlady. As his imagery suggests, he sees himself being destroyed by women, for he did not want to return to Prague and yet felt he could not remain alone in the country. He found it almost impossible to live without some member of his family nearby, either in his parents' apartment or with Ottla, or in the house of one of his other sisters. He was seriously ill now, but the need for family members extended into periods when he was well and might have contemplated independence. Independence, however, would come only in the final stages of the illness, when his body was too far ravaged for any move to matter.

Kafka's panic about being left alone is described in a letter to Brod (September 11), in which he says he will have to drop the "castle story forever, cannot pick it up again since the 'breakdown' which began a week before my trip to Prague [at the end of July], even though the part written in Planá is not quite as bad as the part you know." *The Castle*, of course, has revealed his uneasiness with women, in the images of Frieda with a whip or with her foot on K.'s chest, for starters. Kafka indicates how serene he feels when he is alone with Ottla, without his brother-in-law and guests; and from his remarks, we observe how he wishes Ottla could remain as his wife-mate, the perfect solution to his situation and to his need for female support. But this letter quickly declines into a death-missive: Kafka's roll call of breakdowns, followed by an overwhelming fear not only of being without people but of the loneliness that comes with death and burial. His fear was so powerful that even without trying to sleep, he experienced insomnia. "I was already sleepless, I literally experienced insomnia beforehand as though I had had a sleepless night behind me."[64] That "beforehand insomnia" is, apparently, that fear of sleeping that is linked to a fear of not awakening.

He says he is doomed to a battle with himself, "a battle of annihilation which would have no outcome other than that I stay," although Ottla forbade him to stay because of the raw weather. He was left trembling with indecision: whether he should stay or not, accept their assurances or not, make entirely different decisions or not. It was the kind of dilemma Kafka suffered so intensely he could transform it into fictional terms, into K.'s situation vis-à-vis the castle people, for example. Security and insecurity are separated by a chasm.

Kafka speaks of retreat into his mousehole, where he could test his fear of dying alone. "If I stayed here alone, I would be completely lonely. I cannot talk to the people here, and if I did so, it would only be a heightening of loneliness."[65] These lines can be transposed to K.'s situation, to explain his rapidly developed relationship with Frieda, the barmaid. Kafka says he has a good understanding of loneliness, "not so much of lonely loneliness as of loneliness among people," as it was in Matliary and in Spindlermühle. That lifelong dependence on familial apartments and houses fits this terrible fear.

But, as with nearly everything in Kafka, there is another side or dimension. "Fundamentally, loneliness is my sole aim, my greatest temptation, my opportunity, and assuming it can be said that I have 'arranged' my life, it was always with the view that loneliness can comfortably fit into it." He has the countering fear, "the fear of being robbed of loneliness, which is equally strong. . . . and even more understandable the fear of the torturous middle way, and yet this fear is the weakest of the three, and I am ground between these two fears." He perceives himself as being crushed between fear of loneliness and fear of being robbed of it, ground into dust by some "great miller in the background [who] will growl out that for all his toil, he has not netted much nourishment from me."

He offers as an example his Uncle Rudolf (Löwy), a bookkeeper at a brewery, who remained a bachelor but became a Catholic convert. Kafka sees this as a life of horror, and yet except for the conversion it is reasonably similar to his own. He says he feels good in empty apartments, but not when they are entirely empty. He likes them full of memories of people, but not actually people or objects. His imagination is like a large echo chamber in which memories have replaced more solid elements, and he can deal with echoes, reverberations, vibrations. He likes empty apartments where the mail is addressed to someone else, where someone else's newspaper is thrust into the door. As long as it is unfamiliar, alive with memories of people long gone, he finds it attractive. What Kafka is describing is a tomb that in his imagination is being prepared for him.

Kafka's revelations of self to Brod are extraordinary, most of all because they provide such a close analogue to what he was writing. K. buries himself ever deeper even as he pursues what he thinks is his goal: to locate the correct castle officials so as to define his position in this unfamiliar, unnamed land where he is repeatedly identified as a stranger. His is not quite a quest for death, since he sees his pursuit as part of living; but Kafka perceives it differently, with K. embedding himself in a culture of death while seeing it as life. Some of that "death culture" he assigns to Prague itself. "Prague is more useful if one comes from Berlin. . . . Prague is a medicine against Berlin and Berlin is a medicine against Prague, and since the West European Jew is a sick man and lives on medicines, it is essential for him, if he is to move in these circles, not to pass up Berlin."[66]

He adds he has not himself had sufficient strength to stretch out his hand and "reach for the medicine." He also says that from Berlin one has "a stronger view of Palestine" than from Prague. Kafka's thought here is convoluted. He sees Prague as no longer a friendly host for the Western European Jew. Berlin is the center of culture for him, but Berlin is itself only a jumping-off place for the Jew, who must now consider Palestine. Certainly Berlin in 1922 was the site of constant clashes between left and right, the location of roving fascist bands, the place where Nazism, having incubated in Munich, was now growing, where the Jew could only be the scapegoat and victim for the hardships imposed by the Versailles treaty.* As a result, Berlin, although cosmopolitan and sophisticated in its avant-garde culture, was, in Kafka's eyes, another tomb.

Arrayed against these jejune and depressed thoughts of himself and

---

*Alfred Döblin's *Berlin Alexanderplatz* describes the failure of the Weimar government and the gradual takeover of the city by thugs.

his environment, the actual and the possible, is Kafka's novel, which is keyed into activity, attempts at definition, pursuit of a plan, some determination to follow through, a refusal to succumb to frustration and seeming defeat. K. is not ready to surrender, as Joseph K. was in *The Trial*, even though both become involved with women named Frieda; and K. early on expresses his determination, in a passage (deleted) that foreshadows those wasted gladiators of Samuel Beckett.* Even as he himself deteriorated, Kafka refused to allow K. to decline. Everything around him seems to be fading away, but he retains his grip on purpose and goal, even when he is deflected. There is something of the foolhardiness of the Western European Jew in this: K. as the Jew who still feels that the Gentile world will permit him to live, to carry out his duties, when in fact it has bottled him up, made it impossible for him to function, and diverted him with tempting non-Jewish women. We could see the novel as an allegory of Kafka's view of the Jew doomed in Prague and the entire narrative structure as the passage of a modern-day Moses into the wilderness, seeking his illusory dream and coming away with little except frustration. And beating the drums in the dim background are those who will go beyond frustrating him, those who are preparing the tomb.

Yet we should not settle for this interpretation. While it may have been part of Kafka's recessive thinking, the part in the shadows, the most important part of K.'s quest is that he goes on so that Kafka could himself go on to write his novel. If K. succumbed while confronting one frustration after another, whether assistants, messengers, women, or vague policies, Kafka would in effect be surrendering to his condition. Since writing and, to some extent, his correspondence were now the only things keeping him alive, he needed K.'s persistence to keep himself active. Kafka seems to have recognized that as long as he kept writing (which means as long as he kept K. in contention), he could prolong his own life. Writing had become for him literally a matter of life and death.

When he returned to Prague from Planá, on September 18, he was, as he wrote in his now almost empty diary pages, in a state of "collapse again." He admits to two good months, with some exceptions, and credits Ottla for the better times. Now having returned, he could not evade all the shadows closing in, the ghosts of the city itself, the suspicion Prague meant death for him. In the shape of a letter, Milena loomed, and he responded that he could still chop wood, which was his way of saying he was not yet dead. But what he neglects to mention in his despairing assessment is that he had put a good deal of *The Castle* on paper, and he had been able to capture the sense of the unaccultur-

---

*"For it was clear to him that wasting only a few days here would make him incapable of ever acting decisively" (*The Trial*, p. 14).

ated individual, himself as well as K., trying to gain a foothold in what was essentially alien territory. In brief, he had with a kind of completeness denied most writers captured his world, and he had done so without compromising his beliefs, religious or otherwise.

In October, in the *Neue Rundschau*, he saw the publication of "A Hunger Artist." If he needed any reminder of his mortality he had it in this story, one of the epitomes of his artistic life. It was one of the few pieces (along with "The Judgment," "The Stoker," "The Metamorphosis," "In the Penal Colony," and "A Country Doctor," as well as the few copies remaining of *Meditation*) he would tell Brod not to burn. But even those "five books and a story" he did not want reprinted. He simply felt that while they were "valid" (his word) for his time and place, they were not to be passed on to future generations. He could not, of course, control this, nor could Brod, since once published, the pieces' future belonged to publishers. But Kafka did indicate that if they could be kept from future generations' eyes, he would be pleased; he looks to their disappearance, in much the same way as his hunger artist disappears. Everything else, however, whether manuscripts, letters, papers, or works in periodicals, was to be burned. He would even ask Brod not to look at any of the material, although he eventually permitted him to. There is no mention of *The Trial* or the long manuscript of *The Castle*, so we must assume Kafka felt they were expendable, as was the remainder of *Amerika*, except for "The Stoker."

What has gone unnoticed is what an act of pride this request is. In commenting on Kafka's desire to have nearly everything die with him, most readers have focused on his perfectionism and, therefore, his disappointment at how his work turned out. Following upon that, most critics have cited his humility in the face of the printed word, his recognition that no word on the page could equal what the intention or imagined act was. Yet we can turn all this around and see that Kafka was like the legendary figure who demands that all those around him, wife and servants, for example, die when he dies, on the assumption that with his death nothing else matters. What we then discover is not only pride of accomplishment, but an enormous vanity that once the principal is gone, everything he has touched (here manuscripts and letters) must suffer the same fate — that is, must enter eternity with him. This is not humility, but an expression of accomplishment and a determined effort to locate the self, even as the work speaks of a wandering, homeless, deracinated creature whose only solace may be some form of art. Kafka did not lack self; he had a monstrous sense of self. For if he truly wished everything except a few items burned, then in the time remaining he would have made the effort himself. By leaving the task to Brod, he was, like pharoahs and other tyrants, creating a funeral pyre in his honor.

We recall Kafka's parable/paradox called "The Building of the Temple." Everyone contributes to its building, foreign workers, designers, and so on; the stones rise and are placed according to the calculations of the architect-narrator. "No building ever came into being as easily as did this temple." Yet even as the temple is going up, there is a counter-movement, to create instruments of "a magnificent sharpness" that could be used to scratch on every stone, creating something like modern-day graffiti. These scratches (from "what quarry had they come?") would last for an eternity, in fact would outlast the temple. They were the "clumsy scribblings of senseless children's hands, or rather the entries of barbaric mountain dwellers."[67] Or else they were the memories and echoes any constructed work leaves behind, and those echoes cannot be effaced because they come from a quarry unimaginable even to those who build great temples. The parable here, if we can call it that, serves as an analogue to Kafka and his "destroyed" manuscripts, for by destroying everything, or requesting it of Brod, he was aware of their reverberations — so aware that he could tell from the tracings on the stones or works what magnificence once existed! Kafka did not thrust away his "temple" in a burst of self-hatred; he wanted it burned so that its ashes would live forever, long past the original works.

Now came a fallow period, Kafka in Prague, ill, with a low but steady temperature, enough to enervate him. Probably in this time, toward the end of 1922, he wrote "The Married Couple," mentioned earlier, clearly a despairing sense of Hermann and Julie in their older age, with "N." becoming not the Kafka figure but the father. Another brief piece, "A Commentary," seems directly linked to *The Castle*. In "The Commentary," a man asks his way of a policeman and is told to give up; the policeman turns away laughing. With writing not occupying him, Kafka began to study Hebrew with renewed seriousness. He already knew enough to tutor his niece, Marianne, the daughter of Valli, now ten. Kafka could read the language at least at the level of a newspaper, could speak some, and understood a little. To increase his skill, with the idea of one day emigrating to Palestine, he took lessons from Puah Bentovim, a Palestinian Jew, nineteen, fresh-faced, eager, forward-looking, and dedicated to a Jewish destiny. At this time, she was just about everything Kafka was not, although he was increasingly drawn to the idea of a "return" and an abandonment of his particularly cruel form of diaspora.

Franz Werfel and Otto Pick visited Prague, and Werfel felt obliged to discuss with Kafka his play *Schweiger* (*The Silent* [or "Taciturn"] One), which altogether left Kafka in despair. He had an extraordinary dislike of the play, but furthermore it affected him horribly, because the characters were not people, but hellish figures, creatures of pathology. He tells Brod he still admires Werfel, and even admires his ability to "wade through these three acts of mud."[68] Kafka followed up their meeting with a lengthy letter to Werfel, which he may or may not have sent. He tries to explain his behavior, but in doing so he makes new allegations: that while *Schweiger* may have theatrical merit, it is nevertheless a retreat from leadership and betrays the generation, trivializing it, and therefore cheapening its sufferings. In Kafka's estimation, Werfel had done what he found reprehensible in Schnitzler: that trivialization he associated with Vienna as a whole.

This generally fallow period brought some correspondence with Minze Eisner, who had sent on flowers and wishes for Kafka's eventual recovery. Julie Kafka had been ill and needed a serious operation, from which now, in early 1923, she was recovering. By mid-April, Kafka was awaiting the arrival of Hugo Bergmann, his classmate from the Gymnasium, who was returning to Prague: he had emigrated to Palestine, where he became librarian at the Hebrew National Library and a university professor. Kafka was quite excited and pleased at the news, and eager to be with him. Bergmann, who enjoyed a distinguished career, had always seemed to Kafka to know exactly what his direction should be. An outstanding student, he used his academic gifts and arranged his life for maximum results. As it turned out, Bergmann's visit coincided with the rising arc of Kafka's interest in Palestine, what with his learning Hebrew and attending lectures on Palestinian subjects. Bergmann in fact invited his writer friend to Palestine, and Kafka was tempted. Had the offer come sooner, before he was so ill, he may well have gone, although there was always the question of his need for family and familiar surroundings, however much he railed against them.

Then in May Kafka began a series of trips in and out of Prague, going first to Dobrichovitz (Dobřichovice), where he wrote Milena on May 9 (1923): "This place is so expensive that one should be allowed to stay here only the last days before one's death, then there's nothing else left — and secondly I fear — secondly — Heaven and Hell. Apart from this, the whole world is open to me."*[69] The opening up of the correspondence occurred after Kafka had requested that they cease writing to each other, but after Milena sent greetings to him at Dobrichovitz, Kafka resumed writing, even addressing her with the familiar *du*. After less than two weeks at this resort, pained by the expense and loneliness, he returned to Prague. His diary entry ends with remarks that suggest "final solutions," although he summoned the energy to go with Elli and her children to Müritz, a resort on the Baltic Sea northeast of Rostock.

The diary is so despairing, the ghosts so palpable that one expects Kafka to speak of a hand reaching out and drawing him into the nether world. After saying he is capable of nothing but pain, he indicates it be-

---

*This is almost as mordantly witty as his writing Ottla that at least no doctor had recommended Bavaria: "Besides, they receive foreigners very reluctantly there, and they receive Jews only to kill them" (*Letters to Ottla*, p. 67).

comes more and more "fearful as I write. . . . Every word, twisted in the hands of the spirits [ghosts] — this twist of the hand is their character-istic gesture — becomes a spear turned against the speaker."[70] The image is familiar: a spear or knife thrust, a stabbing, a gashed wound in the flesh, the torment of the spear in the side, elements of martyrdom and of confrontation with demonic forces floating to the surface of con-sciousness. And with this image, the diary entries end.

He continues, however, in a letter to Milena, somewhat later. He mentions leaving in early July for Müritz and stopping off in Berlin — to see Emmy Salveter, whom he found "charming" — and then indi-cates his plans to go to Palestine in October. But this was a dream he could joke about. "If I'm never going to leave my bed again, why shouldn't I travel as far as Palestine?"[71] At Müritz, he met the kind of people, Eastern European Jews, who had always given him pause, part of a group from a Jewish People's Home in Berlin, and this made him consider moving to Berlin. What Kafka omits here is that at a children's holiday camp at Müritz he had met the last of the young women who would fill his life, Dora Dymant. But Kafka could also tell Milena that to "live alone in Berlin was of course impossible, in every respect, not only in Berlin but for that matter anywhere."

Yet even while he tells her this, he still hopes that with Dora he can break the cycle of morbid enervation. The balletic movement of these passages in his letter to Milena, well after the Müritz experience, is characteristic of Kafka not only at this time but during his entire adult life. He whipped back and forth between one hope or another. Those Eastern European Jews from the Berlin Home, the very home where Felice Bauer at his insistence had done volunteer work, brought his life around, as if parallel lines could indeed meet. The vision of Palestine for Kafka was not so much as a Jewish homeland, as it was an opportu-nity for him to discover the community that could relieve his aliena-tion. He was in fact quite acculturated, but in viewing his condition, he saw himself as a wanderer over a part of Europe that had little use for him, a refugee and an émigré who could not even be certain where he came from, much less where he was going to.

While in Berlin, where he met Emmy Salveter, Kafka waited to reacquaint himself with Puah Bentovim, who had given him Hebrew lessons in the spring. She was a supervisor at a children's camp in Eberswalde, but Kafka, accompanied by Emmy Salveter, got no farther than Bernau, about fifteen miles closer to Berlin than Eberswalde. He was disappointed, but tried to put a good face on it, and at the end of his letter telling Brod he had been with his mistress, he sent his regards to Frau Brod. He says the children at the Jewish People's Home had given him great pleasure. But in a letter to Klopstock, three days later (July 13), he speaks of "surviving" the trip to Müritz and the stopover in Ber-lin. He says "any effort that lets us escape the ghosts for a moment is sweet; we literally see ourselves vanishing around the corner and them standing there in perplexity."[72] Relief is only temporary, for "the hounds seem to have picked up the scent already." He says he is learning less Hebrew than in Prague, but he does have contact with many Hebrew-speaking, healthy, and cheerful children.

All the same, several things sweetened the situation for Kafka. Despite his gloomy words to Klopstock, the Müritz experience had its positive sides. He truly enjoyed these children, unlike the Czech children playing outside the house in Planá; he met a sixteen-year-old named Tile Rössler, from Berlin, whom he found pleasant to speak to; and he actually participated in a Shabbos eve celebration, on Friday, July 13. As he told Else Bergmann, this celebration of the Sabbath with the children is "for the first time in my life, I think."[73] But beyond this, he met Dora Dymant, a young woman of twenty-one, born of Eastern European parents, and now kitchen supervisor of a children's summer colony. As a volunteer in the kitchen, she was doing the kind of work for children Felice Bauer had once done for adults at the Berlin Jewish People's Home. Dora Dymant left a memoir of Kafka, an especially important observation for the final year or so of his life. As it deepened, their relationship became analogous to one of those typical Dickens brother-sister couples discussed earlier. Without the combat of sexual consummation, they could be far more companionable than married couples.

Dora saw Kafka on the beach with Elli's children, thought of him as a sympathetic father, and was taken with him even before they met. She particularly liked his ability to put children at ease and comfort them when they had suffered accidents. For his part, Kafka was fascinated by this pleasant-looking young woman from Eastern Europe, who embodied so many of his fantasies about Jewish life, as against his own unfocused existence. Dora speaks of knowing from the first that he fulfilled her idea of what a human being should be; and Kafka, desperate for some relief from morbid self-absorption, was delighted by her open and intelligent manner. Furthermore, Dora was proficient in Hebrew, and though she had come from an Orthodox family (a Hasidic sect), she had sufficiently broken away from that tradition but not from Judaism itself. This was perfect for Kafka, who wanted the commitment but not the practices. Her background had not permitted her to take on any professional work — she had been a seamstress for a while — but she had an independent spirit, which superseded, in his mind, educational or professional achievement.

Dora also knew Berlin, having worked there, and this fitted in perfectly with Kafka's plan, hitherto a fantasy, of moving to the city. He spent the rest of July with Dora, and clearly he was focusing on going to Berlin. His health, however, was unstable: his weight was dangerously low, and his condition was passing into different stages of debilitation. Yet he could summon sufficient interest to tell Klopstock not to remain in Europe, that it was overvalued, both the place and the individuals. He warned Klopstock that one should live differently from the way they live there, and he must rearrange his life, "perhaps leave Prague, go to the dirty Jewish streets of Berlin, for instance."[74]

It is tempting to speculate what Kafka would have done if he had met someone like Dora Dymant earlier; if he had moved to Berlin; and what the effect would have been on his writing if he had been situated squarely in one of the centers, along with Paris and Vienna, of the avant-garde in painting, music, and literature. In Prague, the innovative and experimental filtered in without leading to the development of a large artistic community based on novelty, whereas in Berlin, there were meeting places, cafés, theaters, and cabarets where avant-garde artists met and where their art could be exhibited, discussed, banned, flaunted. Prague had the coffeehouses, but the artists meeting there were mainly traditionalists. Instead of Brod, Werfel, and others like them, Kafka might have come into contact with the Stefan George circle, what came to be called the George *Kreis*, a group that included people as diverse as Buber, Rilke, Thomas Mann, Hofmannsthal, Stefan Zweig; or people who worked in and around George, like Schoenberg, who set several songs based on George poems, or the Blaue Reiter group of painters, which included Kandinsky. Kafka might also have withdrawn from such heady stuff, from that profusion of talent; and he might have preferred doing his art in Prague, where the competition was far less intense. Vienna, we know, was particularly odious to him, and perhaps not only for its perceived frivolity but for its accumulation of talent, which Kafka felt to be threatening. His self-deprecation must not be taken at his own evaluation. Only a man of gigantic ego could have held on as Kafka did in the face of the discouragement he created for himself.

If he had had Dora, perhaps his natural desire for retreat would have been compromised; but in any event, from whatever filtered into Prague from French and German cities Kafka absorbed those elements that seemed innate to him. Freud overtook him, clearly, as did the reverberations from the unconscious in literary narrative, in questions of voice, in tone. As for the sense of the individual deracinated, a refugee in his own family, community, and city — for these feelings he did not require life in Paris or Berlin. He had these qualities merely from his own intense involvement with himself.

Meanwhile, he was spending most of his time with Dora, whom he called "a wonderful person." All his emotional ups and downs are spelled out in a long letter to Tile Rössler, whom Kafka had just met in Müritz. She was only sixteen, but Kafka addresses her as an equal, and while she may have been precocious, his manner indicates how straightforward he was when he liked the person, regardless of her age or achievement. Tile later went on to become a leading choreographer in Tel Aviv; from Kafka she received this letter (August 3, 1923), two other written mementos, and a box of candies, which he called "magic candies."*

Kafka tells her that while the Jewish Home has meant a good deal, some little things have spoiled it, although it could all possibly be ascribed to his fatigue, sleeplessness, and headaches. Noise from the children's dormitory was getting to him, and all those charming little creatures as the result of their howling were now taking on different shapes. He plans to move on once his sister Elli and her children (Felix and Gerti) leave and to go on to Berlin for a day or two, after that journey to Marienbad, where his parents were, ending up in Karlsbad for the Thirteenth Zionist Conference, scheduled for August 6–15. His letter is newsy, with a mention of a visit in Müritz from Puah Bentovim, his Hebrew teacher. He thanks her for a vase she gave him, which is much cherished by the "little white-skinned, red-cheeked" flower of a three-year-old, the landlord's child, that grows "in all the houses around here."[75] What his letter signifies more than anything else is what a perfect touch Kafka had in communicating to someone starting out in life, so different from himself, and yet someone he felt sympathetic toward.

From this point on, Kafka's fortunes become intertwined with Dora's and, in a different respect, with the ever loyal doctor, Robert Klopstock. In lieu of wife or parents or even sisters, they served as support for him when he needed help, not only for the physical aspects of his illness, but for the emotional and psychological reinforcement they provided. That they succeeded in propping him up is evidenced by the fact that he was still able to write two of his most effective stories, "The Burrow," in the winter of 1923–24, and "Josephine the Singer, or the Mouse Folk," in March 1924. In both of these pieces, he continued what had characterized his entire later period, to define not only his art but art itself. They fit well with *The Castle*, "A Hunger Artist," and "Investigations of a Dog." All of these works, short and long, suggest that Kafka's artistic output altered with his illness: that he went from someone personally involved in the psychological working out of his protagonists, whether Georg Bendemann, Gregor Samsa, or Joseph K., to a writer concerned with the very nature of art, the process itself. All these later pieces are explorations, carrying the protagonist into spatial concepts that indicate searching, questing, quarrying. The question, then, becomes not so much a problem of survival, as with Joseph K., as a search for what goes into the problem itself, what creates it, what allows it to maintain itself — that is, how art interacts with ordinary events to reshape itself. Transformation, now, is linked to how art reorganizes matter.

---

*This sweet episode, of the dying writer and the sixteen-year-old girl, was the subject of a brief story in German by Marthe Hofmann, published in 1943 in Tel Aviv, as "Dina and the Writer Kafka: Franz Kafka's Correspondence with a Sixteen-Year-Old Girl."

Eventually, Kafka and Dora Dymant would end up in Berlin, which was not a happy place, with inflation, unemployment, rationing, street riots, and grumbling that was growing into rage. It was a city in which innovative art life clashed with food shortages and starving people. Even as its cabarets, coffeehouses, and theaters blazed with the new, the city was dying. Yet in a short time, after the summer of 1923, Kafka and Dora would try to establish what was, for him, his first household.* It fell to Dora to forage for them, and from what she gathered, as well as from food parcels from his parents, they survived, but barely. As we look ahead to Kafka's final months, we find him in a completely dependent situation, one in which Dora has now replaced, on one hand, his mother, and on the other, his sister Ottla. Although he had finally removed himself from his parents' home, Kafka was as helpless in Dora's care as he had been in theirs. However, now he found mental and emotional peace with someone who, half his age, seemed to understand his needs. At one point, she described him as a solitary man who, somehow, was always in relation to something outside himself.

But the stay in Berlin was still to come. After Elli and her two children left Müritz, Kafka went on, temporarily to Berlin, on August 6. His original plans to visit his parents in Marienbad changed when the Kafkas returned to Prague sooner than expected, but Kafka still intended to go on to Karlsbad, rather than head directly for Prague. He jokingly describes his life as being lived on as imperial a scale as that of the Russian czars, who were not permitted to change their prepared route for fear of assassination. After Prague, he was still not certain where to go, although Berlin was the likely destination. Moving close, he said, "very close to the Jews?"[76]

In Berlin briefly, accompanied by three Eastern European Jewish girls, Kafka attended a performance of Schiller's *The Robbers*, but his own "great fatigue," he told Brod, overwhelmed him. He says he felt too weak to visit Emmy Salveter, and even so, he fears she may think the worst of him, perhaps feeling that Kafka was undermining Brod's attitude toward her. He sees Berlin as "continually menacing,"[77] by which he means it is an unstable, unsettled place, where misery and frivolity exist side by side. We know his health was poor from the report on his weight he sent to Brod from Schelesen, at the end of August (the twenty-ninth), a weight of 54½ kilos (120 pounds), and what he says is the least he has weighed. He finds it difficult, in fact, to maintain even that weight. Before heading for Schelesen (Želízy), however, he had re-

*Kafka suffered the kind of privation, desperation, and discontent in Berlin that made possible Hitler's attempt in Munich, in November, to seize power through a *Putsch*. With the Weimar Republic unable to quell lawlessness and civil discontent, Hitler, with General Erich Ludendorff, forced the local leaders to proclaim a national revolution. Hitler was subsequently imprisoned for nine months, using the time to prepare volume 1 of *Mein Kampf*. As Kafka wrote "The Burrow," about hiding from enemies, the enemy was as close as Munich, planning to flush out moles like Kafka.

turned to Prague, where he met Brod in midmonth (August 16) and made what were for him some unusual demands, requesting his parents' Hebrew prayer book, as well as the traditional phylacteries (the *tefillim* used by Orthodox Jews) from Brod. Although in other respects there appeared little to connect Kafka to formal Jewish worship, these requests are signs that in his final months he was identifying more and more with Eastern European Jewry, perhaps as a result of Dora's Hasidic background and her presence in his mind.

Kafka went to Schelesen because Ottla was already there and he could stay with her, through the third week of September. He tried to calm Brod, who was undergoing storms of rage and predictions of ruin over his relationship with Emmy Salveter. There was in this an ironic chiasmus, or crossover: as Kafka felt himself dwindling, his weight declining slowly, his temperature rising, his condition gradually deteriorating beyond retrieval, his friend — who needed Kafka's help — was heading toward collapse over an unhappy love affair. With acting jobs hard to come by, Emmy talked of taking a position as a nursemaid, and Brod apparently saw this as ruin — his, not hers. His rages, Kafka says, were the outpourings not of a mature man but of a child when his house of cards collapses. Kafka assures Brod that the house did not collapse, although the table was shaken; a real house doesn't collapse even when the table is chopped into firewood.[78] The metaphor doesn't really work, but it indicates how Kafka was trying to support his friend, even as Ottla, Klopstock, then Dora would support him. However close Brod was to Kafka's spirit, these exchanges, only a few weeks after their meeting in Prague, suggest how different they had become in their needs: Brod still priding himself on his philandering, Kafka trying to hang on not to women but to life.

Having chosen to return to Prague for Hermann's birthday on September 14, Kafka then decided against it and stayed on with Ottla. On that very day, he told Brod he noticed his weight was up a little more each day, but that was offset "by some greater defect. . . . There's a trickling in the walls, as Kraus says."[79] On the twenty-first, he returned to Prague, now beginning to show his age, going from youthful looks to the appearance of a man suddenly aged. It was the kind of transformation he had dedicated his writing to capturing; and now it was noticed by others, as well as by himself. His return sent him into anxiety attacks, and after only thirty-six hours he decided he could not bear it and left for Berlin to settle in with Dora. They took a small apartment in the Steglitz section, in the Miquelstrasse, and this became for Kafka the final stage in his odyssey. Although his plans still called for emigration to Palestine, Berlin was his fate. From Prague to Berlin: he was trapped for his entire life in a German-speaking environment, and however much he longed for Eastern Europe or for the Zionist dream of Palestine, he would remain an incompletely assimilated German Jew, as much an alien in Berlin as he had been in Prague.

Needless to add, the Kafkas were not pleased with his move, nor with his association with Dora. But dying, as his letters show, has its advantages, giving Kafka leverage he had never enjoyed previously. In any event, short of restraining him forcibly, it would have been impossible to prevent a man of forty from leaving home. With Berlin and Dora, he now had two of the things he had wanted most: the place itself and an Eastern European Jewish woman. In their very modest apartment, they entertained infrequently, but visitors did come through, including Brod (Emmy Salveter was also in Berlin); Ottla, who did approve of the move; Puah Bentovim, Kafka's Hebrew instructor; Tile Rössler, the young woman from the summer camp; and Ernst Weiss, Kafka's old friend from Prague. Since Hermann and Julie were themselves aging rapidly and not eager to travel, he was safe from the rest of the family. Dora worked extremely hard to provide a home for Kafka, an especially difficult endeavor given the lack of goods in Berlin. Lamp oil, for example, was hard to come by, and yet Kafka required it in order to write, which he did at night; the food was quite simple and prepared on a makeshift stove. In some kind of circular irony, Kafka found himself with Dora in almost the precise situation he had once outlined to Felice Bauer, in another time and place. He was allowed to work undisturbed, not in a cellar but nevertheless in a burrowlike room area, he was waited on by an adoring young woman, and he was involved not with Western Jews but the "real kind," from Eastern Europe.

He and Dora planned marriage, but her father, a Hasid, after consultation with his spiritual guide, the Gerer rebbe, refused to give his permission. The grounds were that Kafka was not a practicing Jew, not even one who minimally observed the holidays. He and Dora continued together, nevertheless, although there is no reason to believe the relationship was sexually consummated. The main reason would be that of health — Kafka simply was too ill by this time to consider any physical act — but also the nature of their companionship seemed to speak more of a deep friendship, like that between siblings or friends or father and daughter.

As he told Ottla (on October 8, 1923), he had finally landed on his feet, however shaky they were, and in Dora, he had his princess, an Eastern Jewess. Although forty, Kafka was not above idealizing her into something symbolic for him: the woman who represented the opposite of everything Felice Bauer had stood for. Dora's innocence and idealism were pitted against Felice's materialism; and, by extension, the idealism of the Eastern European Jew was pitted against the greedy materialism (the "heavy furniture") of the German Jew. Kafka had finally turned against everything his father had advised him about: getting on, competing, winning out over poverty, making one's way. He, Kafka, had now discovered "the true way," and he foresaw that an idealistic, antimaterialistic life in Berlin would be followed by the Zionist dream in Palestine — Berlin was a stage in the move toward Palestine, not only a step away from Prague. All the rage, contempt, and revulsion had now come to the surface; not so much in words as in actions, ironically less than a year before his death. Yet we cannot explain away the rebelliousness by saying it was almost a deathbed act. Kafka saw himself with Dora as reborn, as somehow capable of beating the disease, and as a person transformed by the right woman into a sustained human being. Dora became not only an ideal but a form of salvation; literally, what the doctors had been unable to do, she would accomplish.

For a brief time, even though he felt weak and had to rest a good deal, it did seem as though he would be able to carve out some meaningful existence. All the old ills were still there — trouble breathing, for example, coughing, attacks of terrible anxiety, all signals that his health could not be recovered. His letters to his parents in the fall of 1923, from Berlin, are full of tentative feelings, expressions of work being accomplished accompanied by signs of irreversible physical damage, the usual roller coaster of Kafkan fortunes.

In Berlin, Kafka was visited by Emmy Salveter, and by other friends and relatives. He called it a "housewarming," although when Brod's friend arrived, Kafka was himself asleep, what he calls one of several social slips that she seemed to have overlooked. They discussed attending the Succoth (Sukkot, the Festival of Booths) on the coming Sunday (September 30), but he decided his condition was too weak for that. They all made another date, for the zoo and a walk, but nagging at Kafka, besides the state of his health, was the rising cost of basic goods, especially the rent he and Dora were paying. It was rising exponentially, from 28 crowns a month, to 70, to at least 180, and so on into the stratosphere. Kafka speaks of bad, bad times, and he foresees the fate of Germany heading into some cycle. "But there is," he says to Brod, "a certain justice in being associated with the fate of Germany, like you and me."[80]

A cough continued to bother him, what he considered a minor irritation; it would, however, develop into a fatal stage as tuberculosis of the larynx, making it impossible for him to swallow food or to speak. This worsening condition also helps to explain his "Josephine the Singer," only a few months before his death, with its insistence on the art of voice. Josephine does not even have a good voice, but as a mouse she has a distinctive sound, and that helps to make her a celebrity of sorts. Kafka meanwhile struggled to live some kind of normal life, although spiraling costs seemed a harbinger of a doom-filled future that ran parallel to his physical condition. He depended on money from his mother, who sent on cash in advance of his pension check, but he also enjoyed walks in the lush area where he lived. Yet, as he told Brod, the phantoms of the night had returned. Often, Kafka stayed in his room, and he relates to his friend that he is living exactly the way he did in Prague, although there was no reason to return. His description of his condition, in his room, with the phantoms of the night tracking him down, is very close to how he would describe the mole in "The Burrow."

Further remarks to Brod (October 25), in which he speaks of concealment as having been his life's vocation,[81] strengthen the parallels between Kafka and mole. He is of course concerned about his writing, explaining to Brod he was writing so little because he was continuing his Prague life, by which he means there is little to say. But he was preparing to write two pieces, "The Burrow," toward the end of 1923, and a strangely light story called "A Little Woman," who was, probably, Kafka's landlady in Berlin. Yet even with his strength limited, he thought of attending a gardening school in Dahlem (the State Gardening Institute and Nursery) but was frightened off by what seemed a too demanding curriculum: he felt too weak for the practical classes, too distracted for theoretical instruction. To Klopstock, he indicates he is making slow progress in Hebrew, for he finds it difficult to sustain his studies. He lacks the discipline and regularity that he once had, although when something struck him, like "The Burrow," he would be able to write it in a single sitting. He was reading a novel by Josef Chaim Brenner, written in Hebrew, called *Loss and Stumble* (published in Tel Aviv in 1920), but found it difficult and not very good. Puah Bentovim had been helping him with the reading, but in her absence his progress was slow and discouraging.

"A Little Woman" provides a glimpse into Kafka's Berlin life, with "The Burrow" providing a different kind of view. One is from above, one from below, a perfect blending of his two lives. In one instance, a landlady attempts to control him; in the other, he is restricted not by anyone beyond but by his own fears and inhibitions. We find the external Kafka here and the secretive, phantom Kafka, with the latter by far the greater force, the greater source for art. Even as Kafka hoped to integrate himself through the study of Hebrew and through the fantasy of a "return" to Palestine, his creative self was redividing him, disallowing any effort at integrations of parts. He was, as ever, a man functioning well on the surface of things, but pulled apart and in different directions by the secret self. The secret self, of course, provided the phantoms, but it was also that self which provided the intensity and the ultimate rewards.

"A Little Woman" at first seems a curious piece for Kafka to have written at this juncture in his life. Based on certain squabbles he was having with his landlady, most likely over his excessive use of electricity, Kafka crafts a self-contained piece about a woman who cannot bear the sight of her boarder, neighbor, or tenant, as the case may be.

> This little woman, then, is very ill-pleased with me, she always finds something objectionable in me, I am always doing the wrong thing to her, I annoy her at every step; if a life could be cut into the smallest of small pieces and every scrap of it could be separately assessed, every scrap of my life would certainly be an offense to her. ... It may be that everything

about me outrages her sense of beauty, her feeling for justice, her habits, her traditions, her hopes, there are such completely incompatible natures, but why does that upset her so much?[82]

He recognizes that the discomfort he experiences cannot be compared to the suffering she endures.

The opening of the story (under three thousand words) seems to be a dialectic between the woman who hates and the man who tolerates this hatred. In that respect, it seems anomalous for Kafka. But he soon shifts, and it becomes more characteristic. After several more passages about her vengefulness, her distaste for him, her torment at the sight of him, the narrator changes direction from her to himself. He structures her dislike of him into a more generalized distaste, in which public opinion might rise up against him, even crush him. When he considers whether he can escape this hatred, he enters the world of Joseph K., in *Der Prozess:* not as "the trial," but as a process, a proceeding, a state of mind that becomes a condition. "Public opinion would never find me so infinitely objectionable, even under its most powerful magnifying glass. I am not so altogether useless a creature as she thinks; I don't want to boast and especially not in this connection; but if I am not conspicuous for specially useful qualities, I am certainly not conspicuous for the lack of them."[83]

As the pivot of the story shifts, the narrator thinks how he looks to others, since he appears so tormentingly unpopular to the little woman. Now, all eyes are upon him, not only hers, and he must defend himself against others' attacks, or potential attacks. He fears he may have to transform himself before the world intervenes and condemns him, for whatever it is that the woman has condemned him for. He recognizes that condemnation of him is fundamental, so that even his removal, by suicide, would not alleviate it: "If she heard that I had committed suicide she would fall into transports of rage."[84] A friend counsels him to go away, advice the narrator rejects as missing the point of the affair; since the woman's hatred would remain and reside in the narrator's memory, relocation would solve nothing. Her dislike has become not simply a particularized confrontation, but an experience that transcends the woman and her tenant. It is an event *that must be explained,* as it will be necessary to account for the mouse's voice, the ape's wisdom, the mole's anxiety, and the like. Except to reinforce the narrator's resolution to stay the course and not let her hostility affect his behavior, advice is useless. His resolution is to remain himself, even while all temptations are to change, so as to lighten the burden of her hatred.

The situation is a real "case," like Joseph K.'s, or in more miniature terms, like K.'s futile quest in *The Castle.* The development of the affair does not lead to new insights but to new expectations and assumptions in the narrator; everything is internalized now, from the landlady to him. The tenant once wondered if there would be a "decisive crisis" that would somehow bring everything to a head; but he realizes there are no such decisive moments, and the world has no time to notice such matters. Yet he does fear public opinion, even while he feels such a situation is "beyond its competence." He says that "I certainly won't escape unharmed, but on the other hand people are bound to take into account that I am not unknown to the public, that I have lived for long in the full light of publicity, trustingly and trustworthily."[85] He is desperately seeking some foothold in the world by which he can sustain her unwavering hostility; and yet even as he builds his case, he knows that "a man simply cannot endure being a continual target for someone spiteful, even when he knows well enough that the spite is gratuitous." The target grows uneasy, and, even when he knows none will be forthcoming, he still looks for final decisions. What was in youth an easier expectation becomes in age a different matter. All he can do is continue to live his own life, "untroubled by the world, even with all the outbursts of the woman."[86]

Despite the paranoia the story generates (which is intensified in "The Burrow") there is a good deal of wit in Kafka's description of the woman as slim and tightly laced, with sudden quick movements that characterize her presentation of herself. There is also wit in Kafka's assumption that her eyes will become the eyes of the world — that once he has become the object of her scorn, everyone else is possibly going to follow. Despite the heavy psychological baggage, the story is light, almost amusing.

In this respect, it is quite different from "Der Bau," or "The Burrow." This is one of Kafka's most compelling works, and it is "heavy" in that it portends catastrophe or apocalypse. Even the title suggests heaviness. Like *The Castle*, with its ambiguous German title, "Der Bau" can signify either "burrow" or "building," a location downward or upward; or, in another sense, of someone building downward instead of upward — that is, an underground building. As a burrow, it has multiple meanings depending on the animal involved, such as a burrow for a rabbit, a holt for an otter, or a fortress for a mole — the English title "The Burrow" loses the multiple possibilities of the word. In addition, the title's meaning of a fortress suggests something quite different from a burrow, which neutrally indicates a hole or tunnel that a small animal inhabits.

Kafka is after large themes in this story, and yet an effort to pin down its meaning will lead to confusion and ambiguities. One must read this story intertextually — that is, in connection with other pieces in Kafka's oeuvre that intersect with and reinforce its themes. While this late story seems, biographically, to be of this time (winter 1923) and place (Berlin, a small apartment, a restricted life), it is hardly limited to that. Like "A Hunger Artist," it is a culmination.

The burrow the mole creates has qualities of the artistic product or artifact. Since its qualities go beyond those of merely a place to live and sleep in, it suggests dimensions of a work that requires technique, tone, voice. In its symbolic shaping, it poses the dilemma for the artist: how he or she can make something so tight that it both keeps everything else out and keeps whatever it is, in, while at the same time being accessible. The burrow, for Kafka's mole, must be unique, so that even its entrances, tunnels, and exits cannot be easily spotted. The marks of its creation must not be discernible. The burrow is also a metonymy of the artist-writer: what is his, as distinguished from what others have access to; what he must protect himself against, as much as what he has created, maintained, identified. He must always hover in and around his work to protect it from imitators, invaders, hostile takeover artists. He must consider how much he can give away of his gift before it dwindles to nothing and he is fully exposed to his enemies.

In still another respect, we get the sense of the embattled Jew. Here he has found what seems to be his fortress, and yet at any moment some enemy, having discovered a hitherto unknown entrance, might be at or near his door. The Jew must, traditionally, remain on guard, think ahead, plan his scenarios with great skill, in order to compensate for his vulnerability. By 1923, in Berlin, after his experience with Prague, Kafka knew the Jews' position was not very safe. As Jews became the scapegoat for the humiliating terms of the peace treaty, for the level of joblessness, for the inflationary spiral that made money meaningless, Berlin anti-Semitism was reaching new levels.

But Kafka does not suggest that Jews should merely sequester themselves, on the assumption that if they stay out of sight, things will blow over. He knows they will not, that Jews will pay for whatever historical errors the Germans make. His mole is not merely hidden away; he strikes back. He goes deeper and deeper into the ground, where no one can find him, or where he can confuse his enemies. It is Jewish guile that Kafka celebrates, not Jewish retreat or withdrawal. It is the art of the mole he finds exciting, even when that art is accompanied by fear. The mole is constantly planning strategy: where he can retreat, what areas will be safe, whether his castle keep is secure, and if not, he has in mind other lines of defense, other plans for withdrawal. The mole never has the idea of placing himself at the enemy's mercy. He must find ways to circumvent an enemy that appears to have all the entrances covered, all the exits blocked.

Even as Kafka attempted to transcend his own "hole" in order to create a more generalized experience, this story had considerable significance for him. There is a good deal here of one of his favorite protagonists and situations, Robinson Crusoe on his island, finally alone, fully dependent on his wits to survive. Crusoe seeks psychological reinforcement from his cave full of stores, the packed shelves of his self-created grocery store; in material goods, he finds salvation. What he has achieved is a castle keep, a fastness or resource that almost guarantees his survival. This stronghold or treasure trove is indispensable to his sanity; and for Kafka's mole, a comparable stronghold or fortress is indispensable. Since the mole is as materially oriented as Crusoe and as anxious about being invaded, Kafka can join the two experiences as archetypal, for the materialist and for the artist.

"The place is so spacious," the mole gloats, "that food for half a year scarcely fills it. Consequently I can divide up my stores, walk about among them, play with them, enjoy their plenty and their various smells, and reckon up exactly how much they represent."[87] As for Crusoe, foodstuffs in bulk represent security, although food in individual portions was always perilous for Kafka. Yet the mole's satisfaction at the bulk he observes is undercut by his fear that he may be overrun, and that all his stores will prove unavailing. The materialism of the mole can never prove to be an assurance of safety, for the very nature of stores and bulk is that they can be seized. Kafka is emptying Crusoe to subvert his materialism, and yet he is, in part, beguiled by that materialism, which provides at least temporary satisfaction. The goal, ultimately, is survival: how to outlast one's enemies; and if food is to be a weapon in that quest, then food it must be. Kafka was no stranger to irony.*

In another respect, the building up of stores, the concentration of stuffs, is the artist's accumulation of works, his own treasure trove. The difference is that the artist cannot lose everything, whereas the mole can never be certain if his acquisitions are secure. Yet artist and mole share several conditions in common. For the mole, as for the artist, there is that "still center." "But the most beautiful thing about my burrow is the stillness. . . . For hours I can stroll through my passages and hear nothing except the rustling of some little creature, which I immediately reduce to silence between my jaws."[88] The silence, however potentially threatened, creates the kind of still moment that Kafka sought, the kind of moment intrinsic to all creation. In its earthly manifestations, it is akin to Eden. The entire burrow, as Kafka describes it, has qualities of an earthly paradise, obviously a womblike place. "Every hundred yards I have widened the passage into little round cells; there I can curl myself up in comfort and lie warm. There I sleep the sweet sleep of tranquility, of satisfied desire, of achieved ambition; for I possess a house."

Curled up, fetuslike, the mole has entered another temporal and spatial zone, the ahistorical timelessness and spacelessness of a paradise. But we would be mistaken to see this as precisely Kafka's quest,

---

*We should not forget that in Berlin food was extremely scarce, people were starving, and Kafka and Dora were getting by on food packages from Prague.

although the desire for deathly stillness, as well as for a place of his own, seems congruent with his own needs. Kafka, however, did not retreat; he did not surrender to fetal bliss. He remained outside struggling to put words on paper, battling to continue his life in the outer world so as to accomplish his writing.

Yet that mixture of safety and fear, of seclusion and anxiety, while it seems a form of paranoia, is also the artist's fear of interruption, his anxiety that at any given time something will interfere with his work.* While concerned, the mole continues to build, in an extension of the land-surveyor, K., of *The Castle,* and as more than surveyor, as an architect of underground passages. He creates his own city, something akin to Kafka's "pit of Babel." We recall that the German word *bau* involves both building and burrow, both upward movement and downward activity. The mole's art is seen in the complexity of his labyrinth. He is constantly involved with revisions of his original plan: "My constant preoccupation with defensive measures involves a frequent alteration or modification, though within narrow limits, of my views on how the building can best be organized for that end."[89] He worries he has only one storeroom, but he nevertheless exults in his artwork, what he calls an "idle *tour de force.*" Like the artist, he worries whether his final work is perfect, or whether it is flimsy, full of unavoidable defects, somehow assailable. While for the artist it is only his reputation at stake, for the mole it is life itself: his very existence depends on the perfection of his art. Here, in this equation, we observe Kafka's blending of life and art into one statement.

The mole's attitude toward his artwork, his burrow, parallels Kafka's instructions to Max Brod to burn his manuscripts and letters. The mole, he says, finds "riotous satisfaction there in a labyrinthine burrow which at the time seemed to me the crown of all burrows, but which I judge today, perhaps with more justice, to be too much of an idle *tour de force,* not really worthy of the rest of the burrow, and though perhaps theoretically brilliant . . . is in reality a flimsy piece of jugglery that would hardly withstand a serious attack or the struggles of an enemy fighting for his life."[90] He wonders if he should reconstruct this part of his burrow, but senses he will keep postponing it and it will remain as it is. This is, apparently, the absolutist artist seeking the perfect combination of materials and purpose, but falling short and considering whether to destroy his work, revise it, or let it go as is. In this, there is the inevitable disappointment with anything manmade, because it falls short of what might be divine perfection. Its defects, however, lie not in the object itself, but in the planning and execution, areas where the artist is acutely involved.

---

*This anxiety is surely linked to Kafka's masochism, his submission to privations, and his willingness to embrace sacrifice, even shame and humiliations. (See Theodor Reik, "Masochism in Modern Man," in *Of Love and Lust* [New York: Noonday, 1963], for this view of masochism.)

But Kafka's search for meaning in the labyrinth goes further than the artist seeking the perfect form for his visions. It goes further than a portrayal of the alienated, deracinated, refugee-like Jew seeking protection against his enemies, a protection he can only hope to achieve by going underground. There is, running through all this, a strong sexual component, all intermixed with Kafka's typically ambivalent attitudes toward the human body and toward sex. He had, we know, for the first time moved in with a young woman, and was living with her as if married; and she was attractive, half his age, and apparently eager to meet his needs.

For such a man in such a situation, the sexual dimensions of this are torturous. Although we must assume his physical condition forbade any sexual consummation with Dora, we must not assume Kafka gave up all sexual fantasies, and "The Burrow" is one such fantasy. In schematic terms, it is the "way in" and the "way out," and it is, as a tubelike accommodation, both the source of great pleasure and the source of considerable anxiety and fear. It is, in other words, like sex in Kafka's perception and experience of it. He worries particularly about the labyrinth leading up to the door of his burrow. He dreams of restructuring it, transforming it. That labyrinth is an entrance, as well as an exit, if he needs it. And he fears that once someone gets in, he may be trapped; or in trying to get out, he may be blocked. The sexual potentialities are enormous. With entrances his greatest fear, he must hold on to his castle keep — impregnate it with himself — and make certain no one else can penetrate to his fastness. It was not that he doubted Dora's fidelity, but that he doubted his own ability to fulfill his expected role. He feared penetrating as much as being penetrated.

The mole's hesitation about what to do, whether to remain, whether to rebuild are all hesitations associated with sexual fantasy, sexual performance, sexual doubts and fears. "Also I am not permanently doomed to this free life, for I know that my term is measured, that I do not have to hunt here forever, and that when I am weary of this life and wish to leave it, Someone, whose invitation I shall not be able to withstand, will, so to speak, summon me to him."[91] His "sexual fear," such as it is, must be accompanied by other fears, and when he becomes voyeuristic in his response, he keeps eternal vigil over himself and his works. This "free life" is both trap and refuge, in the way Kafka may have evaluated his life with Dora in Berlin: she as refuge, but Berlin as trap. In order to reshape his life and assert his independence, he had become a stranger in Berlin instead of in Prague; and while the rewards of a "free life" were evident, they also involved a loss of identity. Just as Berlin really had no significance for Kafka, despite Dora's accommodation, so the mole feels "doomed" by a life that appears to offer security and warmth.

The need for vigilance overrides all else, and eternal vigilance is another name for voyeurism; except that, here, he is the subject as well as the object of it: voyeurism that passes into narcissism. Kafka has caught the circuitry of the artistic process; it is so intense he must watch himself sleeping and experience the simultaneous joy of slumbering and keeping vigilant over himself. "I am privileged, as it were, not only to dream about the spectres of the night in all the helplessness and blind trust of sleep, but also at the same time to confront them in actuality with the calm judgment of the fully awake."[92] Watchfulness is all. "Probably it is actually better to hazard the risks of dense traffic whose very impetus carries it past, than to be delivered in complete solitude to the first persistently searching intruder."

As we engage ourselves with what is apparently a tale of Kafka's innermost life, we see not capitulation to fears, sexual or otherwise, or to paranoia, real or imagined, but quite the contrary: the struggle to fight through to some understanding of his situation. It is altogether incorrect to read these stories, from "The Metamorphosis" on, as examples of defeatism or withdrawal into nonentity status. Kafka has, in fact, located the enemy in that post-Freudian world, and the enemy is anxiety, uncertainty, fear. By locating them, he has surveyed the ground on which one must fight one's life battles, not to succumb but to pull through, or at least achieve a balance. Kafka's so-called defeatism rarely involves meek surrender; quite differently, he insists on challenging the specters on the very ground he has laid out, and while he may lose, the battle is, apparently, the main thing.

"The Burrow" is not a tale of a sick, prematurely aging man confronting death, but a story of how such a man has refused to succumb when confronted with all the circumstances that suggest surrender. Kafka was rarely more Nietzschean than he was now, facing down the demons Nietzsche had said were part of that "other" taken from us by civilization. Kafka reintroduces the "other" into life, not to show man as victorious over it, but to reveal, like Nietzsche, that one could transform oneself in struggling with it. For Nietzsche — and here we see clear parallels with Kafka — man is something that must be overcome. Any act of suicide, display of suffering, or manifestation of disease was a form of dying which led to transformation, part of a process through which man could save himself. Kafka's hatred of civilized, modern man, that rational Western European Jew he so often inveighed against, made him fear he might be society's "last man": that individual who lives only to survive and who sacrifices everything meaningful in order to rise to the top of the bottle in which he is contained. For him as for Nietzsche, the "unconscious" must be allowed to express itself, and not to be suppressed because it is too fearful. Neither Nietzsche as a pre-Freudian, nor Kafka as a post-Freudian needed Freud to know about the unconscious. One must, the philosopher warned, live to the moment as "if it would eternally recur," that confrontation with fate that Nietzsche called *amor fati*. From that, the superior man will emerge;

for to embrace the eternal recurrence opens one to the possibility of becoming an Overman.

Kafka did not share Nietzsche's disgust for the weak and pitiful, but he did understand that man must comprehend will and impose it either through himself or through his art. We recognize that Kafka's insistence on writing was not merely a need to leave a record, or to express himself; it was nothing less than a need to survive what would otherwise have pulled him under. Kafka was never free of the suspicion that fate or destiny, or what Nietzsche called "the greatest weight" (*"das grösste Schwergewicht"*), had to be countered by another form of energy. Kafka's attack on the rational Jew, rootless, with nothing to hang on to but his mind, made him realize that energies lost from primitive life left him unprotected. Zarathustra warns, as if speaking directly to Kafka, "You must wish to consume yourself in your own flames: how could you wish to become new unless you had first become ashes!" He adds, "Die at the right time," for "he that consummates his life dies his death victoriously, surrounded by those who hope and promise."[93] Such individuals do not permit themselves to be eaten, even when they taste best; they allow themselves to ripen at their own pace and even to rot when they are ready. Such metaphors of food, of hunger, of eating and being eaten connect nourishment to death, and nowhere more than here do we see Kafka's affiliation.

Virtually all of Kafka's later work falls into the vein of Nietzschean epistemology and rebellion. What set Kafka and his father apart from one another so radically was not the son's weakness, which is what he portrayed in stories, letters, and diaries, but his strength. What Hermann could not tolerate was Kafka's rebelliousness and his refusal to defer to parental authority in areas where it counted. While seeming to signal retreat beyond the reach of Hermann or anyone else (except perhaps Dora and Ottla), "The Burrow" was actually the final battleground of resistance. Kafka had gone "underground" in the sense that those who resist a despicable authority speak of going underground, which is to say, joining the resistance.

Kafka through his mole then raises a considerable philosophical problem, equivalent to whether a tree falling in the forest makes a noise if no one hears it fall. The mole wonders if his enemies can have any "proper awareness" of him if he is not in his burrow; they may, he senses, have a "certain awareness," but not full awareness. He then wonders, along these lines, if he is the one watching over his sleep, or whether he is sleeping while his enemies and destroyers watch. This is, of course, the dilemma of the artist, one posed most prominently, as we have seen, by Thomas Mann in "Tonio Kröger." The mole's fallback position is a paranoia that does not permit him to descend from the entrance, for then he will not know what is occurring behind his back at the door after it is fastened.

The burrow becomes a place of such complex ambiguities that the mole cannot bear the tension. While it appears to provide safety, it means loss of freedom; while it seems to be a refuge, it can also be a perilous trap; while it may be Eden, it is, when anxiety attacks come, hellish and nightmarish. "I almost screw myself to the point of deciding to emigrate to distant parts and take up my old comfortless life again, which had no security whatever, but was one indiscriminate succession of perils, yet in consequence prevented one from perceiving and fearing particular perils, as I am constantly reminded by comparing my secure burrow with ordinary life."[94] This is a typical Kafkan "life sentence," winding around every aspect of his consciousness: his awareness of what constitutes individual freedom, and what leads to the loss of that freedom as soon as one hopes to express or enjoy it.

Every effort at liberation or individualization involves a dialectic with countervailing attempts to prevent disengagement from the general terror of mankind. All efforts at salvation are eventually doomed by the way the world works, and the mole in his burrow, like Kafka in Berlin, has only the semblance of freedom. Like those dwellers in Plato's cave, he is, in this allegory of what is real and what unreal, caught by reflections of freedom. He can no more get close to freedom or liberation than K. can to an understanding of the law in *The Trial*. Whatever motivates the individual is counterbalanced by the will of the world; and Kafka here departs from Nietzschean "will" by reverting to Schopenhauerian will, that force that is too great for the individual to overcome except through art itself.

The mole throws himself into a thorn bush as a "punishment for some sin I do not know of." He senses real danger outside, and while it may be only some innocent little creature, it could be a little beast that, unknowingly, has become the "leader of all the world against me."[95] The mole begins to think of transformation as a form of survival: what if he became the enemy spying out a suitable chance for breaking in, what if he had someone to keep watch, what if he became this or that! Kafka has moved the mole to the edge of peril, and there the mole begins an accounting of what can be his, what is denied him, what possible changes he can look forward to. Yet even as he does this, he resents any intrusion, even from a confidante, on what he has built. "I built it for myself, not for visitors."[96] A trusted companion falls into the same problems as all the rest: he or she provides some peace of mind, but becomes an invader of his work and his privacy.

What remains now, with all these checks and balances dismissed, is the perfect burrow: the dream of Eden, the Earthly Paradise, the privileged moment when everything falls into place. That recognition accompanies his knowledge that he can trust only himself and his burrow. He may chide himself for not having built his burrow more securely, but he also knows that whatever he had done he would find it problematic and unavailing. He can only come back to what he has. Reality beckons. "Now the truth of the matter . . . is that in reality the burrow does provide a considerable degree of security, but by no means enough, for is one free from anxieties inside it?" He also recognizes that "these anxieties are different from ordinary ones, prouder, richer in content, often long repressed, but in their destructive effects they are perhaps much the same as the anxieties that existence in the outer world gives rise to."[97] He knows he is both locked in and locked out, what becomes a general condition. The paradisiacal place is, as it were, decentered, made problematic. It is not possible for any kind of security. Even though he clawed and wrested his castle from the refractory soil himself, he perceives that some mortal enemy can steal it away.

With this, we gain another insight into why Kafka asked Brod to burn his manuscripts and letters after his death. Desire for perfection is a clue, but an equally likely reason is that Kafka saw that by burning he could hold on to what he had written. If the cache of manuscripts were his castle keep, his treasure trove, then it remained forever his, and only his, once it was destroyed. Kafka had always been wary of disseminating his work — his correspondence with Kurt Wolff suggests his hesitancy — and now he saw a way of keeping it all for himself, without the contamination of others' eyes or opinions. The mole's realization that the sole way to protect his burrow is, finally, to destroy it, is part of Kafka's recognition that he needed to protect himself against intruders by destroying whatever was connected to him. This is, incidentally, not too far removed from the would-be suicide, who gives away or destroys his possessions as a means of "cleansing" himself in preparation for the final departure. Kafka's request to Brod has within it something of that desire for a complete and final break: to become invisible to the world as a form of revenge for what it has done to one.

The mole, however, is not quite prepared to succumb, although anxieties undermine his every moment. Besides, the burrow can still restore him.

> It is a new world, endowing me with new powers. . . . I have returned from a journey dog-tired with my wanderings, but the sight of the old house, the thought of all the things that are waiting to be done, the necessity at least to cast a glance at all the rooms, but above all to make my way immediately to the Castle Keep; all this transforms my fatigue into ardent zeal; it is as though at the moment when I set foot in the burrow I had wakened from a long and profound sleep.[98]

This fits Kafka's repeated assertions he felt secure only when anchored to his desk. The mole makes it clear he must not allow any blockage of passages to his castle keep: he must not permit interference with the most significant part of his existence. When he returns to his treasure trove, he "trembles" and describes his return as if to a beloved one. His terms are caressing and romantic: "You belong to me, I to you, we are united; what can harm us?" He embraces his inner castle, as though he had exchanged a wife or sweetheart for it. If we extend this idea, Kafka's lengthy letters to Felice and to Milena and others all indicate strongly that his first passion was his desk, that it was a more than sufficient substitute for what he lost in human relationships. As a memory come alive, he had a priority no woman could fill; and the mole here extends that argument to include the castle keep as a symbol of eternal fidelity. True marriage lies here.

What further entangles Kafka directly in the story is the presence or expectation of noise. Kafka here transfers his long history of sensitivity to noise to the mole's fear of noise as a harbinger of an intruder. The very uniformity of noise disturbs the animal, and as his anxiety and paranoia increase, he senses it may be two noises. All noises suggest "they" are after him. "I know all this, yet that they should have dared to approach the very castle keep itself is incomprehensible to me and fills me with agitation and confuses the faculties which I need so urgently for the work before me."[99] Actual noise must also compete with "potential noise," or the expectation of it, which itself builds into actual noise. He fears crowds of little beasts who smell his stores; he senses they are burrowing in all the passages, not bypassing them. He wishes he had followed a plan, hatched when younger, to isolate from the surroundings his castle keep with all its stores. Then he could have protected it and, at the same time, tempted himself with knowing it was there, close to his body, even when he didn't actually see it. Then, also, instead of lying fearfully in the keep, he could lie outside it, guarding it from invaders.

The noise, he fears, may be of some animal unknown to him. He wonders why he has never seen any of the breed. The intruders may, in fact, be tiny creatures, smaller even than the mice Kafka has written about. Since the noise creates such fear and suspicion, he is tempted to ignore it, but he also knows he must discover the worst. Parallels here are not only to the artist, who must peek around his artwork to see what others think of it, but to the Jew, who while choosing to remain hidden must occasionally assess what his situation is and confront the worst. Kafka's representation of the mole's dilemma spreads out to more general terms. The truth, he knows, will bring him "either peace or despair, but whether the one or the other, it will be beyond doubt or question."[100] In this way, he is prepared to pursue his own doom. Yet an unfamiliar noise, a "faint whistling," still throws him into complete confusion. He wants to consider it a mere nothing, but it disturbs him to the core. He feels he should start digging stubbornly, simply for the sake of clarification.

The mole is never permitted to settle in. Whatever plans he has for himself, he must alter to fit rapidly changing circumstances. "Everything seems difficult, I am too distracted, every now and then, in the middle of my work, I press my ear to the wall and listen."[101] The unfamiliar sounds make him think of starting over, if only he had the vigor of youth. He is confused as to what he had in mind with his original plan, which now seems shoddy and unsafe. "I can find no slightest trace of reason in what had seemed so reasonable." He dismisses his entire youth as a time in which he missed his opportunity; and now he is stuck with what he had wrought. He must settle for lulling himself, since there is no possibility he can alter what exists. He has had enough of discoveries; he will let everything slide, if only he can quiet the conflict going on within him.

Even as he seeks peace, he knows everything has changed. The only safe place is now under the moss covering his burrow, where he can hear nothing, or can convince himself there is no noise. What was once a womb is now a tomblike place. "A complete reversal of things in the burrow; what was once the place of danger has become a place of tranquility, while the Castle Keep has been plunged into the melee of the world and all its perils. Still worse, even here there is no peace in reality . . . silent or vociferous, danger lies in ambush as before above the moss, but I have grown insensitive to it."[102] He must assume there is some great beast waiting to devour him: death? sexual threat? women? personal freedom itself? The beast is everywhere. Possibly, "the beast is not making for me, seeing that the noise never changes; more likely it has a plan in view whose purpose I cannot decipher; I merely assume that the beast — and I make no claim whatever that it knows of my existence — is encircling me."

With these lines, we observe the mole beginning to crack under the strain, as he senses the beast everywhere. He hears an indrawing of breath, which he cannot comprehend, thinking that the beast pauses only for an intake of breath. Breath now becomes a matter of life and death, as it did for Kafka, with his coughing, difficulty in breathing, and near strangulation when the disease began to paralyze his larynx. The mole fears this imaginary or actual beast as a perpetual motion machine, which is now the very opposite of himself, paralyzed as he is by the external disturbance. The mole says he could not have foreseen such an opponent, that his enemy has taken a shape even his nightmares could not have envisioned. The mole can only blame himself, since by being the owner of "this great vulnerable edifice" he has made himself defenseless against any serious attack. "The joy of possessing it has spoilt me, the vulnerability of the burrow has made me vulnerable; any wound to it hurts me as [if] I myself were hit."[103] The analogy with the artist and his works is clear. Had he not written at all, Kafka suggests, he would not be so vulnerable, but since he has displayed himself, there are those eager to attack what he has created. All the more reason to destroy the work, or himself.

The mole feels he has wasted his time, a constant fear. In reference to his failure to create his shelter differently, the mole says, "I have been as thoughtless as a child. I have passed my manhood's years in childish games, I have done nothing but play, even with the thought of danger."[104] The mole is reviewing his life, as he senses its close, whether in actuality or in his nightmarish imagination, in the throes of a breakdown. Assuming matters would work out by themselves, he has avoided the major issues. When youthful, he might not have minded seeing his opponent, for he could have handled it. Now all his defenses are gone. In his maturity, he does not enjoy superior wisdom; anxiety is making him fragment. An "old architect" or "maker," he does not have even the benefits of age. He knows noise now signifies doom, not merely disturbance; it foreshadows the death rattle. He longs for an understanding with the beast, although he knows that is not possible. Obsessed, he listens at ten places at random. "I go once more the long road to the Castle Keep, all my surroundings seem filled with agitation, seem to be looking at me, and then look away again so as not to annoy me."

He is nostalgic for the old days, which, although unpleasant, were relatively more secure than now. He longs for the time when he could enjoy his food, or, in Kafka's case, write. He is fixated on unriddling the beast's plan; but when he dreams, lying on his heap of earth, all he can think of is his failure to understand anything. If only he could return to Eden, when his burrow was an ultimate protection! If we extend this idea, we can suggest that Kafka was looking back on the parental apartment as a true refuge: at least he could write there, despite his hostilities, hatreds, and inability to accommodate himself to their way of life. "If I have peace, and danger does not immediately threaten me, I am still quite fit for all sorts of hard work."[105] Perhaps the beast will give up the idea of extending its own burrow in his direction. Perhaps the beast has never heard of him. He seeks openings that will permit peace. "But all remained unchanged."

The story points in nearly every direction of Kafka's life, both inner and outer. It touches upon deep questions of his work and its relationship to him, as well as to his position as a Jew in a Europe that was making "strange noises." There is also a religious component, for the godless mole has put all his hope in his own works, in his own doing; and yet the world does not permit this, it insists on other recognitions. It poses the question of the degree to which the individual can isolate himself, in the hope of fulfilling some kind of self-fulfillment, with disregard of the world and its makeup. While this can be social and political as well as religious, the question suggests that Kafka was using the story to question everything about himself and his life, and was doing so in a more direct way than he had before. While not forsaking the allegory of the animal or insect, Kafka was cutting the allegory finer, as it were, so as to define himself within the tale. Although "The Metamorphosis," "The Judgment," and "A Hunger Artist" were clearly autobiographical, they came at times when Kafka's life was relatively hopeful. But he wrote "The Burrow" when everything was entrances and exits, when there was little center left.

Since Kafka felt himself to be even more enclosed and cut off than ever, he used his fiction of a mole and his burrow as a means of probing what remained, what he could settle for, what he had to fight for. It is clear he needed ground on which to continue the struggle, even as he discovered that ground shrinking under him, even as he went underground, and then found that threatened too. As more and more was taken from him, Kafka needed to retreat, and the inevitable question was what was left. "The Burrow" in this respect became a kind of land-surveying job: the mole carefully measuring what was his, what was not — only to discover that sharp demarcations of mine and yours no longer existed, not for the mole and certainly not for the man writing. Kafka knew he had to dig in, had to reshape himself, had to seek new identities, but time was getting short for salvation, even for expressions of guilt and suffering. What is remarkable is that with this predicament he had caught not only himself but an era.

By the time Kafka wrote "The Burrow" he and Dora Dymant were living at Grünewaldstrasse 13, Berlin-Steglitz, having moved on November 15.* By now, his remarks on Berlin were not happy ones; he foresaw the troubles to come, which had, in fact, already begun. To his sister Valli (November 1923), he said that when asked how he is the Berliner says, "Rotten, times the index number."[106] The index number was the means by which the inflated mark could be converted to the pre-inflation mark. By this time, 1 trillion marks equaled one U.S. dollar, making German marks in effect useless as currency. Kafka foresees what this will mean, when he writes Brod (on November 5) that there are eruptions and there is no chance of temporary peace developing into real peace. Yet even as he prophesies that the worst is yet to come, he can be familial, asking Valli to thank her daughters, Marianne and Lotte, for their letters, and he responds with remarks about them as individuals.

Twice a week Kafka attended the Lehranstalt für die Wissenschaft des Judentums, or the Educational Establishment (or Academy) for Jewish (or Hebrew) Studies, where he studied the Talmud. At about the

---

*The hostility manifested by the landlady in "A Little Woman" was not Kafkan paranoia but real. Kafka and Dora were forced to move in mid-November (he tells Valli of giving notice). Very possibly the landlady's hostility was grounded on notions of morality, since Kafka and Dora were living together unmarried, although Berlin at this time was hardly the place for moral issues to arise. Their new quarters consisted of two rooms in the house of Dr. Rethburg, a female doctor. Dora, of course, did all the physical moving.

time Dora reported he wrote "The Burrow" in a one-night sitting, he
ordered a list of books from Kurt Wolff, who had generously offered
Kafka whatever he wanted in the elegant Stundenbücher editions.
Kafka was overjoyed and asked for, among other things, Hölderlin's poetry, books on Japanese woodcuts, Chinese landscapes, and Chinese
gods, Georg Simmel's study of Rembrandt, Gaugin's *Before and After*
(all of these art books); Chamisso's famous collection of stories, including the one on Schlemihl, Gottfried August Bürger's *Münchhausen*,
Knut Hamsun's novel *Under the Autumn*; and five stories of his own,
"The Stoker," *Meditation*, "The Metamorphosis," *The Country Doctor*, and "In the Penal Colony."

If, as Dora asserted, Kafka did indeed write "The Burrow" so rapidly, in one sitting, then we may perhaps consider the story complete,
or as complete as he wished to make it. Yet several commentators have
suggested that, if pages are missing, then it was possible some final action did occur: such as the actual invasion of the burrow, or else the
mole's complete breakdown and loss of ability to function, or even an
apocalyptic end, with the mole destroyed by the digging beast or beasts.
But since so much of the story lies in the ambiguity surrounding the
validity of the mole's fears, that uncertain ending, leaving him suspended between life and death, seems fitting as it is. Kafka has made his
point. Dora further indicated that this kind of writing, about parents,
family, home, and the rest, severely depressed Kafka. But while she reports his sadness, his loss of appetite, and his uneasiness, she misses
almost entirely that his response was part of the way he created. To activate his imagination, as in this story, which goes so deeply into past
relationships and into memory, he had to relive his personal history, all
part of the suffering and pain he took upon himself in order to justify
his kind of writing. Sensitive and insightful as she was, Dora seems to
have missed those components of what some have called masochism
but which was, in actuality, the activating of his imagination in the
only way he could.

This is not to deny his depressions. He had reason enough for those.
Although he knew he suffered from his parents' disapproval of the liai-
son with Dora — immoral from their point of view, and she from a Hasidic, Eastern European background to boot — he was dependent on
them for regular checks. Given Berlin's inflation, Kafka's pension
money and savings meant almost nothing; and even when currency reform was introduced, at about the time he and Dora had moved, he still
depended on his parents' aid. To Klopstock, he indicates that what he
wrote in "The Burrow" about the mole fits himself quite well: "There
are abysses into which I sink without even noticing, only as best to
creep up again after a long time." We recall the end of the story: "But
all remained unchanged."[107] He does indicate that the Academy for
Jewish Studies was like a refuge in "wild and woolly Berlin and in the

wild and woolly regions of the mind." Hebrew and Talmudic studies gave Kafka an anchor, but those who see him as moving toward some religious resolution fail to perceive that his Hebrew studies were not religious. They were part of a desire to establish some connection to a people; not to God, but to people, a community of interests, even a way of life.

Strikingly, Kafka failed to be in regular consultation with a doctor and denied himself medical treatment. Except for one visit from a doctor, mentioned to Brod, in mid-January, he let the disease take its course. This was in the face of periodic chills, fever, and general lethargy, all characteristic of a developing tubercular condition. Part of it was the medical cost, which he says was excessive, although fortunately Dora argued it down to half, from 160 crowns to 80 a visit.* He says he fears sickness, since even a second-class bed in the Jewish Hospital costs 64 crowns a day, and that only paid for bed and board, apparently not for doctors or other services. Since cooking facilities were limited to a two-burner, they could not even eat well, and when fuel was lacking Dora had to heat their meals with candle power. Heat itself was missing, and the rent, although modest, was becoming more than they could afford.

Kafka and Dora were caught in the same spiral as most Berliners; and yet both had more ample places to return to, if they so decided. Kafka knew he could always return to far more physically comfortable quarters in Prague, with his parents, although he could not hope to reclaim his room with Dora in tow. What is striking is how, in order to maintain his independence, he lived at or below the poverty level, forsaking his class role as lawyer, insurance executive, even writer. Close to financial collapse, he was in every moment living out the mole's dilemma, measuring insecurity against the desire for liberation.

He was also trying to help Emmy Salveter, Brod's friend, with her acting; he says the mysteries of acting are not as arcane to him as the secrets of "larynx-chest-tongue-nose-and-frontal sinus."[108] He complains of his fever, which limits his freedom of action. Rejecting "warm, well-fed Bohemia," he wonders about where they will go next. Schelesen, little better than Prague, was out of the question. "Besides I had warmth and good feeding for forty years, and the result does not tempt me to go on trying them." Like the mole, Kafka rejects the castle keep with its abundant stores for the mossy ground outside, where he somehow feels safer.

He and Dora soon moved to a single room in Zehlendorf, a further downward spiral in their already impecunious scale of living. He sug-

---

*These amounts cannot be translated into contemporary equivalents, since buying power fluctuated so wildly. In absolute terms, the costs were low, but in relation to pensions and other sources of income they were overwhelming for people like Kafka and Dora.

gests to Brod that if he were not so decrepit, Brod could make a drawing of him. "On the left D., say, supporting him; on the right that man, say; some sort of 'scribbling' might stiffen his neck; now if only the ground beneath him were consolidated, the abyss in front of him filled in, the vultures around his head driven away, the storm in the skies above him quieted down — if all that were to happen, then it might be just barely possible to go on for a while."[109] One recalls that terrible story "The Vulture," in which the bird first hacks at the subject's feet and ends up thrusting its beak, like a javelin-thrower, into the subject's mouth, deep into him. Both subject and vulture drown in the outpouring of blood, "which was filling every depth, flooding every shore."[110]

Brod too was sending food parcels. Kafka says they were ashamed to keep them, and then, with typical honesty, says their contents were "not very tempting either."[111] Brod visited also, and the two old friends discussed emigration to Palestine. Despite his daily fever and loss of energy, Kafka suggested that once there, his health miraculously restored, he would be a waiter and Dora a cook. Brod recognized the determination taking place in his friend, and while they amused themselves with such fantasies, Brod also decided he had to do something drastic. But although Brod was becoming sufficiently worried to send for Kafka's Uncle Siegfried, the country doctor whom he had visited often in Triesch, the patient's condition, paradoxically, was excellent preparation for his final long piece of fiction, "Josephine the Singer, or the Mouse Folk."

This piece, which we can date in, probably, March 1924, carries with it Kafka's peculiar mystique, in which failure becomes to some degree a measure of success. "That she [Josephine] is what she is like always, every trifle, every casual incident, every nuisance, a creaking in the parquet, a grinding of teeth, a failure in the lighting incites her to heighten the effectiveness of her song; she believes anyhow that she is singing to deaf ears; there is lack of enthusiasm and applause, but she has long learned not to expect real understanding, as she conceives it."[112] What one writes for resides within; enthusiasm or applause is not the goal, nor can it be achieved. One *writes:* not for the reader, not to be understood or even misunderstood. Kafka himself wrote out of complete honesty about how the world appeared to him, not about how it should be. His fever fantasies and deliriums did not knock him off his imaginative base but apparently reinforced what was already there.

Uncle Siegfried agreed with Brod that Kafka could not go on as at present; yet given the nature of his disease, it would have made little difference where he stayed. Early in March, Kafka told Klopstock that he thought of coming to either Prague or Vienna, although he did not want to re-enter a sanatorium or a boardinghouse. In his final months, he was insisting on independence from all except Dora, and his general suspicion of doctors dictated his desire not to let them get their hands on him. His contempt went beyond their excessive fees. He says that "100.4° has become my daily bread."[113] The fever extended through all the evening and half the night. Yet he recognized his condition, telling Klopstock he felt strong enough while lying down, but as soon as he attempted to walk, the steps "assume the quality of a grandiose enterprise, so that sometimes the thought of peacefully burying myself alive in the sanatorium is not at all so unpleasant." From the flask in which he deposits his sputum each day, he can tell he is not far from a sanatorium fate. "But then again there is fear, for example, of the horrible compulsory eating there."[114] That final line is so significant, for it suggests that Kafka's fear of heavy eating, of food itself, was more powerful than the impulse toward saving life itself. Rather than undergo the regime of sanatorium eating, he would prefer to die: the obsession is shielded by something stronger than the desire for life.

With Brod in Berlin in mid-March (the fourteenth), Kafka had a traveling companion, and they returned together to Prague on the seventeenth. Klopstock, now along with Brod and Dora the most supportive of Kafka's circle, had come all the way to Berlin to help him to the railroad. Dora accompanied them to the train but did not go to Prague at this time. Even in his present condition, Kafka had to think of his parents' reception of her, either a scene or harsh words. By the next month, he was down to 49 kilos (108 pounds) though he was almost six feet tall. Whereas before he had merely been extremely thin or lanky, his appearance was now approaching the cadaverous. Once back in Prague, ensconced in his parents' apartment, Kafka wrote his final fictional work, "Josephine the Singer," an examination in typically allegorical terms of what art is, what an artist is.

Why does Josephine have such a singular hold on her audience? What quality does she have that makes people defer to her talent? She does not, Kafka admits, have much of a singing voice; she does not even pipe well. Yet she creates something that stands out. The real riddle is to solve the question of the enormous influence she has. It is necessary, however, not only to hear but to see her, and by this, Kafka is suggesting the ceremonial or ritualistic element of art. She is a performer, this singing mouse, and she creates a special rapport with her audience. At the same time, she creates something that we admire in her, but not in ourselves. The difference must be art, the element that remains after both performer and spectator die.

The story is an assessment at the end of Kafka's life of what it all means: work, imagination, creativity, the function of art, its context and significance, the relationship of maker to audience. The sick, feeble writer needed a justification, or explanation, and, accordingly, the transformation into "mouse folk" enabled him to see the larger world through smaller eyes. Josephine struggles to clear the ground so that she can practice her singing: "For a long time back, perhaps since the very beginning of her artistic career, Josephine has been fighting for exemption from all daily work on account of her singing; she should be relieved of all responsibility for earning her daily bread and being involved in the general struggle for existence."[115] As an artist, she is responsible, she feels, only to herself and to her calling. She claims that work will weaken her voice, and yet she does work. She seeks "public, unambiguous, permanent recognition of her art. . . . But while almost everything else seems within her reach, this eludes her persistently."

As a final pursuit, and with an eye toward some ultimate meaning for the artist, Kafka through Josephine was seeking the connection between the triviality of work and the exalted state demanded by art. He was after nothing less than the dissociation of self: life in the ordinary world, life in a transcendent state. He has, he recognizes, not made this point clear. No one, perhaps not even Brod, has glimpsed that inner world of mockery, irony, transformation, intensity, and persistence which has characterized his endeavors. He needs, furthermore, the miniaturization of Josephine, the mouse folk metaphor, as a way of withdrawing: he requires a sense of his own physical inferiority in order to stress the absolute nature of craft, found in unlikely places, even in a mouse. The mouse, after all, is only a beeper, a tiny animal with a sqeaking sound that only approximates singing. It is also a rodent, and by using Josephine, Kafka has erased boundaries between humans and other forms of life. What he had started in "The Metamorphosis" at the very beginning of his writing career has now concluded with another version of it. While humanity has nothing but contempt for rodents and vermin, for Kafka they contain the full range of human responses; and those small creatures reveal their own contempt through their ability to transcend their image.

There is still another dimension to this story. Josephine yearns to be a leader; she sees the artist's role as that of entertainer, but also as that of a guide, in the sense that she can join her people through song. Because of her singing, people become devoted to Josephine, and they give her special powers. But it is not unconditional devotion, which is not known among the mouse folk. "Ours are people who love slyness beyond everything, without any malice to be sure, and childish whispering and chatter, innocent, superficial chatter [Vienna? Prague?], to be sure, but people of such kind cannot go in for unconditional devotion. . . . That is what she is fighting against with all the force of her feeble throat."[116] She feels she protects the people, though the people do not protect her; her singing "saves" them. "The menaces that loom over us make us quieter, more humble, more submissive to Josephine's domination."[117] She is, then, a kind of artistic führer in her effort to bring together the leadership she feels she is capable of and a people who remain just outside her domain.

The people actually prefer silence, and if a real singer were to rise up among them, she would not be endured. They only listen to Josephine *because she is not a real singer.* They want only a poseur, whom they can tolerate because she is so poor. Since the people's sensibility and intelligence are lacking, Josephine, with her thin, piping voice, can be accepted. "May Josephine be spared from perceiving that the mere fact of our listening to her is proof that she is no singer. An intuition of it she must have, else why does she so passionately deny that we do listen."[118] Kafka has created his characteristic conundrum or enigma: the artist pipes away but does not believe anyone is listening; the audience for her or him does listen but only because the artist is so poor. And the serious artist? The serious artist is ground between, neither heard nor accommodated.

She sings with "unusual feeling" but then suddenly disappears, deserting her people entirely. Yet the narrator does not regard her disappearance as a significant event. Her singing was only "a small episode in the eternal history of our people," and they will get over her loss. "So perhaps we shall not miss her very much after all, while Josephine, redeemed from the earthly sorrows which to her thinking lay in wait for all chosen spirits, will happily lose herself in the numberless throng of the heroes of our people, and soon, since we are no historians, will rise to the heights of redemption and be forgotten like all her brothers."[119] Josephine and her so-called art pass into history, forgotten, since the mouse folk do not place much value on the past.

What started as some hope for the artist trying to make her impression on her people ends up with Kafka's characteristic gesture that art really makes no difference. The artist is swallowed up, abandoned by her people, even as she leaves them behind. What counts, perhaps, is not the result but the effort, the thin voice that stirs the people for the time being. There is no more. "And be forgotten like all her brothers" is an epitaph Kafka considered for himself, and it, like so much else, helps explain why he wanted his manuscripts burned.

This story was not just Josephine's swan song, it was also Kafka's. The people do not need a savior of their kind; the artist cannot find a meaningful audience; the artwork itself is less than perfect; memory does not carry much of the past. The "hunger artist" hovers in the shadows. Is this, as some have commented, an expression of Kafka's fears about the Jews? In the light of subsequent history, the mouse folk's abandonment of Josephine would seem prophetic; but in context, in the late winter of 1924, the subject seems not to be Jews but the nature of art and the artist in an elusive world. The chief consideration for this man of forty weighing in at 49 kilos was what he had done with *his* life, and how it would be perceived by people who did not care for him or his work. By the time he commented on "Josephine" to Klopstock, Kafka was at the Sanatorium Wiener Wald, in Ortmann, Austria, about forty-five miles southwest of Vienna. Dora had accompanied him there, in early April, and Klopstock would interrupt his medical studies to help nurse him. Kafka did in fact hope to make a little money from the publication of "Josephine," which appeared in the *Prager Presse* (in Berlin) in the Easter issue for April 20, 1924. He also looked to some modest income from the publication of a volume that included "A Hunger Artist," "A Little Woman," and "First Sorrow," which would be issued by Die Schmiede, a new firm in Berlin. This came about through the auspices of Brod.

As Kafka's days dwindled, so did his circle of friends, so that near the end, there remained only Klopstock and Dora, with Brod of course on the edges but also messily involved in his own life. The patient's letters obviously take up medical matters. He mentions an entire regimen of medication: Demophon for coughing (it didn't help), along with Anästesin lozenges and atropine. He intuits it is the larynx that is affected. But everyone in discussing tuberculosis of the larynx "drops into a shy, evasive, glassy-eyed manner of speech."[120] When they do speak, it is doubletalk: "We cannot yet say anything definite," while they know fully of the malignancy. Kafka was not deceiving himself or letting himself be deceived. He says that pneumothorax, the attempt to get rid of air or gas in the pleural cavity, was out of the question for someone in his poor condition, that destiny-filled weight of "49 kilos in my winter clothes" (which brought him close to 100 pounds naked). His ability to speak and eat was affected: the hunger artist had finally developed an ailment that disallowed food. He was transferred to the University Clinic of Professor M. Hajek in Vienna. "It seems my larynx is so swollen that I cannot eat; they must (they say) undertake alcohol injections into the nerve, probably also surgery."[121] He expected to remain in Vienna for several weeks.

Back in March, before heading for the sanatorium in Ortmann, he had suffered a burning sensation in the throat. His voice now manifested itself as squeaks, very close to the piping he had just written about with Josephine. When his old friend from Gymnasium days, Emil Utitz, came to visit, Kafka had no voice. Once in the Wiener Wald sanatorium, he had to adapt to a condition that would never improve. Sanatorium life was terribly depressing, and Kafka cried when a neighbor of his died during the night. As for himself, "Once the fact of tuberculosis of the larynx is accepted," he tells Brod on April 20, "my condition is bearable; for the present I can swallow again."[122] He is grateful for several "attentions" from Werfel, who, while himself taking a very different literary course from his old friend, venerated Kafka.

Brod observed the progress, or rather the deterioration, of his friend, noting in his diary that Kafka was en route from the Wiener Wald sanatorium to Vienna. Kafka's weight had fallen drastically, to less than 96 pounds, and his throat, as the attending nurse told him, looked like "the witch's kitchen." From the University Clinic, Kafka was trans-

ferred, on April 19 or 20, to a sanatorium run by Dr. Hoffmann, in Kierling, in Klosterneuburg, Lower Austria. Klopstock and Dora insisted on
the move when they felt that Dr. Hajek, at the University Clinic, was
not sufficiently responsive to Kafka's condition, and they were further
disturbed by the doctor's handling of Kafka's room assignment (forbidding a single room) and another patient's condition, which led to his
death. As he was passed from hand to hand in the last weeks of his life,
Kafka's lifelong contempt for doctors and for medical treatment was
being borne out. In the background was a minor conflict, of who loved
Kafka more, Brod or Klopstock. The latter was making himself available, and Brod felt he might himself be pushed aside, so he used Werfel
to try to obtain better conditions at Hajek's clinic, while Klopstock offered to give up everything to stand by Kafka in his need. Kafka told the
medical student not to make any "sudden trip" to Vienna, and Dora
carried out the move without help; then Kafka left for Kierling, his fate
sealed.

As the tuberculosis was clearly settling in the larynx, so that talking as well as eating was becoming almost impossible, Kafka scribbled
brief notes to friends and supporters. These so-called conversation
slips, which fell into the possession of Klopstock, were often mere
phrases or half sentences that indicated the drift of his thought, but
they indicate that Kafka's mind, and wit, remained with him to the
end. We must keep in mind that Kafka was dwindling physically down
to nothing, since the disease did not permit any solid food and even liquids were difficult to administer. Klopstock commented that Kafka
was literally starving to death, even as he was correcting proofs of his
volume *A Hunger Artist*. The ironies are so overwhelming they sound
staged. The "slips" are themselves the sole record remaining of Kafka's
thoughts as he equated his own physical condition with that of the
hunger artist whom he had created. Klopstock says his dying friend
cried, with tears rolling down his face, but otherwise Kafka's stoical
self-control continued.

The "slip" that inspired Klopstock's comment was this: "How
many years will you be able to stand it? How long will I be able to stand
your standing it? Now I want to read it. It will excite me too much, perhaps, and yet I must experience it all over again."[123] Also: "Here, now,
with what strength I have am I to write it? They have waited so long to
send me the material." The question is one of re-experiencing, so that
Kafka's imagination, the creation of the hunger artist, becomes congruent with his present experience. But these remarks are also surrounded by others filled with the pain and anguish of his condition. He
hated injections and preferred medicine, although medication in solid
form could not be swallowed. He says his improvement after lozenges
is greater than after injections: it "shows in the fact that the pain,
which also comes after the injection, is duller, as though the wounds

over which the food flows were sealed a little."[124] He fears there is an obstruction, which should be removed before attempts are made to treat his throat with medicines. Pills stick in the mucus "like splinters of glass."[125] He says wittily, "Maybe it's easier to choke over less."[126] But wit gives way to gallows humor: "If it is true — and it seems probable — that the quantity of food I consume at present is insufficient for the body to mend of its own accord, then there's no hope, apart from miracles."[127]

His contempt for hospitals and doctors pokes through, especially his remark about the Vienna clinic, before he went to Kierling, where he speaks of their killing the man beside him by letting him walk around with pneumonia, with a 106-degree temperature. "Wonderful the way all the assistants were sound asleep in their beds at night and only the priest with his acolytes were there."[128] Fever was consuming him — whatever he ate, even yogurt, needed water to get it down and to quench the fever. Yet the wit again: "Even if I really were to recover a little from it all, I certainly wouldn't recover from the narcotics."[129] "Tremendous amount of sputum, easily, and still pain in the morning. In my daze it went through my head that for such quantities and the ease somehow the Nobel Prize."*

According to Klopstock, some of the "slips" were written at a much earlier period, when Kafka returned to Prague from Berlin, and before he left for the Sanatorium Wiener Wald. This was the time when he wrote "Josephine the Singer," in March 1924. Klopstock reports that when Kafka finished the last page of the story, he said to his friend that he had investigated that animal's squeaking at the right time, for his own larynx was beginning to suffer from his disease. Kafka told Klopstock he felt an "odd burning" in his throat whenever he drank certain beverages: the citrus acid in fruit juices created a particular pain. In one of the "slips" Kafka mentions that he didn't drink beer, only fruit juices, preserves, and cider, all of which irritated his throat but were needed for nourishment. Eating for him had become truly Kafkaesque.

Not unusually, many of the "slips" have to do with swallowing, eating, drinking, even swimming, with its association of water and pools, one of Kafka's favorite recreations, now lost to him. "That cannot be, that a dying man drinks."[130] In connection with water and resorts, he dips back deeply into his relationship with Felice Bauer, in a

---

*The mention of the Nobel Prize brings to mind how it eluded most of the great writers of the age: not only Kafka, but also Proust, Joyce, Conrad, Woolf, Lawrence, Rilke, Tolstoy (still alive when the prize was being awarded), and several others. In this case, however, Kafka simply had not published enough during his lifetime; the failure of the Nobel Prize Committee even to notice him can be explained not only by the fact that his work would not appeal to it, but by its paucity. None of his novels, as we know, appeared in his lifetime, although if we wanted to draw a fine point, we could say that on the basis of his few stories, including "The Metamorphosis," a committee really interested in literature, and not literary politics, might have cited him.

reprise of earlier events. "I was to have gone to the Baltic with her once (along with her girl friend), but was ashamed because of my thinness and other anxieties. . . . She was not beautiful, but slender, fine body, which she has kept according to reports (Max's sister, her girl friend)." Then as he fades away, he asks for someone to put his hand on his forehead to give him courage, and he indicates that every limb is as tired as a person. Finally, wearily, he adds, "So the help goes away without helping."

These slips are all from the final months, not merely from the stay at Kierling, where Kafka died. An immediate question arose of Hermann and Julie Kafka's visiting, caught in a letter Kafka wrote them around May 10, not June 2, as Brod has it. He recalls that once they spent some days together peacefully, in Franzensbad, but that goes back a long way; and most other arguments go against a reunion now. He says his father may not be able to come because of passport difficulties, although that seems a kind way of saying he doesn't want him. As for Julie, Kafka is afraid his mother will concentrate too much on him, "will be too dependent on me, and I am still not very pretty, not at all a sight worth seeing."[131] He was in effect skeletal, as his weight began to move toward 90 pounds, and the pain from the "larynx business" was considerable — a shock, he called it. Dora and Klopstock had insisted on other medical support, not trusting old Dr. Hoffmann; and the two new doctors, Beck and Neumann, from the hospital staff, agreed that relief could come only from injections of alcohol into the upper part of the nerve of the larynx. They foresaw a life expectancy of about three months, which was optimistic, and they said Kafka might as well return to Prague, since they could do nothing more substantial except relieve his discomfort. But Dora felt that a return to Prague was equivalent to telling Kafka he was a dead man, and she was not prepared for that, although Kafka seems not to have been deceived.

In his letter of May 19 to his parents, telling them not to come, he says that all the care — good air and food and attention — has not helped recovery; and, in fact, he was worse off than when he was recently in Prague. He does hold out a forlorn hope, in that one specialist, a Dr. Tschiassny, felt confident the larynx was significantly improved, but though Kafka is grateful for his comforting words, he does not really believe him. He repeats that he doesn't want Hermann and Julie present, even though the sanatorium is owned by a "sick old man" and the resident physician is disagreeable; his parents would not provide much relief. Nevertheless, with Klopstock in constant attendance and other young doctors around, he was receiving the best treatment.* Kaf-

---

*Klopstock himself wrote to his own parents that a visit from Julie Kafka "would be terrible for Franz" (*Letters to Ottla*, pp. 120, 121), and thought that taking Kafka home to Prague would be equally terrible. Klopstock felt that his patient, sick as he was, would penetrate everyone's opaque gaze. Writing to Kafka's relatives in Prague, Klopstock gave

ka's last extant letter, except to his parents, written on May 20, is to Brod, and it takes the form of a kind of farewell, with regards at the end to Felix Weltsch and Oskar Baum.*

Even though he knew otherwise, Kafka held on to Dr. Tschiassny's favorable prognosis about his larynx, to the extent that he wanted to marry Dora — here we must rely on Brod. All the while, however, he was pleading with Klopstock for morphine to relieve his discomfort. In any event, with marriage in mind, he wrote to Dora's father, a Hasid, telling of his intentions and asking the man's permission. Kafka reportedly indicated that while he was not a practicing Jew, he was a repentant one who hoped to return to the fold. He said that with this he hoped to be accepted into such a pious family.[132] As noted earlier, Dymant consulted with his adviser, the rebbe, who said just one word when he read Kafka's letter: No. Kafka received Dymant's own "no" just before he died, but even with a "yes" he could not have managed the ceremony in time. The ironies of Kafka seeking marriage even at this late date confound the spectator; one can find answers, perhaps, only in his fictions. Dora, meanwhile, recognized the omens of his imminent death.

With the rejection in hand, Kafka nevertheless had a powerful desire to hang on; and Brod feels that if he had met Dora sooner, he might have had a stronger will to live, although in the face of his affliction, "will" may have been insufficient. Brod thought the two of them well suited for one another, with Dora's rich storehouse of Jewish lore a perfect complement to Kafka's inquiring but secular mind. Brod said that her knowledge of Polish Jewish religious tradition was a constant source of delight to Kafka. He indicates that when together they could be as playful as children. Of course, a good deal of the suitability was linked to Kafka's condition, which took all pressure off a full male-female relationship, such as he had contemplated with Felice Bauer. Further, Dora's youth — she was half Kafka's age — meant that she hero-worshipped this strange, intelligent, sensitive man, even if she did not fully appreciate his writings. Still further, Kafka's dependence on her gave her a real role in his life, which she might not have had otherwise with a healthy individual. She appears to have been looking for a person or cause that needed her, and in her, Kafka found the perfect embodiment of what he was seeking.

In his last hours, Kafka regretted the trouble he was putting Dora and Klopstock to. For these moments, we must rely on the medical student's account. On Monday, June 2, the day before he died, Kafka appeared to regain some life and asserted he was feeling well. He ate

---

Dora full credit for getting Kafka to eat nourishing food, for catering to his needs, and for acting in effect as full-time nurse.

*In a note written in the margins of a card from Dora to the Kafkas, dated May 26, one week before his death, Kafka announces his diminished craving for liquids and fruit.

strawberries and cherries, enjoyed the fragrance of the fruit, and asked people to drink water and beer in front of him so he could gain vicarious pleasure from something he could no longer do. He talked, in the last days, of drinks and fruit. Consciously or not, he was placing himself in the same position as the hunger artist: starving, watching people eat and drink, gaining his pleasure from observing, knowing he was holding himself back, in this instance physically unable to participate. Even in this condition, he was working, apparently on the final proofs of *A Hunger Artist*, the collection of stories. The letter to his parents that Brod said he wrote the day before his death, on that Monday, was really written almost two weeks before, on May 19 or so.

He fell asleep at midnight, still able to show considerable participation in life, but his body was skeletal. He had even shown some annoyance at his publisher, who had insisted on changing the order of appearance of the stories in the collection, and seemed involved in the details of his life. As he slept, Dora watched over him, and when at 4:00 A.M. she noticed his unusually heavy breathing, she called for Klopstock, who came immediately. Klopstock awoke the attending doctor, who administered a camphor injection, to relieve the difficulty in breathing from the blocked throat passage. Kafka pleaded for morphine to relieve his pain and discomfort. He said Klopstock had been torturing him by denying him sufficient morphine, and he asked for enough to kill him. He was given two injections that Klopstock said were morphine, but Kafka asserted angrily that they were an antidote. Brod reports that he said, amidst all these mixed signals, "Kill me, or else you are a murderer."[133] They then gave him pantopon, but he demanded more, saying it wasn't helping. He slowly drifted off to sleep. With Klopstock holding his head, Kafka in his final moments before sleeping thought Klopstock was Elli and warned her off, fearful of infecting her.

Yet he found the strength to tear off his icepack and throw it on the floor. "Don't torture me any more, why prolong the agony," he told Klopstock. He pleaded with his doctor friend not to leave him, and Klopstock promised not to. "But I am leaving you," Brod, citing Klopstock, reports that Kafka said. That was, in fact, the end. Kafka drifted off to sleep and never awoke. Dora was unable to control herself, whimpering and whispering, "My love, my love, my good one." Kafka had died at forty, on June 3, his body weighing less than 90 pounds, his final collection called *A Hunger Artist*, his reputation yet to come as the most significant writer of the twentieth century. Klopstock promised Dora she could view the body again, in the afternoon.

At his death, Kafka had only Klopstock and Dora. Brod was not there, nor were Hermann and Julie, nor had they been present at any part of their son's decline after his brief stay in Prague. Nor were his sisters, Elli, Valli, and Ottla, all of whom would meet deaths quite different from their brother's, in German concentration camps. Hermann

Kafka lived for another seven years, Julie for another ten. Was it fitting or ironic that all three were buried in the same grave, in the new Jewish cemetery in Prague, their graves now a tourist stop?

Klopstock reported that in death Kafka's face was pure and noble, "a king's face from the oldest and noblest stock. The gentleness of his human existence has gone, only his incomparable soul still forms his stiff, dear face. So beautiful is it as an old marble bust."[134] Klopstock begins to sound like Gustav Janouch, so in awe of Kafka that his prose searches for superhuman metaphors; but his devotion, like Dora's, cannot be disputed.

The body was removed to Prague and buried on June 11, in a simple ceremony. At the burial in Straschnitz (the Jewish section of Prague), Brod gave the funeral oration. Dora threw herself on the grave and fainted, according to one witness. According to other eyewitnesses, Hermann Kafka turned his back, and no one offered to help the young woman. Janouch was there, and he regretted not helping Dora. Hermann and Julie inserted a death notice in the newspaper, with the line that they did not wish to receive condolence visits. In the notice, Kafka's age was given, in both Czech and German versions, as forty-one, when of course he would not be forty-one until the following month. The notice appeared on June 10. Kafka's own final notice was his volume of stories, published by Die Schmiede in 1924, a more fitting memorial than the Kafka family's cold announcement. Even in death, Kafka seemed a stranger to them.

Perhaps Milena Jesenská had the final word: *"He saw a world full of invisible demons that make war on helpless human beings and destroy them"* (July 6, 1924).

Hermann died in 1931, Julie in 1934. Felice Bauer and Franz Werfel emigrated to the United States. German death camps claimed Kafka's three sisters, Grete Bloch, Löwy, Milena, and Julie Wohryzek. Brod and Dora Dymant ended up in Palestine.

Black milk of daybreak we drink it at sundown. . . .

— PAUL CELAN, "DEATH FUGUE"

Epilogue: "Kafkaesque"

K AFKA HAS LENT his name to an entire range of meanings that help interpret the appalling history of the later twentieth century. That word is *Kafkaesque,* and it is as much misused as used. Undeniably, it is connected with Kafka as a representative man of the century. In ways unlike Emerson's representative man, Kafka, the twentieth-century version, is a person who marshals his weaknesses so forcefully he becomes a pillar of strength. He is a man whose passivity and inaction disguise tremendous reserves of inner power. He is marked by a seeming dissociation of self, his being and becoming heading, as it were, in different directions. He lacks unity, or integrity; he divides and subdivides. And yet, withal, he does not collapse or surrender. He has fitted himself to the century.

Kafka was that "representative man," and the word that derives from his name cannot be distinguished from that very dissociation. For *Kafkaesque* at its most meaningful and exalted denotes a world that has its own rules, its own guidelines, its own forms of behavior that cannot be amenable to human will. *Kafkaesque,* in fact, seems to denote a will of its own, and it is, apparently, destructive of human endeavors. Clearly, it runs counter to human directions or goals or aims, and it serves as a form of bedevilment. *Kafkaesque* in our century has replaced the now old-fashioned *fate* or *destiny* or even *circumstance* and *happenstance.* It has become the representative adjective of our times.

No other contemporary or near contemporary literary figure has given his name to such a state of being, to such a majestic sense of demonic forces. *Proustian* or *Joycean* usually suggests a literary style, a manner, even a tone, but not a way of life. T. S. Eliot contributed a sound or rhythm to the language, as did William Butler Yeats, but neither lent his name to a time and place. *Faulknerian* has some wider definition in it, but it still possesses a far narrower sense than *Kafkaesque*. In point of fact, only Kafka comes through as distinctive and definitive. In that, we find his unique ability to create that "representative man" who, while he goes against everything we want to believe, ultimately becomes that man whom we must believe in. Beyond linguistics, he has made the general vocabulary, but further than that, he has achieved a state of mind.

Kafka would have been surprised to learn that he had communicated the century to us. He thought he had died virtually unknown, expecting no major literary figures at his deathbed or graveside. During his lifetime, except for passing recognition from Musil and Rilke, not one major literary figure noted his presence; and that was the way he wanted it, apparently — to slip away underground without giving anything even to friends. He did not want to become a hostage to reputation, nor separated from himself by the wedge of celebrity. All he gave was his name: not to a time or place, but to an entire century.

That word *Kafkaesque* has survived all kinds of criticisms and attacks. Marxism wrote Kafka off as catering to a bourgeois society, claiming that as a purveyor of weakness Kafka offered nothing to a society or state attempting to achieve change through betterment of the masses. As a result, until recently Kafka's works were banned in Czechoslovakia and other iron curtain countries. Freudian criticism was, of course, more sympathetic, but it tended to limit Kafka's work to interpretations of the oedipal struggle between father and son. While this is obviously an important point of reference, it is also, obviously, not one to be emphasized at the expense of all else. Poststructuralist criticism pointed to the lack of center in Kafka, the inability of the reader and critic to find precise meanings. That too was a valuable analysis, although, like the others, it limned only one Kafka, not all. Another way to look at him comes by placing his work within the structures of Modernism, as part of that development of avant-gardes that challenge settled themes and settled techniques. This certainly is a significant way to locate Kafka. As a key force in Modernism, as both its recipient and communicator, Kafka assimilated whatever was developing in Paris, Vienna, Berlin, and Munich. Yet even the subtleties of these arguments, by Marxists, Freudians, poststructuralists, and Modernists, do not adequately explain *Kafkaesque*.

The word eludes us unless we penetrate deeply into the kind of society and world we view ourselves in. *Kafkaesque* now belongs as much to that perception as it does to Kafka; in effect, we have preempted the word. If we view life as somehow overpowering or trapping us, as in some way undermining our will to live as we wish, as strengthening the forces that wait malevolently for human endeavor to falter, then we enter Kafka's world of the Kafkaesque. The adjective really goes back to his own situation in the waning days of the Austro-Hungarian Empire, to the time when the Dual Monarchy was a patchwork of concessions and compromises lacking central power, direction, or even will. From that context, there came the sense of a Kafkaesque world that had little to do with the individual living within it, especially when, as in Kafka's case, that individual was further divided by language and racial/ethnic origin. Caught as he was among the aspects of virtually every defining characteristic — language, race, religion, ethnicity, cultural identification — Kafka was in a prime position to fashion himself as the representative outsider and victim. From that to his adjectival designation is not distant. *Kafkaesque* recalls his own dilemmas, but it also recognizes how thwarted the individual must be by elements seemingly controlling him and his goals.

The world becomes Kafkaesque when it relocates the individual in areas he or she could not have preconceived; when it redefines the terms of existence in unforeseen modes; when it resuscitates the terms of life in ironies and paradoxes that run askew to human will or purpose. Kafkaesque is that mighty juggernaut revving up in the distance, but whose purpose or function cannot be ascertained. It is Yeats's rough beast slouching toward Bethlehem — except that in Kafka's terms, it is already arriving. It defines us. And in our response to the Kafkaesque, we can acquiesce to those elements that reach out malevolently, or we can, like Kafka himself, struggle to the end. The Kafkaesque does claim him, but accompanying its embrace is his refusal to bow to its inevitability. The forces are there, massed; the paranoia is real, but so is the final stand.

Kafkaesque need not be completely inhuman or negative. For Kafka himself, the adjective described conditions that brought out the Sisyphus-like qualities in himself. Without *Kafkaesque*, Kafka would not have been able to energize himself to confront all the terrors he imagined, or to face all the frustrations he saw as inevitable. After his death, and in the development of the adjective, we have turned the word into "the way of the world." And since that way has been so negative, we find *Kafkaesque* a denial, or else the definition of a region waiting to entrap us. Yet even within the catastrophic potentialities of the word, there is another dimension that does not distort Kafka's own quest under the weight of *Kafkaesque*. That is his struggle, even when he believed, especially after his first hemorrhaging in 1917, that what he was had caught up with him, and he faced destruction or annihilation. Given this century's penchant for annihilation, we are tempted to bring out only this side of the word and, indeed, of Kafka's life. But he knew otherwise.

Sisyphus was a bachelor, and he would toil without relief, suffer frustration at every moment, never see his way clear. And yet the bachelorhood of Sisyphus, lonely as it was, enabled him to be himself; and the toil itself, however frustrating, allowed him to be self-contained. Kafka had a horror of Sisyphus — thus his comparison of himself with the martyred figure. But he also found within that suffering figure something heroic, something substantive and redeemable. To that extent, *Kafkaesque* does not always mean surrender to a horrendous destiny; instead, it becomes something to battle against. When we use the adjective, we often lose sight of that.

Kafka, we can speculate, would have concurred with this statement of Mallarmé: "I've created my work only by *elimination*, and any truth I acquired resulted uniquely from the loss of an impression which, having sparkled, burnt itself out and allowed me, thanks to the shadows this created, to advance more deeply in the sensations of the absolute shadows." This too is Kafkaesque.

Notes

Although the notes are self-explanatory, a word about main sources is in order. This listing is only partially complete, since it does not include what I discovered in Prague about Kafka's cultural activities, nor does it include my extensive researches into Modernism and the avant-gardes that Kafka embraced. In all instances, the German editions were used but references are to the English-language texts. Thus the English titles of Kafka's books.

Kafka novels, stories, and related matter:
    Amerika
    The Trial
    The Castle
    The Complete Stories (including *Meditation*)
    Dearest Father (including *Letter to His Father*, "Eight Octavo Notebooks," "Wedding Preparations in the Country," "Reflections on Sin, Suffering, Hope, and the True Way," "Fragments from Notebooks and Loose Pages," "Paralipomena")
Parables and Paradoxes

Kafka diaries:
    Diaries: 1910–1913; Diaries: 1914–1923 (plus the German edition available in 1990, *Tagebücher: Kritische Ausgabe*)

Kafka letters:
    Letters to Friends, Family, and Editors
    Letters to Felice
    Letters to Milena (in two editions)
    Letters to Ottla and the Family

Critical and Biographical: see the Acknowledgments. Also:
  Kafka's Other Trial (Elias Canetti)
  Franz Kafka: Geometrician of Metaphor (Henry Sussman)
  The Kafka Debate (ed. Angel Flores)
  Franz Kafka: The Necessity of Form (Stanley Corngold)
  Reading Kafka: Prague, Politics, and the Fin de Siècle (ed. Mark Anderson)
  Kafka and the Contemporary Critical Performance (ed. Alan Udoff)
  Franz Kafka (Ronald Gray)
  Conversations with Kafka (Gustav Janouch)
  Kafka's Rhetoric: The Passion of Reading (Clayton Koelb)

Introduction

1. *Diaries: 1914–1923* (New York: Schocken, 1949), p. 102.
2. Max Brod, *Franz Kafka: A Biography,* 2d ed. (New York: Schocken, 1963), p. 234.
3. The July 4 letter is to Oskar Baum, the further comments are to Brod on July 5 (1922), *Letters to Friends, Family, and Editors* (New York: Schocken, 1977), pp. 331, 333–34. These two letters are among Kafka's greatest, a kind of autobiographical fiction.

ONE. Prague and Vienna

1. Many details about the Kafka family background come from Klaus Wagenbach's *Franz Kafka: Eine Biographie seiner Jugend, 1883–1912* (Bern: Francke Verlag, 1958). All subsequent biographers of Kafka are indebted to Dr. Wagenbach.

TWO. Prague and Kafka, Kafka and Prague

1. See Bruce E. Pauley, *Hitler and the Forgotten Nazis: A History of Austrian National Socialism* (Chapel Hill: University of North Carolina Press, 1981), p. 17.
2. In his *The Nine Devils.*
3. For the Prague of "Expressionism," see Johannes Urzidil, *There Goes Kafka* (Detroit: Wayne State University Press, 1968), chap. 1, p. 16.

THREE. Early Life in the Austro-Hungarian Empire

1. *Letter to His Father,* in *Dearest Father* (New York: Schocken, 1954), p. 139; next quotation, p. 145.
2. December 2, 1921.
3. Ernst Pawel, in *The Nightmare of Reason: A Life of Franz Kafka* (New York: Farrar, Straus & Giroux, 1984), provides excellent historical background on the Czech and Prague educational system.

4. *Diaries: 1910–1913* (July) (New York: Schocken, 1948), p. 16.
5. Ibid., pp. 15–16.
6. Ibid., pp. 17–18.
7. *Letters to Milena*, ed. Willi Haas (New York: Schocken, 1962), p. 66 (June 21, 1920); new ed., translated by Philip Boehm (New York: Schocken, 1990), p. 54.
8. Ibid., p. 67.
9. See Jacob Katz, *From Prejudice to Destruction: Anti-Semitism, 1700–1933* (Cambridge: Harvard University Press, 1980), for a full discussion of these developments.
10. *Conversations with Kafka* (New York: New Directions, 1971), p. 183. As we shall see, Janouch's transcriptions of Kafka's remarks must be approached with extreme caution.

FOUR. Prague and the Schoolboy

1. See Pawel, *Nightmare of Reason*, p. 36ff.
2. Janouch, *Conversations*, p. 52.
3. Described by Emil Utitz, and cited by Wagenbach in *Franz Kafka*.
4. *Diaries: 1910–1913*, p. 206.
5. *Diaries: 1910–1913*, p. 207 (January 2, 1912).
6. See Heinz Politzer, *Franz Kafka: Parable and Paradox*, rev. ed. (Ithaca, N.Y.: Cornell, 1966), chap. 2.
7. *Diaries: 1910–1913*, pp. 205–6.
8. Ibid., p. 150 (November 14).
9. Ibid., p. 182.
10. Ibid., p. 160.
11. Ibid., p. 197.
12. *Letter to His Father*, p. 157.
13. "Eight Octavo Notebooks," in *Dearest Father*, p. 66.
14. *Letter to His Father*, p. 165.
15. Ibid., pp. 178–79.
16. Ibid., p. 191.
17. For several compelling but eccentric arguments about Kafka and his father, intermixed with oedipal speculations, see Gilles Deleuze and Félix Guattari, *Kafka: Toward a Minor Literature* (1975; Minneapolis: University of Minnesota Press, vol. 30, 1986).
18. Letter to Hermann and Julie Kafka, July 1914, in *Letters to Ottla and the Family* (New York: Schocken, 1982), pp. 9–10.
19. "Octavo Notebooks," p. 87.
20. *Dearest Father*, pp. 385–86.
21. *Letters to Ottla*, p. 73.
22. Quoted by Pawel, *Nightmare of Reason*, p. 52.
23. Quoted by Brod in his German edition of the letters.
24. *Letter to His Father*, p. 172.
25. Ibid., p. 173.
26. Ibid., p. 174.

FIVE. Turn of the Century — Late Adolescence and Fin de Siècle

1. *Letters to Friends, Family, and Editors,* pp. 6–7.
2. Ibid., p. 2 (February 4, 1902).
3. *Letters to Friends,* p. 2.
4. Ibid., p. 7.
5. "Octavo Notebooks," p. 85; also, p. 87.
6. *Letters to Friends,* p. 9.
7. See Pawel, *The Nightmare of Reason,* p. 74.
8. Alfred Wallace, *The Wonderful Century* (New York: Appleton, 1898, 1899). I have covered much of this material in an earlier book, *Modern and Modernism: The Sovereignty of the Artist, 1885–1925* (New York: Atheneum, 1985).
9. *Thus Spake Zarathustra,* trans. Walter Kaufman (New York: Penguin, 1978), p. 206.
10. "Why I Am a Destiny," in *Ecce Homo,* trans. Walter Kaufman (New York: Penguin, 1969), p. 326.
11. Ibid., p. 327.
12. Ibid.
13. See Pawel, *Nightmare of Reason,* p. 69.
14. Dorrit Cohn.
15. Katz, *From Prejudice to Destruction,* p. 52.
16. See Allan Janik and Stephen Toulmin, *Wittgenstein's Vienna* (New York: Touchstone Books, 1973), especially pp. 197–98, 219–20, for the Wittgenstein half of this analogy.
17. See Richard Gilman's brief but trenchant *Decadence.* For a more historically based study, see Jean Pierrot, *The Decadent Imagination: 1880–1900,* trans. Derek Coltman (Chicago: University of Chicago Press, 1981). Pierrot ranges widely through both painting and literature, in the process creating a "decadent aesthetics."
18. *Psychopathia Sexualis* (New York: Putnam, 1965), p. 23; also, the next quotation.
19. *Myth, Religion and Mother Right* (Princeton: Princeton University Press, 1967), p. 71; originally published as *Das Mutterrecht* (1861). Following material is from pp. 83, 103.
20. *A Madman's Defense,* trans. Evert Sprinchorn (New York: Anchor Books, 1967), pp. 42–43.
21. *Diaries: 1914–1923,* p. 78 (August 7, 1914).
22. *Letters to Friends,* p. 4.
23. *Letter to His Father,* p. 145.
24. Ibid., p. 166.
25. Ibid., p. 178.
26. *Letters to Milena,* p. 164 (August 8–9, 1920); Boehm ed., p. 148.

SIX. The Advent of High Modernism

1. *Parables and Paradoxes* (New York: Schocken, 1975), pp. 97–99.
2. Ibid., pp. 85–86.

3. "Octavo Notebooks," p. 87.

4. Ibid., p. 99.

5. Ibid., p. 118.

6. *Letter to His Father*, p. 181, and repeated through the *Diaries* and letters.

7. See Wagenbach, *Franz Kafka*.

8. *Memoirs of My Nervous Illness* (Cambridge: Harvard University Press, 1988), p. 133.

9. *Letters to Friends*, p. 4.

10. See Carl E. Schorske, *Fin-de-Siècle Vienna: Politics and Culture* (New York: Knopf, 1980), especially chap. 2, for a brilliant analysis of Viennese and Dual Monarchy architecture.

11. *Letters to Friends*, p. 5 (Autumn 1902).

12. Ibid., p. 8.

13. November 9, 1903.

14. *Letters to Friends*, p. 12 (December 21, 1903).

15. Max Brod, *Franz Kafka: A Biography*, 2d ed. (New York: Schocken, 1963), pp. 53–54. The German edition (1937) differs somewhat from the English translation by G. Humphreys Roberts and Richard Winston.

SEVEN. Young Kafka and Modernism

1. To Pollak, *Letters to Friends*, p. 16 (January 27, 1904).

2. Ibid., p. 17 (August 28, 1904).

3. Ibid., pp. 18–19.

4. "Description of a Struggle," in *Franz Kafka: The Complete Stories*, ed. Nahum N. Glatzer (New York: Schocken, 1971), p. 16.

5. Ibid., p. 17.

6. Ibid., p. 21.

7. Brod, *Franz Kafka*, p. 107; following quotation, p. 108.

8. Ibid., pp. 66–67.

9. Ibid., p. 67.

10. *Conversations with Kafka*, p. 86.

11. Wagenbach, *Franz Kafka*, pp. 162–64.

12. As with so many of Kafka's short pieces, the dating of "The Animal in the Synagogue" is only approximate.

13. *Parables and Paradoxes*, p. 57.

14. For suggestive remarks on such a response, see William B. Ober, *Boswell's Clap and Other Essays: Medical Analyses of Literary Men's Afflictions* (New York: Harper & Row, 1988). Ober does not write directly about Kafka, but many of his comments on Boswell, Swinburne, D. H. Lawrence, Keats, and others can be carried over.

15. *Letters to Friends*, p. 25.

16. Ibid., p. 23.

17. *The Complete Stories*, p. 56.

18. Ibid., pp. 53–54.

19. Ibid., pp. 56–57.

20. *The Complete Stories*, p. 55.

21. Ibid., p. 65.

22. Ibid., p. 71.

23. Ibid., p. 53.

24. Ibid., p. 55.

25. *Letters to Friends*, p. 24 (May 1907).

26. Ibid.

27. Ibid., p. 26; also, following quotation.

28. Ibid., p. 25.

29. Ibid., p. 27; also, following quotation.

30. Ernst Pawel believes that the relationship was sexually consummated, but in the absence of proof, the "friendship" seems to be of the usual kind Kafka entered into, flirtation without results.

31. *Letters to Friends*, p. 29.

32. Ibid.

33. Ibid., p. 31.

34. Ibid., p. 33.

35. *The Complete Stories*, p. 384.

36. Ibid., p. 35; also, following quotation.

37. *Letters to Friends*, p. 36.

38. Ibid., pp. 38–39.

39. Ibid., p. 41.

40. Ibid., p. 53; also preceding and following quotations.

41. The December 20 issue.

42. *The Complete Stories*, p. 385.

43. Addressed to Arsene Houssaye, *Paris Spleen 1969*, trans. Louise Varèse (New York: New Directions, 1970); all following quotations are from this edition.

44. *The Complete Stories*, p. 387.

45. Ibid., p. 382.

46. *Letters to Friends*, p. 39.

47. Ibid., p. 43.

48. Pawel, *Nightmare of Reason*, following Wagenbach's biography, recreates the institute, particularly pp. 184–85.

49. Wagenbach quotes this report; also, Ronald Hayman, *Kafka: A Biography* (New York: Oxford University Press, 1982), p. 70.

50. *Conversations with Kafka*, p. 65.

51. Ibid., p. 18.

52. Ibid., p. 19; also, following quotation.

53. *Letters to Friends*, p. 48.

54. *The Complete Stories*, p. 384.

55. *Diaries: 1910–1913*, p. 150.

56. *Conversations with Kafka*, p. 70.

57. Ibid., p. 48.

58. *The Complete Stories*, pp. 390–91.

59. Ibid., p. 394.

60. Ibid., p. 398.

61. Ibid., p. 390.

62. Ibid., p. 396.

EIGHT. *Early Years of Achievement in an Age of Hostility*

1. *Conversations with Kafka*, p. 111.
2. *Letters to Friends*, p. 52.
3. Ibid., p. 53.
4. Ibid., p. 56.
5. Ibid., p. 57 (July 19, 1909).
6. Ibid., p. 58.
7. Requested on August 19, approved the following day.
8. *Franz Kafka*, p. 104.
9. *The Metamorphosis, The Penal Colony and Other Stories* (New York: Schocken, 1961), p. 298; also, for previous quotation.
10. Ibid., p. 306.
11. *Letters to Friends*, p. 63 (postmarked March 12, 1910).
12. Ibid., p. 61.
13. Ibid., p. 63.
14. Ibid., p. 65.
15. Ibid., p. 67.
16. *Diaries: 1910–1913*, pp. 14–15; also, following quotation.
17. Ibid., p. 18.
18. Ibid., p. 27.
19. Ibid., p. 33.
20. *Letters to Friends*, p. 71 (January 27, 1911).
21. *Franz Kafka*, p. 44.
22. *Letters to Friends*, p. 70 (December 17); also, following quotation.
23. *Letters to Felice* (New York: Schocken, 1973), p. 146 (January 8–9, 1913 [misdated 1912]).
24. Ibid., p. 147.
25. Ibid., p. 148.
26. Ibid.
27. So he tells Brod, December 15, 1910.
28. *Diaries: 1910–1913*, pp. 18–19.
29. Ibid., p. 10.
30. Ibid., p. 86.
31. Ibid., p. 39.
32. Ibid., p. 12.
33. *Letters to Friends*, p. 69 (postcard dated December 9, 1910); also, following quotation.
34. *Diaries: 1910–1913*, p. 39; also, following quotation.
35. Ibid., p. 41 (January 12).
36. *Diaries: 1914–1923*, pp. 239–40 ("Trip to Friedland and Reichenberg, 1911").
37. *Diaries: 1910–1913*, p. 43.
38. Ibid., p. 44.
39. Ibid., p. 45.
40. Ibid., p. 50 (February 21, 1911, or shortly thereafter).
41. Ibid.; all subsequent quotations from "The Urban World," p. 50ff.
42. Those entries directly following "The Urban World."
43. Ibid., p. 57 (March 28, 1911).

44. Ibid., p. 58.
45. *Nightmare of Reason*, p. 205; quoted from Christoph Stölzl, *Kafkas böses Böhmen* (Munich: Text + Kritik, 1975), p. 134.
46. *Franz Kafka*, p. 109; also, following quotations.
47. *Parables and Paradoxes*, pp. 13–15.
48. *Diaries: 1910–1913*, p. 61 (August 20, 1911).
49. Ibid., p. 60.
50. Ibid., p. 62.
51. *Diaries: 1914–1923*, p. 246 (part of the Travel Diaries).
52. Ibid., p. 253; also, following quotation.
53. Ibid., pp. 258–59, for this and following quotations.
54. Ibid., p. 263; following quotation, p. 267.
55. Ibid., pp. 265–66.
56. *Diaries: 1910–1913*, p. 63 (August 26, 1911); also, following quotation.
57. Ibid., p. 122.
58. Ibid., p. 123 (November 19, 1911).
59. *Letters to Friends*, p. 73 (September 17, 1911).
60. *Diaries: 1910–1913*, p. 123.
61. *Letters to Friends*, p. 73.
62. Ibid.
63. *Diaries: 1910–1913*, p. 156.
64. Ibid., pp. 70–71.
65. Ibid., p. 73; see, also, p. 72.
66. Ibid., pp. 128–29.
67. Ibid., pp. 73–74.
68. Ibid., p. 77 (October 3, 1911).
69. Ibid., p. 79.
70. Ibid.
71. Ibid., p. 80; also, following quotations.
72. Ibid., p. 87 (October 9, 1911).
73. Ibid., pp. 89–90.
74. Ibid., by December 14.
75. Ibid., p. 103.
76. Ibid., p. 104 (October 16, 1911).
77. Ibid., p. 201 (December 28, 1911).
78. Ibid., p. 107; also, preceding and following quotations.
79. Ibid., pp. 110, 111.
80. Ibid., p. 115.
81. Ibid., p. 121.
82. Ibid., p. 131.
83. Ibid., p. 133.
84. Ibid., p. 134.
85. Ibid., p. 137.
86. Ibid., p. 138.
87. Ibid., p. 139.
88. Ibid., p. 146.
89. Ibid., pp. 147–48.
90. Ibid., pp. 151–52.
91. Ibid., pp. 158–59.

92. Ibid., p. 160.
93. Ibid., p. 167.
94. Ibid., p. 170.
95. Ibid., pp. 171, 172 (December 8, 1911).
96. Ibid., p. 173.
97. Ibid.
98. Ibid.; also, following quotation.
99. Ibid., p. 183.
100. Ibid., pp. 184–85; also, following quotation.
101. Ibid., pp. 187–88.
102. Ibid., p. 190.
103. Ibid., p. 191.
104. Ibid., pp. 191–92.
105. Ibid., pp. 192–93.
106. Ibid., p. 194; following quotation, p. 197.

NINE. Franz, Felice, and the Great War

1. *Dearest Father*, p. 139.
2. *Diaries: 1910–1913*, pp. 268–69.
3. *Letters to Felice*, p. 5.
4. Ibid.
5. Ibid., pp. 6–7 (September 28, 1912).
6. Ibid., p. 8 (the volume *Letters to Felice* contains Kafka letters to others as well as to Felice Bauer).
7. Ibid., p. 19.
8. Ibid., p. 22.
9. Ibid.
10. Ibid., p. 25 (November 3, 1912).
11. Ibid., p. 27 (November 4, 1912).
12. Ibid., pp. 30–31.
13. Ibid.
14. Ibid., p. 32.
15. Ibid.
16. Ibid., p. 33.
17. Ibid., p. 36.
18. Ibid.; also, following quotation.
19. Ibid., p. 37.
20. Ibid.
21. Ibid., p. 39.
22. Ibid., p. 40 (November 14, 1912); also, following quotation.
23. Ibid., p. 46.
24. Ibid., p. 47.
25. Ibid., p. 49.
26. Ibid., p. 52.
27. Ibid., p. 53 (November 21, 1912).
28. Ibid.
29. Ibid., p. 54.

30. Ibid., p. 55.
31. Ibid., p. 56.
32. *Letters to Felice*, p. 57 (November 22, 1912); also, following quotations.
33. Ibid., p. 58.
34. Ibid.
35. Ibid., p. 59.
36. Ibid., p. 60; also, following quotation.
37. Ibid., p. 66.
38. Ibid., p. 67.
39. Ibid., p. 72.
40. Ibid., p. 73.
41. Ibid., p. 87.
42. Ibid., p. 88.
43. Ibid., p. 89; also, following quotation.
44. Ibid., p. 97.
45. Ibid., p. 101; also, following quotations.
46. Ibid., p. 103 (December 13–14, 1912).
47. Ibid., p. 112 (December 18–19, 1912).
48. Ibid., p. 113 (December 19–20, 1912).
49. Ibid.; also, following quotation.
50. Ibid., p. 119.
51. Ibid., p. 127 (December 27–28, 1912).
52. Ibid., p. 133.
53. Ibid.
54. Ibid., p. 139.
55. Ibid., p. 140.
56. Ibid., p. 145 (January 7, 1913).
57. Ibid., p. 152 (January 10–11, 1913); also, following quotation.
58. Ibid., p. 154 (January 12–13, 1913).
59. Ibid., p. 156.
60. Ibid.; also, following quotation.
61. Ibid., p. 161 (January 19, 1913).
62. Ibid.
63. Ibid., p. 166.
64. Ibid., p. 168 (January 22–23, 1913).
65. Ibid., p. 175 (January 29–30, 1913).
66. Ibid., p. 176.
67. In his February 2 letter, p. 180.
68. *Letters to Felice*, p. 185.
69. Ibid., p. 184.
70. Ibid., p. 193.
71. Ibid., p. 195 (February 16, 1913).
72. Ibid., p. 200 (February 20–21, 1913).
73. Ibid., p. 201 (February 21–22, 1913).
74. Ibid.
75. Ibid., p. 202 (February 23, 1913).
76. Ibid.
77. Ibid., p. 205.
78. Ibid.

79. Ibid., p. 208; also, following quotation.
80. *Diaries: 1910–1913*, p. 280.
81. *Letters to Felice*, p. 211 (March 2–3, 1913); also, following quotation.
82. Ibid., p. 212 (March 3–4, 1913).
83. Ibid., p. 215.
84. Ibid., p. 223 (March 16, 1913).
85. Ibid., p. 224.
86. Ibid., p. 228.
87. Ibid., p. 230.
88. Ibid., p. 233.
89. Ibid., p. 235.
90. Ibid., p. 236.
91. Ibid., p. 242 (April 13, 1913).
92. Ibid., p. 243 (April 14, 1913); also, following quotation.
93. Ibid., p. 245.
94. Ibid., p. 247 (April 26, 1913).
95. Ibid., p. 250.
96. Ibid., p. 252.
97. Ibid., p. 255 (May 12–13, 1913).
98. Ibid., p. 258.
99. Ibid., p. 260.
100. Ibid., p. 261; also, following quotation.
101. Ibid., p. 263 (May 27, 1913); also, following quotation.
102. Ibid., p. 264.
103. Ibid., p. 265 (June 2, 1913).
104. Ibid., p. 267.
105. Ibid., p. 269; also, following quotation.
106. Ibid., p. 270.
107. Ibid., p. 271.
108. Ibid.; also following quotation.
109. Ibid., p. 272.
110. Ibid., p. 275 (June 21–23, 1913); also, following quotations.
111. Ibid., p. 276; also, following quotation.
112. Ibid., p. 279 (June 26, 1913).
113. Ibid.
114. Ibid., p. 283 (July 1, 1913).
115. Ibid.
116. Ibid., p. 284.
117. Ibid., p. 286 (July 7, 1913).
118. Ibid.
119. Ibid., pp. 286–87.
120. Ibid., p. 288 (July 8, 1913).
121. Ibid., p. 289 (July 10, 1913).
122. Ibid., p. 290.
123. Ibid., p. 291 (July 28, 1913).
124. Ibid., p. 292 (August 1, 1913).
125. Ibid., p. 293 (misdated July, but really August 1, 1913).
126. Ibid., p. 294.
127. Ibid., p. 297.

128. Ibid., p. 301 (August 9, 1913).

129. Ibid., p. 302 (August 11, 1913); also, following quotation.

130. Ibid., p. 304.

131. Ibid., p. 306.

132. Ibid., p. 307.

133. Ibid., p. 308.

134. Ibid.

135. *Diaries: 1910–1913*, p. 299; also, following quotations.

136. *Letters to Felice*, p. 309 (August 24, 1913); also, following quotations.

137. Ibid.

138. Ibid., p. 310.

139. Ibid., p. 311.

140. Ibid., p. 314 (August 30, 1913); also, following quotations.

141. Ibid., p. 315; also, following quotation.

142. Ibid., p. 317 (September 9, 1913).

143. *Letters to Friends*, pp. 101–2.

144. Ibid., p. 101.

145. *Letters to Felice*, p. 320.

146. *Diaries: 1910–1913*, p. 300 (October 15, 1913).

147. *Letters to Friends*, p. 102.

148. *Letters to Felice*, p. 321.

149. Ibid., p. 327; also, following quotation.

150. Ibid.

151. Ibid., p. 329; also, following quotation.

152. Ibid., p. 333 (December 29).

153. Ibid., p. 334.

154. Ibid., p. 335; also, following quotations.

155. Ibid., p. 336.

156. Ibid., p. 337.

157. Ibid., p. 338.

158. Ibid., p. 339 (January 23, 1914); also, following quotation.

159. Ibid., p. 344 (February 7, 1914).

160. Ibid., p. 347 (February 11, 1914).

161. Ibid., p. 349 (February 14, 1914).

162. Ibid., p. 381.

163. Ibid., p. 349 (February 19, 1914).

164. Ibid., p. 352 (March 1, 1914).

165. Ibid., p. 352.

166. Ibid., p. 353.

167. Ibid., p. 354.

168. Ibid., p. 355.

169. *Diaries: 1914–1923*, p. 24.

170. Ibid.

171. *Letters to Felice*, p. 358 (March 7, 1914).

172. Ibid., p. 361.

173. Ibid., p. 362.

174. Ibid., p. 365.

175. Ibid., p. 366.

176. Ibid., pp. 367–68 (March 21, 1914).

177. Ibid., p. 368.
178. Ibid., p. 369 (March 21, 1914, letter).
179. Ibid.
180. Ibid., p. 370.
181. Ibid., p. 371.
182. Ibid., p. 371.
183. Ibid., p. 372.
184. Ibid., p. 406 (May 16, 1914).
185. Ibid.
186. Ibid., p. 373 (March 14, 1914).
187. Ibid., p. 374.
188. Ibid., p. 376 (April 3, 1914).
189. Ibid., p. 382.
190. Ibid., p. 385 (April 14, 1914).
191. Ibid., p. 386 (April 15, 1914).
192. Ibid., p. 391 (April 19, 1914).
193. Ibid., p. 393 (April 21, 1914).
194. Ibid., p. 395; also, following quotation.
195. Ibid.
196. Ibid., p. 402 (May 7, 1914).
197. Ibid., p. 403 (May 8, 1914).
198. Ibid., p. 406 (May 16, 1914).
199. Ibid., p. 408 (May 18, 1914); also, following quotation.
200. Ibid., p. 414 (May 24, 1914).
201. Ibid., p. 411 (May 21, 1914).
202. Ibid., p. 417.
203. Ibid., p. 418.
204. Ibid., p. 420 (June 6, 1914); also, following quotations.
205. Ibid.; also, following quotation.
206. Ibid., p. 422 (June 8, 1914).
207. Ibid.
208. Ibid., p. 423 (June 11, 1914).
209. Ibid., p. 425 (June 14, 1914).
210. Ibid., p. 426 (June 18, 1914).
211. Ibid., p. 429 (June 26, 1914).
212. Ibid., p. 431 (July 3, 1914); also, following quotations.
213. Ibid., p. 437; also, following quotation.
214. Ibid.
215. Ibid., p. 438; also, following quotations.
216. Ibid., p. 440.
217. Ibid., p. 441.
218. Ibid., p. 443 (January 25, 1915).
219. Ibid., p. 443.
220. Ibid., p. 445 (February 11, 1915).
221. Ibid.
222. Ibid., p. 448 (March 21, 1915).
223. Ibid.
224. Ibid., p. 451.
225. Ibid., p. 453 (postmarked Berlin, May 6, 1915).

226. Ibid., p. 455 (postmarked May 26, 1915).

227. Ibid., p. 456 (August 9, 1915).

228. Ibid., p. 458.

229. Ibid., p. 459.

230. Ibid., p. 460 (postmarked January 18, 1916).

231. Ibid.; also, following quotation.

232. Ibid., p. 461 (January 24, 1916).

233. Ibid., in the letter of March 16, 1916.

234. Ibid., p. 462 (March 16); also, following quotation.

235. Ibid.

236. Ibid., p. 463; also, following quotations.

237. Ibid., p. 464.

238. Ibid., p. 465 (April 19, 1916).

239. Ibid., p. 467 (May 14).

240. Ibid., p. 468.

241. *Letters to Friends*, p. 117.

242. Ibid., p. 118.

243. Ibid., p. 121 (mid-July 1916); also, following quotation.

244. *Letters to Felice*, p. 482 (August 2, 1916).

245. Ibid., August 13, 1916.

246. Ibid., p. 487.

247. Ibid.

248. Ibid., p. 490 (August 19, 1916); also, following quotation.

249. Ibid., p. 491 (August 21, 1916).

250. Ibid., p. 499 (September 11, 1916).

251. Ibid., p. 502 (September 16, 1916); also, following quotations.

252. Ibid., p. 509 (September 26, 1916).

253. Ibid., p. 513 (October 1, 1916).

254. Ibid., p. 515; also, following quotations, pp. 515–16.

255. Ibid., p. 516.

256. Ibid., p. 518 (October 8, 1916).

257. Ibid., p. 520 (October 12, 1916).

258. Ibid., p. 525 (October 19, 1916).

259. Ibid.

260. Ibid.; also, following quotations.

261. Ibid.

262. Ibid., p. 526.

263. Ibid., p. 529 (October 26, 1916).

264. Ibid., p. 531 (October 30, 1916).

265. Ibid., p. 577; see note 97.

266. Ibid., p. 534 (November 21, 1916).

267. Ibid., pp. 540–41.

268. Ibid., p. 542 (December 16–January 17, 1917).

269. Ibid., p. 543; also, following quotations. The information, like the blood itself, gushes forth from Kafka, as though he cannot get it out fast enough.

270. *Diaries: 1914–1923*, p. 183.

271. Ibid., p. 185.

272. *Letters to Friends*, p. 140 (mid-September 1917).

273. Ibid.

274. Ibid., p. 142.
275. Ibid., p. 144.
276. *Letters to Felice*, p. 544.
277. Ibid., p. 545.
278. Ibid.
279. Ibid.
280. Ibid.
281. Ibid., p. 546.
282. Ibid.
283. *Letters to Friends*, p. 156; a letter from October 12, 1916.
284. *Letters to Felice*, p. 549.

TEN. Kafka's Maturity and the Beginning of a New Era

1. *Franz Kafka*, p. 112.
2. Ritchie Robertson, in *Kafka: Judaism, Politics, and Literature* (New York: Oxford University Press, 1985).
3. Ibid., pp. 147, 152.
4. *Diaries: 1910–1913*, p. 233. See Anderson, ed., *Reading Kafka* (New York: Pantheon, 1989), p. 263ff.
5. See *Reading Kafka*, p. 266.
6. *Diaries: 1910–1913*, p. 211 (January 3, 1912); also, following quotations.
7. Ibid., p. 249.
8. Ibid., p. 264 (June 6, 1912).
9. Ibid.
10. *Franz Kafka*, p. 122.
11. *Diaries: 1914–1923*, p. 289.
12. Ibid., p. 303.
13. Ibid., p. 305.
14. *Letters to Family*, pp. 82–83 (August 22, 1912).
15. *The Complete Stories*, p. 85.
16. *Diaries: 1910–1913*, pp. 278–79.
17. Ibid., p. 47ff. (February 21, 1911).
18. *Letters to Friends*, pp. 89–90; also, following quotations.
19. Ibid., p. 92 (November 13, 1912).
20. *Amerika*, trans. Willa and Edwin Muir (New York: New Directions, 1946), pp. 26, 27.
21. Ibid., p. 31; also, following quotations, pp. 31, 33.
22. Ibid., p. 48.
23. Ibid., p. 55.
24. Ibid., p. 59; also, following quotations, p. 61.
25. Ibid., p. 67.
26. Ibid., p. 71.
27. Ibid., p. 88.
28. Ibid., p. 98.
29. Ibid., p. 107, for a typical example.
30. Ibid., p. 157.
31. Ibid., p. 180.

32. Ibid., p. 184; also, following quotation, p. 186.
33. *Letters to Felice*, p. 47.
34. *Amerika*, p. 192; also, following quotations, p. 202.
35. Ibid., p. 214.
36. Ibid., p. 242.
37. Probably between August and October.
38. *Amerika*, p. 252.
39. Ibid., p. 254.
40. Ibid., p. 264.
41. Ibid., p. 268.
42. *The Complete Stories*. All references to "The Metamorphosis" are from the centennial bilingual edition, 1988.
43. "The Metamorphosis," p. 45.
44. Ibid., p. 51.
45. This of course fits well with Kafka's identification with his names suggesting a carrion-eater, something already close to vermin.
46. *Diaries: 1910–1913*, p. 284 (February 28, 1913).
47. Ibid., p. 287.
48. *Letters to Friends*, p. 99.
49. Ibid., p. 99 (August 29, 1913).
50. *Diaries: 1910–1913*, p. 301 (October 14, 1913).
51. *Letters to Friends*, p. 102 (September 13, 1913).
52. *Letters to Felice*, p. 327.
53. Ibid., p. 328.
54. *Diaries: 1910–1913*, p. 309.
55. Ibid.
56. Ibid., p. 316 (December 4, 1913).
57. Ibid., p. 319 (December 10, 1913); following quotations, p. 321.
58. *Diaries: 1914–1923*, pp. 13–14.
59. Ibid., p. 18 (February 10, 1914).
60. Ibid., p. 20 (February 14, 1914).
61. Ibid., p. 22 (February 23, 1914).
62. Ibid., pp. 24–25.
63. Ibid., p. 27 (March 9, 1914).
64. *Diaries: 1910–1913*, p. 182.
65. *Diaries: 1914–1923*, pp. 35–36 (May 27, 1914).
66. Ibid., p. 36.
67. Ibid., p. 41 (May 29, 1914).
68. Ibid., p. 42; also, following quotations.
69. *Letters to Friends*, p. 107 (June 6, 1914).
70. *Diaries: 1914–1923*, p. 68 (July 28, 1914).
71. Ibid., p. 71.
72. Ibid., p. 75 (July 31, 1914).
73. Ibid.
74. Ibid., pp. 76–77.
75. Ibid., p. 77; also, following two quotations.
76. Ibid., p. 87.
77. References to *The Trial* in English will be to three editions, to the earlier Knopf edition, originally published in 1937; to the Schocken edition, with

revisions by E. M. Butler of Willa and Edwin Muir's translation; and, coinciding with the recent sale of the *Trial* manuscript, the definitive edition, by Sir Malcolm Pasley, insofar as any is possible with an incomplete novel. His editing model for *The Trial* was his edition of *The Castle*, in two volumes, in German. The differences in translation between the Knopf and Schocken editions begin with the very first line, for in the Schocken *verleumdet* is translated into English as "telling lies."

78. "Essential Solitude," pp. 64, 69.
79. *The Complete Stories*, p. 144.
80. Ibid., p. 150.
81. Ibid., p. 154.
82. *Diaries: 1914–1923*, pp. 12, 13, 14, for this and following quotations.
83. *The Complete Stories*, p. 168.
84. Ibid., p. 172.
85. *Diaries: 1914–1923*, p. 104 (December 20, 1914).

ELEVEN. Kafka as Prophet, 1915–1917

1. *The Metamorphosis, The Penal Colony, and Other Stories* (New York: Schocken, 1961), bringing together everything published during Kafka's lifetime, p. 172.
2. Knopf ed., p. 184ff.; Schocken ed., p. 148ff.
3. Knopf ed., p. 106; Schocken ed., p. 85.
4. *Diaries: 1914–1923*, p. 107 (January 4, 1915).
5. Ibid., p. 109 (January 18, 1915).
6. Ibid. (January 19, 1915).
7. Ibid., p. 111 (January 24, 1915).
8. Ibid.
9. Ibid., p. 112.
10. *Letters to Felice*, p. 443 (January 25, 1915).
11. *The Complete Stories*, p. 183.
12. Ibid., p. 185.
13. *Diaries: 1914–1923*, p. 118 (March 13, 1915).
14. On March 21 and April 5, 1915.
15. *Diaries: 1914–1923*, p. 120 (April 27, 1915).
16. Ibid., p. 121 (May 3, 1915).
17. *Letters to Felice*, p. 457.
18. Ibid., p. 458, for all quotations.
19. *Diaries: 1914–1923*, p. 130 (September 16, 1915).
20. Ibid., p. 132.
21. Ibid., p. 138 (October 6, 1915).
22. Ibid., p. 140 (October 7, 1915).
23. Ibid., p. 142 (November 5, 1915).
24. Ibid., p. 143 (November 6, 1915).
25. *Letters to Felice*, p. 459 (December 5, 1915).
26. Ibid., p. 460 (January 18, 1916).
27. Ibid., p. 461.
28. *Diaries: 1914–1923*, p. 155 (June 2, 1916).

29. Ibid., p. 157 (July 5, 1916).
30. Ibid., p. 161.
31. *Letters to Friends*, p. 126.
32. *Letters to Felice*, p. 495.
33. *Diaries: 1914–1923*, p. 165 (August 27, 1916).
34. Ibid., p. 166.
35. Ibid., p. 165 (October 8, 1916).
36. *Letters to Felice*, p. 502 (September 16, 1916); also, following quotations.
37. *Diaries: 1914–1923*, pp. 168–69; also, preceding quotations.
38. *Letters to Friends*, p. 127 (October 11, 1916).
39. *Letters to Felice*, p. 534 (November 23, 1916).
40. Ibid., p. 536 (December 7, 1916).
41. "The Guardian of the Tomb," in *Seven Expressionist Plays* (London: Calder, 1968), p. 55. (Also in *The Complete Stories*.)
42. *The Complete Stories*, p. 230.
43. Ibid., p. 234.
44. Ibid., p. 225.
45. Ibid., p. 412.
46. Ibid., p. 402.
47. Ibid., p. 403.
48. Ibid., p. 404.
49. Ibid., p. 415.
50. *Parables and Paradoxes*, p. 95.
51. Very possibly the spring of 1917.
52. *The Complete Stories*, p. 255.
53. Ibid., p. 257.
54. Ibid., p. 258.
55. Ibid., p. 402.
56. Ibid., p. 417.
57. Ibid., p. 409.
58. Ibid., p. 428.
59. Ibid., p. 429; also, following quotation.
60. Hayman, for example, in *Kafka*, p. 220.
61. *The Complete Stories*, p. 243.
62. Ibid., p. 244.
63. Ibid., p. 245.
64. *Diaries: 1914–1923*, pp. 173–74.
65. *Letters to Felice*, p. 543.
66. Ibid., p. 544.
67. Ibid., p. 545.
68. Ibid., p. 546.
69. *Letters to Friends*, p. 141 (mid-September 1917).
70. Ibid., p. 138 (mid-September 1917).
71. *Letters to Milena*, p. 22 (April 1920); Boehm ed., p. 6.
72. An August 8–9 entry, *Diaries: 1914–1923*, pp. 178–79.
73. Ibid., p. 182.
74. Ibid., p. 185.
75. *Letters to Friends*, p. 140 (mid-September 1917); also, following quotation.
76. Ibid., p. 142; also, following quotation.

77. Ibid., p. 144 (September 22, 1917).

78. Ibid., p. 146 (late September 1917).

79. Ibid., p. 151, to the Brods.

80. Ibid., p. 151 (early October); also, following quotation.

81. Ibid., p. 155 (October 12, 1917), to Brod.

82. Ibid., p. 156.

83. Available in *Dearest Father* (New York: Schocken, 1954), p. 34.

84. Number 5.

85. Number 13.

86. Number 20.

87. Number 29, second part.

88. Number 38.

89. Number 47.

90. Number 52.

91. Number 66.

92. Numbers 75, 93, 82, and 83 respectively.

93. Number 86; also, following quotation.

94. Number 109.

95. *Letters to Friends* (to Brod), p. 166 (mid-November 1917); also, following quotations.

96. Ibid., p. 163 (early November 1917).

97. Ibid., p. 169 (mid-November 1917).

98. Ibid.

99. Ibid., p. 171 (November 24, 1917), to Brod.

100. Ibid., p. 173.

101. *Letters to Friends*, p. 179 (postmarked December 17, 1917).

102. Ibid., p. 186 (January 13, 1918).

103. Felice departed on December 27. Kafka wrote in his "Octavo Notebooks," p. 77.

104. "Octavo Notebooks," December 25, 26, 27.

105. Ibid., p. 84 (January 17, 1918).

106. Ibid., p. 85 (January 18, 1918).

107. Ibid., p. 84 (January 17, 1918).

108. Ibid., p. 87 (January 25, 1918).

109. Ibid., p. 88.

110. *Letters to Friends*, p. 194.

111. Ibid.

112. "Octavo Notebooks," p. 94 (February 10, 1918).

113. Ibid., p. 95.

114. *Letters to Friends*, p. 201 (late March).

115. Ibid., p. 202; following remarks on Kierkegaard, pages 202–3.

116. "Octavo Notebooks," p. 99 (February 25, 1918).

117. Ibid., p. 100.

118. Ibid., p. 101.

119. Ibid., p. 109.

120. Ibid., p. 118.

121. Ibid., p. 118; also, following quotation.

122. Ibid., p. 121.

123. Ibid., p. 129, the "Eighth Octavo."

124. *Letters to Friends*, p. 213 (February 6, 1919), to Brod.
125. *Letter to His Father*, p. 187.
126. *Diaries: 1914–1923*, p. 191.
127. *Letters to Friends*, p. 216 (November 24, 1919); following quotation, p. 217.
128. Ibid., p. 218; following quotations from pp. 219, 220.
129. Ibid., pp. 218–19; also, following quotations.
130. Ibid., p. 219; following two quotations, p. 220.
131. *Diaries: 1914–1923*, p. 192.

TWELVE. *Modernism and Death, Kafka and Death*

1. *Letters to Friends*, p. 237 (early May 1920).
2. Brod's description.
3. *Letter to His Father*, in *Dearest Father*, pp. 138–39.
4. Ibid., p. 140.
5. Ibid.
6. Ibid., p. 145.
7. Ibid., p. 191.
8. Ibid., p. 148.
9. Ibid., p. 150.
10. Ibid., p. 152.
11. Ibid., pp. 152–53.
12. Ibid., p. 154.
13. *Letters to Milena*, pp. 204–5 (September 1920); Boehm ed., p. 201.
14. *Letter to His Father*, p. 157.
15. *Diaries: 1910–1913*, p. 200.
16. Ibid., p. 159; following quotations, pp. 160, 161.
17. *Letter to His Father*, p. 163.
18. Ibid., p. 166; also, following quotations.
19. Ibid., p. 167.
20. Ibid., p. 170; also, following quotation.
21. Ibid., p. 172.
22. Ibid., p. 174.
23. Ibid.
24. Ibid., p. 176.
25. Ibid.
26. Ibid., p. 177.
27. Ibid., p. 178.
28. Ibid., p. 179; also, following quotation.
29. Ibid., p. 180.
30. Ibid., p. 181.
31. Ibid., p. 183; also, following quotation.
32. Ibid., p. 189.
33. Ibid., p. 190; also, following quotations.
34. Ibid., p. 191; also, following quotations.
35. *Letters to Friends*, p. 273 (mid-April 1921).
36. Ibid., p. 270.

37. *Letter to His Father*, p. 192.
38. Ibid., p. 193.
39. Ibid., p. 195; also, following quotation.
40. Ibid.
41. Ibid., p. 196.
42. *Diaries: 1914–1923*, p. 209 (January 23, 1922).
43. *The Complete Stories*, p. 446.
44. Ibid., p. 448.
45. *Letters to Friends*, p. 229 (March 1920).
46. Ibid., p. 267; also, following quotations.
47. *Diaries: 1914–1923*, p. 192 (January 9, 1920).
48. Ibid., p. 193.
49. *Franz Kafka*, p. 75.
50. "Paralipomena," in *Dearest Father*, p. 378.
51. Ibid., p. 379.
52. Ibid.
53. *The Complete Stories*, p. 449; following quotations, pp. 450, 451.
54. *Letters to Friends*, p. 233; also, following quotations about this incident.
55. See Brod's original German biography, p. 280ff.
56. *Diaries: 1914–1923*, p. 203 (January 18, 1922).
57. *Milena: The Story of a Remarkable Friendship*, by Margarete Buber-Neumann (New York: Seaver Books, 1988), p. 66. Buber-Neumann became very close to Milena when both were imprisoned in the Ravensbrück concentration camp, where Milena died.
58. Ibid.
59. Ibid., p. 69.
60. Ibid., p. 70.
61. *Letters to Milena*, p. 21 (April 1920); Boehm ed., p. 5.
62. Ibid., p. 22.
63. Ibid., p. 25.
64. Ibid., p. 37. The comments on Ernst Polak appear on p. 36.
65. Ibid., p. 48.
66. Ibid., p. 49.
67. Ibid., p. 50.
68. Ibid. See also a letter to Brod, *Letters to Friends*, pp. 236–37 (early May 1920).
69. Ibid., p. 51.
70. Ibid., p. 52.
71. Ibid., p. 59.
72. *Letters to Friends*, p. 236.
73. Ibid., p. 237.
74. Ibid.
75. Ibid., p. 238 (June 1920).
76. Ibid., p. 239.
77. *Letters to Milena*, p. 55.
78. Ibid.
79. Ibid., p. 164.
80. Ibid., p. 165.
81. Ibid., p. 105.

82. Ibid., p. 108.

83. Ibid., p. 110.

84. Ibid., p. 115 (July 29, 1920); Boehm ed., p. 116, with the passage connected to a different letter from Haas.

85. "Fragments from Notebooks and Loose Pages," in *Dearest Father*, pp. 347–48.

86. Ibid., p. 349.

87. Ibid., p. 312.

88. Ibid., p. 271.

89. *The Complete Stories*, p. 437.

90. Ibid., p. 438.

91. *Dearest Father*, p. 41.

92. *Letters to Milena*, p. 133; also, following quotation.

93. Ibid., p. 147.

94. Ibid., p. 148.

95. Ibid., p. 150.

96. Ibid., p. 157.

97. Ibid., p. 159.

98. *The Complete Stories*, p. 263.

99. Ibid., p. 267.

100. Ibid., p. 265.

101. Ibid., p. 454.

102. Ibid., p. 456.

103. *Letters to Milena*, p. 177 (August 13, 1920); Boehm ed., p. 160.

104. Ibid., p. 176; Boehm ed., p. 159.

105. Ibid., p. 179 (August 17–18, 1920); Boehm ed., p. 161.

106. *Letters to Friends*, p. 247 (December 31, 1920).

107. Ibid., pp. 272–73.

108. Ibid., pp. 273–74.

109. Ibid., p. 249 (January 13, 1921).

110. Ibid., p. 250.

111. Ibid.

112. Ibid., p. 253.

113. Ibid.; also, following quotations.

114. Ibid., p. 254.

115. *Letters to Milena*, p. 192.

116. Ibid., p. 194 (September 5, 1920); Boehm ed., p. 187.

117. Ibid., p. 195; Boehm ed., p. 187.

118. Ibid., p. 196 (September 7, 1920); Boehm ed., p. 196.

119. Ibid., p. 199 (September 14, 1920); Boehm ed., pp. 193–94.

120. Ibid., p. 200; also, following quotation.

121. Ibid., p. 207.

122. Ibid., p. 208.

123. Ibid., p. 216.

124. Ibid., p. 217.

125. Ibid., p. 219.

126. Ibid., p. 235.

127. *Letters to Friends*, p. 263 (early March 1921).

128. Ibid., p. 264 (March 11, 1921).

129. Ibid., p. 275 (April 1921).

130. Ibid., p. 280 (early May 1921).

131. Ibid., p. 281 (early June 1921).

132. Ibid., p. 285.

133. Ibid.

134. Ibid., p. 286.

135. Ibid., p. 287 (to Brod, June 1921). "I can only watch with disgust when the others bring up sputum, and I myself don't have a sputum jar, as I should have."

136. Ibid., p. 289 (to Brod, June 1921).

137. Ibid.

138. Ibid., p. 291 (Autumn 1921); also, following quotation.

139. Ibid., p. 293.

140. Ibid., p. 294.

141. Ibid., p. 295; also, following quotation.

142. Ibid.; also, following quotations.

143. Ibid., p. 296; also, preceding and following quotations.

144. Ibid., p. 297.

145. Ibid., p. 302.

146. *Diaries: 1914–1923*, p. 193 (October 15, 1921).

147. Ibid., p. 195 (October 17, 1921).

148. Ibid.; also, following quotation.

149. Ibid., p. 196.

150. Ibid., p. 197 (October 20, 1921).

151. Ibid., p. 198 (October 29, 1921); also, following quotation.

152. Ibid., p. 201 (December 6, 1921).

153. Ibid., p. 202.

154. Ibid.

155. Ibid.

156. Ibid., p. 203; also, following quotation.

157. Ibid.

158. Ibid., p. 204.

159. Ibid., p. 205.

160. Ibid.

161. Ibid., p. 207.

162. Ibid.; also, following quotation.

163. *Letters to Friends*, p. 333. Like so many other Kafka letters, this one must be seen as an attempt on Kafka's part to put his internal life in a dialogic relationship with his public life, a struggle that could not be resolved.

164. Ibid., p. 208.

165. Ibid., p. 213 (January 27, 1922).

166. Ibid., p. 212.

167. Ibid., p. 213; also, preceding quotation.

168. Ibid., p. 214.

169. Ibid., p. 215.

170. Ibid.; also, preceding quotations.

171. Ibid., p. 216.

172. Ibid., p. 217.

173. Ibid., pp. 217–18 (January 30, 1922).

174. Ibid., p. 219.
175. Ibid., pp. 220–21 (February 10, 1922).
176. *Letters to Friends*, p. 320, to Klopstock (March 1, 1922).
177. *Concerning the Spiritual in Art* (New York: Dover, 1977), p. 8.
178. *The Complete Stories*, p. 277.
179. Ibid.

THIRTEEN. *Kafka, Jews, and Other Solutions: The Kafka Presence*

1. *Diaries: 1914–1923*, p. 222.
2. Ibid., p. 224 (c. February 20, 1922).
3. *Letters to Friends*, p. 321 (March 1, 1922).
4. Ibid. (late March 1922).
5. Ibid., p. 323 (early April 1922).
6. See Hayman, for example, in *Kafka*, p. 273.
7. *The Complete Stories*, p. 451.
8. Ibid., p. 450.
9. *Diaries: 1914–1923*, p. 223 (February 20, 1922); also, following quotation.
10. *Letters to Friends*, p. 324.
11. *The Complete Stories*, p. 278.
12. Ibid., p. 279.
13. Ibid., p. 283.
14. Ibid., p. 286.
15. Ibid., p. 291.
16. Ibid., p. 294; also, preceding quotations.
17. Ibid., p. 295.
18. Ibid., p. 299.
19. Ibid.
20. Ibid., p. 309.
21. Ibid.
22. Ibid., p. 310; also, following quotations.
23. Ibid., p. 314; also, following quotation.
24. *Diaries: 1914–1923*, p. 227 (April 13, 1922).
25. Ibid., p. 239 (May 19, 1922).
26. *Conversations with Kafka*, p. 190.
27. *Letters to Friends*, p. 326, to Brod (postmarked June 26, 1922).
28. *Parables and Paradoxes*, p. 185.
29. *Letters to Friends*, p. 328, to Brod.
30. *Diaries: 1914–1923*, p. 231.
31. *Letters to Friends*, p. 330 (June 30, 1922).
32. Ibid., p. 331 (July 4, 1922).
33. Ibid., pp. 331–32.
34. Ibid., p. 332; also, following quotations.
35. Ibid., p. 333 (July 5, 1922).
36. Ibid.; also, following quotations.
37. Ibid.
38. Ibid., p. 334; also, following quotation.

39. Ibid.; also, following quotation.
40. Ibid.; also, following quotation.
41. Ibid., p. 335; also, following quotation.
42. Ibid.
43. Ibid., p. 337 (early July 1922), to Weltsch.
44. Ibid.
45. Ibid., p. 338 (July 12, 1922); also, following quotation.
46. Ibid., p. 339; also, following quotation.
47. Ibid.
48. Ibid., p. 341.
49. Ibid., to Brod, p. 343 (July 20, 1922).
50. For the American reader, the most accessible edition is the Schocken paperback of 1974, translated by Willa and Edwin Muir, with additional material translated by Eithne Wilkins and Ernst Kaiser. The German original of *The Castle* was published two years after Kafka's death, in 1926, with the first English edition appearing four years later. The so-called definitive English edition was issued in 1954 and follows the German editions of 1935 and 1951. According to Brod, although there was no concluding chapter, Kafka told him what it was. The land-surveyor was to find partial satisfaction, in that he did not give up his struggle but would die worn out by it. At the time of his death, he was vindicated, for he was to be permitted to live and work in the village.
51. *The Castle* (Schocken paperback ed.), p. 140.
52. *Letters to Friends*, p. 336 (July 5, 1922).
53. Dorrit Cohn.
54. *The Castle*, p. 351.
55. *Letters to Friends*, to Brod, p. 346 (late July 1922).
56. Ibid., p. 347.
57. Ibid., to Brod, p. 349 (postmarked July 31, 1922).
58. Ibid., to Brod, p. 351 (early August 1922).
59. Ibid.
60. Ibid.; also, following quotation.
61. Ibid., p. 353.
62. Ibid., p. 355 (postmarked August 6, 1922). Kafka's fascination with the Emmy Salveter affair really goes beyond biography itself into areas of wild speculation. The "loss" of Brod to a mistress was quite different from "losing" him to a wife. But beyond that, Kafka could enjoy the deprivation of precisely what Brod possessed: an exogamous relationship that allowed him, Kafka, to revel in what he knew he was missing from life. The situation was, in this respect, simply another form of masochism.
63. Ibid., to Emmy Salveter, p. 356 (August 1922).
64. Ibid., p. 358.
65. Ibid., p. 359.
66. Ibid., to Klopstock, p. 361 (September 1922).
67. *Parables and Paradoxes*, p. 47.
68. *Letters to Friends*, p. 365 (December 1922).
69. *Letters to Milena*, p. 235 (late November 1923); Boehm ed., p. 236.
70. *Diaries: 1914–1923*, p. 232 (June 12, 1923).
71. *Letters to Milena*, p. 236.

72. *Letters to Friends*, p. 372 (July 13, 1923).
73. Ibid., p. 373 (July 13, 1923).
74. Ibid., p. 374 (July 24, 1923).
75. Ibid., p. 376.
76. Ibid., to Klopstock, p. 378 (early August 1923).
77. Ibid., p. 378 (August 8, 1923).
78. Ibid., p. 379 (September 6, 1923).
79. Ibid., p. 381 (September 14, 1923).
80. Ibid., p. 384 (postmarked October 2, 1923).
81. Ibid., p. 387.
82. *The Complete Stories*, p. 317.
83. Ibid., p. 319.
84. Ibid., p. 320.
85. Ibid., p. 323; also, following quotation.
86. Ibid., p. 324.
87. *The Complete Stories*, p. 328.
88. Ibid., p. 327; also, following quotation.
89. Ibid., pp. 328–29.
90. Ibid., p. 331.
91. Ibid., p. 334.
92. Ibid.; also, following quotations.
93. *Thus Spake Zarathustra* (Kaufman translation) (New York: Viking, 1970), p. 204, all quotations.
94. *The Complete Stories*, p. 336.
95. Ibid.; also, following quotation.
96. Ibid., p. 338.
97. Ibid., p. 339.
98. Ibid., p. 341.
99. Ibid., p. 345.
100. Ibid., p. 348.
101. Ibid., p. 349; also, following quotation.
102. Ibid., p. 352.
103. Ibid., p. 355.
104. Ibid.
105. Ibid., pp. 358–59; also, following quotation.
106. *Letters to Friends*, p. 490, note 67.
107. Ibid., p. 402 (December 19, 1923); also, following quotation.
108. Ibid., to Brod, p. 404 (mid-January 1924); also, following quotations.
109. Ibid., p. 405.
110. *Parables and Paradoxes*, p. 149.
111. *Letters to Friends*, p. 405.
112. *The Complete Stories*, p. 363.
113. *Letters to Friends*, p. 409.
114. Ibid., p. 410.
115. *The Complete Stories*, p. 371; also, following quotation.
116. Ibid., p. 365.
117. Ibid., p. 366.
118. Ibid., pp. 367–68.
119. Ibid., p. 376.

120. *Letters to Friends*, to Klopstock, p. 411 (April 7, 1924); also, following quotation.
121. Ibid., to Klopstock, p. 412 (April 13, 1924).
122. Ibid., to Brod, p. 413 (April 20, 1924).
123. Ibid., p. 419; also, following quotation.
124. Ibid., p. 418.
125. Ibid., p. 416.
126. Ibid., p. 417.
127. Ibid., p. 419.
128. Ibid., p. 418.
129. Ibid., p. 421; also, following quotation.
130. Ibid., p. 422; also, following quotation.
131. Ibid., p. 414.
132. *Franz Kafka*, p. 208.
133. Ibid., pp. 212–13, for the details of Kafka's final moments.
134. Ibid., p. 213.

Index